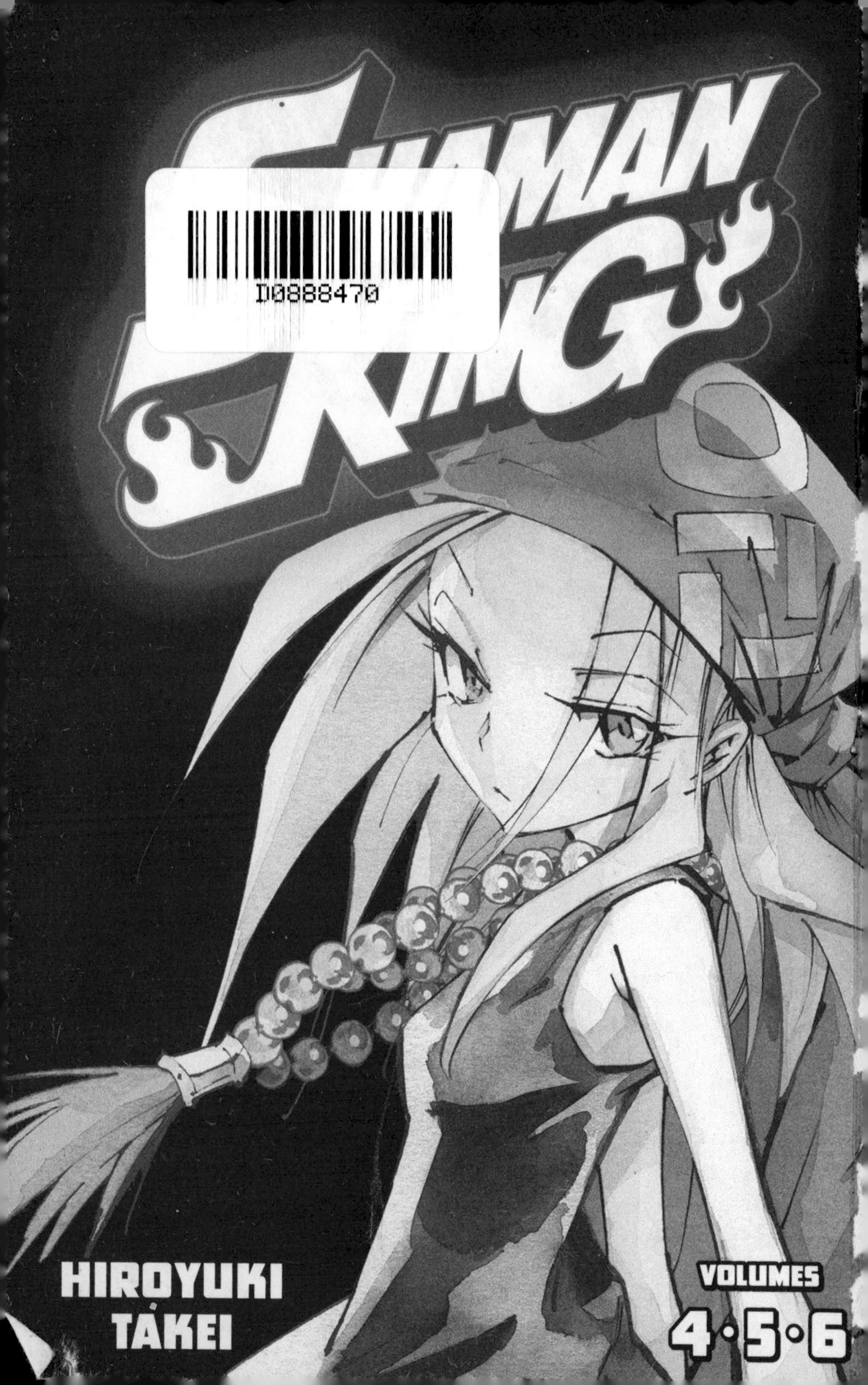
SHAMAN KING
HIROYUKI TAKEI
VOLUMES
4·5·6

SHAMAN KING

VOLUMES

4·5·6

TABLE OF CONTENTS

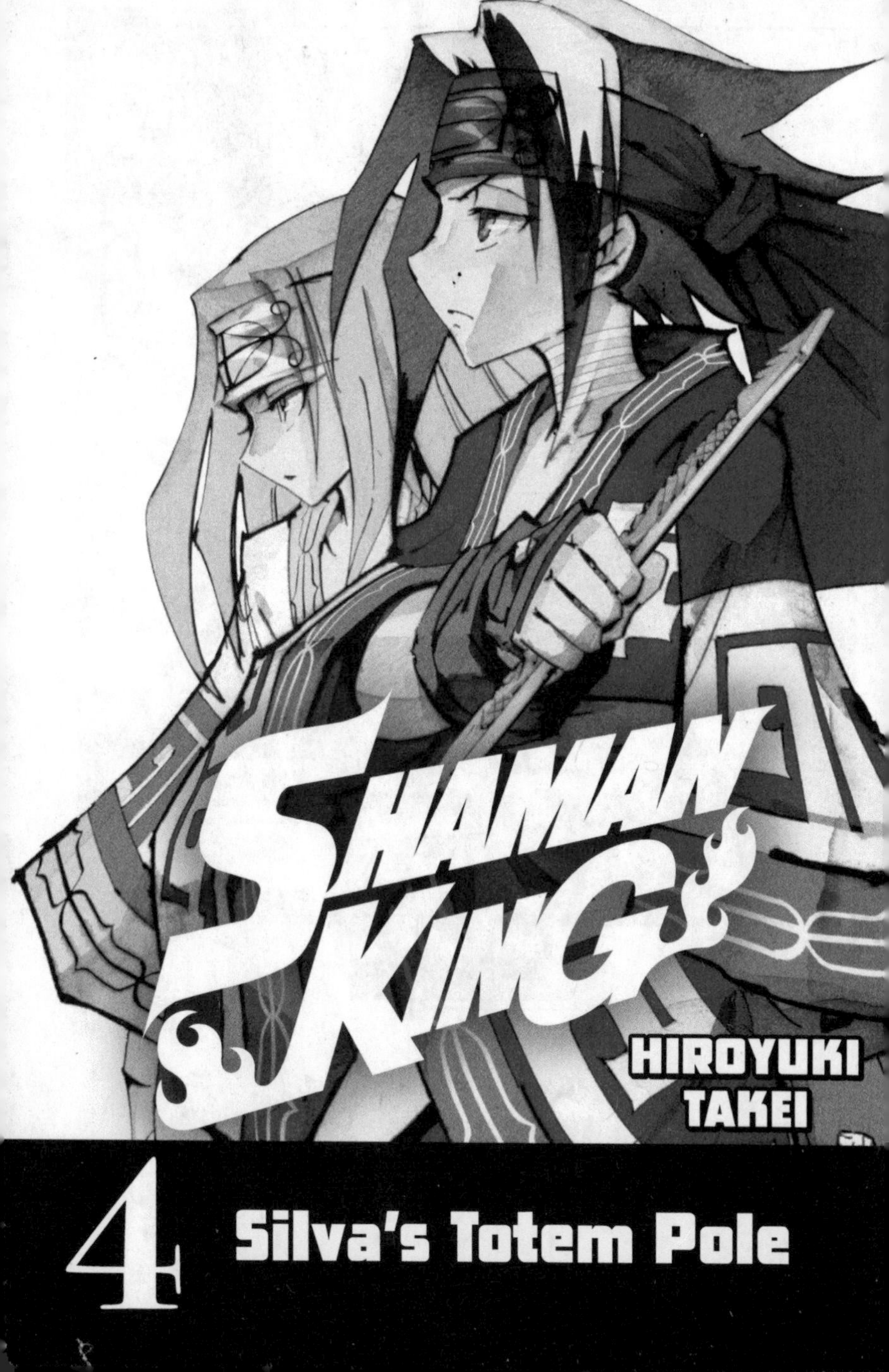
SHAMAN KING
HIROYUKI TAKEI

4 Silva's Totem Pole

SHAMAN KING

Volume 4
Characters

Amidamaru
The spirit of a samurai who died 600 years ago. Yoh's spirit companion.

Amidamaru
Spirit Flame Mode

Yoh Asakura
A boy who bridges the gap between our world and the spirit world... In other words, a shaman (in training).

Anna Kyoyama
An *itako* from Mt. Osore. Yoh's arranged fiancée.

Manta Oyamada
Yoh's friend. You'll never see him without a dictionary tucked under his arm.

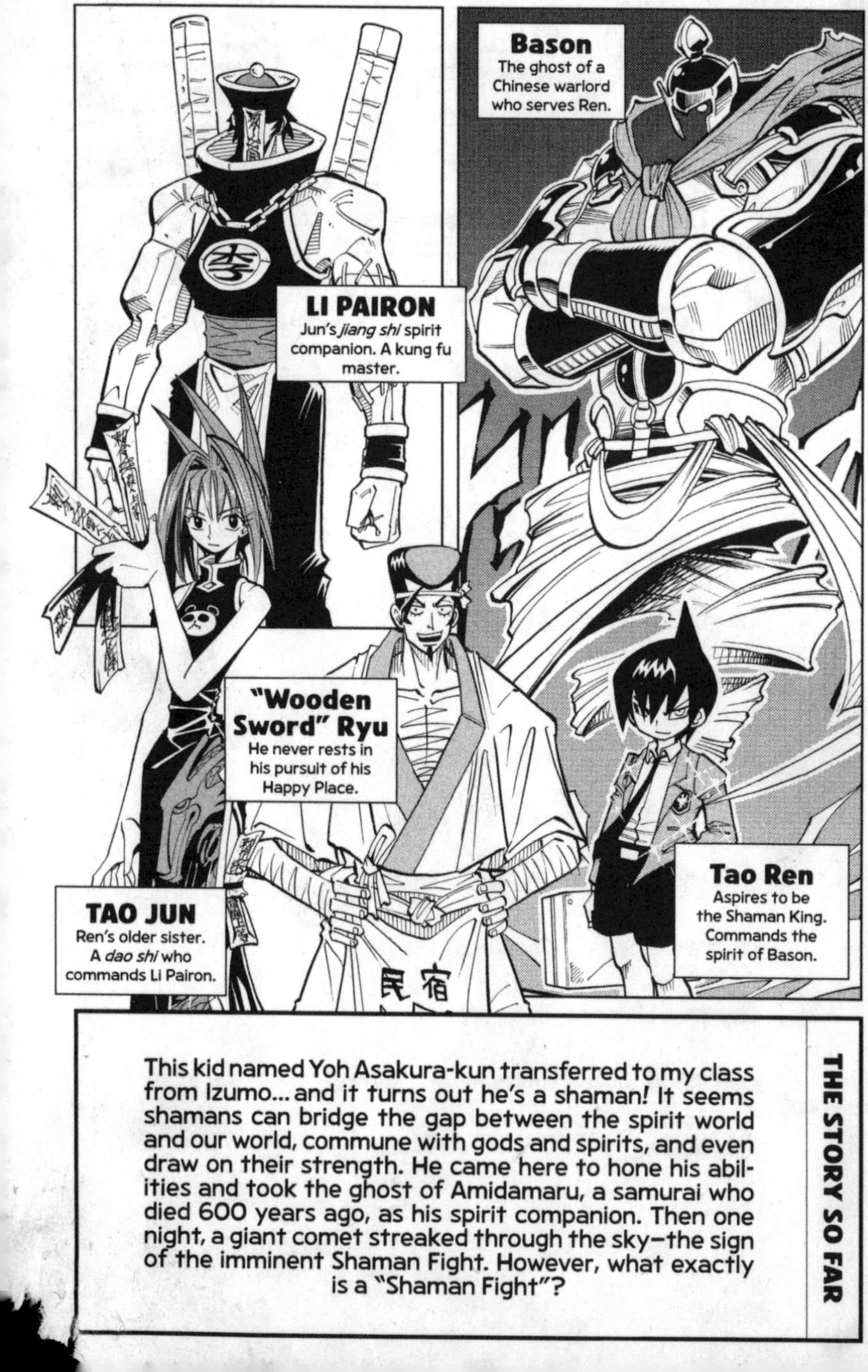
Bason
The ghost of a Chinese warlord who serves Ren.
LI PAIRON
Jun's *jiang shi* spirit companion. A kung fu master.
Tao Ren
Aspires to be the Shaman King. Commands the spirit of Bason.
"Wooden Sword" Ryu
He never rests in his pursuit of his Happy Place.
民宿
TAO JUN
Ren's older sister. A *dao shi* who commands Li Pairon.

THE STORY SO FAR

This kid named Yoh Asakura-kun transferred to my class from Izumo... and it turns out he's a shaman! It seems shamans can bridge the gap between the spirit world and our world, commune with gods and spirits, and even draw on their strength. He came here to hone his abilities and took the ghost of Amidamaru, a samurai who died 600 years ago, as his spirit companion. Then one night, a giant comet streaked through the sky—the sign of the imminent Shaman Fight. However, what exactly is a "Shaman Fight"?

SHAMAN KING 4

Silva's Totem Pole

4

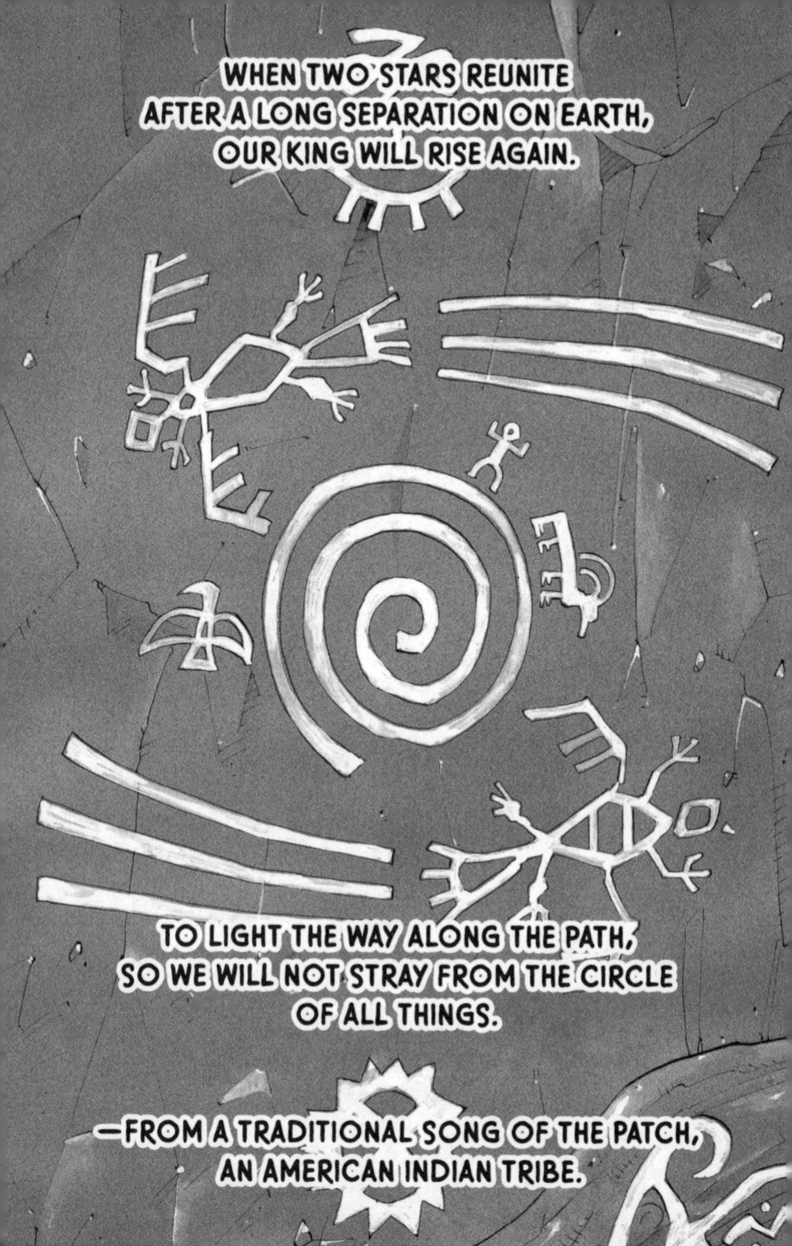
WHEN TWO STARS REUNITE
AFTER A LONG SEPARATION ON EARTH,
OUR KING WILL RISE AGAIN.
TO LIGHT THE WAY ALONG THE PATH,
SO WE WILL NOT STRAY FROM THE CIRCLE
OF ALL THINGS.
—FROM A TRADITIONAL SONG OF THE PATCH,
AN AMERICAN INDIAN TRIBE.

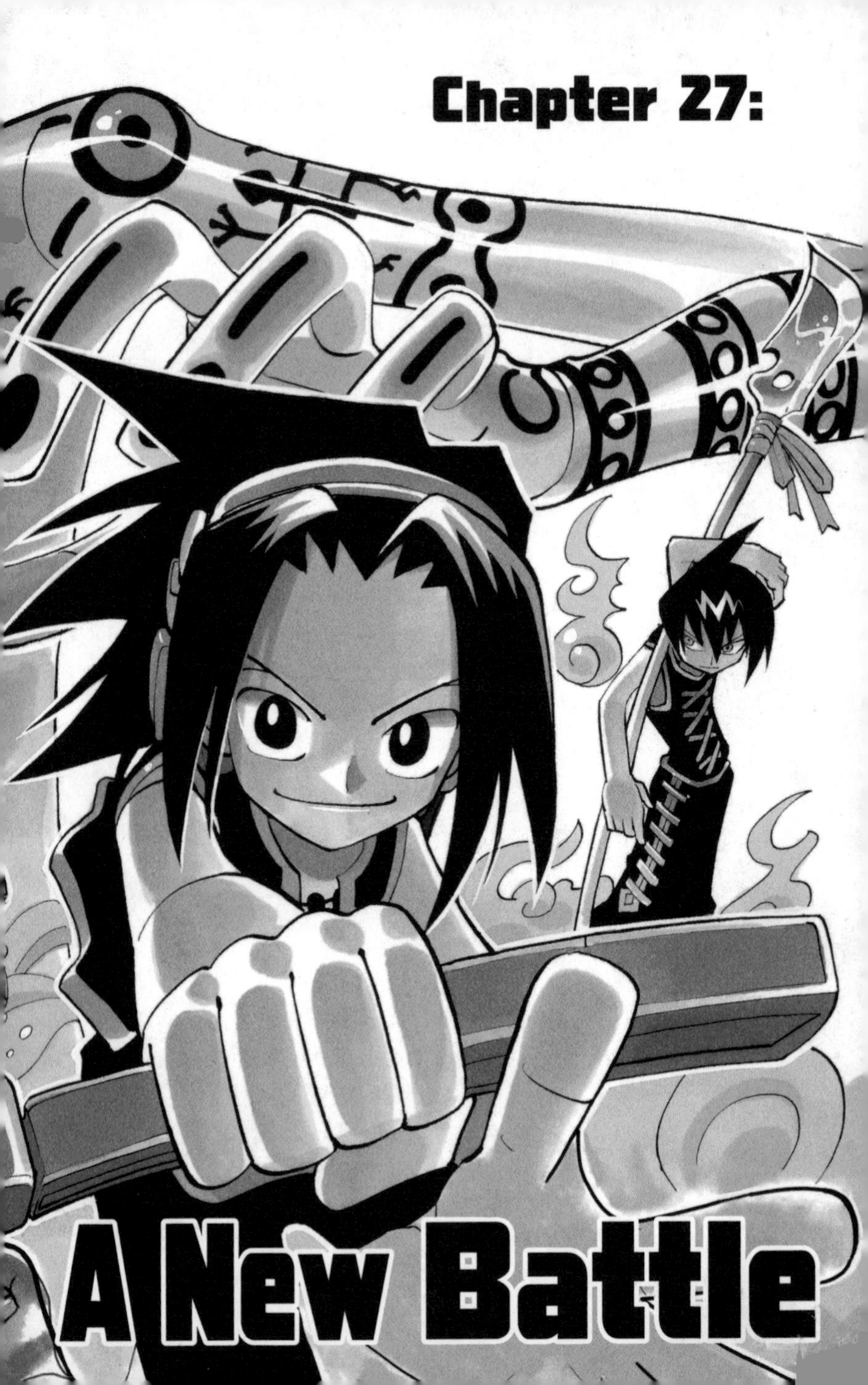
Chapter 27:
A New Battle

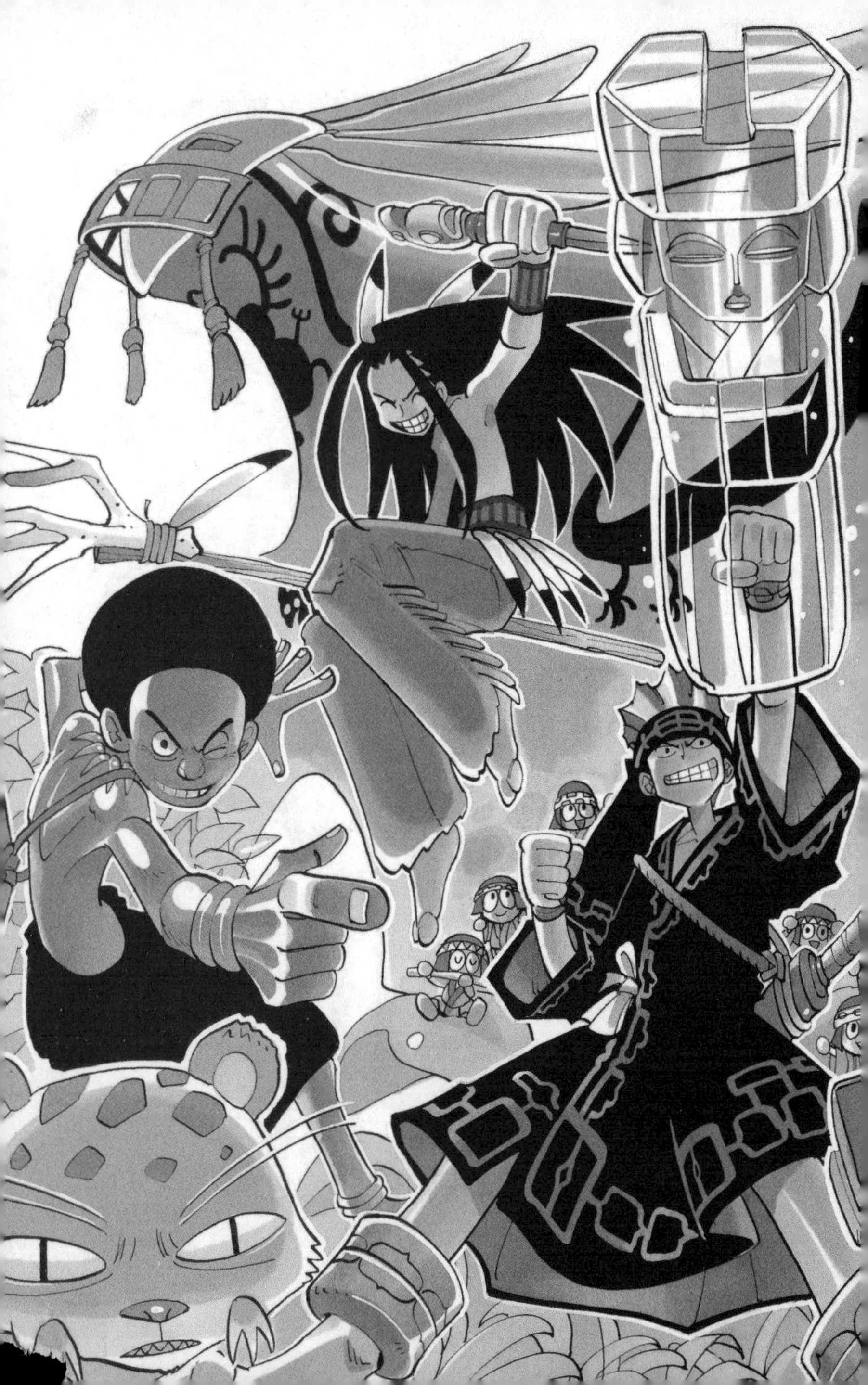

SHAMAN KING CHARACTER FILE No.14

Goldva

July 1999

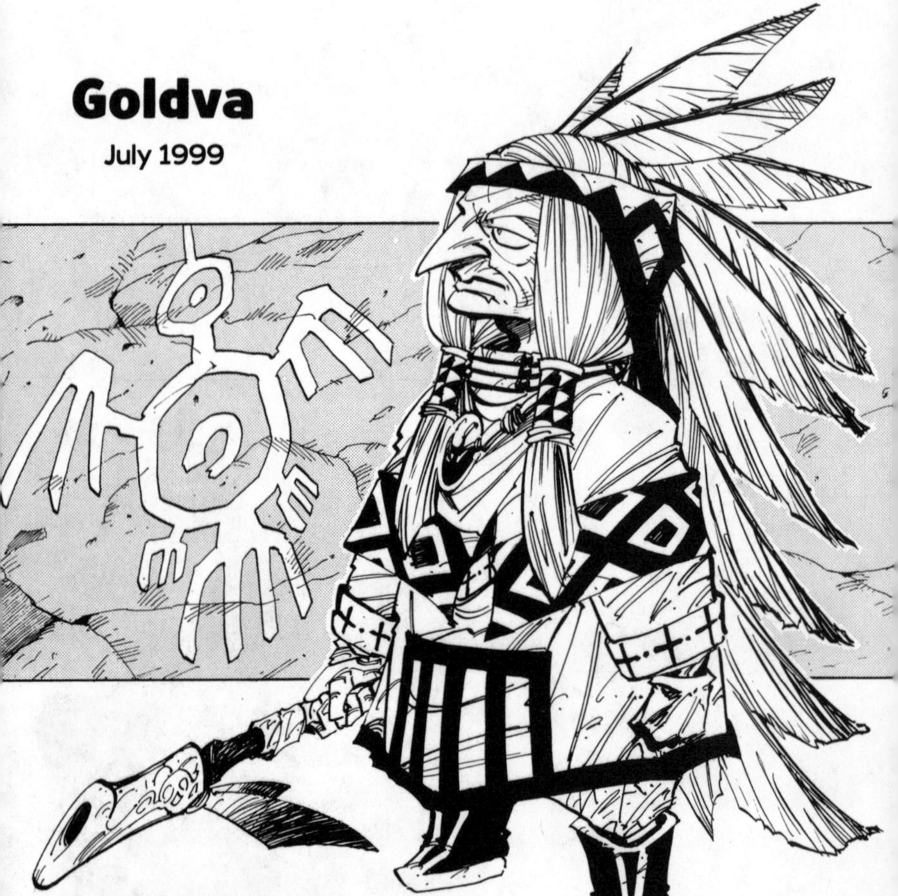

Age:77
Date of Birth: October 1, 1921
Astrological Sign: Libra
Blood Type: O

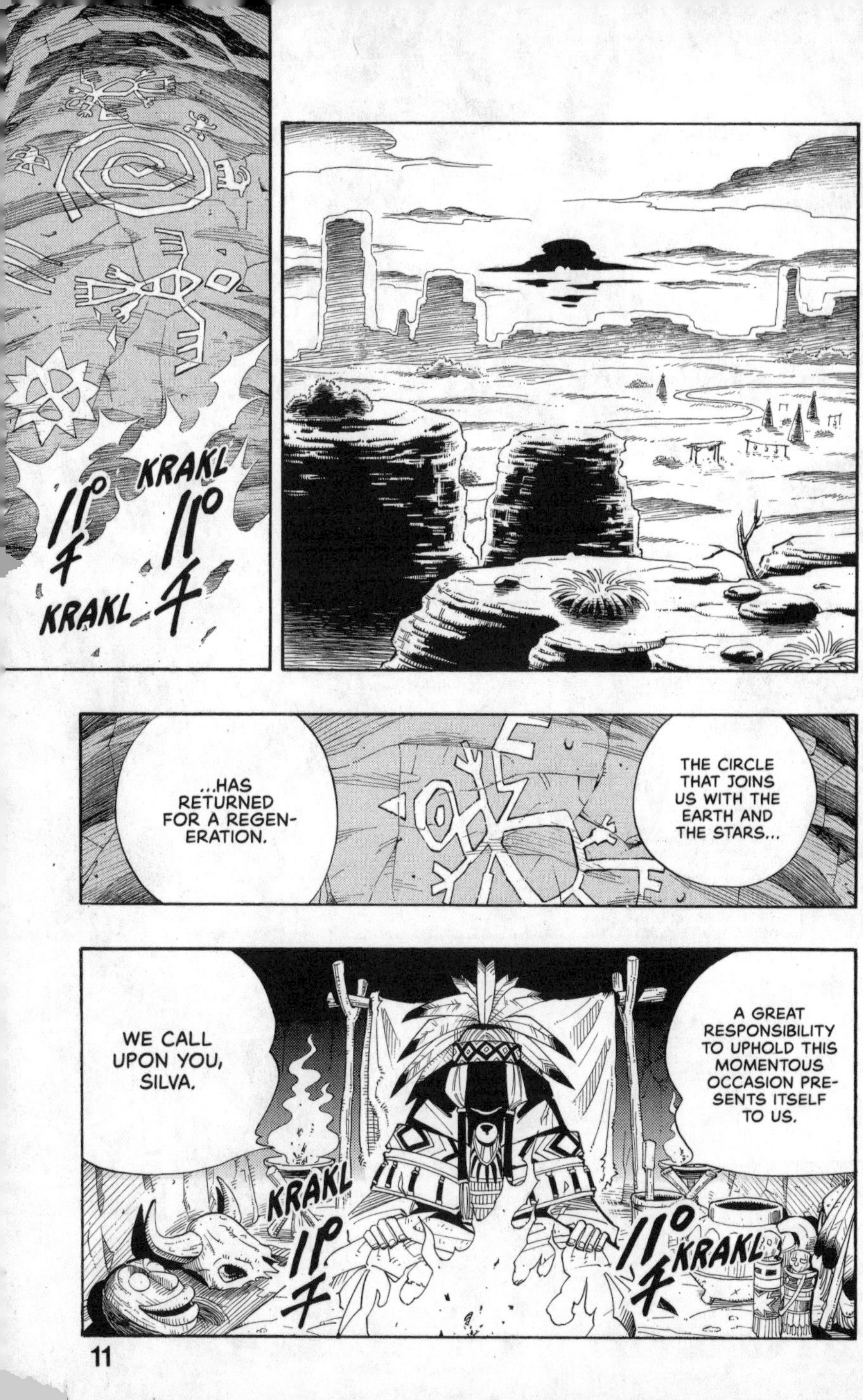
パチ
KRAKL
パチ
KRAKL
THE CIRCLE THAT JOINS US WITH THE EARTH AND THE STARS...
...HAS RETURNED FOR A REGEN-ERATION.
A GREAT RESPONSIBILITY TO UPHOLD THIS MOMENTOUS OCCASION PRE-SENTS ITSELF TO US.
WE CALL UPON YOU, SILVA.
パチ
KRAKL
KRAKL
パチ

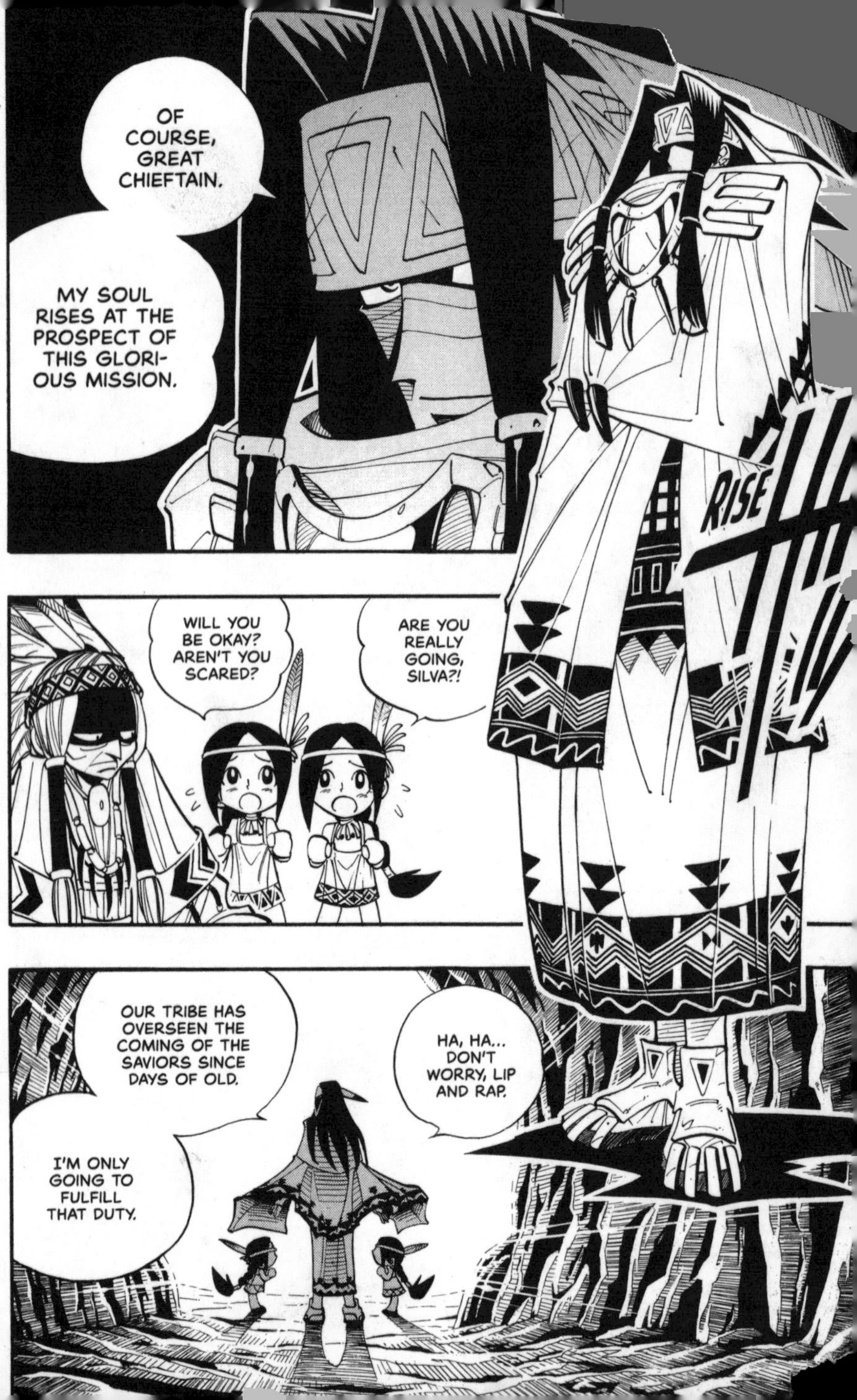
RISE
OF COURSE, GREAT CHIEFTAIN.
MY SOUL RISES AT THE PROSPECT OF THIS GLORI-OUS MISSION.
ARE YOU REALLY GOING, SILVA?!
WILL YOU BE OKAY? AREN'T YOU SCARED?
HA, HA... DON'T WORRY, LIP AND RAP.
OUR TRIBE HAS OVERSEEN THE COMING OF THE SAVIORS SINCE DAYS OF OLD.
I'M ONLY GOING TO FULFILL THAT DUTY.

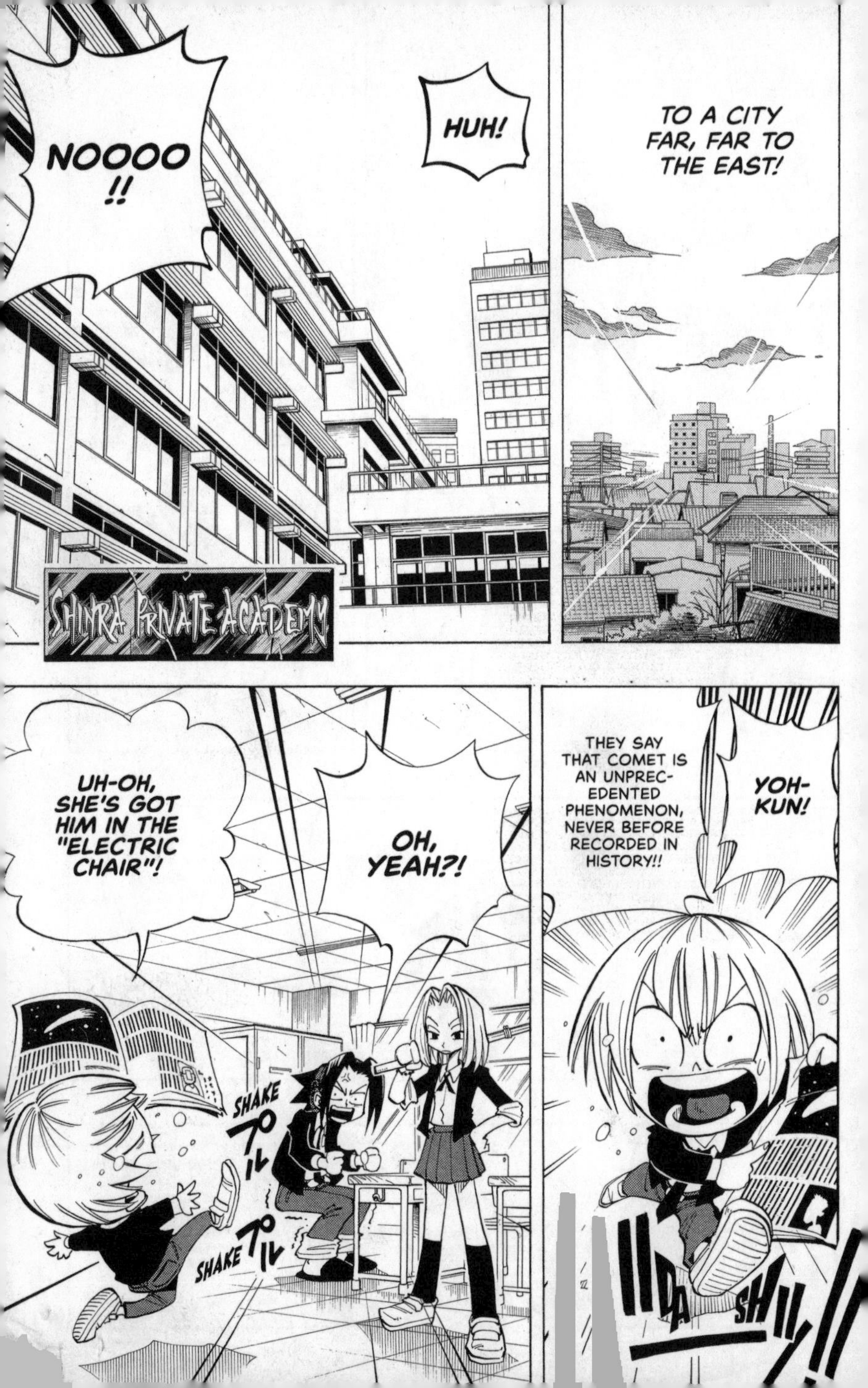
TO A CITY FAR, FAR TO THE EAST!
HUH!
NOOOO!!
SHINRA PRIVATE ACADEMY
YOH-KUN!
THEY SAY THAT COMET IS AN UNPREC-EDENTED PHENOMENON, NEVER BEFORE RECORDED IN HISTORY!!
DASH!!
OH, YEAH?!
UH-OH, SHE'S GOT HIM IN THE "ELECTRIC CHAIR"!
SHAKE プル
SHAKE プル

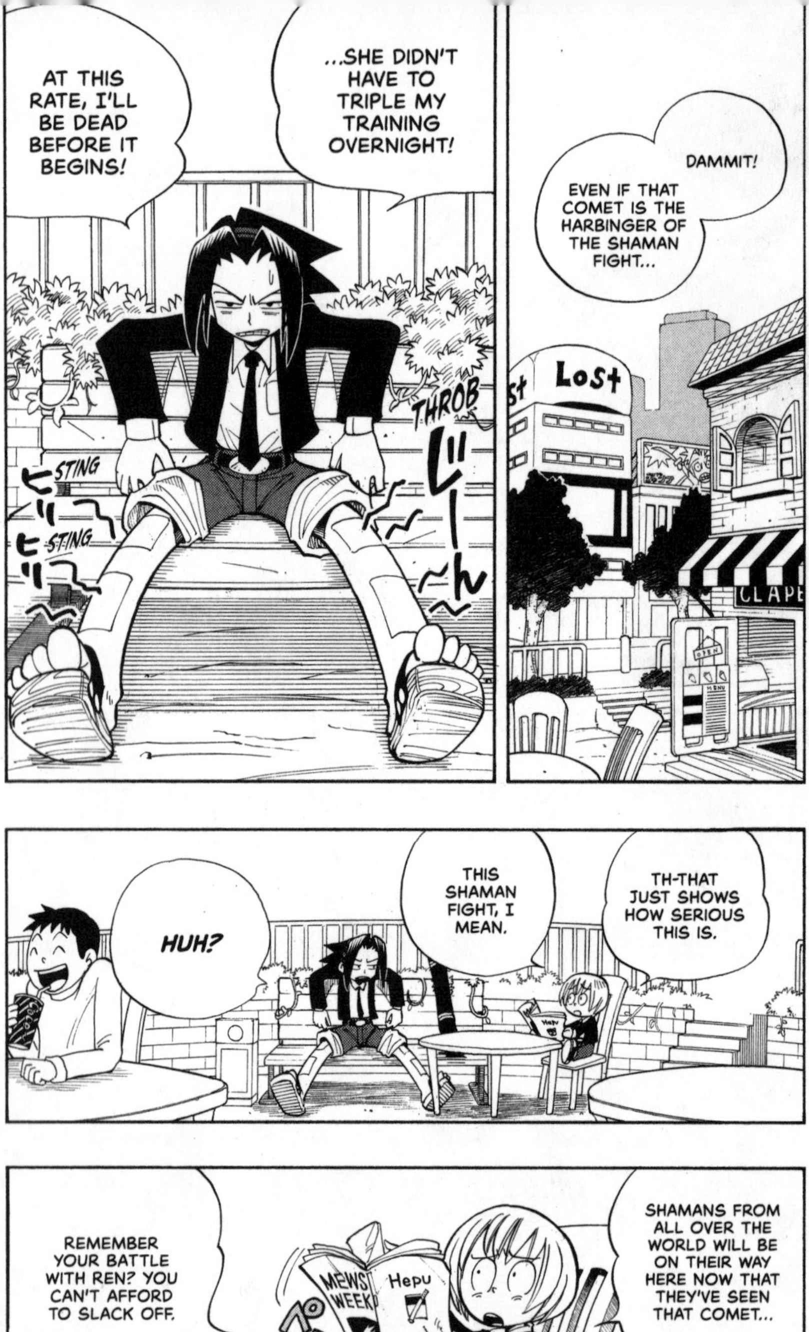
DAMMIT!
EVEN IF THAT COMET IS THE HARBINGER OF THE SHAMAN FIGHT...
Lost
CLAPE
...SHE DIDN'T HAVE TO TRIPLE MY TRAINING OVERNIGHT!
AT THIS RATE, I'LL BE DEAD BEFORE IT BEGINS!
THROB
ジーん
STING
ヒリ
STING
ヒリ
TH-THAT JUST SHOWS HOW SERIOUS THIS IS.
THIS SHAMAN FIGHT, I MEAN.
HUH?
SHAMANS FROM ALL OVER THE WORLD WILL BE ON THEIR WAY HERE NOW THAT THEY'VE SEEN THAT COMET...
Hepu
MEWS WEEK
ペら
FWIP
REMEMBER YOUR BATTLE WITH REN? YOU CAN'T AFFORD TO SLACK OFF.

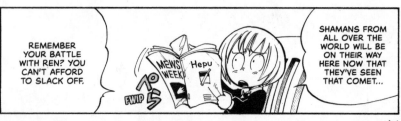

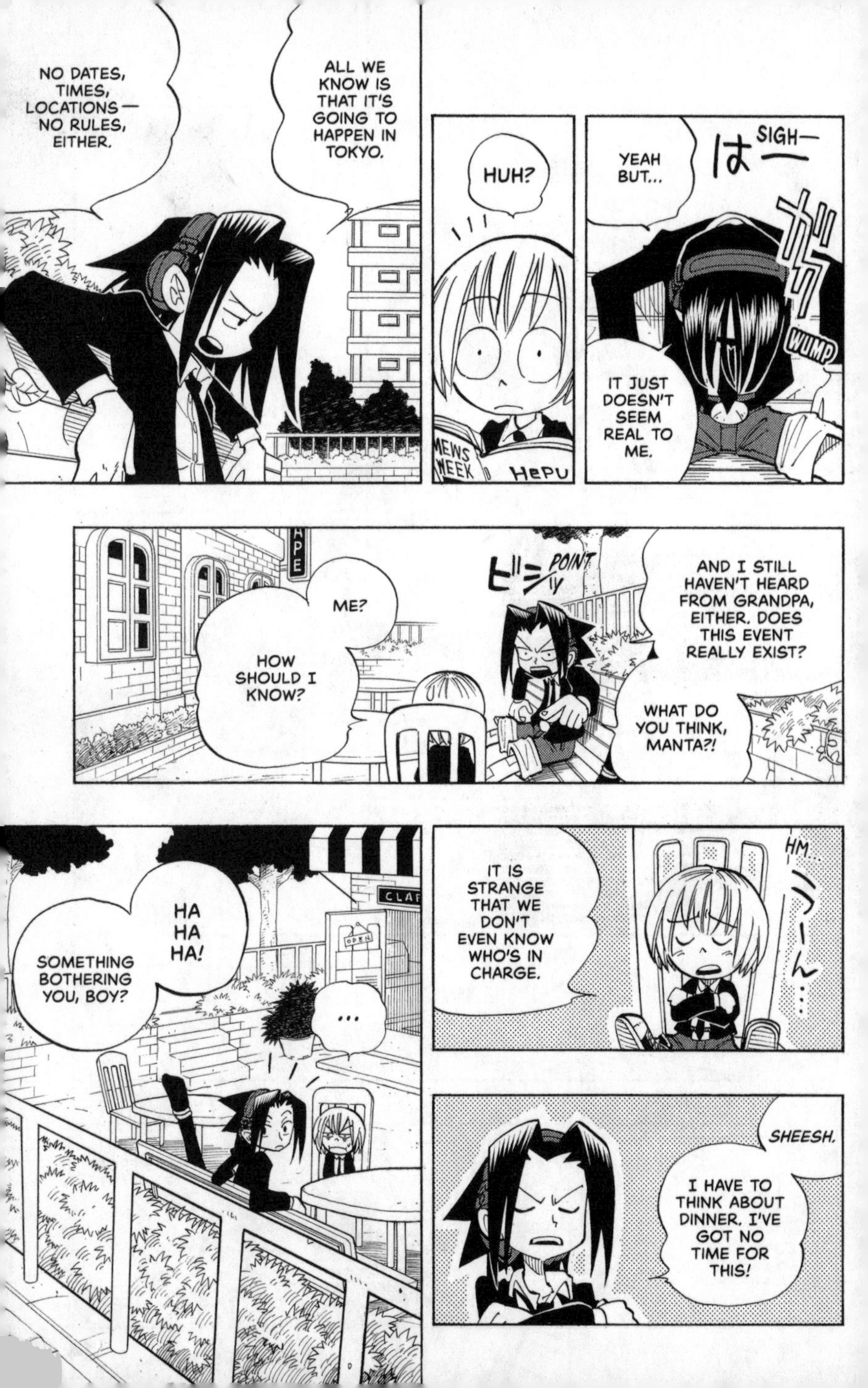
YEAH BUT...
SIGH—
は一
WUMP
IT JUST DOESN'T SEEM REAL TO ME.
HUH?
NEWS WEEK
HePU
ALL WE KNOW IS THAT IT'S GOING TO HAPPEN IN TOKYO.
NO DATES, TIMES, LOCATIONS— NO RULES, EITHER.
AND I STILL HAVEN'T HEARD FROM GRANDPA, EITHER. DOES THIS EVENT REALLY EXIST?
WHAT DO YOU THINK, MANTA?!
POINT
ME?
HOW SHOULD I KNOW?
HM...
IT IS STRANGE THAT WE DON'T EVEN KNOW WHO'S IN CHARGE.
SHEESH.
I HAVE TO THINK ABOUT DINNER. I'VE GOT NO TIME FOR THIS!
HA HA HA!
SOMETHING BOTHERING YOU, BOY?
...
OPEN

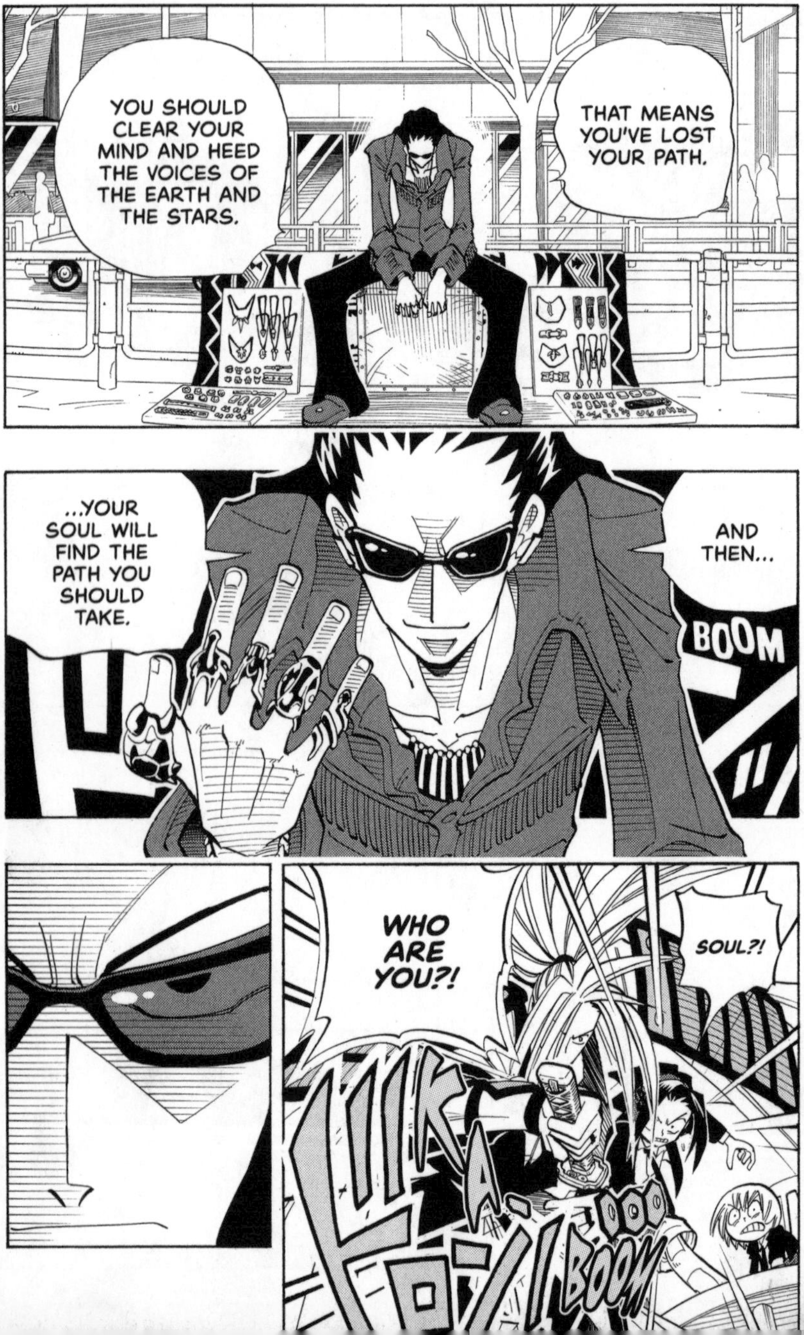
THAT MEANS YOU'VE LOST YOUR PATH.
YOU SHOULD CLEAR YOUR MIND AND HEED THE VOICES OF THE EARTH AND THE STARS.
AND THEN...
BOOM
...YOUR SOUL WILL FIND THE PATH YOU SHOULD TAKE.
SOUL?!
WHO ARE YOU?!
BOOM

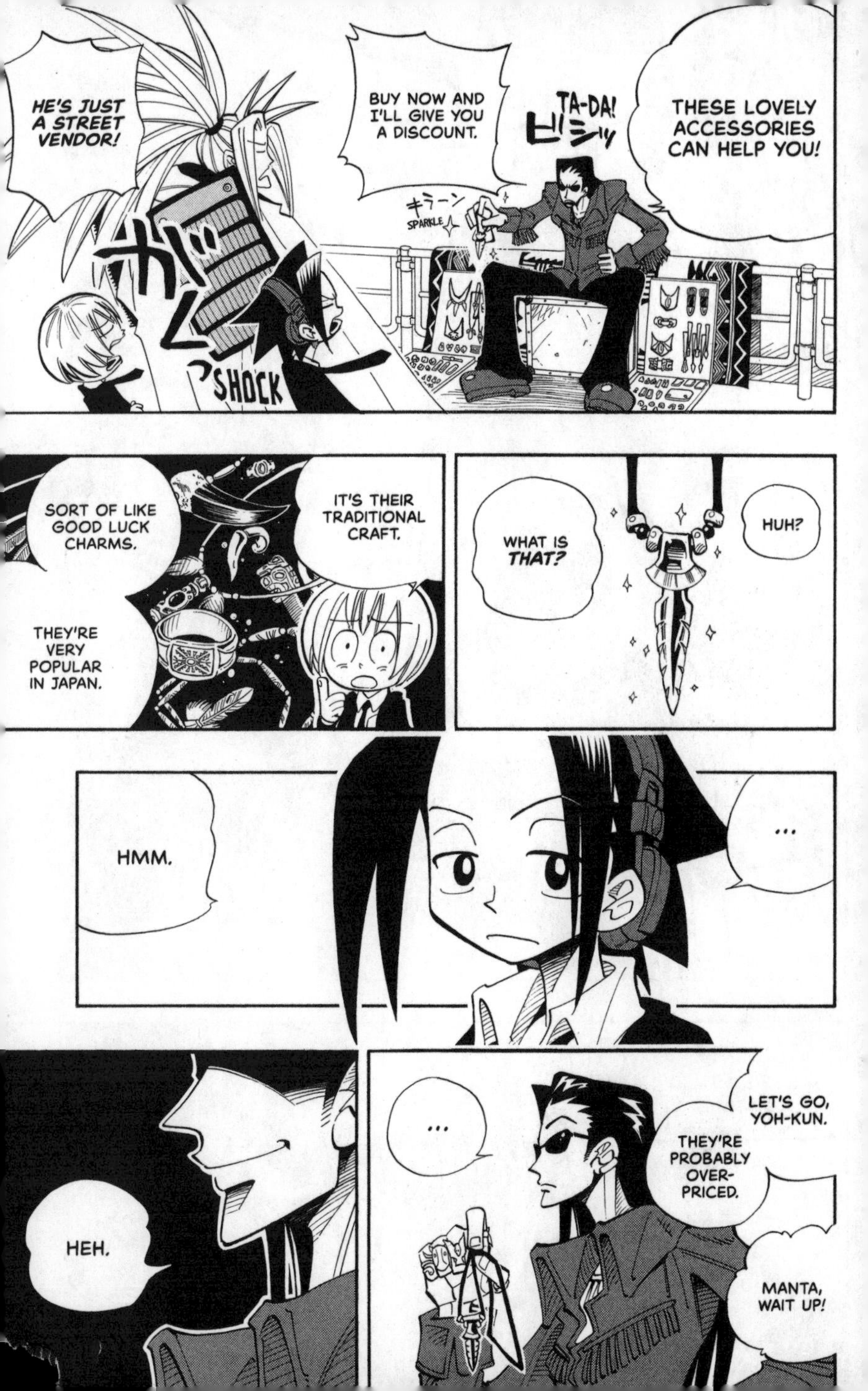
THESE LOVELY ACCESSORIES CAN HELP YOU!
TA-DA! ビシッ
BUY NOW AND I'LL GIVE YOU A DISCOUNT.
キラーン SPARKLE
HE'S JUST A STREET VENDOR!
SHOCK
HUH?
WHAT IS *THAT?*
IT'S THEIR TRADITIONAL CRAFT.
SORT OF LIKE GOOD LUCK CHARMS.
THEY'RE VERY POPULAR IN JAPAN.
...
HMM.
LET'S GO, YOH-KUN.
THEY'RE PROBABLY OVER-PRICED.
...
MANTA, WAIT UP!
HEH.

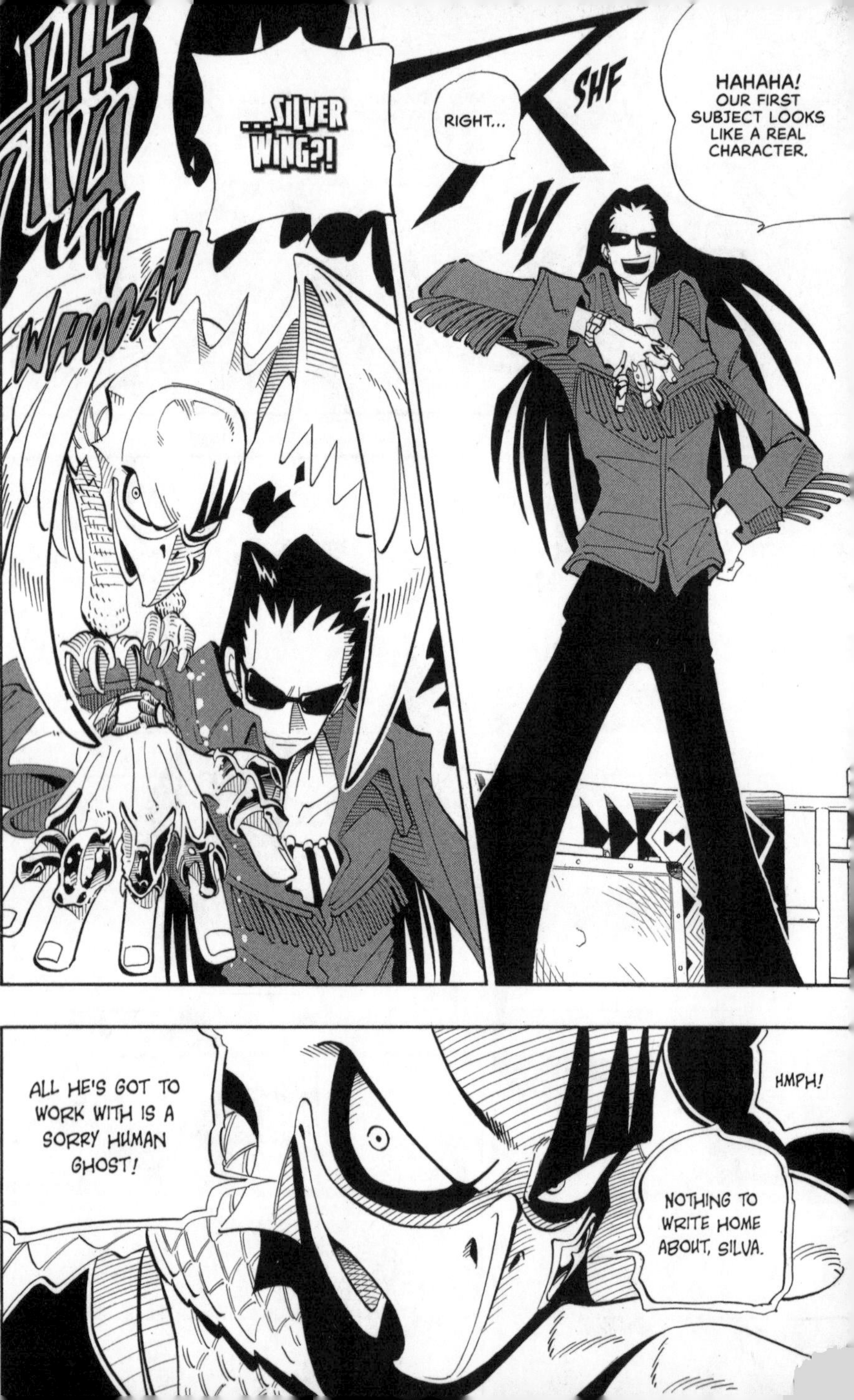
HAHAHA! OUR FIRST SUBJECT LOOKS LIKE A REAL CHARACTER.
SHF
RIGHT...
...SILVER WING?!
WHOOSH
HMPH!
NOTHING TO WRITE HOME ABOUT, SILVA.
ALL HE'S GOT TO WORK WITH IS A SORRY HUMAN GHOST!

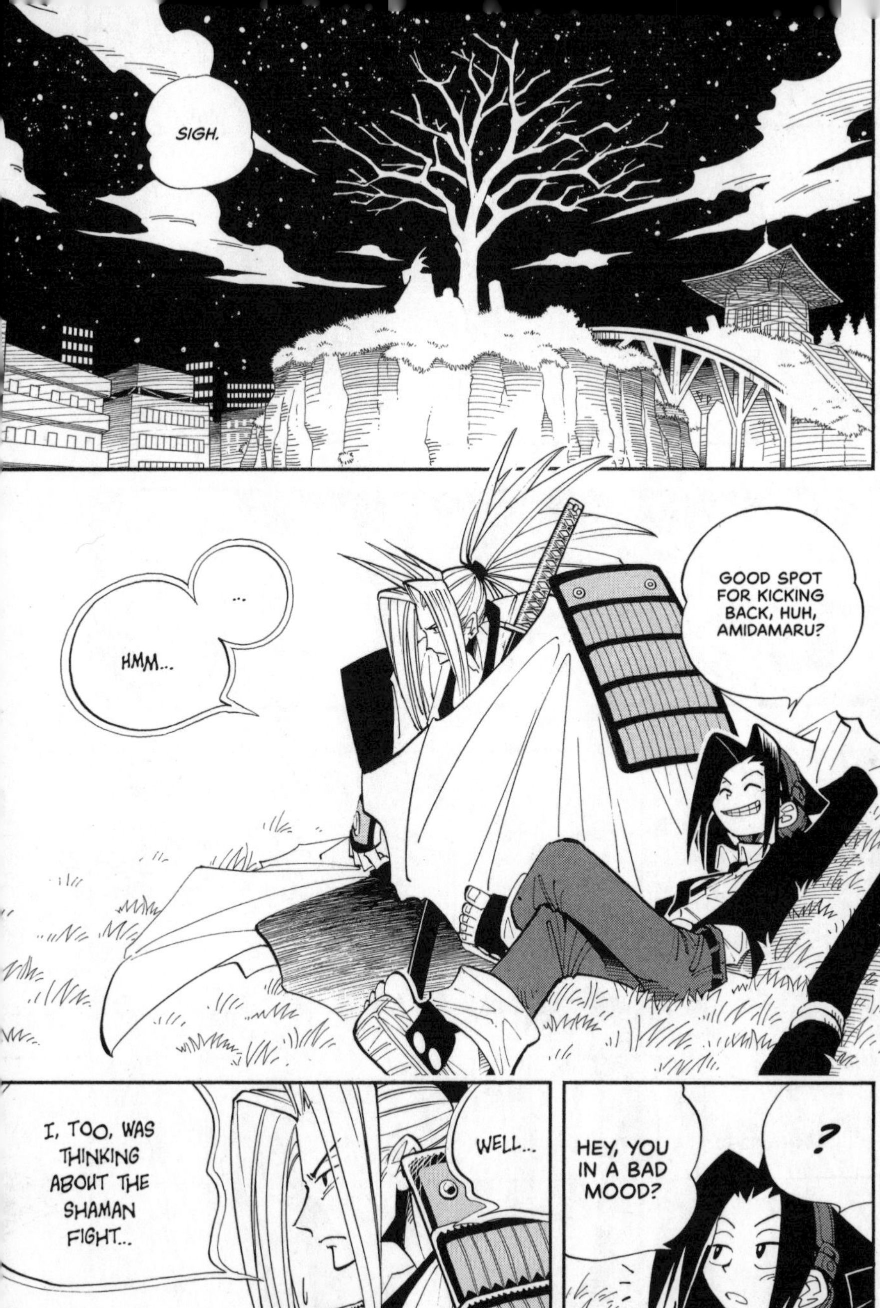

SIGH.
GOOD SPOT FOR KICKING BACK, HUH, AMIDAMARU?
...
HMM...
?
HEY, YOU IN A BAD MOOD?
WELL...
I, TOO, WAS THINKING ABOUT THE SHAMAN FIGHT...

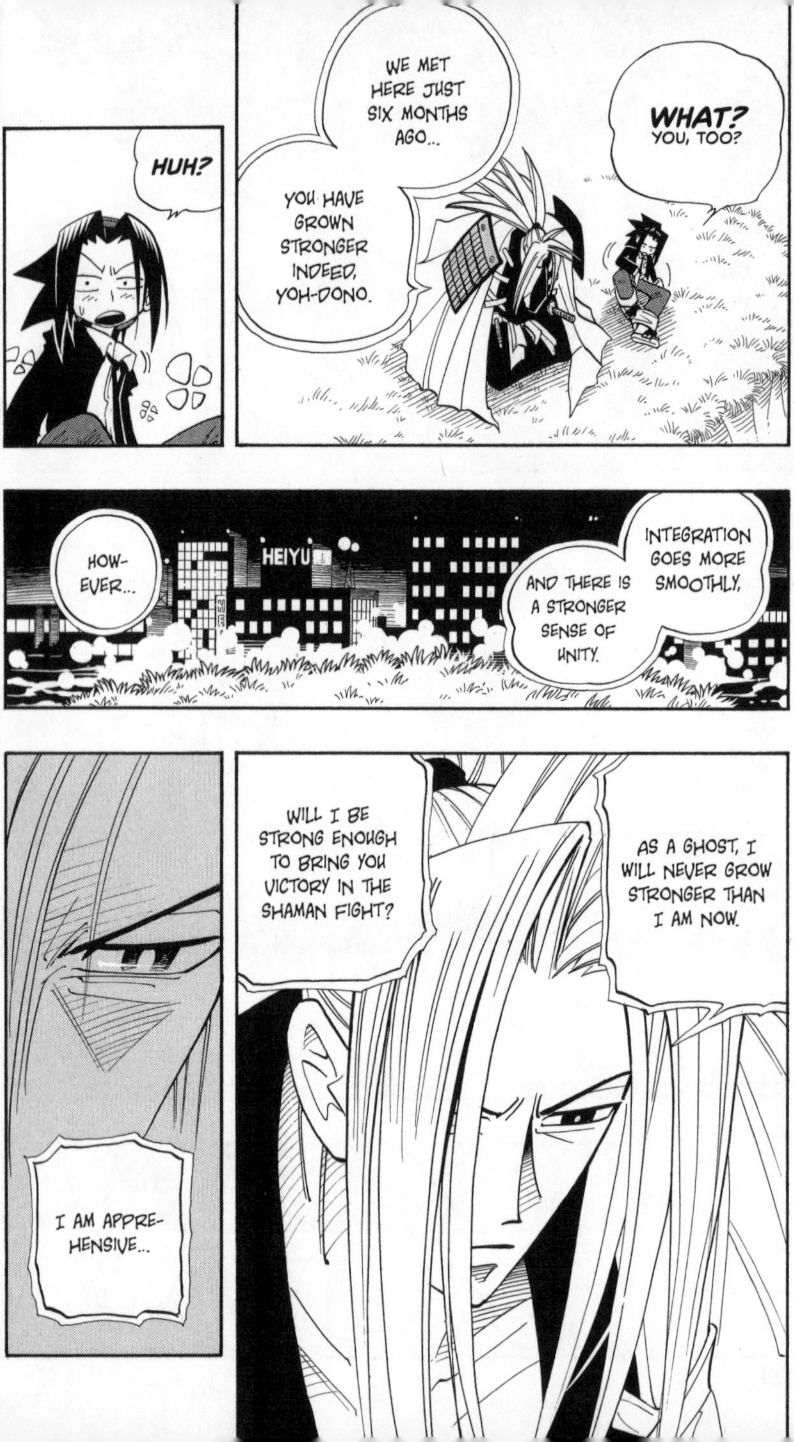
WHAT? YOU, TOO?
WE MET HERE JUST SIX MONTHS AGO...
YOU HAVE GROWN STRONGER INDEED, YOH-DONO.
HUH?
INTEGRATION GOES MORE SMOOTHLY,
AND THERE IS A STRONGER SENSE OF UNITY.
HEIYU
HOW-EVER...
AS A GHOST, I WILL NEVER GROW STRONGER THAN I AM NOW.
WILL I BE STRONG ENOUGH TO BRING YOU VICTORY IN THE SHAMAN FIGHT?
I AM APPRE-HENSIVE...

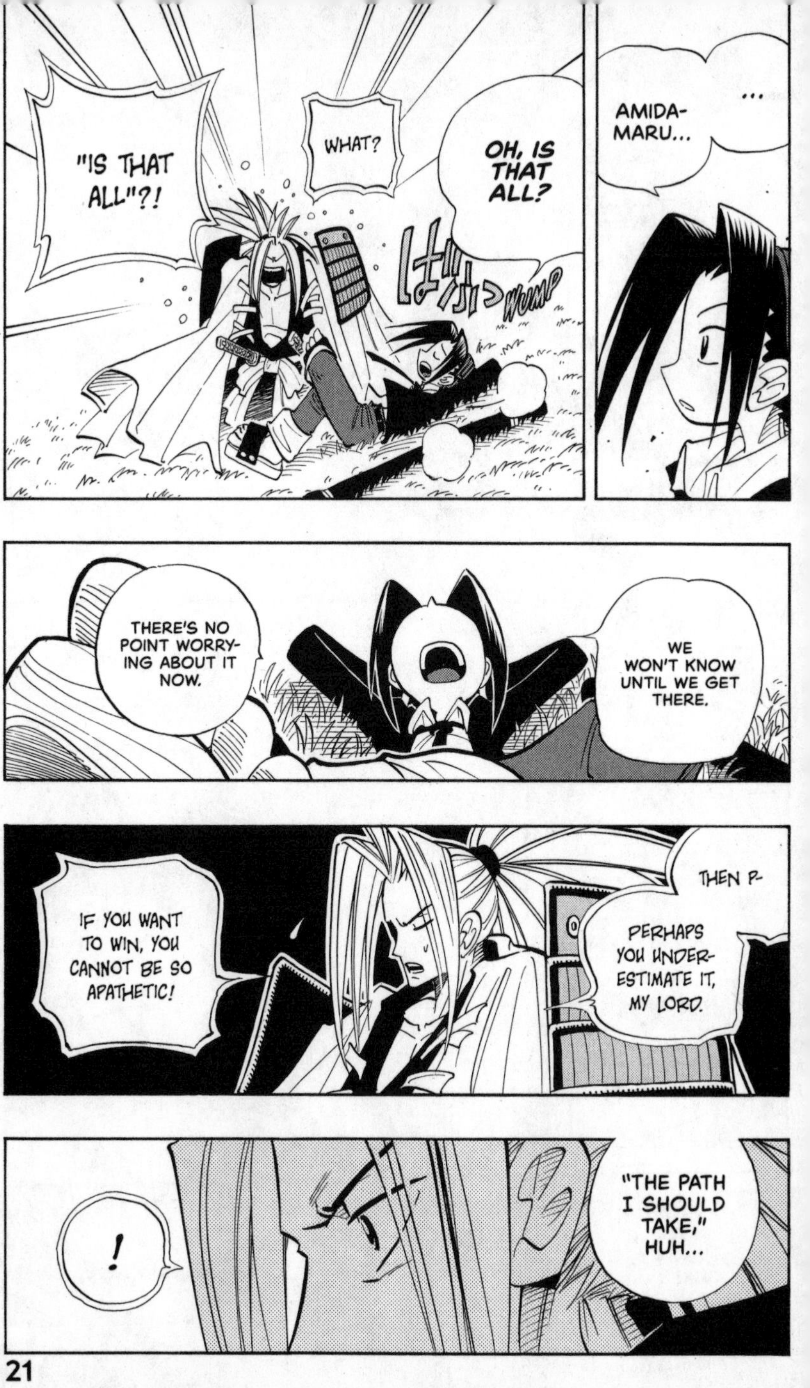
...
AMIDA-MARU...
OH, IS THAT ALL?
WHAT?
"IS THAT ALL"?!
WUMP
WE WON'T KNOW UNTIL WE GET THERE.
THERE'S NO POINT WORRYING ABOUT IT NOW.
THEN P-
PERHAPS YOU UNDERESTIMATE IT, MY LORD.
IF YOU WANT TO WIN, YOU CANNOT BE SO APATHETIC!
"THE PATH I SHOULD TAKE," HUH...
!

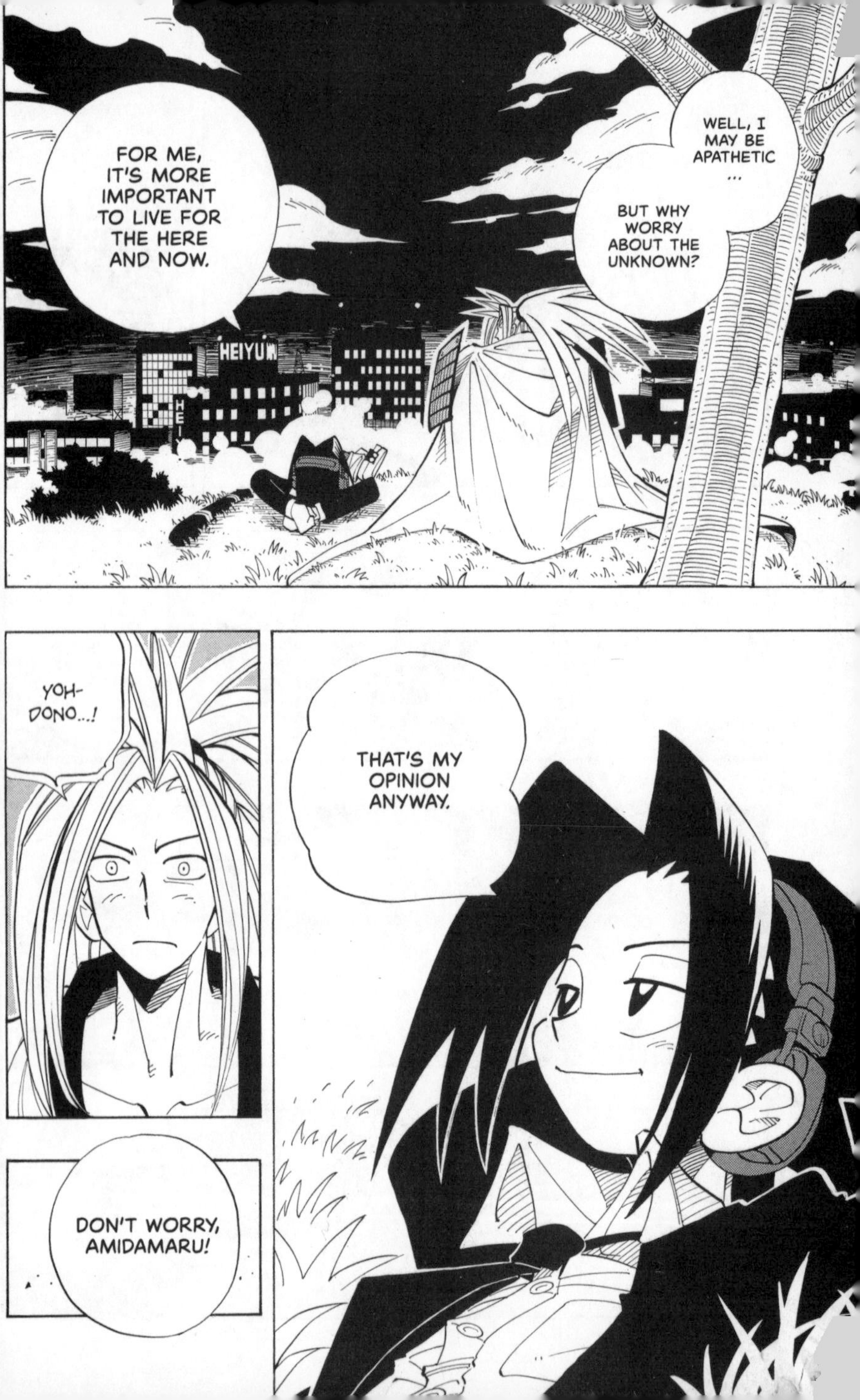
WELL, I MAY BE APATHETIC ...
BUT WHY WORRY ABOUT THE UNKNOWN?
FOR ME, IT'S MORE IMPORTANT TO LIVE FOR THE HERE AND NOW.
THAT'S MY OPINION ANYWAY.
YOH-DONO...!
DON'T WORRY, AMIDAMARU!

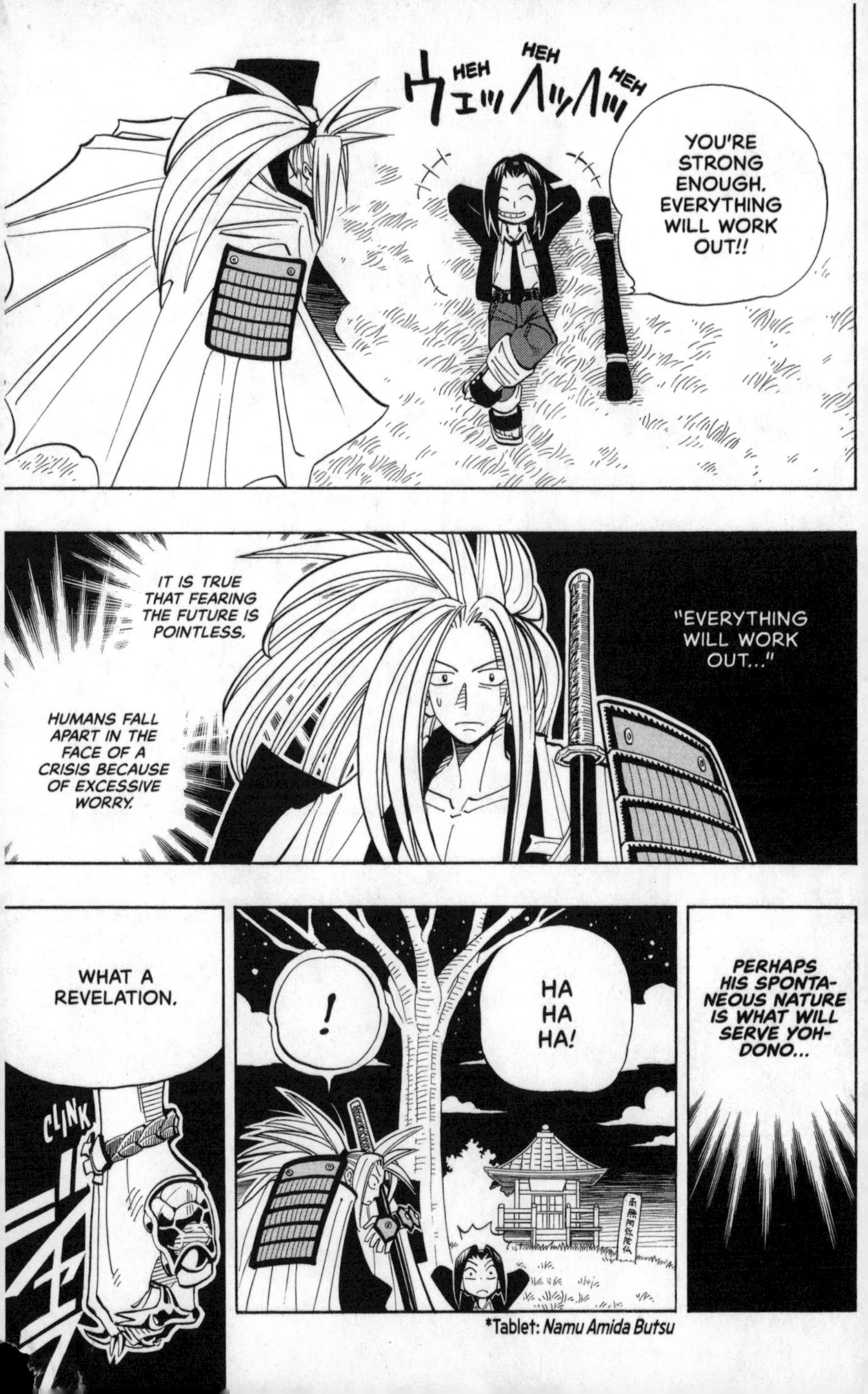
ウェッヘッヘッ
HEH HEH HEH
YOU'RE STRONG ENOUGH. EVERYTHING WILL WORK OUT!!
"EVERYTHING WILL WORK OUT..."
IT IS TRUE THAT FEARING THE FUTURE IS POINTLESS.
HUMANS FALL APART IN THE FACE OF A CRISIS BECAUSE OF EXCESSIVE WORRY.
PERHAPS HIS SPONTANEOUS NATURE IS WHAT WILL SERVE YOH-DONO...
HA HA HA!
!
WHAT A REVELATION.
CLINK
*Tablet: Namu Amida Butsu

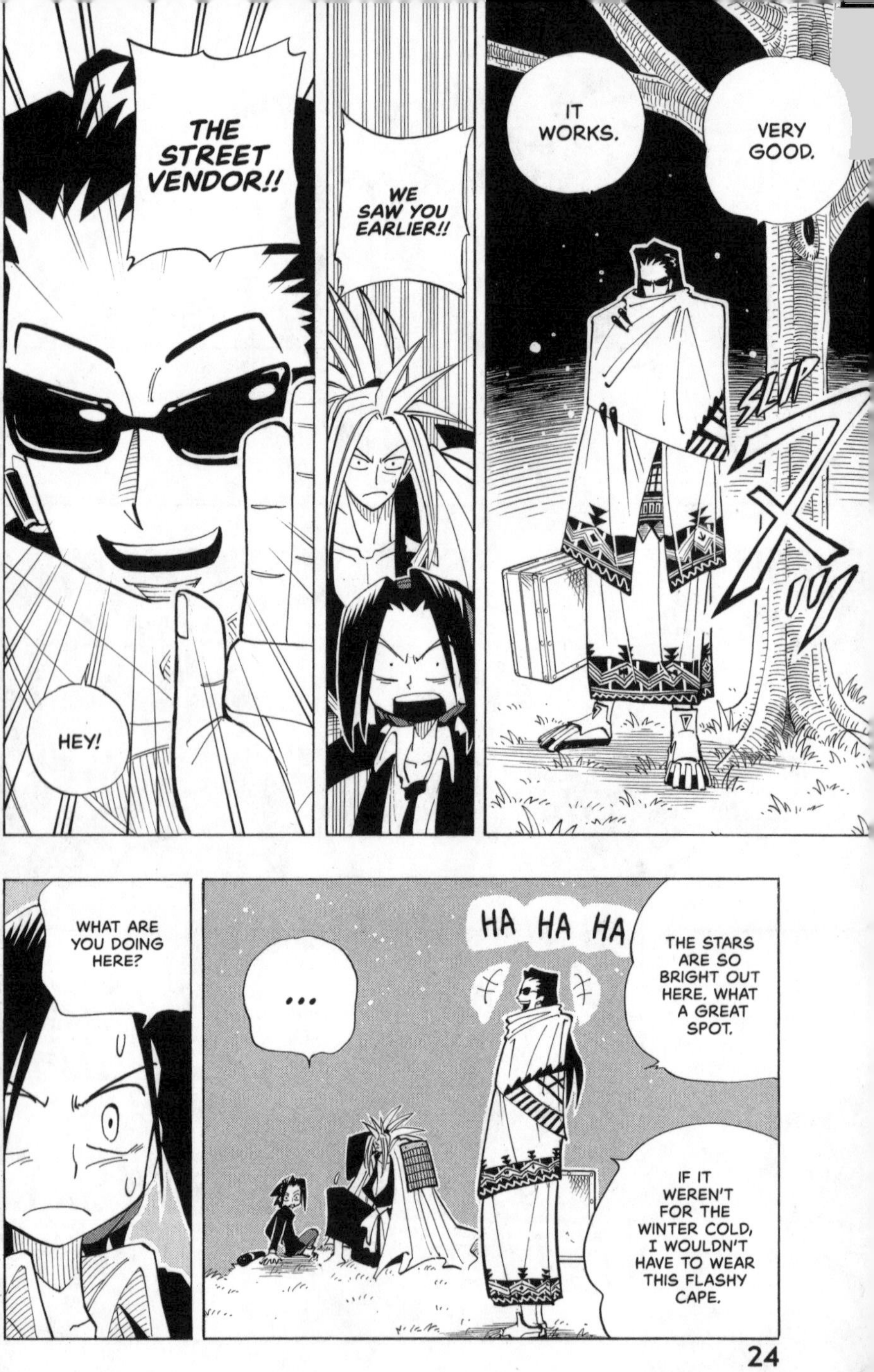
VERY GOOD.
IT WORKS.
SLIP
WE SAW YOU EARLIER!!
THE STREET VENDOR!!
HEY!
THE STARS ARE SO BRIGHT OUT HERE. WHAT A GREAT SPOT.
HA HA HA
...
IF IT WEREN'T FOR THE WINTER COLD, I WOULDN'T HAVE TO WEAR THIS FLASHY CAPE.
WHAT ARE YOU DOING HERE?

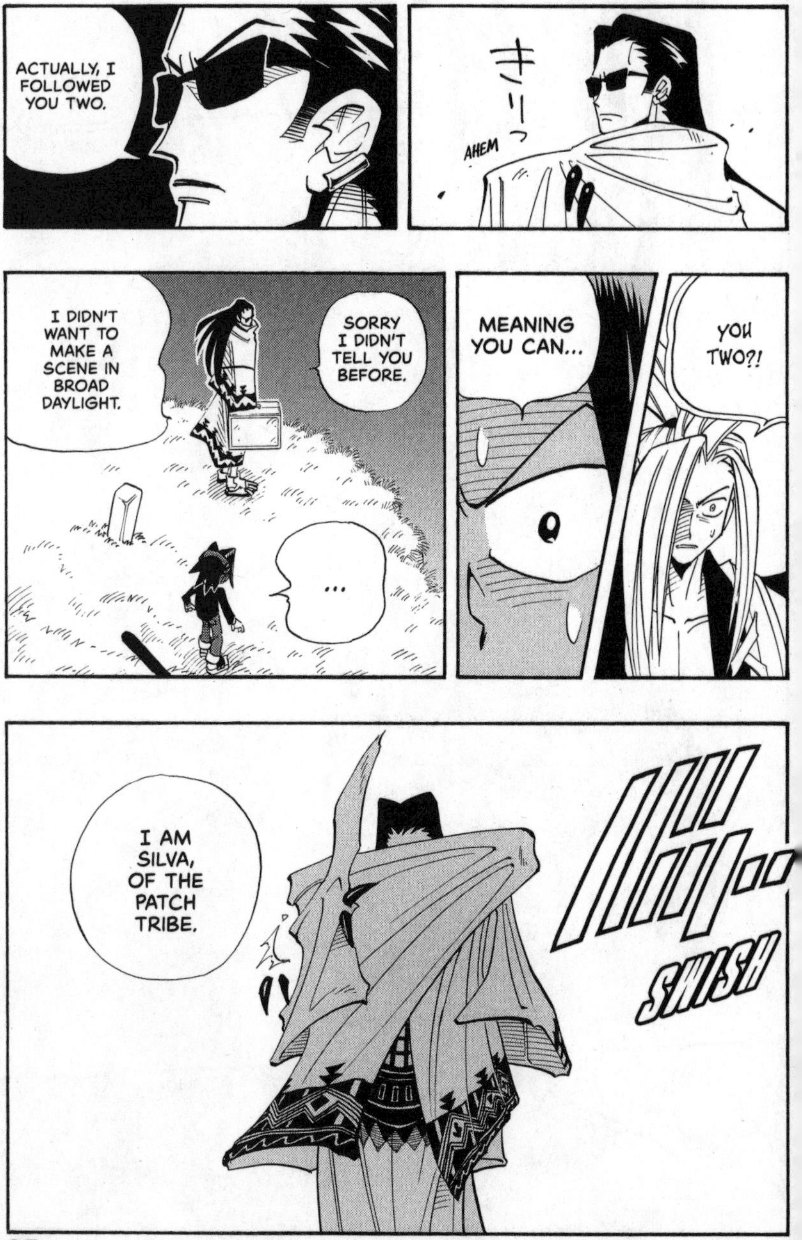
きりっ
AHEM
ACTUALLY, I FOLLOWED YOU TWO.
YOU TWO?!
MEANING YOU CAN...
SORRY I DIDN'T TELL YOU BEFORE.
I DIDN'T WANT TO MAKE A SCENE IN BROAD DAYLIGHT.
...
SWISH
I AM SILVA, OF THE PATCH TRIBE.

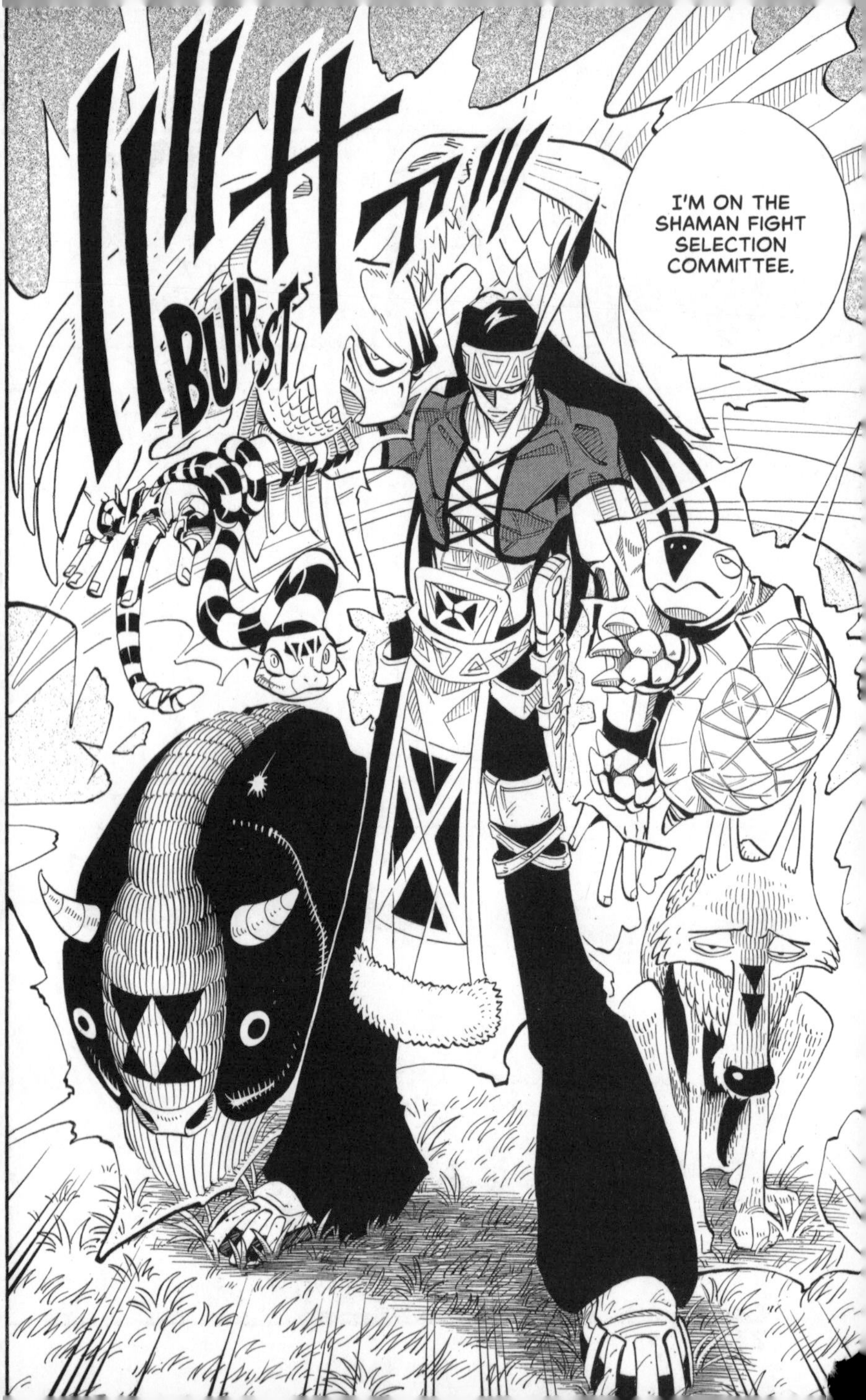
I'M ON THE SHAMAN FIGHT SELECTION COMMITTEE.
BURST

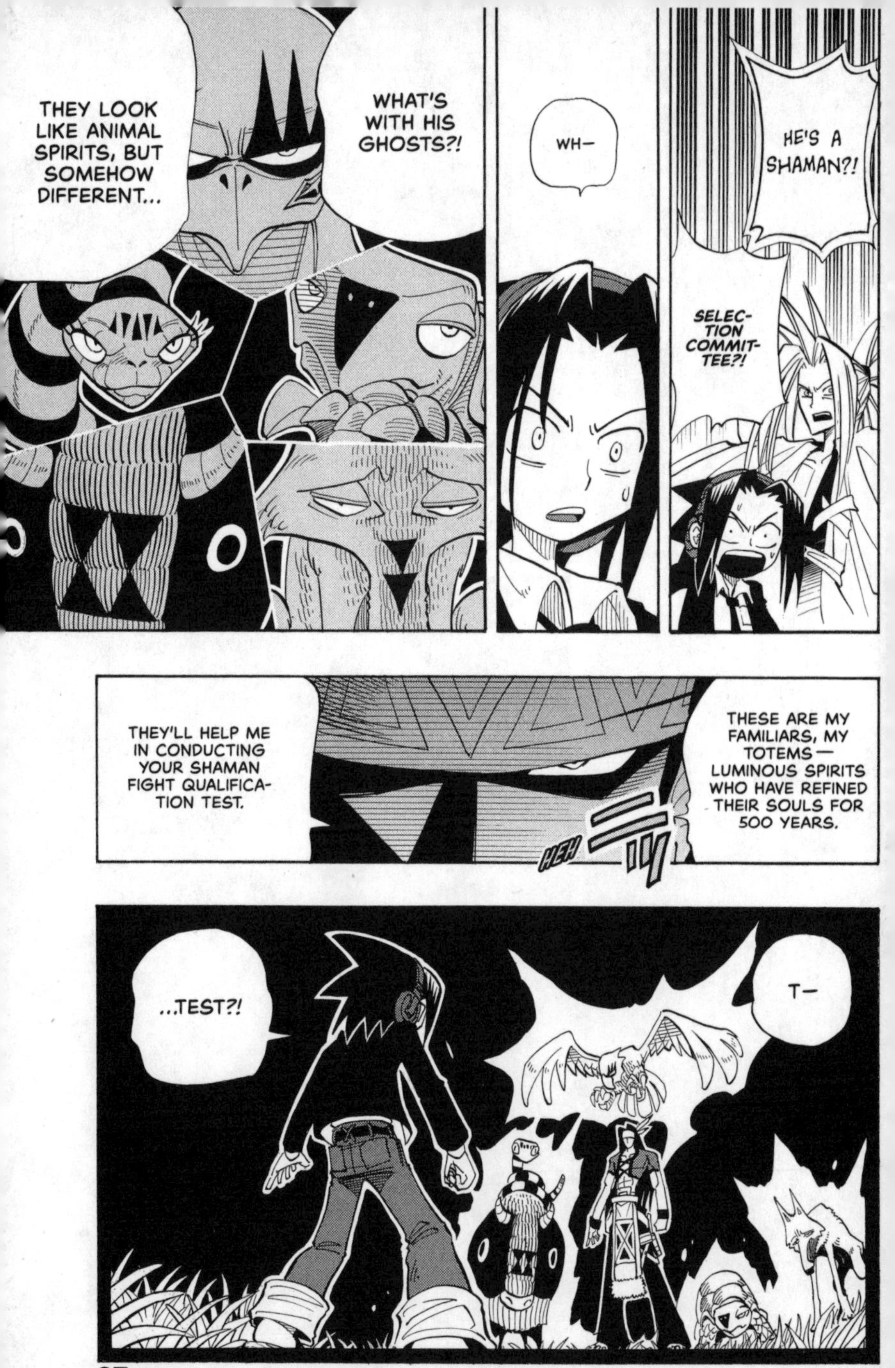

HE'S A SHAMAN?!
SELECTION COMMITTEE?!
WH—
WHAT'S WITH HIS GHOSTS?!
THEY LOOK LIKE ANIMAL SPIRITS, BUT SOMEHOW DIFFERENT...
THESE ARE MY FAMILIARS, MY TOTEMS— LUMINOUS SPIRITS WHO HAVE REFINED THEIR SOULS FOR 500 YEARS.
HEH
THEY'LL HELP ME IN CONDUCTING YOUR SHAMAN FIGHT QUALIFICATION TEST.
T—
...TEST?!

SHAMAN
KING
4

Rahu

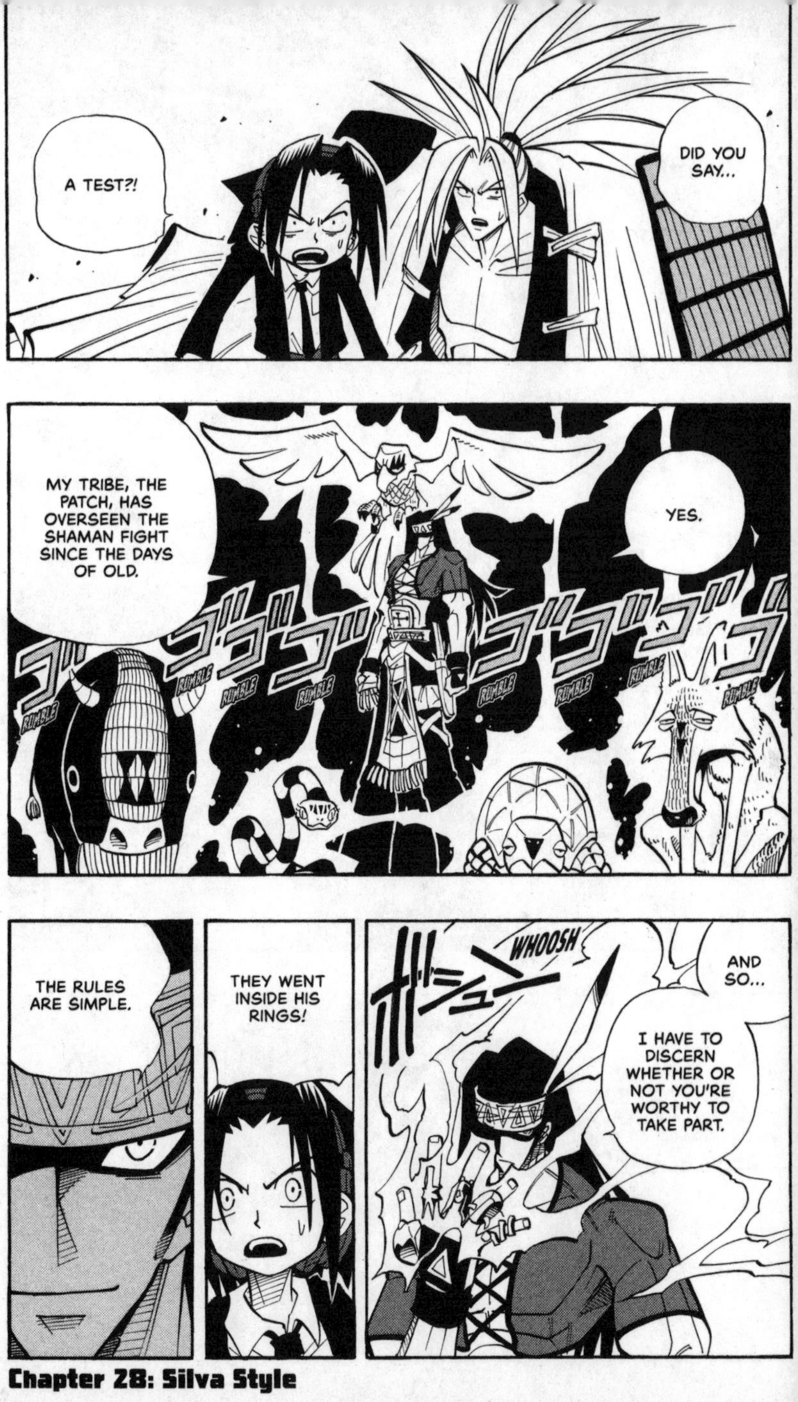
DID YOU SAY...
A TEST?!
YES.
MY TRIBE, THE PATCH, HAS OVERSEEN THE SHAMAN FIGHT SINCE THE DAYS OF OLD.
RUMBLE RUMBLE RUMBLE RUMBLE RUMBLE RUMBLE RUMBLE RUMBLE
WHOOSH
AND SO...
I HAVE TO DISCERN WHETHER OR NOT YOU'RE WORTHY TO TAKE PART.
THEY WENT INSIDE HIS RINGS!
THE RULES ARE SIMPLE.

Chapter 28: Silva Style

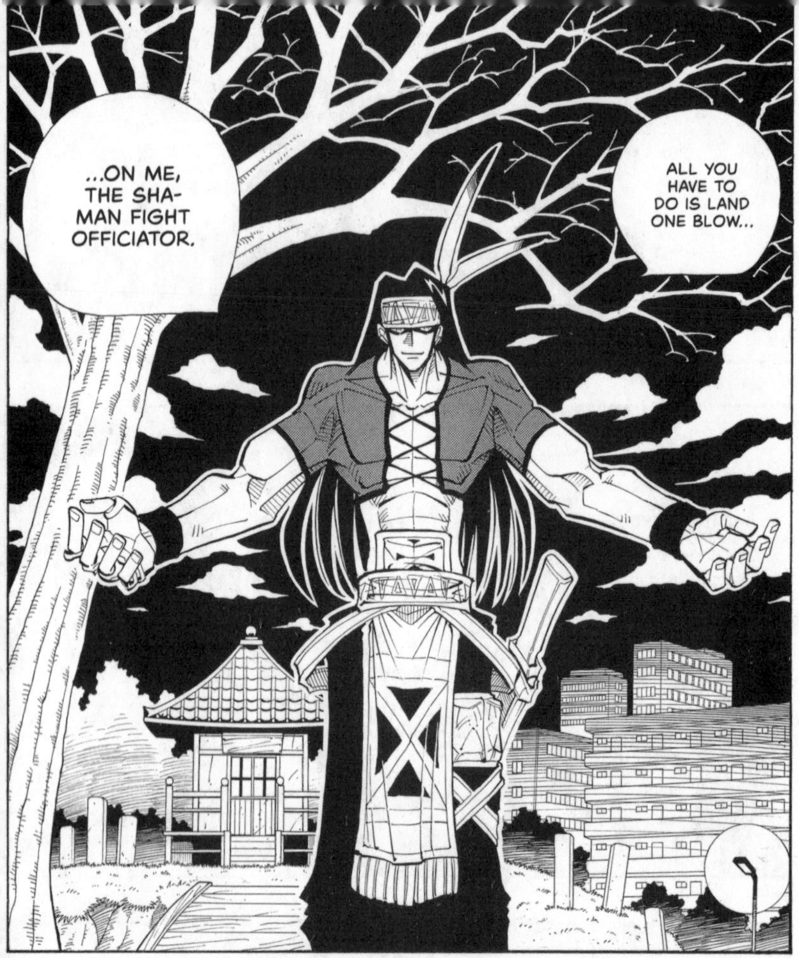
ALL YOU HAVE TO DO IS LAND ONE BLOW...
...ON ME, THE SHA-MAN FIGHT OFFICIATOR.

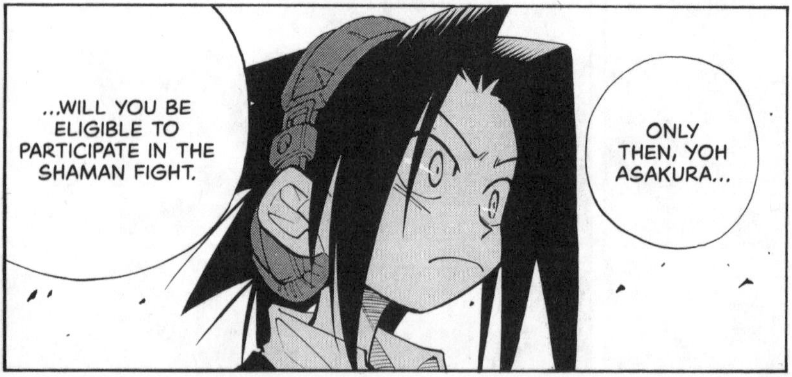
ONLY THEN, YOH ASAKURA...
...WILL YOU BE ELIGIBLE TO PARTICIPATE IN THE SHAMAN FIGHT.

Chapter 28:

Silva Style

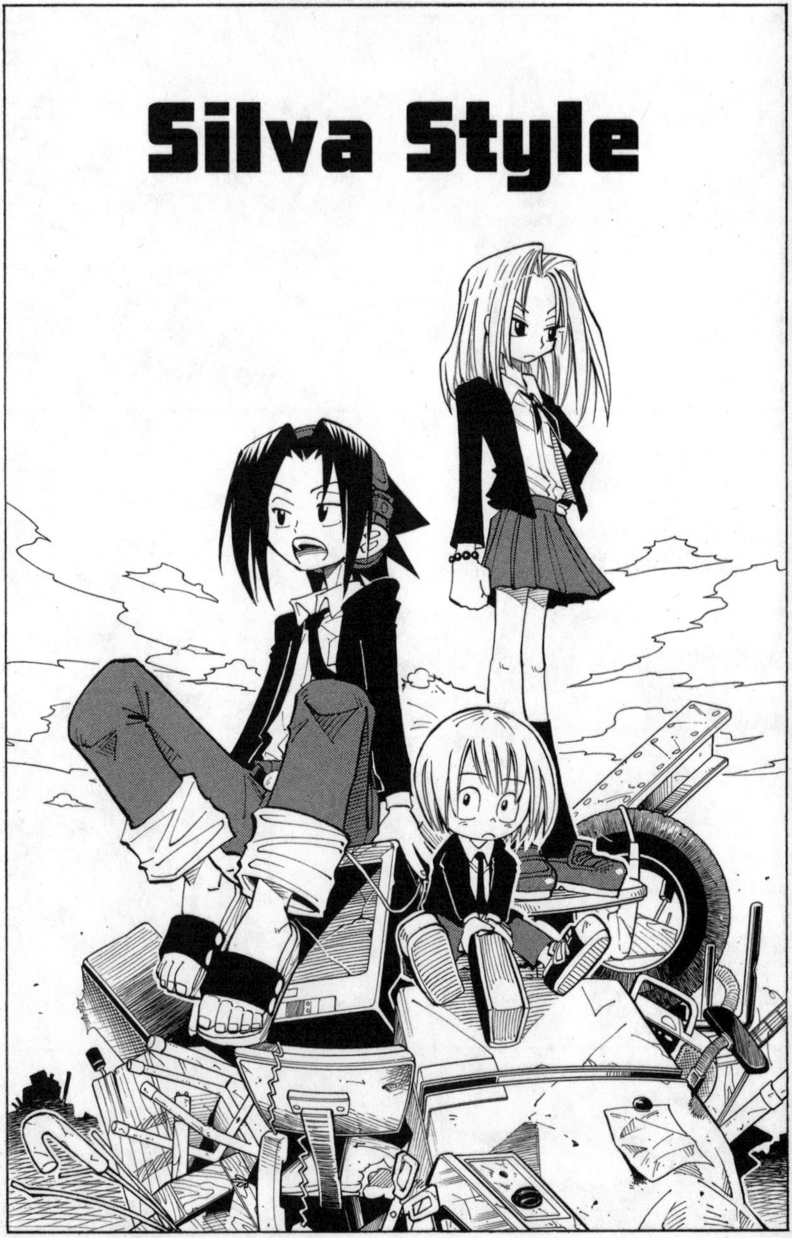

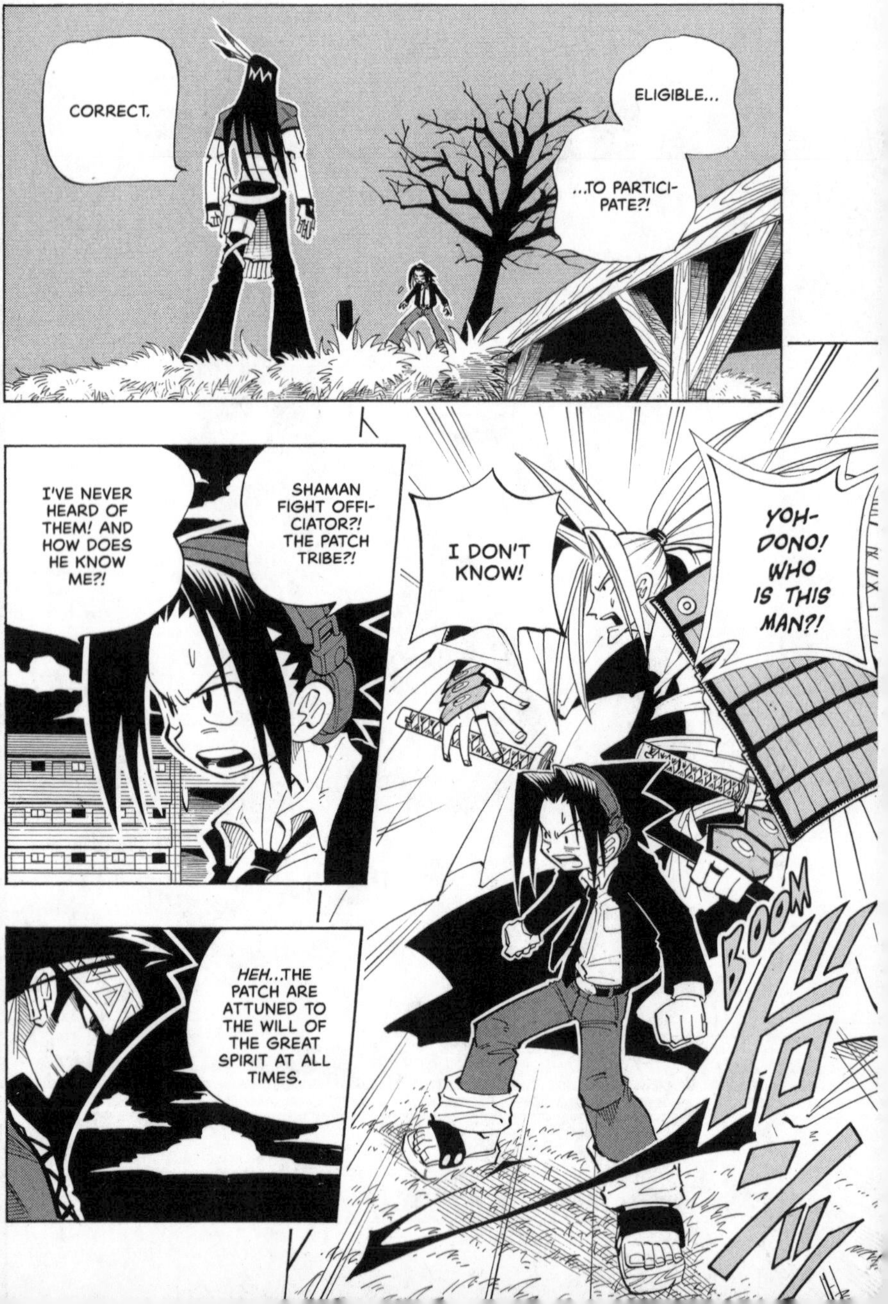
ELIGIBLE...
...TO PARTICIPATE?!
CORRECT.
YOH-DONO! WHO IS THIS MAN?!
I DON'T KNOW!
BOOM
SHAMAN FIGHT OFFICIATOR?! THE PATCH TRIBE?!
I'VE NEVER HEARD OF THEM! AND HOW DOES HE KNOW ME?!
HEH...THE PATCH ARE ATTUNED TO THE WILL OF THE GREAT SPIRIT AT ALL TIMES.

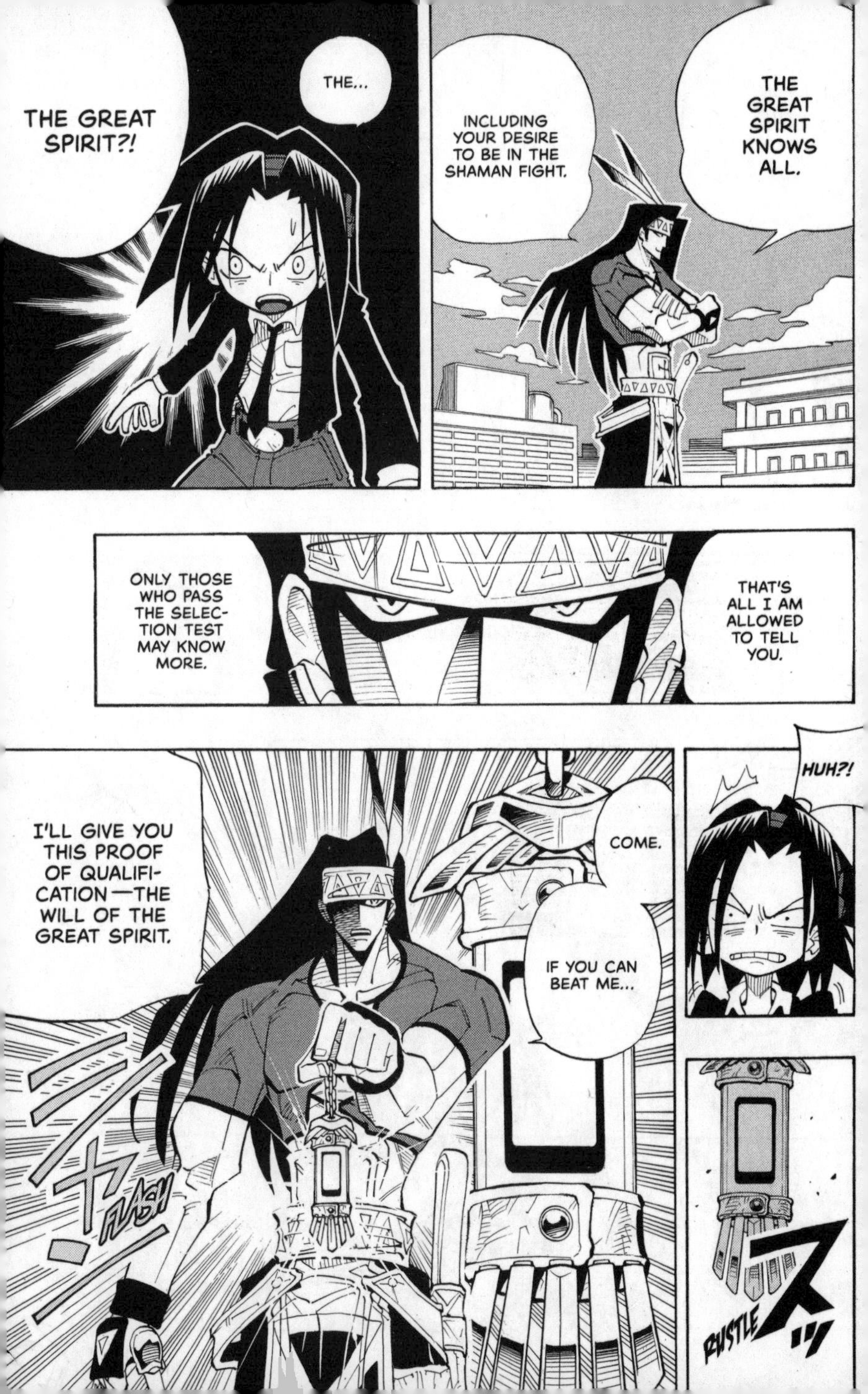
THE GREAT SPIRIT KNOWS ALL.
INCLUDING YOUR DESIRE TO BE IN THE SHAMAN FIGHT.
THE...
THE GREAT SPIRIT?!
THAT'S ALL I AM ALLOWED TO TELL YOU.
ONLY THOSE WHO PASS THE SELECTION TEST MAY KNOW MORE.
HUH?!
RUSTLE
COME.
IF YOU CAN BEAT ME...
I'LL GIVE YOU THIS PROOF OF QUALIFICATION—THE WILL OF THE GREAT SPIRIT.
FLASH

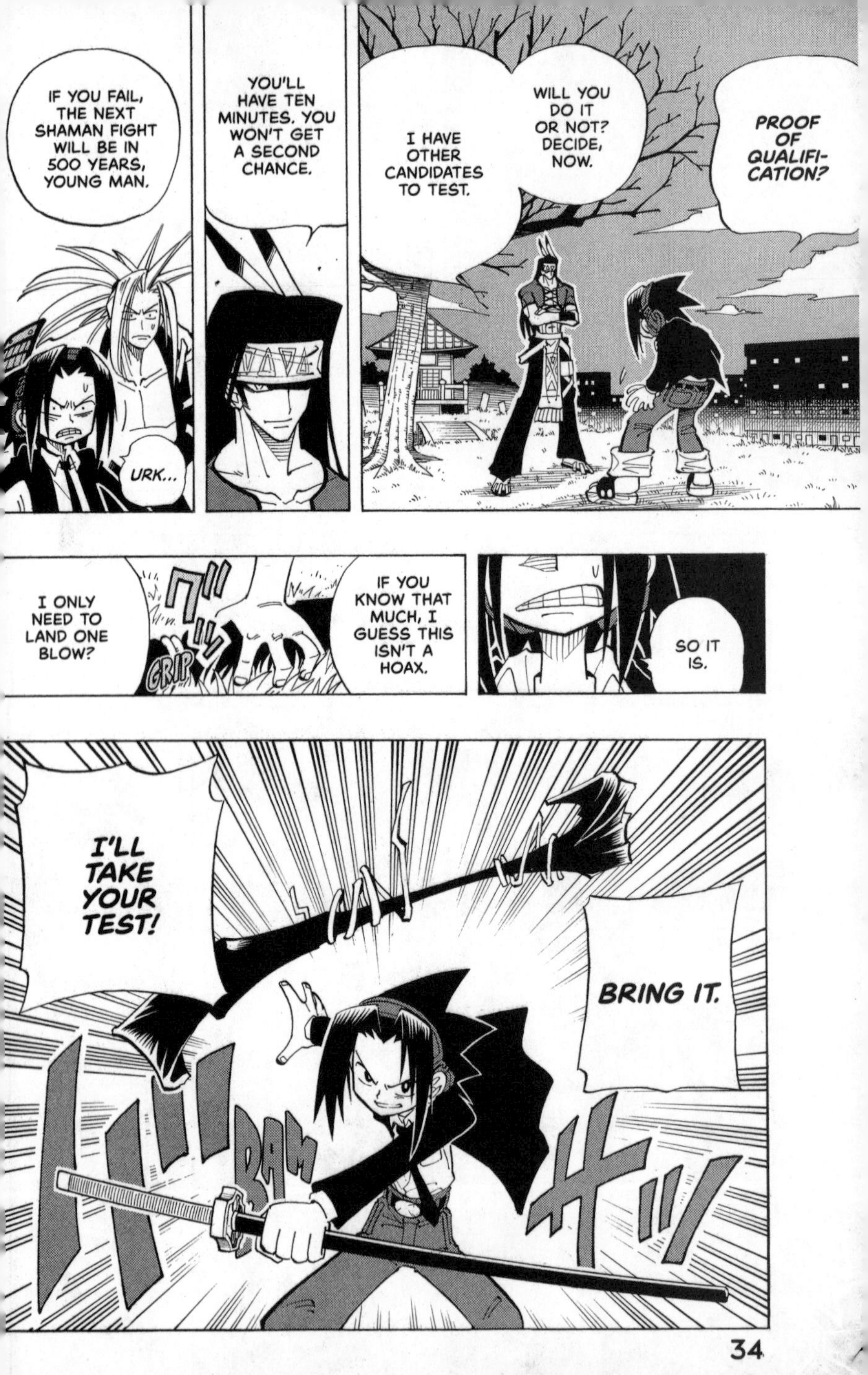
PROOF OF QUALIFICATION?
WILL YOU DO IT OR NOT? DECIDE, NOW.
I HAVE OTHER CANDIDATES TO TEST.
YOU'LL HAVE TEN MINUTES. YOU WON'T GET A SECOND CHANCE.
IF YOU FAIL, THE NEXT SHAMAN FIGHT WILL BE IN 500 YEARS, YOUNG MAN.
URK...
SO IT IS.
IF YOU KNOW THAT MUCH, I GUESS THIS ISN'T A HOAX.
GRIP
I ONLY NEED TO LAND ONE BLOW?
BRING IT.
I'LL TAKE YOUR TEST!
BAM

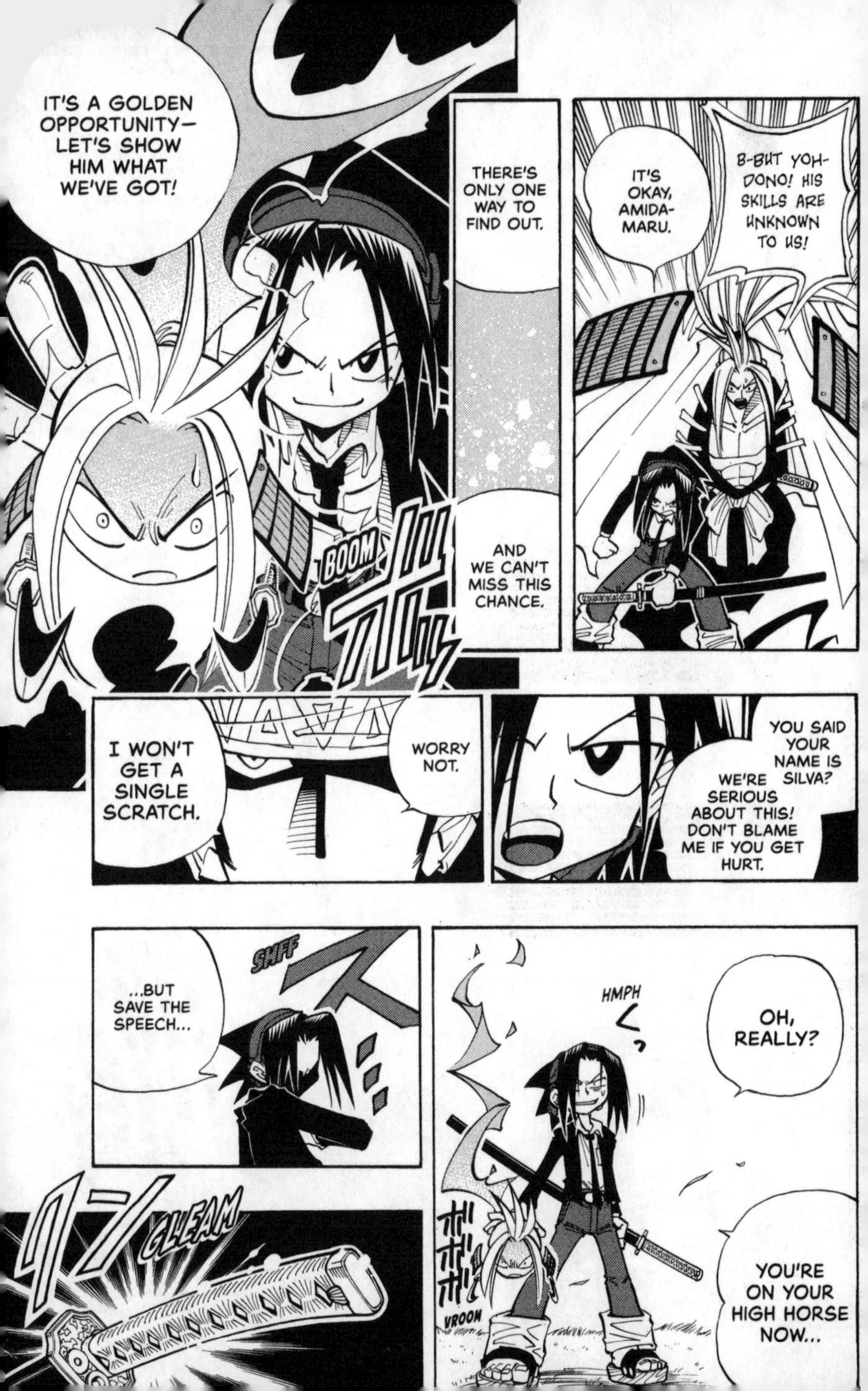
B-BUT YOH-DONO! HIS SKILLS ARE UNKNOWN TO US!
IT'S OKAY, AMIDA-MARU.
THERE'S ONLY ONE WAY TO FIND OUT.
AND WE CAN'T MISS THIS CHANCE.
IT'S A GOLDEN OPPORTUNITY—LET'S SHOW HIM WHAT WE'VE GOT!
BOOM
YOU SAID YOUR NAME IS SILVA?
WE'RE SERIOUS ABOUT THIS! DON'T BLAME ME IF YOU GET HURT.
WORRY NOT.
I WON'T GET A SINGLE SCRATCH.
OH, REALLY?
HMPH
YOU'RE ON YOUR HIGH HORSE NOW...
VROOM
SHFF
...BUT SAVE THE SPEECH...
GLEAM

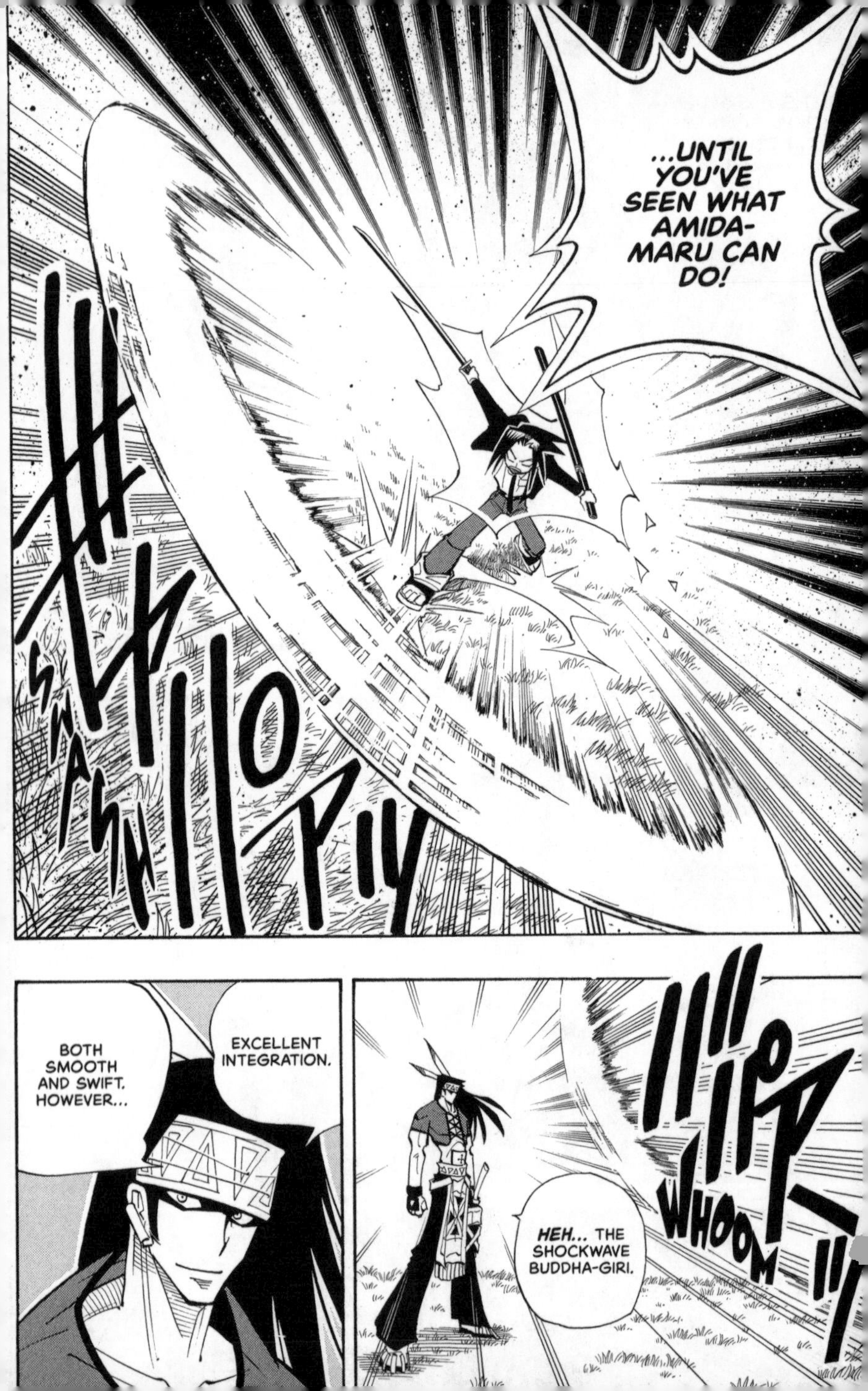
...UNTIL YOU'VE SEEN WHAT AMIDA-MARU CAN DO!
SWASH
WHOOM
HEH... THE SHOCKWAVE BUDDHA-GIRI.
EXCELLENT INTEGRATION.
BOTH SMOOTH AND SWIFT. HOWEVER...

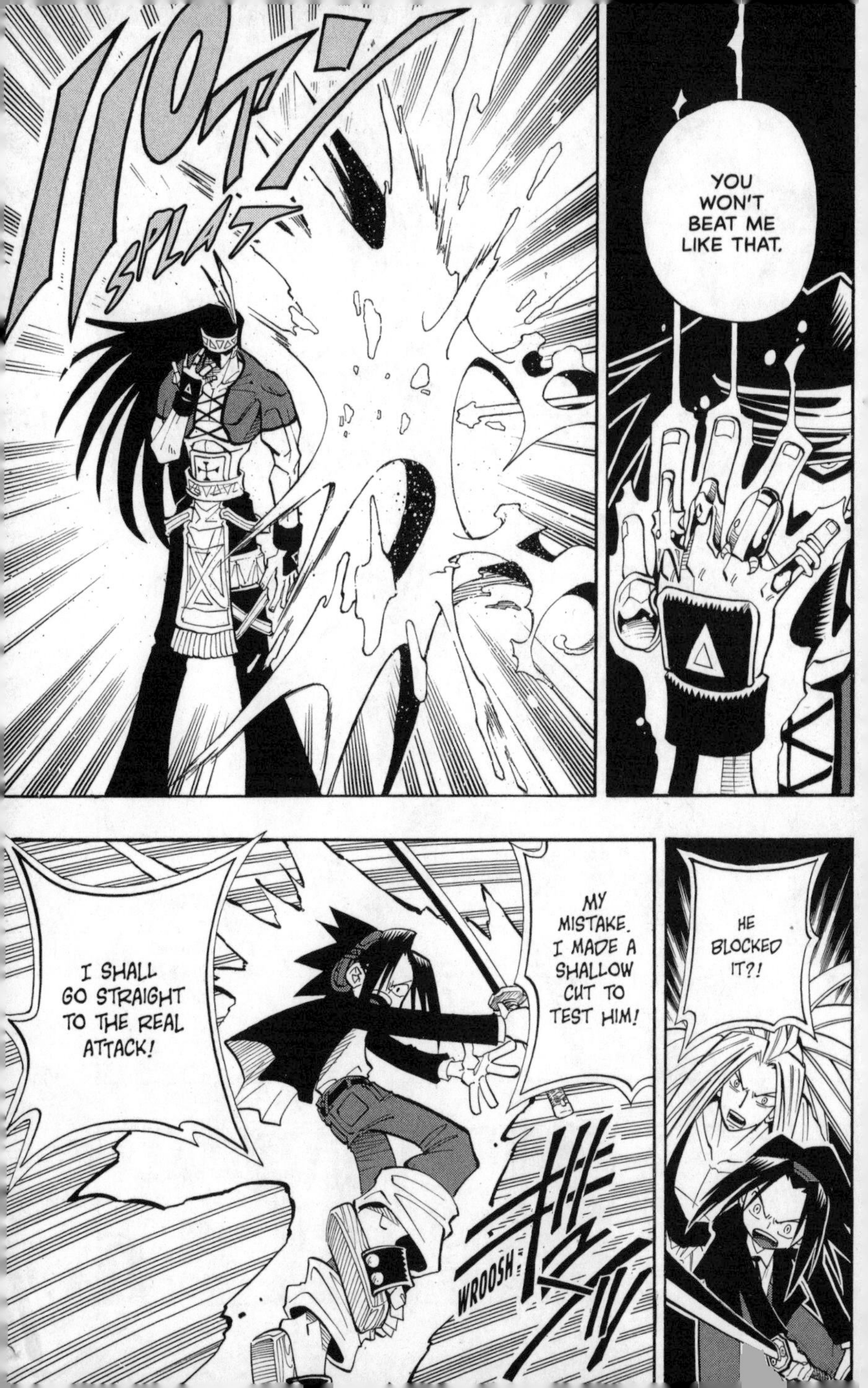
YOU WON'T BEAT ME LIKE THAT.
SPLAT
HE BLOCKED IT?!
MY MISTAKE. I MADE A SHALLOW CUT TO TEST HIM!
I SHALL GO STRAIGHT TO THE REAL ATTACK!
WROOSH

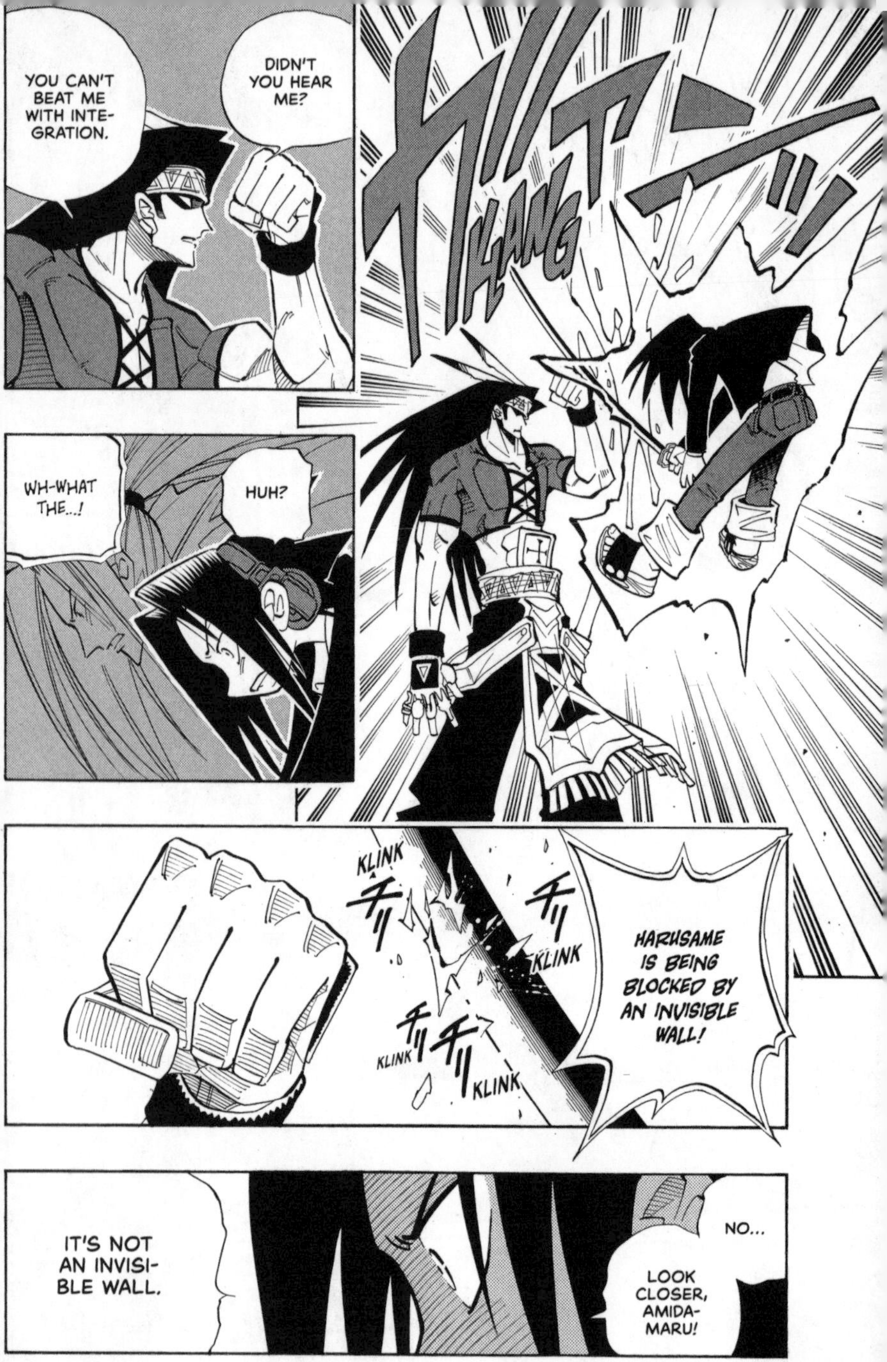
KHANG
DIDN'T YOU HEAR ME?
YOU CAN'T BEAT ME WITH INTE-GRATION.
HUH?
WH-WHAT THE...!
HARUSAME IS BEING BLOCKED BY AN INVISIBLE WALL!
KLINK
KLINK
KLINK
KLINK
NO...
LOOK CLOSER, AMIDA-MARU!
IT'S NOT AN INVISI-BLE WALL.

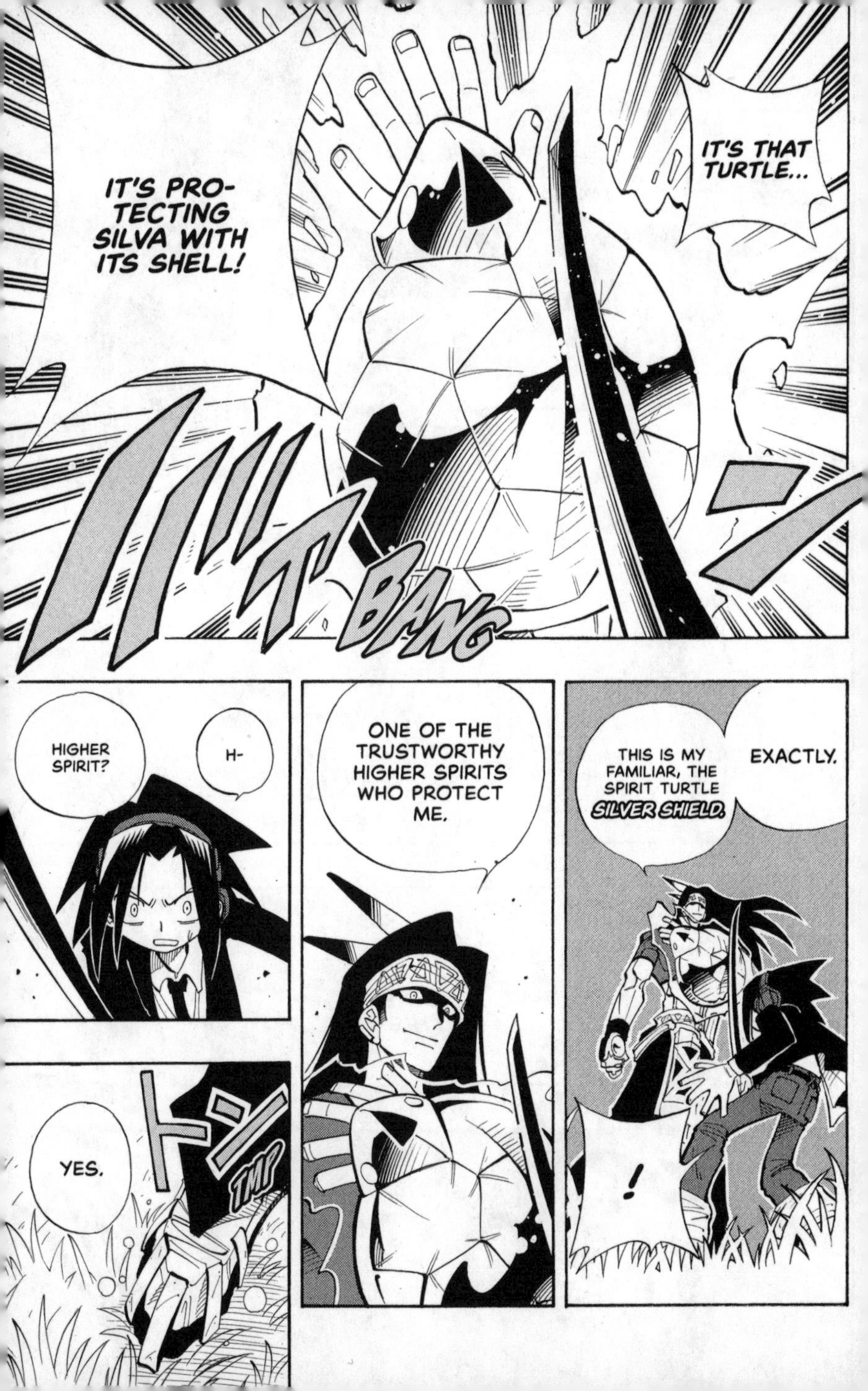
IT'S THAT TURTLE...
IT'S PROTECTING SILVA WITH ITS SHELL!
BANG
EXACTLY.
THIS IS MY FAMILIAR, THE SPIRIT TURTLE SILVER SHIELD.
!
ONE OF THE TRUSTWORTHY HIGHER SPIRITS WHO PROTECT ME.
H-
HIGHER SPIRIT?
YES.
TMP

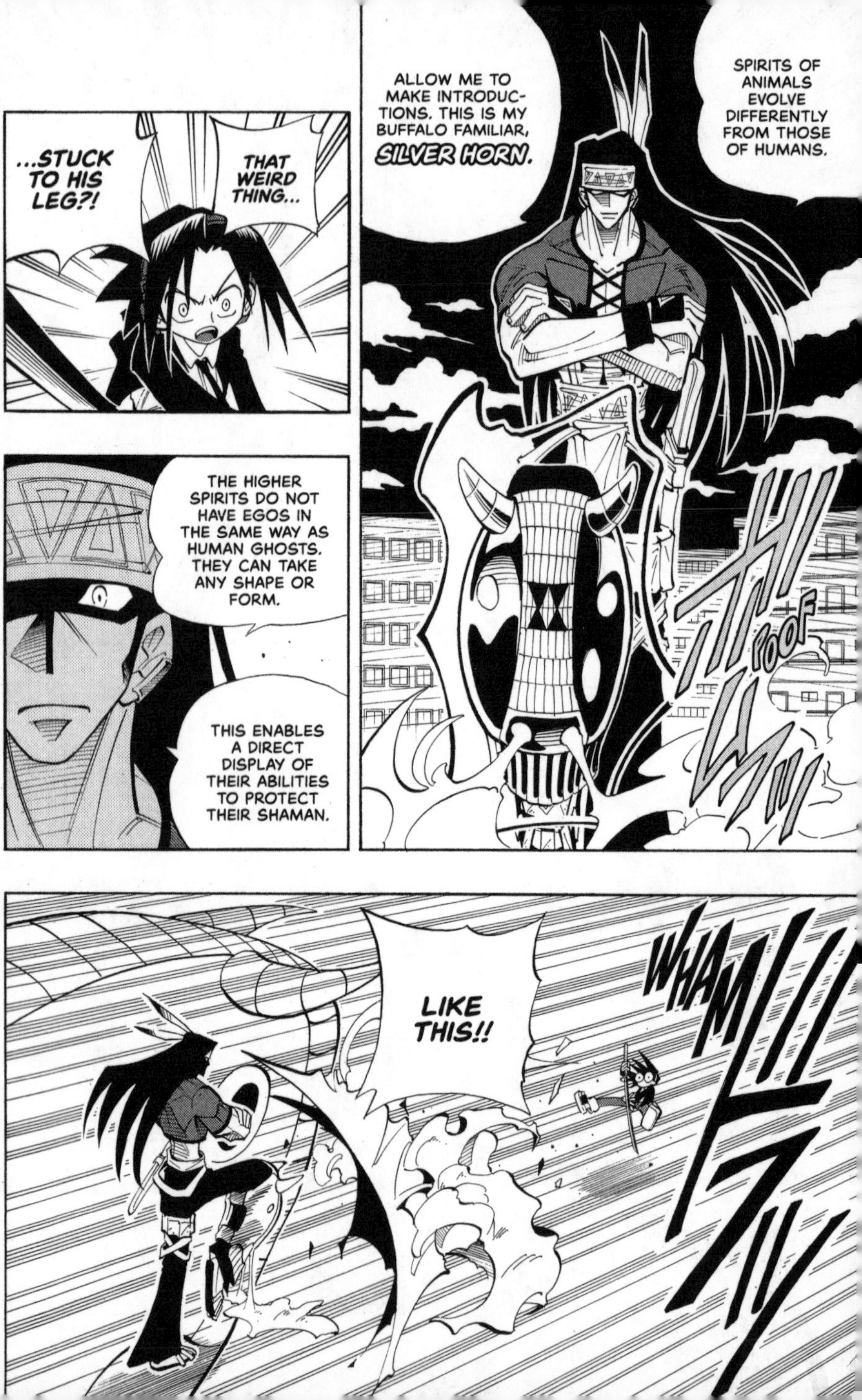
SPIRITS OF ANIMALS EVOLVE DIFFERENTLY FROM THOSE OF HUMANS.
ALLOW ME TO MAKE INTRODUC-TIONS. THIS IS MY BUFFALO FAMILIAR, SILVER HORN.
POOF
THAT WEIRD THING...
...STUCK TO HIS LEG?!
THE HIGHER SPIRITS DO NOT HAVE EGOS IN THE SAME WAY AS HUMAN GHOSTS. THEY CAN TAKE ANY SHAPE OR FORM.
THIS ENABLES A DIRECT DISPLAY OF THEIR ABILITIES TO PROTECT THEIR SHAMAN.
WHAM
LIKE THIS!!

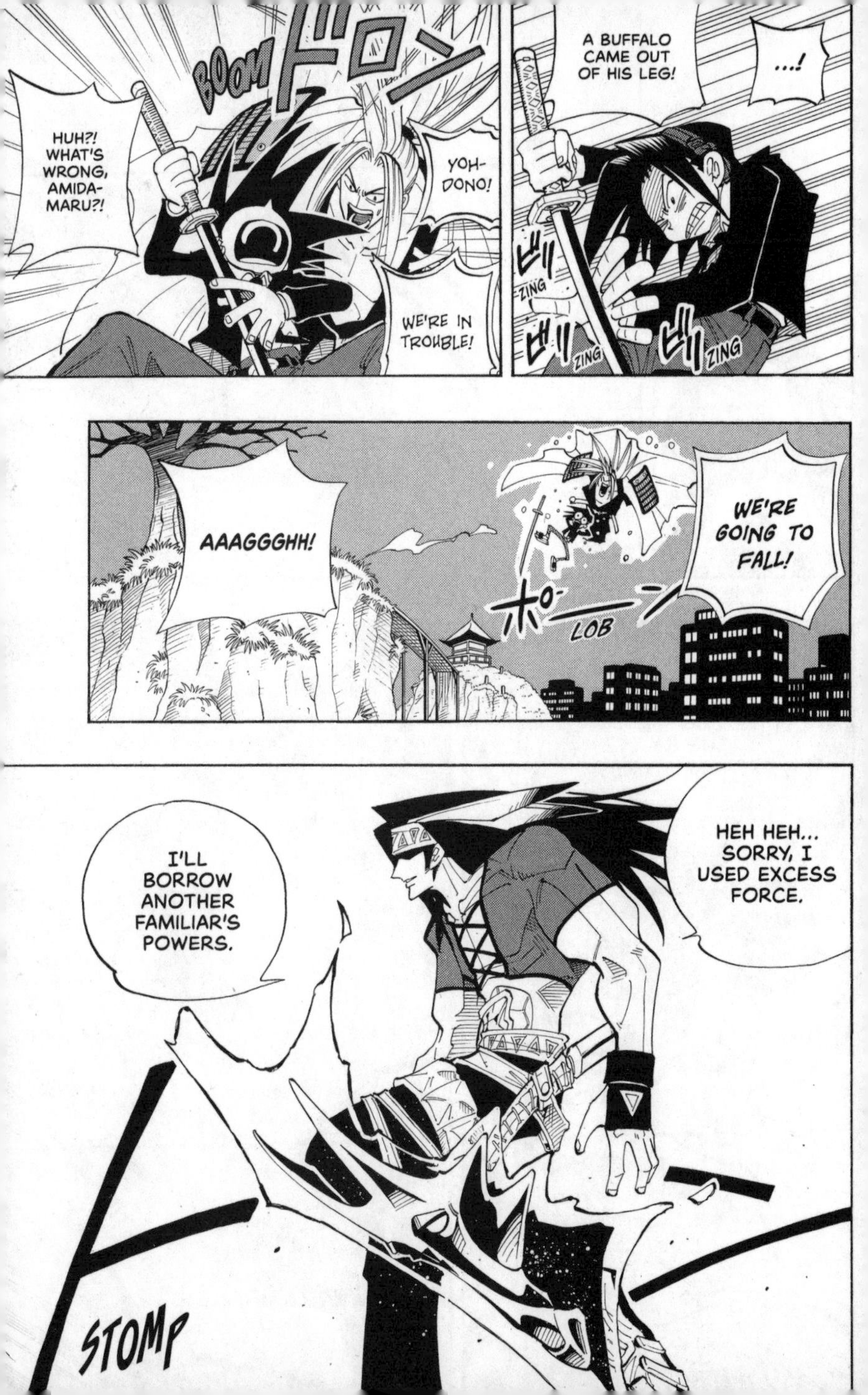
A BUFFALO CAME OUT OF HIS LEG!
...!
ZING
ZING
ZING
BOOM
YOH-DONO!
HUH?! WHAT'S WRONG, AMIDA-MARU?!
WE'RE IN TROUBLE!
WE'RE GOING TO FALL!
LOB
AAAGGGHH!
HEH HEH... SORRY, I USED EXCESS FORCE.
I'LL BORROW ANOTHER FAMILIAR'S POWERS.
STOMP

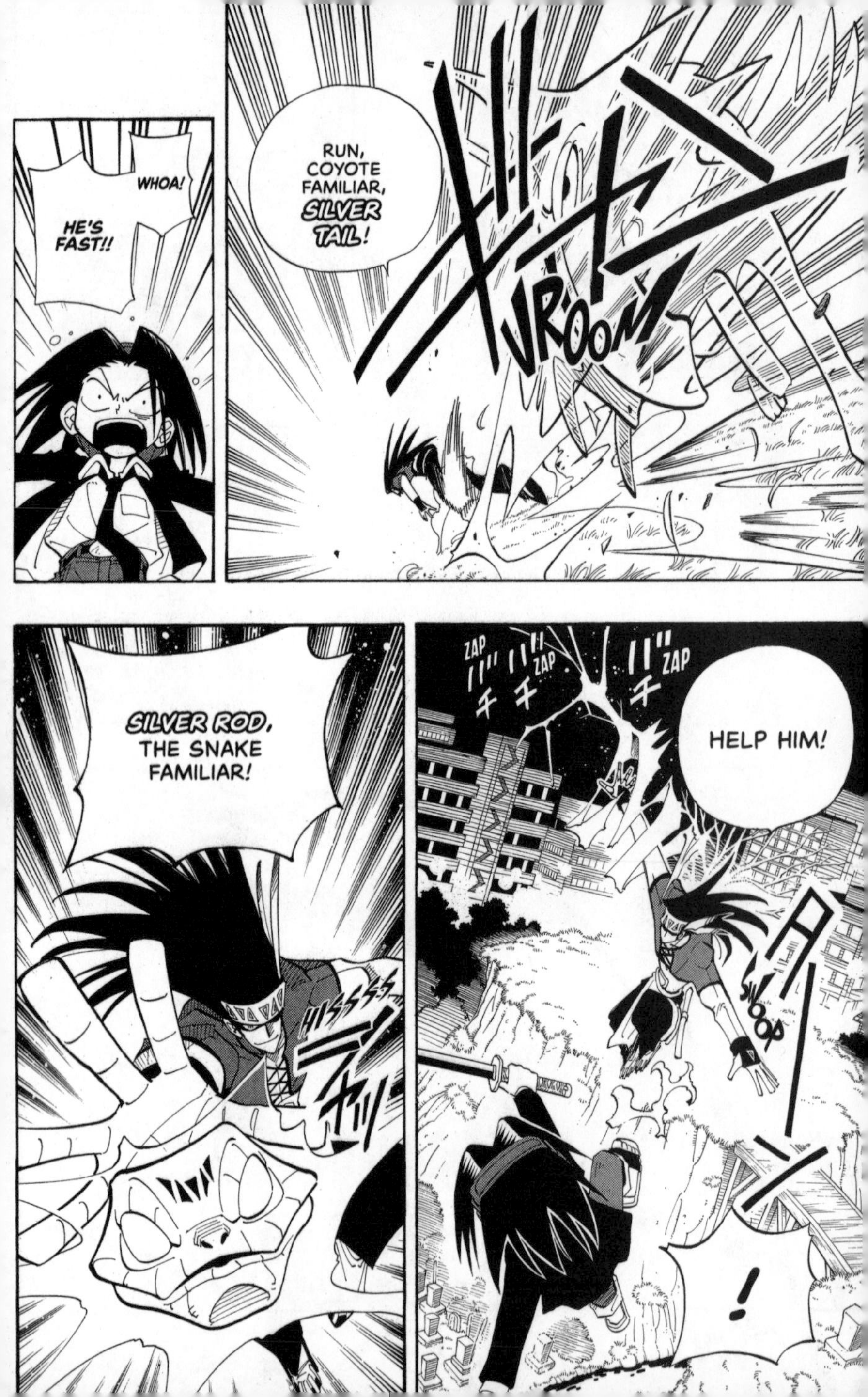

RUN, COYOTE FAMILIAR, SILVER TAIL!
VROOM
WHOA!
HE'S FAST!!
ZAP
ZAP
ZAP
HELP HIM!
SWOOP
!
SILVER ROD, THE SNAKE FAMILIAR!
HISSSSS

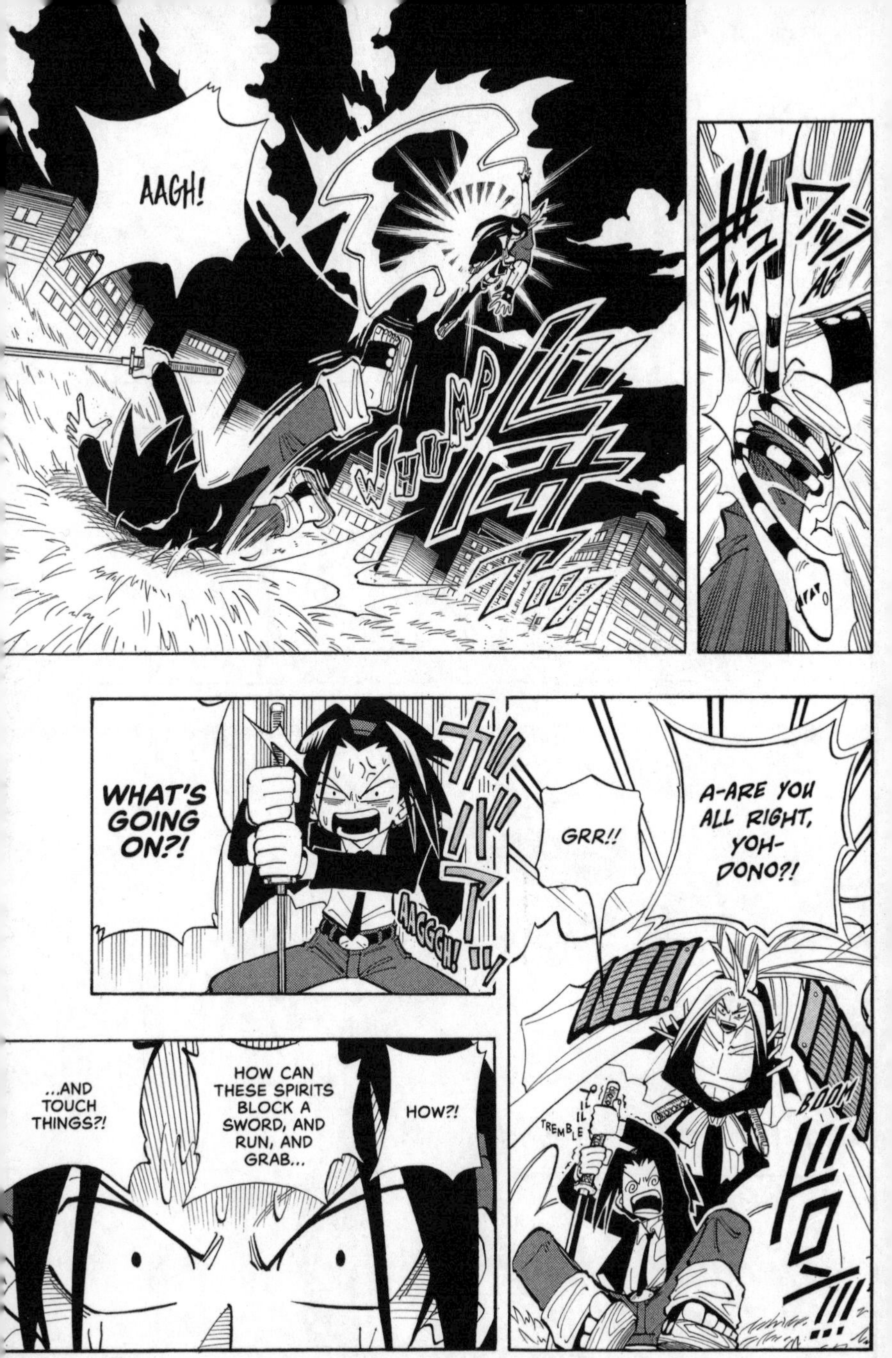
AAGH!
WHUMP
A-ARE YOU ALL RIGHT, YOH-DONO?!
GRR!!
TREMBLE
BOOM
WHAT'S GOING ON?!
AAGGH!!
HOW?!
HOW CAN THESE SPIRITS BLOCK A SWORD, AND RUN, AND GRAB...
...AND TOUCH THINGS?!

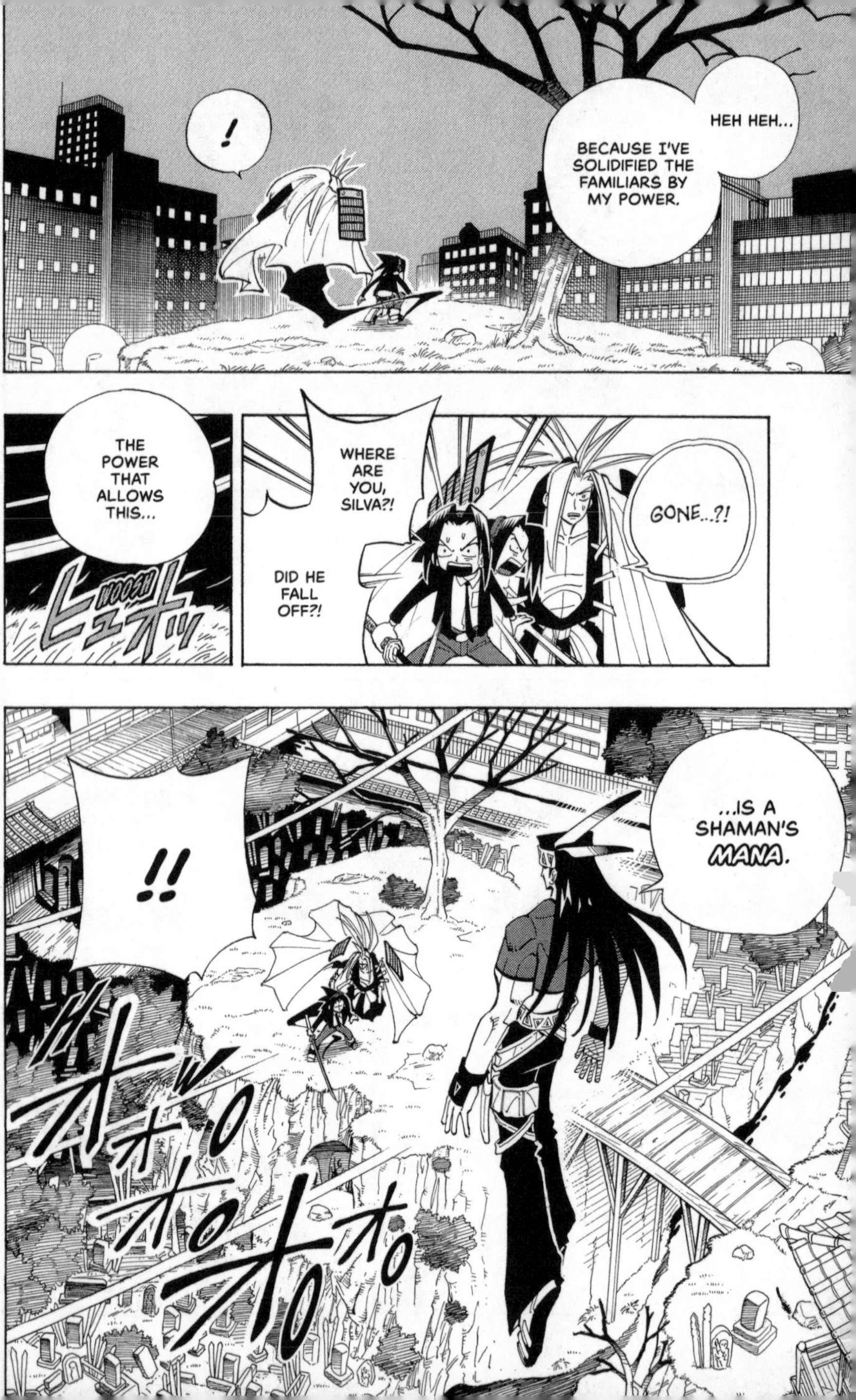
HEH HEH...
BECAUSE I'VE SOLIDIFIED THE FAMILIARS BY MY POWER.
!
GONE..?!
WHERE ARE YOU, SILVA?!
DID HE FALL OFF?!
THE POWER THAT ALLOWS THIS...
...IS A SHAMAN'S MANA.
!!

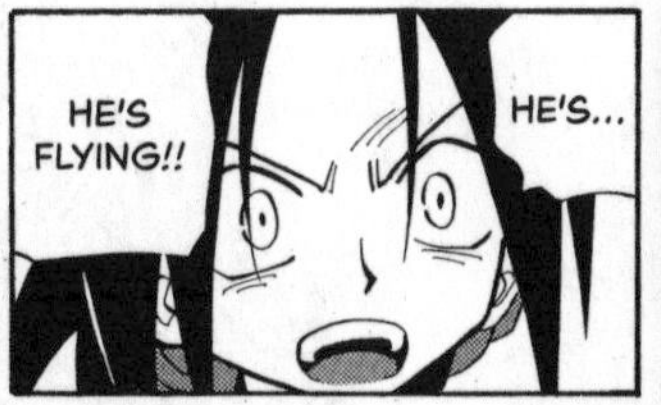
HE'S...
HE'S FLYING!!

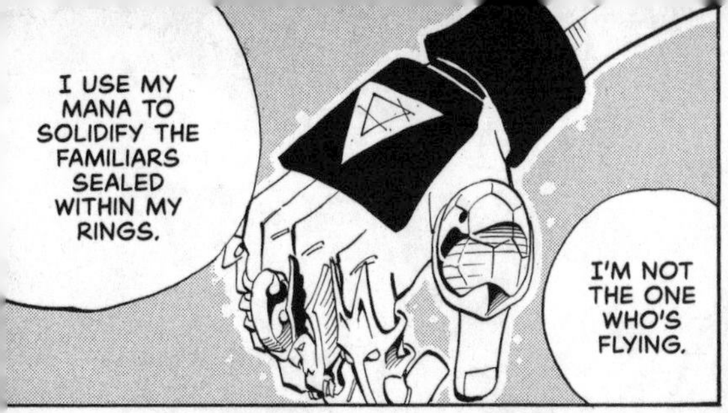
I'M NOT THE ONE WHO'S FLYING.
I USE MY MANA TO SOLIDIFY THE FAMILIARS SEALED WITHIN MY RINGS.

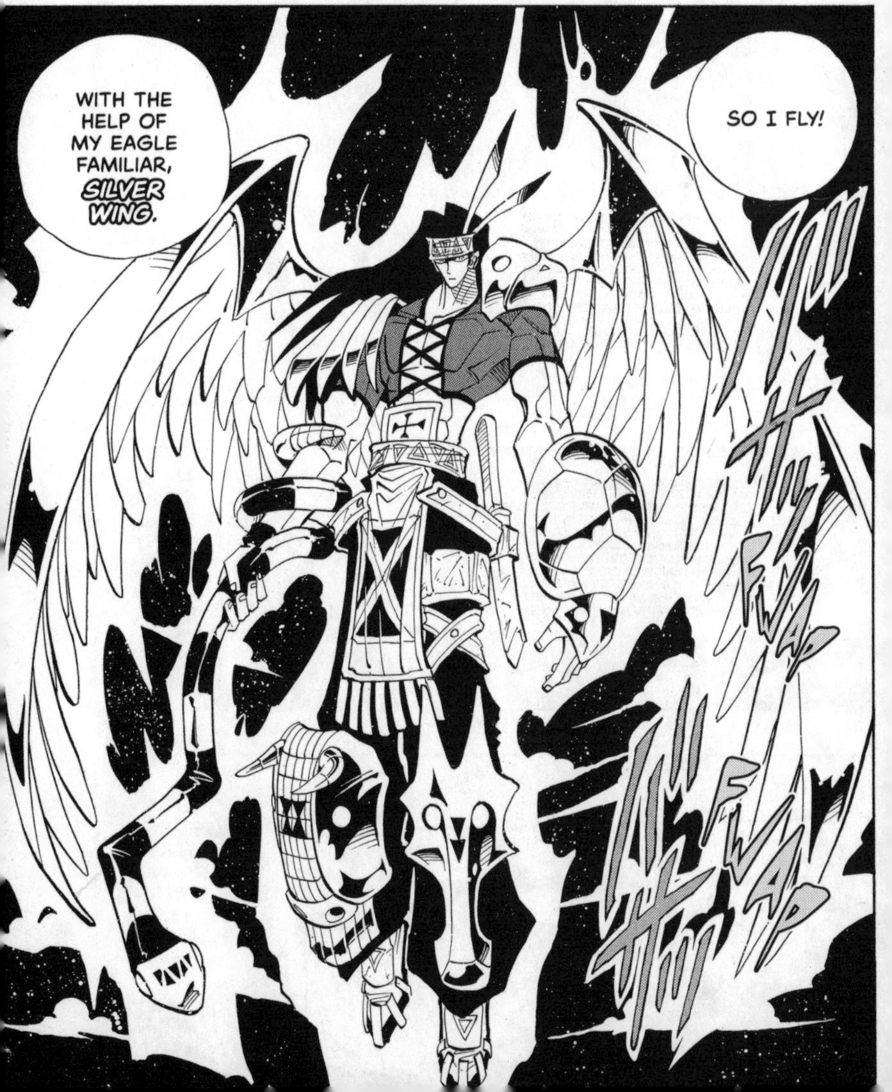
SO I FLY!
WITH THE HELP OF MY EAGLE FAMILIAR, SILVER WING.
FWAP
FWAP

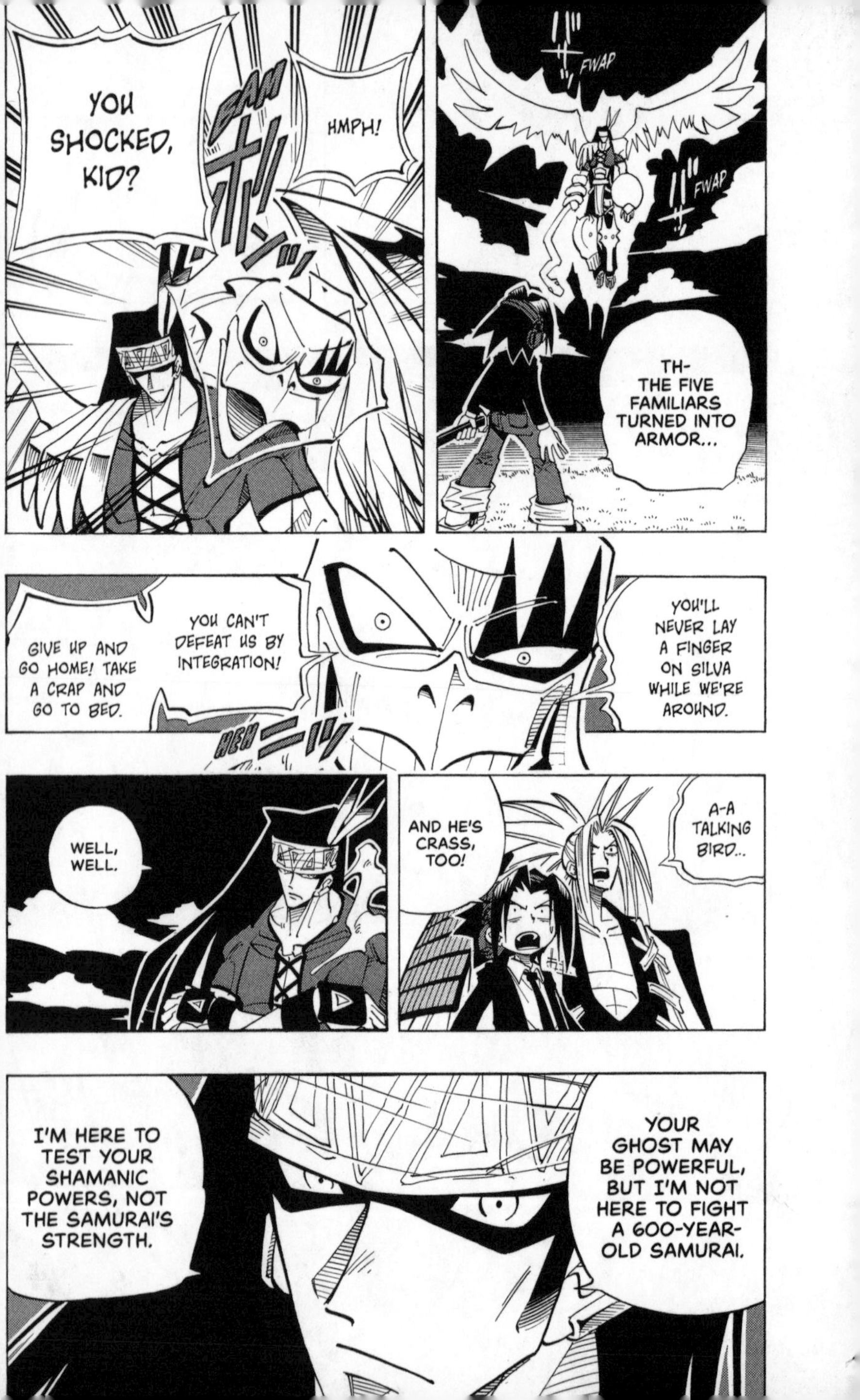
FWAP
FWAP
TH- THE FIVE FAMILIARS TURNED INTO ARMOR...
HMPH!
BAM
YOU SHOCKED, KID?
YOU'LL NEVER LAY A FINGER ON SILVA WHILE WE'RE AROUND.
HEH
YOU CAN'T DEFEAT US BY INTEGRATION!
GIVE UP AND GO HOME! TAKE A CRAP AND GO TO BED.
A-A TALKING BIRD...
AND HE'S CRASS, TOO!
WELL, WELL.
YOUR GHOST MAY BE POWERFUL, BUT I'M NOT HERE TO FIGHT A 600-YEAR-OLD SAMURAI.
I'M HERE TO TEST YOUR SHAMANIC POWERS, NOT THE SAMURAI'S STRENGTH.

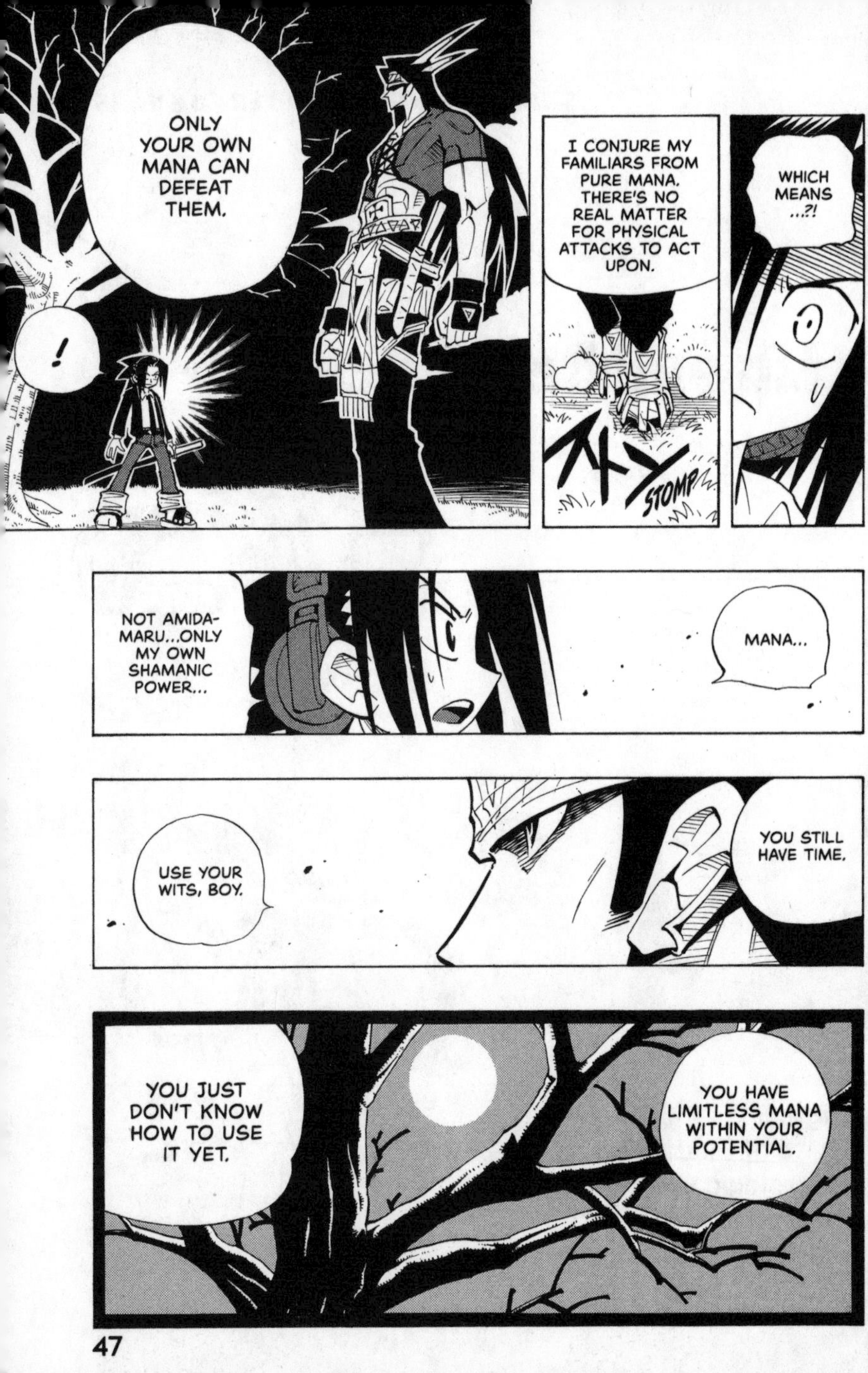
WHICH MEANS ...?!
I CONJURE MY FAMILIARS FROM PURE MANA. THERE'S NO REAL MATTER FOR PHYSICAL ATTACKS TO ACT UPON.
STOMP
ONLY YOUR OWN MANA CAN DEFEAT THEM.
!
MANA...
NOT AMIDA-MARU...ONLY MY OWN SHAMANIC POWER...
YOU STILL HAVE TIME.
USE YOUR WITS, BOY.
YOU HAVE LIMITLESS MANA WITHIN YOUR POTENTIAL.
YOU JUST DON'T KNOW HOW TO USE IT YET.

SHAMAN KING CHARACTER FILE No.15

Lip and Rap

July 1999

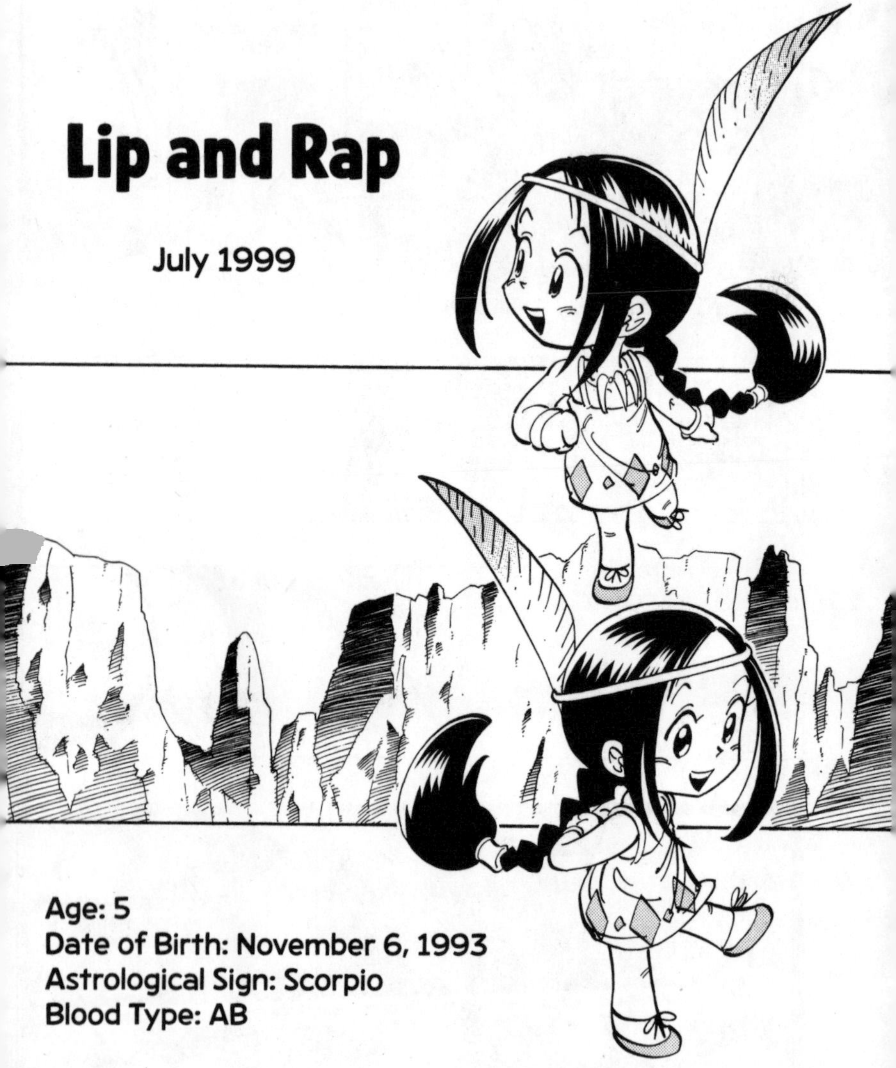

Age: 5
Date of Birth: November 6, 1993
Astrological Sign: Scorpio
Blood Type: AB

Chapter 29: Over Soul

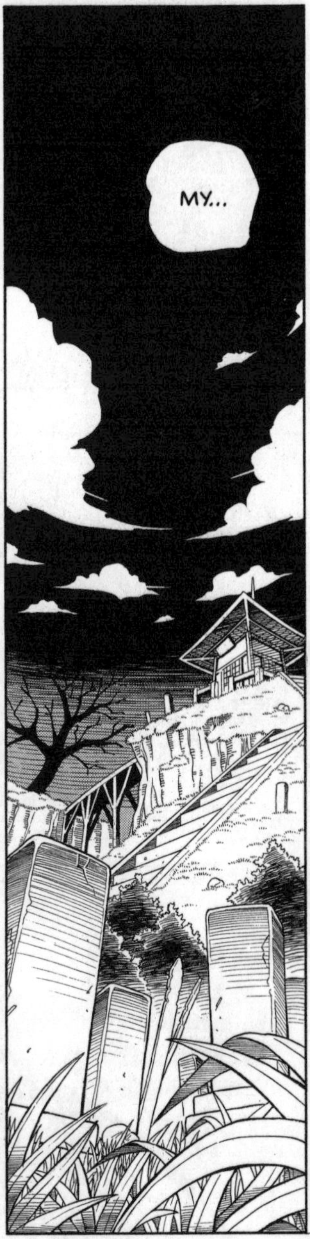
MY...

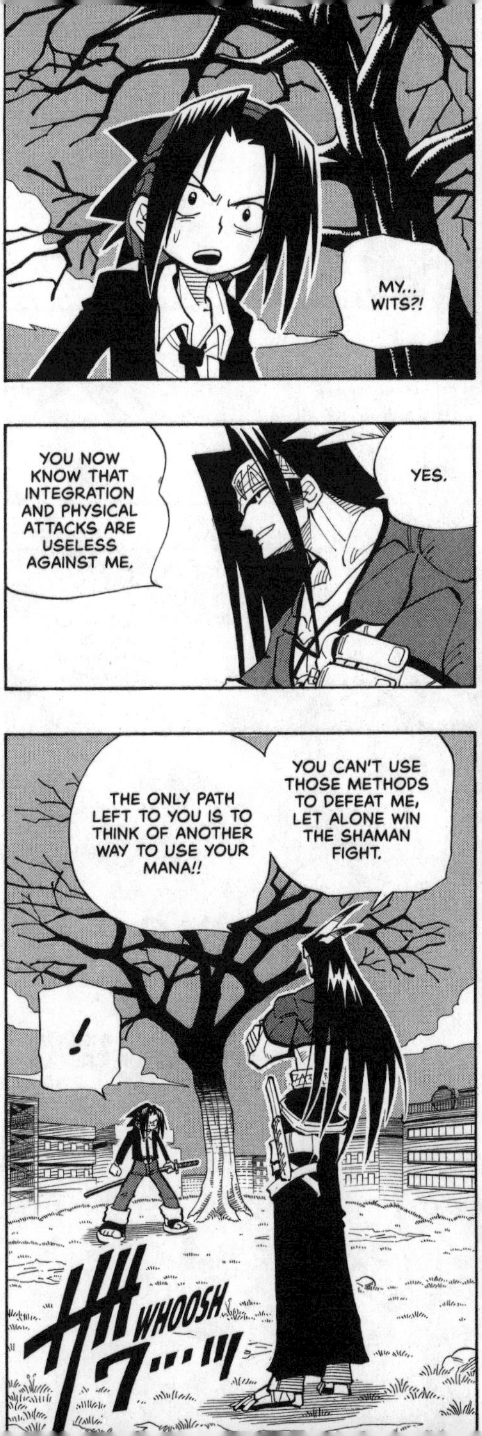
MY... WITS?!
YES.
YOU NOW KNOW THAT INTEGRATION AND PHYSICAL ATTACKS ARE USELESS AGAINST ME.
YOU CAN'T USE THOSE METHODS TO DEFEAT ME, LET ALONE WIN THE SHAMAN FIGHT.
THE ONLY PATH LEFT TO YOU IS TO THINK OF ANOTHER WAY TO USE YOUR MANA!!
!
WHOOSH

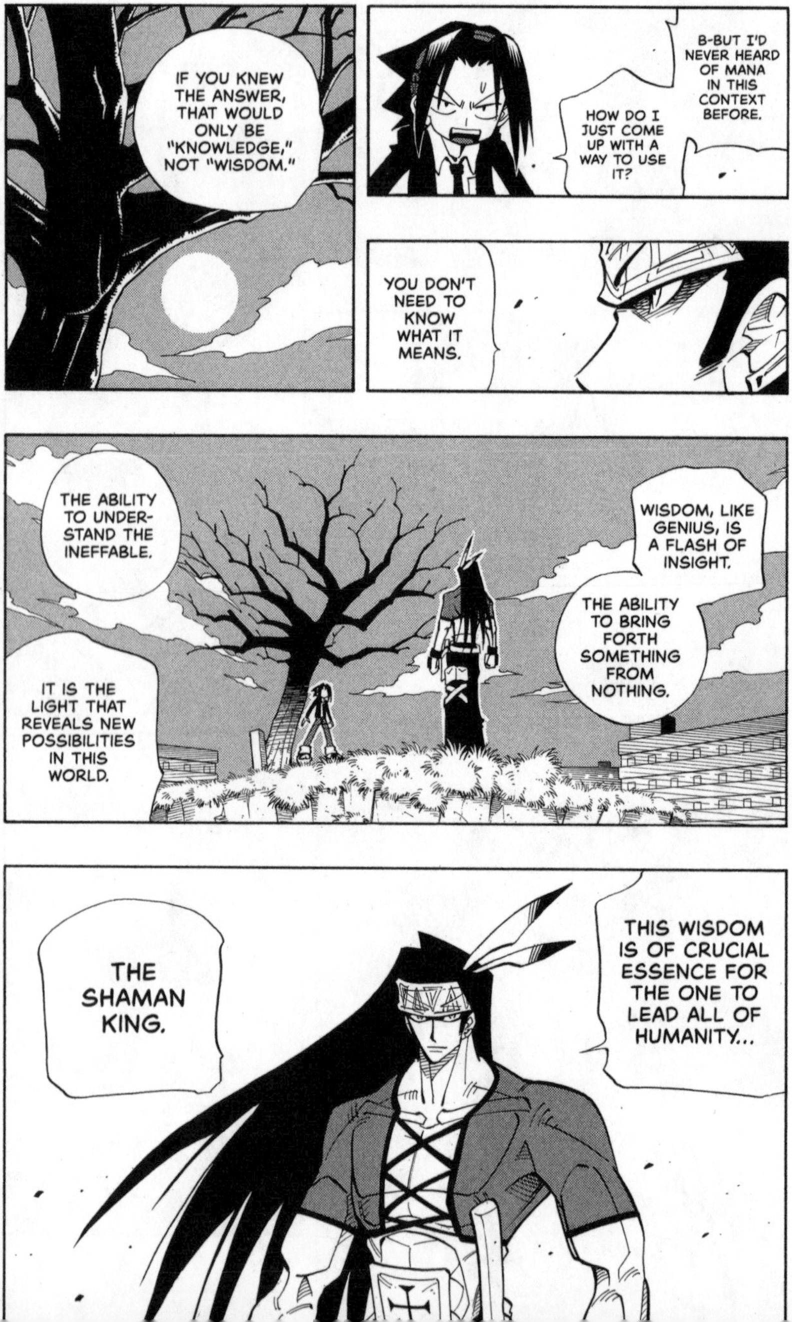
B-BUT I'D NEVER HEARD OF MANA IN THIS CONTEXT BEFORE.
HOW DO I JUST COME UP WITH A WAY TO USE IT?
YOU DON'T NEED TO KNOW WHAT IT MEANS.
IF YOU KNEW THE ANSWER, THAT WOULD ONLY BE "KNOWLEDGE," NOT "WISDOM."
WISDOM, LIKE GENIUS, IS A FLASH OF INSIGHT.
THE ABILITY TO BRING FORTH SOMETHING FROM NOTHING.
THE ABILITY TO UNDER-STAND THE INEFFABLE.
IT IS THE LIGHT THAT REVEALS NEW POSSIBILITIES IN THIS WORLD.
THIS WISDOM IS OF CRUCIAL ESSENCE FOR THE ONE TO LEAD ALL OF HUMANITY...
THE SHAMAN KING.

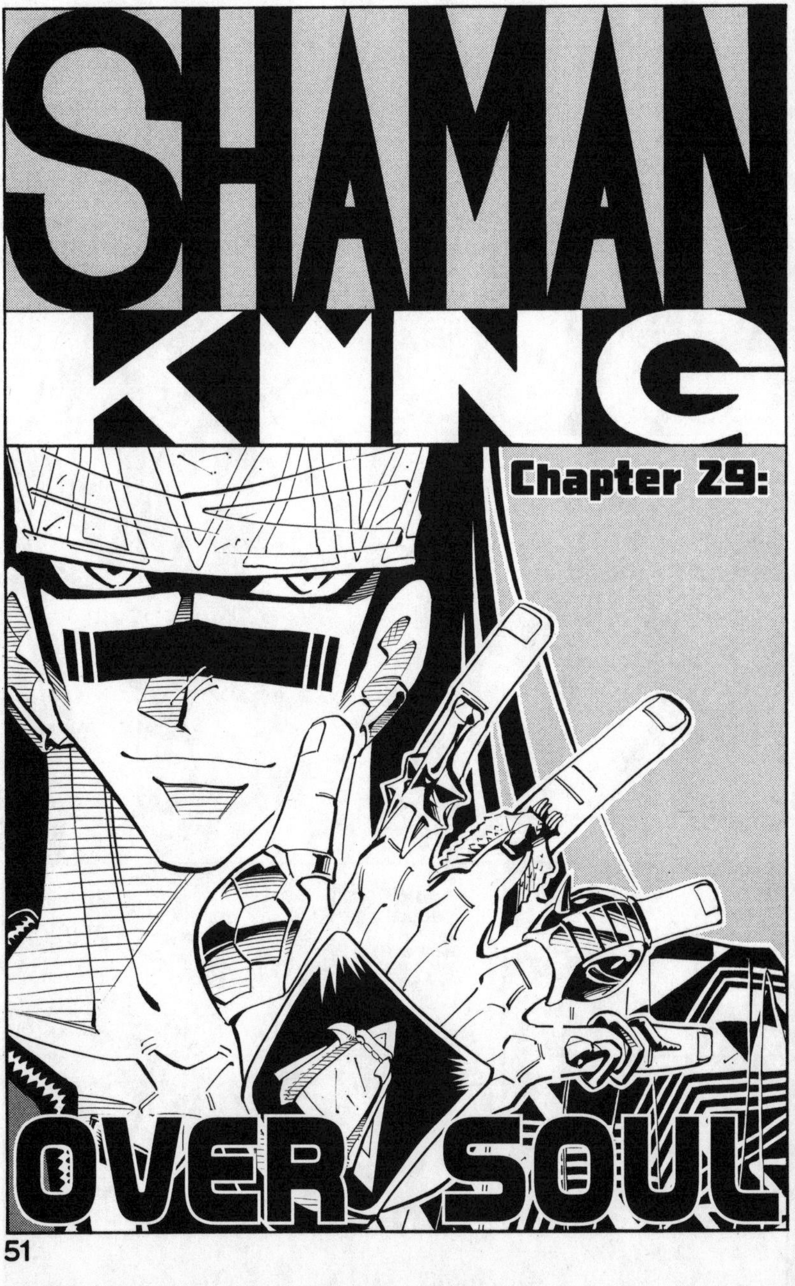
SHAMAN KING
Chapter 29:
OVER SOUL

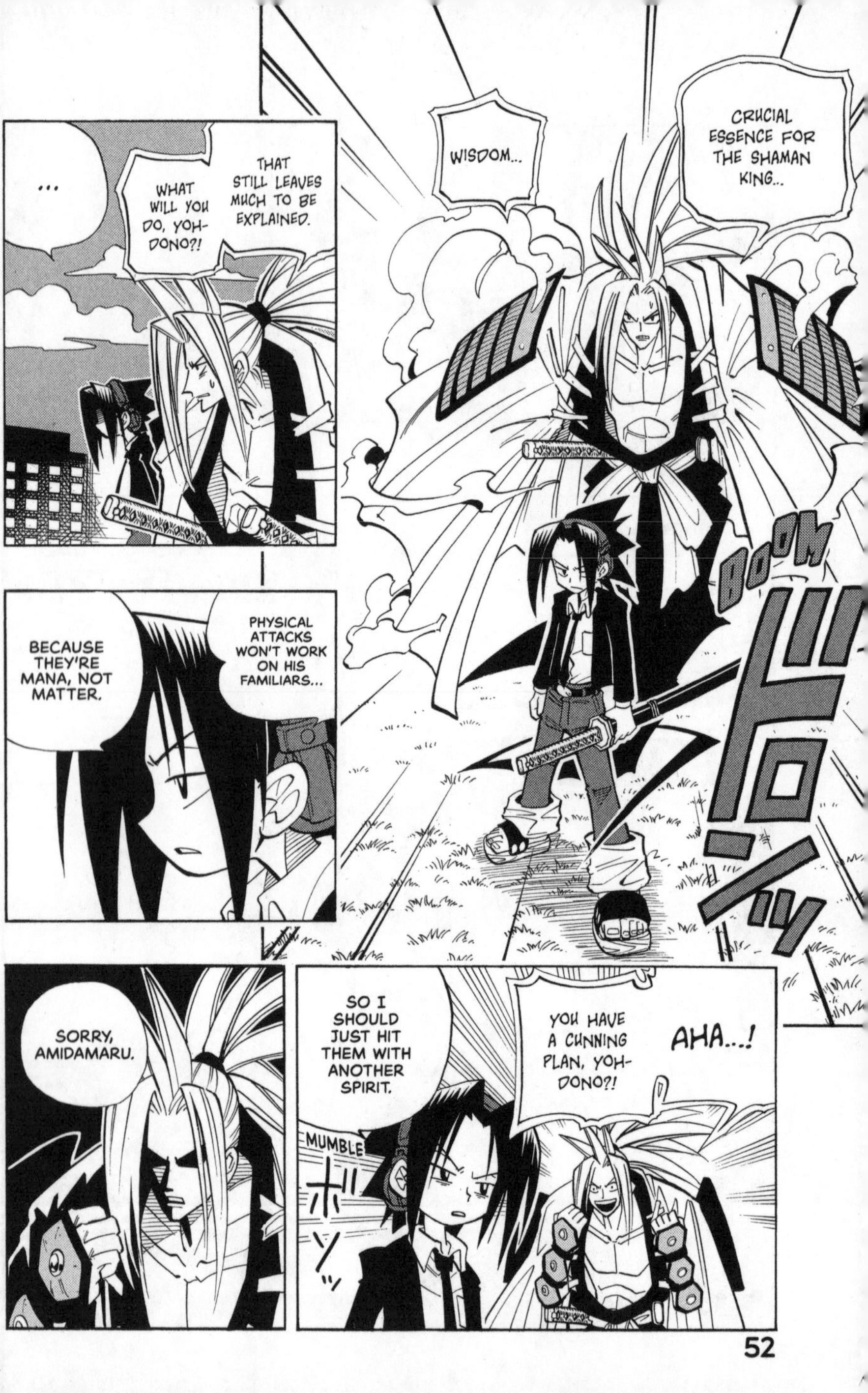
WISDOM...
CRUCIAL ESSENCE FOR THE SHAMAN KING...
BOOM
...
THAT STILL LEAVES MUCH TO BE EXPLAINED.
WHAT WILL YOU DO, YOH-DONO?!
PHYSICAL ATTACKS WON'T WORK ON HIS FAMILIARS...
BECAUSE THEY'RE MANA, NOT MATTER.
AHA...!
YOU HAVE A CUNNING PLAN, YOH-DONO?!
SO I SHOULD JUST HIT THEM WITH ANOTHER SPIRIT.
MUMBLE
SORRY, AMIDAMARU.

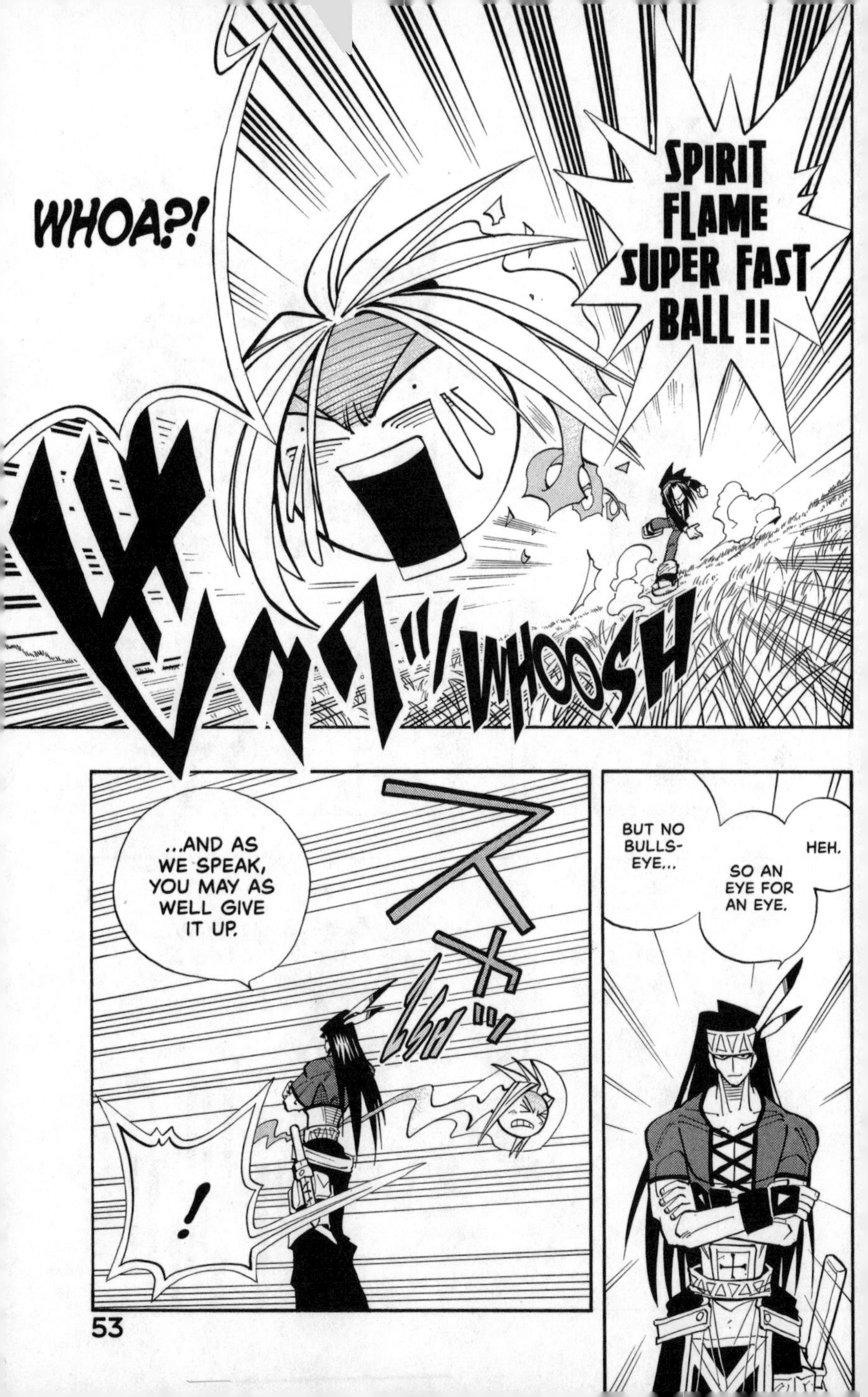
SPIRIT FLAME SUPER FAST BALL !!
WHOA?!
WHOOSH
HEH.
SO AN EYE FOR AN EYE.
BUT NO BULLS-EYE...
...AND AS WE SPEAK, YOU MAY AS WELL GIVE IT UP.
!

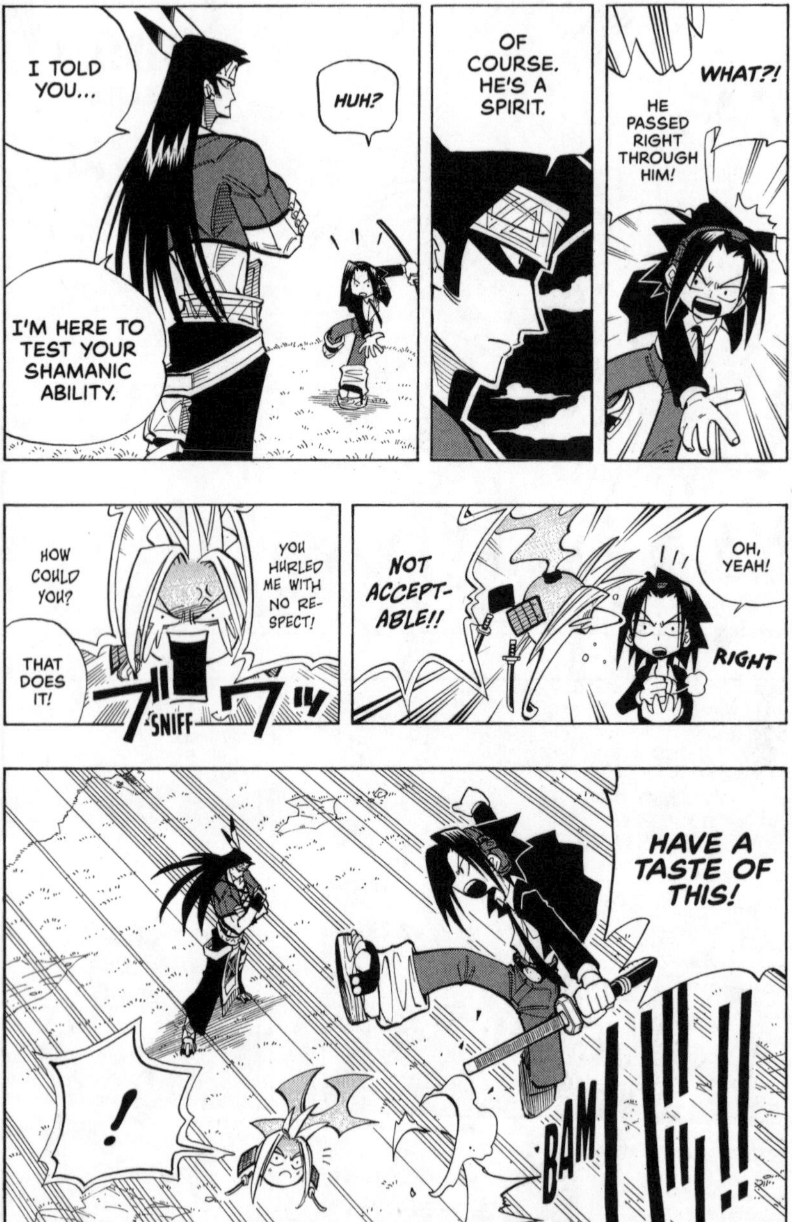
WHAT?!
HE PASSED RIGHT THROUGH HIM!
OF COURSE. HE'S A SPIRIT.
HUH?
I TOLD YOU...
I'M HERE TO TEST YOUR SHAMANIC ABILITY.
OH, YEAH!
RIGHT
NOT ACCEPT-ABLE!!
YOU HURLED ME WITH NO RE-SPECT!
HOW COULD YOU?
THAT DOES IT!
SNIFF
HAVE A TASTE OF THIS!
BAM
!

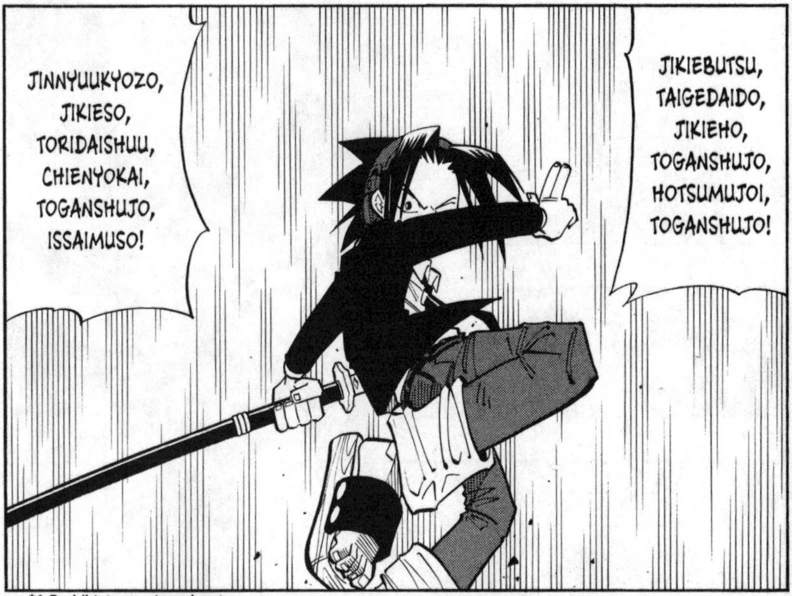
JIKIEBUTSU, TAIGEDAIDO, JIKIEHO, TOGANSHUJO, HOTSUMUJOI, TOGANSHUJO!
JINNYUUKYOZO, JIKIESO, TORIDAISHUU, CHIENYOKAI, TOGANSHUJO, ISSAIMUSO!

*A Buddhist exorcism chant

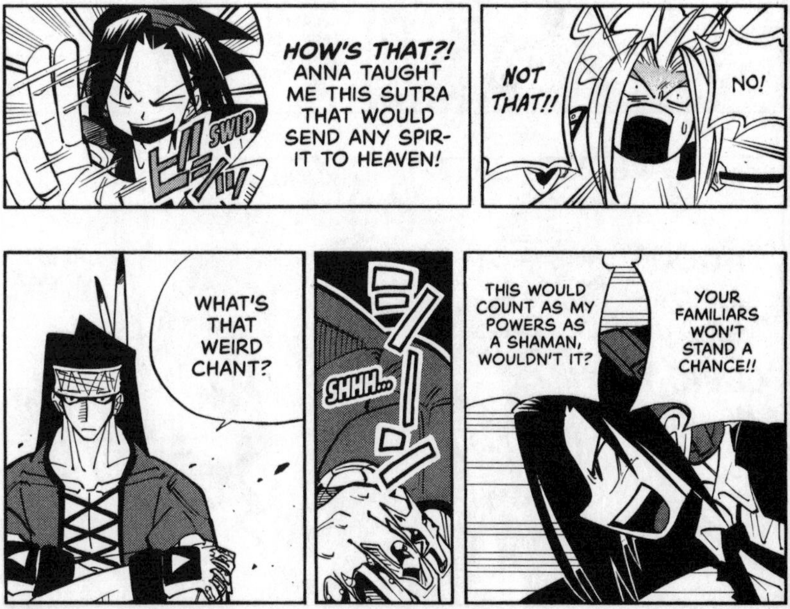
NO!
NOT THAT!!
HOW'S THAT?! ANNA TAUGHT ME THIS SUTRA THAT WOULD SEND ANY SPIR-IT TO HEAVEN!
SWIP
YOUR FAMILIARS WON'T STAND A CHANCE!!
THIS WOULD COUNT AS MY POWERS AS A SHAMAN, WOULDN'T IT?
SHHH...
WHAT'S THAT WEIRD CHANT?

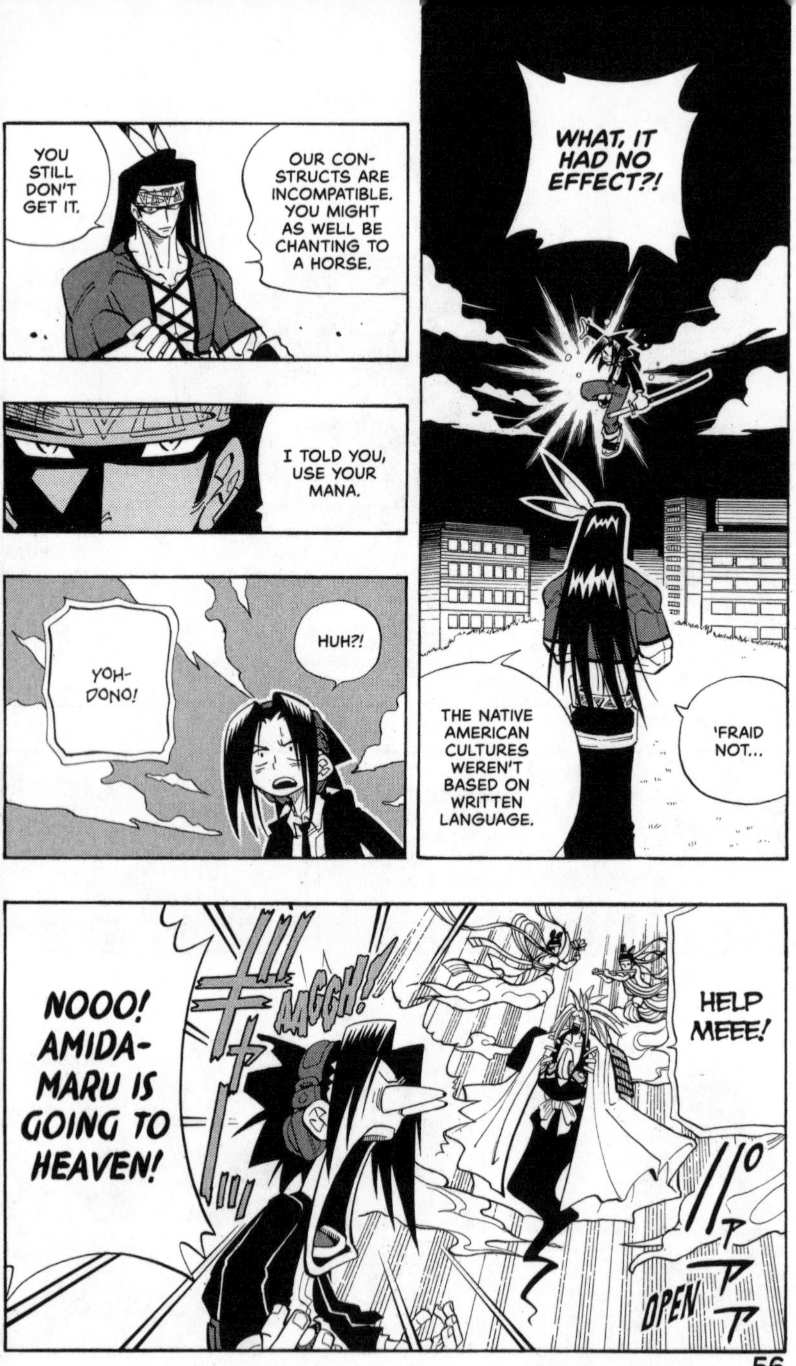
WHAT, IT HAD NO EFFECT?!
'FRAID NOT...
THE NATIVE AMERICAN CULTURES WEREN'T BASED ON WRITTEN LANGUAGE.
OUR CON-STRUCTS ARE INCOMPATIBLE. YOU MIGHT AS WELL BE CHANTING TO A HORSE.
YOU STILL DON'T GET IT.
I TOLD YOU, USE YOUR MANA.
HUH?!
YOH-DONO!
HELP MEEE!
OPEN
AAGGH!!
NOOO! AMIDA-MARU IS GOING TO HEAVEN!

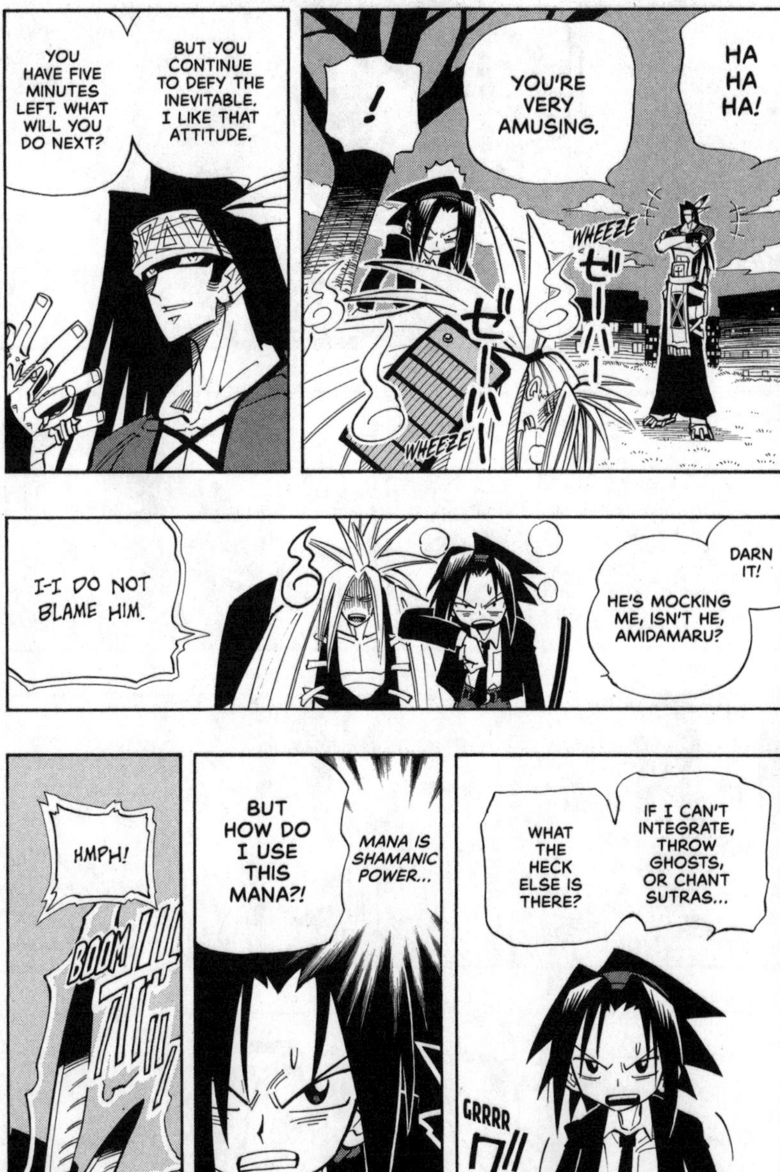
HA HA HA!
YOU'RE VERY AMUSING.
!
WHEEZE
WHEEZE
BUT YOU CONTINUE TO DEFY THE INEVITABLE. I LIKE THAT ATTITUDE.
YOU HAVE FIVE MINUTES LEFT. WHAT WILL YOU DO NEXT?
DARN IT!
HE'S MOCKING ME, ISN'T HE, AMIDAMARU?
I-I DO NOT BLAME HIM.
IF I CAN'T INTEGRATE, THROW GHOSTS, OR CHANT SUTRAS...
WHAT THE HECK ELSE IS THERE?
GRRRR
MANA IS SHAMANIC POWER...
BUT HOW DO I USE THIS MANA?!
HMPH!
BOOM

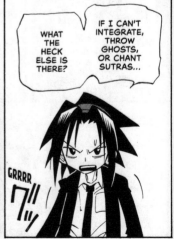

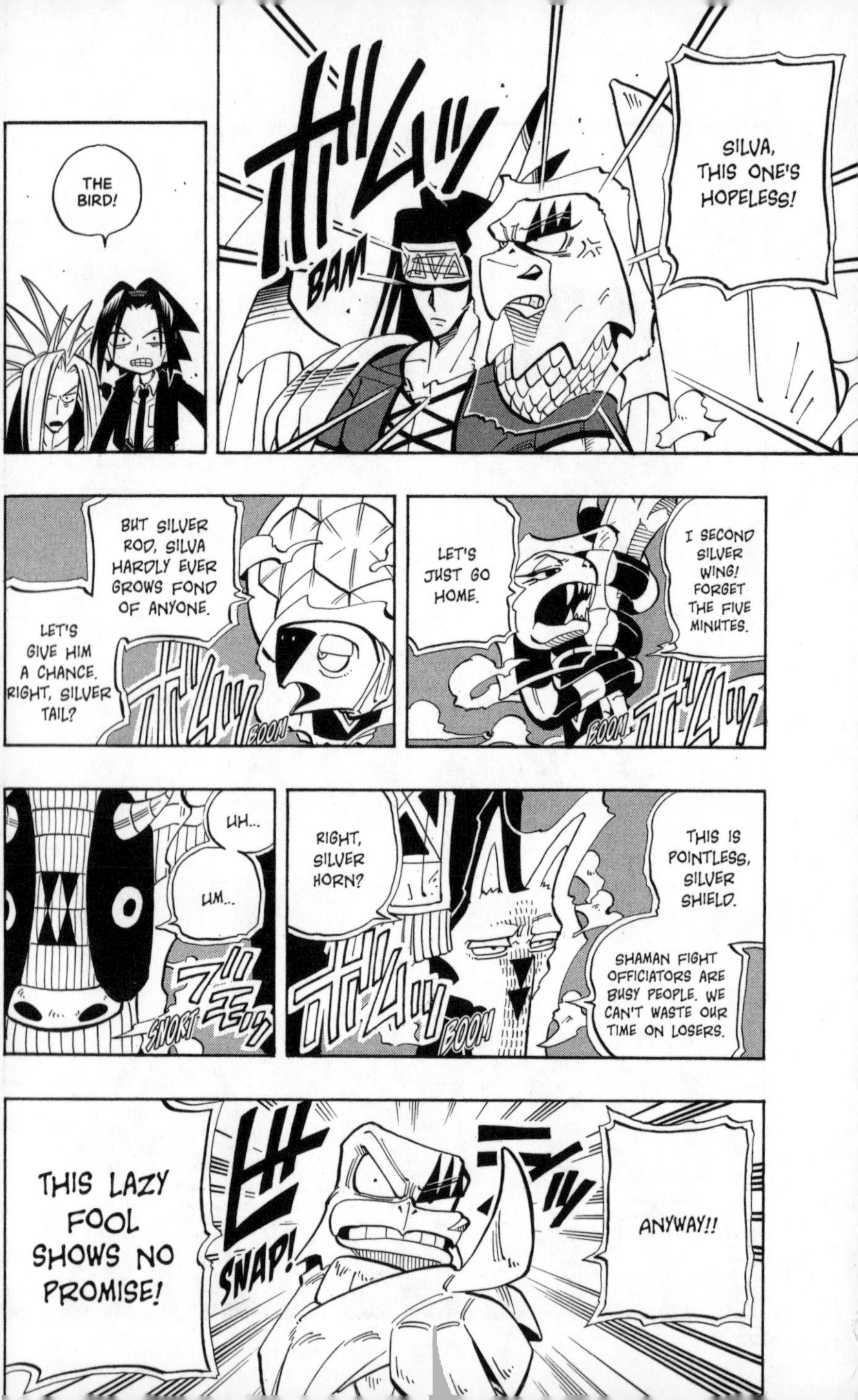
SILVA, THIS ONE'S HOPELESS!
BAM
THE BIRD!
I SECOND SILVER WING! FORGET THE FIVE MINUTES.
LET'S JUST GO HOME.
BOOM
BUT SILVER ROD, SILVA HARDLY EVER GROWS FOND OF ANYONE.
LET'S GIVE HIM A CHANCE. RIGHT, SILVER TAIL?
BOOM
THIS IS POINTLESS, SILVER SHIELD.
SHAMAN FIGHT OFFICIATORS ARE BUSY PEOPLE. WE CAN'T WASTE OUR TIME ON LOSERS.
RIGHT, SILVER HORN?
BOOM
UH...
UM...
SNORT
ANYWAY!!
SNAP!
THIS LAZY FOOL SHOWS NO PROMISE!

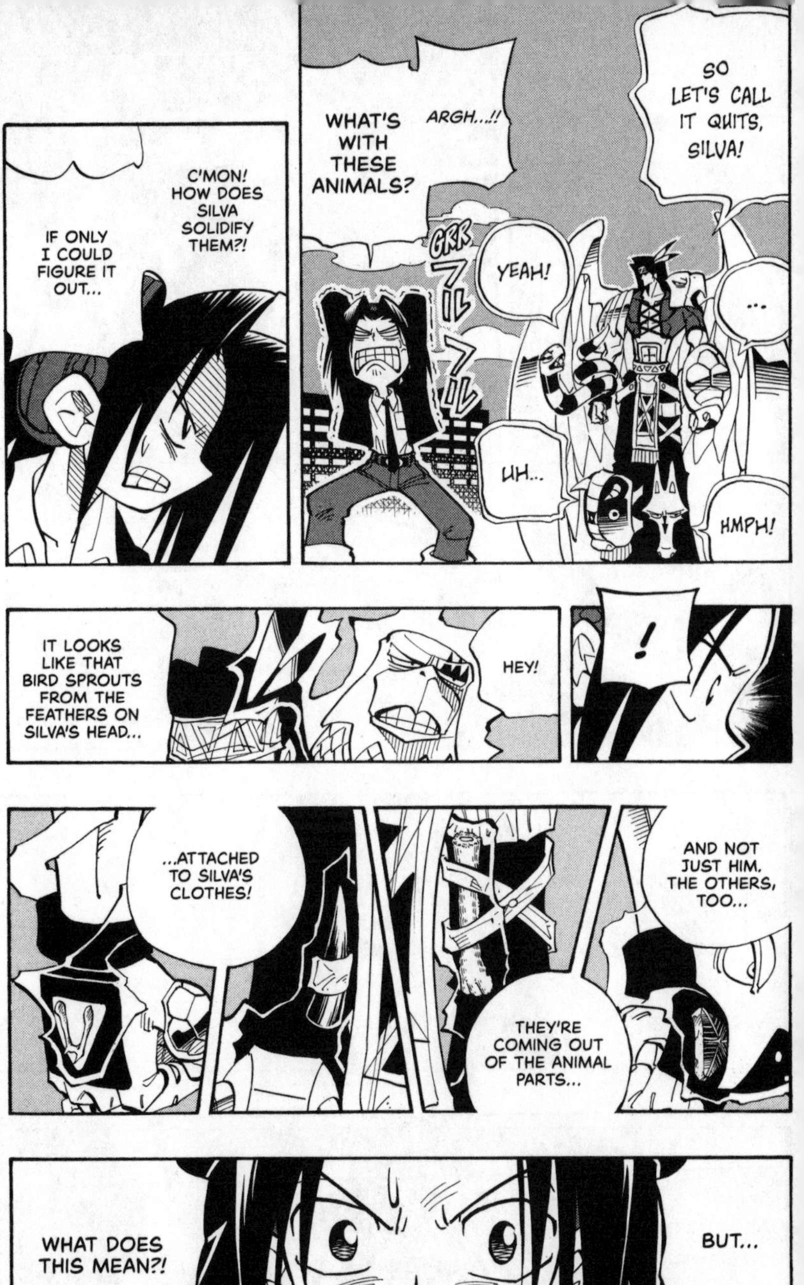
SO LET'S CALL IT QUITS, SILVA!
ARGH...!!
WHAT'S WITH THESE ANIMALS?
...
YEAH!
GRR
UH...
HMPH!
C'MON! HOW DOES SILVA SOLIDIFY THEM?!
IF ONLY I COULD FIGURE IT OUT...
!
HEY!
IT LOOKS LIKE THAT BIRD SPROUTS FROM THE FEATHERS ON SILVA'S HEAD...
AND NOT JUST HIM. THE OTHERS, TOO...
THEY'RE COMING OUT OF THE ANIMAL PARTS...
...ATTACHED TO SILVA'S CLOTHES!
BUT...
WHAT DOES THIS MEAN?!

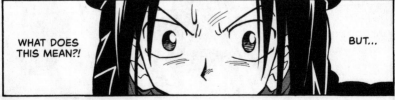

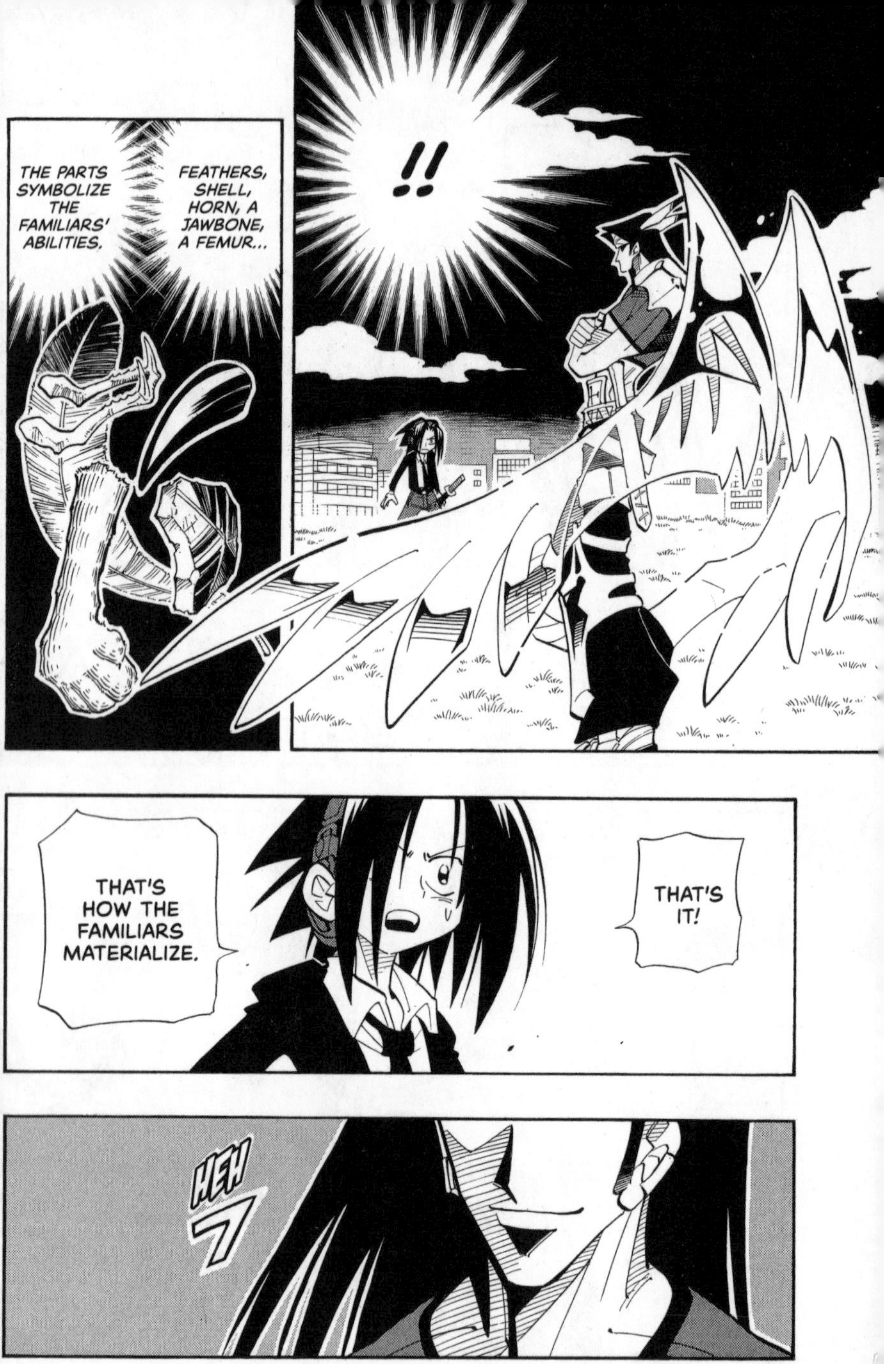
!!
FEATHERS, SHELL, HORN, A JAWBONE, A FEMUR...
THE PARTS SYMBOLIZE THE FAMILIARS' ABILITIES.
THAT'S IT!
THAT'S HOW THE FAMILIARS MATERIALIZE.
HEH

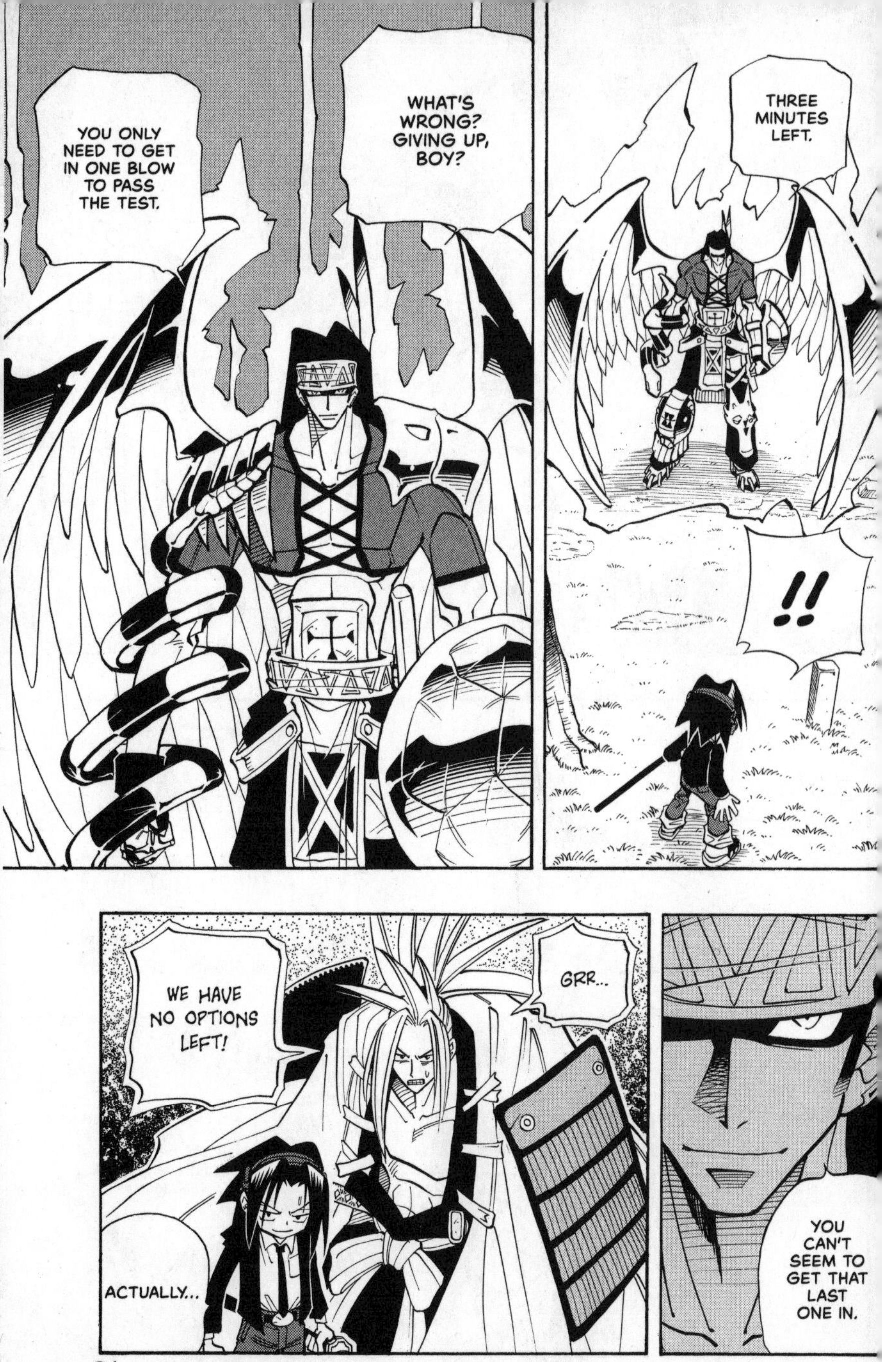
THREE MINUTES LEFT.
!!
WHAT'S WRONG? GIVING UP, BOY?
YOU ONLY NEED TO GET IN ONE BLOW TO PASS THE TEST.
YOU CAN'T SEEM TO GET THAT LAST ONE IN.
GRR...
WE HAVE NO OPTIONS LEFT!
ACTUALLY...

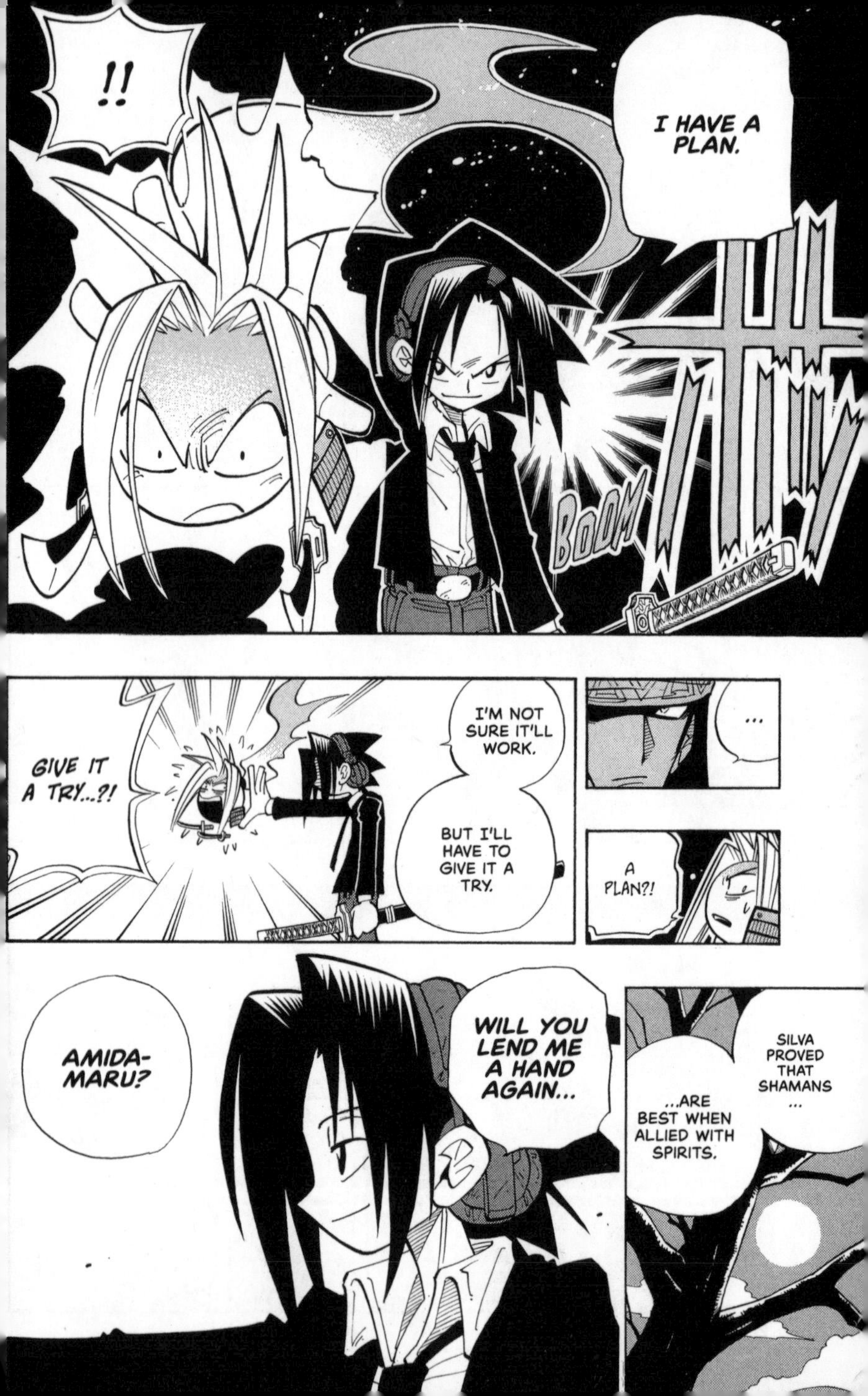
I HAVE A PLAN.
!!
BOOM
...
A PLAN?!
I'M NOT SURE IT'LL WORK.
BUT I'LL HAVE TO GIVE IT A TRY.
GIVE IT A TRY...?!
SILVA PROVED THAT SHAMANS ...
...ARE BEST WHEN ALLIED WITH SPIRITS.
WILL YOU LEND ME A HAND AGAIN...
AMIDA-MARU?

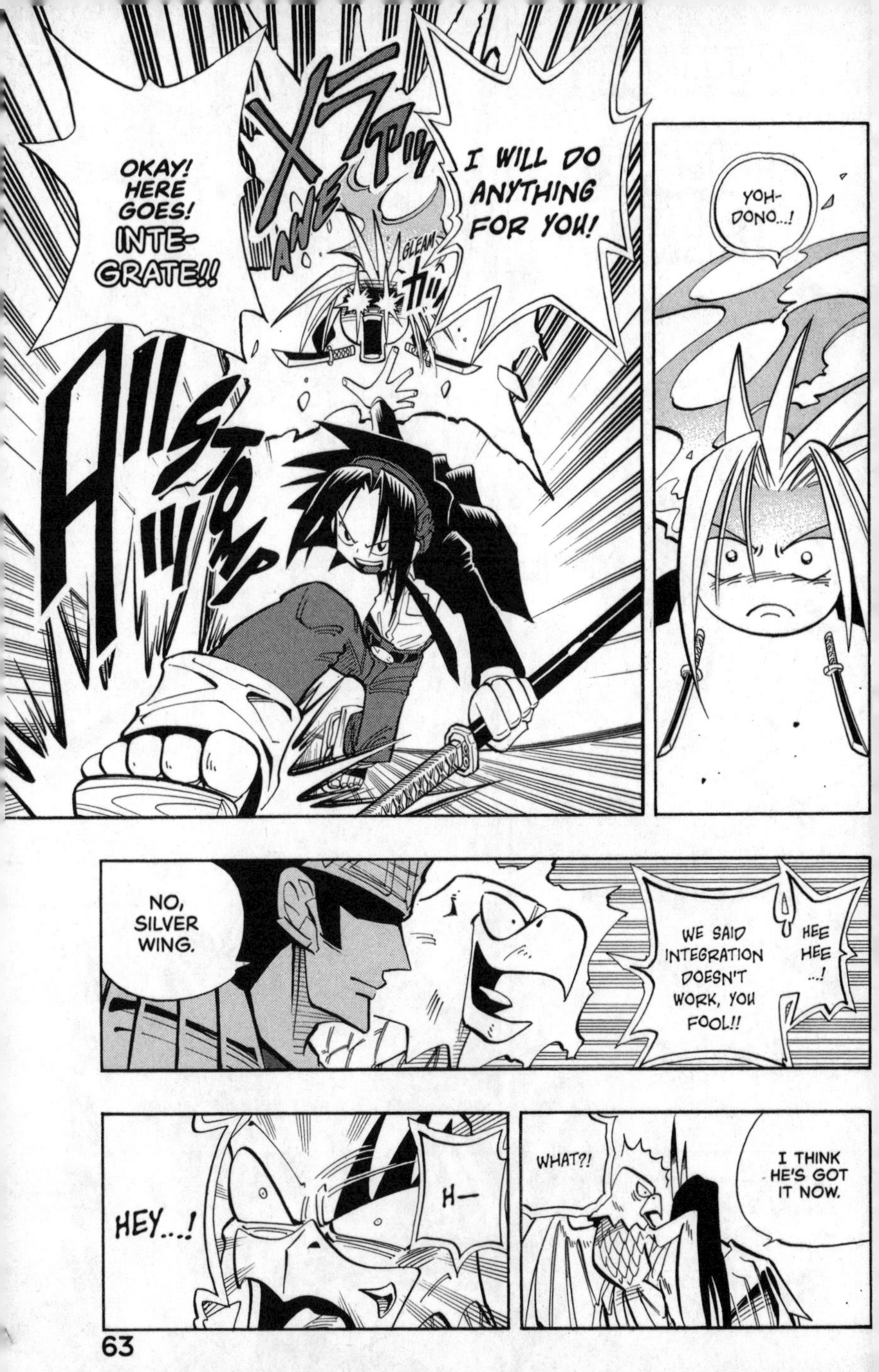

YOH-DONO...!
I WILL DO ANYTHING FOR YOU!
GLEAM
OKAY! HERE GOES! INTEGRATE!!
STOMP
HEE HEE ...!
WE SAID INTEGRATION DOESN'T WORK, YOU FOOL!!
NO, SILVER WING.
I THINK HE'S GOT IT NOW.
WHAT?!
H—
HEY...!

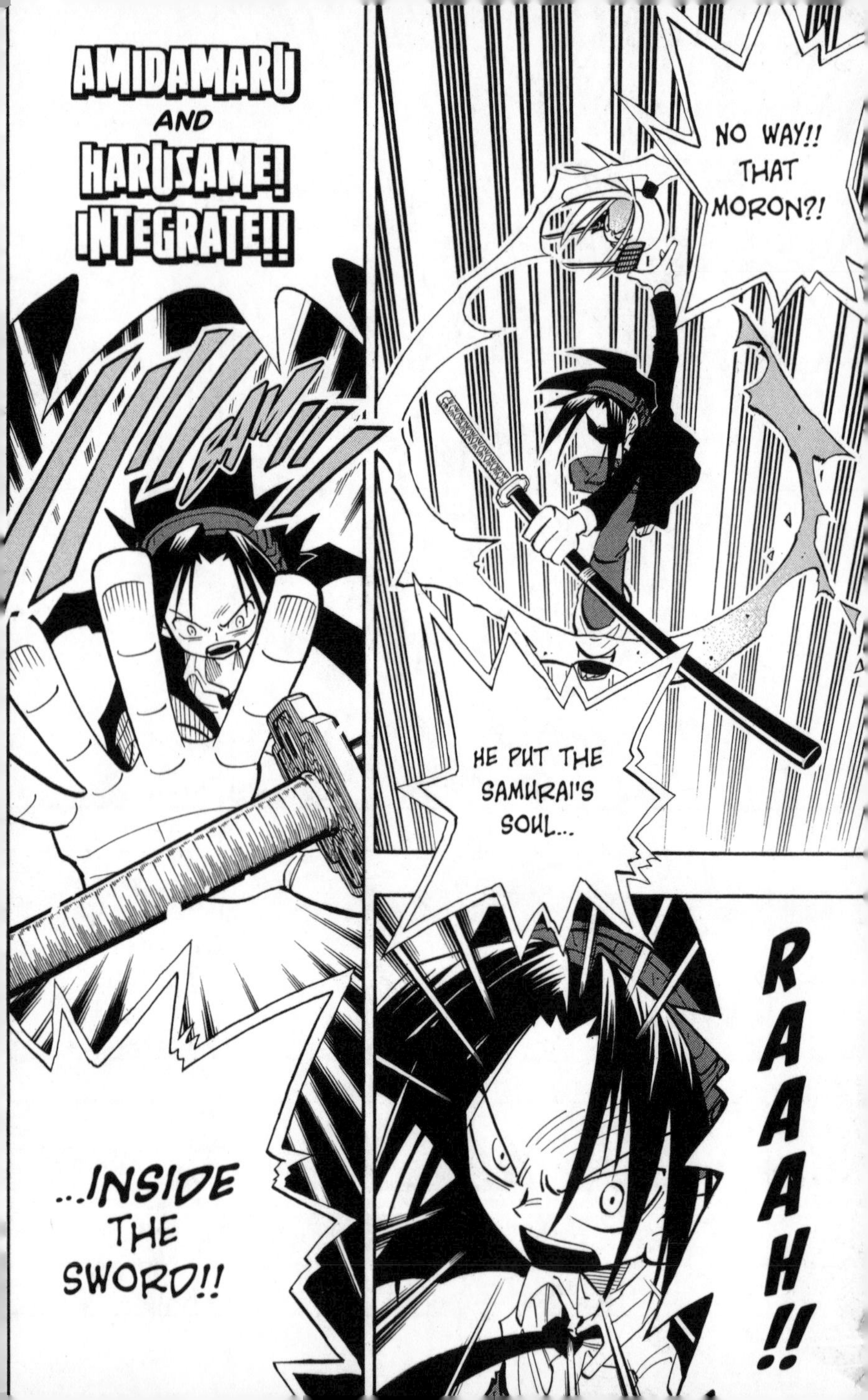
NO WAY!! THAT MORON?!
HE PUT THE SAMURAI'S SOUL...
RAAAAH!!
AMIDAMARU AND HARUSAME! INTEGRATE!!
BAM!!
...INSIDE THE SWORD!!

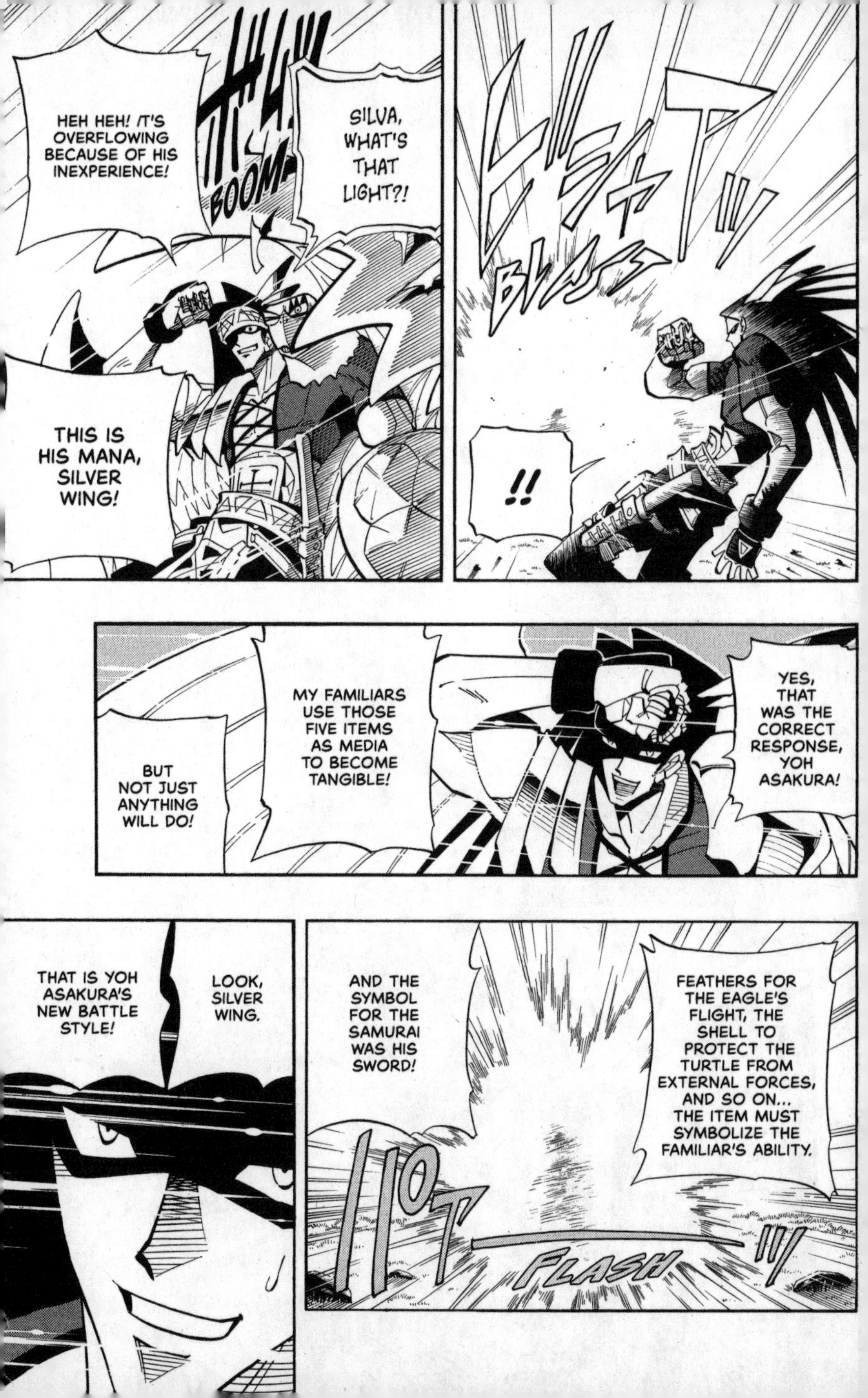
BLAST
!!
SILVA, WHAT'S THAT LIGHT?!
BOOM
HEH HEH! IT'S OVERFLOWING BECAUSE OF HIS INEXPERIENCE!
THIS IS HIS MANA, SILVER WING!
YES, THAT WAS THE CORRECT RESPONSE, YOH ASAKURA!
MY FAMILIARS USE THOSE FIVE ITEMS AS MEDIA TO BECOME TANGIBLE!
BUT NOT JUST ANYTHING WILL DO!
FEATHERS FOR THE EAGLE'S FLIGHT, THE SHELL TO PROTECT THE TURTLE FROM EXTERNAL FORCES, AND SO ON... THE ITEM MUST SYMBOLIZE THE FAMILIAR'S ABILITY.
AND THE SYMBOL FOR THE SAMURAI WAS HIS SWORD!
FLASH
LOOK, SILVER WING.
THAT IS YOH ASAKURA'S NEW BATTLE STYLE!

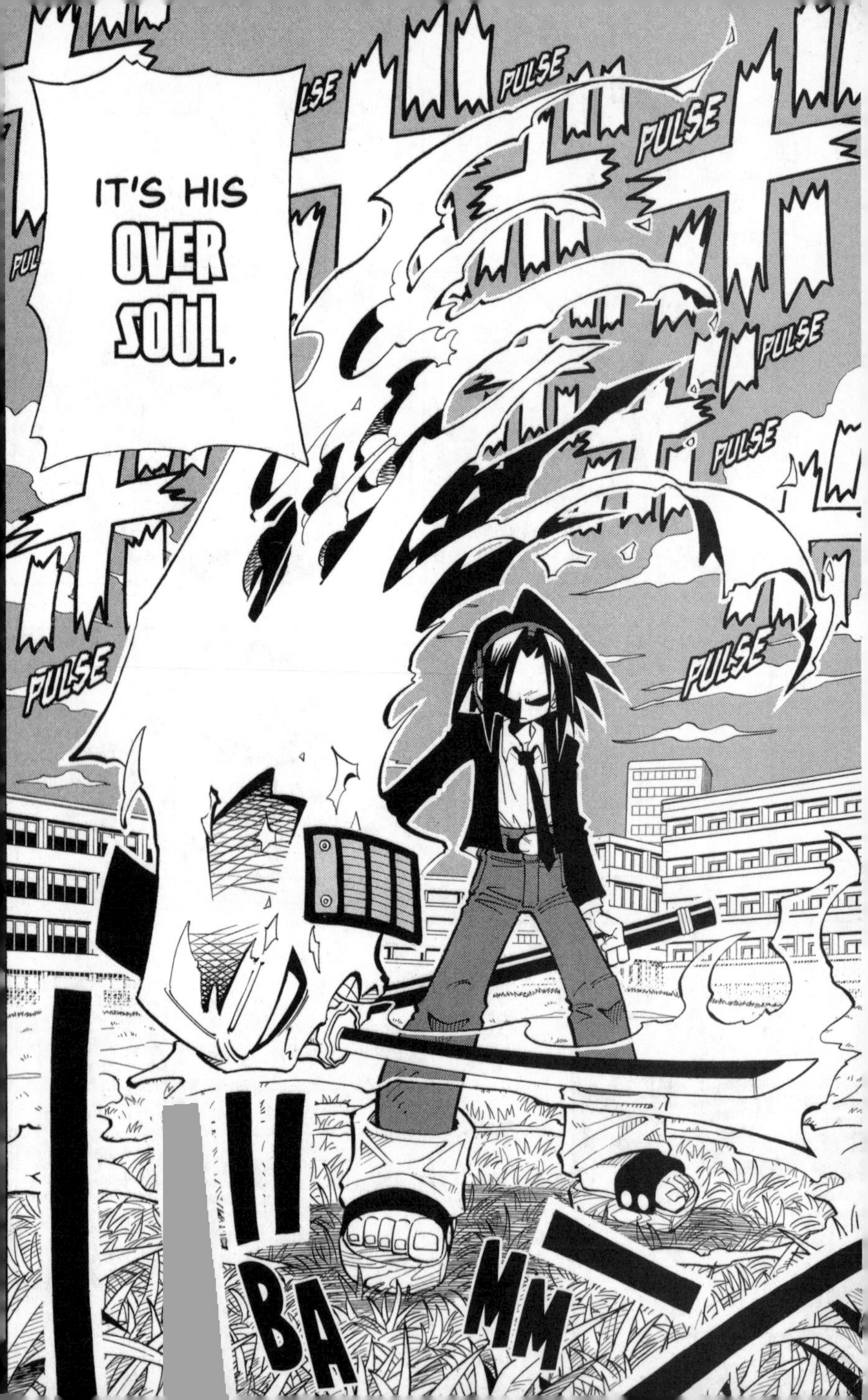
IT'S HIS OVER SOUL.
PULSE
PULSE
PULSE
PULSE
PULSE
PULSE
BAMM

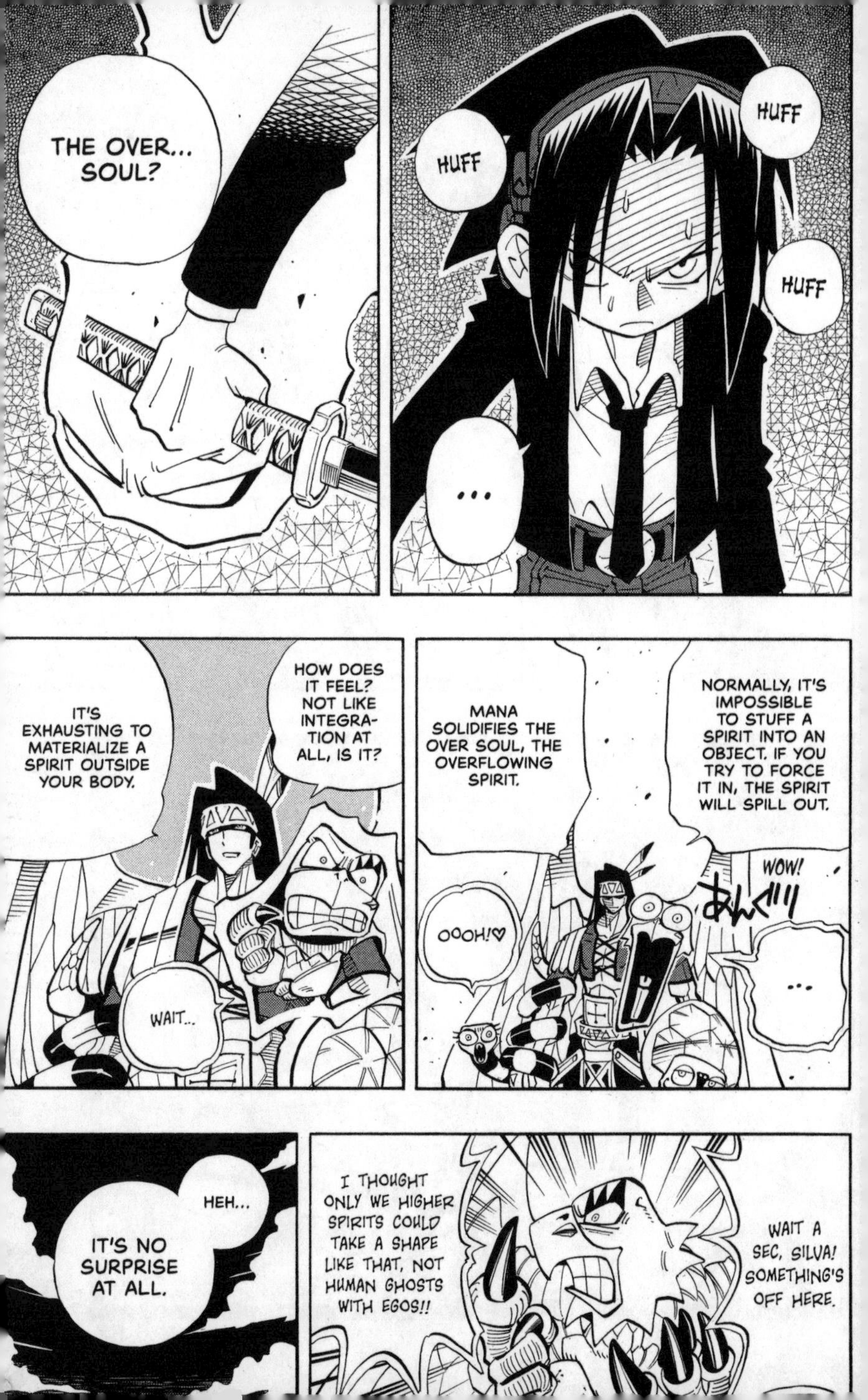
HUFF
HUFF
HUFF
...
THE OVER... SOUL?
NORMALLY, IT'S IMPOSSIBLE TO STUFF A SPIRIT INTO AN OBJECT. IF YOU TRY TO FORCE IT IN, THE SPIRIT WILL SPILL OUT.
MANA SOLIDIFIES THE OVER SOUL, THE OVERFLOWING SPIRIT.
WOW!
あんぐり
...
OOOH!♡
HOW DOES IT FEEL? NOT LIKE INTEGRATION AT ALL, IS IT?
IT'S EXHAUSTING TO MATERIALIZE A SPIRIT OUTSIDE YOUR BODY.
WAIT...
WAIT A SEC, SILVA! SOMETHING'S OFF HERE.
I THOUGHT ONLY WE HIGHER SPIRITS COULD TAKE A SHAPE LIKE THAT, NOT HUMAN GHOSTS WITH EGOS!!
HEH...
IT'S NO SURPRISE AT ALL.

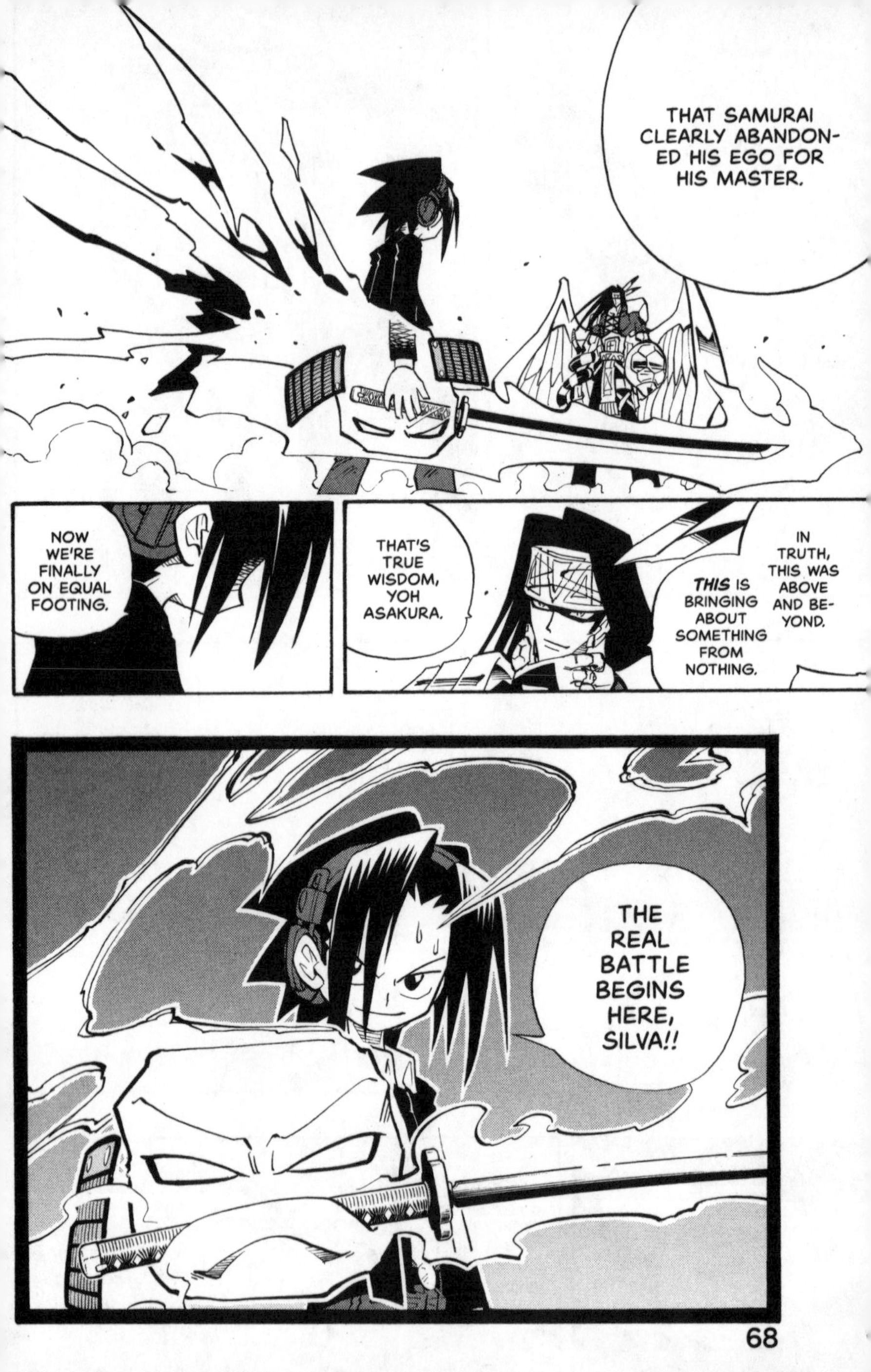
THAT SAMURAI CLEARLY ABANDONED HIS EGO FOR HIS MASTER.
IN TRUTH, THIS WAS ABOVE AND BEYOND.
THIS IS BRINGING ABOUT SOMETHING FROM NOTHING.
THAT'S TRUE WISDOM, YOH ASAKURA.
NOW WE'RE FINALLY ON EQUAL FOOTING.
THE REAL BATTLE BEGINS HERE, SILVA!!

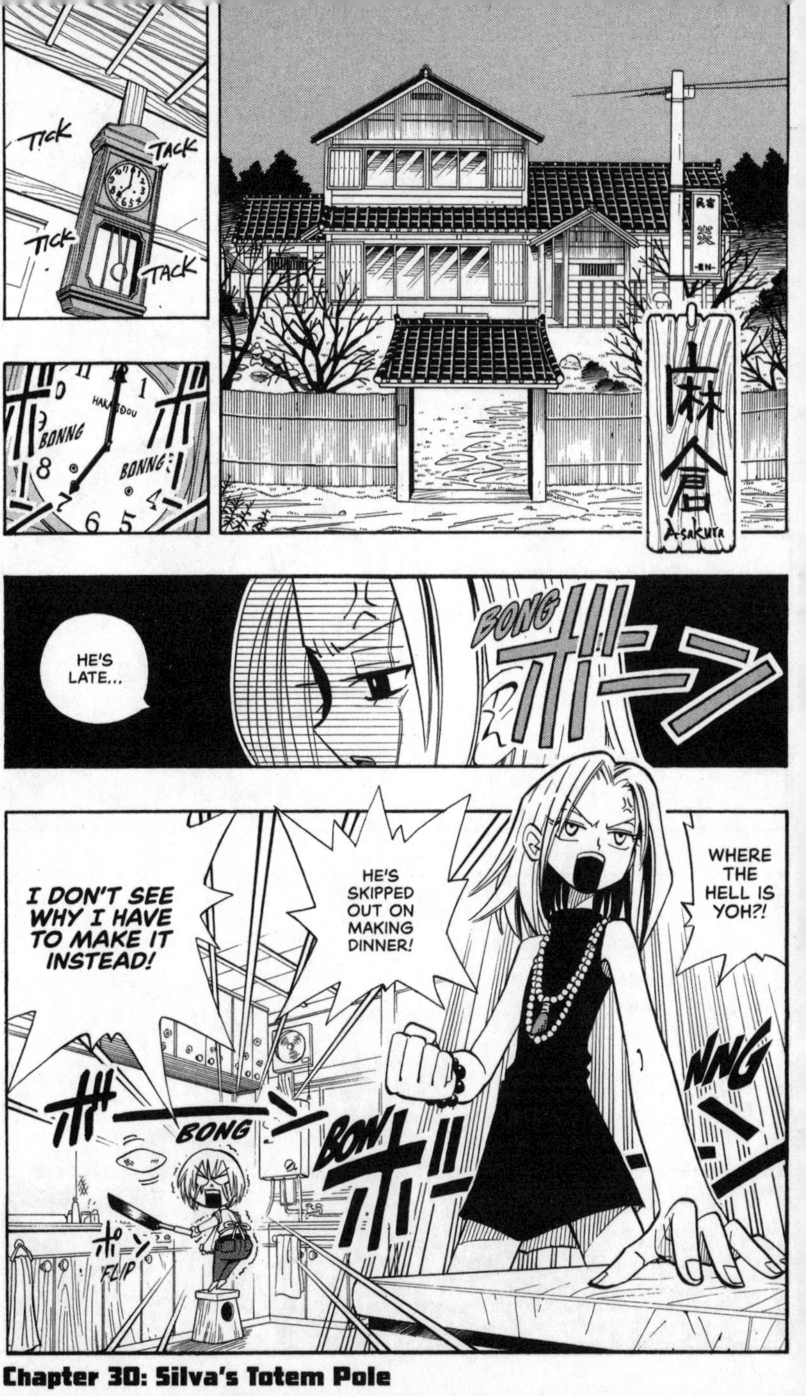

麻倉
ASAKURA
TICK
TACK
TICK
TACK
BONNG
BONNG
HE'S LATE...
BONG
WHERE THE HELL IS YOH?!
HE'S SKIPPED OUT ON MAKING DINNER!
I DON'T SEE WHY I HAVE TO MAKE IT INSTEAD!
NNG
BON
BONG
FLIP

Chapter 30: Silva's Totem Pole

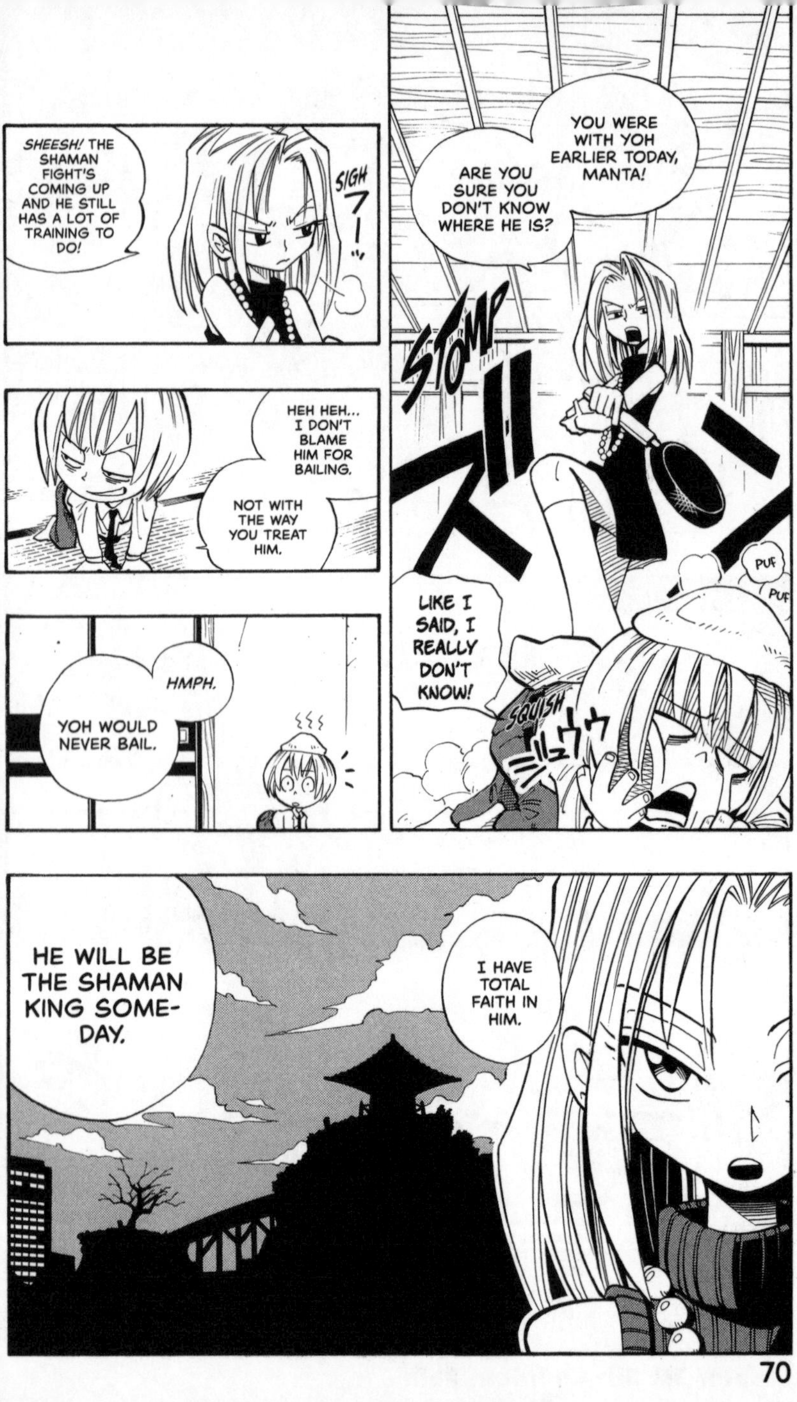
YOU WERE WITH YOH EARLIER TODAY, MANTA!
ARE YOU SURE YOU DON'T KNOW WHERE HE IS?
STOMP
PUF
PUF
LIKE I SAID, I REALLY DON'T KNOW!
SQUISH
SHEESH! THE SHAMAN FIGHT'S COMING UP AND HE STILL HAS A LOT OF TRAINING TO DO!
SIGH
HEH HEH... I DON'T BLAME HIM FOR BAILING.
NOT WITH THE WAY YOU TREAT HIM.
HMPH.
YOH WOULD NEVER BAIL.
I HAVE TOTAL FAITH IN HIM.
HE WILL BE THE SHAMAN KING SOME-DAY.

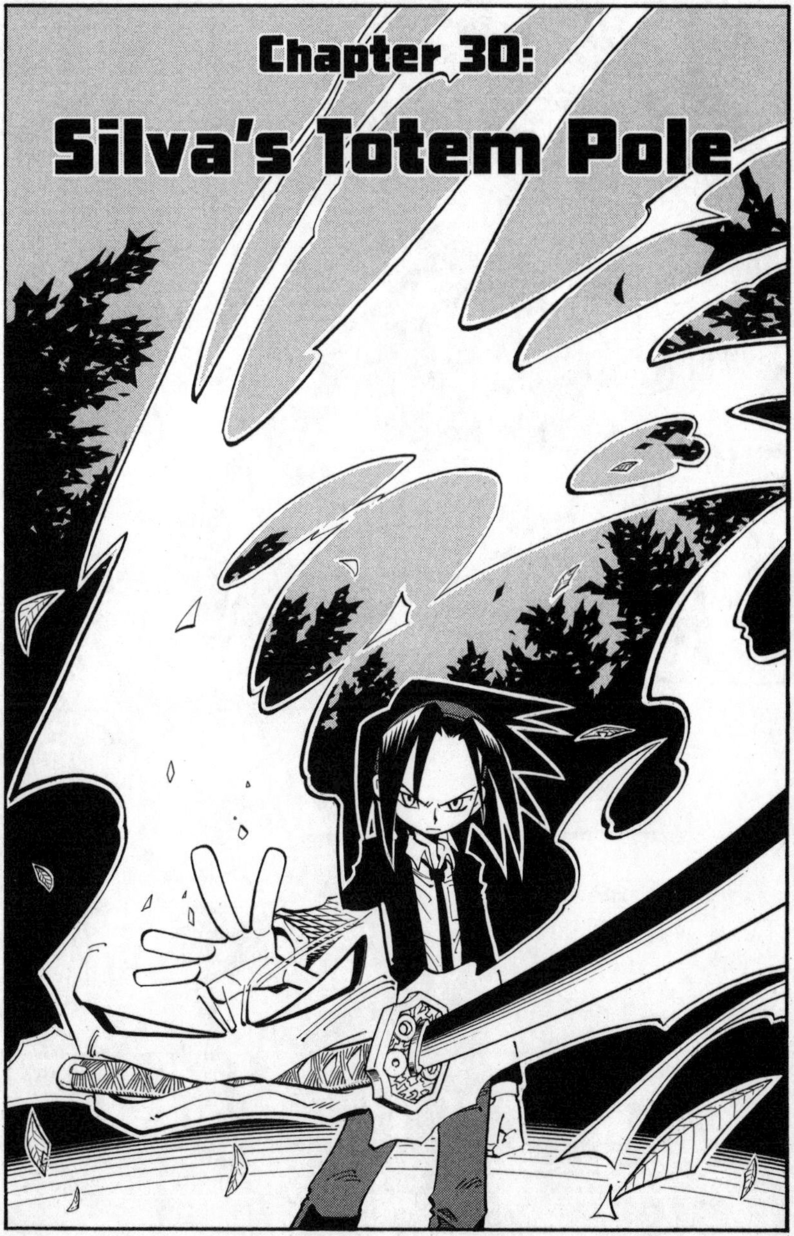
Chapter 30:
Silva's Totem Pole

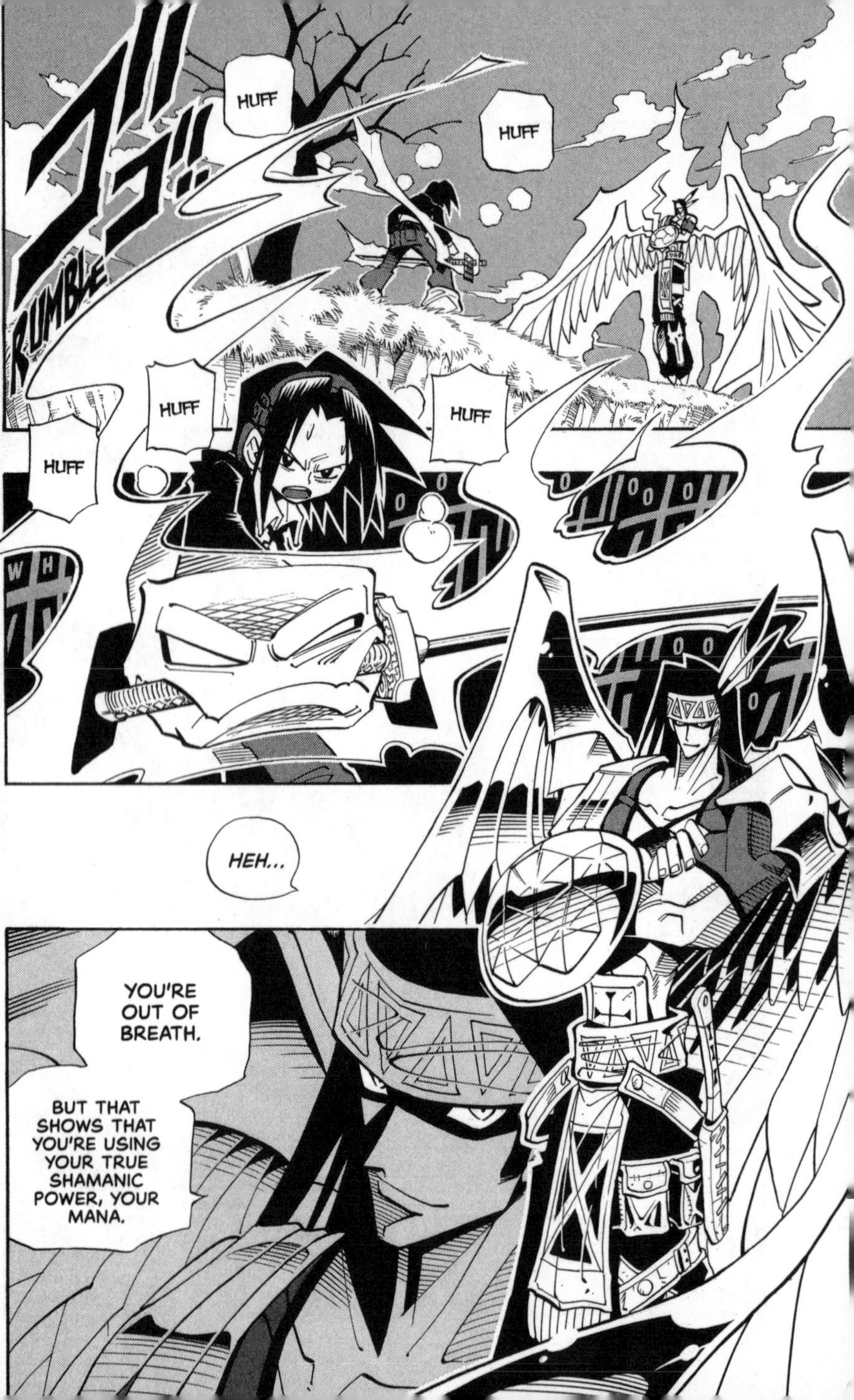
HUFF
HUFF
RUMBLE
HUFF
HUFF
HUFF
HEH...
YOU'RE OUT OF BREATH.
BUT THAT SHOWS THAT YOU'RE USING YOUR TRUE SHAMANIC POWER, YOUR MANA.

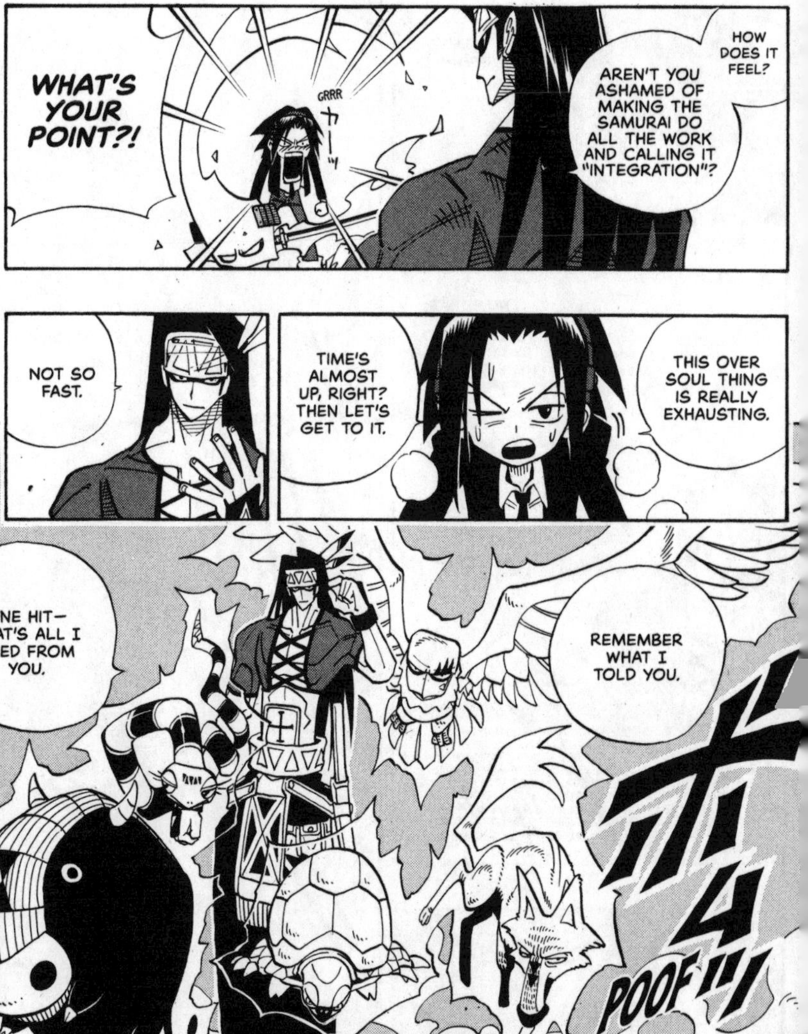
HOW DOES IT FEEL?
AREN'T YOU ASHAMED OF MAKING THE SAMURAI DO ALL THE WORK AND CALLING IT "INTEGRATION"?
GRRR
WHAT'S YOUR POINT?!
THIS OVER SOUL THING IS REALLY EXHAUSTING.
TIME'S ALMOST UP, RIGHT? THEN LET'S GET TO IT.
NOT SO FAST.
REMEMBER WHAT I TOLD YOU.
ONE HIT— THAT'S ALL I NEED FROM YOU.
POOF!!!
ONE HIT?
WHY DID HE DIS-ARM HIS ANIMALS?
THAT'S RIGHT...

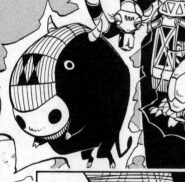

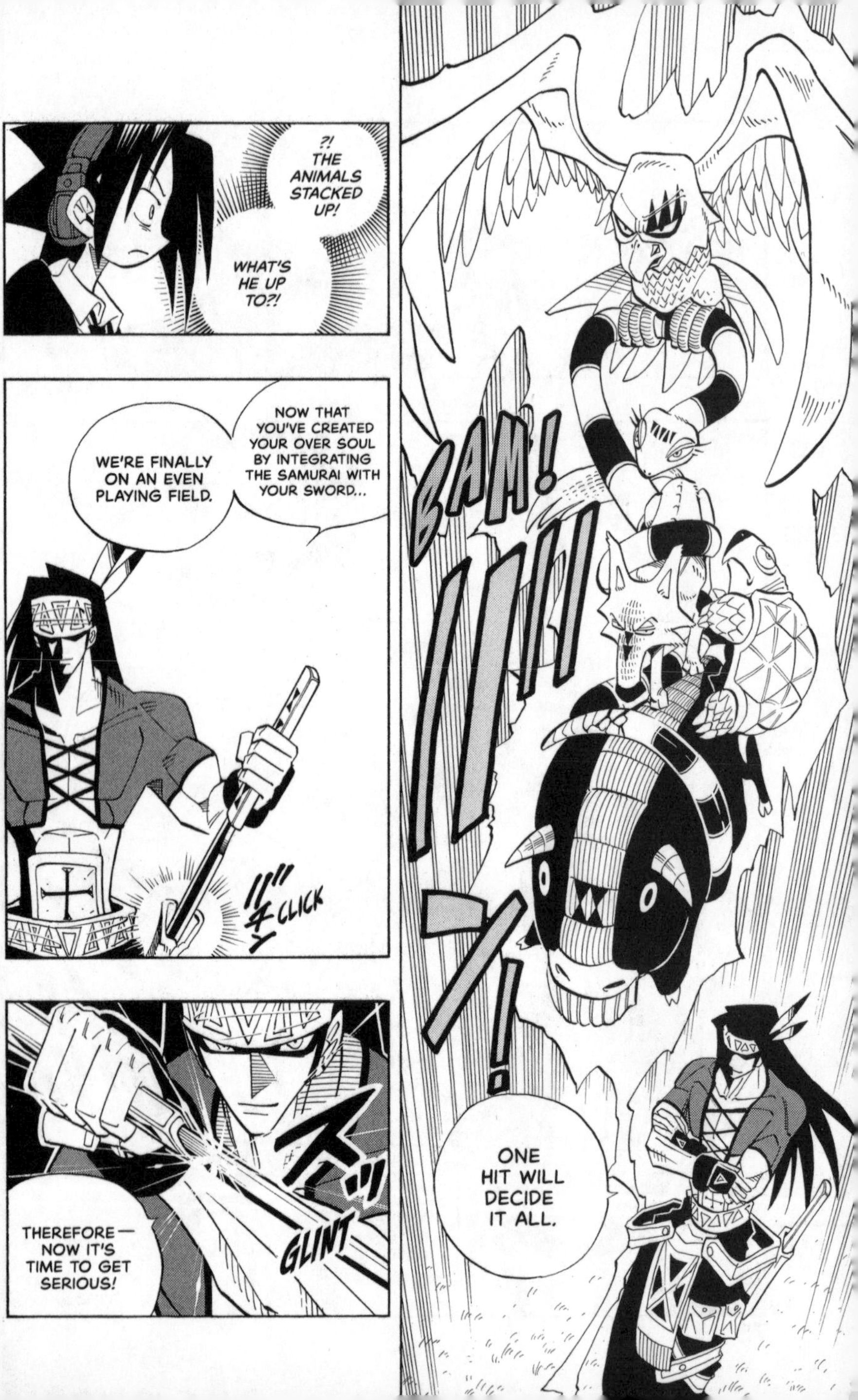
BAM!
ONE HIT WILL DECIDE IT ALL.
?! THE ANIMALS STACKED UP!
WHAT'S HE UP TO?!
NOW THAT YOU'VE CREATED YOUR OVER SOUL BY INTEGRATING THE SAMURAI WITH YOUR SWORD...
WE'RE FINALLY ON AN EVEN PLAYING FIELD.
CLICK
THEREFORE— NOW IT'S TIME TO GET SERIOUS!
GLINT

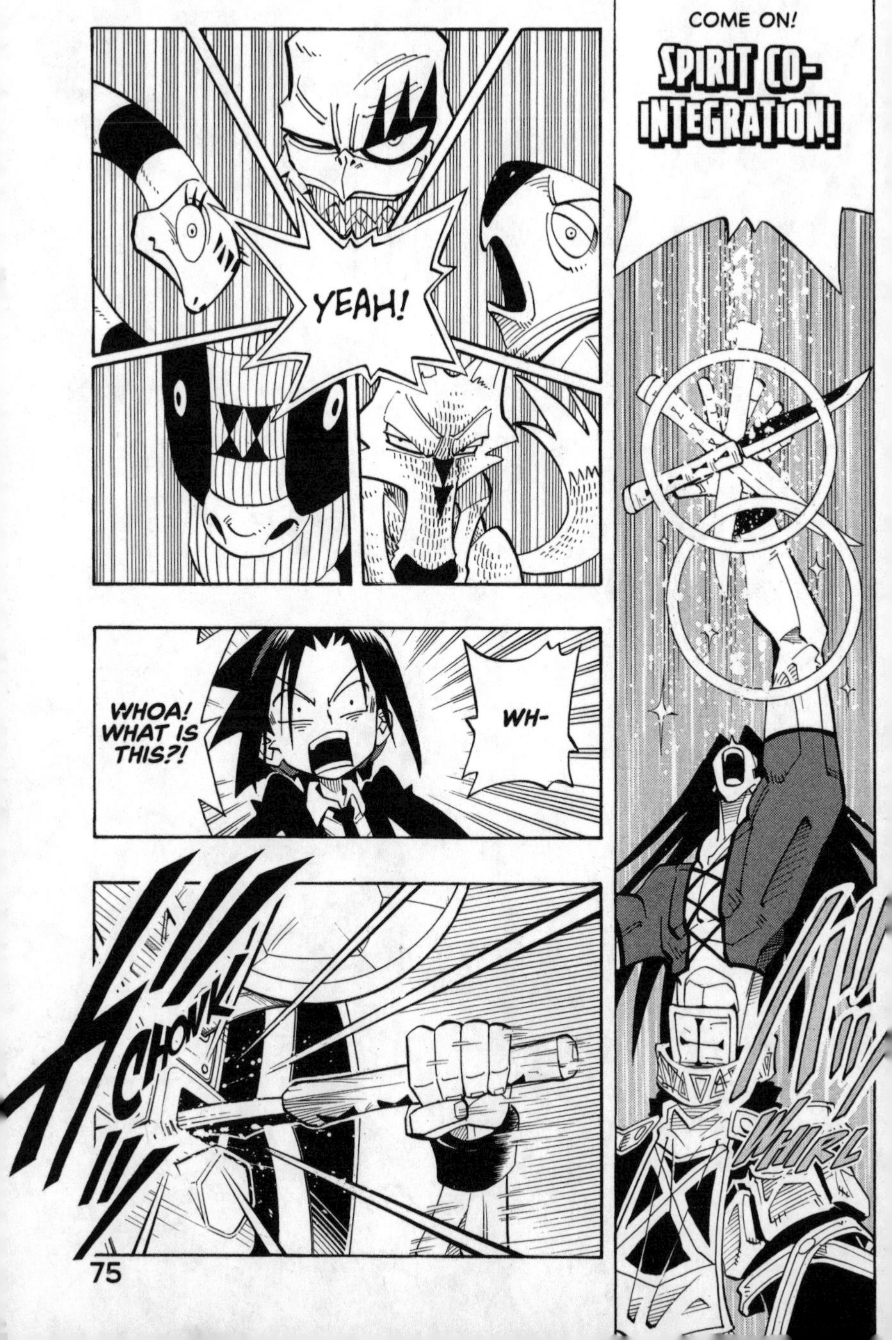
COME ON!
SPIRIT CO-INTEGRATION!
WHIRL
YEAH!
WH-
WHOA! WHAT IS THIS?!
CHONK

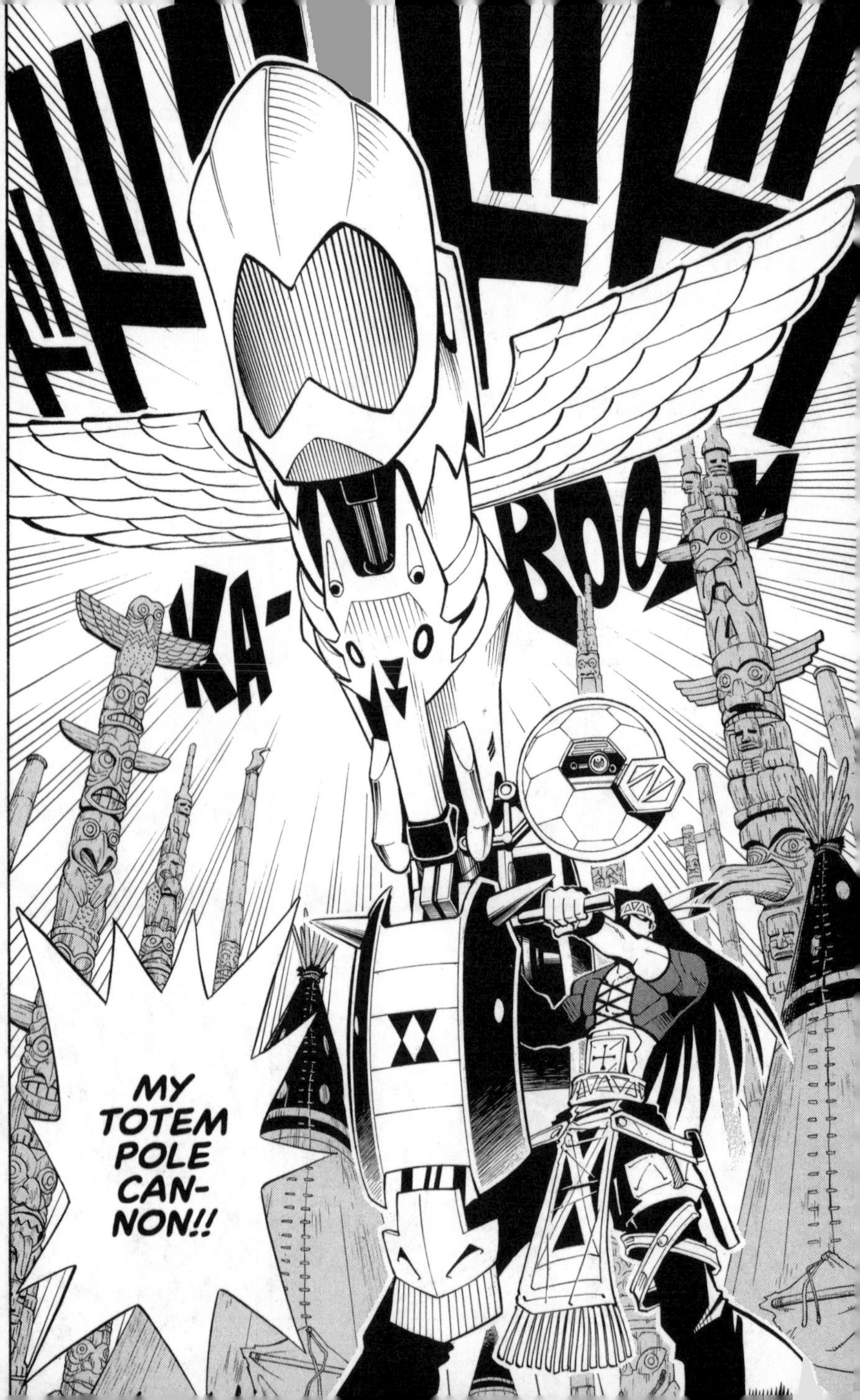
KA-BOOM
MY TOTEM POLE CAN-NON!!

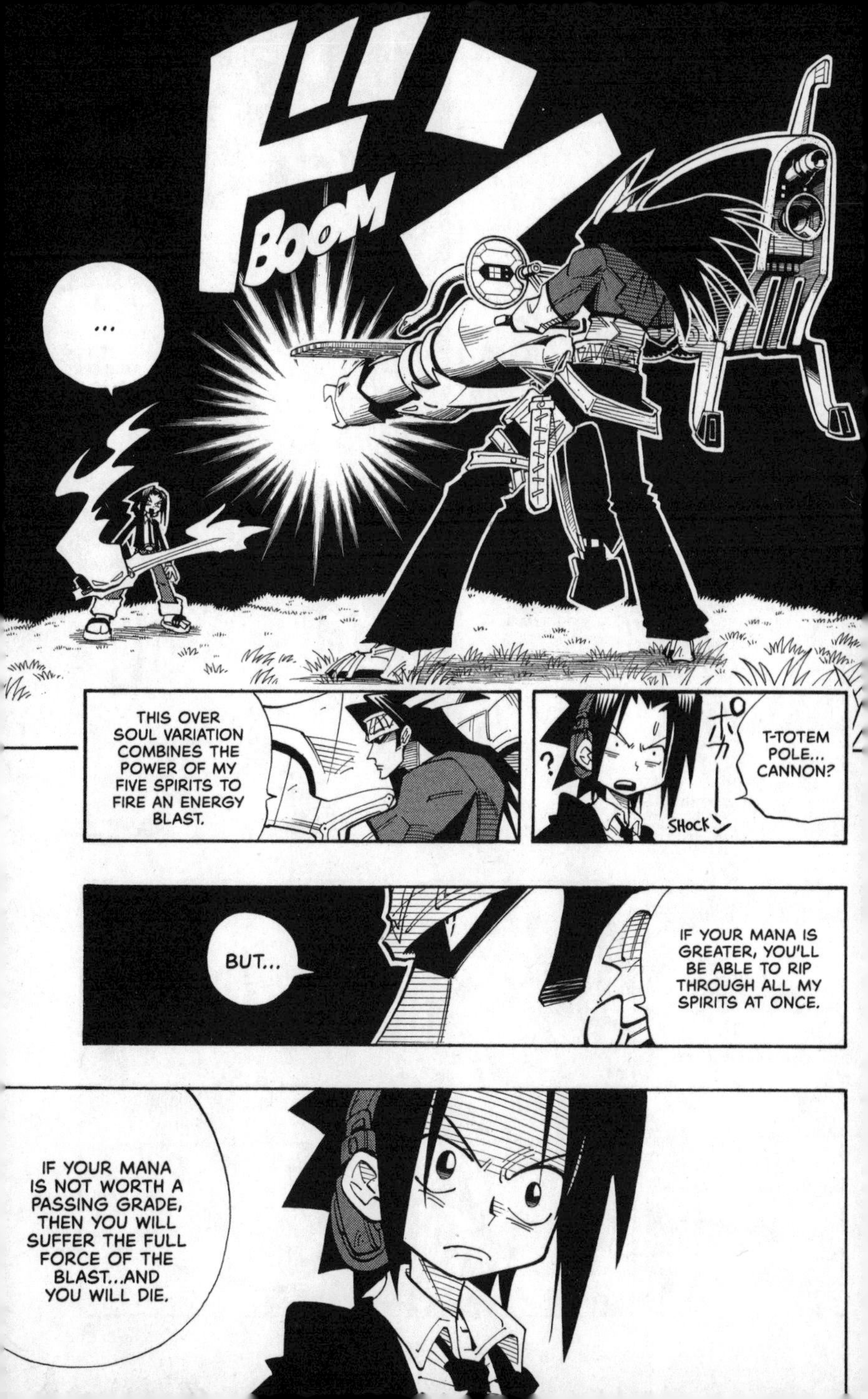
BOOM
...
T-TOTEM POLE... CANNON?
SHOCK
THIS OVER SOUL VARIATION COMBINES THE POWER OF MY FIVE SPIRITS TO FIRE AN ENERGY BLAST.
IF YOUR MANA IS GREATER, YOU'LL BE ABLE TO RIP THROUGH ALL MY SPIRITS AT ONCE.
BUT...
IF YOUR MANA IS NOT WORTH A PASSING GRADE, THEN YOU WILL SUFFER THE FULL FORCE OF THE BLAST...AND YOU WILL DIE.

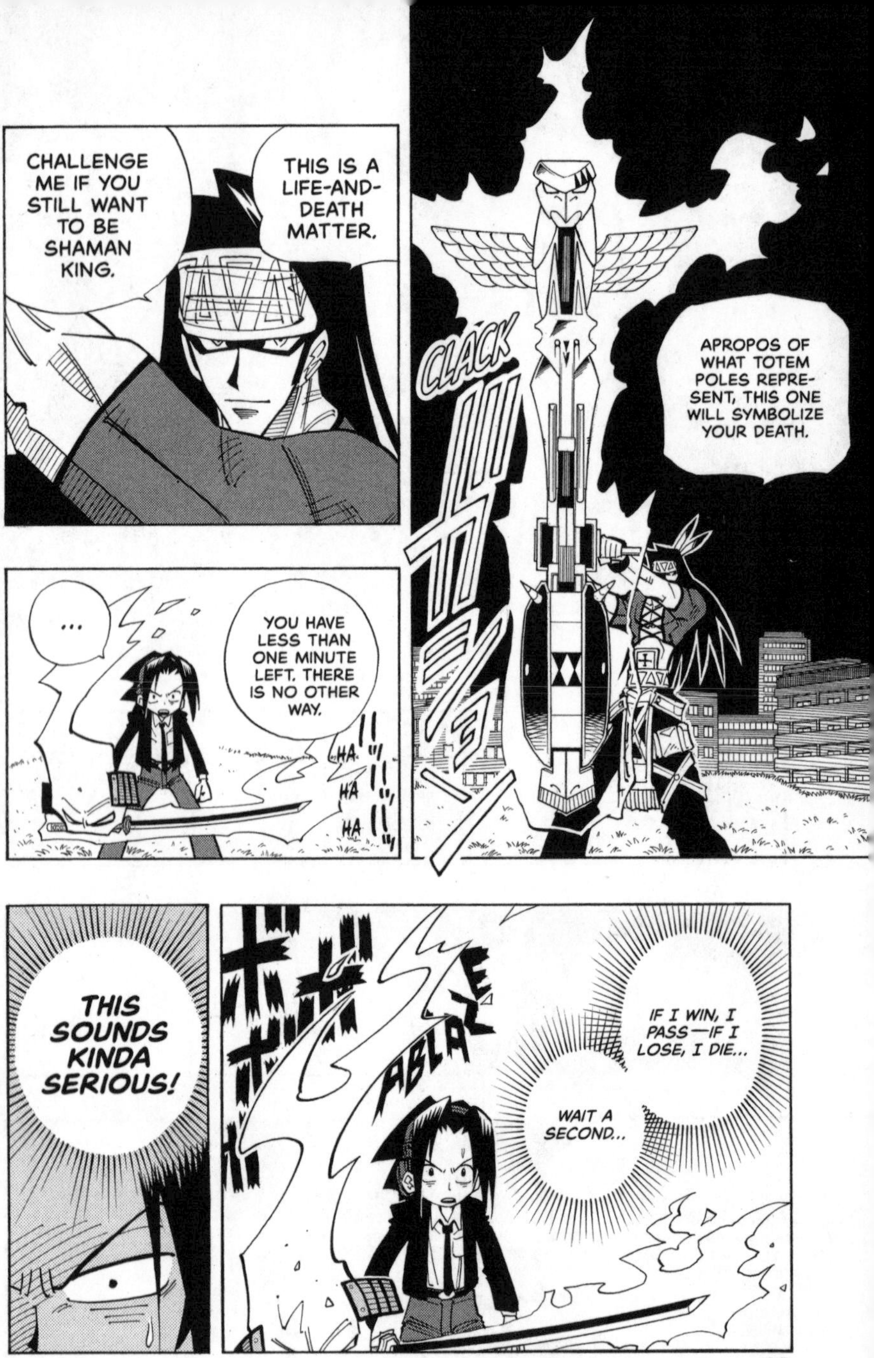
CLACK
APROPOS OF WHAT TOTEM POLES REPRESENT, THIS ONE WILL SYMBOLIZE YOUR DEATH.
THIS IS A LIFE-AND-DEATH MATTER.
CHALLENGE ME IF YOU STILL WANT TO BE SHAMAN KING.
YOU HAVE LESS THAN ONE MINUTE LEFT. THERE IS NO OTHER WAY.
...
HA
HA
HA
IF I WIN, I PASS—IF I LOSE, I DIE...
WAIT A SECOND...
ABLAZE
THIS SOUNDS KINDA SERIOUS!

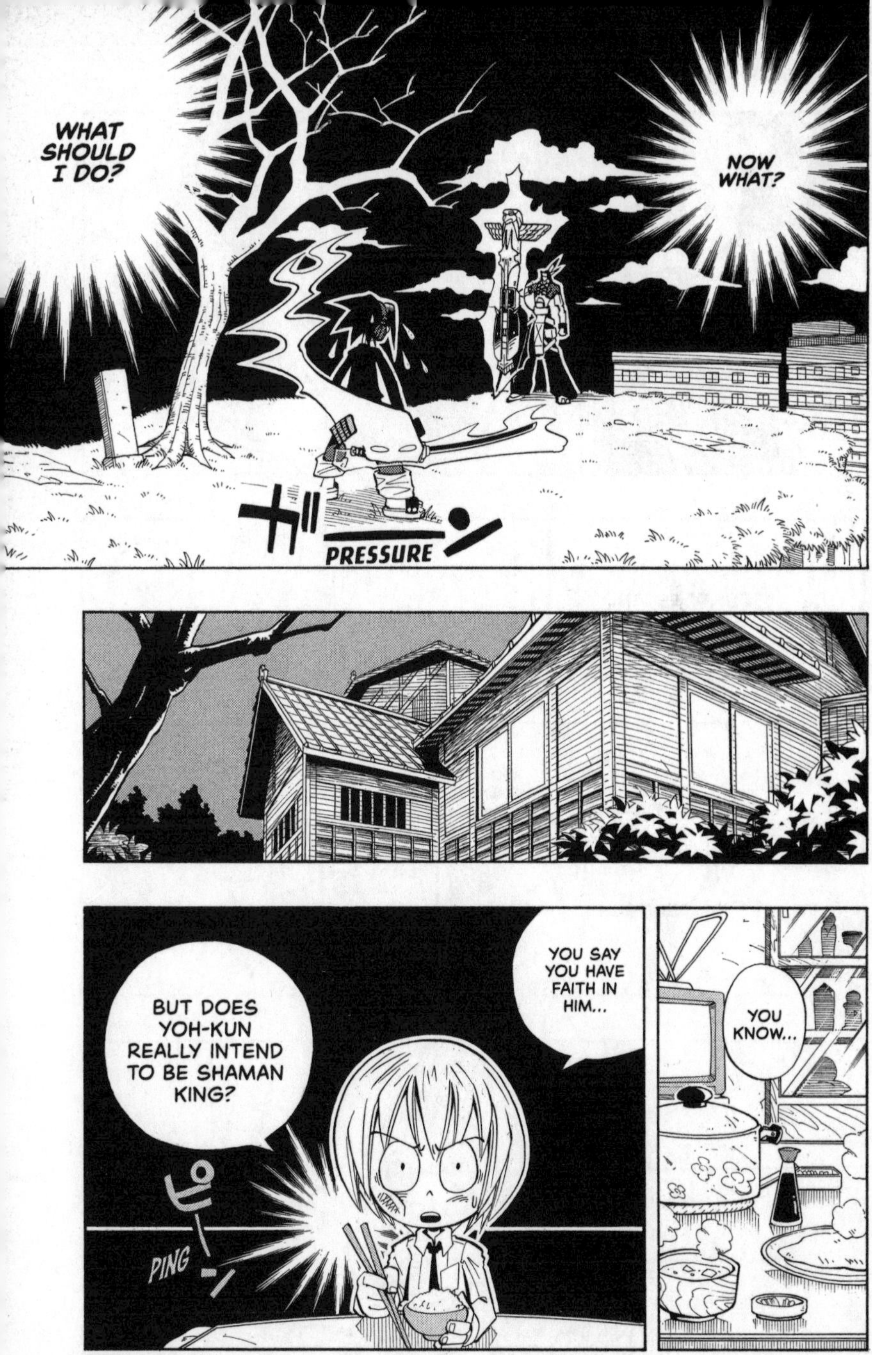
NOW WHAT?
WHAT SHOULD I DO?
PRESSURE
YOU KNOW...
YOU SAY YOU HAVE FAITH IN HIM...
BUT DOES YOH-KUN REALLY INTEND TO BE SHAMAN KING?
PING

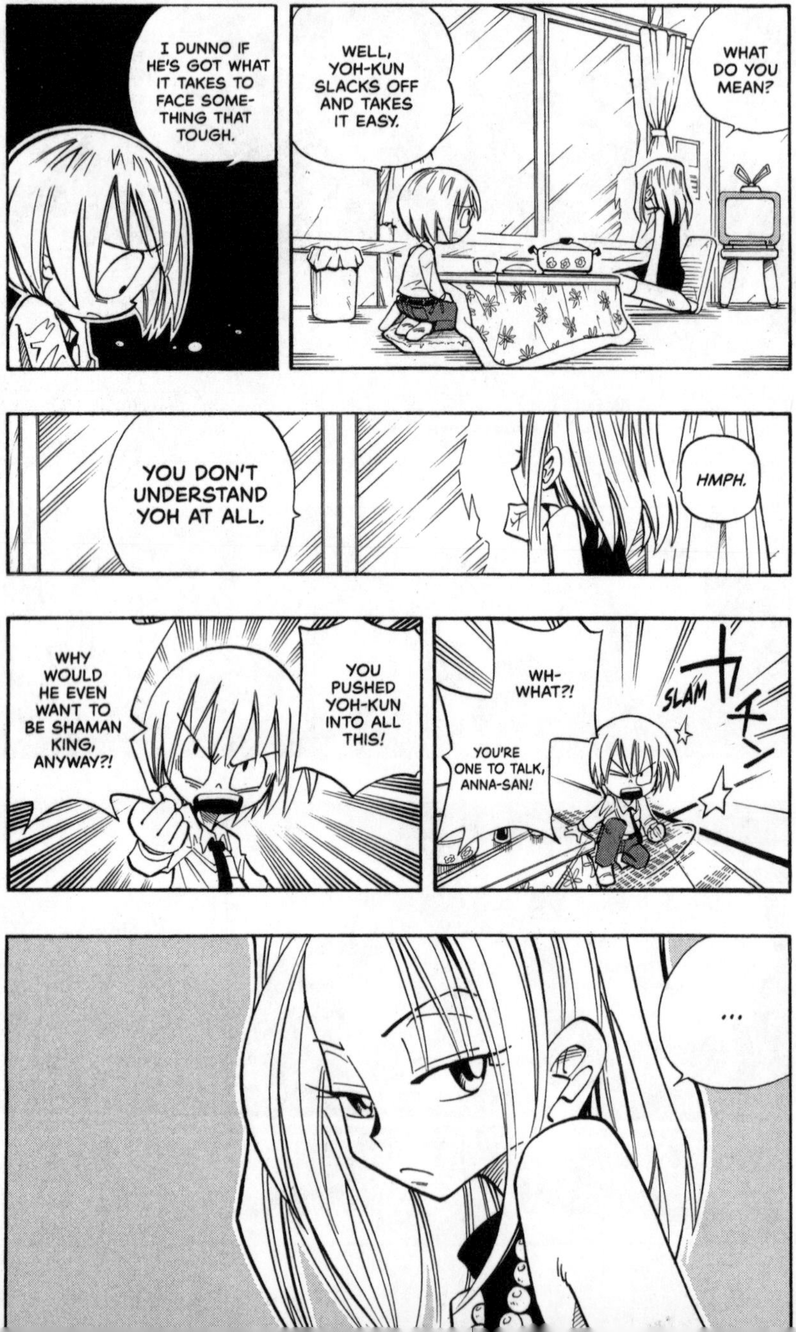
WHAT DO YOU MEAN?
WELL, YOH-KUN SLACKS OFF AND TAKES IT EASY.
I DUNNO IF HE'S GOT WHAT IT TAKES TO FACE SOME-THING THAT TOUGH.
HMPH.
YOU DON'T UNDERSTAND YOH AT ALL.
カチン
SLAM
WH-WHAT?!
YOU'RE ONE TO TALK, ANNA-SAN!
YOU PUSHED YOH-KUN INTO ALL THIS!
WHY WOULD HE EVEN WANT TO BE SHAMAN KING, ANYWAY?!
...

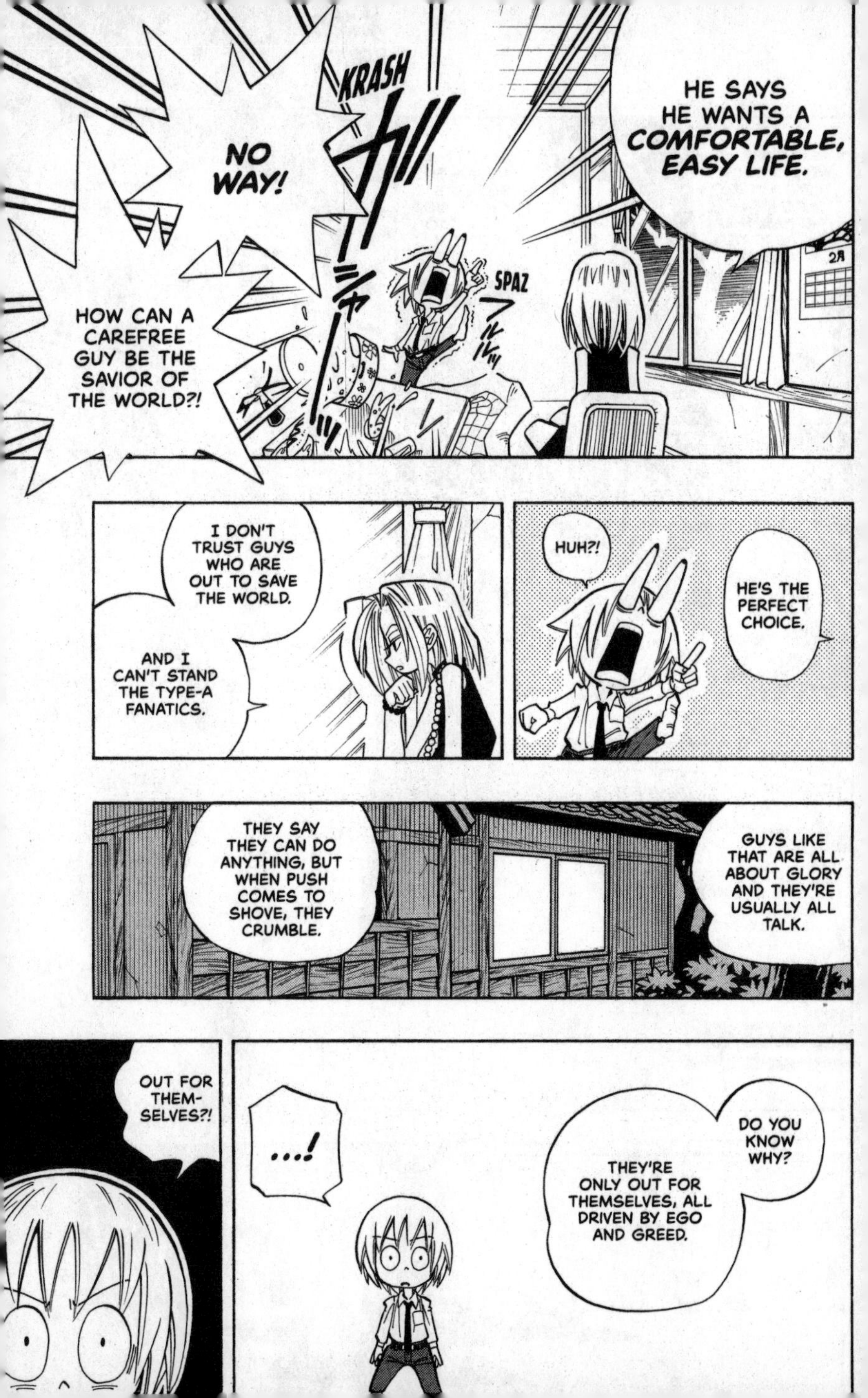
HE SAYS HE WANTS A **COMFORTABLE, EASY LIFE.**
KRASH
SPAZ
NO WAY!
HOW CAN A CAREFREE GUY BE THE SAVIOR OF THE WORLD?!
HE'S THE PERFECT CHOICE.
HUH?!
I DON'T TRUST GUYS WHO ARE OUT TO SAVE THE WORLD.
AND I CAN'T STAND THE TYPE-A FANATICS.
GUYS LIKE THAT ARE ALL ABOUT GLORY AND THEY'RE USUALLY ALL TALK.
THEY SAY THEY CAN DO ANYTHING, BUT WHEN PUSH COMES TO SHOVE, THEY CRUMBLE.
DO YOU KNOW WHY?
THEY'RE ONLY OUT FOR THEMSELVES, ALL DRIVEN BY EGO AND GREED.
...!
OUT FOR THEM-SELVES?!

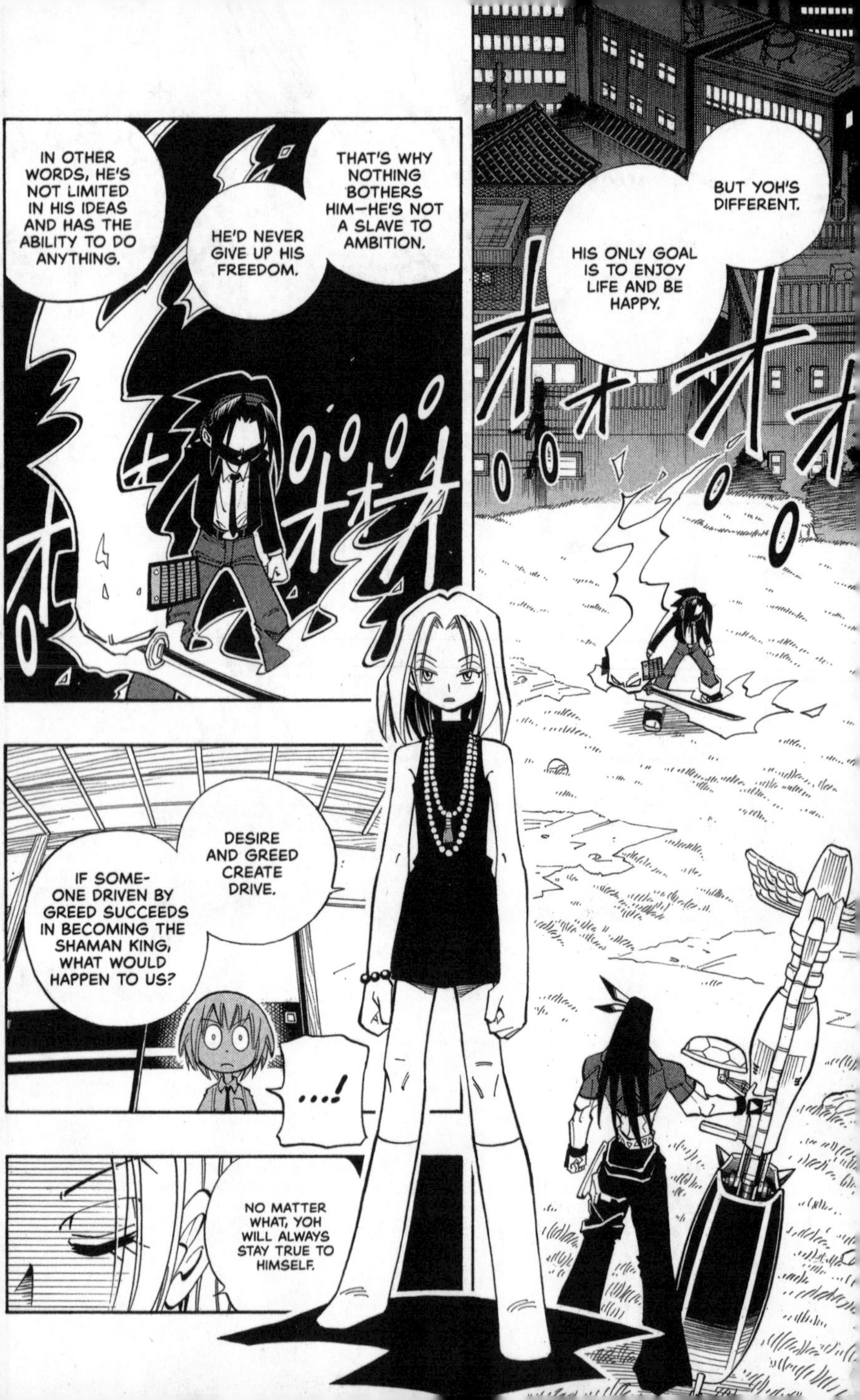
BUT YOH'S DIFFERENT.
HIS ONLY GOAL IS TO ENJOY LIFE AND BE HAPPY.
THAT'S WHY NOTHING BOTHERS HIM—HE'S NOT A SLAVE TO AMBITION.
HE'D NEVER GIVE UP HIS FREEDOM.
IN OTHER WORDS, HE'S NOT LIMITED IN HIS IDEAS AND HAS THE ABILITY TO DO ANYTHING.
DESIRE AND GREED CREATE DRIVE.
IF SOME-ONE DRIVEN BY GREED SUCCEEDS IN BECOMING THE SHAMAN KING, WHAT WOULD HAPPEN TO US?
...!
NO MATTER WHAT, YOH WILL ALWAYS STAY TRUE TO HIMSELF.

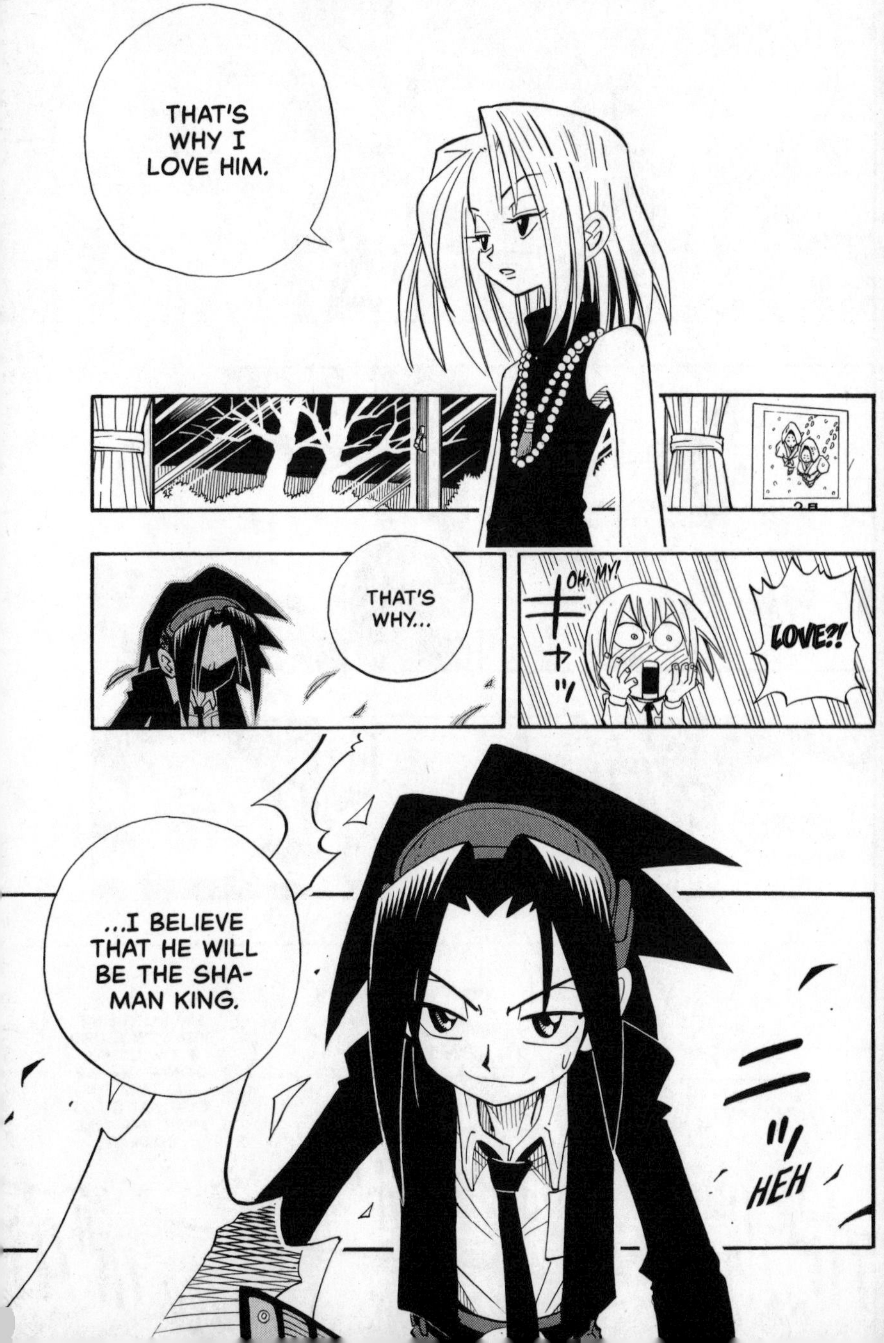
THAT'S WHY I LOVE HIM.
OH, MY!
キャッ
LOVE?!
THAT'S WHY...
...I BELIEVE THAT HE WILL BE THE SHA-MAN KING.
ニッ
HEH

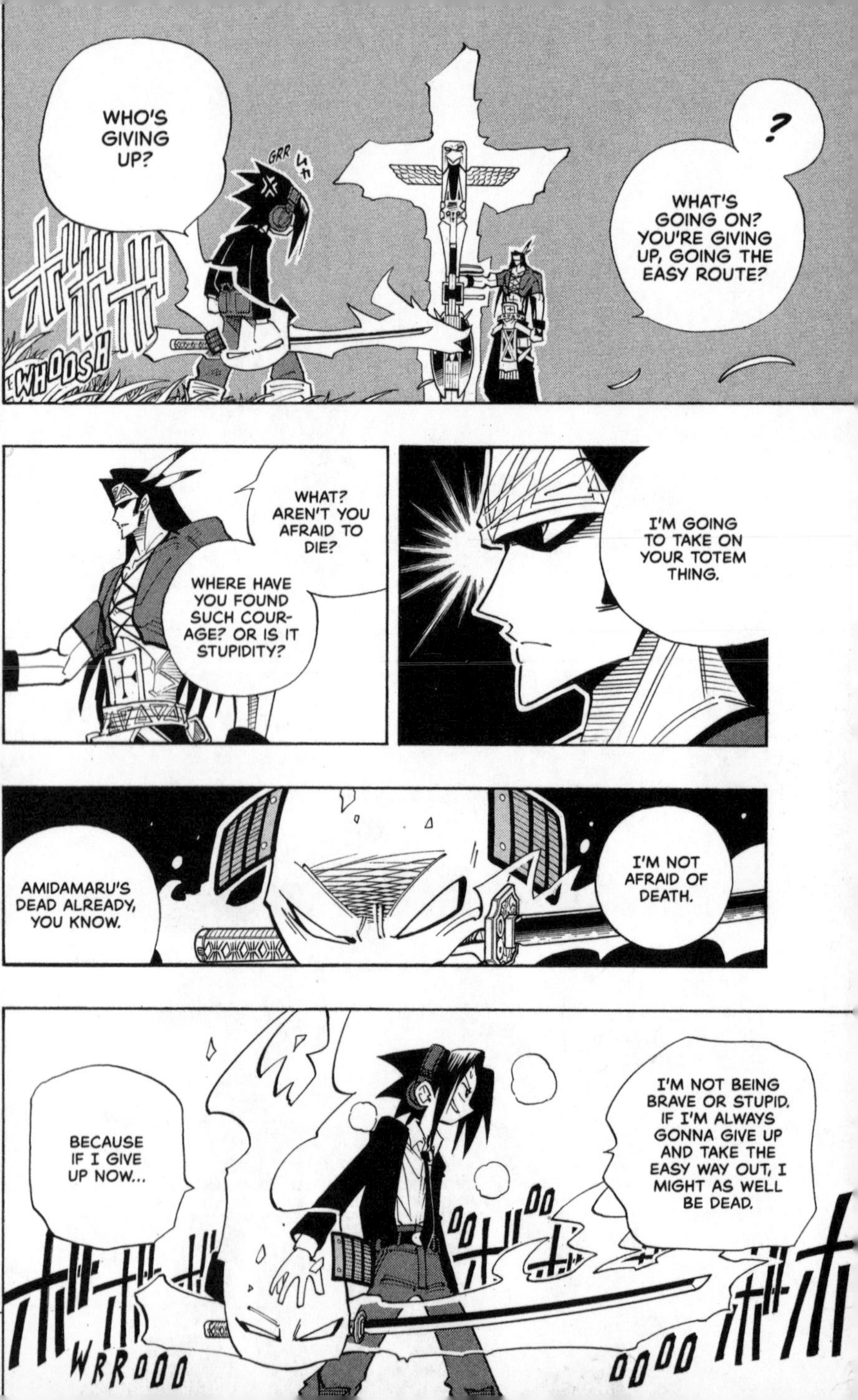
?
WHAT'S GOING ON? YOU'RE GIVING UP, GOING THE EASY ROUTE?
WHO'S GIVING UP?
GRR
WHOOSH
I'M GOING TO TAKE ON YOUR TOTEM THING.
WHAT? AREN'T YOU AFRAID TO DIE?
WHERE HAVE YOU FOUND SUCH COURAGE? OR IS IT STUPIDITY?
I'M NOT AFRAID OF DEATH.
AMIDAMARU'S DEAD ALREADY, YOU KNOW.
I'M NOT BEING BRAVE OR STUPID. IF I'M ALWAYS GONNA GIVE UP AND TAKE THE EASY WAY OUT, I MIGHT AS WELL BE DEAD.
BECAUSE IF I GIVE UP NOW...
OOOO
WRROOO

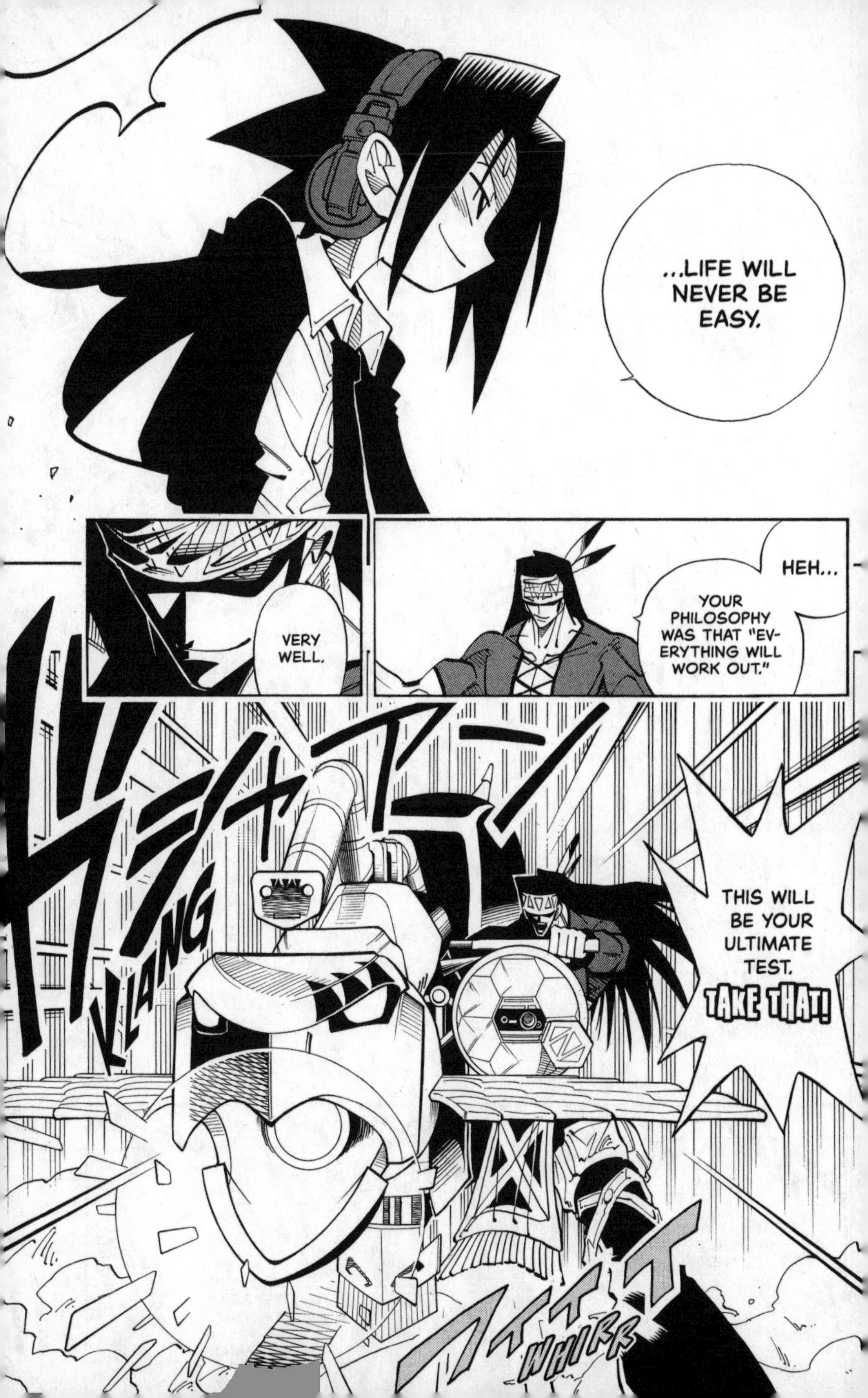
...LIFE WILL NEVER BE EASY.
HEH...
YOUR PHILOSOPHY WAS THAT "EV-ERYTHING WILL WORK OUT."
VERY WELL.
THIS WILL BE YOUR ULTIMATE TEST.
TAKE THAT!
KLANG
WHIRR

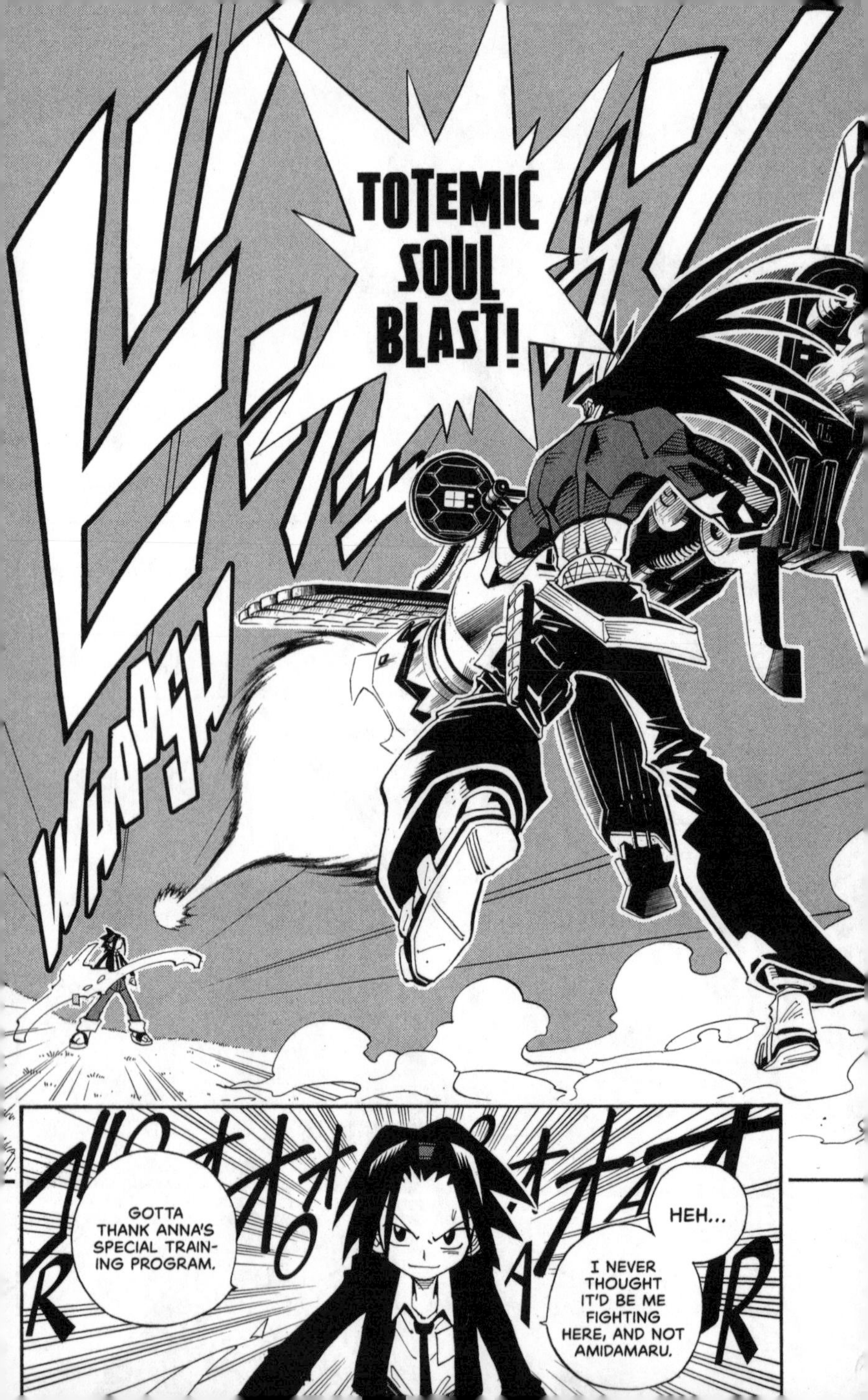
TOTEMIC SOUL BLAST!
WHOOSH
HEH...
I NEVER THOUGHT IT'D BE ME FIGHTING HERE, AND NOT AMIDAMARU.
GOTTA THANK ANNA'S SPECIAL TRAIN-ING PROGRAM.
ROAR

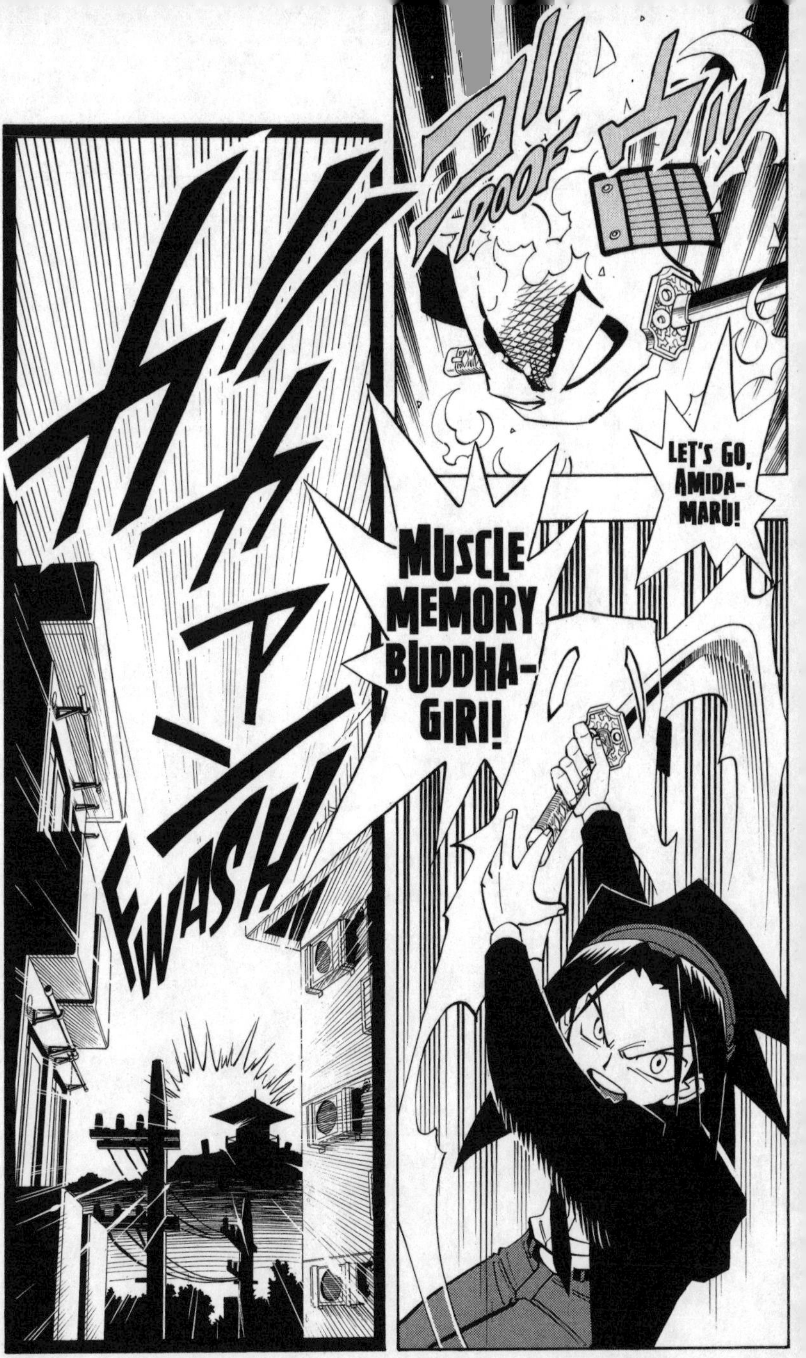
POOF
LET'S GO, AMIDA-MARU!
MUSCLE MEMORY BUDDHA-GIRI!
FWASH

SHAMAN
KING
4

**The Oracle
Pager**

Chapter 31: The Oracle Pager

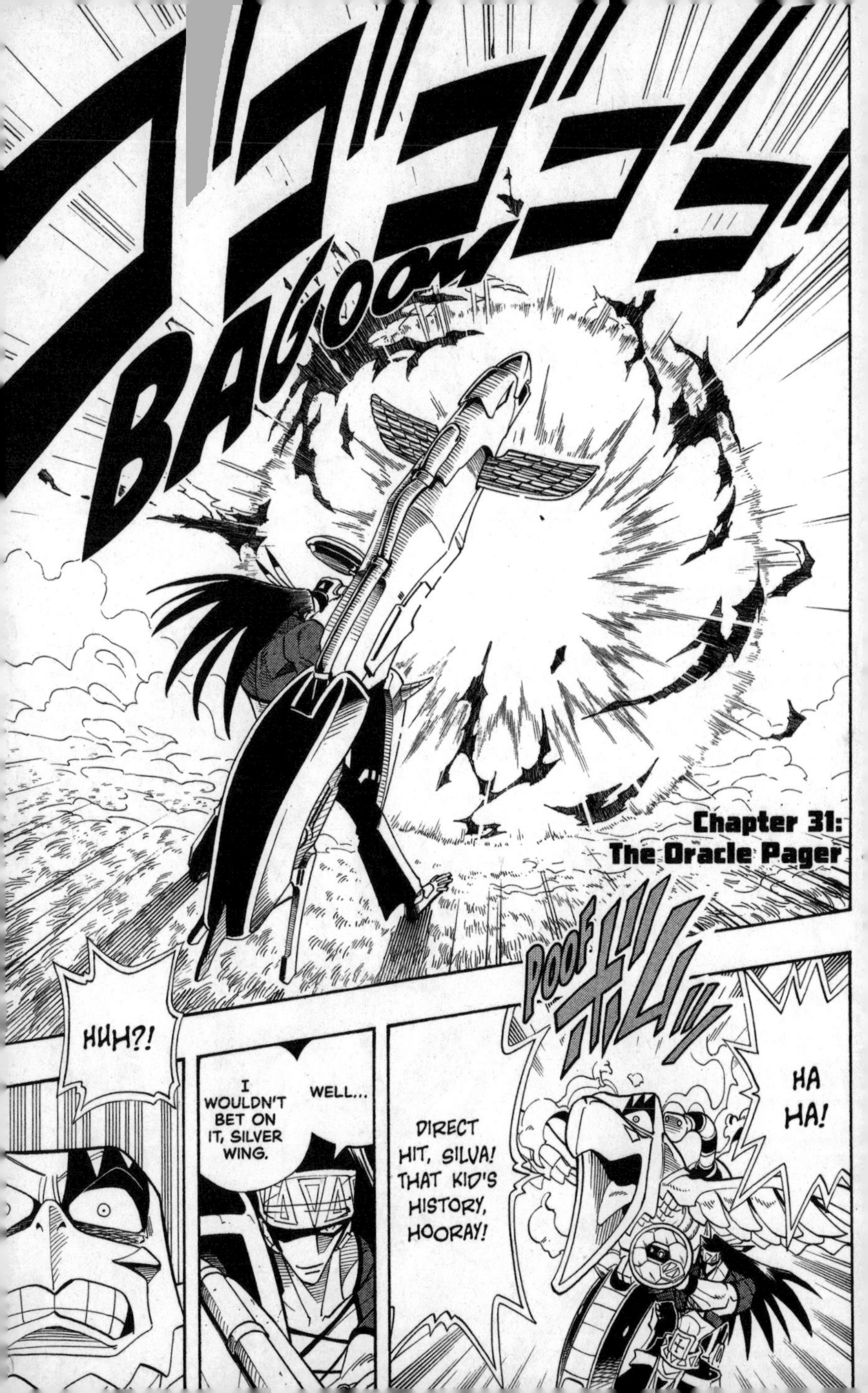
BAGOOM
POOF
HA HA!
DIRECT HIT, SILVA! THAT KID'S HISTORY, HOORAY!
WELL...
I WOULDN'T BET ON IT, SILVER WING.
HUH?!

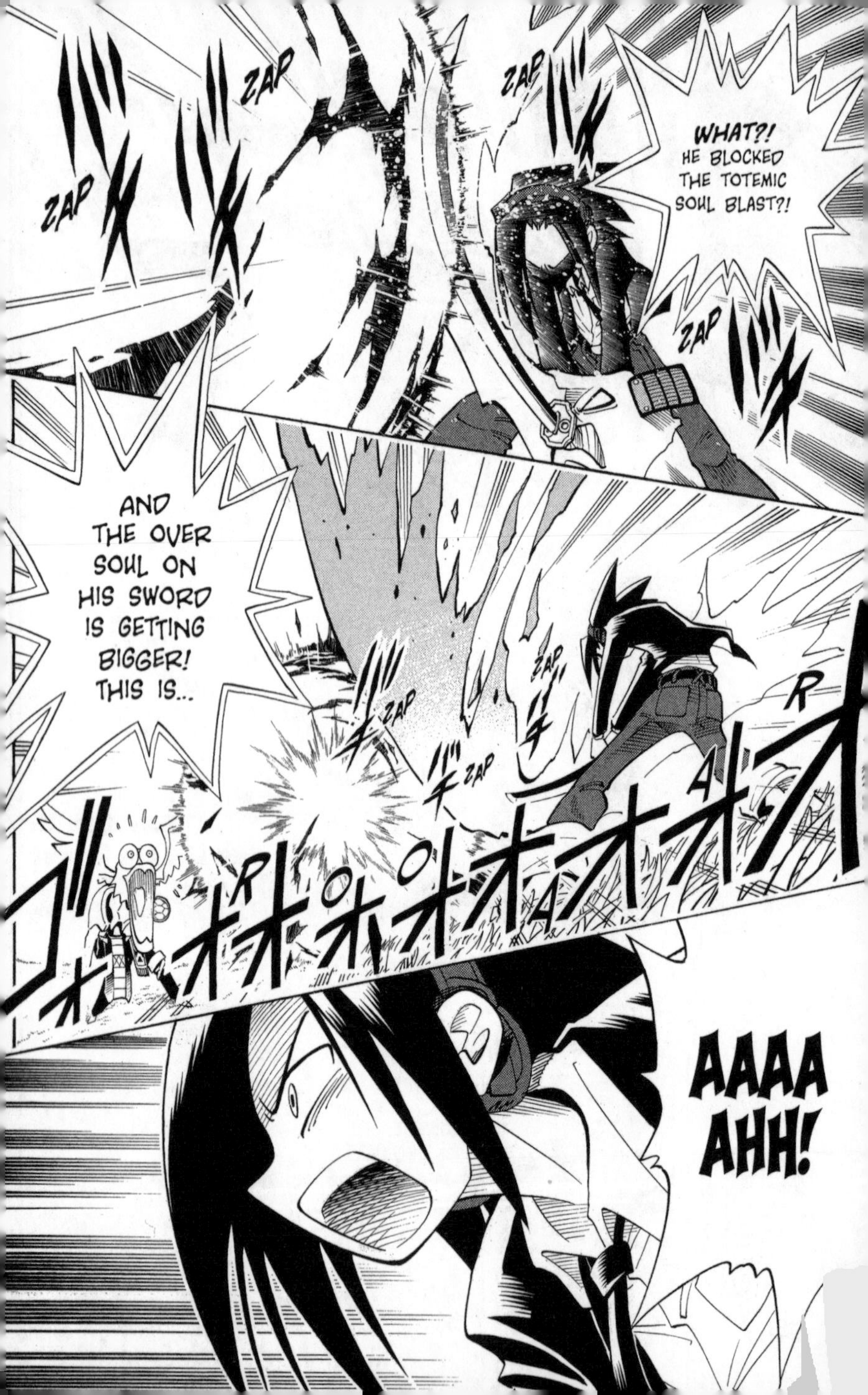
ZAP
WHAT?! HE BLOCKED THE TOTEMIC SOUL BLAST?!
ZAP
ZAP
ZAP
AND THE OVER SOUL ON HIS SWORD IS GETTING BIGGER! THIS IS...
ZAP
ZAP
ZAP
R
A
A
R
O
AAAA AHH!

Chapter 31:

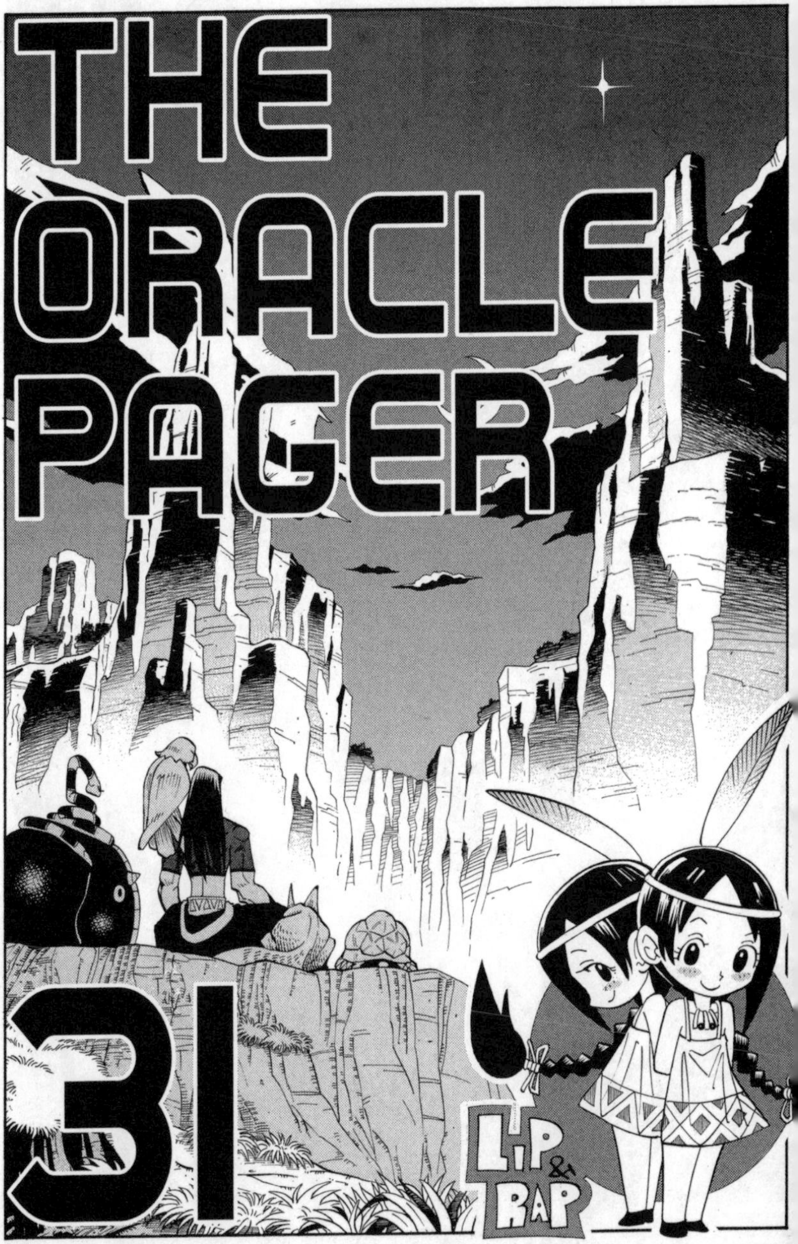
THE ORACLE PAGER
31
LIP & RAP

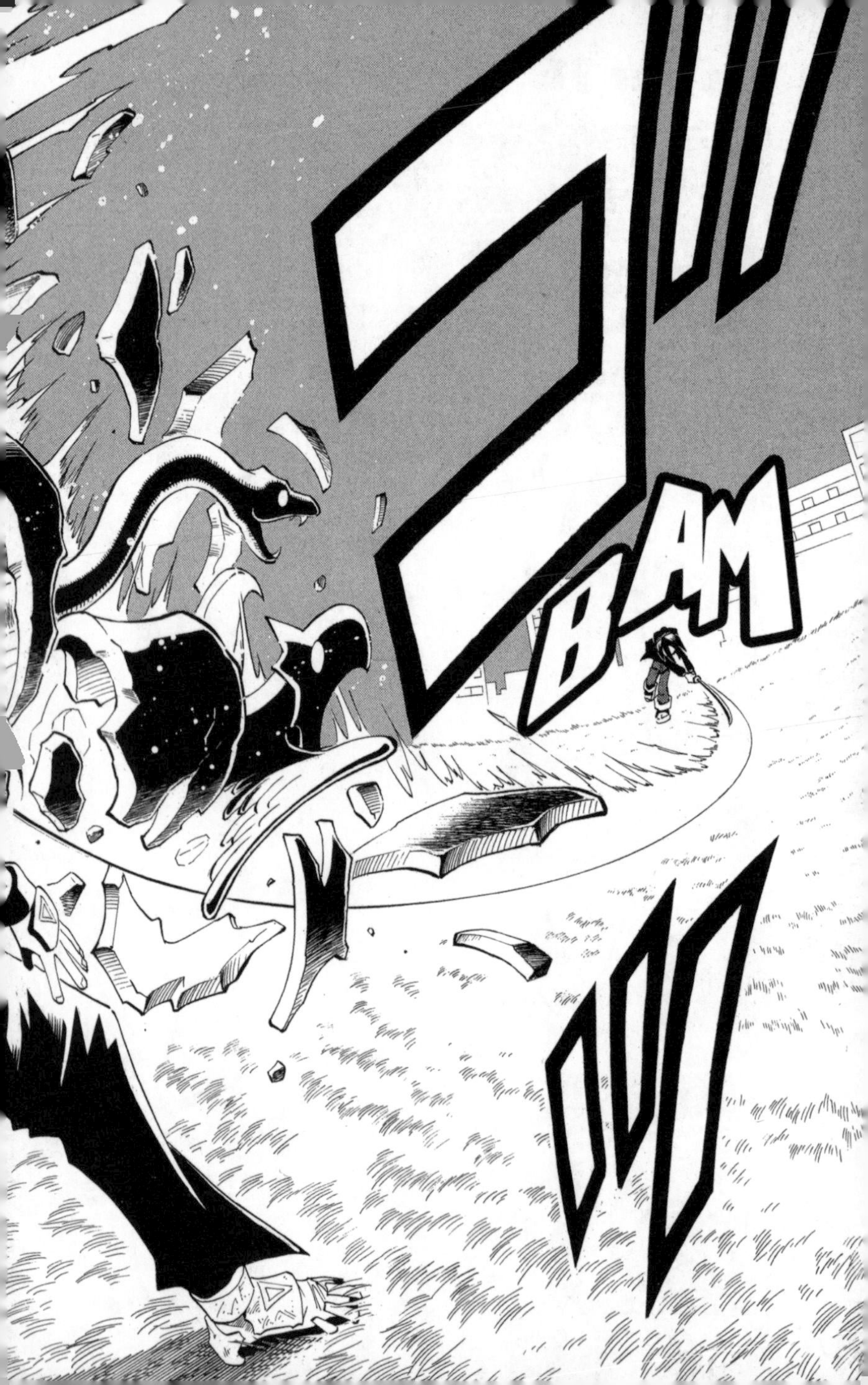
BAM

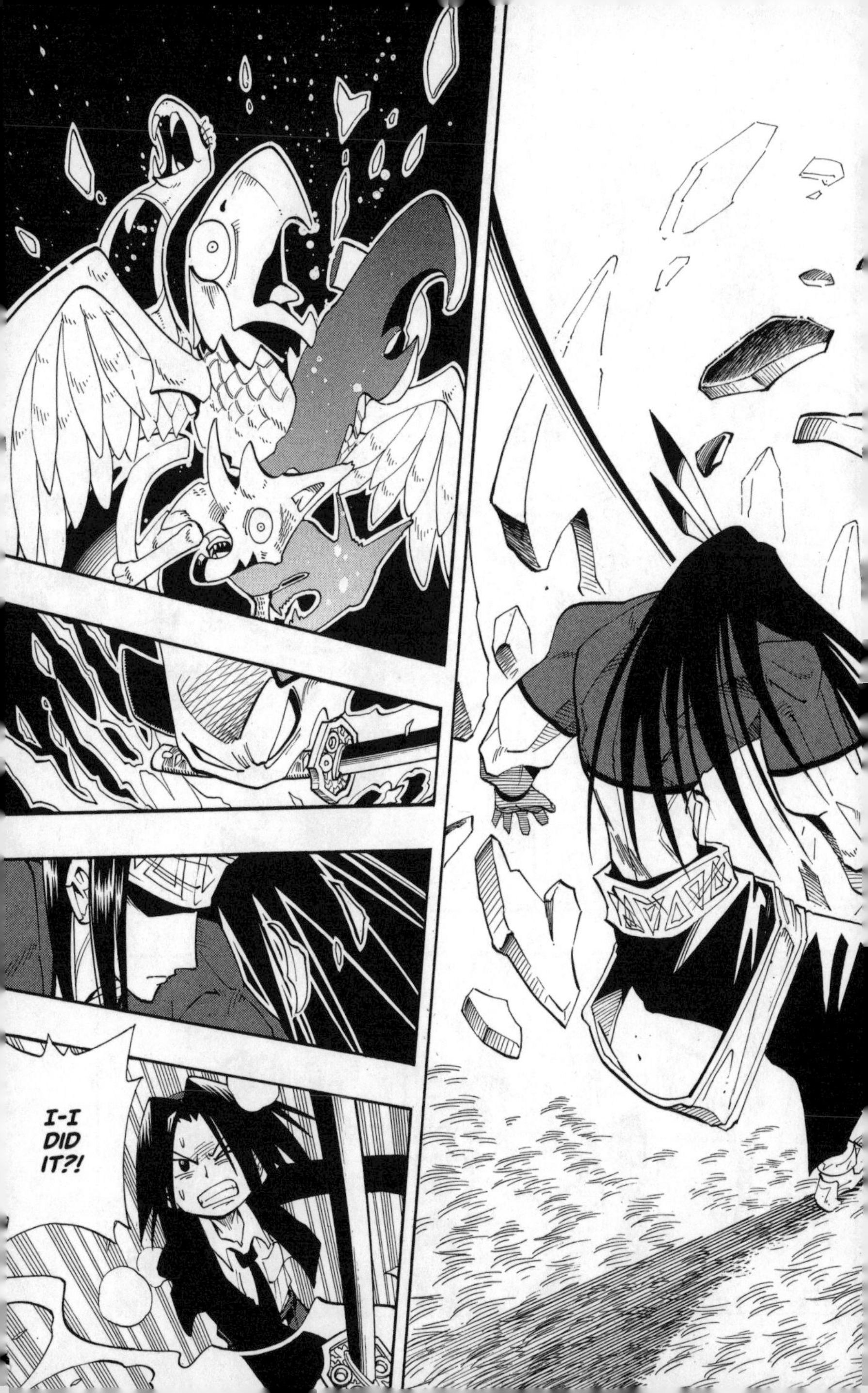
I-I DID IT?!

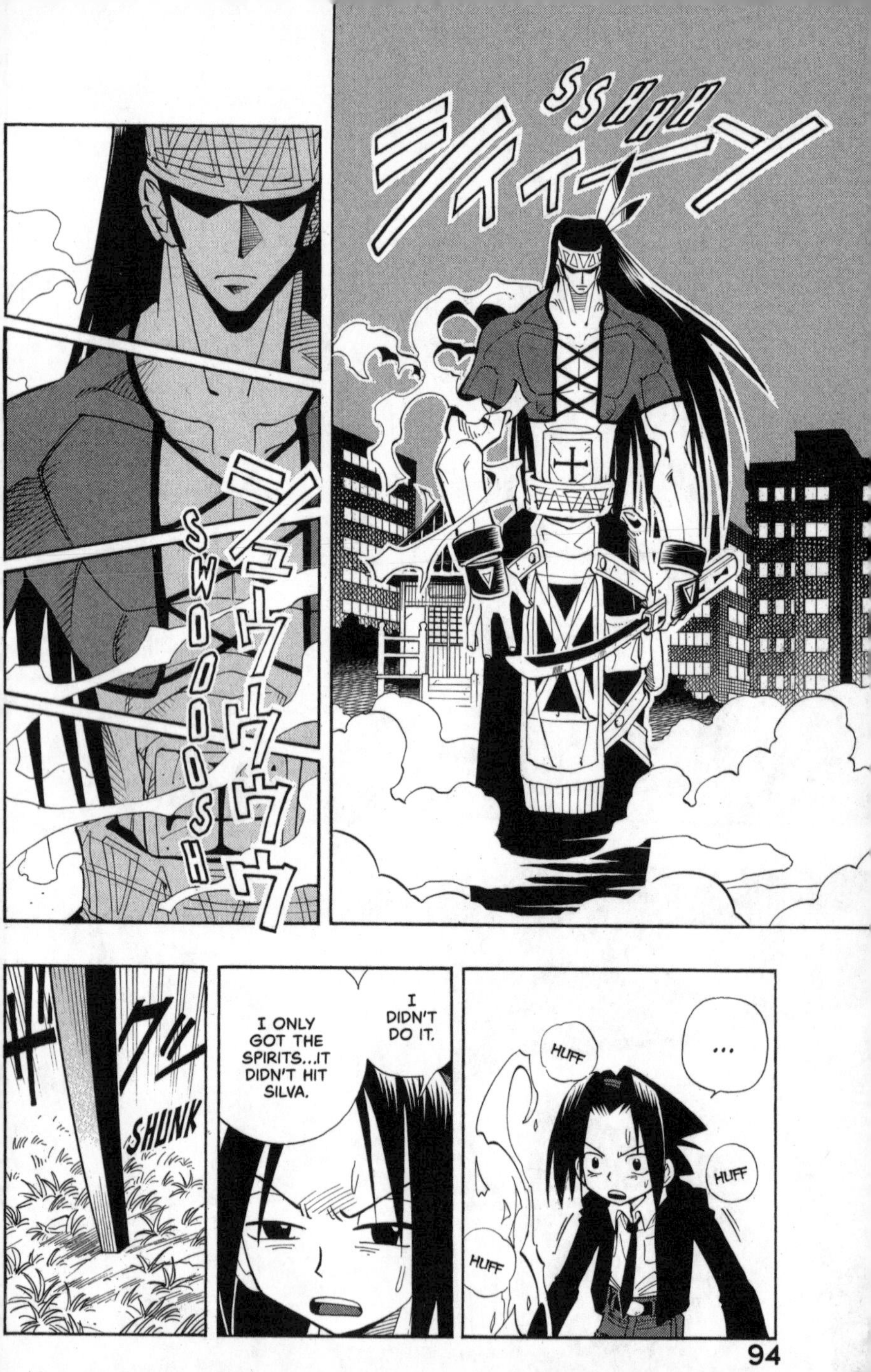

SSHHH
SWOOOOSH
...
HUFF
HUFF
HUFF
I DIDN'T DO IT.
I ONLY GOT THE SPIRITS...IT DIDN'T HIT SILVA.
SHUNK

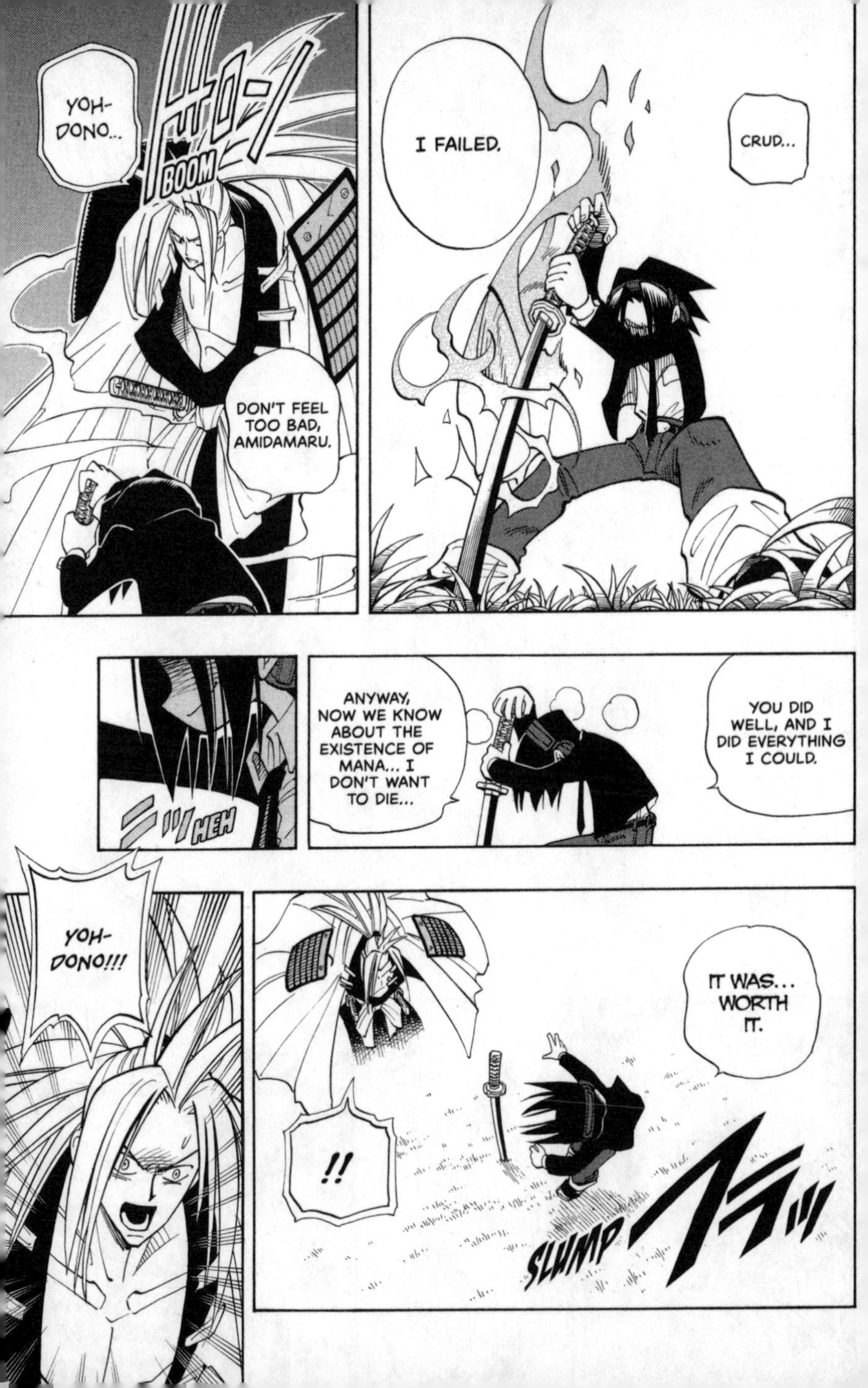
CRUD...
I FAILED.
YOH-DONO...
BOOM
DON'T FEEL TOO BAD, AMIDAMARU.
YOU DID WELL, AND I DID EVERYTHING I COULD.
ANYWAY, NOW WE KNOW ABOUT THE EXISTENCE OF MANA... I DON'T WANT TO DIE...
HEH
IT WAS... WORTH IT.
!!
SLUMP
YOH-DONO!!!

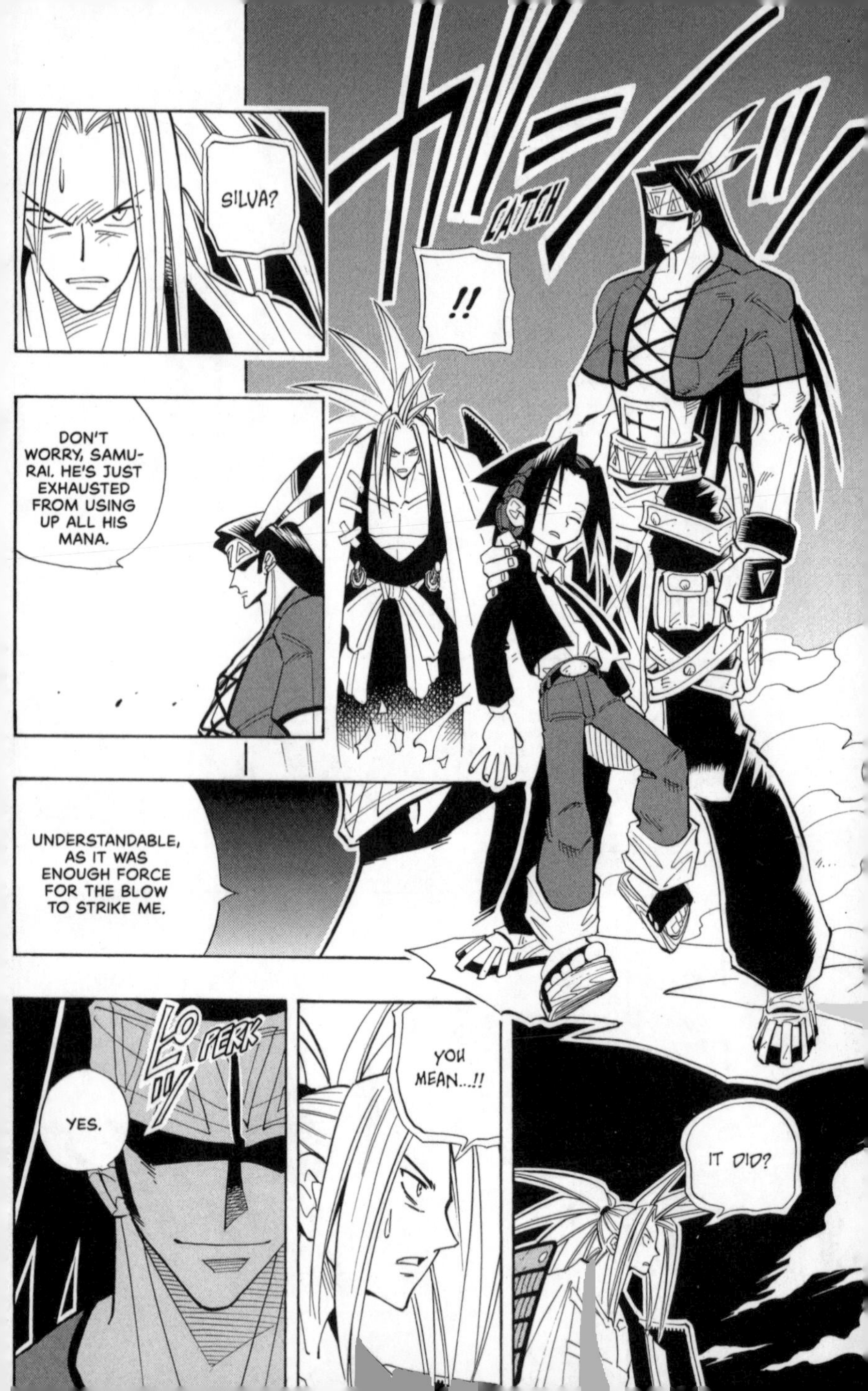
CATCH
!!
SILVA?
DON'T WORRY, SAMURAI. HE'S JUST EXHAUSTED FROM USING UP ALL HIS MANA.
UNDERSTANDABLE, AS IT WAS ENOUGH FORCE FOR THE BLOW TO STRIKE ME.
IT DID?
YOU MEAN...!!
PERK
YES.

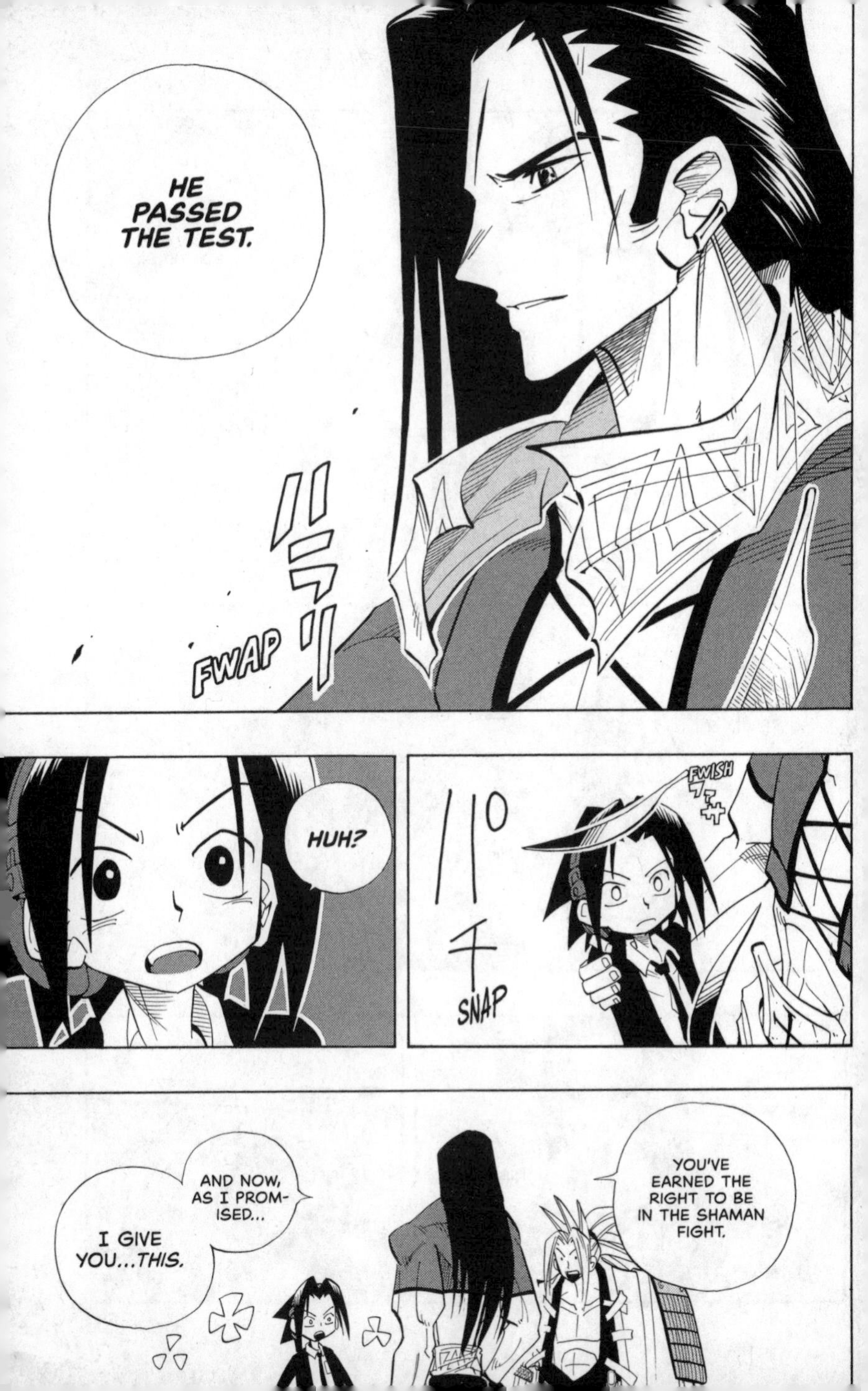
HE PASSED THE TEST.
ハラリ
FWAP
FWISH
パチ
SNAP
HUH?
YOU'VE EARNED THE RIGHT TO BE IN THE SHAMAN FIGHT.
AND NOW, AS I PROM-ISED...
I GIVE YOU...THIS.

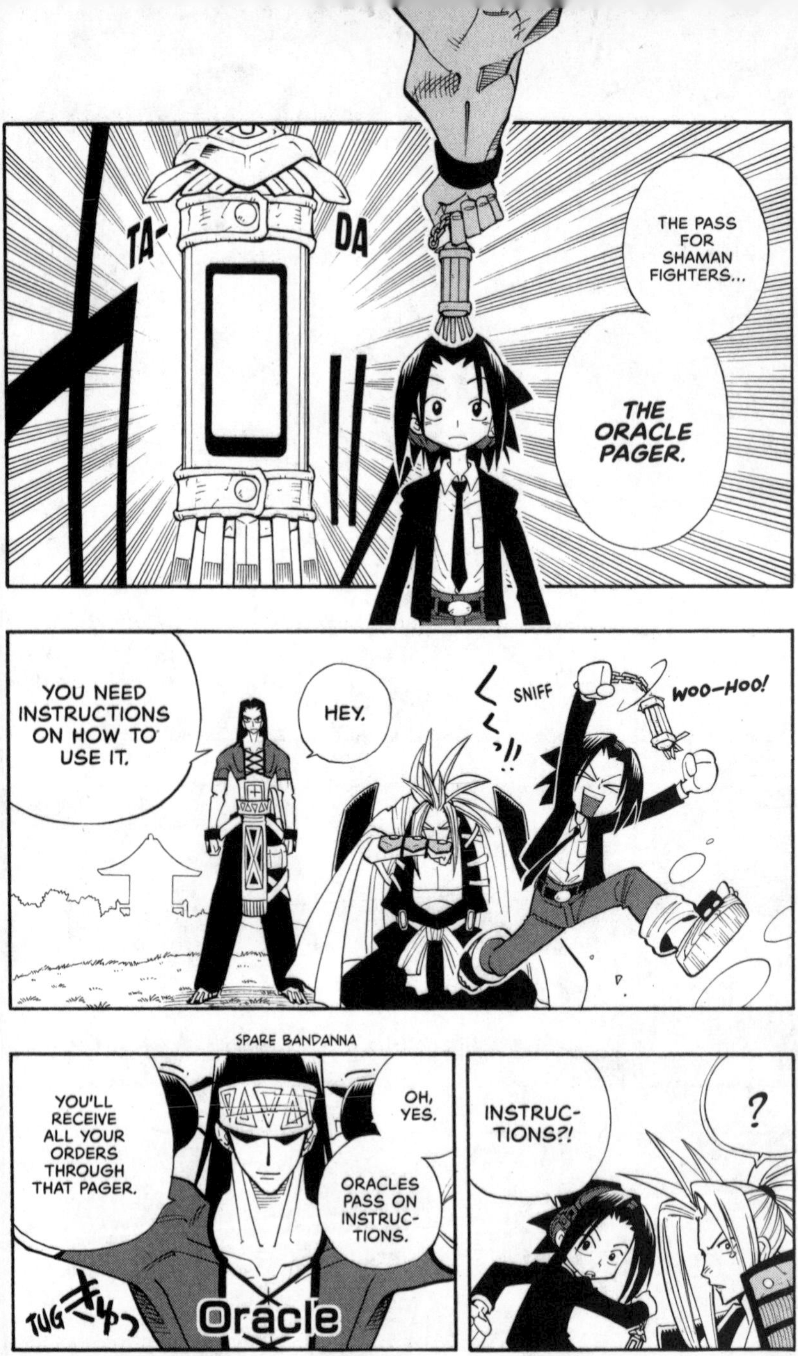
THE PASS FOR SHAMAN FIGHTERS...
THE ORACLE PAGER.
TA-
DA
WOO-HOO!
SNIFF
HEY.
YOU NEED INSTRUCTIONS ON HOW TO USE IT.
?
INSTRUCTIONS?!
OH, YES.
ORACLES PASS ON INSTRUCTIONS.
SPARE BANDANNA
YOU'LL RECEIVE ALL YOUR ORDERS THROUGH THAT PAGER.
Oracle
TUG

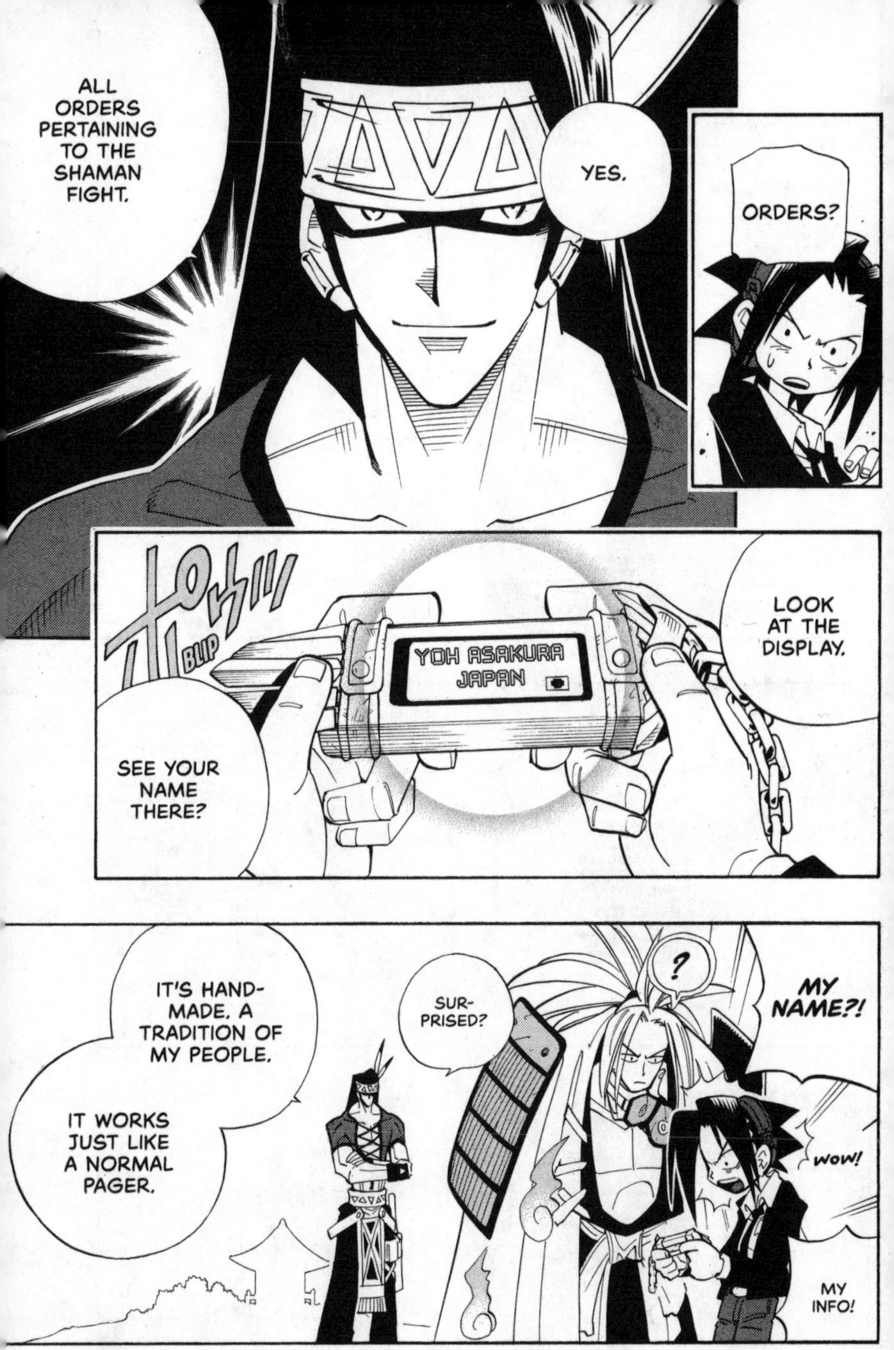
ORDERS?
YES.
ALL ORDERS PERTAINING TO THE SHAMAN FIGHT.
LOOK AT THE DISPLAY.
YOH ASAKURA
JAPAN
BLIP
SEE YOUR NAME THERE?
MY NAME?!
WOW!
MY INFO!
?
SUR-PRISED?
IT'S HAND-MADE. A TRADITION OF MY PEOPLE.
IT WORKS JUST LIKE A NORMAL PAGER.

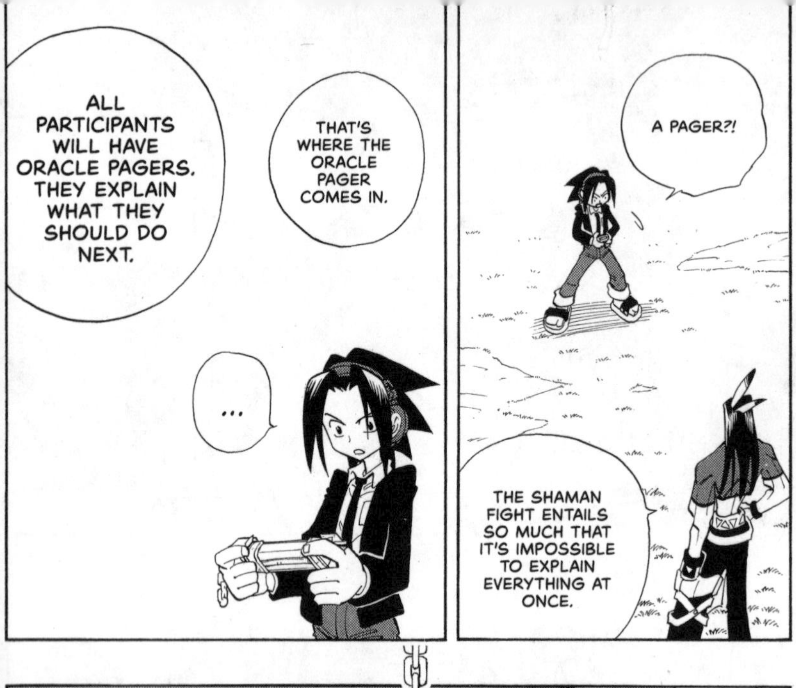

A PAGER?!
THE SHAMAN FIGHT ENTAILS SO MUCH THAT IT'S IMPOSSIBLE TO EXPLAIN EVERYTHING AT ONCE.
THAT'S WHERE THE ORACLE PAGER COMES IN.
ALL PARTICIPANTS WILL HAVE ORACLE PAGERS. THEY EXPLAIN WHAT THEY SHOULD DO NEXT.
...
IT MAY TELL YOU THE TIME AND PLACE OF YOUR NEXT BATTLE, AND YOUR OPPONENT'S NAME...
...SPECIAL RULES, OR CONFIRMATION OF THE RESULTS.
IT MAY GIVE YOU MISSIONS TO ACCOM-PLISH.
YOU WILL BE JUDGED BASED ON YOUR LEVEL OF SHAMANIC STANDARDS.
THE WINNER AT THE END WILL BECOME THE SHAMAN KING.
THAT'S ALL I CAN TELL YOU FOR NOW.

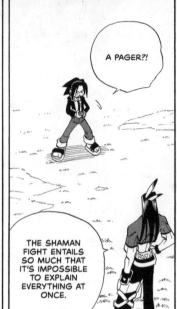

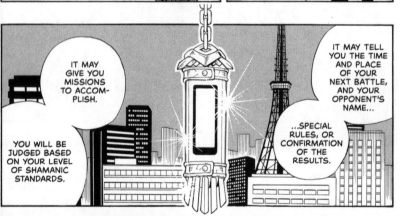

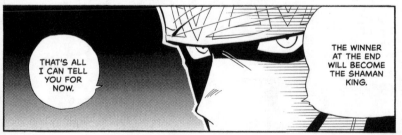

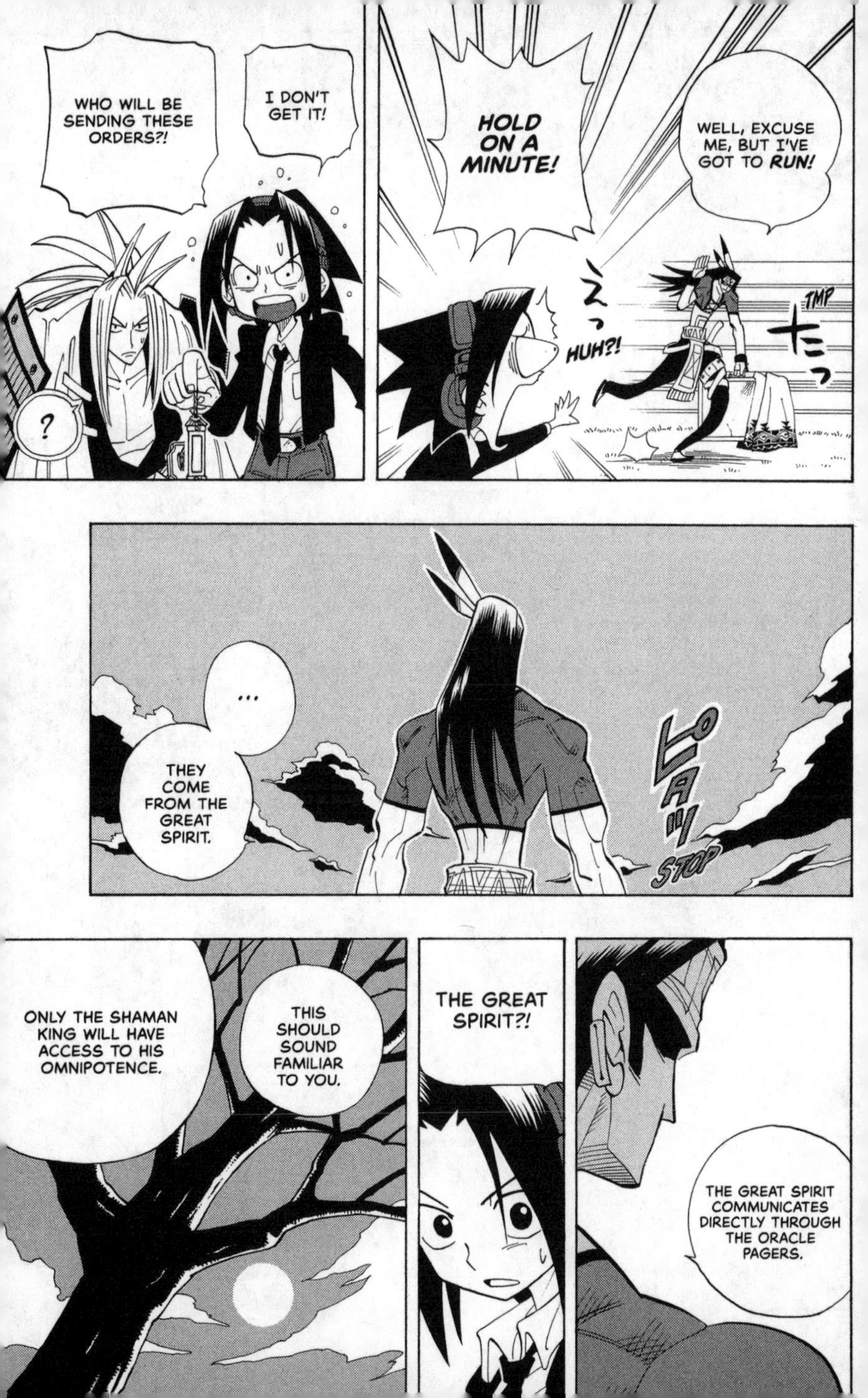

WELL, EXCUSE ME, BUT I'VE GOT TO RUN!
TMP
HOLD ON A MINUTE!
HUH?!
I DON'T GET IT!
WHO WILL BE SENDING THESE ORDERS?!
?
STOP
...
THEY COME FROM THE GREAT SPIRIT.
THE GREAT SPIRIT COMMUNICATES DIRECTLY THROUGH THE ORACLE PAGERS.
THE GREAT SPIRIT?!
THIS SHOULD SOUND FAMILIAR TO YOU.
ONLY THE SHAMAN KING WILL HAVE ACCESS TO HIS OMNIPOTENCE.

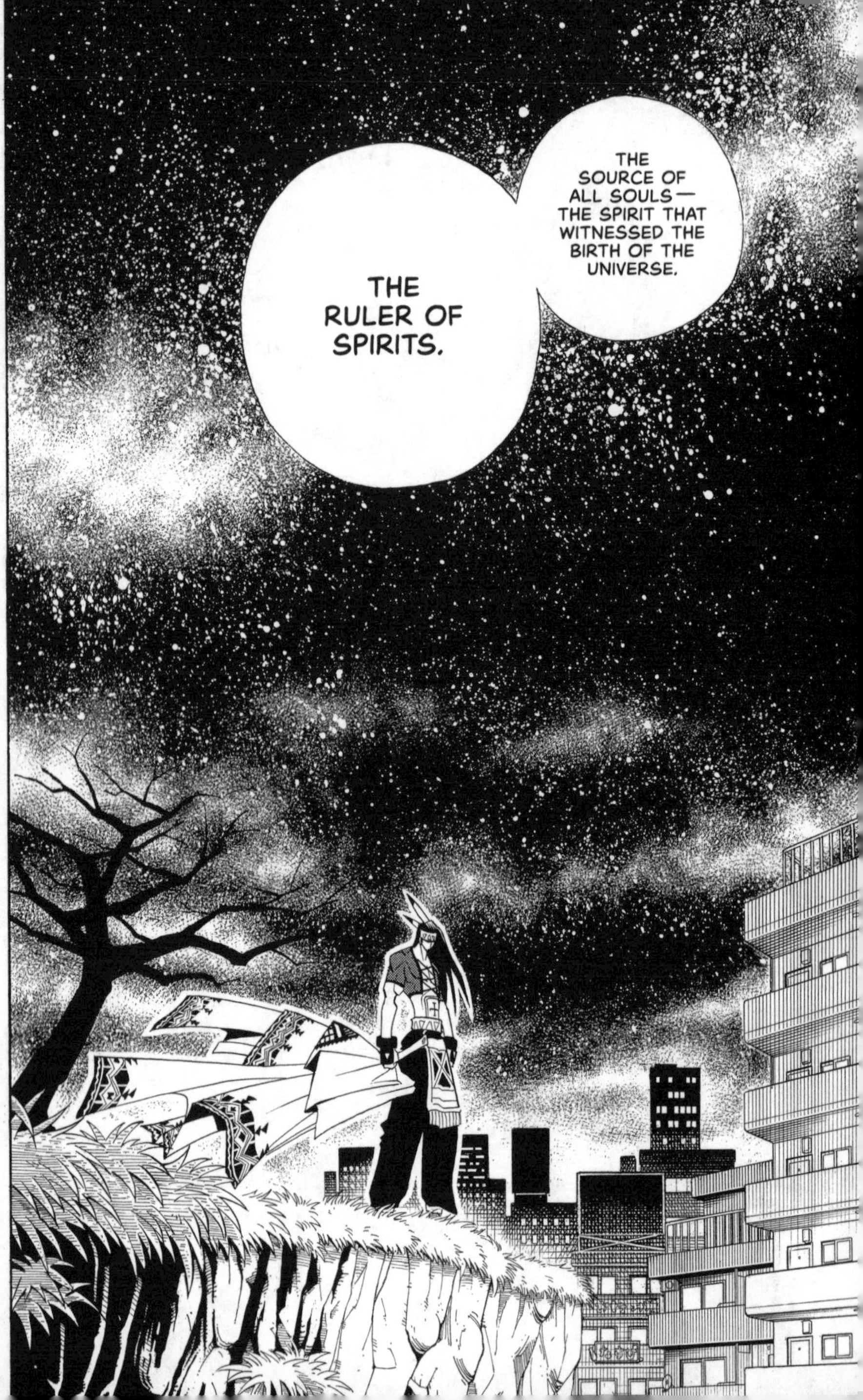
THE SOURCE OF ALL SOULS— THE SPIRIT THAT WITNESSED THE BIRTH OF THE UNIVERSE.
THE RULER OF SPIRITS.

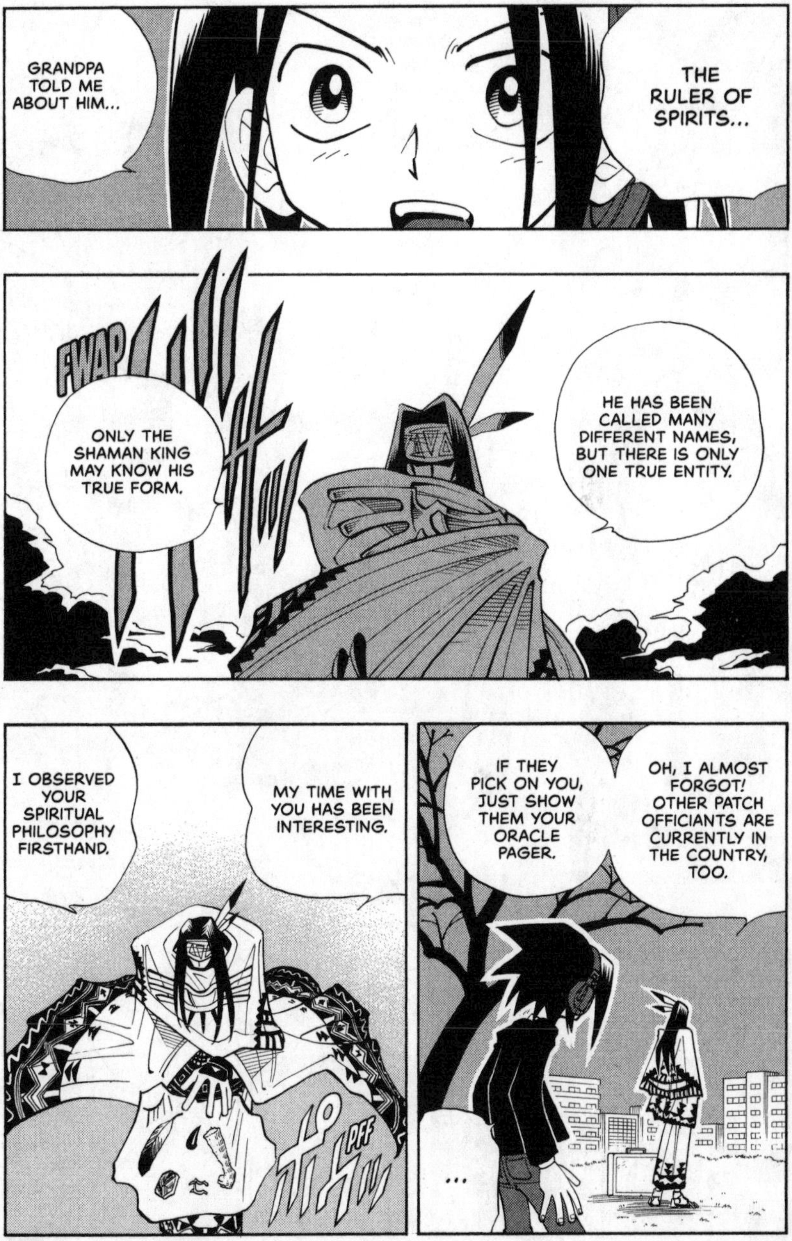

THE RULER OF SPIRITS...
GRANDPA TOLD ME ABOUT HIM...
HE HAS BEEN CALLED MANY DIFFERENT NAMES, BUT THERE IS ONLY ONE TRUE ENTITY.
ONLY THE SHAMAN KING MAY KNOW HIS TRUE FORM.
FWAP
OH, I ALMOST FORGOT! OTHER PATCH OFFICIANTS ARE CURRENTLY IN THE COUNTRY, TOO.
IF THEY PICK ON YOU, JUST SHOW THEM YOUR ORACLE PAGER.
...
MY TIME WITH YOU HAS BEEN INTERESTING.
I OBSERVED YOUR SPIRITUAL PHILOSOPHY FIRSTHAND.
PFF

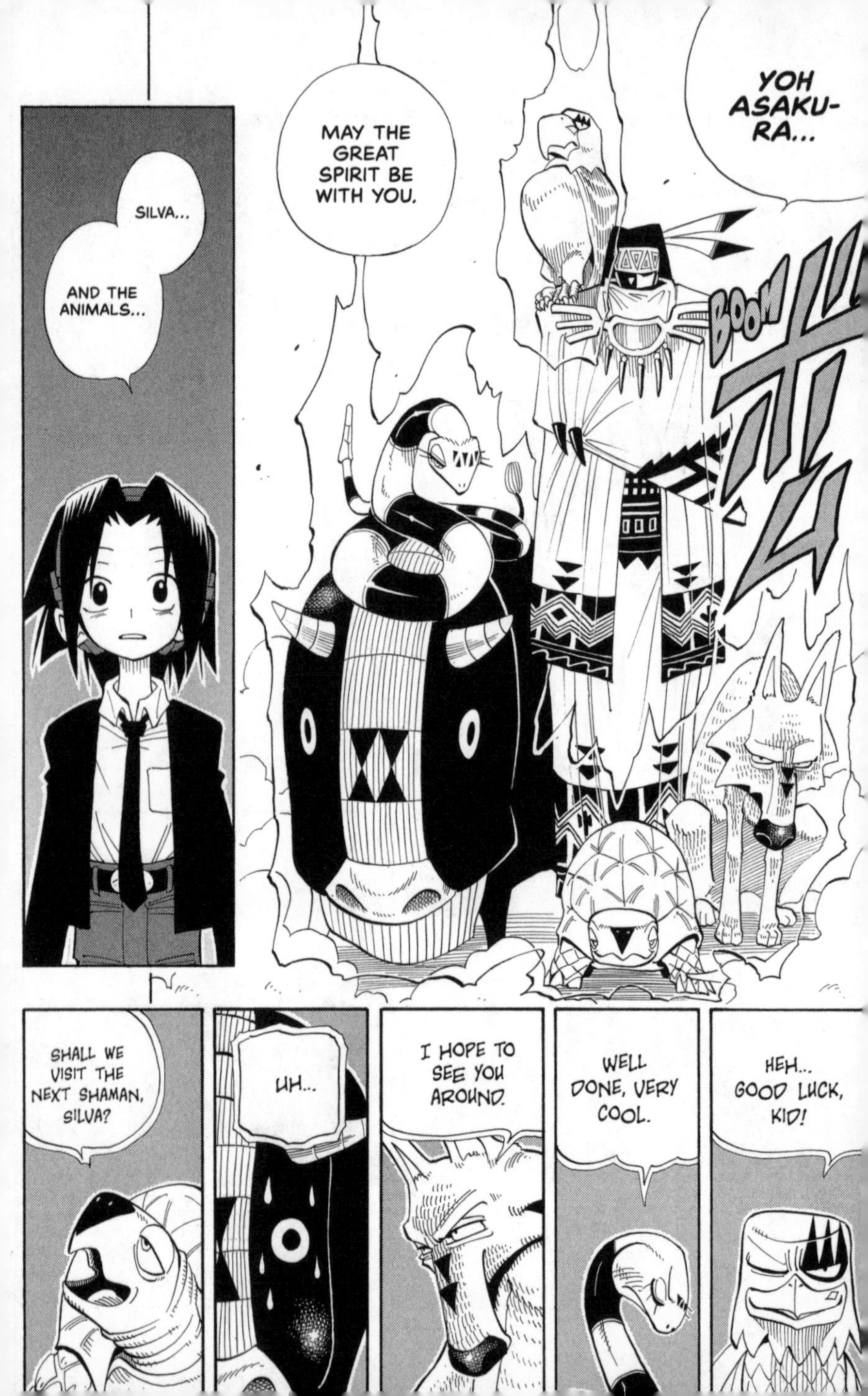
YOH ASAKURA...
BOOM
MAY THE GREAT SPIRIT BE WITH YOU.
SILVA...
AND THE ANIMALS...
HEH... GOOD LUCK, KID!
WELL DONE, VERY COOL.
I HOPE TO SEE YOU AROUND.
UH...
SHALL WE VISIT THE NEXT SHAMAN, SILVA?

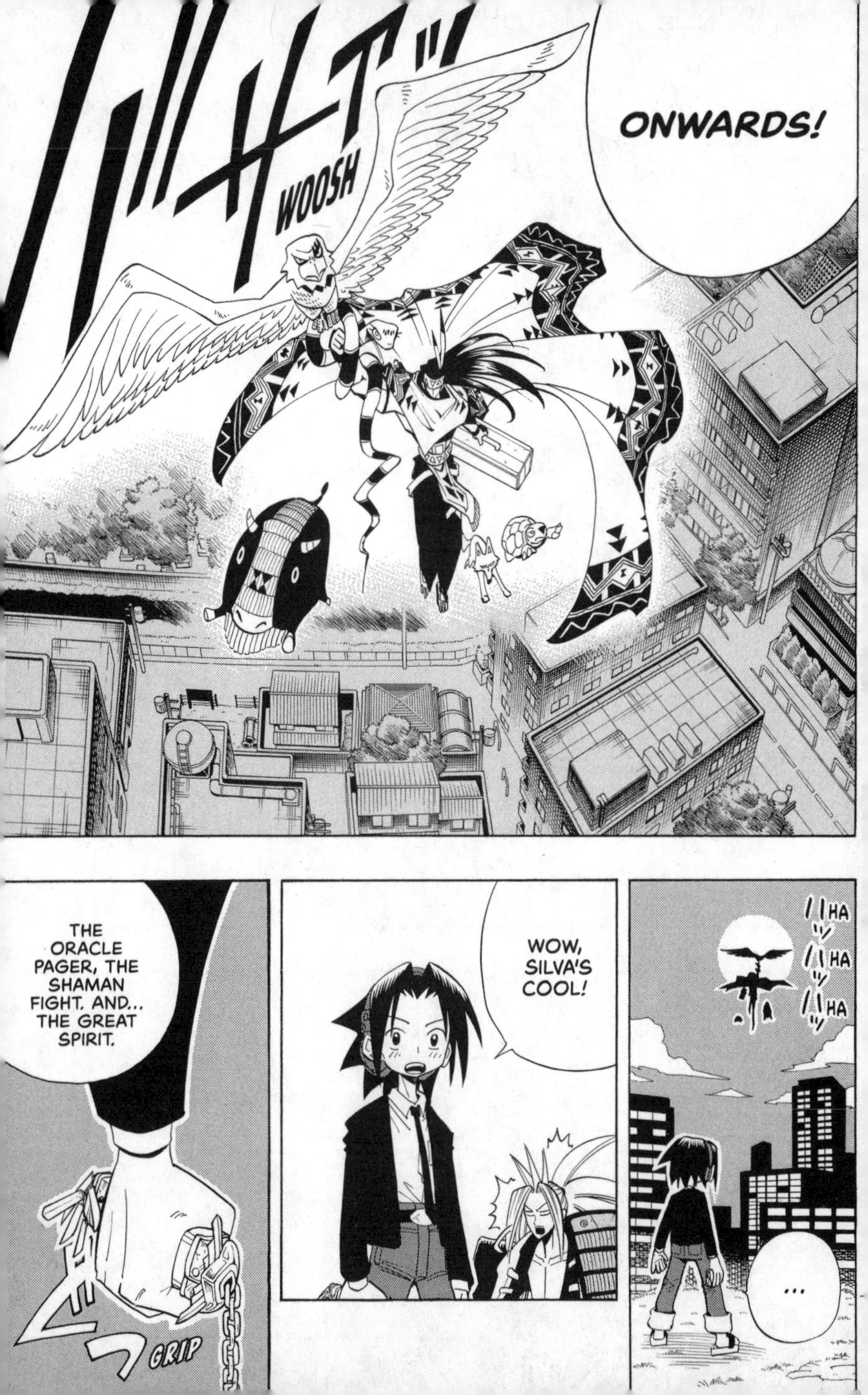

ONWARDS!
WOOSH
HA HA HA
...
WOW, SILVA'S COOL!
THE ORACLE PAGER, THE SHAMAN FIGHT, AND... THE GREAT SPIRIT.
GRIP

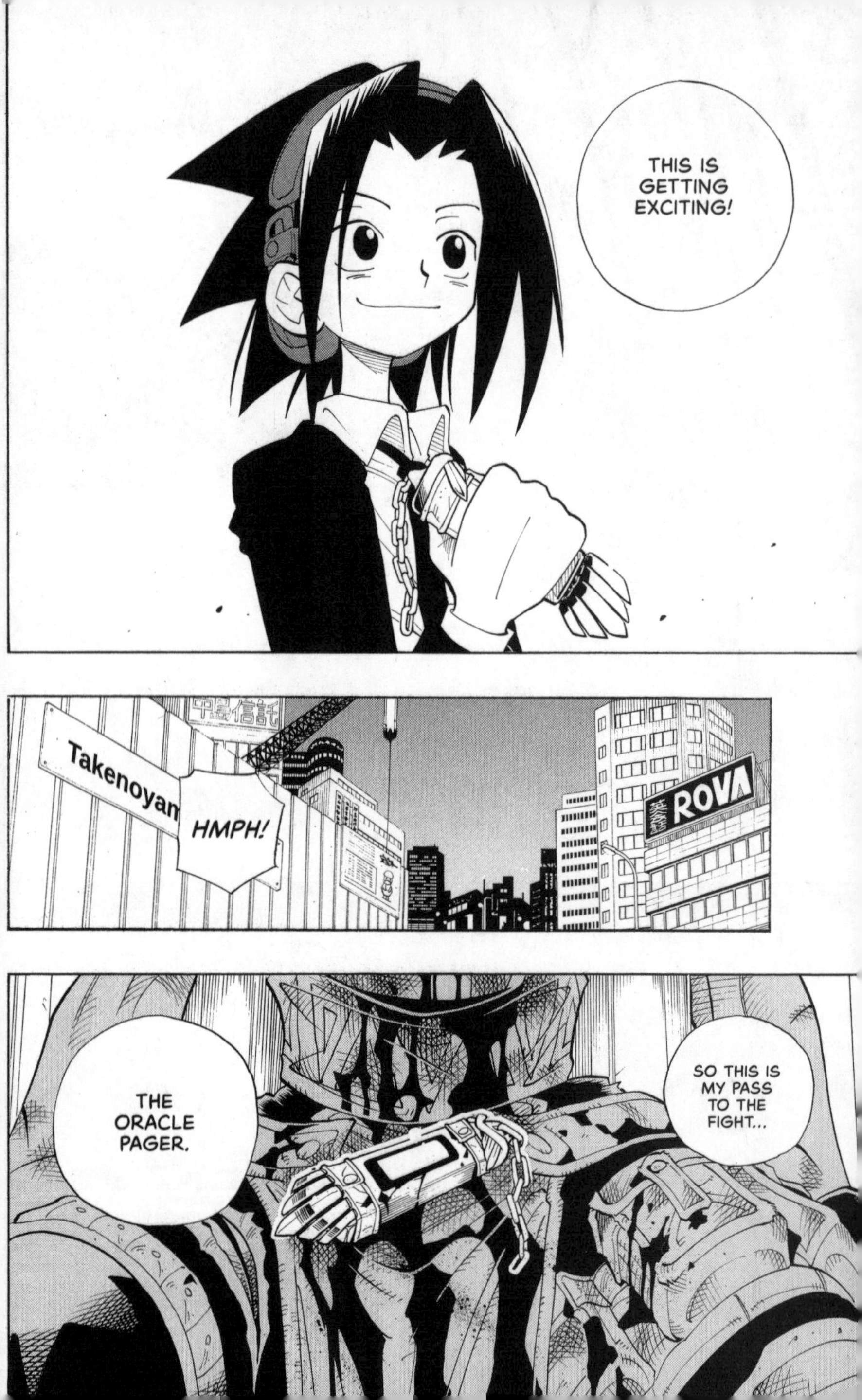
THIS IS GETTING EXCITING!
Takenoyam
HMPH!
ROVA
SO THIS IS MY PASS TO THE FIGHT...
THE ORACLE PAGER.

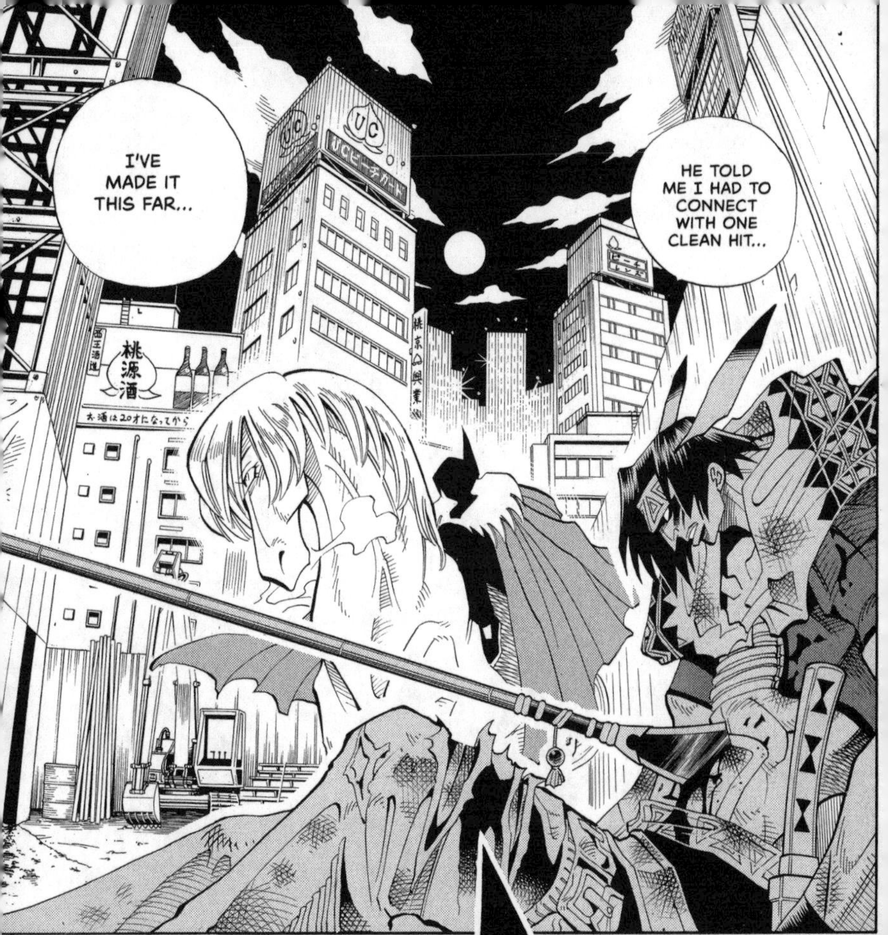
HE TOLD ME I HAD TO CONNECT WITH ONE CLEAN HIT...
I'VE MADE IT THIS FAR...
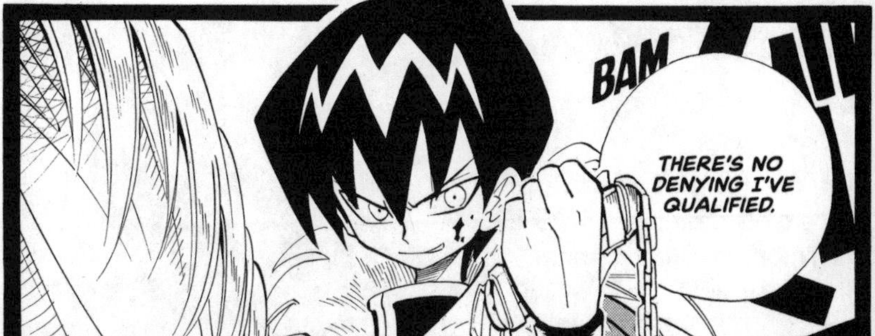
BAM
THERE'S NO DENYING I'VE QUALIFIED.

SHAMAN KING CHARACTER FILE No.16

Chrom

July 1999

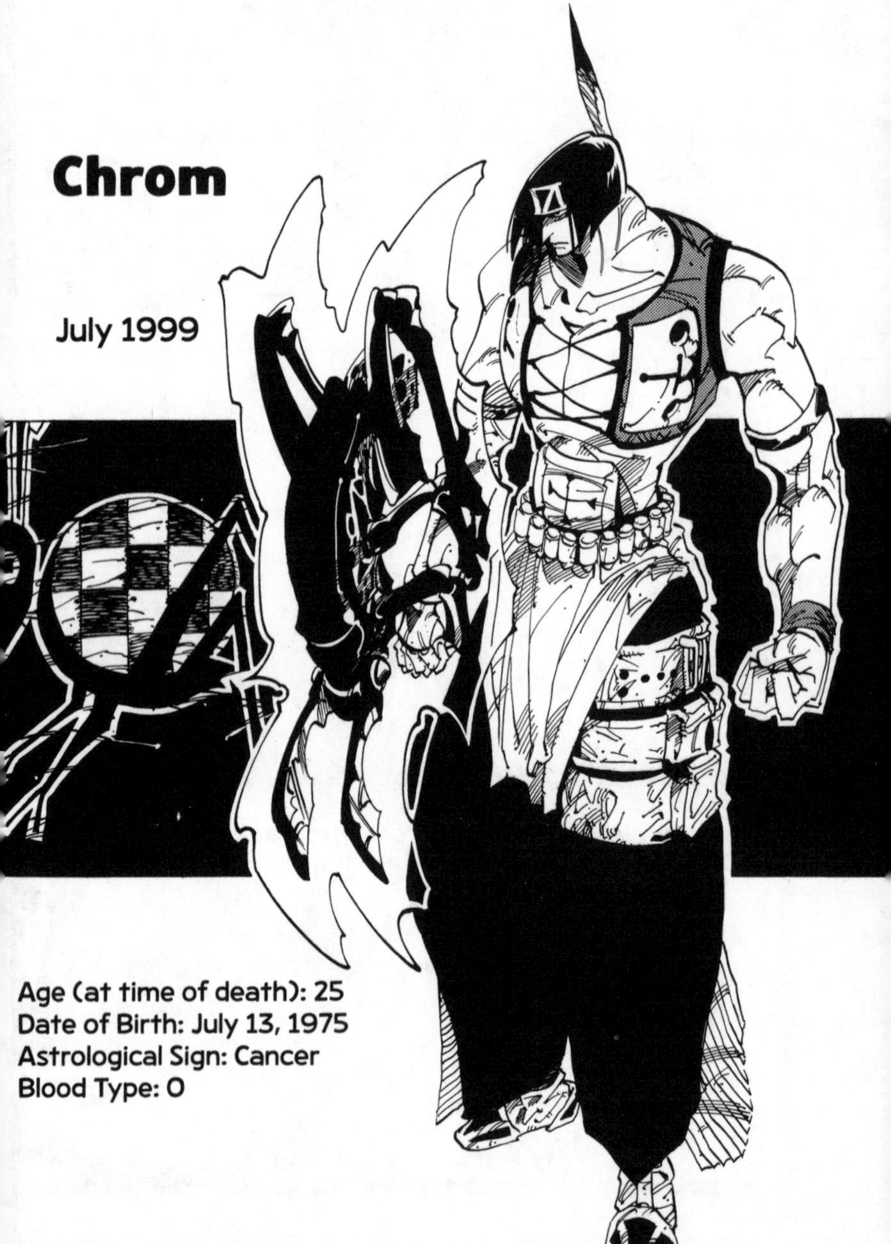

Age (at time of death): 25
Date of Birth: July 13, 1975
Astrological Sign: Cancer
Blood Type: O

Chapter 32: The Way of the Patch

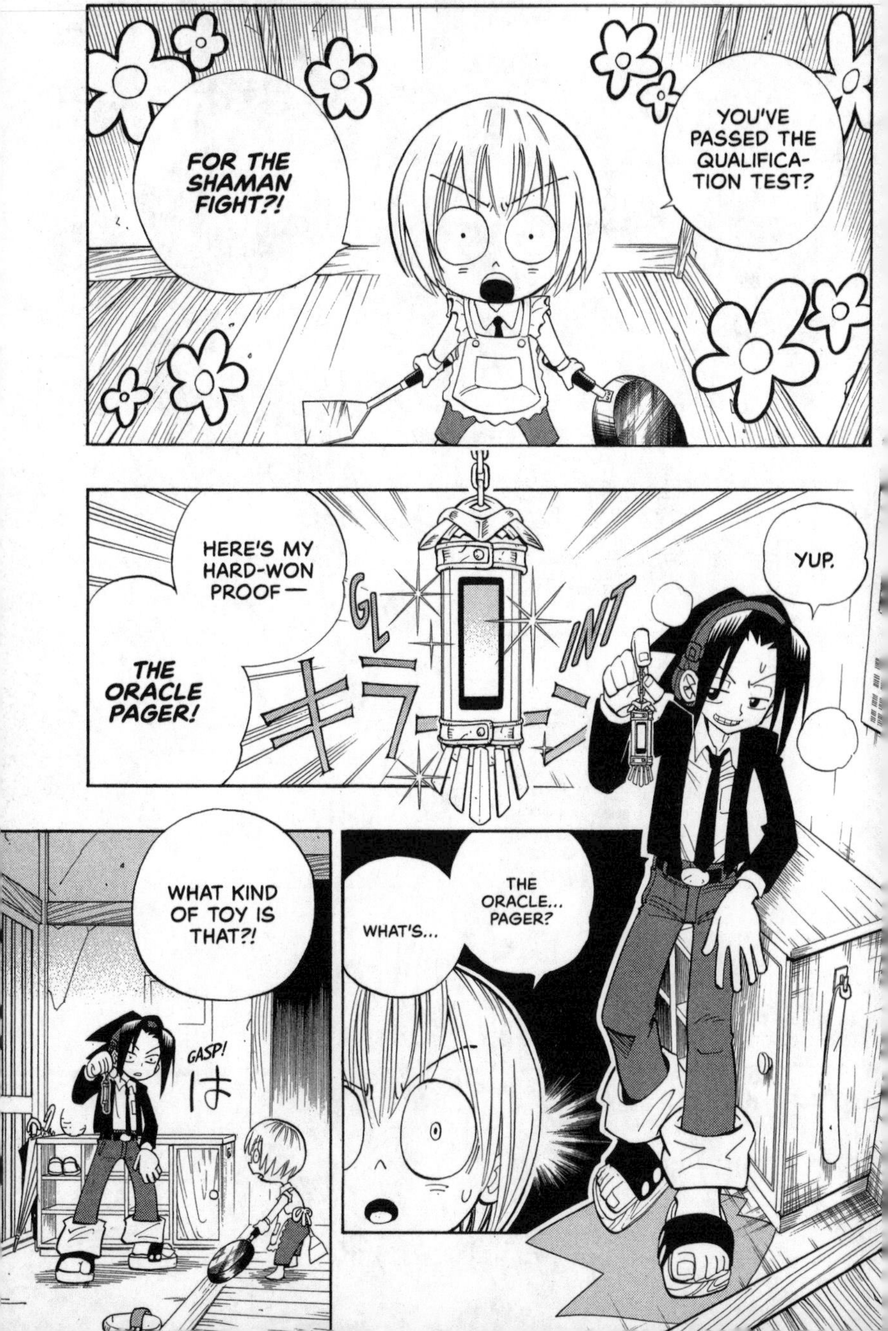

YOU'VE PASSED THE QUALIFICA-TION TEST?
FOR THE SHAMAN FIGHT?!
YUP.
HERE'S MY HARD-WON PROOF—
THE ORACLE PAGER!
GLINT
THE ORACLE... PAGER?
WHAT'S...
WHAT KIND OF TOY IS THAT?!
GASP!

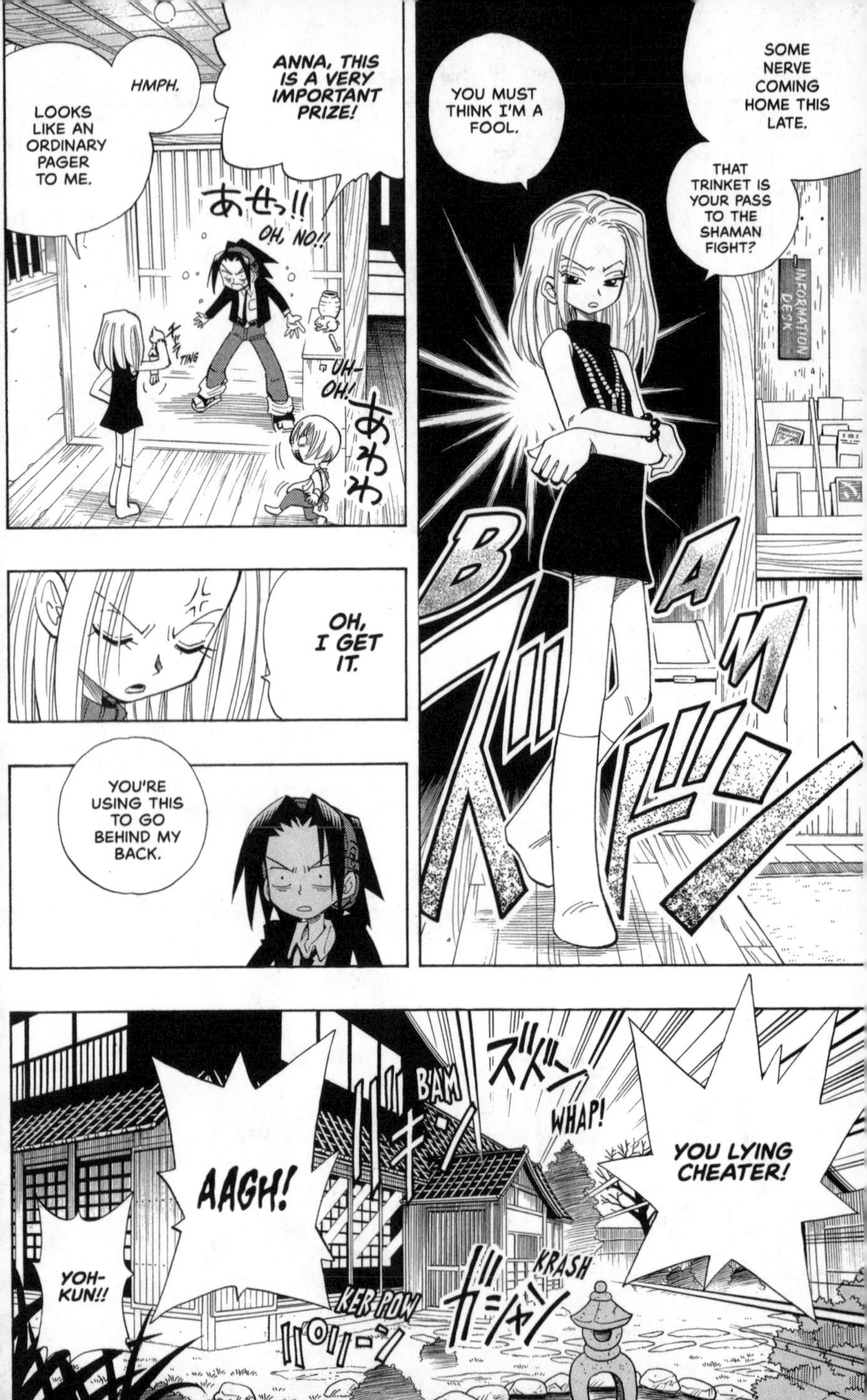
SOME NERVE COMING HOME THIS LATE.
THAT TRINKET IS YOUR PASS TO THE SHAMAN FIGHT?
YOU MUST THINK I'M A FOOL.
INFORMATION DESK
BAM
ANNA, THIS IS A VERY IMPORTANT PRIZE!
HMPH.
LOOKS LIKE AN ORDINARY PAGER TO ME.
あせっ!!
OH, NO!!
TING
UH-OH!
あわわ
OH, I GET IT.
YOU'RE USING THIS TO GO BEHIND MY BACK.
YOU LYING CHEATER!
WHAP!
BAM
AAGH!
KRASH
ガシャン
KER POW
バリーン
YOH-KUN!!

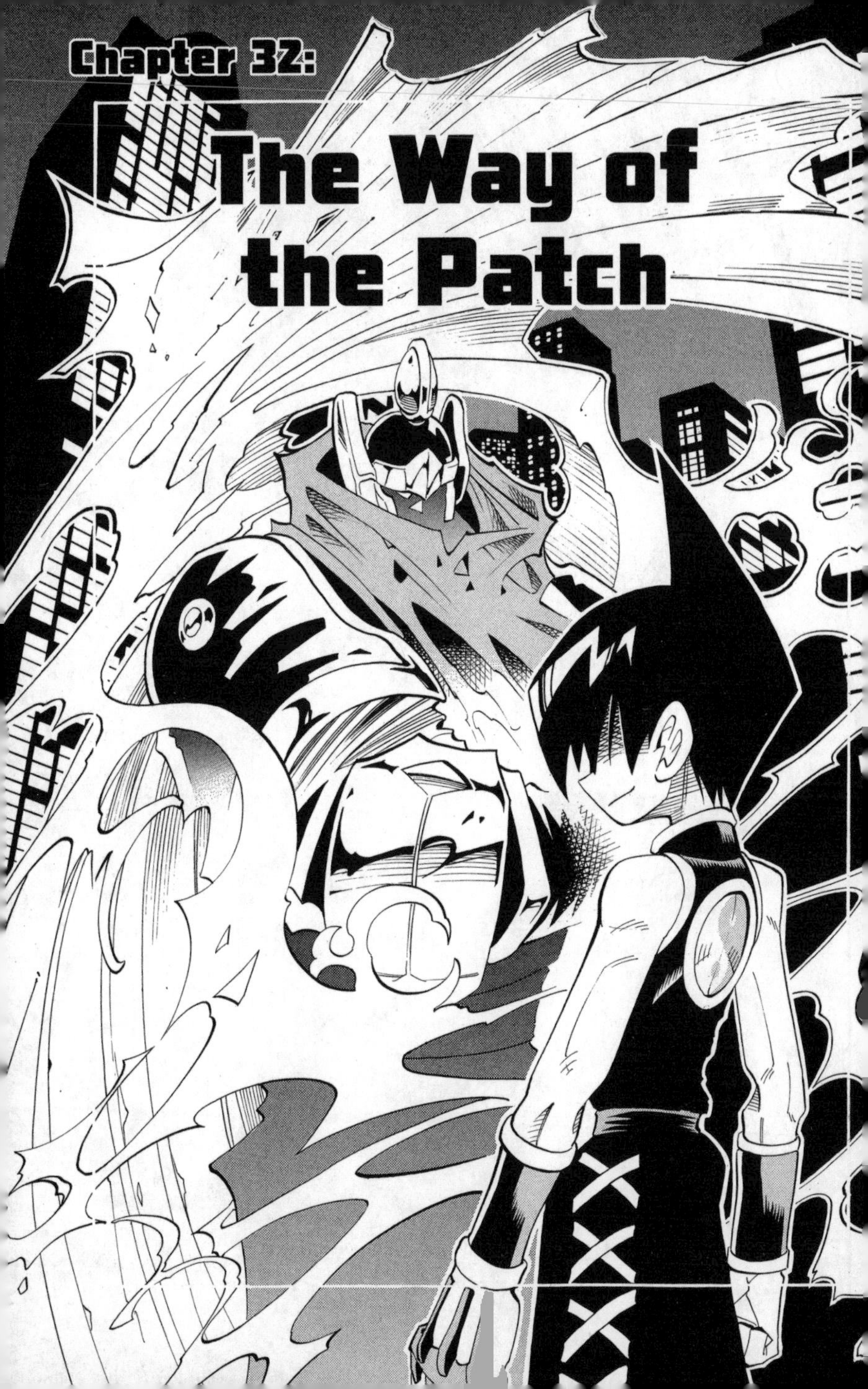
Chapter 32:
The Way of the Patch

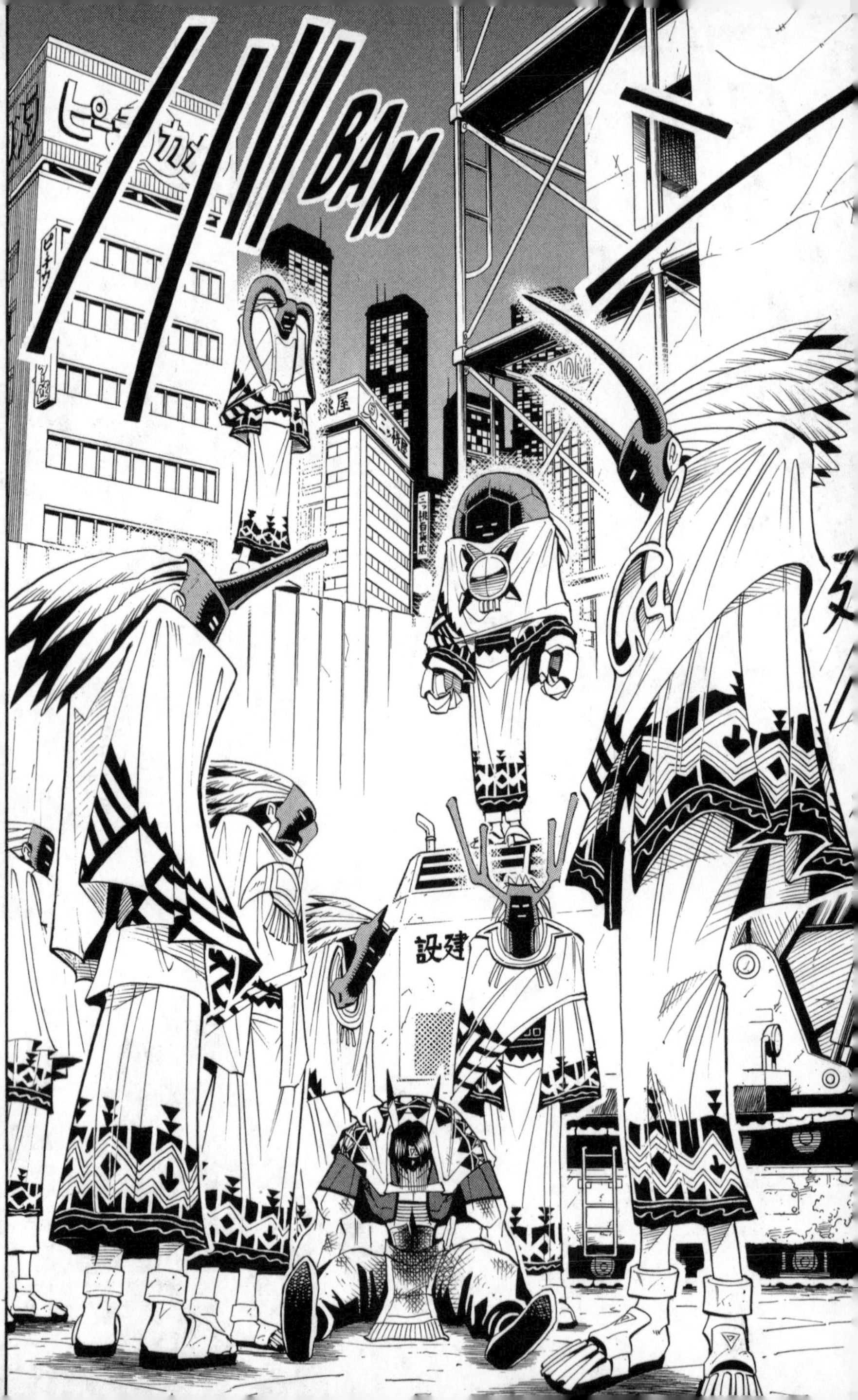
BAM

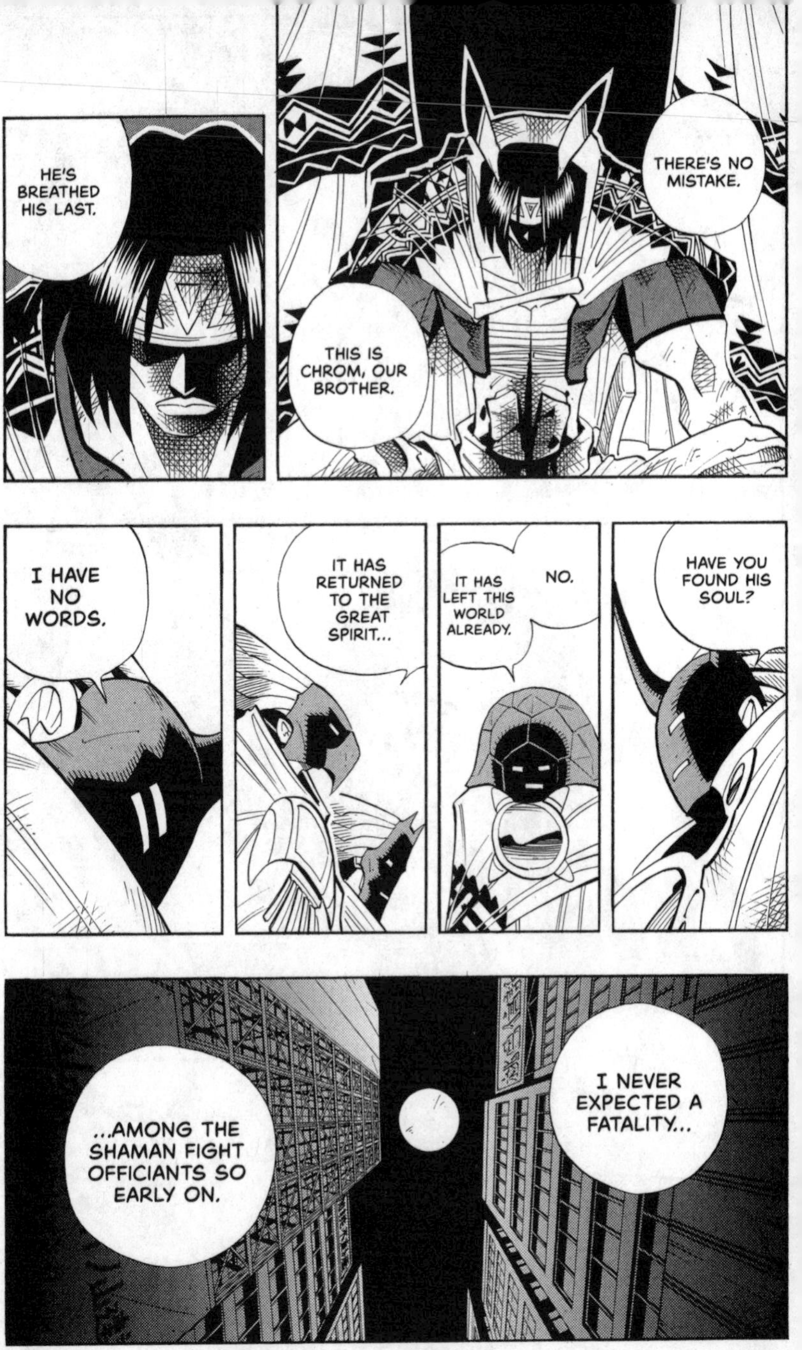
THERE'S NO MISTAKE.
THIS IS CHROM, OUR BROTHER.
HE'S BREATHED HIS LAST.
HAVE YOU FOUND HIS SOUL?
NO.
IT HAS LEFT THIS WORLD ALREADY.
IT HAS RETURNED TO THE GREAT SPIRIT...
I HAVE NO WORDS.
I NEVER EXPECTED A FATALITY...
...AMONG THE SHAMAN FIGHT OFFICIANTS SO EARLY ON.

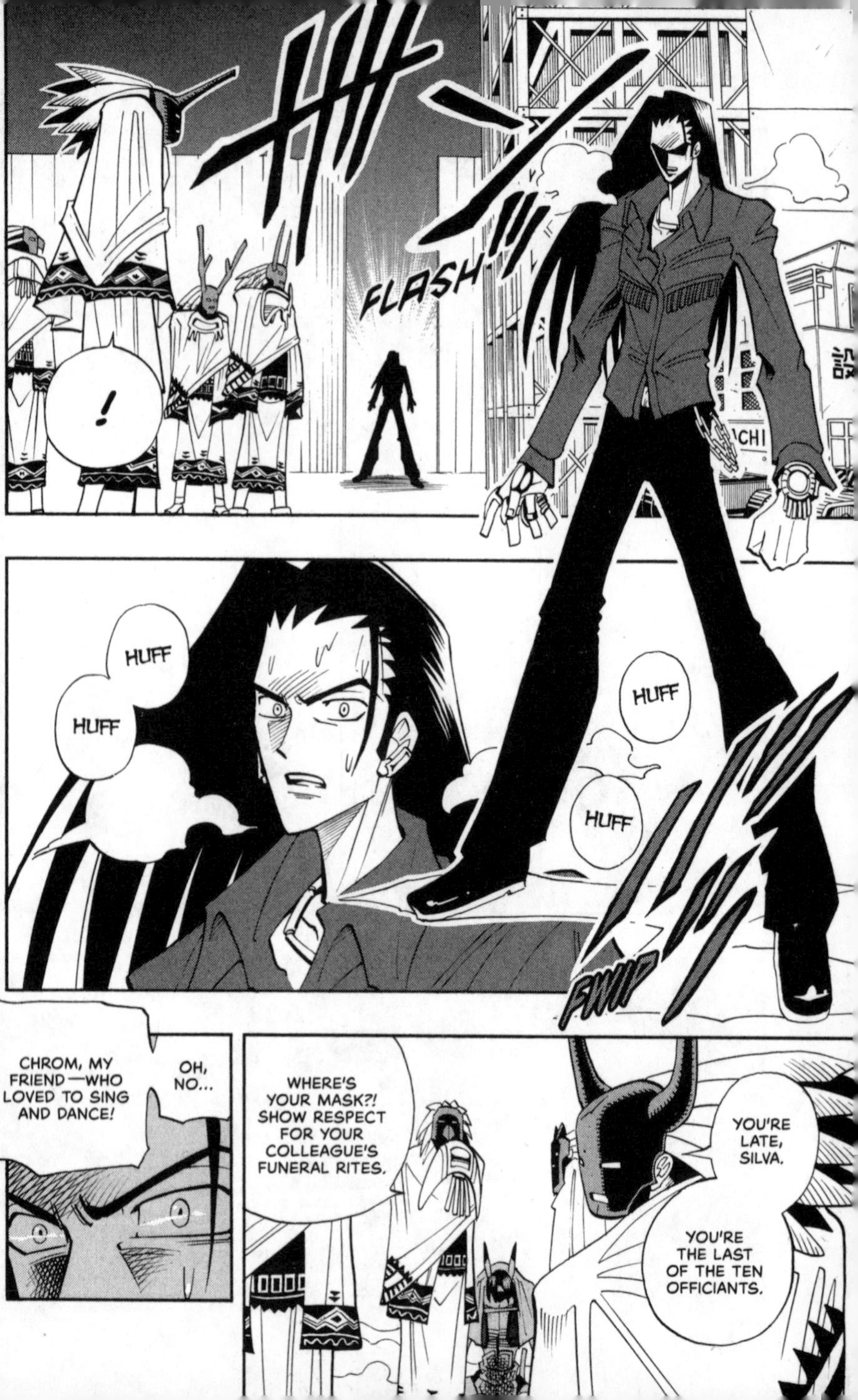
FLASH
!
HUFF
HUFF
FWIP
HUFF
HUFF
YOU'RE LATE, SILVA.
YOU'RE THE LAST OF THE TEN OFFICIANTS.
WHERE'S YOUR MASK?! SHOW RESPECT FOR YOUR COLLEAGUE'S FUNERAL RITES.
OH, NO...
CHROM, MY FRIEND—WHO LOVED TO SING AND DANCE!

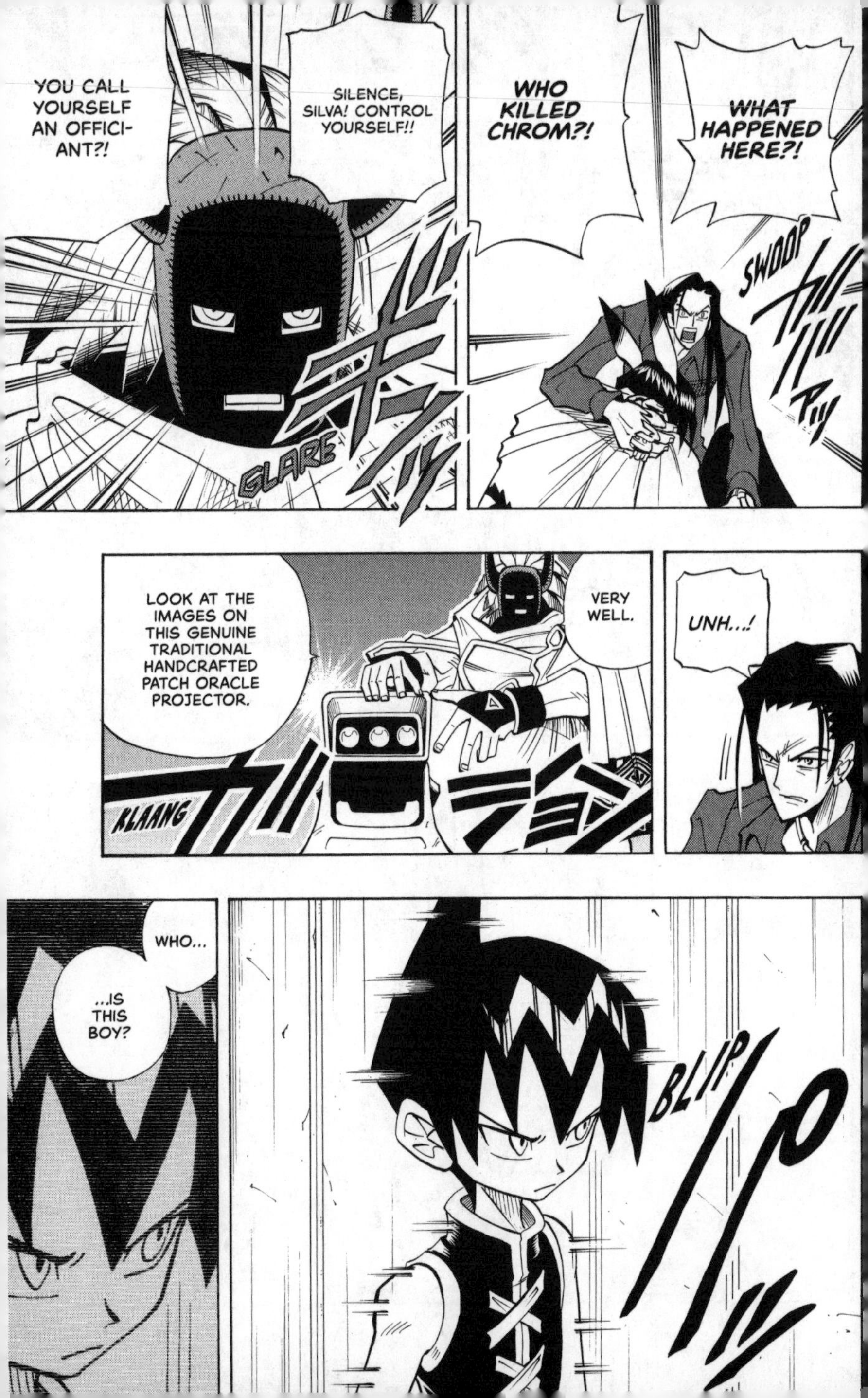
WHAT HAPPENED HERE?!
WHO KILLED CHROM?!
SWOOP
SILENCE, SILVA! CONTROL YOURSELF!!
YOU CALL YOURSELF AN OFFICI-ANT?!
GLARE
UNH...!
VERY WELL.
LOOK AT THE IMAGES ON THIS GENUINE TRADITIONAL HANDCRAFTED PATCH ORACLE PROJECTOR.
KLAANG
BLIP
WHO...
...IS THIS BOY?

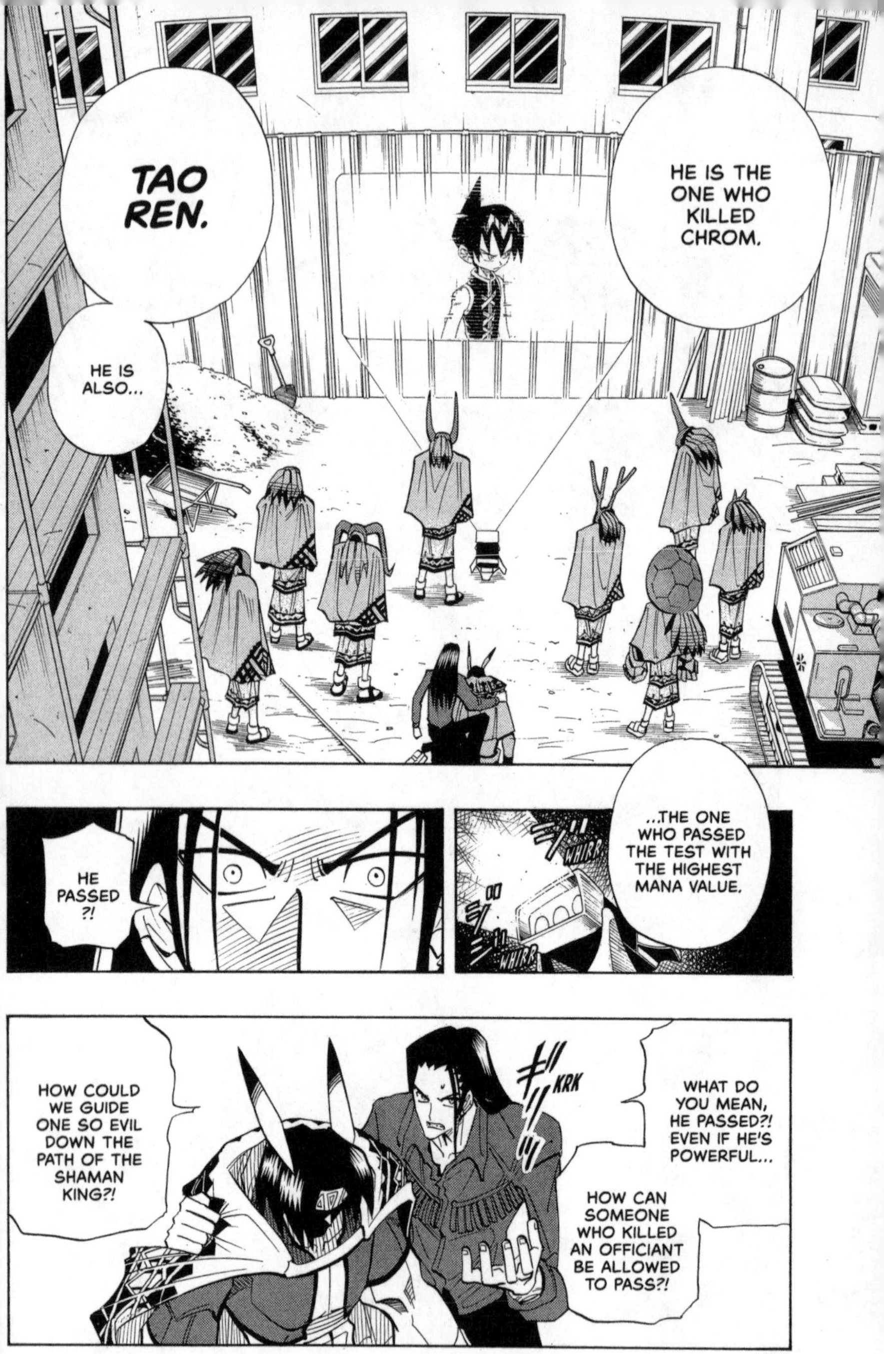
HE IS THE ONE WHO KILLED CHROM.
TAO REN.
HE IS ALSO...
WHIRR
WHIRR
...THE ONE WHO PASSED THE TEST WITH THE HIGHEST MANA VALUE.
HE PASSED ?!
WHAT DO YOU MEAN, HE PASSED?! EVEN IF HE'S POWERFUL...
KRK
HOW CAN SOMEONE WHO KILLED AN OFFICIANT BE ALLOWED TO PASS?!
HOW COULD WE GUIDE ONE SO EVIL DOWN THE PATH OF THE SHAMAN KING?!

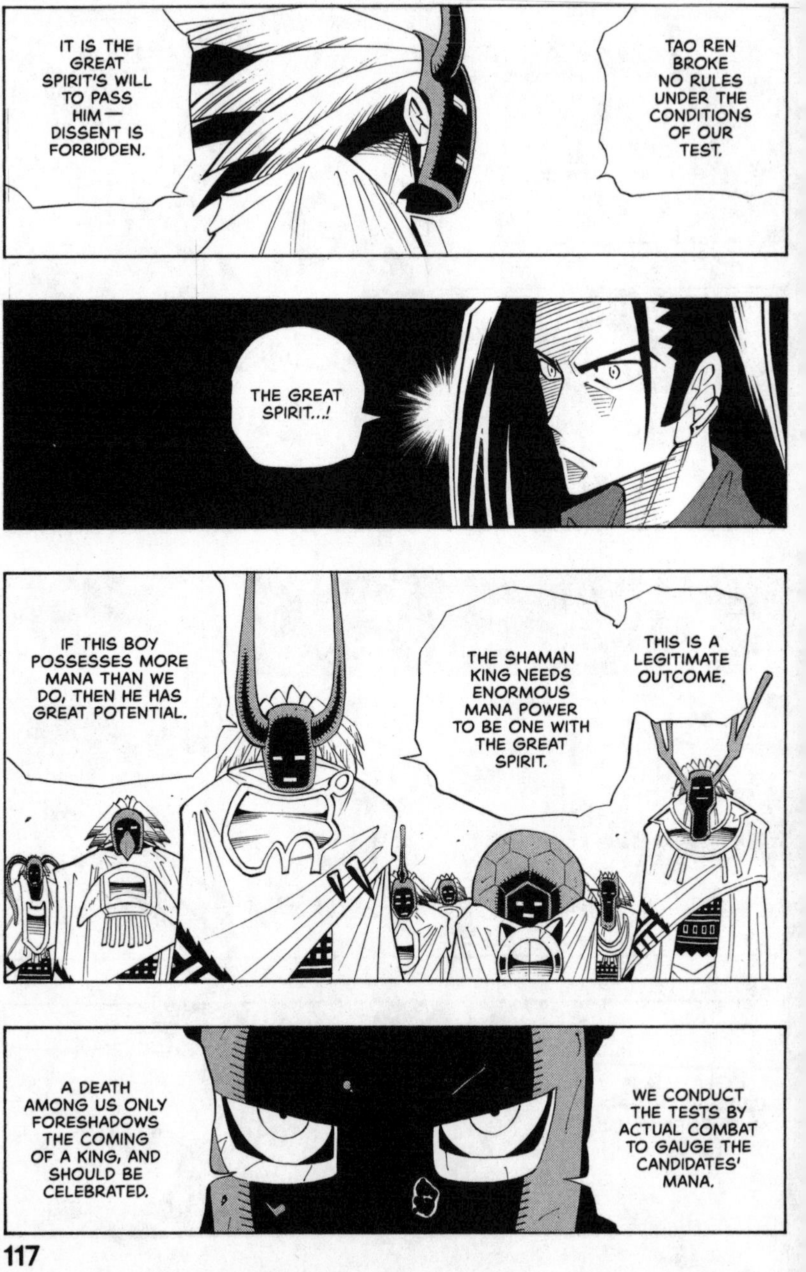
TAO REN BROKE NO RULES UNDER THE CONDITIONS OF OUR TEST.
IT IS THE GREAT SPIRIT'S WILL TO PASS HIM— DISSENT IS FORBIDDEN.
THE GREAT SPIRIT...!
THIS IS A LEGITIMATE OUTCOME.
THE SHAMAN KING NEEDS ENORMOUS MANA POWER TO BE ONE WITH THE GREAT SPIRIT.
IF THIS BOY POSSESSES MORE MANA THAN WE DO, THEN HE HAS GREAT POTENTIAL.
WE CONDUCT THE TESTS BY ACTUAL COMBAT TO GAUGE THE CANDIDATES' MANA.
A DEATH AMONG US ONLY FORESHADOWS THE COMING OF A KING, AND SHOULD BE CELEBRATED.

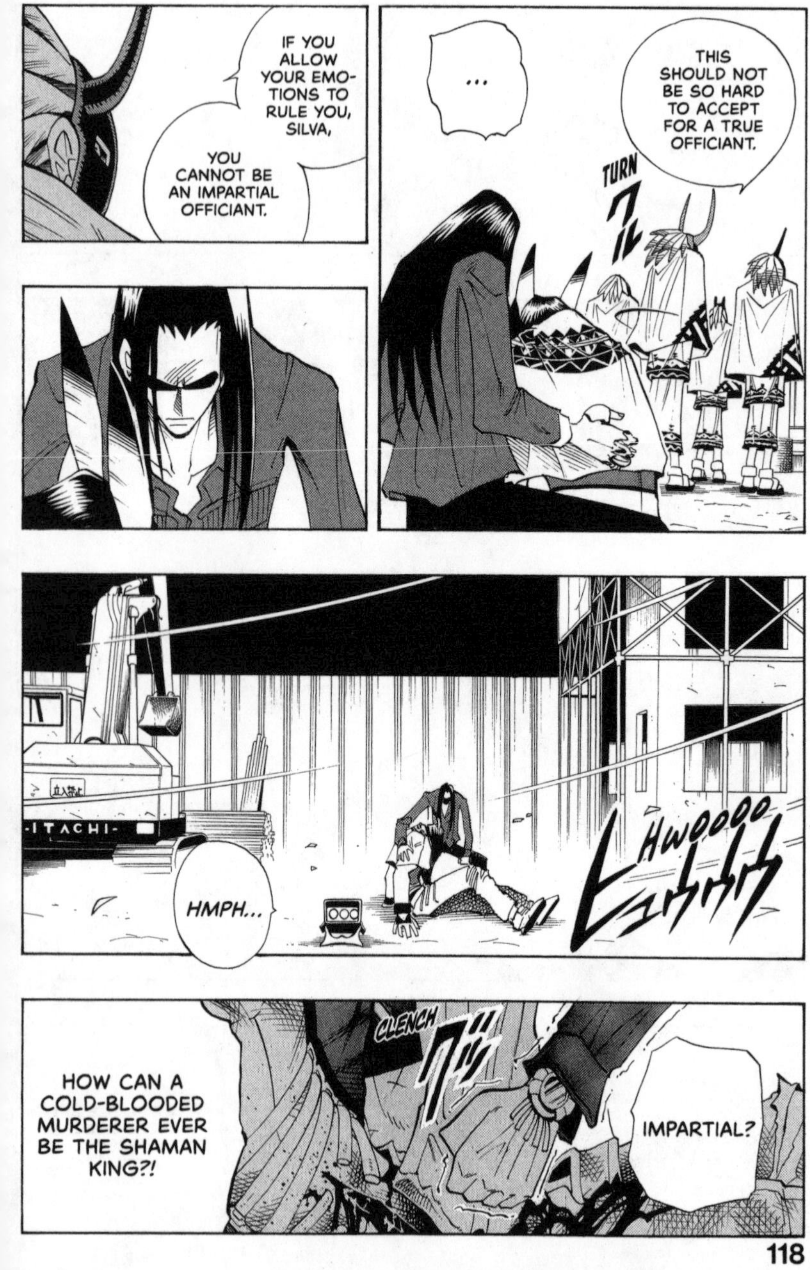
THIS SHOULD NOT BE SO HARD TO ACCEPT FOR A TRUE OFFICIANT.
...
TURN
IF YOU ALLOW YOUR EMO-TIONS TO RULE YOU, SILVA,
YOU CANNOT BE AN IMPARTIAL OFFICIANT.
HWOOOO
HMPH...
-ITACHI-
IMPARTIAL?
CLENCH
HOW CAN A COLD-BLOODED MURDERER EVER BE THE SHAMAN KING?!

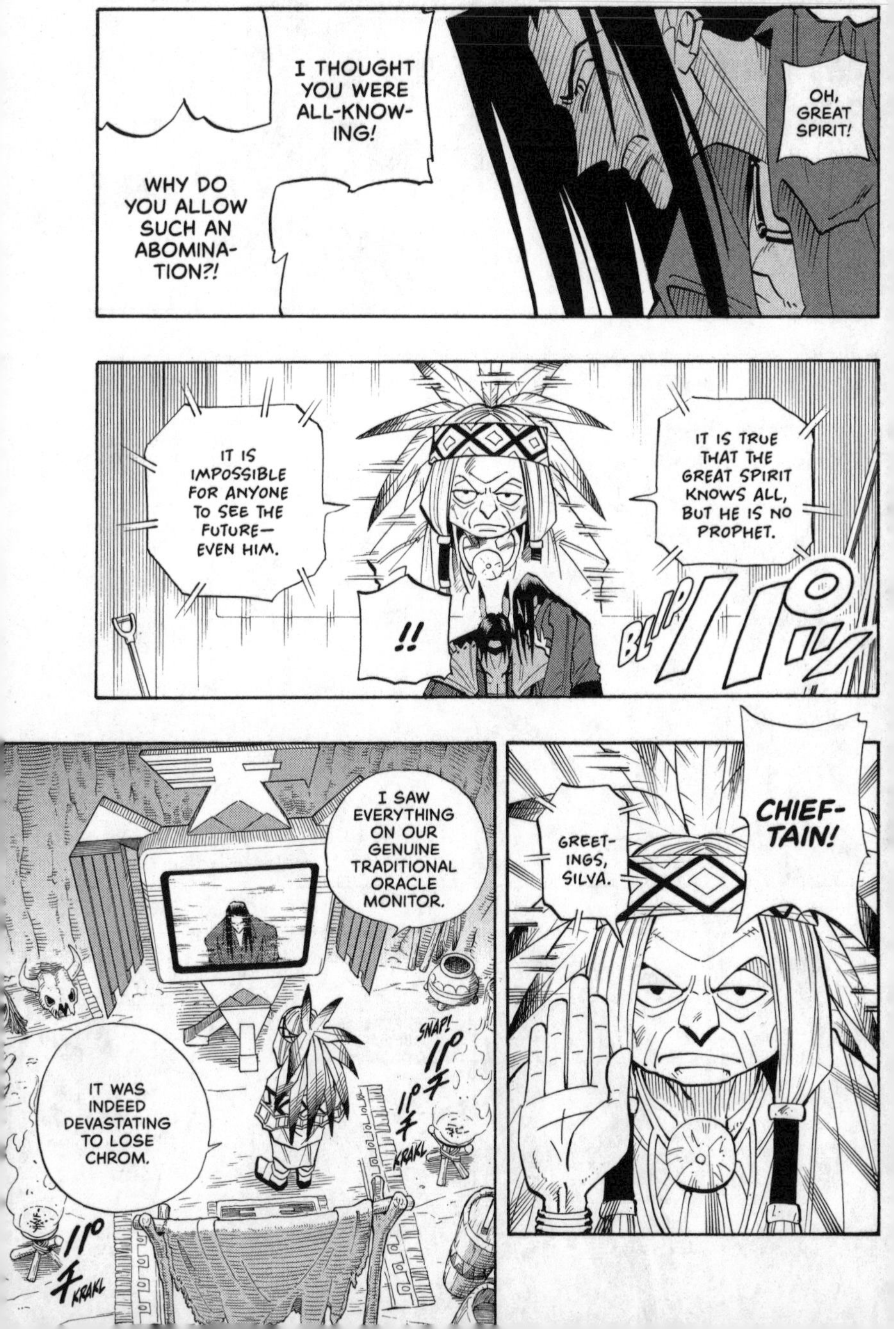
OH, GREAT SPIRIT!
I THOUGHT YOU WERE ALL-KNOWING!
WHY DO YOU ALLOW SUCH AN ABOMINATION?!
IT IS TRUE THAT THE GREAT SPIRIT KNOWS ALL, BUT HE IS NO PROPHET.
BLIP
IT IS IMPOSSIBLE FOR ANYONE TO SEE THE FUTURE—EVEN HIM.
!!
CHIEF-TAIN!
GREET-INGS, SILVA.
I SAW EVERYTHING ON OUR GENUINE TRADITIONAL ORACLE MONITOR.
SNAP!
KRAKL
IT WAS INDEED DEVASTATING TO LOSE CHROM.
KRAKL

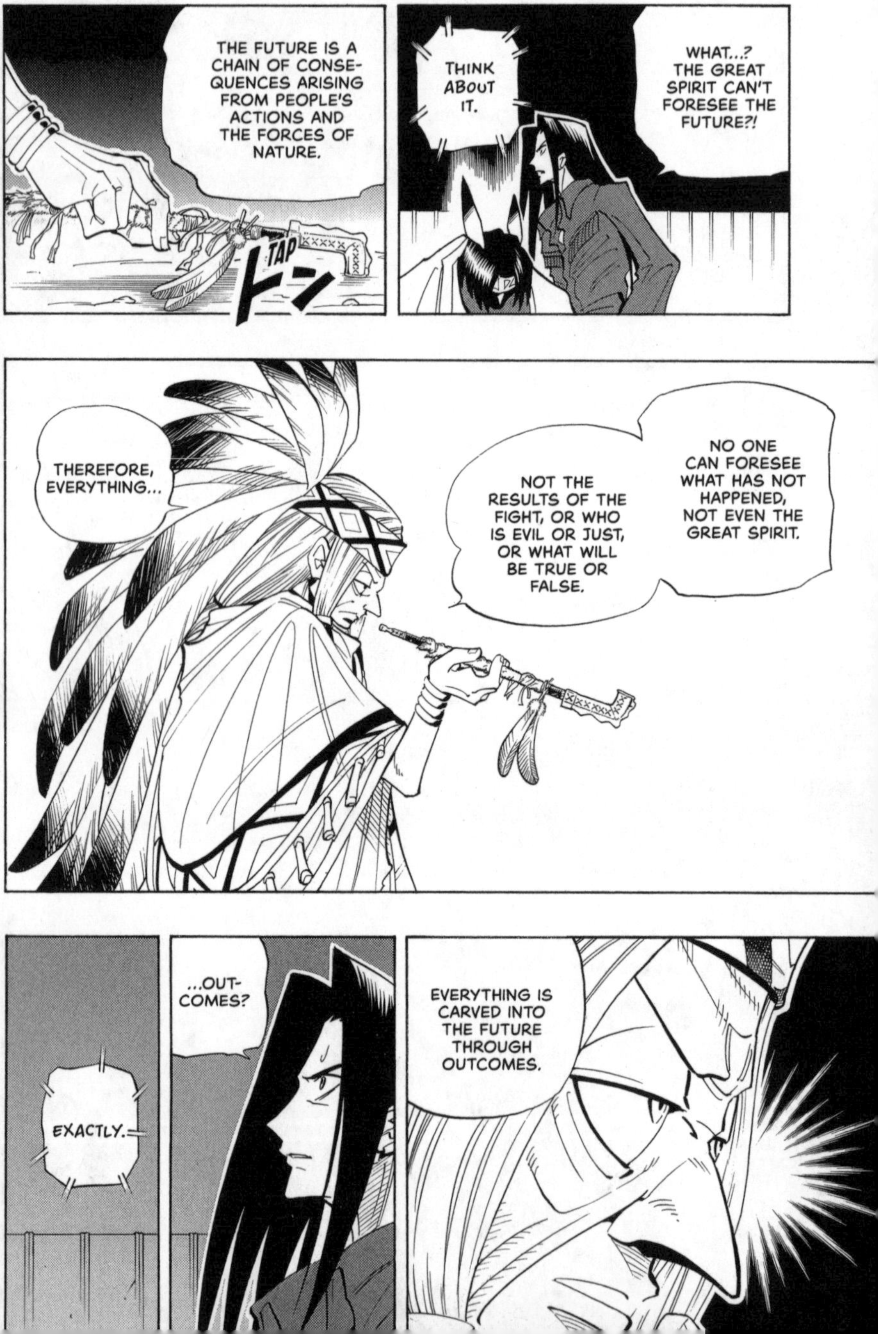
WHAT...? THE GREAT SPIRIT CAN'T FORESEE THE FUTURE?!
THINK ABOUT IT.
THE FUTURE IS A CHAIN OF CONSE-QUENCES ARISING FROM PEOPLE'S ACTIONS AND THE FORCES OF NATURE.
TAP トン
NO ONE CAN FORESEE WHAT HAS NOT HAPPENED, NOT EVEN THE GREAT SPIRIT.
NOT THE RESULTS OF THE FIGHT, OR WHO IS EVIL OR JUST, OR WHAT WILL BE TRUE OR FALSE.
THEREFORE, EVERYTHING...
EVERYTHING IS CARVED INTO THE FUTURE THROUGH OUTCOMES.
...OUT-COMES?
EXACTLY.

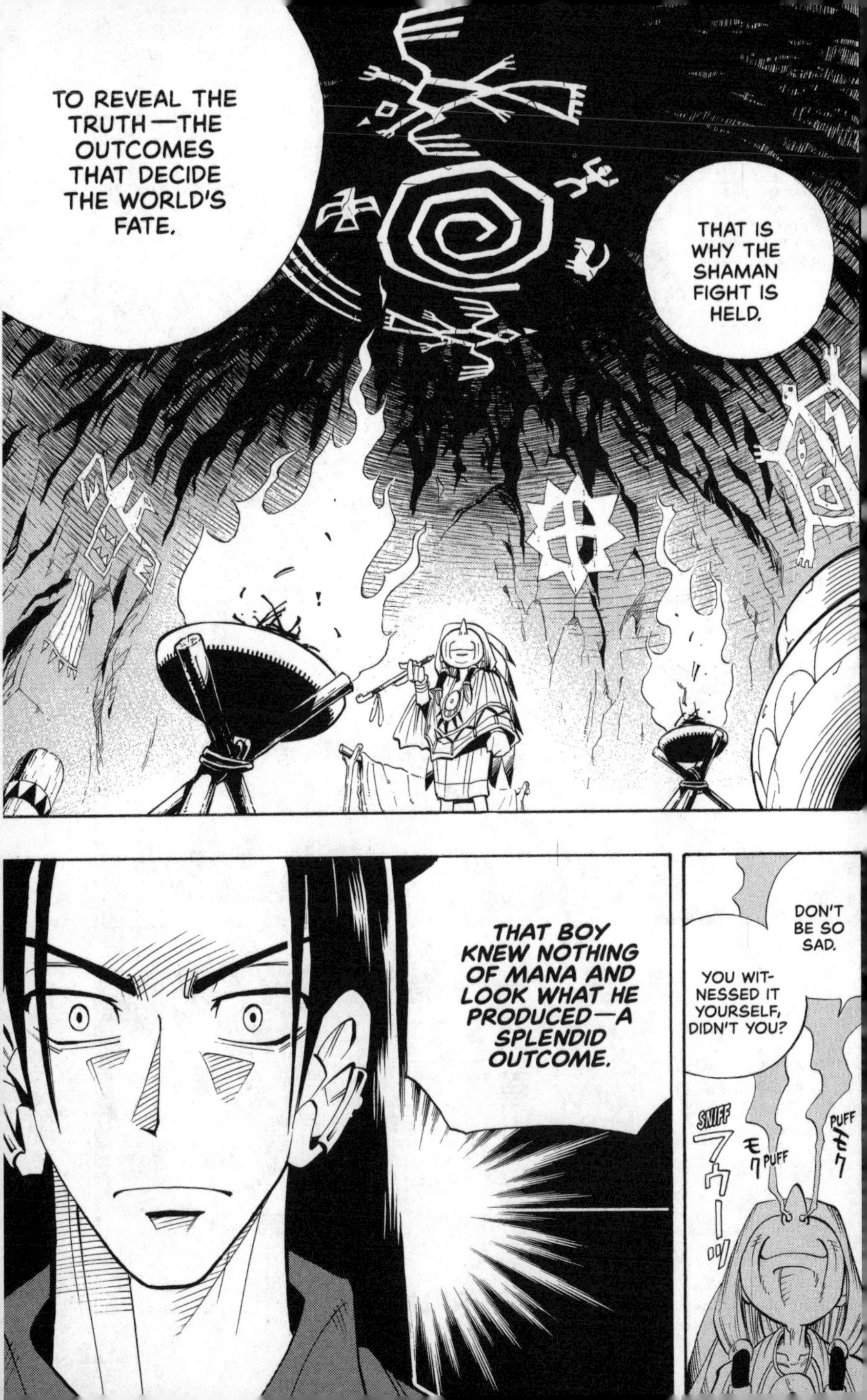
TO REVEAL THE TRUTH—THE OUTCOMES THAT DECIDE THE WORLD'S FATE.
THAT IS WHY THE SHAMAN FIGHT IS HELD.
DON'T BE SO SAD.
YOU WIT- NESSED IT YOURSELF, DIDN'T YOU?
SNIFF
フウーッ
PUFF
モク
PUFF
モク
THAT BOY KNEW NOTHING OF MANA AND LOOK WHAT HE PRODUCED—A SPLENDID OUTCOME.

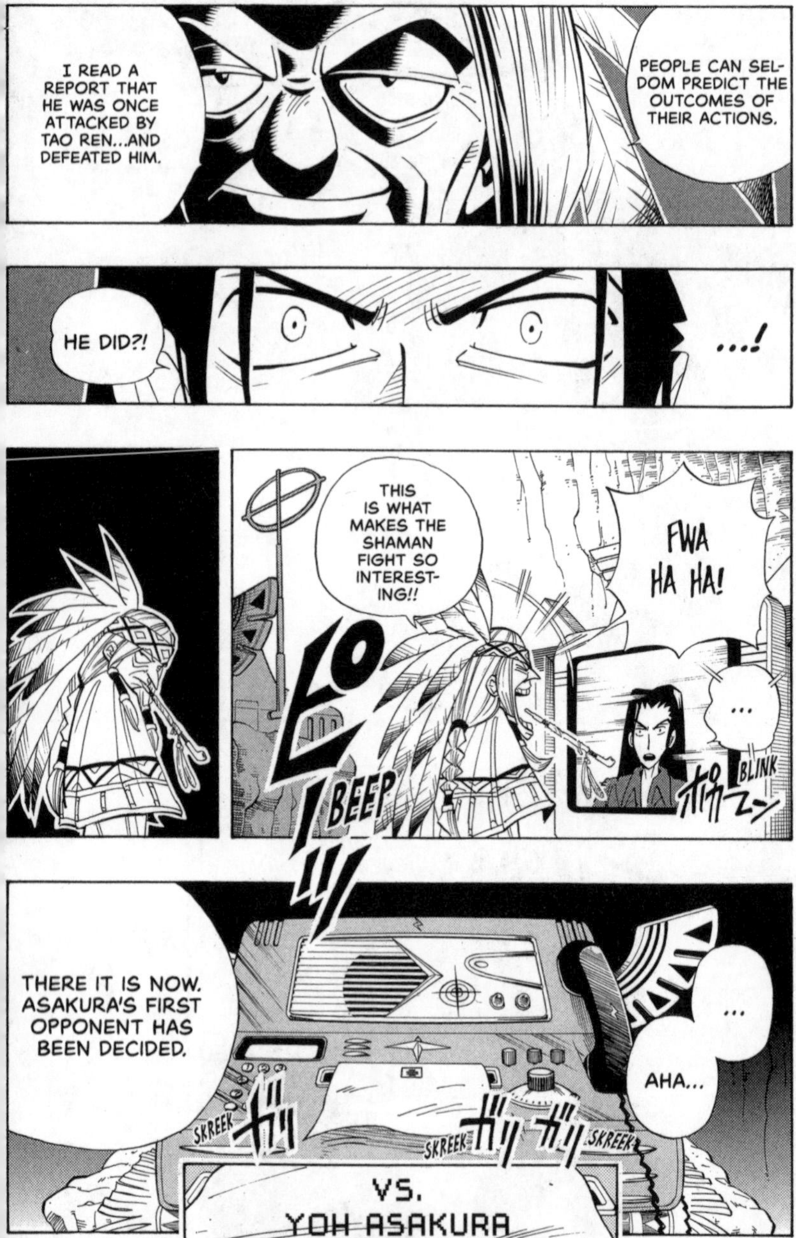
PEOPLE CAN SEL-DOM PREDICT THE OUTCOMES OF THEIR ACTIONS.
I READ A REPORT THAT HE WAS ONCE ATTACKED BY TAO REN...AND DEFEATED HIM.
...!
HE DID?!
FWA HA HA!
...
BLINK
THIS IS WHAT MAKES THE SHAMAN FIGHT SO INTEREST-ING!!
BEEP
...
AHA...
THERE IT IS NOW. ASAKURA'S FIRST OPPONENT HAS BEEN DECIDED.
SKREEK
SKREEK
SKREEK
VS.
YOH ASAKURA

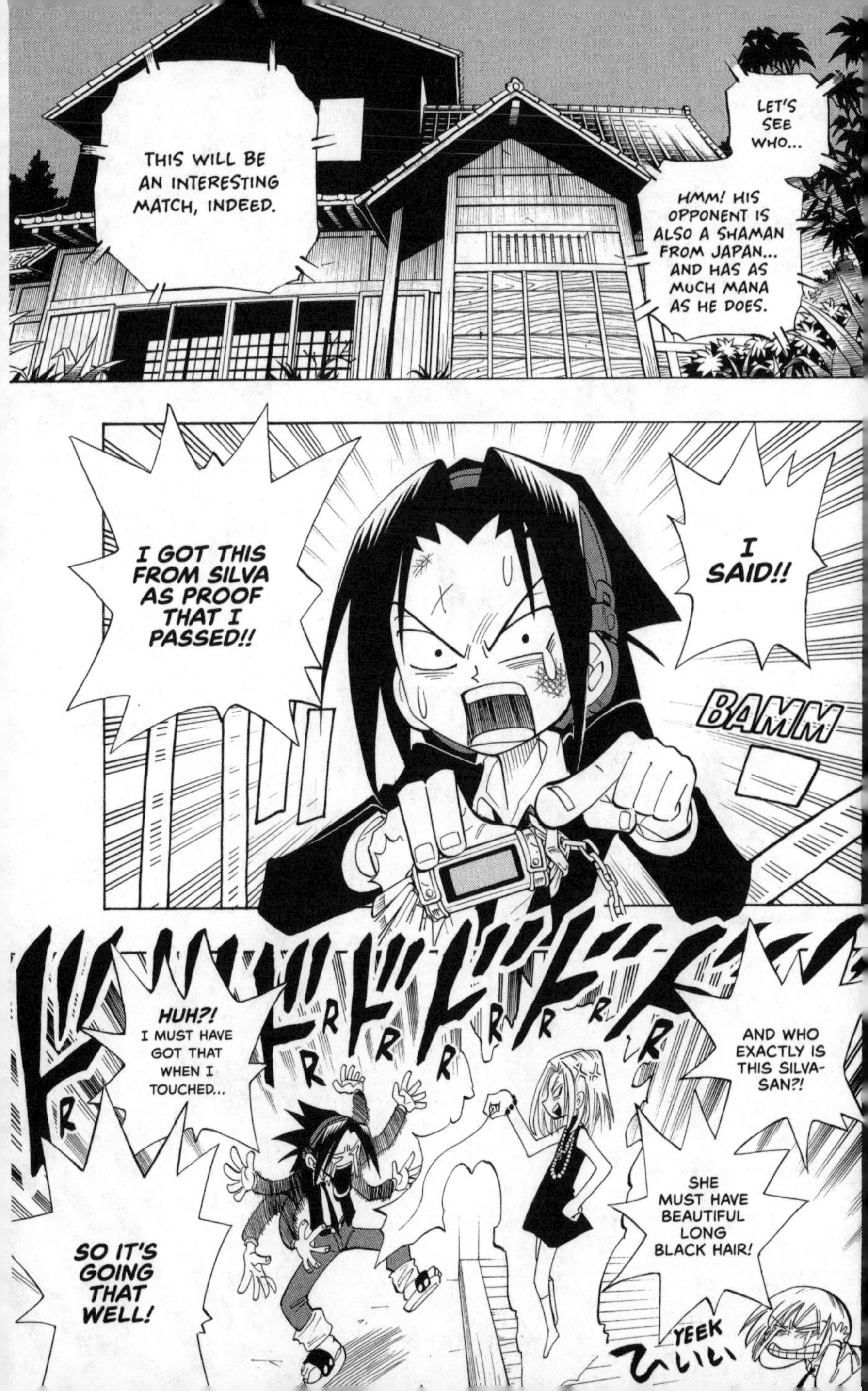
LET'S SEE WHO...
HMM! HIS OPPONENT IS ALSO A SHAMAN FROM JAPAN... AND HAS AS MUCH MANA AS HE DOES.
THIS WILL BE AN INTERESTING MATCH, INDEED.
I SAID!!
BAMM
I GOT THIS FROM SILVA AS PROOF THAT I PASSED!!
KRRRRRRRRR
AND WHO EXACTLY IS THIS SILVA-SAN?!
HUH?! I MUST HAVE GOT THAT WHEN I TOUCHED...
SHE MUST HAVE BEAUTIFUL LONG BLACK HAIR!
YEEK
ひいい
SO IT'S GOING THAT WELL!

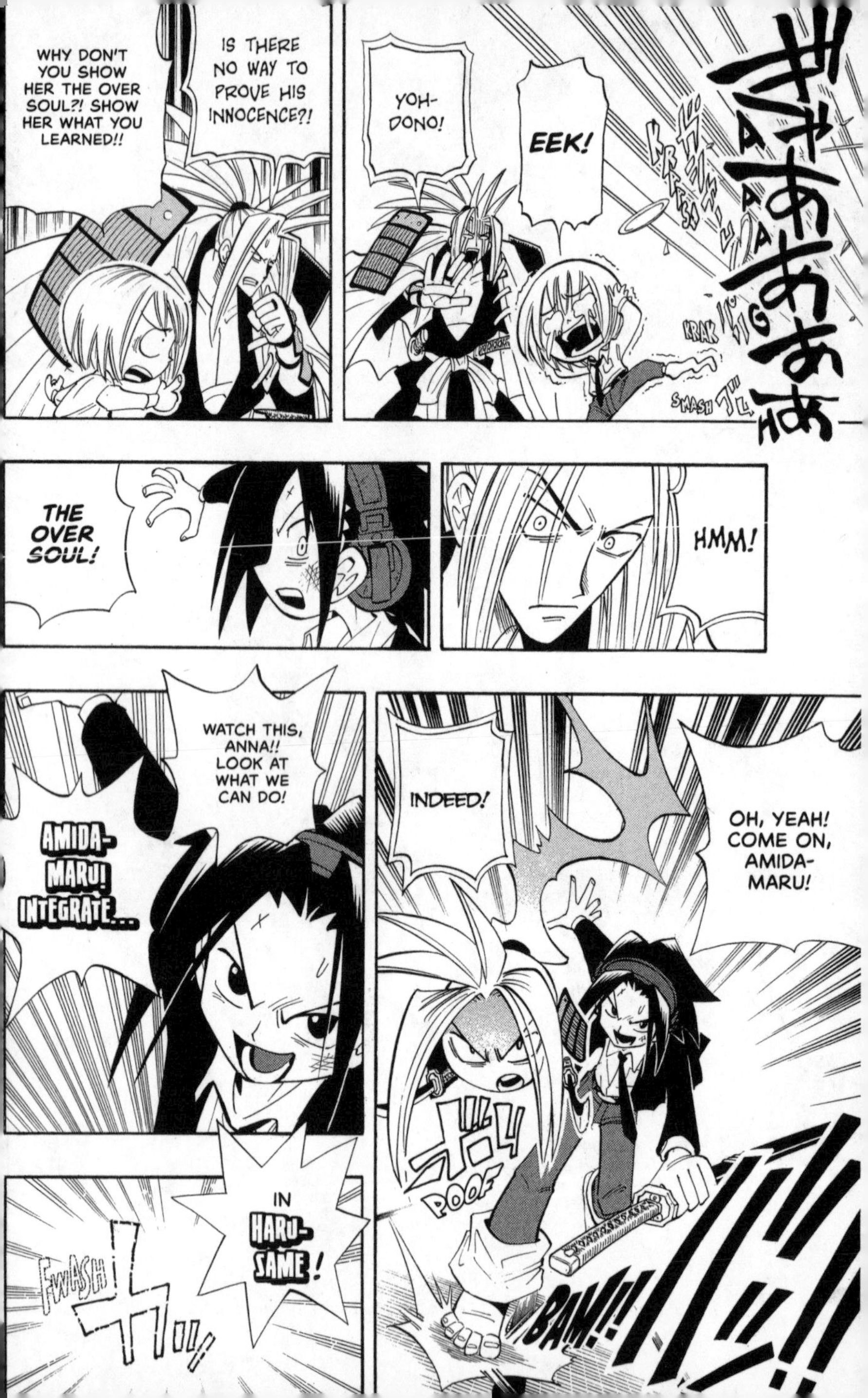
EEK!
YOH-DONO!
KRAK
SMASH
IS THERE NO WAY TO PROVE HIS INNOCENCE?!
WHY DON'T YOU SHOW HER THE OVER SOUL?! SHOW HER WHAT YOU LEARNED!!
HMM!
THE OVER SOUL!
OH, YEAH! COME ON, AMIDA-MARU!
INDEED!
POOF
BAM!!
WATCH THIS, ANNA!! LOOK AT WHAT WE CAN DO!
AMIDA-MARU! INTEGRATE...
IN HARU-SAME!
FWASH!

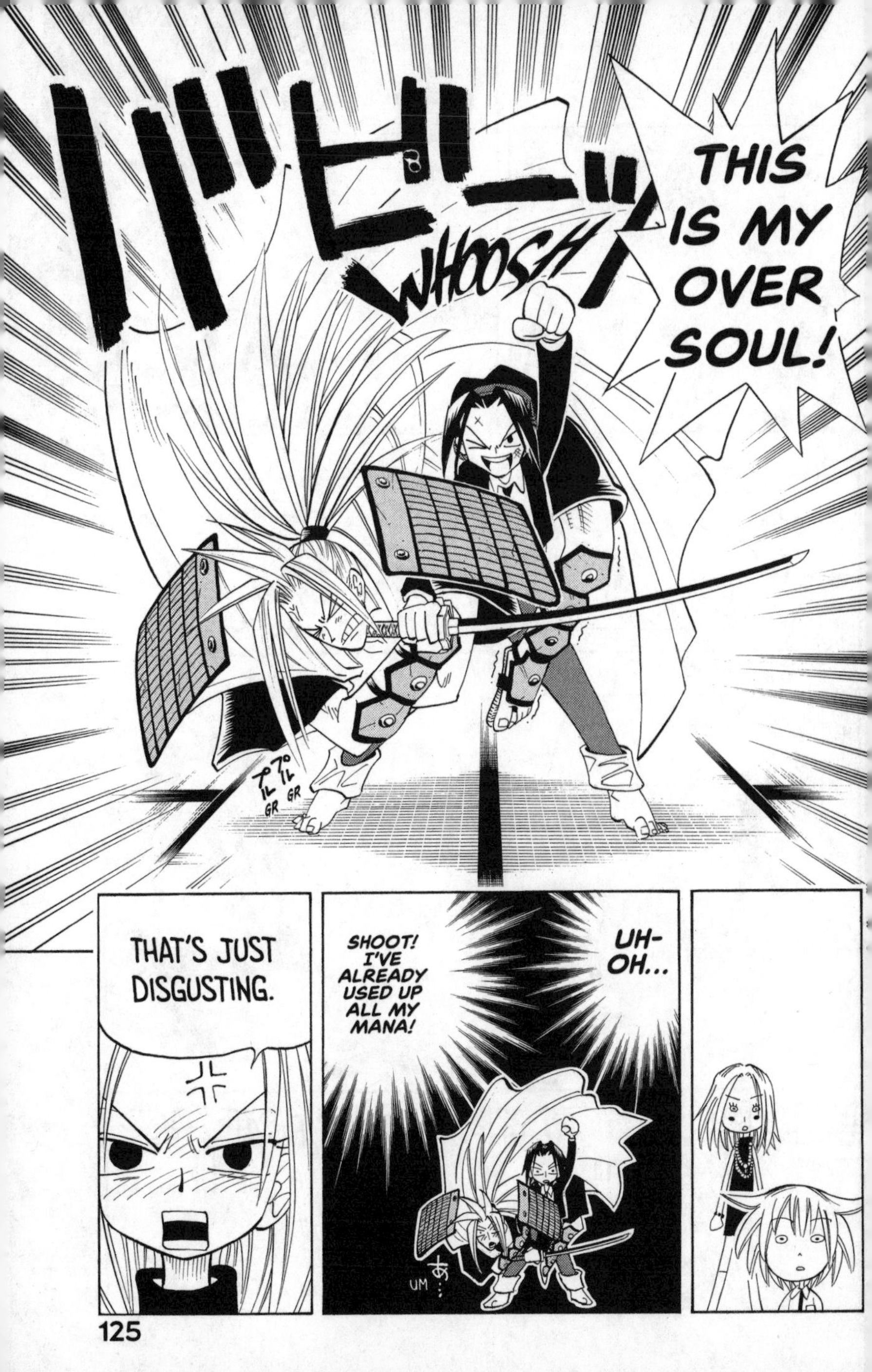
WHOOSH
THIS IS MY OVER SOUL!
プルプル
GR GR
UH-OH...
SHOOT! I'VE ALREADY USED UP ALL MY MANA!
あ…
UM...
THAT'S JUST DISGUSTING.

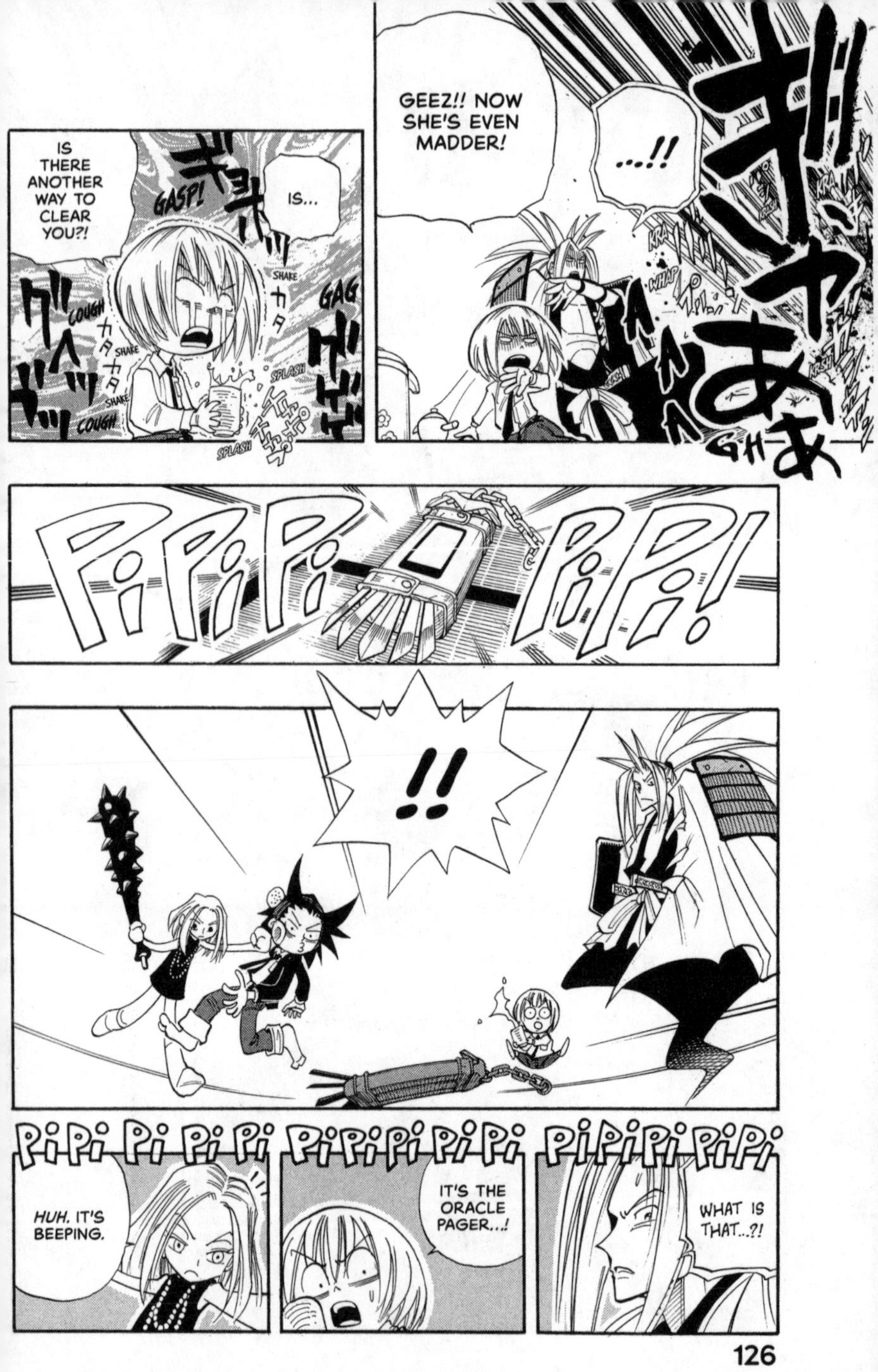
...!!
GEEZ!! NOW SHE'S EVEN MADDER!
KRA
KRASH
WHAP
KRSH
GH
IS...
GASP!
IS THERE ANOTHER WAY TO CLEAR YOU?!
GAG
SHAKE
SPLASH
COUGH
SHAKE
SHAKE
COUGH
SPLASH
PiPiPi PiPi!
!!
PiPiPiPiPiPi
WHAT IS THAT...?!
PiPiPiPiPiPi
IT'S THE ORACLE PAGER...!
PiPi Pi Pi Pi
HUH. IT'S BEEPING.

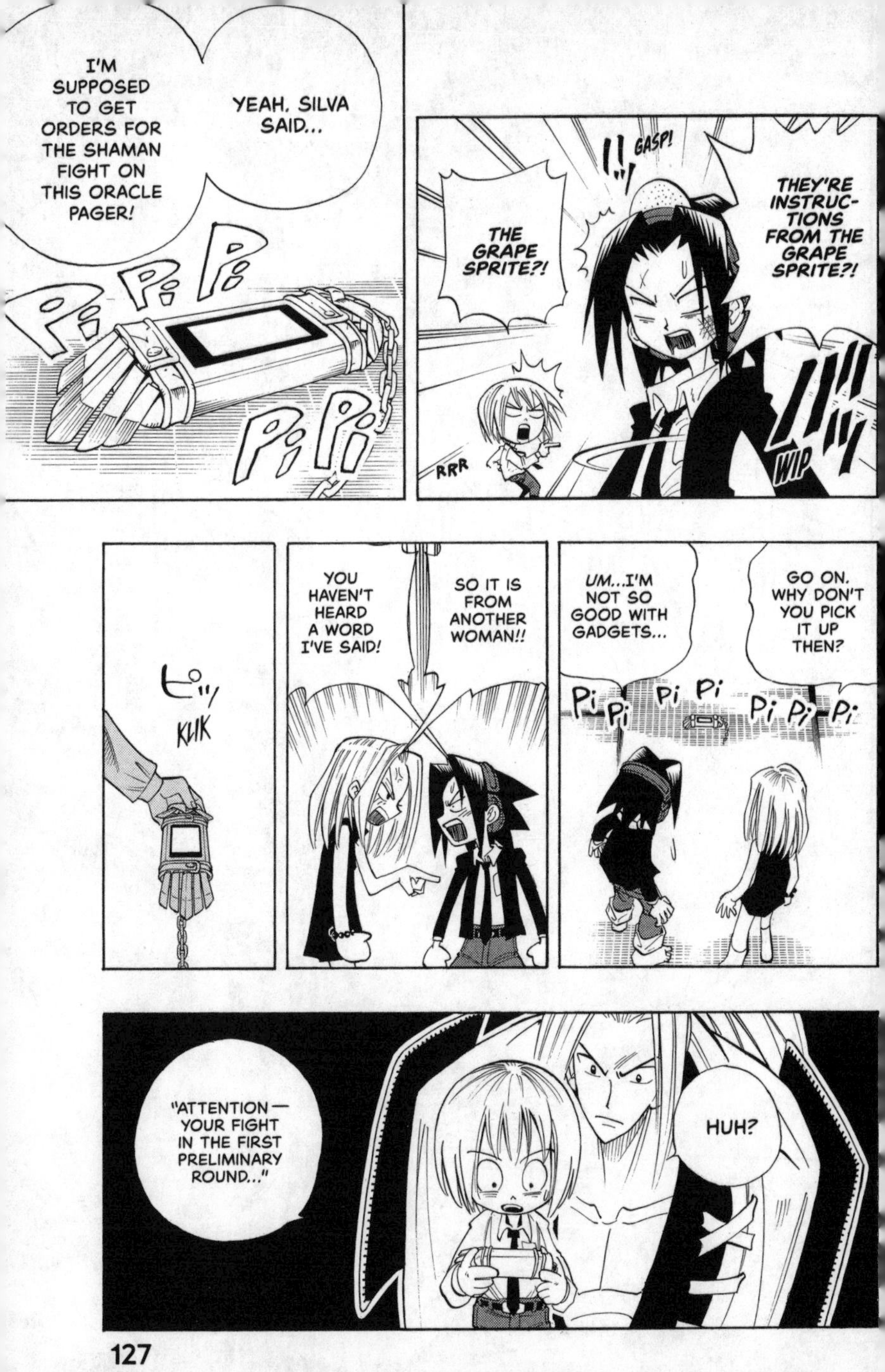
GASP!
THEY'RE INSTRUCTIONS FROM THE GRAPE SPRITE?!
THE GRAPE SPRITE?!
WIP
RRR
YEAH, SILVA SAID...
I'M SUPPOSED TO GET ORDERS FOR THE SHAMAN FIGHT ON THIS ORACLE PAGER!
Pi Pi Pi
Pi Pi
GO ON. WHY DON'T YOU PICK IT UP THEN?
UM...I'M NOT SO GOOD WITH GADGETS...
Pi Pi Pi Pi Pi Pi Pi
SO IT IS FROM ANOTHER WOMAN!!
YOU HAVEN'T HEARD A WORD I'VE SAID!
ピッ
KLIK
HUH?
"ATTENTION— YOUR FIGHT IN THE FIRST PRELIMINARY ROUND..."

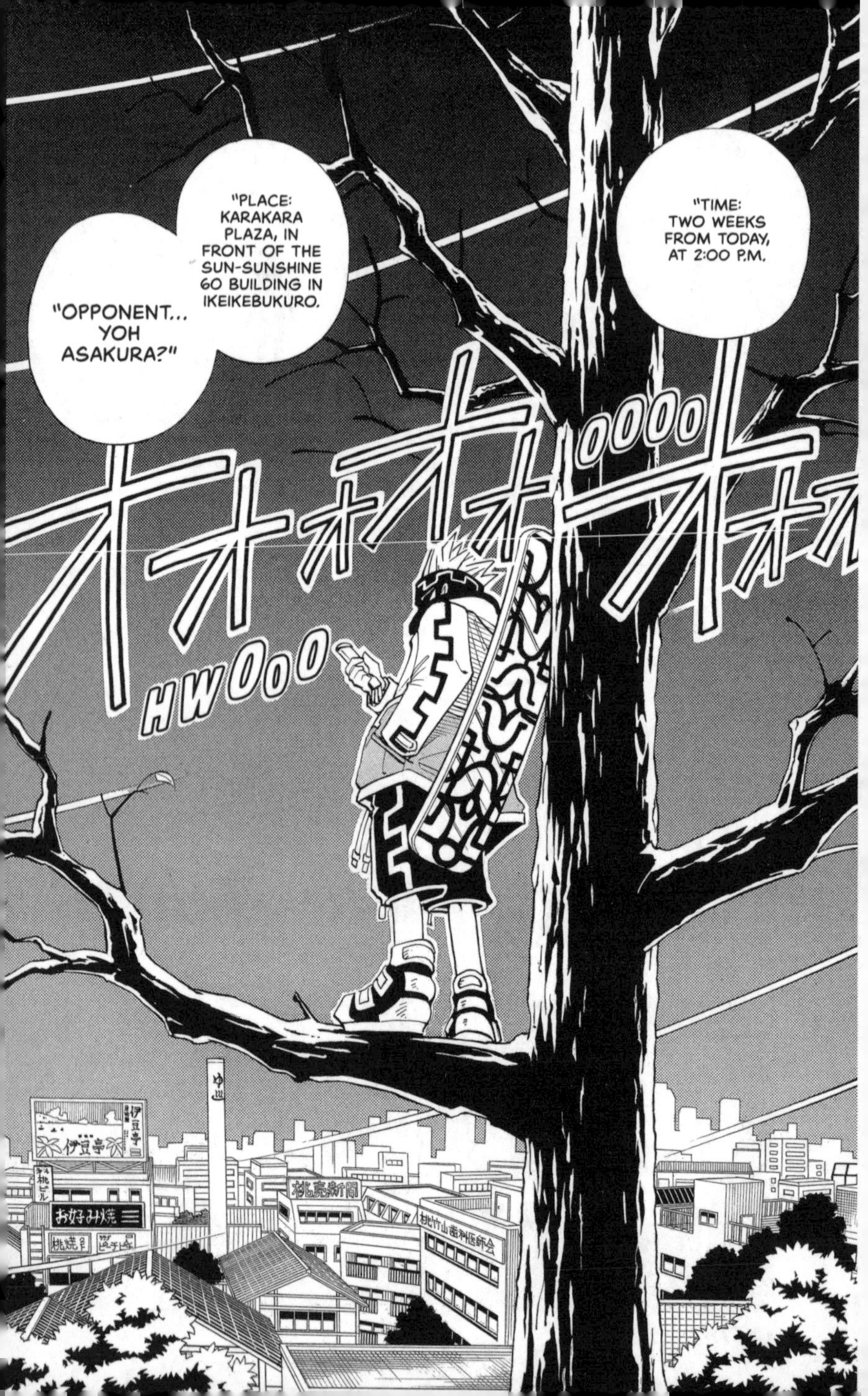
"TIME: TWO WEEKS FROM TODAY, AT 2:00 P.M.
"PLACE: KARAKARA PLAZA, IN FRONT OF THE SUN-SUNSHINE 60 BUILDING IN IKEIKEBUKURO.
"OPPONENT... YOH ASAKURA?"
OOOOO
HWOOO

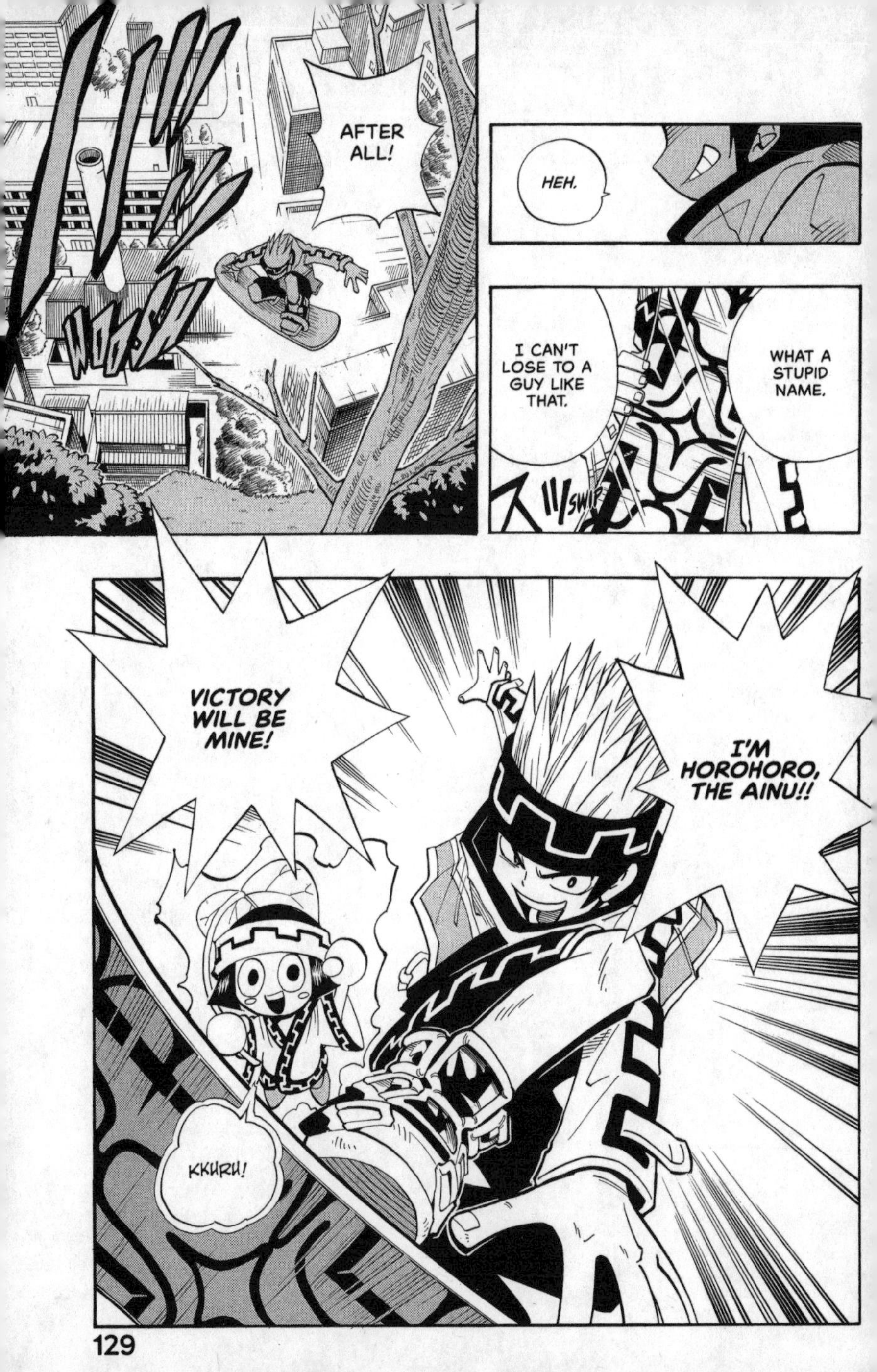
HEH.
WHAT A STUPID NAME.
I CAN'T LOSE TO A GUY LIKE THAT.
SWIP
AFTER ALL!
I'M HOROHORO, THE AINU!!
VICTORY WILL BE MINE!
KKURU!

SHAMAN KING
KING
4

Oracle Projector

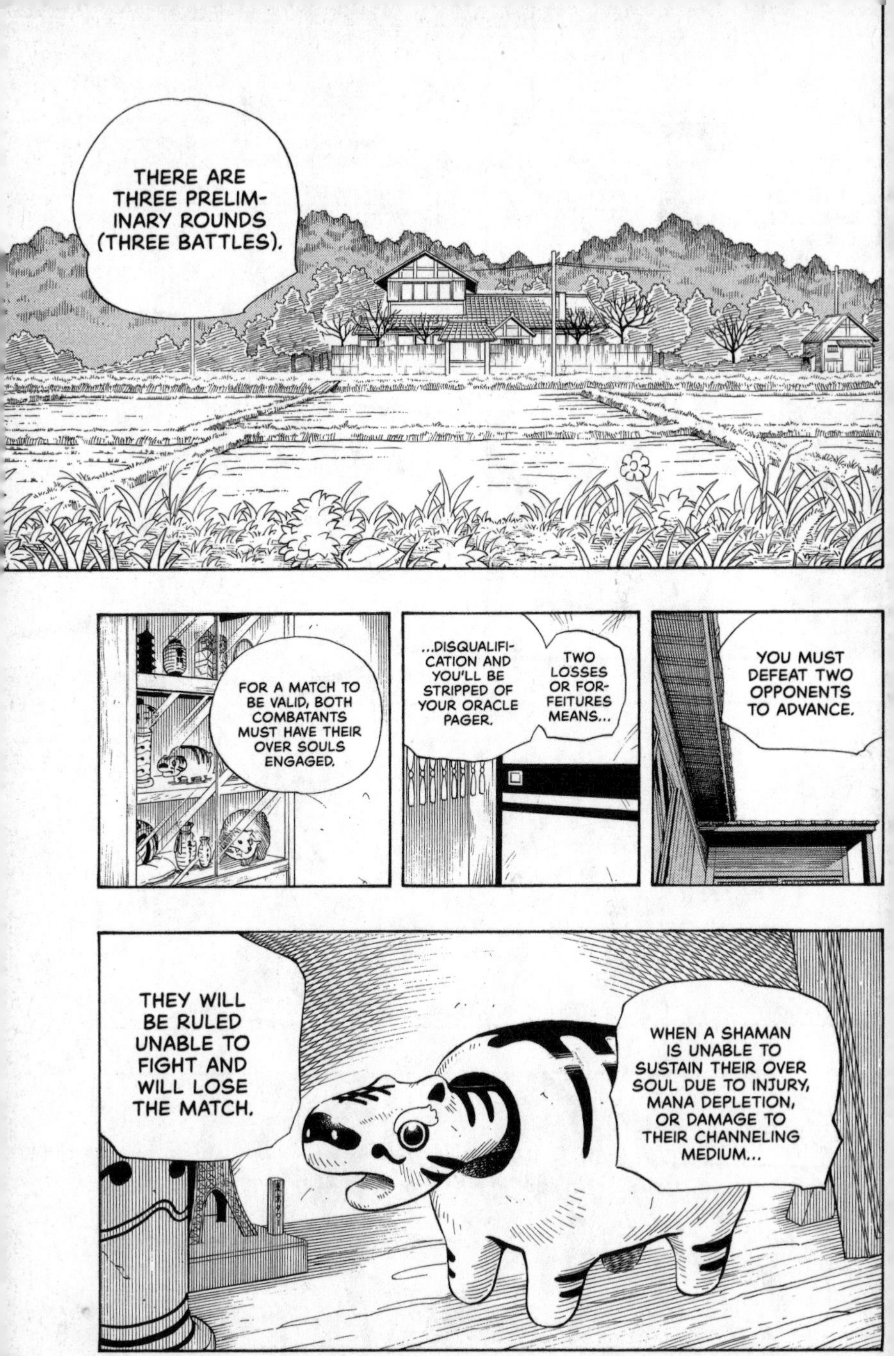
THERE ARE THREE PRELIMINARY ROUNDS (THREE BATTLES).
YOU MUST DEFEAT TWO OPPONENTS TO ADVANCE.
TWO LOSSES OR FORFEITURES MEANS...
...DISQUALIFICATION AND YOU'LL BE STRIPPED OF YOUR ORACLE PAGER.
FOR A MATCH TO BE VALID, BOTH COMBATANTS MUST HAVE THEIR OVER SOULS ENGAGED.
WHEN A SHAMAN IS UNABLE TO SUSTAIN THEIR OVER SOUL DUE TO INJURY, MANA DEPLETION, OR DAMAGE TO THEIR CHANNELING MEDIUM...
THEY WILL BE RULED UNABLE TO FIGHT AND WILL LOSE THE MATCH.

Chapter 33: Horohoro

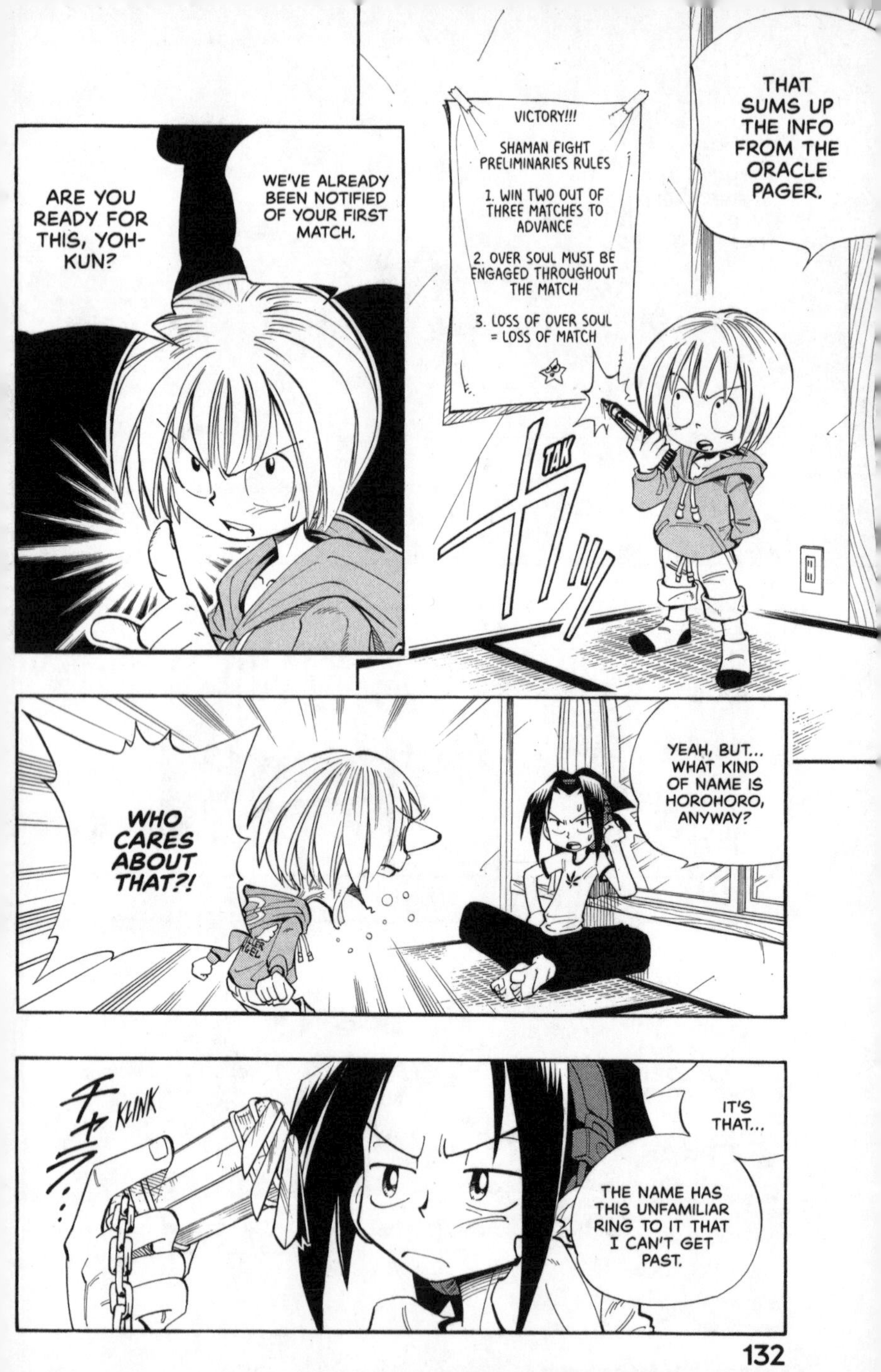
THAT SUMS UP THE INFO FROM THE ORACLE PAGER.
VICTORY!!!
SHAMAN FIGHT PRELIMINARIES RULES
1. WIN TWO OUT OF THREE MATCHES TO ADVANCE
2. OVER SOUL MUST BE ENGAGED THROUGHOUT THE MATCH
3. LOSS OF OVER SOUL = LOSS OF MATCH
TAK
WE'VE ALREADY BEEN NOTIFIED OF YOUR FIRST MATCH.
ARE YOU READY FOR THIS, YOH-KUN?
YEAH, BUT... WHAT KIND OF NAME IS HOROHORO, ANYWAY?
WHO CARES ABOUT THAT?!
IT'S THAT...
THE NAME HAS THIS UNFAMILIAR RING TO IT THAT I CAN'T GET PAST.
KLINK

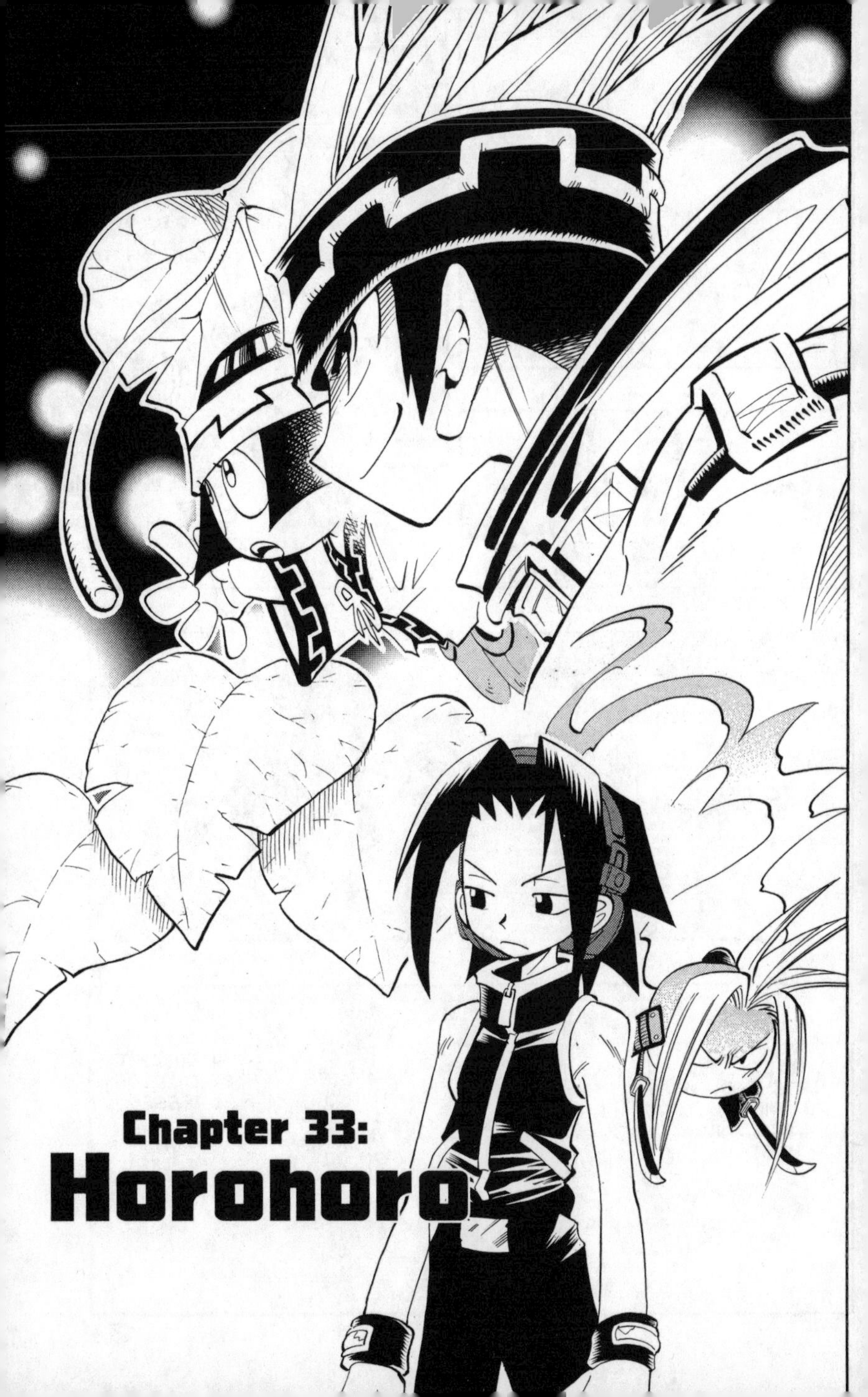
Chapter 33:
Horohoro

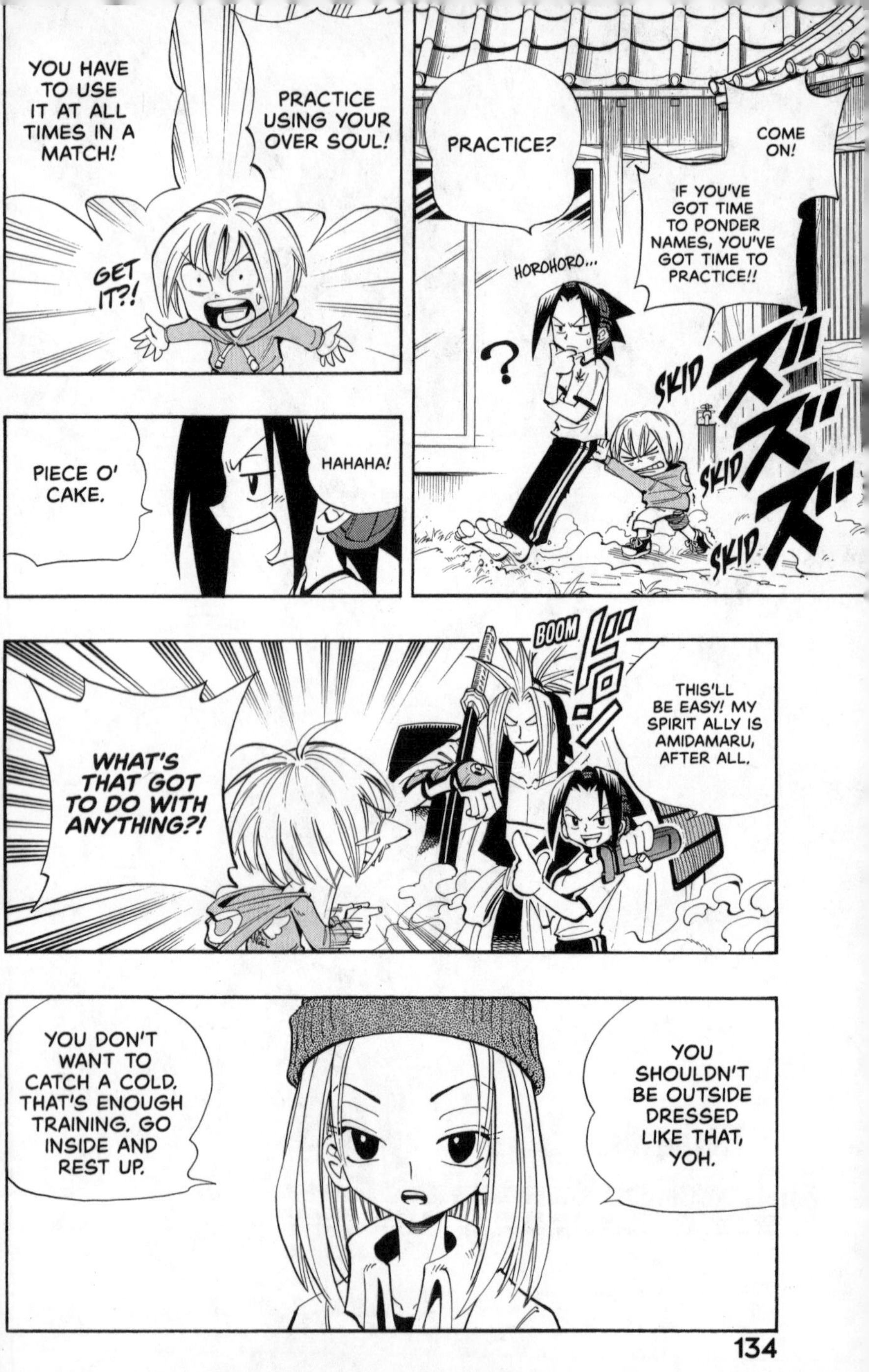
PRACTICE?
COME ON!
IF YOU'VE GOT TIME TO PONDER NAMES, YOU'VE GOT TIME TO PRACTICE!!
HOROHORO...
SKID
SKID
SKID
PRACTICE USING YOUR OVER SOUL!
YOU HAVE TO USE IT AT ALL TIMES IN A MATCH!
GET IT?!
HAHAHA!
PIECE O' CAKE.
BOOM
THIS'LL BE EASY! MY SPIRIT ALLY IS AMIDAMARU, AFTER ALL.
WHAT'S THAT GOT TO DO WITH ANYTHING?!
YOU SHOULDN'T BE OUTSIDE DRESSED LIKE THAT, YOH.
YOU DON'T WANT TO CATCH A COLD. THAT'S ENOUGH TRAINING. GO INSIDE AND REST UP.

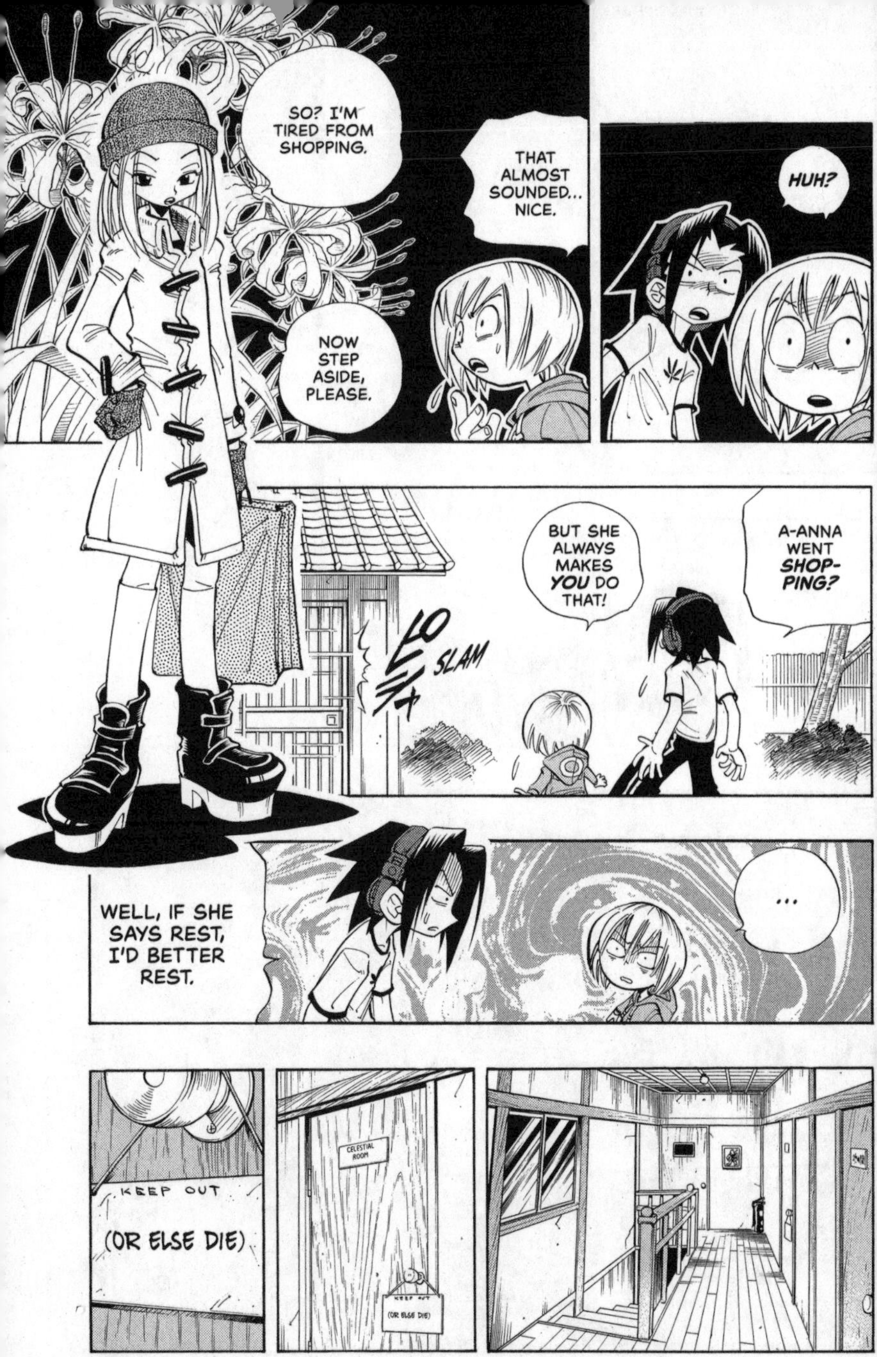

SO? I'M TIRED FROM SHOPPING.
THAT ALMOST SOUNDED... NICE.
NOW STEP ASIDE, PLEASE.
HUH?
SLAM
A-ANNA WENT SHOPPING?
BUT SHE ALWAYS MAKES YOU DO THAT!
...
WELL, IF SHE SAYS REST, I'D BETTER REST.
CELESTIAL ROOM
KEEP OUT
(OR ELSE DIE)
KEEP OUT
(OR ELSE DIE)

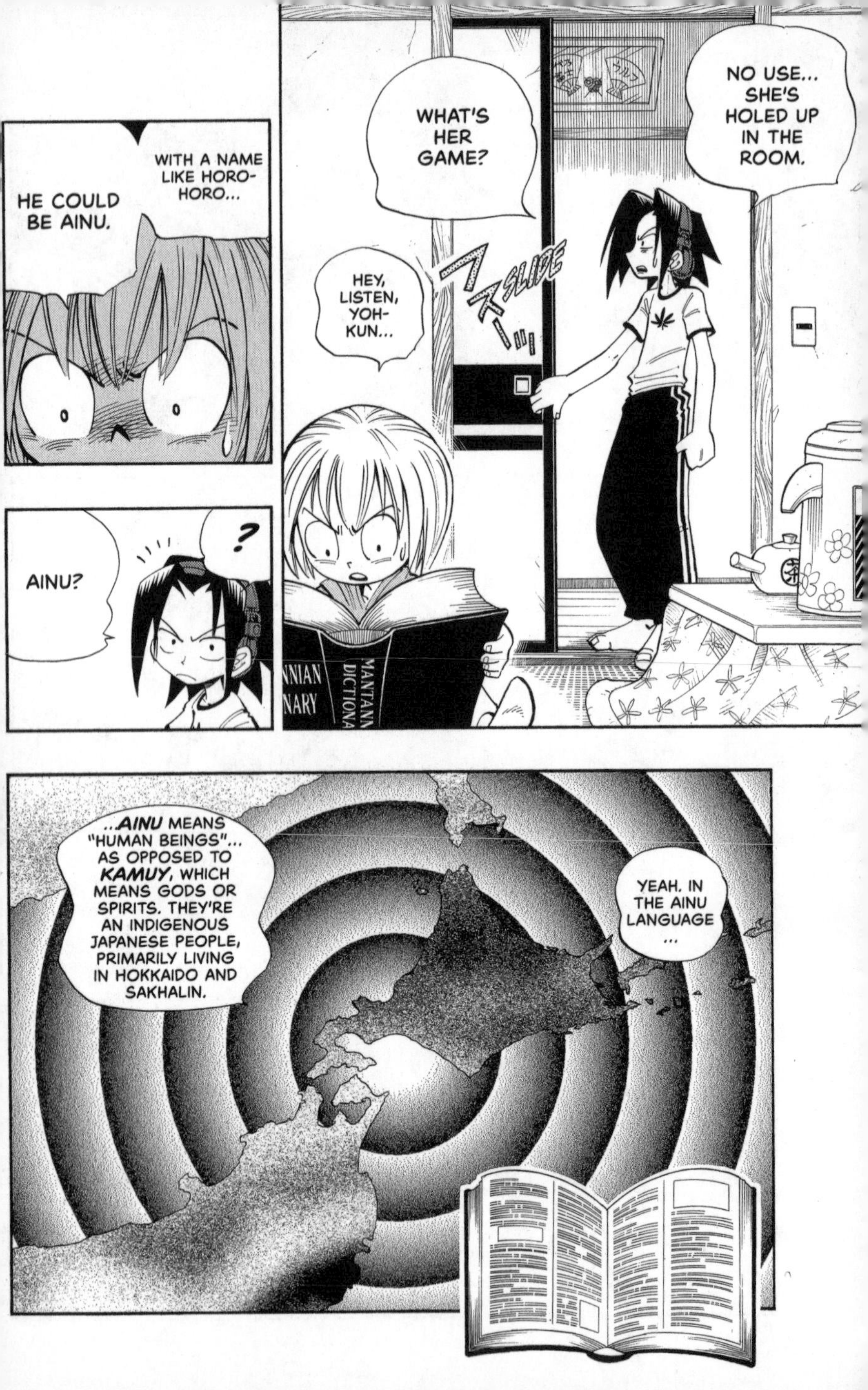
NO USE... SHE'S HOLED UP IN THE ROOM.
WHAT'S HER GAME?
SLIDE
HEY, LISTEN, YOH-KUN...
WITH A NAME LIKE HORO-HORO...
HE COULD BE AINU.
?
AINU?
YEAH. IN THE AINU LANGUAGE ...
...AINU MEANS "HUMAN BEINGS"... AS OPPOSED TO KAMUY, WHICH MEANS GODS OR SPIRITS. THEY'RE AN INDIGENOUS JAPANESE PEOPLE, PRIMARILY LIVING IN HOKKAIDO AND SAKHALIN.

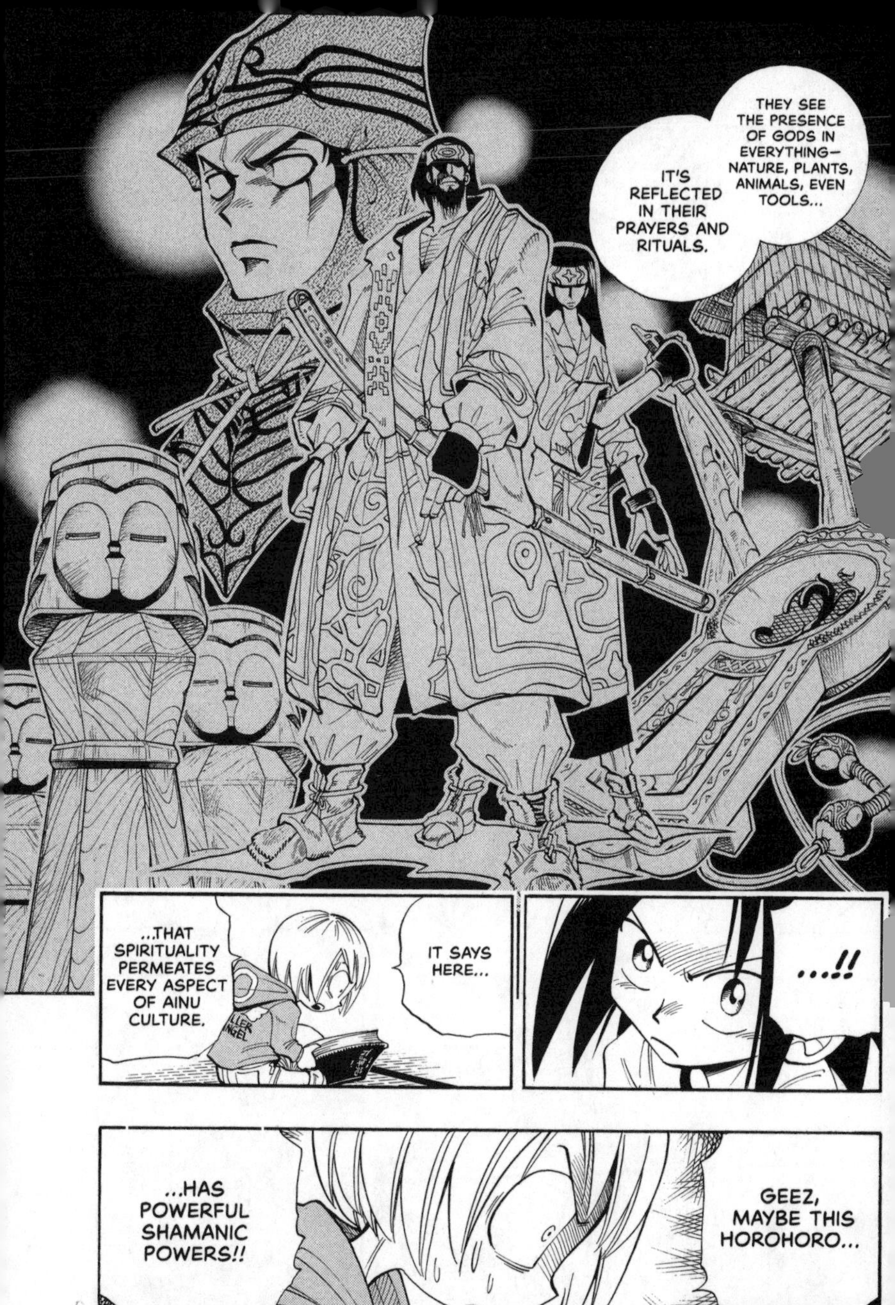
THEY SEE THE PRESENCE OF GODS IN EVERYTHING— NATURE, PLANTS, ANIMALS, EVEN TOOLS...
IT'S REFLECTED IN THEIR PRAYERS AND RITUALS.
...!!
IT SAYS HERE...
...THAT SPIRITUALITY PERMEATES EVERY ASPECT OF AINU CULTURE.
GEEZ, MAYBE THIS HOROHORO...
...HAS POWERFUL SHAMANIC POWERS!!

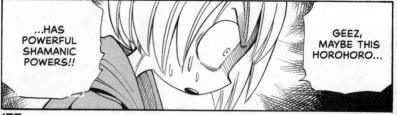

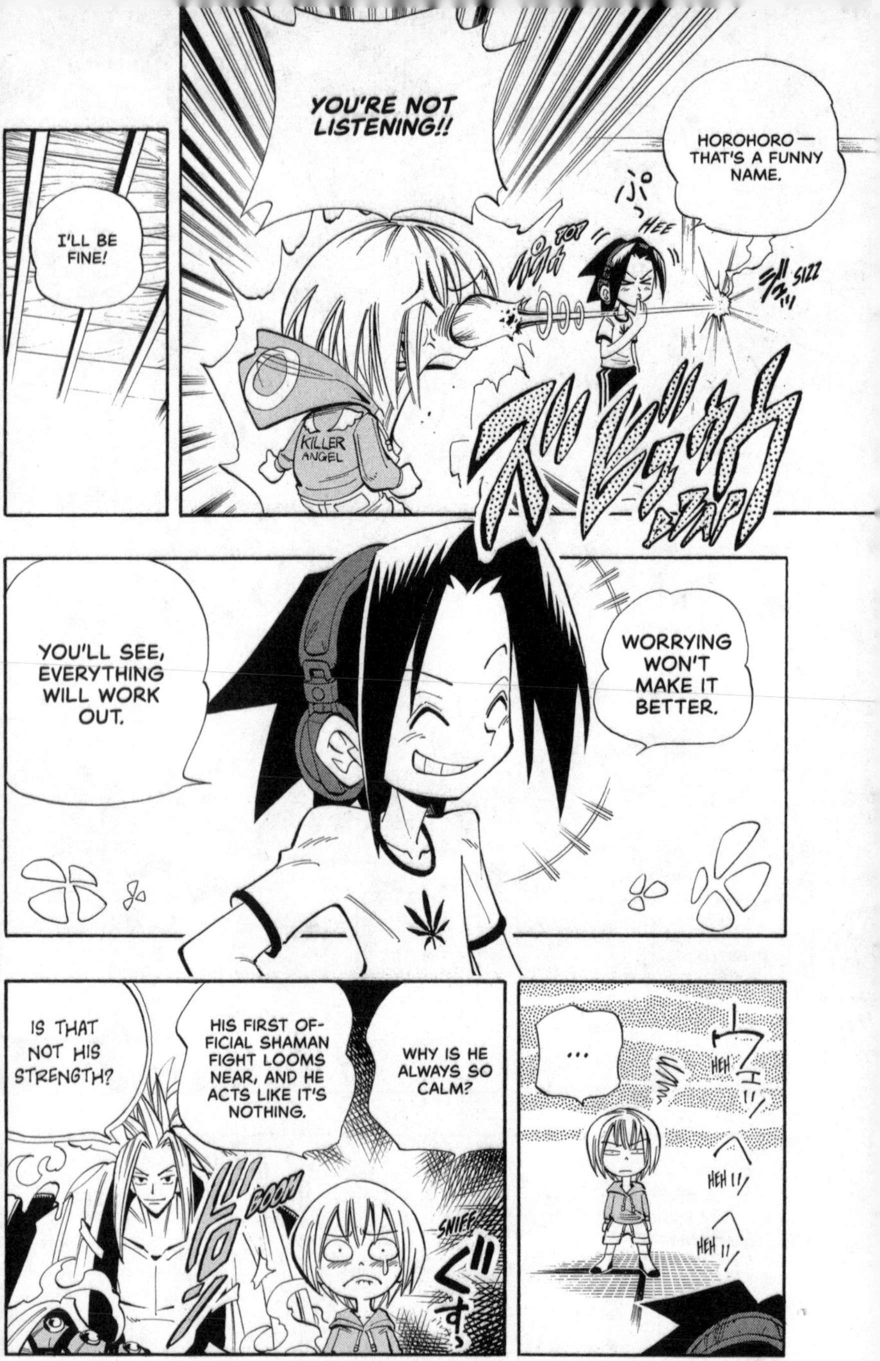
HOROHORO—THAT'S A FUNNY NAME.
HEE
TOT
SIZZ
YOU'RE NOT LISTENING!!
KILLER ANGEL
ZAP
I'LL BE FINE!
WORRYING WON'T MAKE IT BETTER.
YOU'LL SEE, EVERYTHING WILL WORK OUT.
...
HEH!!
HEH!!
HEH!!
WHY IS HE ALWAYS SO CALM?
HIS FIRST OF-FICIAL SHAMAN FIGHT LOOMS NEAR, AND HE ACTS LIKE IT'S NOTHING.
IS THAT NOT HIS STRENGTH?
SNIFF
BOOM

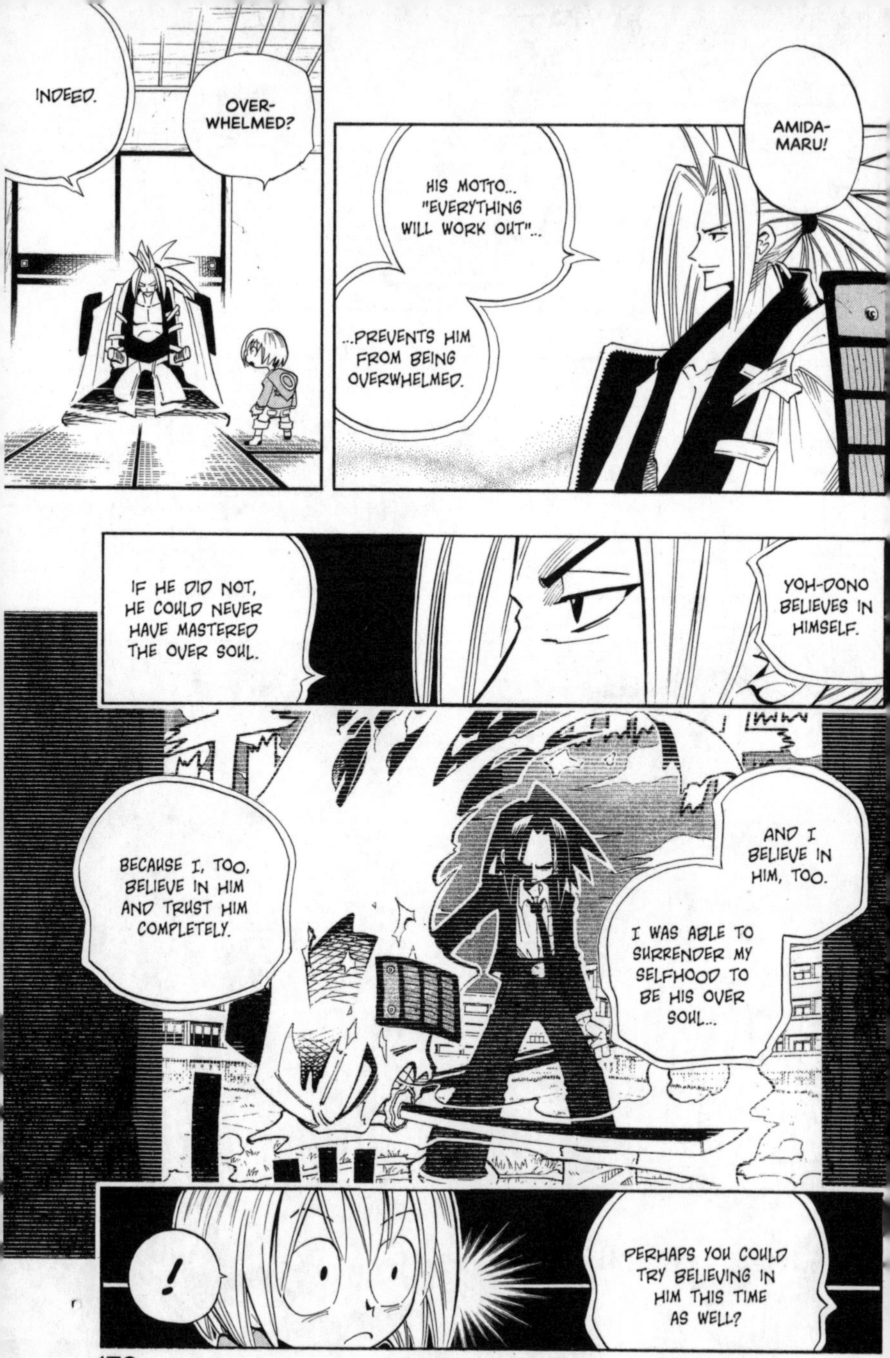
AMIDA-MARU!
HIS MOTTO... "EVERYTHING WILL WORK OUT"...
...PREVENTS HIM FROM BEING OVERWHELMED.
OVER-WHELMED?
INDEED.
YOH-DONO BELIEVES IN HIMSELF.
IF HE DID NOT, HE COULD NEVER HAVE MASTERED THE OVER SOUL.
AND I BELIEVE IN HIM, TOO.
I WAS ABLE TO SURRENDER MY SELFHOOD TO BE HIS OVER SOUL...
BECAUSE I, TOO, BELIEVE IN HIM AND TRUST HIM COMPLETELY.
PERHAPS YOU COULD TRY BELIEVING IN HIM THIS TIME AS WELL?
!

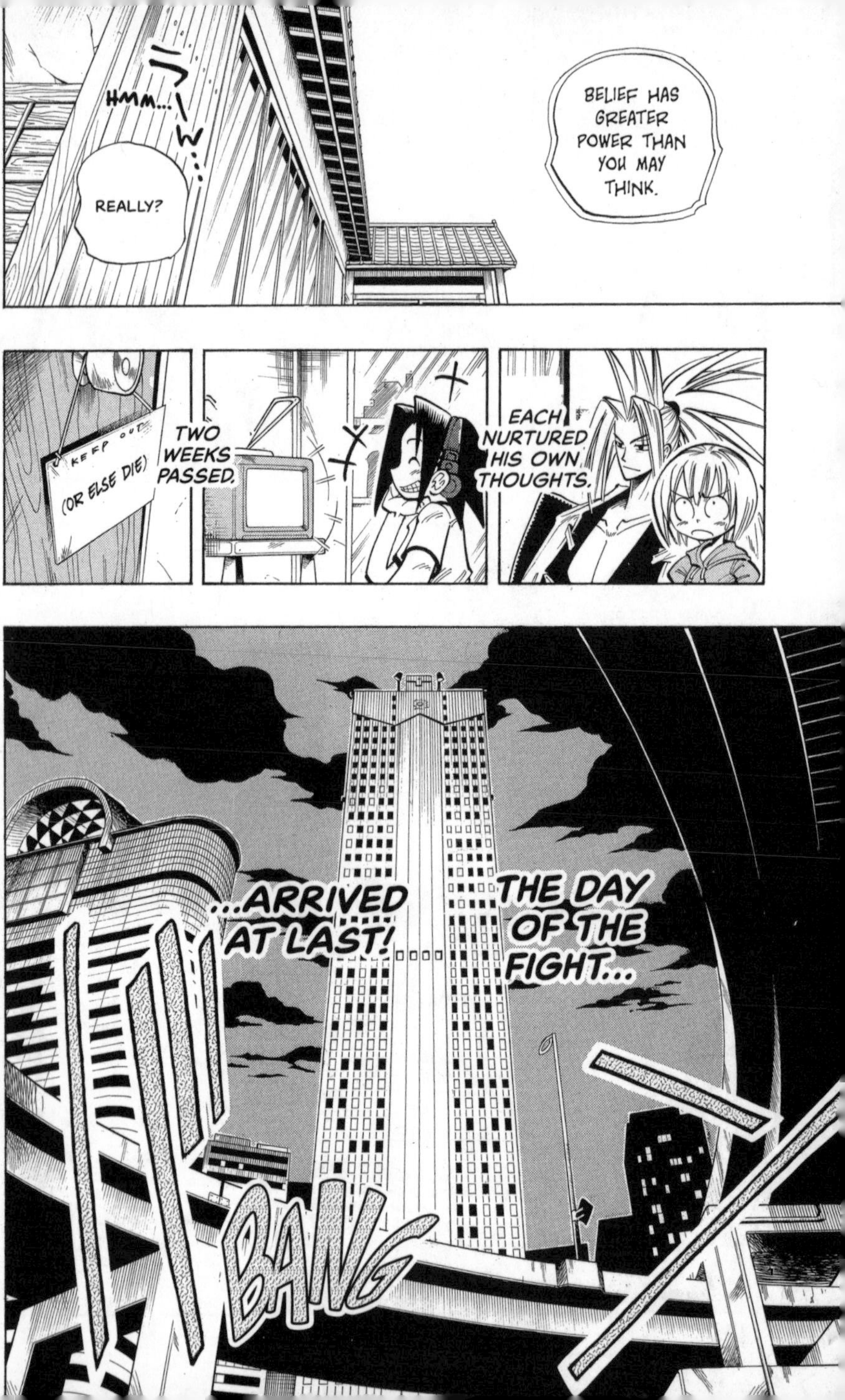
BELIEF HAS GREATER POWER THAN YOU MAY THINK.
HMM...
REALLY?
EACH NURTURED HIS OWN THOUGHTS.
TWO WEEKS PASSED.
KEEP OUT
(OR ELSE DIE)
THE DAY OF THE FIGHT...
...ARRIVED AT LAST!
BANG

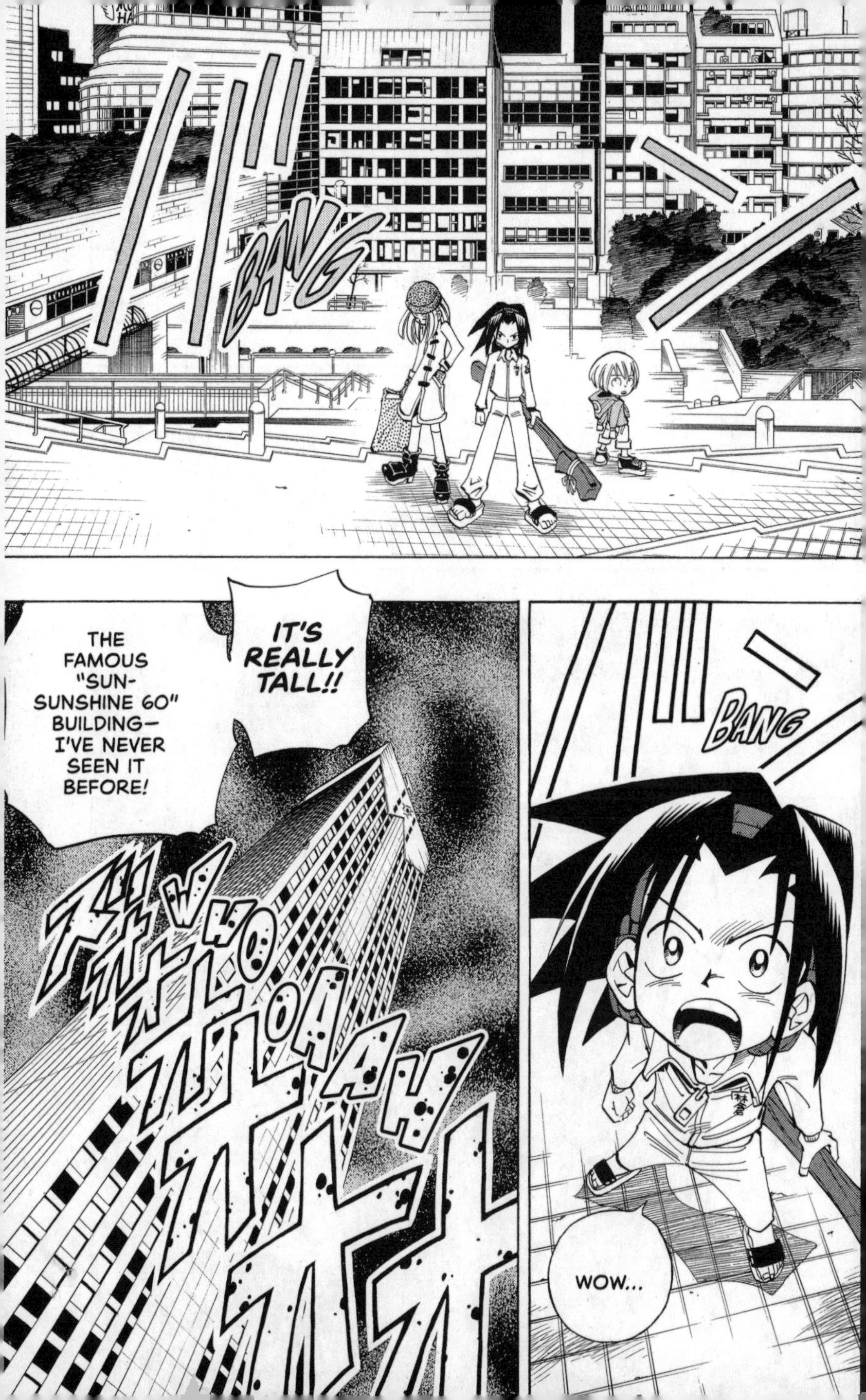
BANG
BANG
WOW...
IT'S REALLY TALL!!
THE FAMOUS "SUN-SUNSHINE 60" BUILDING— I'VE NEVER SEEN IT BEFORE!
WHOOOAH

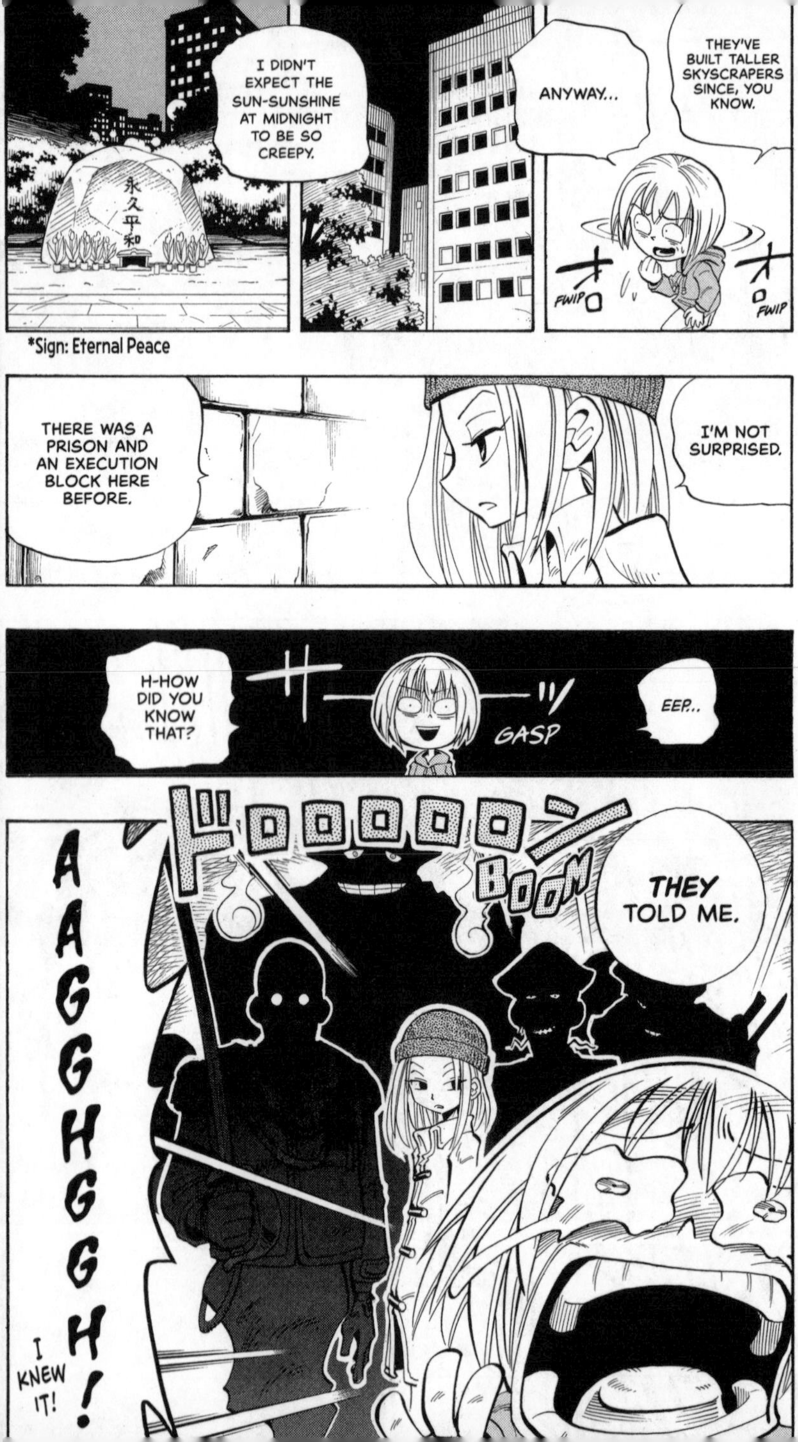

THEY'VE BUILT TALLER SKYSCRAPERS SINCE, YOU KNOW.
ANYWAY...
FWIP
FWIP
I DIDN'T EXPECT THE SUN-SUNSHINE AT MIDNIGHT TO BE SO CREEPY.
永久平和
*Sign: Eternal Peace
I'M NOT SURPRISED.
THERE WAS A PRISON AND AN EXECUTION BLOCK HERE BEFORE.
EEP...
GASP
H-HOW DID YOU KNOW THAT?
BOOM
THEY TOLD ME.
AAGGHHGGGH!
I KNEW IT!

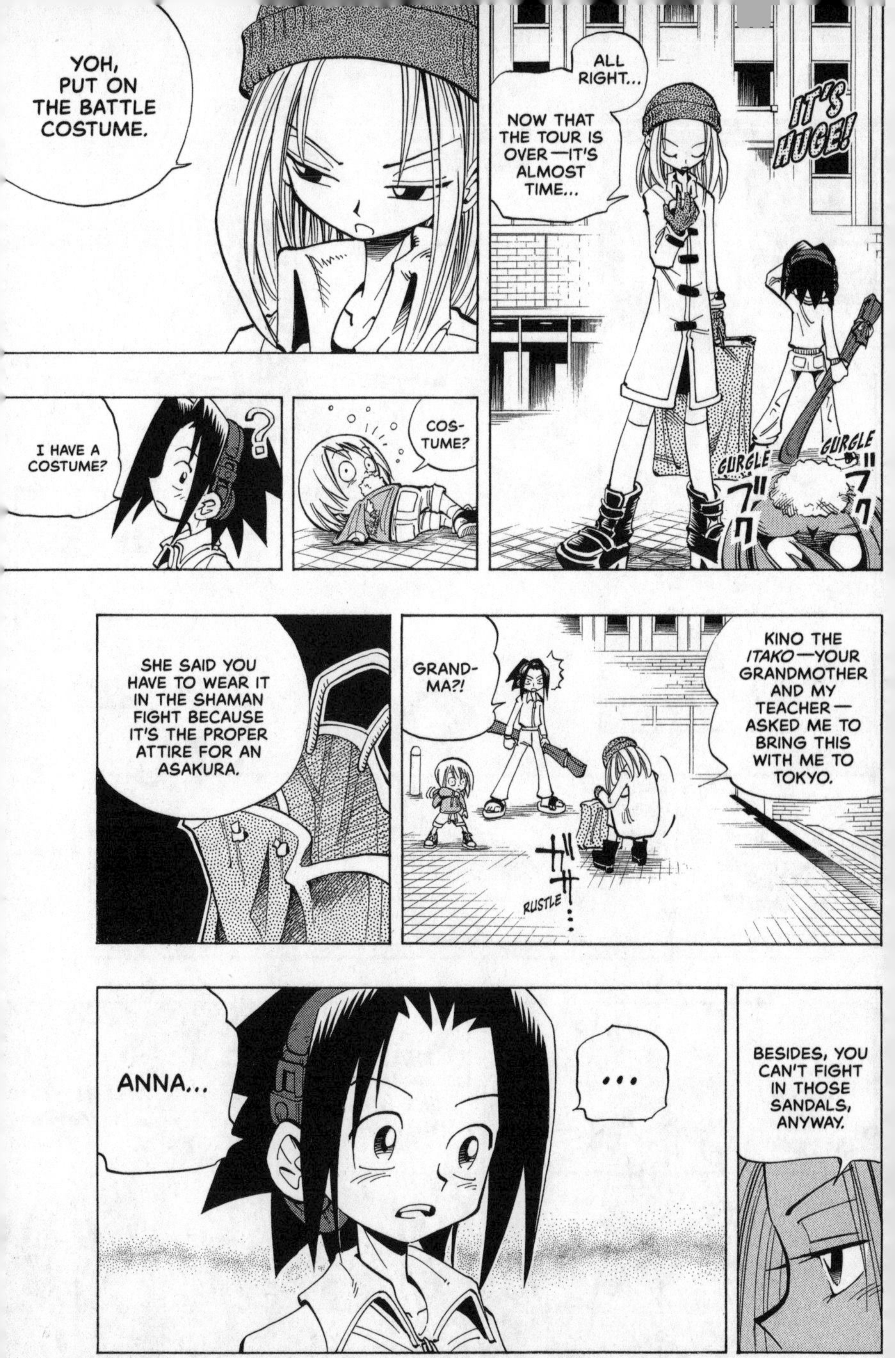
ALL RIGHT...
NOW THAT THE TOUR IS OVER—IT'S ALMOST TIME...
IT'S HUGE!
GURGLE
GURGLE
YOH, PUT ON THE BATTLE COSTUME.
COS-TUME?
I HAVE A COSTUME?
KINO THE *ITAKO*—YOUR GRANDMOTHER AND MY TEACHER—ASKED ME TO BRING THIS WITH ME TO TOKYO.
GRAND-MA?!
RUSTLE
SHE SAID YOU HAVE TO WEAR IT IN THE SHAMAN FIGHT BECAUSE IT'S THE PROPER ATTIRE FOR AN ASAKURA.
BESIDES, YOU CAN'T FIGHT IN THOSE SANDALS, ANYWAY.
...
ANNA...

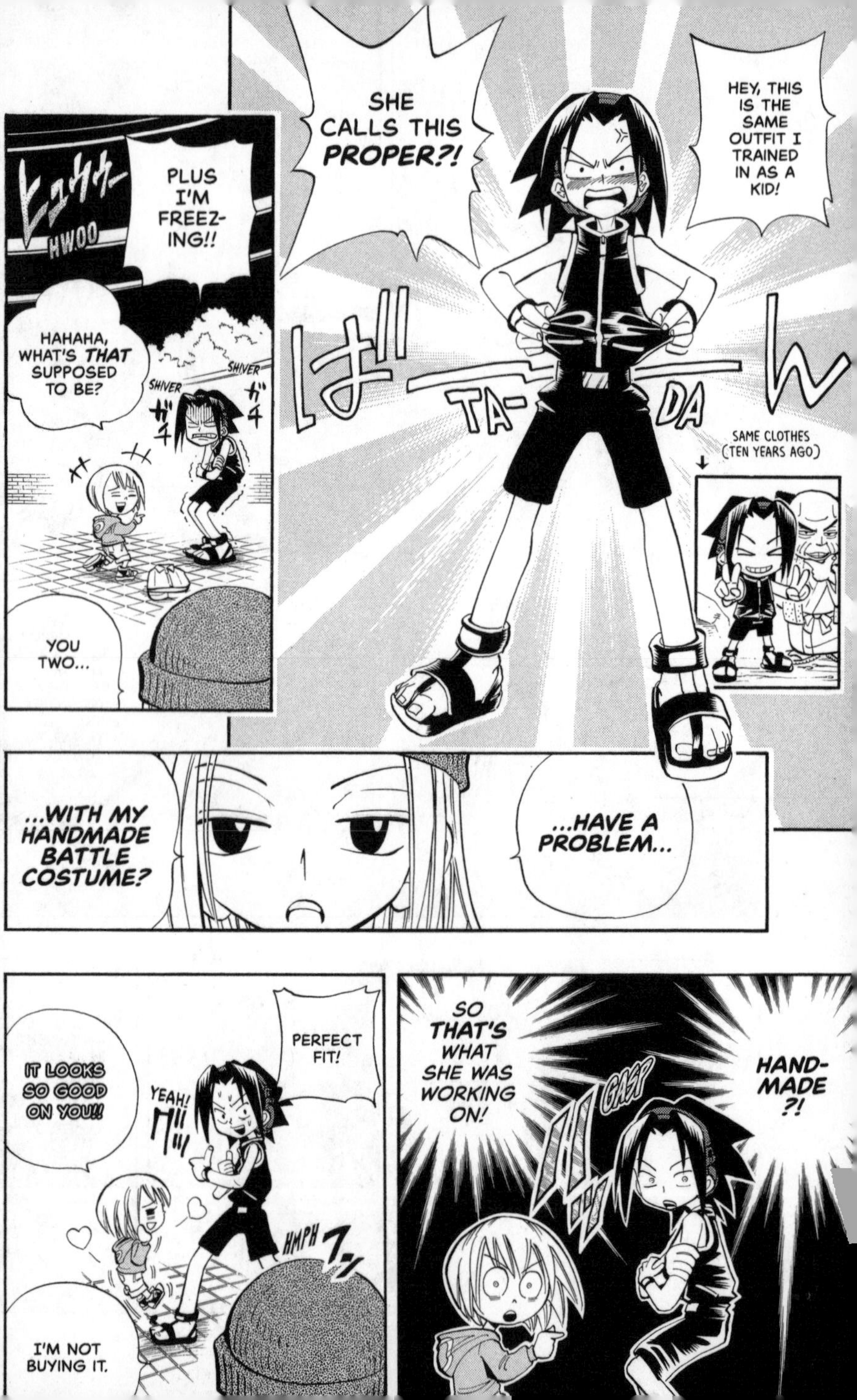
HEY, THIS IS THE SAME OUTFIT I TRAINED IN AS A KID!
SHE CALLS THIS PROPER?!
TA-DA
SAME CLOTHES (TEN YEARS AGO)
PLUS I'M FREEZING!!
HW.OO
HAHAHA, WHAT'S THAT SUPPOSED TO BE?
SHIVER
SHIVER
YOU TWO...
...HAVE A PROBLEM...
...WITH MY HANDMADE BATTLE COSTUME?
HANDMADE?!
SO THAT'S WHAT SHE WAS WORKING ON!
GASP
PERFECT FIT!
YEAH!
IT LOOKS SO GOOD ON YOU!!
HMPH
I'M NOT BUYING IT.

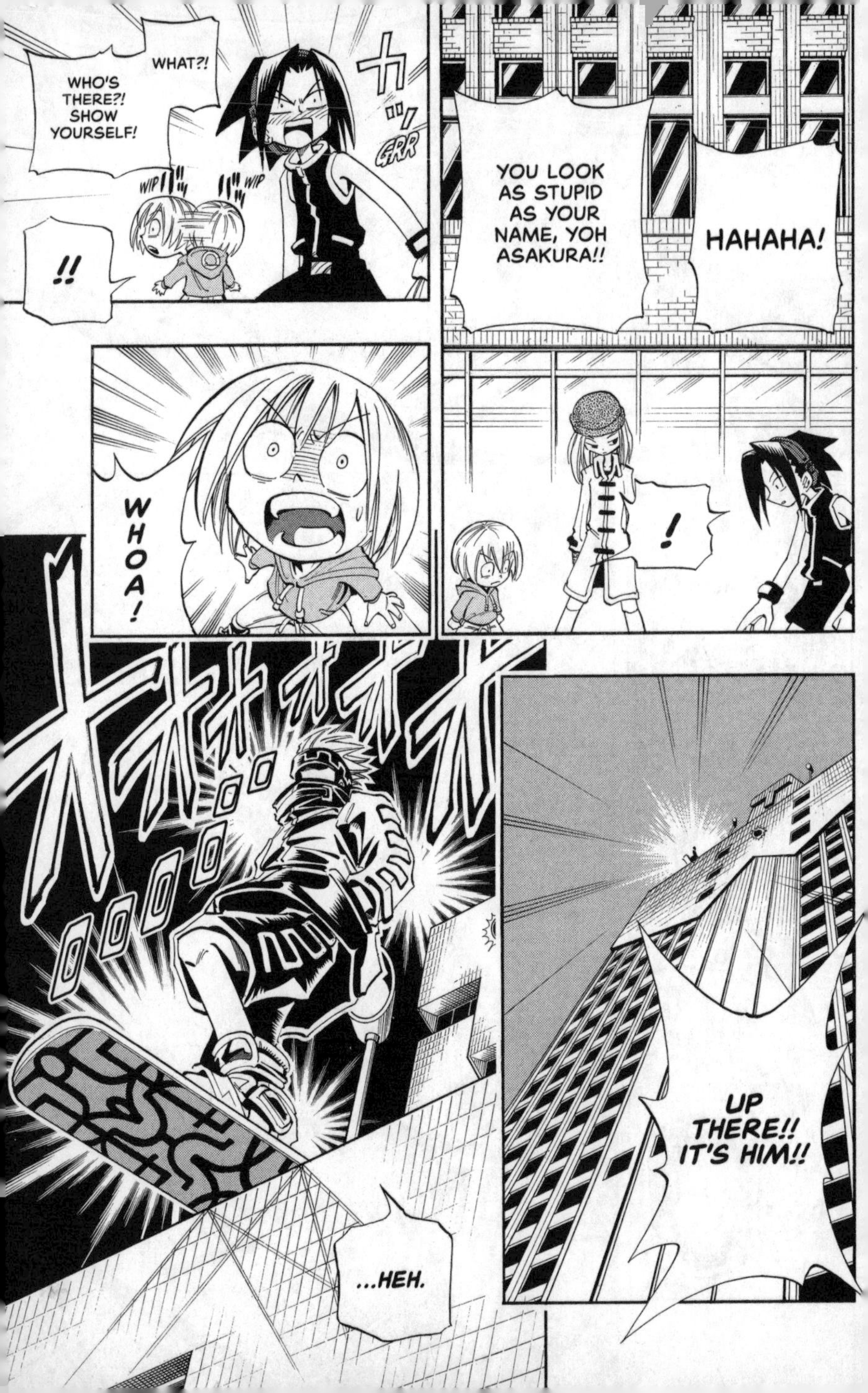
YOU LOOK AS STUPID AS YOUR NAME, YOH ASAKURA!!
HAHAHA!
WHAT?!
WHO'S THERE?! SHOW YOURSELF!
GRR
WIP
WIP
!!
!
WHOA!
UP THERE!! IT'S HIM!!
...HEH.

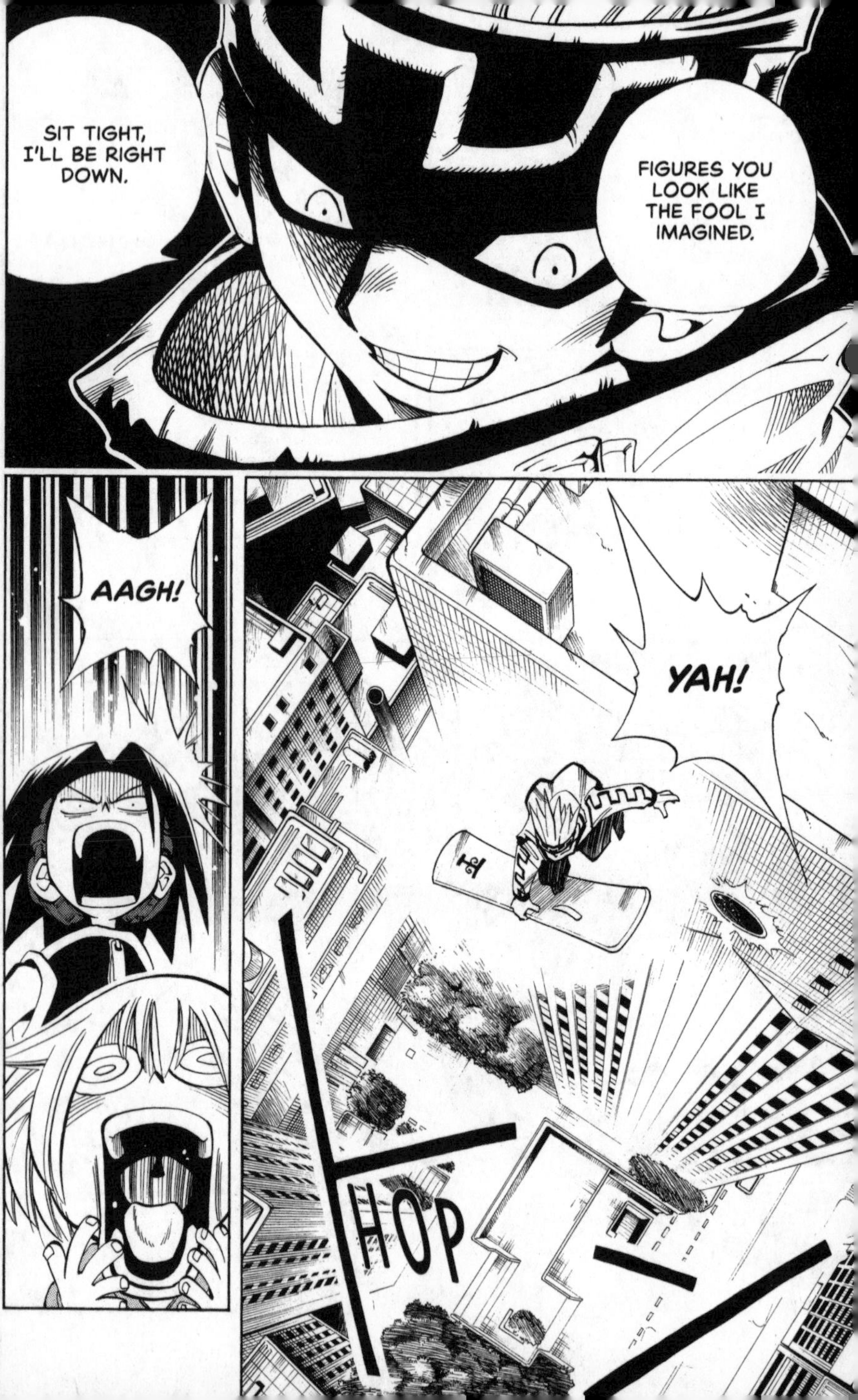
FIGURES YOU LOOK LIKE THE FOOL I IMAGINED.
SIT TIGHT, I'LL BE RIGHT DOWN.
YAH!
HOP
AAGH!

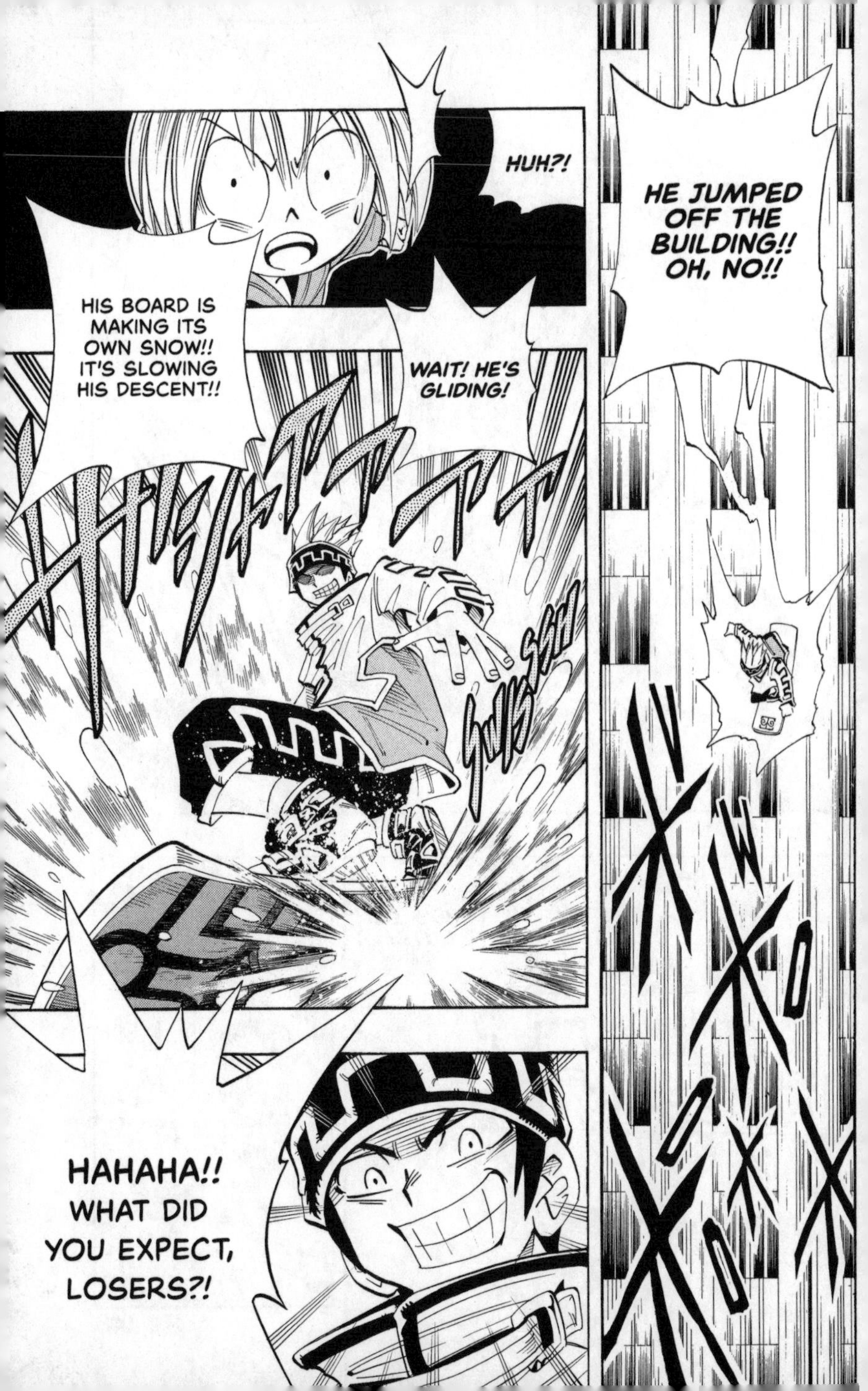
HE JUMPED OFF THE BUILDING!! OH, NO!!
HUH?!
WAIT! HE'S GLIDING!
HIS BOARD IS MAKING ITS OWN SNOW!! IT'S SLOWING HIS DESCENT!!
HAHAHA!! WHAT DID YOU EXPECT, LOSERS?!

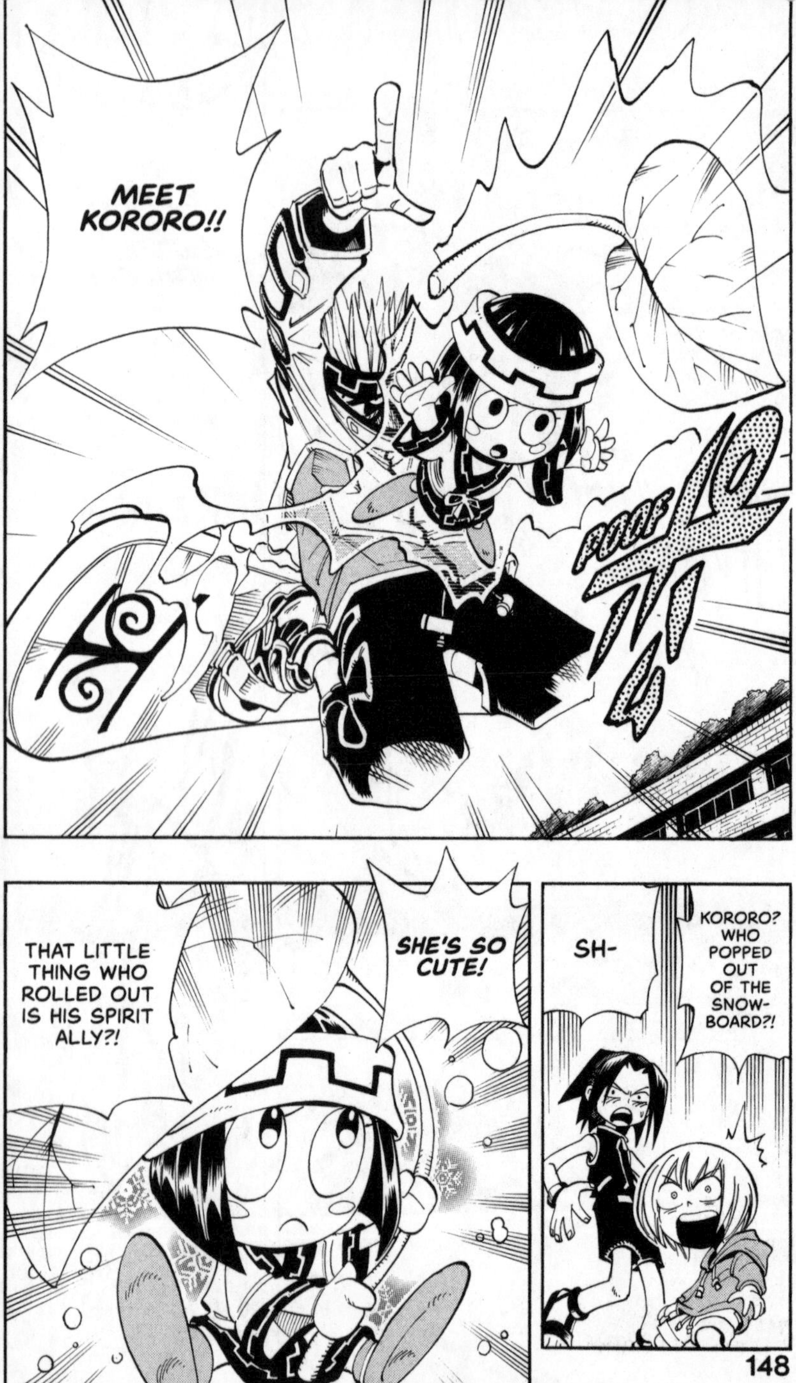
MEET KORORO!!
POOF
KORORO? WHO POPPED OUT OF THE SNOW-BOARD?!
SH-
SHE'S SO CUTE!
THAT LITTLE THING WHO ROLLED OUT IS HIS SPIRIT ALLY?!

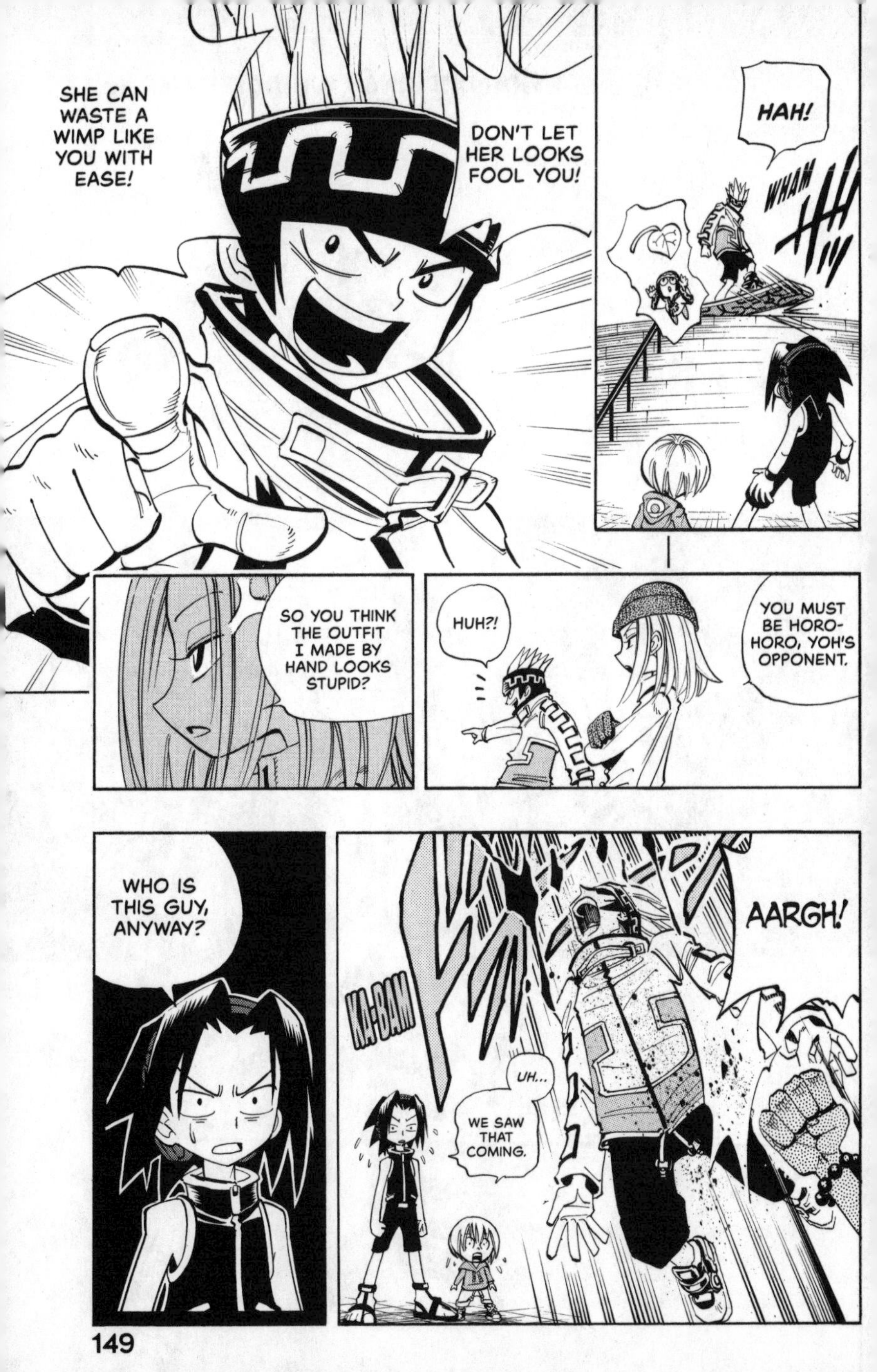
HAH!
WHAM
DON'T LET HER LOOKS FOOL YOU!
SHE CAN WASTE A WIMP LIKE YOU WITH EASE!
YOU MUST BE HORO-HORO, YOH'S OPPONENT.
HUH?!
SO YOU THINK THE OUTFIT I MADE BY HAND LOOKS STUPID?
AARGH!
KA-BAM
UH...
WE SAW THAT COMING.
WHO IS THIS GUY, ANYWAY?

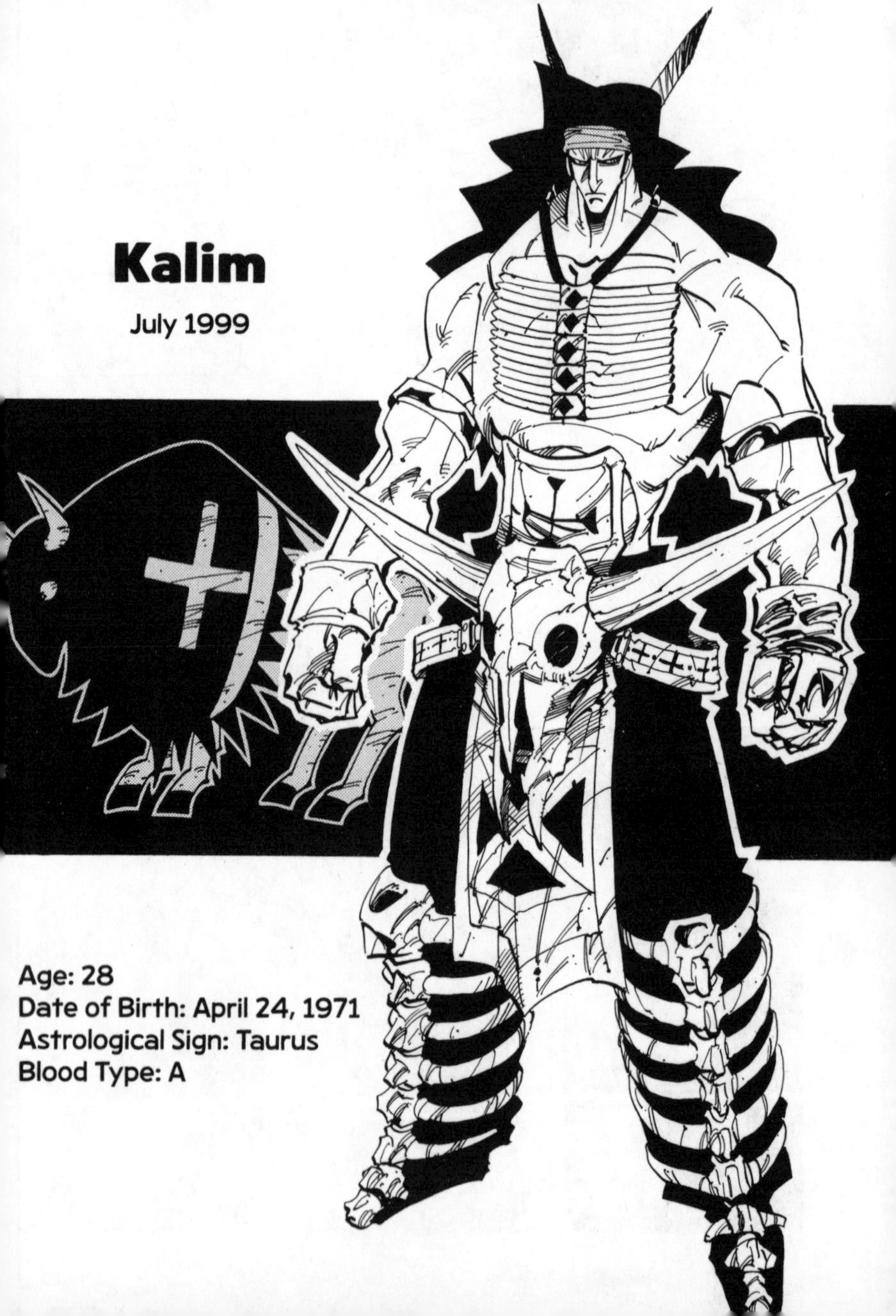

Kalim

July 1999

Age: 28
Date of Birth: April 24, 1971
Astrological Sign: Taurus
Blood Type: A

Chapter 34: The Powers of Kororo

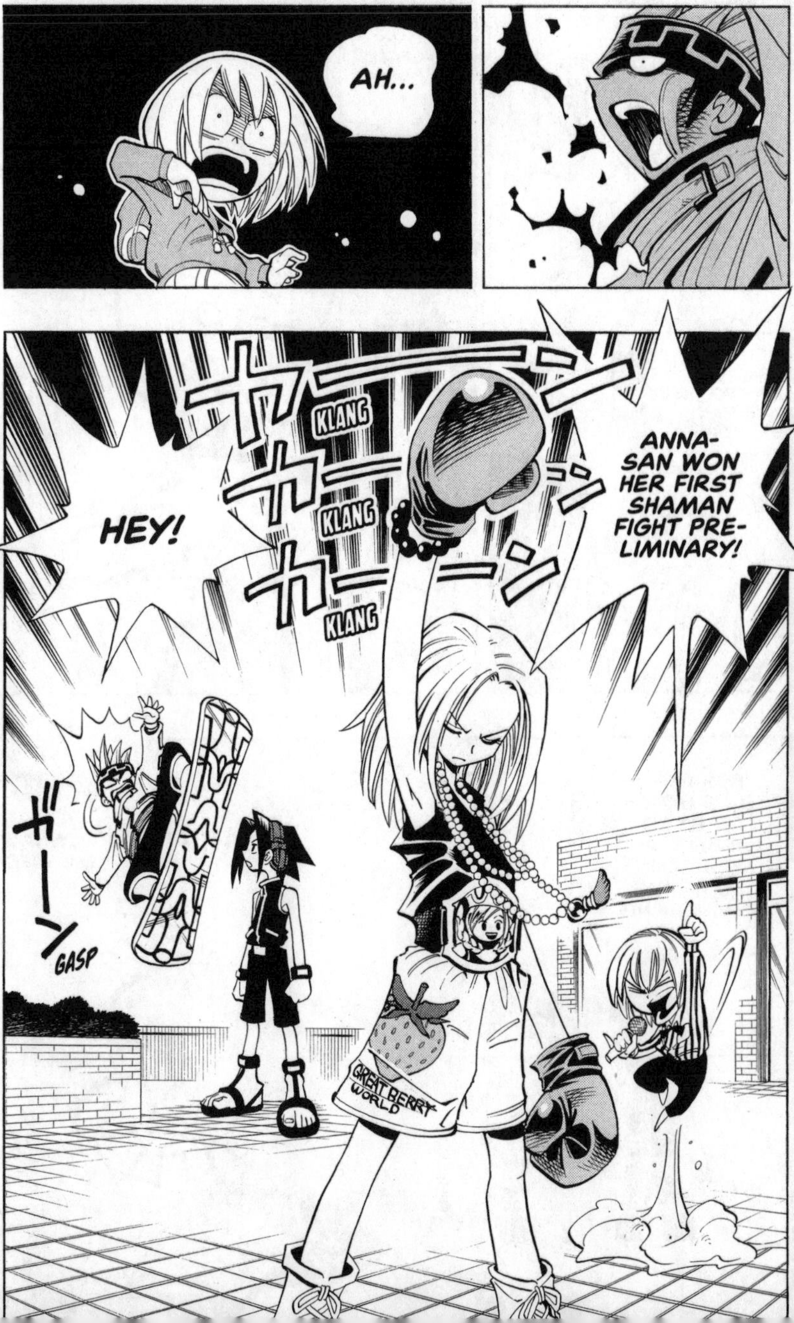
AH...
ANNA-SAN WON HER FIRST SHAMAN FIGHT PRE-LIMINARY!
KLANG
KLANG
KLANG
HEY!
GASP
GREAT BERRY WORLD

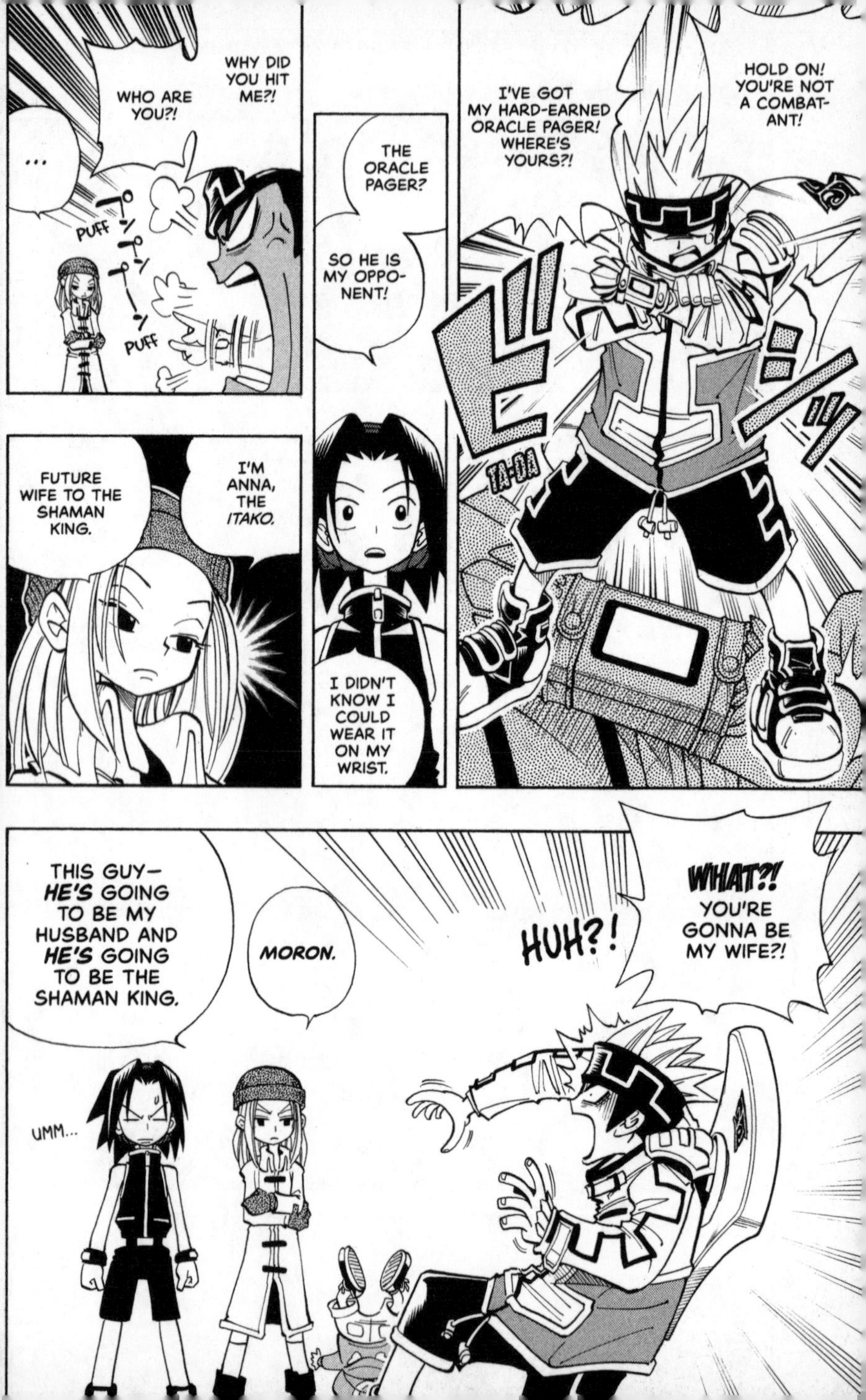
HOLD ON! YOU'RE NOT A COMBAT-ANT!
I'VE GOT MY HARD-EARNED ORACLE PAGER! WHERE'S YOURS?!
TA-DA
THE ORACLE PAGER?
SO HE IS MY OPPO-NENT!
I DIDN'T KNOW I COULD WEAR IT ON MY WRIST.
WHY DID YOU HIT ME?!
WHO ARE YOU?!
...
PUFF
PUFF
I'M ANNA, THE *ITAKO.*
FUTURE WIFE TO THE SHAMAN KING.
WHAT?! YOU'RE GONNA BE MY WIFE?!
HUH?!
MORON.
THIS GUY— ***HE'S*** GOING TO BE MY HUSBAND AND ***HE'S*** GOING TO BE THE SHAMAN KING.
UMM...

The Powers of Kororo

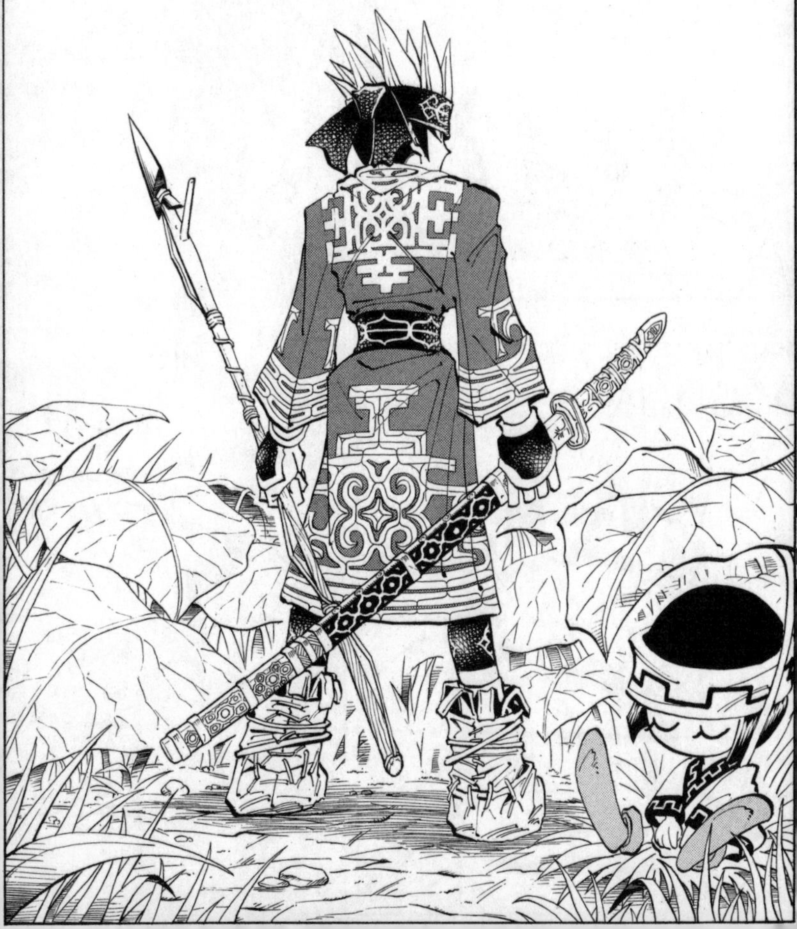

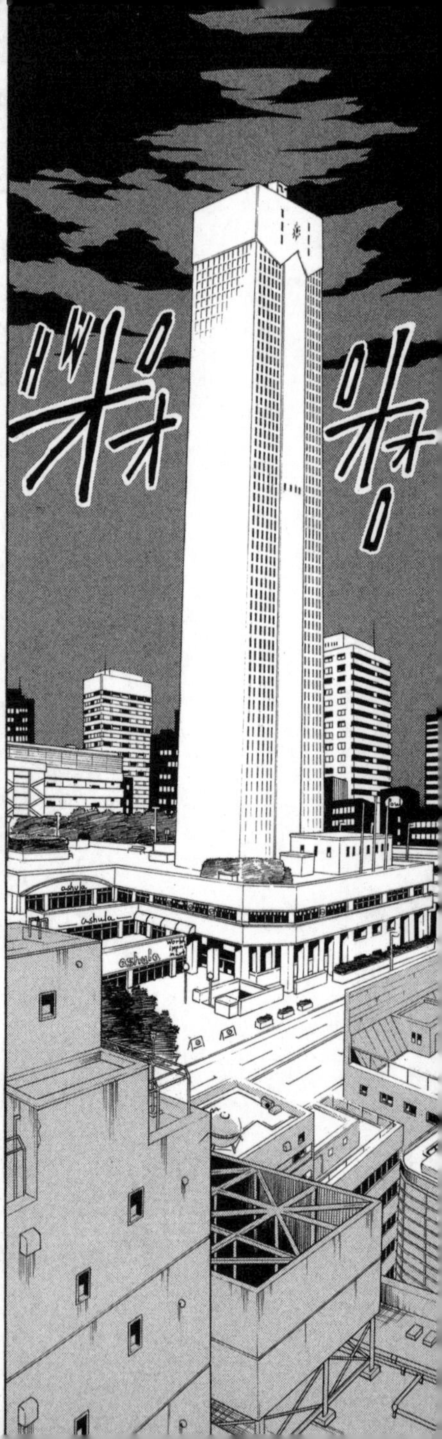
HWOOOO
ashula
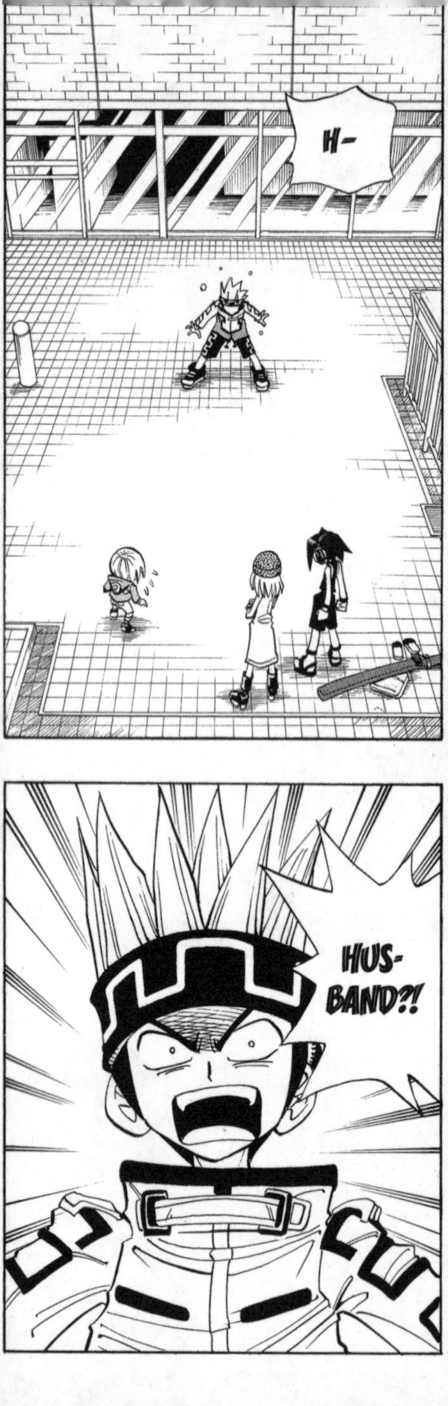
H-
HUS-
BAND?!

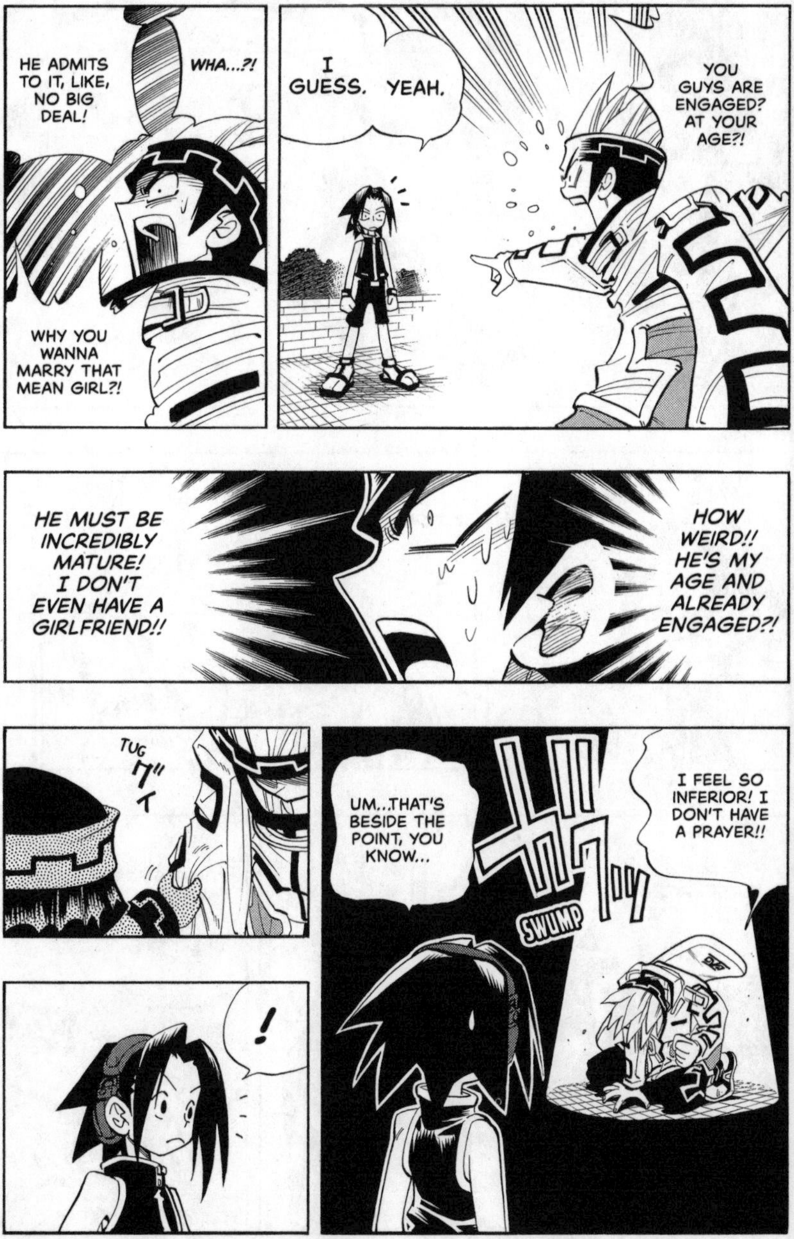
YOU GUYS ARE ENGAGED? AT YOUR AGE?!
I GUESS. YEAH.
WHA...?!
HE ADMITS TO IT, LIKE, NO BIG DEAL!
WHY YOU WANNA MARRY THAT MEAN GIRL?!
HOW WEIRD!! HE'S MY AGE AND ALREADY ENGAGED?!
HE MUST BE INCREDIBLY MATURE! I DON'T EVEN HAVE A GIRLFRIEND!!
I FEEL SO INFERIOR! I DON'T HAVE A PRAYER!!
SWUMP
UM...THAT'S BESIDE THE POINT, YOU KNOW...
TUG
!

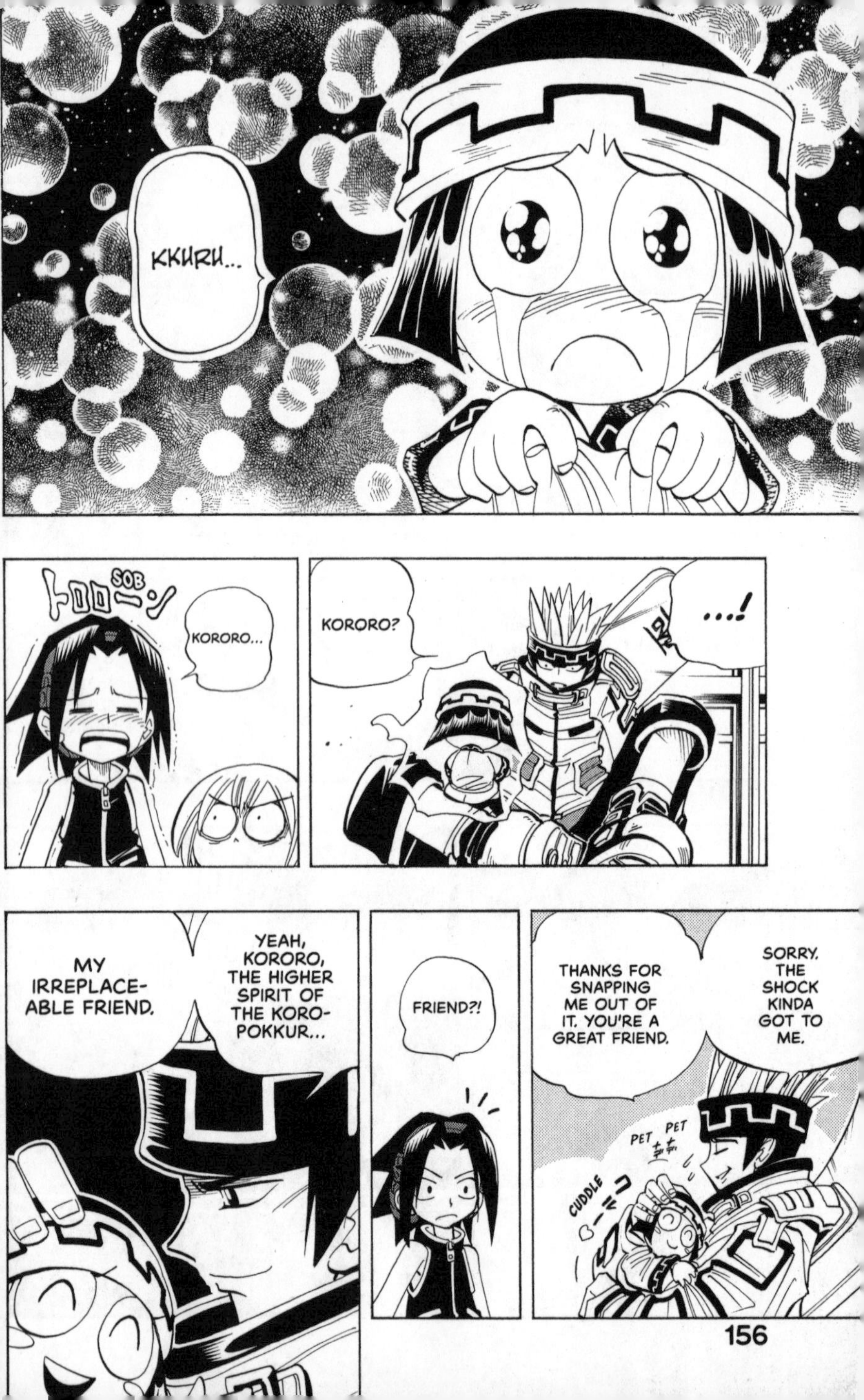
KKURU...
...!
KORORO?
SOB
KORORO...
SORRY. THE SHOCK KINDA GOT TO ME.
THANKS FOR SNAPPING ME OUT OF IT. YOU'RE A GREAT FRIEND.
PET PET
CUDDLE
FRIEND?!
YEAH, KORORO, THE HIGHER SPIRIT OF THE KORO-POKKUR...
MY IRREPLACE-ABLE FRIEND.

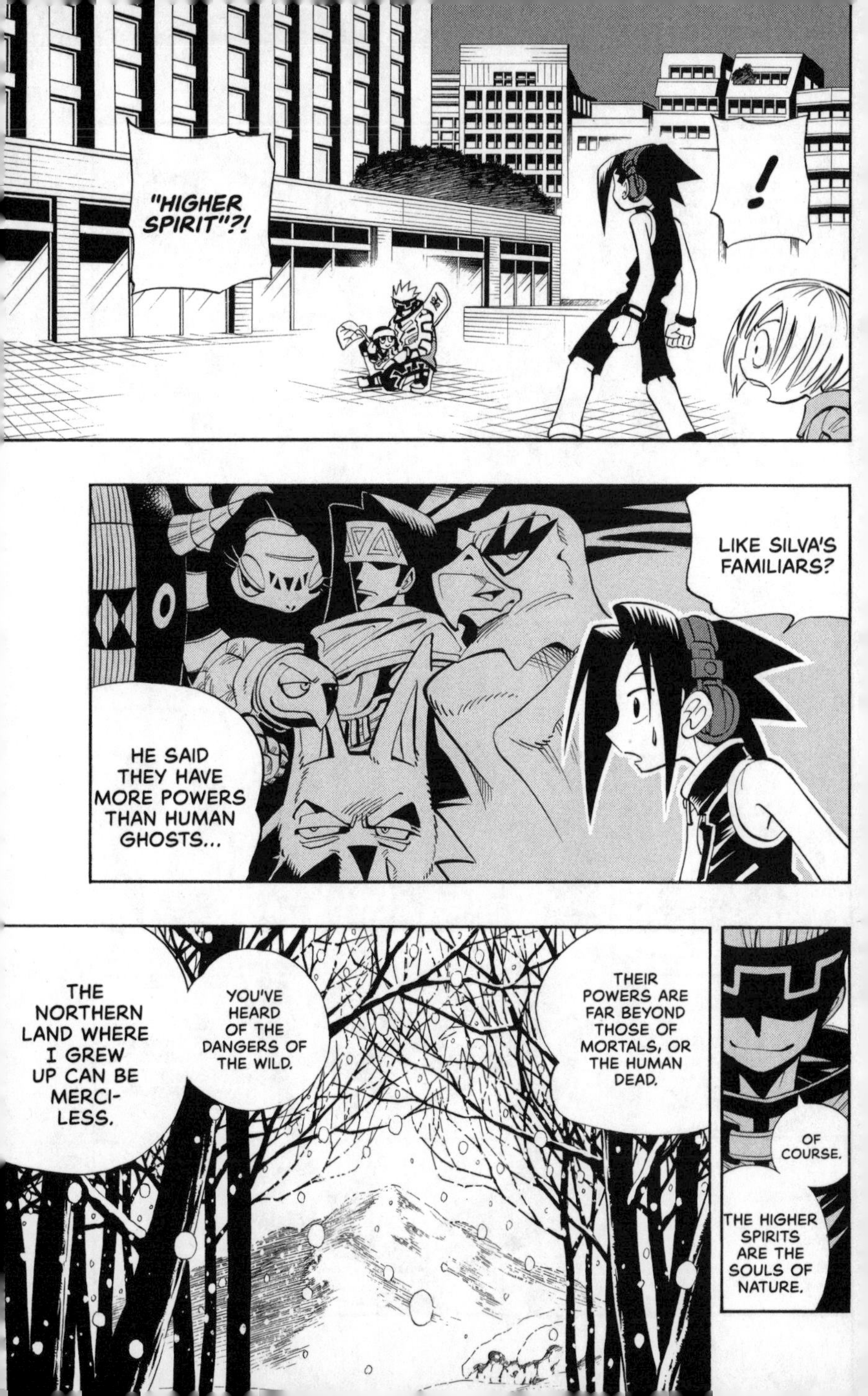
!
"HIGHER SPIRIT"?!
LIKE SILVA'S FAMILIARS?
HE SAID THEY HAVE MORE POWERS THAN HUMAN GHOSTS...
OF COURSE.
THE HIGHER SPIRITS ARE THE SOULS OF NATURE.
THEIR POWERS ARE FAR BEYOND THOSE OF MORTALS, OR THE HUMAN DEAD.
YOU'VE HEARD OF THE DANGERS OF THE WILD.
THE NORTHERN LAND WHERE I GREW UP CAN BE MERCI-LESS.

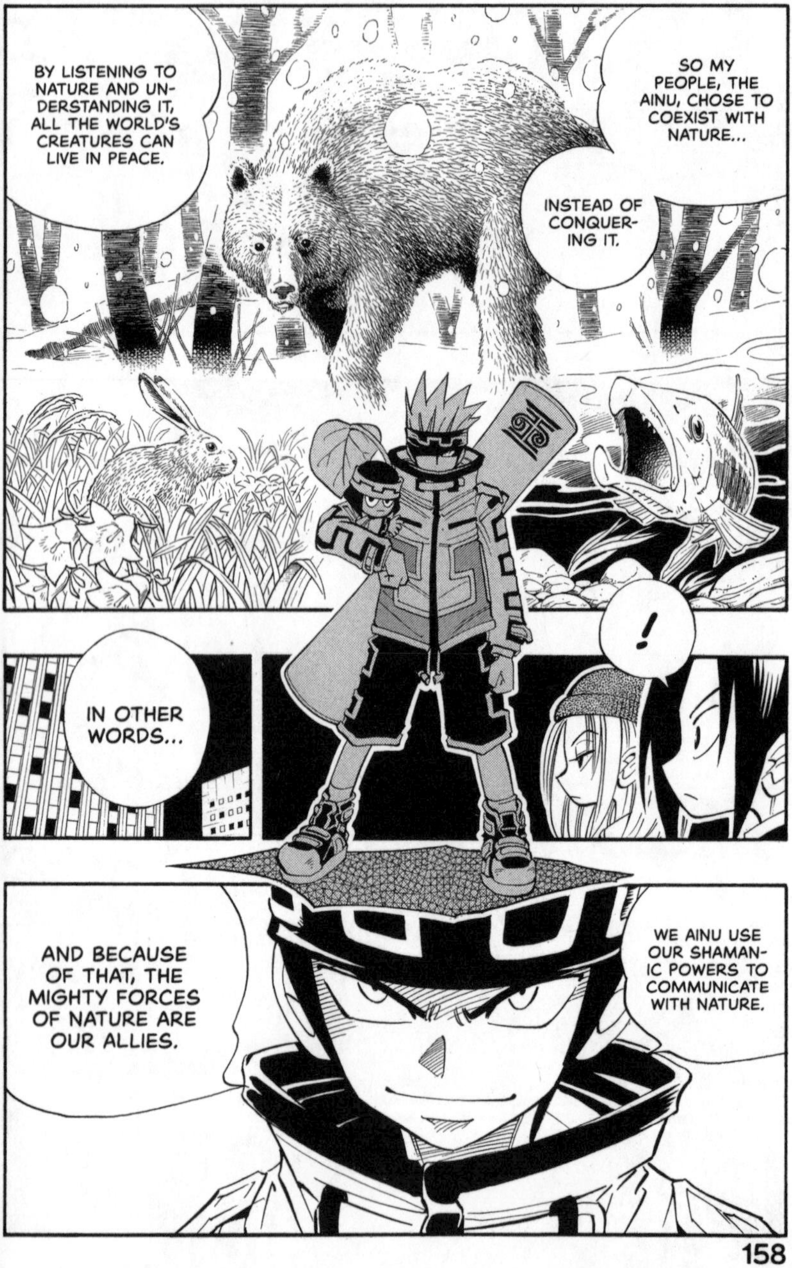
SO MY PEOPLE, THE AINU, CHOSE TO COEXIST WITH NATURE...
INSTEAD OF CONQUERING IT.
BY LISTENING TO NATURE AND UNDERSTANDING IT, ALL THE WORLD'S CREATURES CAN LIVE IN PEACE.
!
IN OTHER WORDS...
WE AINU USE OUR SHAMANIC POWERS TO COMMUNICATE WITH NATURE.
AND BECAUSE OF THAT, THE MIGHTY FORCES OF NATURE ARE OUR ALLIES.

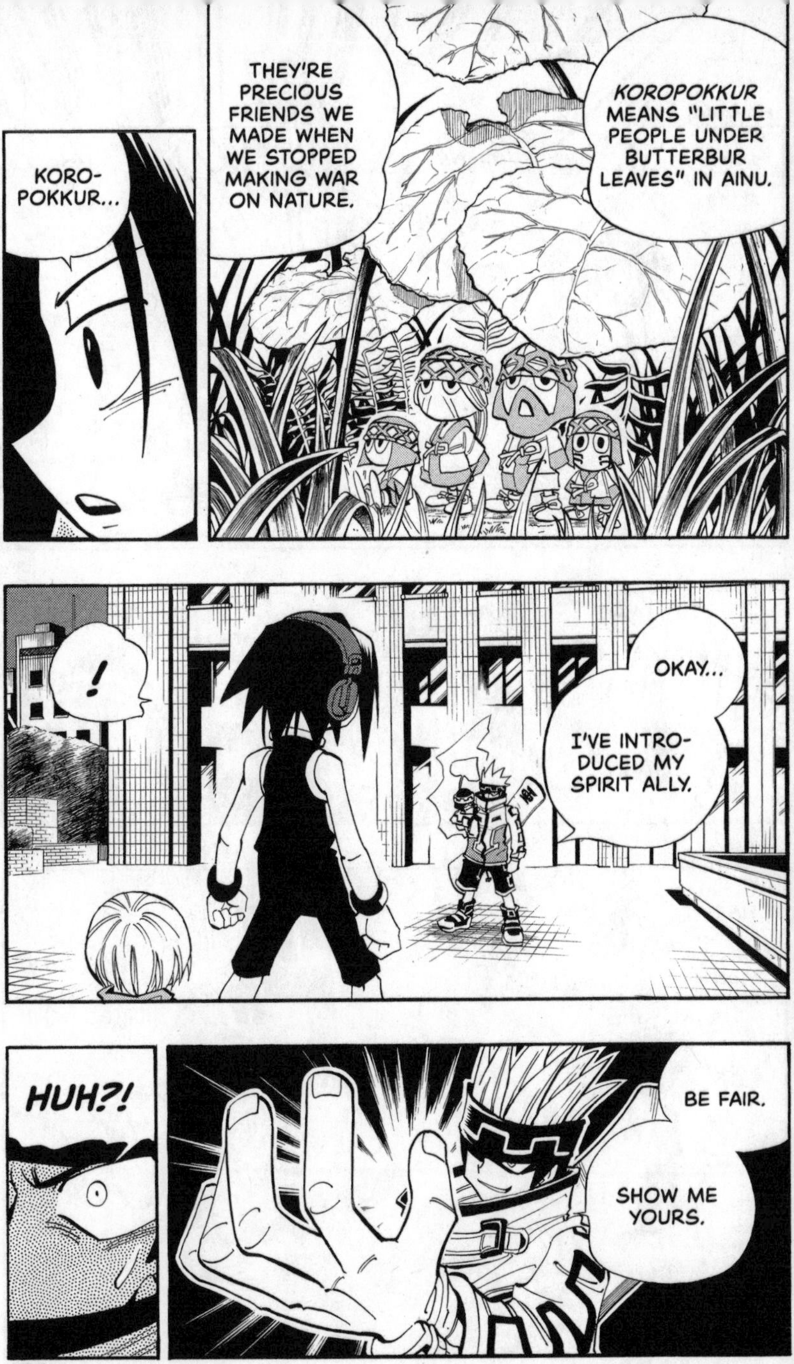
KOROPOKKUR MEANS "LITTLE PEOPLE UNDER BUTTERBUR LEAVES" IN AINU.
THEY'RE PRECIOUS FRIENDS WE MADE WHEN WE STOPPED MAKING WAR ON NATURE.
KORO-POKKUR...
OKAY...
I'VE INTRODUCED MY SPIRIT ALLY.
!
BE FAIR.
SHOW ME YOURS.
HUH?!

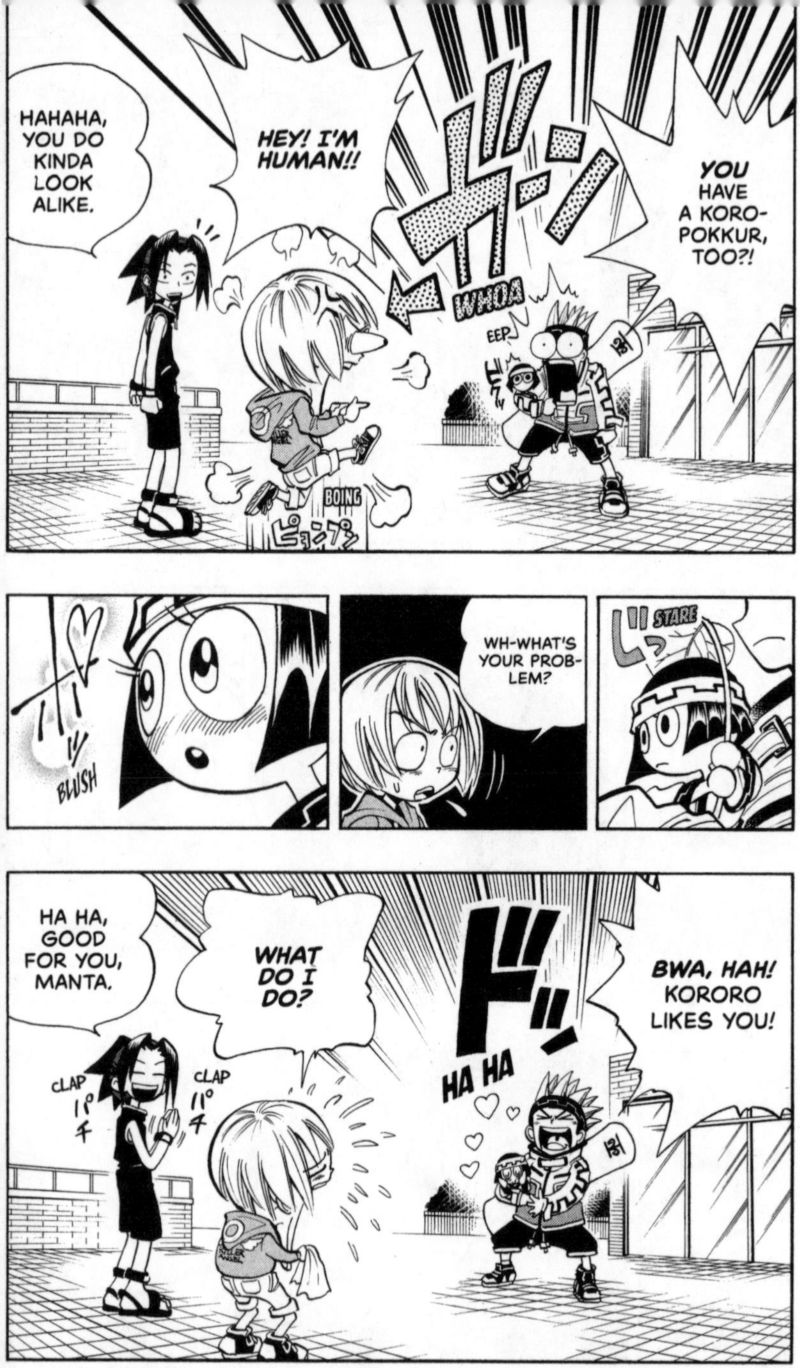
YOU HAVE A KORO-POKKUR, TOO?!
WHOA
EEP
HEY! I'M HUMAN!!
BOING
HAHAHA, YOU DO KINDA LOOK ALIKE.
STARE
WH-WHAT'S YOUR PROB-LEM?
BLUSH
BWA, HAH! KORORO LIKES YOU!
HA HA
WHAT DO I DO?
CLAP
CLAP
HA HA, GOOD FOR YOU, MANTA.

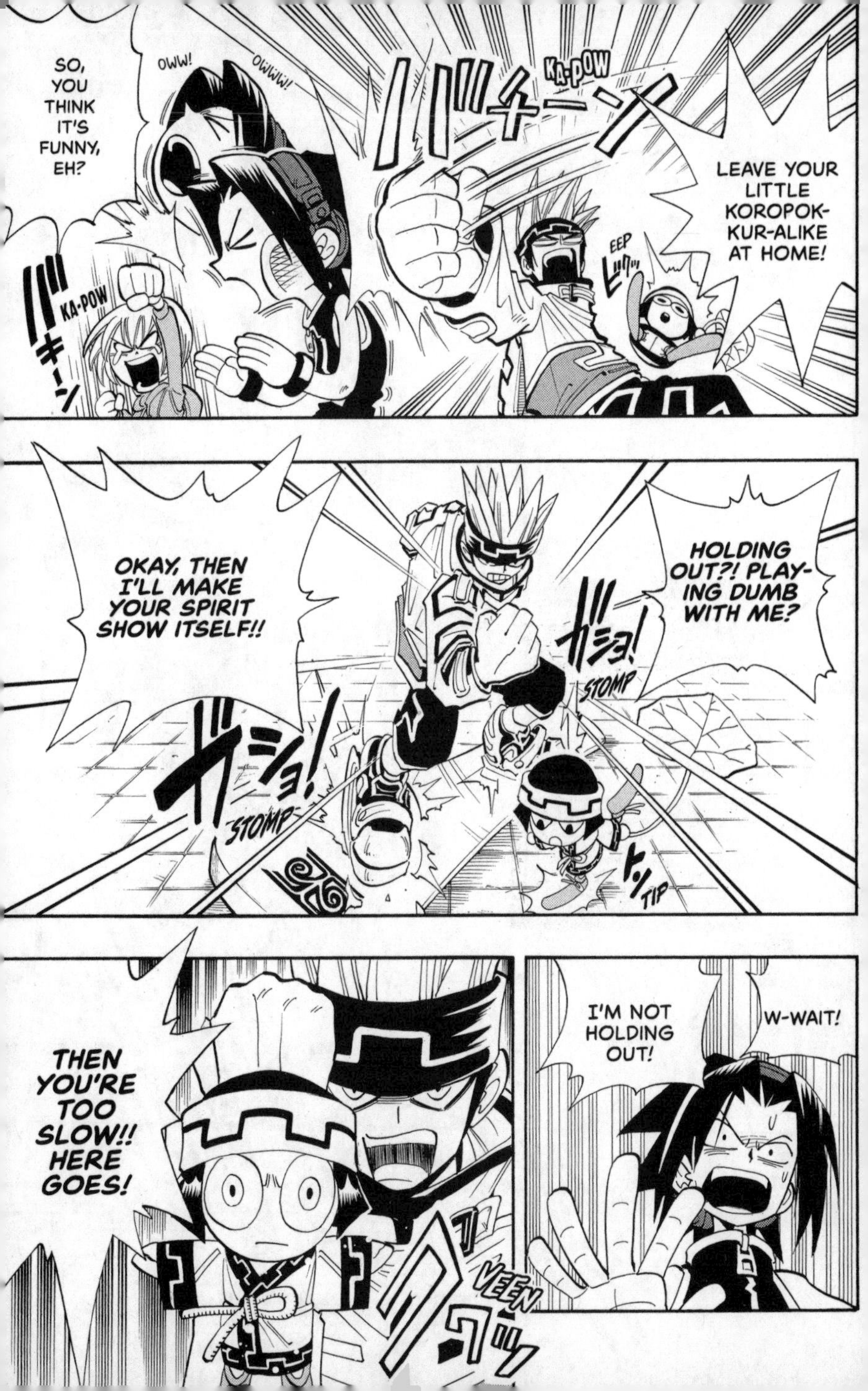
LEAVE YOUR LITTLE KOROPOK-KUR-ALIKE AT HOME!
KA-POW
EEP
OWWW!
OWW!
SO, YOU THINK IT'S FUNNY, EH?
KA-POW
HOLDING OUT?! PLAY-ING DUMB WITH ME?
STOMP
OKAY, THEN I'LL MAKE YOUR SPIRIT SHOW ITSELF!!
STOMP
TIP
W-WAIT!
I'M NOT HOLDING OUT!
THEN YOU'RE TOO SLOW!! HERE GOES!
VEEN

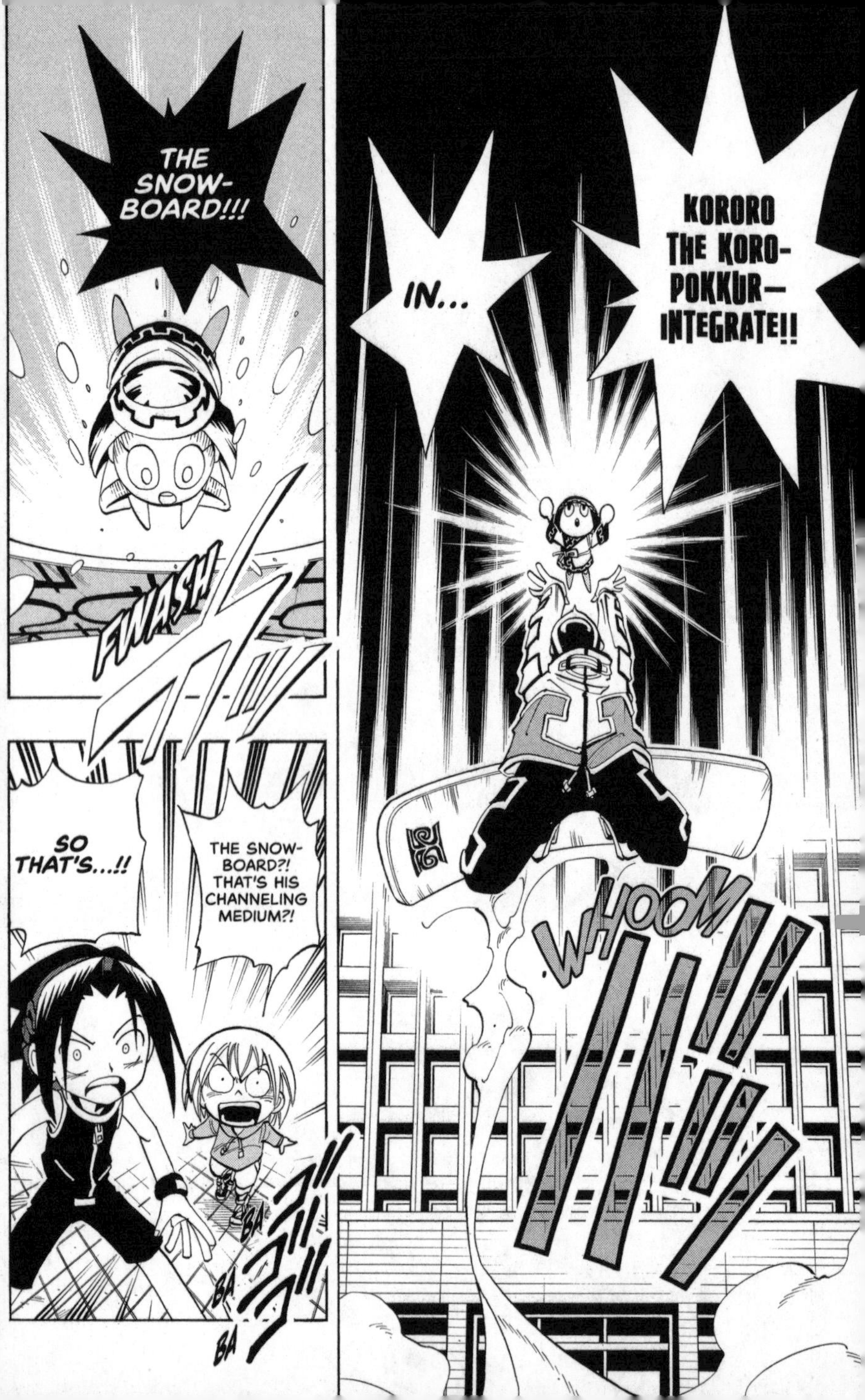
KORORO THE KORO-POKKUR— INTEGRATE!!
IN...
WHOOM
THE SNOW-BOARD!!!
FWASH
THE SNOW-BOARD?! THAT'S HIS CHANNELING MEDIUM?!
SO THAT'S...!!
BA
BA
BA

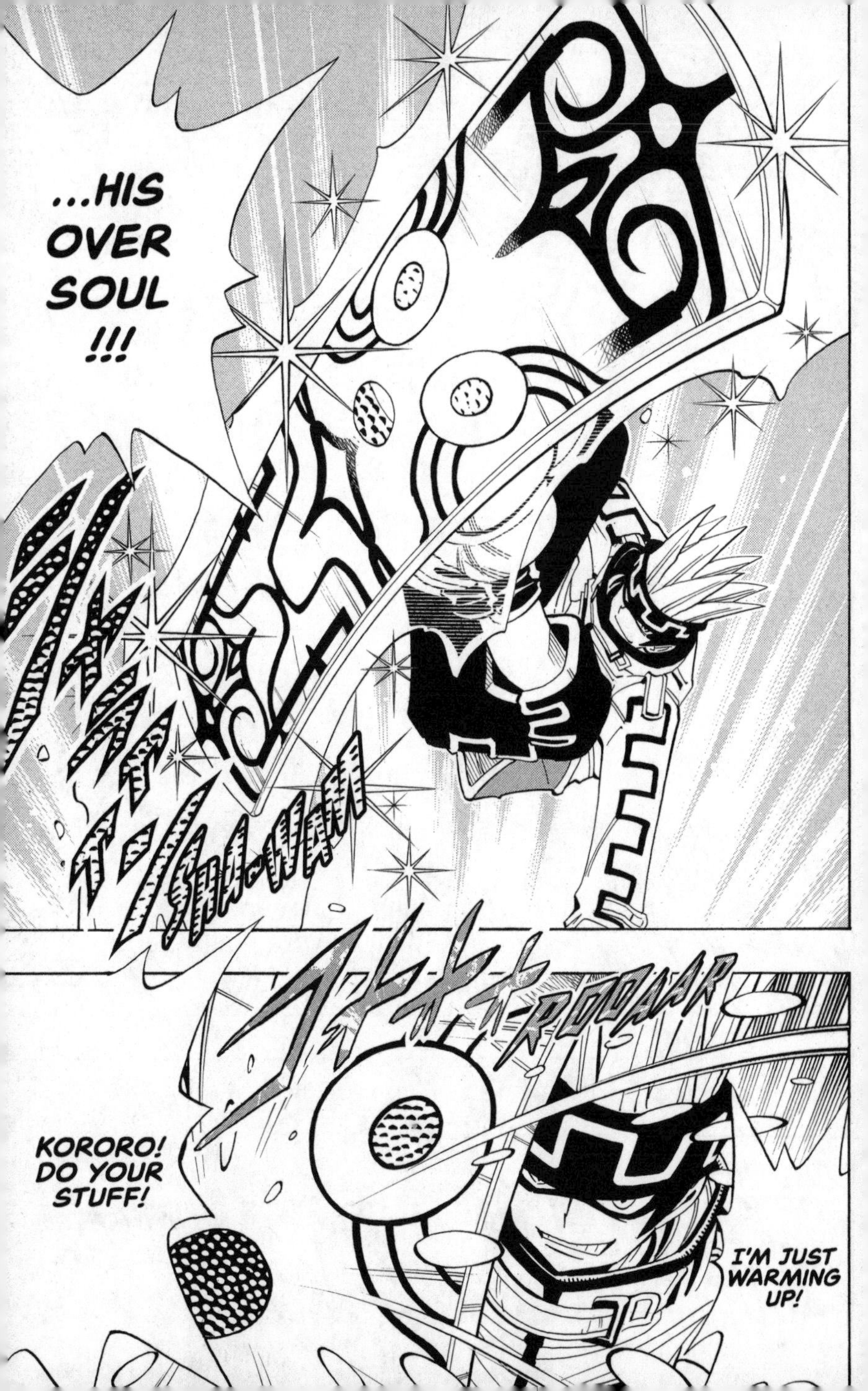
...HIS OVER SOUL !!!
SHA-WAAH
ROOAAR
KORORO! DO YOUR STUFF!
I'M JUST WARMING UP!

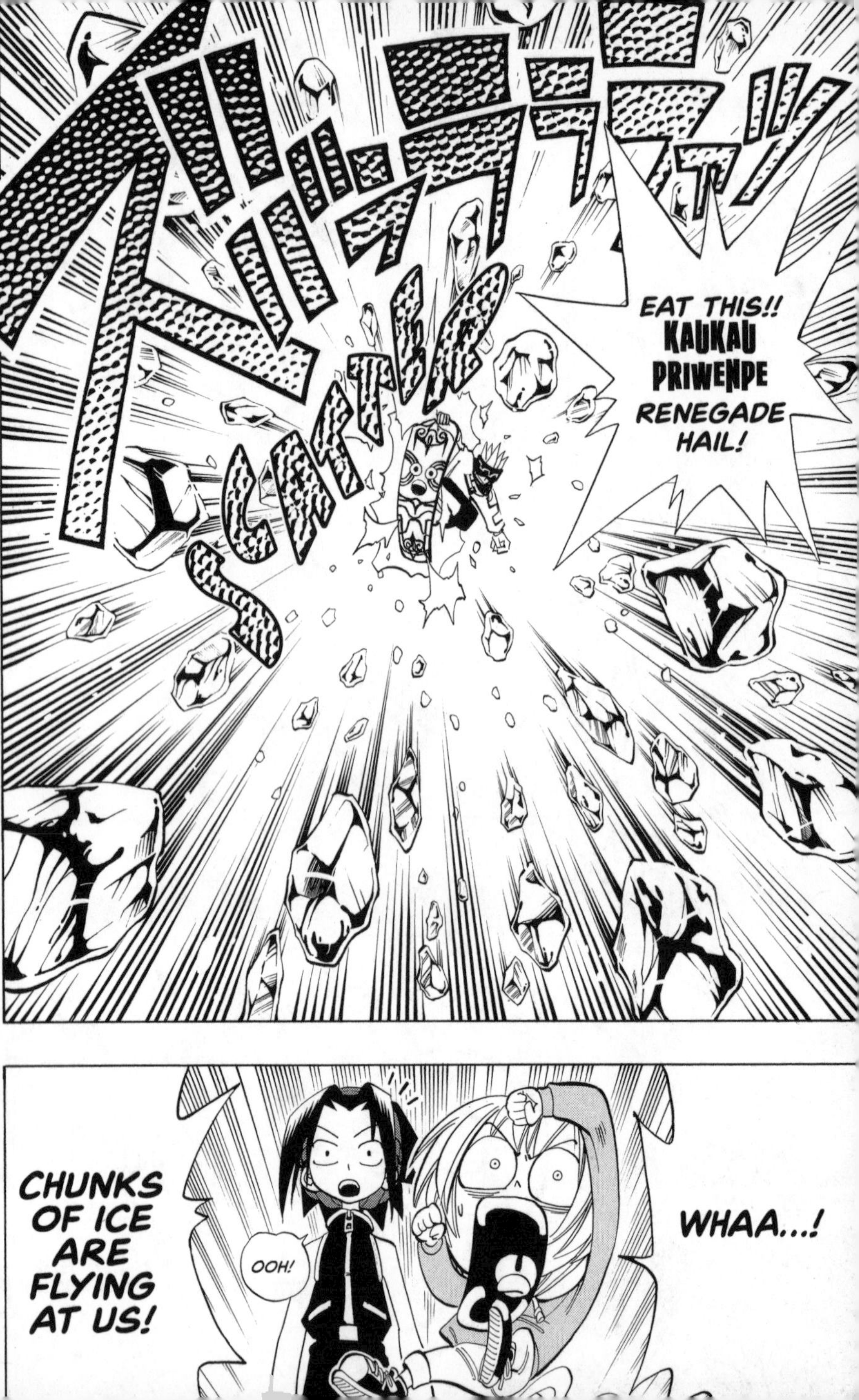
SCATTER
EAT THIS!! KAUKAU PRIWENPE RENEGADE HAIL!
WHAA...!
OOH!
CHUNKS OF ICE ARE FLYING AT US!

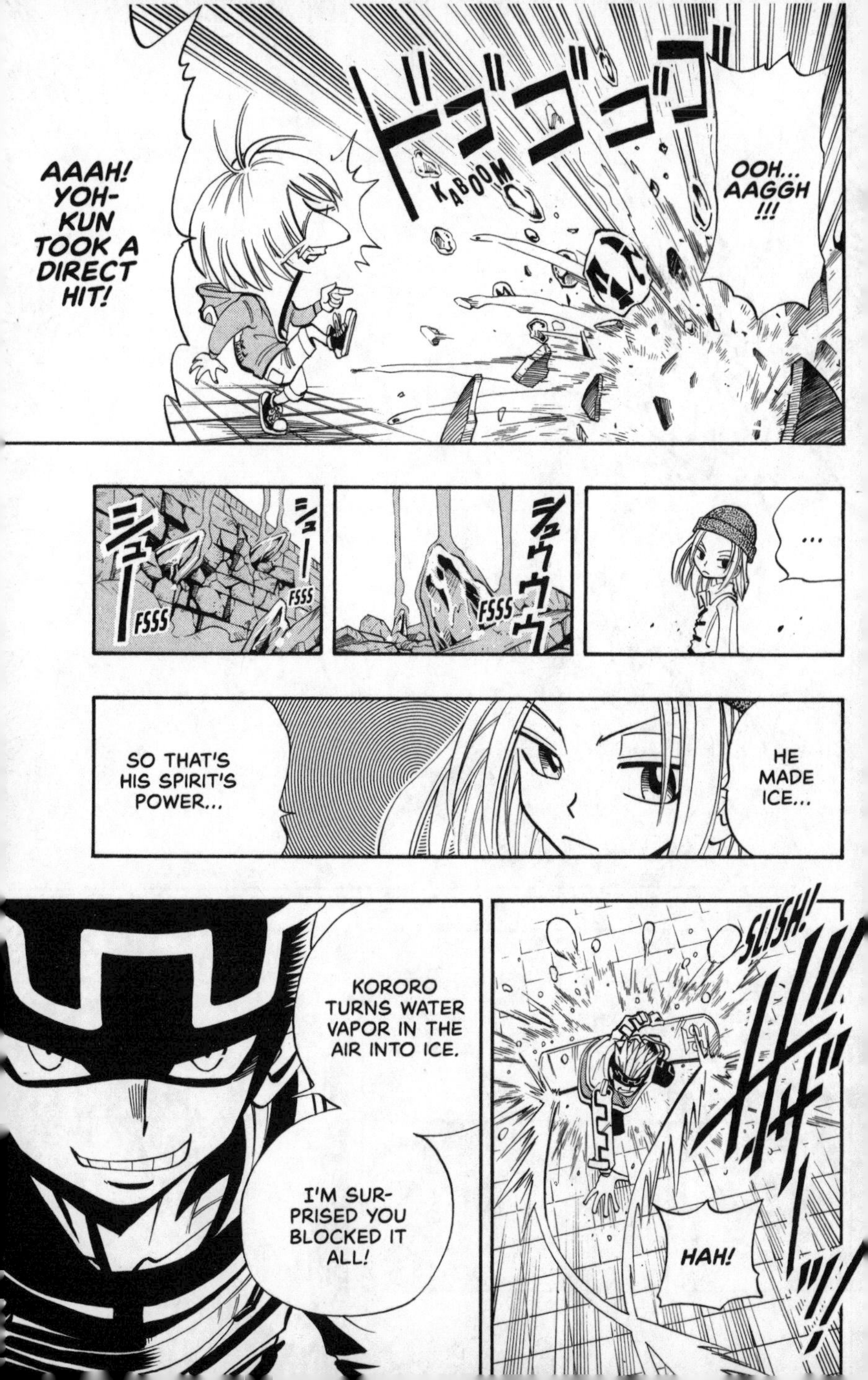
OOH... AAGGH!!!
KABOOM
AAAH! YOH-KUN TOOK A DIRECT HIT!
...
FSSS
FSSS
FSSS
HE MADE ICE...
SO THAT'S HIS SPIRIT'S POWER...
SLISH!
HAH!
KORORO TURNS WATER VAPOR IN THE AIR INTO ICE.
I'M SURPRISED YOU BLOCKED IT ALL!

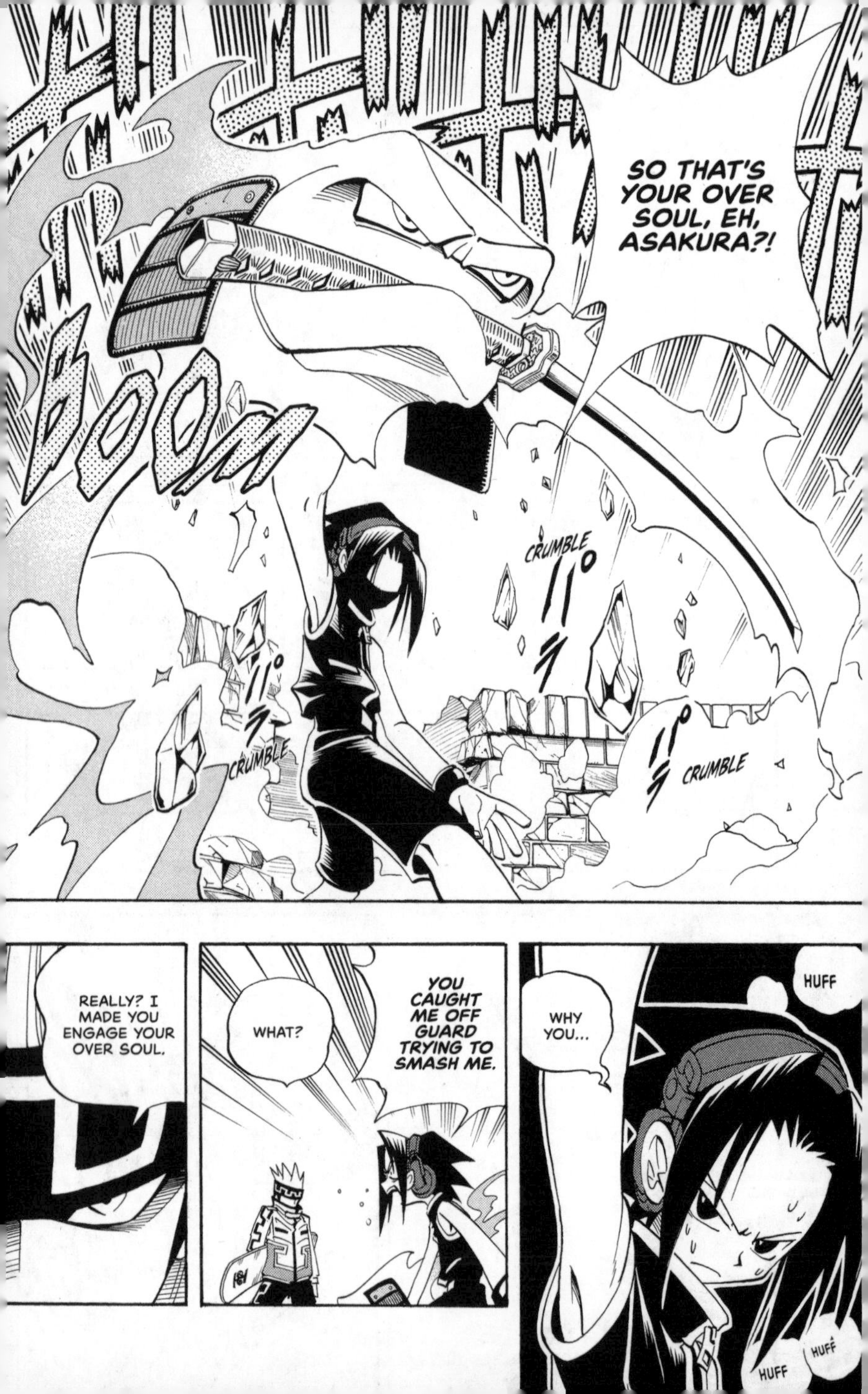
SO THAT'S YOUR OVER SOUL, EH, ASAKURA?!
BOOM
CRUMBLE
CRUMBLE
CRUMBLE
HUFF
WHY YOU...
HUFF
HUFF
YOU CAUGHT ME OFF GUARD TRYING TO SMASH ME.
WHAT?
REALLY? I MADE YOU ENGAGE YOUR OVER SOUL.

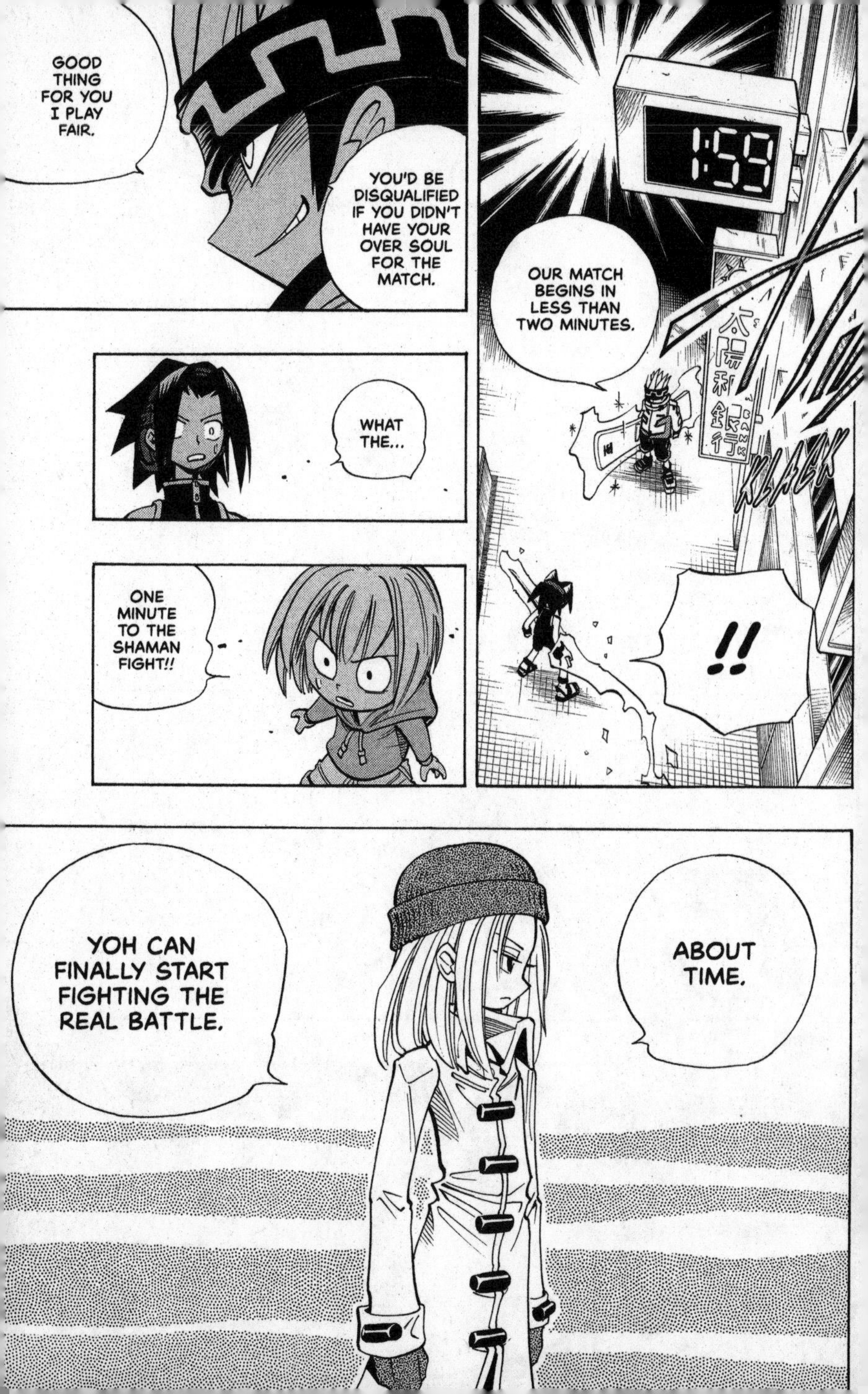
1:59
OUR MATCH BEGINS IN LESS THAN TWO MINUTES.
KLACK
!!
YOU'D BE DISQUALIFIED IF YOU DIDN'T HAVE YOUR OVER SOUL FOR THE MATCH.
GOOD THING FOR YOU I PLAY FAIR.
WHAT THE...
ONE MINUTE TO THE SHAMAN FIGHT!!
ABOUT TIME.
YOH CAN FINALLY START FIGHTING THE REAL BATTLE.

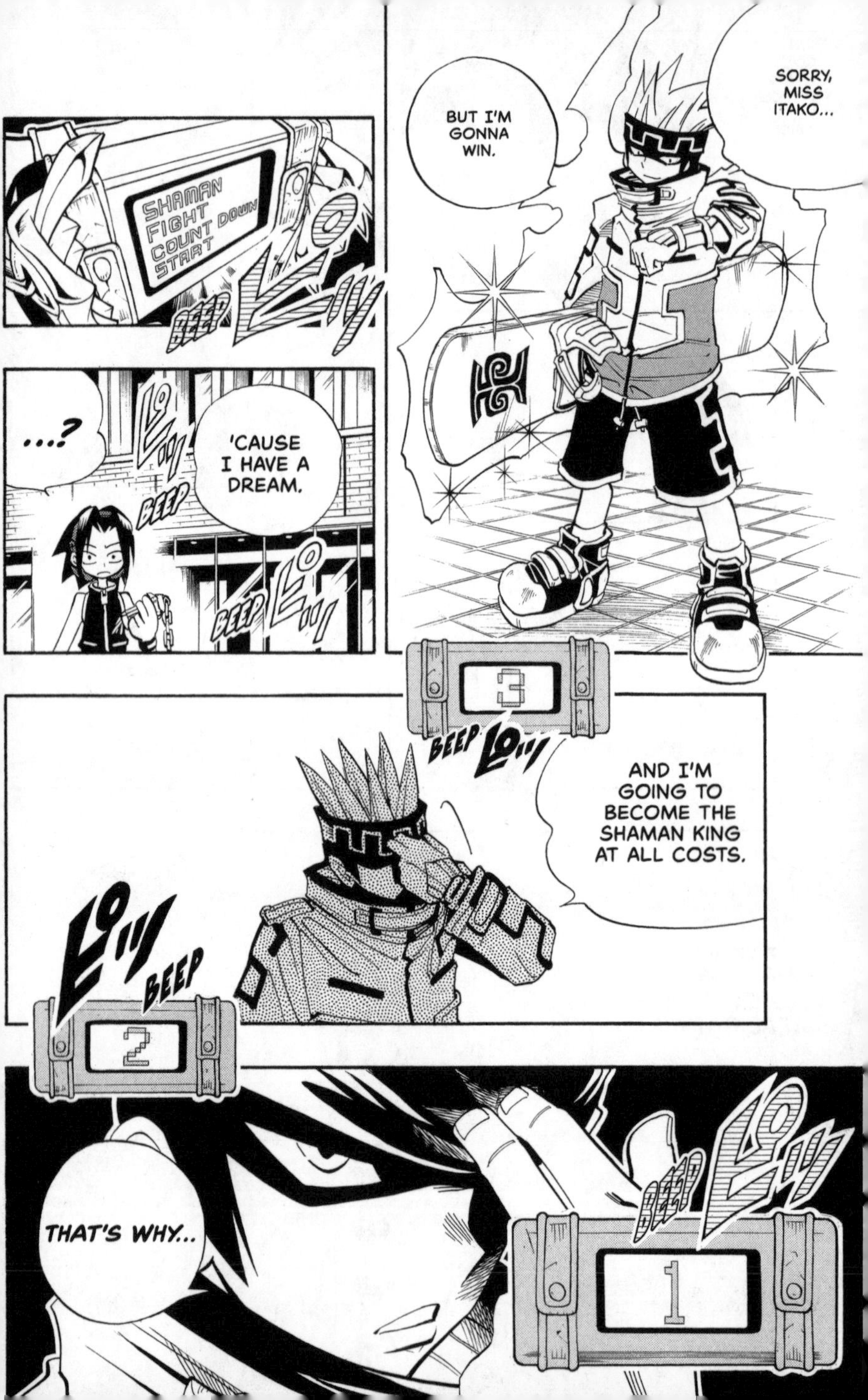
SORRY, MISS ITAKO...
BUT I'M GONNA WIN.
SHAMAN FIGHT COUNT DOWN START
BEEP
'CAUSE I HAVE A DREAM.
...?
BEEP
BEEP
3
BEEP
AND I'M GOING TO BECOME THE SHAMAN KING AT ALL COSTS.
BEEP
2
BEEP
1
THAT'S WHY...

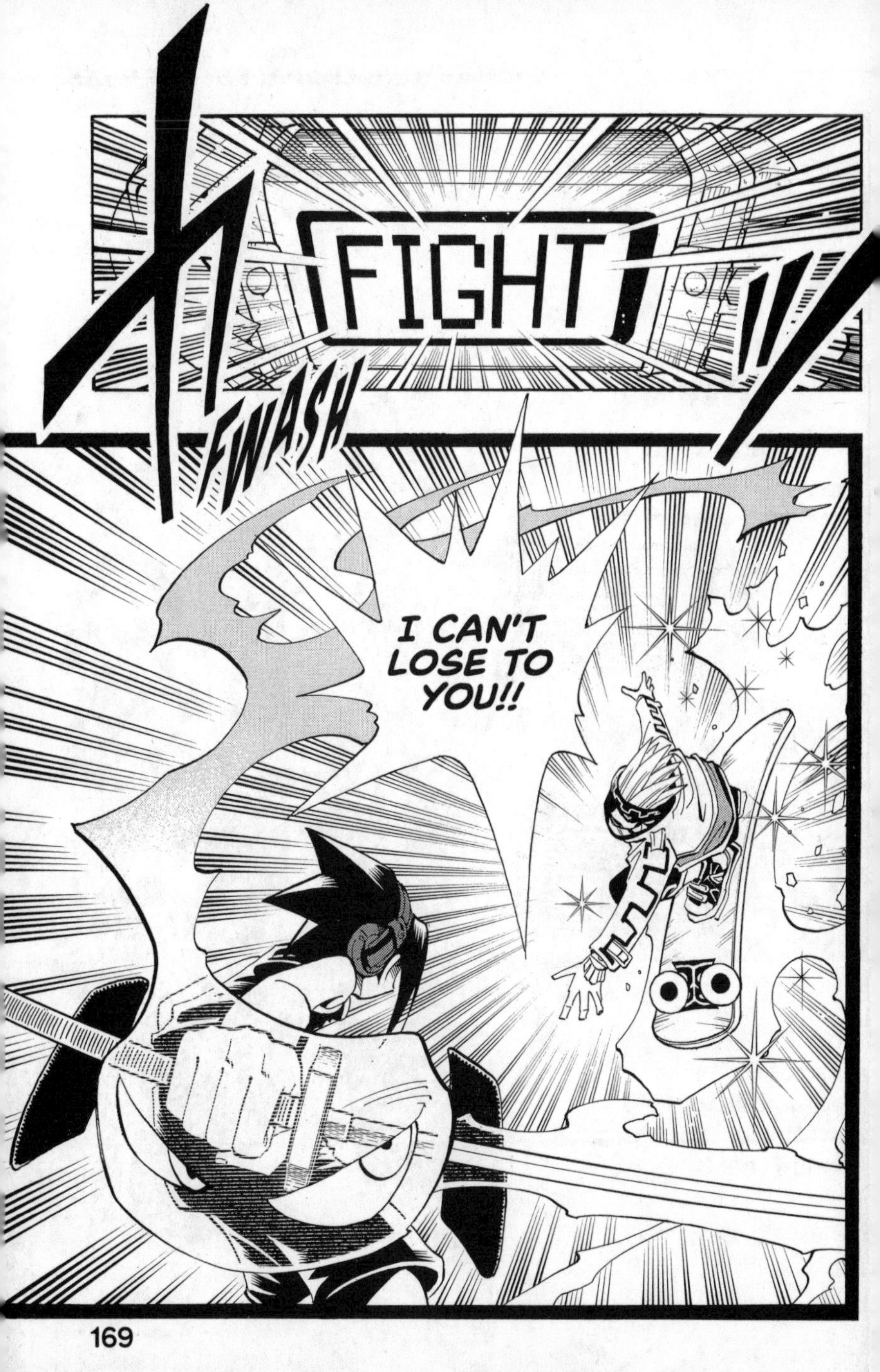
FIGHT
FWASH
I CAN'T LOSE TO YOU!!

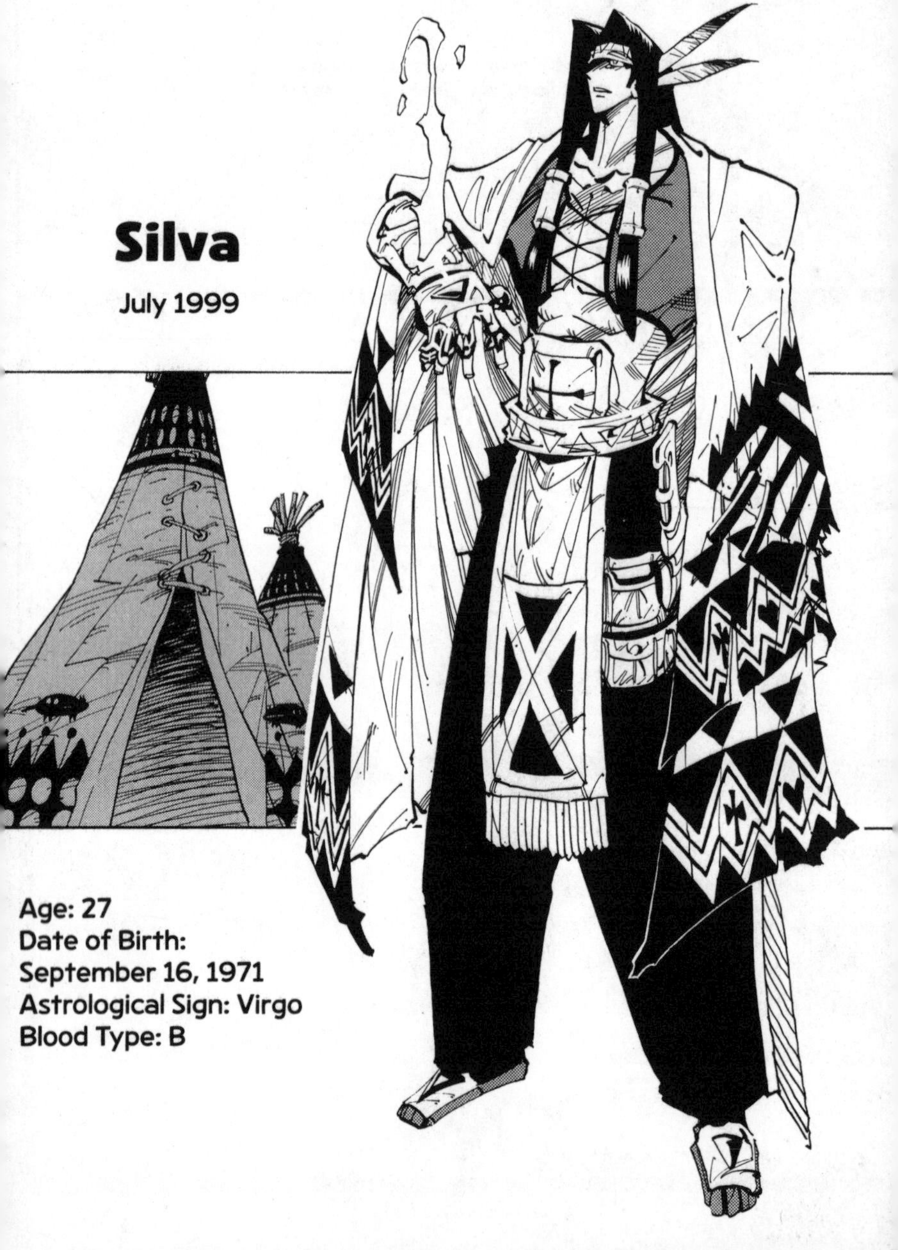

Silva

July 1999

Age: 27
Date of Birth:
September 16, 1971
Astrological Sign: Virgo
Blood Type: B

Chapter 35: Horohoro's Dream

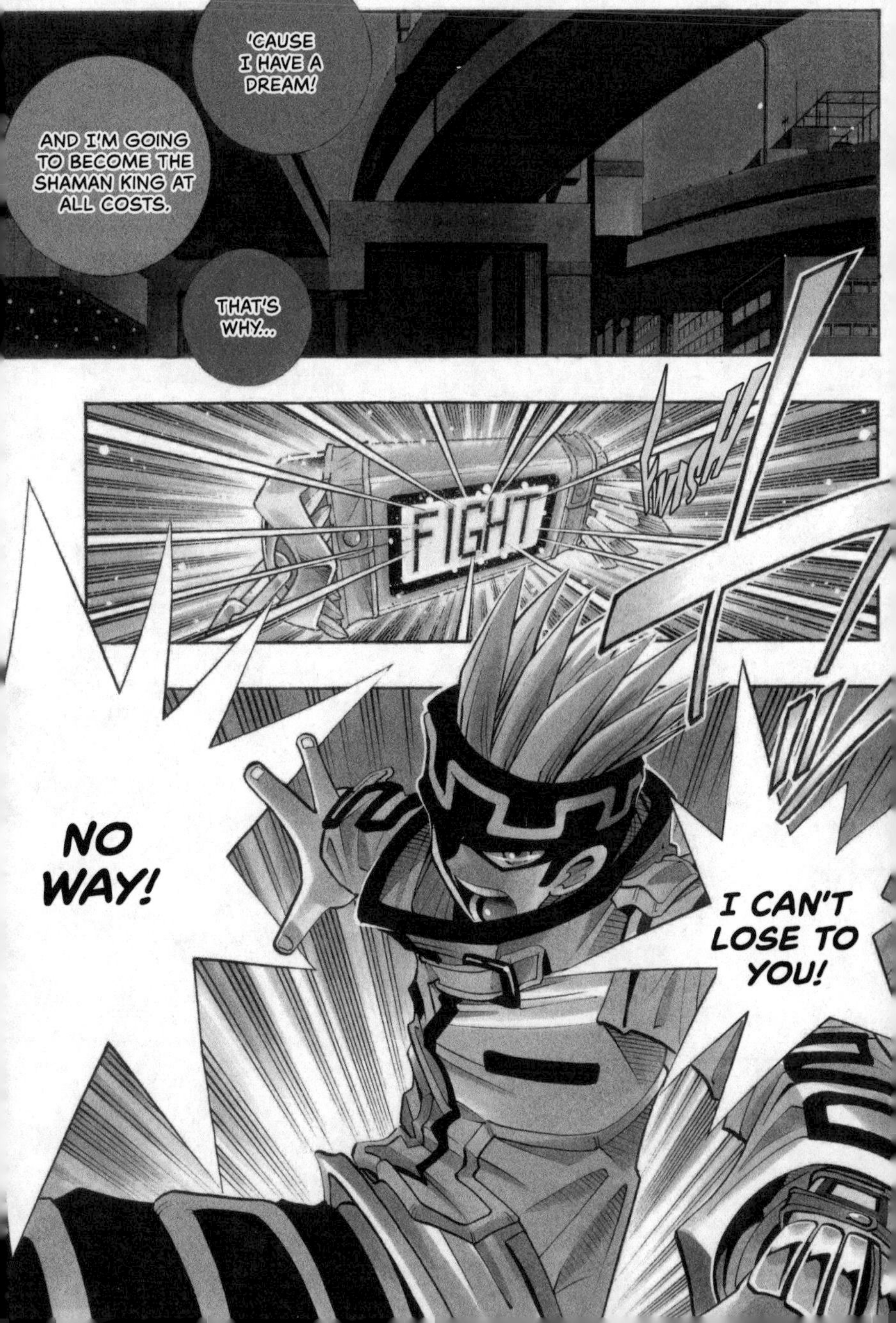
'CAUSE I HAVE A DREAM!
AND I'M GOING TO BECOME THE SHAMAN KING AT ALL COSTS.
THAT'S WHY...
FIGHT
NO WAY!
I CAN'T LOSE TO YOU!

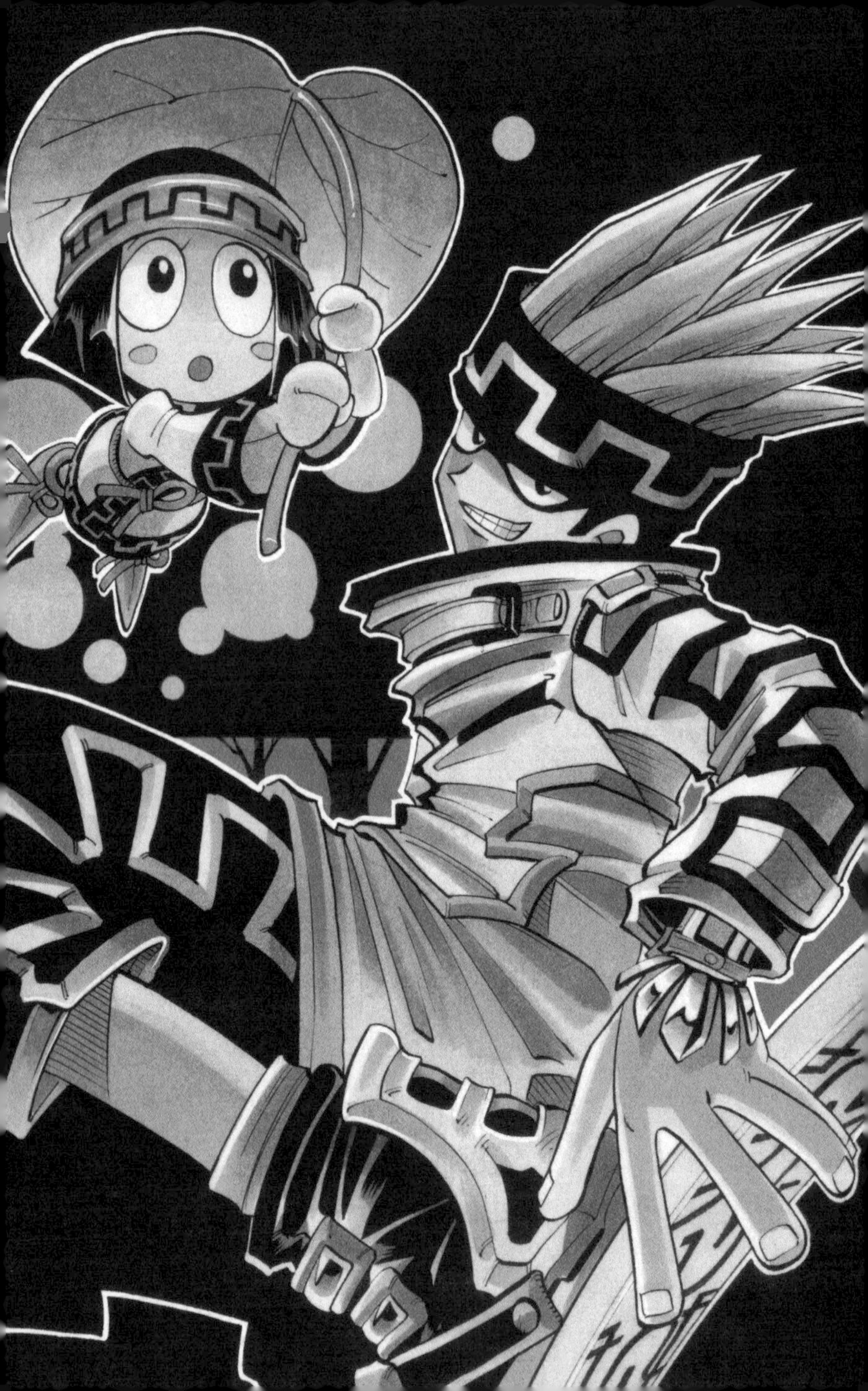

Chapter 35:

HOROHORO'S DREAM

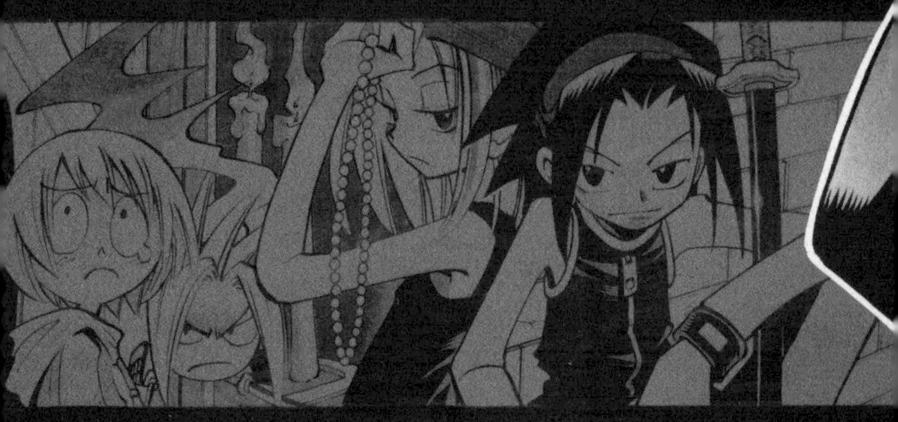

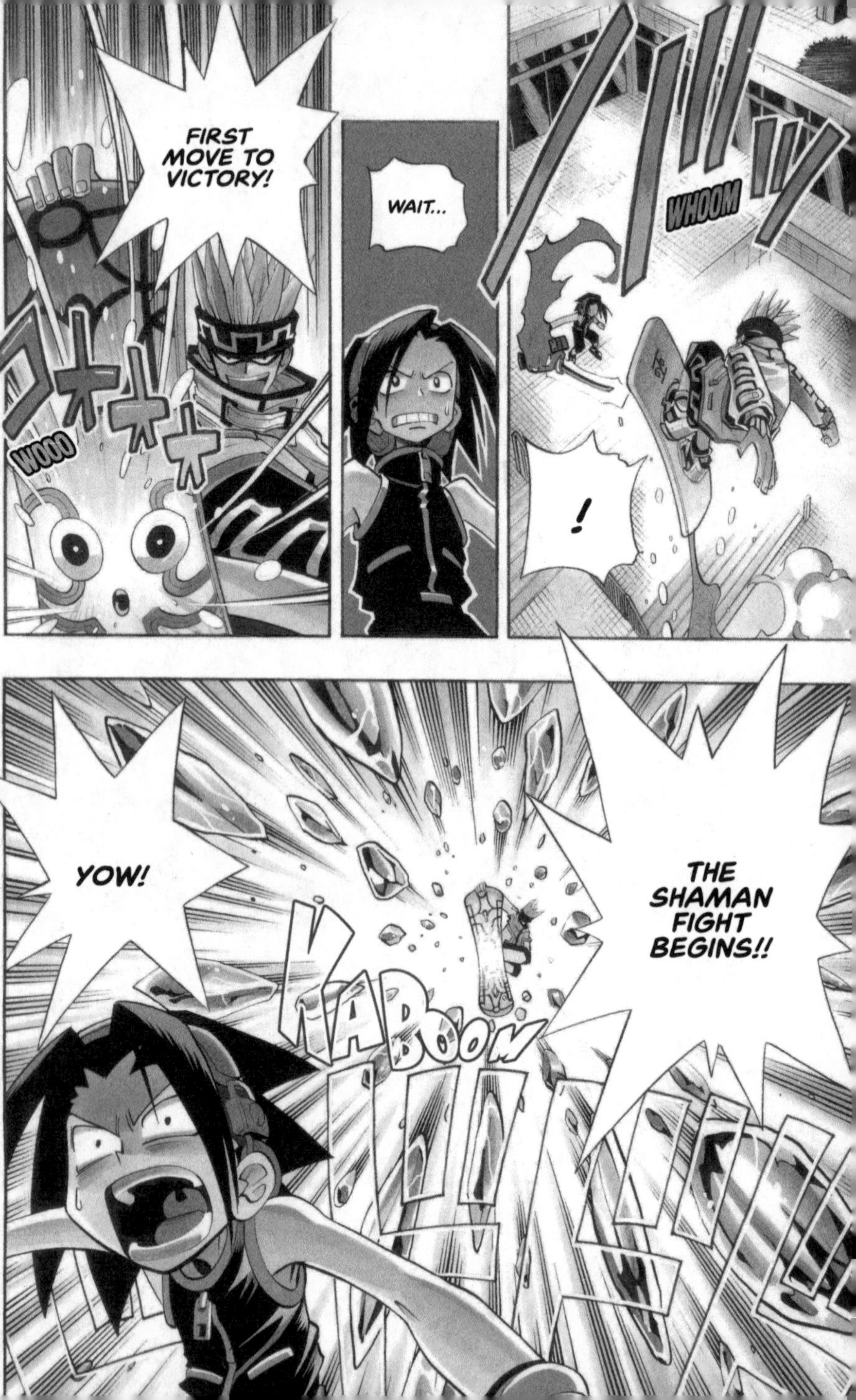
WHOOM
!
WAIT...
FIRST MOVE TO VICTORY!
WOOO
THE SHAMAN FIGHT BEGINS!!
KABOOM
YOW!

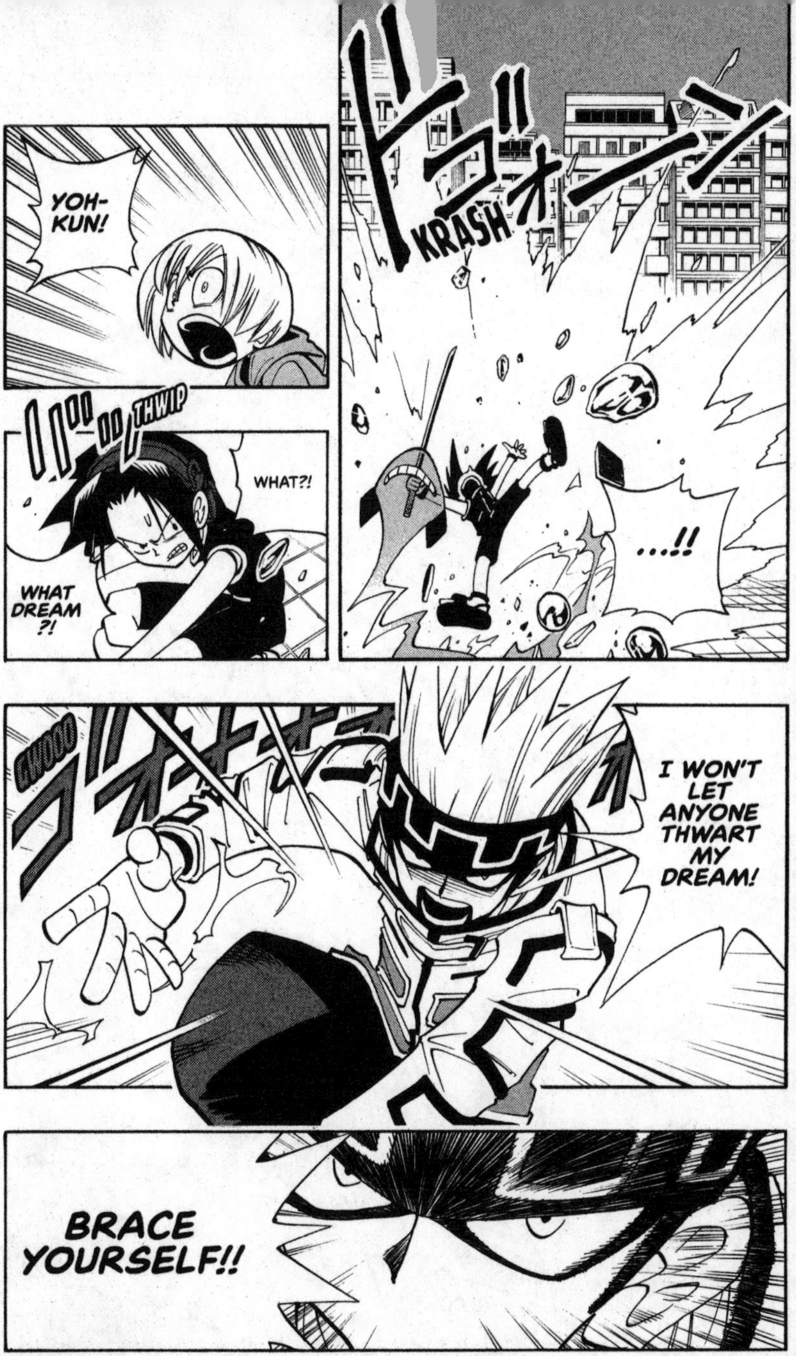
KRASH
...!!
YOH-KUN!
THWIP
WHAT?!
WHAT DREAM ?!
GWOOO
I WON'T LET ANYONE THWART MY DREAM!
BRACE YOURSELF!!

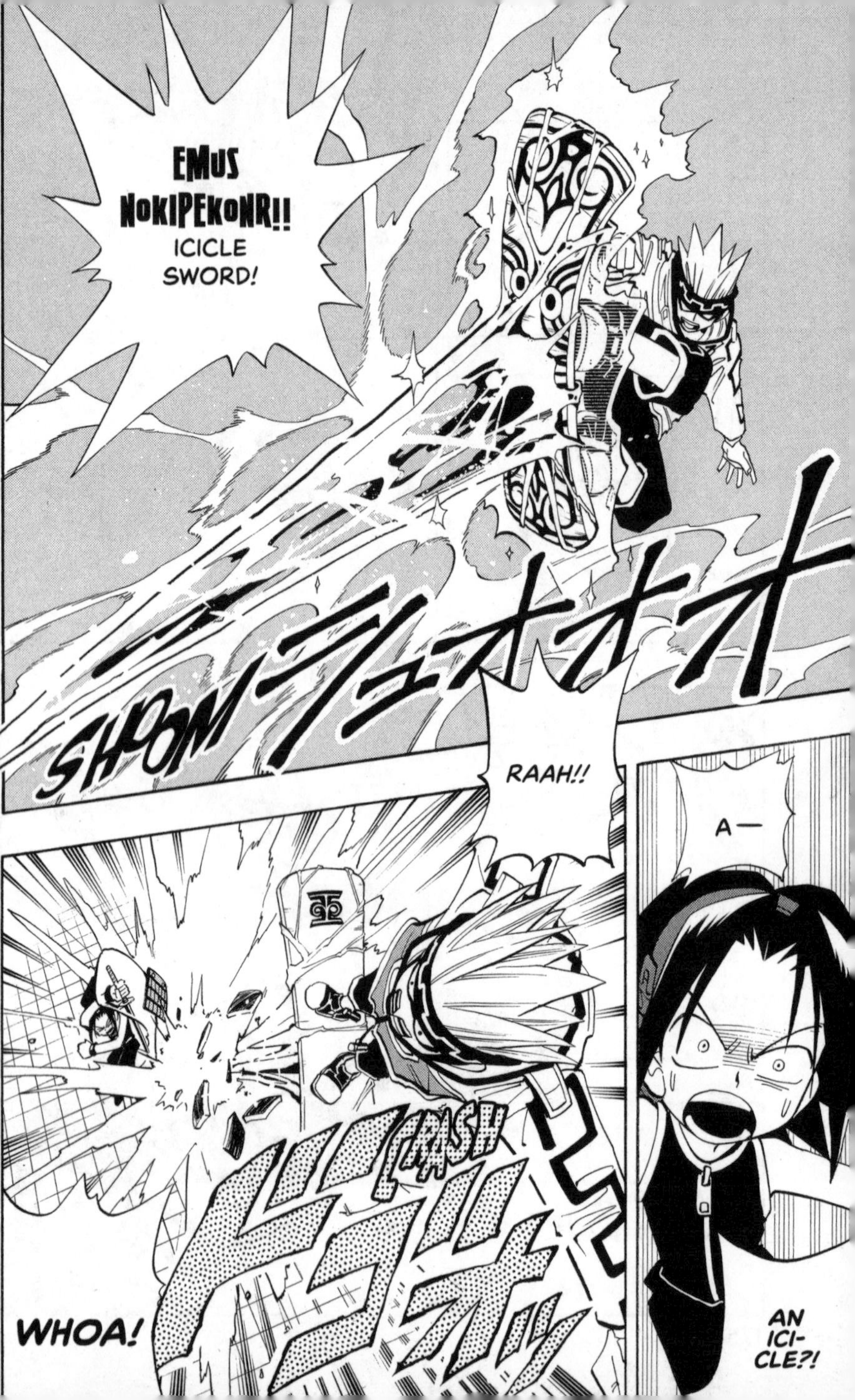
EMUS NOKIPEKONR!!
ICICLE SWORD!
SHOOM
A—
AN ICI-CLE?!
RAAH!!
CRASH
WHOA!

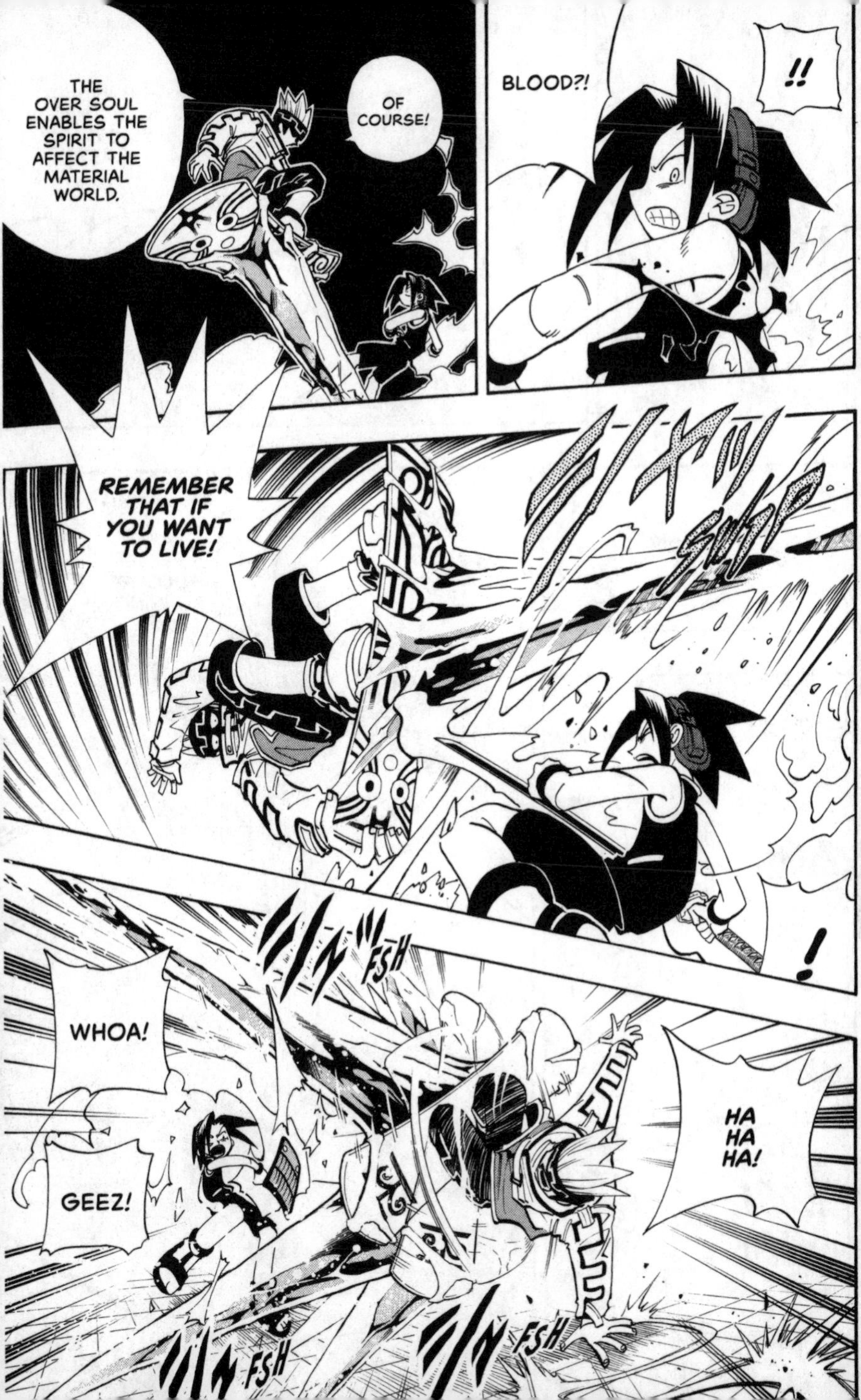
!!
BLOOD?!
OF COURSE!
THE OVER SOUL ENABLES THE SPIRIT TO AFFECT THE MATERIAL WORLD.
REMEMBER THAT IF YOU WANT TO LIVE!
!
HA HA HA!
FSH
WHOA!
GEEZ!
FSH
FSH

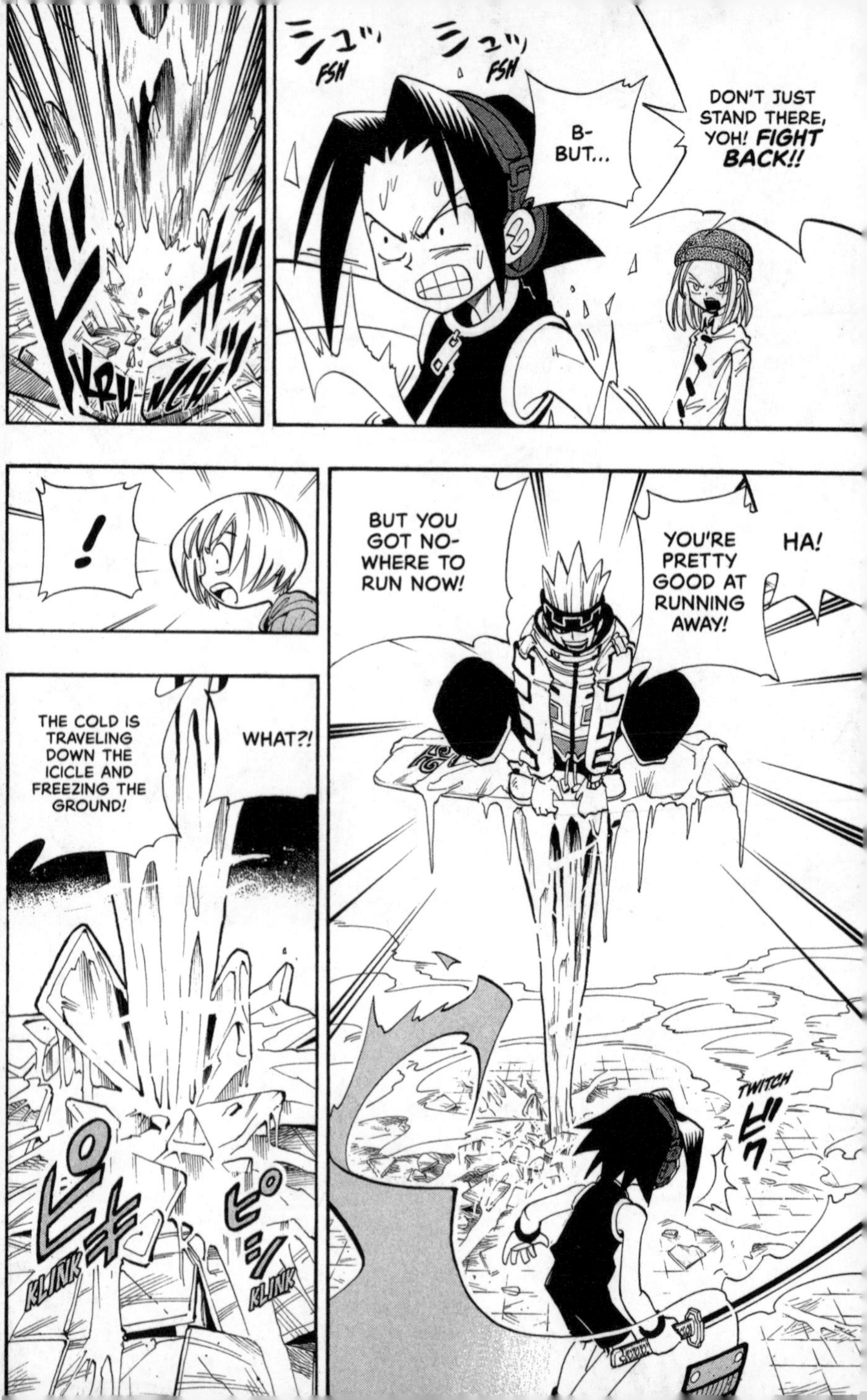

DON'T JUST STAND THERE, YOH! **FIGHT BACK!!**
FSH
FSH
B-BUT...
KRUNCH
HA!
YOU'RE PRETTY GOOD AT RUNNING AWAY!
BUT YOU GOT NO-WHERE TO RUN NOW!
TWITCH
!
WHAT?!
THE COLD IS TRAVELING DOWN THE ICICLE AND FREEZING THE GROUND!
KLINK
KLINK

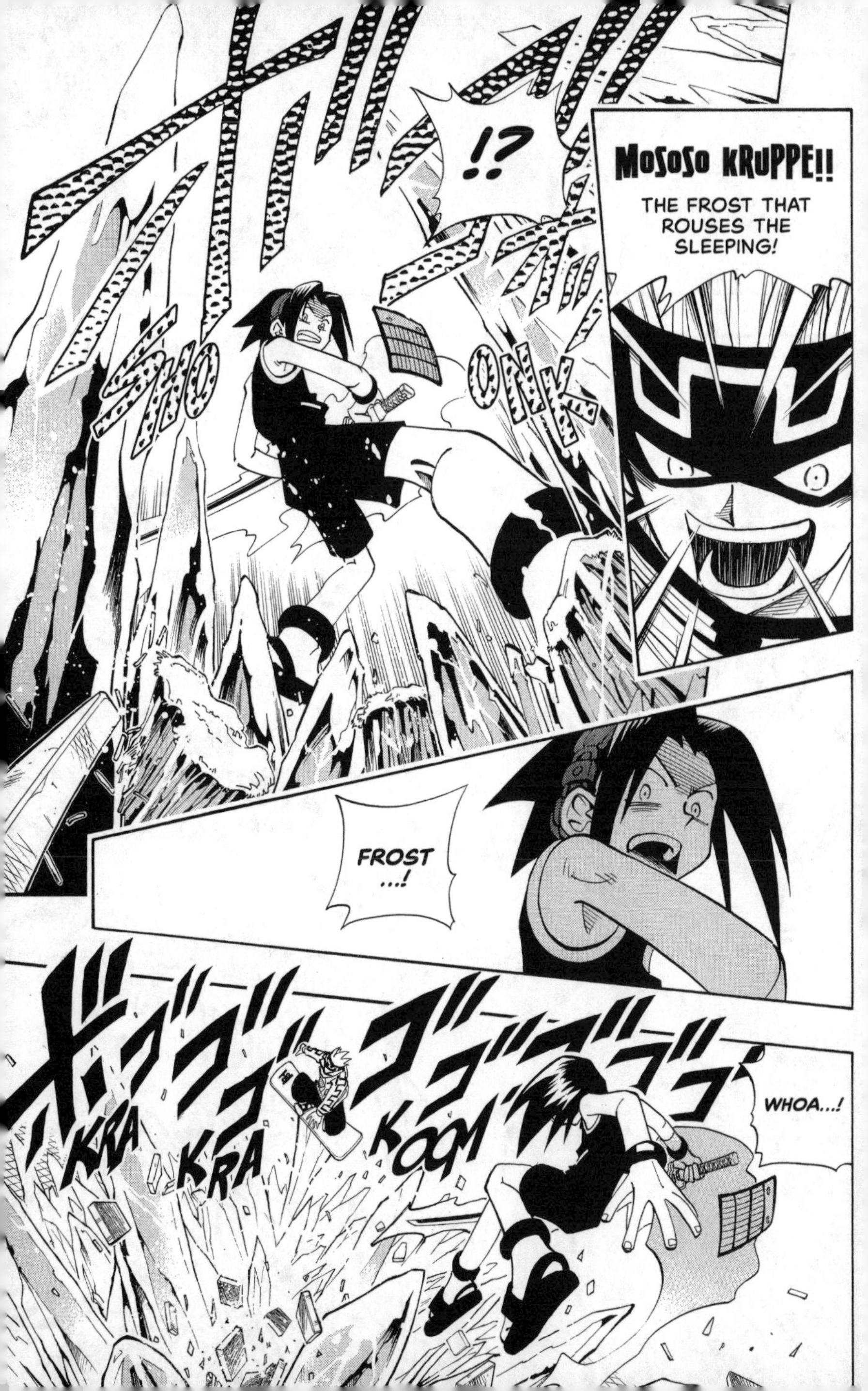
MOSOSO KRUPPE!!
THE FROST THAT ROUSES THE SLEEPING!
!?
SHO
ONK
FROST ...!
WHOA...!
KRA
KRA
KOOM

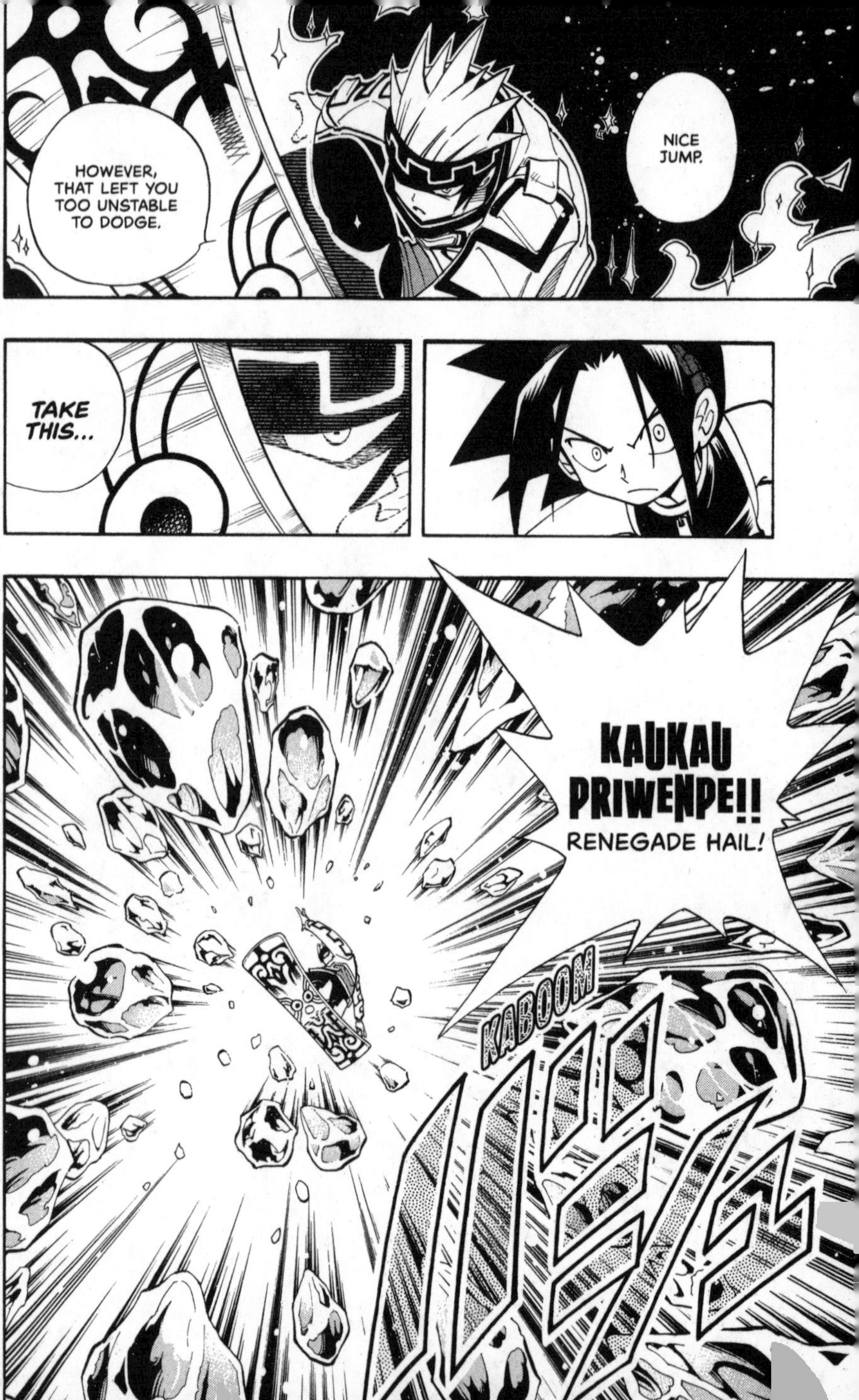
NICE JUMP.
HOWEVER, THAT LEFT YOU TOO UNSTABLE TO DODGE.
TAKE THIS...
KAUKAU PRIWENPE!!
RENEGADE HAIL!
KABOOM

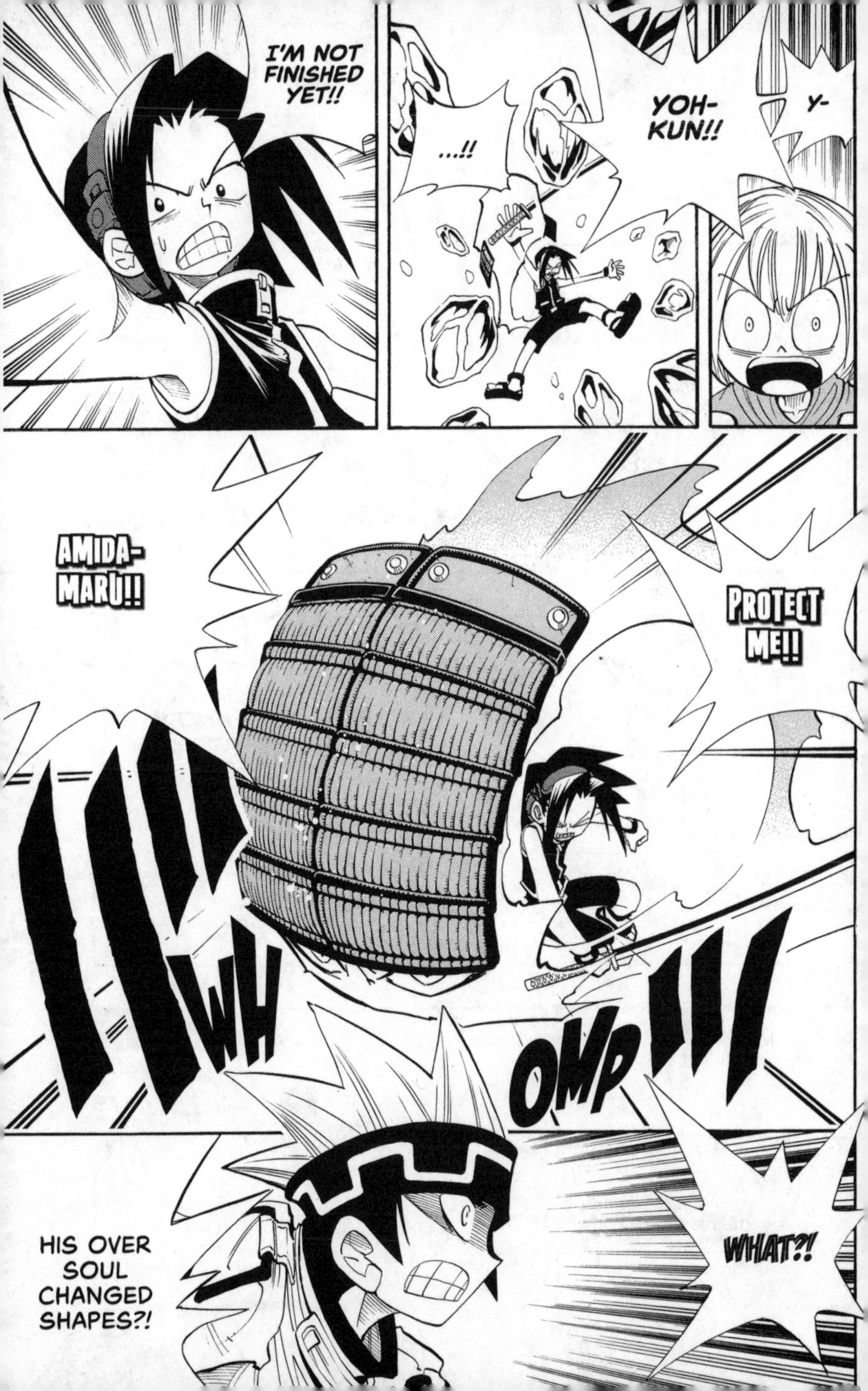
Y-
YOH-KUN!!
...!!
I'M NOT FINISHED YET!!
AMIDA-MARU!!
PROTECT ME!!
WHOMP!!!
WHAT?!
HIS OVER SOUL CHANGED SHAPES?!

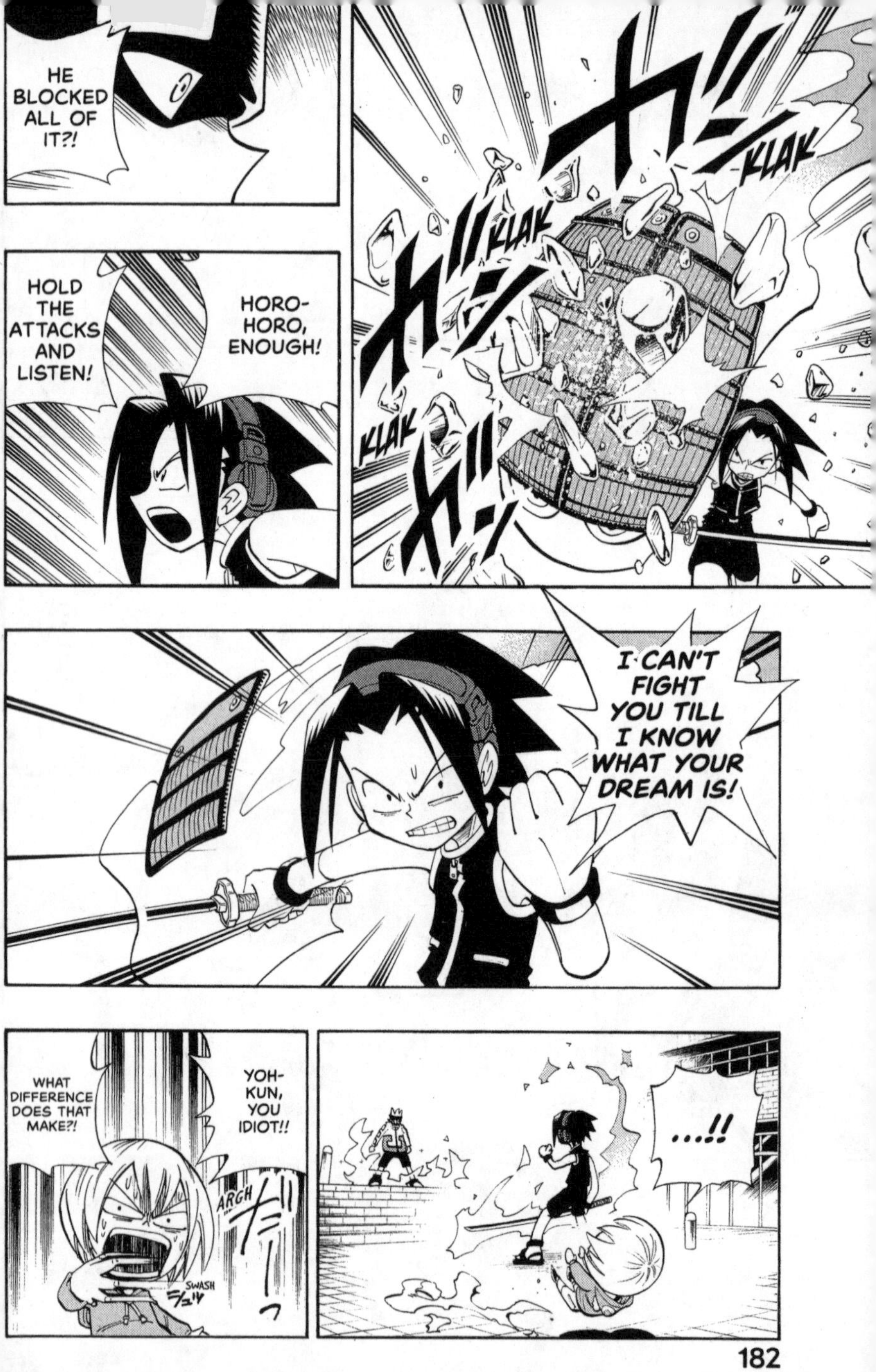
KLAK
KLAK
KLAK
HE BLOCKED ALL OF IT?!
HORO-HORO, ENOUGH!
HOLD THE ATTACKS AND LISTEN!
I CAN'T FIGHT YOU TILL I KNOW WHAT YOUR DREAM IS!
...!!
YOH-KUN, YOU IDIOT!!
WHAT DIFFERENCE DOES THAT MAKE?!
ARGH
SWASH

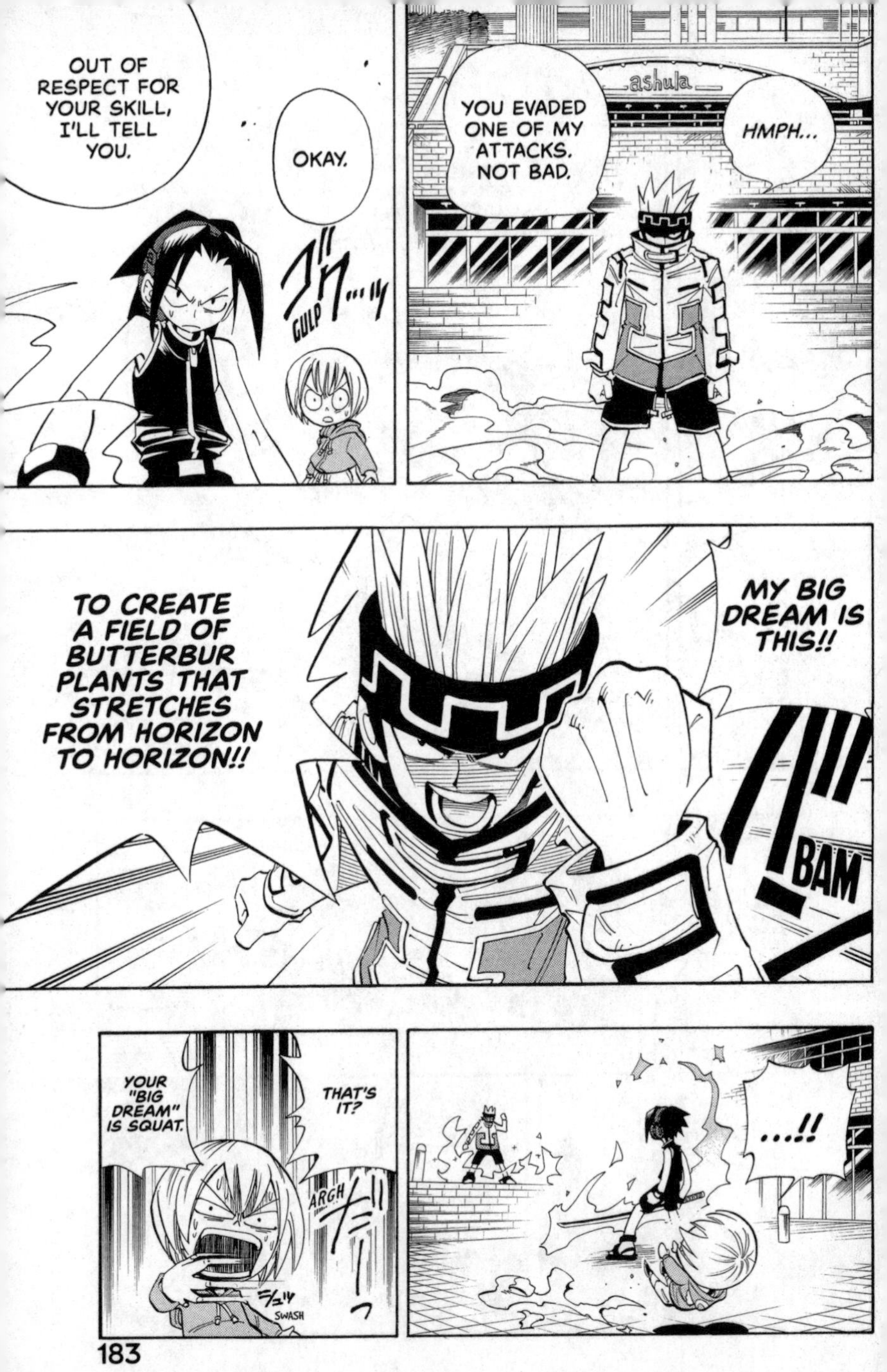
HMPH...
YOU EVADED ONE OF MY ATTACKS. NOT BAD.
OUT OF RESPECT FOR YOUR SKILL, I'LL TELL YOU.
OKAY.
GULP
MY BIG DREAM IS THIS!!
TO CREATE A FIELD OF BUTTERBUR PLANTS THAT STRETCHES FROM HORIZON TO HORIZON!!
BAM
...!!
THAT'S IT?
YOUR "BIG DREAM" IS SQUAT.
ARGH
SWASH

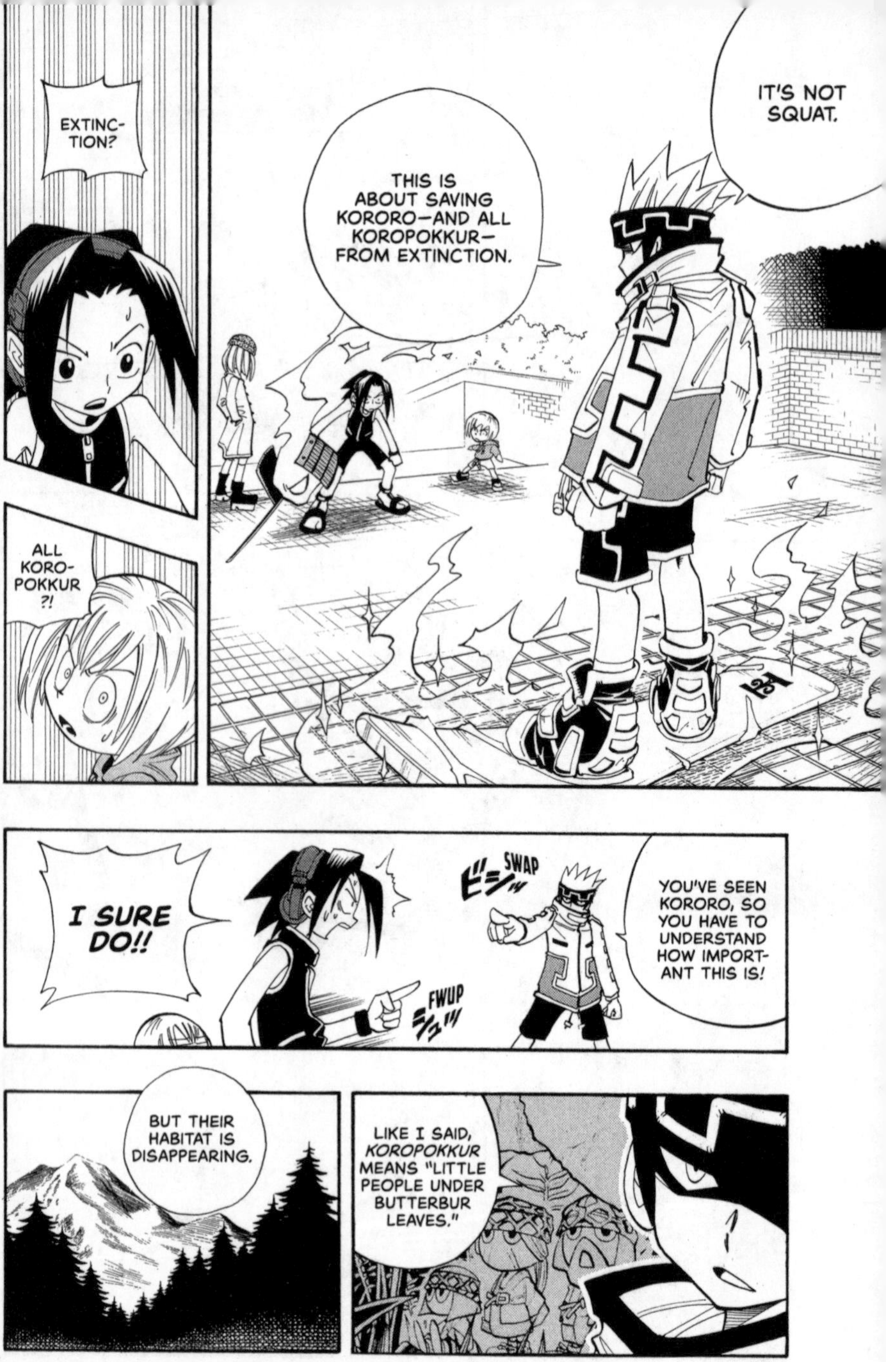
IT'S NOT SQUAT.
THIS IS ABOUT SAVING KORORO—AND ALL KOROPOKKUR—FROM EXTINCTION.
EXTINC-TION?
ALL KORO-POKKUR?!
YOU'VE SEEN KORORO, SO YOU HAVE TO UNDERSTAND HOW IMPORT-ANT THIS IS!
SWAP
FWUP
I SURE DO!!
LIKE I SAID, *KOROPOKKUR* MEANS "LITTLE PEOPLE UNDER BUTTERBUR LEAVES."
BUT THEIR HABITAT IS DISAPPEARING.

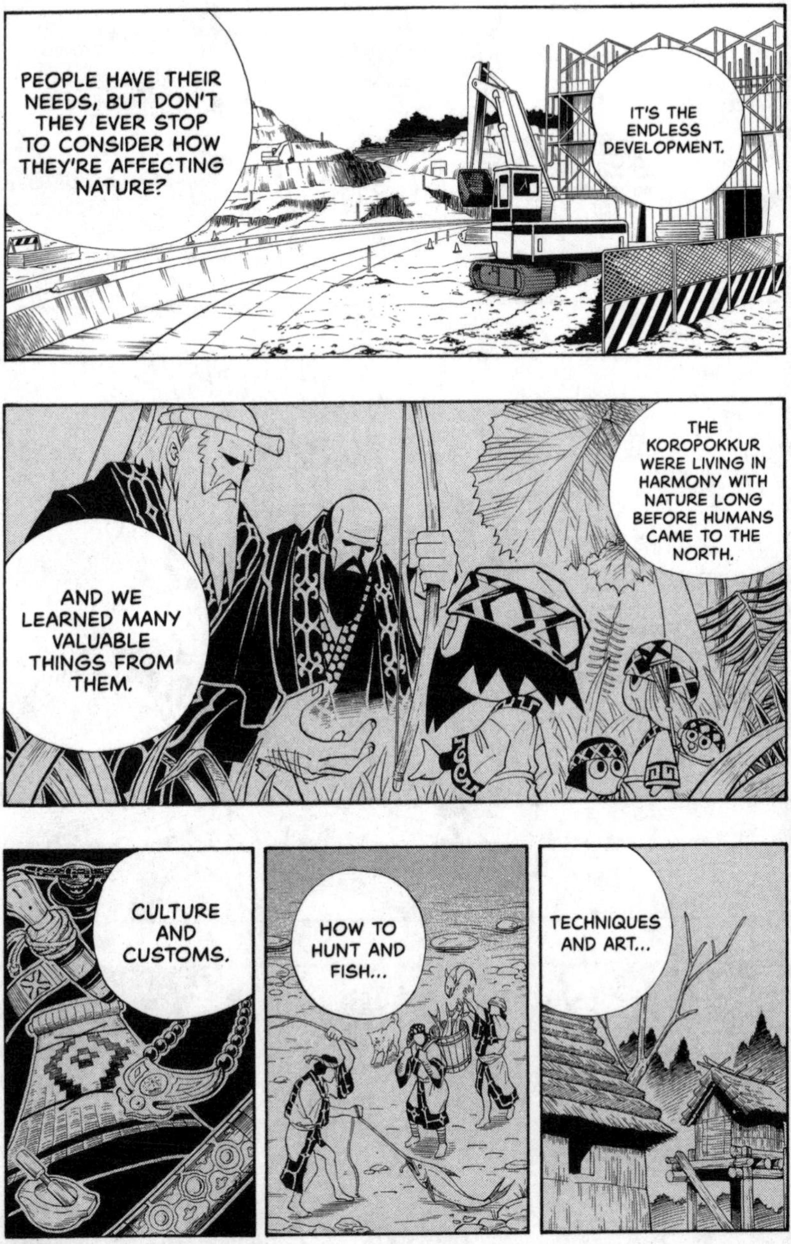
IT'S THE ENDLESS DEVELOPMENT.
PEOPLE HAVE THEIR NEEDS, BUT DON'T THEY EVER STOP TO CONSIDER HOW THEY'RE AFFECTING NATURE?
THE KOROPOKKUR WERE LIVING IN HARMONY WITH NATURE LONG BEFORE HUMANS CAME TO THE NORTH.
AND WE LEARNED MANY VALUABLE THINGS FROM THEM.
TECHNIQUES AND ART...
HOW TO HUNT AND FISH...
CULTURE AND CUSTOMS.

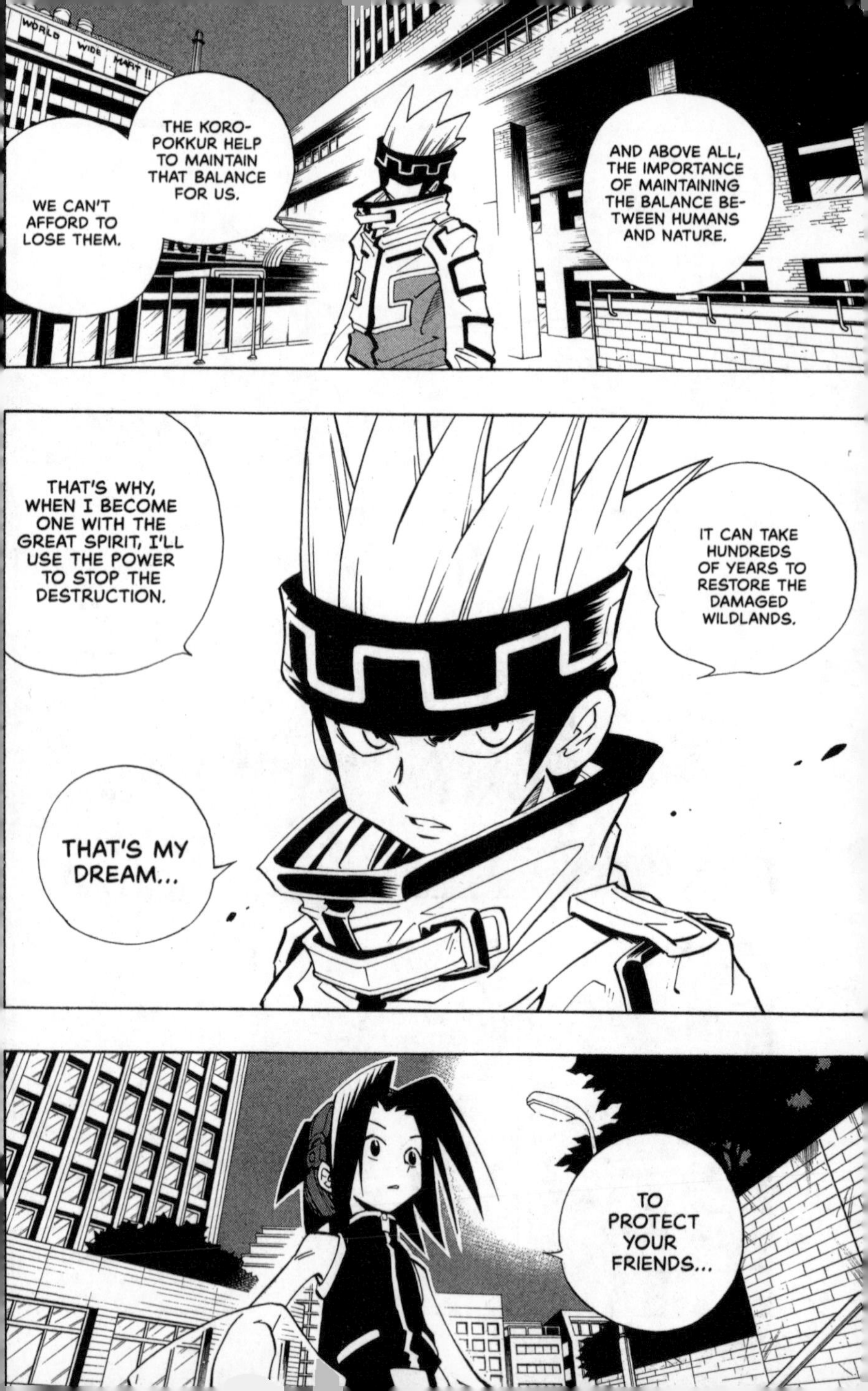

AND ABOVE ALL, THE IMPORTANCE OF MAINTAINING THE BALANCE BETWEEN HUMANS AND NATURE.
THE KORO-POKKUR HELP TO MAINTAIN THAT BALANCE FOR US.
WE CAN'T AFFORD TO LOSE THEM.
WORLD WIDE MART!!
IT CAN TAKE HUNDREDS OF YEARS TO RESTORE THE DAMAGED WILDLANDS.
THAT'S WHY, WHEN I BECOME ONE WITH THE GREAT SPIRIT, I'LL USE THE POWER TO STOP THE DESTRUCTION.
THAT'S MY DREAM...
TO PROTECT YOUR FRIENDS...

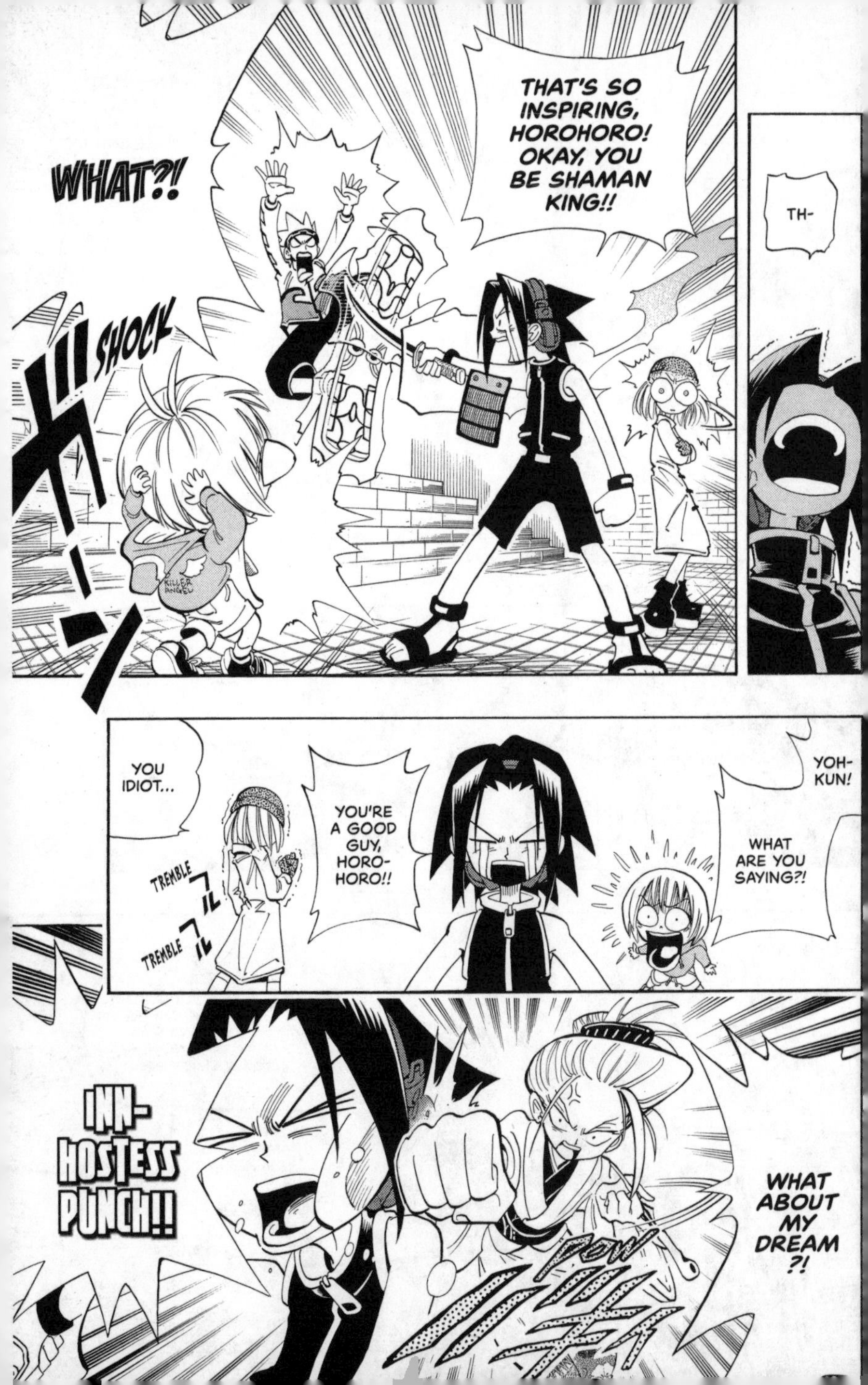
TH-
THAT'S SO INSPIRING, HOROHORO! OKAY, YOU BE SHAMAN KING!!
WHAT?!
SHOCK
YOH-KUN!
WHAT ARE YOU SAYING?!
YOU'RE A GOOD GUY, HORO-HORO!!
YOU IDIOT...
TREMBLE
TREMBLE
WHAT ABOUT MY DREAM?!
POW
INN-HOSTESS PUNCH!!

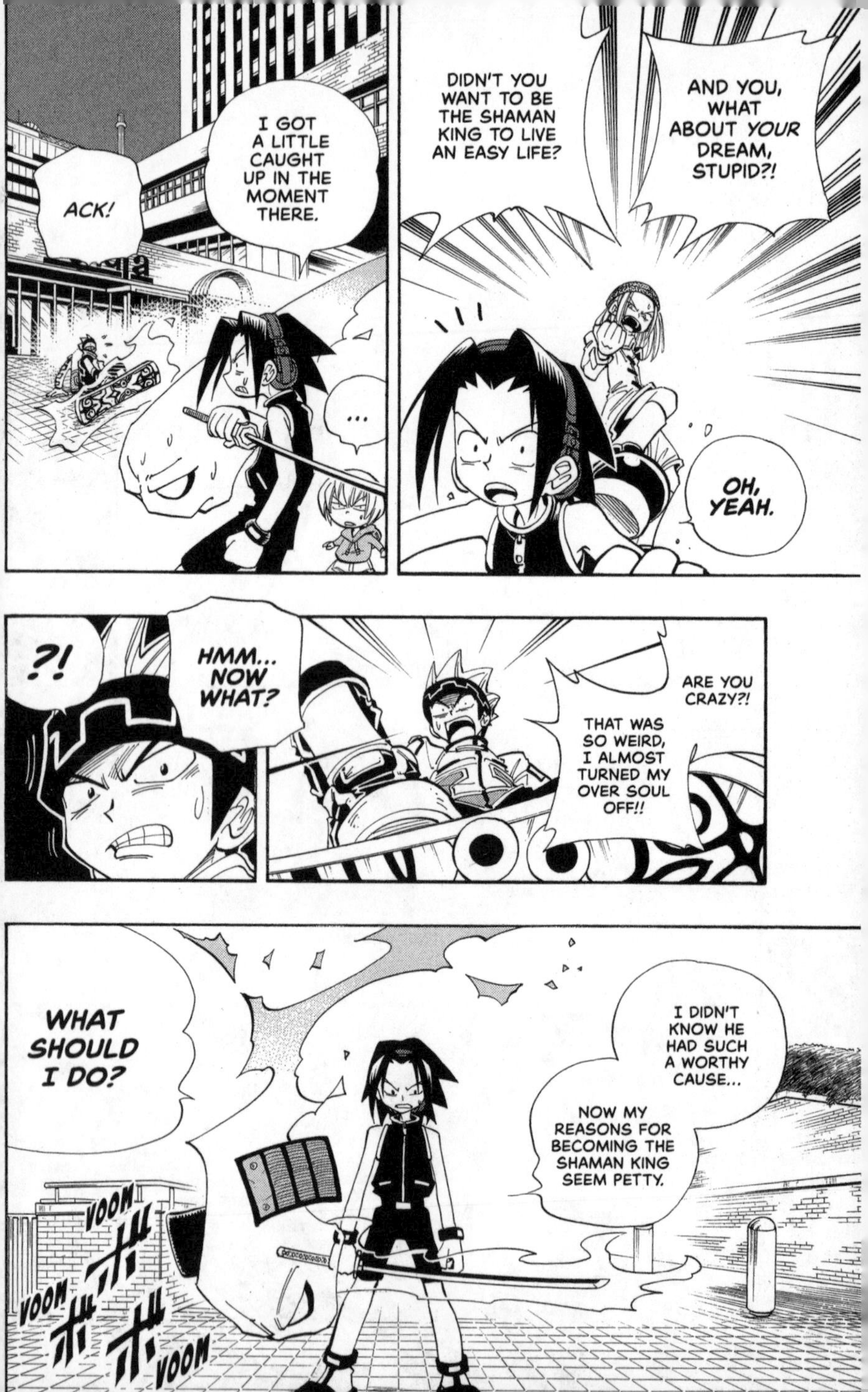
AND YOU, WHAT ABOUT *YOUR* DREAM, STUPID?!
DIDN'T YOU WANT TO BE THE SHAMAN KING TO LIVE AN EASY LIFE?
OH, YEAH.
I GOT A LITTLE CAUGHT UP IN THE MOMENT THERE.
ACK!
...
ARE YOU CRAZY?!
THAT WAS SO WEIRD, I ALMOST TURNED MY OVER SOUL OFF!!
HMM... NOW WHAT?
?!
I DIDN'T KNOW HE HAD SUCH A WORTHY CAUSE...
NOW MY REASONS FOR BECOMING THE SHAMAN KING SEEM PETTY.
WHAT SHOULD I DO?
VOOM
VOOM
VOOM

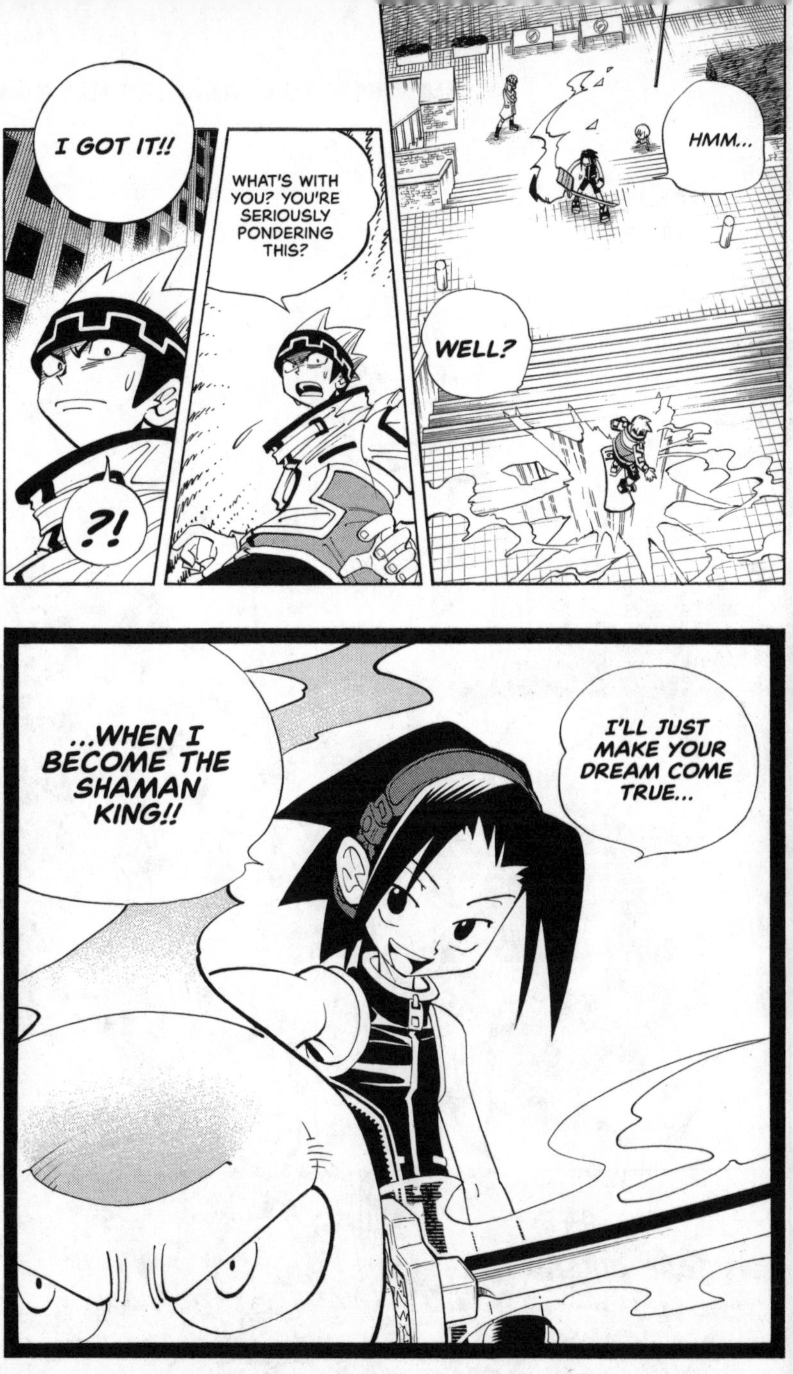
HMM...
WELL?
WHAT'S WITH YOU? YOU'RE SERIOUSLY PONDERING THIS?
I GOT IT!!
?!
I'LL JUST MAKE YOUR DREAM COME TRUE...
...WHEN I BECOME THE SHAMAN KING!!

SHAMAN KING CHARACTER FILE No.19

Silver Arms

500 years postmortem

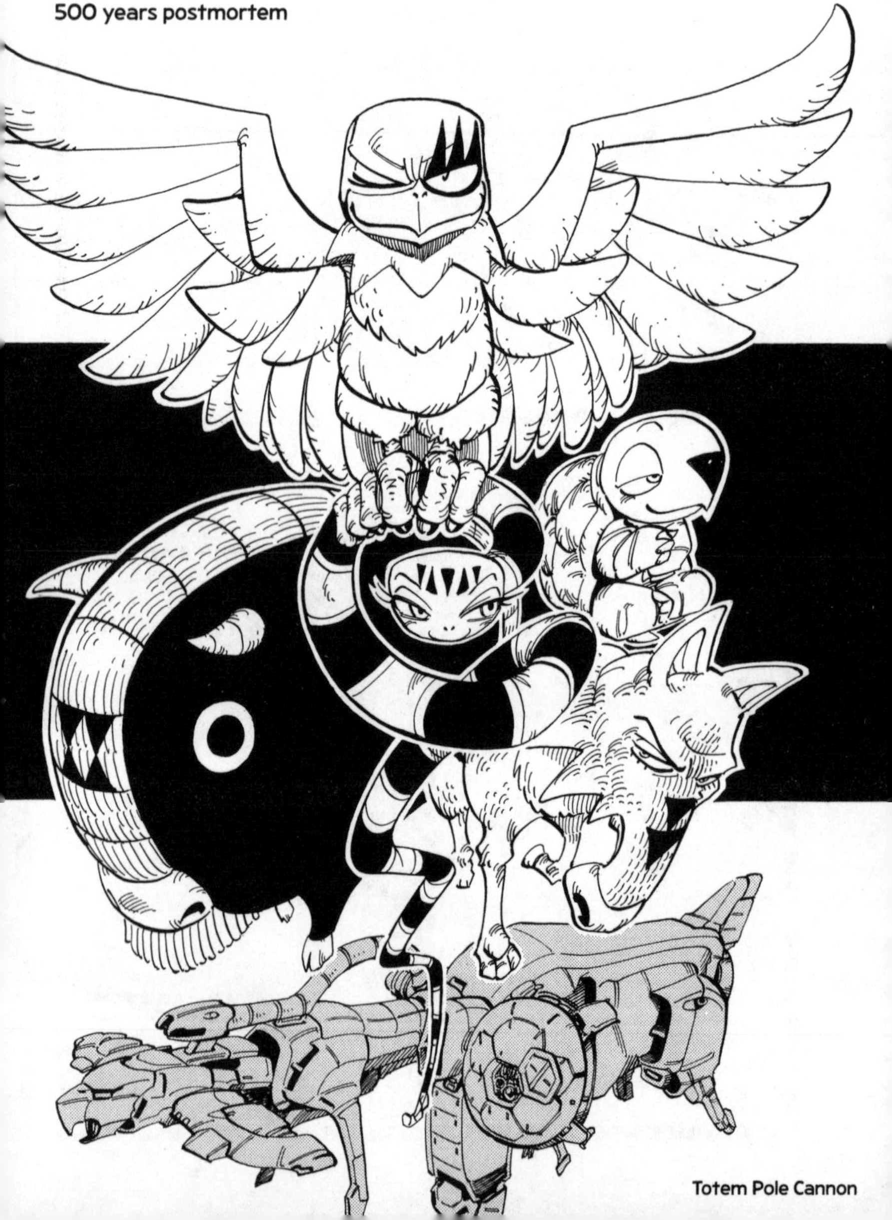

Totem Pole Cannon

-Special Bonus -

Diagram of the Totem Pole Cannon

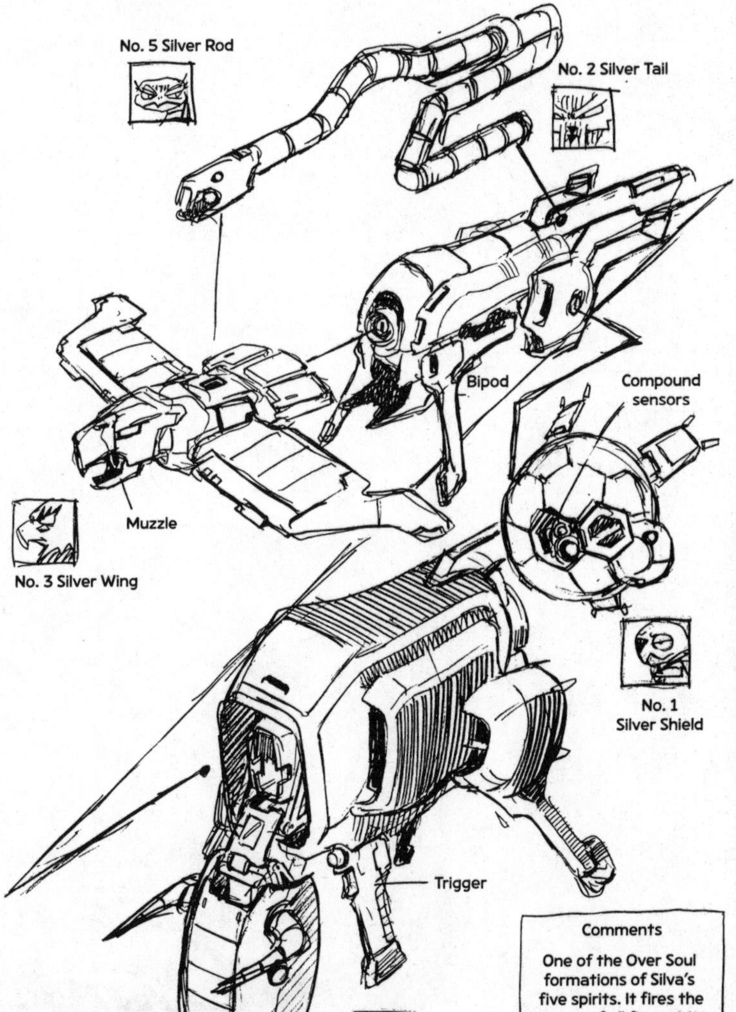
No. 5 Silver Rod
No. 2 Silver Tail
Bipod
Compound sensors
Muzzle
No. 3 Silver Wing
No. 1 Silver Shield
Trigger
Looks something like this!!
No. 4 Silver Horn

Comments

One of the Over Soul formations of Silva's five spirits. It fires the energy of all five spirits at once, so it packs a pretty powerful punch. However, that means it also consumes a corresponding amount of mana. Use caution!

SHAMAN KING

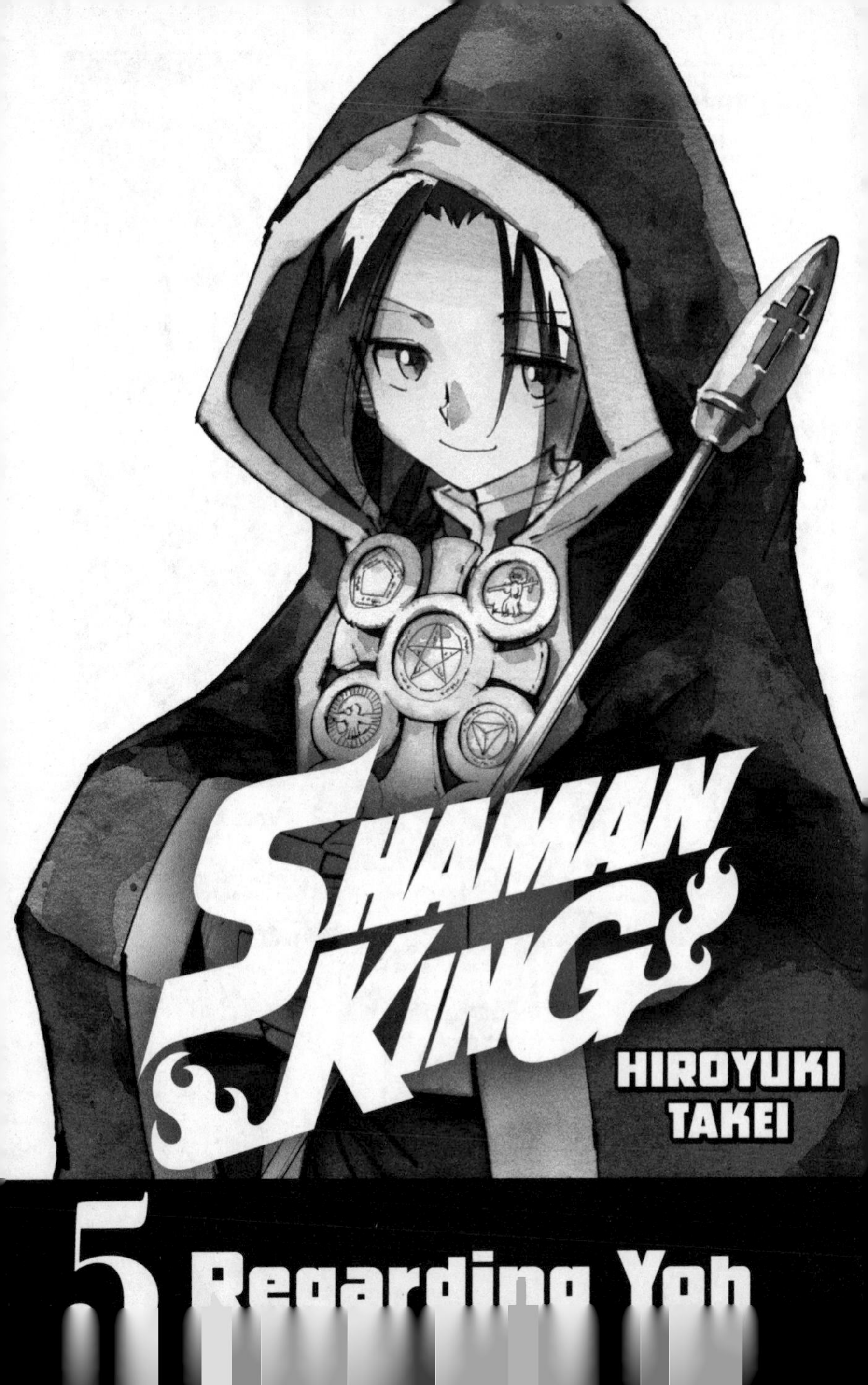

SHAMAN KING

HIROYUKI TAKEI

5 Regarding Yoh

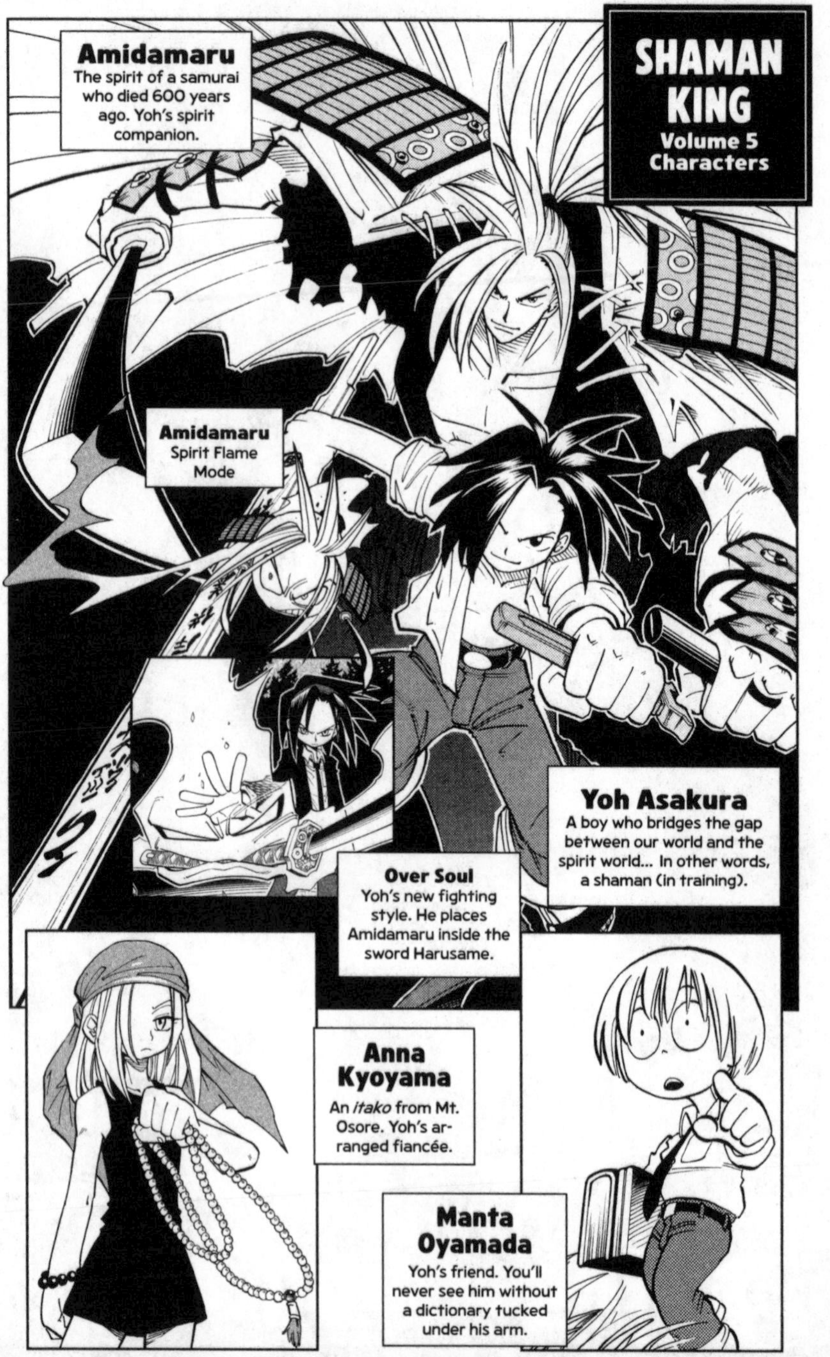
SHAMAN KING
Volume 5 Characters
Amidamaru
The spirit of a samurai who died 600 years ago. Yoh's spirit companion.
Amidamaru
Spirit Flame Mode
Yoh Asakura
A boy who bridges the gap between our world and the spirit world... In other words, a shaman (in training).
Over Soul
Yoh's new fighting style. He places Amidamaru inside the sword Harusame.
Manta Oyamada
Yoh's friend. You'll never see him without a dictionary tucked under his arm.
Anna Kyoyama
An *itako* from Mt. Osore. Yoh's arranged fiancée.

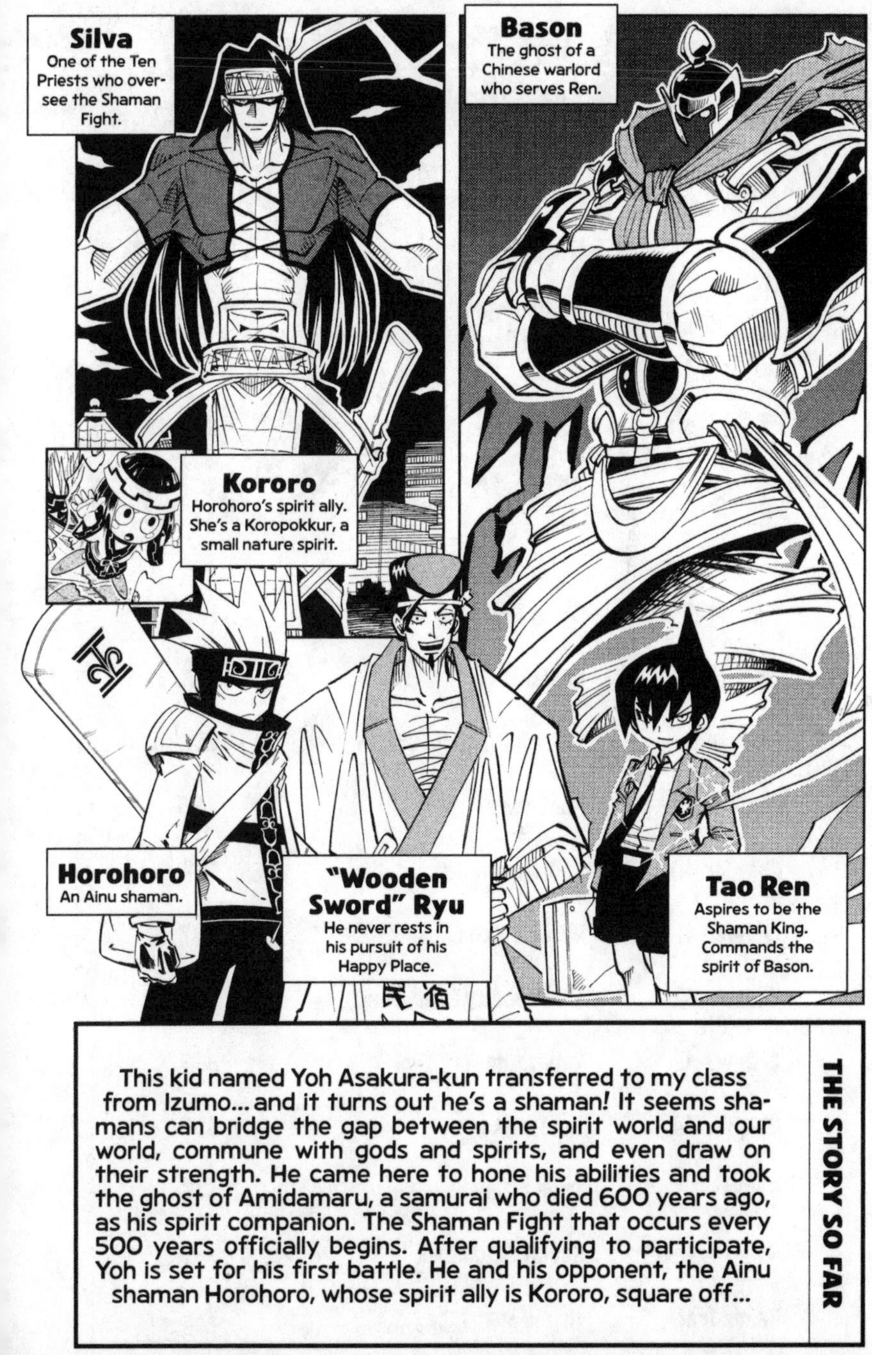
Bason
The ghost of a Chinese warlord who serves Ren.
Silva
One of the Ten Priests who over-see the Shaman Fight.
Kororo
Horohoro's spirit ally. She's a Koropokkur, a small nature spirit.
Tao Ren
Aspires to be the Shaman King. Commands the spirit of Bason.
"Wooden Sword" Ryu
He never rests in his pursuit of his Happy Place.
Horohoro
An Ainu shaman.
民 宿

THE STORY SO FAR

This kid named Yoh Asakura-kun transferred to my class from Izumo... and it turns out he's a shaman! It seems shamans can bridge the gap between the spirit world and our world, commune with gods and spirits, and even draw on their strength. He came here to hone his abilities and took the ghost of Amidamaru, a samurai who died 600 years ago, as his spirit companion. The Shaman Fight that occurs every 500 years officially begins. After qualifying to participate, Yoh is set for his first battle. He and his opponent, the Ainu shaman Horohoro, whose spirit ally is Kororo, square off...

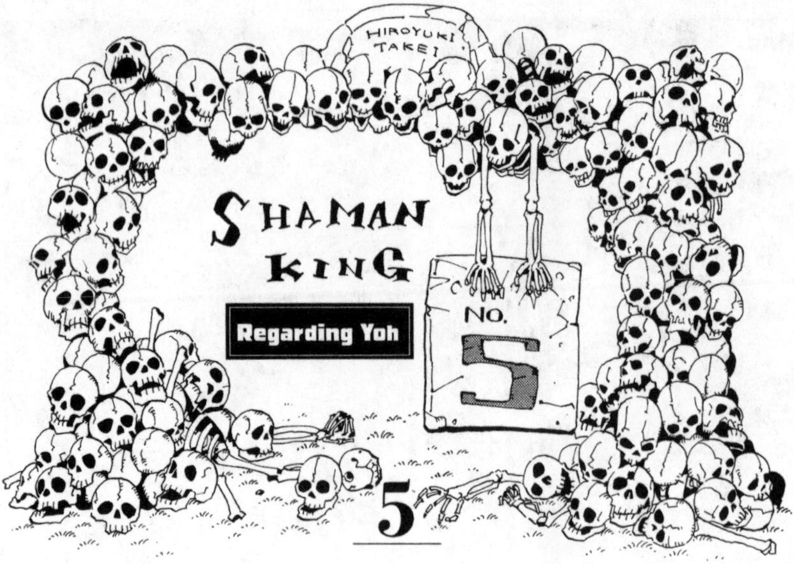
HIROYUKI TAKEI
SHAMAN KING
Regarding Yoh
NO.
5
5

Chapter 36: Great Ghost, Great Sword

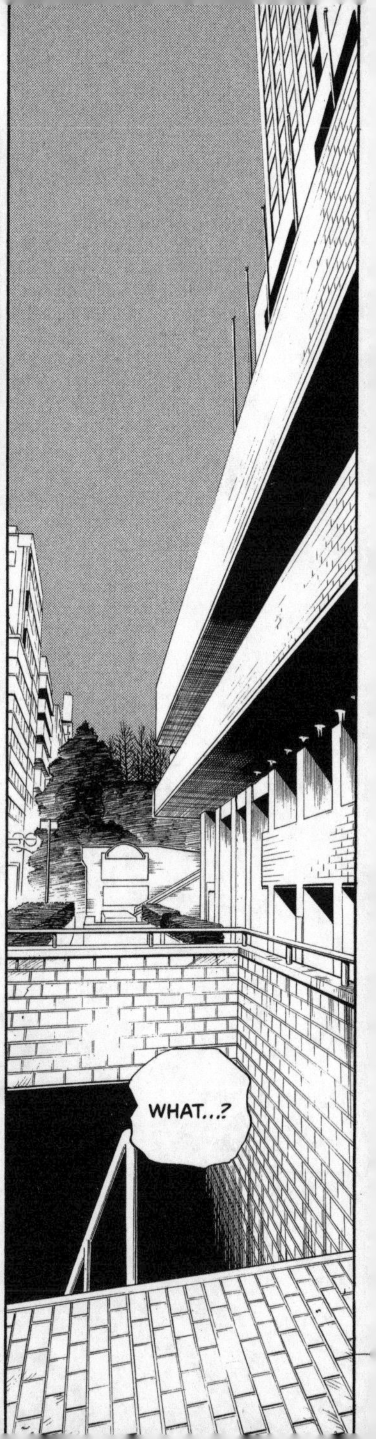
WHAT...?

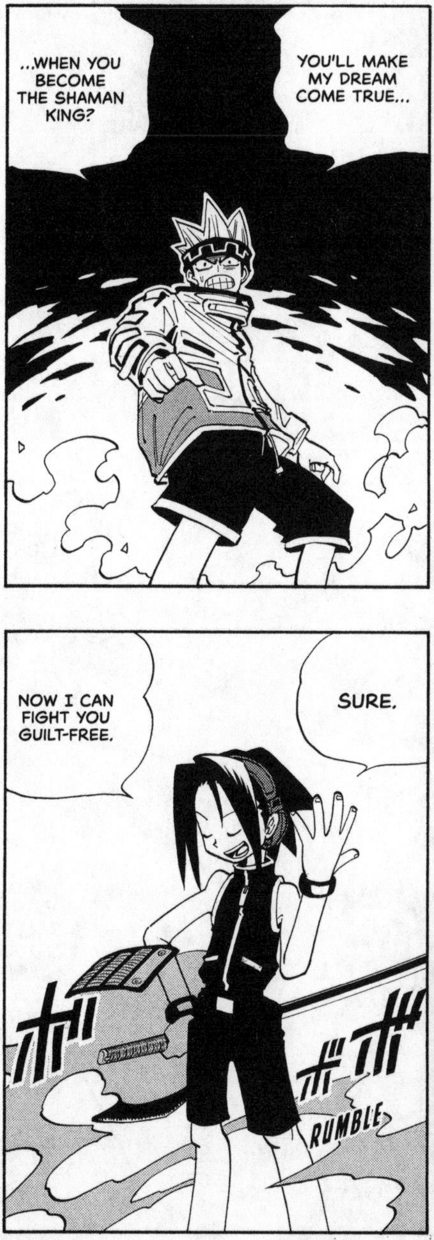
YOU'LL MAKE MY DREAM COME TRUE...
...WHEN YOU BECOME THE SHAMAN KING?
SURE.
NOW I CAN FIGHT YOU GUILT-FREE.
RUMBLE

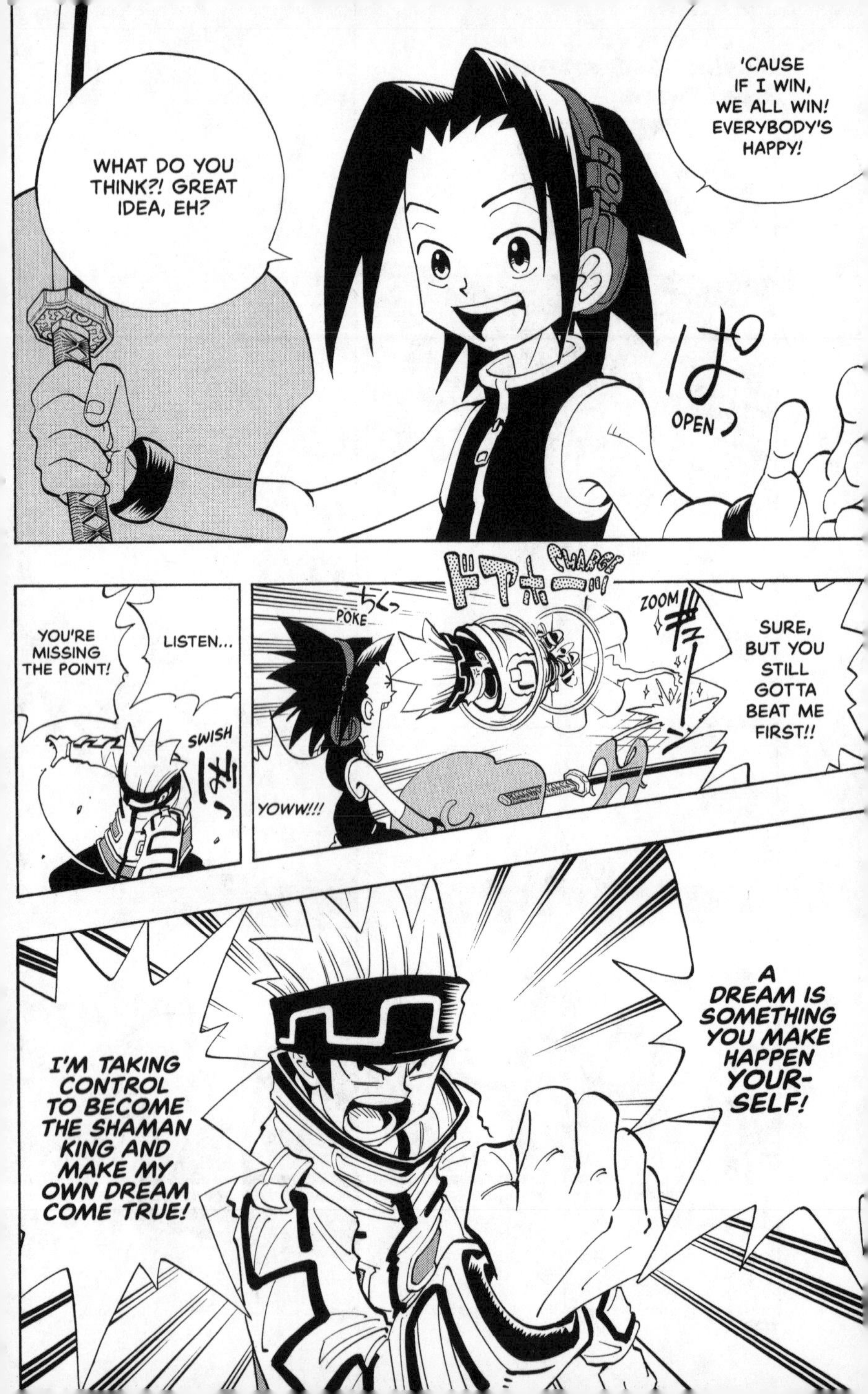
'CAUSE IF I WIN, WE ALL WIN! EVERYBODY'S HAPPY!
WHAT DO YOU THINK?! GREAT IDEA, EH?
OPEN
SURE, BUT YOU STILL GOTTA BEAT ME FIRST!!
ZOOM
CHARGE
POKE
YOWW!!!
LISTEN...
YOU'RE MISSING THE POINT!
SWISH
A DREAM IS SOMETHING YOU MAKE HAPPEN YOURSELF!
I'M TAKING CONTROL TO BECOME THE SHAMAN KING AND MAKE MY OWN DREAM COME TRUE!

Chapter 36:

Great Ghost, Great Sword

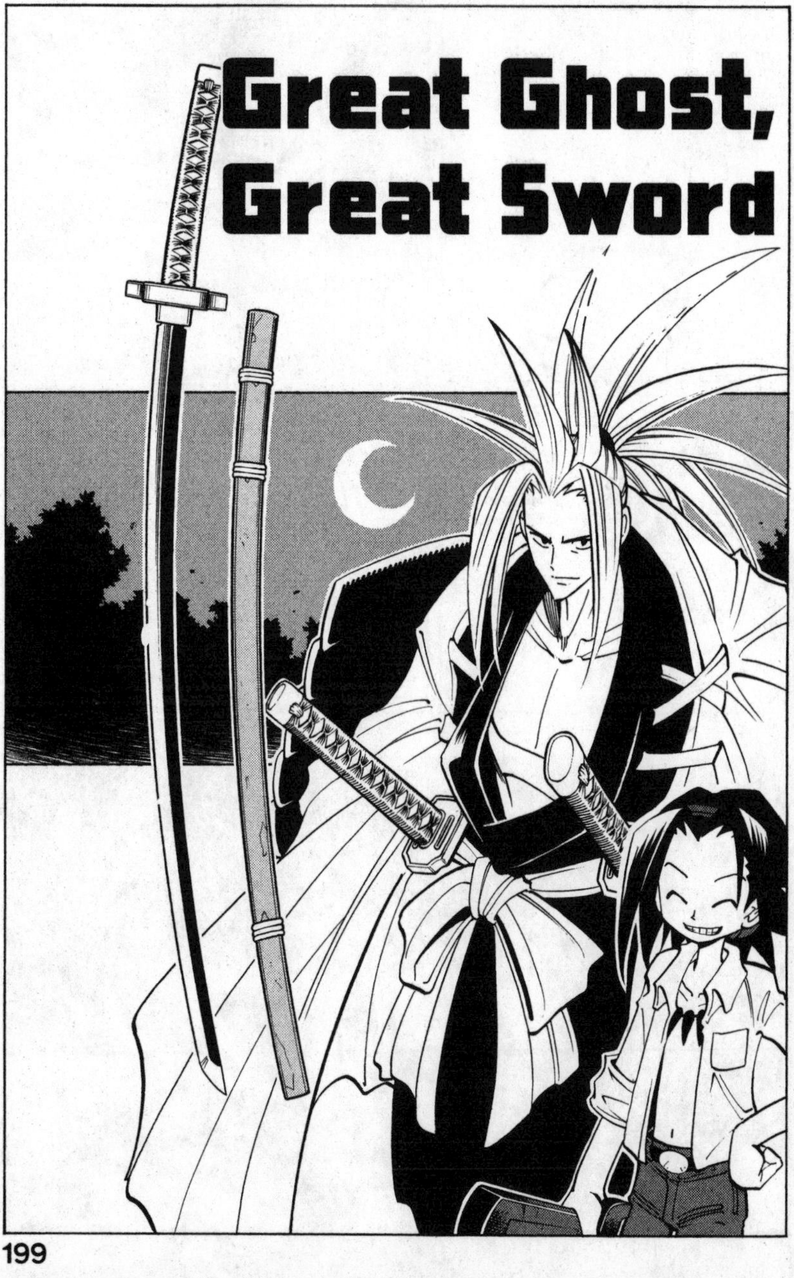

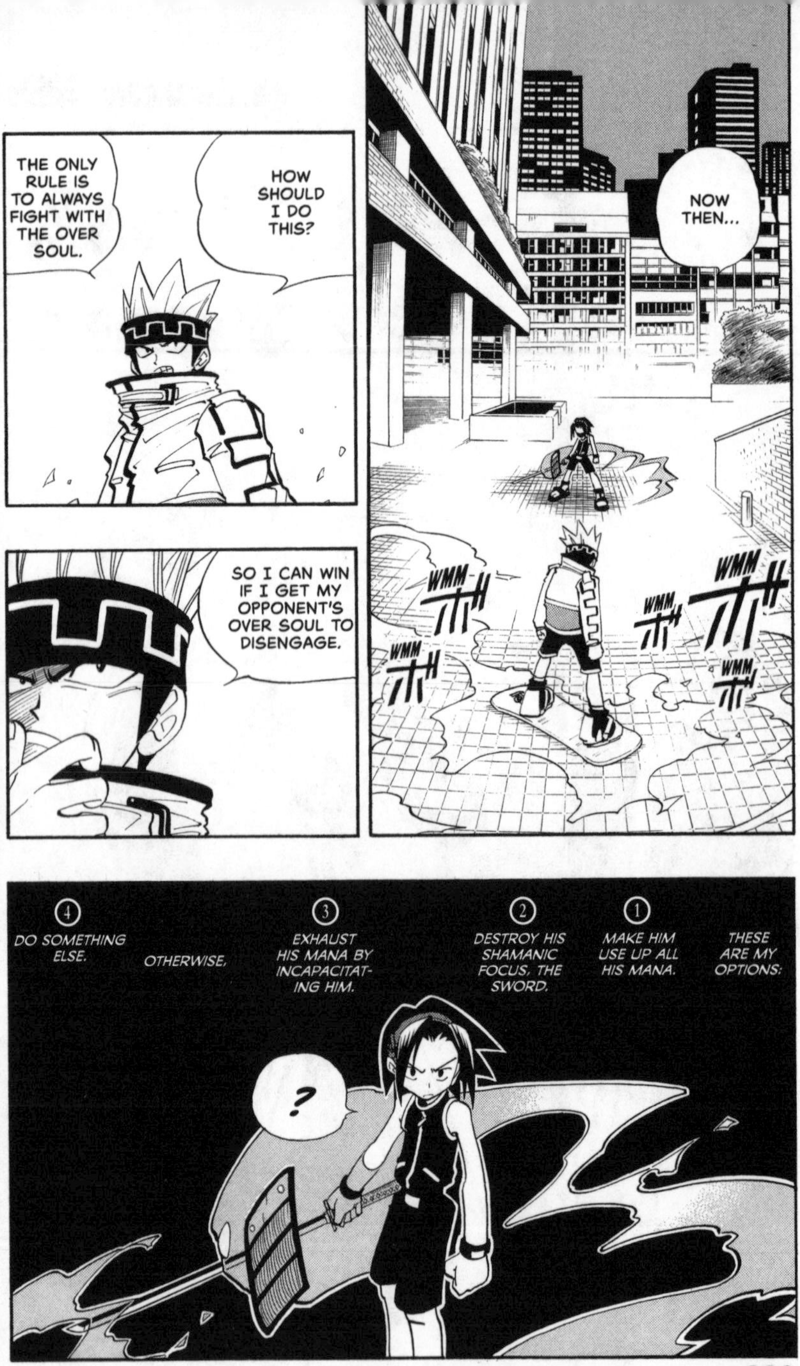
NOW THEN...
WMM
WMM
WMM
WMM-
WMM
HOW SHOULD I DO THIS?
THE ONLY RULE IS TO ALWAYS FIGHT WITH THE OVER SOUL.
SO I CAN WIN IF I GET MY OPPONENT'S OVER SOUL TO DISENGAGE.
THESE ARE MY OPTIONS:
① MAKE HIM USE UP ALL HIS MANA.
② DESTROY HIS SHAMANIC FOCUS, THE SWORD.
③ EXHAUST HIS MANA BY INCAPACITATING HIM.
OTHERWISE,
④ DO SOMETHING ELSE.
?

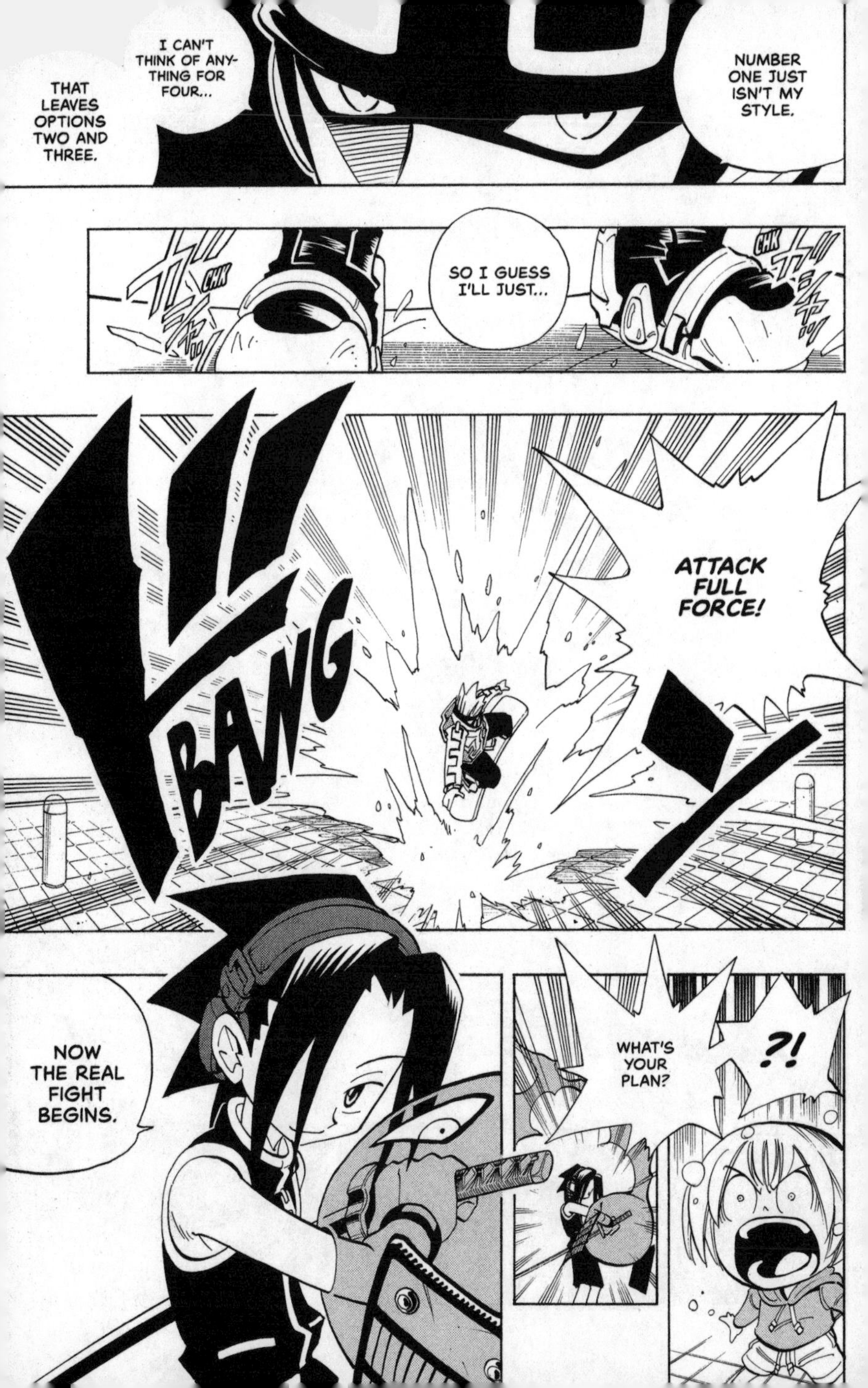
NUMBER ONE JUST ISN'T MY STYLE.
I CAN'T THINK OF ANY-THING FOR FOUR...
THAT LEAVES OPTIONS TWO AND THREE.
CHK
SO I GUESS I'LL JUST...
CHK
ATTACK FULL FORCE!
BANG
?!
WHAT'S YOUR PLAN?
NOW THE REAL FIGHT BEGINS.

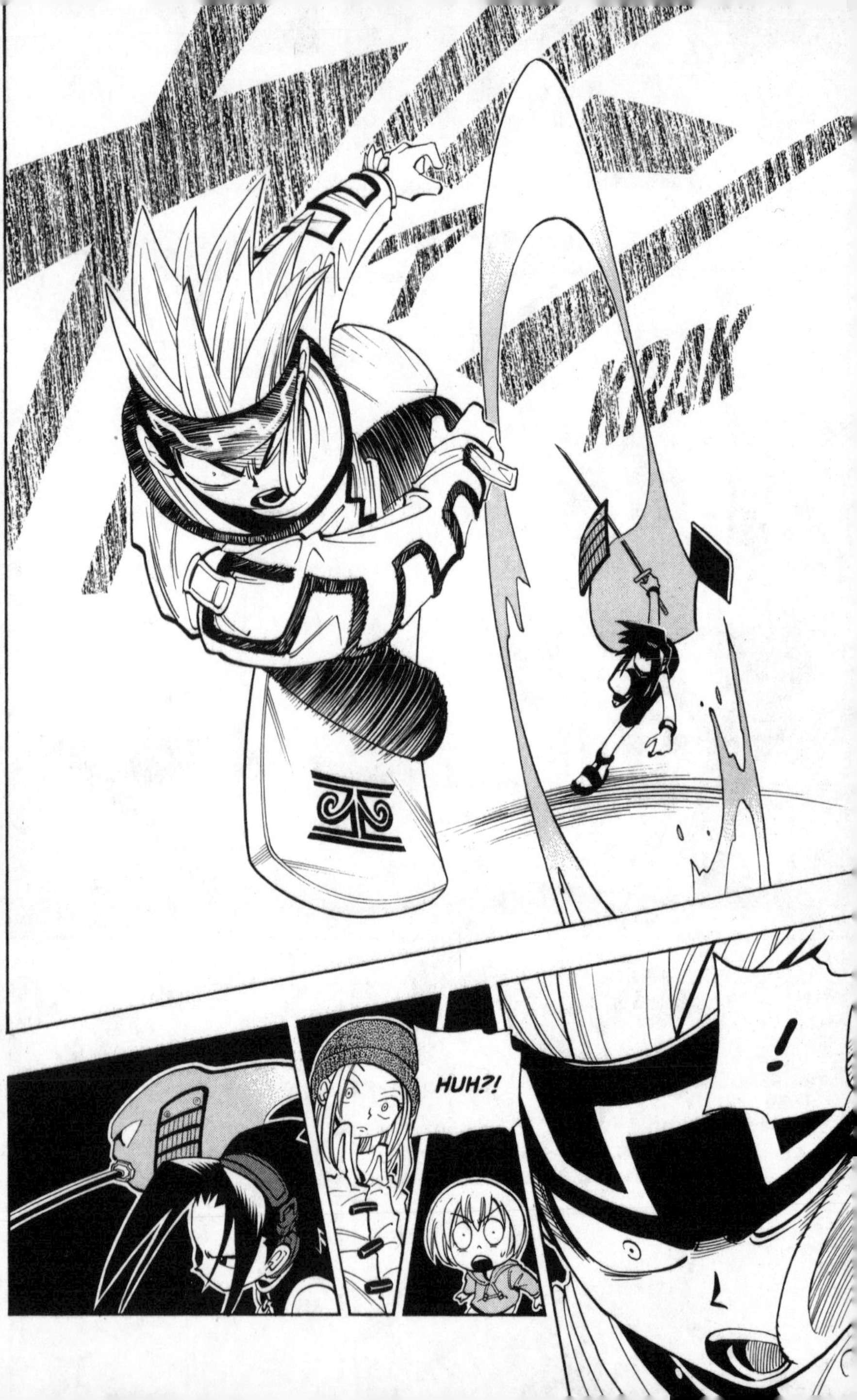
KRAK
!
HUH?!

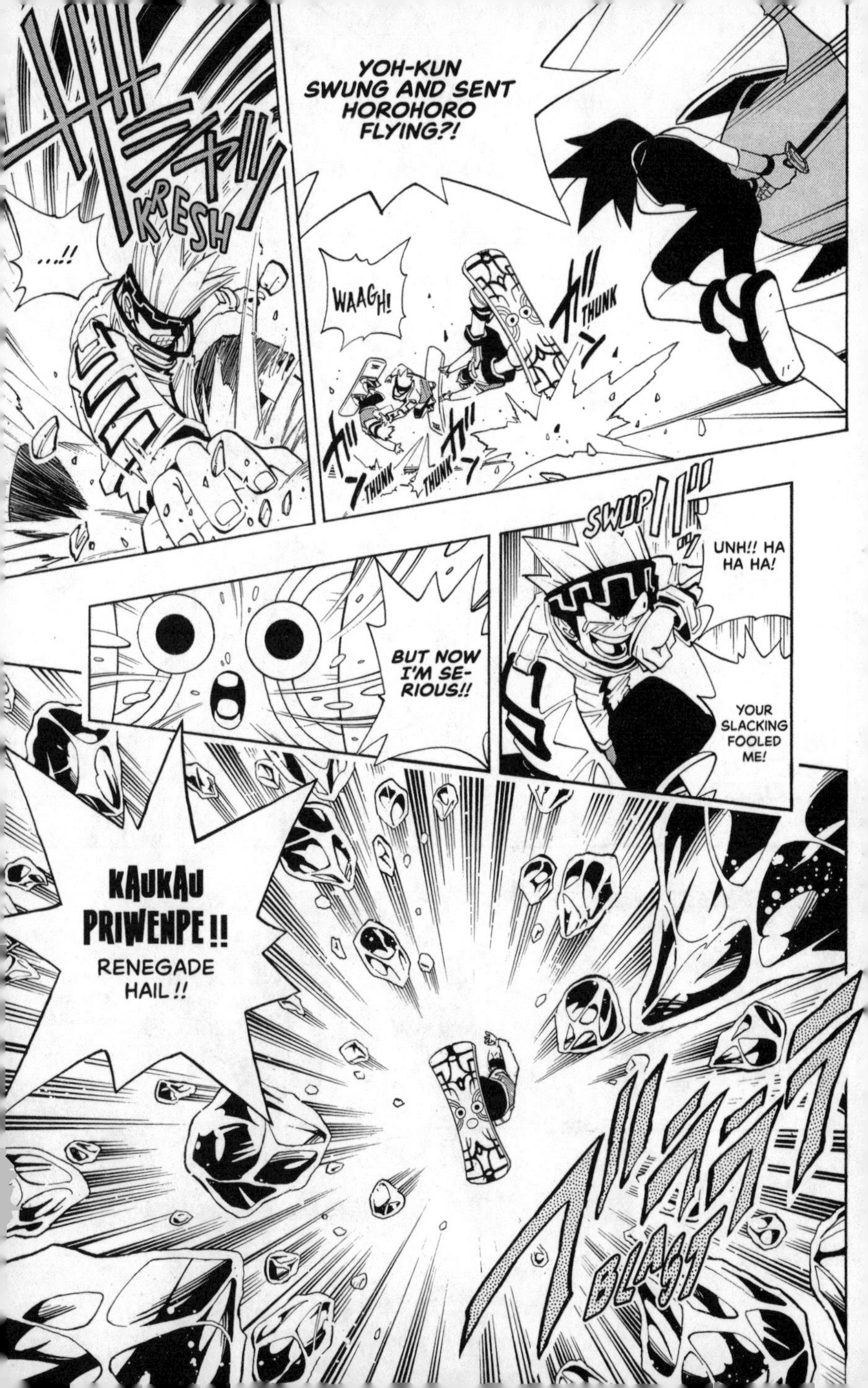
YOH-KUN SWUNG AND SENT HOROHORO FLYING?!
THUNK
WAAGH!
THUNK
THUNK
KRESH
...!!
SWUP
UNH!! HA HA HA!
YOUR SLACKING FOOLED ME!
BUT NOW I'M SE-RIOUS!!
KAUKAU PRIWENPE!!
RENEGADE HAIL!!
BLAST

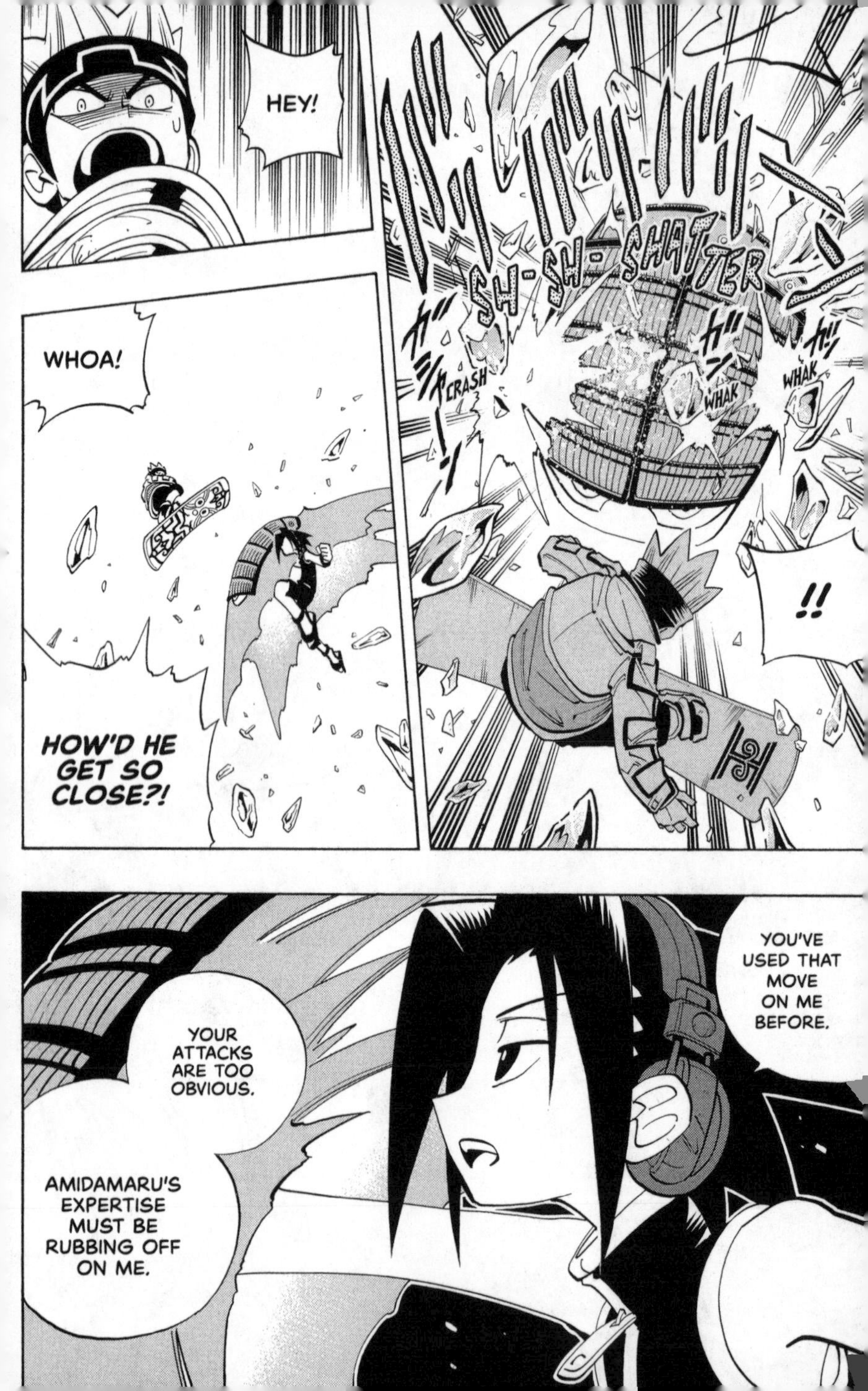
SH-SH-SHATTER
WHAK
WHAK
CRASH
!!
HEY!
WHOA!
HOW'D HE GET SO CLOSE?!
YOU'VE USED THAT MOVE ON ME BEFORE.
YOUR ATTACKS ARE TOO OBVIOUS.
AMIDAMARU'S EXPERTISE MUST BE RUBBING OFF ON ME.

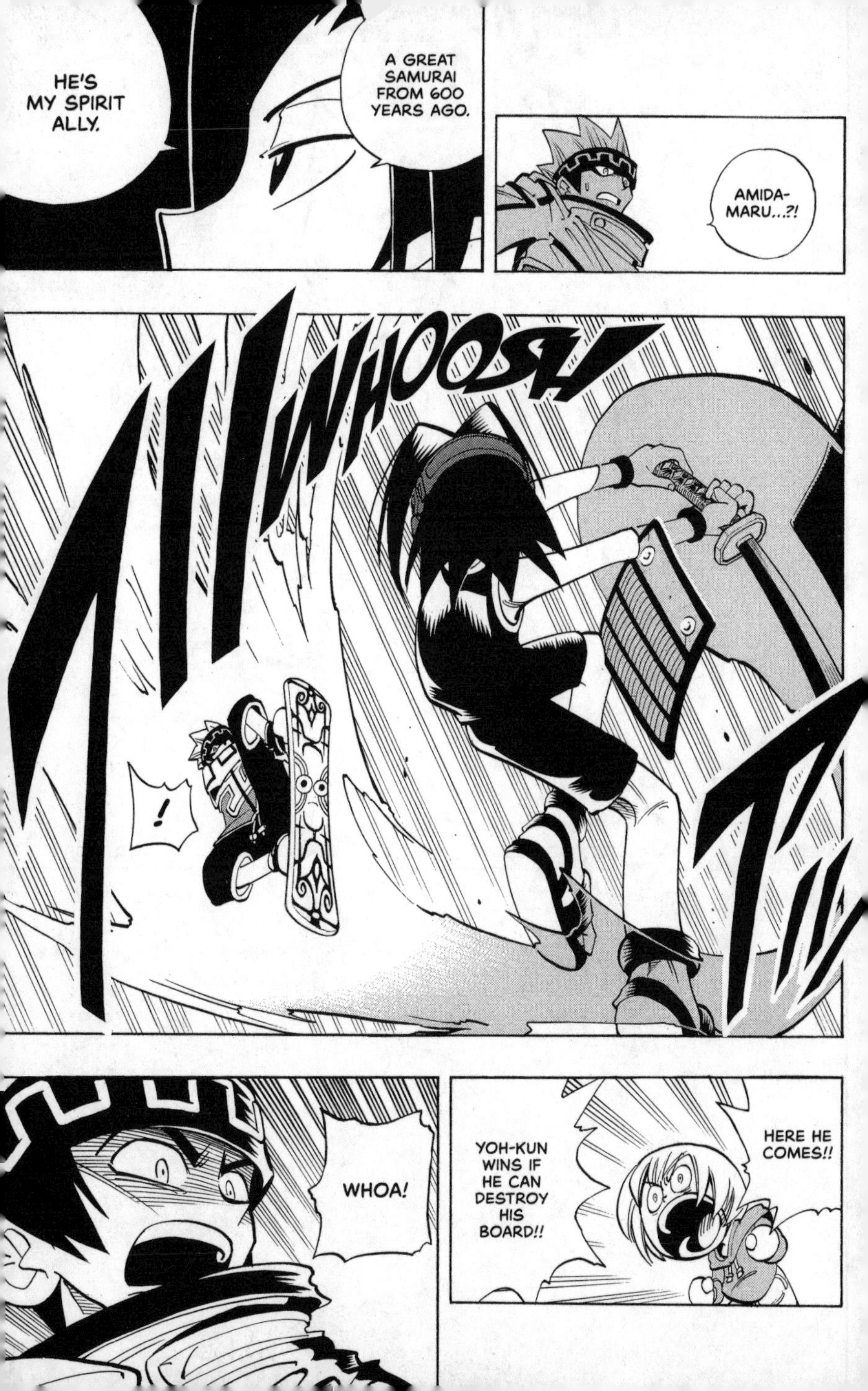
AMIDA-MARU...?!
A GREAT SAMURAI FROM 600 YEARS AGO.
HE'S MY SPIRIT ALLY.
WHOOSH
!
HERE HE COMES!!
YOH-KUN WINS IF HE CAN DESTROY HIS BOARD!!
WHOA!

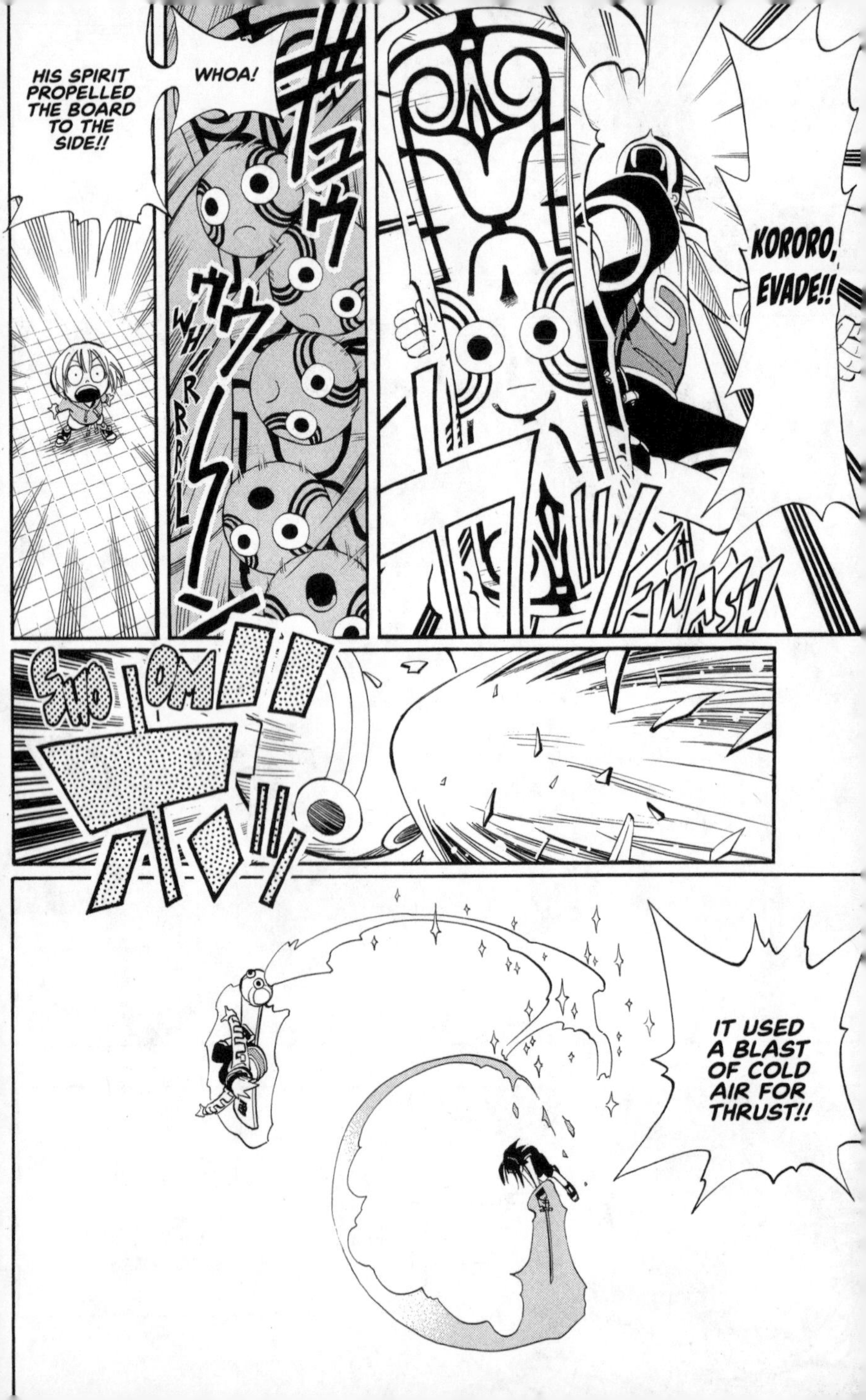
KORORO, EVADE!!
FWASH
WHOA!
WHIRRRL
HIS SPIRIT PROPELLED THE BOARD TO THE SIDE!!
SWOOM!!
IT USED A BLAST OF COLD AIR FOR THRUST!!

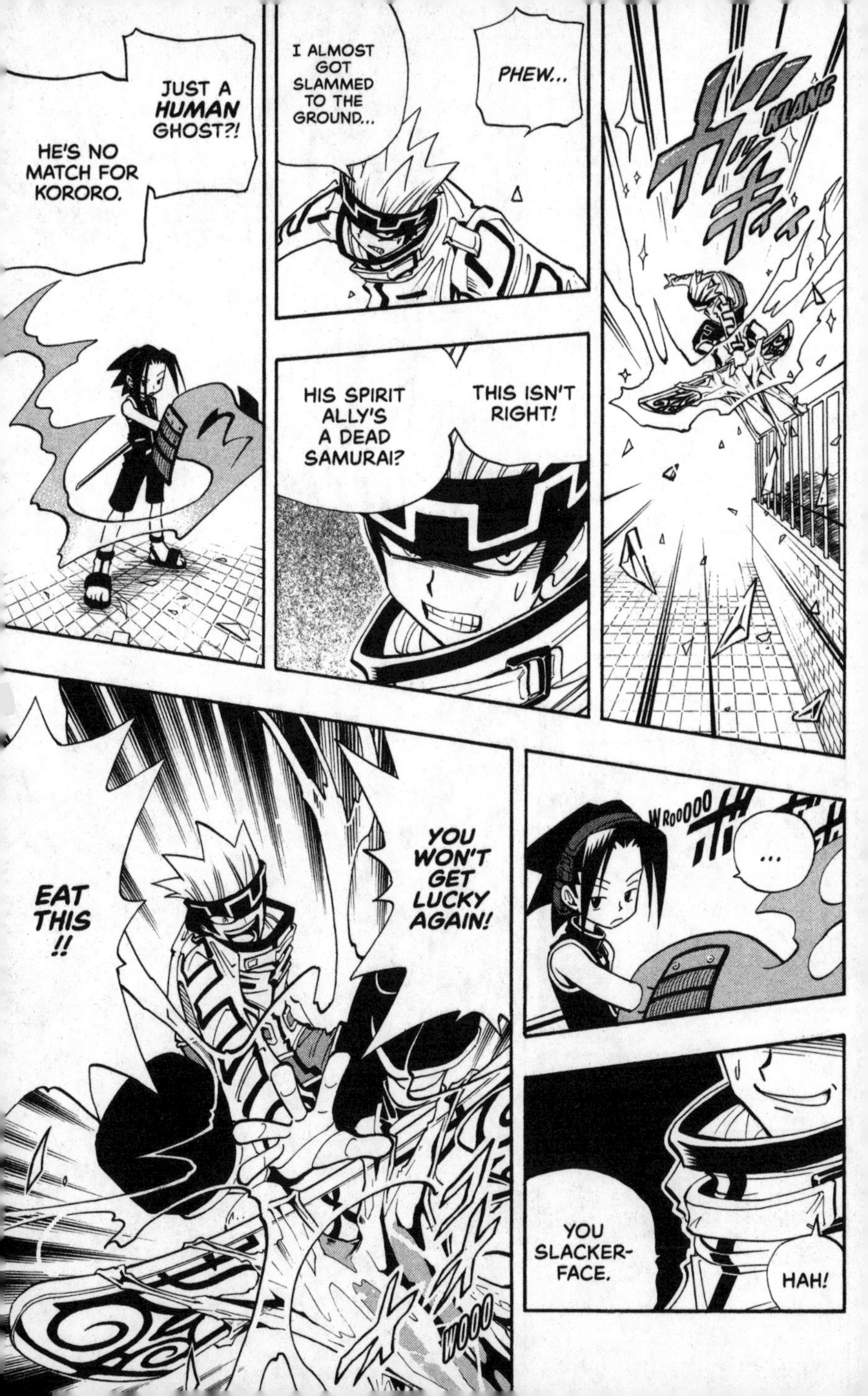
KLANG
PHEW...
I ALMOST GOT SLAMMED TO THE GROUND...
THIS ISN'T RIGHT!
HIS SPIRIT ALLY'S A DEAD SAMURAI?
JUST A HUMAN GHOST?!
HE'S NO MATCH FOR KORORO.
WROOOOO
...
HAH!
YOU SLACKER-FACE.
YOU WON'T GET LUCKY AGAIN!
EAT THIS!!
WOOO

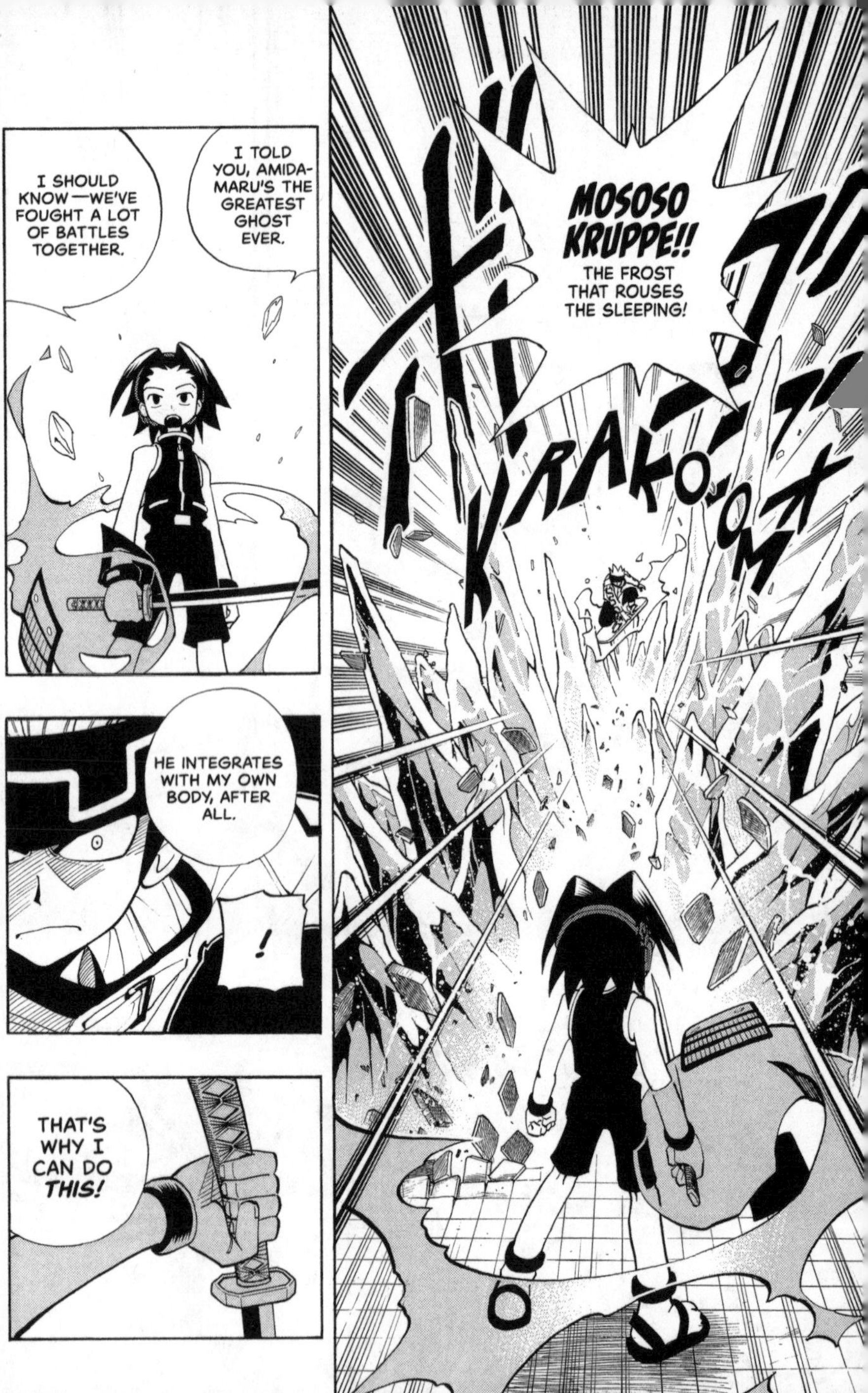
MOSOSO KRUPPE!!
THE FROST THAT ROUSES THE SLEEPING!
KRAKOOOM
I TOLD YOU, AMIDA-MARU'S THE GREATEST GHOST EVER.
I SHOULD KNOW—WE'VE FOUGHT A LOT OF BATTLES TOGETHER.
HE INTEGRATES WITH MY OWN BODY, AFTER ALL.
!
THAT'S WHY I CAN DO *THIS!*

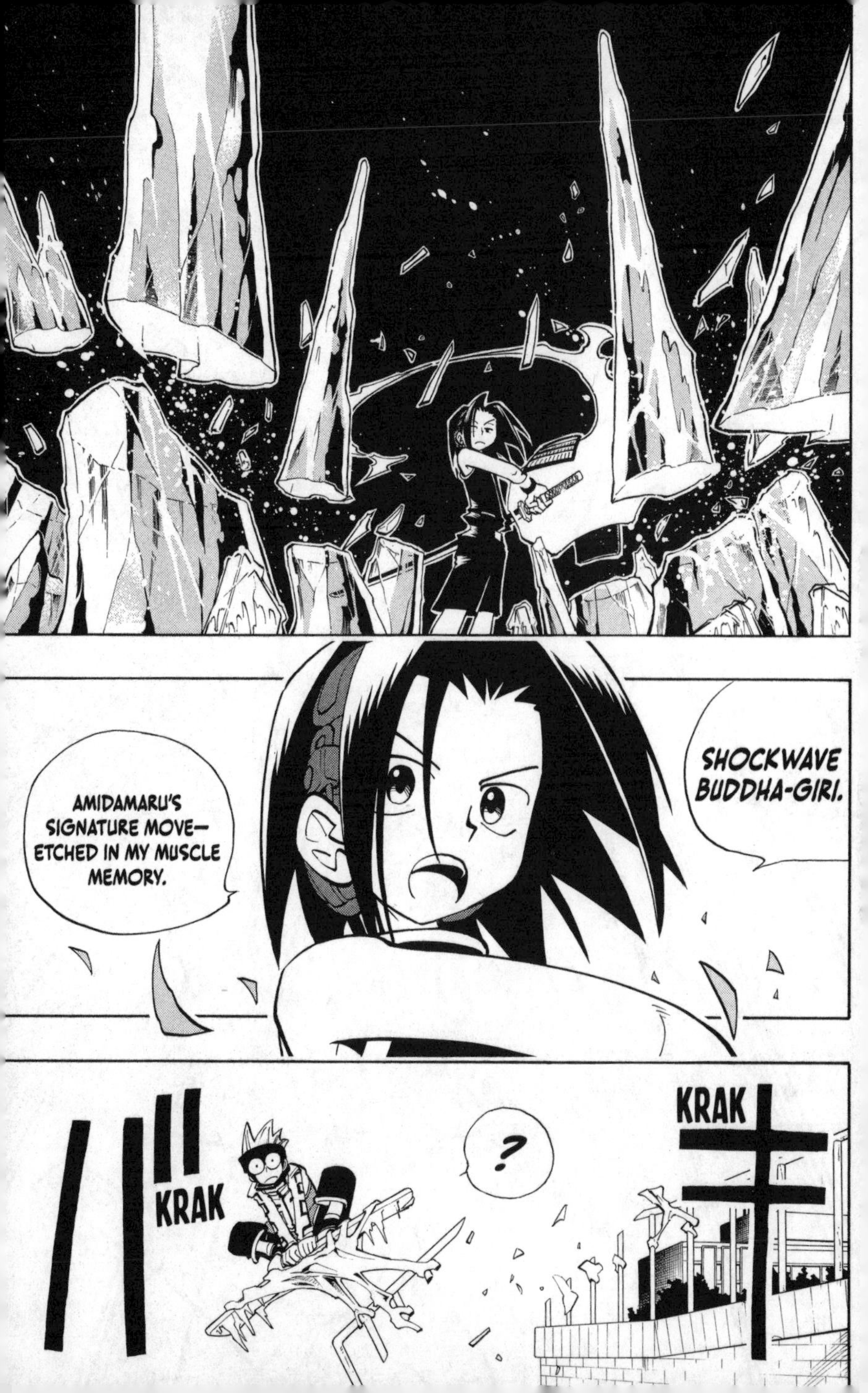
SHOCKWAVE BUDDHA-GIRI.
AMIDAMARU'S SIGNATURE MOVE—ETCHED IN MY MUSCLE MEMORY.
KRAK
?
KRAK

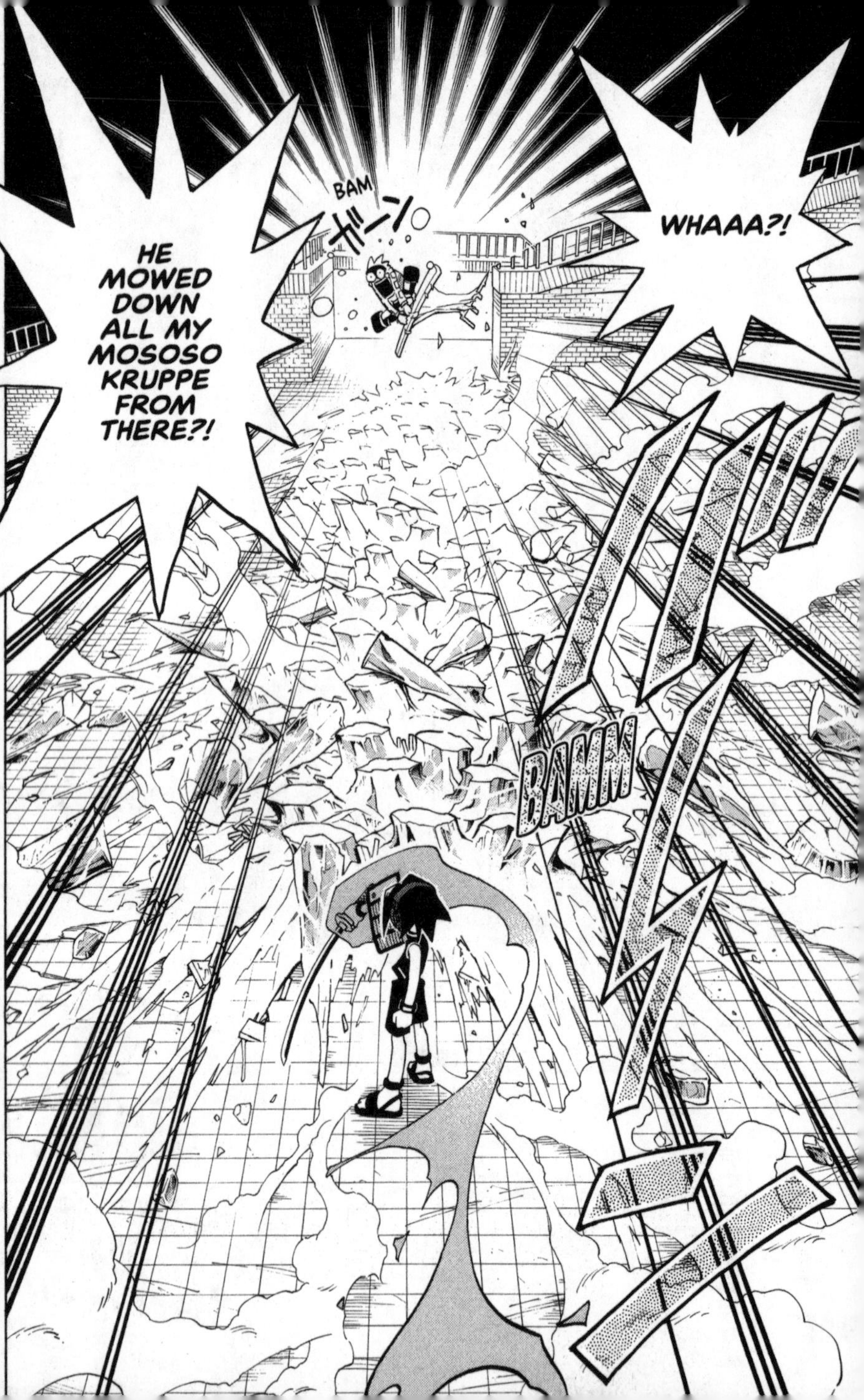
WHAAA?!
BAM
ガーン!
HE MOWED DOWN ALL MY MOSOSO KRUPPE FROM THERE?!
BAMM

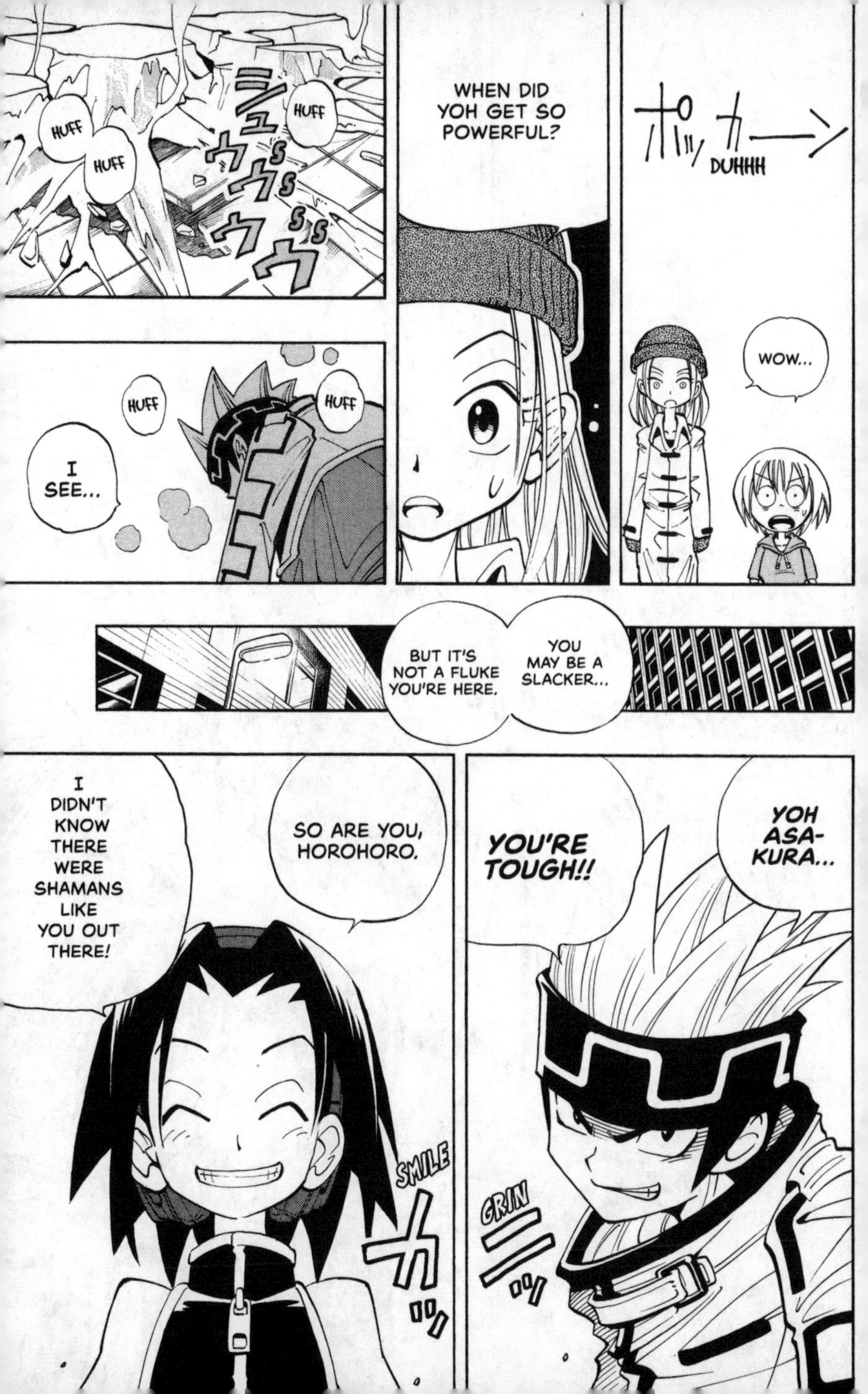
ポッカーン
DUHHH
WOW...
WHEN DID YOH GET SO POWERFUL?
HUFF
HUFF
HUFF
シュウウウウ
SSSSS
HUFF
HUFF
I SEE...
YOU MAY BE A SLACKER...
BUT IT'S NOT A FLUKE YOU'RE HERE.
YOH ASA-KURA...
YOU'RE TOUGH!!
GRIN
SO ARE YOU, HOROHORO.
I DIDN'T KNOW THERE WERE SHAMANS LIKE YOU OUT THERE!
SMILE

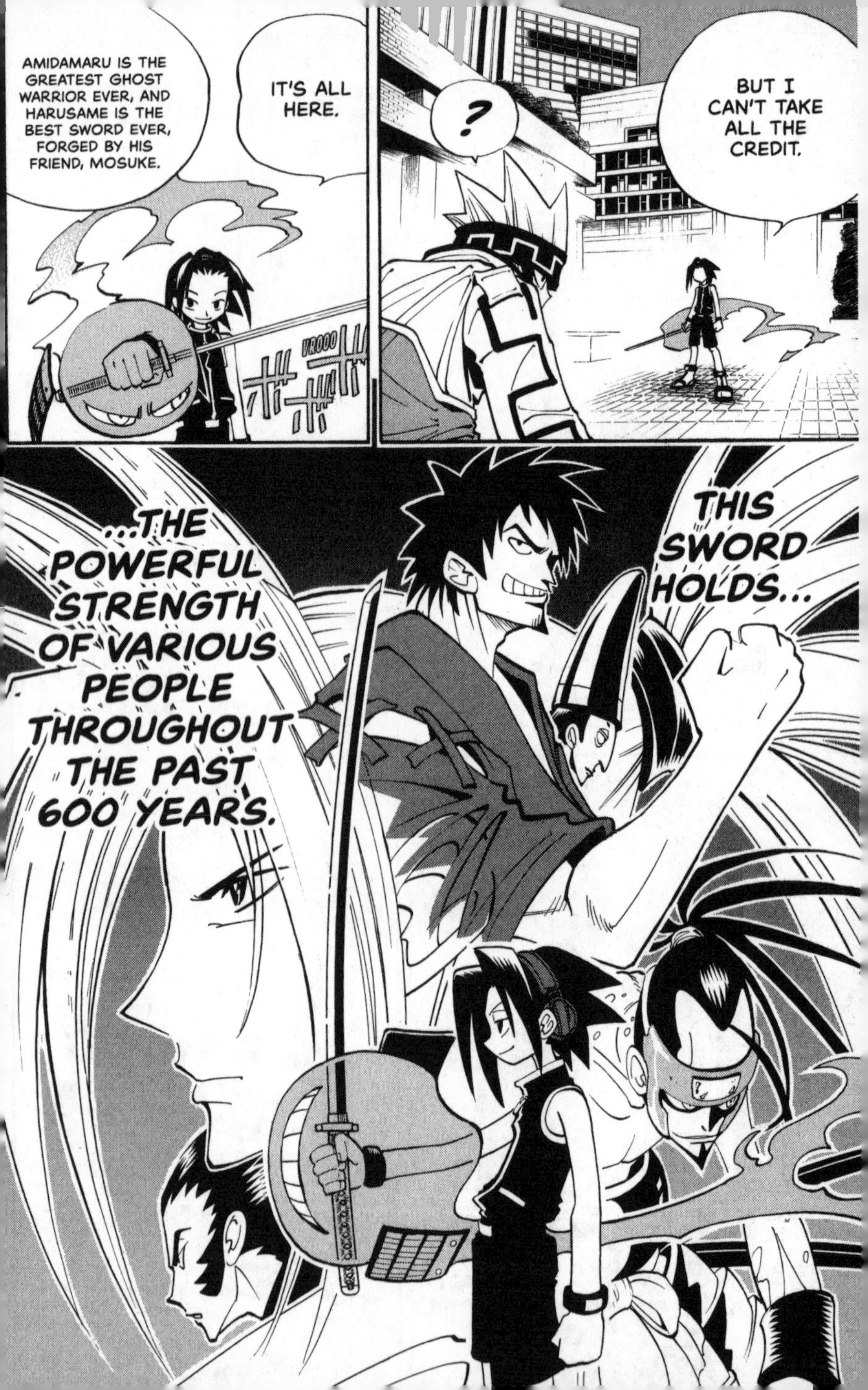
BUT I CAN'T TAKE ALL THE CREDIT.
?
IT'S ALL HERE.
AMIDAMARU IS THE GREATEST GHOST WARRIOR EVER, AND HARUSAME IS THE BEST SWORD EVER, FORGED BY HIS FRIEND, MOSUKE.
VROOO
THIS SWORD HOLDS...
...THE POWERFUL STRENGTH OF VARIOUS PEOPLE THROUGHOUT THE PAST 600 YEARS.

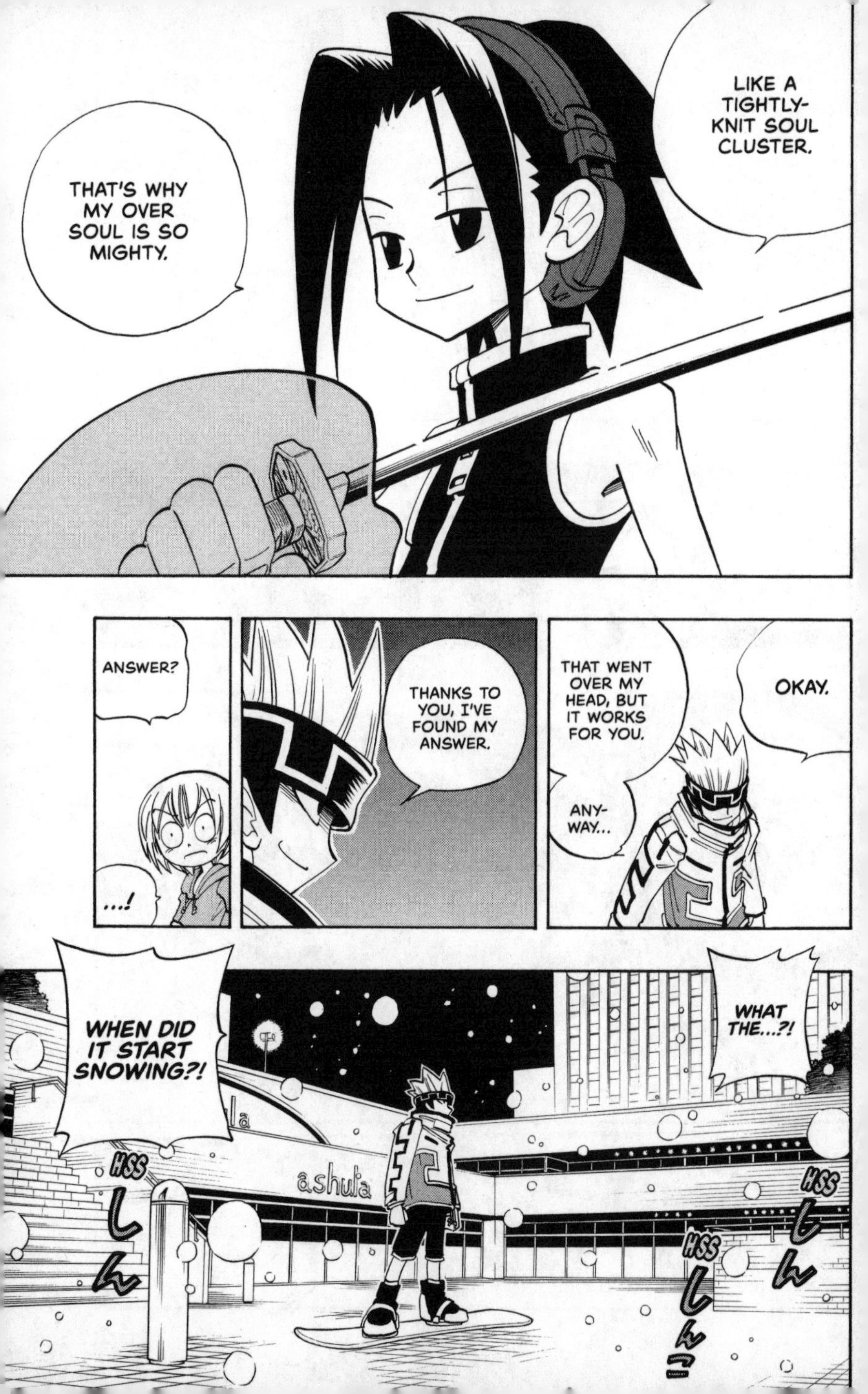
LIKE A TIGHTLY-KNIT SOUL CLUSTER.
THAT'S WHY MY OVER SOUL IS SO MIGHTY.
OKAY.
THAT WENT OVER MY HEAD, BUT IT WORKS FOR YOU.
ANY-WAY...
THANKS TO YOU, I'VE FOUND MY ANSWER.
ANSWER?
...!
WHAT THE...?!
WHEN DID IT START SNOWING?!
HSS
HSS
ashula
HSS

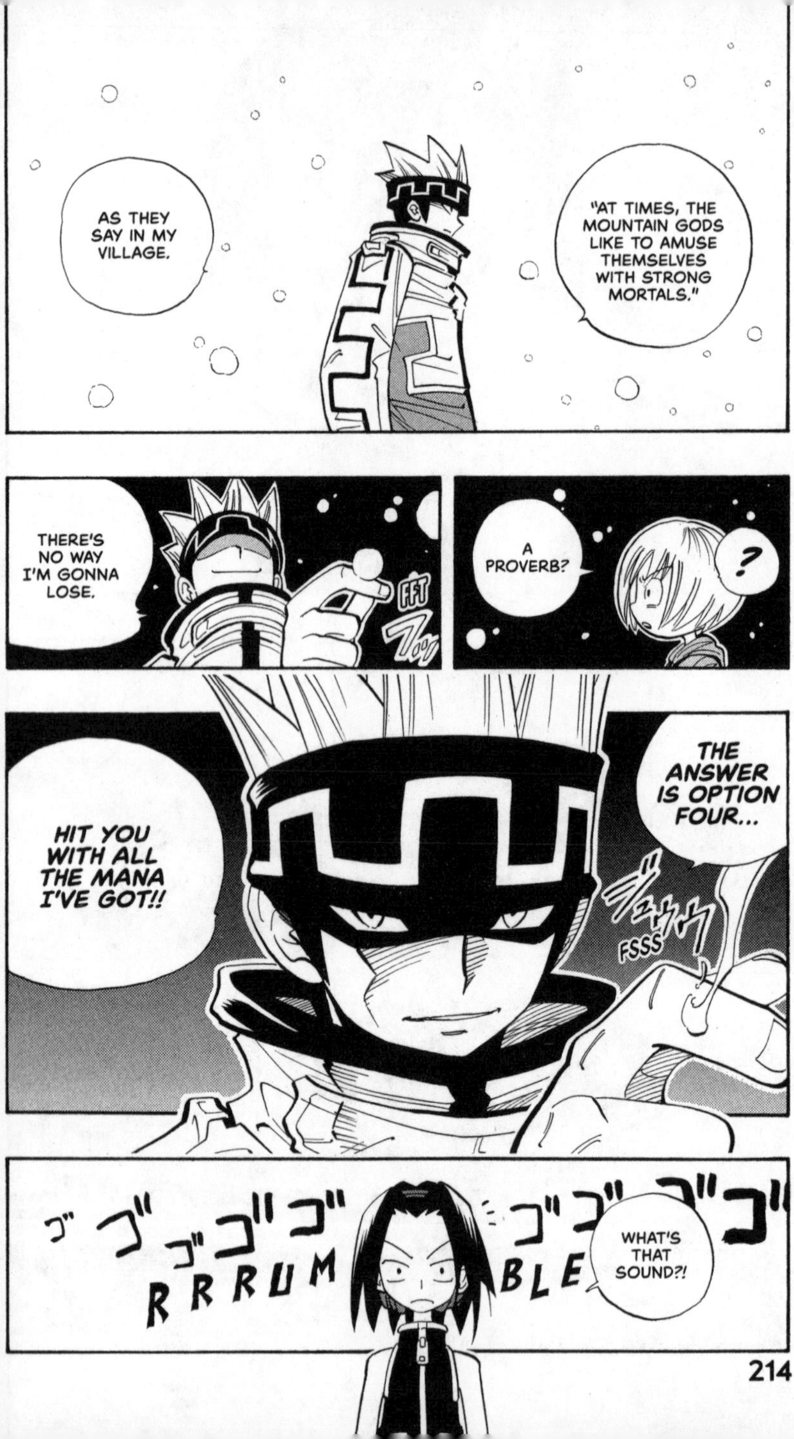
"AT TIMES, THE MOUNTAIN GODS LIKE TO AMUSE THEMSELVES WITH STRONG MORTALS."
AS THEY SAY IN MY VILLAGE.
?
A PROVERB?
THERE'S NO WAY I'M GONNA LOSE.
FFT
THE ANSWER IS OPTION FOUR...
FSSS
HIT YOU WITH ALL THE MANA I'VE GOT!!
WHAT'S THAT SOUND?!
RRRUMBLE

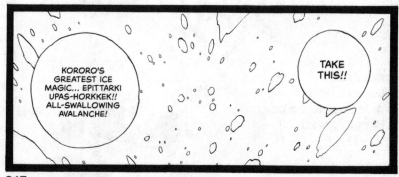

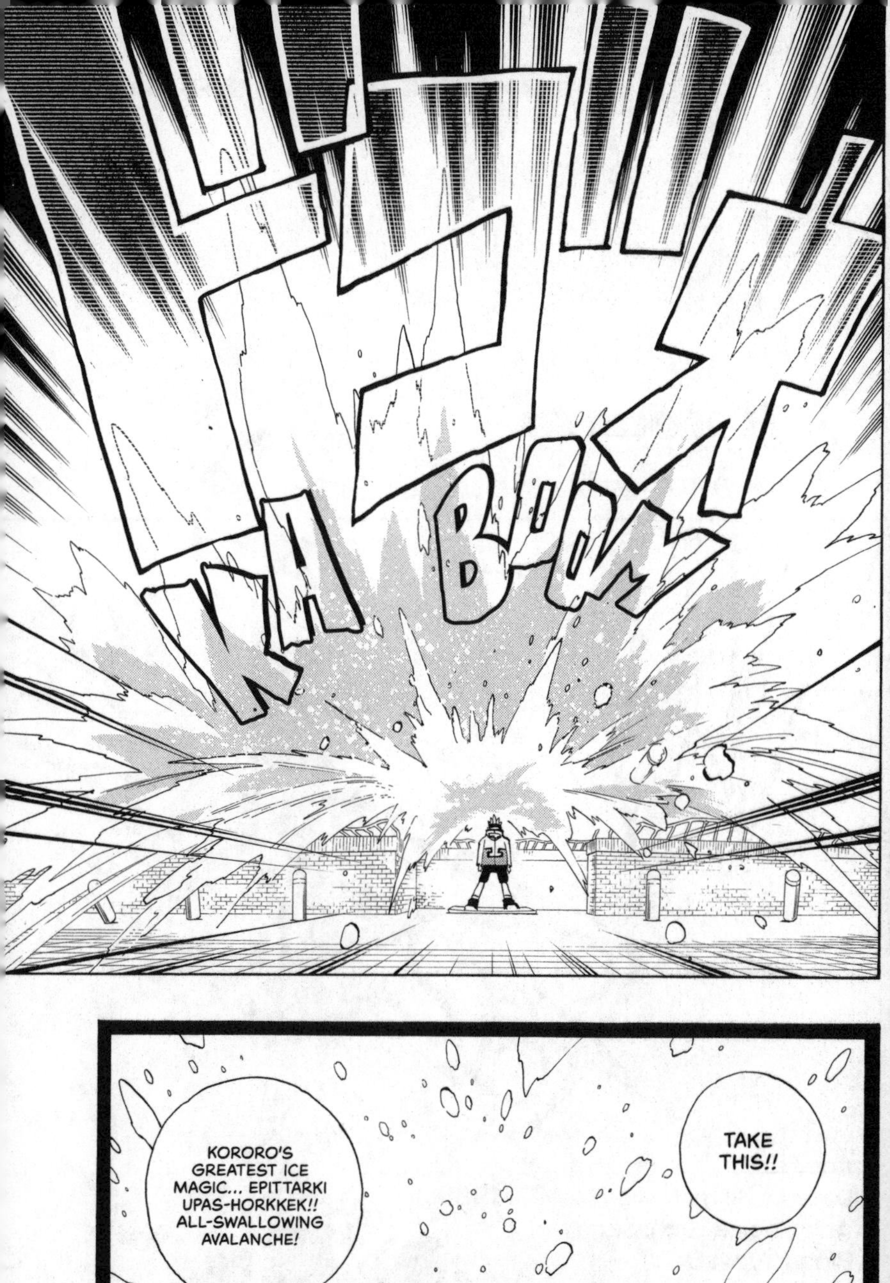
KA-BOOM
TAKE THIS!!
KORORO'S GREATEST ICE MAGIC... EPITTARKI UPAS-HORKKEK!! ALL-SWALLOWING AVALANCHE!

Horohoro

August 1999

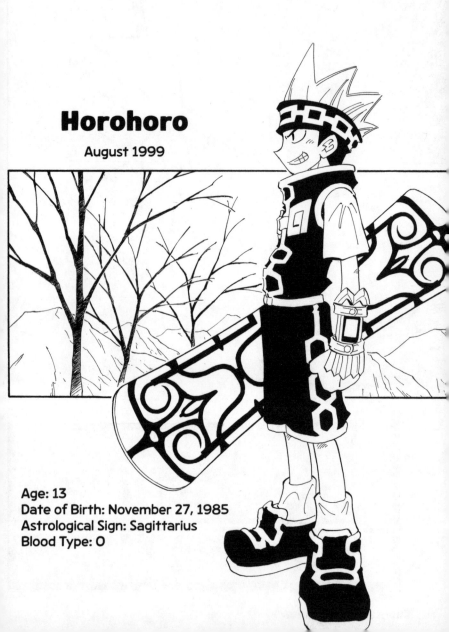

Age: 13
Date of Birth: November 27, 1985
Astrological Sign: Sagittarius
Blood Type: O

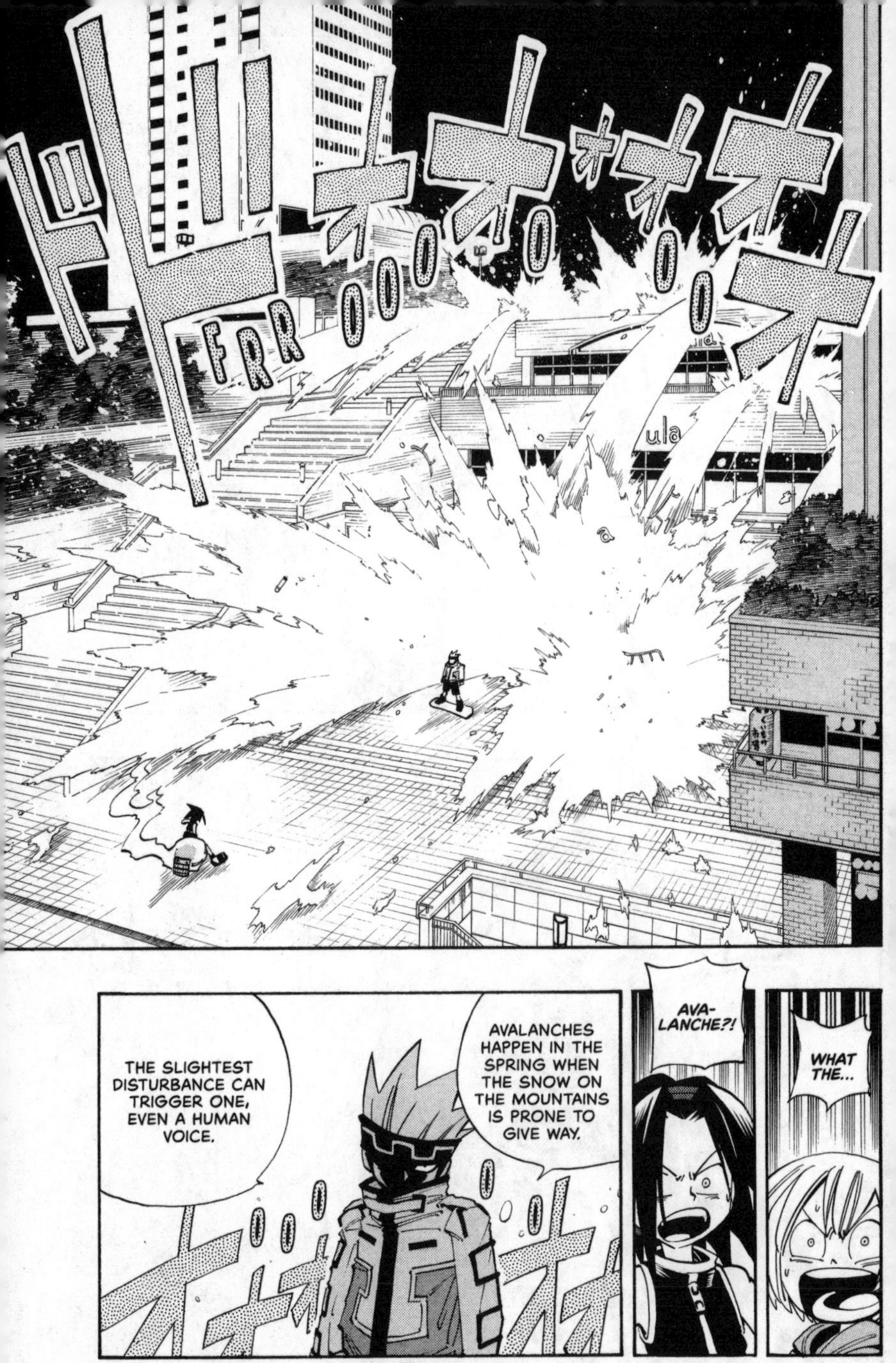
FRROOOOOOO
WHAT THE...
AVA-LANCHE?!
AVALANCHES HAPPEN IN THE SPRING WHEN THE SNOW ON THE MOUNTAINS IS PRONE TO GIVE WAY.
THE SLIGHTEST DISTURBANCE CAN TRIGGER ONE, EVEN A HUMAN VOICE.

Chapter 37: Decision

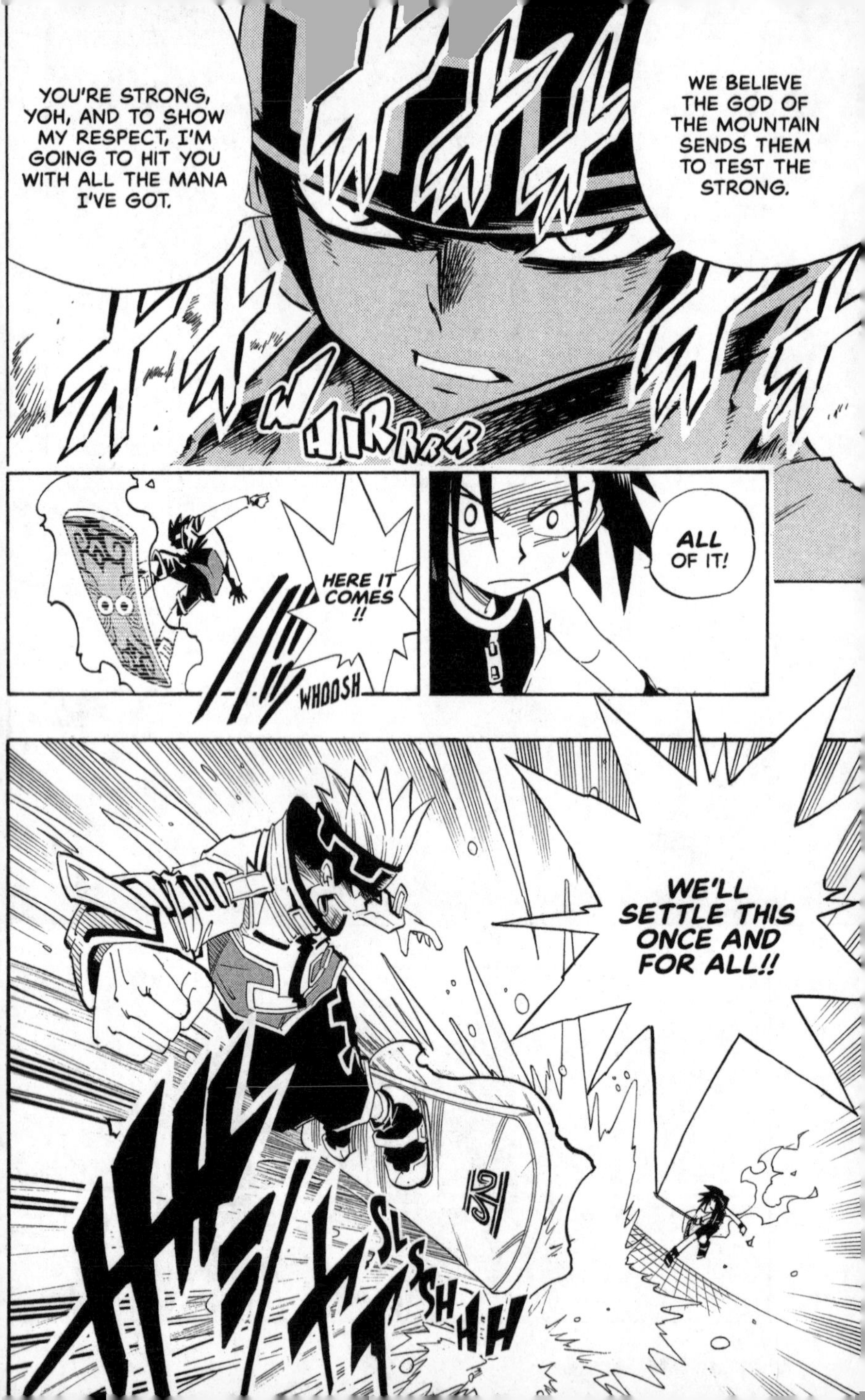
WE BELIEVE THE GOD OF THE MOUNTAIN SENDS THEM TO TEST THE STRONG.
YOU'RE STRONG, YOH, AND TO SHOW MY RESPECT, I'M GOING TO HIT YOU WITH ALL THE MANA I'VE GOT.
WHIRRRRR
ALL OF IT!
HERE IT COMES!!
WHOOSH
WE'LL SETTLE THIS ONCE AND FOR ALL!!
SLSSHHH

Chapter 37: Decision

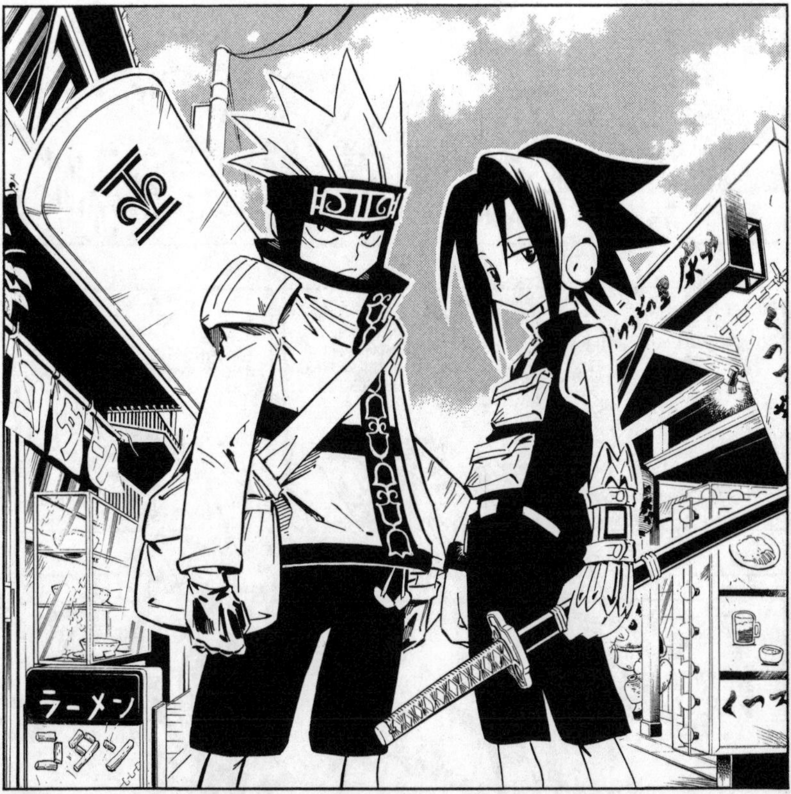
ラーメン
コタン

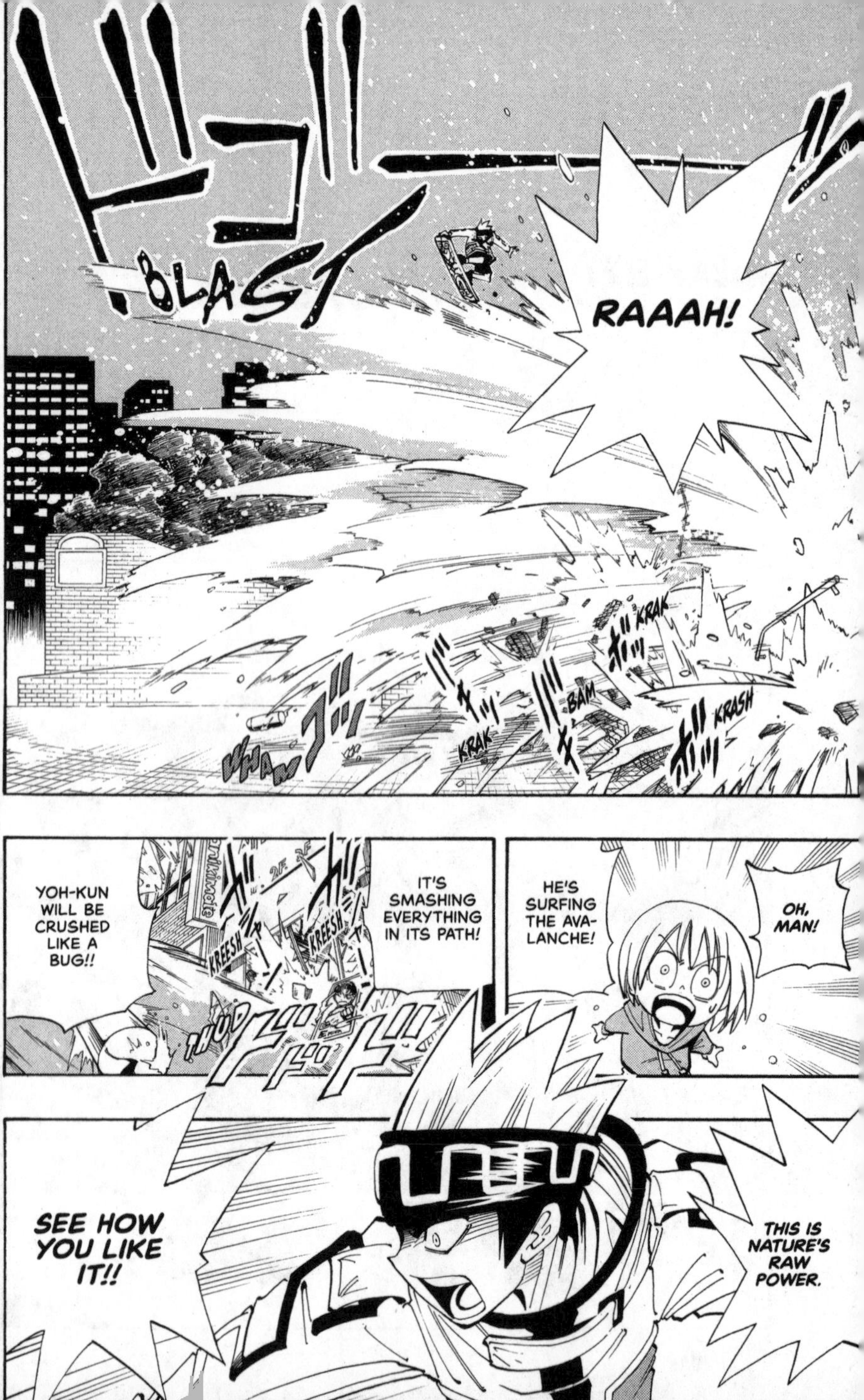
RAAAH!
BLAST
KRAK
KRASH
BAM
KRAK
WHAM
OH, MAN!
HE'S SURFING THE AVA-LANCHE!
IT'S SMASHING EVERYTHING IN ITS PATH!
KREESH
KREESH
YOH-KUN WILL BE CRUSHED LIKE A BUG!!
THUD
THIS IS NATURE'S RAW POWER.
SEE HOW YOU LIKE IT!!

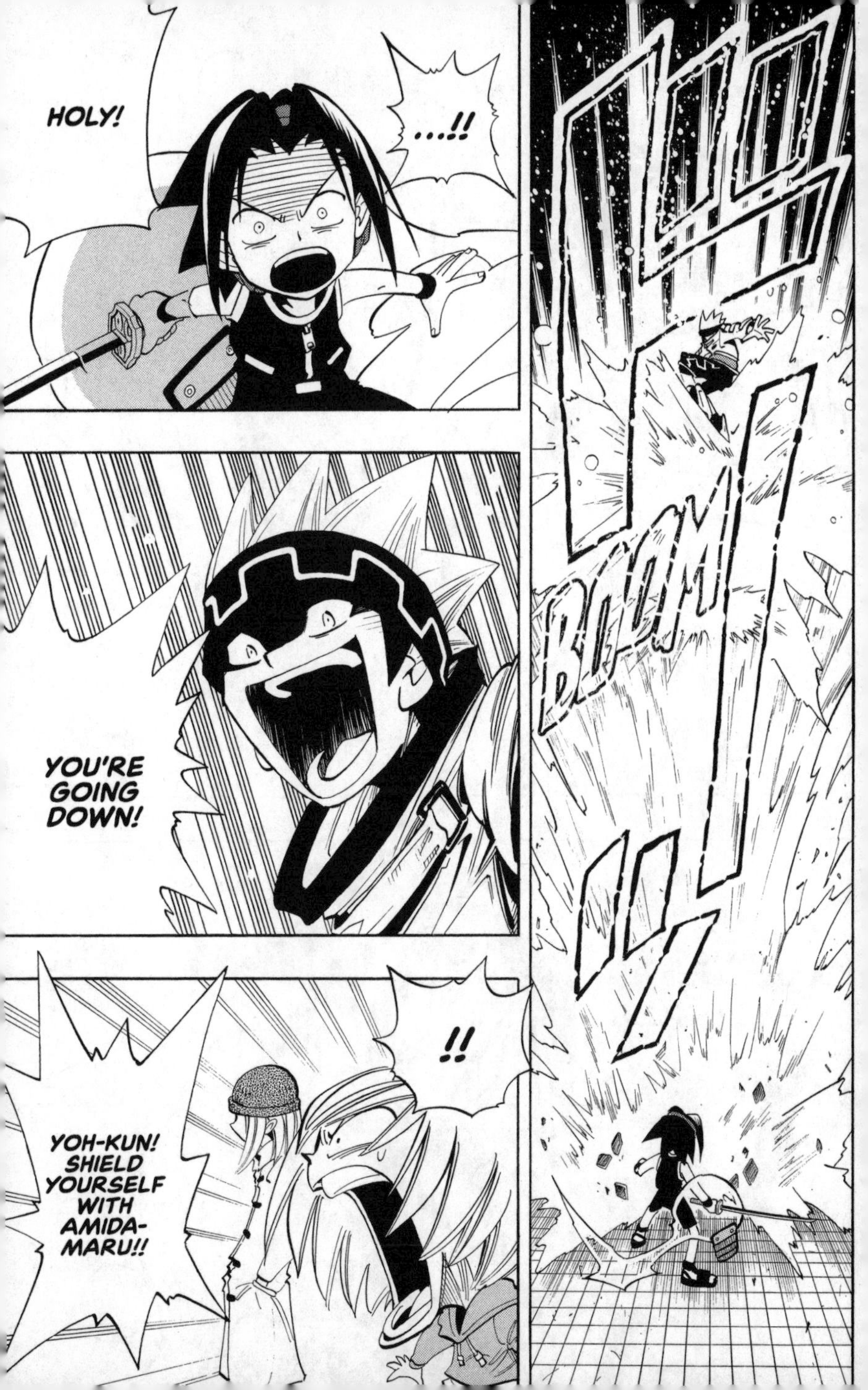
BOOM
...!!
HOLY!
YOU'RE GOING DOWN!
!!
YOH-KUN! SHIELD YOURSELF WITH AMIDA-MARU!!

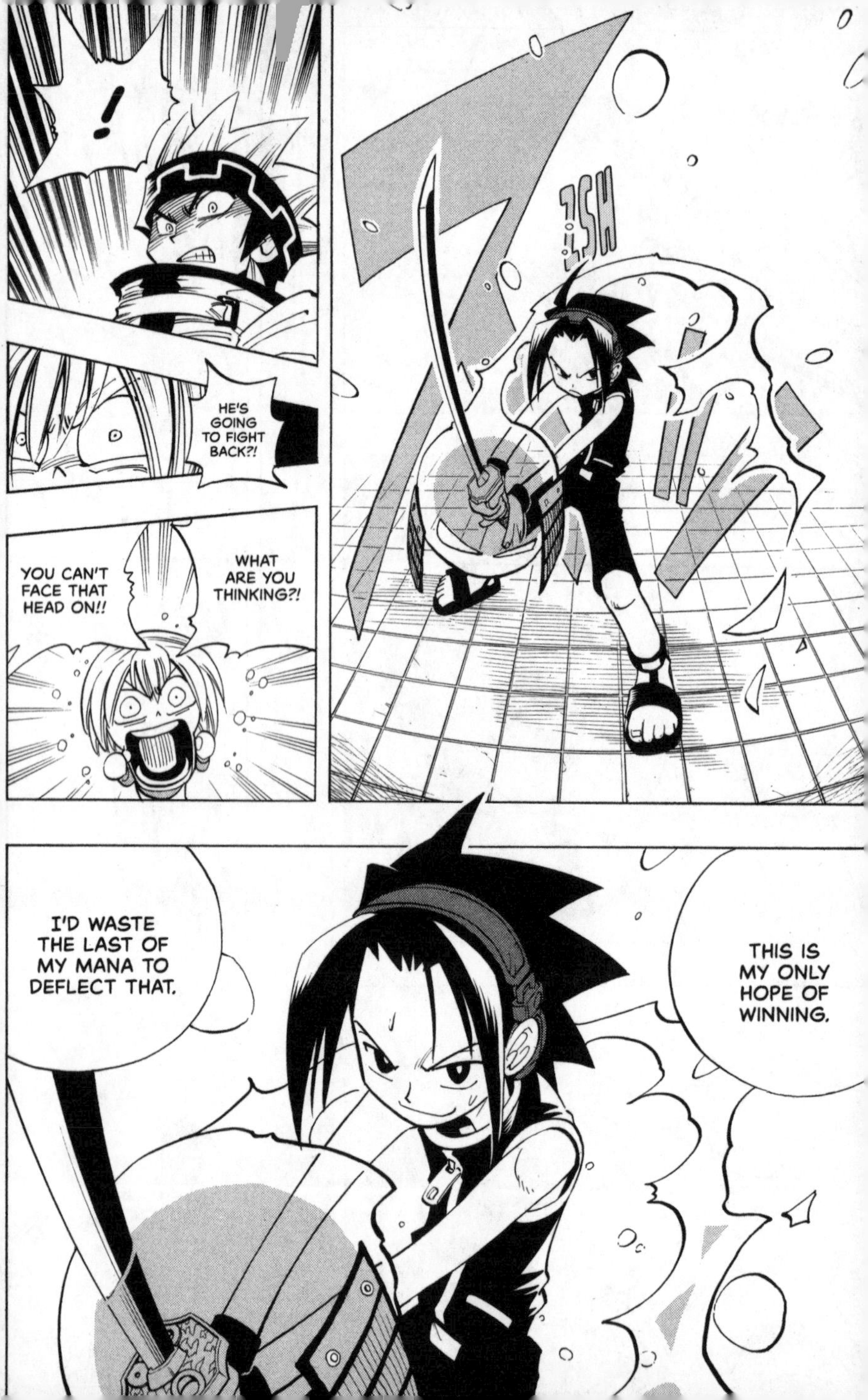
!
HE'S GOING TO FIGHT BACK?!
WHAT ARE YOU THINKING?!
YOU CAN'T FACE THAT HEAD ON!!
THIS IS MY ONLY HOPE OF WINNING.
I'D WASTE THE LAST OF MY MANA TO DEFLECT THAT.

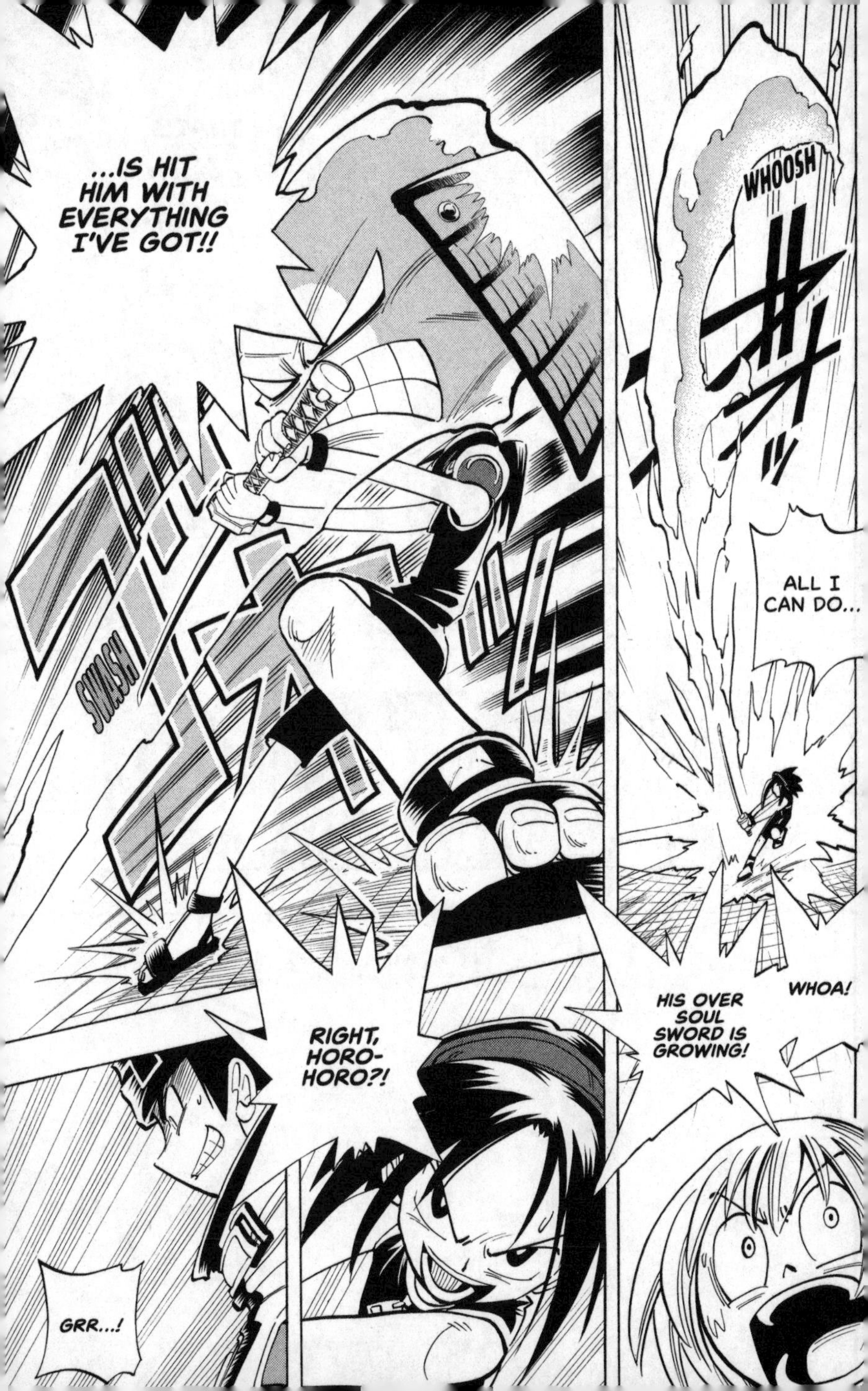
WHOOSH
ALL I CAN DO...
...IS HIT HIM WITH EVERYTHING I'VE GOT!!
SWASH
WHOA!
HIS OVER SOUL SWORD IS GROWING!
RIGHT, HORO-HORO?!
GRR...!

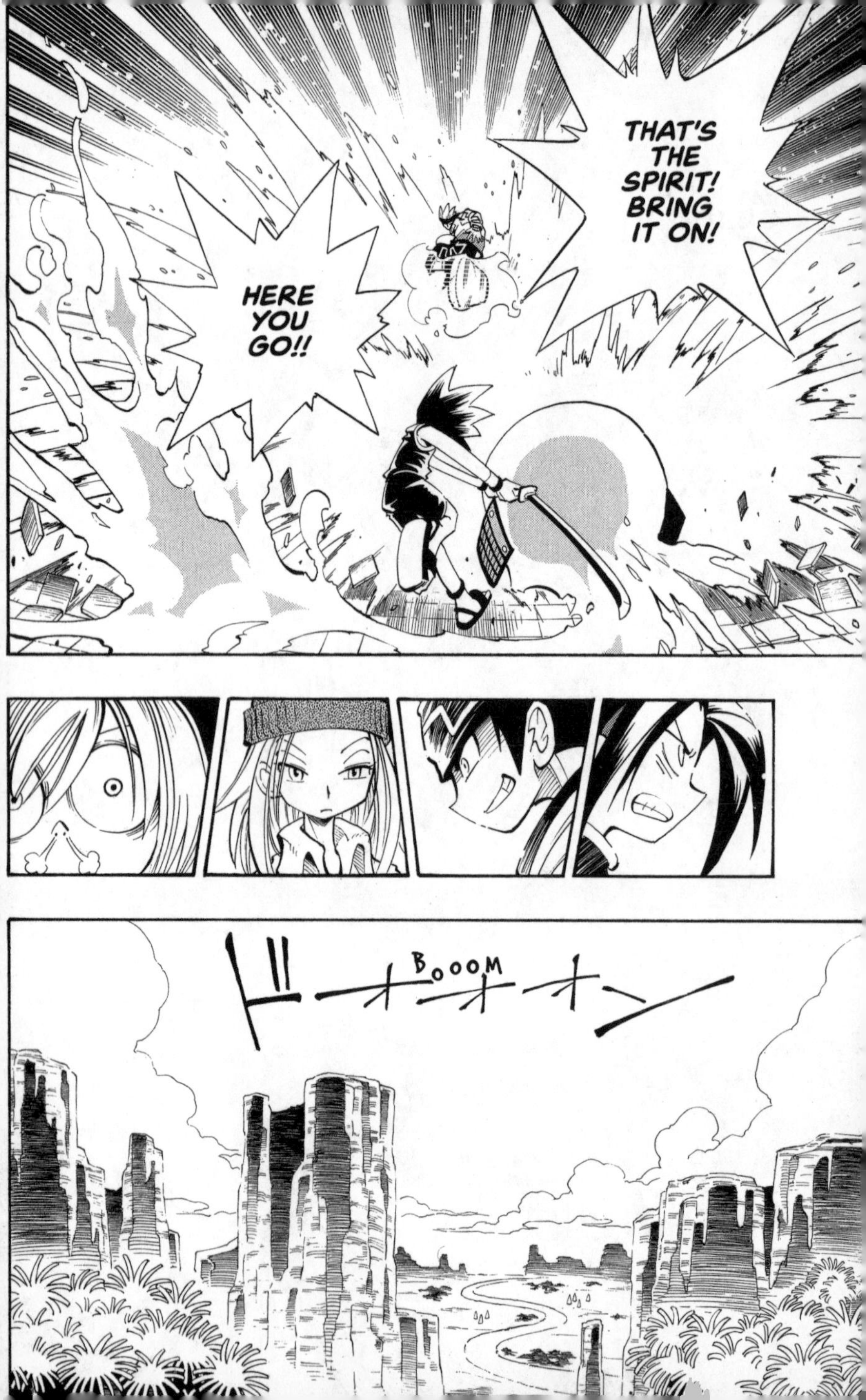
THAT'S THE SPIRIT! BRING IT ON!
HERE YOU GO!!
ドーオーオーオン
BOOOM

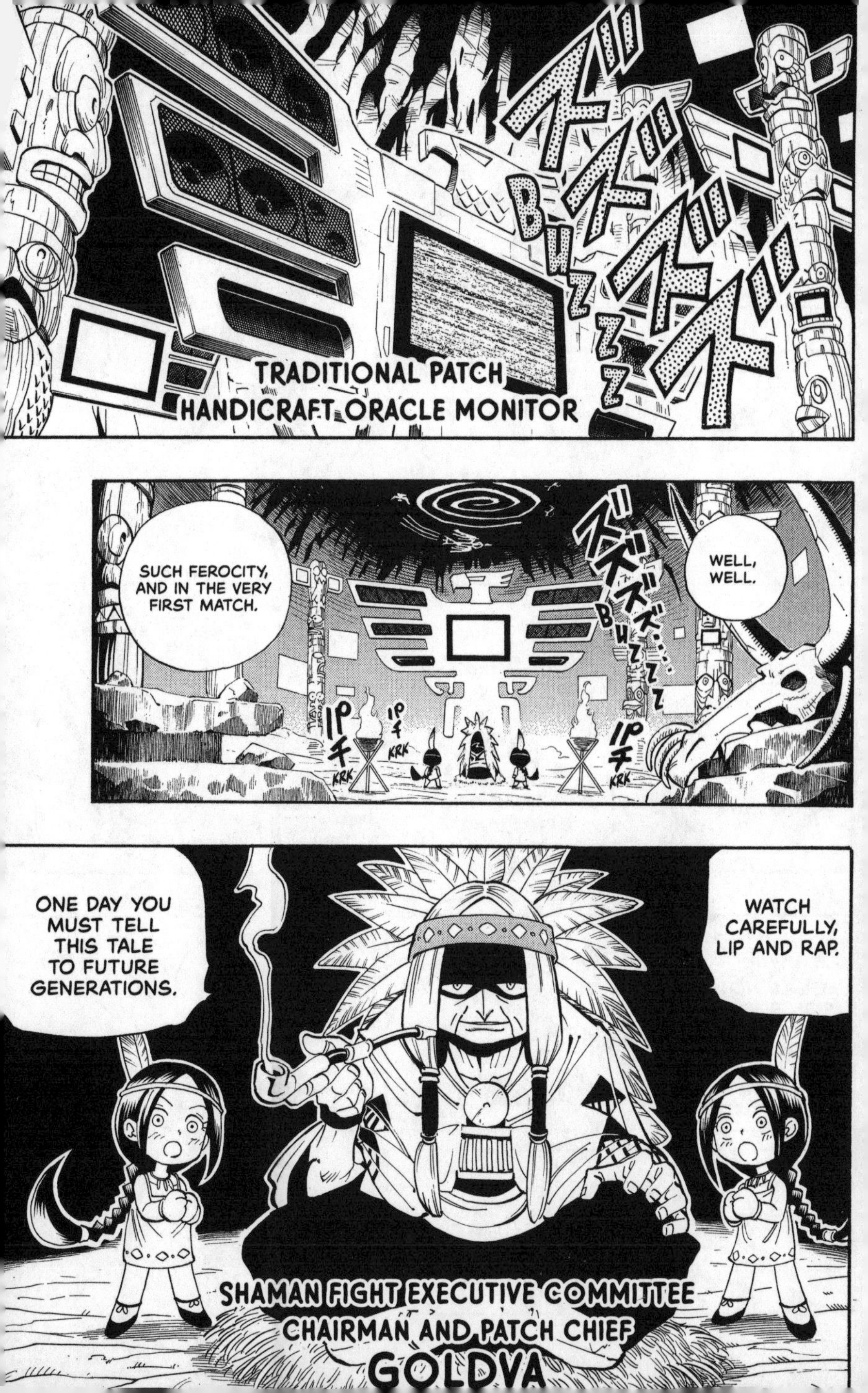
ズズズズ
BUZZZZ
TRADITIONAL PATCH
HANDICRAFT ORACLE MONITOR
WELL, WELL.
ズズズズ…
BUZZZZ
SUCH FEROCITY, AND IN THE VERY FIRST MATCH.
パチ
KRK
パチ
KRK
パチ
KRK
WATCH CAREFULLY, LIP AND RAP.
ONE DAY YOU MUST TELL THIS TALE TO FUTURE GENERATIONS.
SHAMAN FIGHT EXECUTIVE COMMITTEE
CHAIRMAN AND PATCH CHIEF
GOLDVA

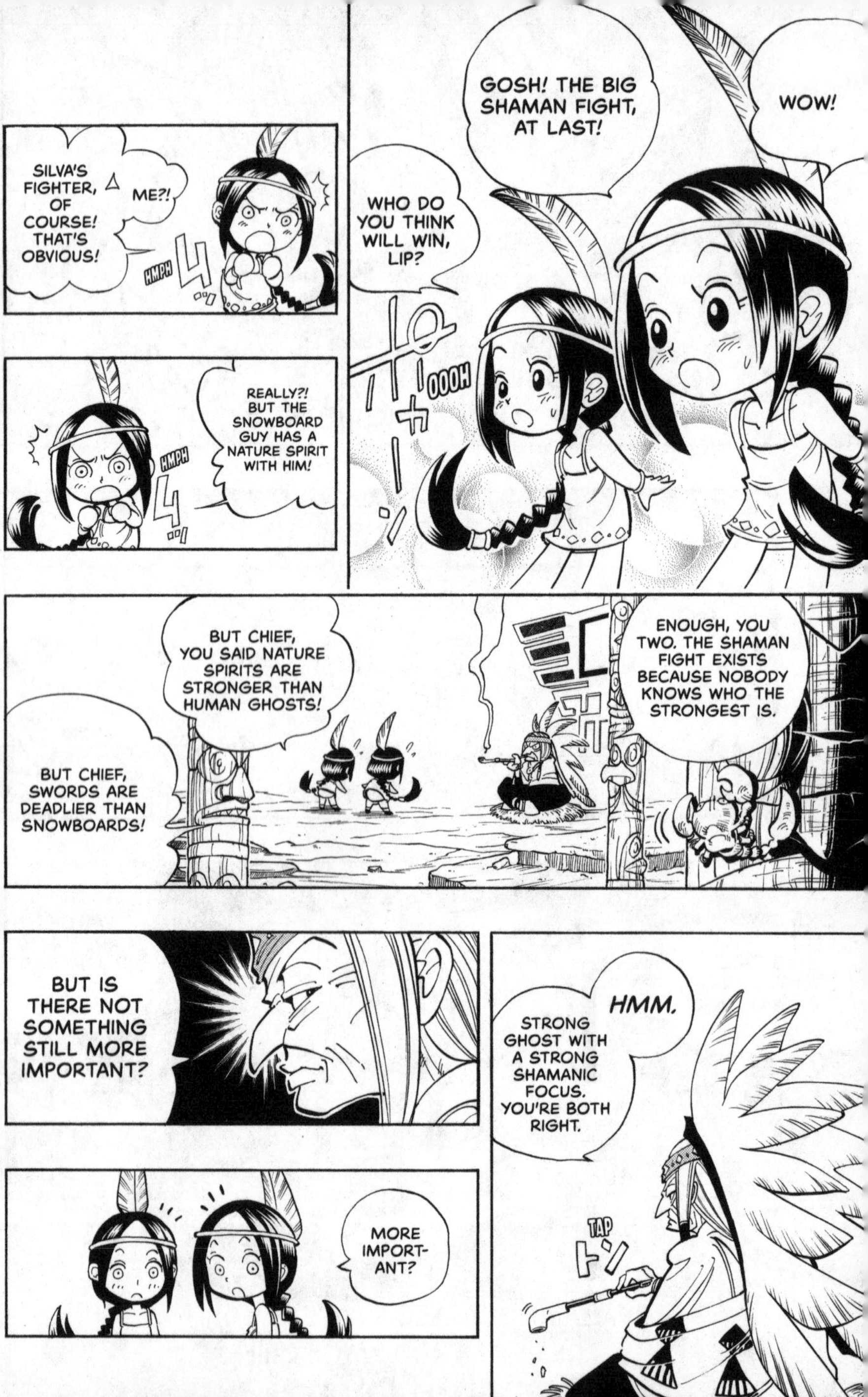
GOSH! THE BIG SHAMAN FIGHT, AT LAST!
WOW!
WHO DO YOU THINK WILL WIN, LIP?
OOOH
ME?!
SILVA'S FIGHTER, OF COURSE! THAT'S OBVIOUS!
HMPH
REALLY?! BUT THE SNOWBOARD GUY HAS A NATURE SPIRIT WITH HIM!
HMPH
BUT CHIEF, YOU SAID NATURE SPIRITS ARE STRONGER THAN HUMAN GHOSTS!
BUT CHIEF, SWORDS ARE DEADLIER THAN SNOWBOARDS!
ENOUGH, YOU TWO. THE SHAMAN FIGHT EXISTS BECAUSE NOBODY KNOWS WHO THE STRONGEST IS.
HMM.
STRONG GHOST WITH A STRONG SHAMANIC FOCUS. YOU'RE BOTH RIGHT.
TAP
BUT IS THERE NOT SOMETHING STILL MORE IMPORTANT?
MORE IMPORT-ANT?

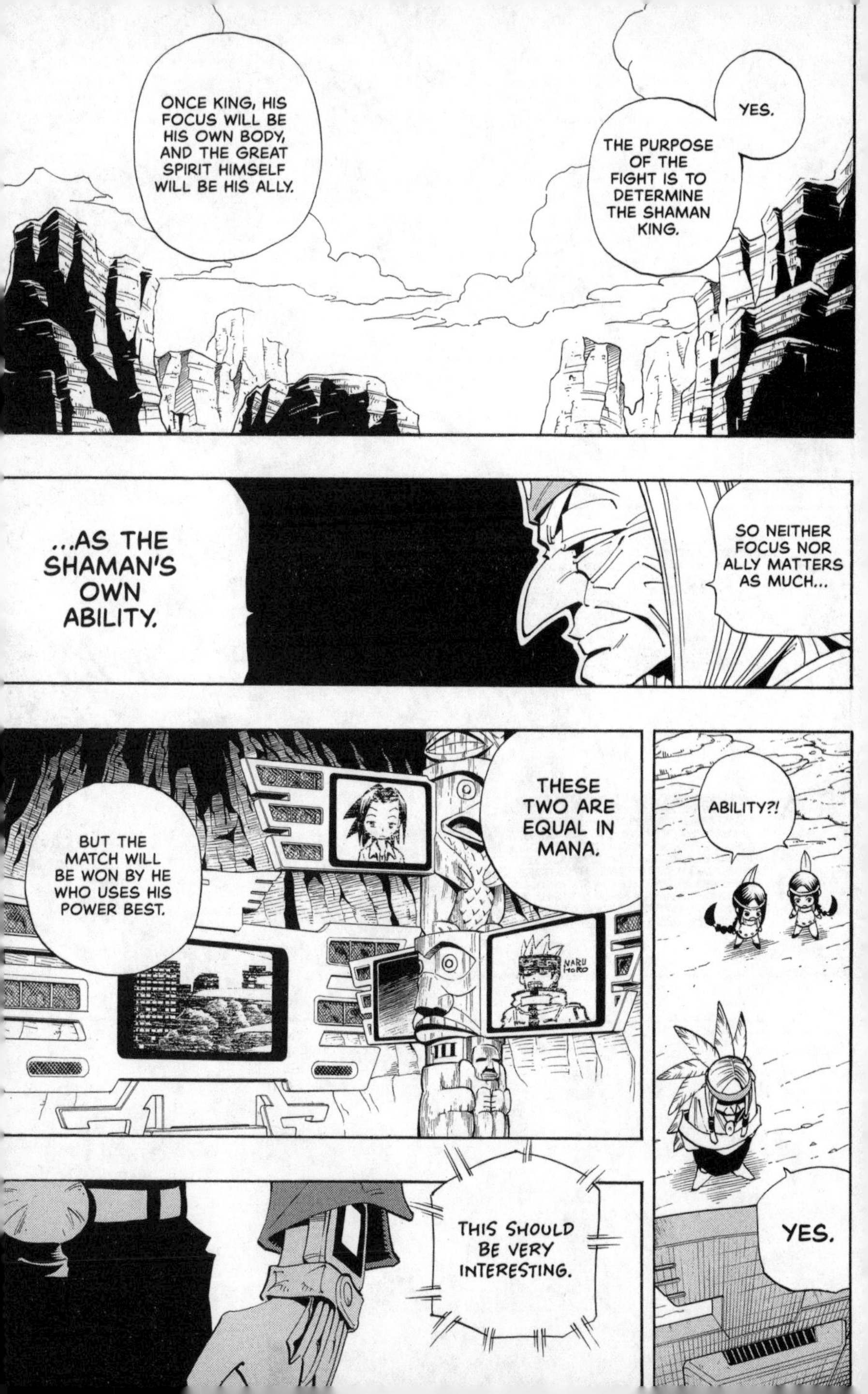
YES.
THE PURPOSE OF THE FIGHT IS TO DETERMINE THE SHAMAN KING.
ONCE KING, HIS FOCUS WILL BE HIS OWN BODY, AND THE GREAT SPIRIT HIMSELF WILL BE HIS ALLY.
SO NEITHER FOCUS NOR ALLY MATTERS AS MUCH...
...AS THE SHAMAN'S OWN ABILITY.
ABILITY?!
YES.
THESE TWO ARE EQUAL IN MANA.
BUT THE MATCH WILL BE WON BY HE WHO USES HIS POWER BEST.
THIS SHOULD BE VERY INTERESTING.

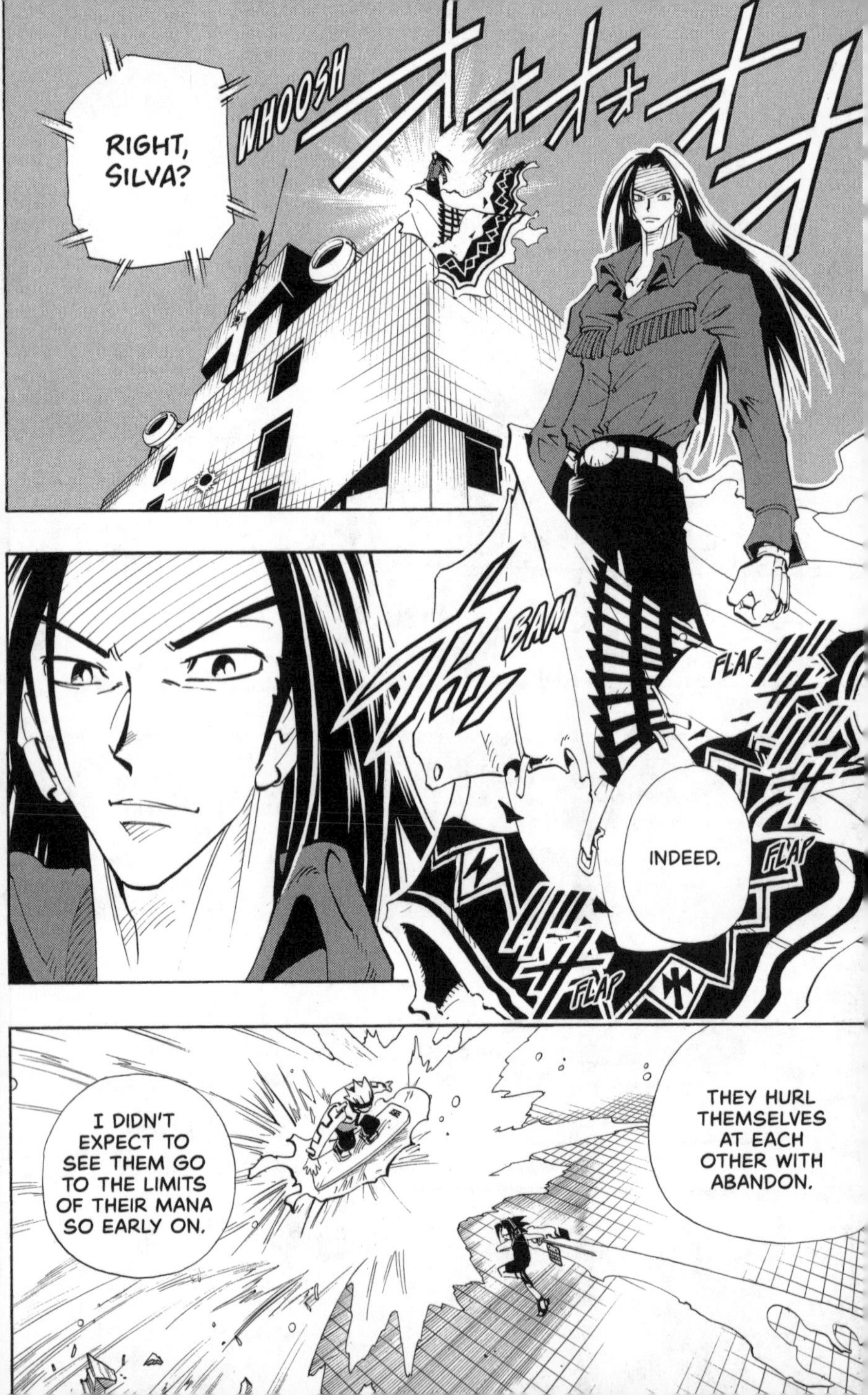
WHOOSH
RIGHT, SILVA?
FLAP-
FLAP
INDEED.
FLAP
BAM
THEY HURL THEMSELVES AT EACH OTHER WITH ABANDON.
I DIDN'T EXPECT TO SEE THEM GO TO THE LIMITS OF THEIR MANA SO EARLY ON.

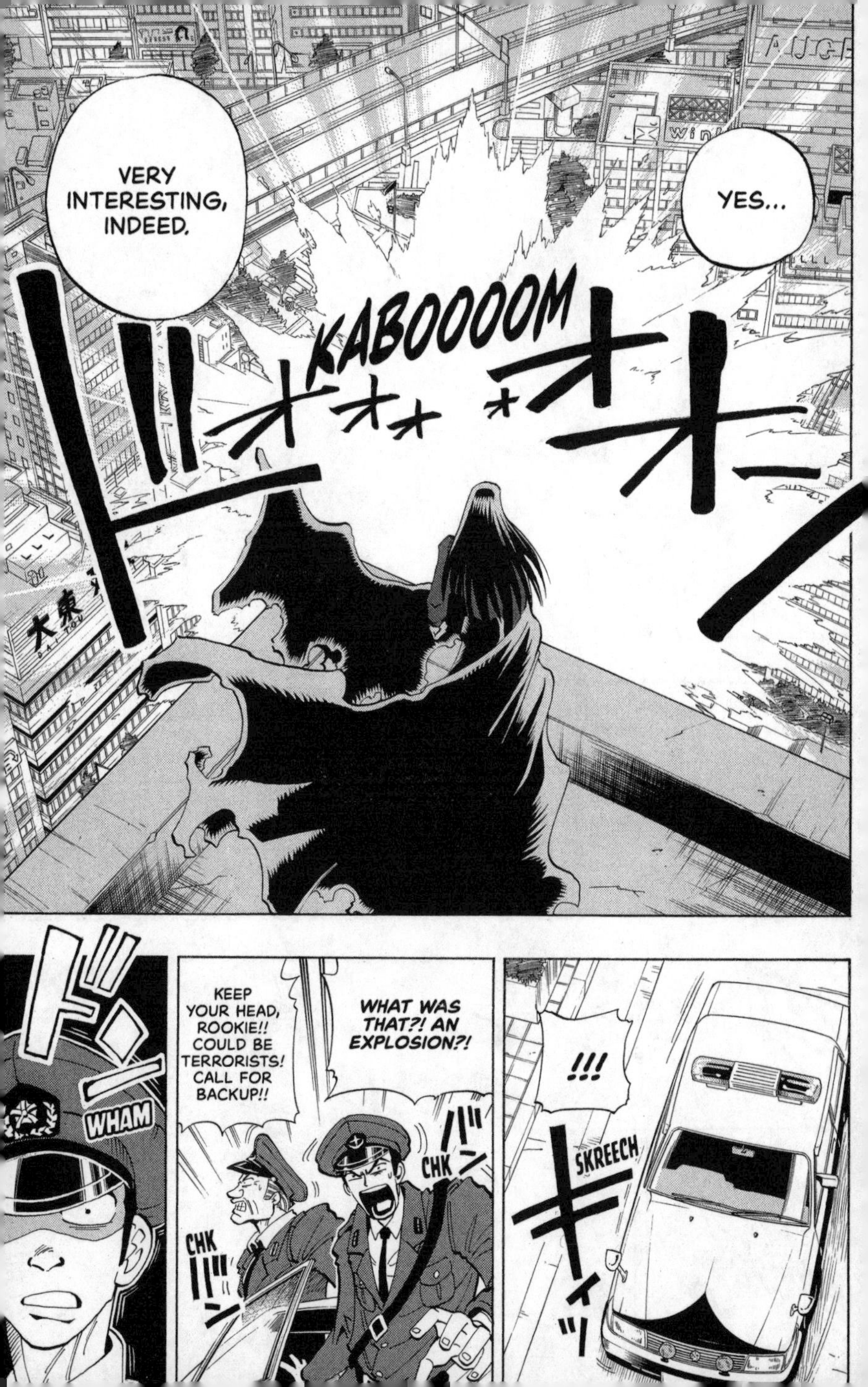
YES...
VERY INTERESTING, INDEED.
KABOOOOM
!!!
SKREECH
WHAT WAS THAT?! AN EXPLOSION?!
KEEP YOUR HEAD, ROOKIE!! COULD BE TERRORISTS! CALL FOR BACKUP!!
CHK
CHK
WHAM

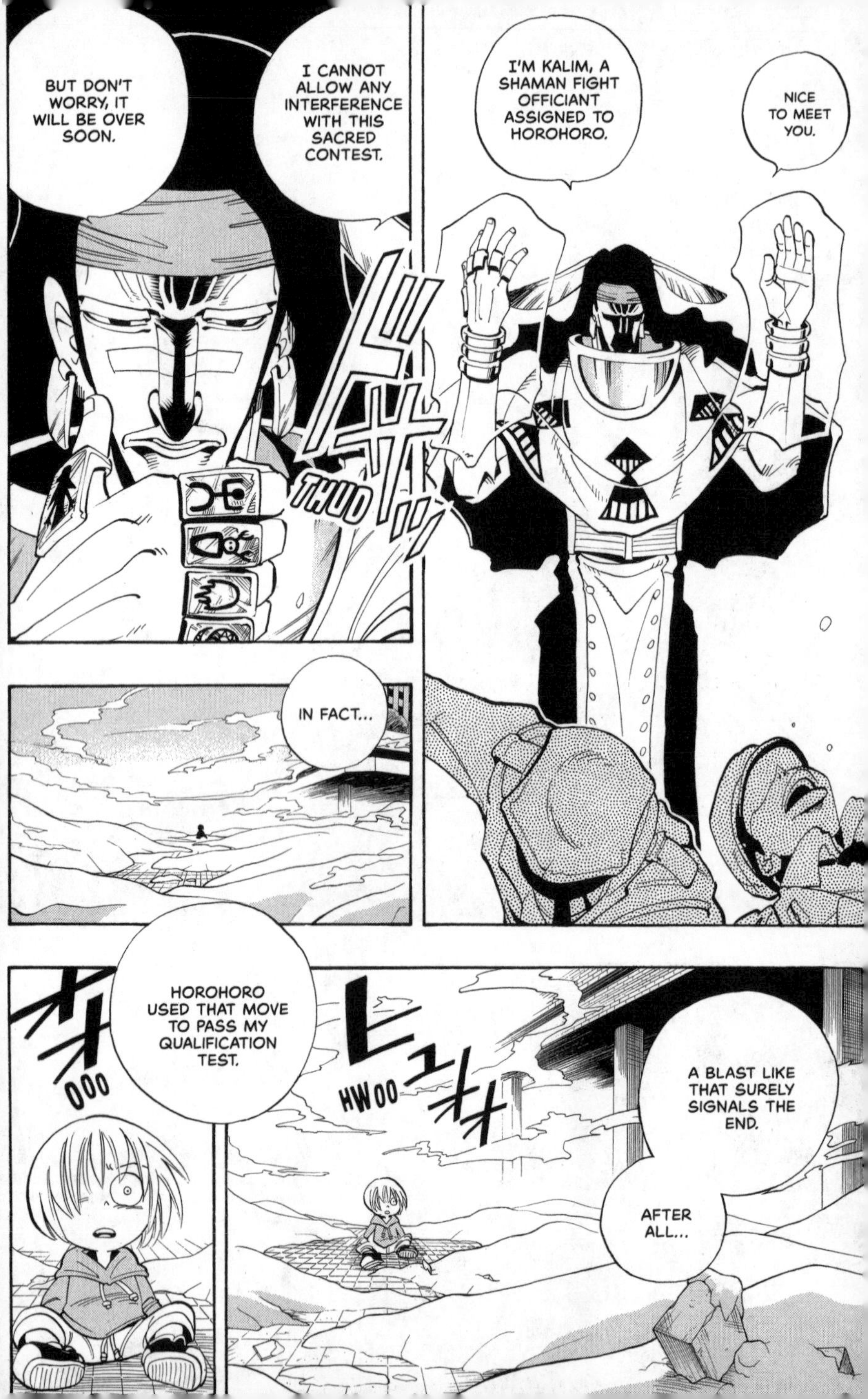

I'M KALIM, A SHAMAN FIGHT OFFICIANT ASSIGNED TO HOROHORO.
NICE TO MEET YOU.
I CANNOT ALLOW ANY INTERFERENCE WITH THIS SACRED CONTEST.
BUT DON'T WORRY, IT WILL BE OVER SOON.
THUD
IN FACT...
A BLAST LIKE THAT SURELY SIGNALS THE END.
AFTER ALL...
HWOO
HOROHORO USED THAT MOVE TO PASS MY QUALIFICATION TEST.
OOO

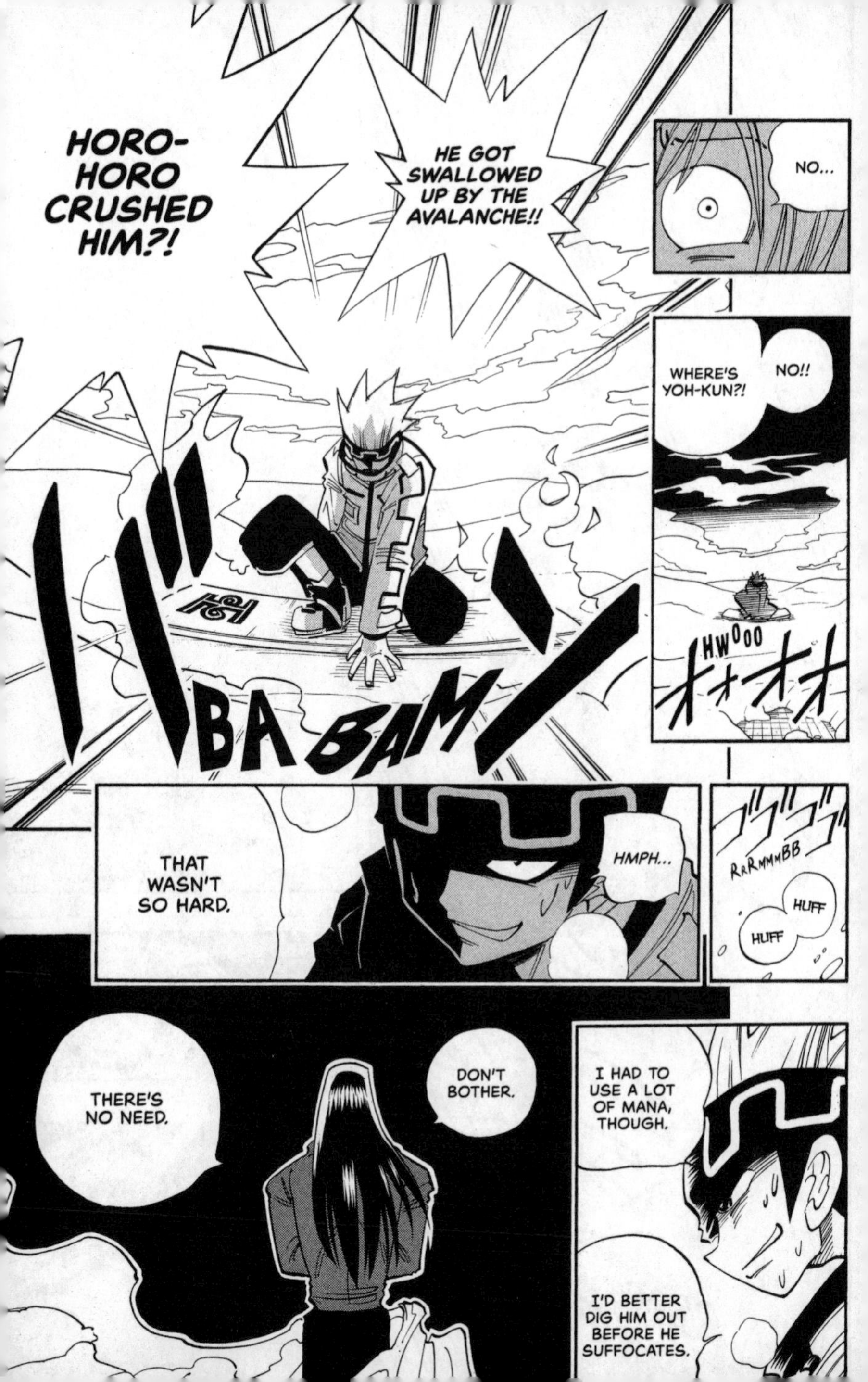
NO...
NO!!
WHERE'S YOH-KUN?!
HWOOO
HE GOT SWALLOWED UP BY THE AVALANCHE!!
HORO-HORO CRUSHED HIM?!
BABAM
RRRMMMBB
HUFF
HUFF
HMPH...
THAT WASN'T SO HARD.
I HAD TO USE A LOT OF MANA, THOUGH.
I'D BETTER DIG HIM OUT BEFORE HE SUFFOCATES.
DON'T BOTHER.
THERE'S NO NEED.

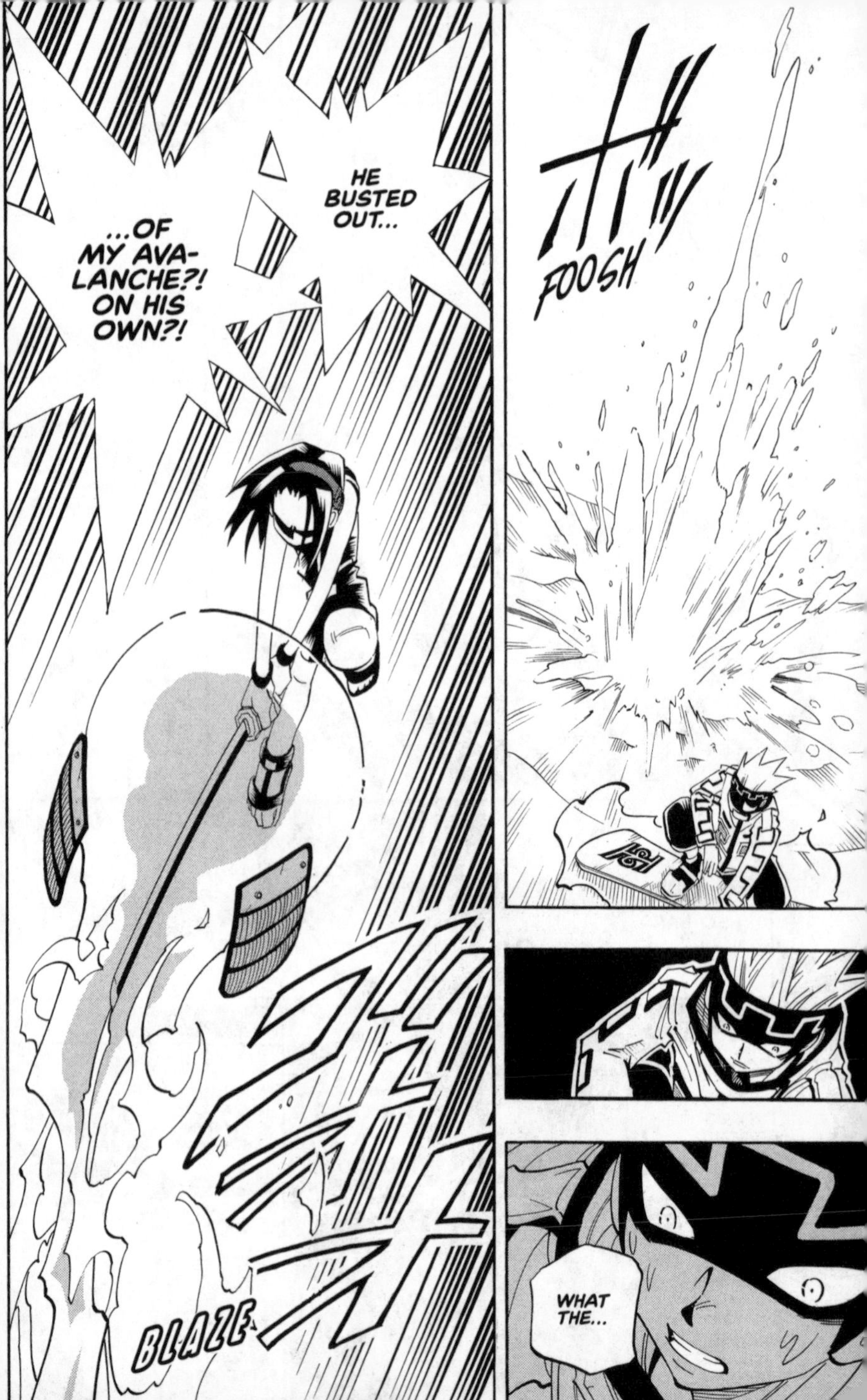
FOOSH
WHAT THE...
HE BUSTED OUT...
...OF MY AVA-LANCHE?! ON HIS OWN?!
BLAZE

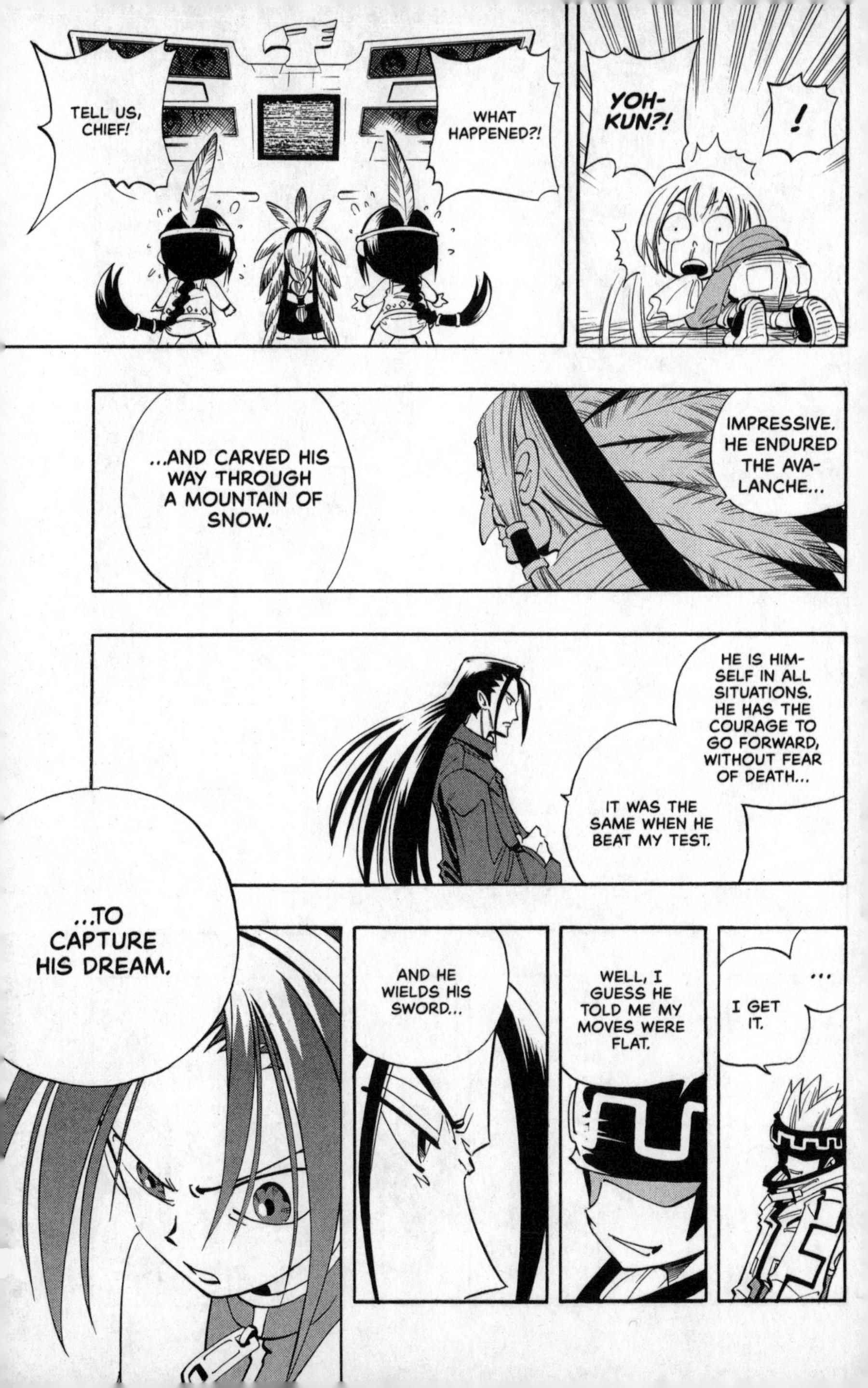
!
YOH-KUN?!
WHAT HAPPENED?!
TELL US, CHIEF!
IMPRESSIVE. HE ENDURED THE AVA-LANCHE...
...AND CARVED HIS WAY THROUGH A MOUNTAIN OF SNOW.
HE IS HIM-SELF IN ALL SITUATIONS. HE HAS THE COURAGE TO GO FORWARD, WITHOUT FEAR OF DEATH...
IT WAS THE SAME WHEN HE BEAT MY TEST.
...
I GET IT.
WELL, I GUESS HE TOLD ME MY MOVES WERE FLAT.
AND HE WIELDS HIS SWORD...
...TO CAPTURE HIS DREAM.

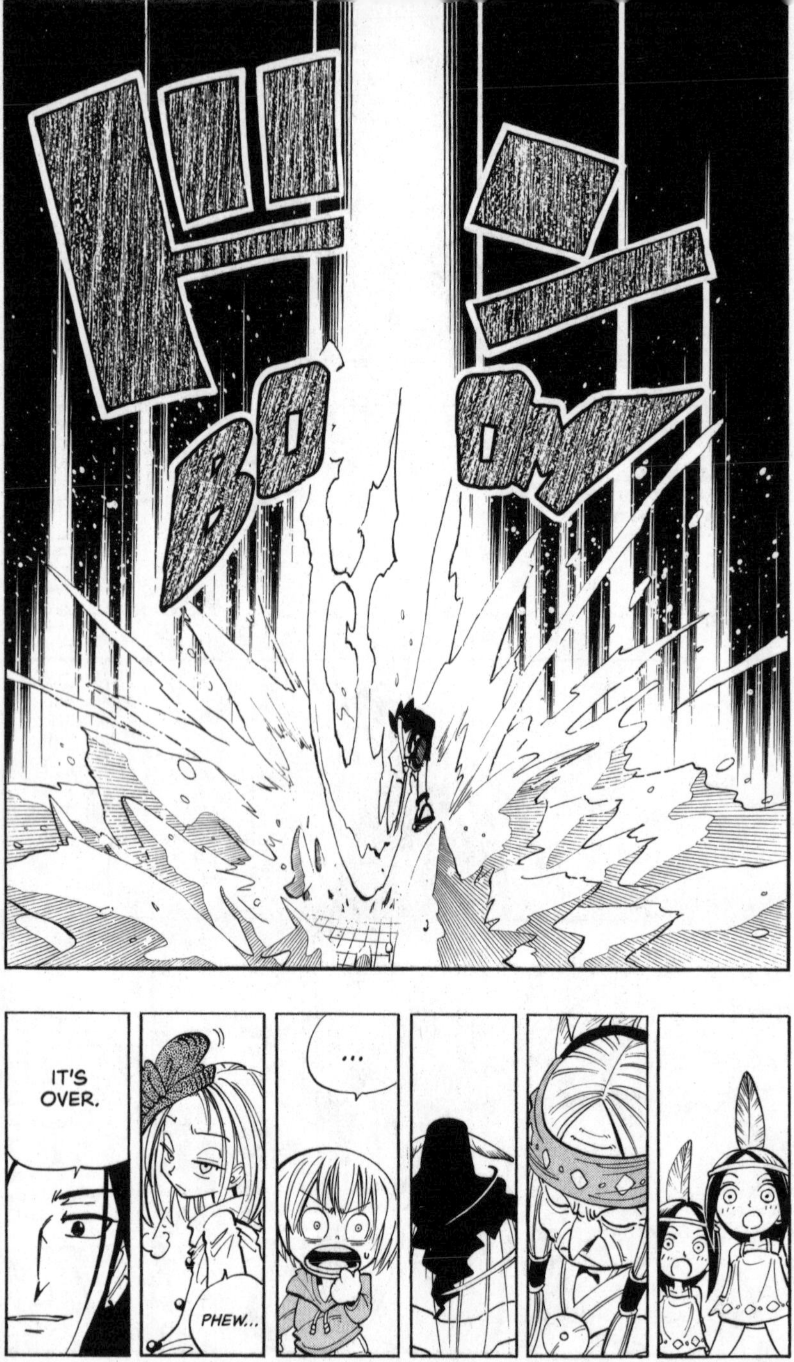
BOOM
...
PHEW...
IT'S OVER.

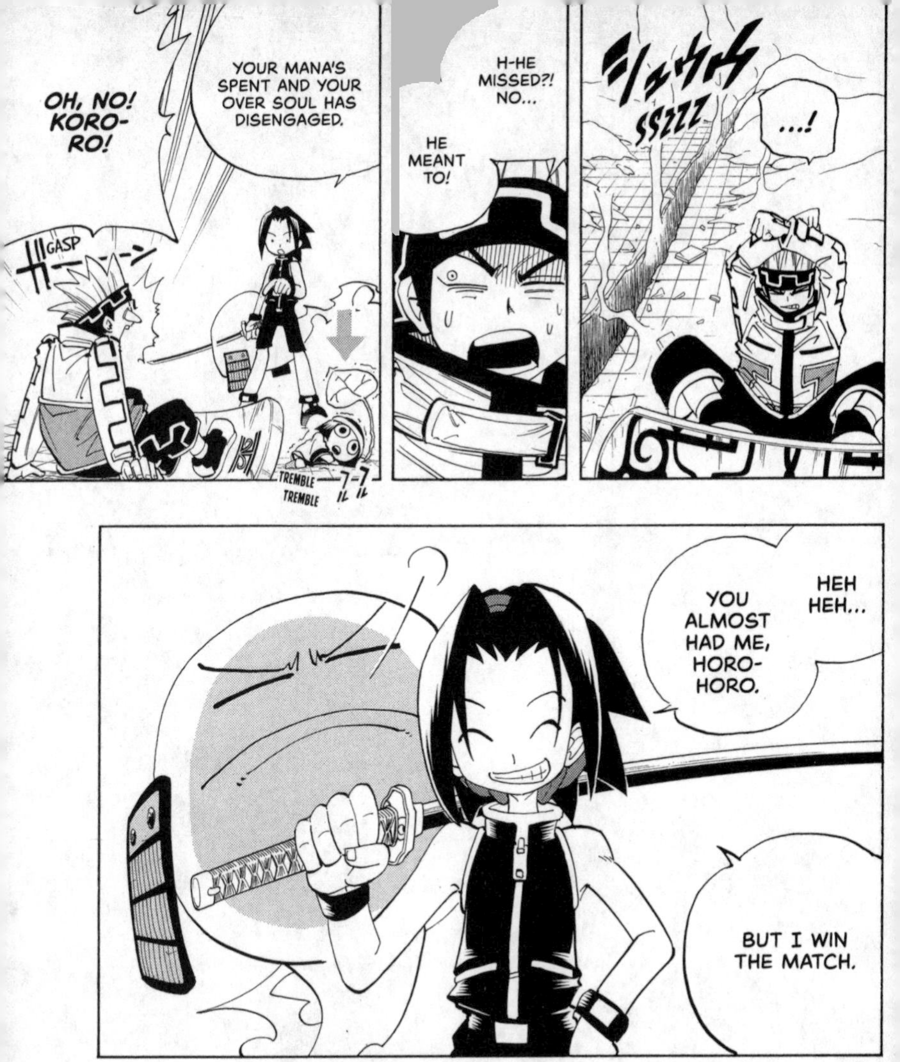
SSZZZ
...!
H-HE MISSED?! NO...
HE MEANT TO!
YOUR MANA'S SPENT AND YOUR OVER SOUL HAS DISENGAGED.
OH, NO! KORO-RO!
GASP
TREMBLE TREMBLE
HEH HEH...
YOU ALMOST HAD ME, HORO-HORO.
BUT I WIN THE MATCH.

SHAMAN FIGHT PRELIMINARIES

MATCH #1

○ YOH ASAKURA VS. HOROHORO ●

SPIRIT ALLIES	**AMIDAMARU**	**KORORO**

SHAMAN
KING
5

Snowboard

Chapter 38: A Hot Bath and a Starry Sky

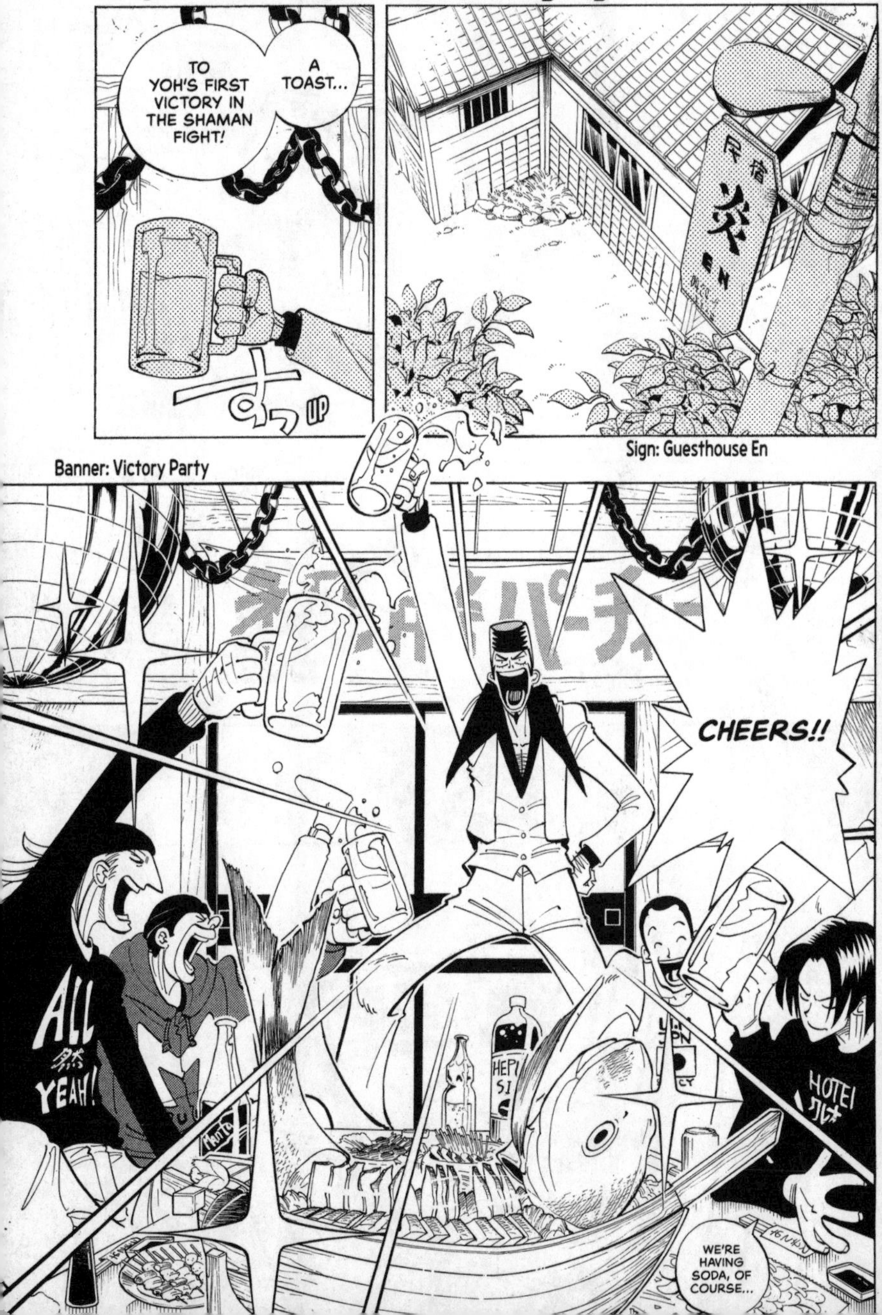

Sign: Guesthouse En
A TOAST...
TO YOH'S FIRST VICTORY IN THE SHAMAN FIGHT!
すっ UP
Banner: Victory Party
CHEERS!!
WE'RE HAVING SODA, OF COURSE...

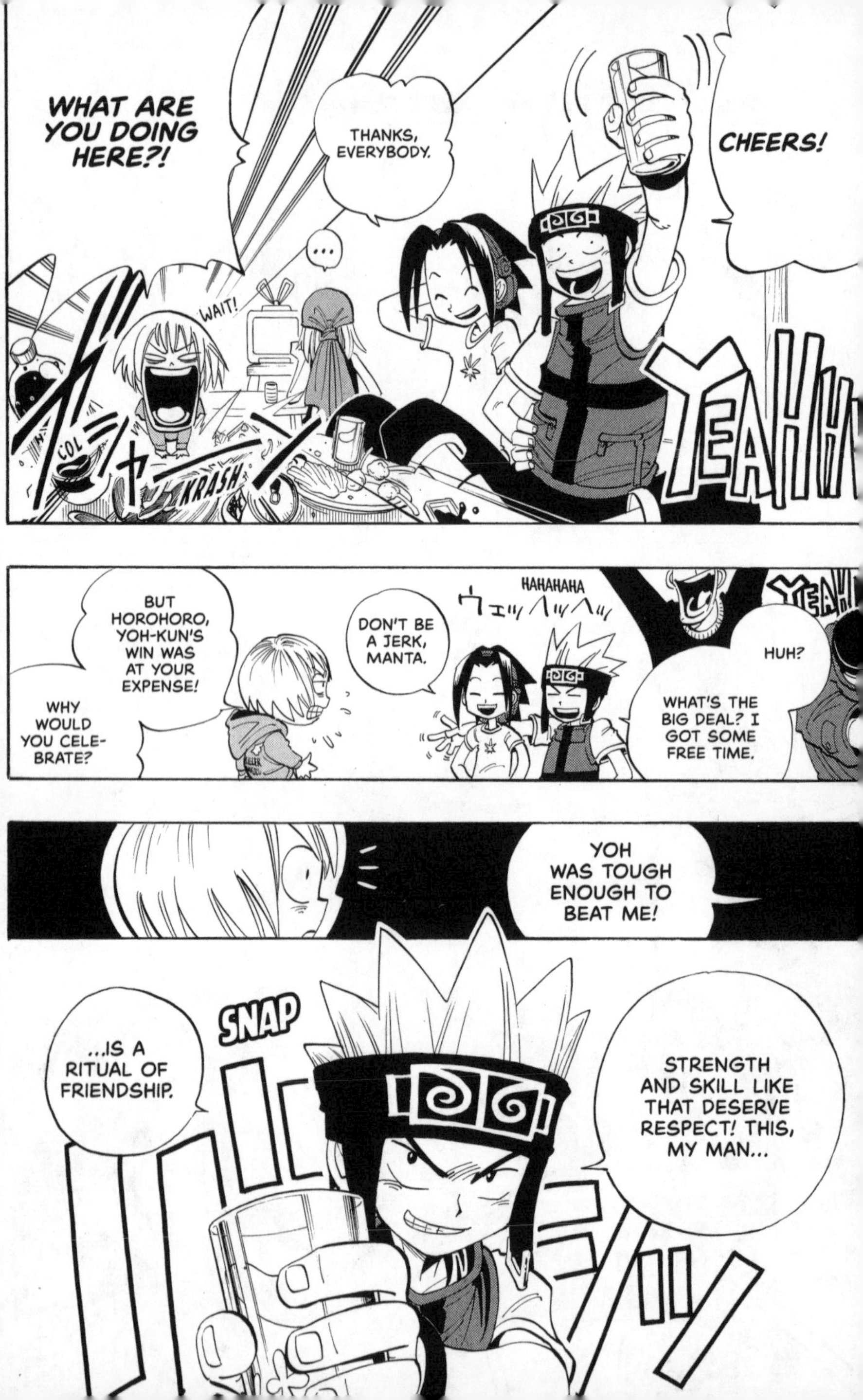
CHEERS!
YEAHH
THANKS, EVERYBODY.
...
WHAT ARE YOU DOING HERE?!
WAIT!
KRASH
COL
YEAH
HUH?
WHAT'S THE BIG DEAL? I GOT SOME FREE TIME.
HAHAHAHA
DON'T BE A JERK, MANTA.
BUT HOROHORO, YOH-KUN'S WIN WAS AT YOUR EXPENSE!
WHY WOULD YOU CELE-BRATE?
YOH WAS TOUGH ENOUGH TO BEAT ME!
STRENGTH AND SKILL LIKE THAT DESERVE RESPECT! THIS, MY MAN...
SNAP
...IS A RITUAL OF FRIENDSHIP.

Chapter 38:

A Hot Bath and a Starry Sky

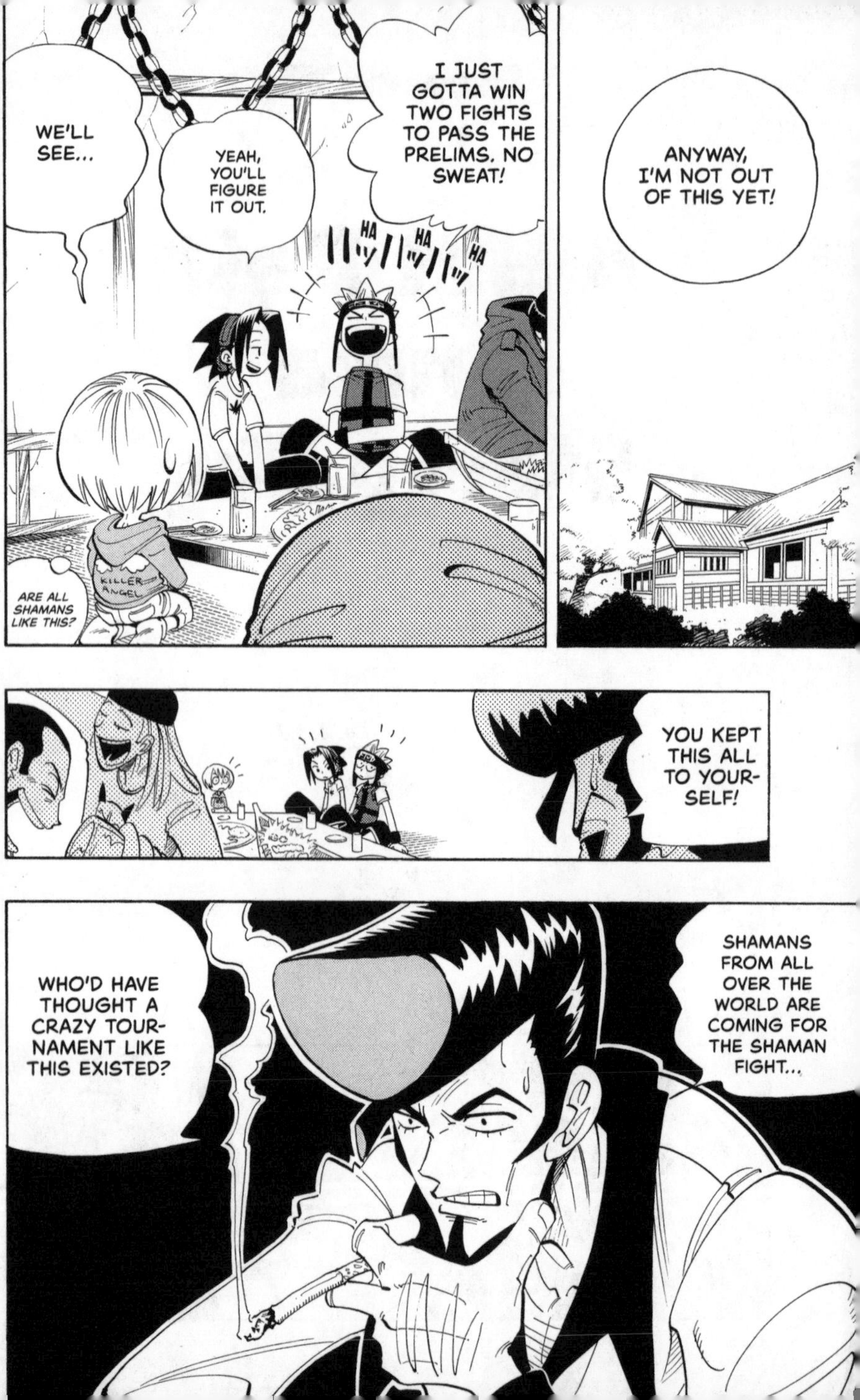
ANYWAY, I'M NOT OUT OF THIS YET!
I JUST GOTTA WIN TWO FIGHTS TO PASS THE PRELIMS. NO SWEAT!
HA HA HA
YEAH, YOU'LL FIGURE IT OUT.
WE'LL SEE...
ARE ALL SHAMANS LIKE THIS?
KILLER ANGEL
YOU KEPT THIS ALL TO YOUR-SELF!
SHAMANS FROM ALL OVER THE WORLD ARE COMING FOR THE SHAMAN FIGHT...
WHO'D HAVE THOUGHT A CRAZY TOUR-NAMENT LIKE THIS EXISTED?

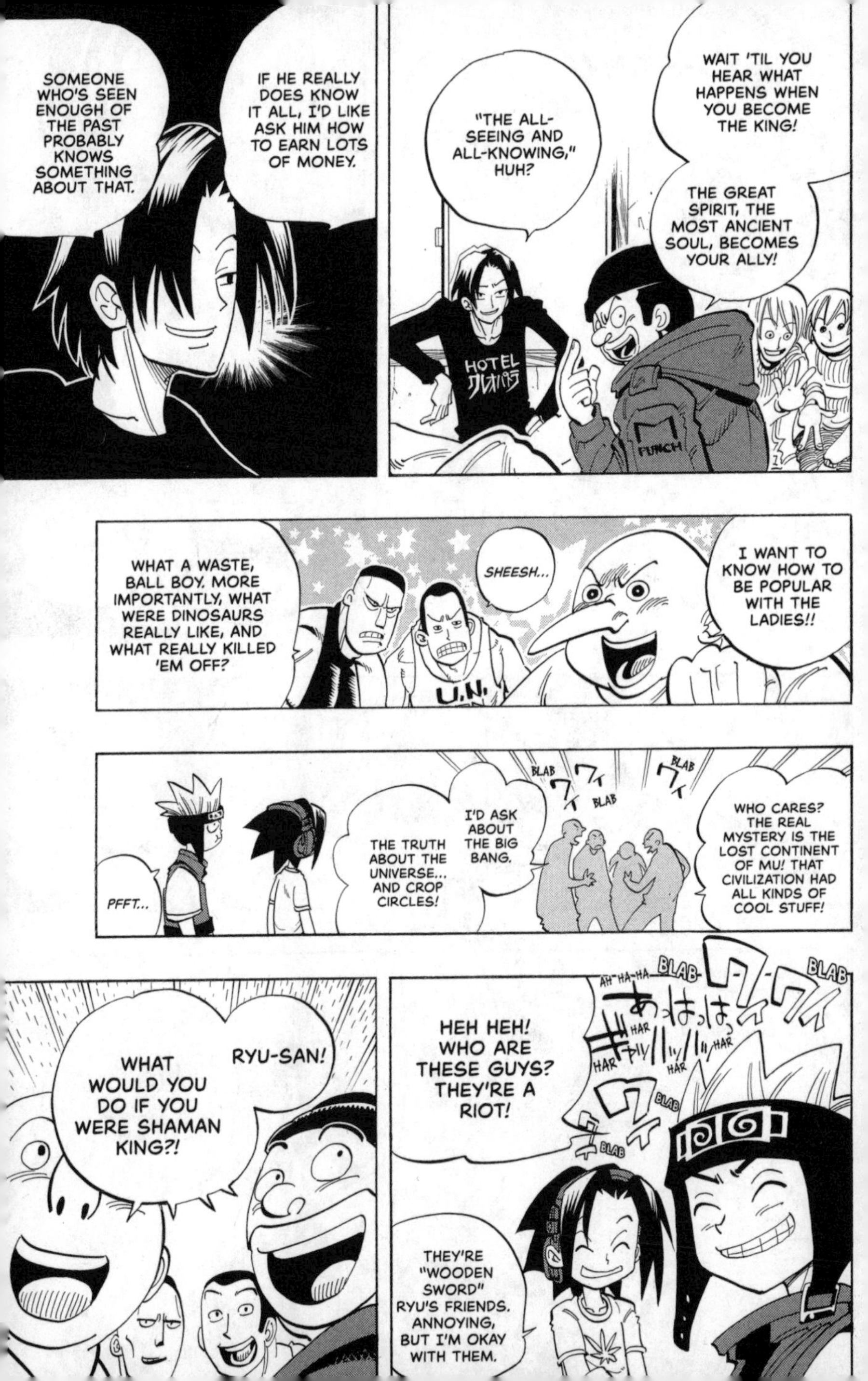
WAIT 'TIL YOU HEAR WHAT HAPPENS WHEN YOU BECOME THE KING!
THE GREAT SPIRIT, THE MOST ANCIENT SOUL, BECOMES YOUR ALLY!
"THE ALL-SEEING AND ALL-KNOWING," HUH?
HOTEL
FUNCH
IF HE REALLY DOES KNOW IT ALL, I'D LIKE ASK HIM HOW TO EARN LOTS OF MONEY.
SOMEONE WHO'S SEEN ENOUGH OF THE PAST PROBABLY KNOWS SOMETHING ABOUT THAT.
I WANT TO KNOW HOW TO BE POPULAR WITH THE LADIES!!
SHEESH...
U.N.
WHAT A WASTE, BALL BOY. MORE IMPORTANTLY, WHAT WERE DINOSAURS REALLY LIKE, AND WHAT REALLY KILLED 'EM OFF?
BLAB BLAB
BLAB BLAB
WHO CARES? THE REAL MYSTERY IS THE LOST CONTINENT OF MU! THAT CIVILIZATION HAD ALL KINDS OF COOL STUFF!
I'D ASK ABOUT THE BIG BANG.
THE TRUTH ABOUT THE UNIVERSE... AND CROP CIRCLES!
PFFT...
AH-HA-HA BLAB BLAB
HAR HAR HAR HAR HAR
BLAB BLAB
HEH HEH! WHO ARE THESE GUYS? THEY'RE A RIOT!
THEY'RE "WOODEN SWORD" RYU'S FRIENDS. ANNOYING, BUT I'M OKAY WITH THEM.
RYU-SAN!
WHAT WOULD YOU DO IF YOU WERE SHAMAN KING?!

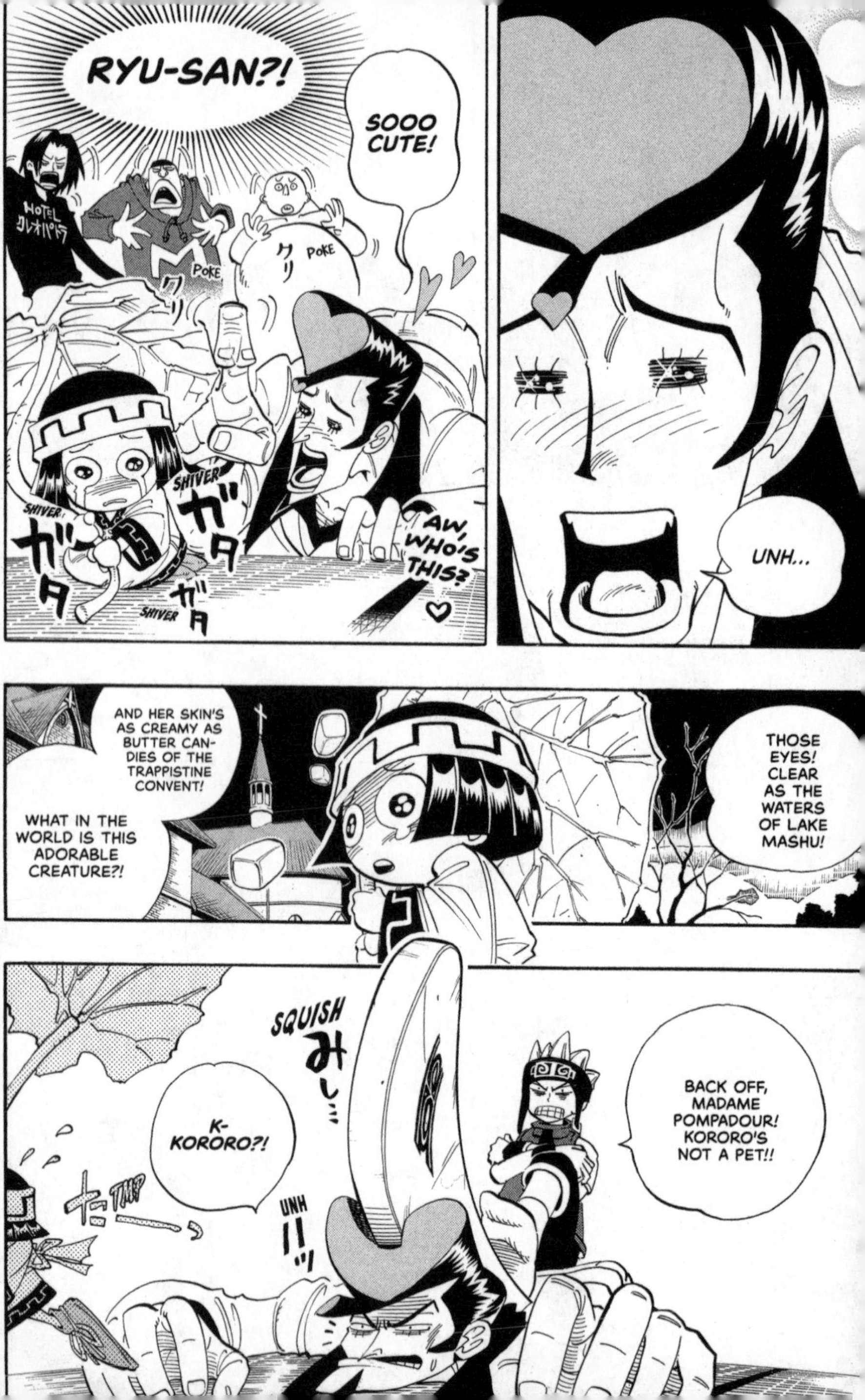

UNH...
RYU-SAN?!
SOOO CUTE!
HOTEL
クレオパトラ
POKE
グリ
POKE
グリ
AW, WHO'S THIS?
SHIVER
ガタ
SHIVER
ガタ
SHIVER
ガタ
THOSE EYES! CLEAR AS THE WATERS OF LAKE MASHU!
AND HER SKIN'S AS CREAMY AS BUTTER CANDIES OF THE TRAPPISTINE CONVENT!
WHAT IN THE WORLD IS THIS ADORABLE CREATURE?!
BACK OFF, MADAME POMPADOUR! KORORO'S NOT A PET!!
UNH
SQUISH
みし
K-KORORO?!
TMP

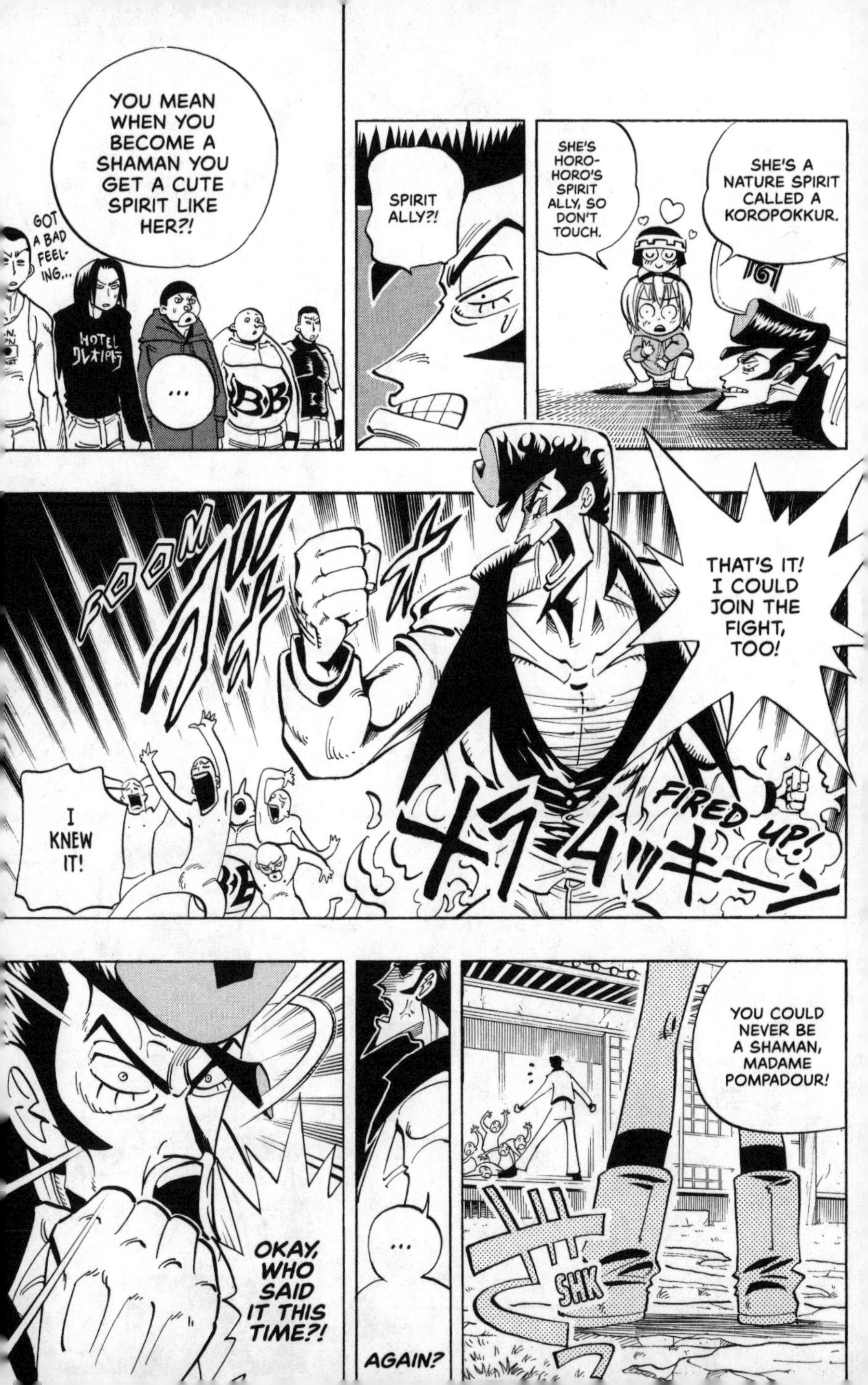
SHE'S A NATURE SPIRIT CALLED A KOROPOKKUR.
SHE'S HORO-HORO'S SPIRIT ALLY, SO DON'T TOUCH.
SPIRIT ALLY?!
YOU MEAN WHEN YOU BECOME A SHAMAN YOU GET A CUTE SPIRIT LIKE HER?!
GOT A BAD FEEL-ING...
...
THAT'S IT! I COULD JOIN THE FIGHT, TOO!
FIRED UP!
FOOM
I KNEW IT!
YOU COULD NEVER BE A SHAMAN, MADAME POMPADOUR!
SHK
...
AGAIN?
OKAY, WHO SAID IT THIS TIME?!

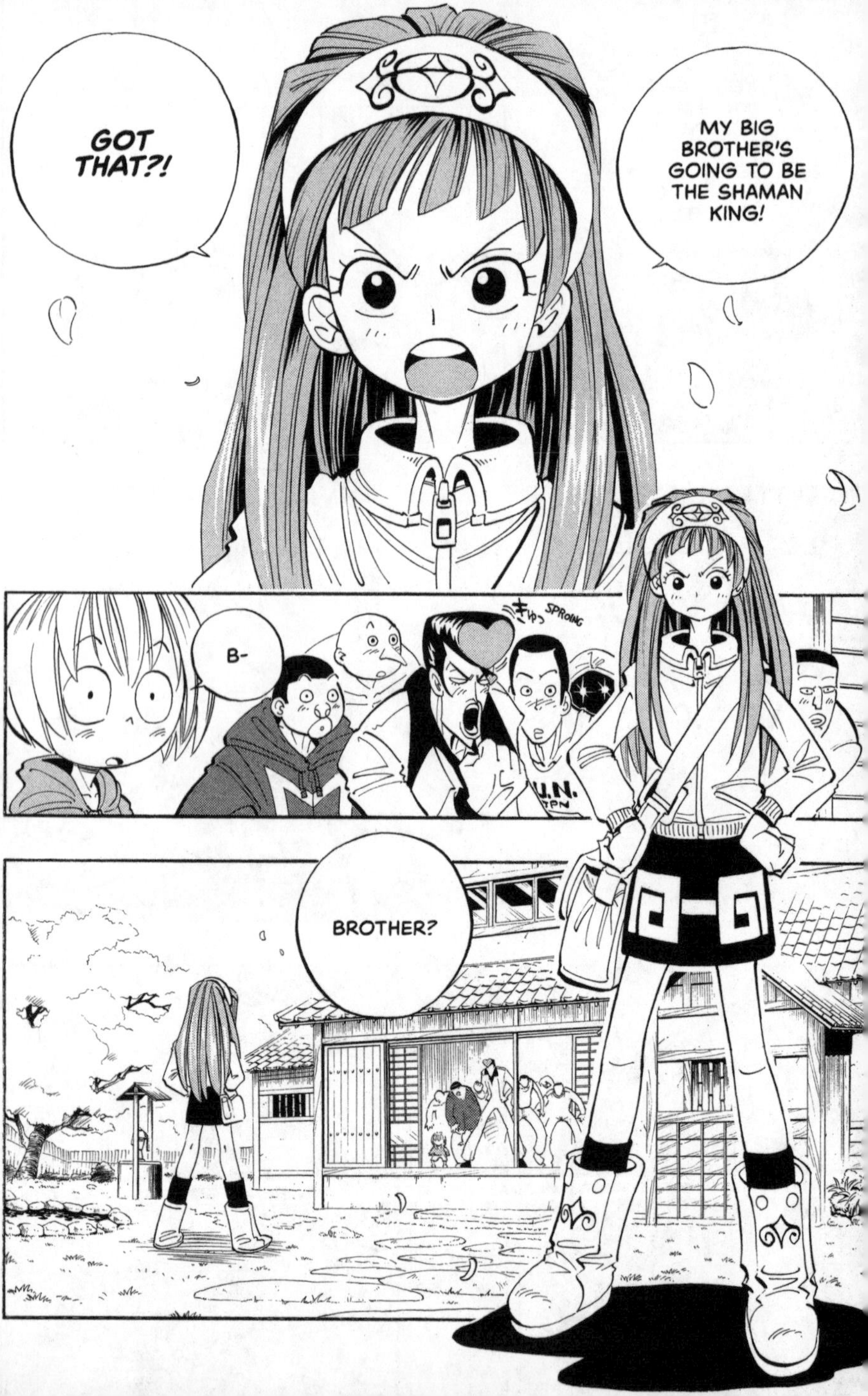
MY BIG BROTHER'S GOING TO BE THE SHAMAN KING!
GOT THAT?!
SPROING
B-
BROTHER?

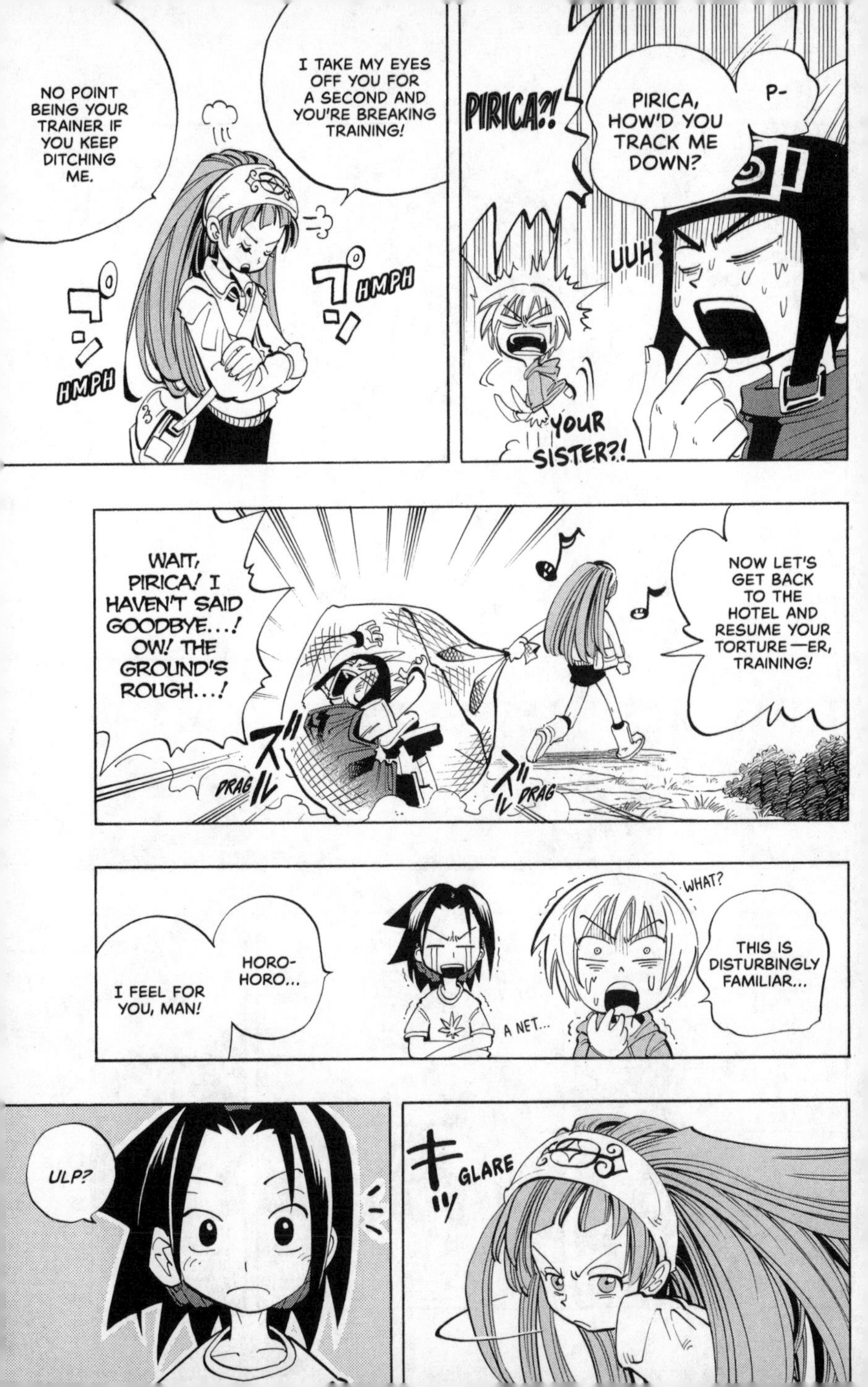
P-
PIRICA, HOW'D YOU TRACK ME DOWN?
PIRICA?!
UUH
YOUR SISTER?!
I TAKE MY EYES OFF YOU FOR A SECOND AND YOU'RE BREAKING TRAINING!
NO POINT BEING YOUR TRAINER IF YOU KEEP DITCHING ME.
HMPH
HMPH
NOW LET'S GET BACK TO THE HOTEL AND RESUME YOUR TORTURE—ER, TRAINING!
WAIT, PIRICA! I HAVEN'T SAID GOODBYE...! OW! THE GROUND'S ROUGH...!
DRAG
DRAG
WHAT?
THIS IS DISTURBINGLY FAMILIAR...
A NET...
HORO-HORO...
I FEEL FOR YOU, MAN!
GLARE
ULP?

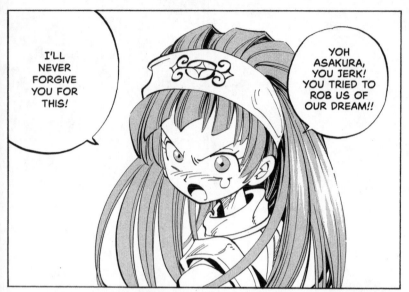

YOH ASAKURA, YOU JERK! YOU TRIED TO ROB US OF OUR DREAM!!
I'LL NEVER FORGIVE YOU FOR THIS!
BANG
GONG
SHAKE
SHAKE
WHAT?
HEY!
!
SORRY, YOH!
DON'T WORRY ABOUT WHAT MY SISTER SAYS.
HORO-HORO!!
HMPH...
SO I LOST THIS ONE ROUND.

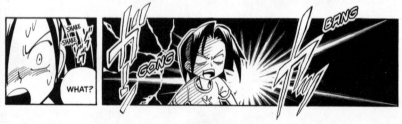

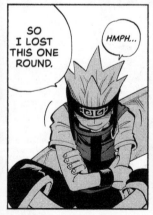

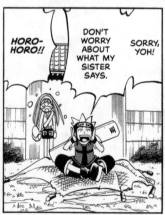

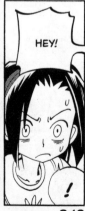

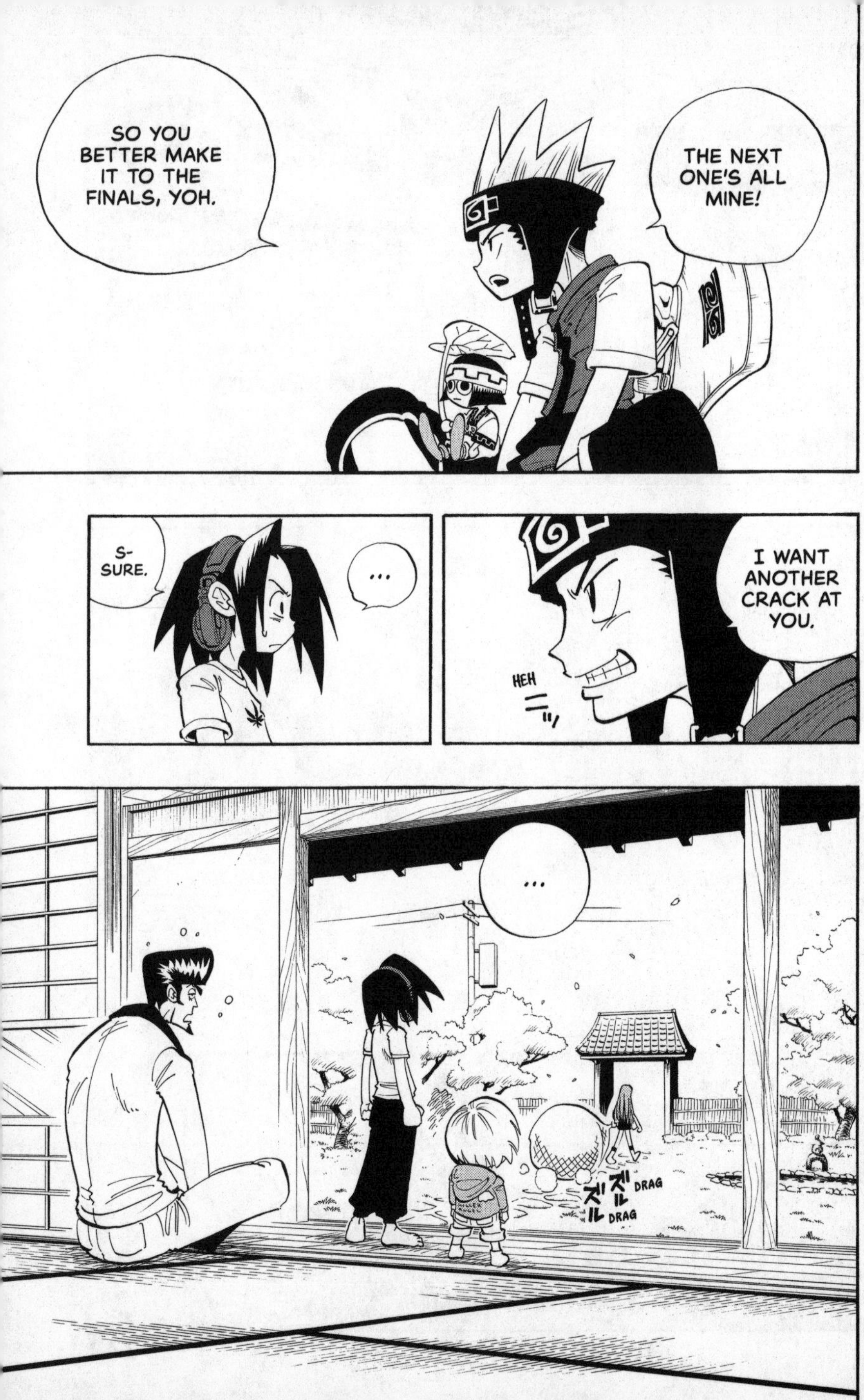
THE NEXT ONE'S ALL MINE!
SO YOU BETTER MAKE IT TO THE FINALS, YOH.
I WANT ANOTHER CRACK AT YOU.
HEH
...
S-SURE.
...
ズルズル
DRAG DRAG

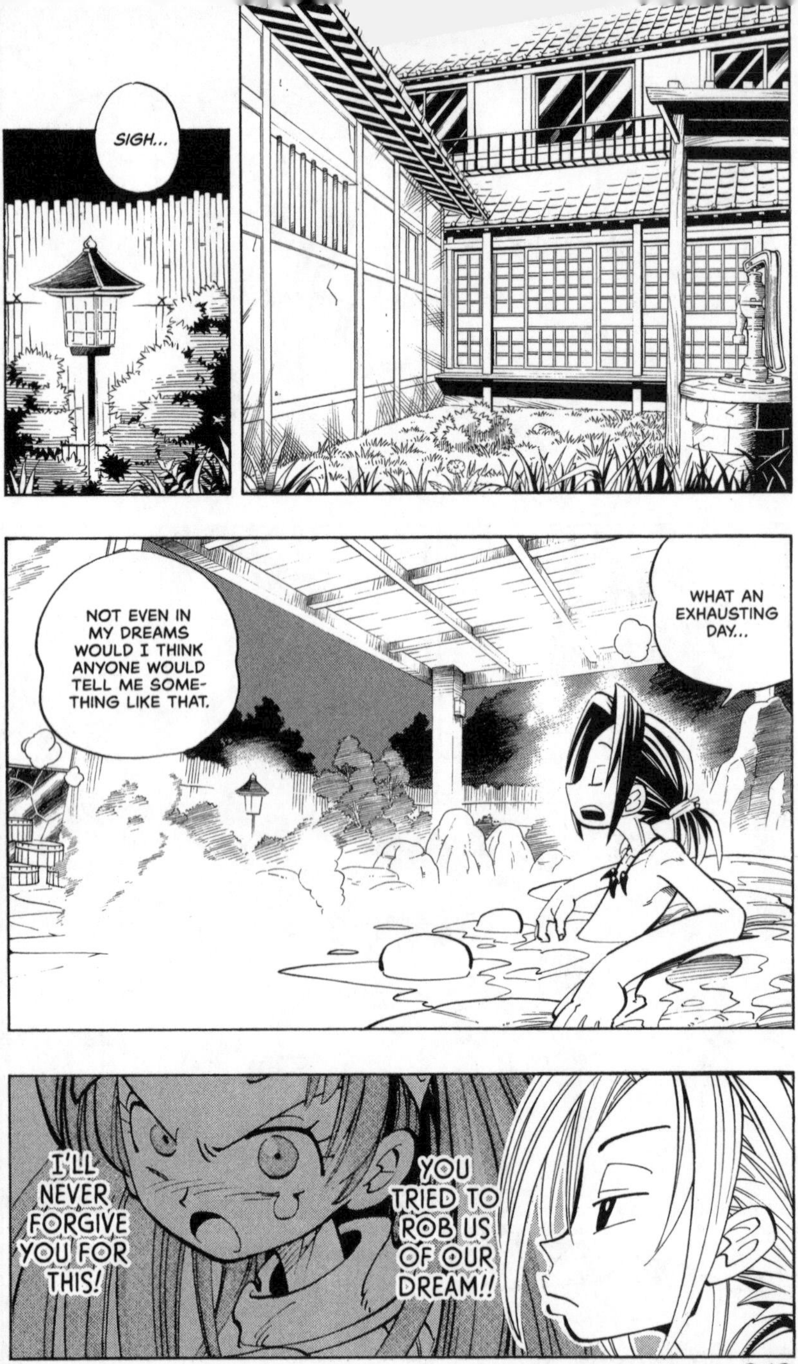
SIGH...
WHAT AN EXHAUSTING DAY...
NOT EVEN IN MY DREAMS WOULD I THINK ANYONE WOULD TELL ME SOME-THING LIKE THAT.
YOU TRIED TO ROB US OF OUR DREAM!!
I'LL NEVER FORGIVE YOU FOR THIS!

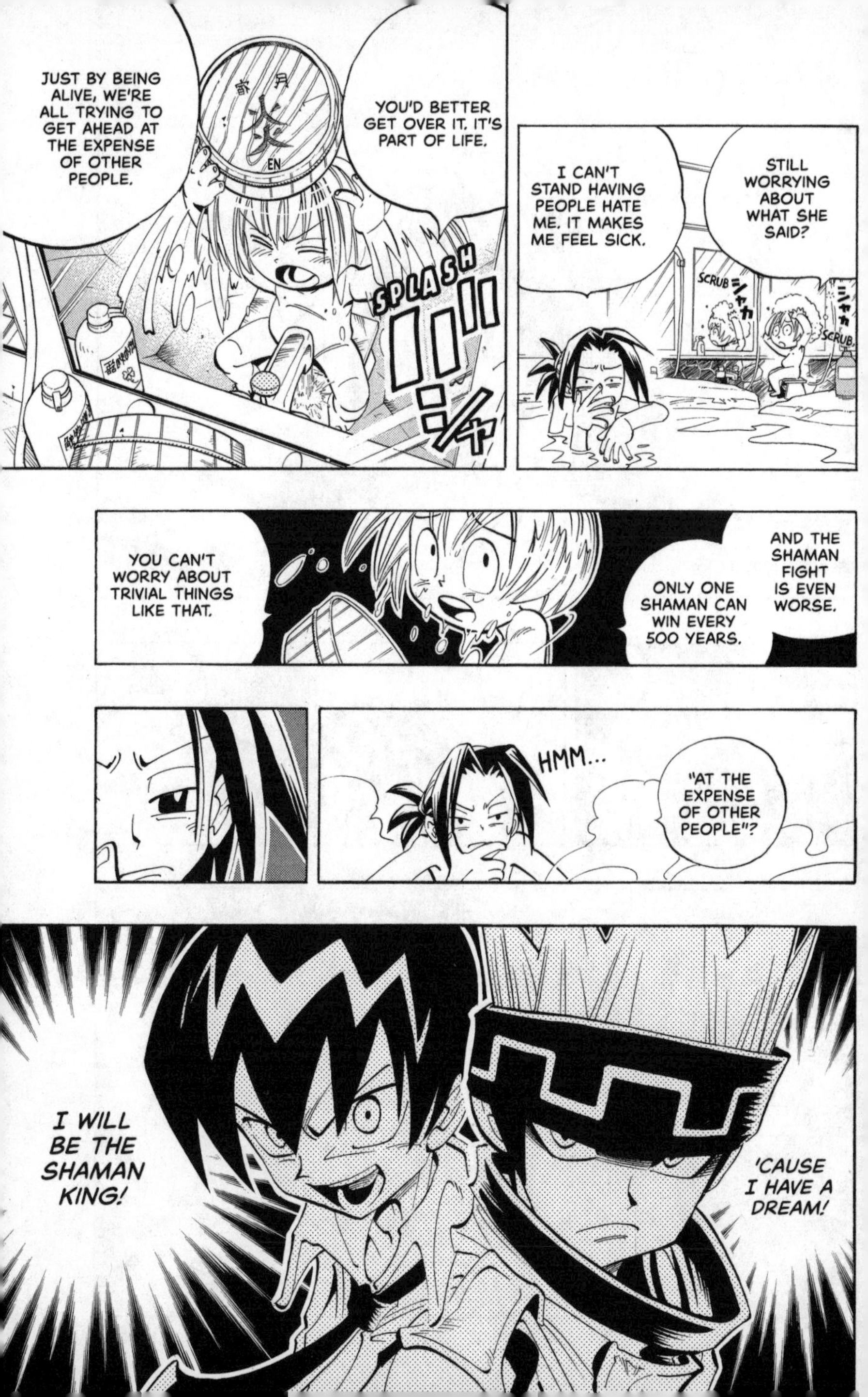
STILL WORRYING ABOUT WHAT SHE SAID?
I CAN'T STAND HAVING PEOPLE HATE ME. IT MAKES ME FEEL SICK.
SCRUB シャカ
SCRUB シャカ
YOU'D BETTER GET OVER IT. IT'S PART OF LIFE.
JUST BY BEING ALIVE, WE'RE ALL TRYING TO GET AHEAD AT THE EXPENSE OF OTHER PEOPLE.
EN
SPLASH
AND THE SHAMAN FIGHT IS EVEN WORSE.
ONLY ONE SHAMAN CAN WIN EVERY 500 YEARS.
YOU CAN'T WORRY ABOUT TRIVIAL THINGS LIKE THAT.
"AT THE EXPENSE OF OTHER PEOPLE"?
HMM...
'CAUSE I HAVE A DREAM!
I WILL BE THE SHAMAN KING!

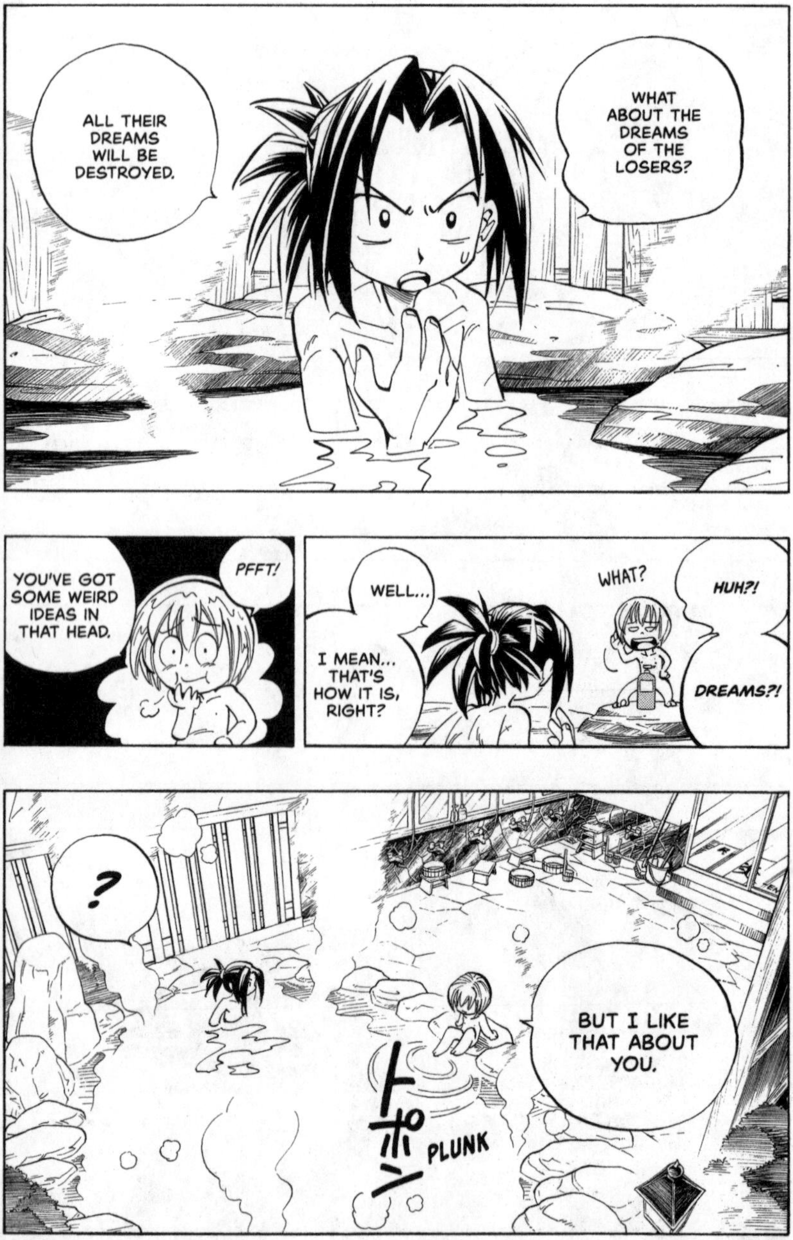
WHAT ABOUT THE DREAMS OF THE LOSERS?
ALL THEIR DREAMS WILL BE DESTROYED.
HUH?! DREAMS?!
WHAT?
WELL...
I MEAN... THAT'S HOW IT IS, RIGHT?
PFFT!
YOU'VE GOT SOME WEIRD IDEAS IN THAT HEAD.
BUT I LIKE THAT ABOUT YOU.
?
トポン PLUNK

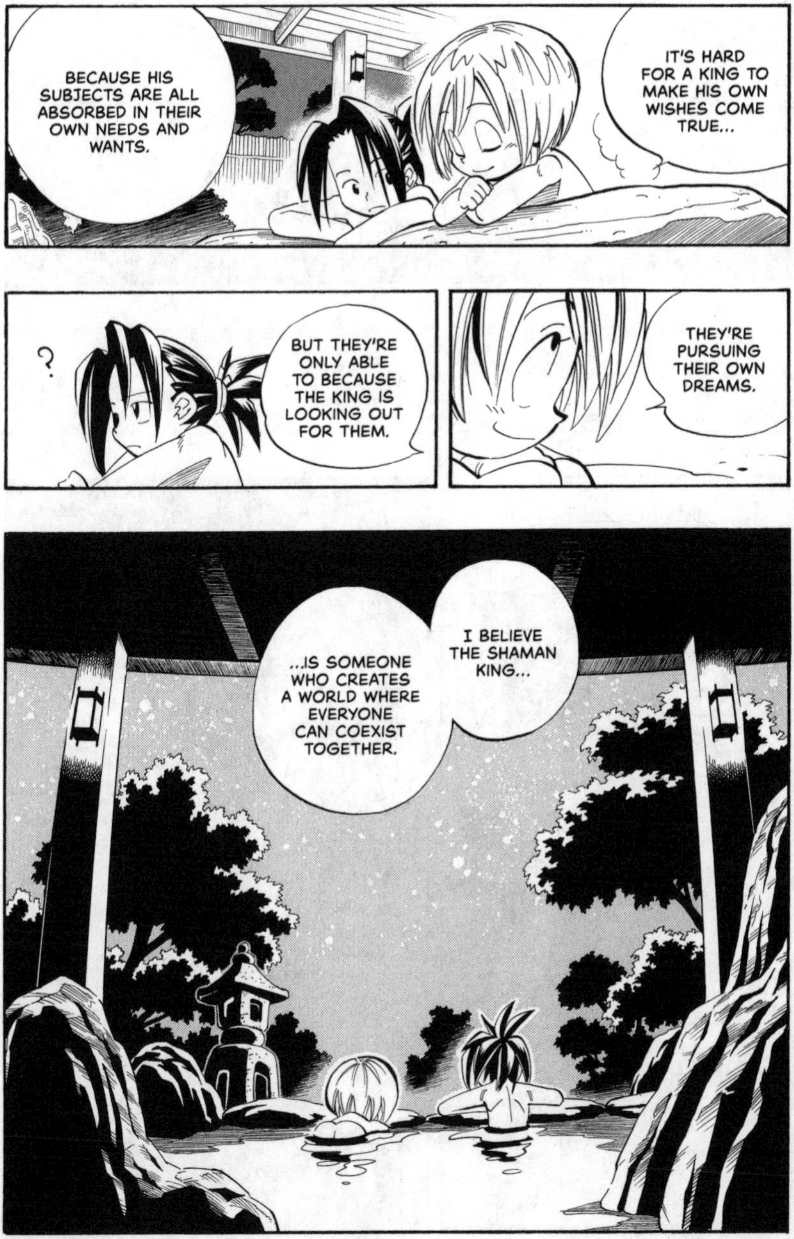

IT'S HARD FOR A KING TO MAKE HIS OWN WISHES COME TRUE...
BECAUSE HIS SUBJECTS ARE ALL ABSORBED IN THEIR OWN NEEDS AND WANTS.
THEY'RE PURSUING THEIR OWN DREAMS.
BUT THEY'RE ONLY ABLE TO BECAUSE THE KING IS LOOKING OUT FOR THEM.
?
I BELIEVE THE SHAMAN KING...
...IS SOMEONE WHO CREATES A WORLD WHERE EVERYONE CAN COEXIST TOGETHER.

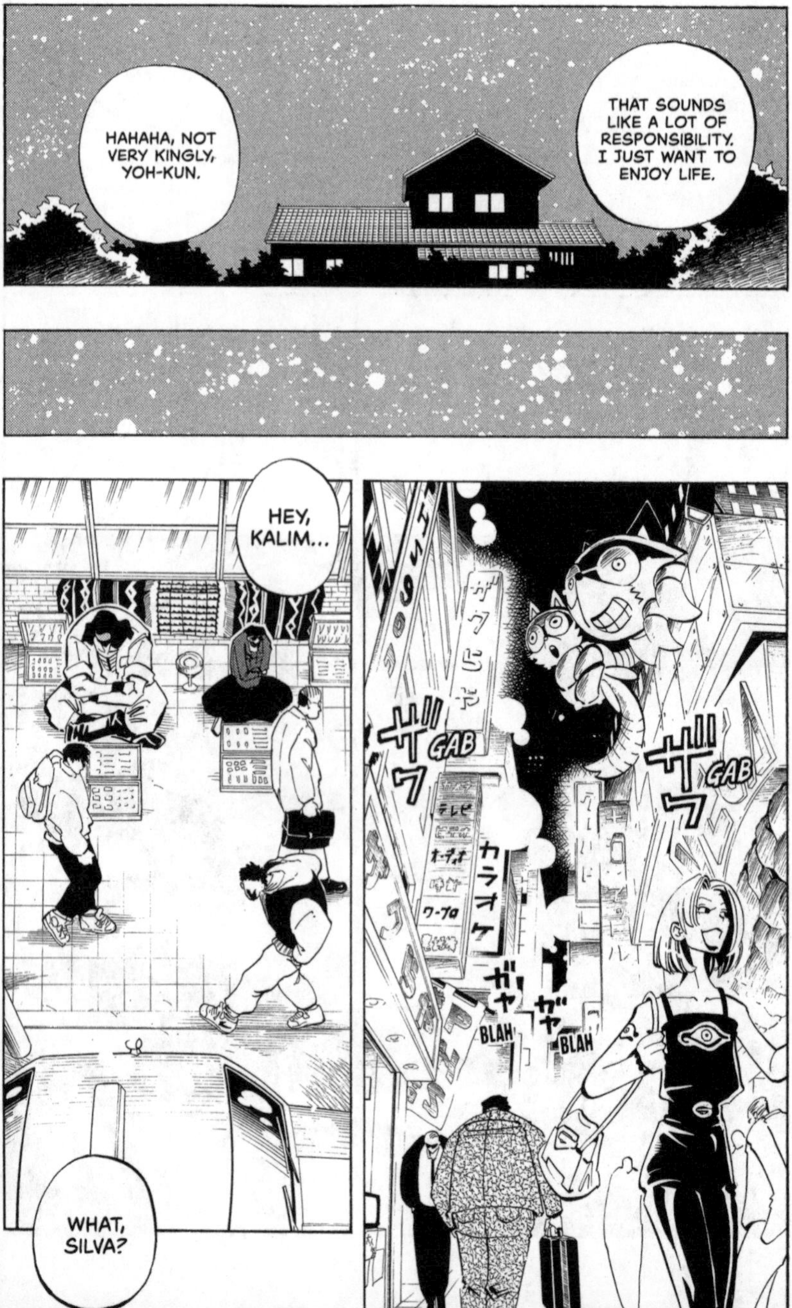
THAT SOUNDS LIKE A LOT OF RESPONSIBILITY. I JUST WANT TO ENJOY LIFE.
HAHAHA, NOT VERY KINGLY, YOH-KUN.
GAB
GAB
BLAH
BLAH
HEY, KALIM...
WHAT, SILVA?

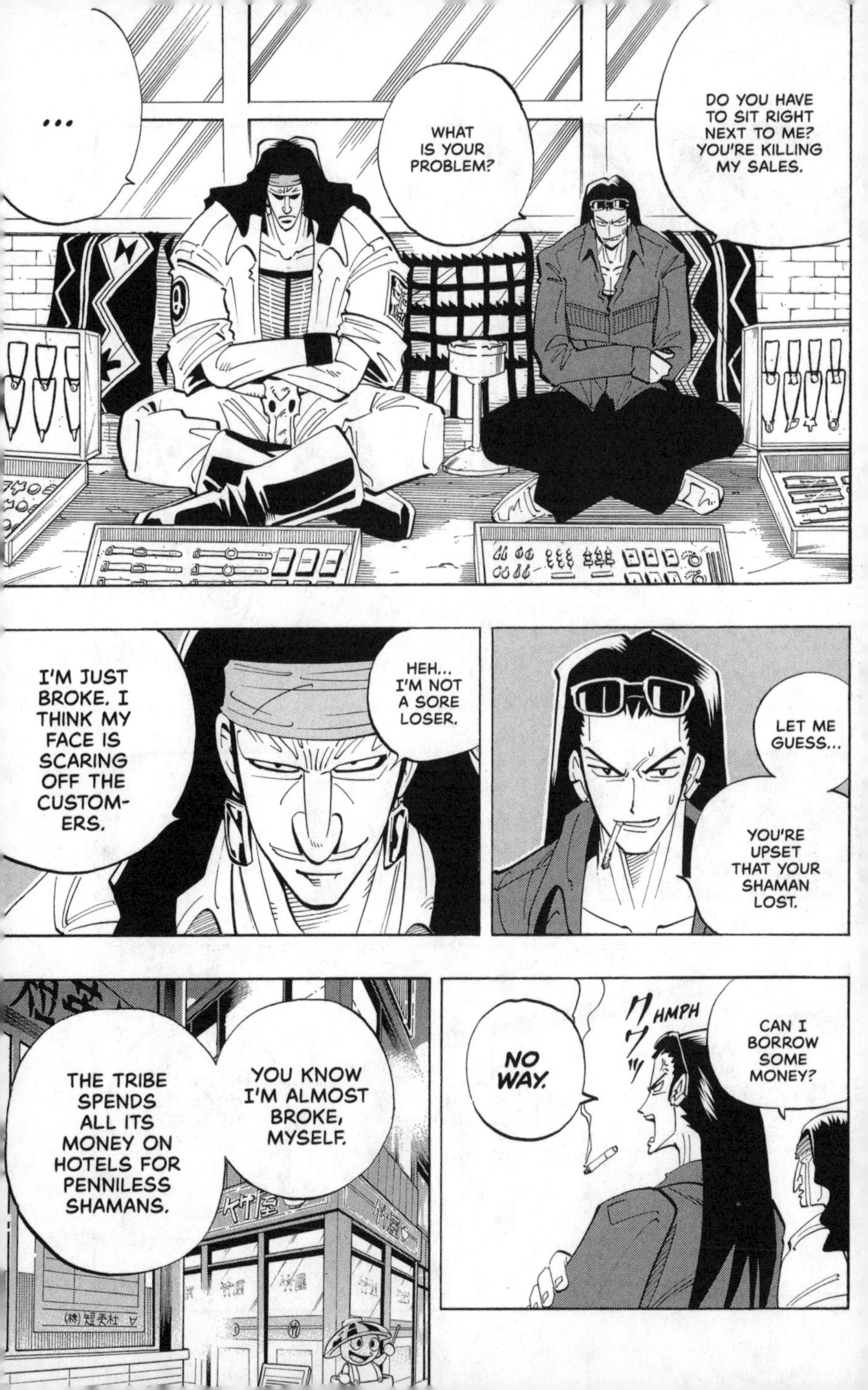
DO YOU HAVE TO SIT RIGHT NEXT TO ME? YOU'RE KILLING MY SALES.
WHAT IS YOUR PROBLEM?
...
LET ME GUESS...
YOU'RE UPSET THAT YOUR SHAMAN LOST.
HEH... I'M NOT A SORE LOSER.
I'M JUST BROKE. I THINK MY FACE IS SCARING OFF THE CUSTOM-ERS.
CAN I BORROW SOME MONEY?
HMPH
NO WAY.
YOU KNOW I'M ALMOST BROKE, MYSELF.
THE TRIBE SPENDS ALL ITS MONEY ON HOTELS FOR PENNILESS SHAMANS.

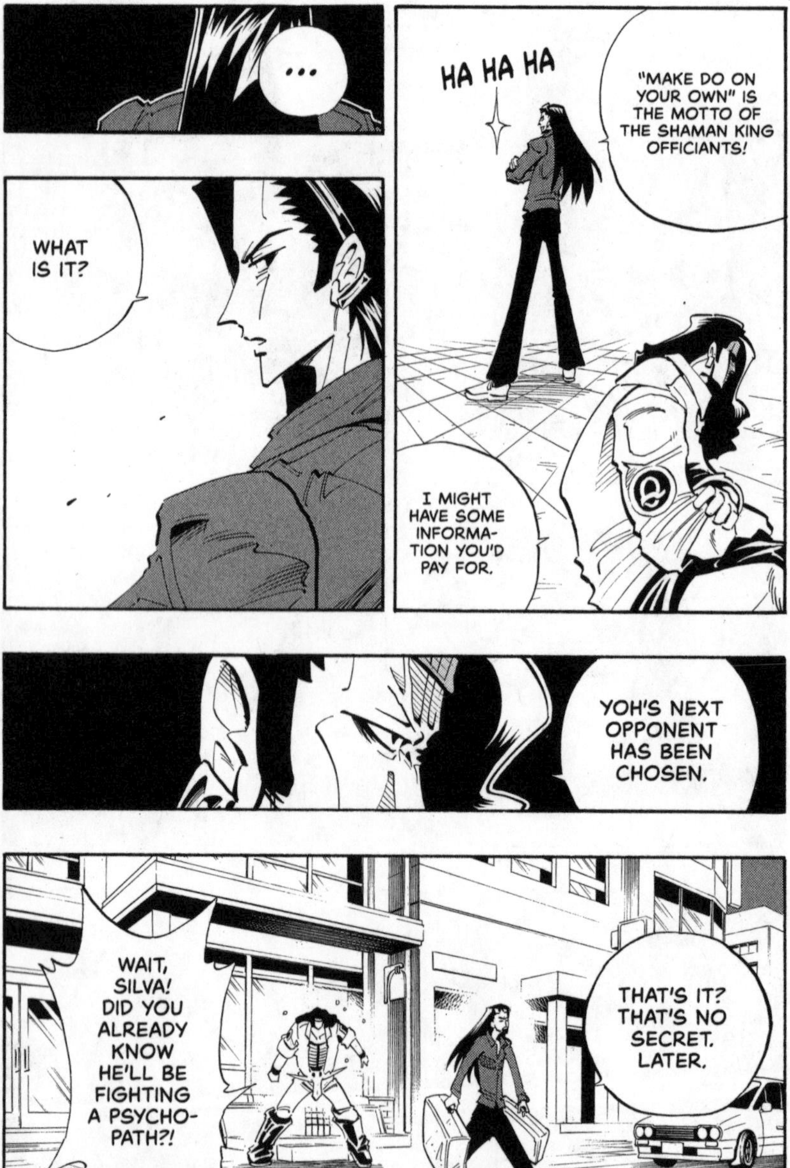
"MAKE DO ON YOUR OWN" IS THE MOTTO OF THE SHAMAN KING OFFICIANTS!
HA HA HA
I MIGHT HAVE SOME INFORMATION YOU'D PAY FOR.
...
WHAT IS IT?
YOH'S NEXT OPPONENT HAS BEEN CHOSEN.
THAT'S IT? THAT'S NO SECRET. LATER.
WAIT, SILVA! DID YOU ALREADY KNOW HE'LL BE FIGHTING A PSYCHOPATH?!

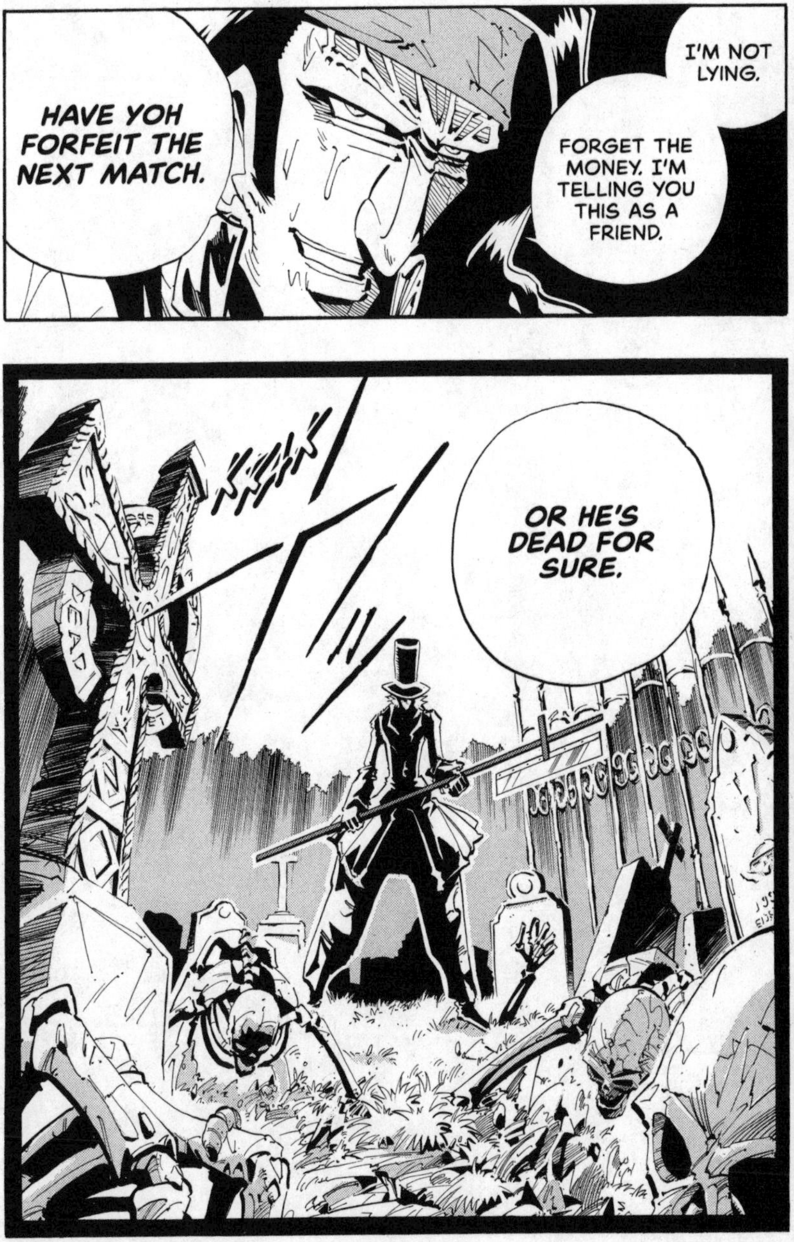
I'M NOT LYING.
FORGET THE MONEY. I'M TELLING YOU THIS AS A FRIEND.
HAVE YOH FORFEIT THE NEXT MATCH.
OR HE'S DEAD FOR SURE.

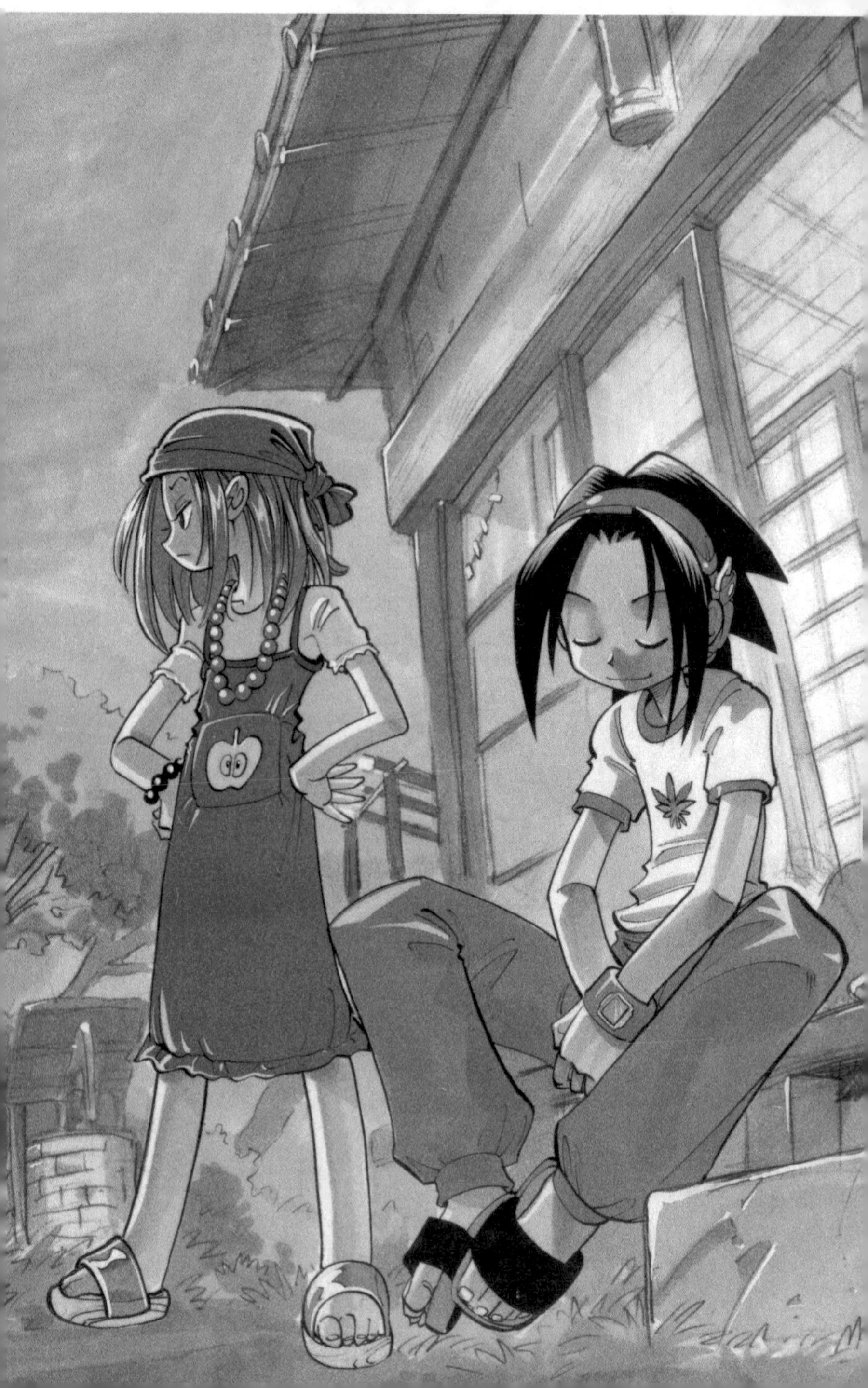

Chapter 39: Backbone

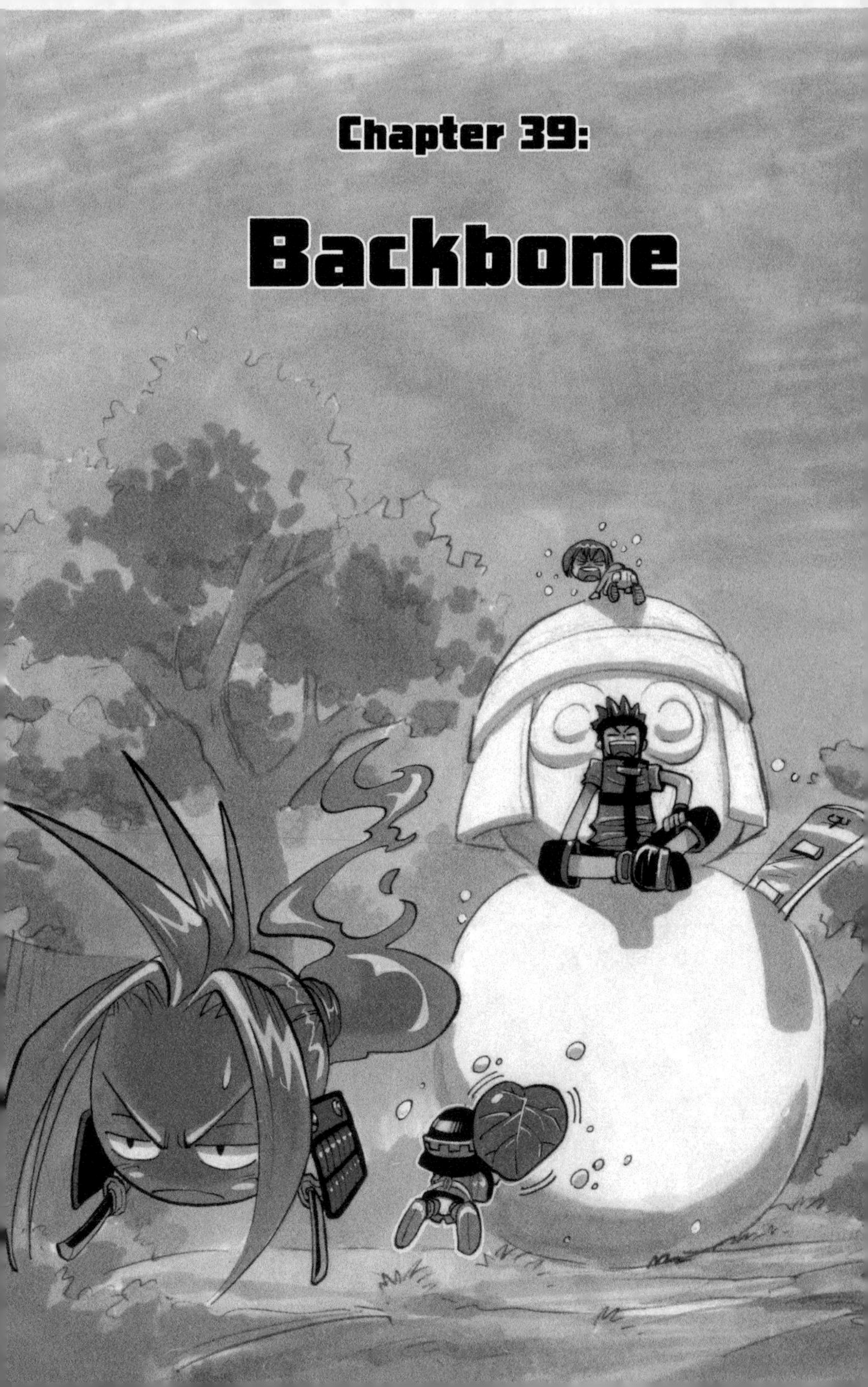

Kororo

August 1999

?

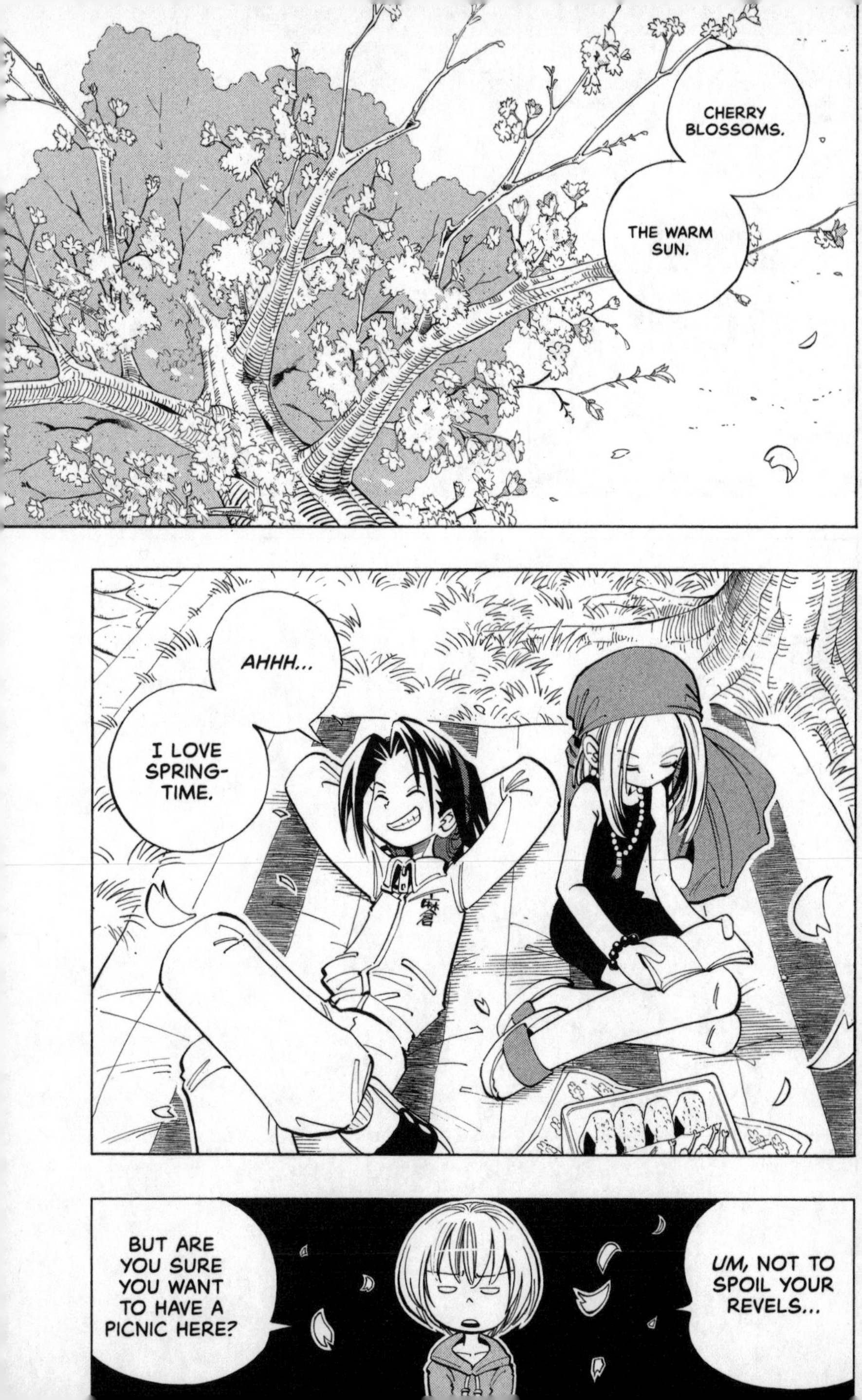
CHERRY BLOSSOMS.
THE WARM SUN.
AHHH...
I LOVE SPRING-TIME.
UM, NOT TO SPOIL YOUR REVELS...
BUT ARE YOU SURE YOU WANT TO HAVE A PICNIC HERE?

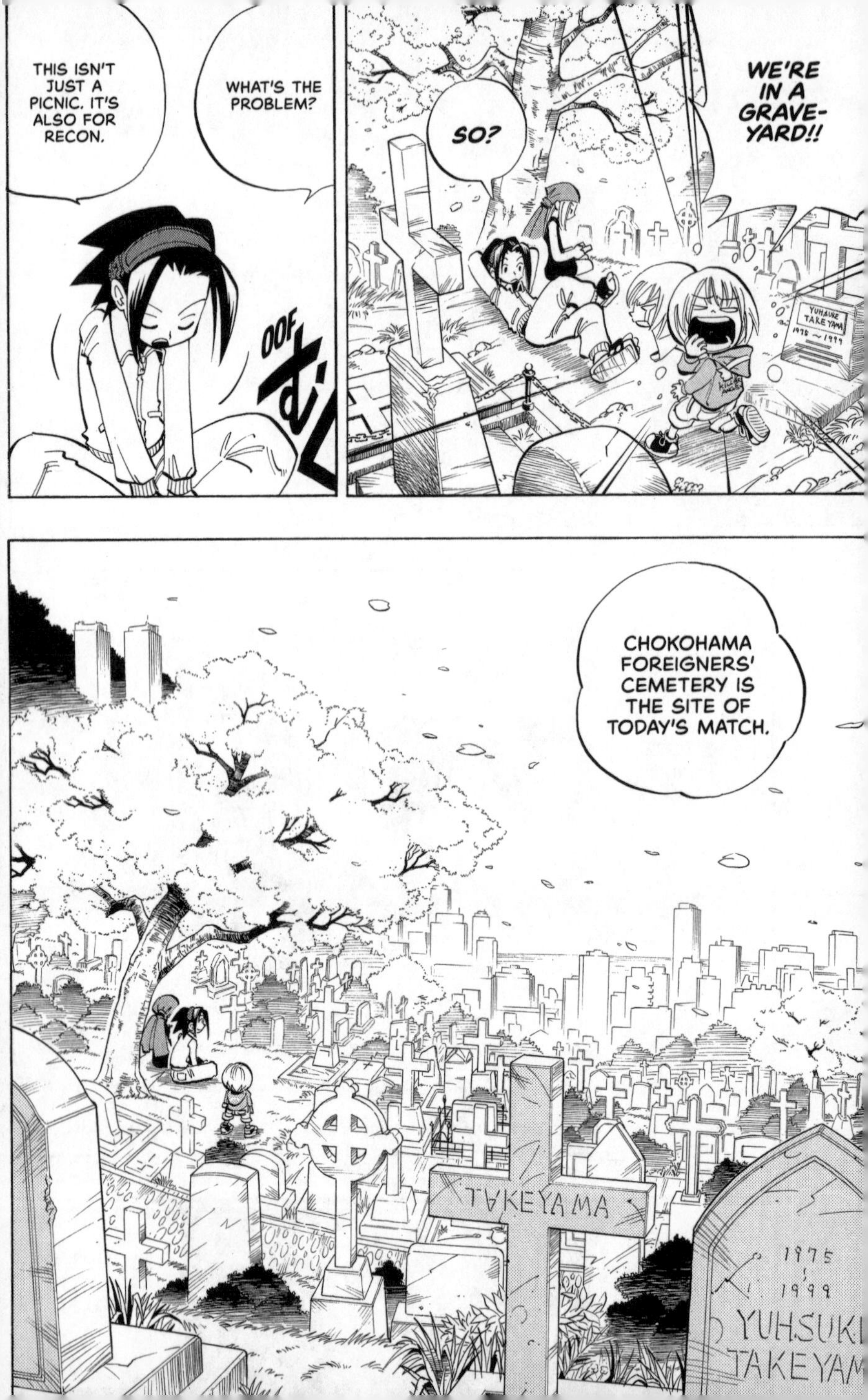
WE'RE IN A GRAVEYARD!!
SO?
WHAT'S THE PROBLEM?
THIS ISN'T JUST A PICNIC. IT'S ALSO FOR RECON.
OOF
CHOKOHAMA FOREIGNERS' CEMETERY IS THE SITE OF TODAY'S MATCH.
TAKEYAMA
1975
1999

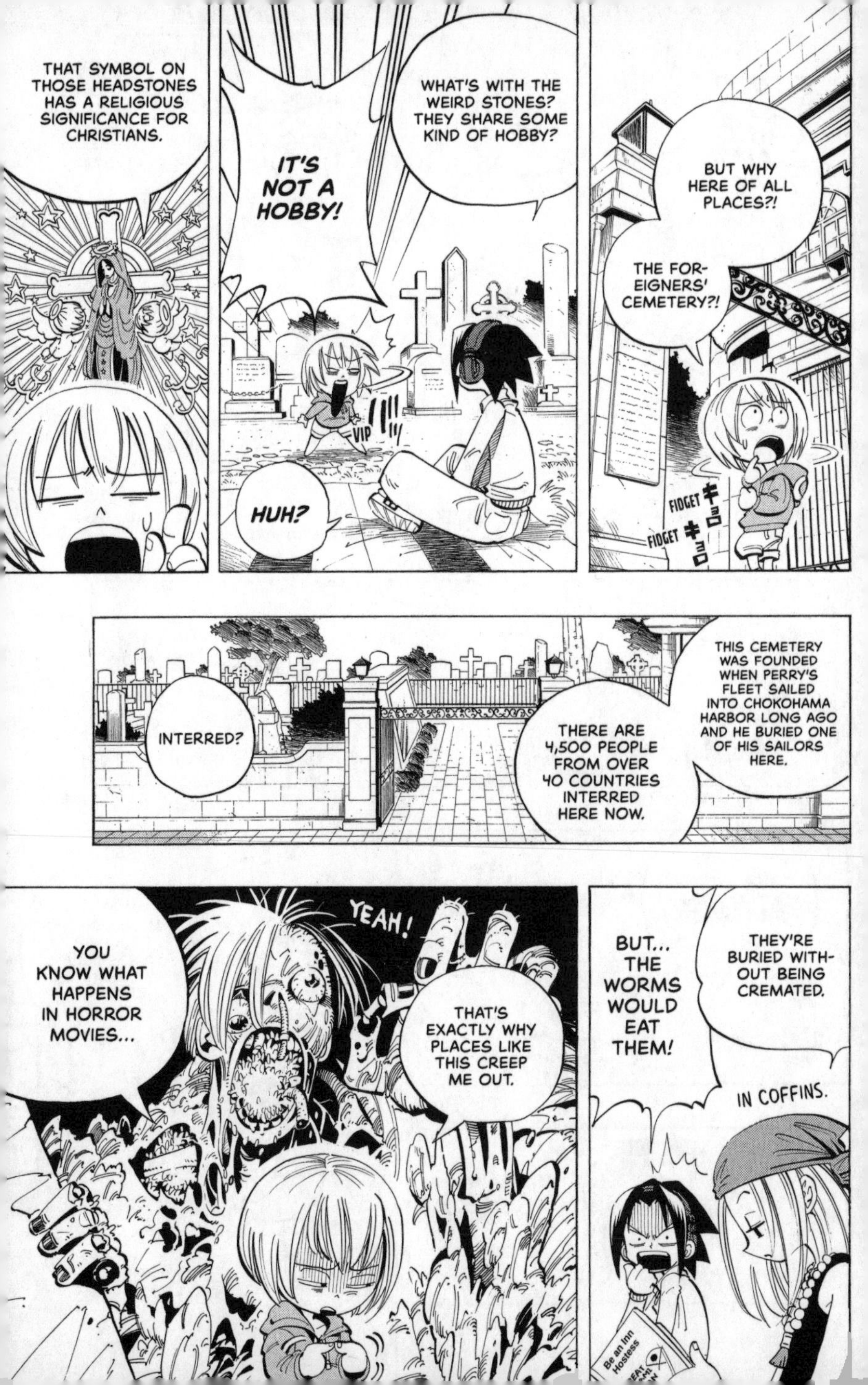
BUT WHY HERE OF ALL PLACES?!
THE FOR-EIGNERS' CEMETERY?!
FIDGET
FIDGET
WHAT'S WITH THE WEIRD STONES? THEY SHARE SOME KIND OF HOBBY?
IT'S NOT A HOBBY!
VIP
HUH?
THAT SYMBOL ON THOSE HEADSTONES HAS A RELIGIOUS SIGNIFICANCE FOR CHRISTIANS.
THIS CEMETERY WAS FOUNDED WHEN PERRY'S FLEET SAILED INTO CHOKOHAMA HARBOR LONG AGO AND HE BURIED ONE OF HIS SAILORS HERE.
THERE ARE 4,500 PEOPLE FROM OVER 40 COUNTRIES INTERRED HERE NOW.
INTERRED?
THEY'RE BURIED WITH-OUT BEING CREMATED.
IN COFFINS.
BUT... THE WORMS WOULD EAT THEM!
Be an Inn Hostess
YEAH!
THAT'S EXACTLY WHY PLACES LIKE THIS CREEP ME OUT.
YOU KNOW WHAT HAPPENS IN HORROR MOVIES...

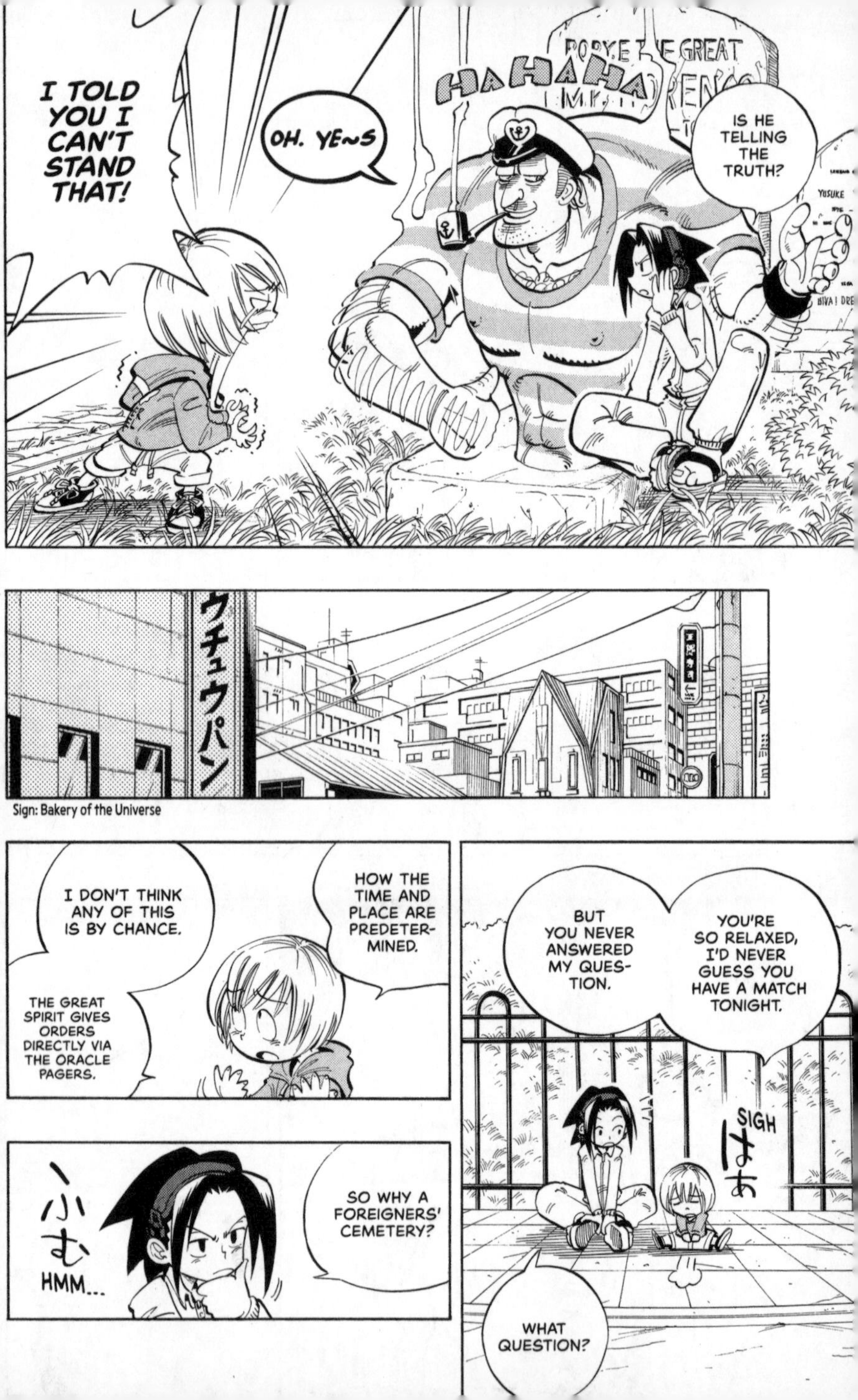
IS HE TELLING THE TRUTH?
HAHAHA
OH. YE~S
I TOLD YOU I CAN'T STAND THAT!
ウチュウパン
YOU'RE SO RELAXED, I'D NEVER GUESS YOU HAVE A MATCH TONIGHT.
BUT YOU NEVER ANSWERED MY QUESTION.
SIGH
はぁ
WHAT QUESTION?
HOW THE TIME AND PLACE ARE PREDETERMINED.
I DON'T THINK ANY OF THIS IS BY CHANCE.
THE GREAT SPIRIT GIVES ORDERS DIRECTLY VIA THE ORACLE PAGERS.
SO WHY A FOREIGNERS' CEMETERY?
ふむ
HMM...
Sign: Bakery of the Universe

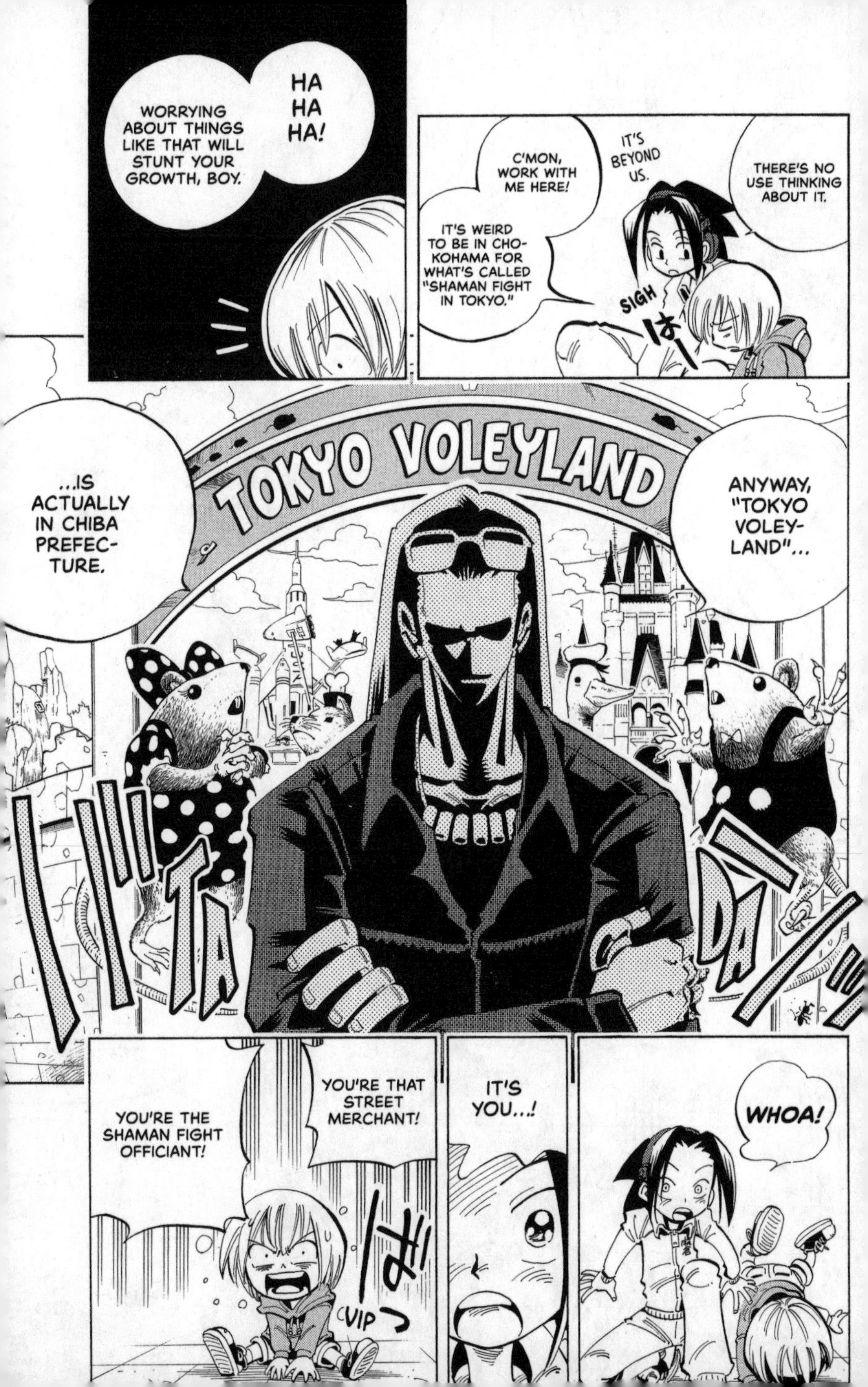
THERE'S NO USE THINKING ABOUT IT.
IT'S BEYOND US.
C'MON, WORK WITH ME HERE!
IT'S WEIRD TO BE IN CHO-KOHAMA FOR WHAT'S CALLED "SHAMAN FIGHT IN TOKYO."
SIGH
HA HA HA!
WORRYING ABOUT THINGS LIKE THAT WILL STUNT YOUR GROWTH, BOY.
ANYWAY, "TOKYO VOLEY-LAND"...
TOKYO VOLEYLAND
...IS ACTUALLY IN CHIBA PREFEC-TURE.
DA
TA
WHOA!
IT'S YOU...!
YOU'RE THAT STREET MERCHANT!
YOU'RE THE SHAMAN FIGHT OFFICIANT!
VIP

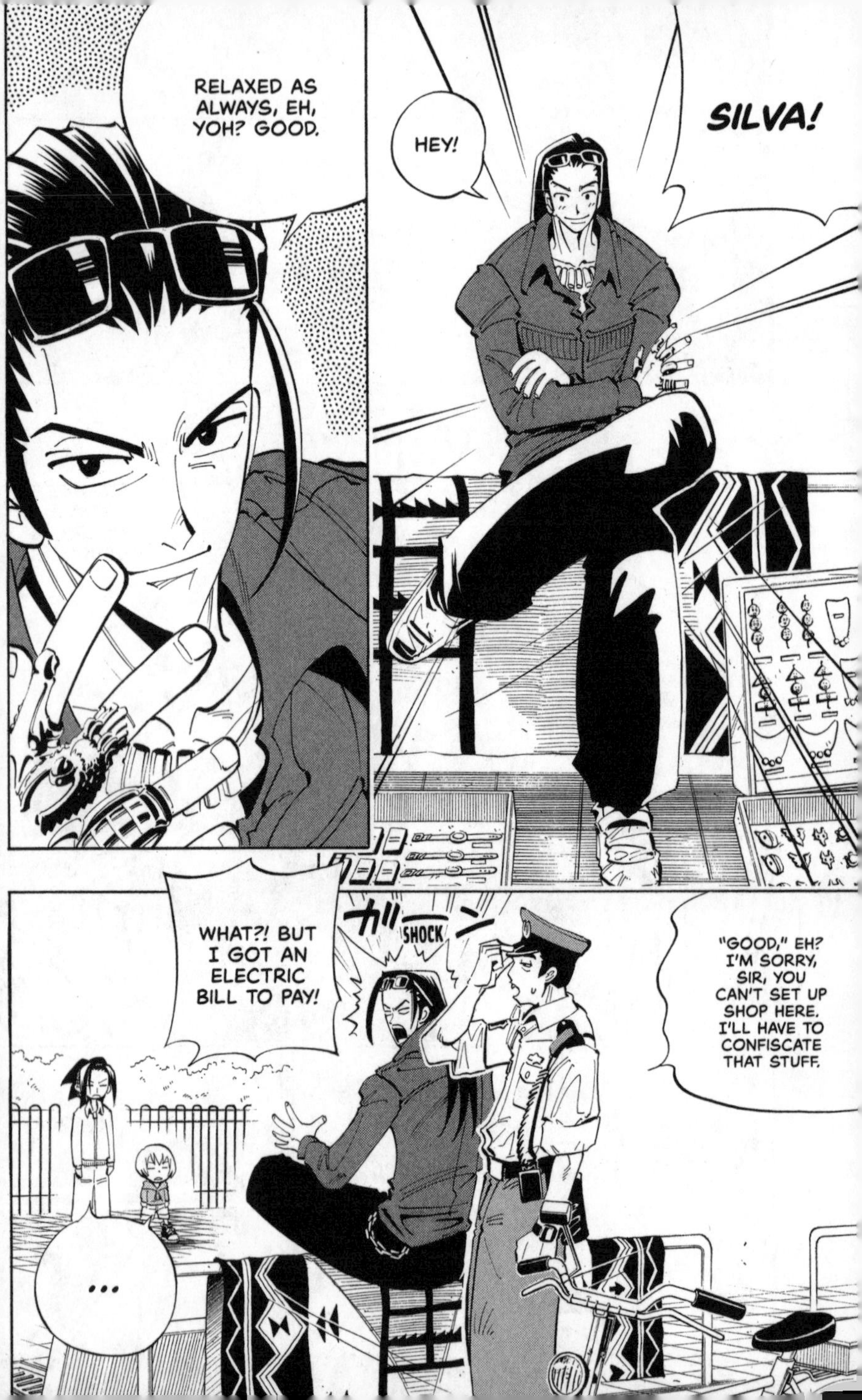
SILVA!
HEY!
RELAXED AS ALWAYS, EH, YOH? GOOD.
"GOOD," EH? I'M SORRY, SIR, YOU CAN'T SET UP SHOP HERE. I'LL HAVE TO CONFISCATE THAT STUFF.
SHOCK
WHAT?! BUT I GOT AN ELECTRIC BILL TO PAY!
...

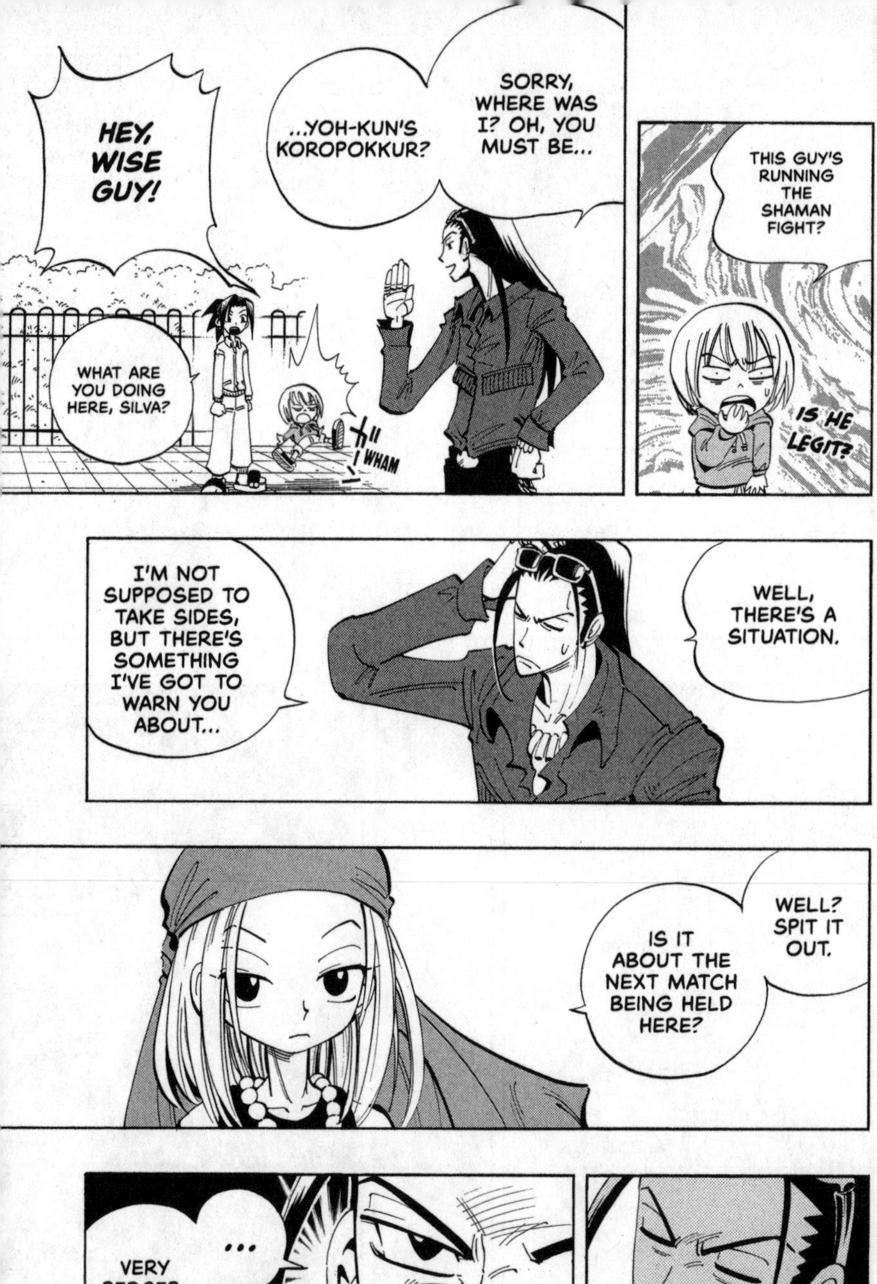

THIS GUY'S RUNNING THE SHAMAN FIGHT?
IS HE LEGIT?
SORRY, WHERE WAS I? OH, YOU MUST BE...
...YOH-KUN'S KOROPOKKUR?
HEY, WISE GUY!
WHAM
WHAT ARE YOU DOING HERE, SILVA?
WELL, THERE'S A SITUATION.
I'M NOT SUPPOSED TO TAKE SIDES, BUT THERE'S SOMETHING I'VE GOT TO WARN YOU ABOUT...
WELL? SPIT IT OUT.
IS IT ABOUT THE NEXT MATCH BEING HELD HERE?
...
VERY PERCEPTIVE.

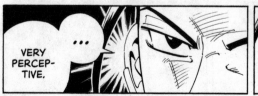

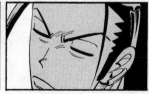

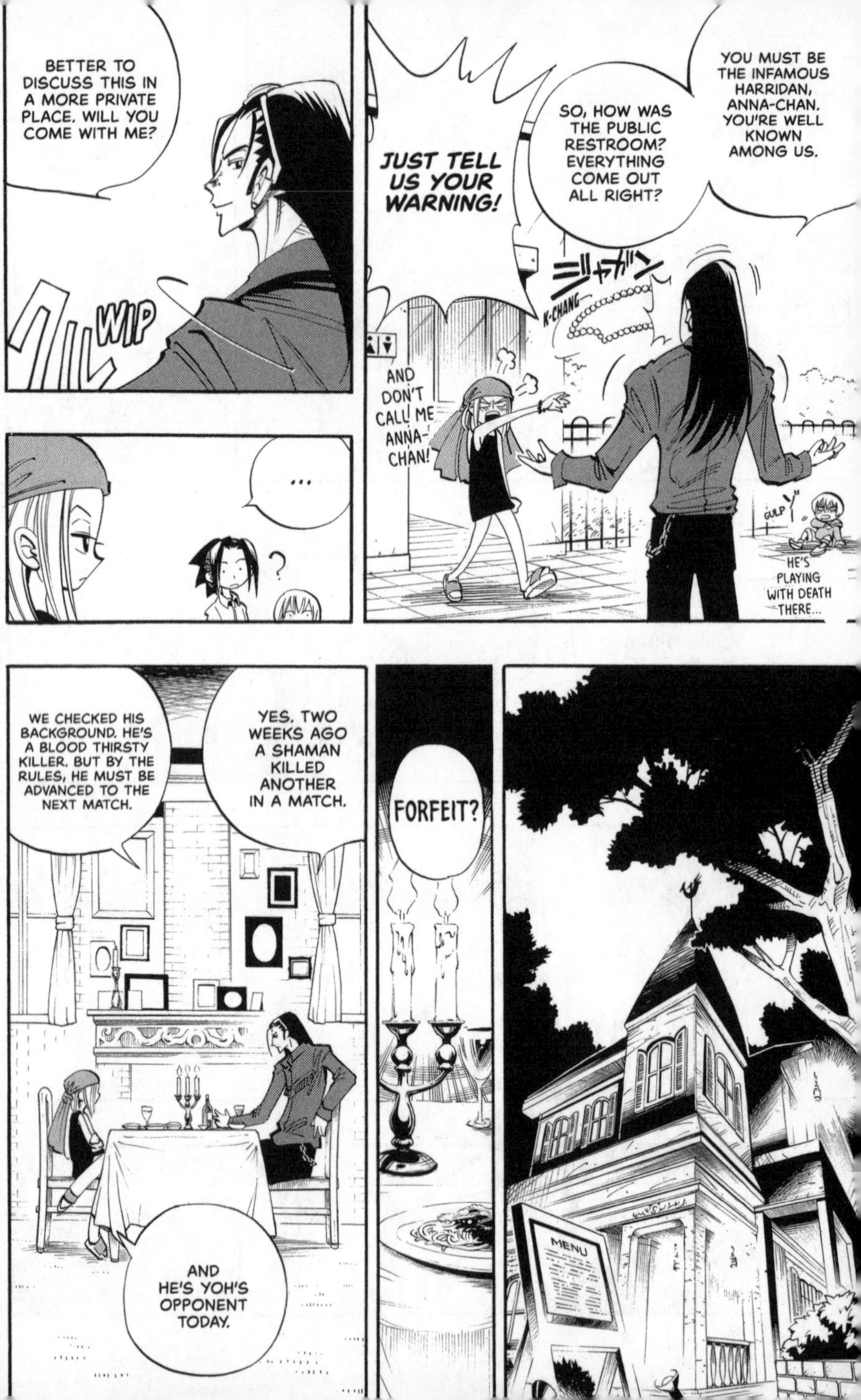
YOU MUST BE THE INFAMOUS HARRIDAN, ANNA-CHAN. YOU'RE WELL KNOWN AMONG US.
SO, HOW WAS THE PUBLIC RESTROOM? EVERYTHING COME OUT ALL RIGHT?
JUST TELL US YOUR WARNING!
K-CHANG
AND DON'T CALL ME ANNA-CHAN!
GULP
HE'S PLAYING WITH DEATH THERE...
BETTER TO DISCUSS THIS IN A MORE PRIVATE PLACE. WILL YOU COME WITH ME?
WIP
...
MENU
FORFEIT?
YES. TWO WEEKS AGO A SHAMAN KILLED ANOTHER IN A MATCH.
WE CHECKED HIS BACKGROUND. HE'S A BLOOD THIRSTY KILLER. BUT BY THE RULES, HE MUST BE ADVANCED TO THE NEXT MATCH.
AND HE'S YOH'S OPPONENT TODAY.

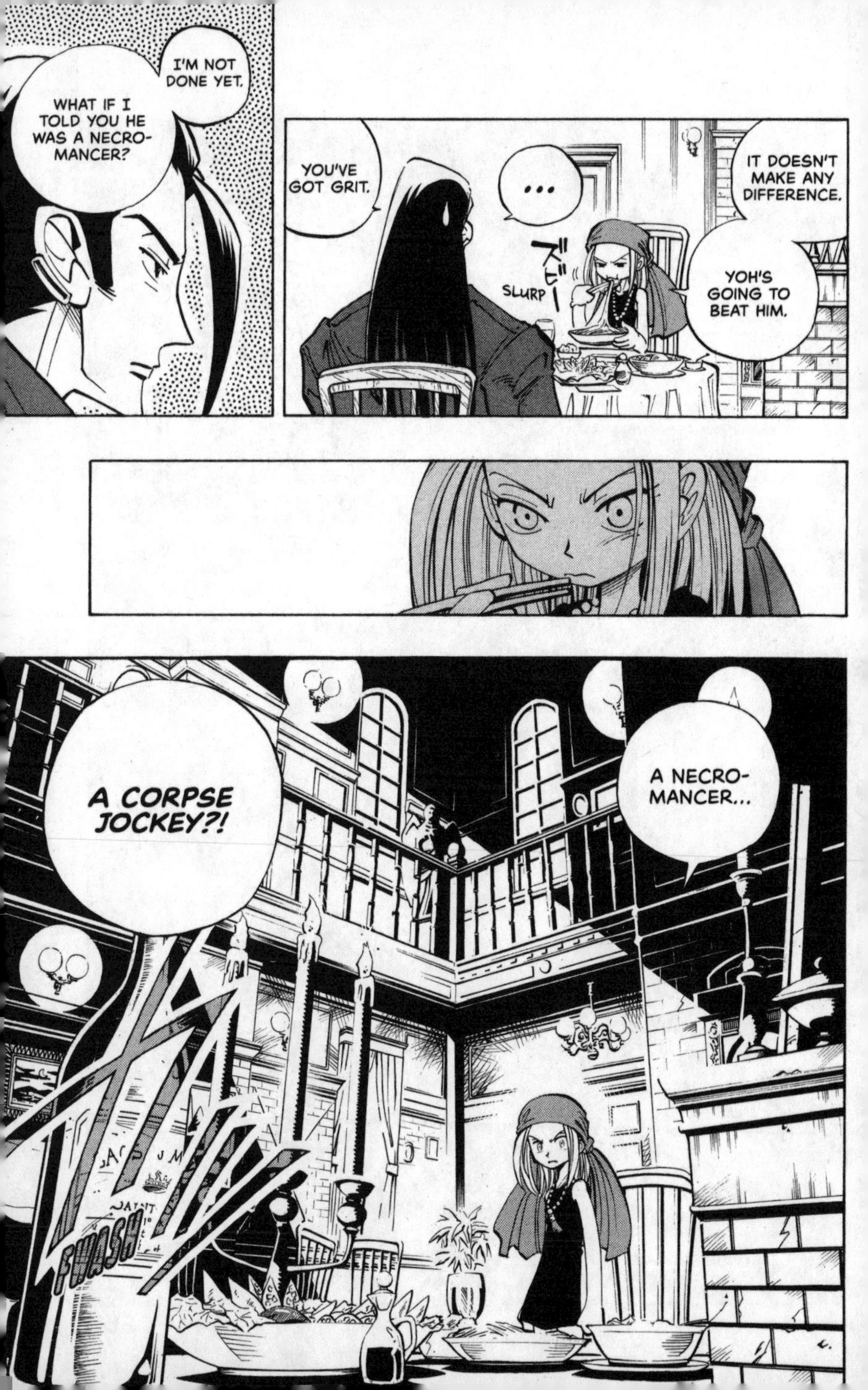
IT DOESN'T MAKE ANY DIFFERENCE.
YOH'S GOING TO BEAT HIM.
...
SLURP
YOU'VE GOT GRIT.
I'M NOT DONE YET.
WHAT IF I TOLD YOU HE WAS A NECRO-MANCER?
A NECRO-MANCER...
A CORPSE JOCKEY?!
FWASH

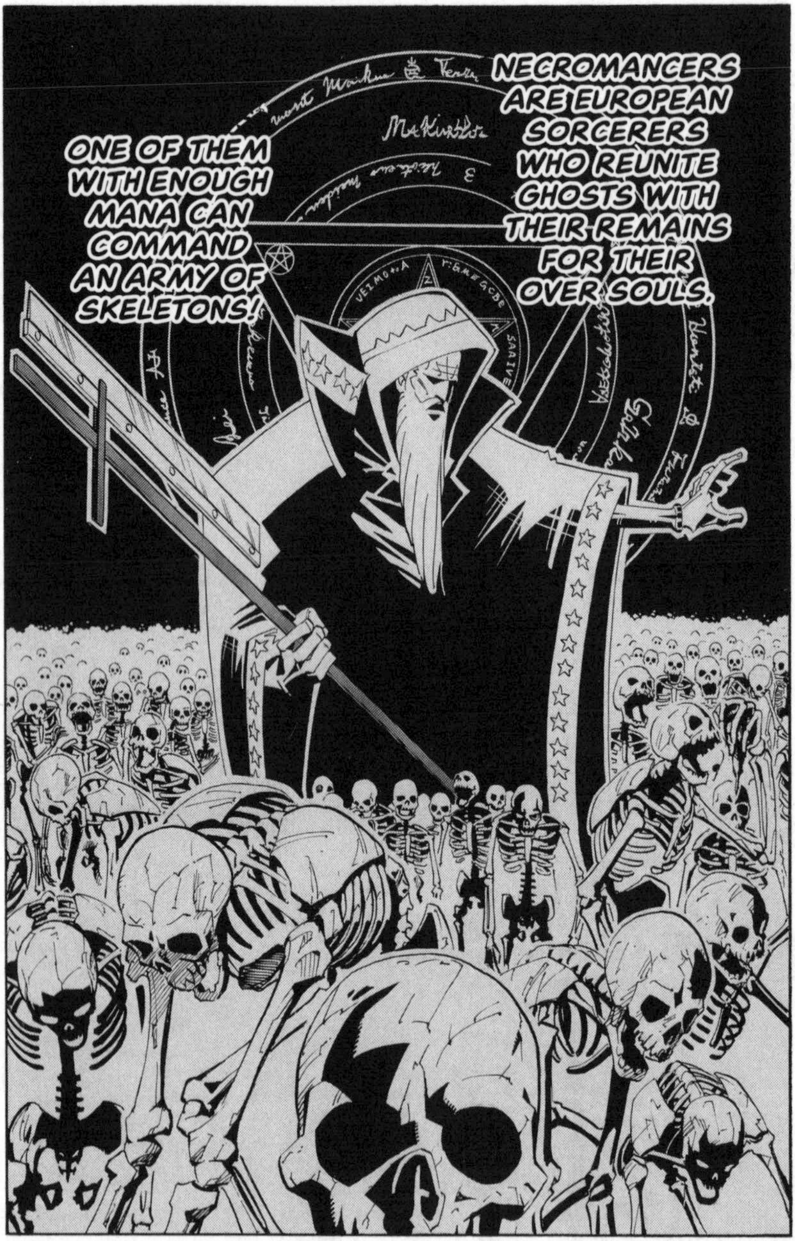
NECROMANCERS ARE EUROPEAN SORCERERS WHO REUNITE GHOSTS WITH THEIR REMAINS FOR THEIR OVER SOULS.
ONE OF THEM WITH ENOUGH MANA CAN COMMAND AN ARMY OF SKELETONS!

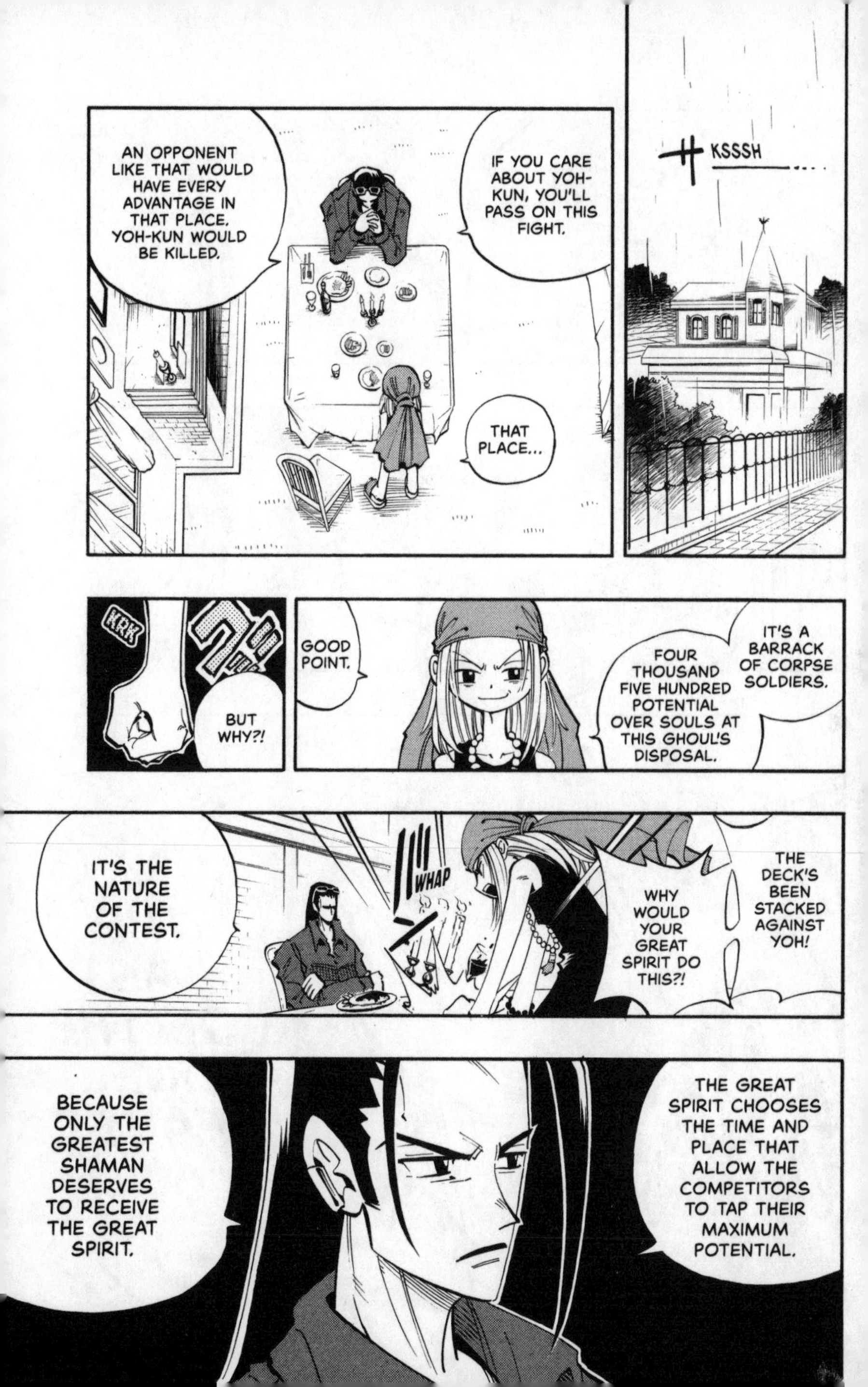
KSSSH
IF YOU CARE ABOUT YOH-KUN, YOU'LL PASS ON THIS FIGHT.
AN OPPONENT LIKE THAT WOULD HAVE EVERY ADVANTAGE IN THAT PLACE. YOH-KUN WOULD BE KILLED.
THAT PLACE...
IT'S A BARRACK OF CORPSE SOLDIERS.
FOUR THOUSAND FIVE HUNDRED POTENTIAL OVER SOULS AT THIS GHOUL'S DISPOSAL.
GOOD POINT.
KRK
BUT WHY?!
THE DECK'S BEEN STACKED AGAINST YOH!
WHY WOULD YOUR GREAT SPIRIT DO THIS?!
WHAP
IT'S THE NATURE OF THE CONTEST.
THE GREAT SPIRIT CHOOSES THE TIME AND PLACE THAT ALLOW THE COMPETITORS TO TAP THEIR MAXIMUM POTENTIAL.
BECAUSE ONLY THE GREATEST SHAMAN DESERVES TO RECEIVE THE GREAT SPIRIT.

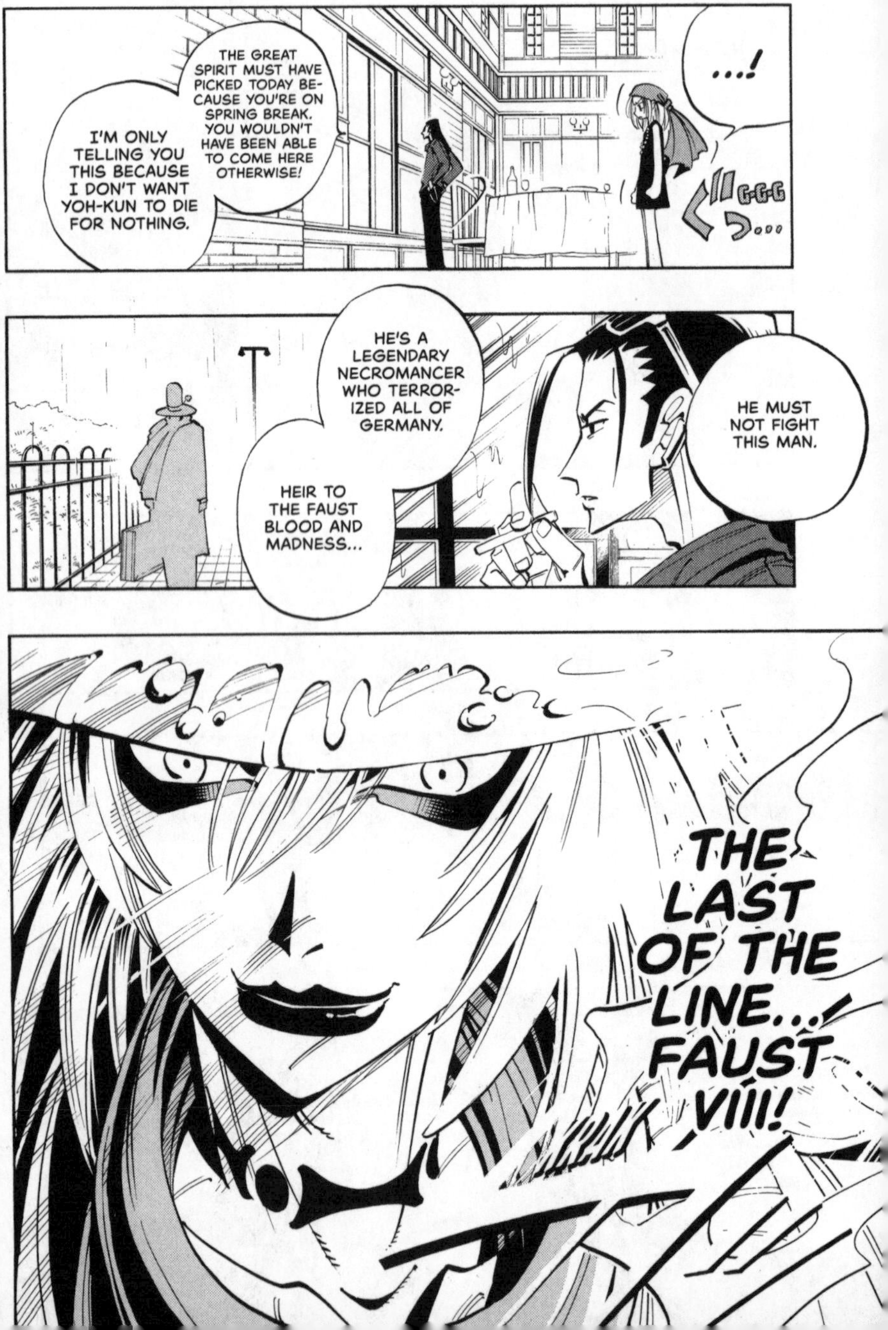
...!
G-G-G...
THE GREAT SPIRIT MUST HAVE PICKED TODAY BECAUSE YOU'RE ON SPRING BREAK. YOU WOULDN'T HAVE BEEN ABLE TO COME HERE OTHERWISE!
I'M ONLY TELLING YOU THIS BECAUSE I DON'T WANT YOH-KUN TO DIE FOR NOTHING.
HE MUST NOT FIGHT THIS MAN.
HE'S A LEGENDARY NECROMANCER WHO TERRORIZED ALL OF GERMANY.
HEIR TO THE FAUST BLOOD AND MADNESS...
THE LAST OF THE LINE...! FAUST VIII!

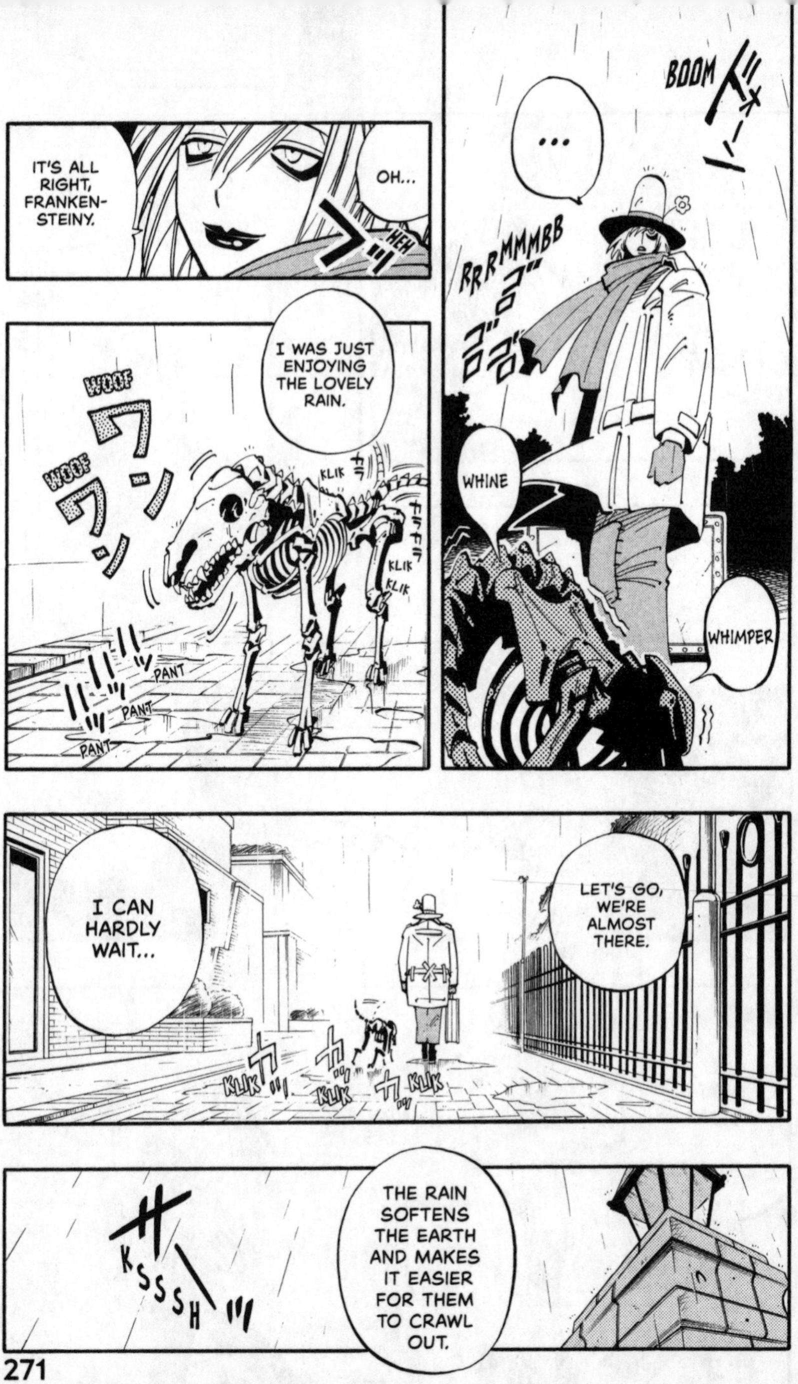
BOOM
...
RRRMMMBB
WHINE
WHIMPER
OH...
HEH
IT'S ALL RIGHT, FRANKEN-STEINY.
I WAS JUST ENJOYING THE LOVELY RAIN.
WOOF
WOOF
KLIK
KLIK
KLIK
PANT
PANT
PANT
LET'S GO, WE'RE ALMOST THERE.
I CAN HARDLY WAIT...
KLIK
KLIK
KLIK
THE RAIN SOFTENS THE EARTH AND MAKES IT EASIER FOR THEM TO CRAWL OUT.
KSSSH

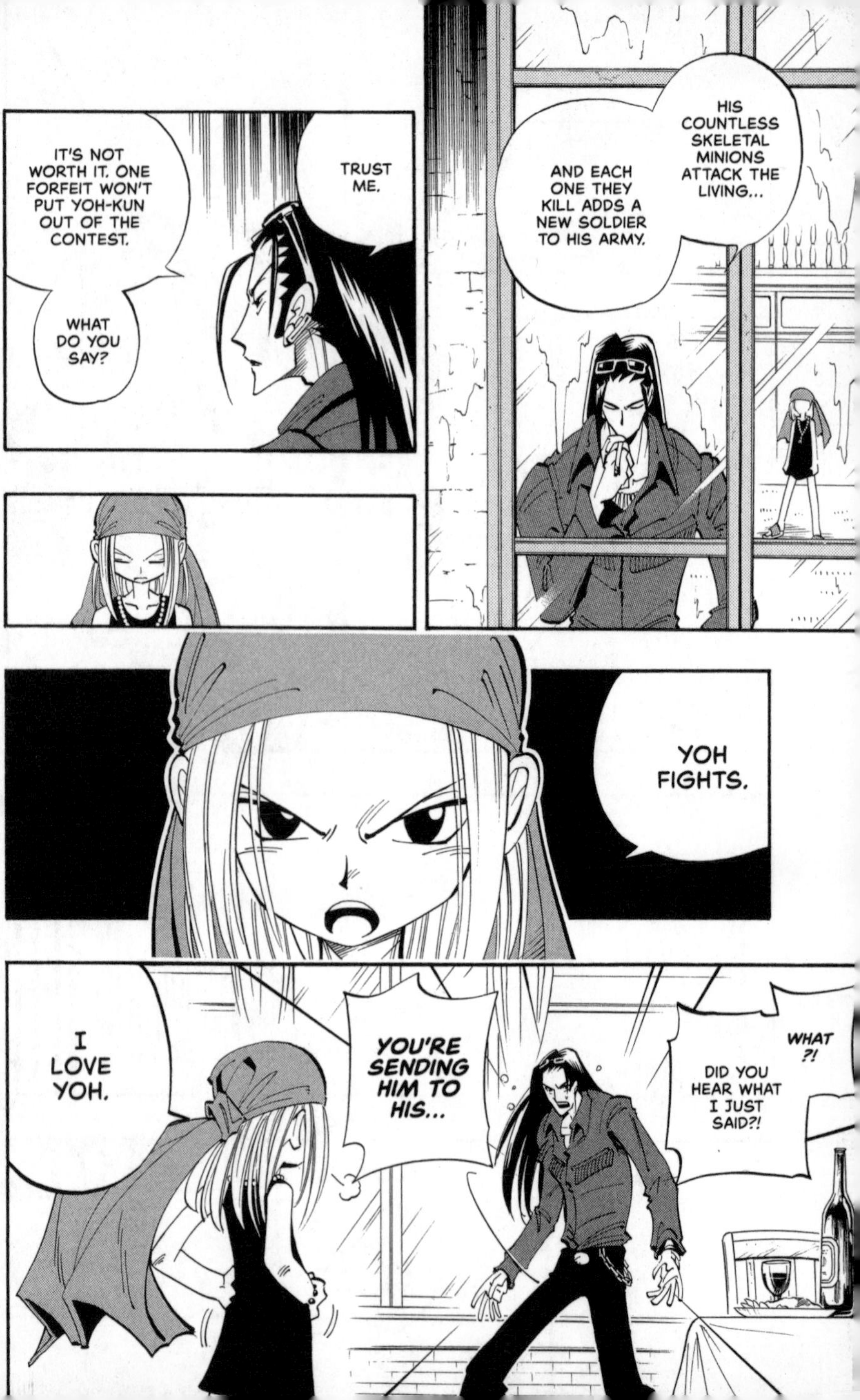
HIS COUNTLESS SKELETAL MINIONS ATTACK THE LIVING...
AND EACH ONE THEY KILL ADDS A NEW SOLDIER TO HIS ARMY.
TRUST ME.
IT'S NOT WORTH IT. ONE FORFEIT WON'T PUT YOH-KUN OUT OF THE CONTEST.
WHAT DO YOU SAY?
YOH FIGHTS.
WHAT?!
DID YOU HEAR WHAT I JUST SAID?!
YOU'RE SENDING HIM TO HIS...
I LOVE YOH.

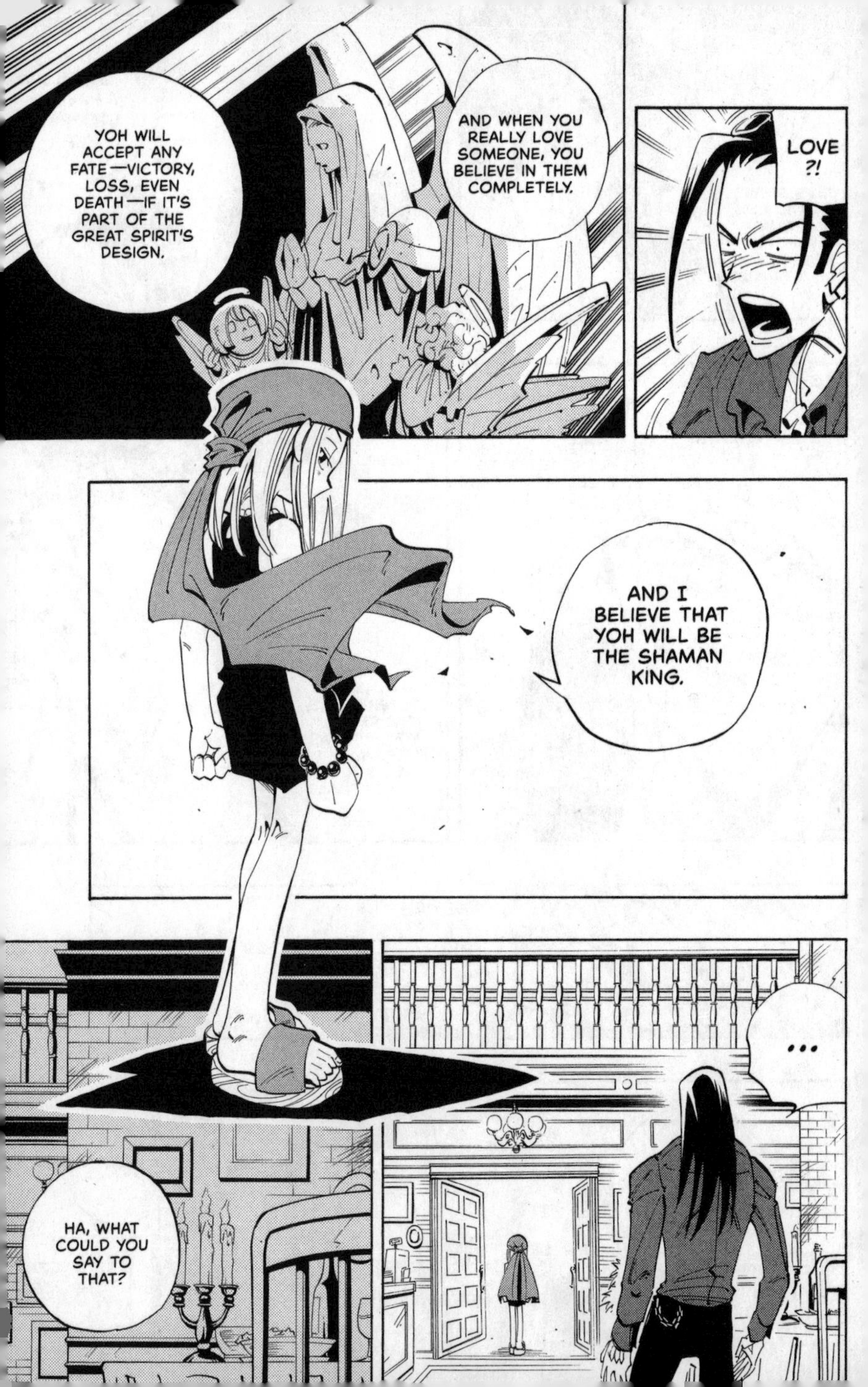
LOVE ?!
YOH WILL ACCEPT ANY FATE—VICTORY, LOSS, EVEN DEATH—IF IT'S PART OF THE GREAT SPIRIT'S DESIGN.
AND WHEN YOU REALLY LOVE SOMEONE, YOU BELIEVE IN THEM COMPLETELY.
AND I BELIEVE THAT YOH WILL BE THE SHAMAN KING.
...
HA, WHAT COULD YOU SAY TO THAT?

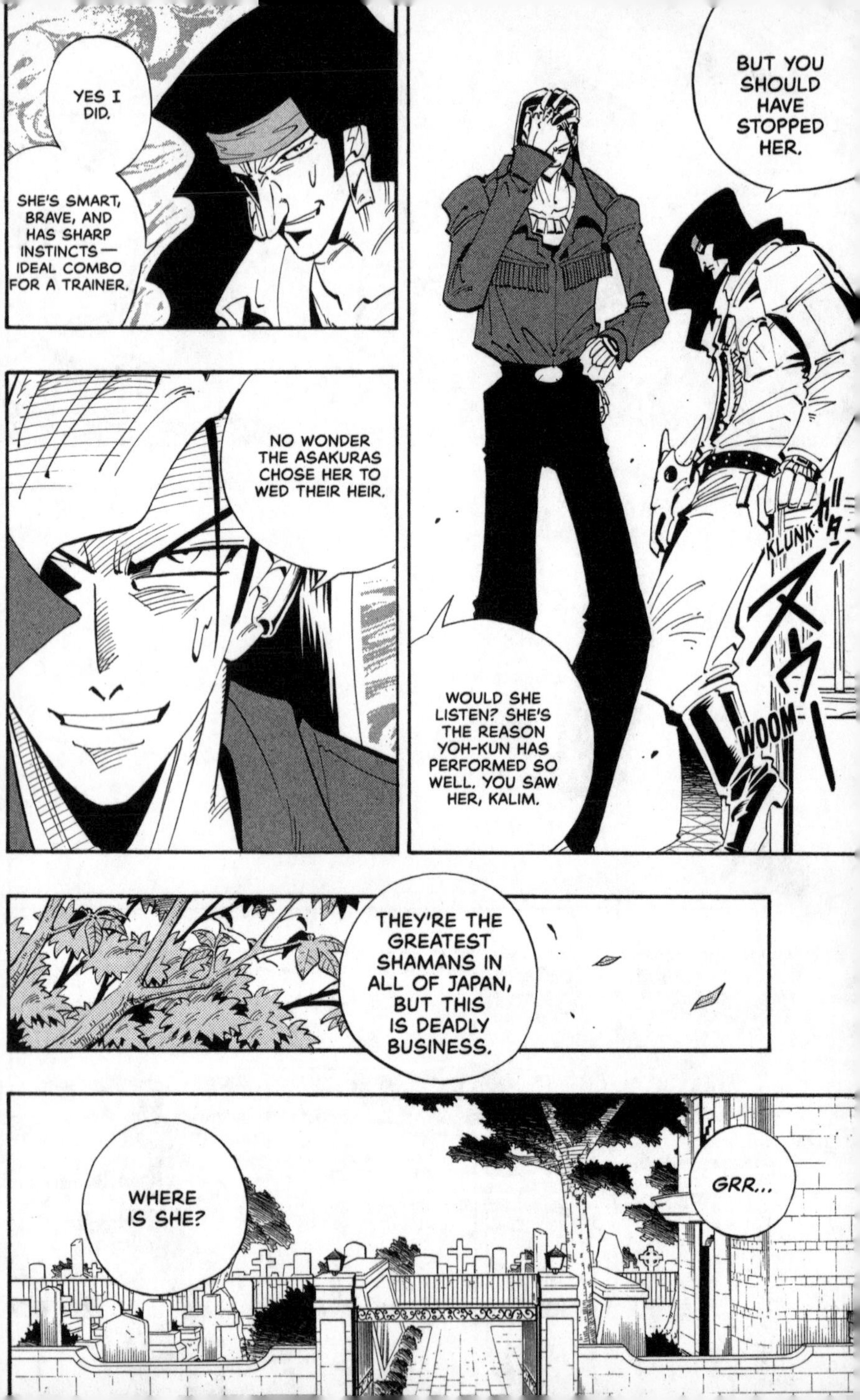
BUT YOU SHOULD HAVE STOPPED HER.
KLUNK
WOULD SHE LISTEN? SHE'S THE REASON YOH-KUN HAS PERFORMED SO WELL. YOU SAW HER, KALIM.
WOOM
YES I DID.
SHE'S SMART, BRAVE, AND HAS SHARP INSTINCTS— IDEAL COMBO FOR A TRAINER.
NO WONDER THE ASAKURAS CHOSE HER TO WED THEIR HEIR.
THEY'RE THE GREATEST SHAMANS IN ALL OF JAPAN, BUT THIS IS DEADLY BUSINESS.
GRR...
WHERE IS SHE?

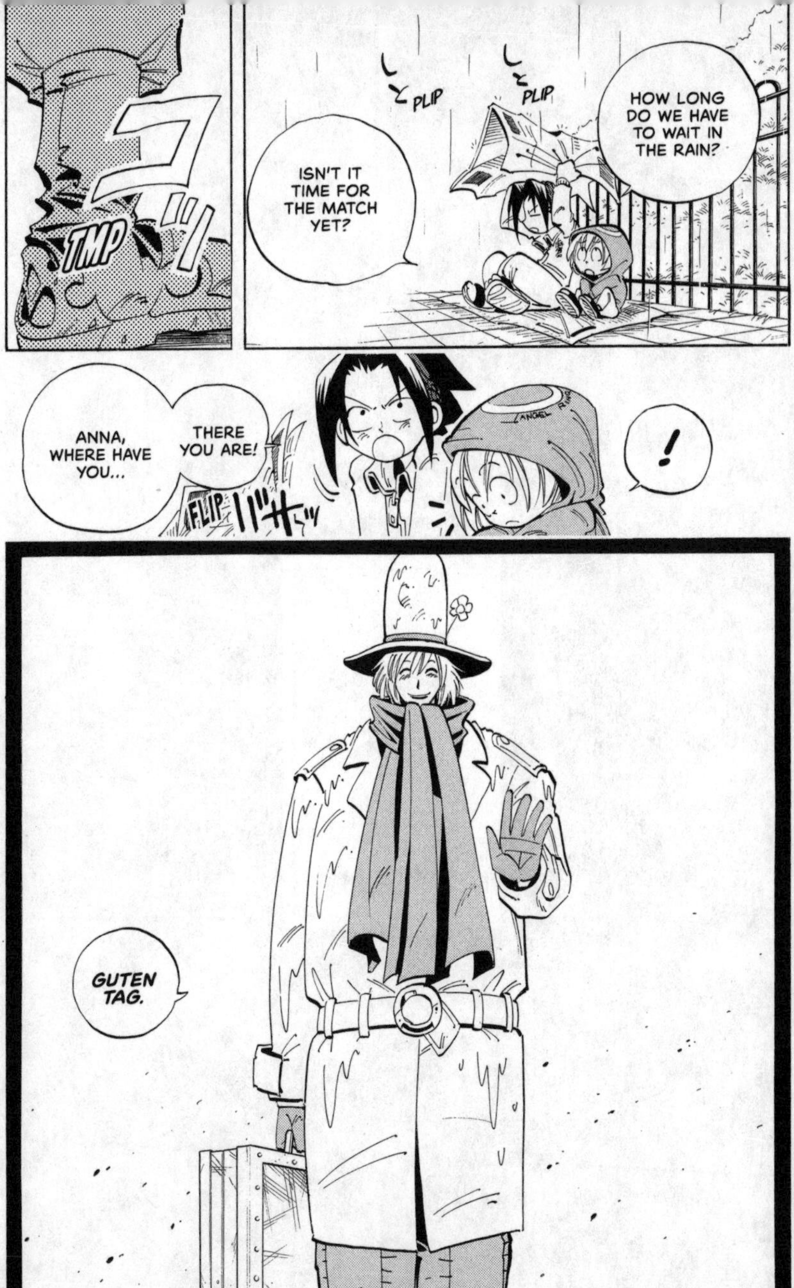
HOW LONG DO WE HAVE TO WAIT IN THE RAIN?
PLIP
PLIP
ISN'T IT TIME FOR THE MATCH YET?
TMP
!
THERE YOU ARE!
ANNA, WHERE HAVE YOU...
FLIP
GUTEN TAG.

SHAMAN
KING
5

Butterbur

Chapter 40: Spill Your Guts

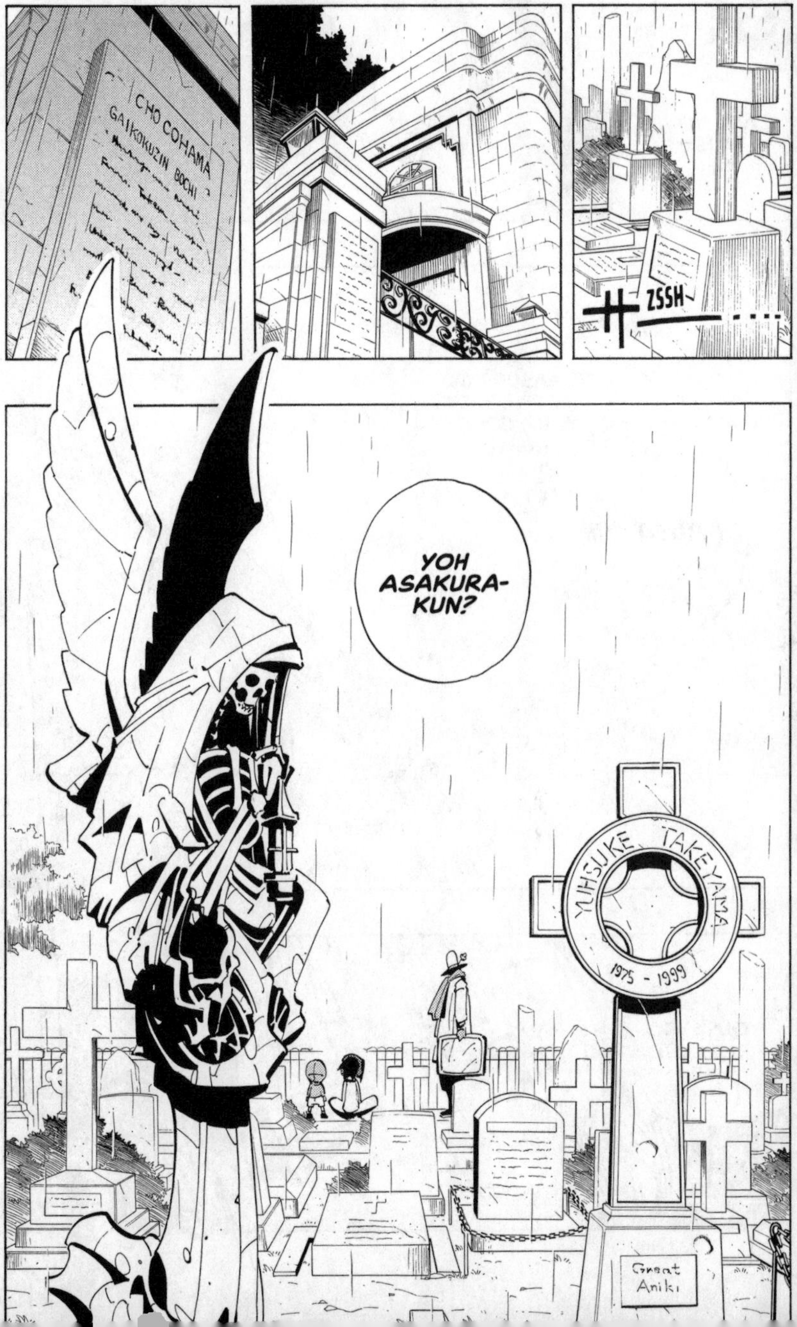
ZSSH
CHO COHAMA
GAIKOKUZIN BOCHI
YOH ASAKURA-KUN?
YUHSUKE TAKEYAMA
1975 - 1999
Great Aniki

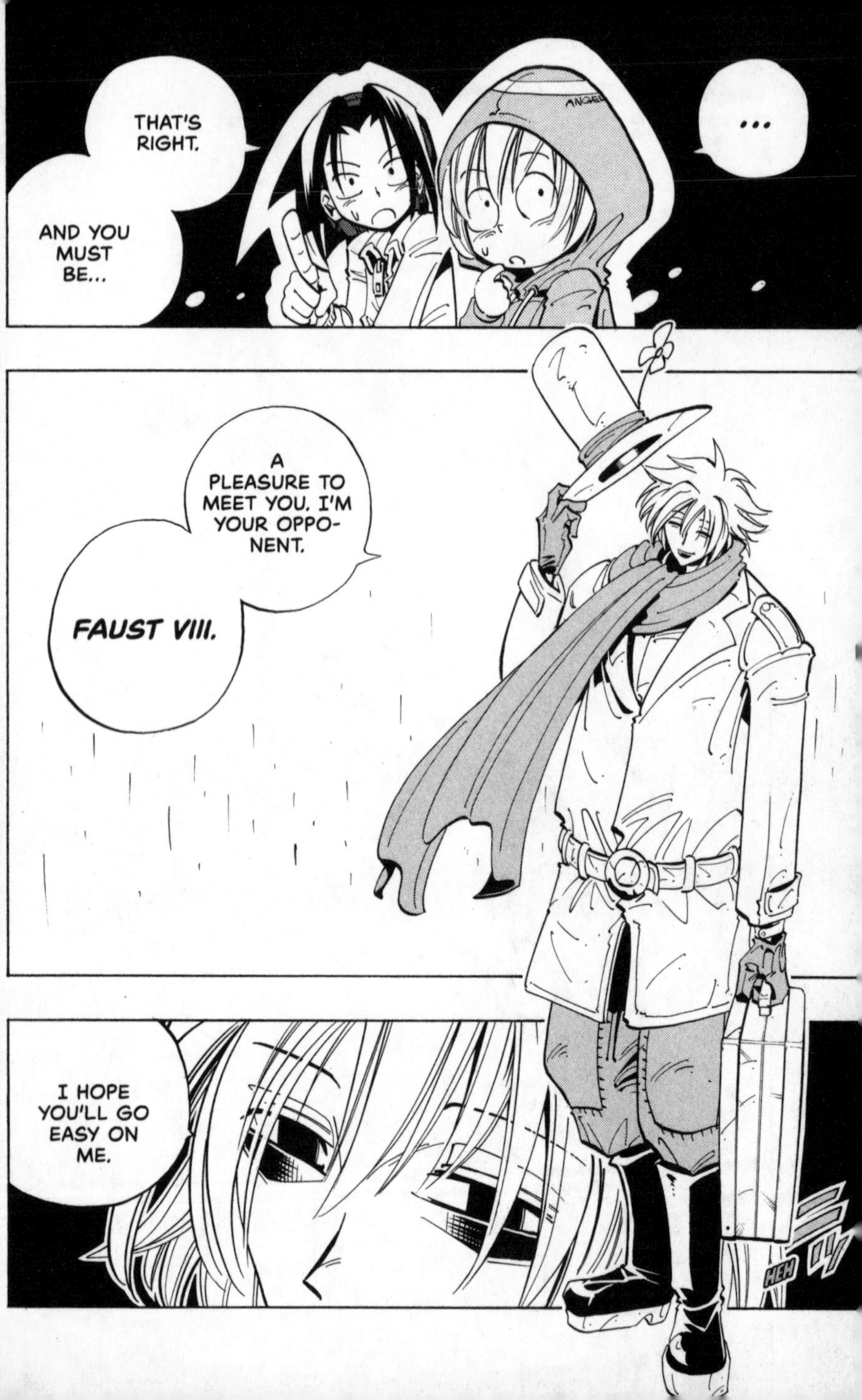
...
THAT'S RIGHT.
AND YOU MUST BE...
A PLEASURE TO MEET YOU. I'M YOUR OPPO-NENT.
FAUST VIII.
I HOPE YOU'LL GO EASY ON ME.
HEH

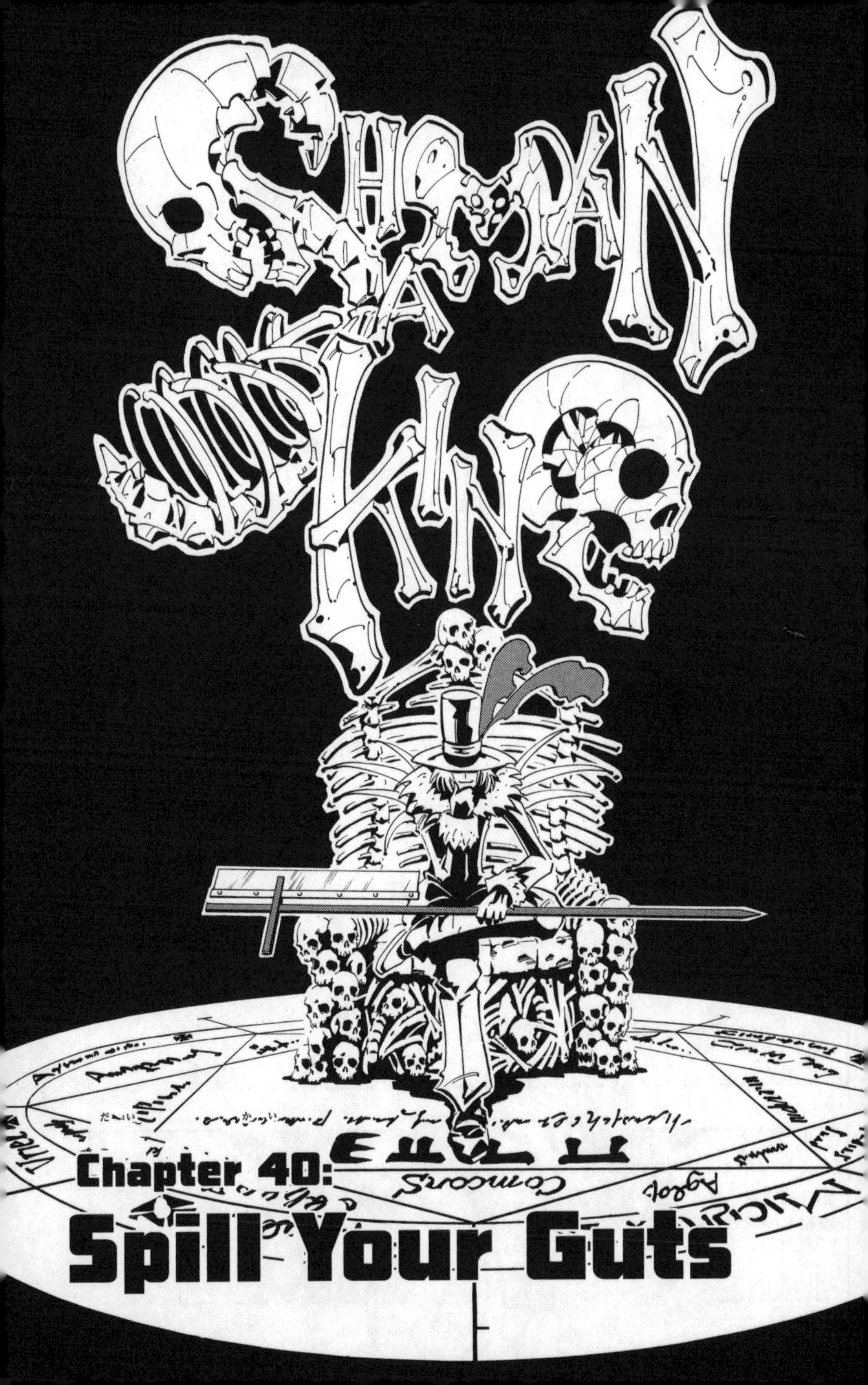
SHAMAN KING
Chapter 40:
Spill Your Guts

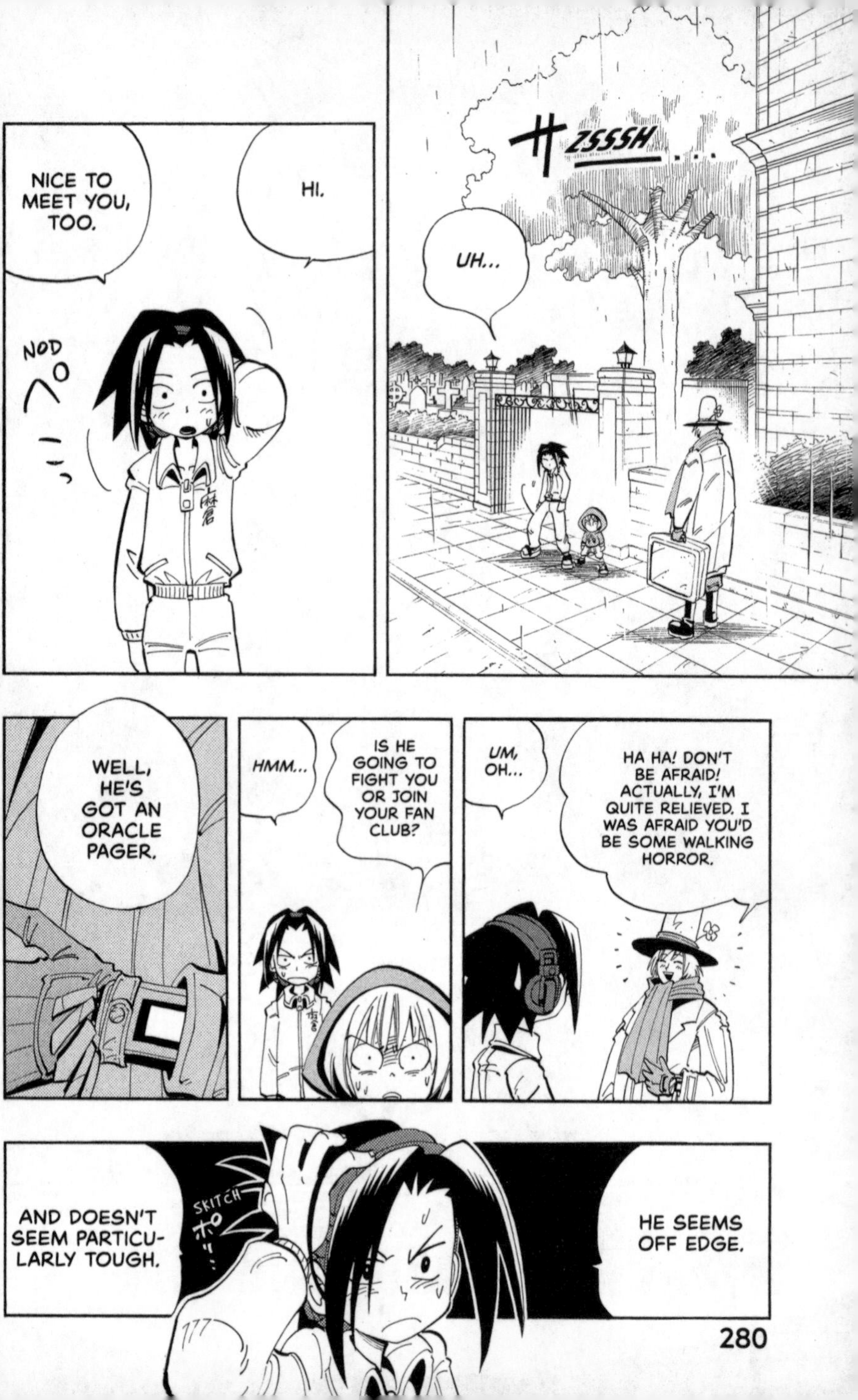
ZSSSH...
UH...
HI.
NICE TO MEET YOU, TOO.
NOD
HA HA! DON'T BE AFRAID! ACTUALLY, I'M QUITE RELIEVED. I WAS AFRAID YOU'D BE SOME WALKING HORROR.
UM, OH...
IS HE GOING TO FIGHT YOU OR JOIN YOUR FAN CLUB?
HMM...
WELL, HE'S GOT AN ORACLE PAGER.
HE SEEMS OFF EDGE.
SKITCH
AND DOESN'T SEEM PARTICU-LARLY TOUGH.

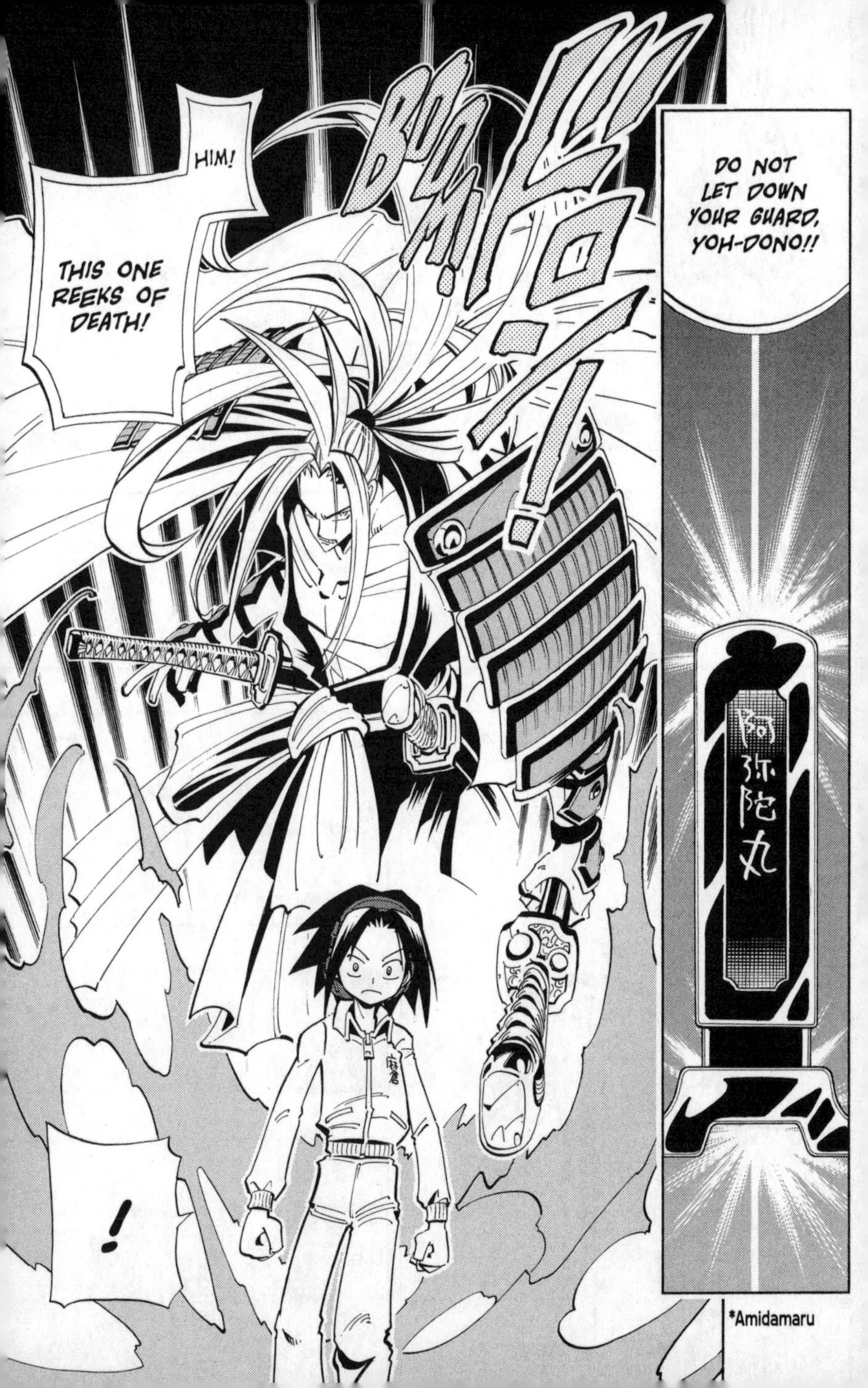
DO NOT LET DOWN YOUR GUARD, YOH-DONO!!
阿弥陀丸
HIM!
THIS ONE REEKS OF DEATH!
!
*Amidamaru

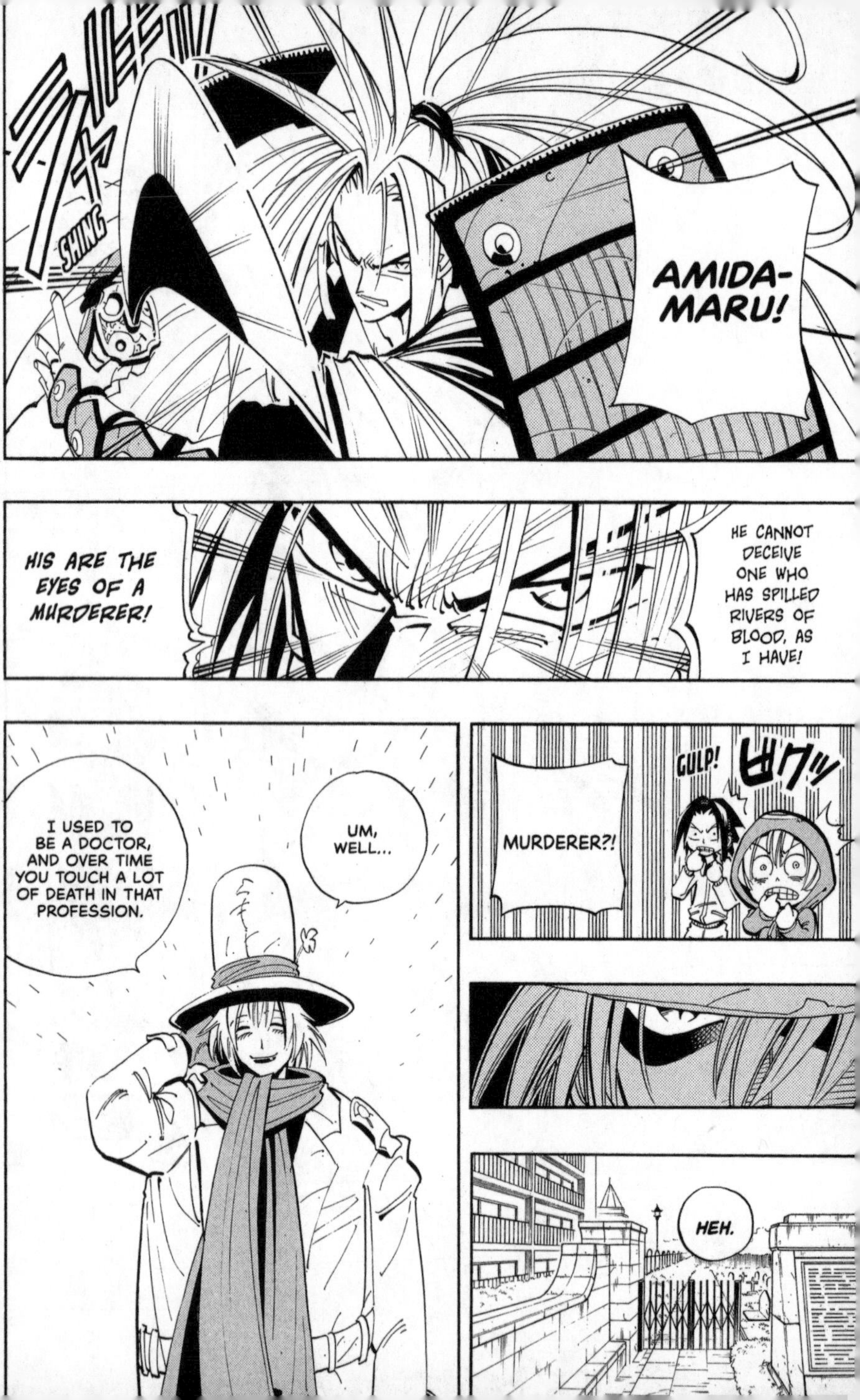
AMIDA-MARU!
SHING
HE CANNOT DECEIVE ONE WHO HAS SPILLED RIVERS OF BLOOD, AS I HAVE!
HIS ARE THE EYES OF A MURDERER!
GULP!
MURDERER?!
HEH.
UM, WELL...
I USED TO BE A DOCTOR, AND OVER TIME YOU TOUCH A LOT OF DEATH IN THAT PROFESSION.

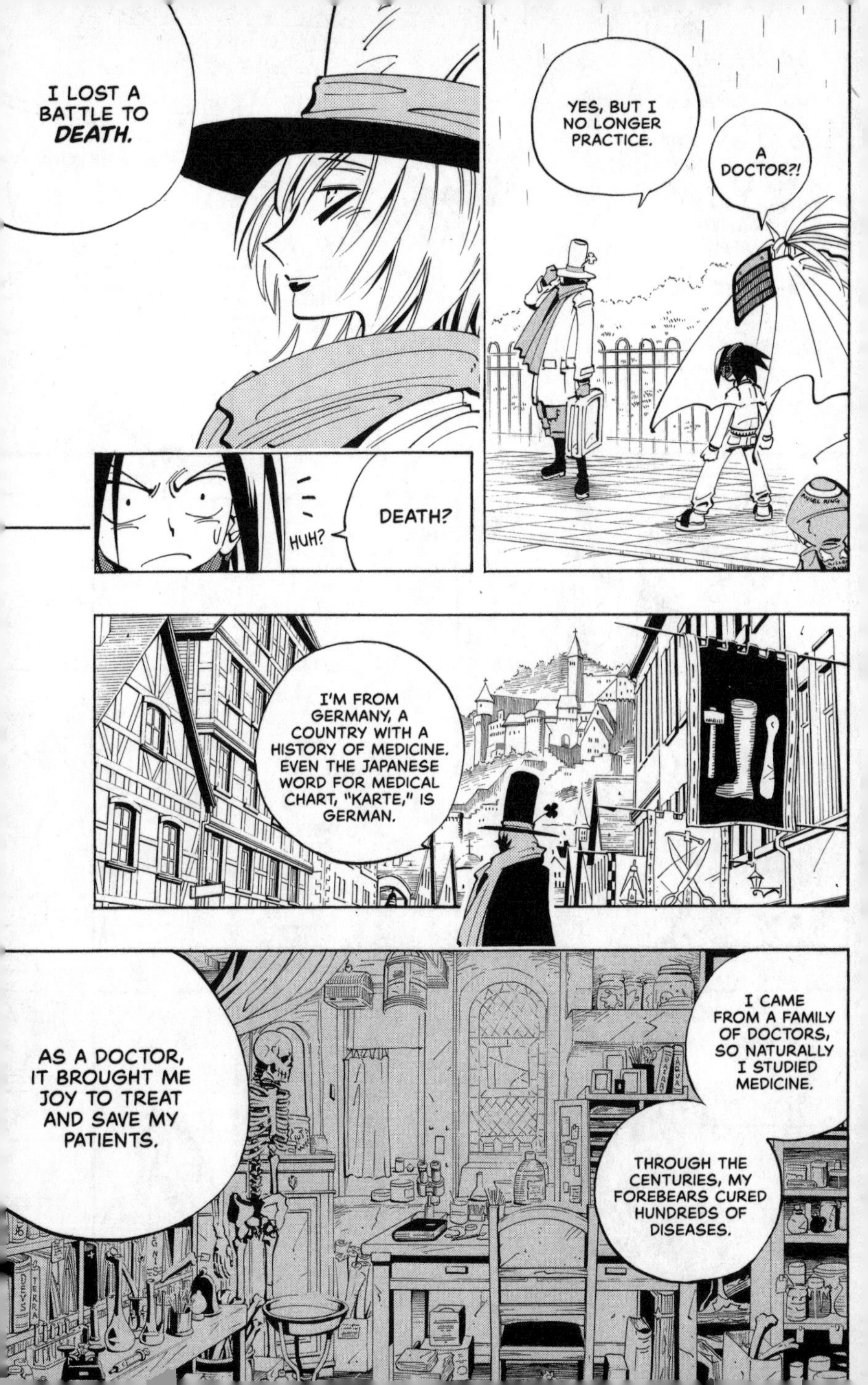
A DOCTOR?!
YES, BUT I NO LONGER PRACTICE.
I LOST A BATTLE TO *DEATH.*
DEATH?
HUH?
I'M FROM GERMANY, A COUNTRY WITH A HISTORY OF MEDICINE. EVEN THE JAPANESE WORD FOR MEDICAL CHART, "KARTE," IS GERMAN.
I CAME FROM A FAMILY OF DOCTORS, SO NATURALLY I STUDIED MEDICINE.
THROUGH THE CENTURIES, MY FOREBEARS CURED HUNDREDS OF DISEASES.
AS A DOCTOR, IT BROUGHT ME JOY TO TREAT AND SAVE MY PATIENTS.

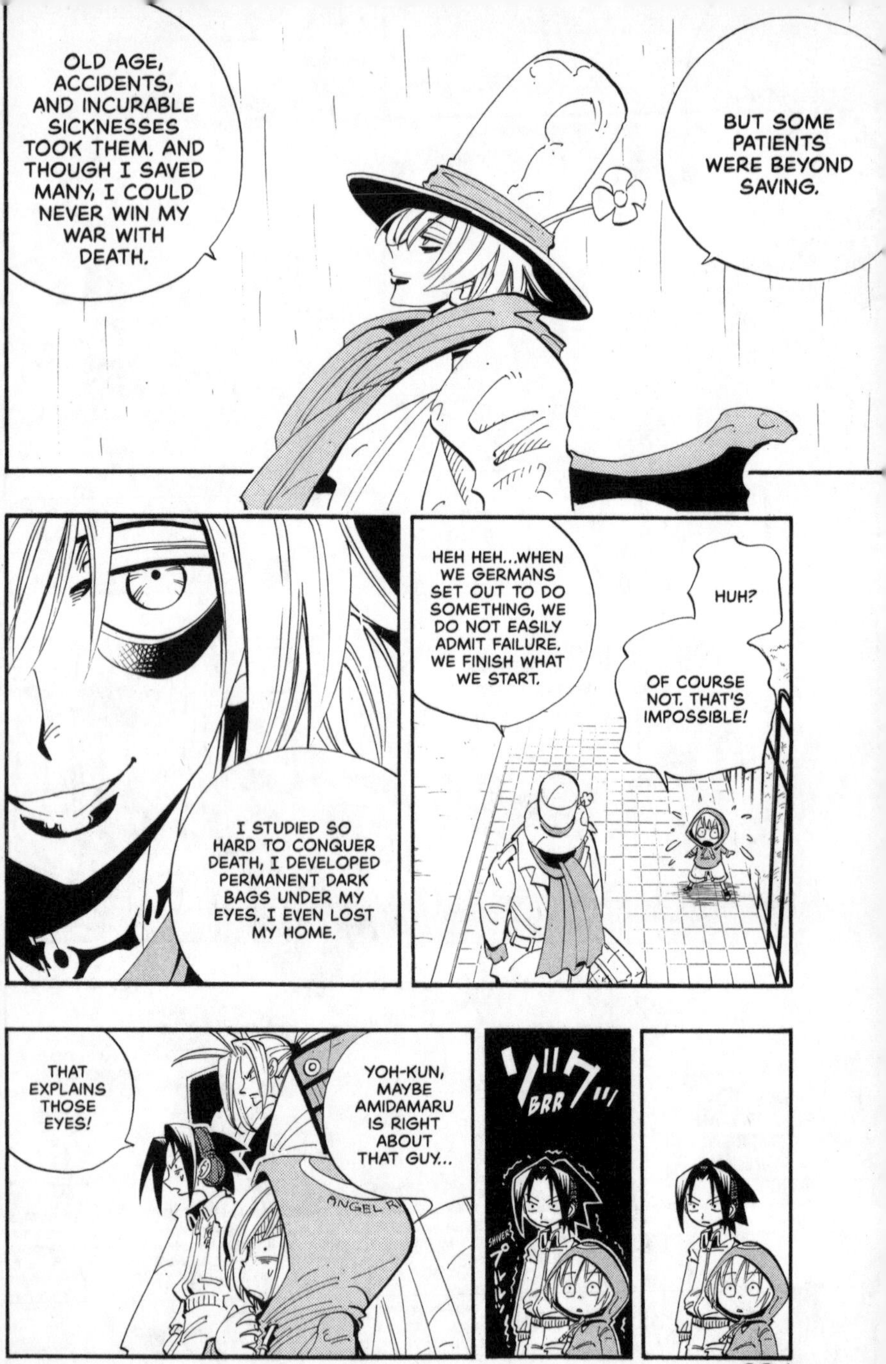
BUT SOME PATIENTS WERE BEYOND SAVING.
OLD AGE, ACCIDENTS, AND INCURABLE SICKNESSES TOOK THEM. AND THOUGH I SAVED MANY, I COULD NEVER WIN MY WAR WITH DEATH.
HUH?
OF COURSE NOT. THAT'S IMPOSSIBLE!
HEH HEH...WHEN WE GERMANS SET OUT TO DO SOMETHING, WE DO NOT EASILY ADMIT FAILURE. WE FINISH WHAT WE START.
I STUDIED SO HARD TO CONQUER DEATH, I DEVELOPED PERMANENT DARK BAGS UNDER MY EYES. I EVEN LOST MY HOME.
BRR
SHIVER
YOH-KUN, MAYBE AMIDAMARU IS RIGHT ABOUT THAT GUY...
THAT EXPLAINS THOSE EYES!
ANGEL R

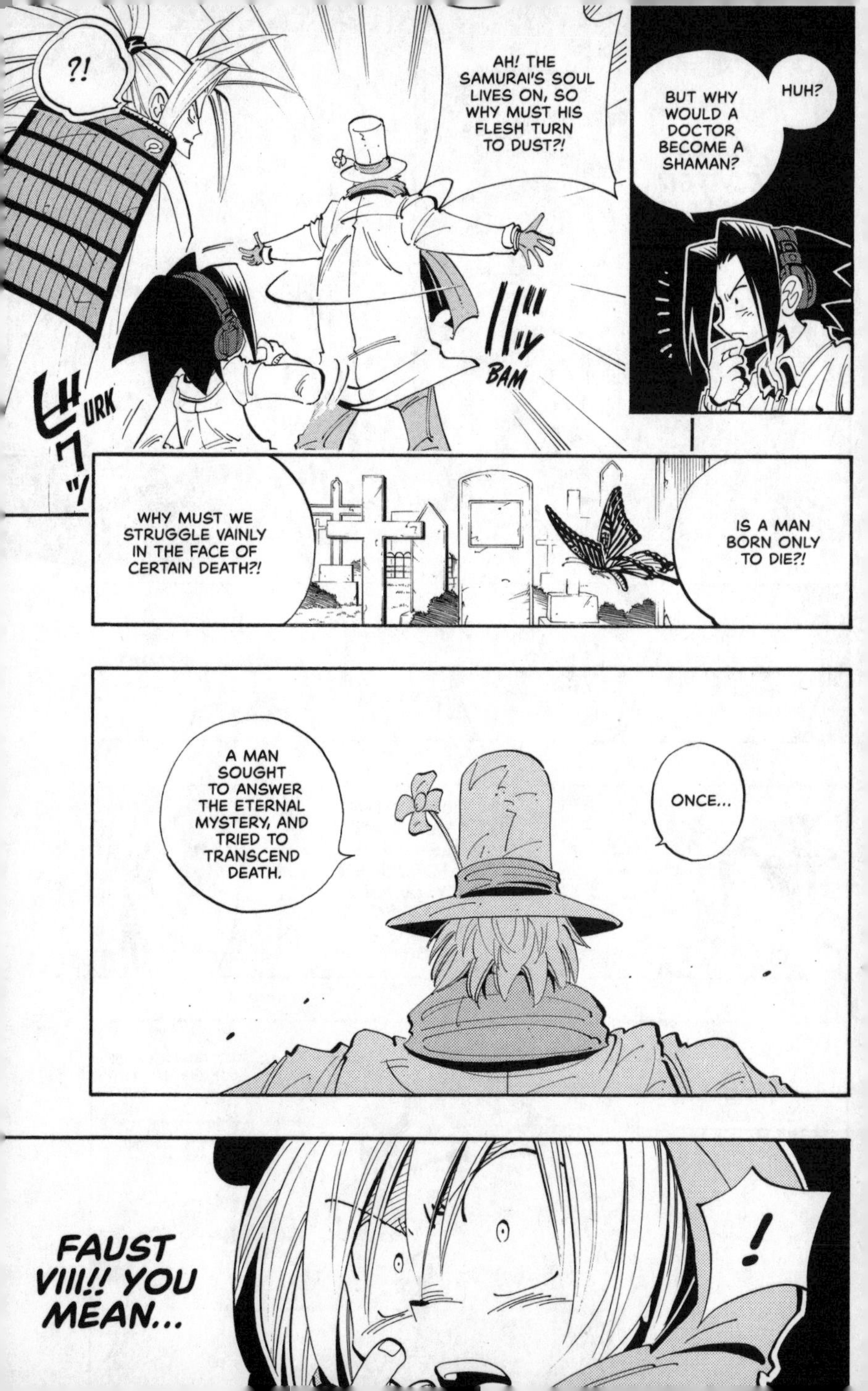
HUH?
BUT WHY WOULD A DOCTOR BECOME A SHAMAN?
AH! THE SAMURAI'S SOUL LIVES ON, SO WHY MUST HIS FLESH TURN TO DUST?!
?!
BAM
URK
IS A MAN BORN ONLY TO DIE?!
WHY MUST WE STRUGGLE VAINLY IN THE FACE OF CERTAIN DEATH?!
ONCE...
A MAN SOUGHT TO ANSWER THE ETERNAL MYSTERY, AND TRIED TO TRANSCEND DEATH.
!
FAUST VIII!! YOU MEAN...

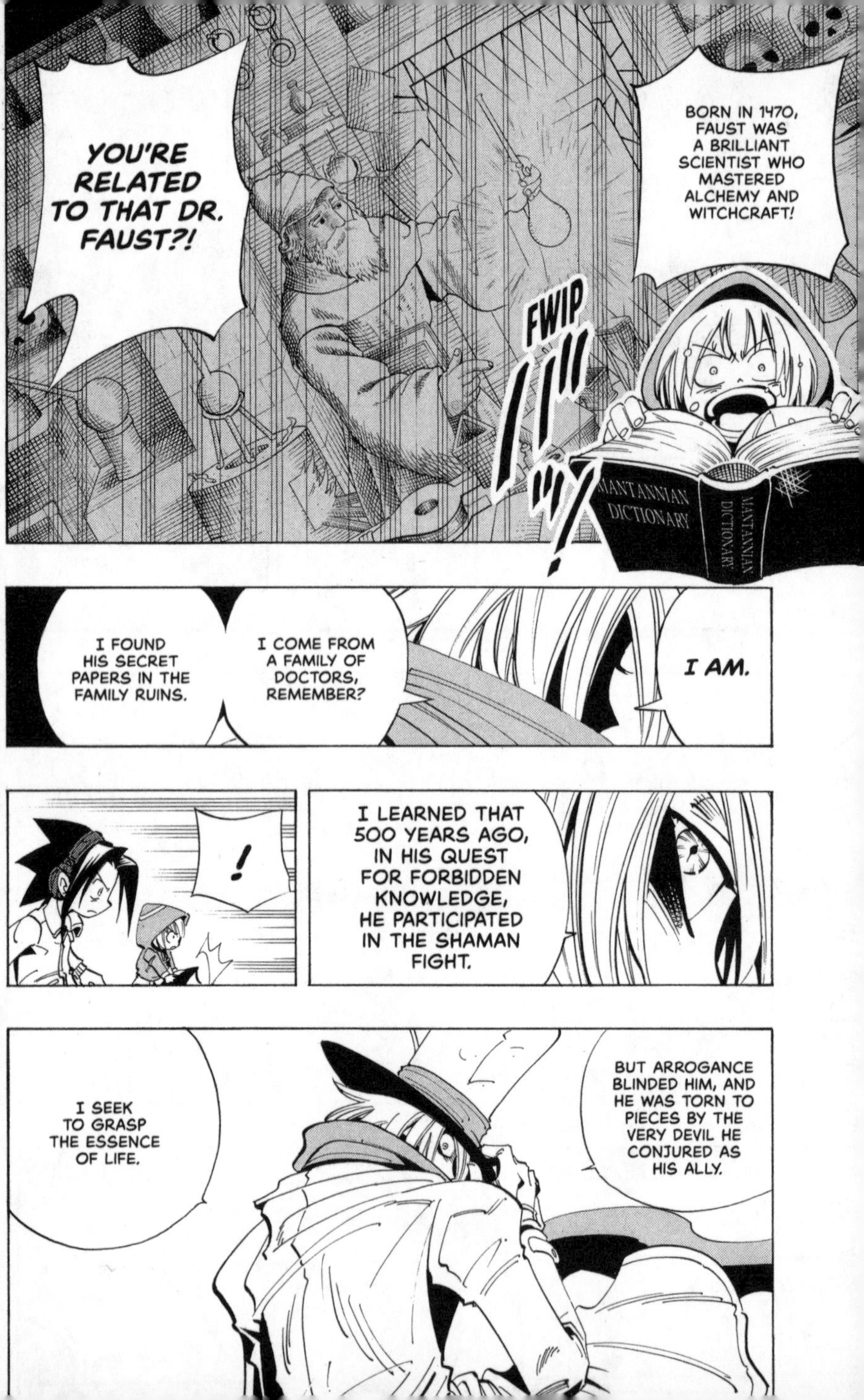
BORN IN 1470, FAUST WAS A BRILLIANT SCIENTIST WHO MASTERED ALCHEMY AND WITCHCRAFT!
FWIP
MANTANNIAN DICTIONARY
YOU'RE RELATED TO THAT DR. FAUST?!
I AM.
I COME FROM A FAMILY OF DOCTORS, REMEMBER?
I FOUND HIS SECRET PAPERS IN THE FAMILY RUINS.
I LEARNED THAT 500 YEARS AGO, IN HIS QUEST FOR FORBIDDEN KNOWLEDGE, HE PARTICIPATED IN THE SHAMAN FIGHT.
!
BUT ARROGANCE BLINDED HIM, AND HE WAS TORN TO PIECES BY THE VERY DEVIL HE CONJURED AS HIS ALLY.
I SEEK TO GRASP THE ESSENCE OF LIFE.

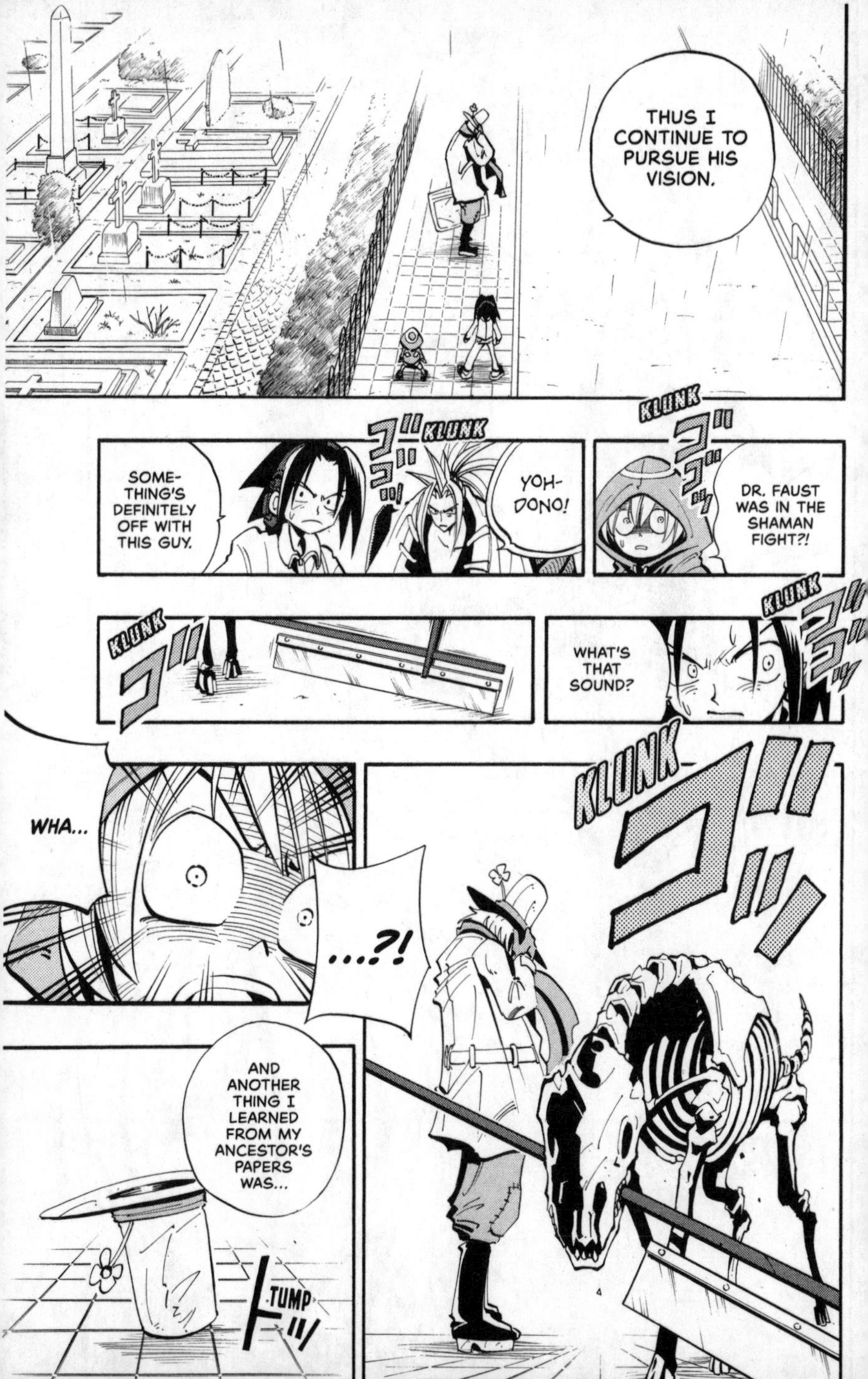
THUS I CONTINUE TO PURSUE HIS VISION.
KLUNK
DR. FAUST WAS IN THE SHAMAN FIGHT?!
KLUNK
YOH-DONO!
SOME-THING'S DEFINITELY OFF WITH THIS GUY.
KLUNK
WHAT'S THAT SOUND?
KLUNK
KLUNK
WHA...
...?!
AND ANOTHER THING I LEARNED FROM MY ANCESTOR'S PAPERS WAS...
TUMP

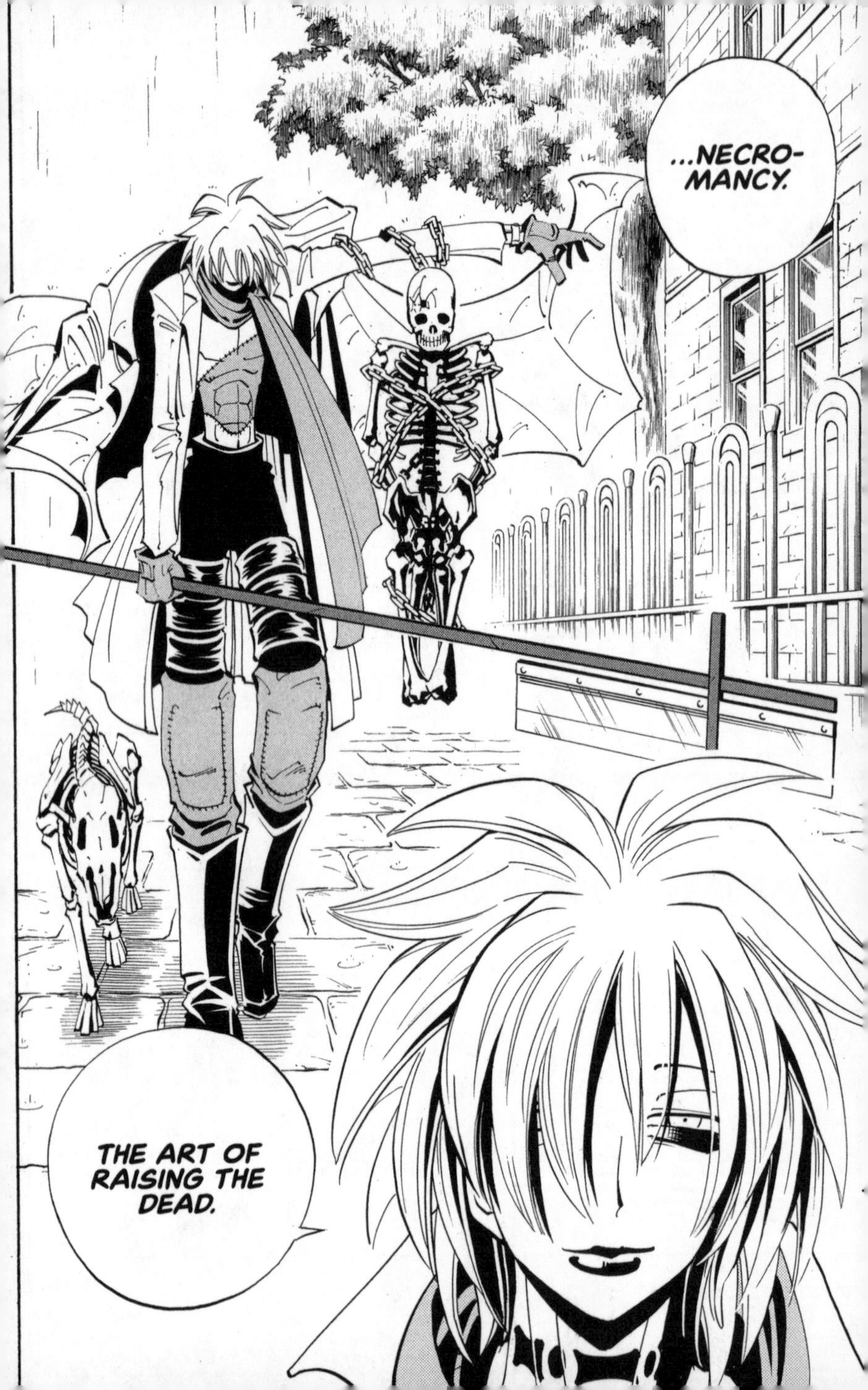
...NECRO-MANCY.
THE ART OF RAISING THE DEAD.

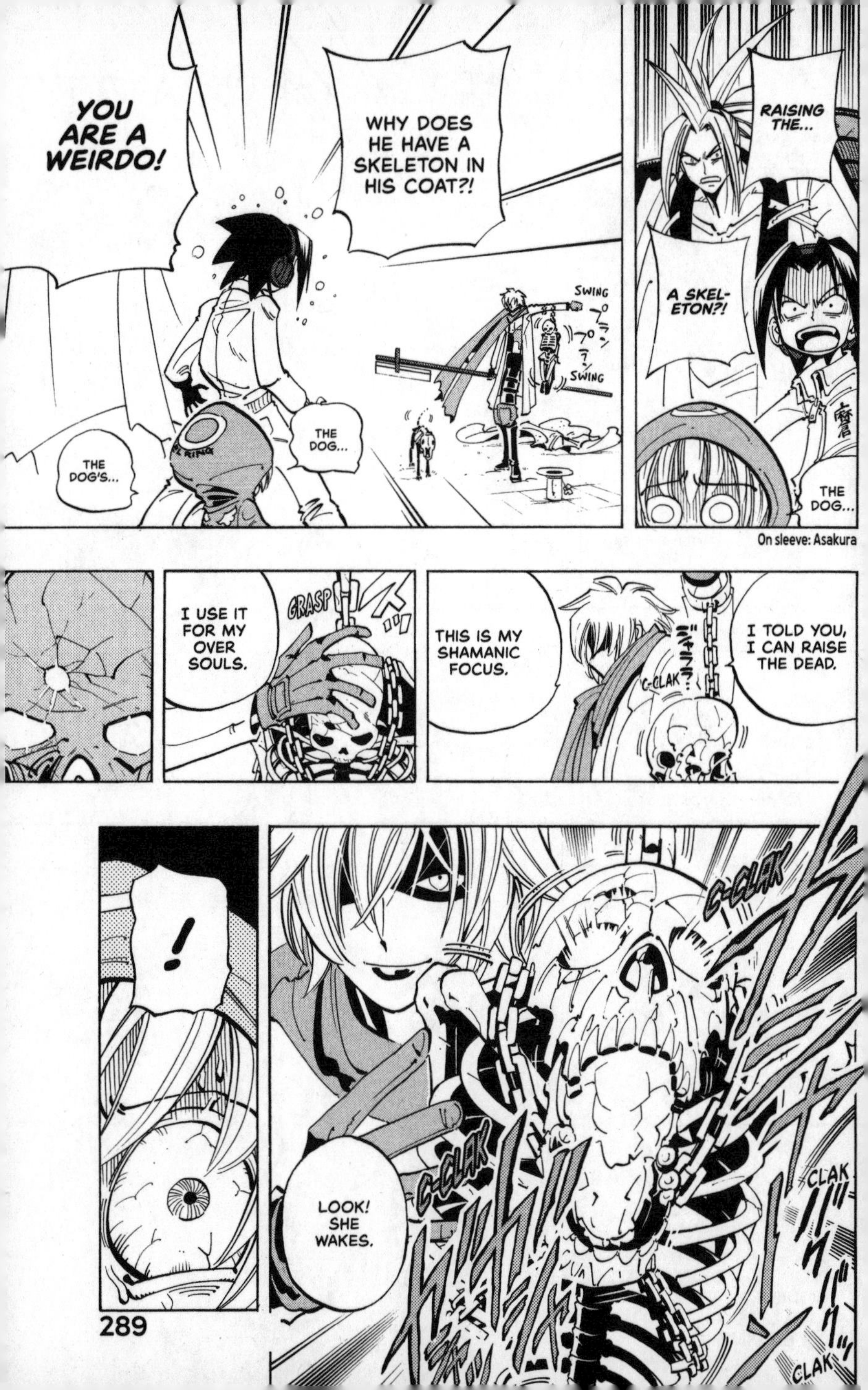
RAISING THE...
A SKEL-ETON?!
THE DOG...
WHY DOES HE HAVE A SKELETON IN HIS COAT?!
YOU ARE A WEIRDO!
SWING
SWING
THE DOG...
THE DOG'S...
I TOLD YOU, I CAN RAISE THE DEAD.
C-CLAK
THIS IS MY SHAMANIC FOCUS.
GRASP
I USE IT FOR MY OVER SOULS.
C-CLAK
CLAK
LOOK! SHE WAKES.
C-CLAK
CLAK
!

On sleeve: Asakura

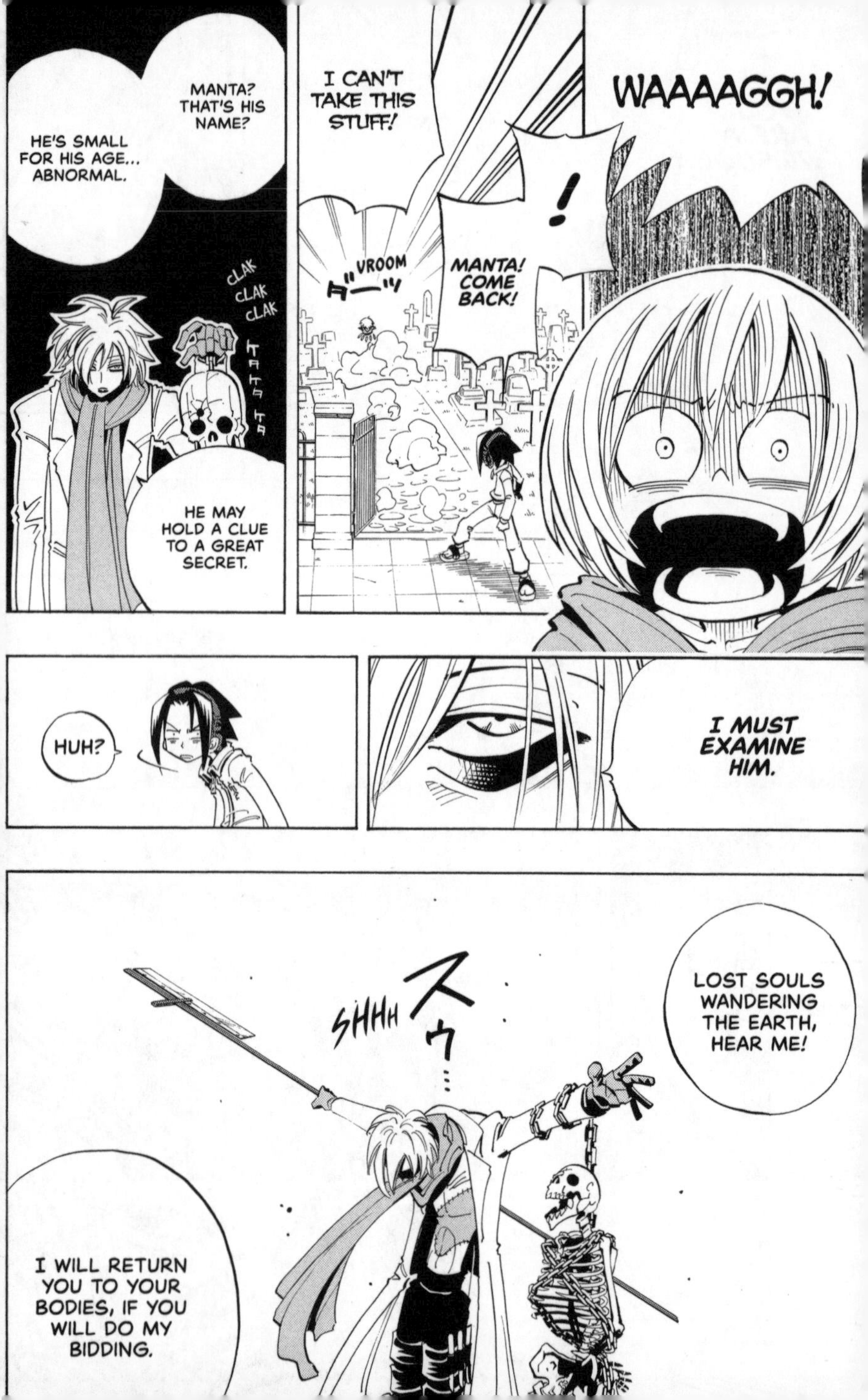
WAAAAGGH!
!
I CAN'T TAKE THIS STUFF!
VROOM
ダーッ
MANTA! COME BACK!
MANTA? THAT'S HIS NAME?
HE'S SMALL FOR HIS AGE... ABNORMAL.
CLAK CLAK CLAK
カタカタ カタ
HE MAY HOLD A CLUE TO A GREAT SECRET.
I MUST EXAMINE HIM.
HUH?
LOST SOULS WANDERING THE EARTH, HEAR ME!
SHHH
スゥ…
I WILL RETURN YOU TO YOUR BODIES, IF YOU WILL DO MY BIDDING.

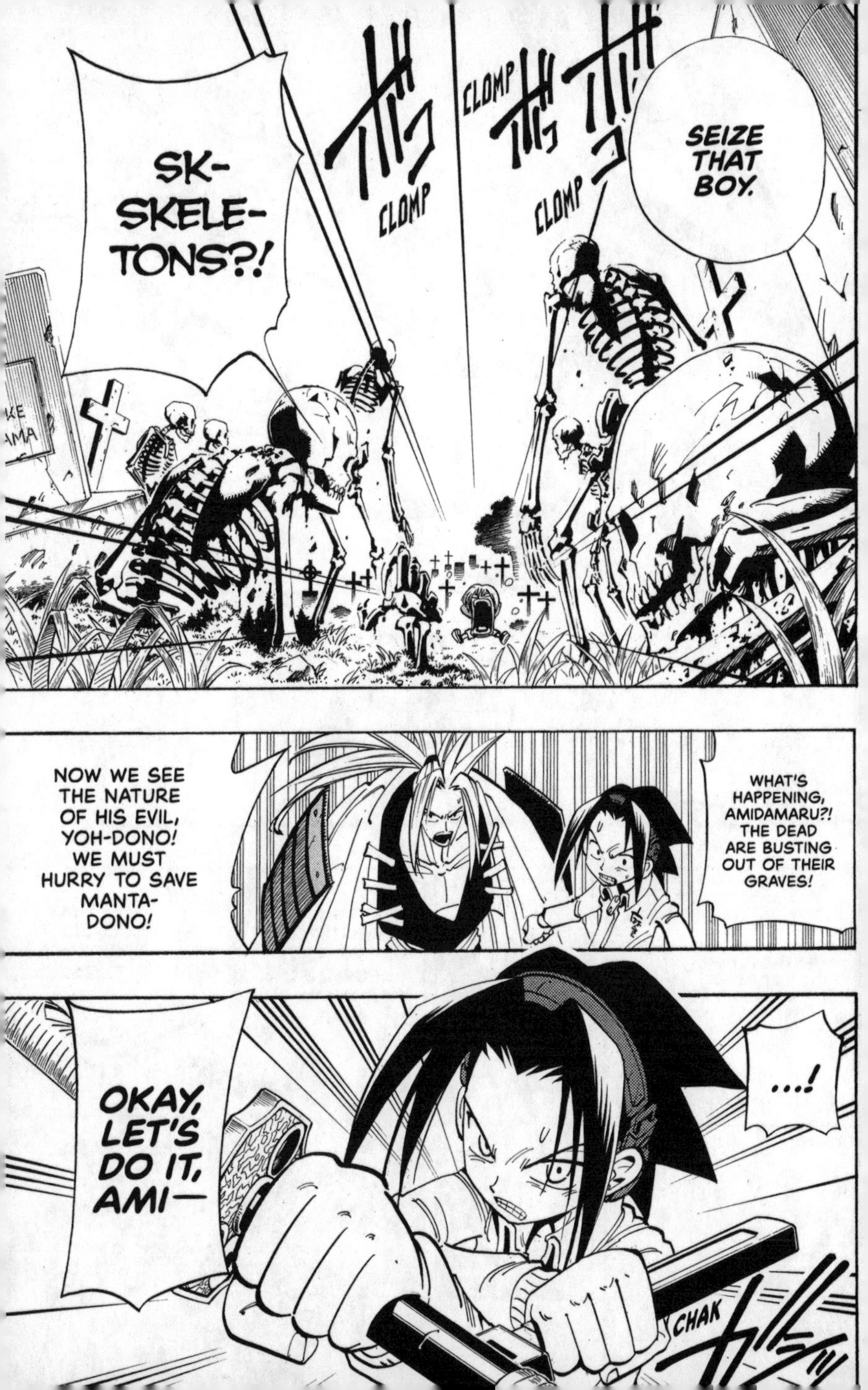
SEIZE THAT BOY.
CLOMP
CLOMP
CLOMP
SK- SKELE- TONS?!
WHAT'S HAPPENING, AMIDAMARU?! THE DEAD ARE BUSTING OUT OF THEIR GRAVES!
NOW WE SEE THE NATURE OF HIS EVIL, YOH-DONO! WE MUST HURRY TO SAVE MANTA-DONO!
...!
OKAY, LET'S DO IT, AMI—
CHAK

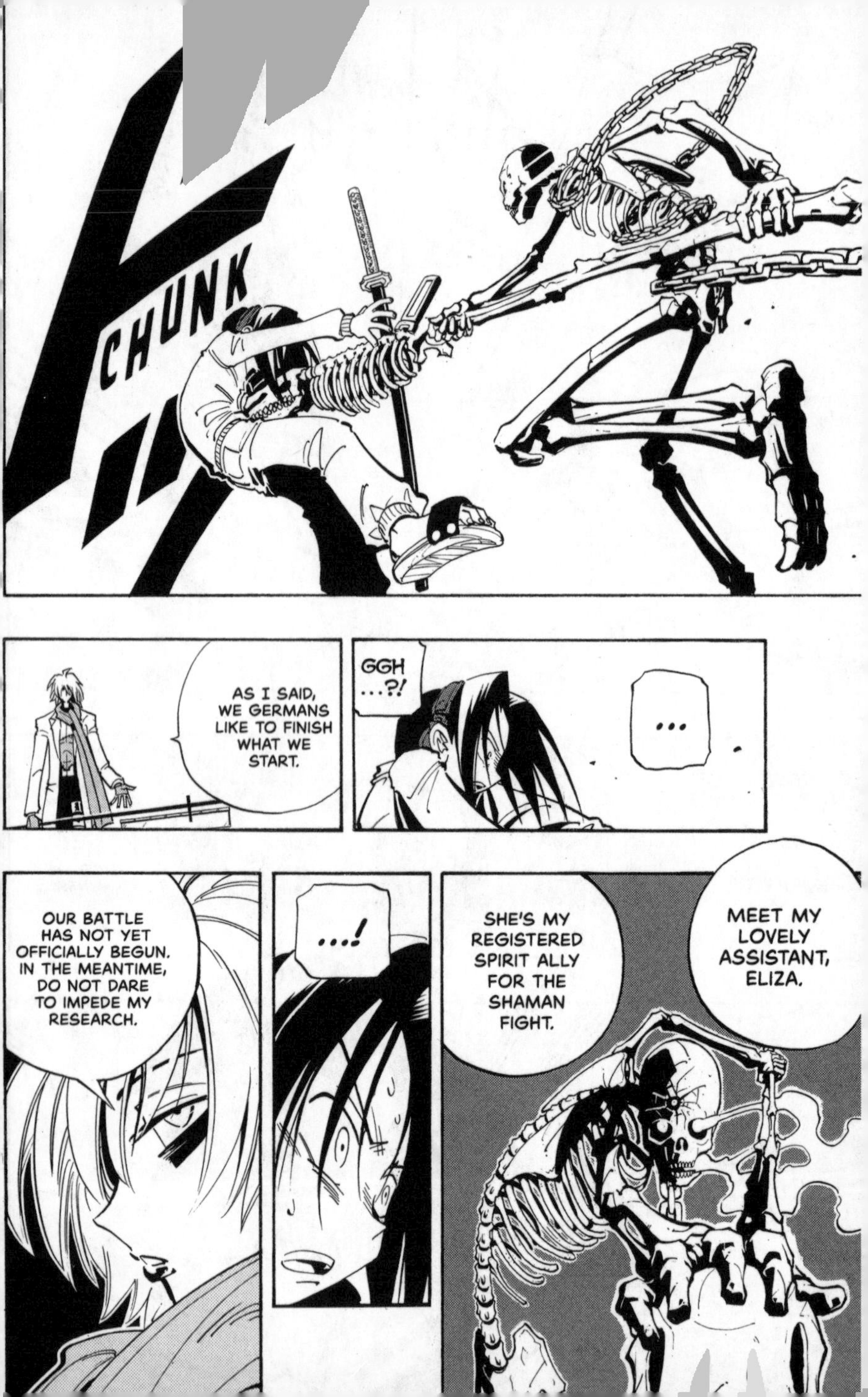
CHUNK
GGH ...?!
...
AS I SAID, WE GERMANS LIKE TO FINISH WHAT WE START.
MEET MY LOVELY ASSISTANT, ELIZA.
SHE'S MY REGISTERED SPIRIT ALLY FOR THE SHAMAN FIGHT.
...!
OUR BATTLE HAS NOT YET OFFICIALLY BEGUN. IN THE MEANTIME, DO NOT DARE TO IMPEDE MY RESEARCH.

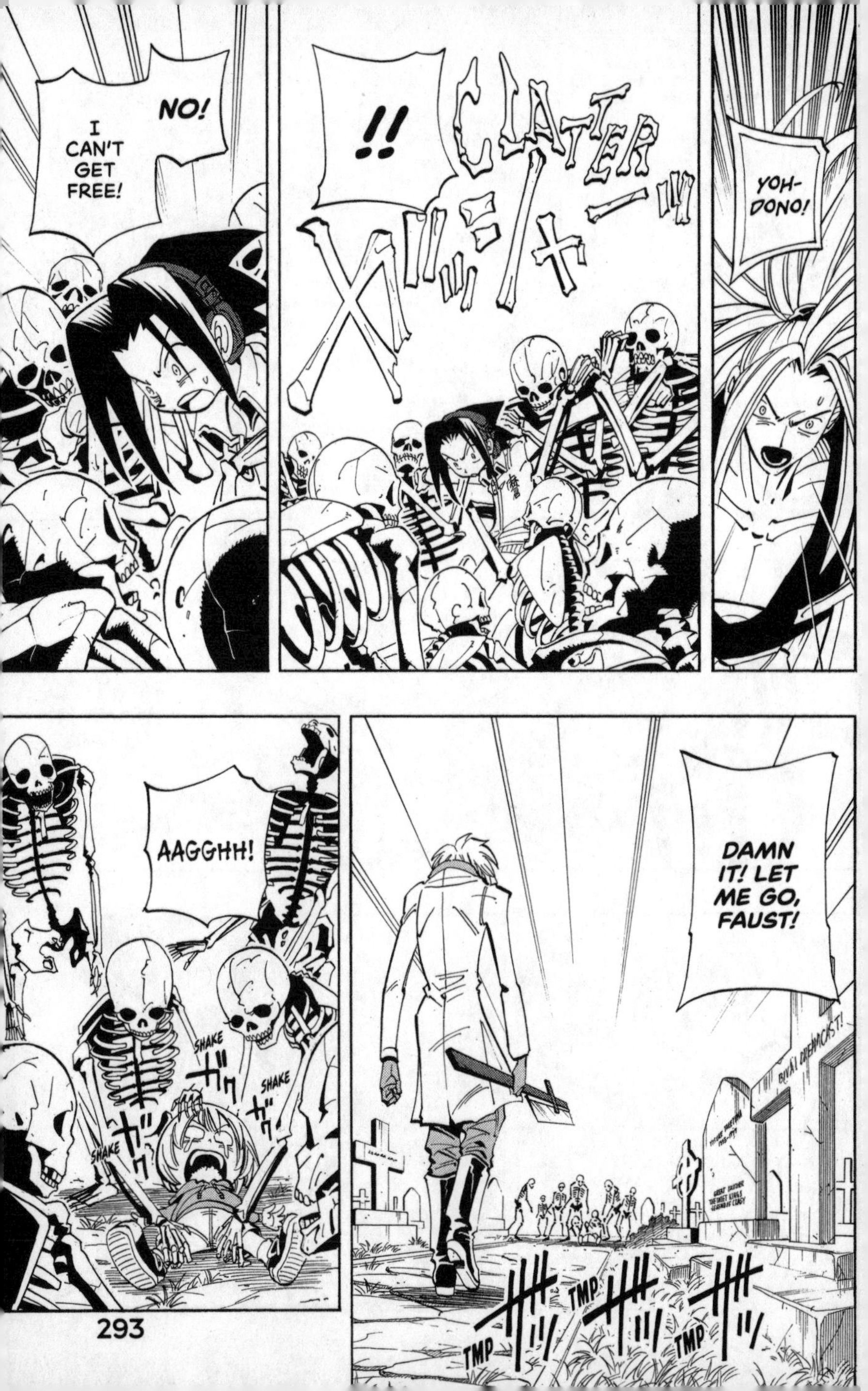
YOH-DONO!
!!
CLATTER
NO!
I CAN'T GET FREE!
DAMN IT! LET ME GO, FAUST!
TMP
TMP
TMP
AAGGHH!
SHAKE
SHAKE
SHAKE

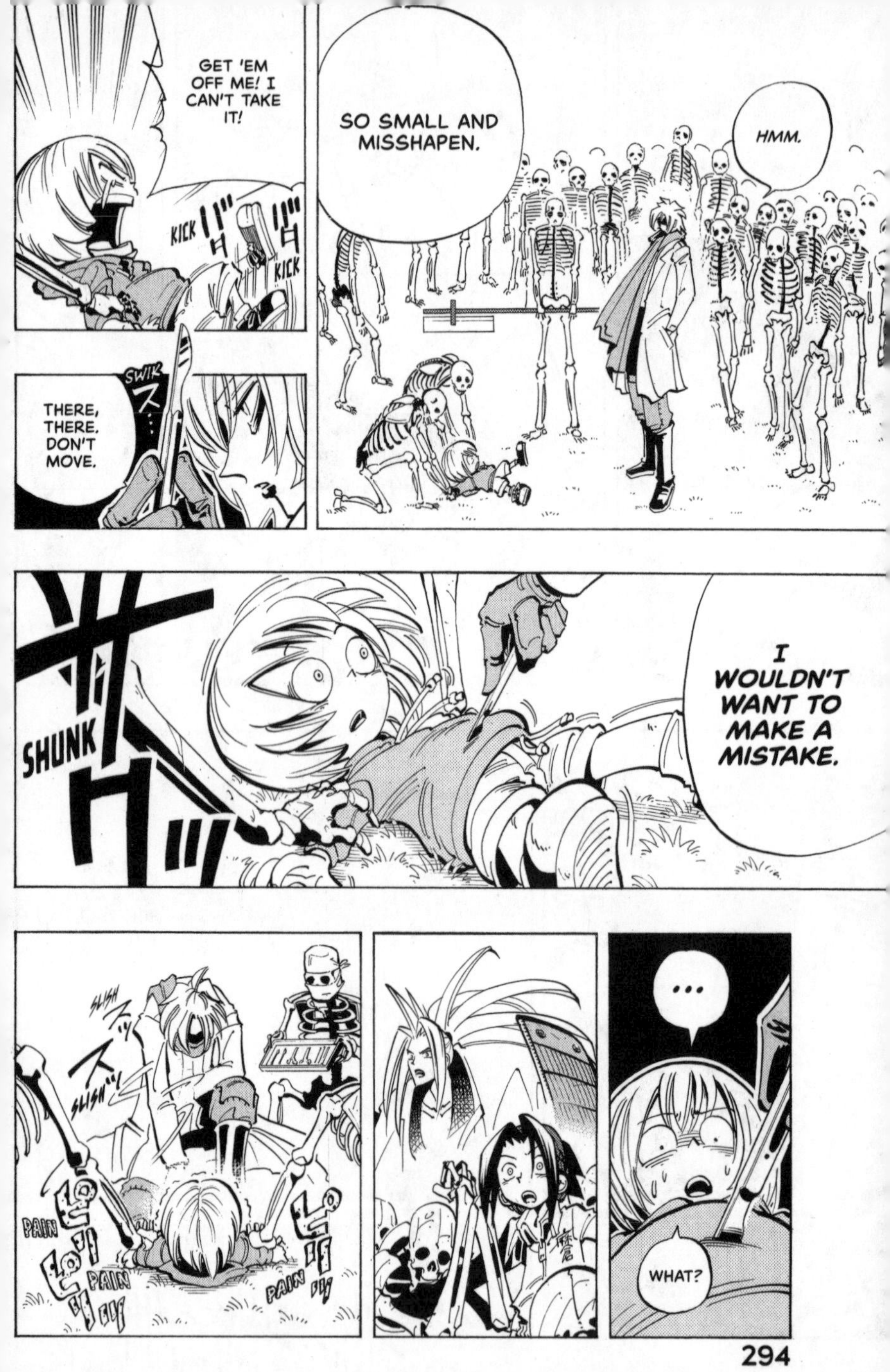
HMM.
SO SMALL AND MISSHAPEN.
GET 'EM OFF ME! I CAN'T TAKE IT!
KICK
KICK
SWIK
THERE, THERE. DON'T MOVE.
I WOULDN'T WANT TO MAKE A MISTAKE.
SHUNK
...
WHAT?
SLISH
SLISH
PAIN
PAIN
PAIN

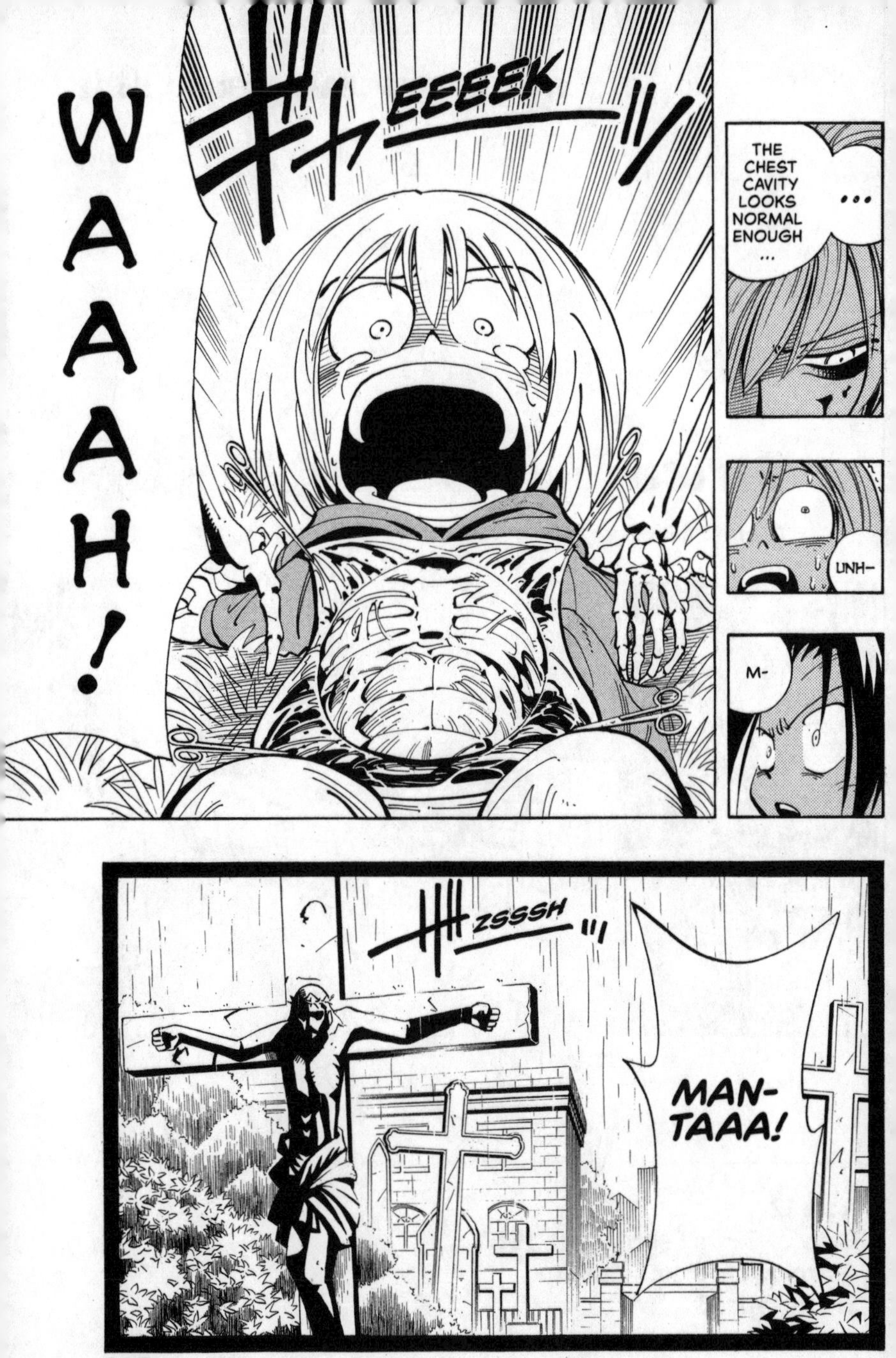
THE CHEST CAVITY LOOKS NORMAL ENOUGH ...
...
UNH-
M-
WAAAAH!
EEEEEK
ZSSSH
MAN-TAAA!

SHAMAN KING CHARACTER FILE No.22

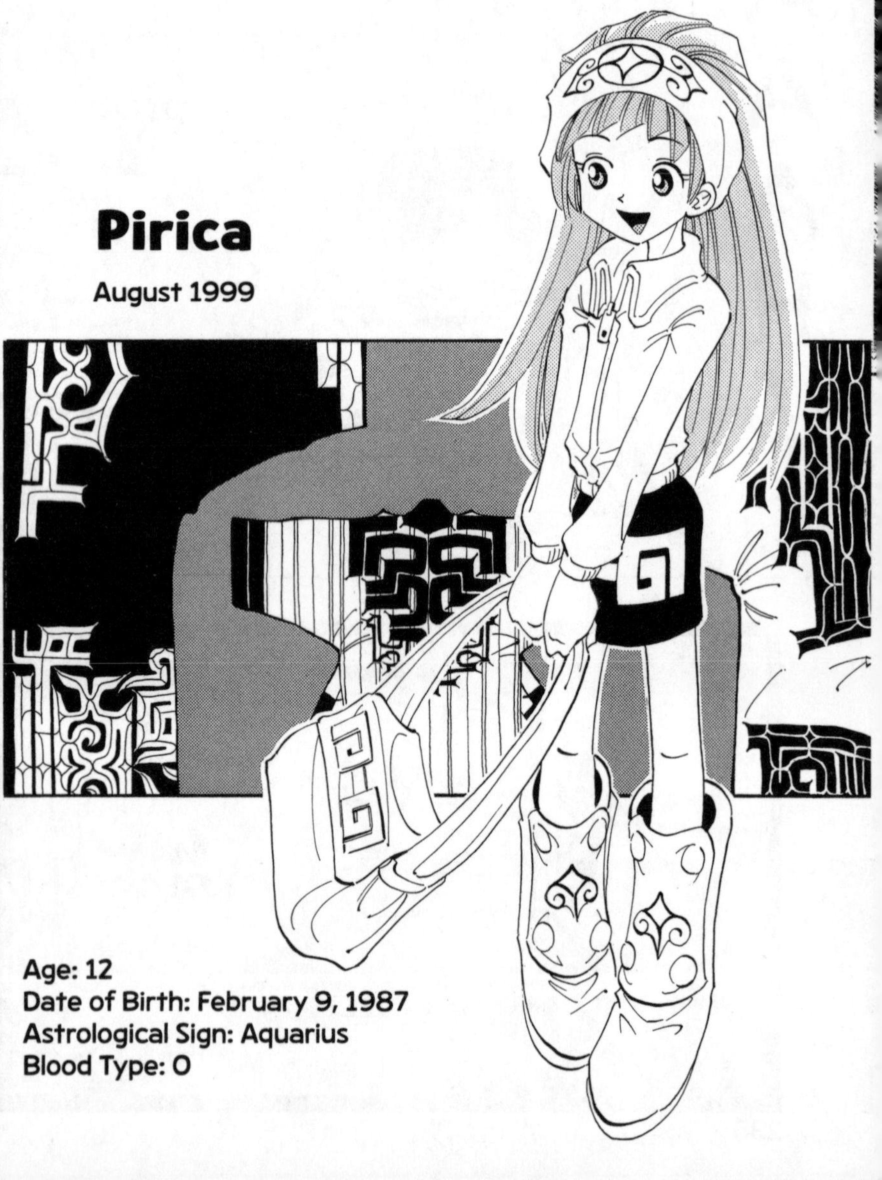

Pirica

August 1999

Age: 12
Date of Birth: February 9, 1987
Astrological Sign: Aquarius
Blood Type: O

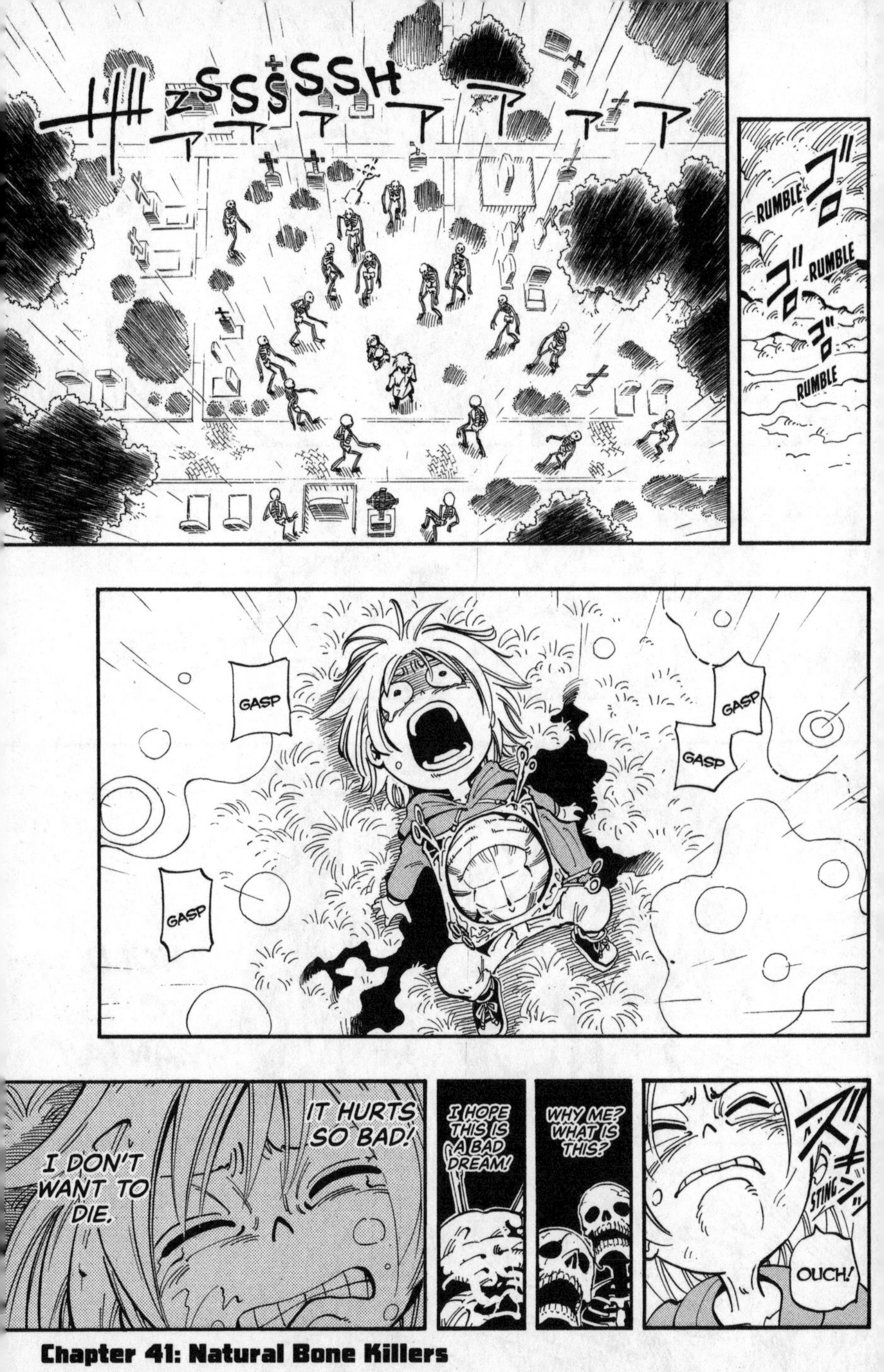
RUMBLE
RUMBLE
RUMBLE
ZSSSSSH
GASP
GASP
GASP
GASP
STING
OUCH!
WHY ME? WHAT IS THIS?
I HOPE THIS IS A BAD DREAM!
IT HURTS SO BAD!
I DON'T WANT TO DIE.

Chapter 41: Natural Bone Killers

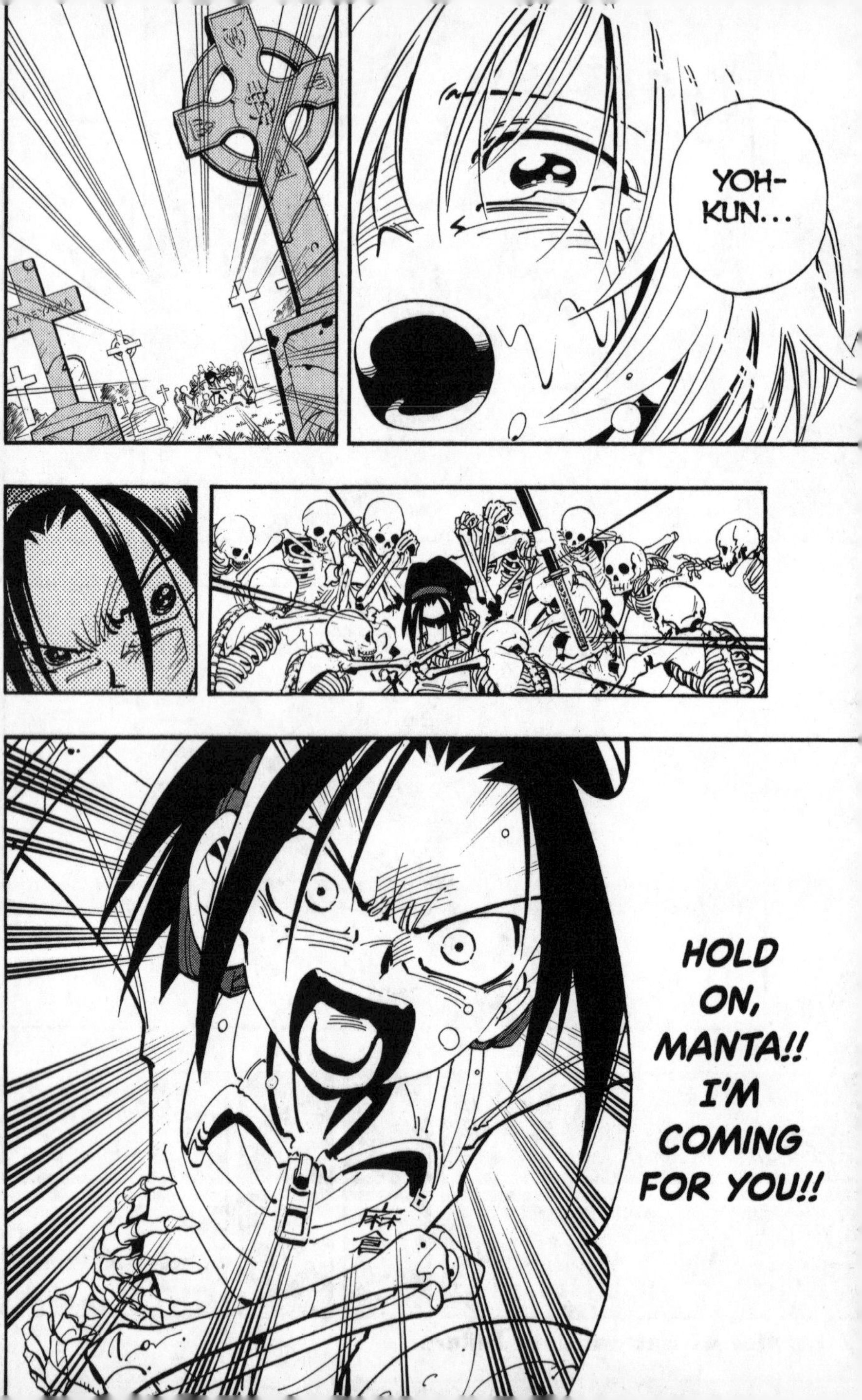
YOH-KUN...
HOLD ON, MANTA!! I'M COMING FOR YOU!!

Chapter 41:

NATURAL BONE KILLERS

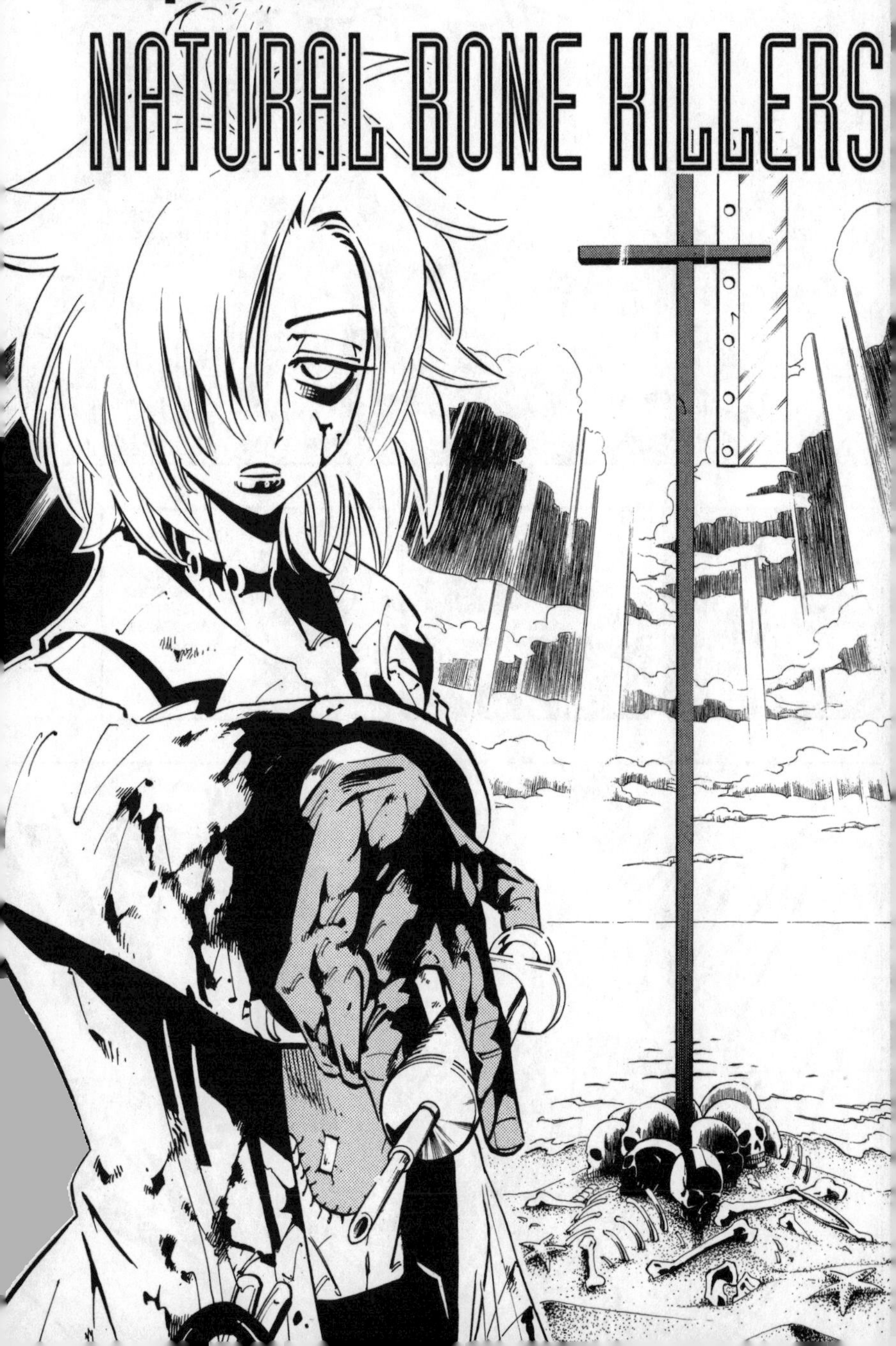

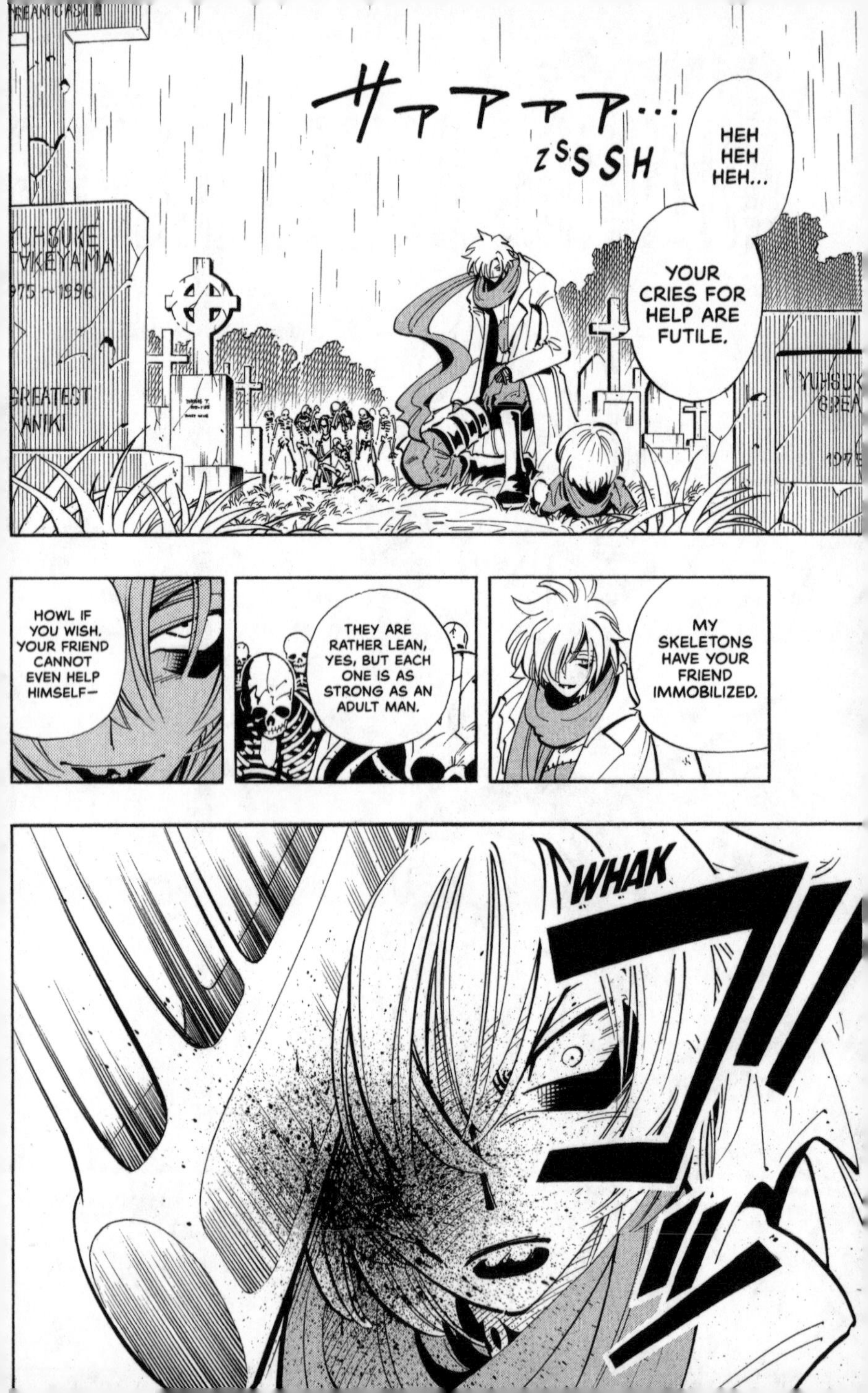
YUHSUKE TAKEYAMA
1975 ~ 1996
GREATEST ANIKI
サァァァァ…
ZSSSH
HEH HEH HEH...
YOUR CRIES FOR HELP ARE FUTILE.
MY SKELETONS HAVE YOUR FRIEND IMMOBILIZED.
THEY ARE RATHER LEAN, YES, BUT EACH ONE IS AS STRONG AS AN ADULT MAN.
HOWL IF YOU WISH. YOUR FRIEND CANNOT EVEN HELP HIMSELF—
WHAK
ゴ

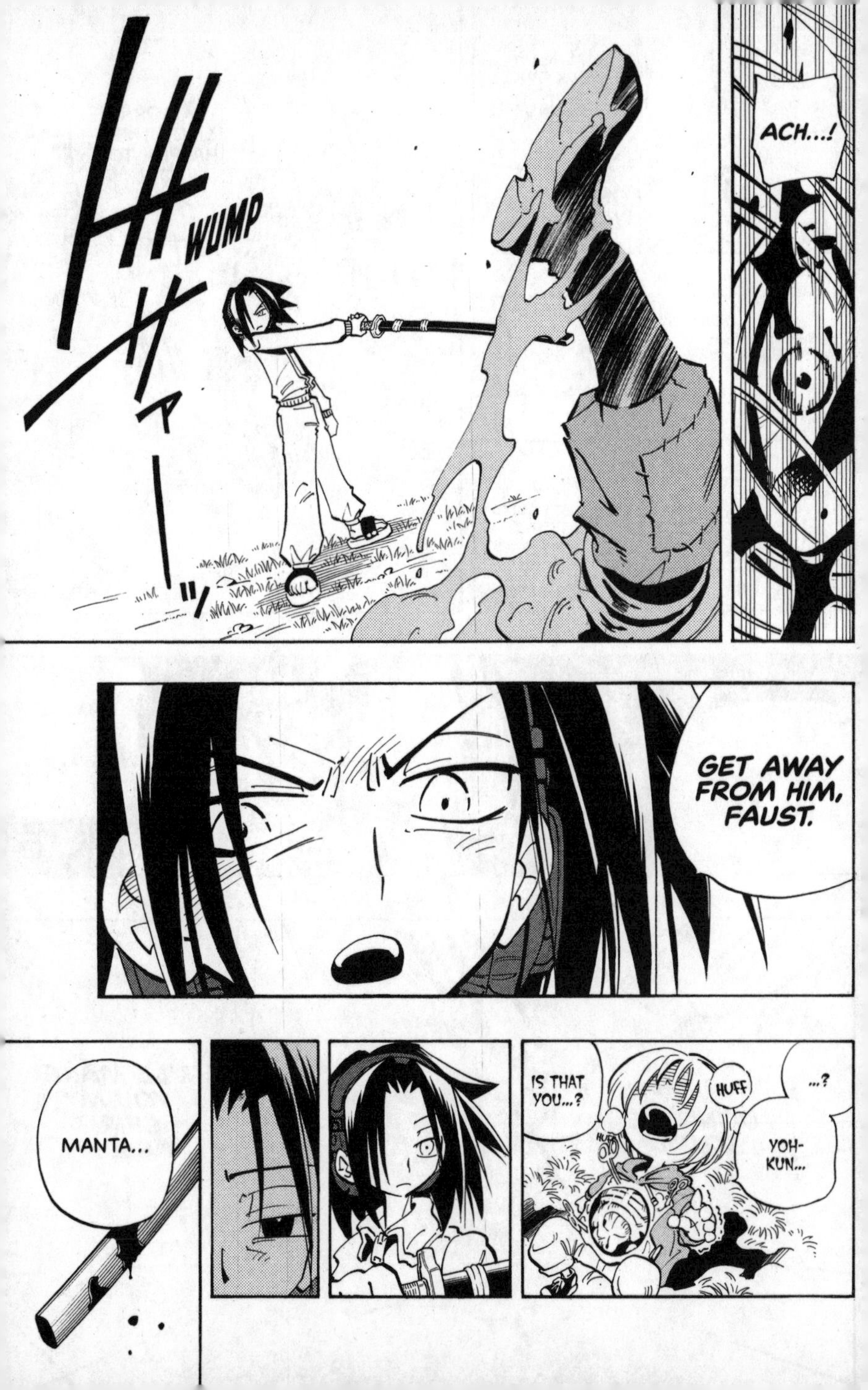
ACH...!
WUMP
GET AWAY FROM HIM, FAUST.
...?
YOH-KUN...
HUFF
IS THAT YOU...?
HUFF
MANTA...

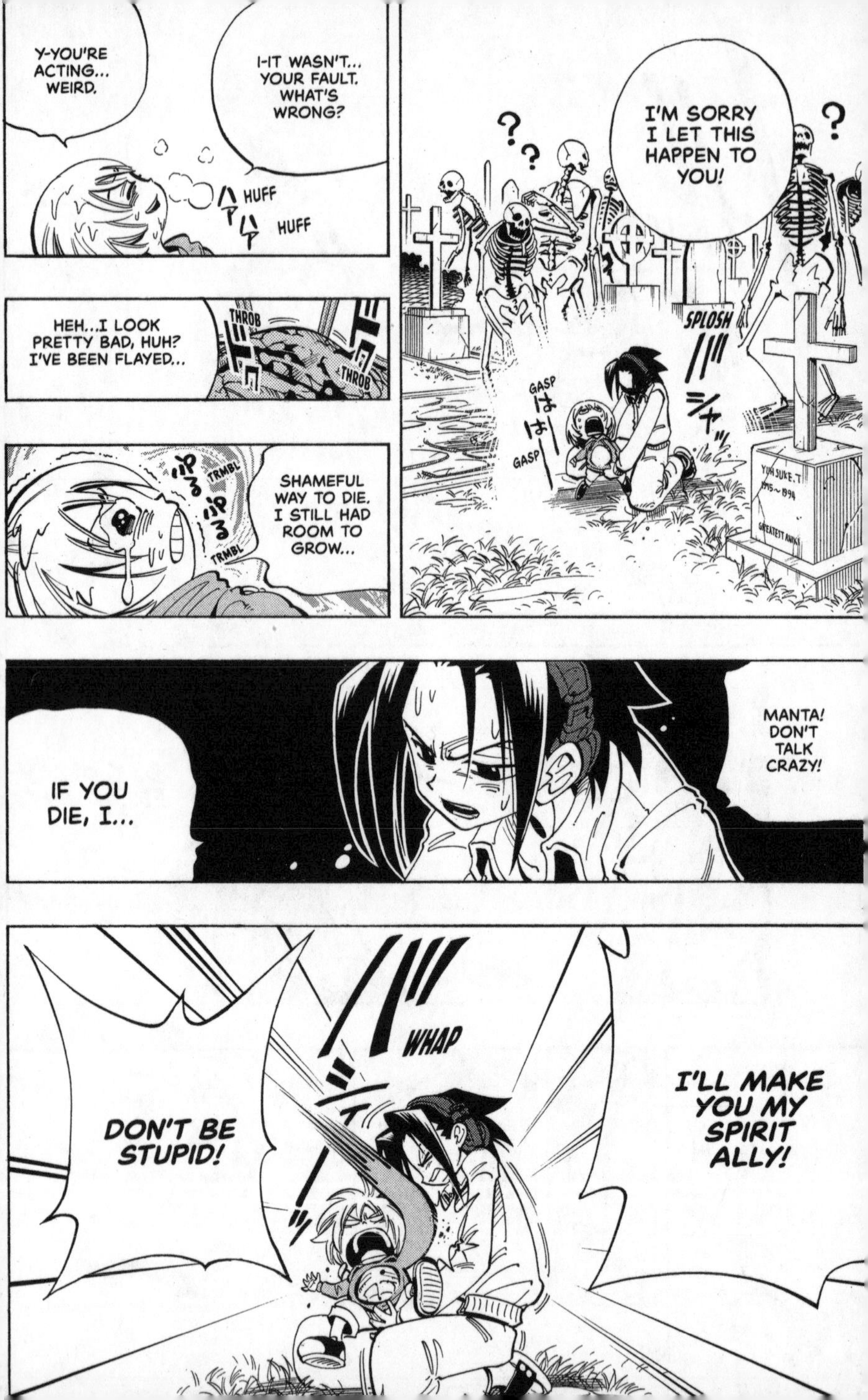
I'M SORRY I LET THIS HAPPEN TO YOU!
SPLOSH
GASP
GASP
I-IT WASN'T... YOUR FAULT. WHAT'S WRONG?
Y-YOU'RE ACTING... WEIRD.
HUFF
HUFF
THROB
THROB
HEH...I LOOK PRETTY BAD, HUH? I'VE BEEN FLAYED...
SHAMEFUL WAY TO DIE. I STILL HAD ROOM TO GROW...
TRMBL
TRMBL
MANTA! DON'T TALK CRAZY!
IF YOU DIE, I...
I'LL MAKE YOU MY SPIRIT ALLY!
WHAP
DON'T BE STUPID!

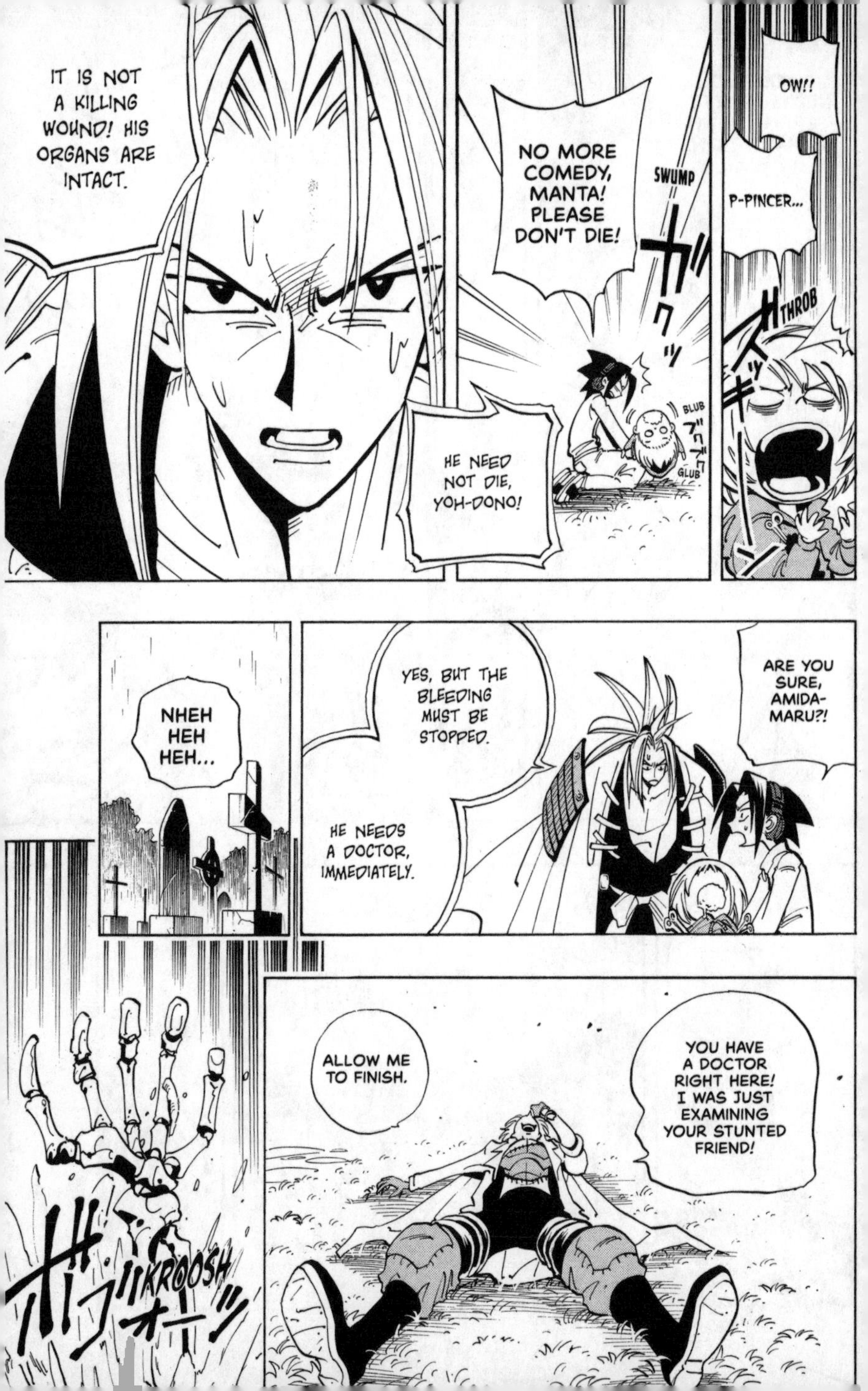
OW!!
P-PINCER...
THROB
NO MORE COMEDY, MANTA! PLEASE DON'T DIE!
SWUMP
BLUB
GLUB
HE NEED NOT DIE, YOH-DONO!
IT IS NOT A KILLING WOUND! HIS ORGANS ARE INTACT.
ARE YOU SURE, AMIDA-MARU?!
YES, BUT THE BLEEDING MUST BE STOPPED.
HE NEEDS A DOCTOR, IMMEDIATELY.
NHEH HEH HEH...
YOU HAVE A DOCTOR RIGHT HERE! I WAS JUST EXAMINING YOUR STUNTED FRIEND!
ALLOW ME TO FINISH.
KROOSH

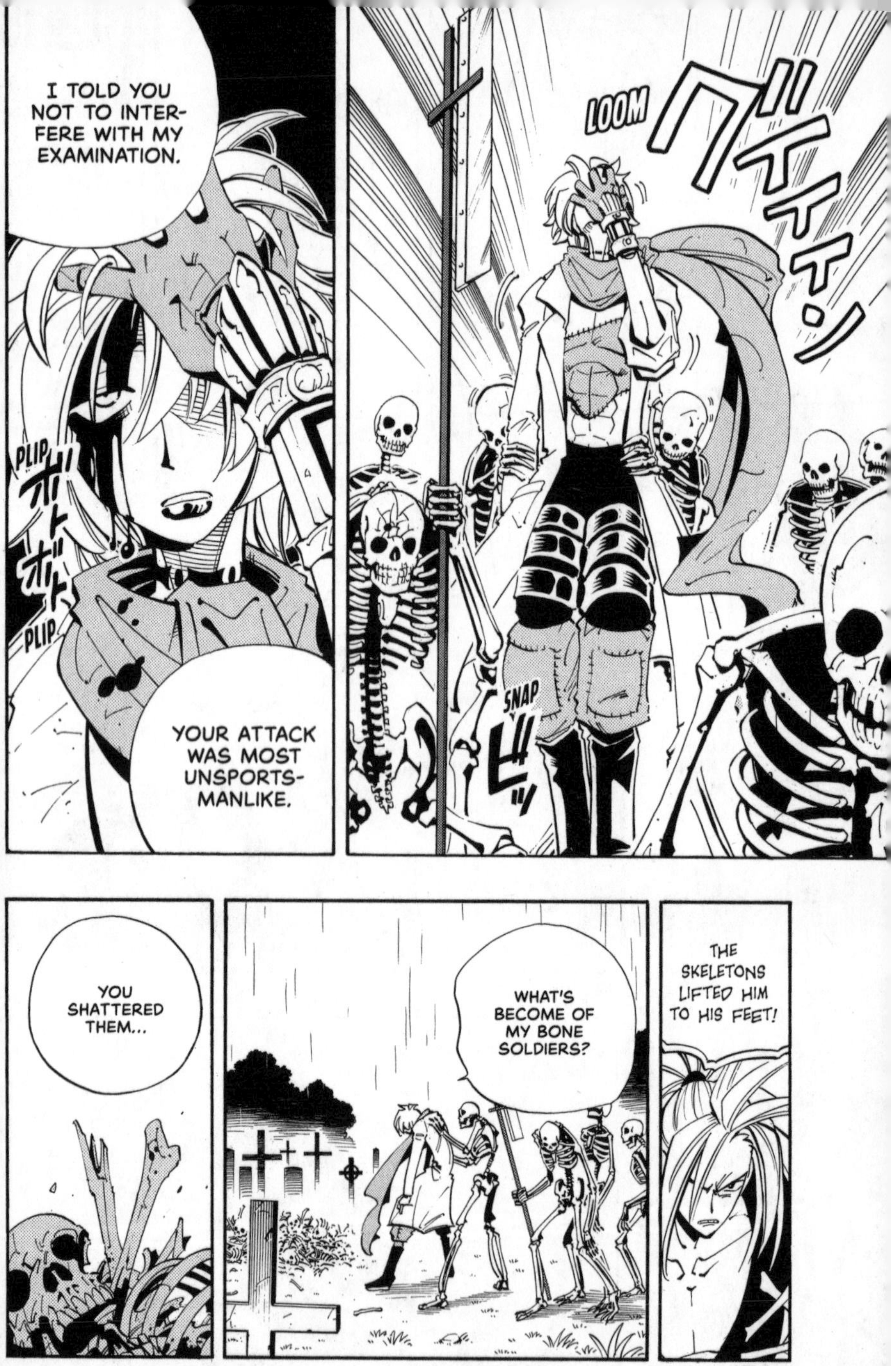
LOOM
SNAP
I TOLD YOU NOT TO INTERFERE WITH MY EXAMINATION.
PLIP
PLIP
YOUR ATTACK WAS MOST UNSPORTSMANLIKE.
THE SKELETONS LIFTED HIM TO HIS FEET!
WHAT'S BECOME OF MY BONE SOLDIERS?
YOU SHATTERED THEM...

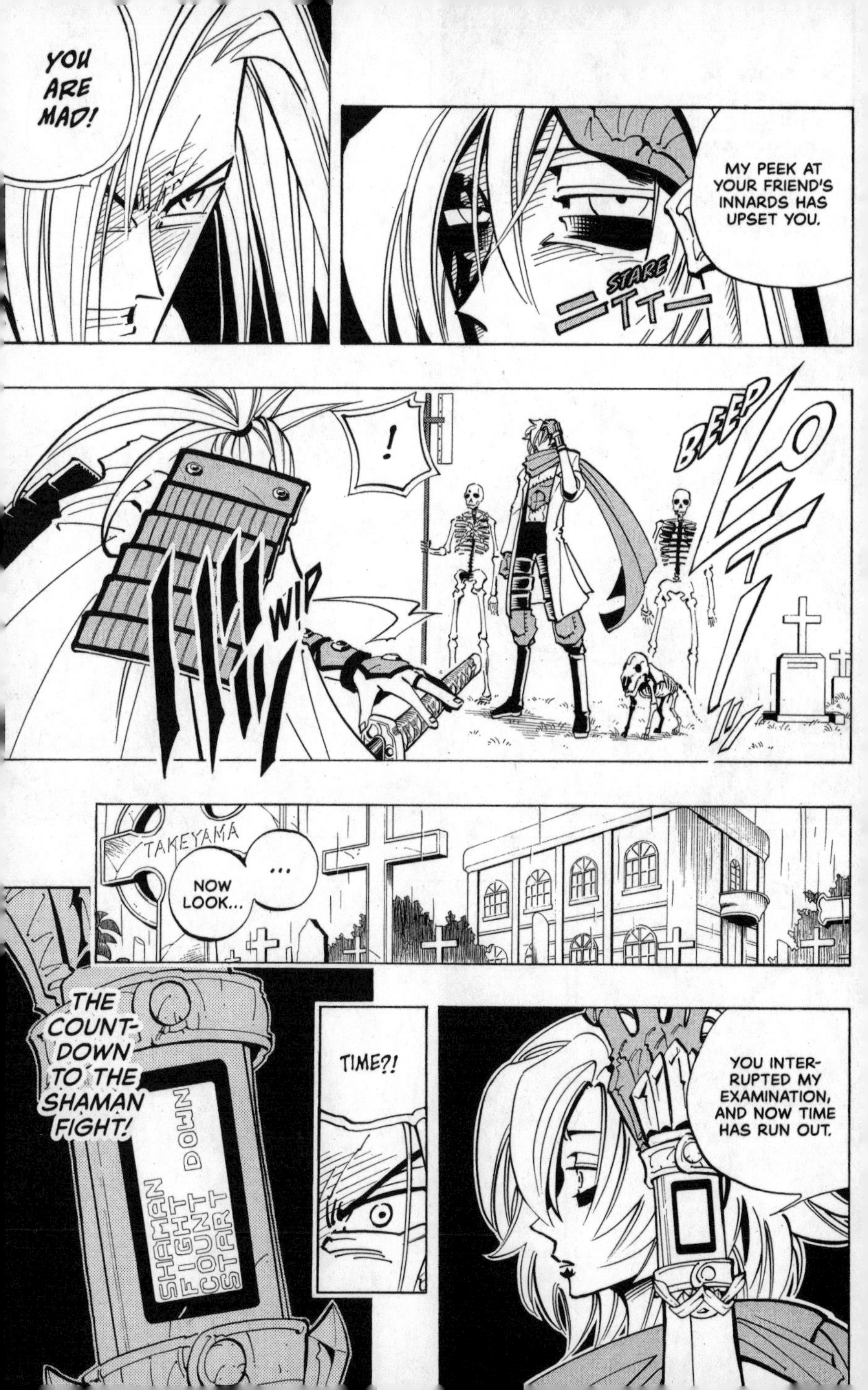
MY PEEK AT YOUR FRIEND'S INNARDS HAS UPSET YOU.
STARE
YOU ARE MAD!
BEEP
!
WIP
TAKEYAMA
...
NOW LOOK...
YOU INTER-RUPTED MY EXAMINATION, AND NOW TIME HAS RUN OUT.
TIME?!
THE COUNT-DOWN TO THE SHAMAN FIGHT!
SHAMAN FIGHT COUNT DOWN START

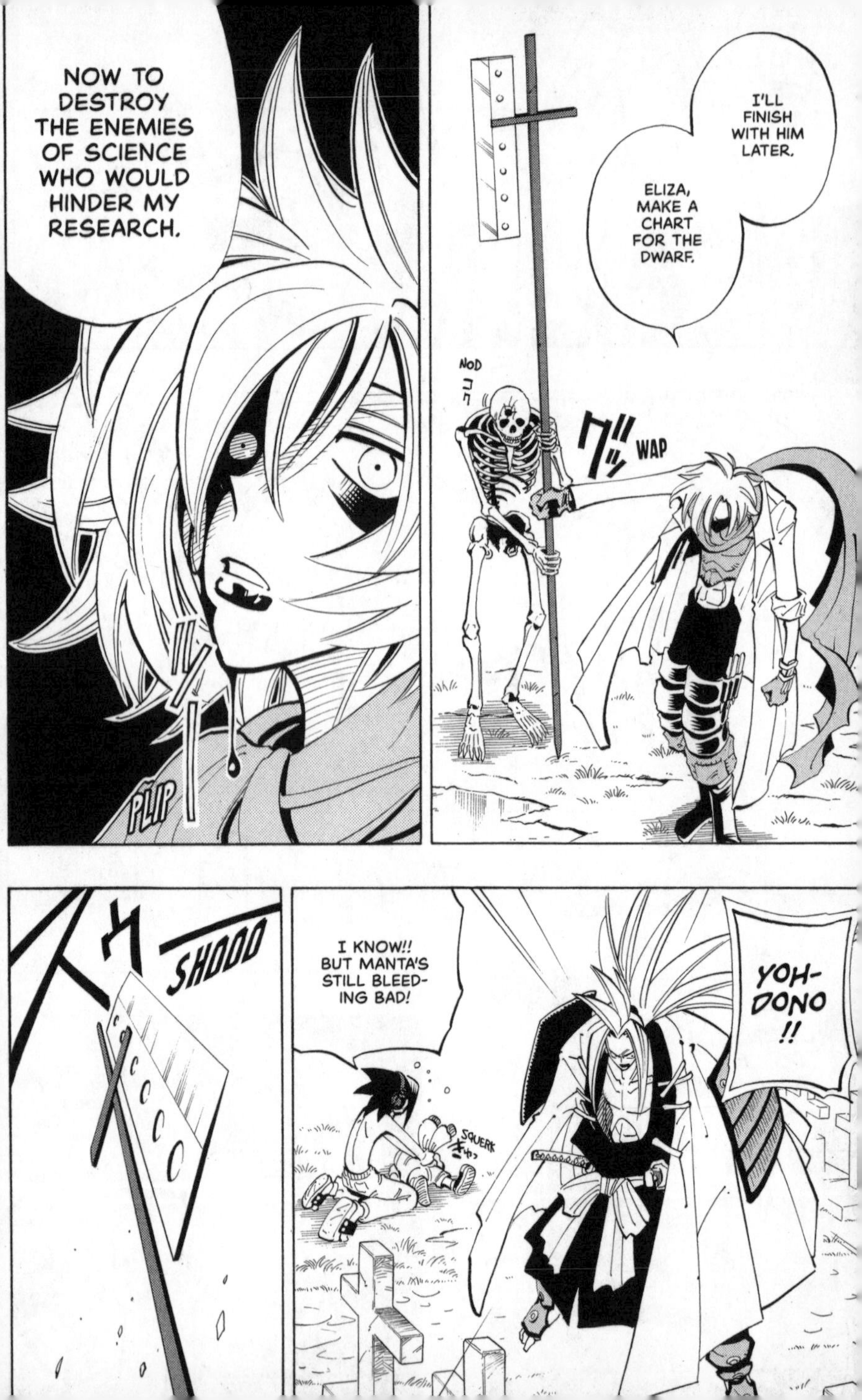
I'LL FINISH WITH HIM LATER.
ELIZA, MAKE A CHART FOR THE DWARF.
WAP
NOD
NOW TO DESTROY THE ENEMIES OF SCIENCE WHO WOULD HINDER MY RESEARCH.
PLIP
YOH-DONO !!
I KNOW!! BUT MANTA'S STILL BLEED-ING BAD!
SQUERK
SHOOO

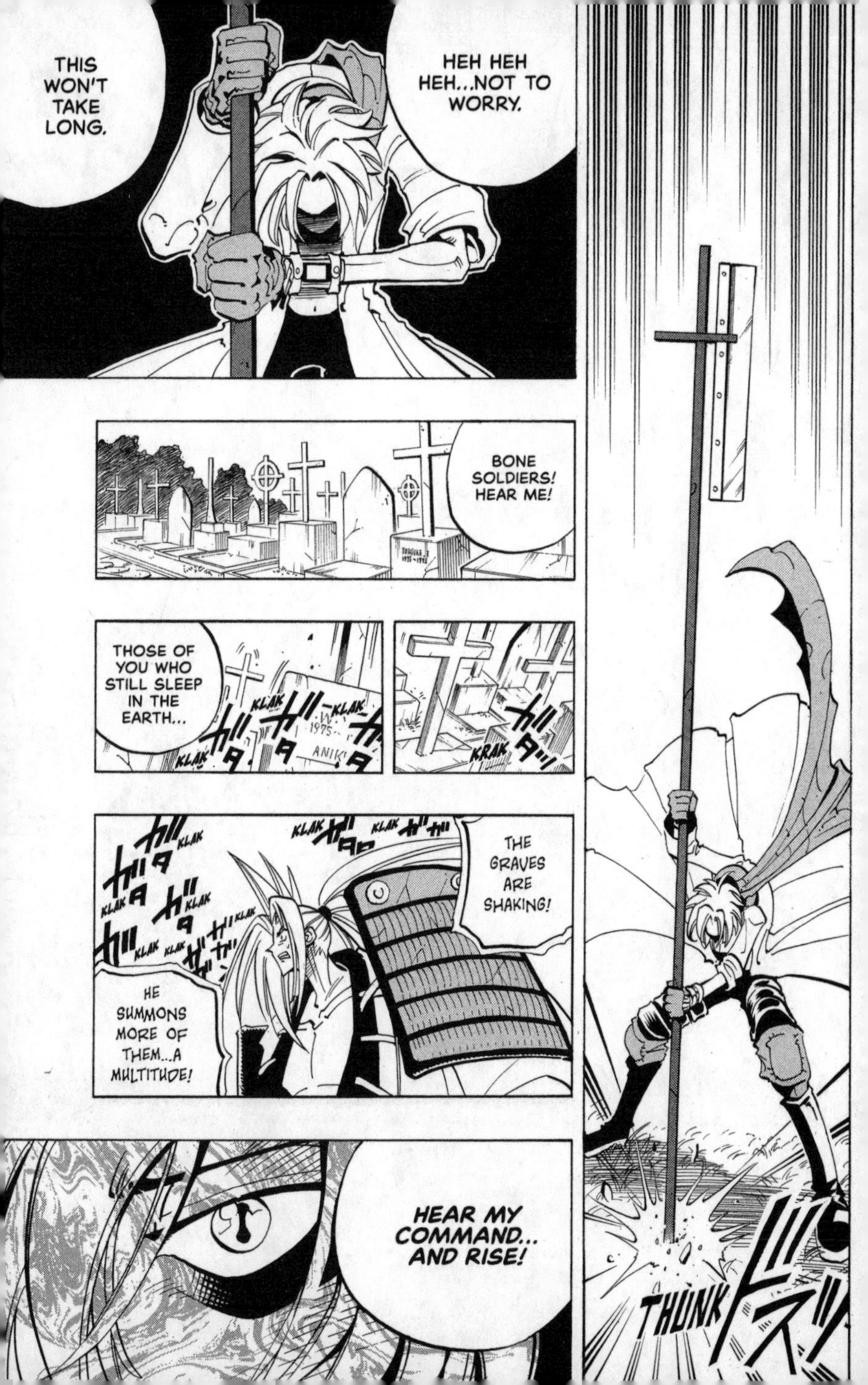
THUNK
HEH HEH HEH...NOT TO WORRY.
THIS WON'T TAKE LONG.
BONE SOLDIERS! HEAR ME!
KRAK
THOSE OF YOU WHO STILL SLEEP IN THE EARTH...
KLAK
KLAK
KLAK
KLAK
THE GRAVES ARE SHAKING!
HE SUMMONS MORE OF THEM...A MULTITUDE!
HEAR MY COMMAND... AND RISE!

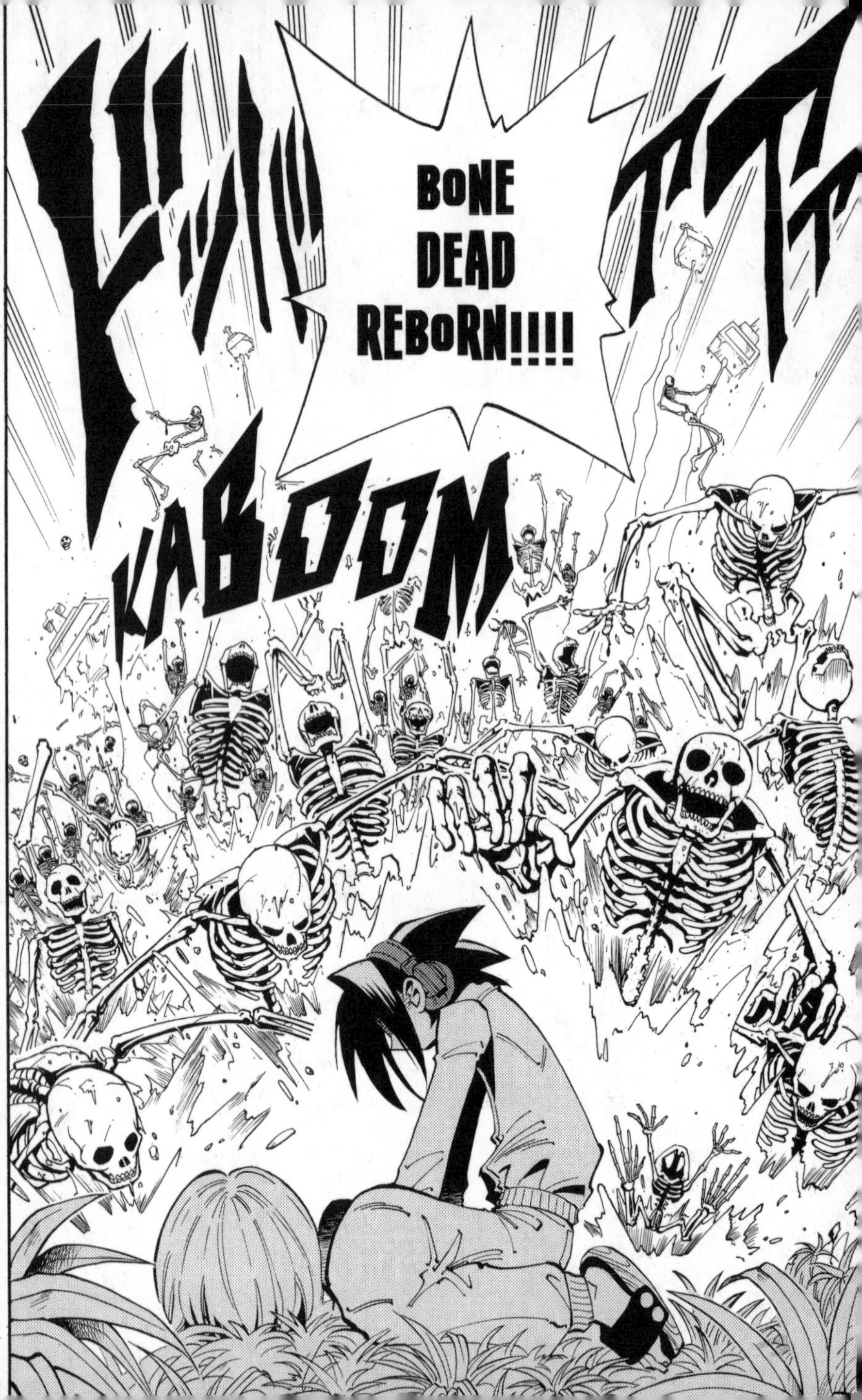
BONE DEAD REBORN!!!!!
KABOOM

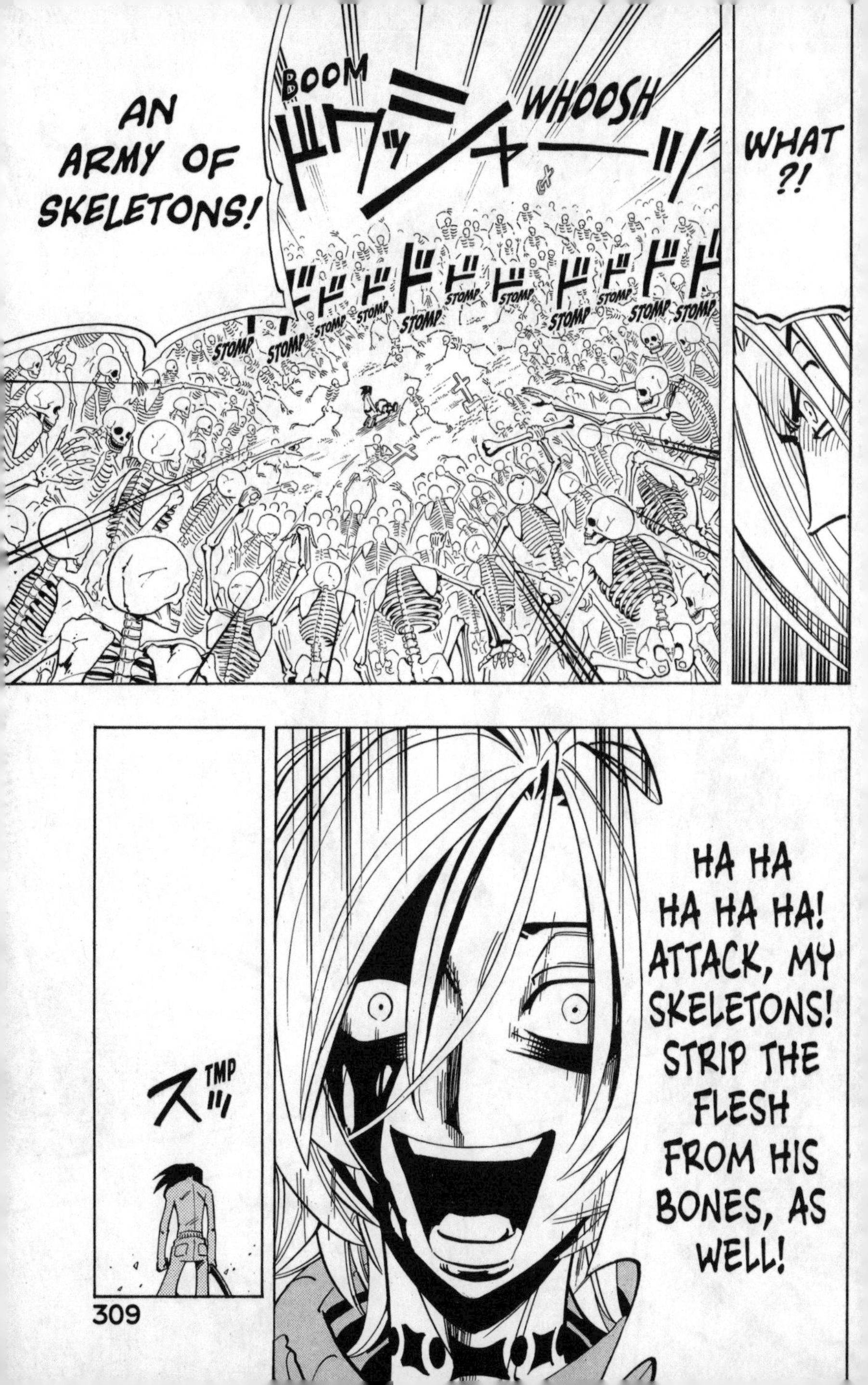
WHAT?!
BOOM
WHOOSH
AN ARMY OF SKELETONS!
STOMP STOMP STOMP STOMP STOMP STOMP STOMP STOMP STOMP STOMP STOMP STOMP
HA HA HA HA HA! ATTACK, MY SKELETONS! STRIP THE FLESH FROM HIS BONES, AS WELL!
TMP

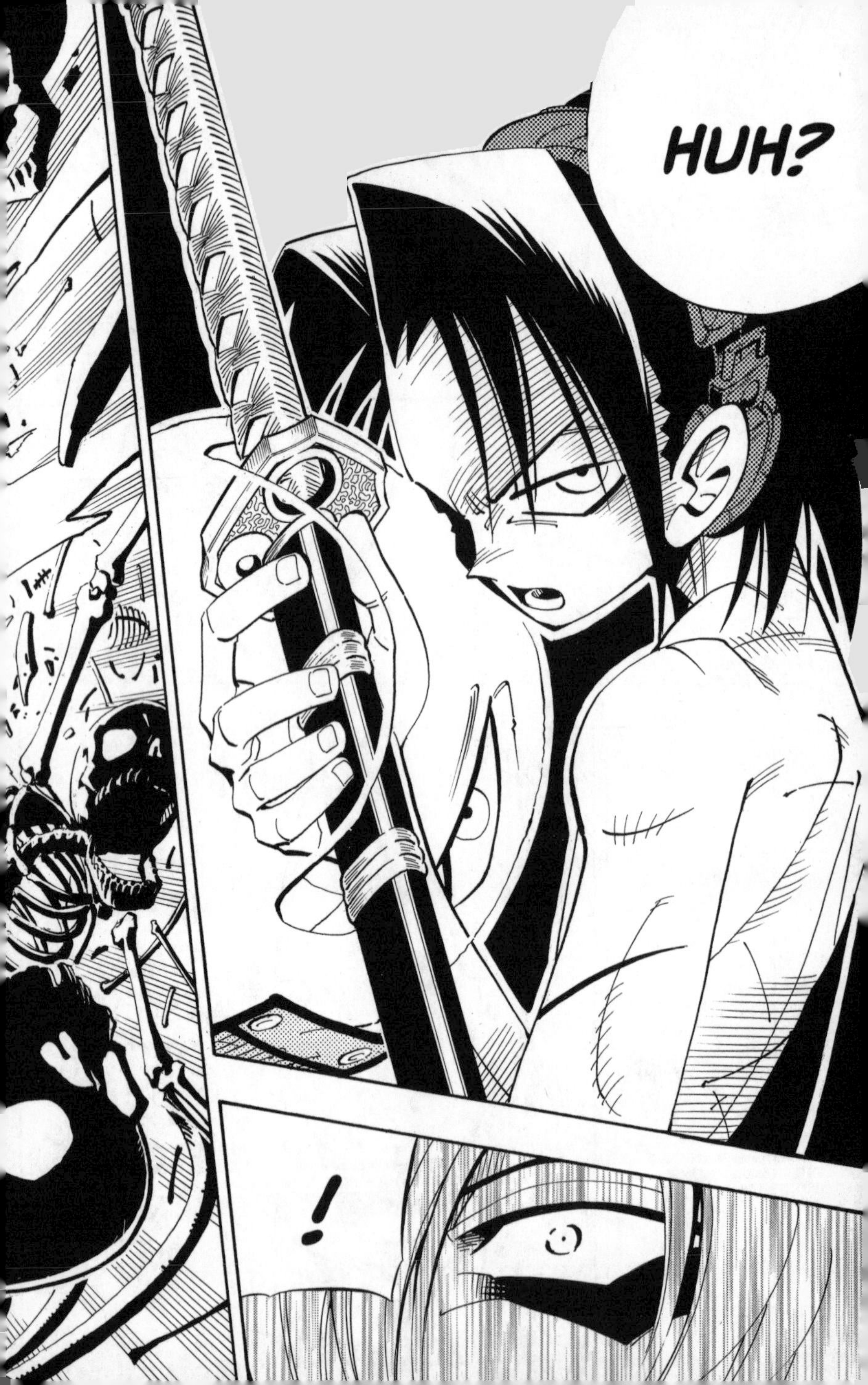
HUH?
!

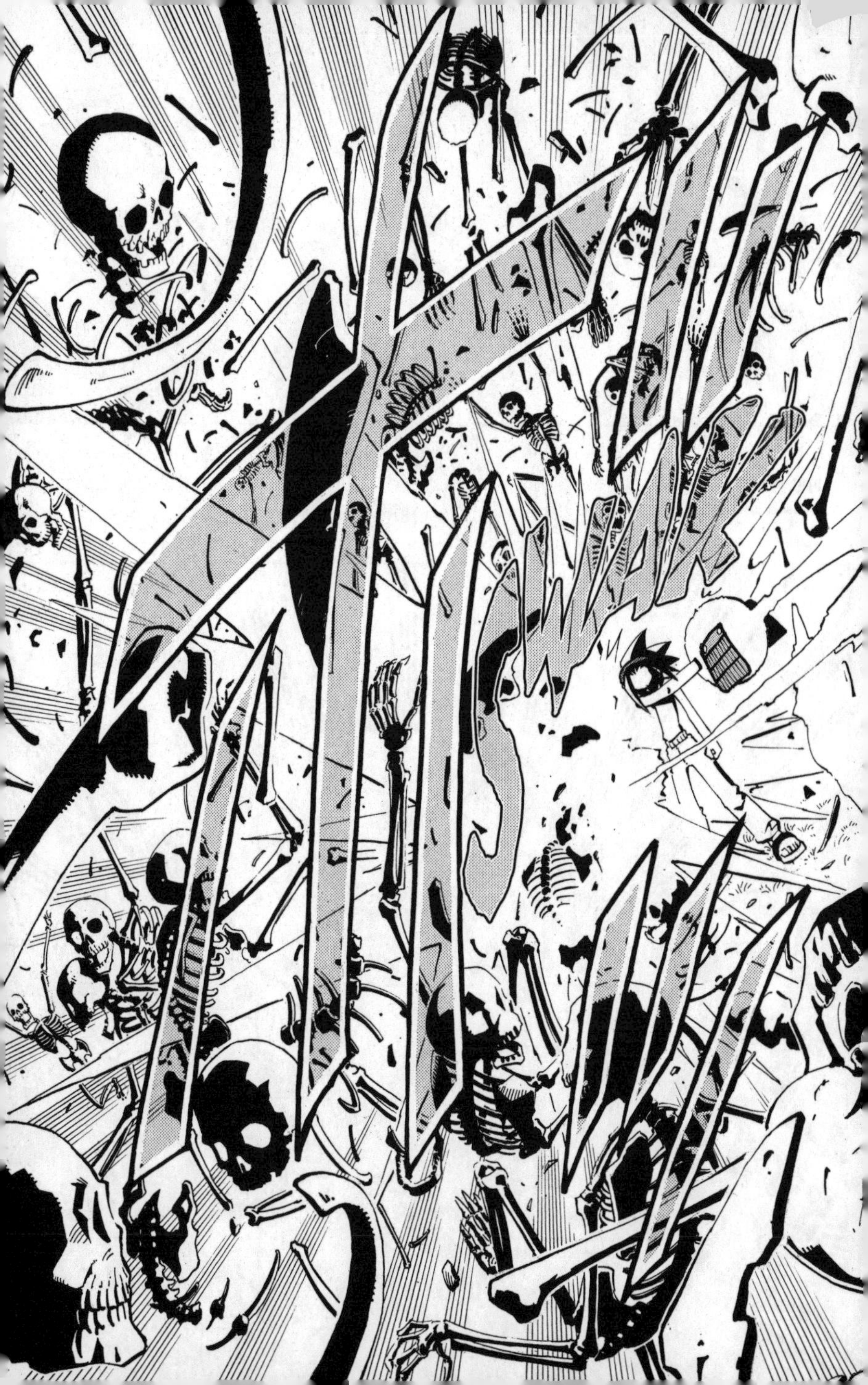

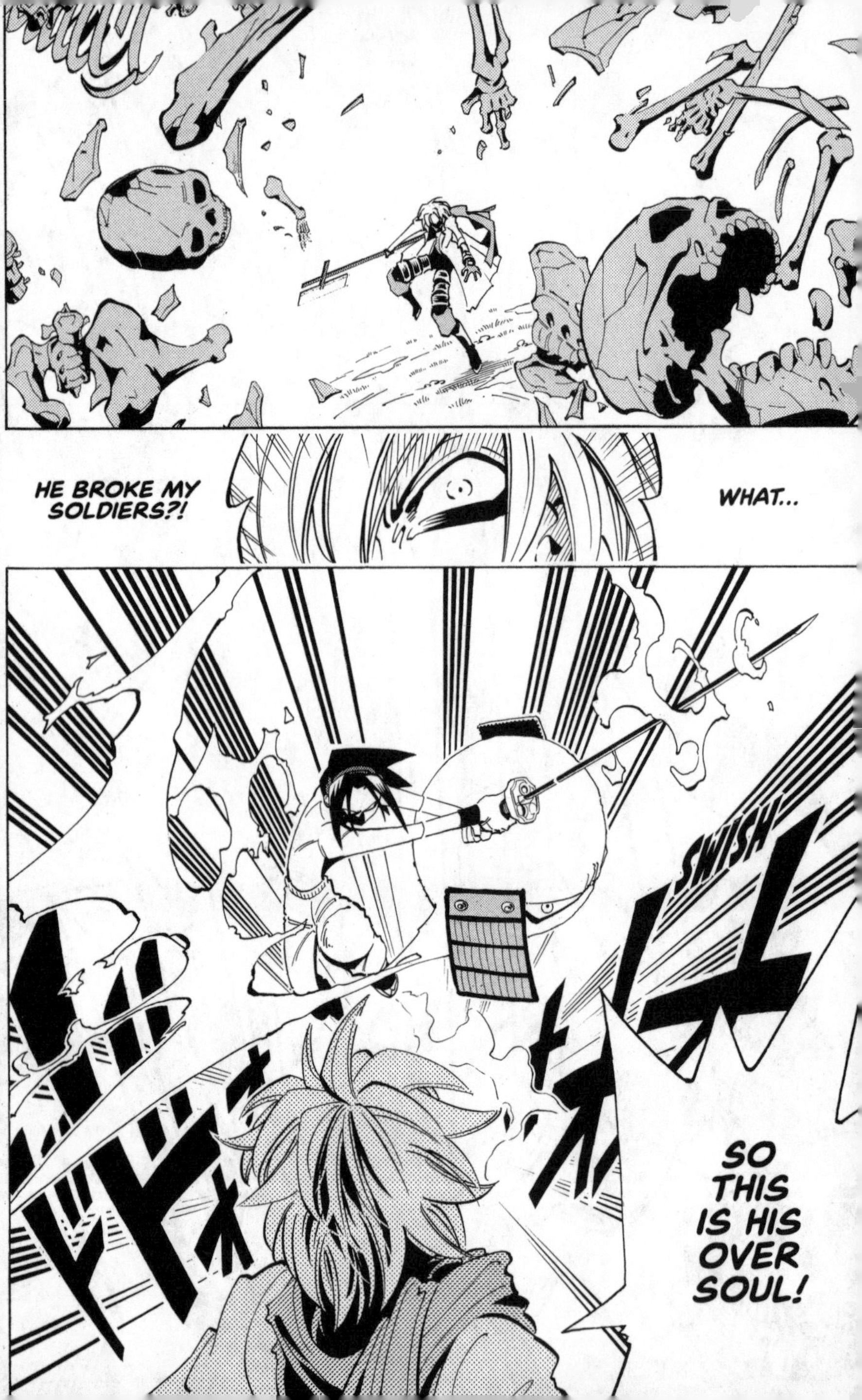
WHAT...
HE BROKE MY SOLDIERS?!
SWISH
SO THIS IS HIS OVER SOUL!

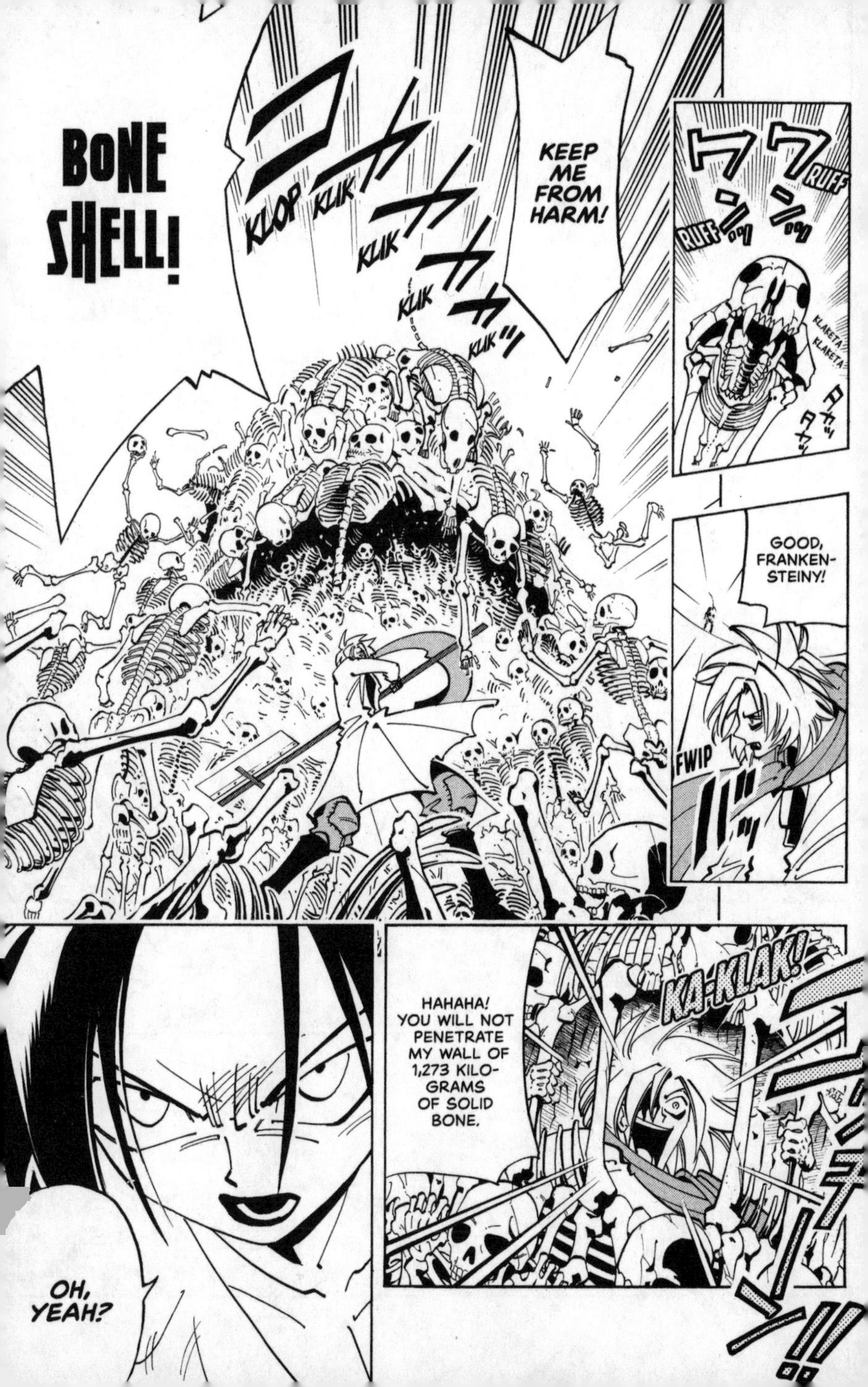
RUFF
RUFF
KLAKETA KLAKETA
GOOD, FRANKEN-STEINY!
FWIP
KEEP ME FROM HARM!
KLOP
KLIK
KLIK
KLIK
KLIK
BONE SHELL!
KA-KLAK!
HAHAHA! YOU WILL NOT PENETRATE MY WALL OF 1,273 KILO-GRAMS OF SOLID BONE.
OH, YEAH?

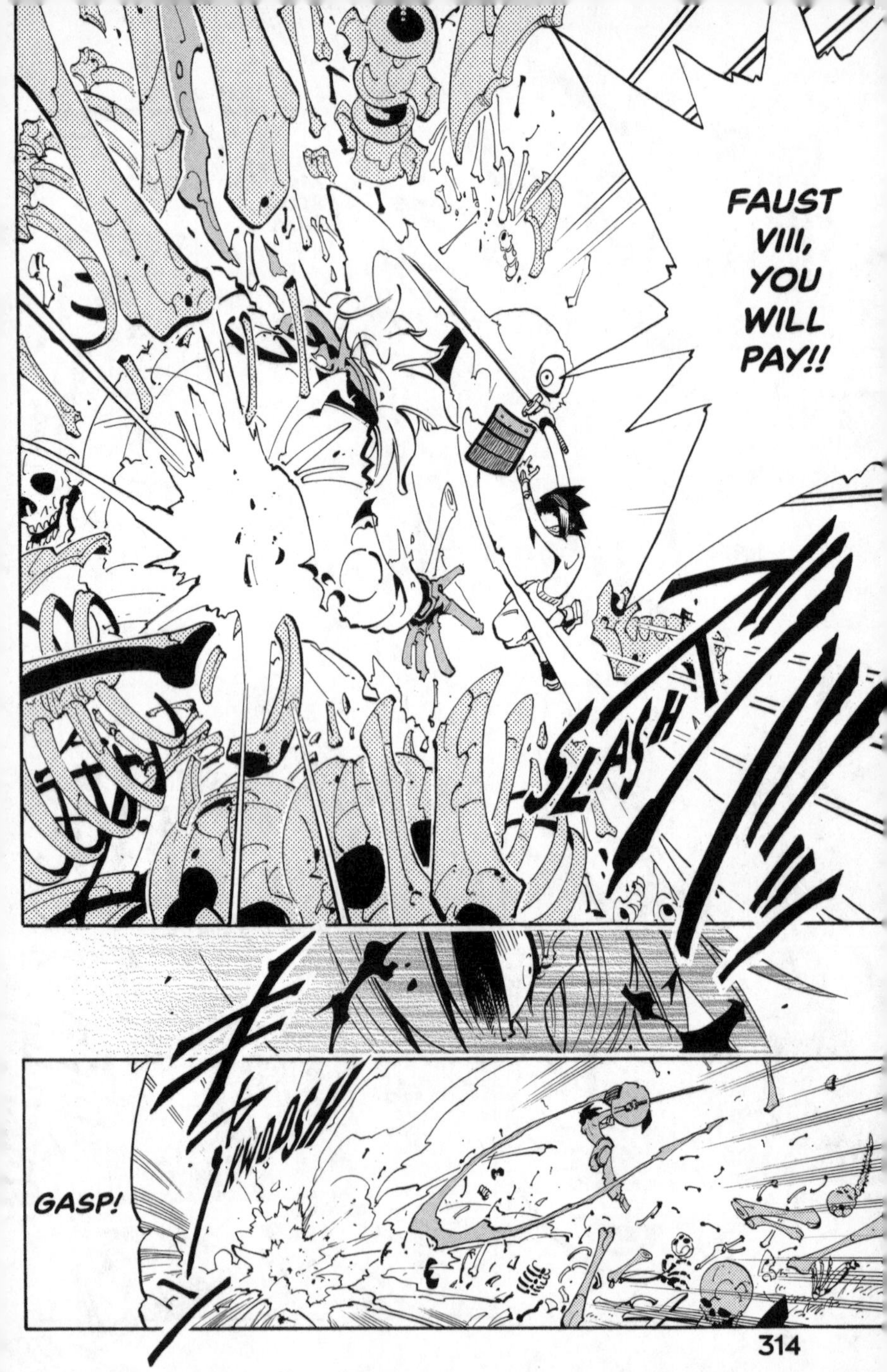
FAUST VIII, YOU WILL PAY!!
SLASH
KWOOSH
GASP!

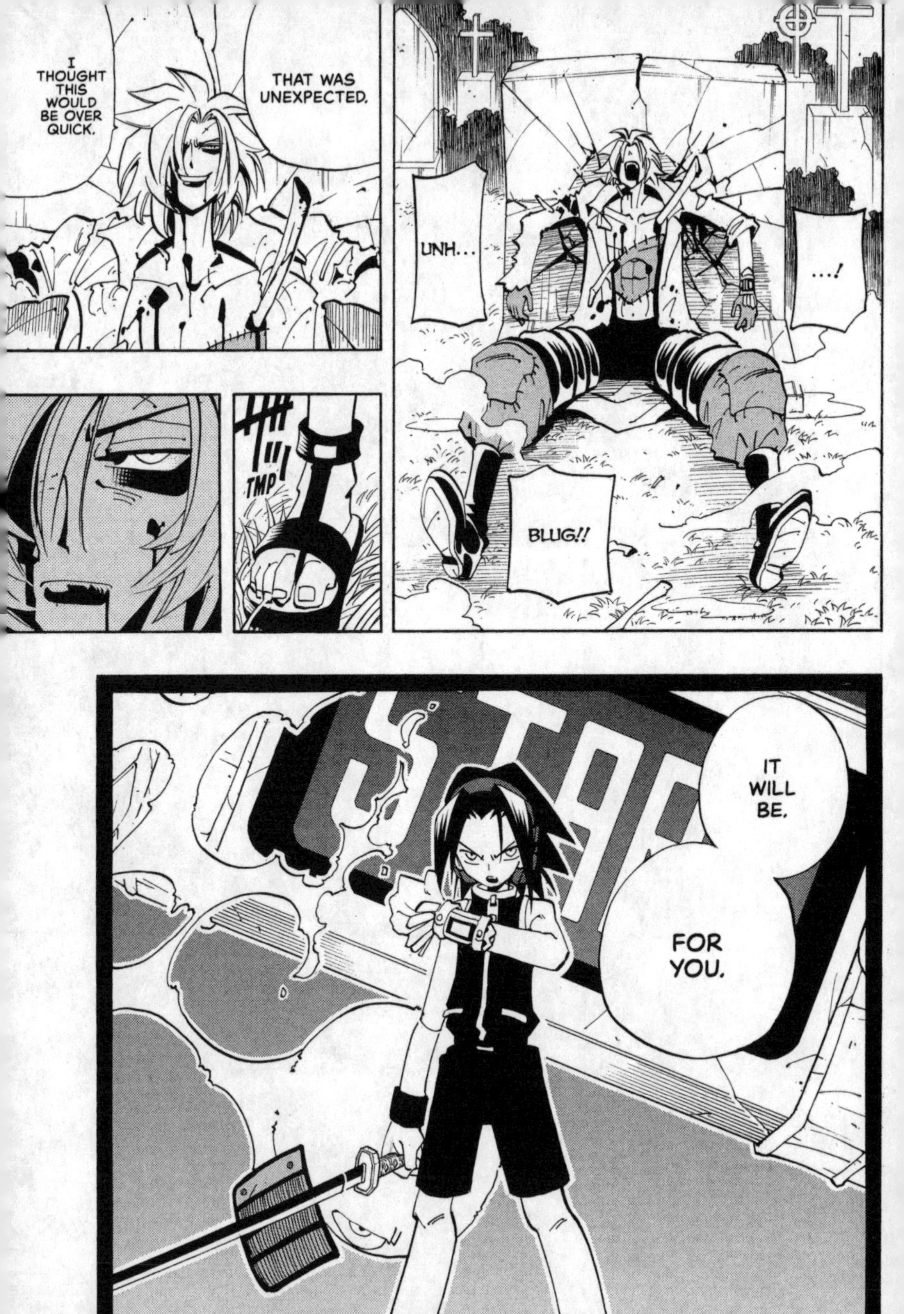
...!
UNH...
BLUG!!
THAT WAS UNEXPECTED.
I THOUGHT THIS WOULD BE OVER QUICK.
TMP
IT WILL BE.
FOR YOU.

SHAMAN KING
5

**The
Sun-Sunshine
Building**

Chapter 42: The Atrocity Exhibition

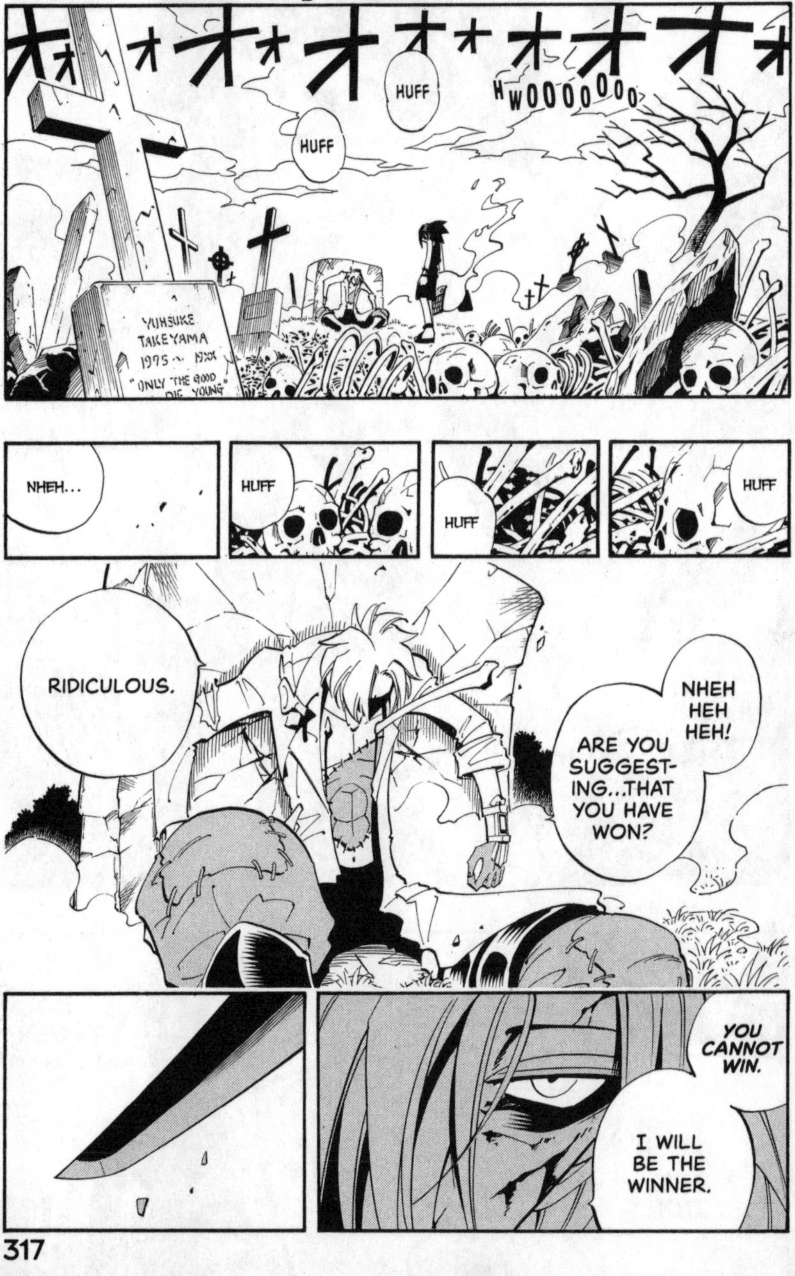

オォォオォオオォォオオォ
HWOOOOOOO
HUFF
HUFF
YUHSUKE TAKEYAMA 1975 ~ 19XX "ONLY THE GOOD DIE YOUNG"
HUFF
HUFF
HUFF
NHEH...
RIDICULOUS.
NHEH HEH HEH!
ARE YOU SUGGESTING...THAT YOU HAVE WON?
YOU CANNOT WIN.
I WILL BE THE WINNER.

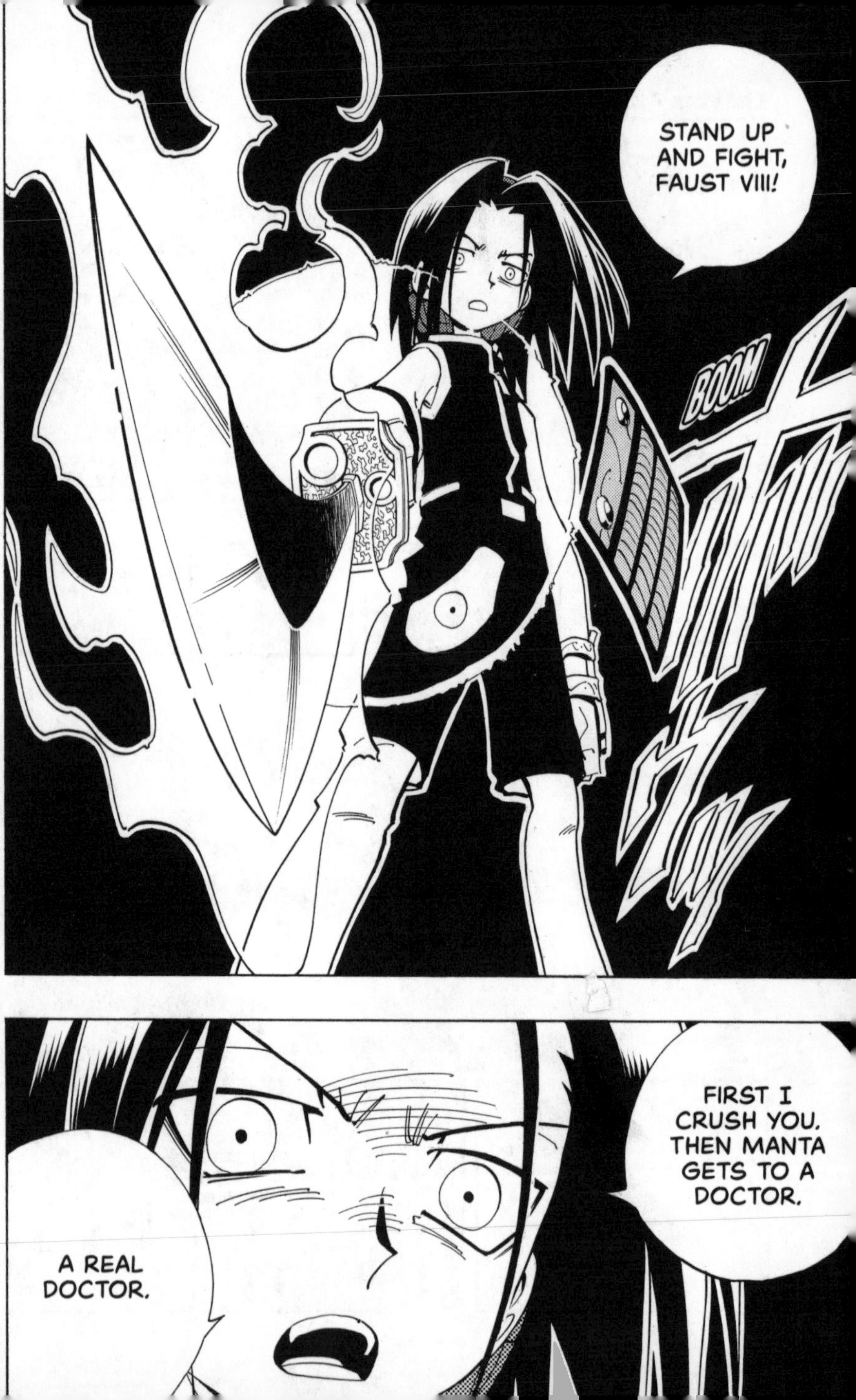
STAND UP AND FIGHT, FAUST VIII!
BOOM
FIRST I CRUSH YOU. THEN MANTA GETS TO A DOCTOR.
A REAL DOCTOR.

Chapter 42:

The Atrocity Exhibition

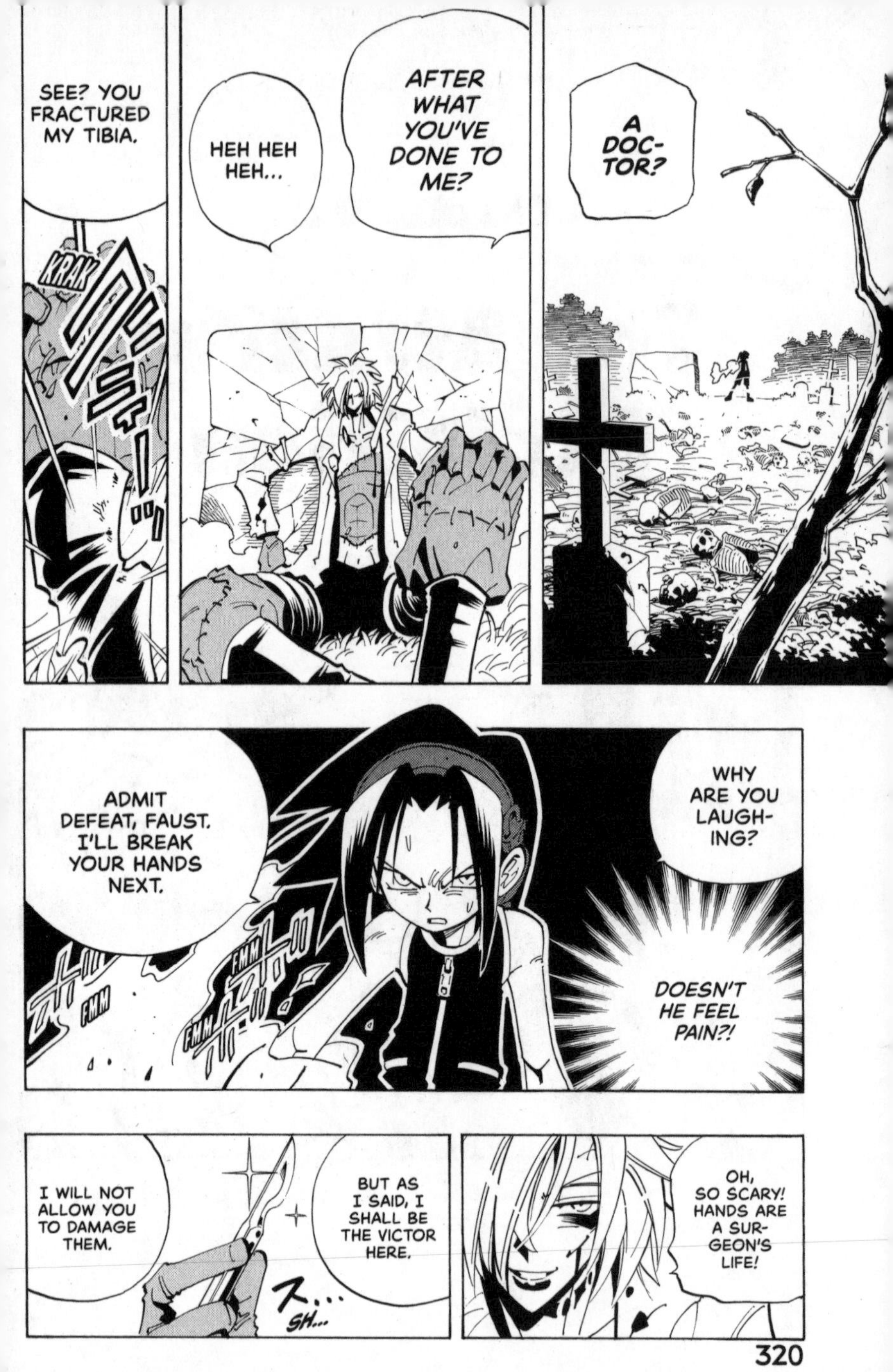
A DOC-TOR?
AFTER WHAT YOU'VE DONE TO ME?
HEH HEH HEH...
SEE? YOU FRACTURED MY TIBIA.
KRAK
WHY ARE YOU LAUGH-ING?
DOESN'T HE FEEL PAIN?!
ADMIT DEFEAT, FAUST. I'LL BREAK YOUR HANDS NEXT.
FMM
FMM
FMM
OH, SO SCARY! HANDS ARE A SUR-GEON'S LIFE!
BUT AS I SAID, I SHALL BE THE VICTOR HERE.
I WILL NOT ALLOW YOU TO DAMAGE THEM.
SH...

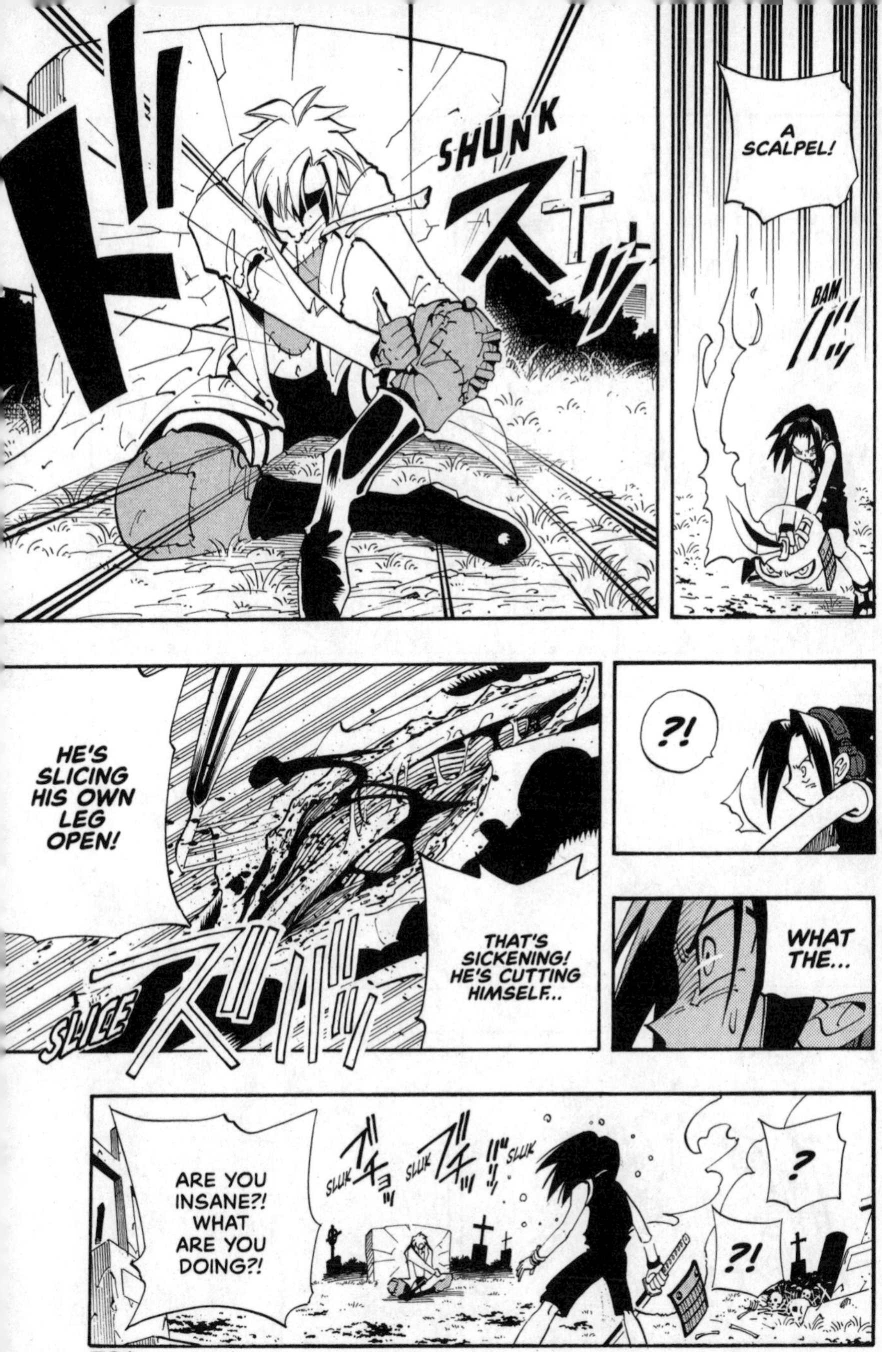
A SCALPEL!
BAM
SHUNK
?!
WHAT THE...
HE'S SLICING HIS OWN LEG OPEN!
THAT'S SICKENING! HE'S CUTTING HIMSELF...
SLICE
?
?!
SLUK
SLUK
SLUK
ARE YOU INSANE?! WHAT ARE YOU DOING?!

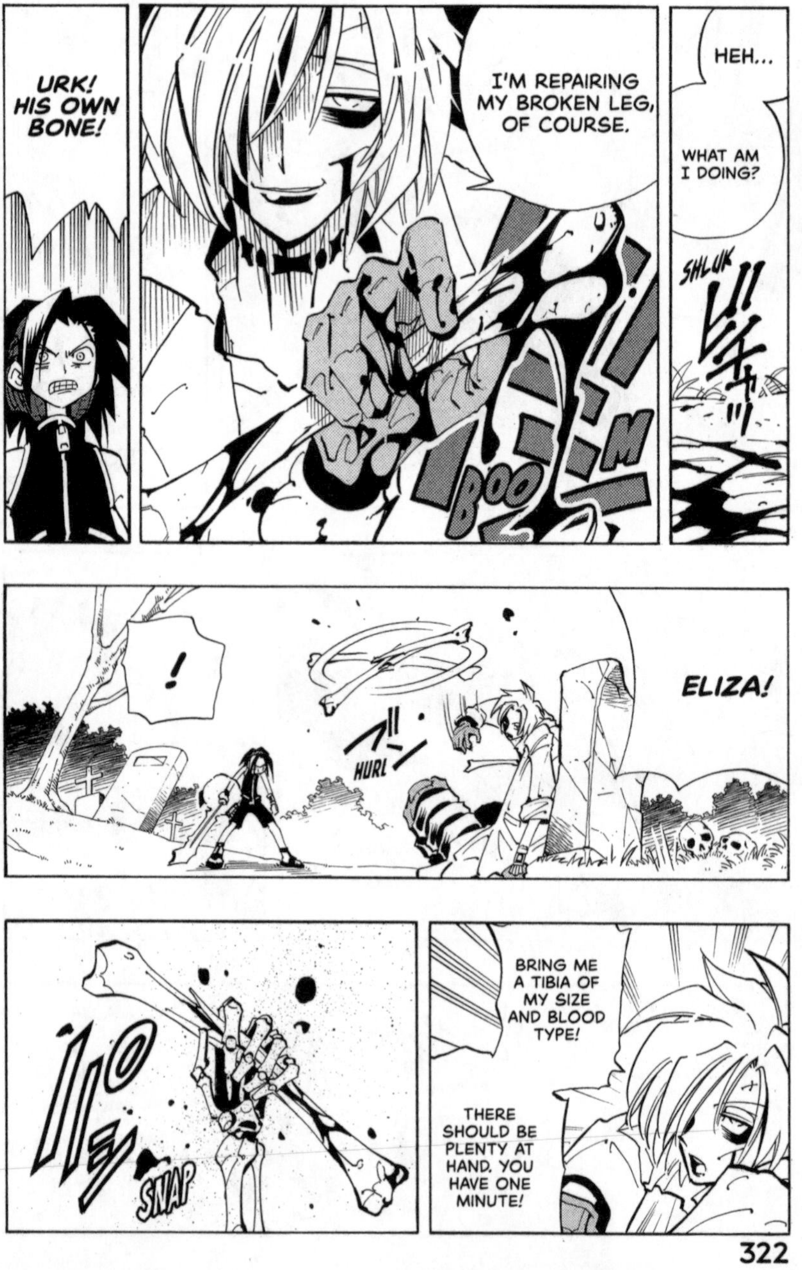
HEH...
WHAT AM I DOING?
SHLUK
I'M REPAIRING MY BROKEN LEG, OF COURSE.
BOOM
URK! HIS OWN BONE!
ELIZA!
!
HURL
BRING ME A TIBIA OF MY SIZE AND BLOOD TYPE!
THERE SHOULD BE PLENTY AT HAND. YOU HAVE ONE MINUTE!
SNAP

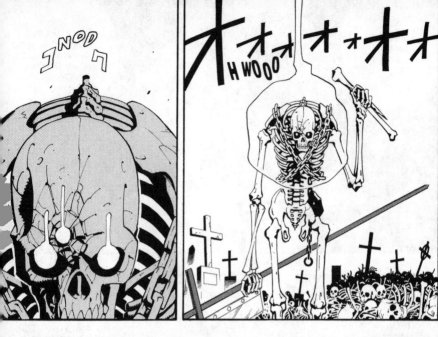

THE SHOCK ON YOUR FACE!

IT'S VERY SIMPLE. I'M TRANS- PLANTING THE WHOLE TIBIA.

HUFF

HUFF

...

NHEH HEH HEH.

...

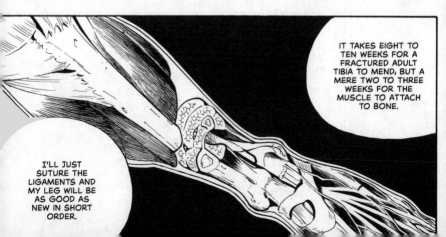

IT TAKES EIGHT TO TEN WEEKS FOR A FRACTURED ADULT TIBIA TO MEND, BUT A MERE TWO TO THREE WEEKS FOR THE MUSCLE TO ATTACH TO BONE.

I'LL JUST SUTURE THE LIGAMENTS AND MY LEG WILL BE AS GOOD AS NEW IN SHORT ORDER.

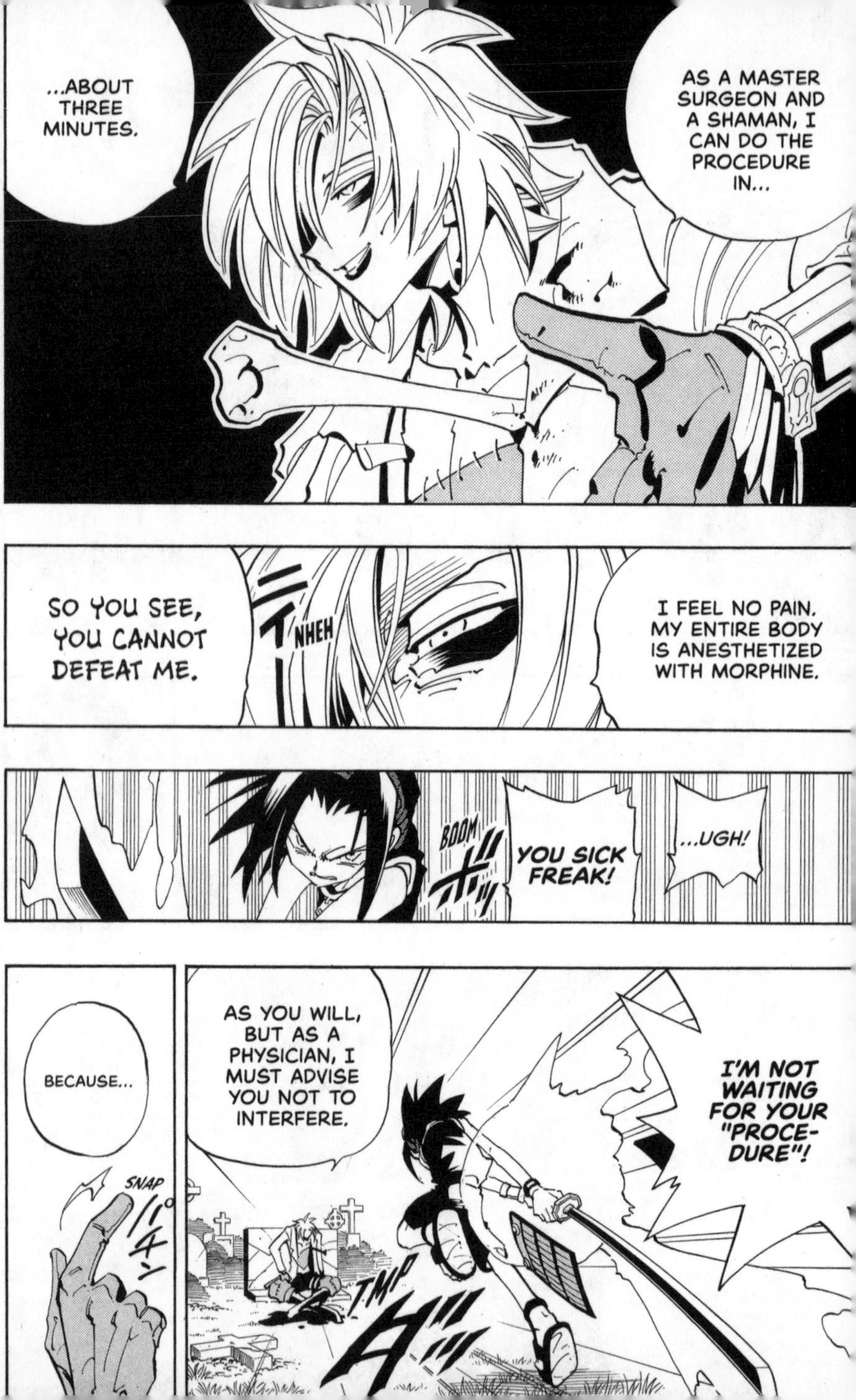
AS A MASTER SURGEON AND A SHAMAN, I CAN DO THE PROCEDURE IN...
...ABOUT THREE MINUTES.
I FEEL NO PAIN. MY ENTIRE BODY IS ANESTHETIZED WITH MORPHINE.
NHEH
SO YOU SEE, YOU CANNOT DEFEAT ME.
...UGH!
YOU SICK FREAK!
BOOM
I'M NOT WAITING FOR YOUR "PROCE-DURE"!
AS YOU WILL, BUT AS A PHYSICIAN, I MUST ADVISE YOU NOT TO INTERFERE.
TMP
BECAUSE...
SNAP

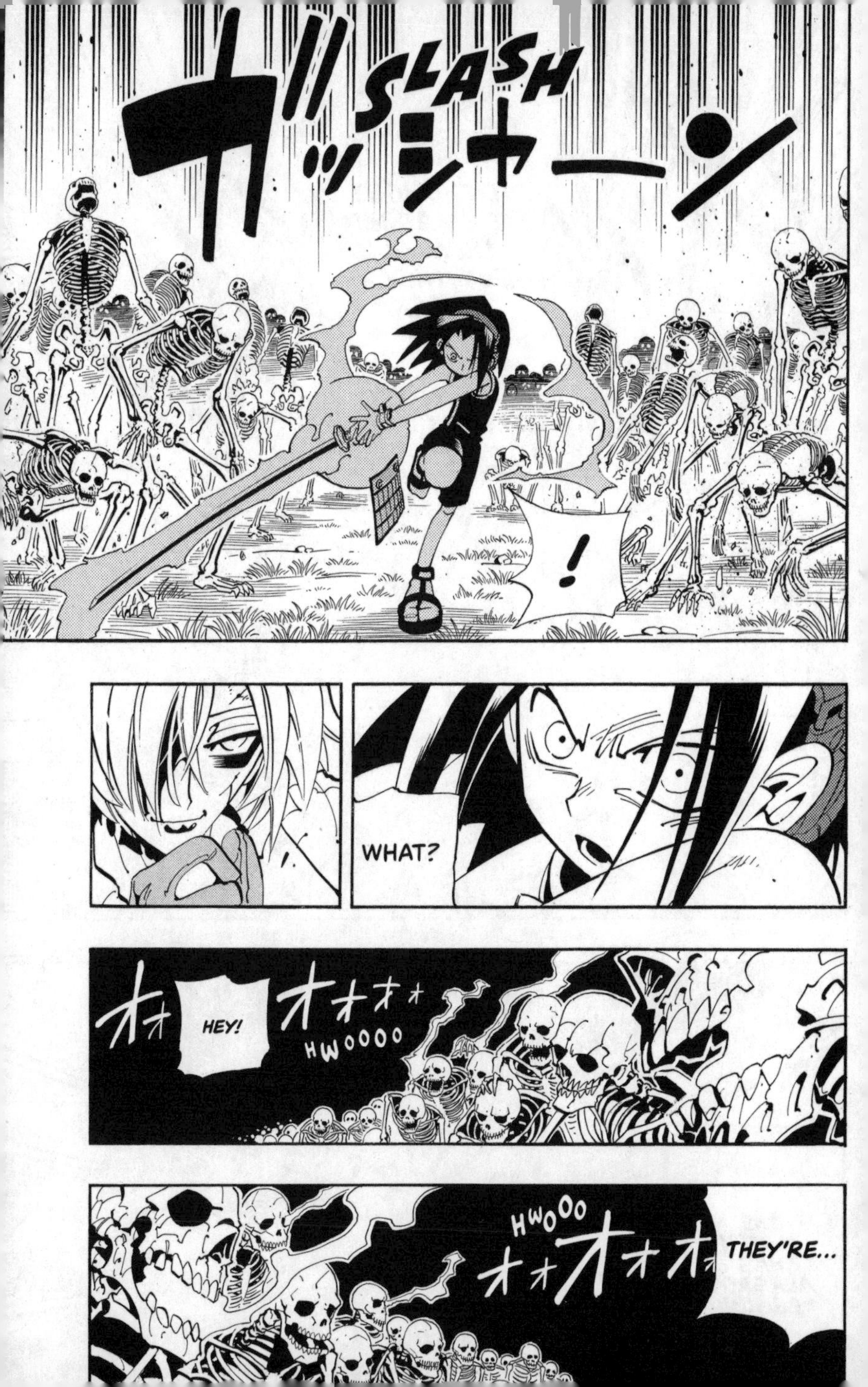

ガッシャーン
SLASH
!
WHAT?
オオオオオオ
HWOOOO
HEY!
THEY'RE...
オオオオオオ
HWOOO

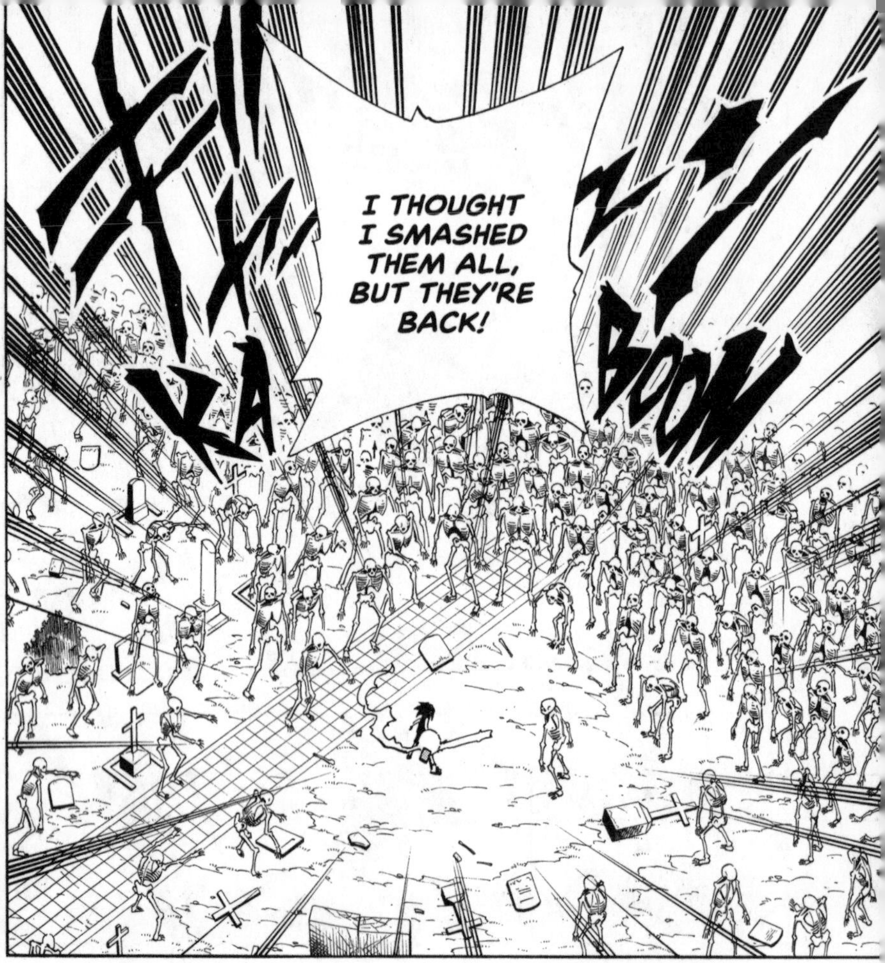
BOOM
I THOUGHT I SMASHED THEM ALL, BUT THEY'RE BACK!
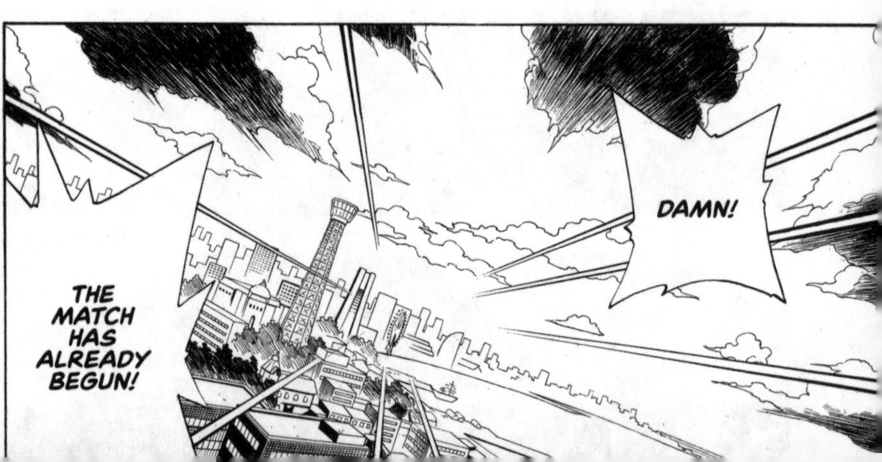
DAMN!
THE MATCH HAS ALREADY BEGUN!

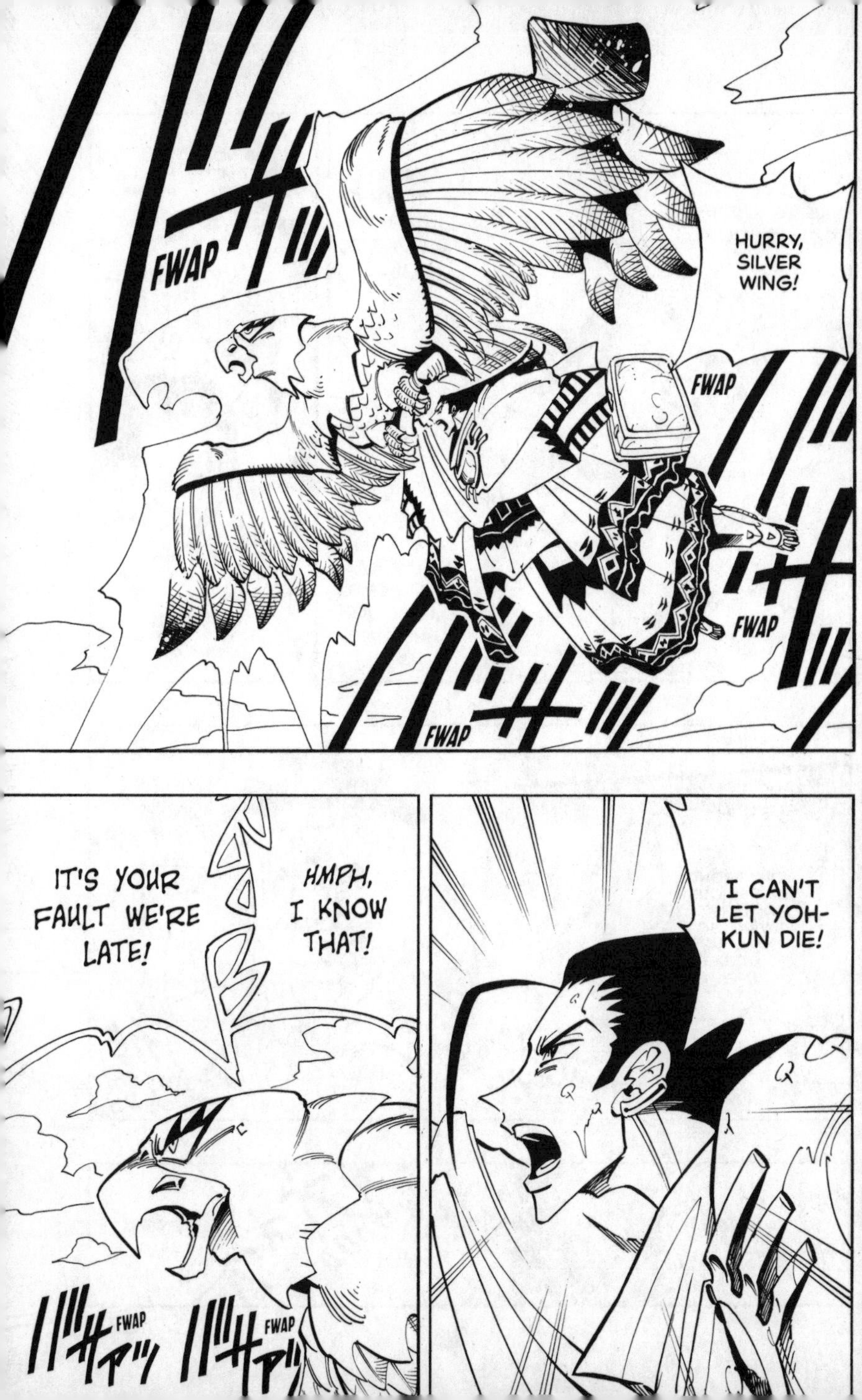
HURRY, SILVER WING!
FWAP
FWAP
FWAP
FWAP
I CAN'T LET YOH-KUN DIE!
HMPH, I KNOW THAT!
IT'S YOUR FAULT WE'RE LATE!
FWAP
FWAP

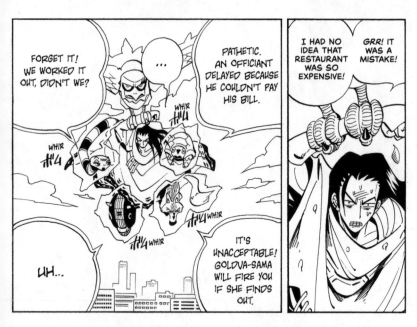

GRR! IT WAS A MISTAKE!
I HAD NO IDEA THAT RESTAURANT WAS SO EXPENSIVE!
PATHETIC. AN OFFICIANT DELAYED BECAUSE HE COULDN'T PAY HIS BILL.
...
FORGET IT! WE WORKED IT OUT, DIDN'T WE?
WHIR
WHIR
WHIR
WHIR
IT'S UNACCEPTABLE! GOLDVA-SAMA WILL FIRE YOU IF SHE FINDS OUT.
UH...
HOW THEY "WORKED IT OUT."
...
YOUR FRIEND SKIPPED OUT WITHOUT PAYING, SO YOU'LL HAVE TO WORK IT OFF!
Ristrante
SCRUB
SCRUB
SCRUB
ANYWAY, SILVA...
HWOOO
WHY DO YOU CARE SO MUCH ABOUT YOH?

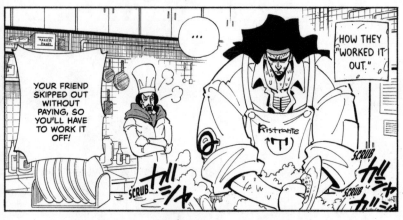

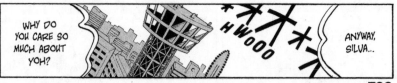

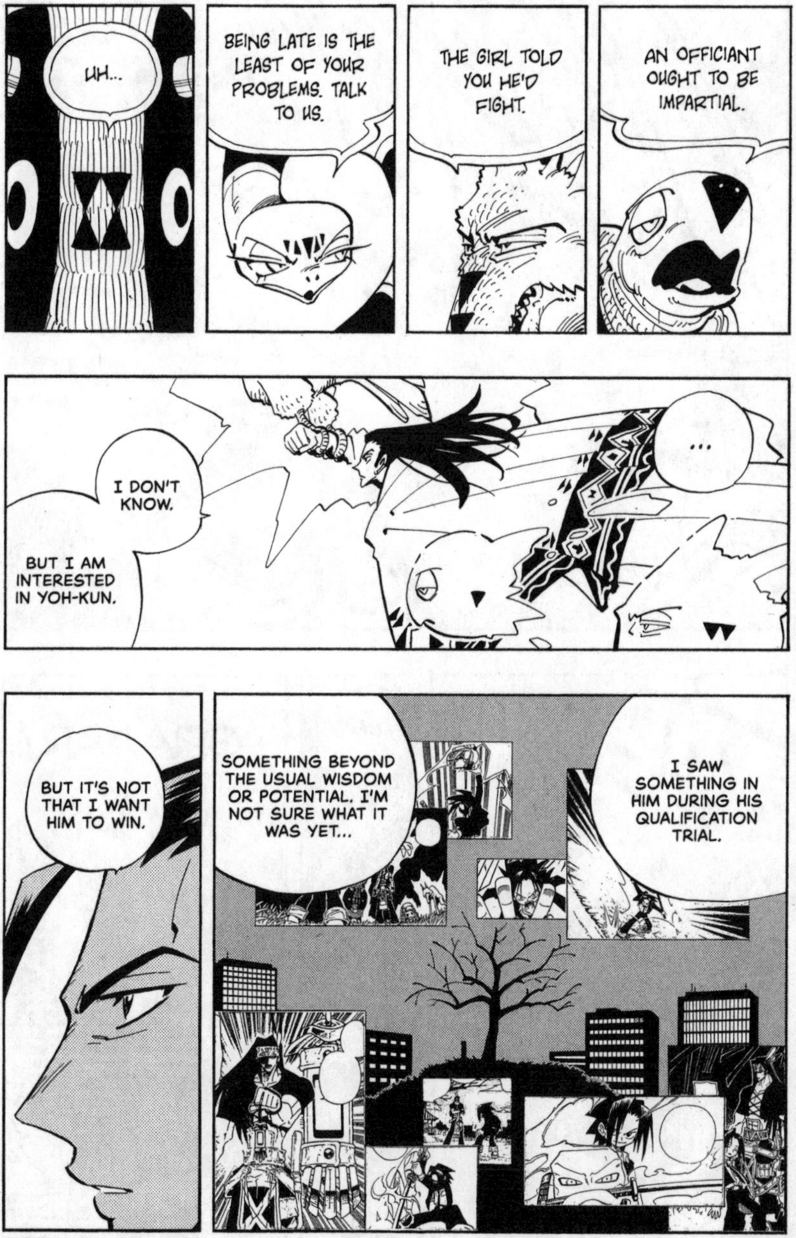
AN OFFICIANT OUGHT TO BE IMPARTIAL.
THE GIRL TOLD YOU HE'D FIGHT.
BEING LATE IS THE LEAST OF YOUR PROBLEMS. TALK TO US.
UH...
...
I DON'T KNOW.
BUT I AM INTERESTED IN YOH-KUN.
I SAW SOMETHING IN HIM DURING HIS QUALIFICATION TRIAL.
SOMETHING BEYOND THE USUAL WISDOM OR POTENTIAL. I'M NOT SURE WHAT IT WAS YET...
BUT IT'S NOT THAT I WANT HIM TO WIN.

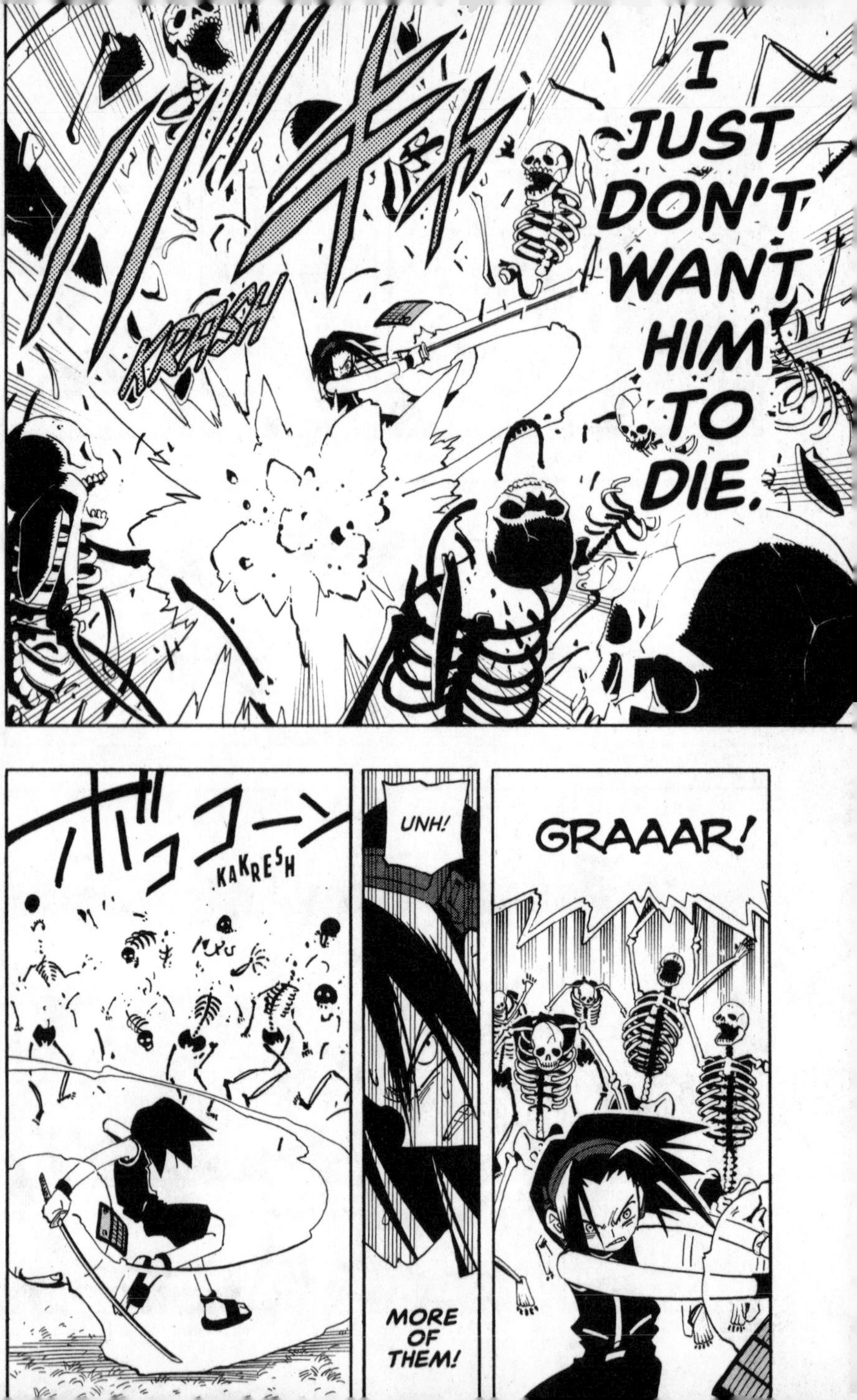
I JUST DON'T WANT HIM TO DIE.
KRASH
GRAAAR!
UNH!
MORE OF THEM!
KAKRESH

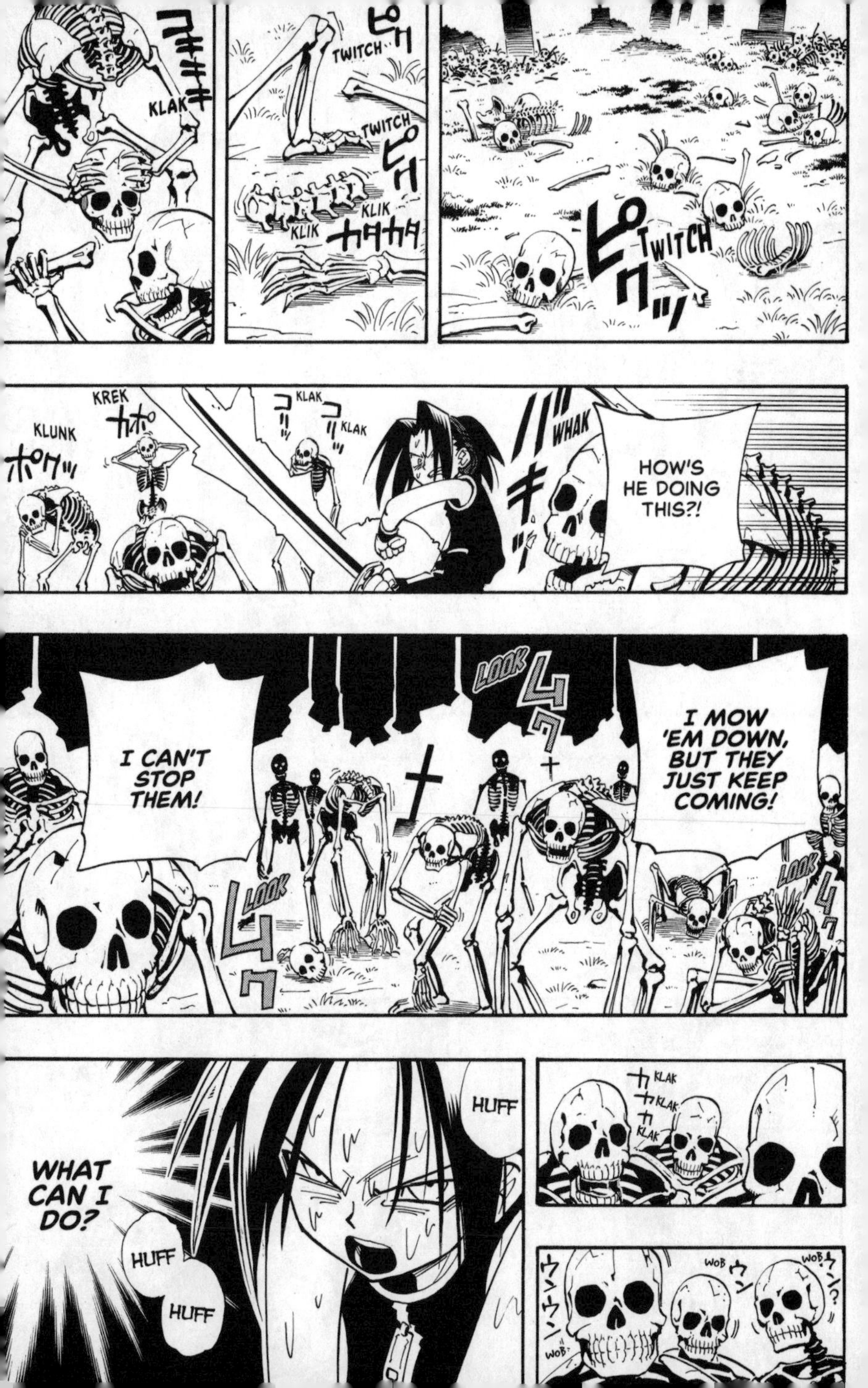

TWITCH
TWITCH
TWITCH
KLIK
KLIK
KLAK
HOW'S HE DOING THIS?!
WHAK
KLAK
KLAK
KREK
KLUNK
I MOW 'EM DOWN, BUT THEY JUST KEEP COMING!
LOOK
LOOK
LOOK
I CAN'T STOP THEM!
KLAK
KLAK
KLAK
WOB
WOB
WOB
HUFF
WHAT CAN I DO?
HUFF
HUFF

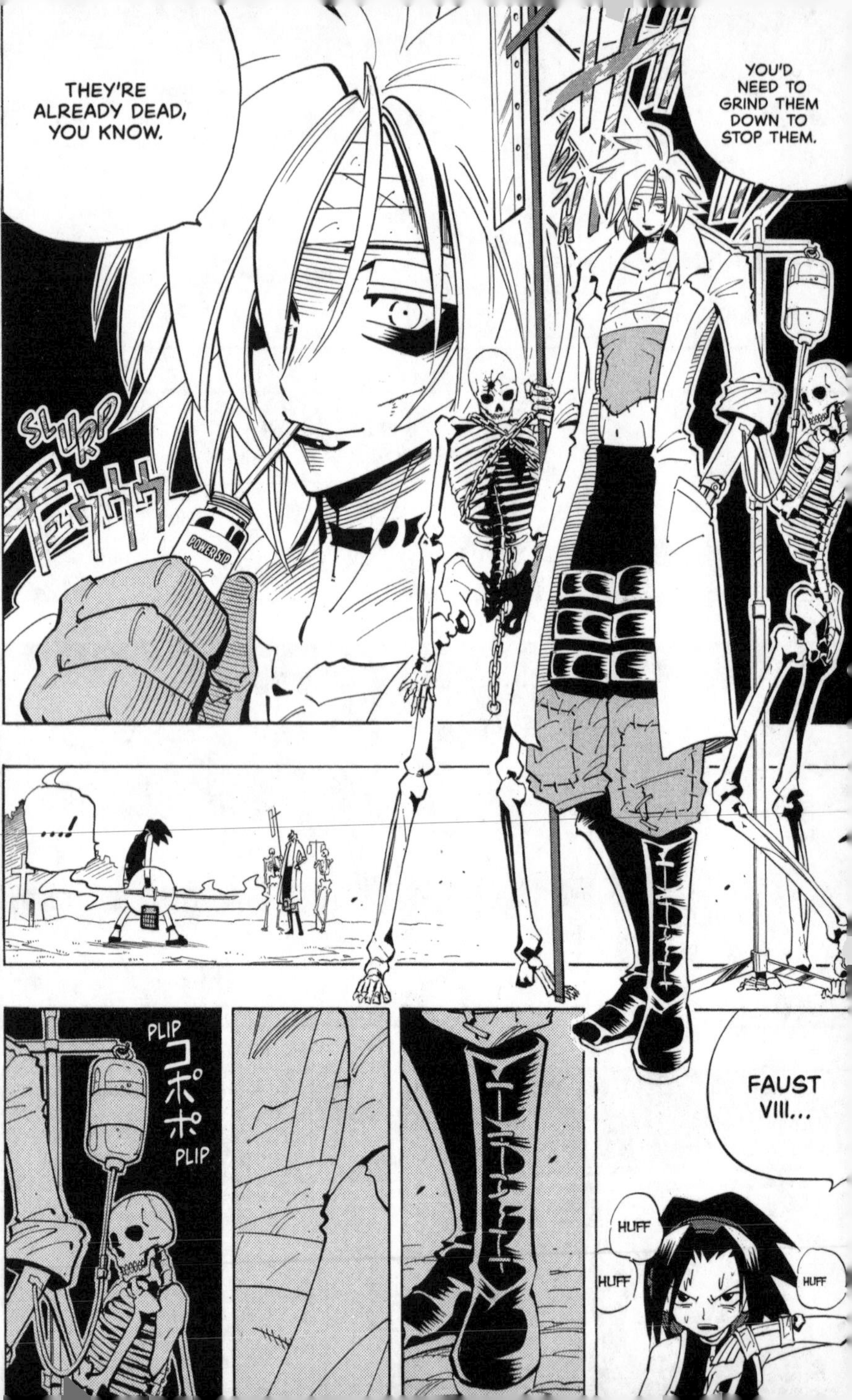
YOU'D NEED TO GRIND THEM DOWN TO STOP THEM.
THEY'RE ALREADY DEAD, YOU KNOW.
SLURP
チューウウウ
POWER SIP
...!
FAUST VIII...
HUFF
HUFF
HUFF
PLIP
コポポ
PLIP

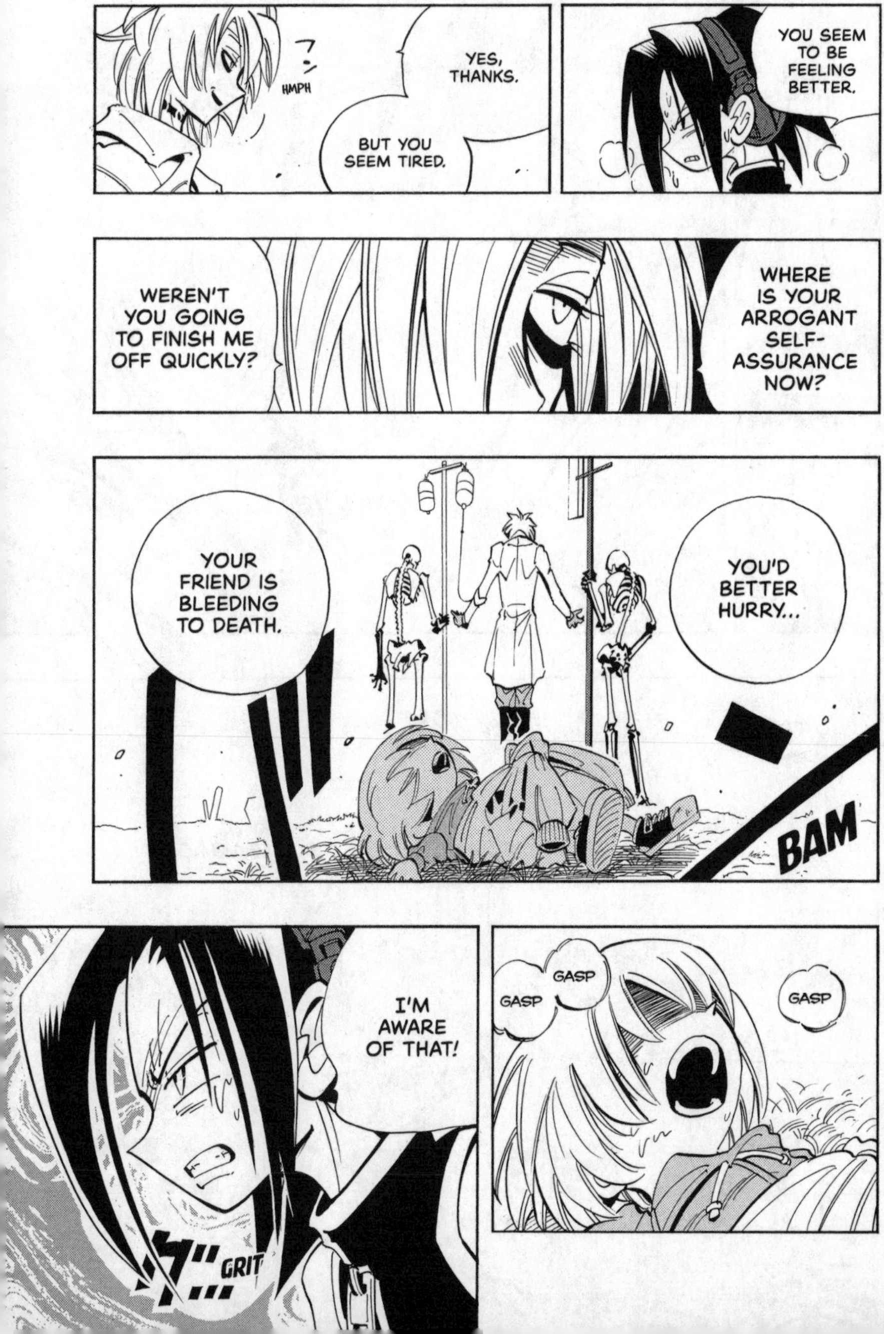
YOU SEEM TO BE FEELING BETTER.
YES, THANKS.
HMPH
BUT YOU SEEM TIRED.
WHERE IS YOUR ARROGANT SELF-ASSURANCE NOW?
WEREN'T YOU GOING TO FINISH ME OFF QUICKLY?
YOU'D BETTER HURRY...
BAM
YOUR FRIEND IS BLEEDING TO DEATH.
GASP
GASP
GASP
I'M AWARE OF THAT!
GRIT

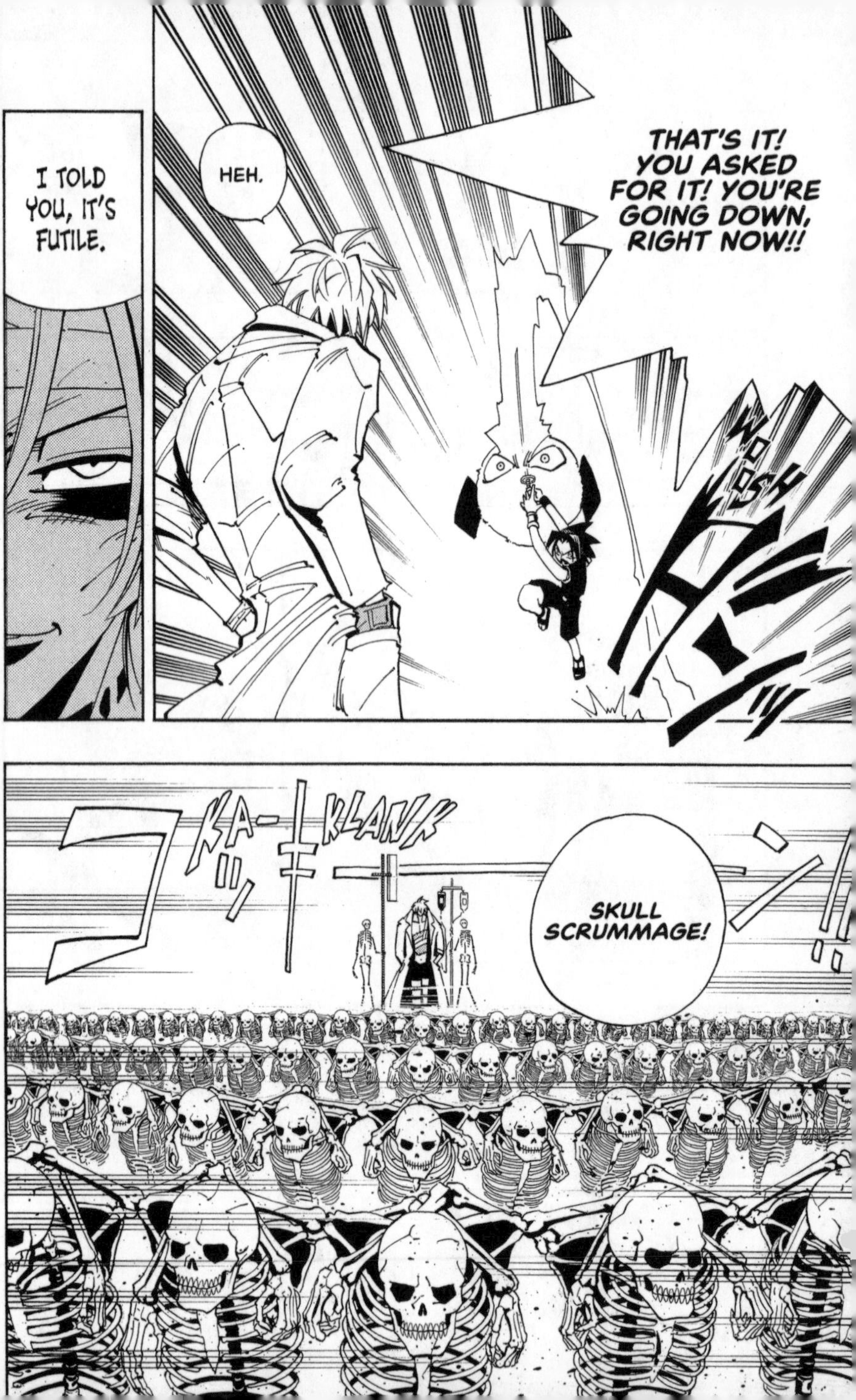
THAT'S IT! YOU ASKED FOR IT! YOU'RE GOING DOWN, RIGHT NOW!!
WOOSH
HEH.
I TOLD YOU, IT'S FUTILE.
SKULL SCRUMMAGE!
KA-KLANK

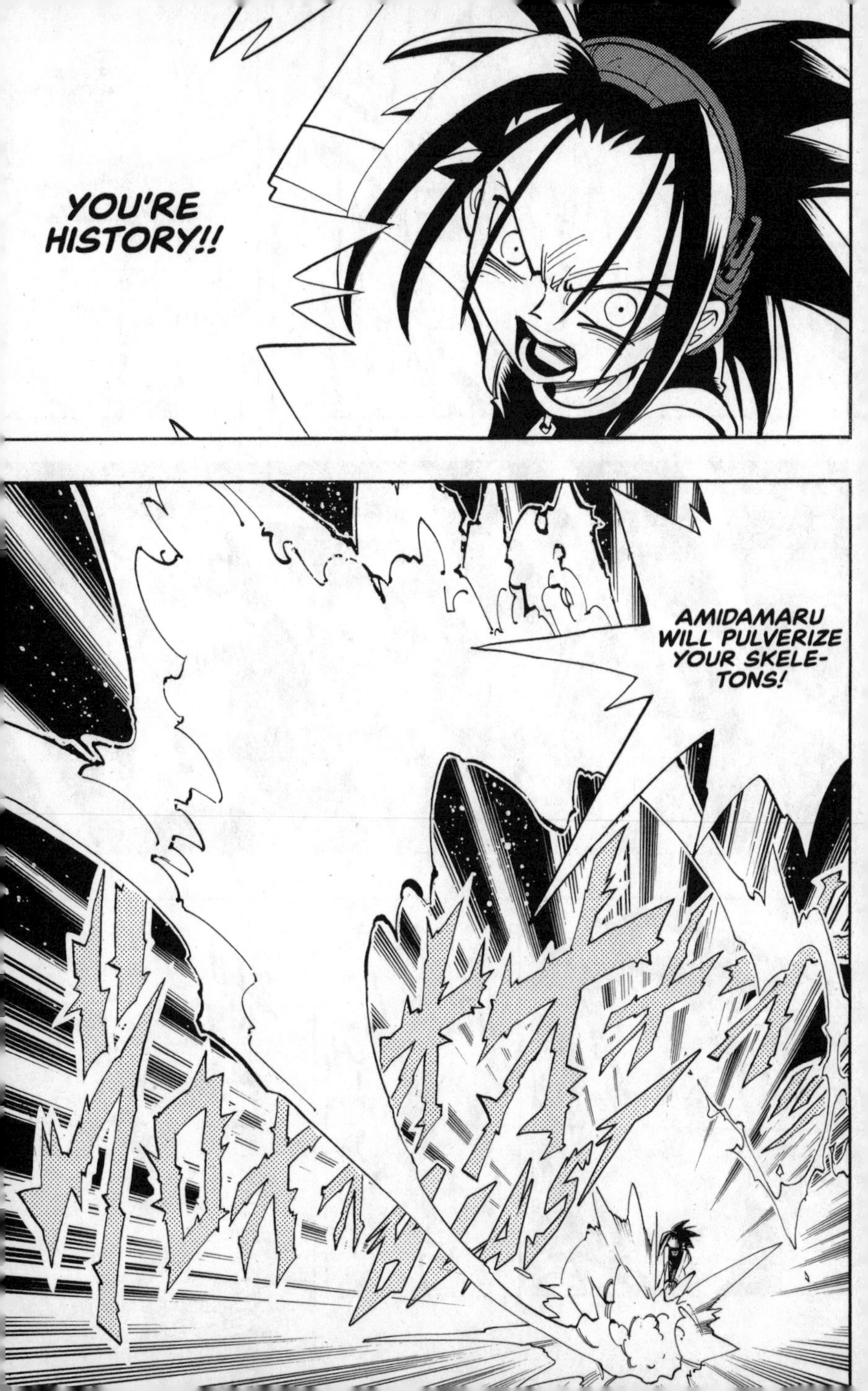
YOU'RE HISTORY!!
AMIDAMARU WILL PULVERIZE YOUR SKELE- TONS!

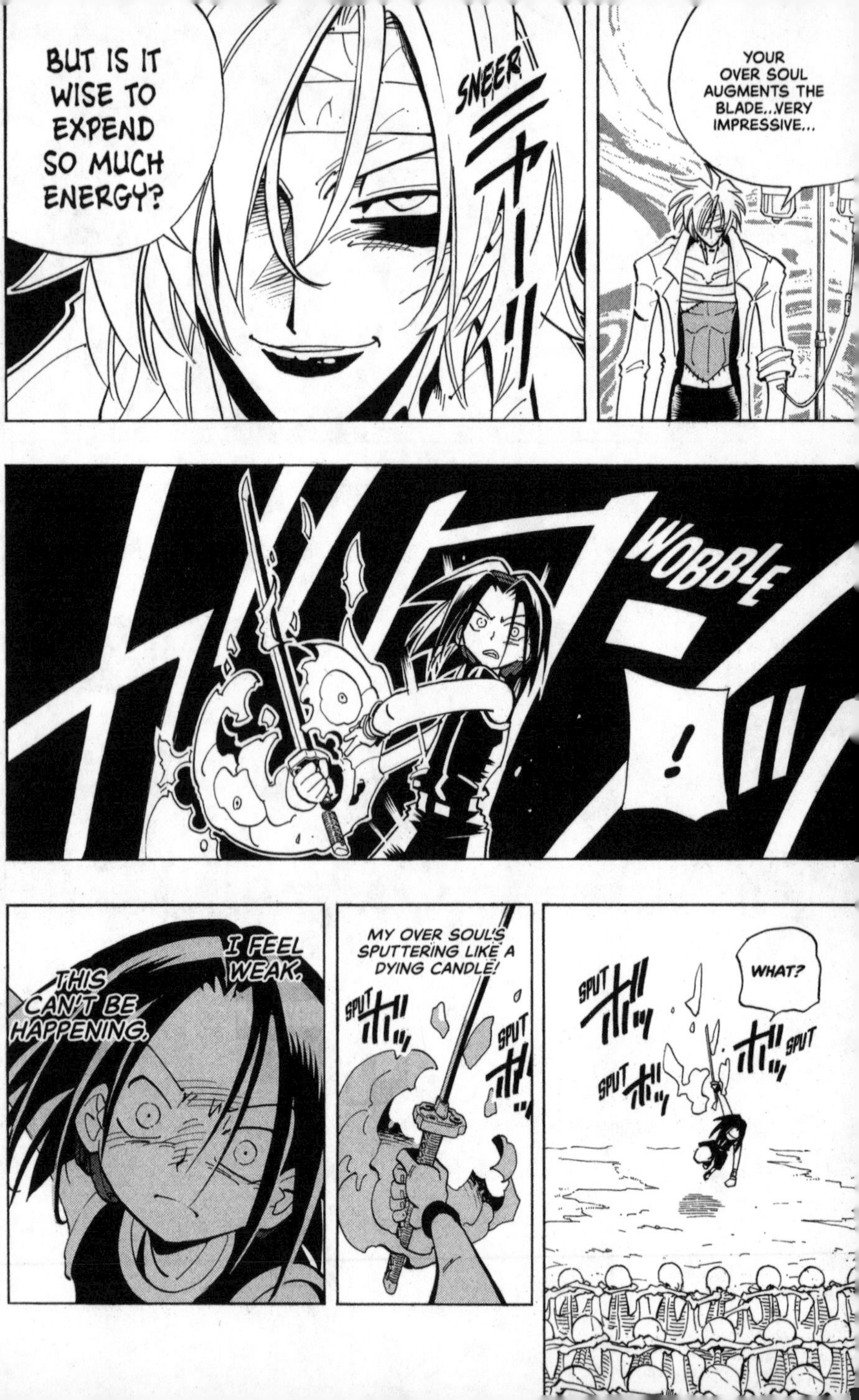
YOUR OVER SOUL AUGMENTS THE BLADE...VERY IMPRESSIVE...
SNEER
BUT IS IT WISE TO EXPEND SO MUCH ENERGY?
WOBBLE
!
WHAT?
SPUT
SPUT
SPUT
MY OVER SOUL'S SPUTTERING LIKE A DYING CANDLE!
SPUT
SPUT
I FEEL WEAK.
THIS CAN'T BE HAPPENING.

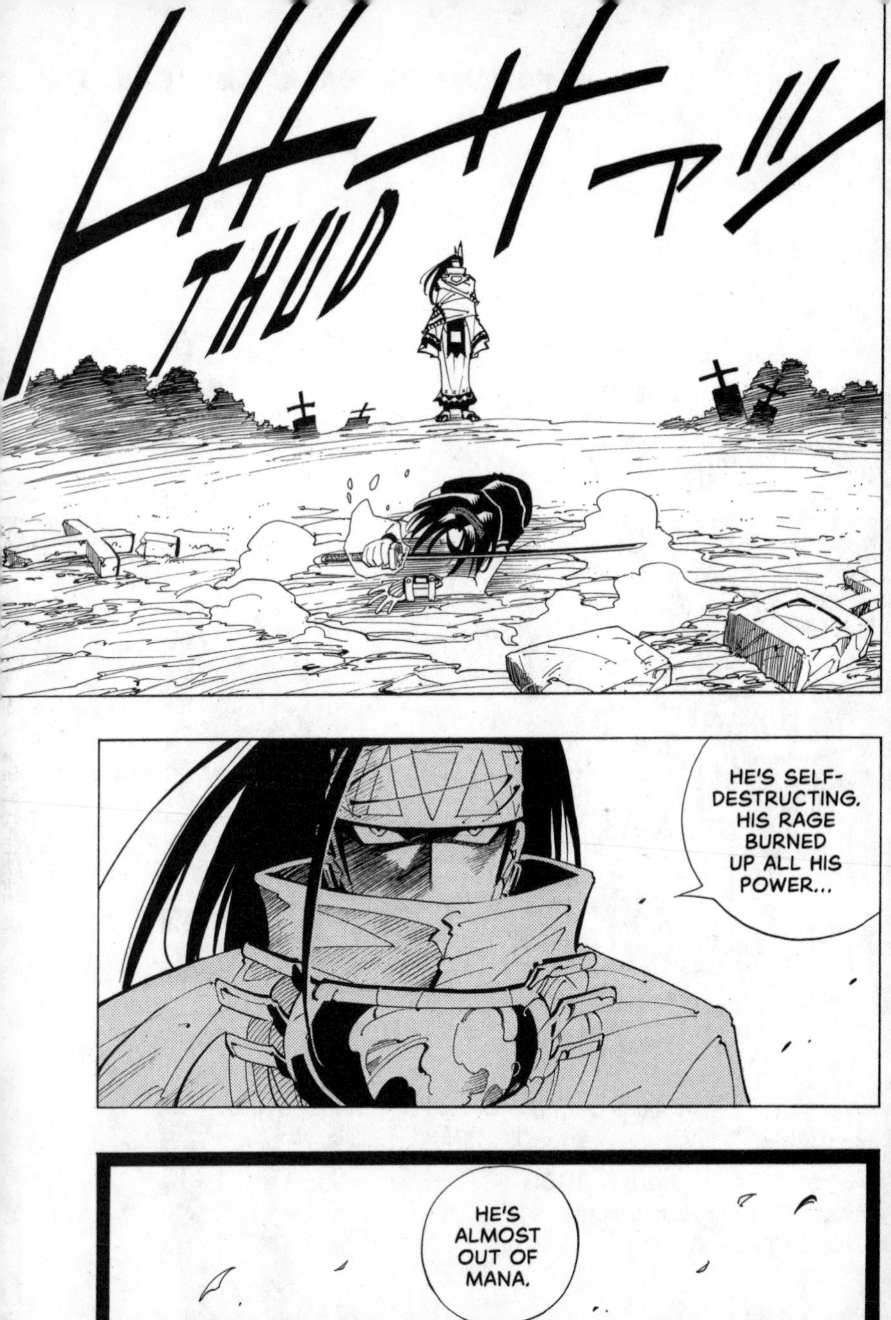
THUD
HE'S SELF-DESTRUCTING. HIS RAGE BURNED UP ALL HIS POWER...
HE'S ALMOST OUT OF MANA.

SHAMAN KING CHARACTER FILE No.23

Faust VIII

August 1999

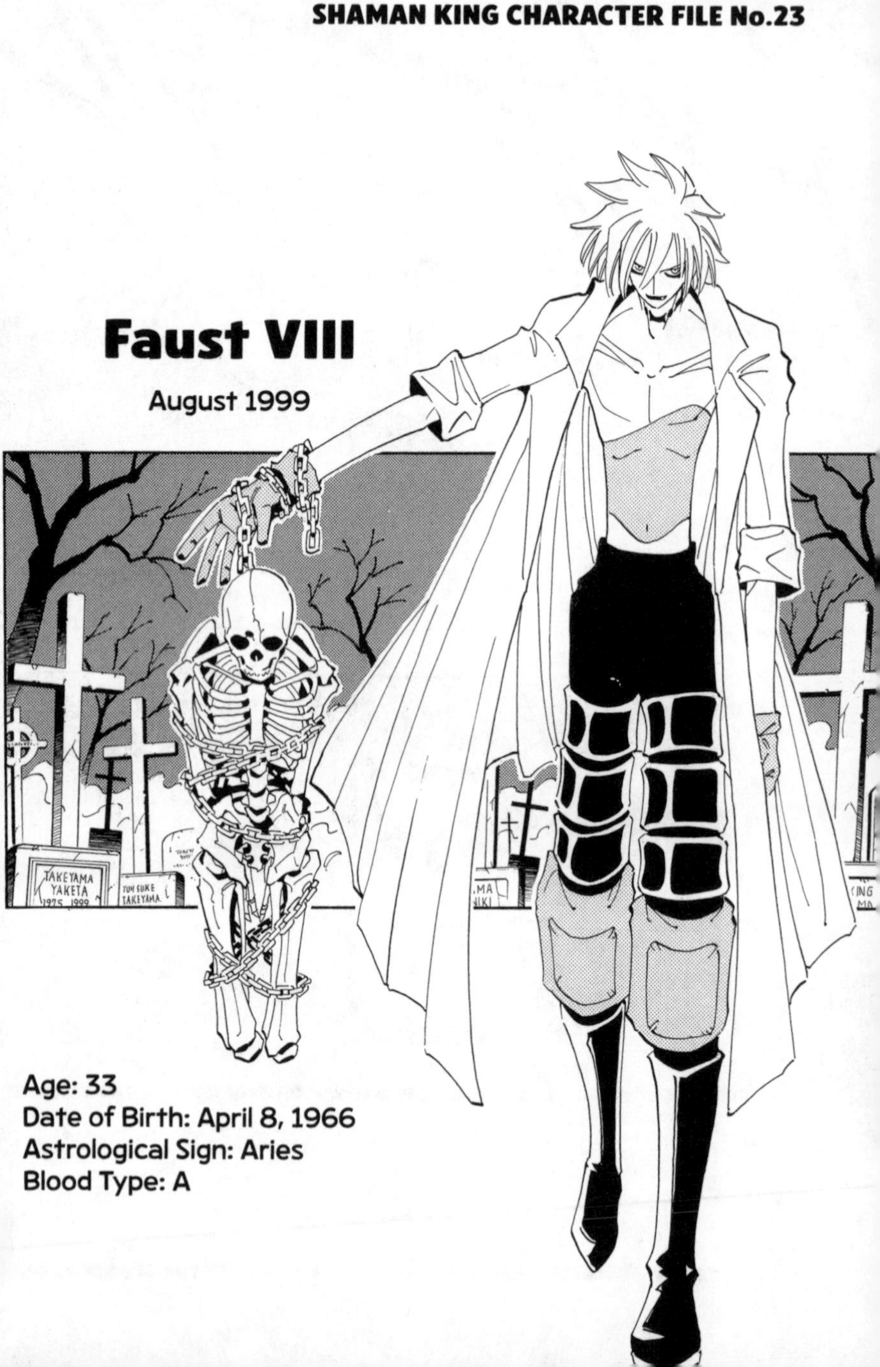
TAKEYAMA
YAKETA

Age: 33
Date of Birth: April 8, 1966
Astrological Sign: Aries
Blood Type: A

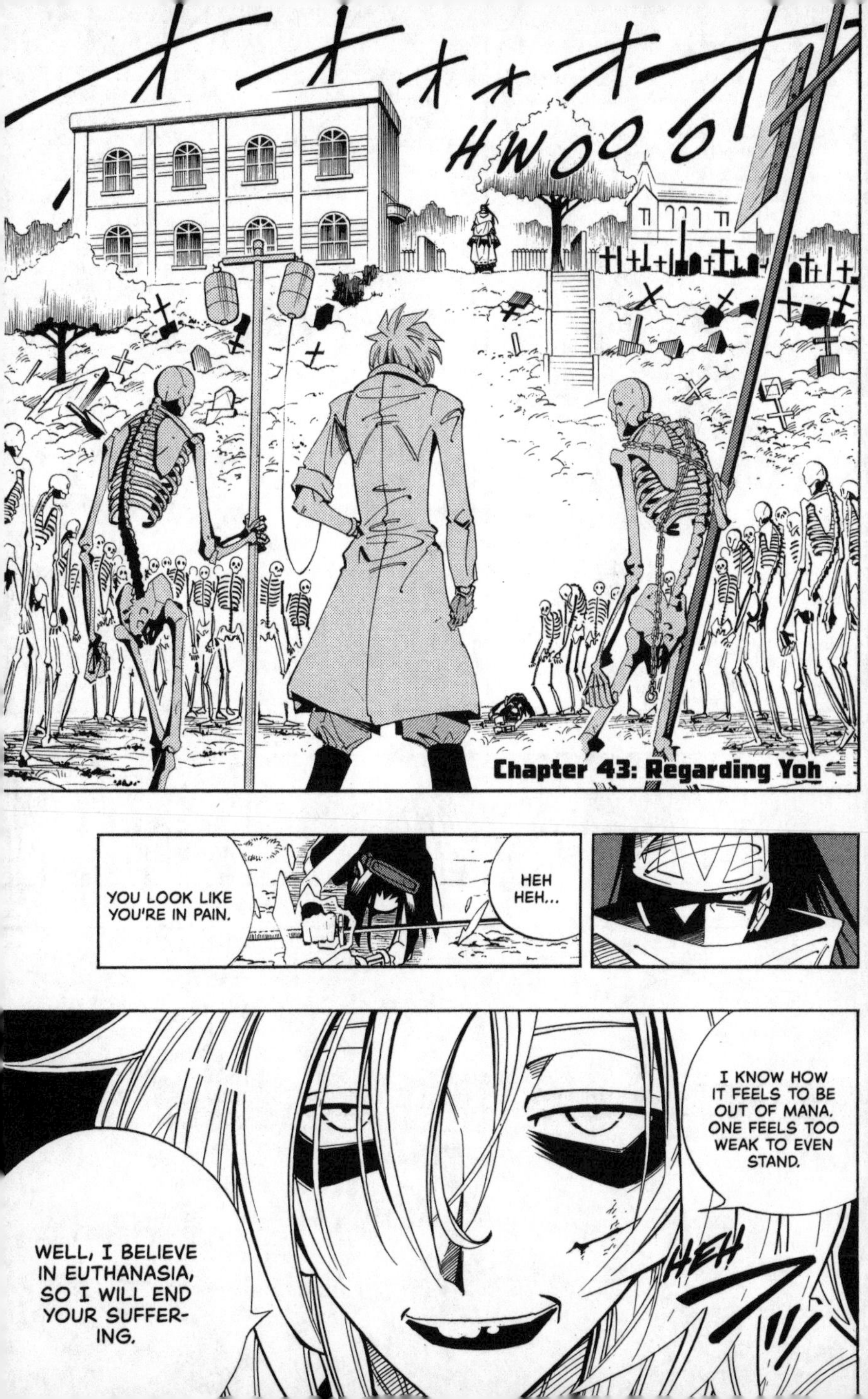
HWOOO
Chapter 43: Regarding Yoh
HEH HEH...
YOU LOOK LIKE YOU'RE IN PAIN.
I KNOW HOW IT FEELS TO BE OUT OF MANA. ONE FEELS TOO WEAK TO EVEN STAND.
HEH
WELL, I BELIEVE IN EUTHANASIA, SO I WILL END YOUR SUFFER-ING.

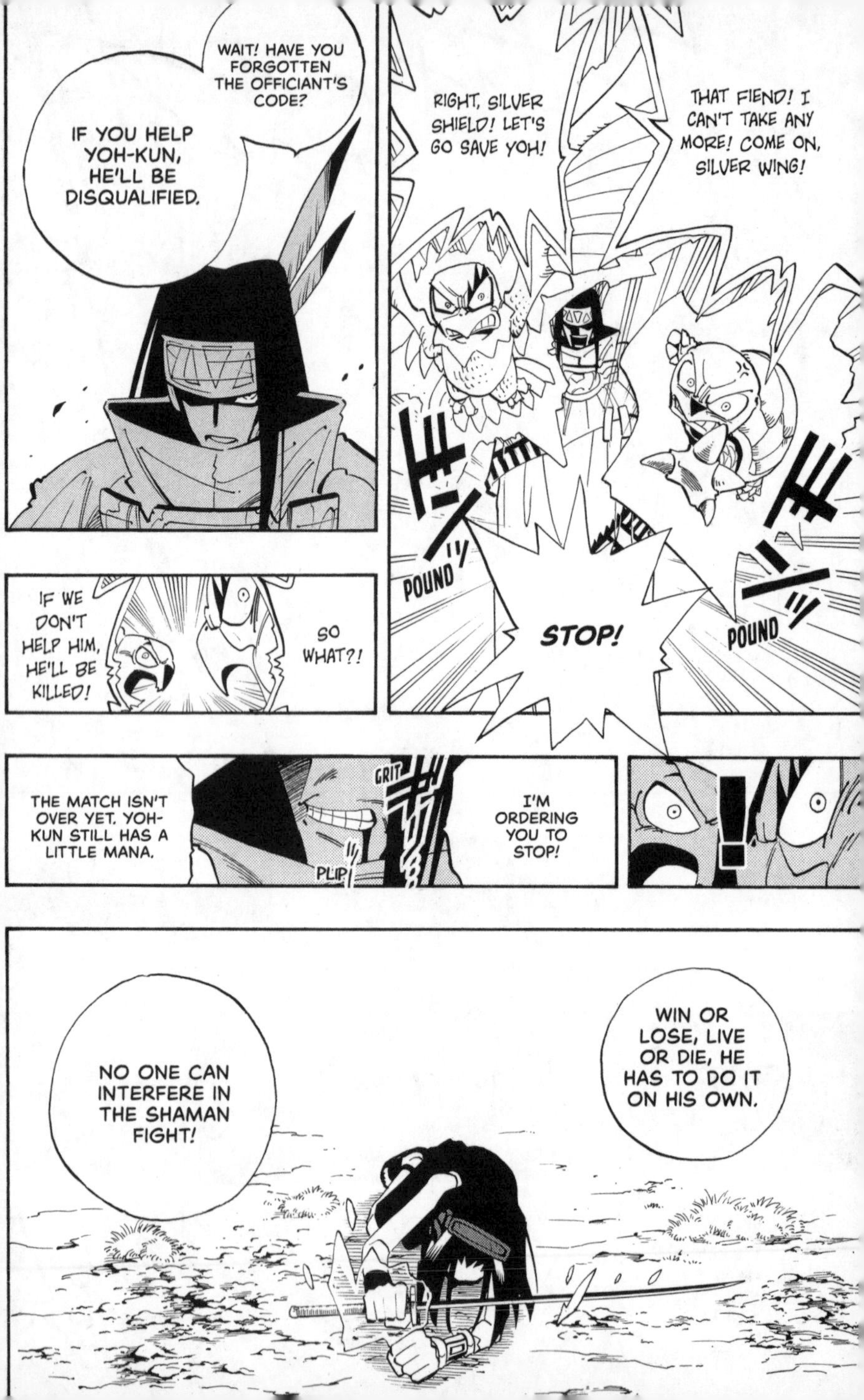
THAT FIEND! I CAN'T TAKE ANY MORE! COME ON, SILVER WING!
RIGHT, SILVER SHIELD! LET'S GO SAVE YOH!
POUND
POUND
STOP!
WAIT! HAVE YOU FORGOTTEN THE OFFICIANT'S CODE?
IF YOU HELP YOH-KUN, HE'LL BE DISQUALIFIED.
SO WHAT?!
IF WE DON'T HELP HIM, HE'LL BE KILLED!
!
I'M ORDERING YOU TO STOP!
GRIT
THE MATCH ISN'T OVER YET. YOH-KUN STILL HAS A LITTLE MANA.
PLIP
WIN OR LOSE, LIVE OR DIE, HE HAS TO DO IT ON HIS OWN.
NO ONE CAN INTERFERE IN THE SHAMAN FIGHT!

Chapter 43:

Regarding Yoh

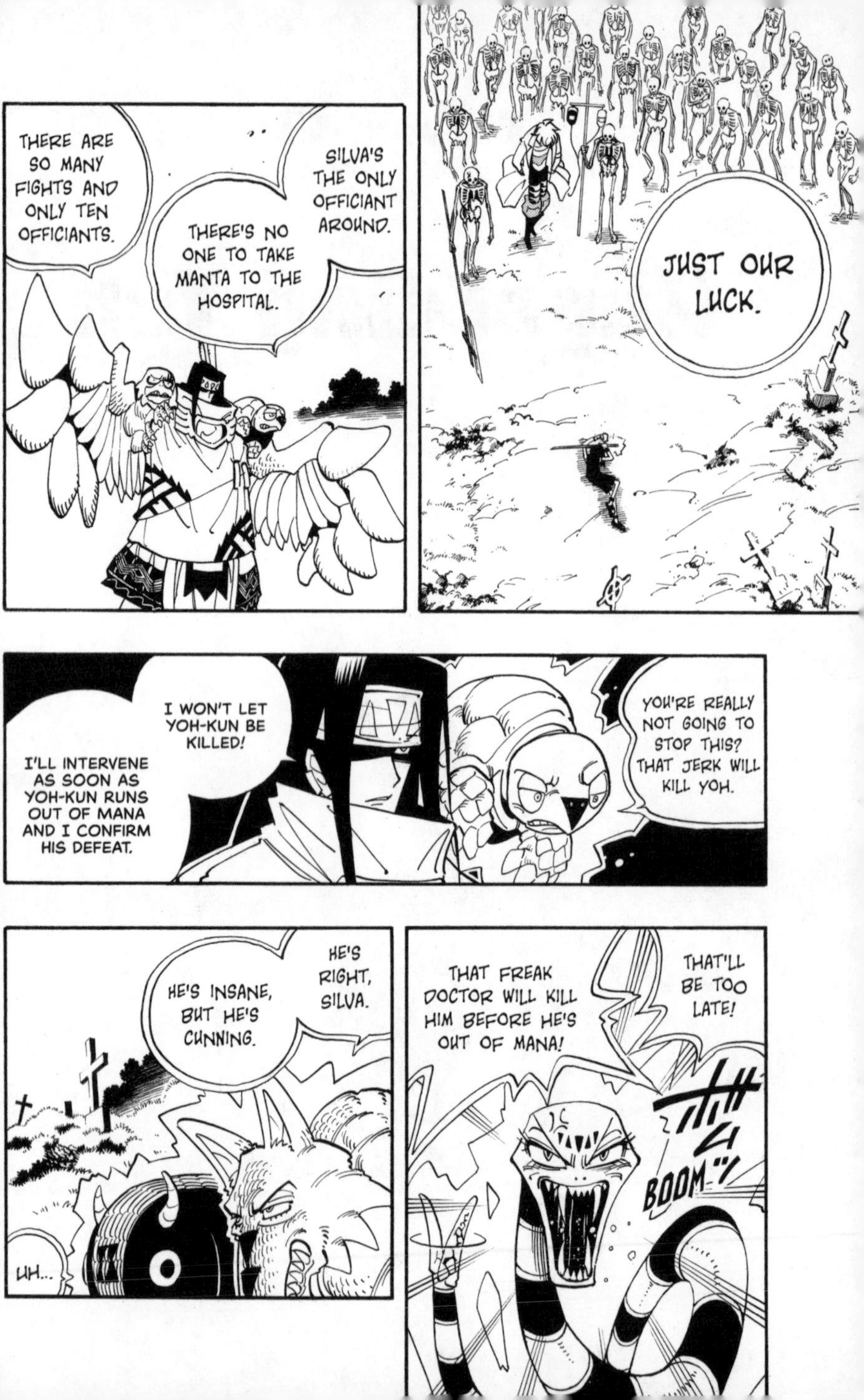
JUST OUR LUCK.
SILVA'S THE ONLY OFFICIANT AROUND.
THERE ARE SO MANY FIGHTS AND ONLY TEN OFFICIANTS.
THERE'S NO ONE TO TAKE MANTA TO THE HOSPITAL.
YOU'RE REALLY NOT GOING TO STOP THIS? THAT JERK WILL KILL YOH.
I WON'T LET YOH-KUN BE KILLED!
I'LL INTERVENE AS SOON AS YOH-KUN RUNS OUT OF MANA AND I CONFIRM HIS DEFEAT.
THAT'LL BE TOO LATE!
THAT FREAK DOCTOR WILL KILL HIM BEFORE HE'S OUT OF MANA!
BOOM
HE'S RIGHT, SILVA.
HE'S INSANE, BUT HE'S CUNNING.
UH...

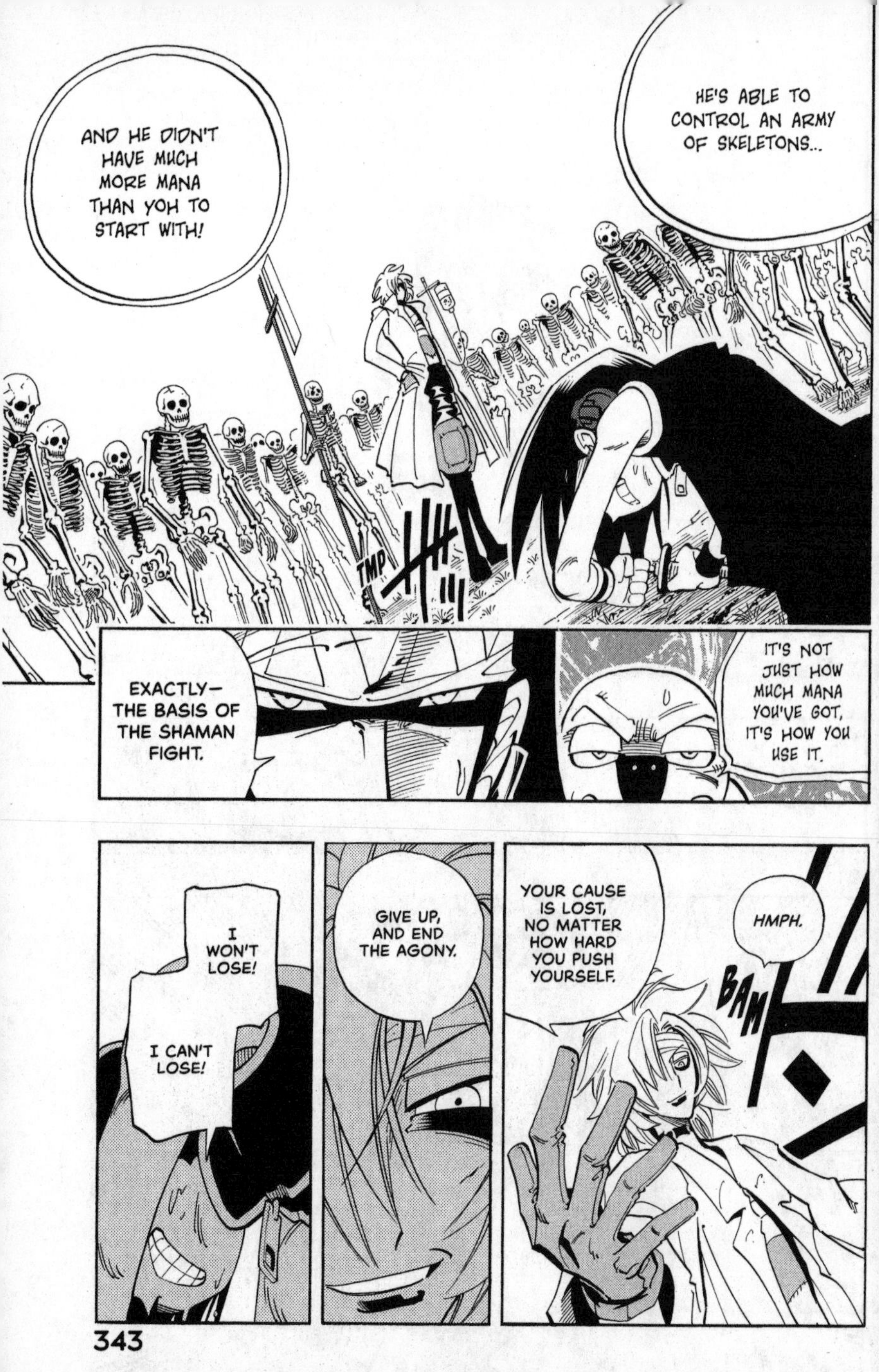
HE'S ABLE TO CONTROL AN ARMY OF SKELETONS...
AND HE DIDN'T HAVE MUCH MORE MANA THAN YOH TO START WITH!
TMP
IT'S NOT JUST HOW MUCH MANA YOU'VE GOT, IT'S HOW YOU USE IT.
EXACTLY— THE BASIS OF THE SHAMAN FIGHT.
HMPH.
BAM
YOUR CAUSE IS LOST, NO MATTER HOW HARD YOU PUSH YOURSELF.
GIVE UP, AND END THE AGONY.
I WON'T LOSE!
I CAN'T LOSE!

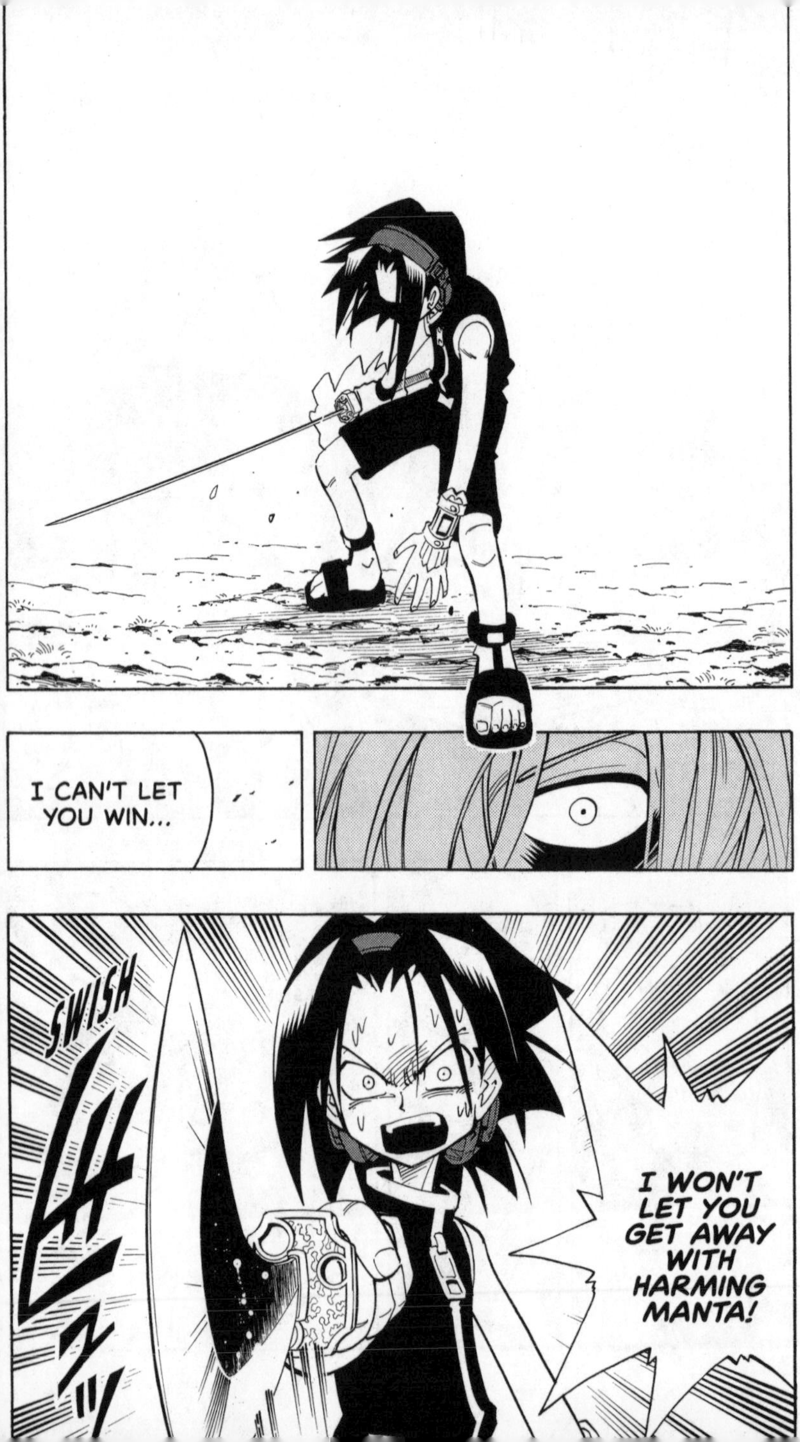
I CAN'T LET YOU WIN...
I WON'T LET YOU GET AWAY WITH HARMING MANTA!
SWISH

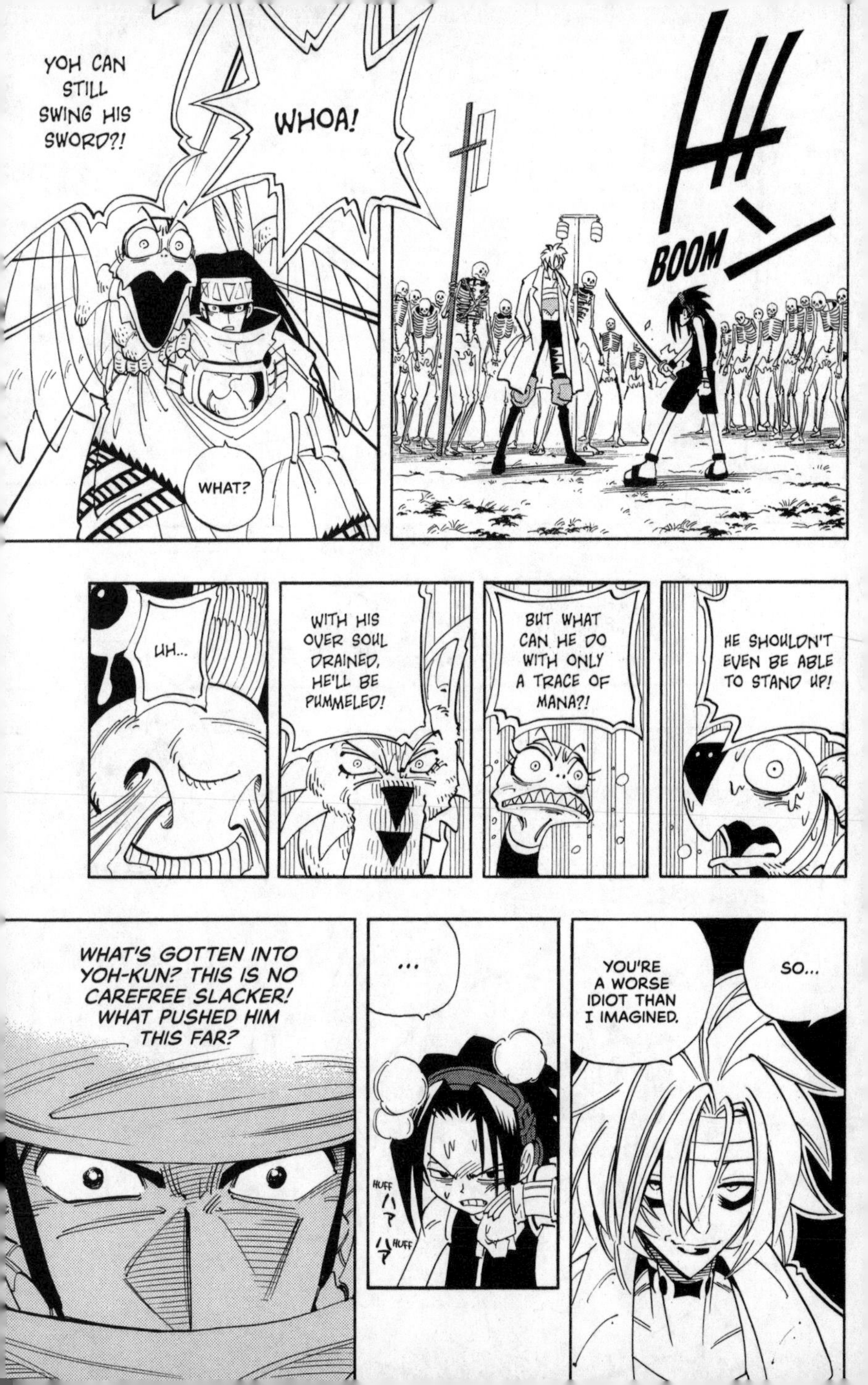
BOOM
WHOA!
YOH CAN STILL SWING HIS SWORD?!
WHAT?
HE SHOULDN'T EVEN BE ABLE TO STAND UP!
BUT WHAT CAN HE DO WITH ONLY A TRACE OF MANA?!
WITH HIS OVER SOUL DRAINED, HE'LL BE PUMMELED!
UH...
SO...
YOU'RE A WORSE IDIOT THAN I IMAGINED.
...
HUFF
HUFF
WHAT'S GOTTEN INTO YOH-KUN? THIS IS NO CAREFREE SLACKER! WHAT PUSHED HIM THIS FAR?

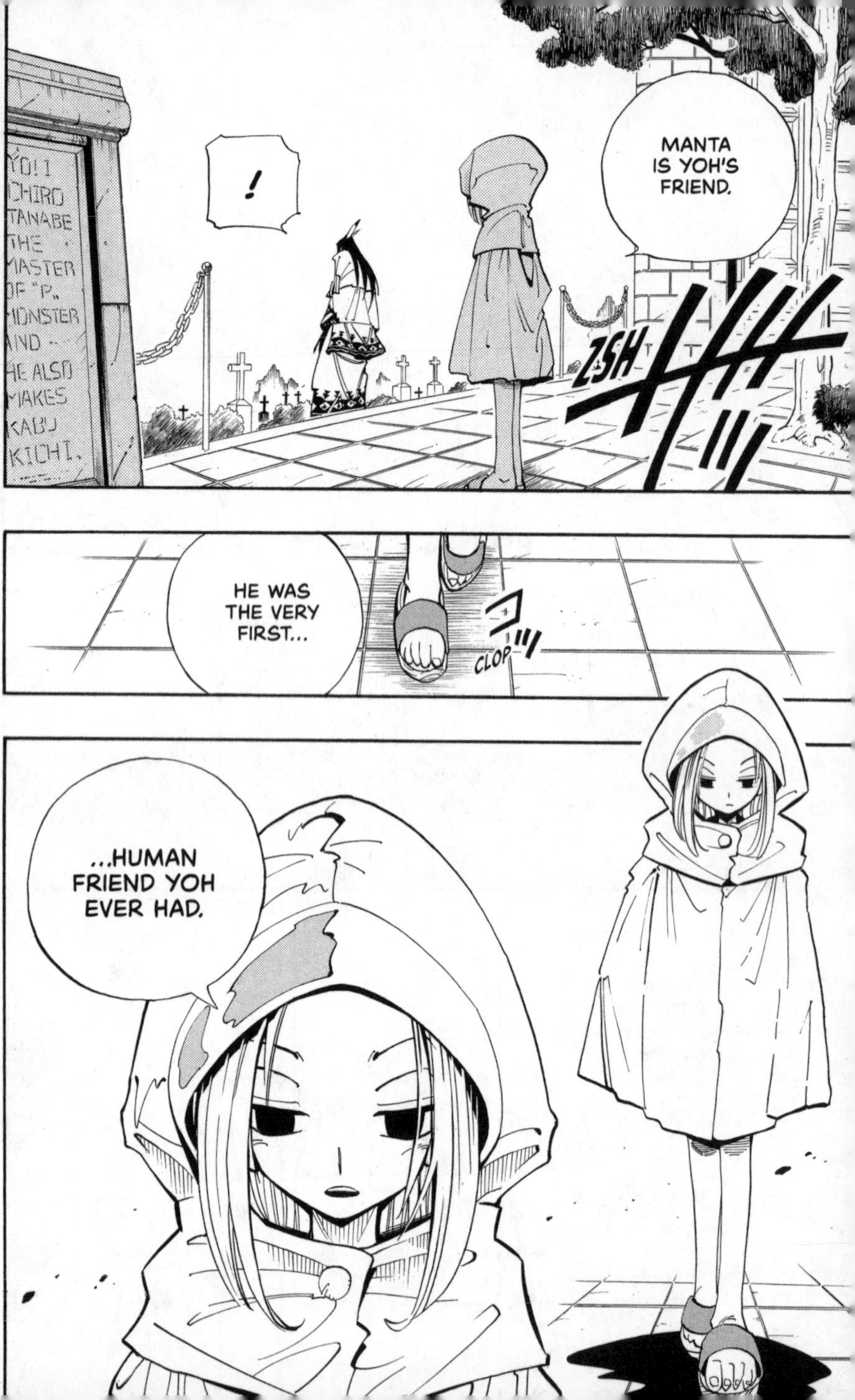
MANTA IS YOH'S FRIEND.
ZSH
!
YOH ICHIRO TANABE THE MASTER OF "P. MONSTER AND -- HE ALSO MAKES KABU KICHI.
CLOP
HE WAS THE VERY FIRST...
...HUMAN FRIEND YOH EVER HAD.

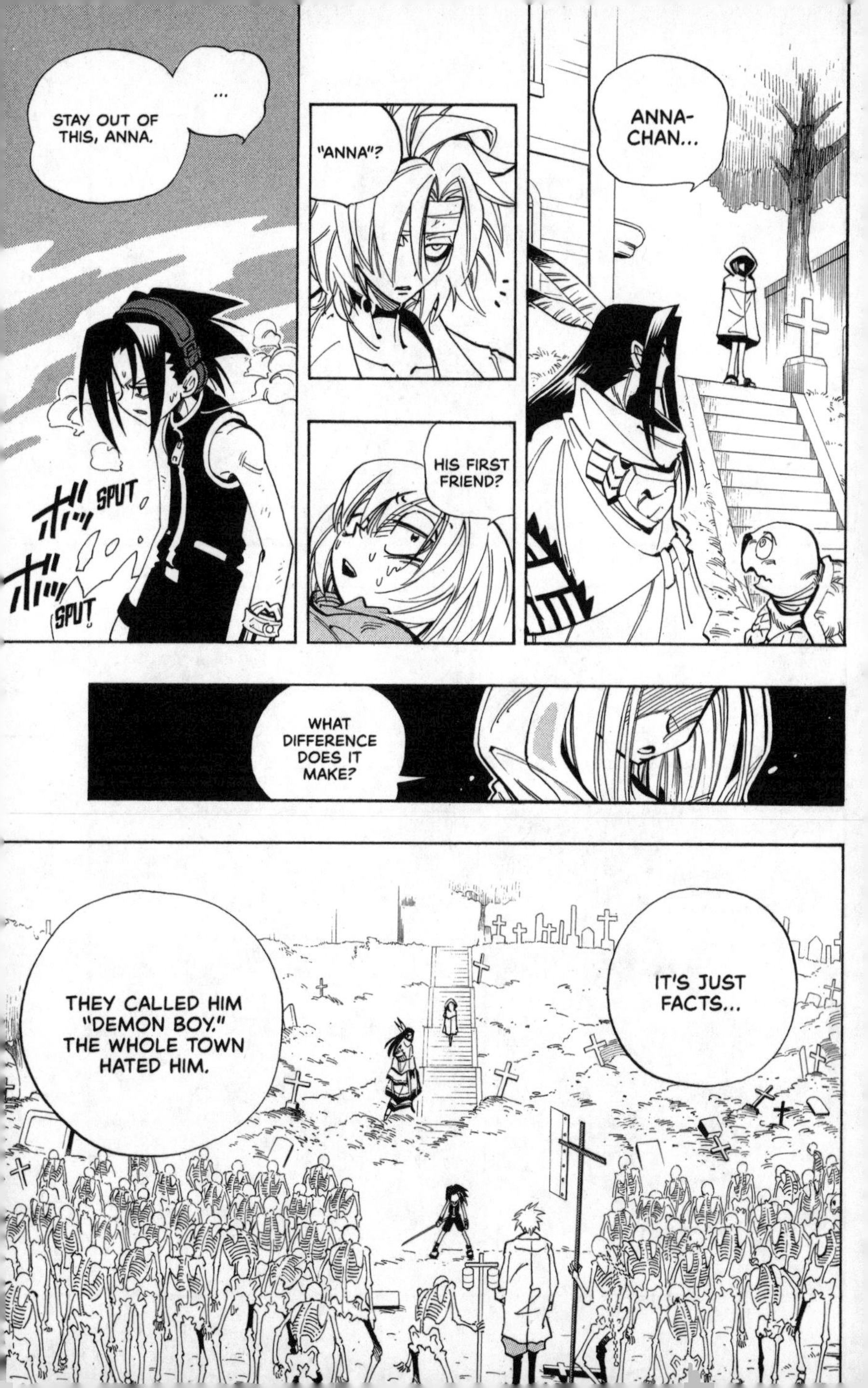
ANNA-CHAN...
"ANNA"?
HIS FIRST FRIEND?
...
STAY OUT OF THIS, ANNA.
SPUT
SPUT
WHAT DIFFERENCE DOES IT MAKE?
IT'S JUST FACTS...
THEY CALLED HIM "DEMON BOY." THE WHOLE TOWN HATED HIM.

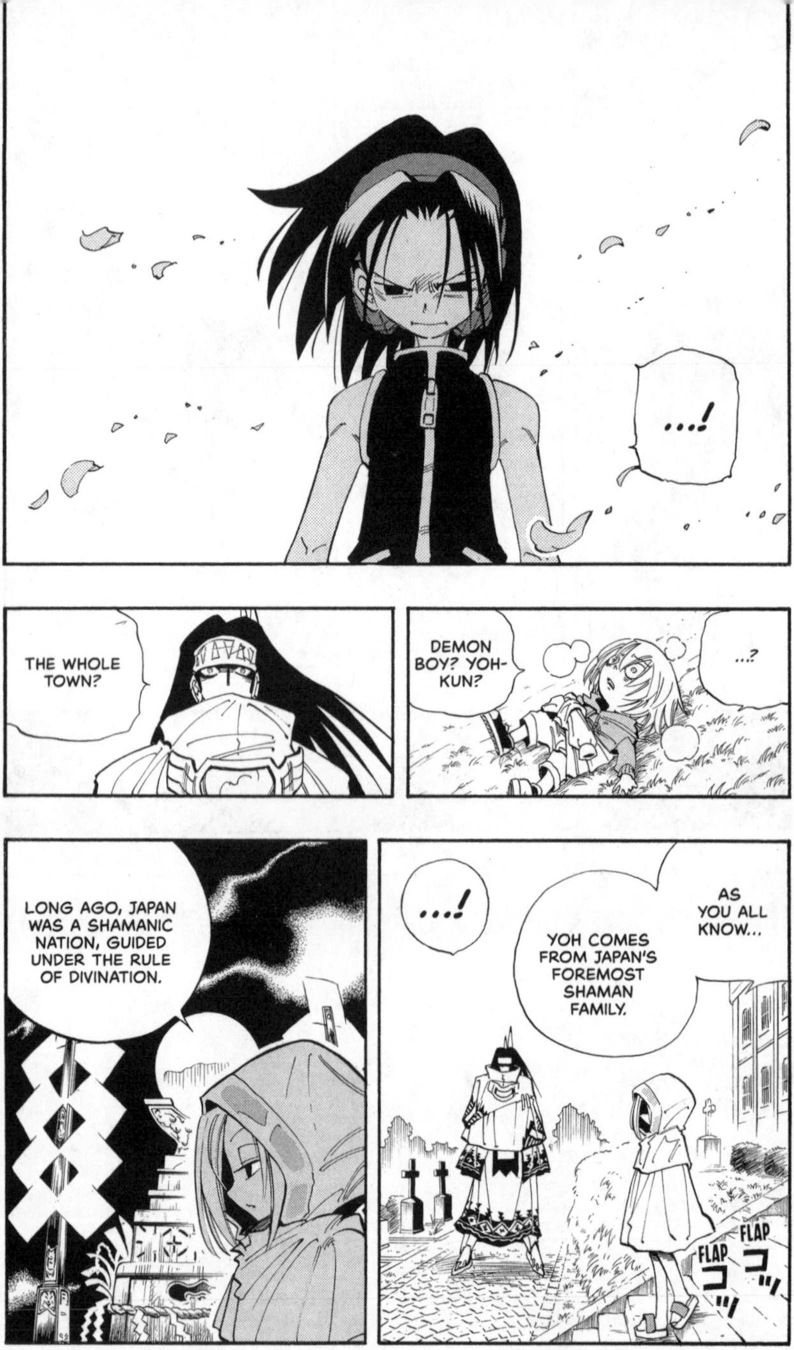
...!
...?
DEMON BOY? YOH-KUN?
THE WHOLE TOWN?
AS YOU ALL KNOW...
YOH COMES FROM JAPAN'S FOREMOST SHAMAN FAMILY.
...!
FLAP
FLAP
LONG AGO, JAPAN WAS A SHAMANIC NATION, GUIDED UNDER THE RULE OF DIVINATION.

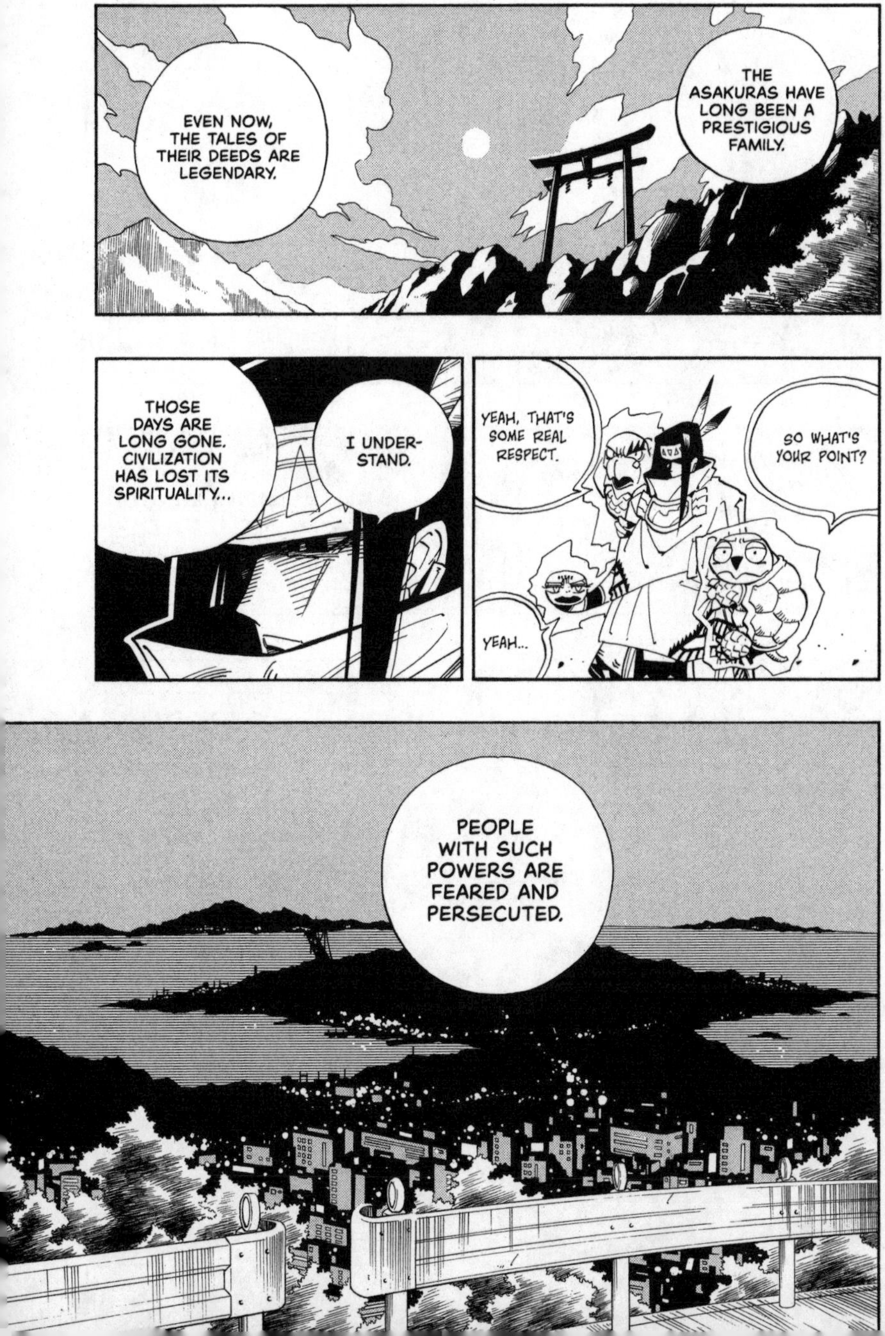
THE ASAKURAS HAVE LONG BEEN A PRESTIGIOUS FAMILY.
EVEN NOW, THE TALES OF THEIR DEEDS ARE LEGENDARY.
SO WHAT'S YOUR POINT?
YEAH, THAT'S SOME REAL RESPECT.
YEAH...
I UNDER-STAND.
THOSE DAYS ARE LONG GONE. CIVILIZATION HAS LOST ITS SPIRITUALITY...
PEOPLE WITH SUCH POWERS ARE FEARED AND PERSECUTED.

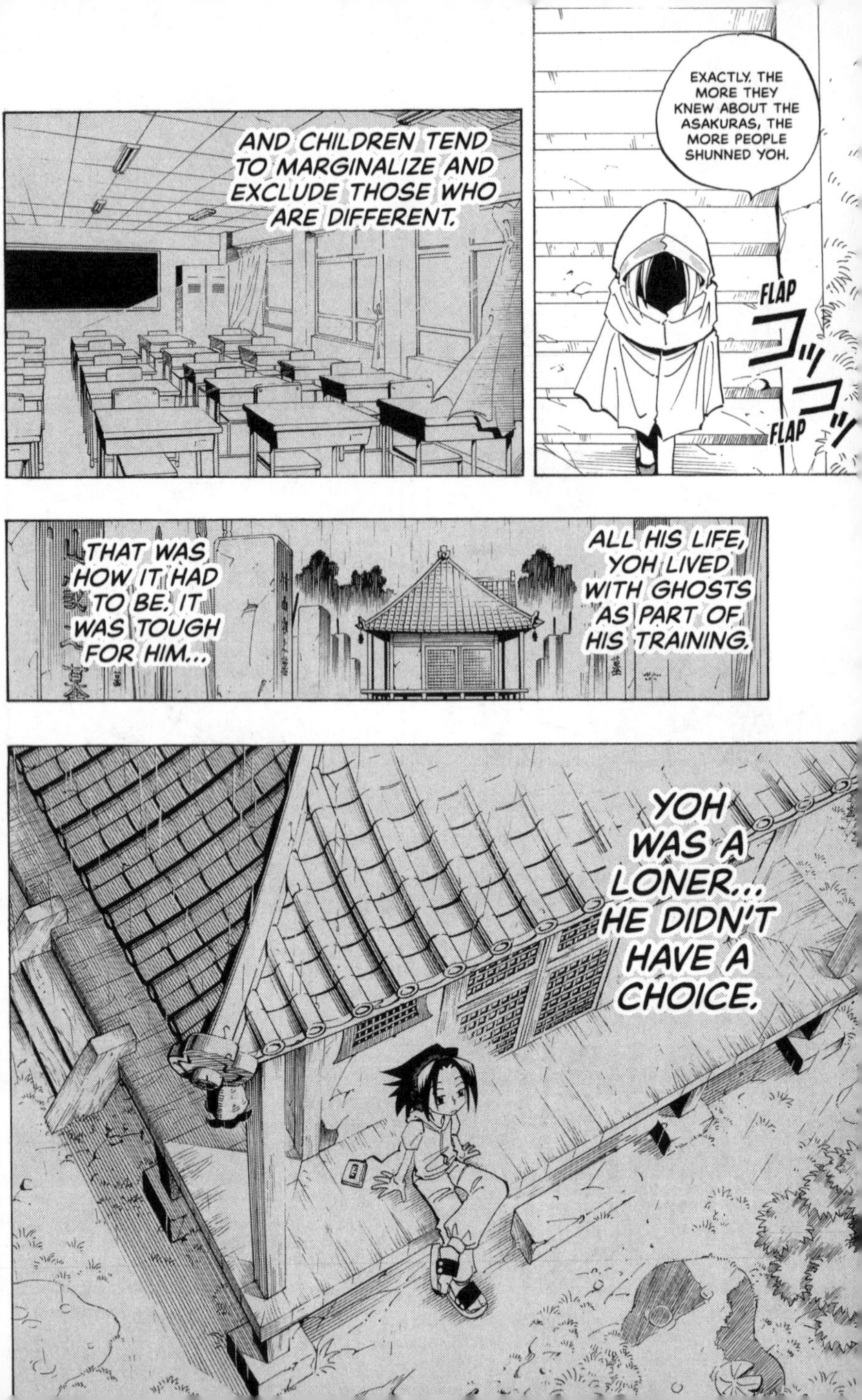
EXACTLY. THE MORE THEY KNEW ABOUT THE ASAKURAS, THE MORE PEOPLE SHUNNED YOH.
FLAP
FLAP
AND CHILDREN TEND TO MARGINALIZE AND EXCLUDE THOSE WHO ARE DIFFERENT.
ALL HIS LIFE, YOH LIVED WITH GHOSTS AS PART OF HIS TRAINING.
THAT WAS HOW IT HAD TO BE. IT WAS TOUGH FOR HIM...
YOH WAS A LONER... HE DIDN'T HAVE A CHOICE.

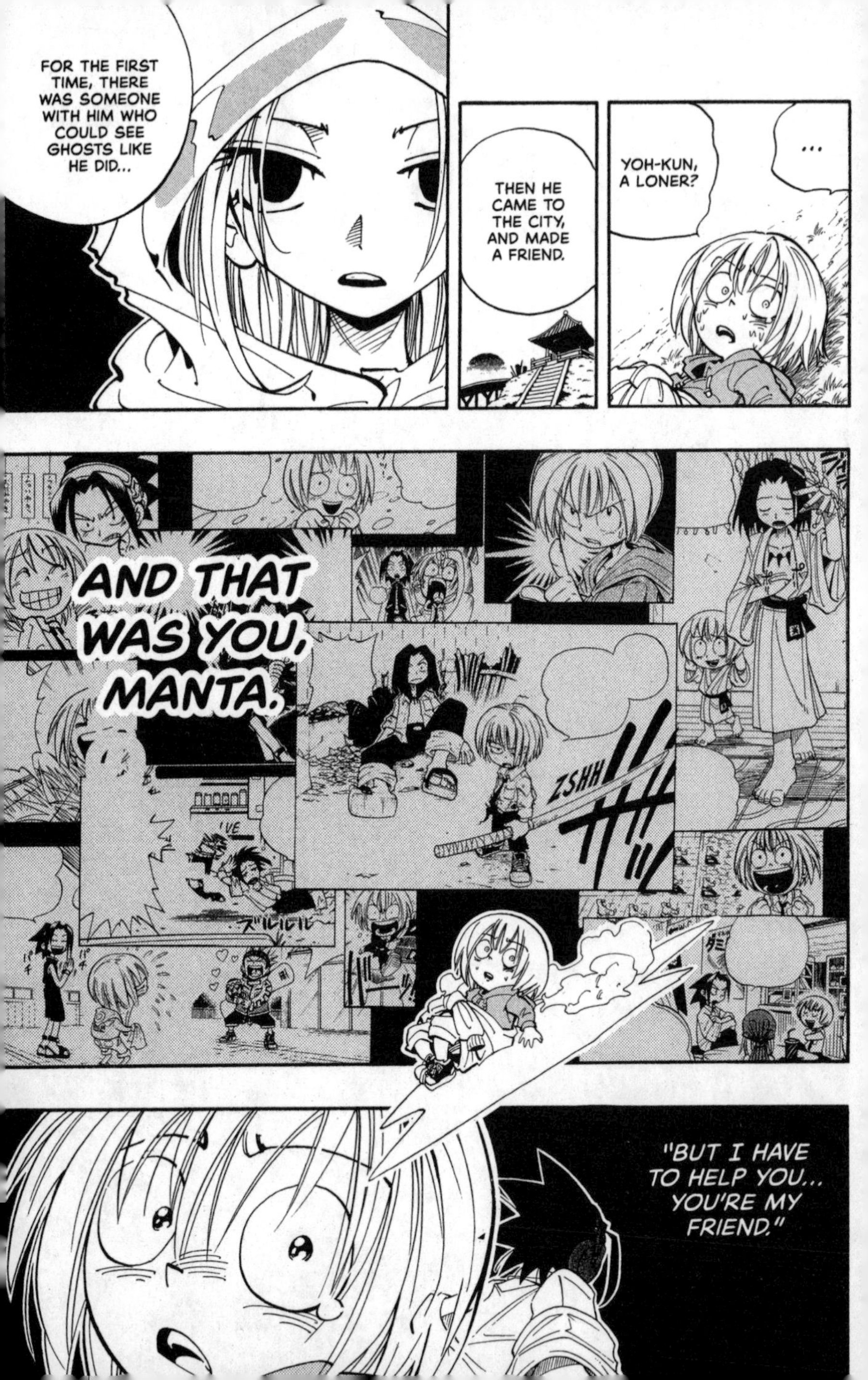
...
YOH-KUN, A LONER?
THEN HE CAME TO THE CITY, AND MADE A FRIEND.
FOR THE FIRST TIME, THERE WAS SOMEONE WITH HIM WHO COULD SEE GHOSTS LIKE HE DID...
AND THAT WAS YOU, MANTA.
ZSHH
"BUT I HAVE TO HELP YOU... YOU'RE MY FRIEND."

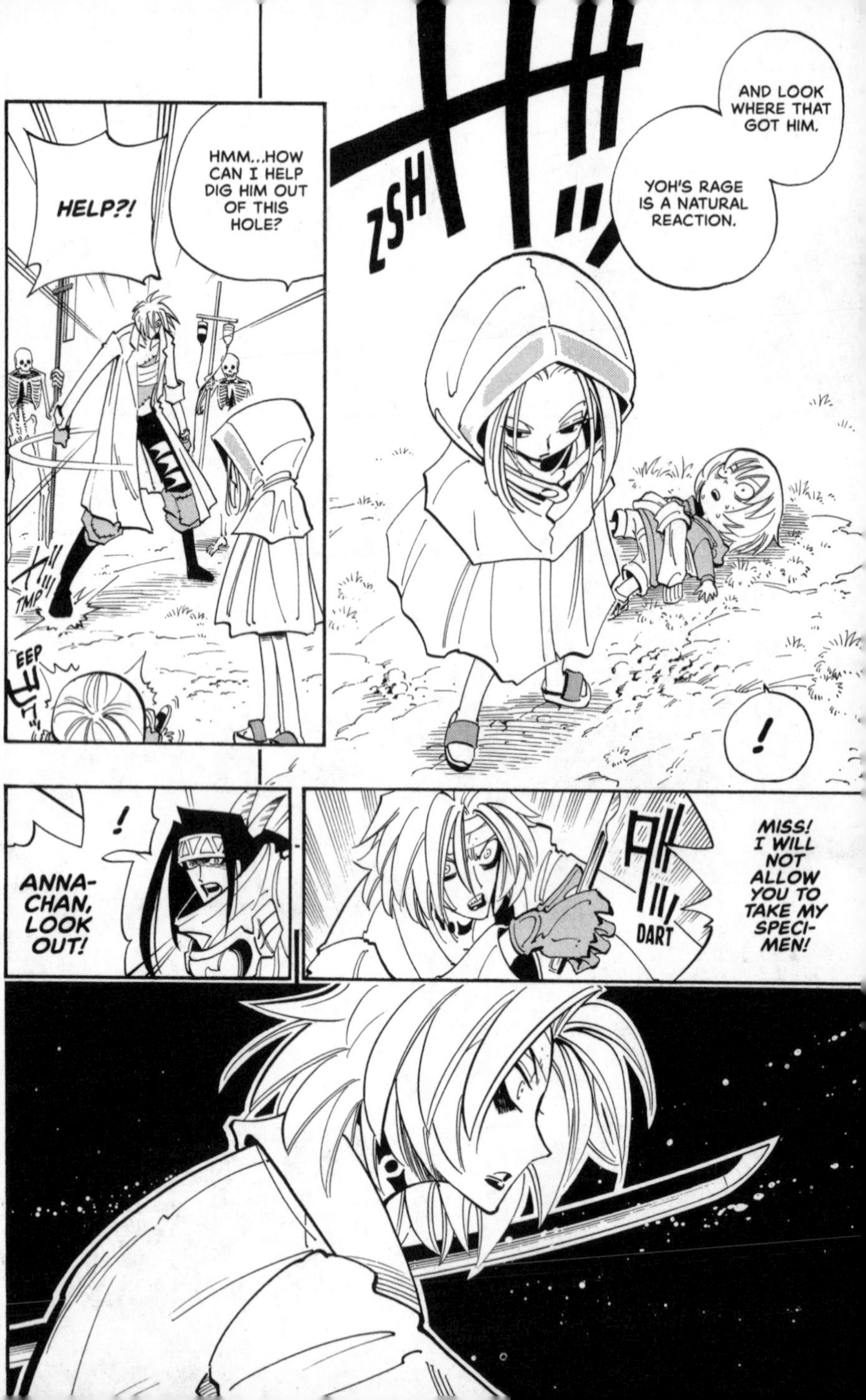
AND LOOK WHERE THAT GOT HIM.
YOH'S RAGE IS A NATURAL REACTION.
ZSH
!
HMM...HOW CAN I HELP DIG HIM OUT OF THIS HOLE?
HELP?!
TMP
EEP
MISS! I WILL NOT ALLOW YOU TO TAKE MY SPECIMEN!
DART
!
ANNA-CHAN, LOOK OUT!

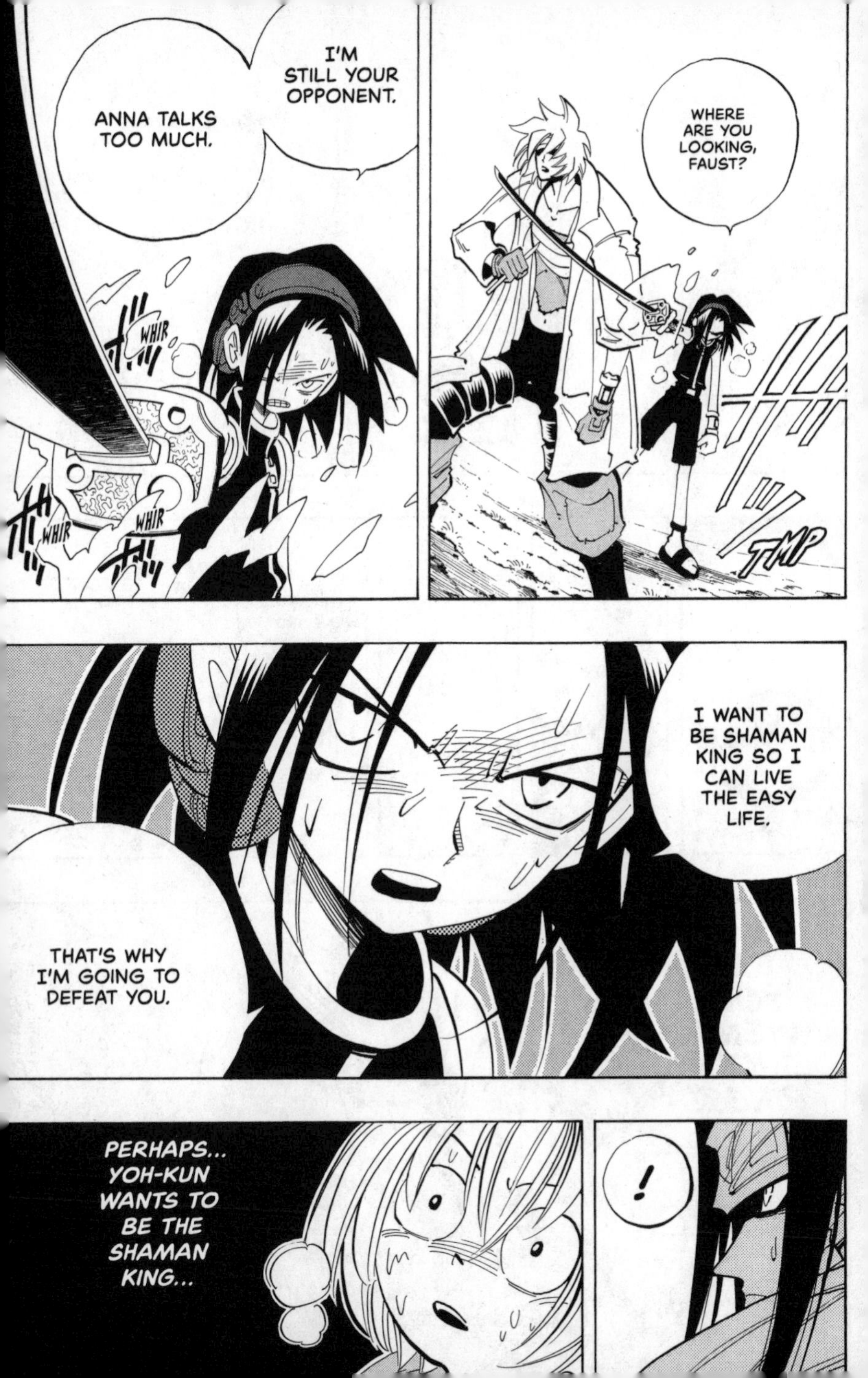
WHERE ARE YOU LOOKING, FAUST?
TMP
I'M STILL YOUR OPPONENT.
ANNA TALKS TOO MUCH.
WHIR
WHIR
WHIR
I WANT TO BE SHAMAN KING SO I CAN LIVE THE EASY LIFE.
THAT'S WHY I'M GOING TO DEFEAT YOU.
!
PERHAPS... YOH-KUN WANTS TO BE THE SHAMAN KING...

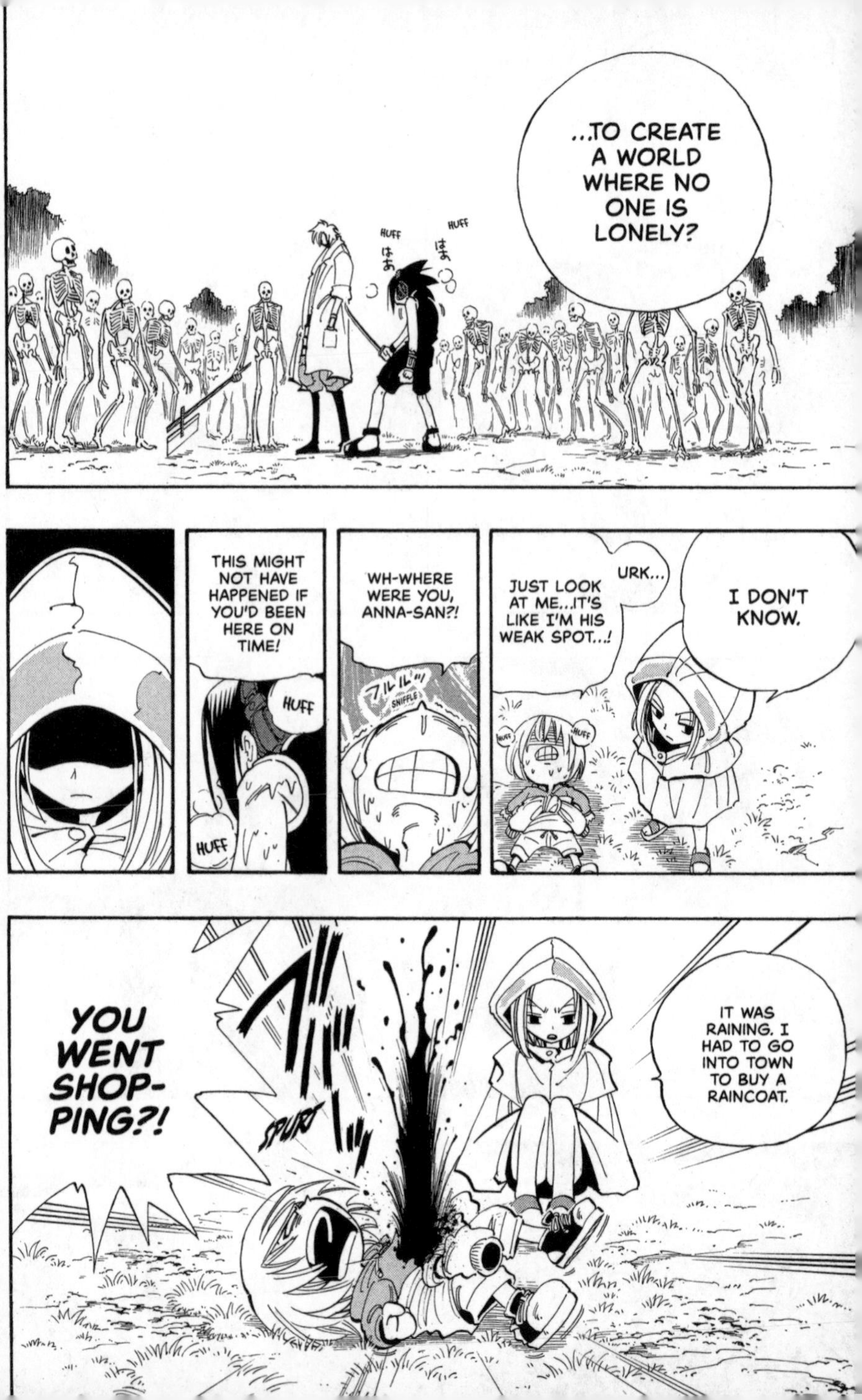
...TO CREATE A WORLD WHERE NO ONE IS LONELY?
HUFF
はあ
HUFF
はあ
I DON'T KNOW.
URK...
JUST LOOK AT ME...IT'S LIKE I'M HIS WEAK SPOT...!
HUFF
HUFF
WH-WHERE WERE YOU, ANNA-SAN?!
SNIFFLE
THIS MIGHT NOT HAVE HAPPENED IF YOU'D BEEN HERE ON TIME!
HUFF
HUFF
IT WAS RAINING. I HAD TO GO INTO TOWN TO BUY A RAINCOAT.
YOU WENT SHOP-PING?!
SPURT

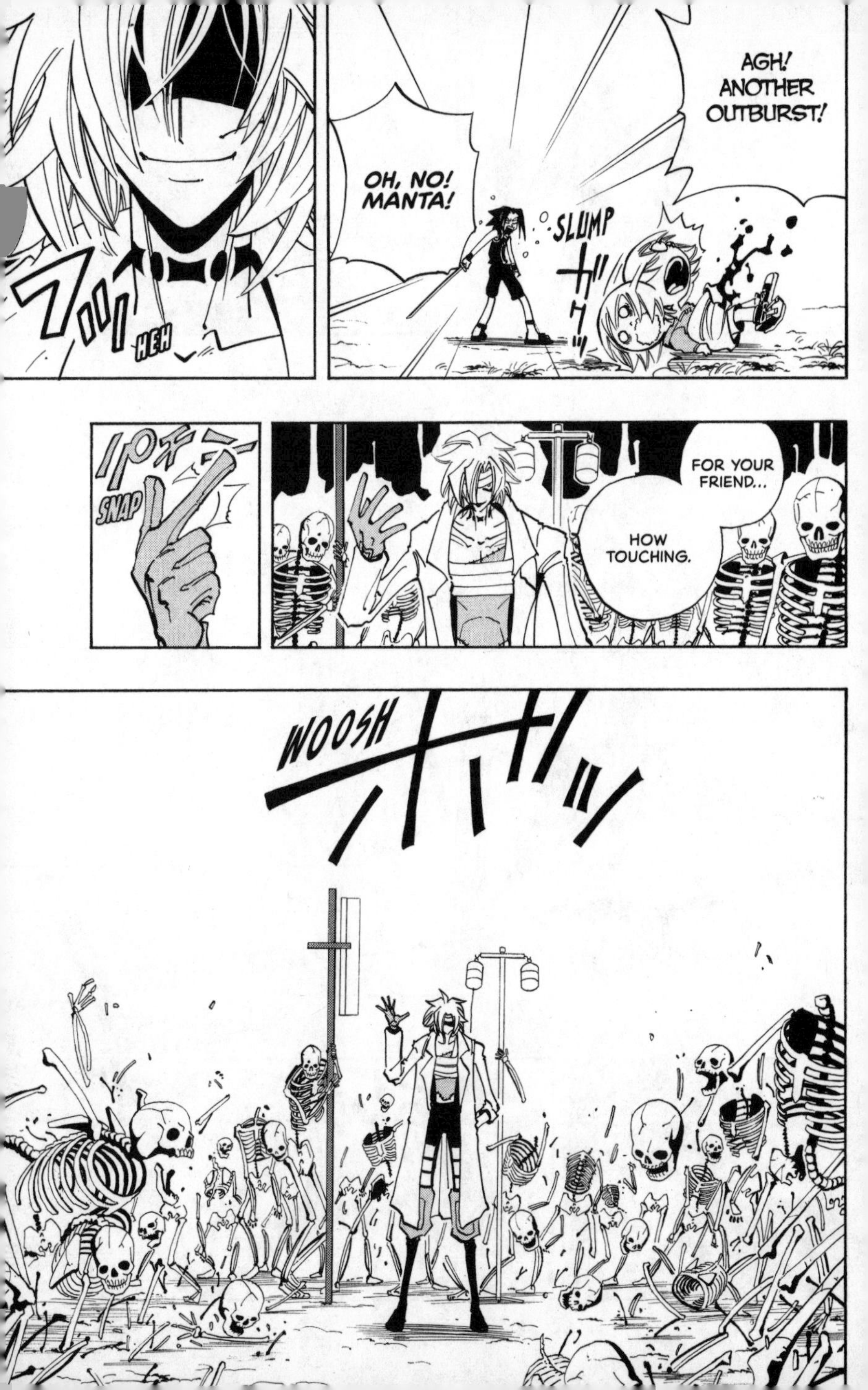
AGH! ANOTHER OUTBURST!
OH, NO! MANTA!
SLUMP
HEH
FOR YOUR FRIEND...
HOW TOUCHING.
SNAP
WOOSH

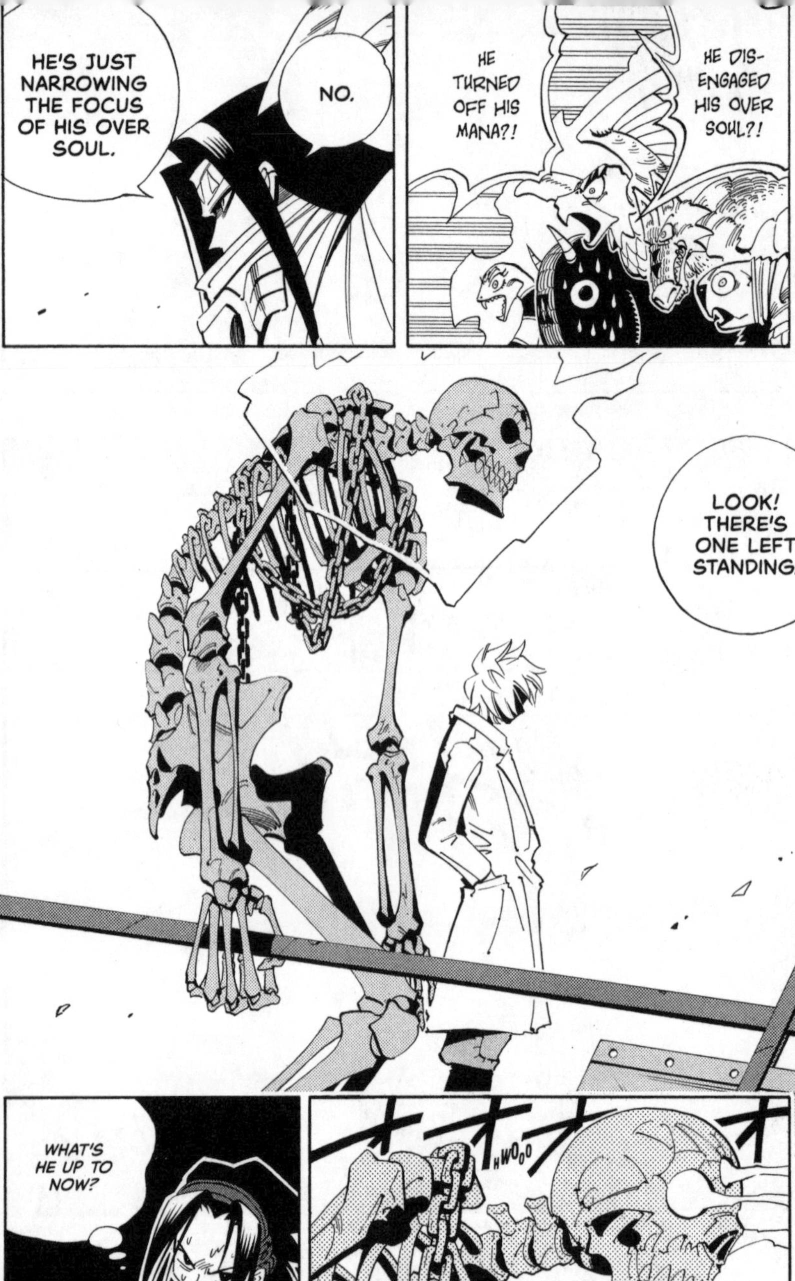
HE DIS-ENGAGED HIS OVER SOUL?!
HE TURNED OFF HIS MANA?!
NO.
HE'S JUST NARROWING THE FOCUS OF HIS OVER SOUL.
LOOK! THERE'S ONE LEFT STANDING.
HWOOO
WHAT'S HE UP TO NOW?

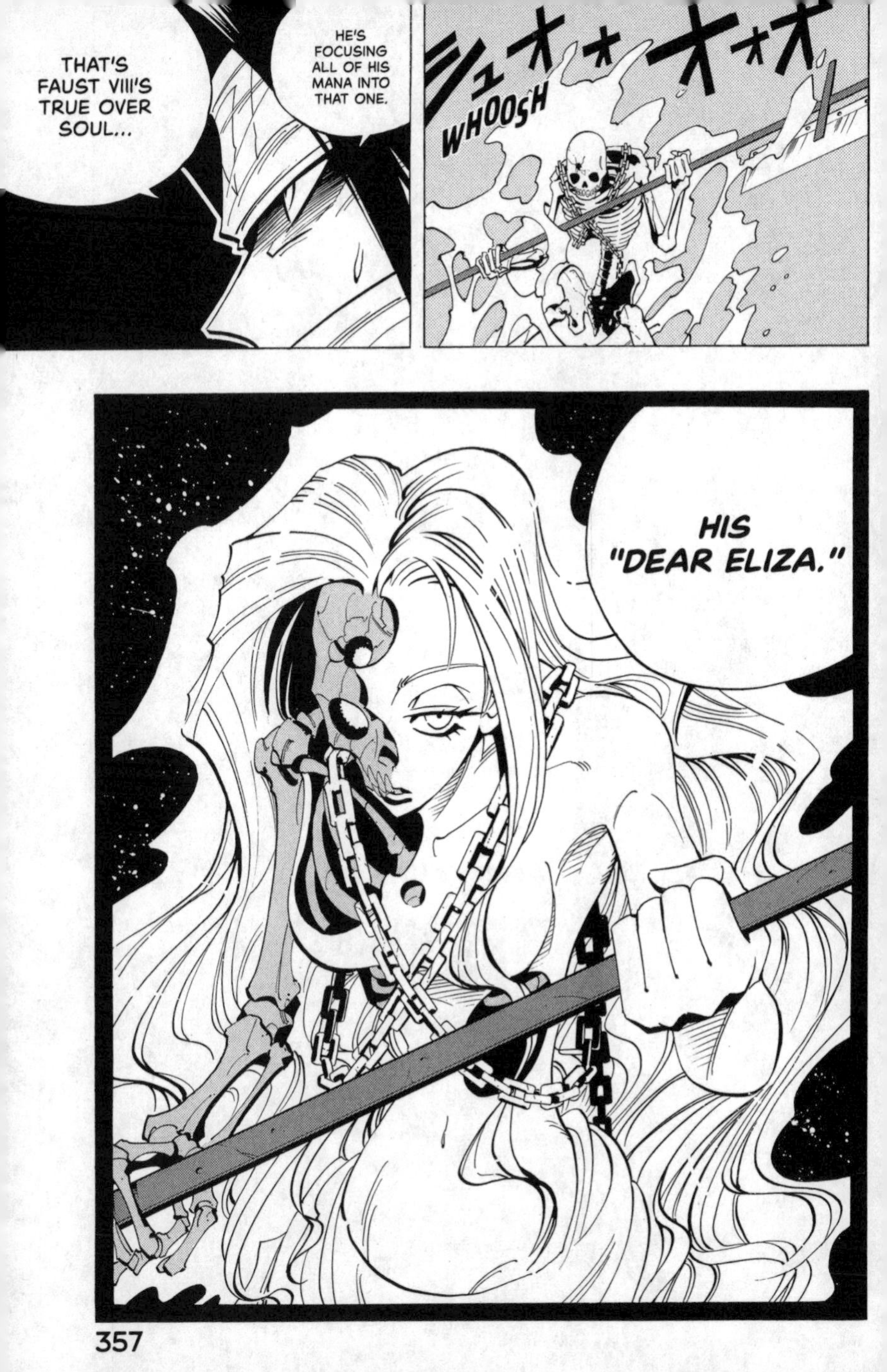
シュオォオォオ
WHOOSH
HE'S FOCUSING ALL OF HIS MANA INTO THAT ONE.
THAT'S FAUST VIII'S TRUE OVER SOUL...
HIS "DEAR ELIZA."

SHAMAN
KING
5

Doctor's Kit

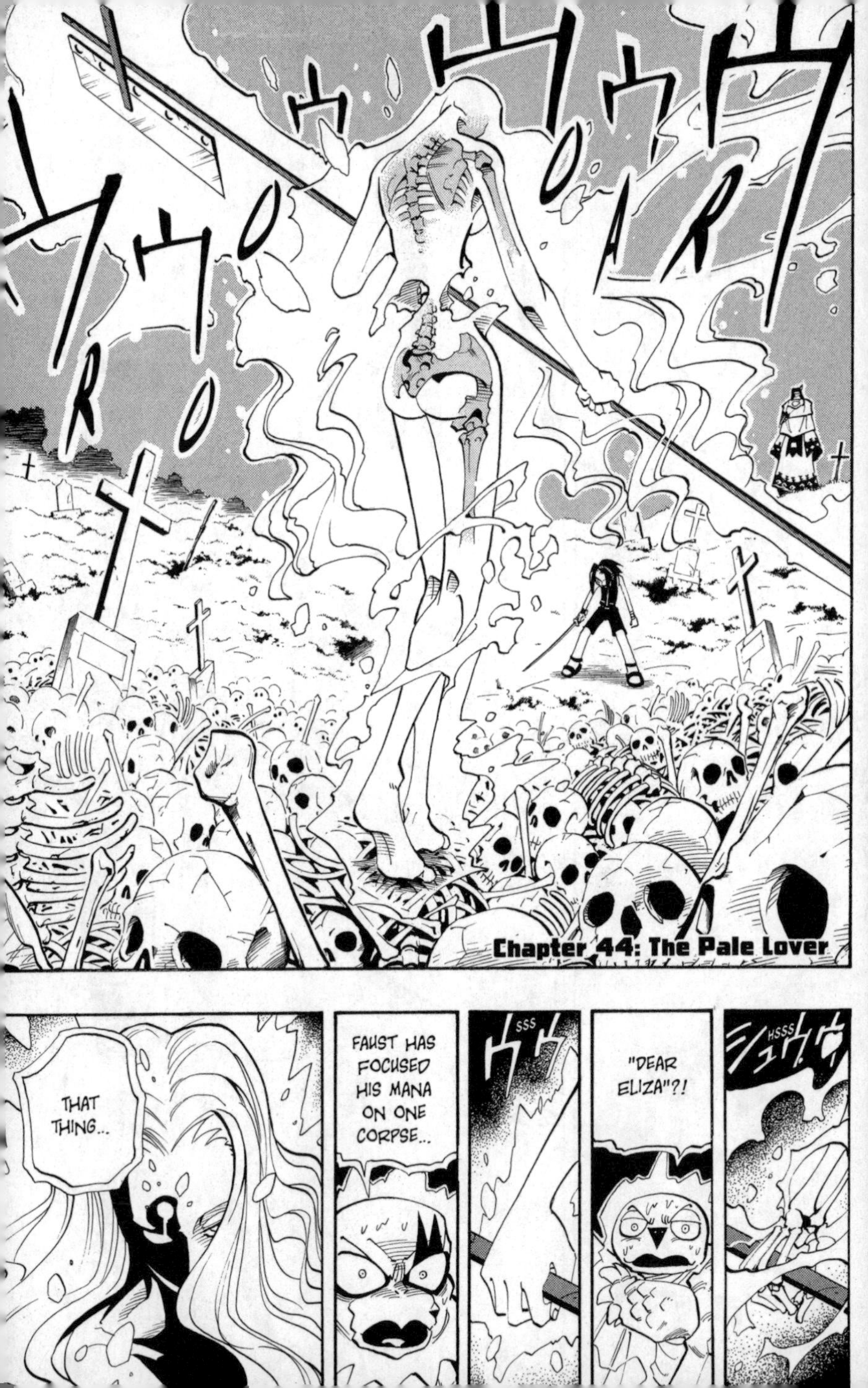
Chapter 44: The Pale Lover
HSSS
"DEAR ELIZA"?!
SSS
FAUST HAS FOCUSED HIS MANA ON ONE CORPSE...
THAT THING...

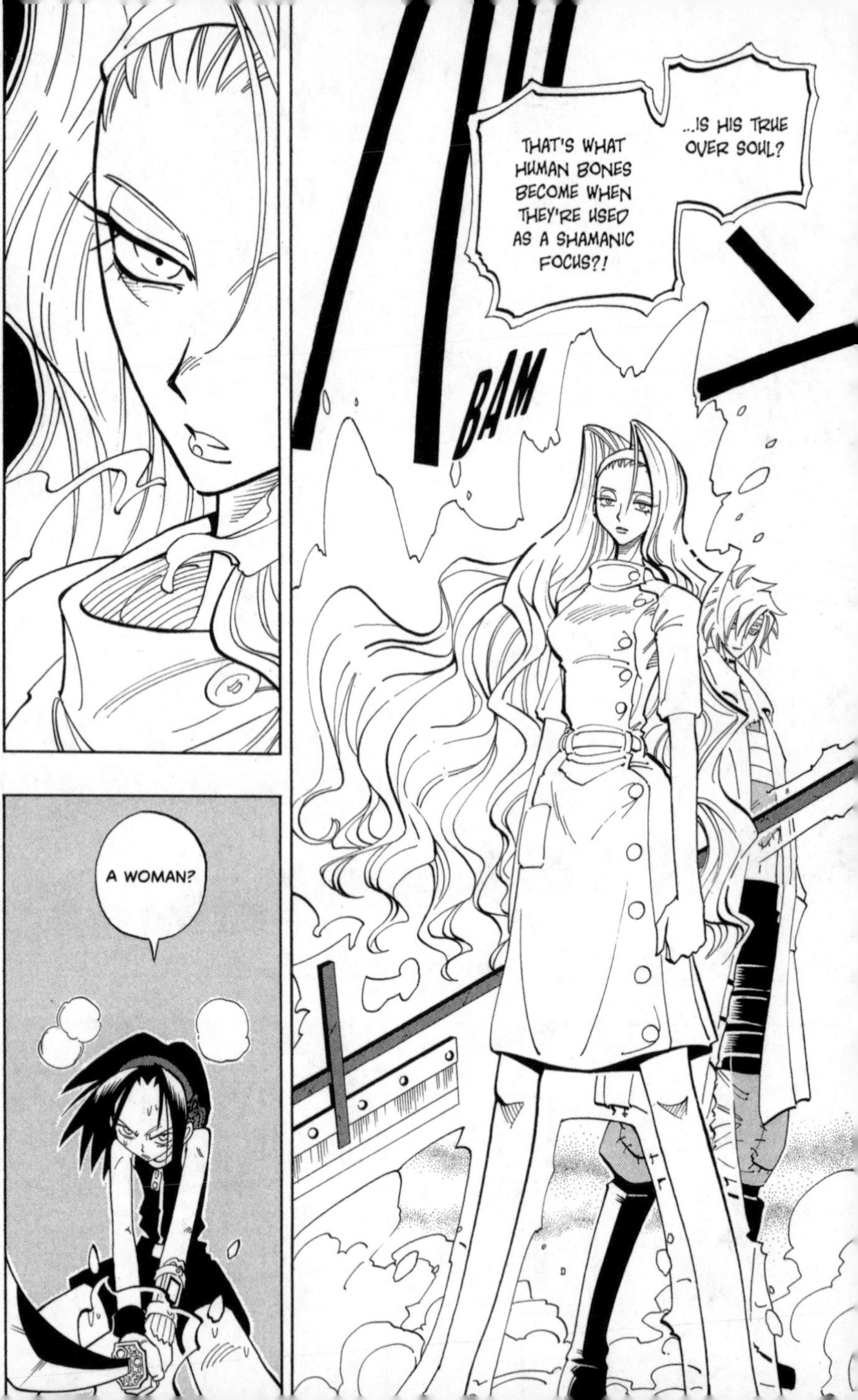
THAT'S WHAT HUMAN BONES BECOME WHEN THEY'RE USED AS A SHAMANIC FOCUS?!
...IS HIS TRUE OVER SOUL?
BAM
A WOMAN?

Chapter 44:

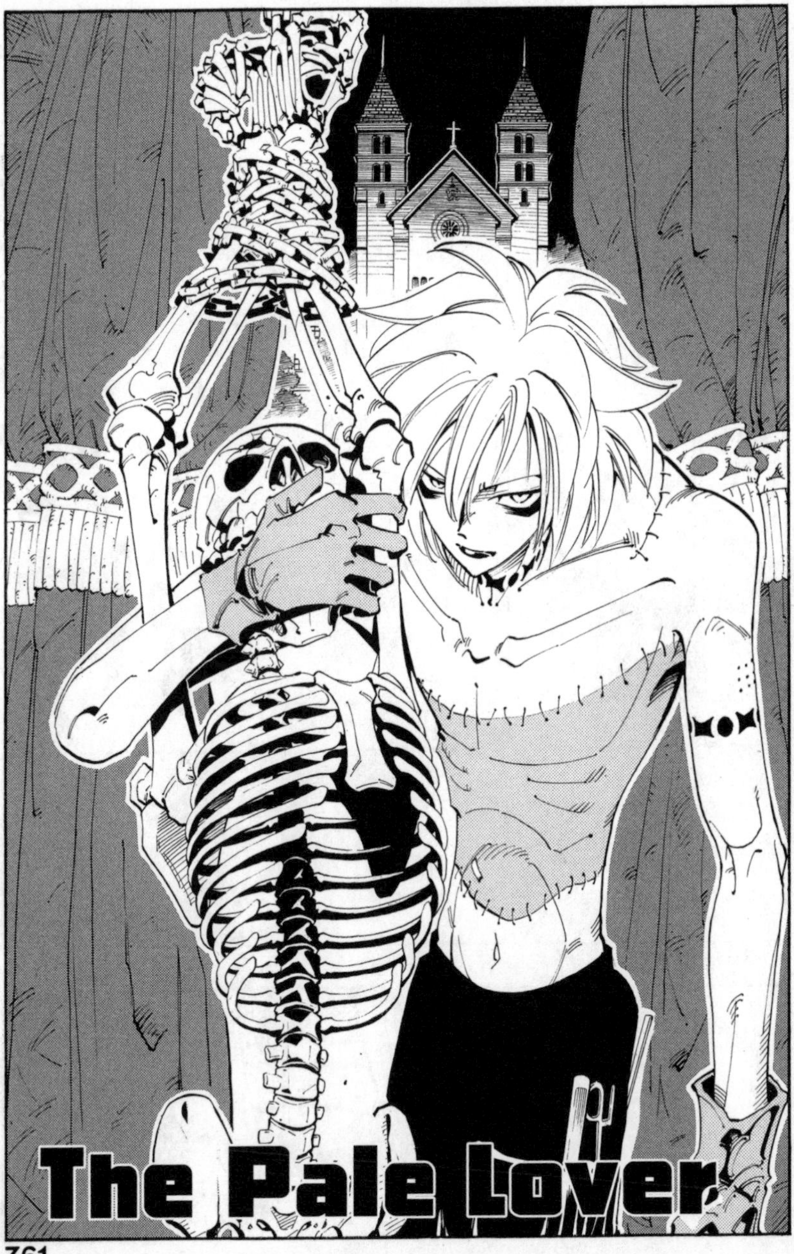
The Pale Lover

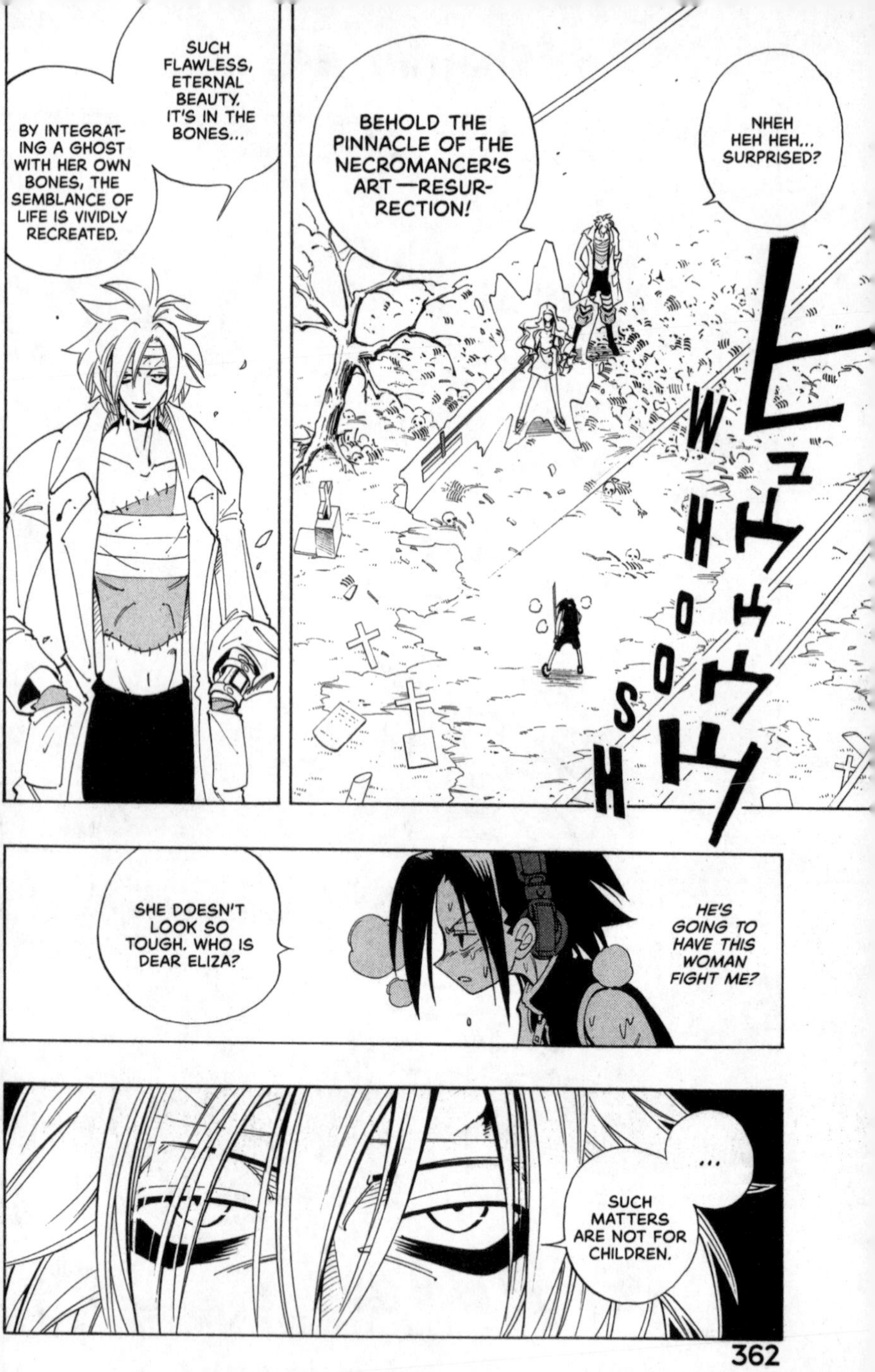
NHEH HEH HEH... SURPRISED?
BEHOLD THE PINNACLE OF THE NECROMANCER'S ART—RESURRECTION!
WHOOSH
SUCH FLAWLESS, ETERNAL BEAUTY. IT'S IN THE BONES...
BY INTEGRATING A GHOST WITH HER OWN BONES, THE SEMBLANCE OF LIFE IS VIVIDLY RECREATED.
HE'S GOING TO HAVE THIS WOMAN FIGHT ME?
SHE DOESN'T LOOK SO TOUGH. WHO IS DEAR ELIZA?
...
SUCH MATTERS ARE NOT FOR CHILDREN.

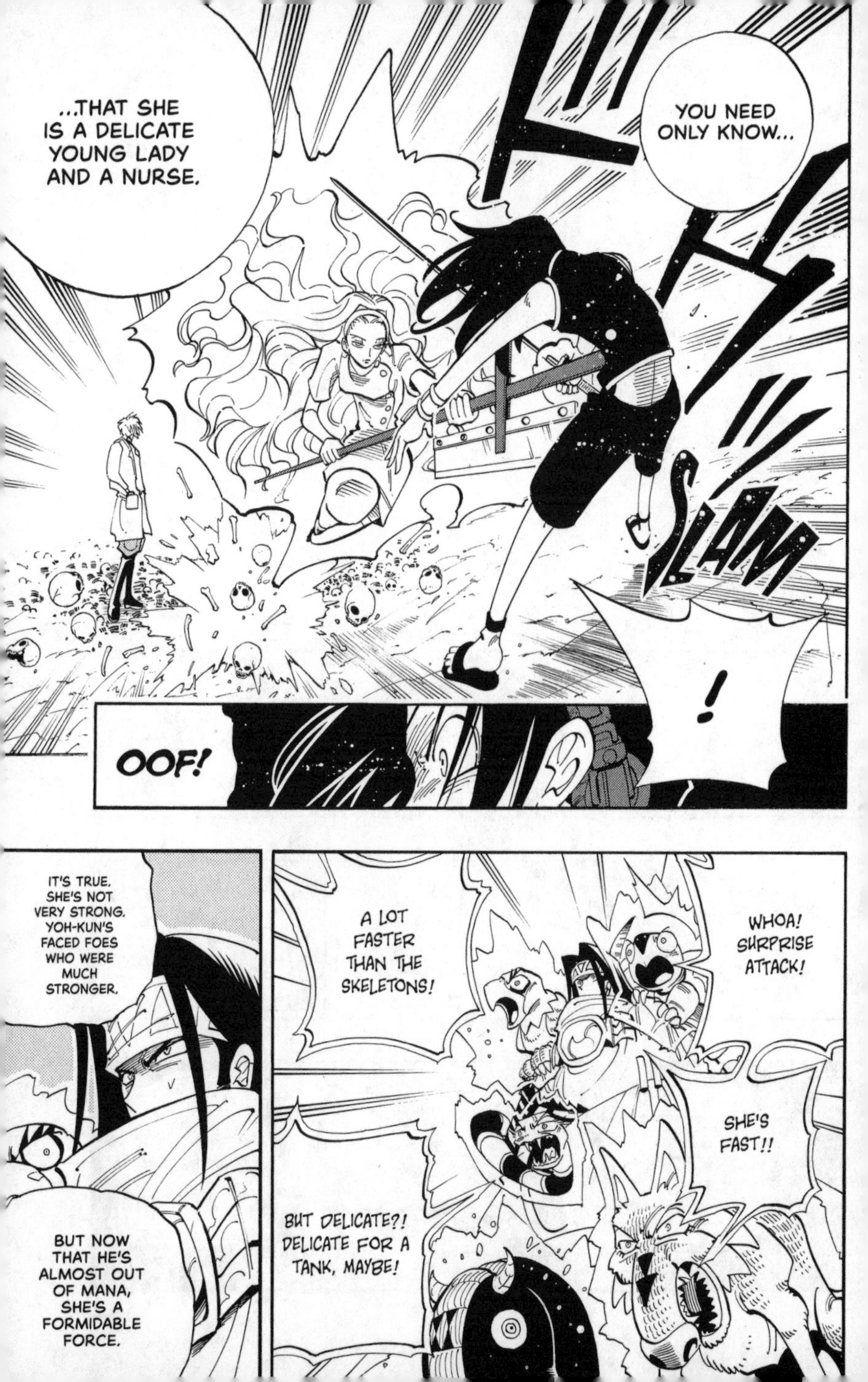
YOU NEED ONLY KNOW...
...THAT SHE IS A DELICATE YOUNG LADY AND A NURSE.
SLAM
!
OOF!
WHOA! SURPRISE ATTACK!
A LOT FASTER THAN THE SKELETONS!
SHE'S FAST!!
BUT DELICATE?! DELICATE FOR A TANK, MAYBE!
IT'S TRUE. SHE'S NOT VERY STRONG. YOH-KUN'S FACED FOES WHO WERE MUCH STRONGER.
BUT NOW THAT HE'S ALMOST OUT OF MANA, SHE'S A FORMIDABLE FORCE.

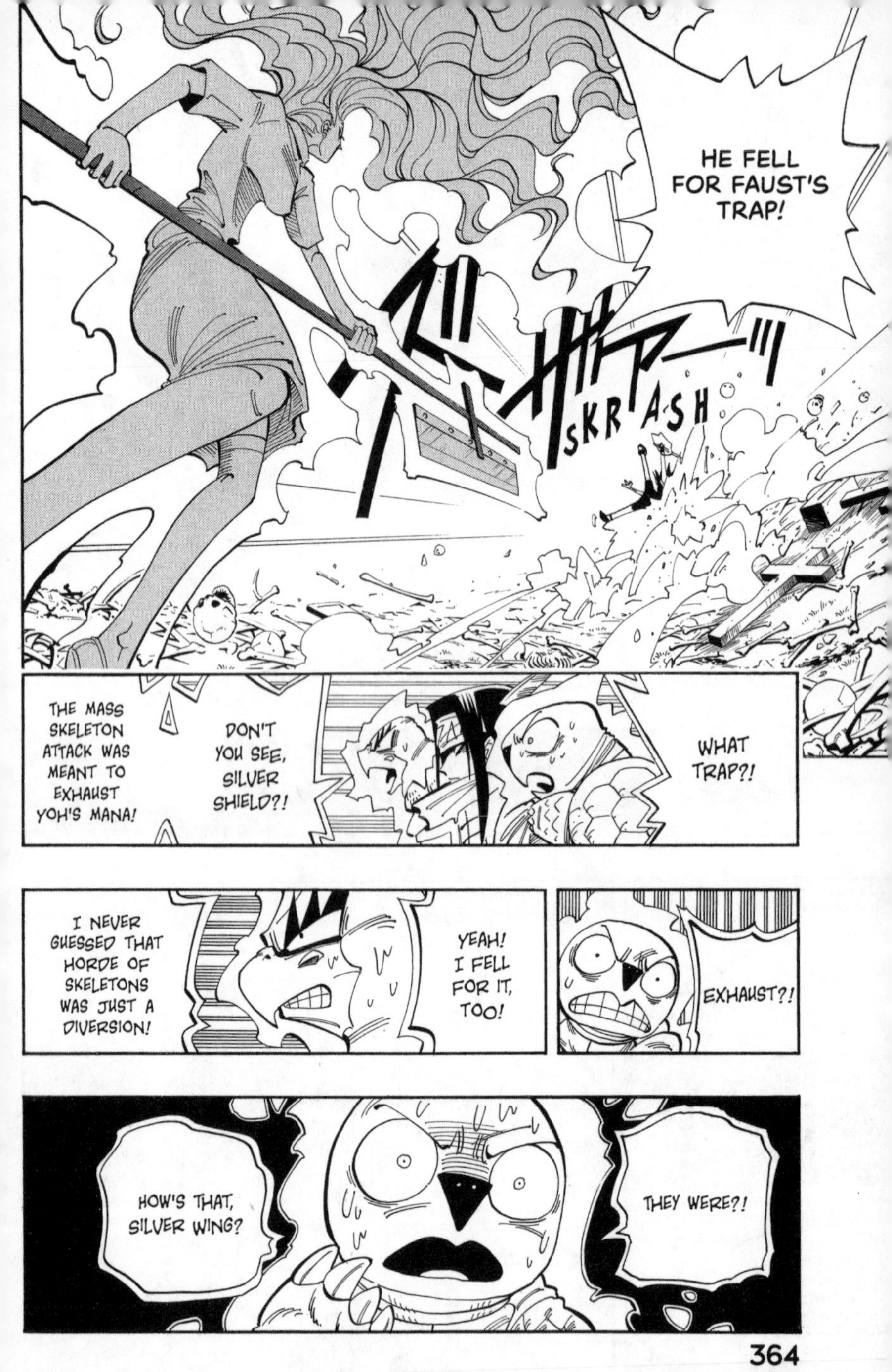
HE FELL FOR FAUST'S TRAP!
SKRASH
WHAT TRAP?!
DON'T YOU SEE, SILVER SHIELD?!
THE MASS SKELETON ATTACK WAS MEANT TO EXHAUST YOH'S MANA!
EXHAUST?!
YEAH! I FELL FOR IT, TOO!
I NEVER GUESSED THAT HORDE OF SKELETONS WAS JUST A DIVERSION!
THEY WERE?!
HOW'S THAT, SILVER WING?

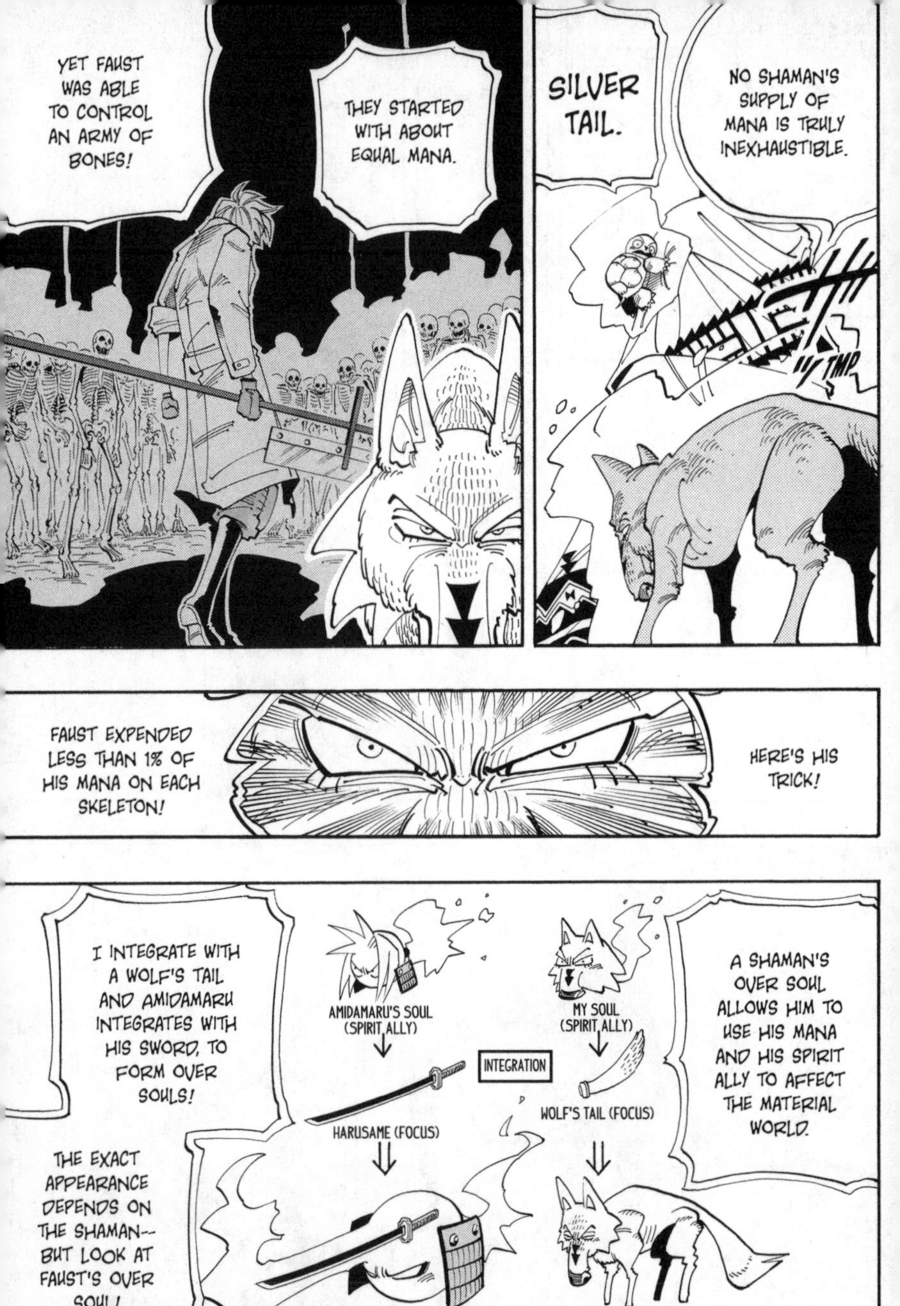
NO SHAMAN'S SUPPLY OF MANA IS TRULY INEXHAUSTIBLE.
SILVER TAIL.
TMP
THEY STARTED WITH ABOUT EQUAL MANA.
YET FAUST WAS ABLE TO CONTROL AN ARMY OF BONES!
HERE'S HIS TRICK!
FAUST EXPENDED LESS THAN 1% OF HIS MANA ON EACH SKELETON!
A SHAMAN'S OVER SOUL ALLOWS HIM TO USE HIS MANA AND HIS SPIRIT ALLY TO AFFECT THE MATERIAL WORLD.
MY SOUL (SPIRIT ALLY)
WOLF'S TAIL (FOCUS)
OVER SOUL (ME)
INTEGRATION
AMIDAMARU'S SOUL (SPIRIT ALLY)
HARUSAME (FOCUS)
OVER SOUL (AMIDAMARU)
I INTEGRATE WITH A WOLF'S TAIL AND AMIDAMARU INTEGRATES WITH HIS SWORD, TO FORM OVER SOULS!
THE EXACT APPEARANCE DEPENDS ON THE SHAMAN-- BUT LOOK AT FAUST'S OVER SOUL!

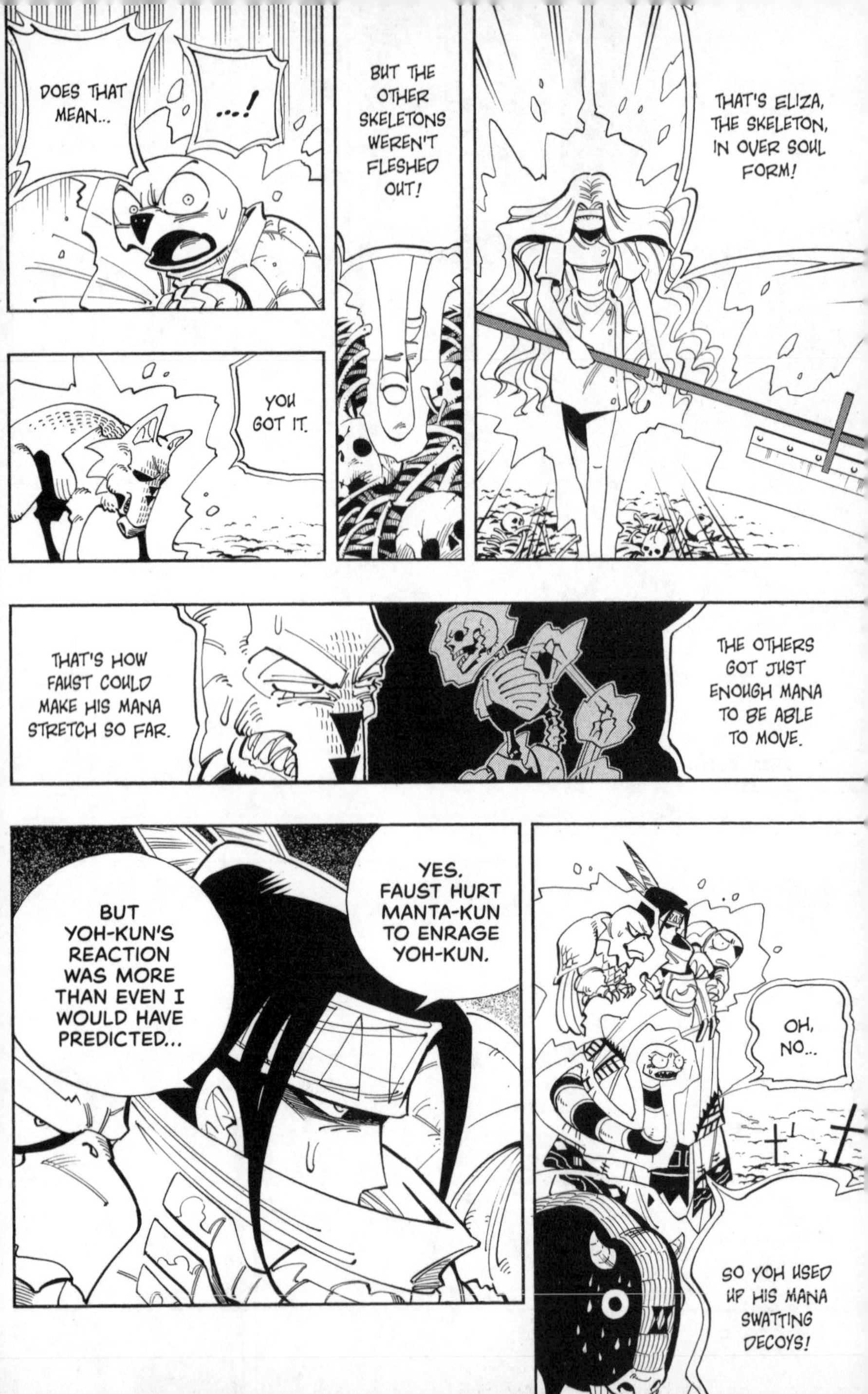
THAT'S ELIZA, THE SKELETON, IN OVER SOUL FORM!
BUT THE OTHER SKELETONS WEREN'T FLESHED OUT!
...!
DOES THAT MEAN...
YOU GOT IT.
THE OTHERS GOT JUST ENOUGH MANA TO BE ABLE TO MOVE.
THAT'S HOW FAUST COULD MAKE HIS MANA STRETCH SO FAR.
OH, NO...
SO YOH USED UP HIS MANA SWATTING DECOYS!
YES. FAUST HURT MANTA-KUN TO ENRAGE YOH-KUN.
BUT YOH-KUN'S REACTION WAS MORE THAN EVEN I WOULD HAVE PREDICTED...

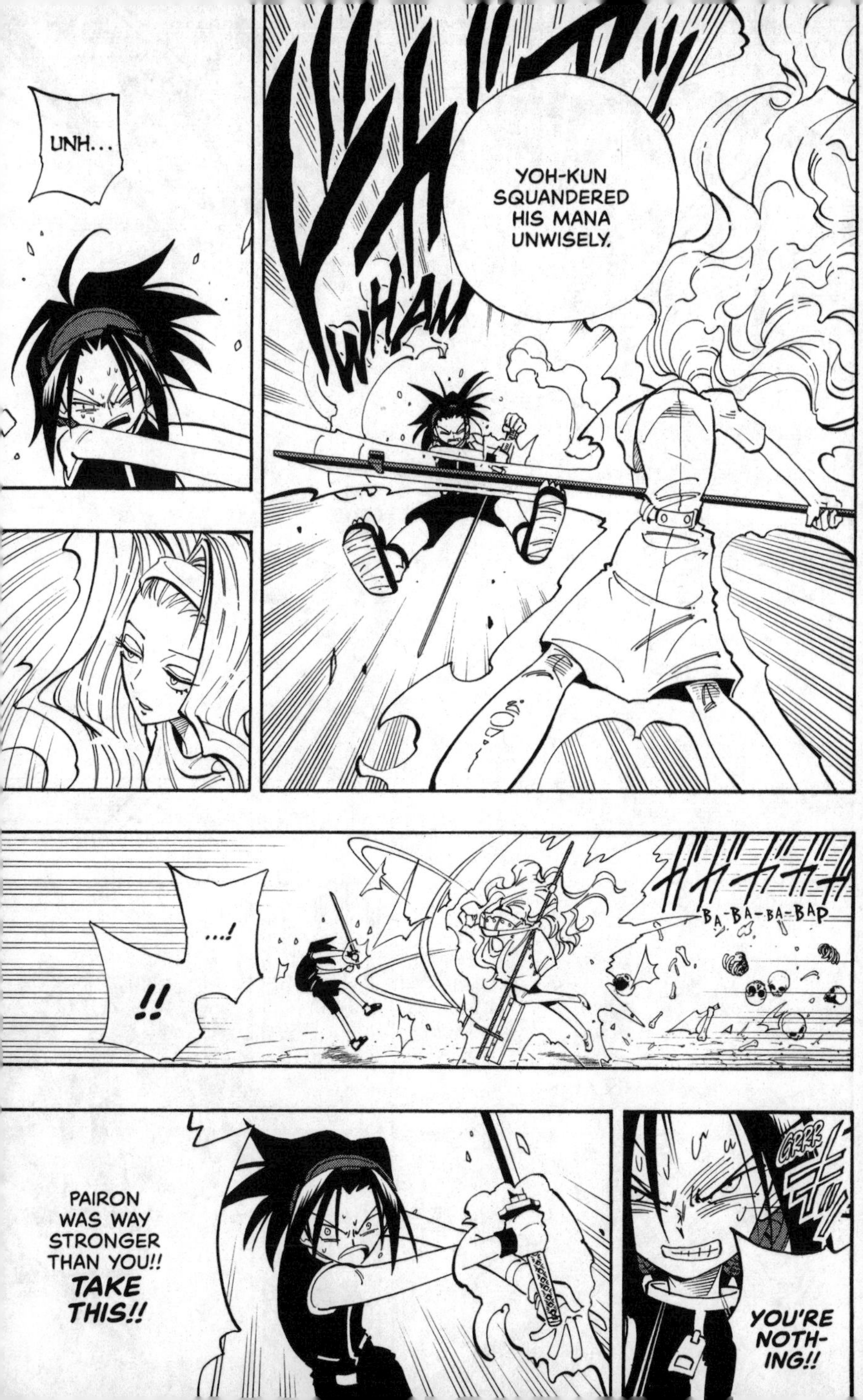
WHAM
YOH-KUN SQUANDERED HIS MANA UNWISELY.
UNH...
BA-BA-BA-BAP
...!
!!
GRRR
YOU'RE NOTH-ING!!
PAIRON WAS WAY STRONGER THAN YOU!! TAKE THIS!!

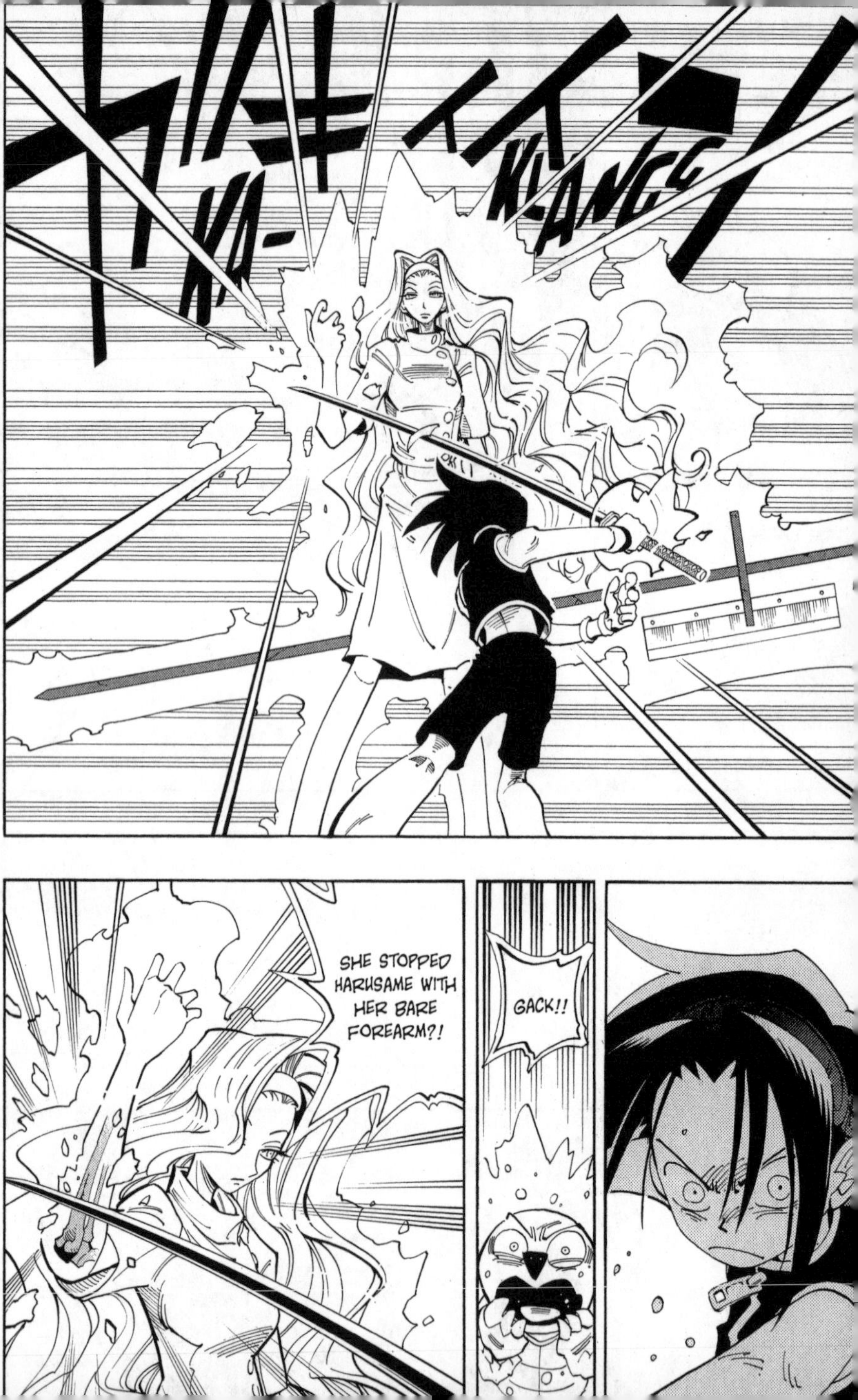
KA-
KLANGG
GACK!!
SHE STOPPED HARUSAME WITH HER BARE FOREARM?!

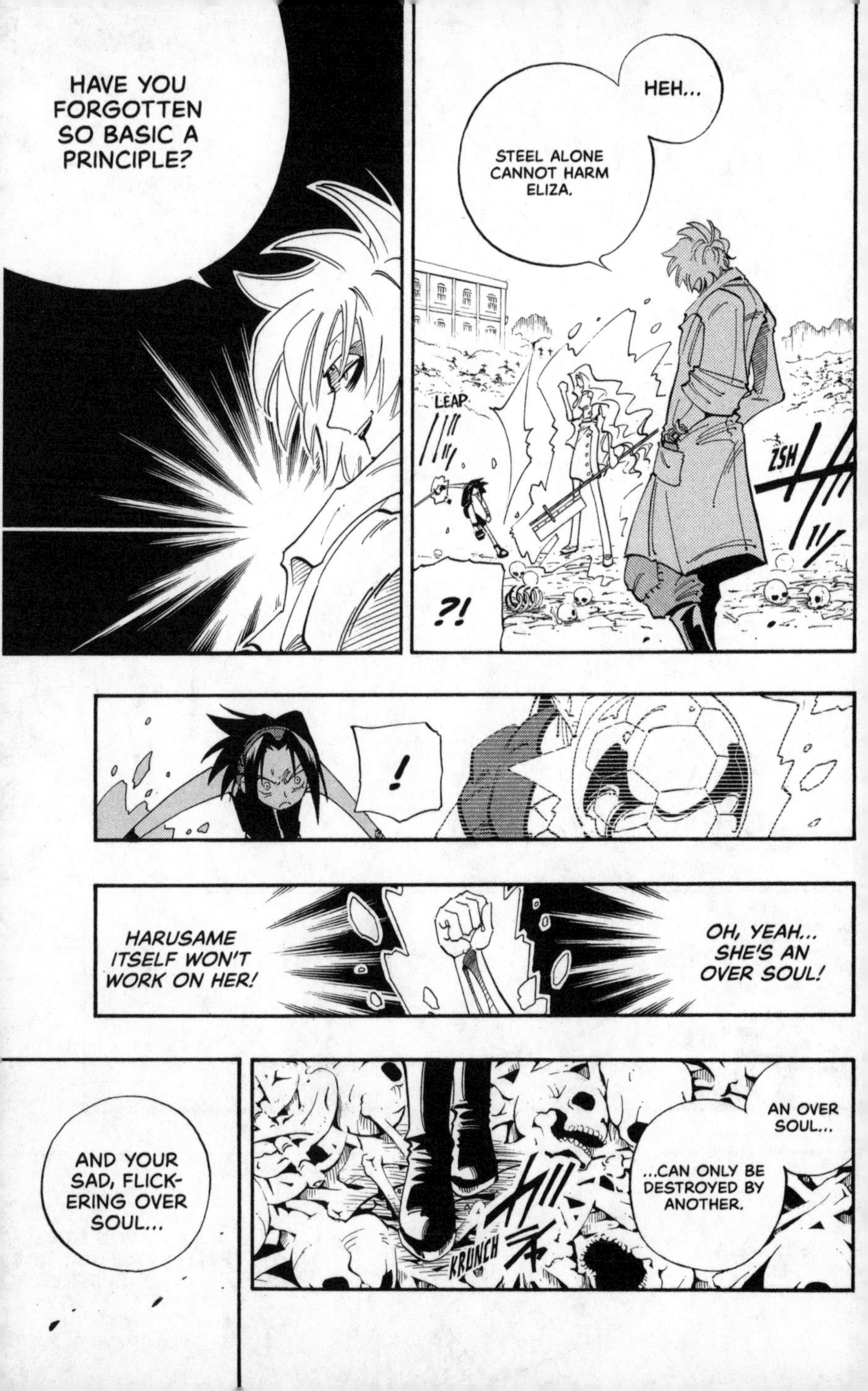
HEH...
STEEL ALONE CANNOT HARM ELIZA.
ZSH
LEAP
?!
HAVE YOU FORGOTTEN SO BASIC A PRINCIPLE?
!
OH, YEAH... SHE'S AN OVER SOUL!
HARUSAME ITSELF WON'T WORK ON HER!
AN OVER SOUL...
...CAN ONLY BE DESTROYED BY ANOTHER.
KRUNCH
AND YOUR SAD, FLICKERING OVER SOUL...

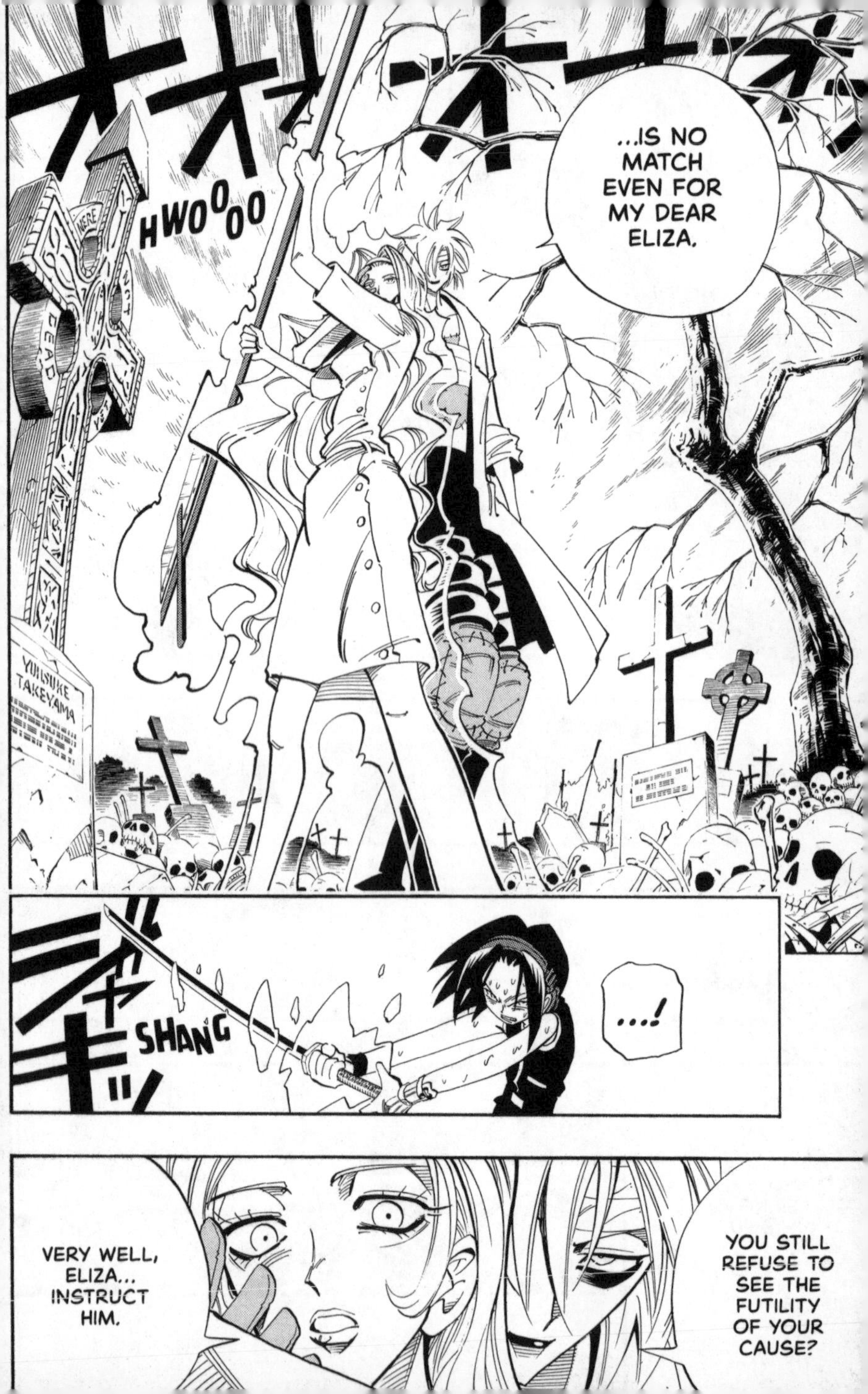
...IS NO MATCH EVEN FOR MY DEAR ELIZA.
HWOOOO
YOHSUKE TAKEYAMA
...!
SHANG
YOU STILL REFUSE TO SEE THE FUTILITY OF YOUR CAUSE?
VERY WELL, ELIZA... INSTRUCT HIM.

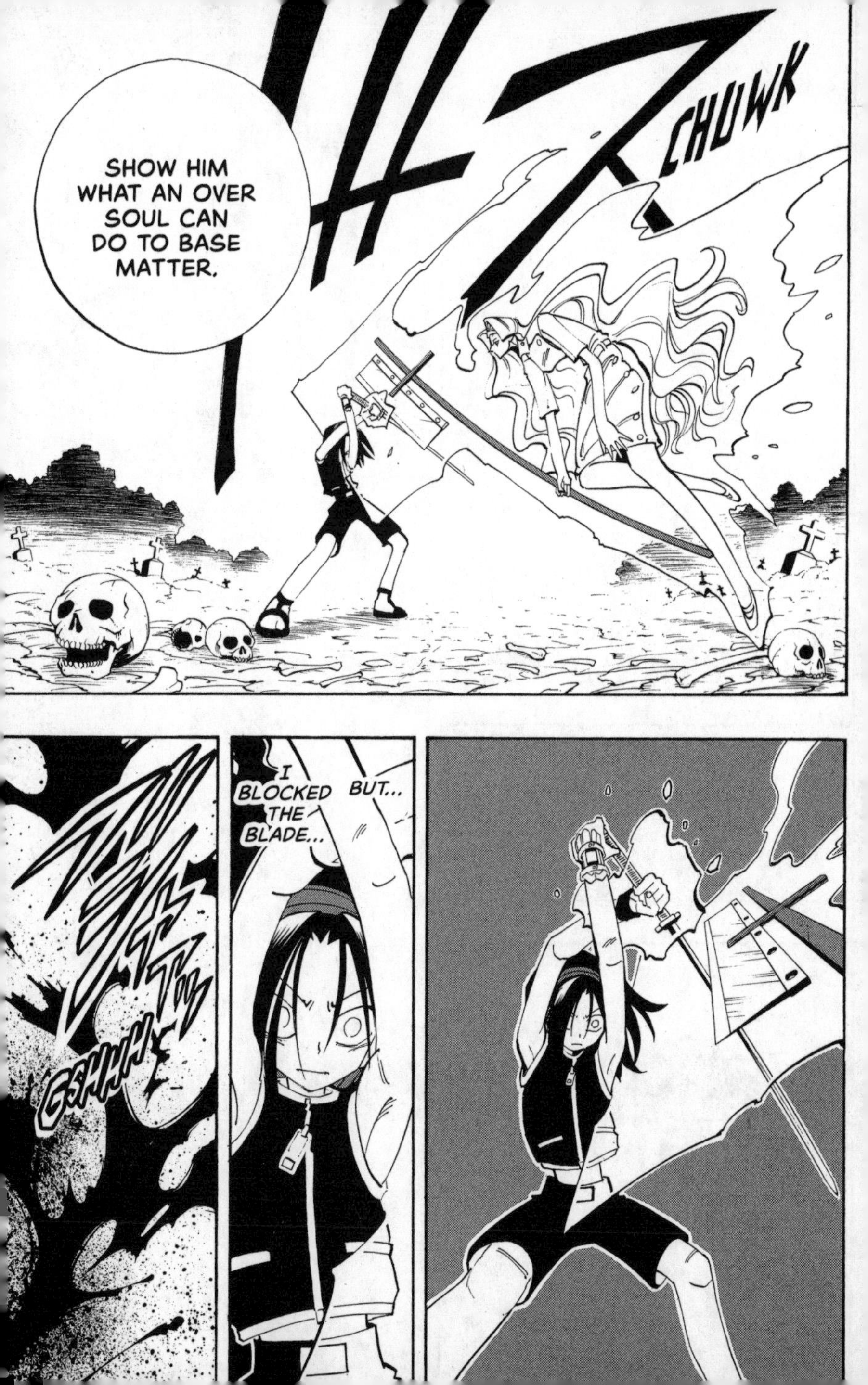
CHUWK
SHOW HIM WHAT AN OVER SOUL CAN DO TO BASE MATTER.
I BLOCKED THE BLADE...
BUT...

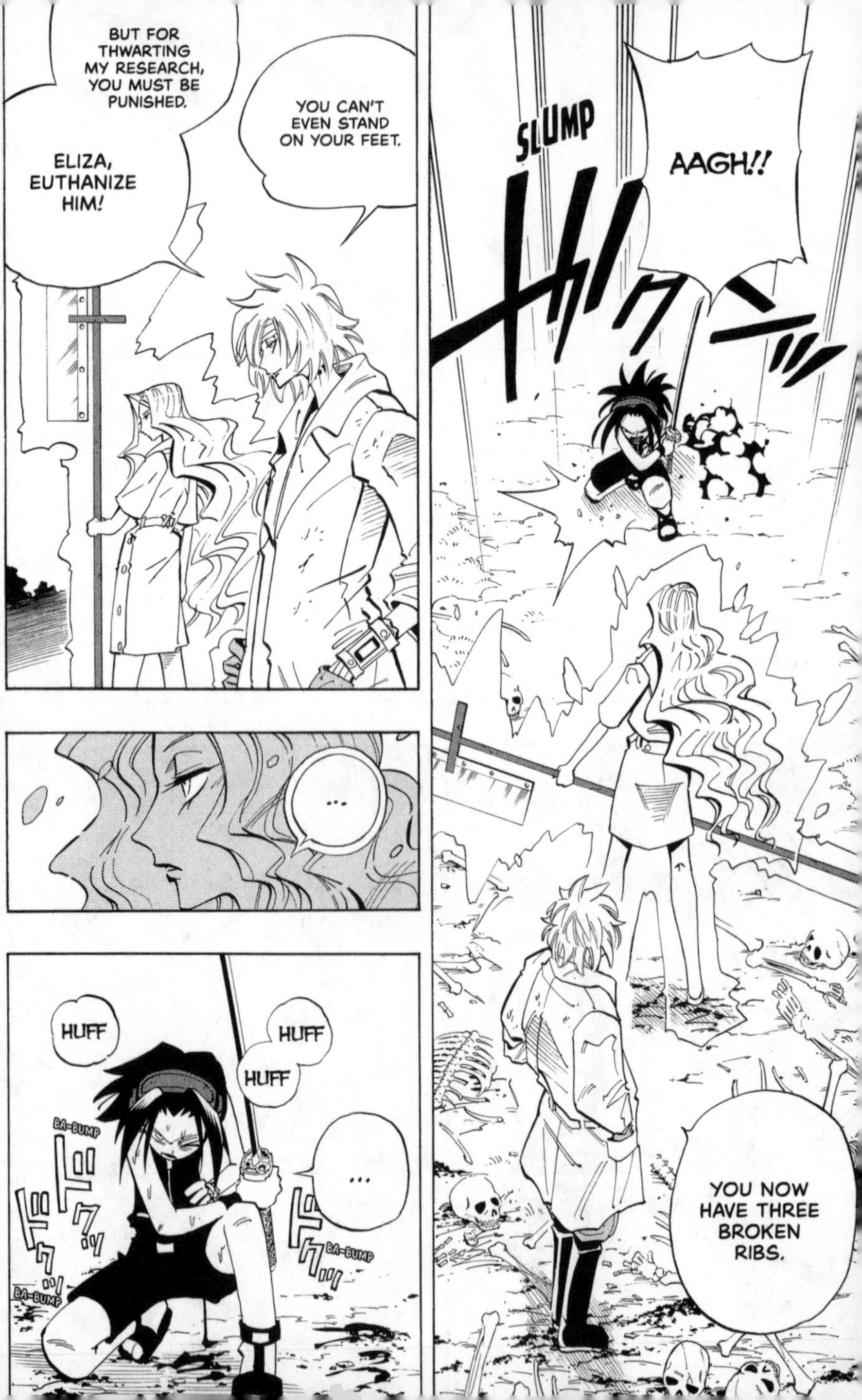
AAGH!!
SLUMP
YOU NOW HAVE THREE BROKEN RIBS.
YOU CAN'T EVEN STAND ON YOUR FEET.
BUT FOR THWARTING MY RESEARCH, YOU MUST BE PUNISHED.
ELIZA, EUTHANIZE HIM!
...
HUFF
HUFF
HUFF
...
BA-BUMP
BA-BUMP
BA-BUMP

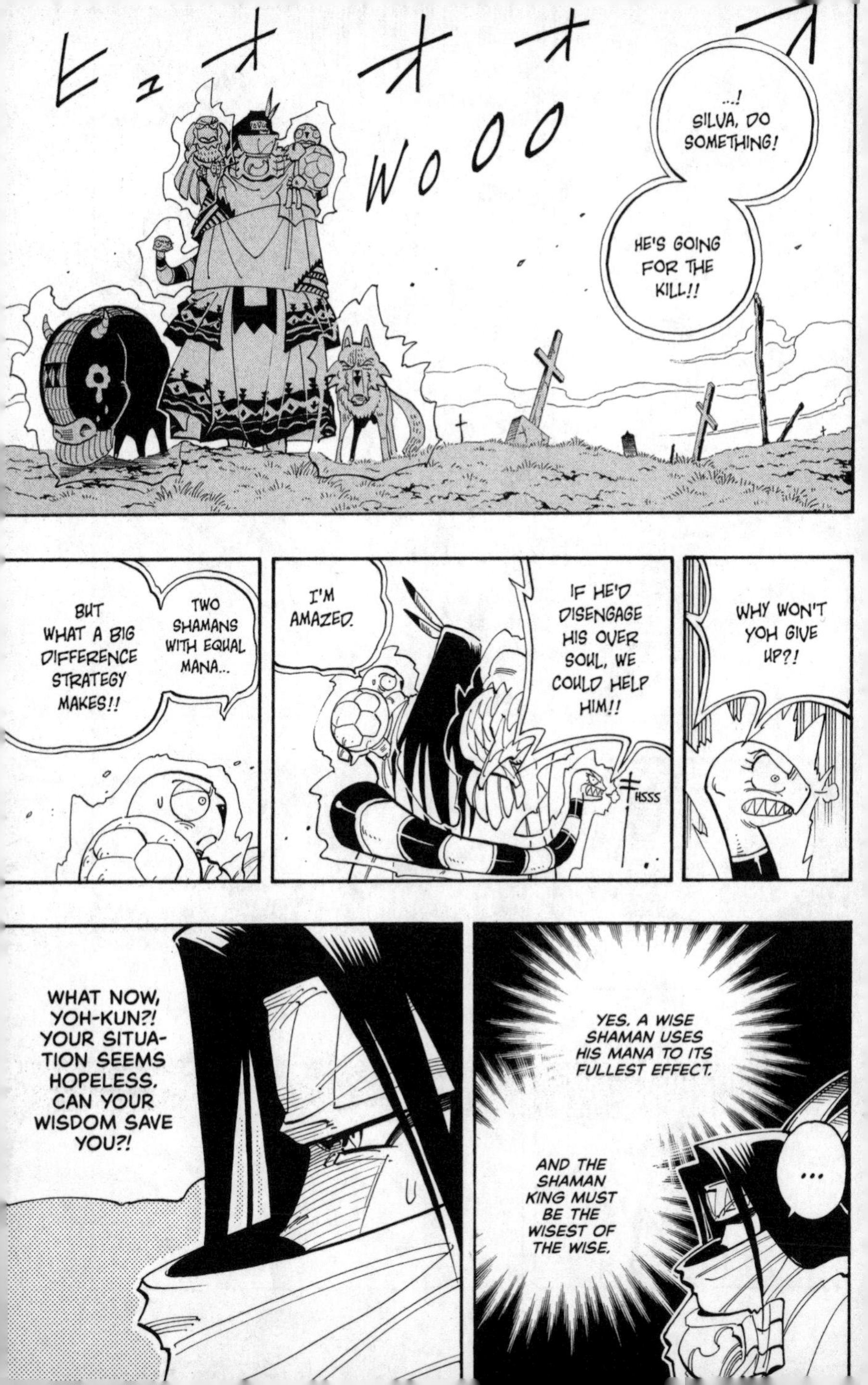
ヒュオオオオ
WOOO
...! SILVA, DO SOMETHING!
HE'S GOING FOR THE KILL!!
WHY WON'T YOH GIVE UP?!
IF HE'D DISENGAGE HIS OVER SOUL, WE COULD HELP HIM!!
HSSS
I'M AMAZED.
TWO SHAMANS WITH EQUAL MANA...
BUT WHAT A BIG DIFFERENCE STRATEGY MAKES!!
YES. A WISE SHAMAN USES HIS MANA TO ITS FULLEST EFFECT.
...
AND THE SHAMAN KING MUST BE THE WISEST OF THE WISE.
WHAT NOW, YOH-KUN?! YOUR SITUATION SEEMS HOPELESS. CAN YOUR WISDOM SAVE YOU?!

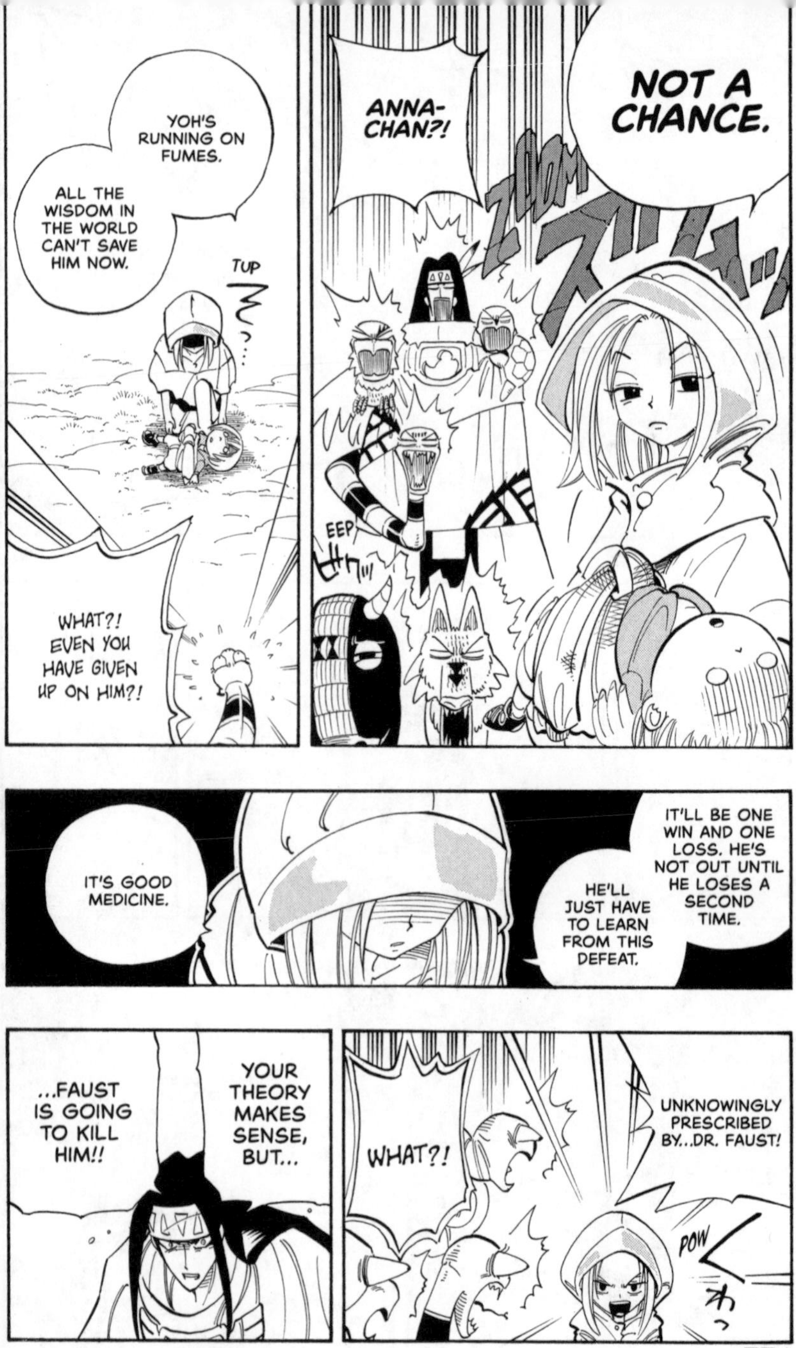
NOT A CHANCE.
ANNA-CHAN?!
ZOOM
スッ
EEP
ギクッ
YOH'S RUNNING ON FUMES.
ALL THE WISDOM IN THE WORLD CAN'T SAVE HIM NOW.
TUP
WHAT?! EVEN YOU HAVE GIVEN UP ON HIM?!
IT'LL BE ONE WIN AND ONE LOSS. HE'S NOT OUT UNTIL HE LOSES A SECOND TIME.
HE'LL JUST HAVE TO LEARN FROM THIS DEFEAT.
IT'S GOOD MEDICINE.
UNKNOWINGLY PRESCRIBED BY...DR. FAUST!
POW
WHAT?!
YOUR THEORY MAKES SENSE, BUT...
...FAUST IS GOING TO KILL HIM!!

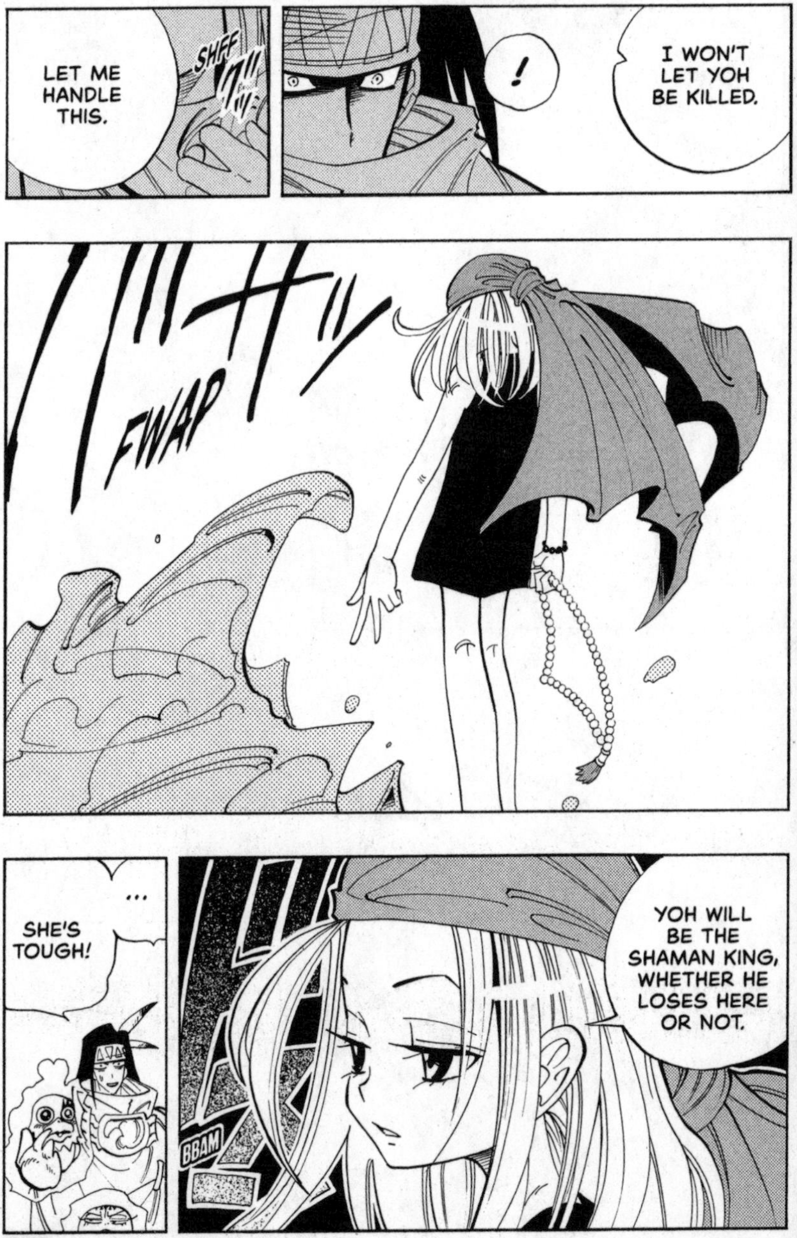
I WON'T LET YOH BE KILLED.
!
SHFF
LET ME HANDLE THIS.
FWAP
YOH WILL BE THE SHAMAN KING, WHETHER HE LOSES HERE OR NOT.
BBAM
...
SHE'S TOUGH!

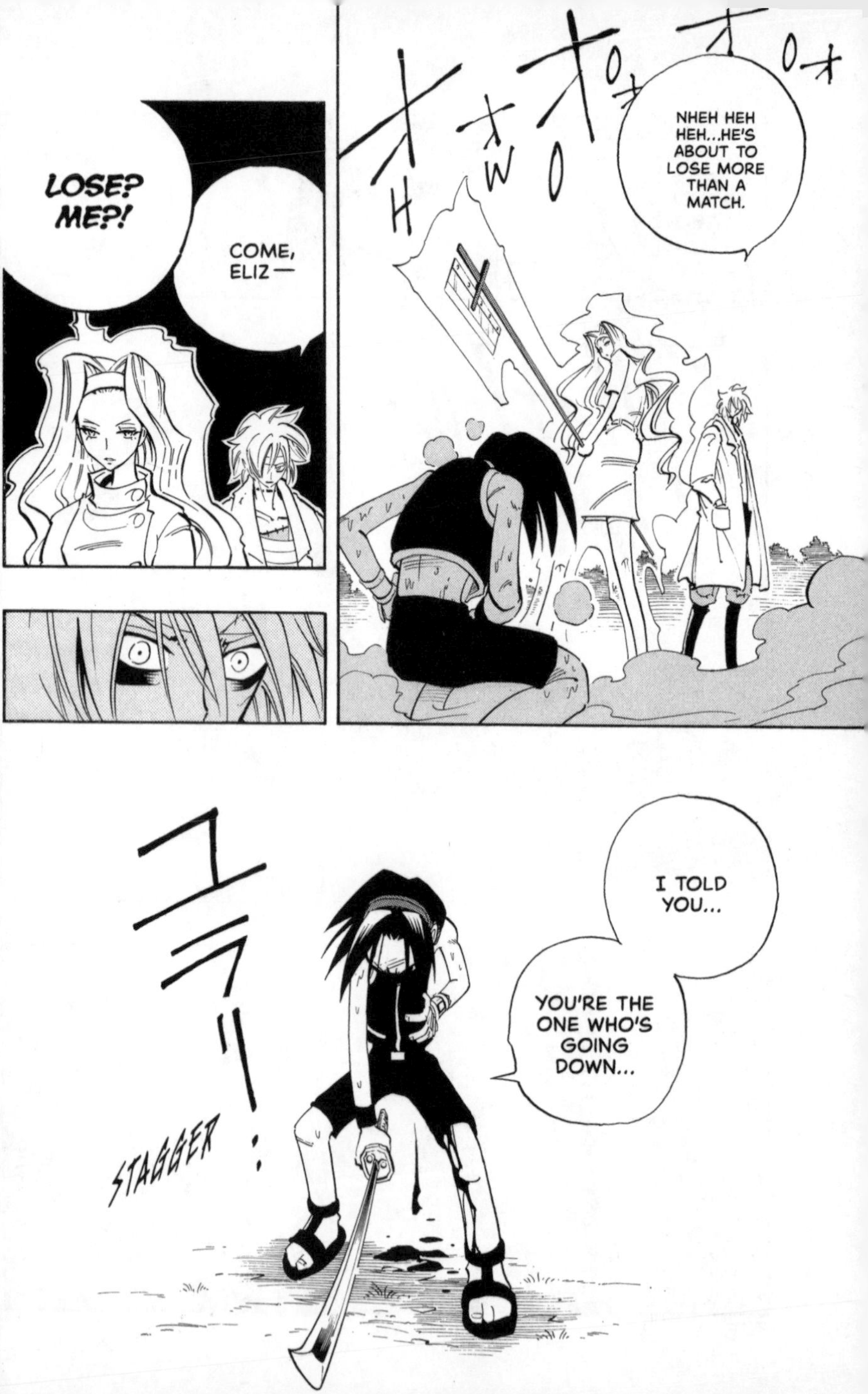
HWO
NHEH HEH HEH...HE'S ABOUT TO LOSE MORE THAN A MATCH.
COME, ELIZ—
LOSE? ME?!
I TOLD YOU...
YOU'RE THE ONE WHO'S GOING DOWN...
STAGGER

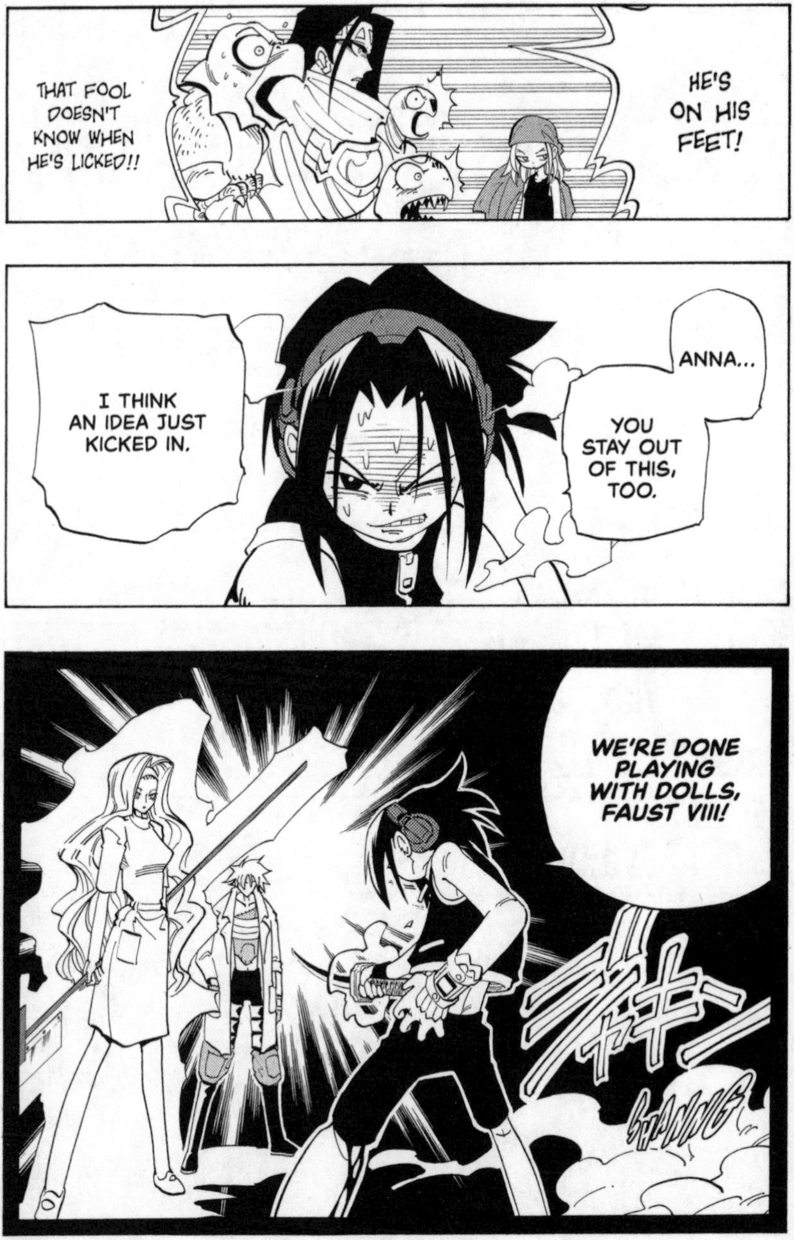
HE'S ON HIS FEET!
THAT FOOL DOESN'T KNOW WHEN HE'S LICKED!!
ANNA...
YOU STAY OUT OF THIS, TOO.
I THINK AN IDEA JUST KICKED IN.
WE'RE DONE PLAYING WITH DOLLS, FAUST VIII!

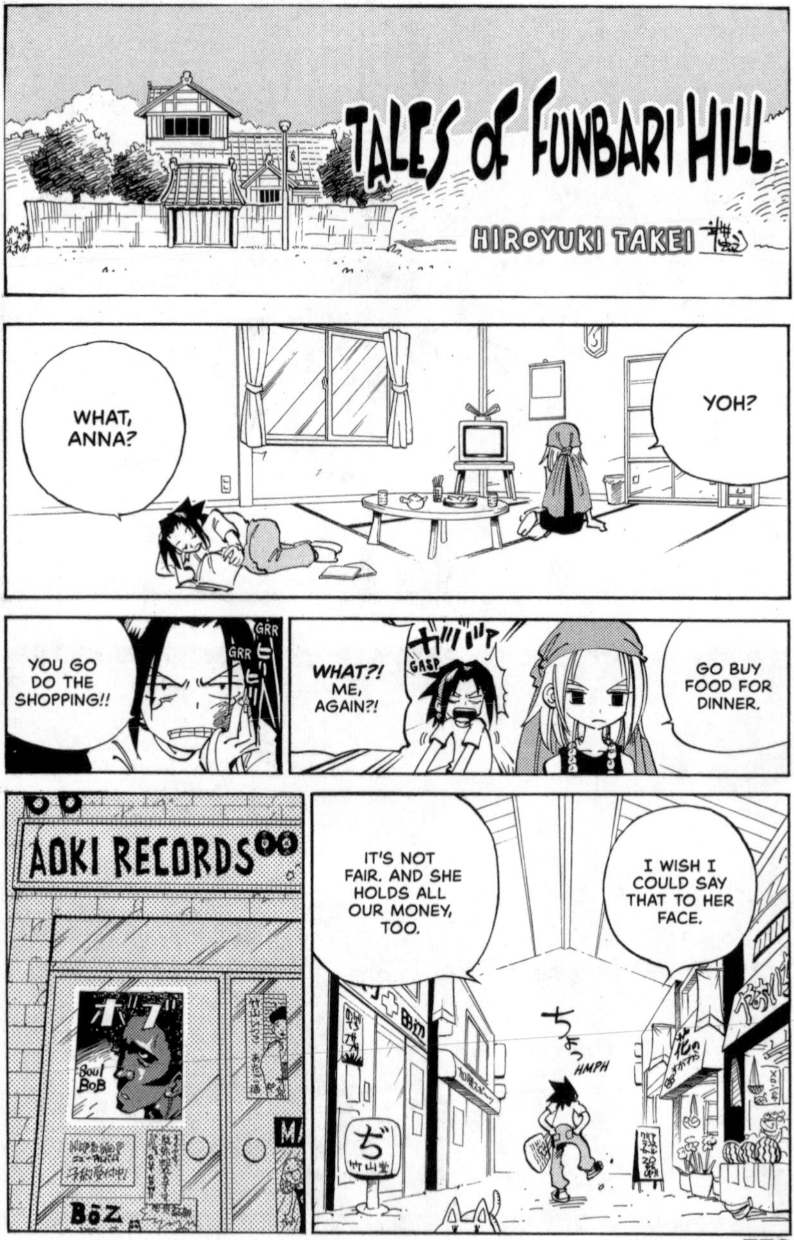
TALES OF FUNBARI HILL
HIROYUKI TAKEI
YOH?
WHAT, ANNA?
GO BUY FOOD FOR DINNER.
WHAT?! ME, AGAIN?!
GASP
GRR
GRR
YOU GO DO THE SHOPPING!!
I WISH I COULD SAY THAT TO HER FACE.
IT'S NOT FAIR. AND SHE HOLDS ALL OUR MONEY, TOO.
HMPH
AOKI RECORDS
Soul BOB
BōZ

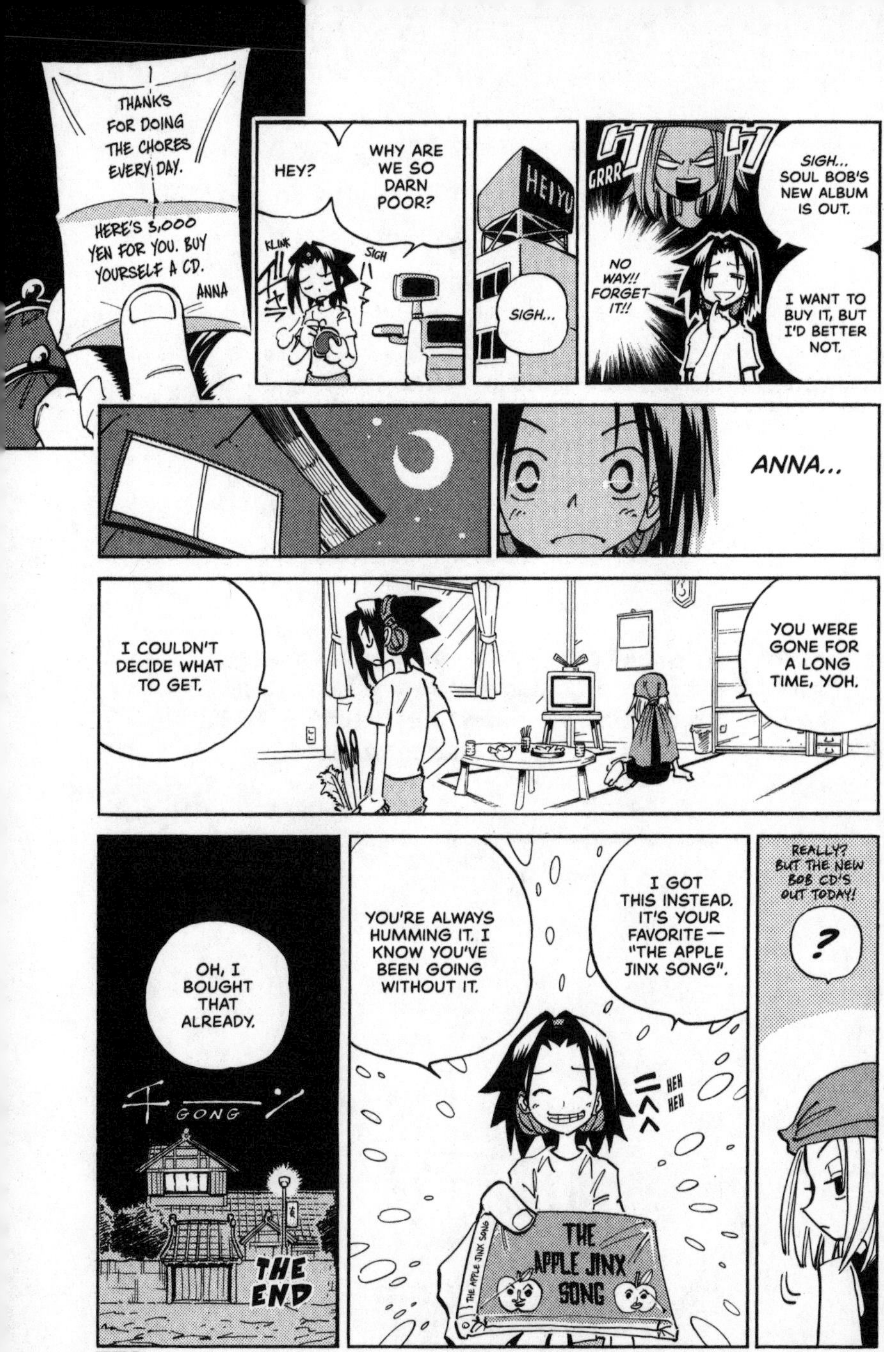
SIGH... SOUL BOB'S NEW ALBUM IS OUT.
I WANT TO BUY IT, BUT I'D BETTER NOT.
GRRR
NO WAY!! FORGET IT!!
HEIYU
SIGH...
WHY ARE WE SO DARN POOR?
HEY?
KLINK
SIGH
THANKS FOR DOING THE CHORES EVERY DAY.
HERE'S 3,000 YEN FOR YOU. BUY YOURSELF A CD.
ANNA
ANNA...
YOU WERE GONE FOR A LONG TIME, YOH.
I COULDN'T DECIDE WHAT TO GET.
REALLY? BUT THE NEW BOB CD'S OUT TODAY!
?
I GOT THIS INSTEAD. IT'S YOUR FAVORITE—"THE APPLE JINX SONG".
YOU'RE ALWAYS HUMMING IT. I KNOW YOU'VE BEEN GOING WITHOUT IT.
HEH HEH
THE APPLE JINX SONG
THE APPLE JINX SONG
OH, I BOUGHT THAT ALREADY.
GONG
THE END

Following this page are the first two *Shaman King* Remix Tracks, bonus chapters first published in 2011, about 13 years after the series began in 1998. This edition presents them alongside the individual volumes that originally included them. Enjoy this alternate take on the story!

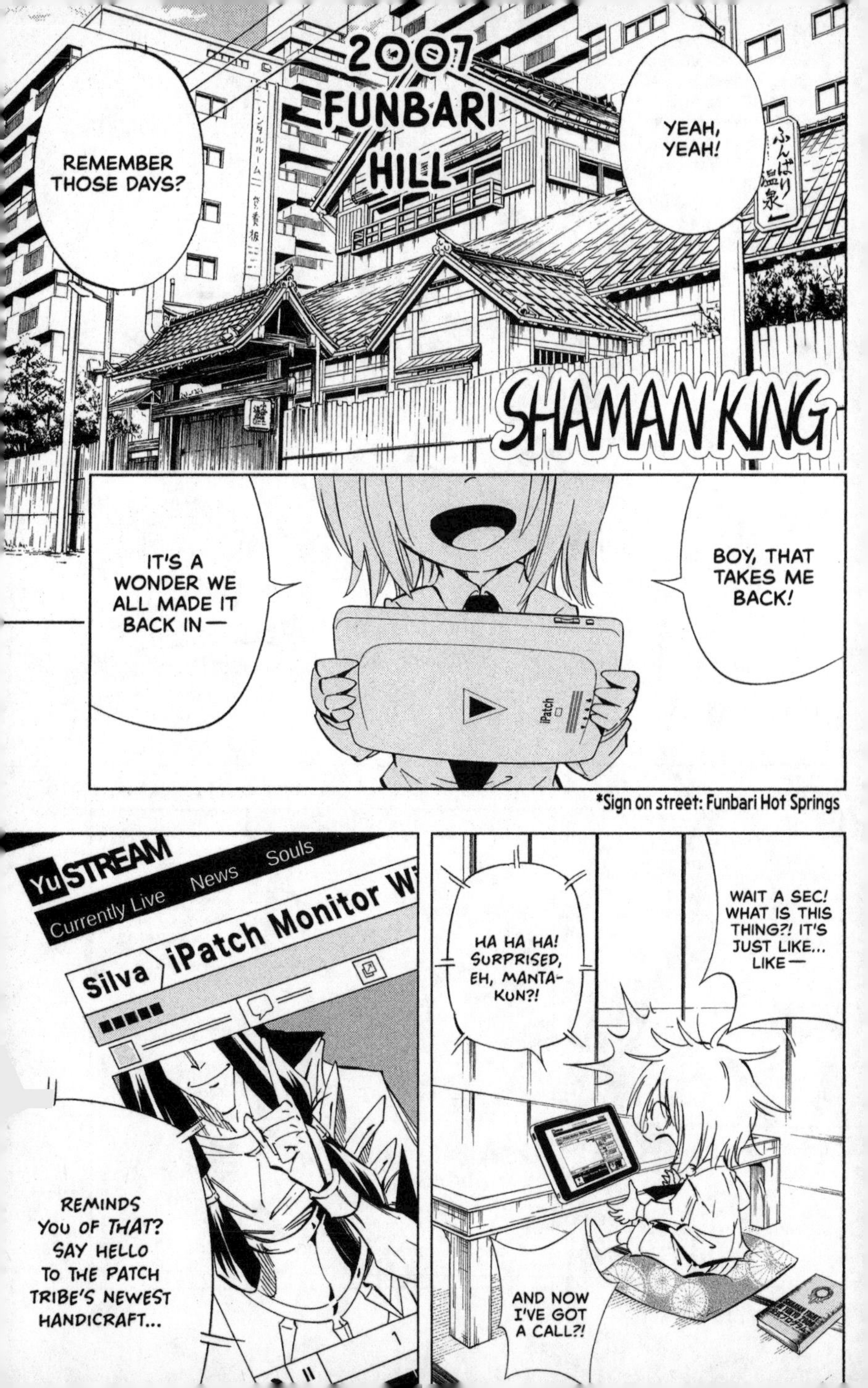
2007 FUNBARI HILL
REMEMBER THOSE DAYS?
YEAH, YEAH!
ふんばり温泉
SHAMAN KING
BOY, THAT TAKES ME BACK!
IT'S A WONDER WE ALL MADE IT BACK IN—
iPatch
WAIT A SEC! WHAT IS THIS THING?! IT'S JUST LIKE... LIKE—
HA HA HA! SURPRISED, EH, MANTA-KUN?!
AND NOW I'VE GOT A CALL?!
YuSTREAM
News
Souls
Currently Live
iPatch Monitor
Silva
REMINDS YOU OF THAT? SAY HELLO TO THE PATCH TRIBE'S NEWEST HANDICRAFT...

*Sign on street: Funbari Hot Springs

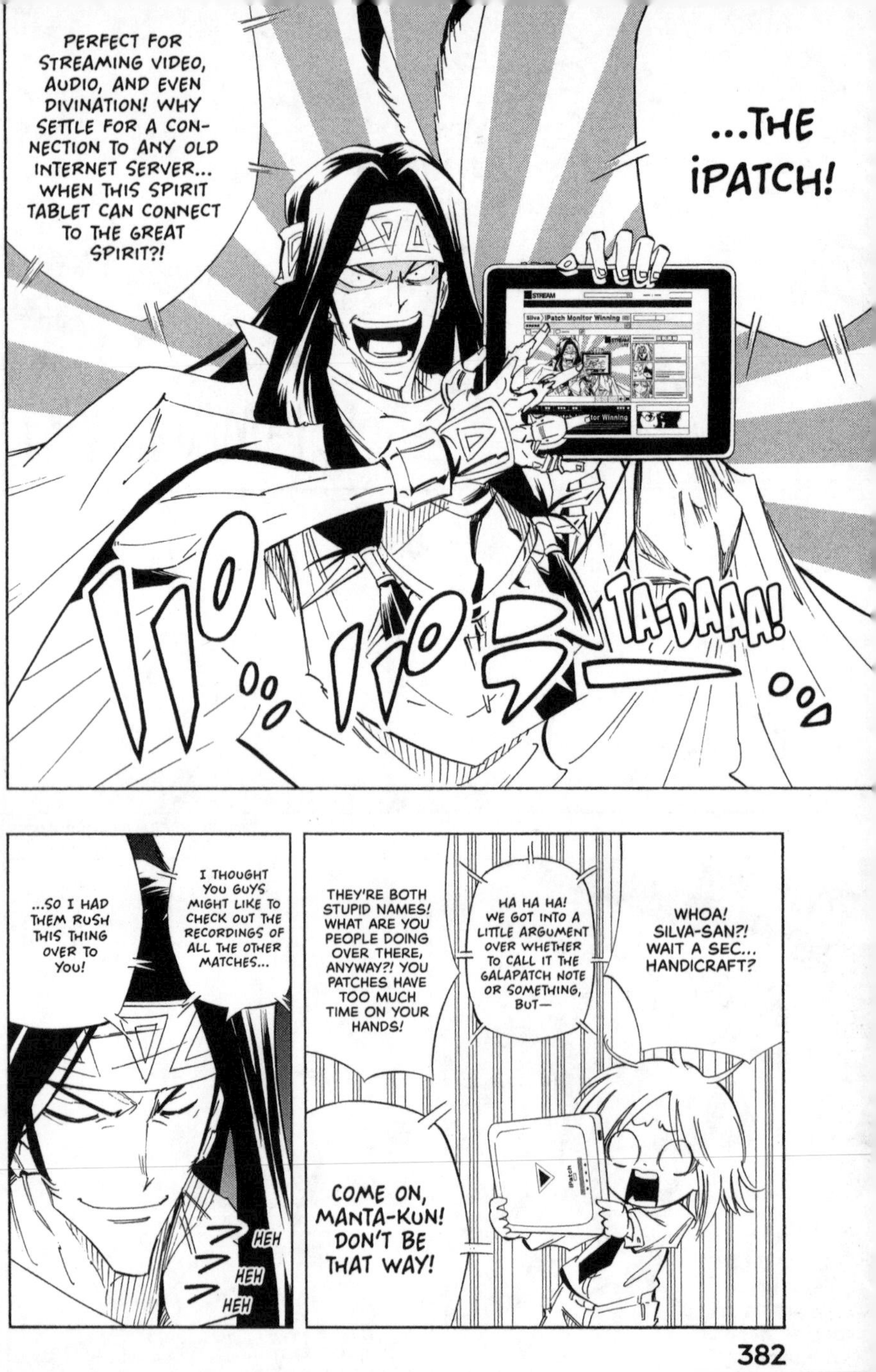
...THE iPATCH!
PERFECT FOR STREAMING VIDEO, AUDIO, AND EVEN DIVINATION! WHY SETTLE FOR A CON-NECTION TO ANY OLD INTERNET SERVER... WHEN THIS SPIRIT TABLET CAN CONNECT TO THE GREAT SPIRIT?!
TA-DAAA!
WHOA! SILVA-SAN?! WAIT A SEC... HANDICRAFT?
HA HA HA! WE GOT INTO A LITTLE ARGUMENT OVER WHETHER TO CALL IT THE GALAPATCH NOTE OR SOMETHING, BUT—
THEY'RE BOTH STUPID NAMES! WHAT ARE YOU PEOPLE DOING OVER THERE, ANYWAY?! YOU PATCHES HAVE TOO MUCH TIME ON YOUR HANDS!
COME ON, MANTA-KUN! DON'T BE THAT WAY!
I THOUGHT YOU GUYS MIGHT LIKE TO CHECK OUT THE RECORDINGS OF ALL THE OTHER MATCHES...
...SO I HAD THEM RUSH THIS THING OVER TO YOU!
HEH
HEH
HEH

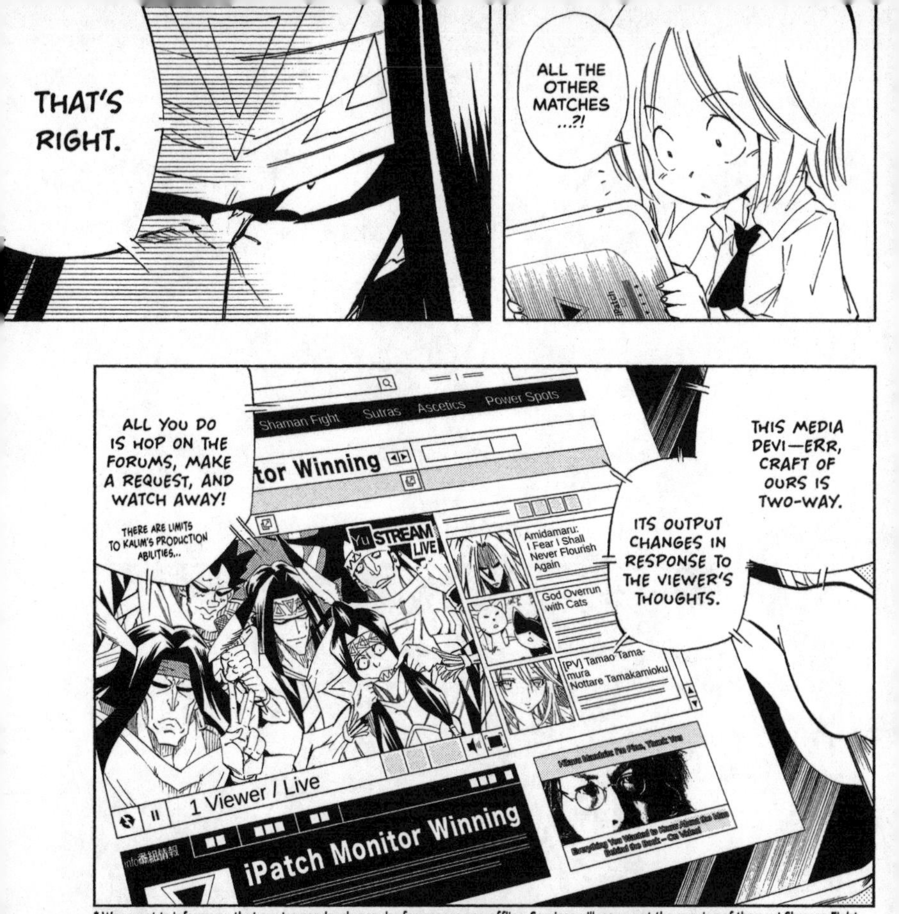
ALL THE OTHER MATCHES ...?!
THAT'S RIGHT.
THIS MEDIA DEVI—ERR, CRAFT OF OURS IS TWO-WAY.
ITS OUTPUT CHANGES IN RESPONSE TO THE VIEWER'S THOUGHTS.
ALL YOU DO IS HOP ON THE FORUMS, MAKE A REQUEST, AND WATCH AWAY!
THERE ARE LIMITS TO KALIM'S PRODUCTION ABILITIES...
Shaman Fight
Sutras
Ascetics
Power Spots
tor Winning
YU STREAM LIVE
Amidamaru: I Fear I Shall Never Flourish Again
God Overrun with Cats
[PV] Tamao Tamamura Nottare Tamakamioku
1 Viewer / Live
info番組情報
iPatch Monitor Winning

* We regret to inform you that our tremendously popular forums are now offline. Services will resume at the opening of the next Shaman Fight (approx. 500 years from date of publication).

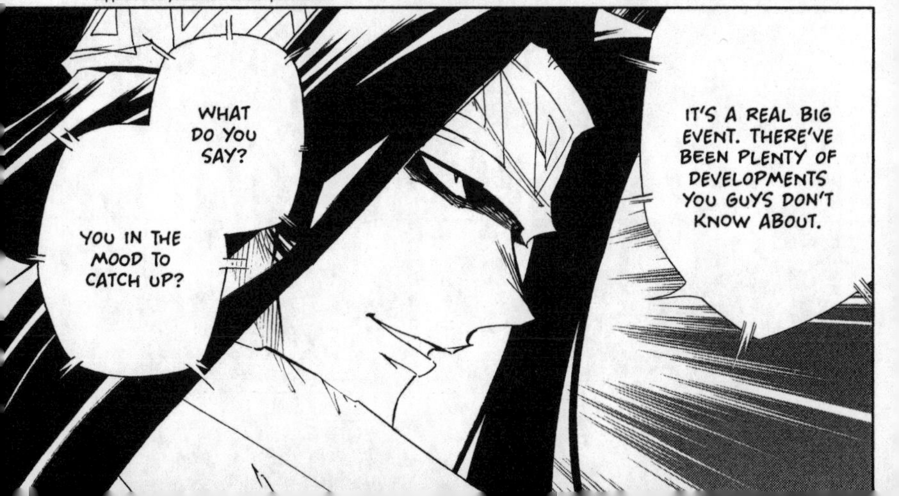
IT'S A REAL BIG EVENT. THERE'VE BEEN PLENTY OF DEVELOPMENTS YOU GUYS DON'T KNOW ABOUT.
WHAT DO YOU SAY?
YOU IN THE MOOD TO CATCH UP?

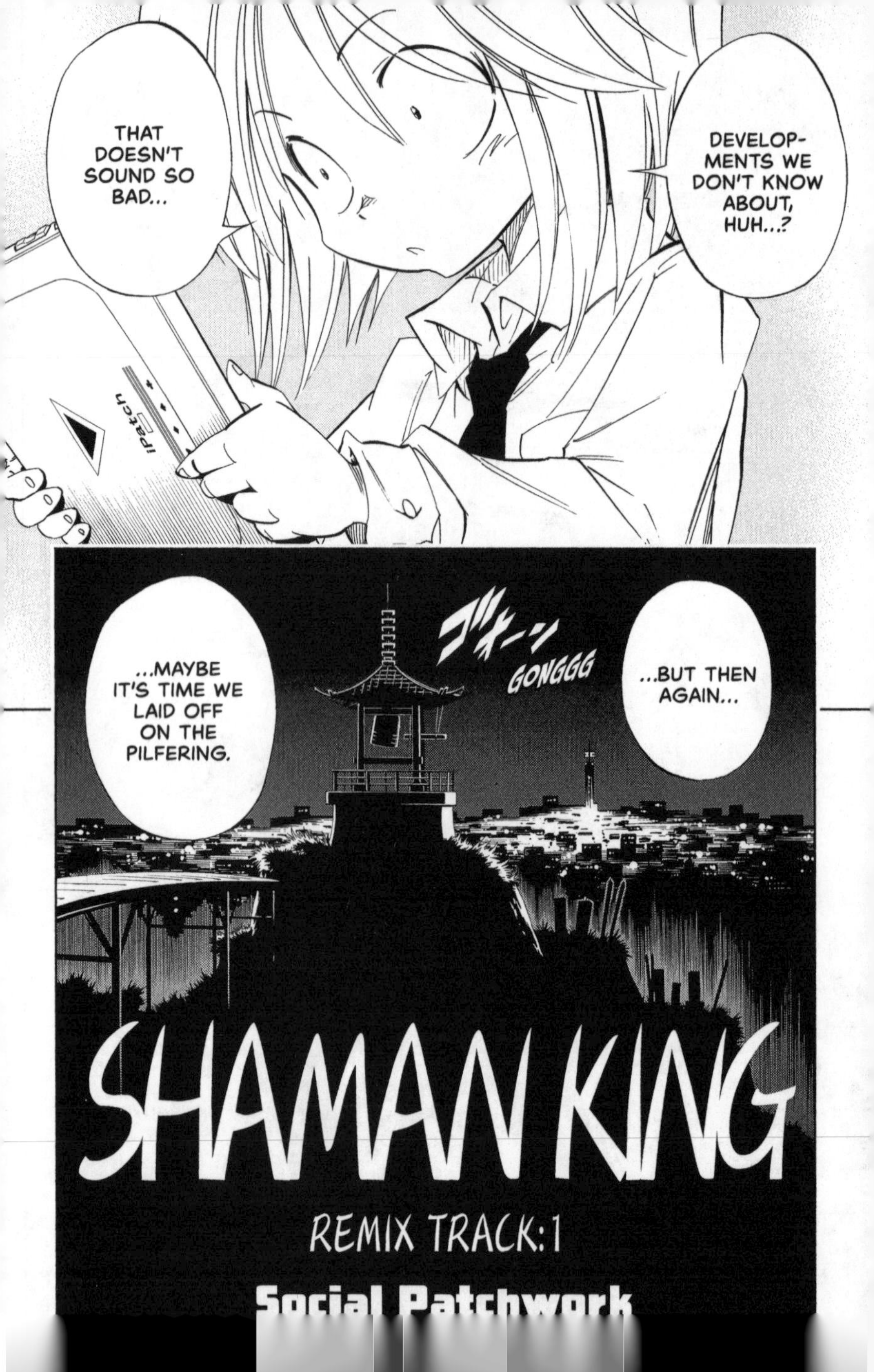
DEVELOPMENTS WE DON'T KNOW ABOUT, HUH...?
THAT DOESN'T SOUND SO BAD...
iPatch
...BUT THEN AGAIN...
GONGGG
...MAYBE IT'S TIME WE LAID OFF ON THE PILFERING.
SHAMAN KING
REMIX TRACK:1
Social Patchwork

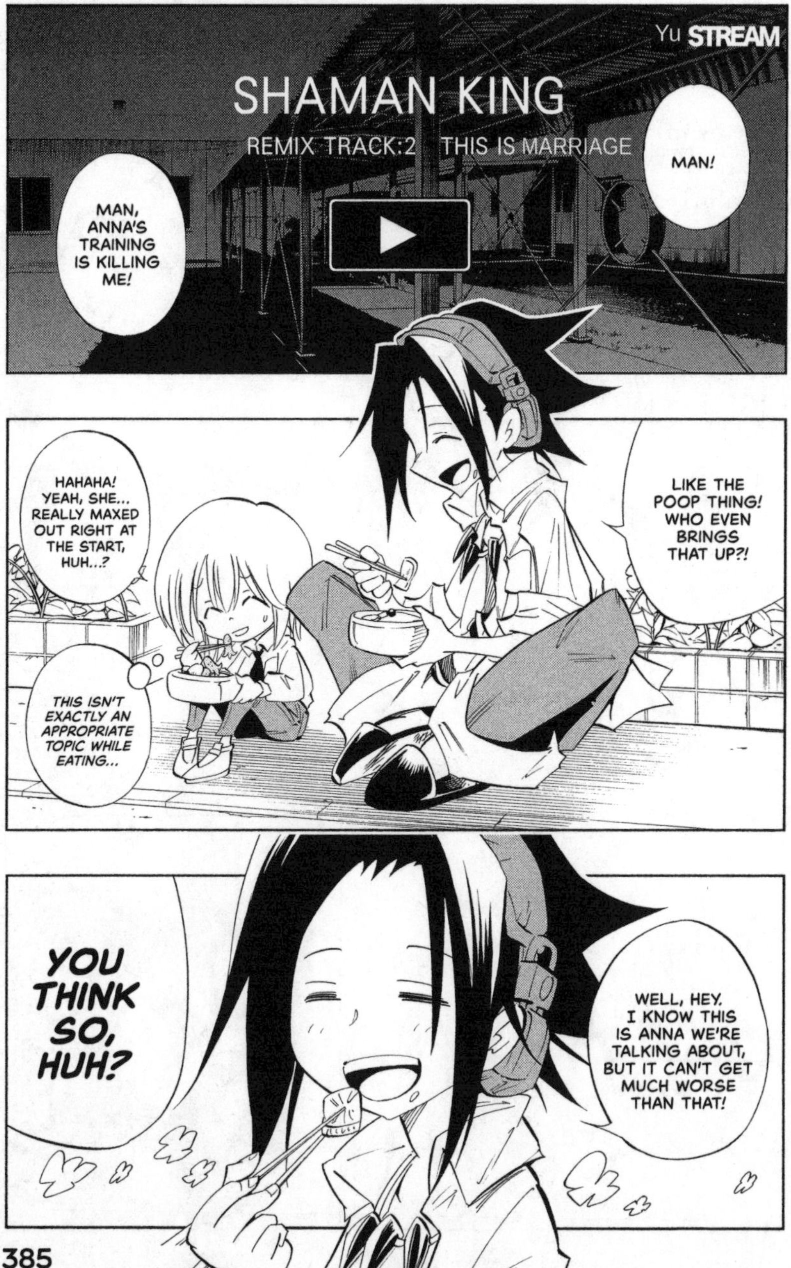
Yu STREAM
SHAMAN KING
REMIX TRACK:2 THIS IS MARRIAGE
MAN!
MAN, ANNA'S TRAINING IS KILLING ME!
LIKE THE POOP THING! WHO EVEN BRINGS THAT UP?!
HAHAHA! YEAH, SHE... REALLY MAXED OUT RIGHT AT THE START, HUH...?
THIS ISN'T EXACTLY AN APPROPRIATE TOPIC WHILE EATING...
WELL, HEY. I KNOW THIS IS ANNA WE'RE TALKING ABOUT, BUT IT CAN'T GET MUCH WORSE THAN THAT!
YOU THINK SO, HUH?

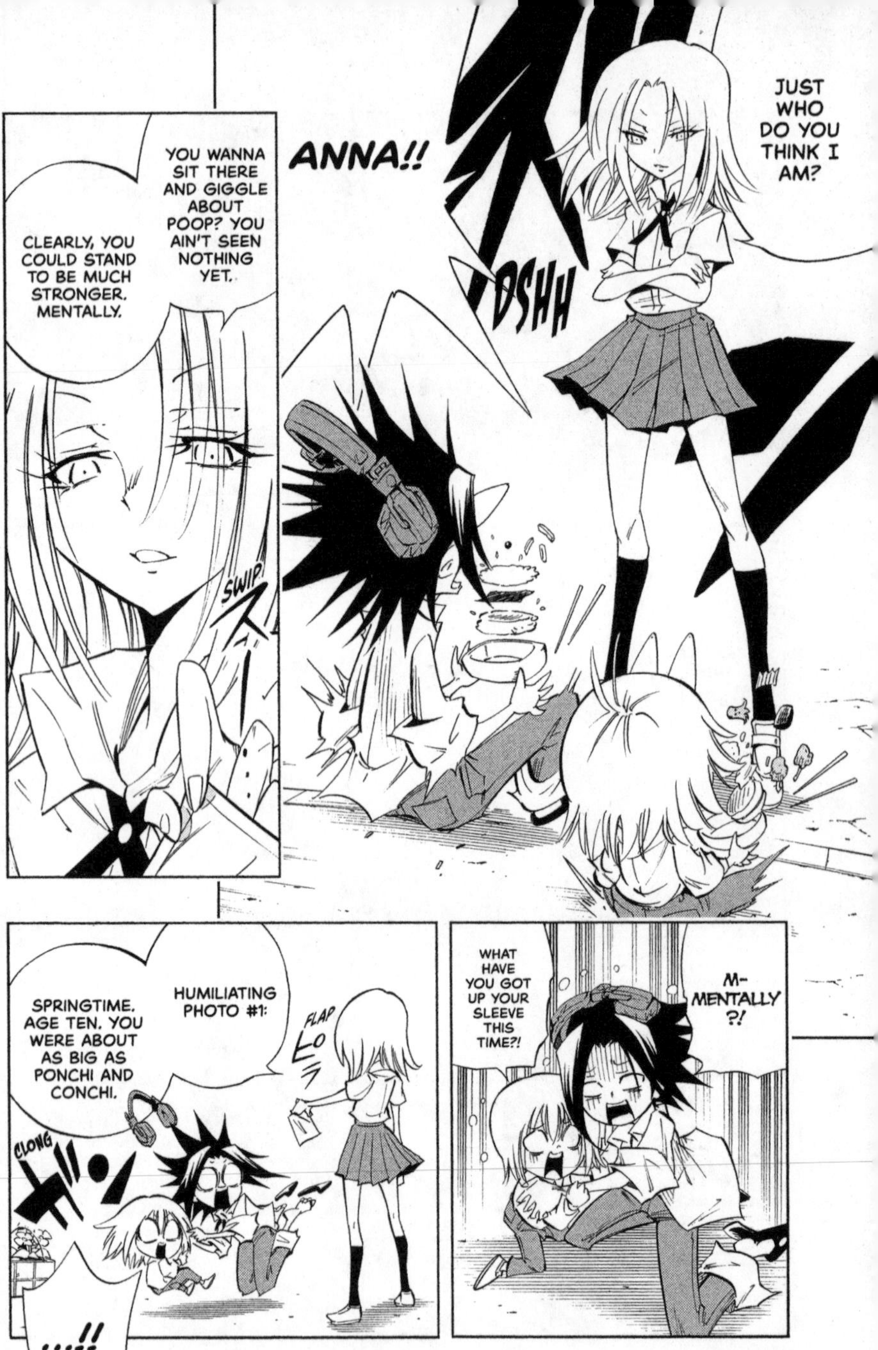
JUST WHO DO YOU THINK I AM?
ANNA!!
DSHH
YOU WANNA SIT THERE AND GIGGLE ABOUT POOP? YOU AIN'T SEEN NOTHING YET.
CLEARLY, YOU COULD STAND TO BE MUCH STRONGER. MENTALLY.
SWIP
M-MENTALLY?!
WHAT HAVE YOU GOT UP YOUR SLEEVE THIS TIME?!
HUMILIATING PHOTO #1:
SPRINGTIME. AGE TEN. YOU WERE ABOUT AS BIG AS PONCHI AND CONCHI.
FLAP
CLONG
...!!

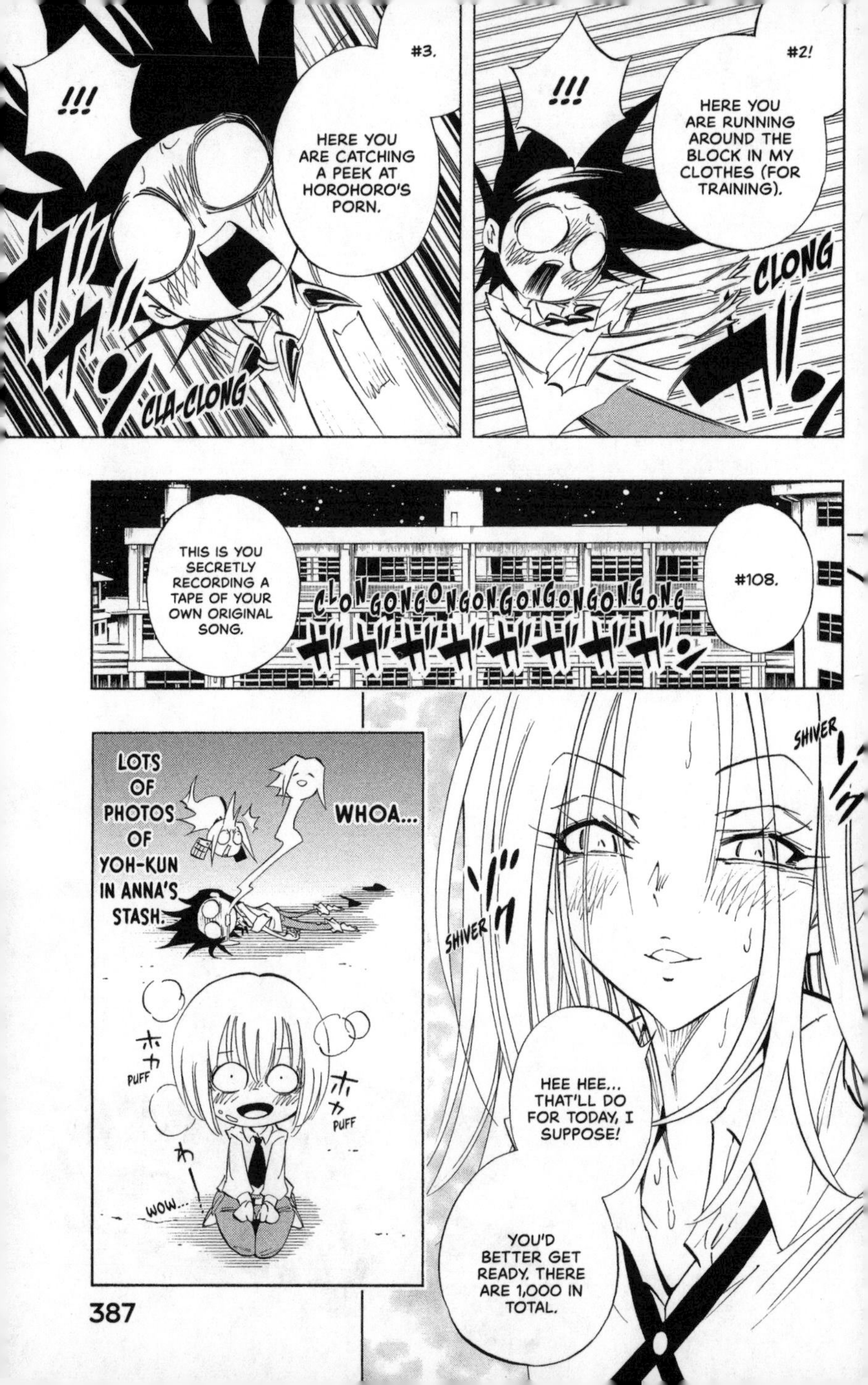
#2!
!!!
HERE YOU ARE RUNNING AROUND THE BLOCK IN MY CLOTHES (FOR TRAINING).
CLONG
#3.
!!!
HERE YOU ARE CATCHING A PEEK AT HOROHORO'S PORN.
CLA-CLONG
#108.
THIS IS YOU SECRETLY RECORDING A TAPE OF YOUR OWN ORIGINAL SONG.
CLONGONGONGONGONGONGONGONG
SHIVER
SHIVER
HEE HEE... THAT'LL DO FOR TODAY, I SUPPOSE!
YOU'D BETTER GET READY. THERE ARE 1,000 IN TOTAL.
LOTS OF PHOTOS OF YOH-KUN IN ANNA'S STASH.
WHOA...
PUFF
PUFF
WOW...

SHAMAN KING

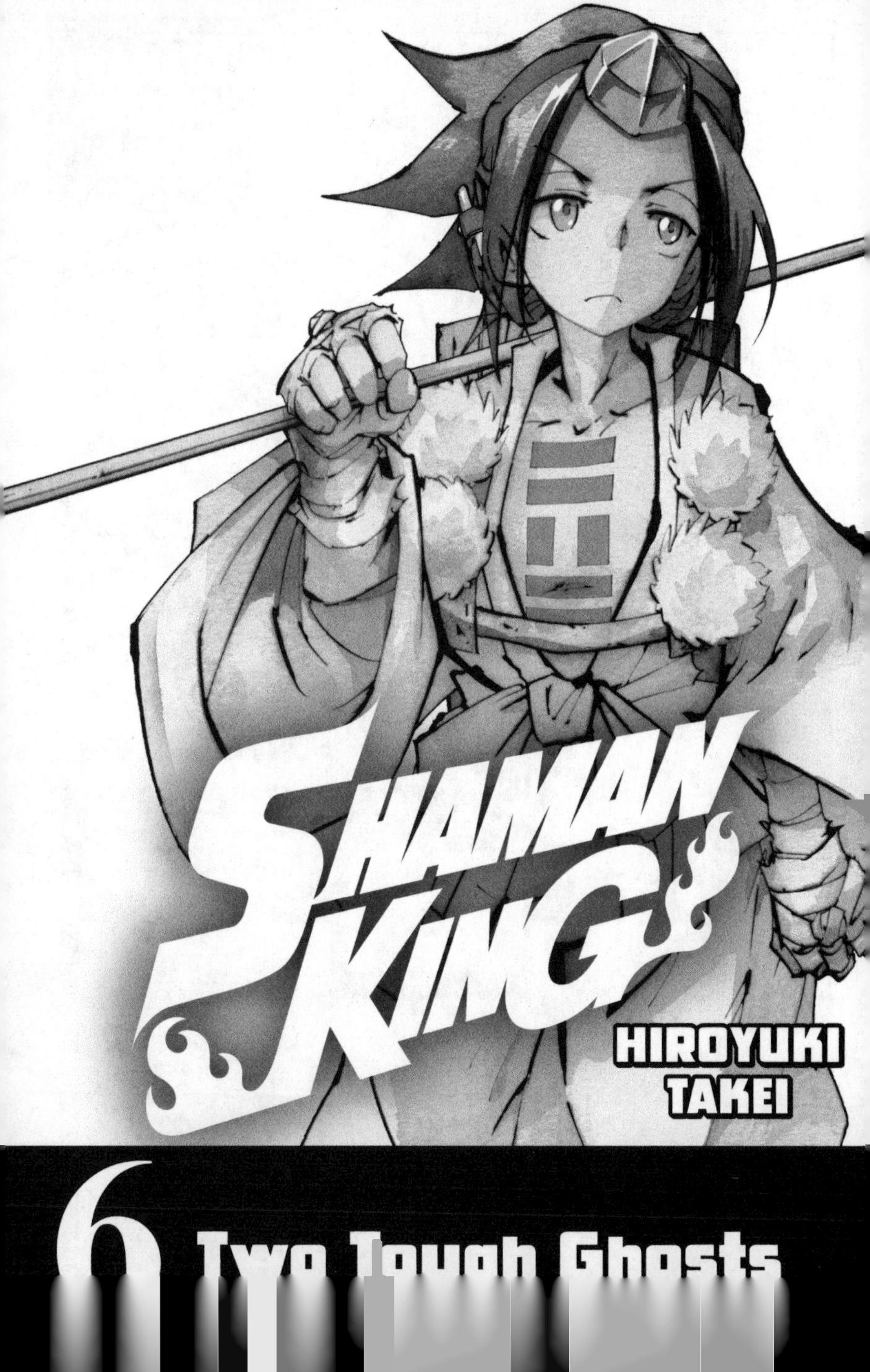

SHAMAN KING

HIROYUKI TAKEI

6 Two Tough Ghosts

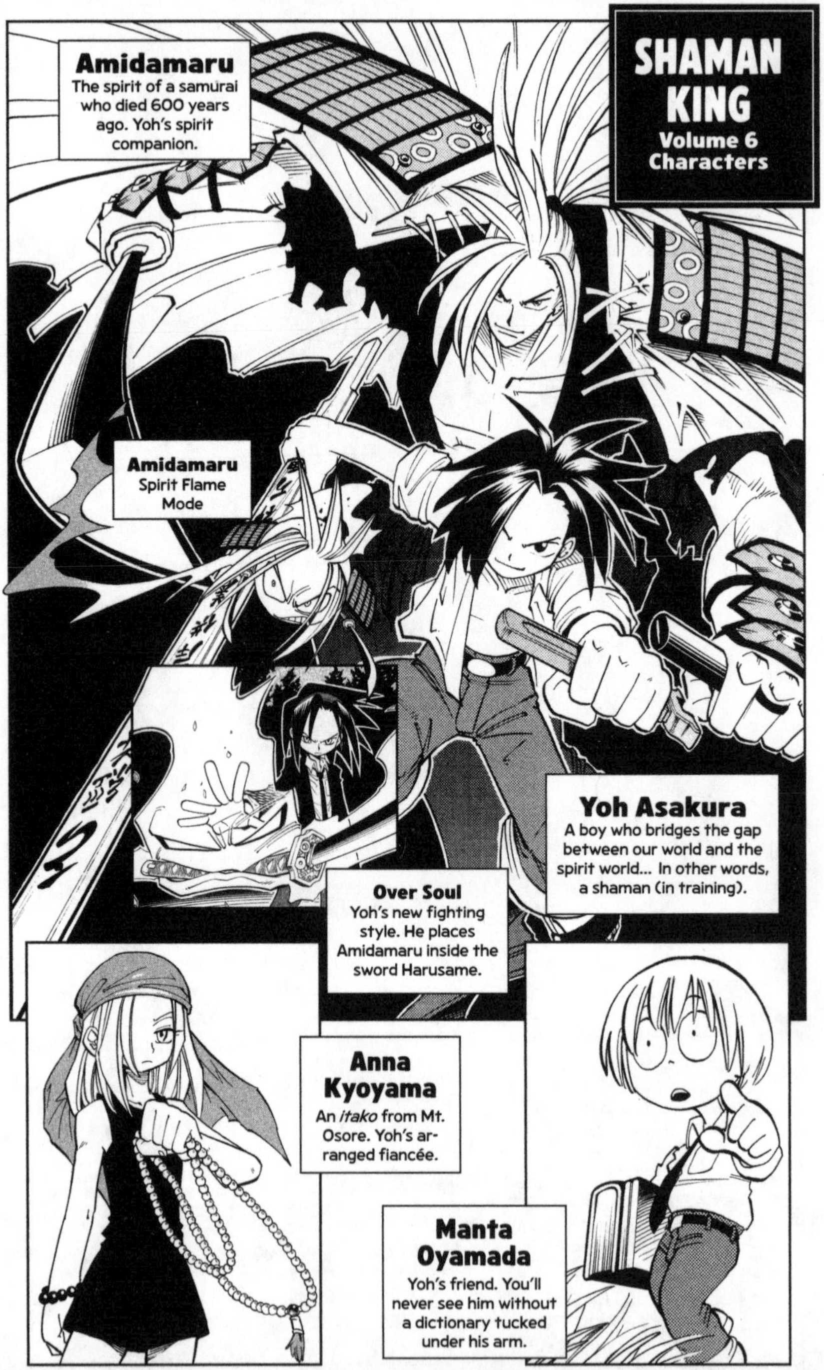
SHAMAN KING
Volume 6 Characters
Amidamaru
The spirit of a samurai who died 600 years ago. Yoh's spirit companion.
Amidamaru
Spirit Flame Mode
Yoh Asakura
A boy who bridges the gap between our world and the spirit world... In other words, a shaman (in training).
Over Soul
Yoh's new fighting style. He places Amidamaru inside the sword Harusame.
Anna Kyoyama
An *itako* from Mt. Osore. Yoh's arranged fiancée.
Manta Oyamada
Yoh's friend. You'll never see him without a dictionary tucked under his arm.

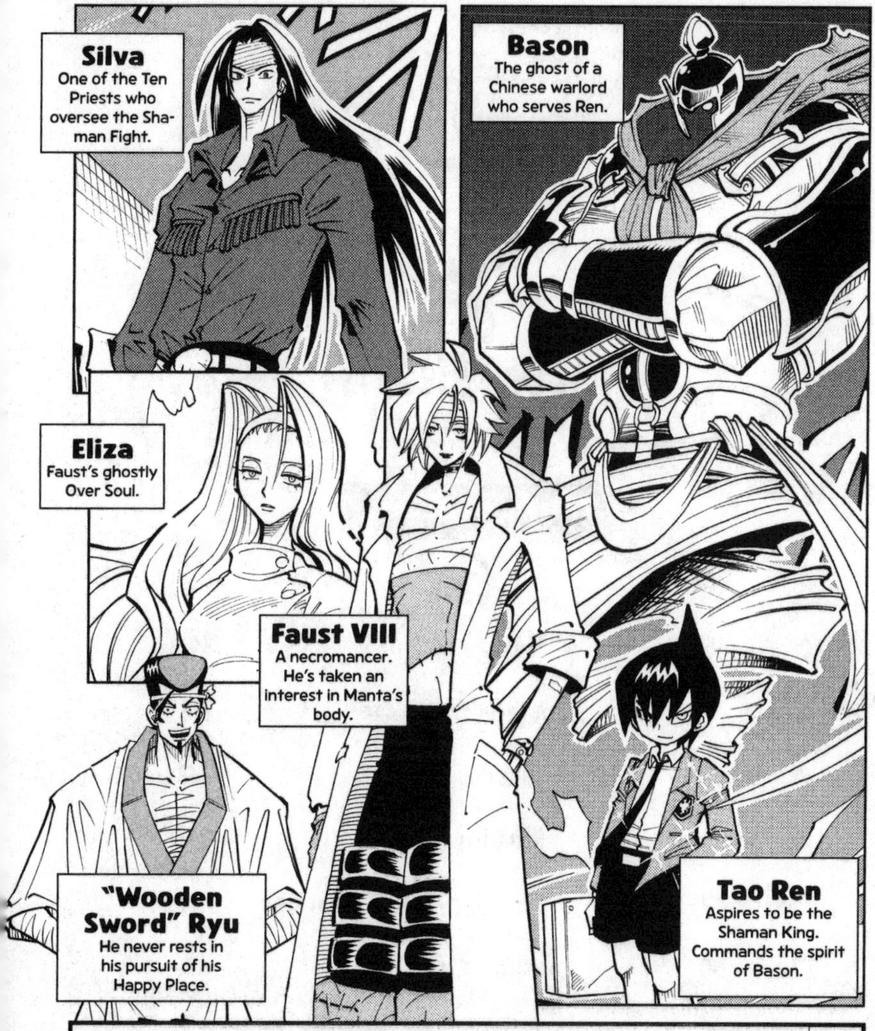
Bason
The ghost of a Chinese warlord who serves Ren.
Silva
One of the Ten Priests who oversee the Shaman Fight.
Eliza
Faust's ghostly Over Soul.
Faust VIII
A necromancer. He's taken an interest in Manta's body.
Tao Ren
Aspires to be the Shaman King. Commands the spirit of Bason.
"Wooden Sword" Ryu
He never rests in his pursuit of his Happy Place.

THE STORY SO FAR

This kid named Yoh Asakura-kun transferred to my class from Izumo... and it turns out he's a shaman! It seems shamans can bridge the gap between the spirit world and our world, commune with gods and spirits, and even draw on their strength. He came here to hone his abilities and took the ghost of Amidamaru, a samurai who died 600 years ago, as his spirit companion. The Shaman Fight that occurs every 500 years has officially begun. Yoh advanced to the next round and now faces his second battle. His opponent, Faust VIII, unleashes deadly tactics that deplete Yoh of his mana, putting his chances—and his life—at serious risk.

SHAMAN KING

6
TABLE OF CONTENTS

Two Tough Ghosts

6

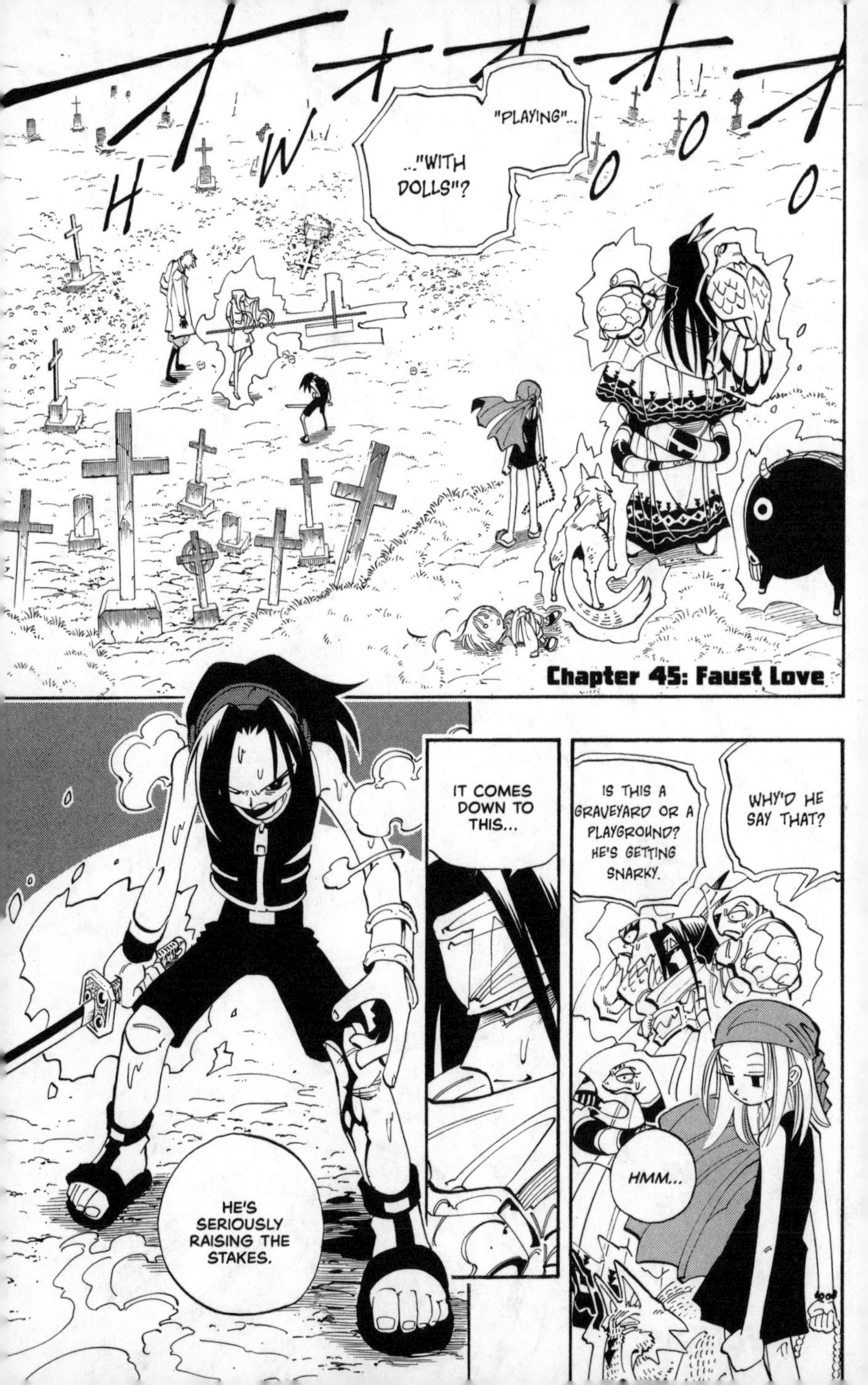
HWOOOO
"PLAYING"...
..."WITH DOLLS"?
Chapter 45: Faust Love
WHY'D HE SAY THAT?
IS THIS A GRAVEYARD OR A PLAYGROUND? HE'S GETTING SNARKY.
HMM...
IT COMES DOWN TO THIS...
HE'S SERIOUSLY RAISING THE STAKES.

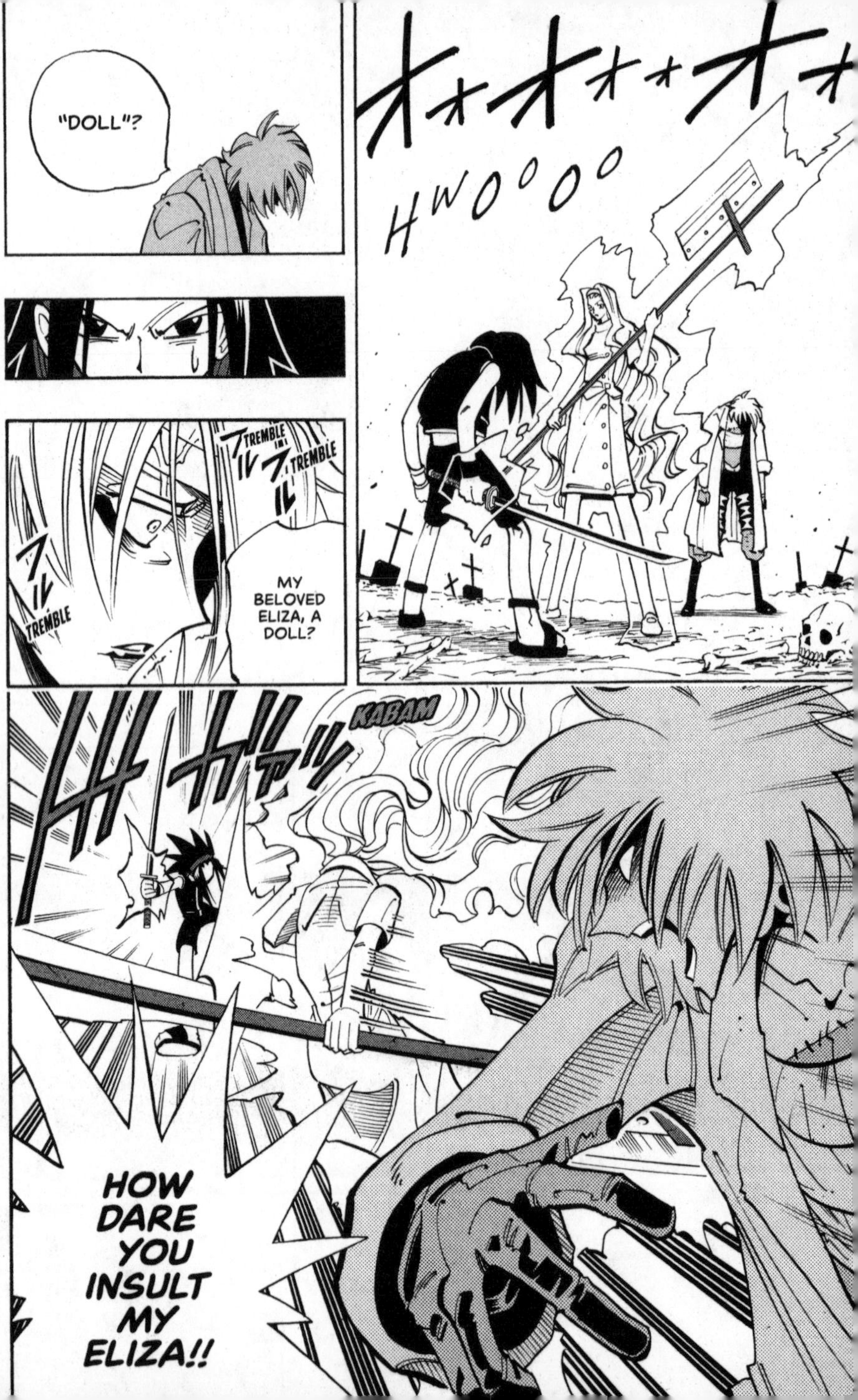

オォオォォオォ
HWOOOO
"DOLL"?
ブル
TREMBLE
ブル
TREMBLE
ブル
TREMBLE
MY BELOVED ELIZA, A DOLL?
ドガァッ
KABAM
HOW DARE YOU INSULT MY ELIZA!!

Chapter 45:
Faust Love

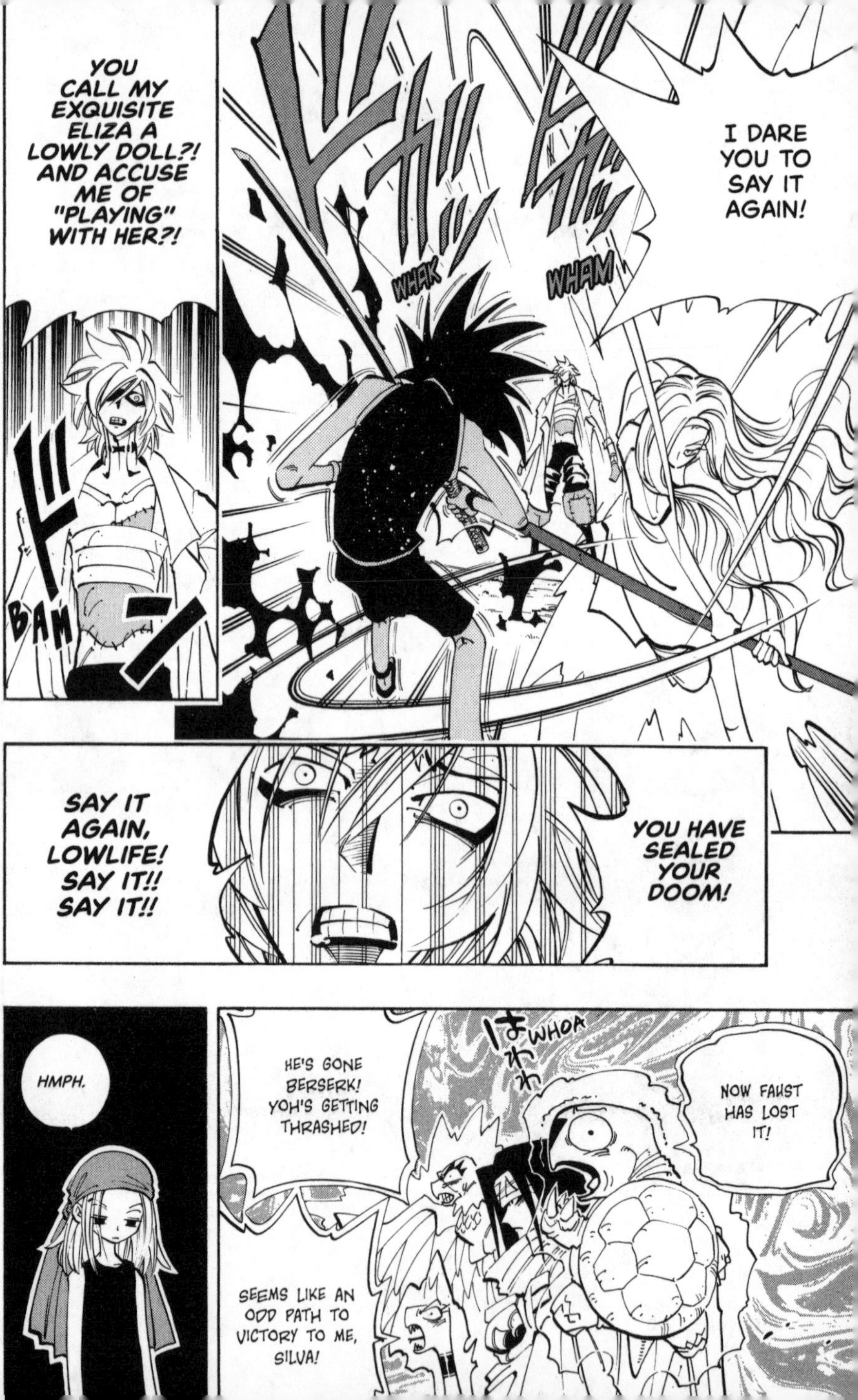
I DARE YOU TO SAY IT AGAIN!
WHAM
WHAK
YOU CALL MY EXQUISITE ELIZA A LOWLY DOLL?! AND ACCUSE ME OF "PLAYING" WITH HER?!
BAM
YOU HAVE SEALED YOUR DOOM!
SAY IT AGAIN, LOWLIFE! SAY IT!! SAY IT!!
WHOA
NOW FAUST HAS LOST IT!
HE'S GONE BERSERK! YOH'S GETTING THRASHED!
SEEMS LIKE AN ODD PATH TO VICTORY TO ME, SILVA!
HMPH.

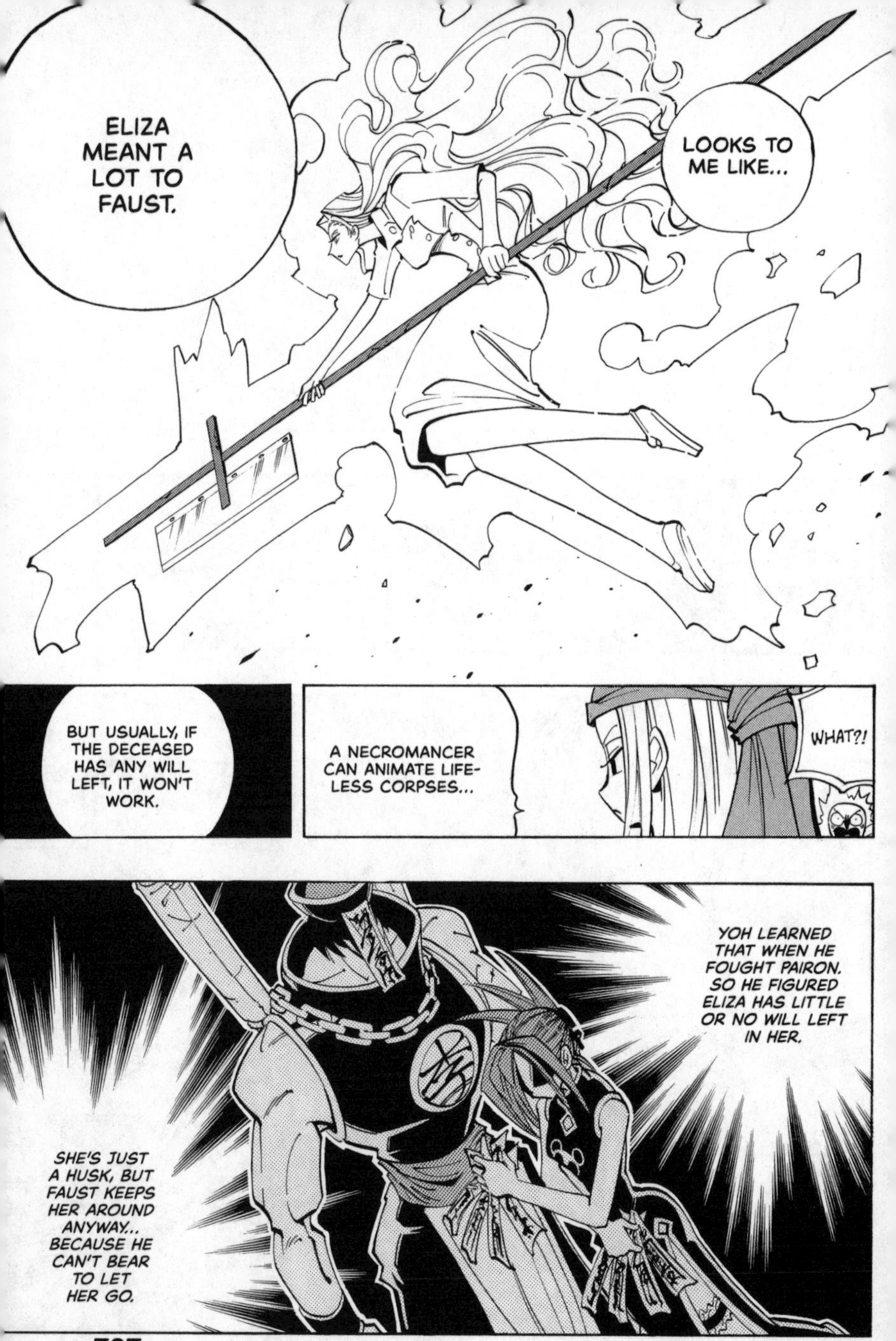
LOOKS TO ME LIKE...
ELIZA MEANT A LOT TO FAUST.
WHAT?!
A NECROMANCER CAN ANIMATE LIFE-LESS CORPSES...
BUT USUALLY, IF THE DECEASED HAS ANY WILL LEFT, IT WON'T WORK.
YOH LEARNED THAT WHEN HE FOUGHT PAIRON. SO HE FIGURED ELIZA HAS LITTLE OR NO WILL LEFT IN HER.
SHE'S JUST A HUSK, BUT FAUST KEEPS HER AROUND ANYWAY... BECAUSE HE CAN'T BEAR TO LET HER GO.

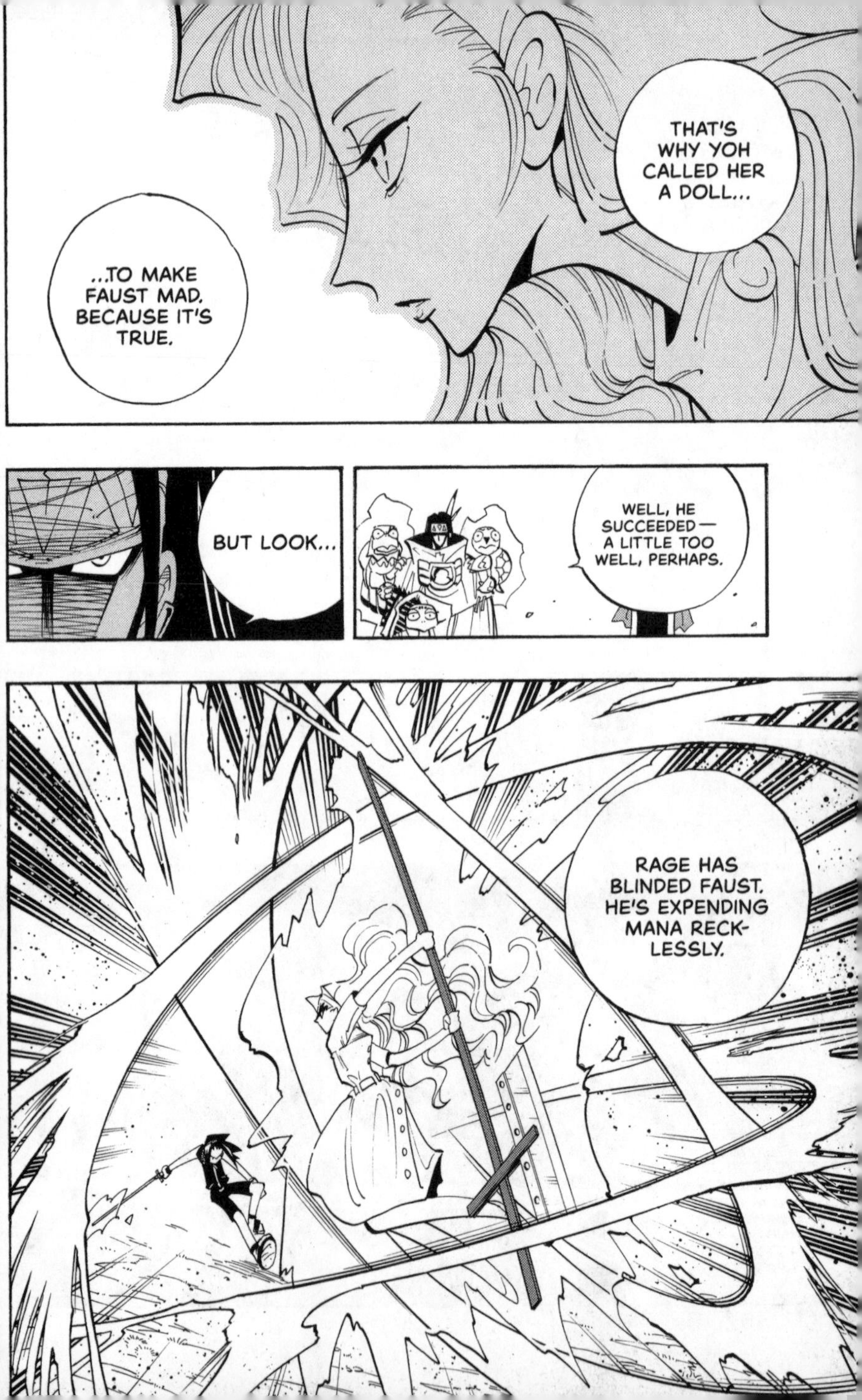
THAT'S WHY YOH CALLED HER A DOLL...
...TO MAKE FAUST MAD. BECAUSE IT'S TRUE.
WELL, HE SUCCEEDED— A LITTLE TOO WELL, PERHAPS.
BUT LOOK...
RAGE HAS BLINDED FAUST. HE'S EXPENDING MANA RECK-LESSLY.

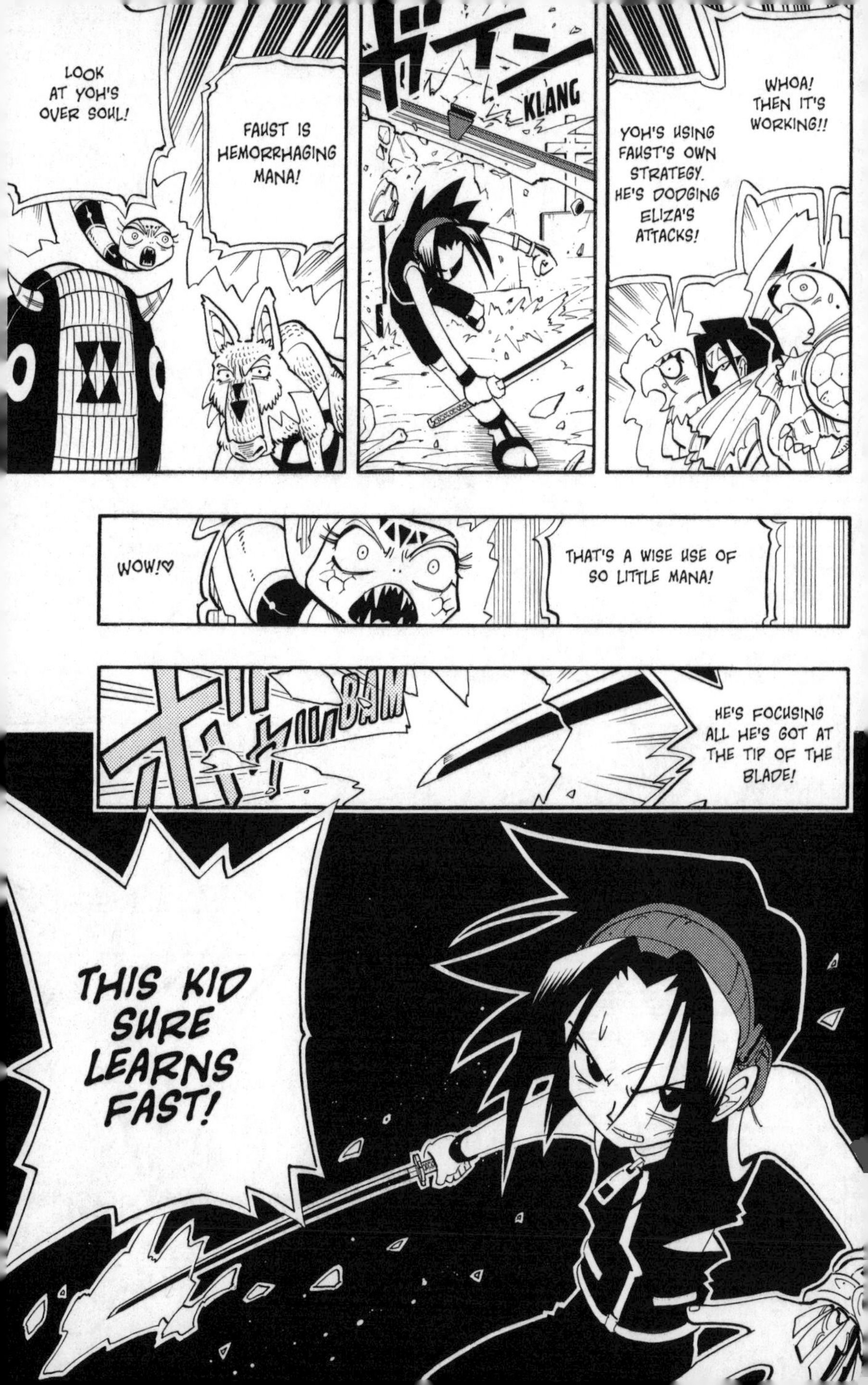
WHOA! THEN IT'S WORKING!!
YOH'S USING FAUST'S OWN STRATEGY. HE'S DODGING ELIZA'S ATTACKS!
KLANG
FAUST IS HEMORRHAGING MANA!
LOOK AT YOH'S OVER SOUL!
THAT'S A WISE USE OF SO LITTLE MANA!
WOW!♡
HE'S FOCUSING ALL HE'S GOT AT THE TIP OF THE BLADE!
BAM
THIS KID SURE LEARNS FAST!

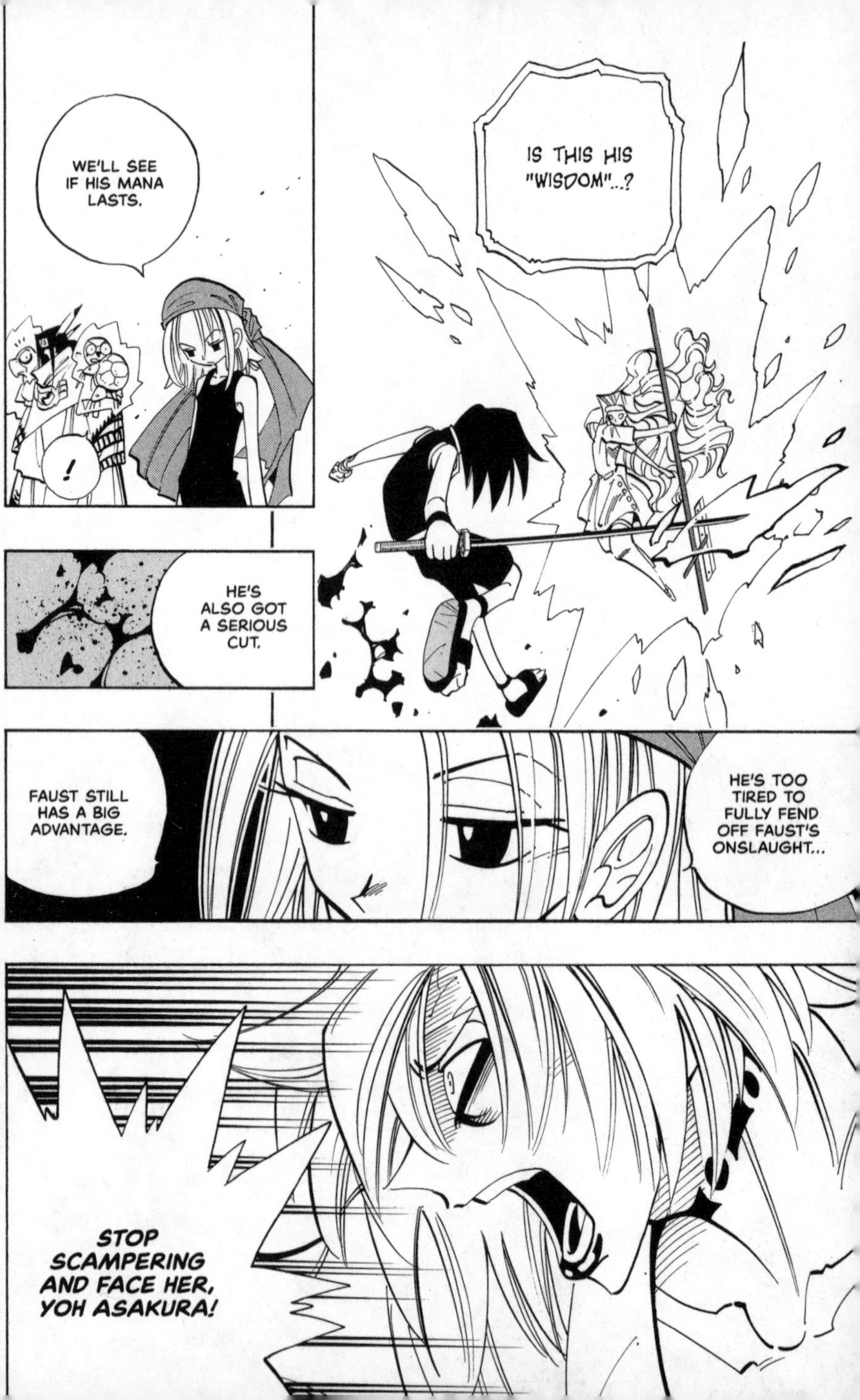
IS THIS HIS "WISDOM"...?
WE'LL SEE IF HIS MANA LASTS.
!
HE'S ALSO GOT A SERIOUS CUT.
HE'S TOO TIRED TO FULLY FEND OFF FAUST'S ONSLAUGHT...
FAUST STILL HAS A BIG ADVANTAGE.
STOP SCAMPERING AND FACE HER, YOH ASAKURA!

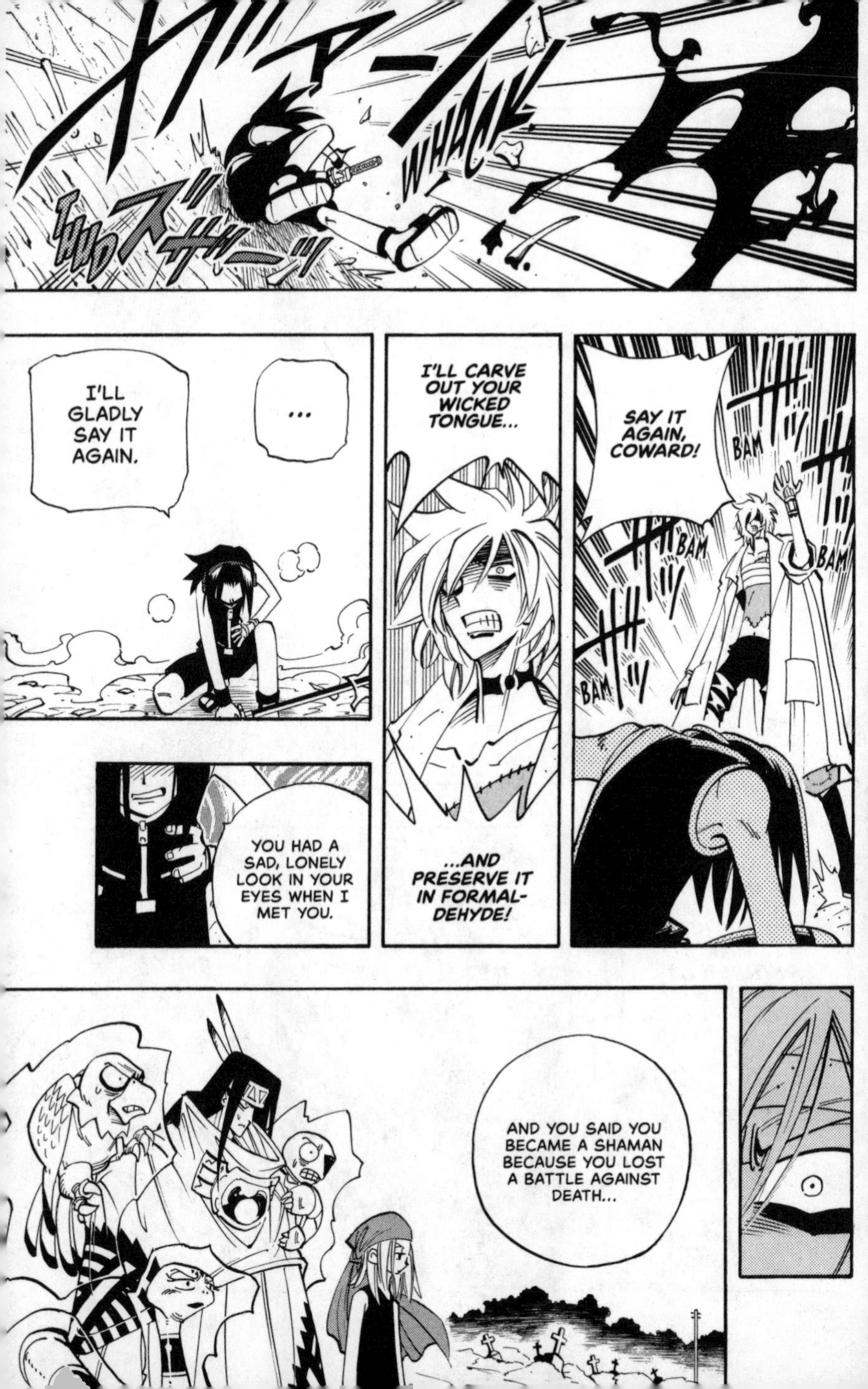
WHACK
THUD
SAY IT AGAIN, COWARD!
BAM
BAM
BAM
BAM
I'LL CARVE OUT YOUR WICKED TONGUE...
...AND PRESERVE IT IN FORMAL-DEHYDE!
...
I'LL GLADLY SAY IT AGAIN.
YOU HAD A SAD, LONELY LOOK IN YOUR EYES WHEN I MET YOU.
AND YOU SAID YOU BECAME A SHAMAN BECAUSE YOU LOST A BATTLE AGAINST DEATH...

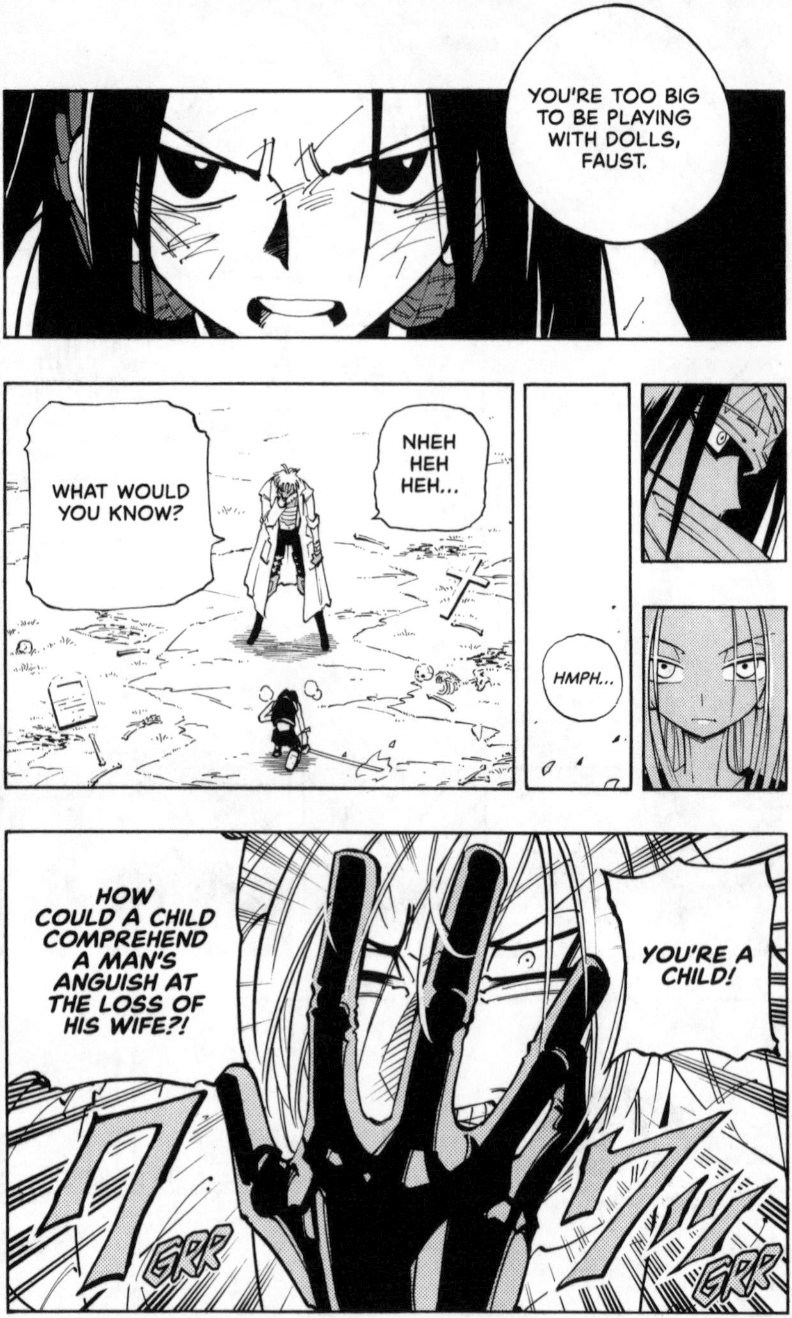
YOU'RE TOO BIG TO BE PLAYING WITH DOLLS, FAUST.
HMPH...
NHEH HEH HEH...
WHAT WOULD YOU KNOW?
YOU'RE A CHILD!
HOW COULD A CHILD COMPREHEND A MAN'S ANGUISH AT THE LOSS OF HIS WIFE?!
GRR
GRR

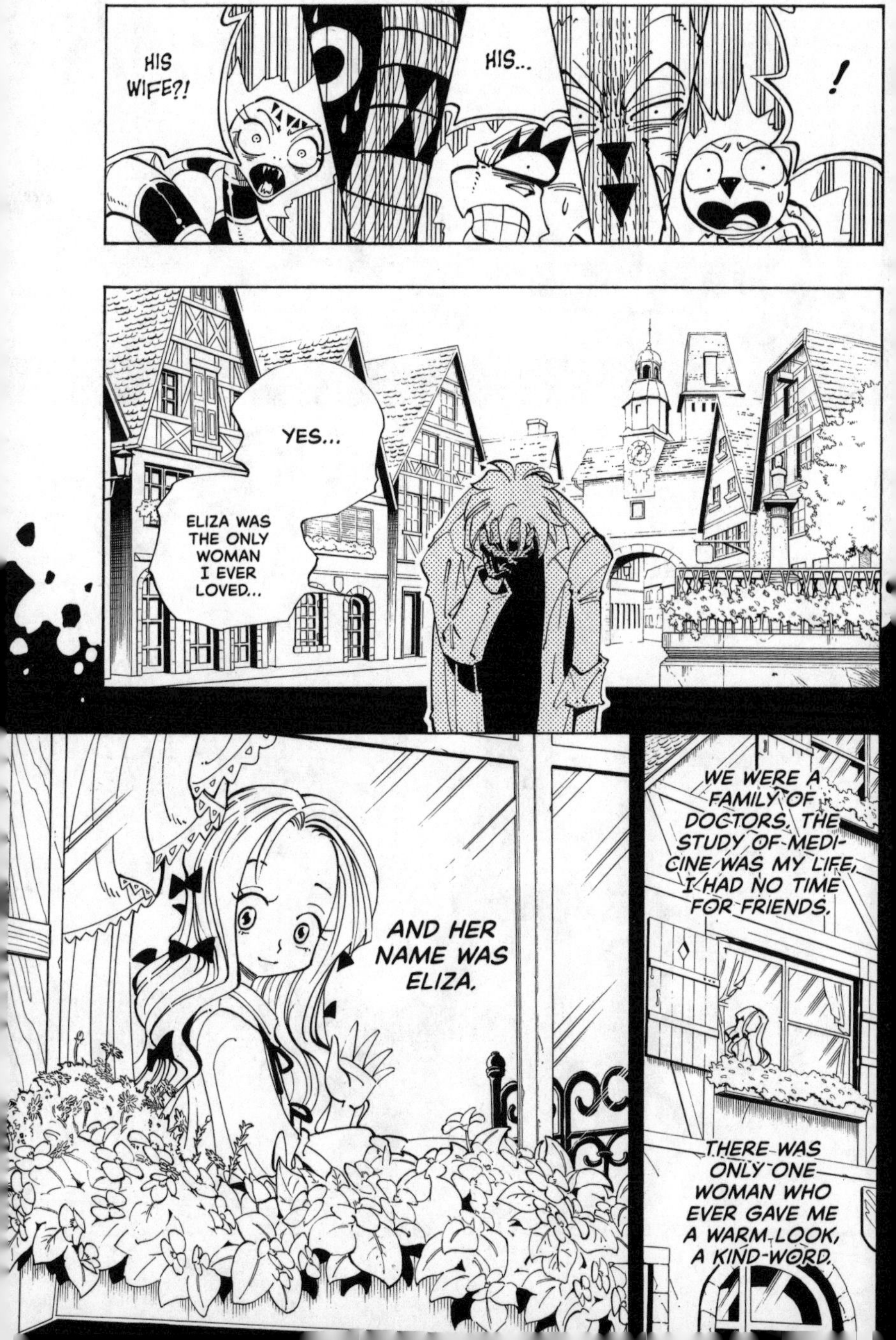
!
HIS...
HIS WIFE?!
YES...
ELIZA WAS THE ONLY WOMAN I EVER LOVED...
WE WERE A FAMILY OF DOCTORS. THE STUDY OF MEDICINE WAS MY LIFE. I HAD NO TIME FOR FRIENDS.
THERE WAS ONLY ONE WOMAN WHO EVER GAVE ME A WARM LOOK, A KIND WORD.
AND HER NAME WAS ELIZA.

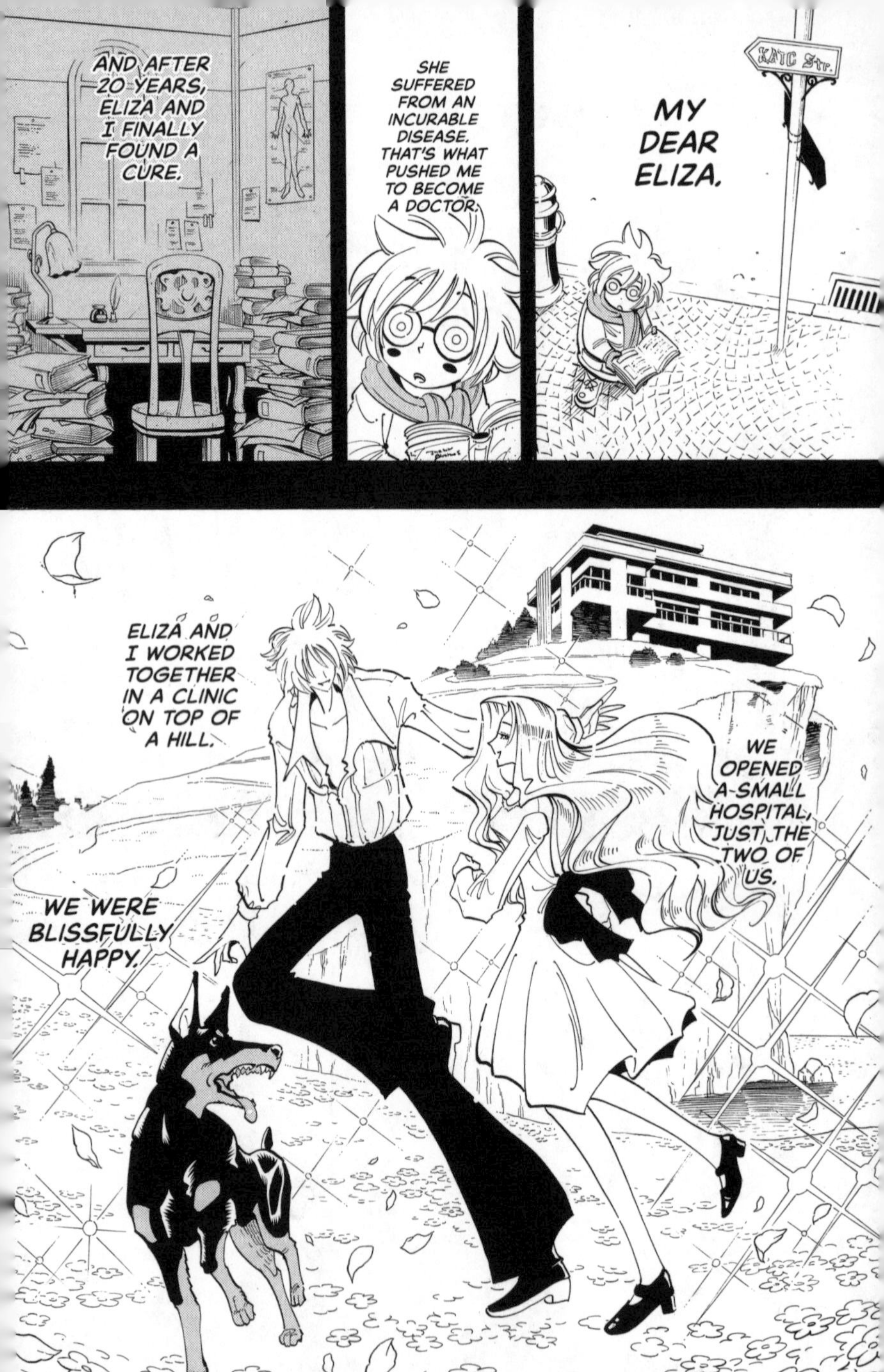
MY DEAR ELIZA.
SHE SUFFERED FROM AN INCURABLE DISEASE. THAT'S WHAT PUSHED ME TO BECOME A DOCTOR.
AND AFTER 20 YEARS, ELIZA AND I FINALLY FOUND A CURE.
WE OPENED A SMALL HOSPITAL, JUST THE TWO OF US.
ELIZA AND I WORKED TOGETHER IN A CLINIC ON TOP OF A HILL.
WE WERE BLISSFULLY HAPPY.

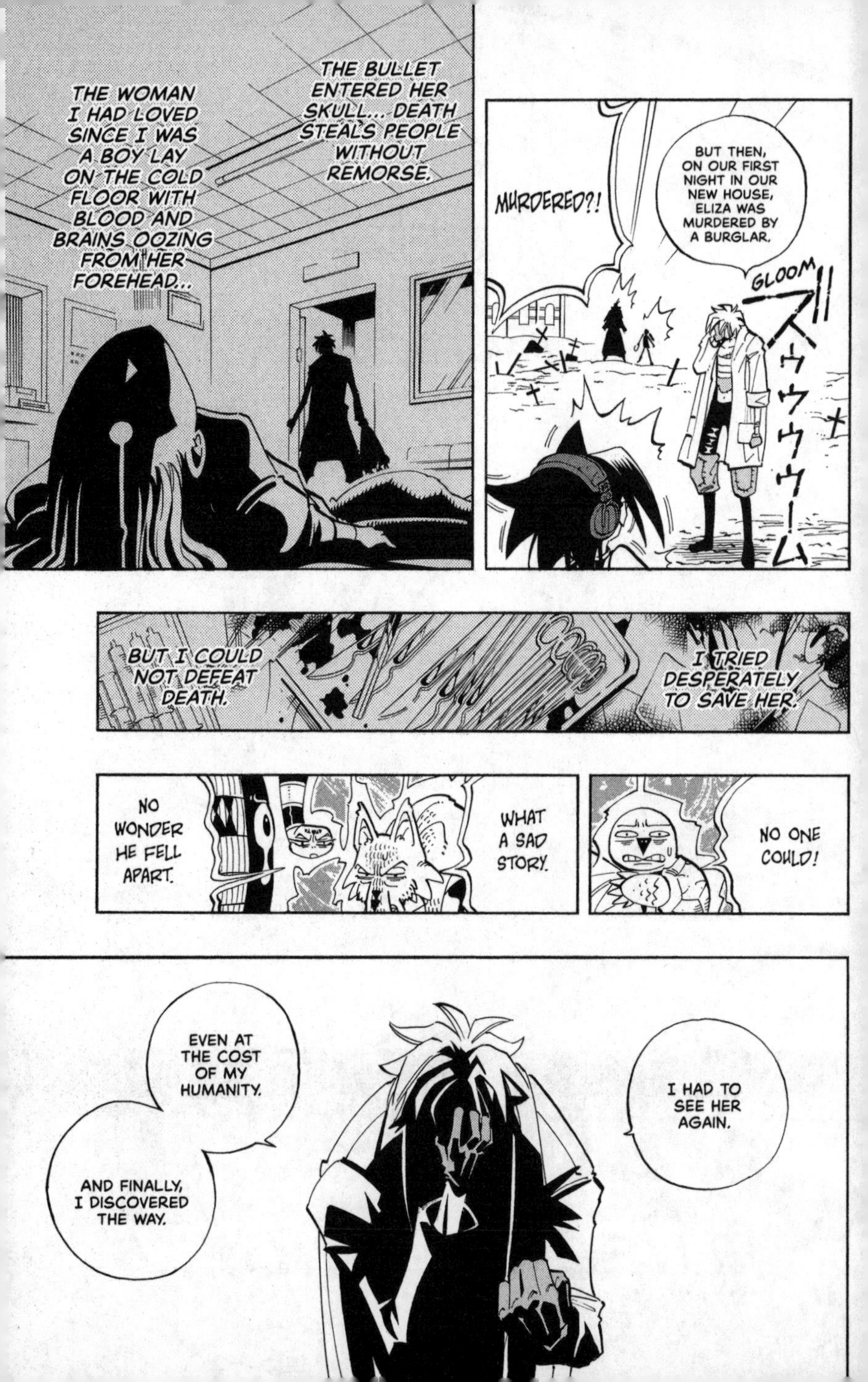
BUT THEN, ON OUR FIRST NIGHT IN OUR NEW HOUSE, ELIZA WAS MURDERED BY A BURGLAR.
MURDERED?!
GLOOM
ズウウウウーム
THE BULLET ENTERED HER SKULL... DEATH STEALS PEOPLE WITHOUT REMORSE.
THE WOMAN I HAD LOVED SINCE I WAS A BOY LAY ON THE COLD FLOOR WITH BLOOD AND BRAINS OOZING FROM HER FOREHEAD...
I TRIED DESPERATELY TO SAVE HER.
BUT I COULD NOT DEFEAT DEATH.
NO ONE COULD!
WHAT A SAD STORY.
NO WONDER HE FELL APART.
I HAD TO SEE HER AGAIN.
EVEN AT THE COST OF MY HUMANITY.
AND FINALLY, I DISCOVERED THE WAY.

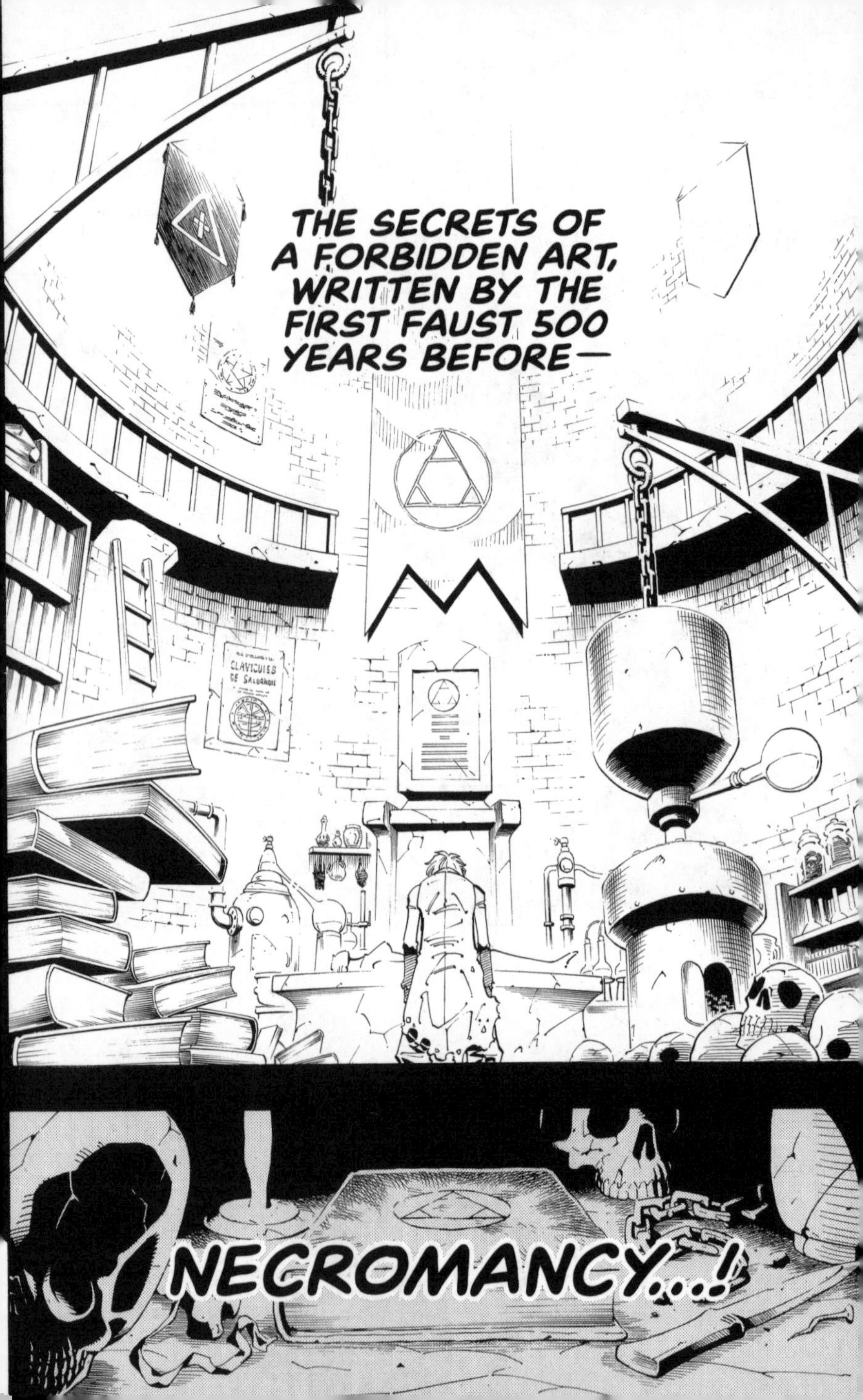
THE SECRETS OF A FORBIDDEN ART, WRITTEN BY THE FIRST FAUST 500 YEARS BEFORE—
NECROMANCY...!

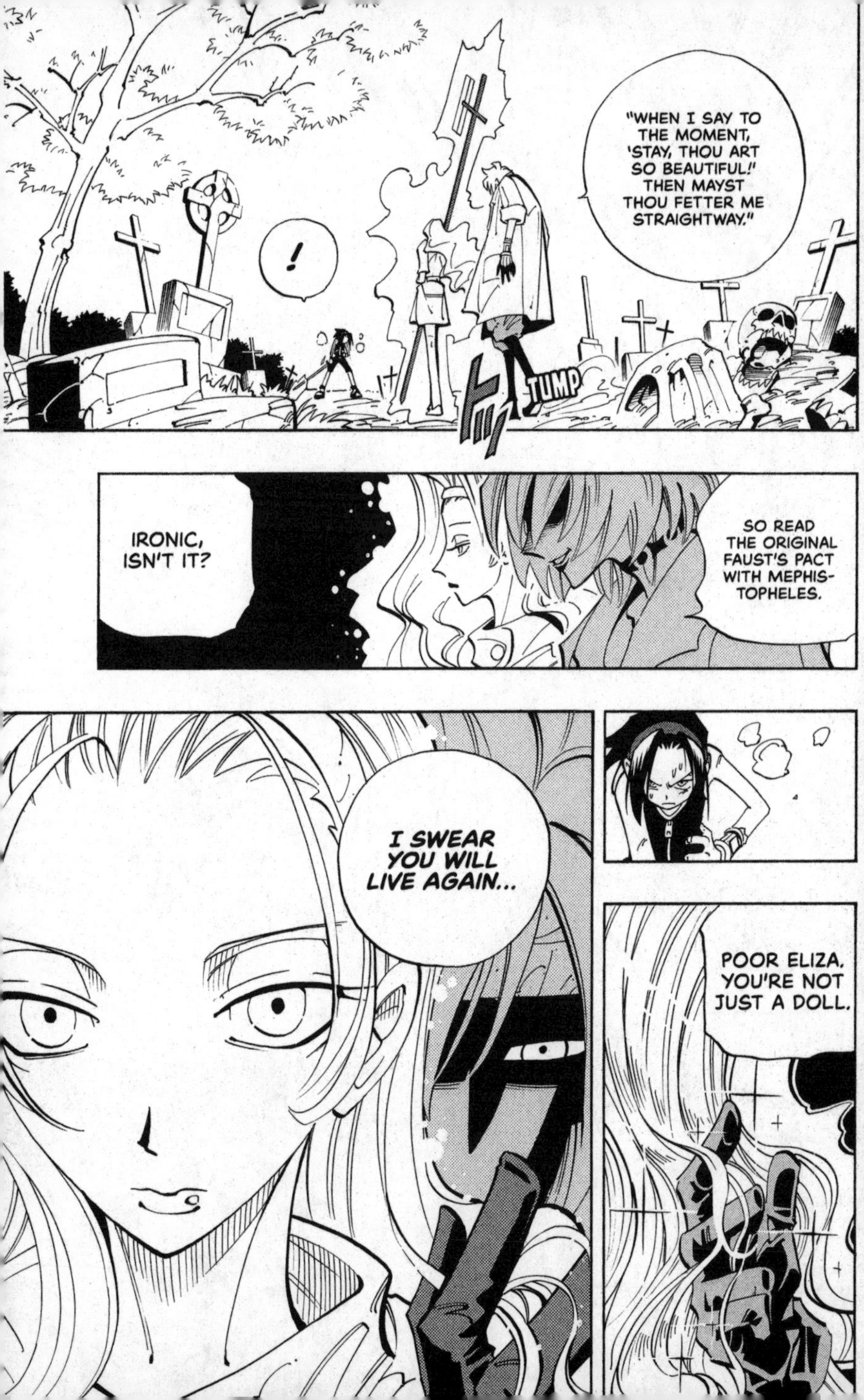
"WHEN I SAY TO THE MOMENT, 'STAY, THOU ART SO BEAUTIFUL!' THEN MAYST THOU FETTER ME STRAIGHTWAY."
!
TUMP
SO READ THE ORIGINAL FAUST'S PACT WITH MEPHISTOPHELES.
IRONIC, ISN'T IT?
POOR ELIZA, YOU'RE NOT JUST A DOLL.
I SWEAR YOU WILL LIVE AGAIN...

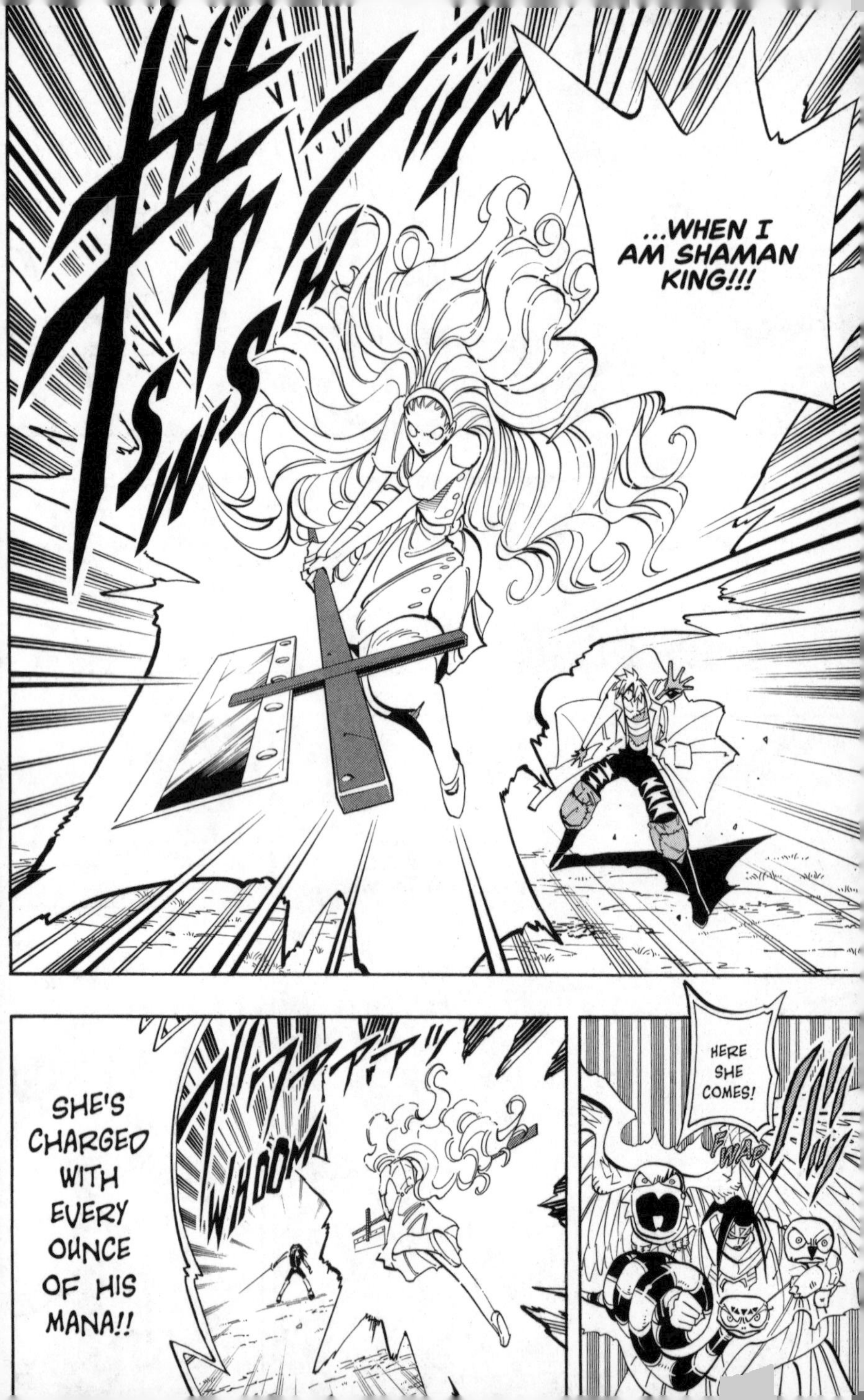
SWISH
...WHEN I AM SHAMAN KING!!!
HERE SHE COMES!
FWAP
SHE'S CHARGED WITH EVERY OUNCE OF HIS MANA!!
WHOOM

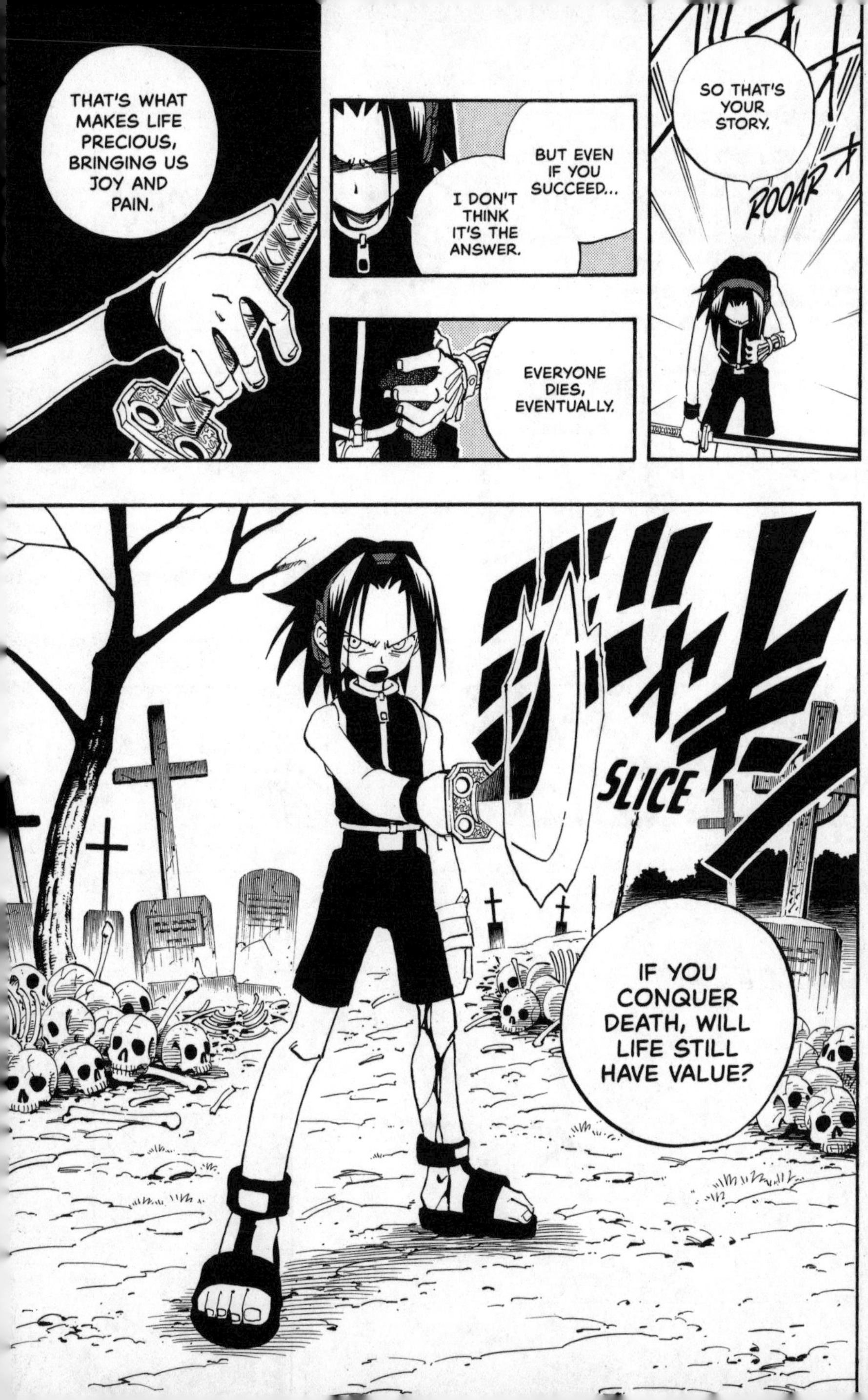
SO THAT'S YOUR STORY.
ROOAR
BUT EVEN IF YOU SUCCEED...
I DON'T THINK IT'S THE ANSWER.
EVERYONE DIES, EVENTUALLY.
THAT'S WHAT MAKES LIFE PRECIOUS, BRINGING US JOY AND PAIN.
SLICE
IF YOU CONQUER DEATH, WILL LIFE STILL HAVE VALUE?

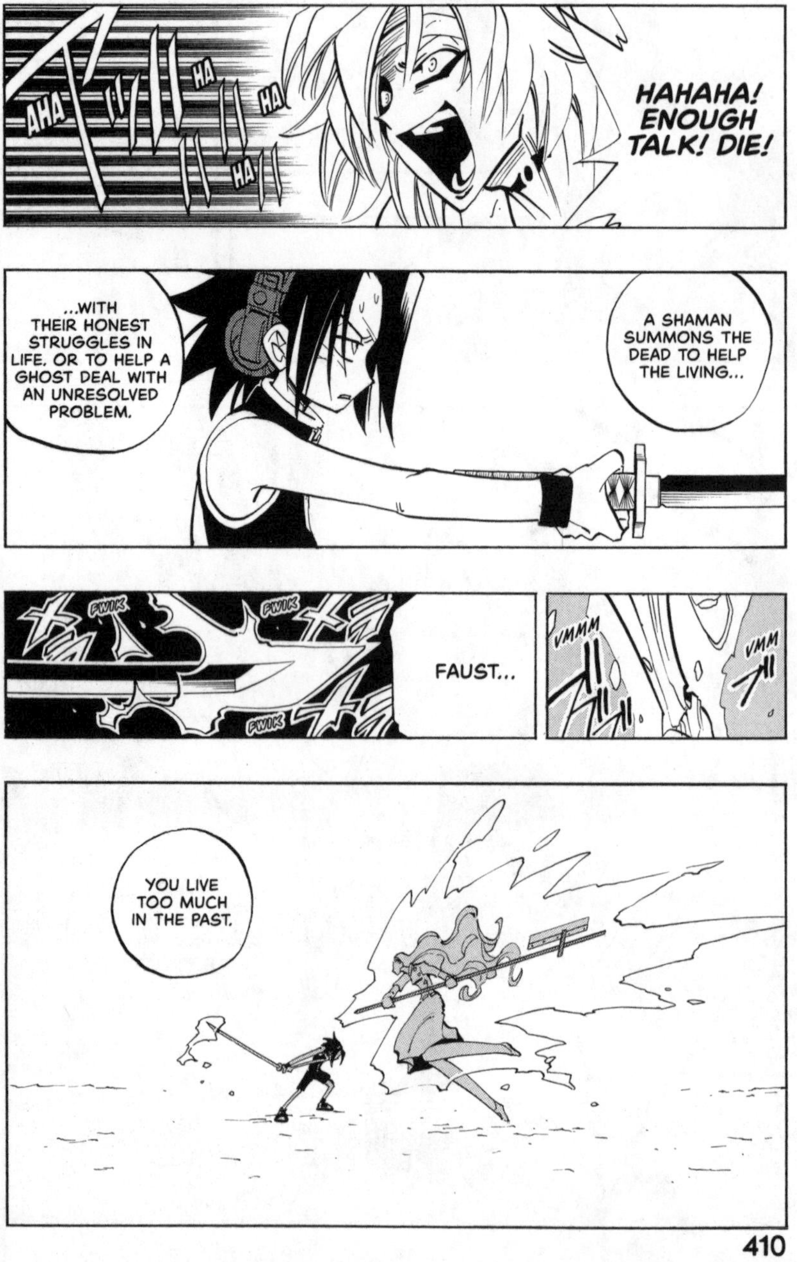
HAHAHA! ENOUGH TALK! DIE!
HA
HA
HA
AHA
A SHAMAN SUMMONS THE DEAD TO HELP THE LIVING...
...WITH THEIR HONEST STRUGGLES IN LIFE, OR TO HELP A GHOST DEAL WITH AN UNRESOLVED PROBLEM.
VMM
VMMM
FAUST...
FWIK
FWIK
FWIK
YOU LIVE TOO MUCH IN THE PAST.

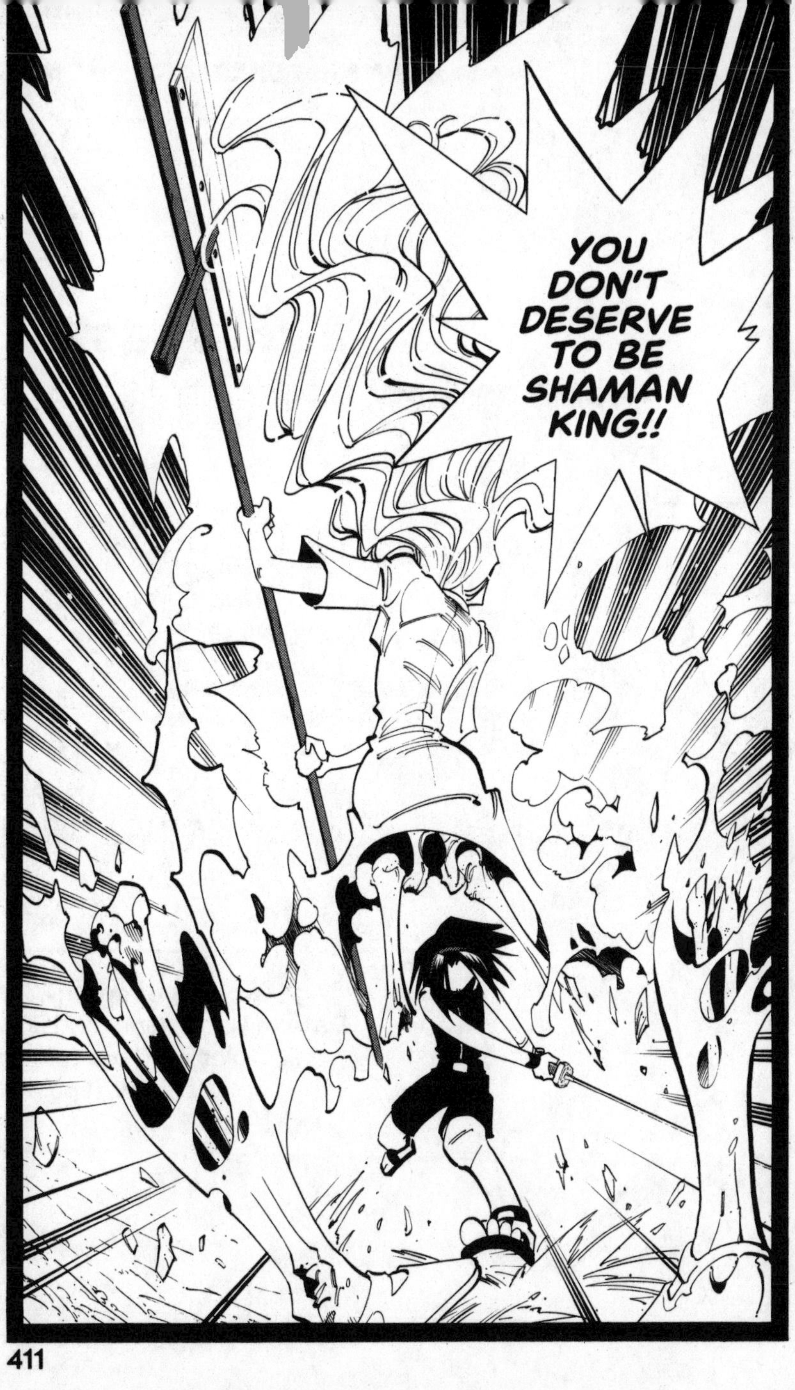
YOU DON'T DESERVE TO BE SHAMAN KING!!

SHAMAN KING CHARACTER FILE No.24

Eliza Faust

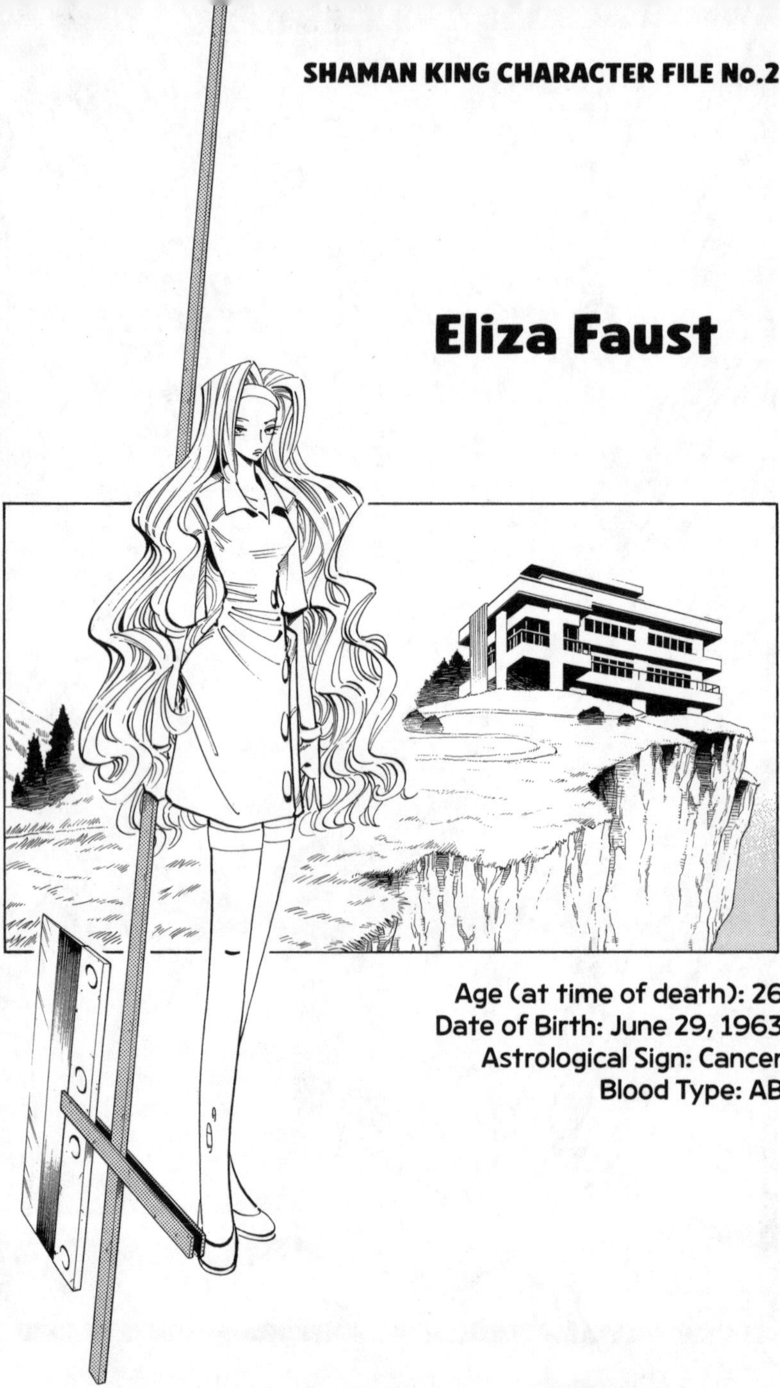

Age (at time of death): 26
Date of Birth: June 29, 1963
Astrological Sign: Cancer
Blood Type: AB

Chapter 46: A Form of Courage

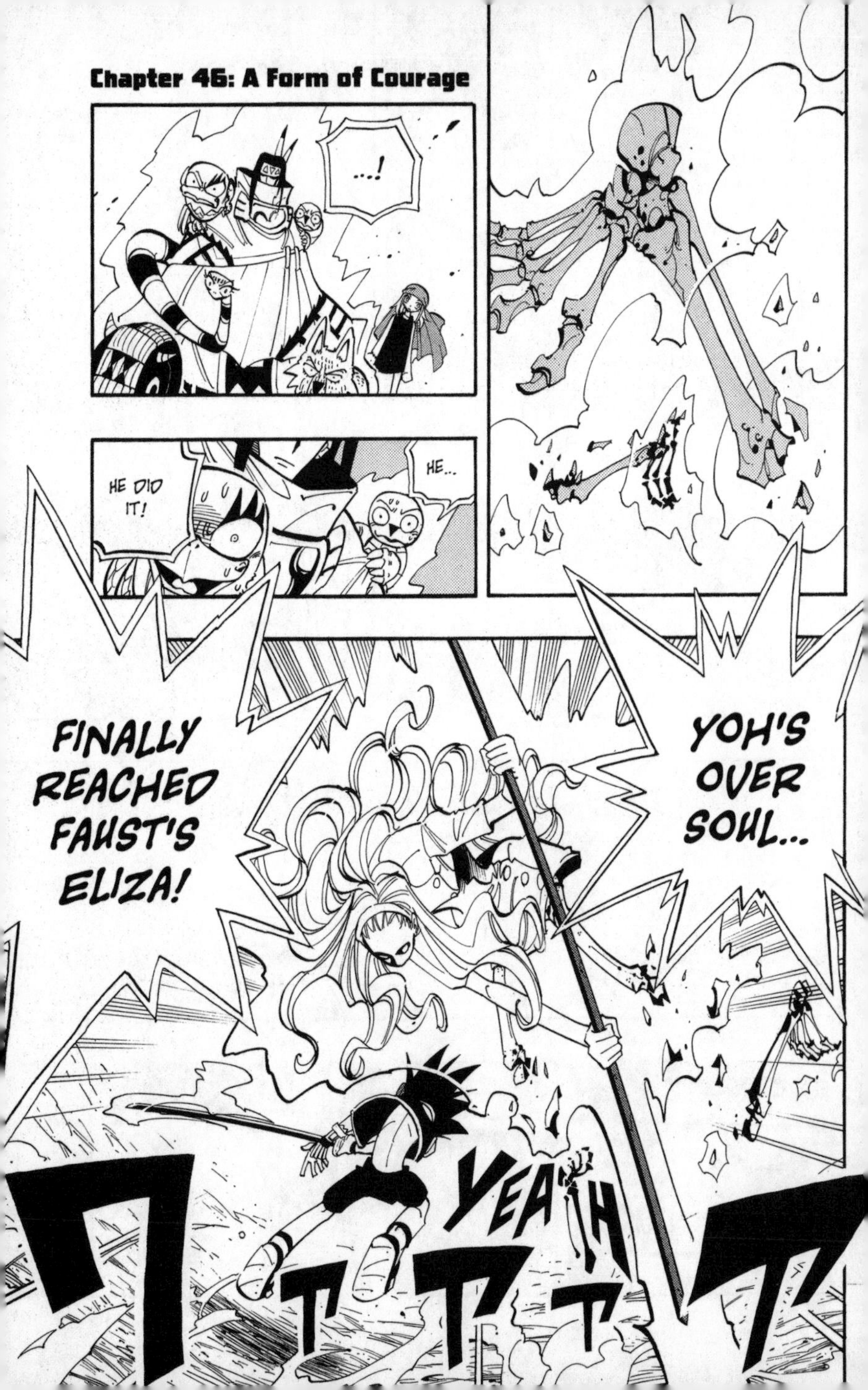

...!
HE...
HE DID IT!
YOH'S OVER SOUL...
FINALLY REACHED FAUST'S ELIZA!
YEAH

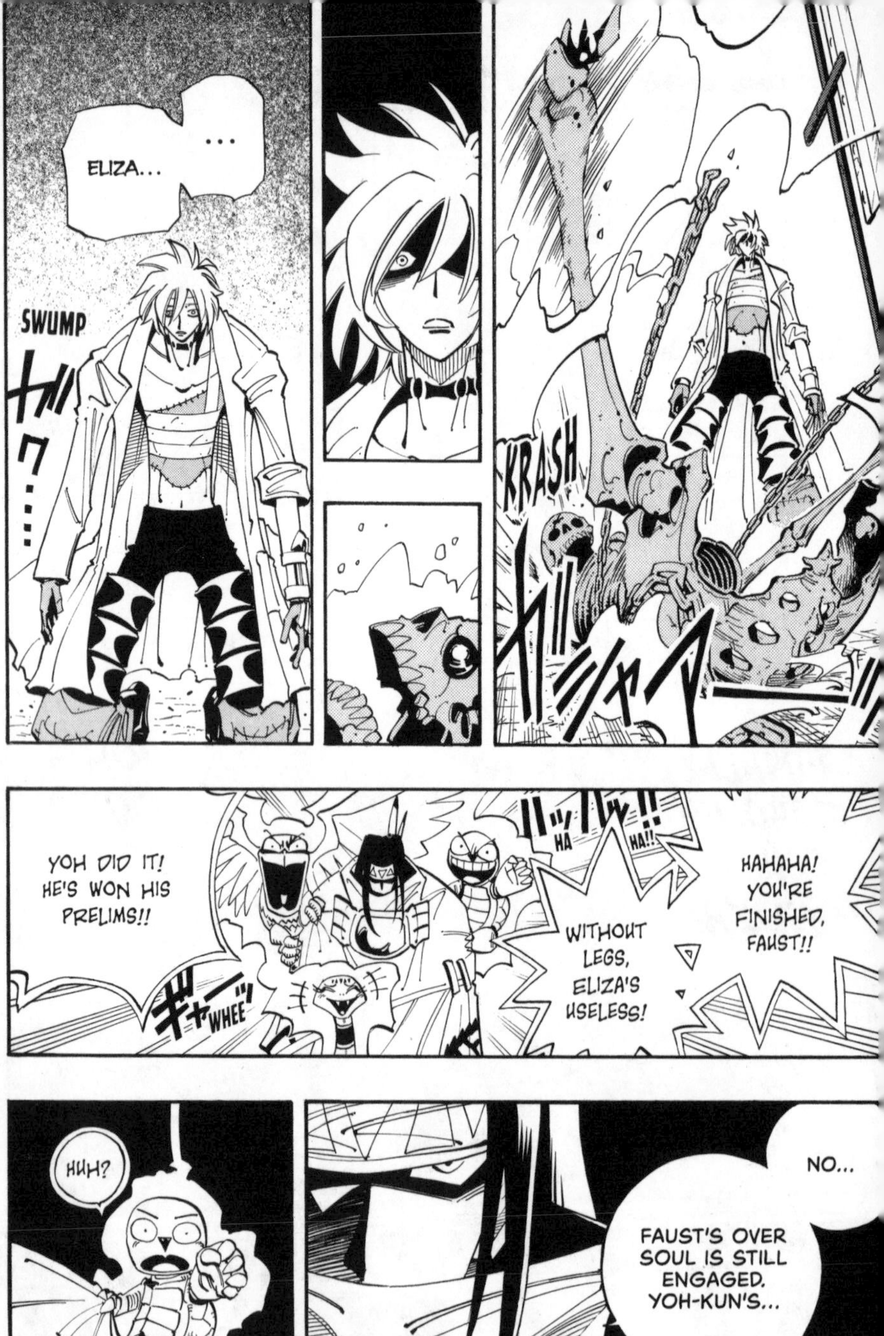
KRASH
...
ELIZA...
SWUMP
HAHAHA! YOU'RE FINISHED, FAUST!!
HA HA!!
WITHOUT LEGS, ELIZA'S USELESS!
WHEE
YOH DID IT! HE'S WON HIS PRELIMS!!
NO...
FAUST'S OVER SOUL IS STILL ENGAGED. YOH-KUN'S...
HUH?

Chapter 46:

A Form of Courage

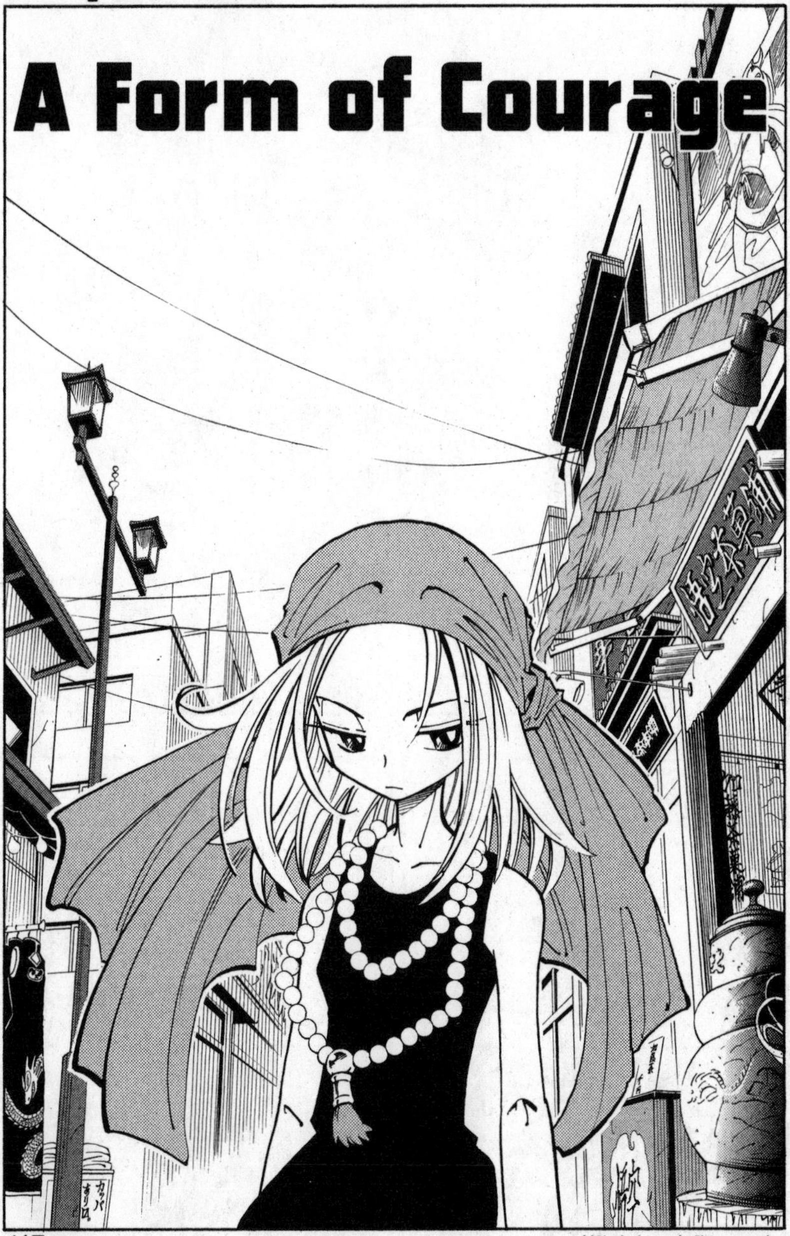

*(Chokohama's Chinatown)

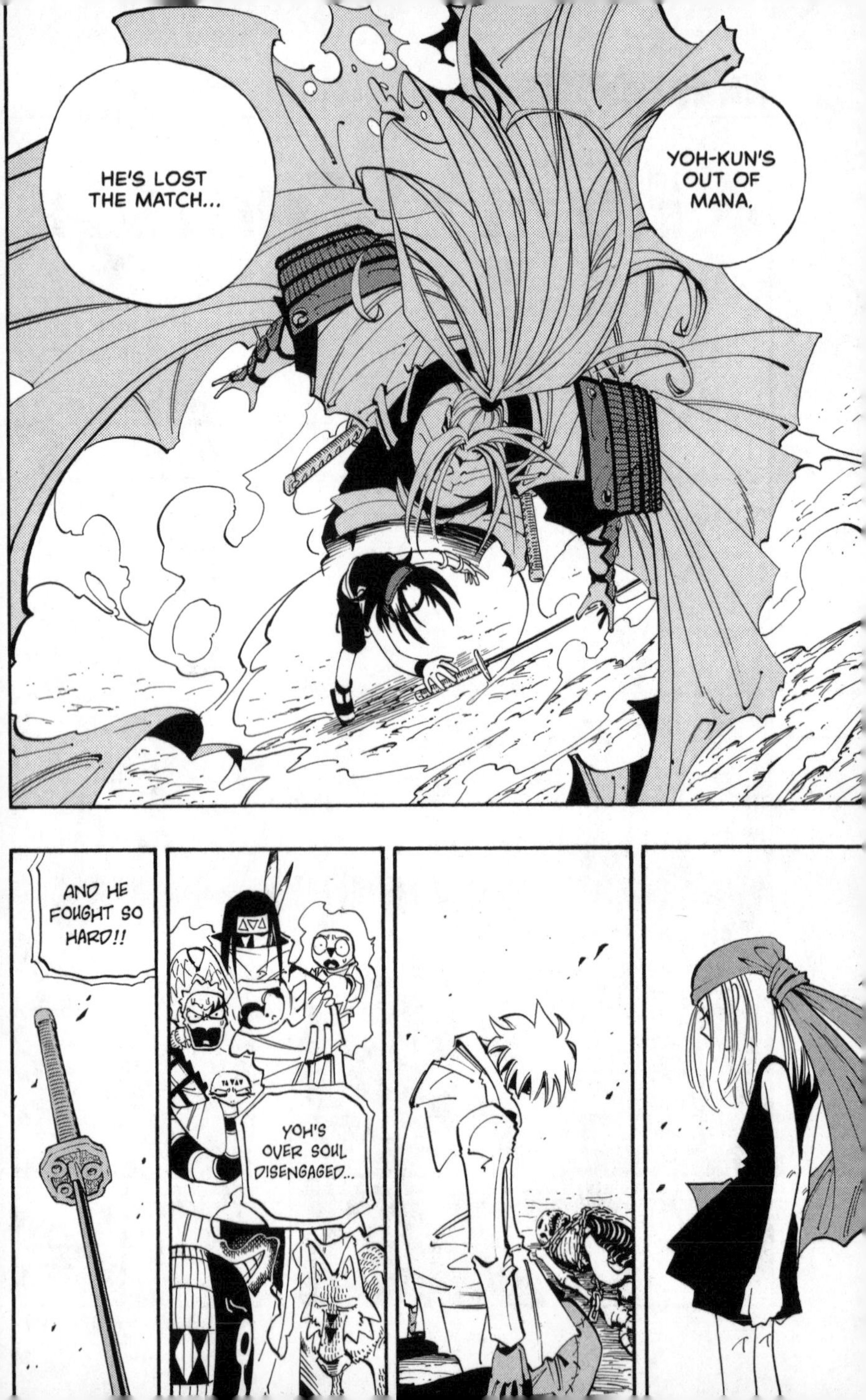
YOH-KUN'S OUT OF MANA,
HE'S LOST THE MATCH...
YOH'S OVER SOUL DISENGAGED...
AND HE FOUGHT SO HARD!!

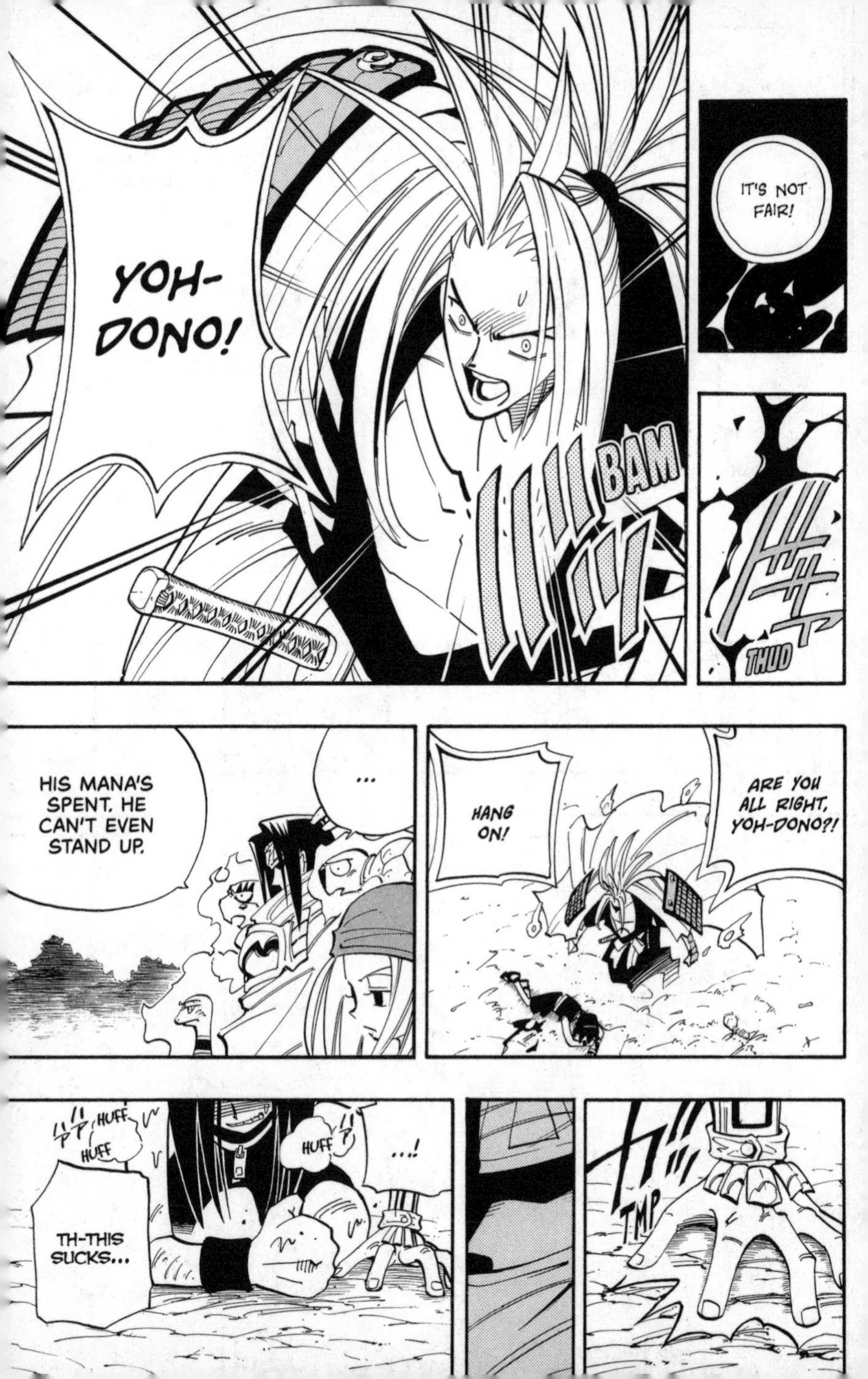
IT'S NOT FAIR!
THUD
YOH-DONO!
BAM
ARE YOU ALL RIGHT, YOH-DONO?!
HANG ON!
...
HIS MANA'S SPENT. HE CAN'T EVEN STAND UP.
TMP
...!
HUFF
HUFF HUFF
TH-THIS SUCKS...

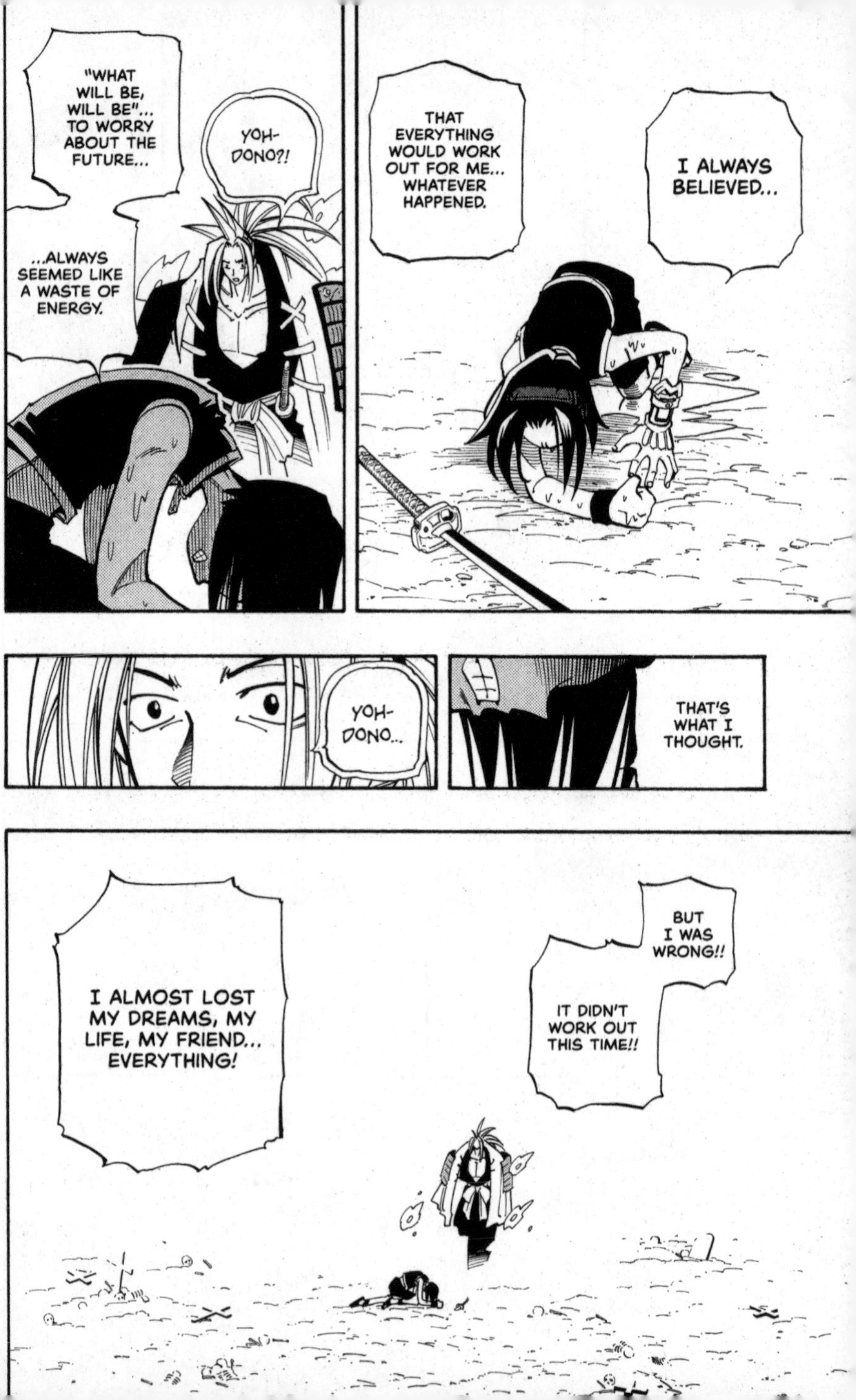
I ALWAYS BELIEVED...
THAT EVERYTHING WOULD WORK OUT FOR ME... WHATEVER HAPPENED.
YOH-DONO?!
"WHAT WILL BE, WILL BE"... TO WORRY ABOUT THE FUTURE...
...ALWAYS SEEMED LIKE A WASTE OF ENERGY.
THAT'S WHAT I THOUGHT.
YOH-DONO...
BUT I WAS WRONG!!
IT DIDN'T WORK OUT THIS TIME!!
I ALMOST LOST MY DREAMS, MY LIFE, MY FRIEND... EVERYTHING!

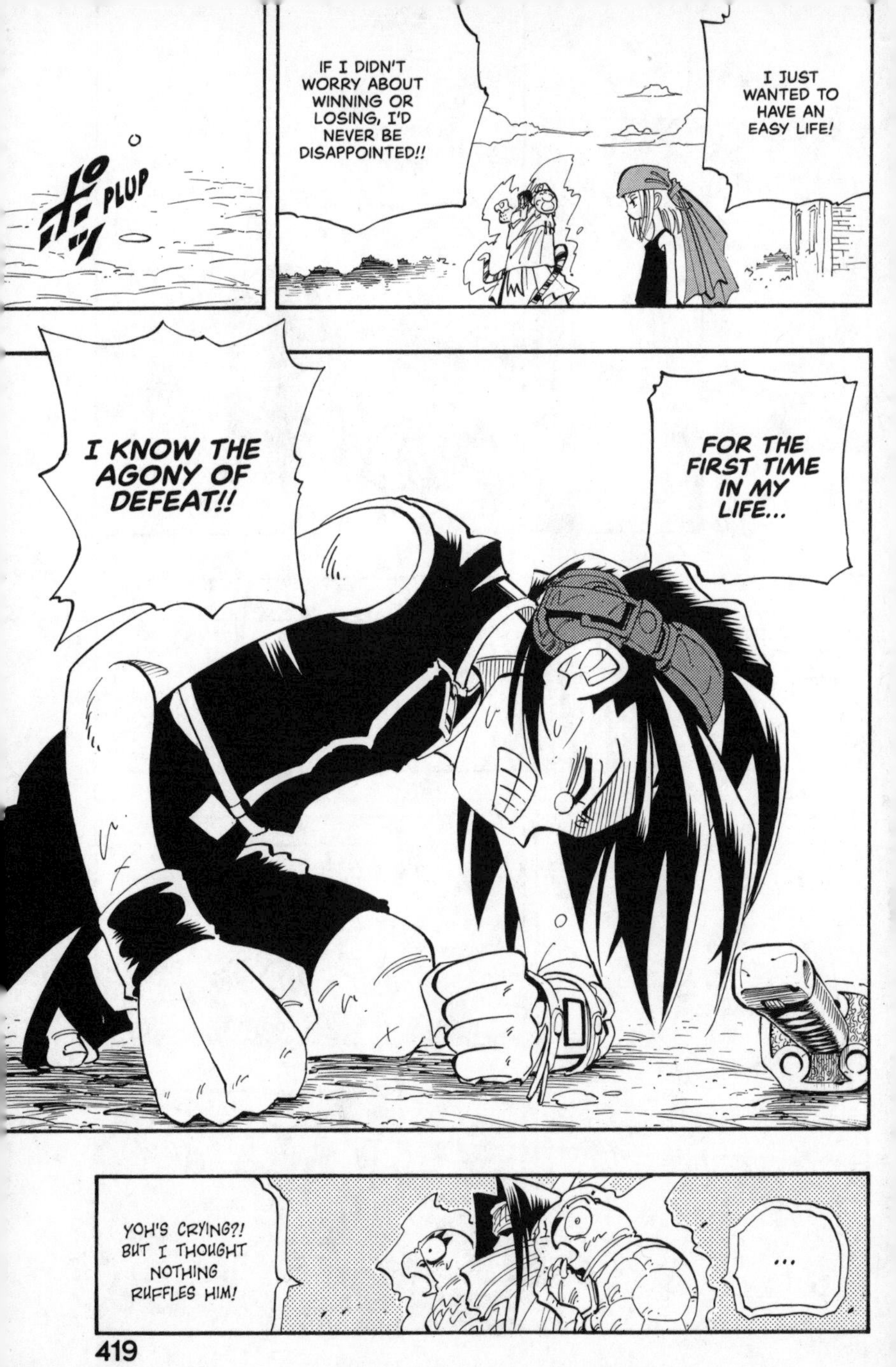
I JUST WANTED TO HAVE AN EASY LIFE!
IF I DIDN'T WORRY ABOUT WINNING OR LOSING, I'D NEVER BE DISAPPOINTED!!
ポッ
PLUP
FOR THE FIRST TIME IN MY LIFE...
I KNOW THE AGONY OF DEFEAT!!
...
YOH'S CRYING?! BUT I THOUGHT NOTHING RUFFLES HIM!

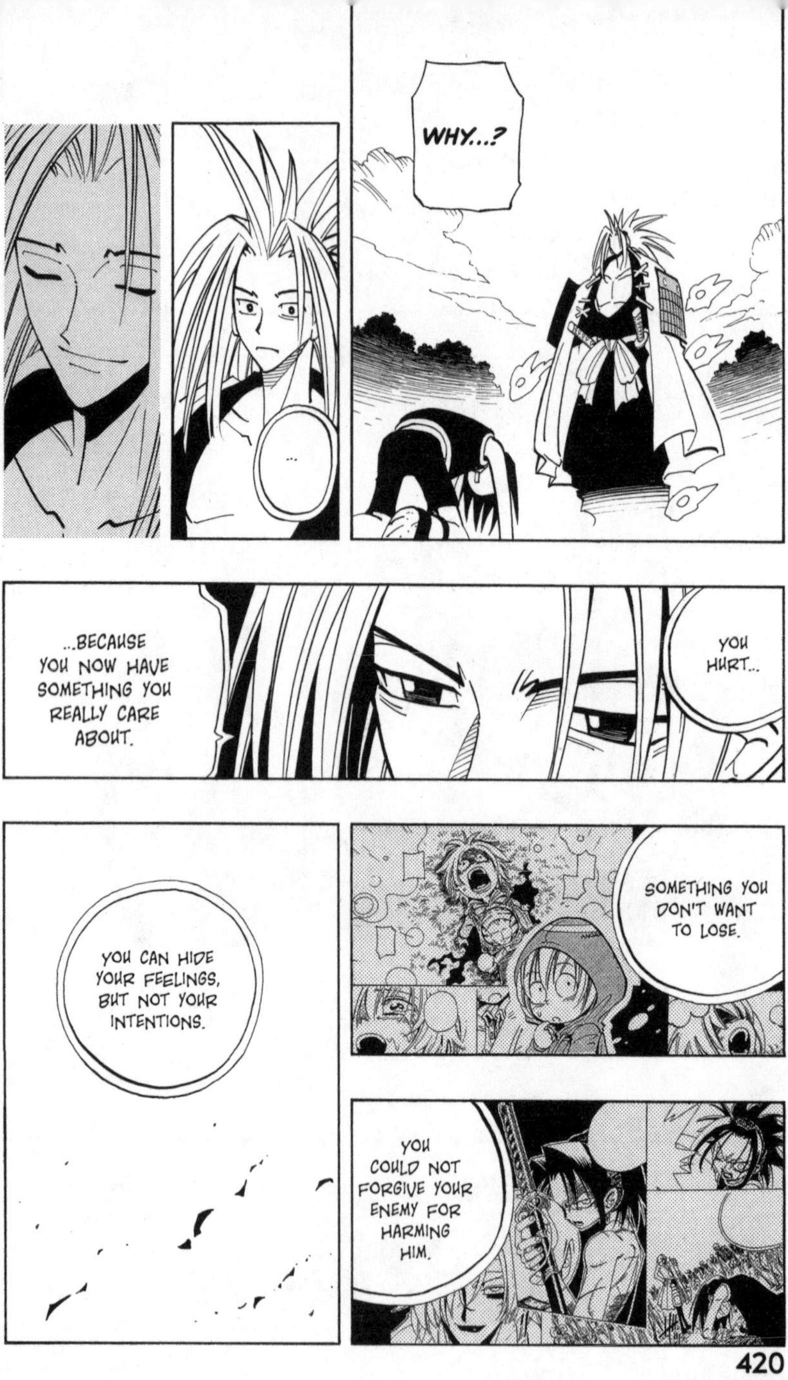
WHY...?
...
YOU HURT...
...BECAUSE YOU NOW HAVE SOMETHING YOU REALLY CARE ABOUT.
SOMETHING YOU DON'T WANT TO LOSE.
YOU COULD NOT FORGIVE YOUR ENEMY FOR HARMING HIM.
YOU CAN HIDE YOUR FEELINGS, BUT NOT YOUR INTENTIONS.

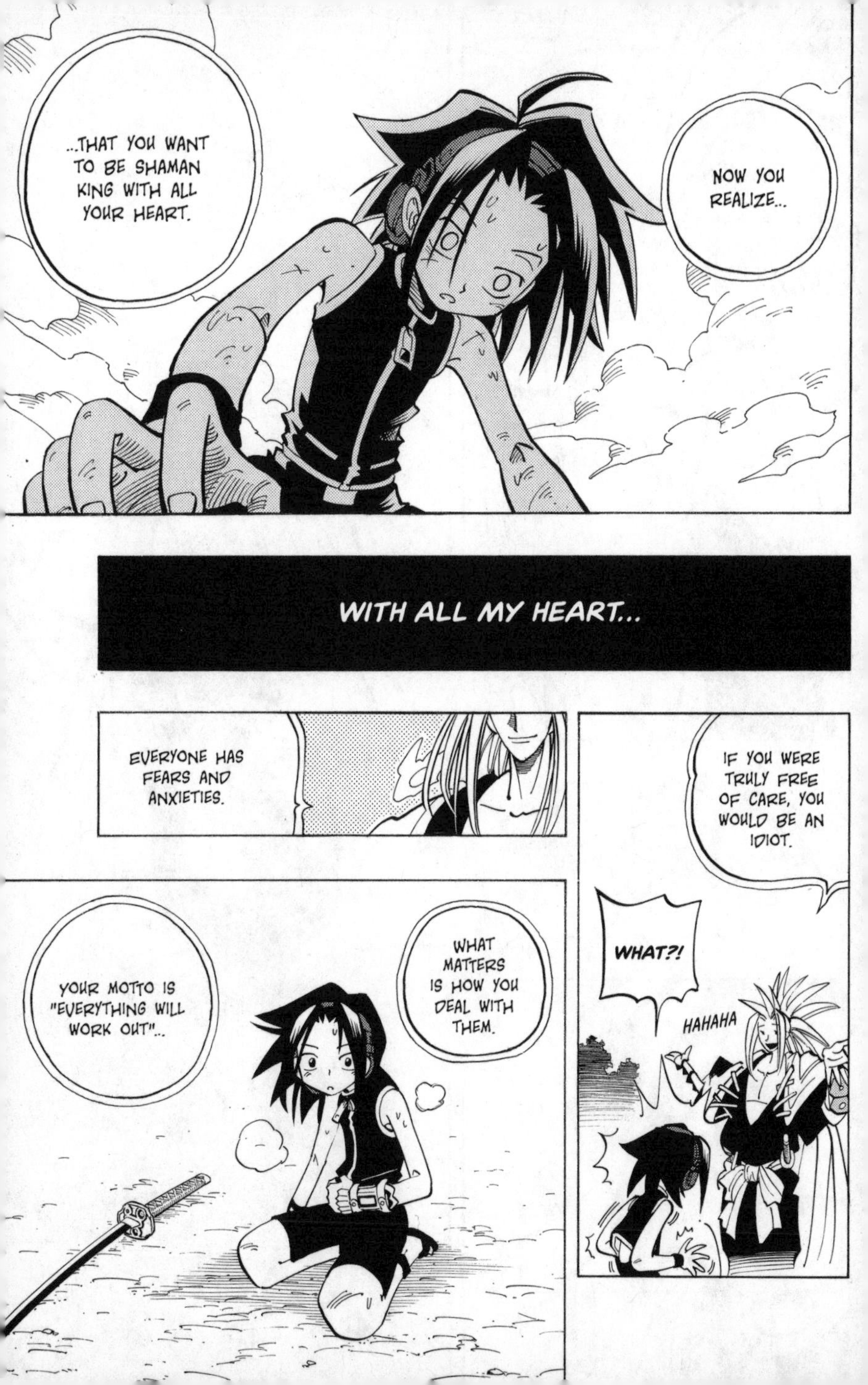
NOW YOU REALIZE...
...THAT YOU WANT TO BE SHAMAN KING WITH ALL YOUR HEART.
WITH ALL MY HEART...
IF YOU WERE TRULY FREE OF CARE, YOU WOULD BE AN IDIOT.
WHAT?!
HAHAHA
EVERYONE HAS FEARS AND ANXIETIES.
WHAT MATTERS IS HOW YOU DEAL WITH THEM.
YOUR MOTTO IS "EVERYTHING WILL WORK OUT"...

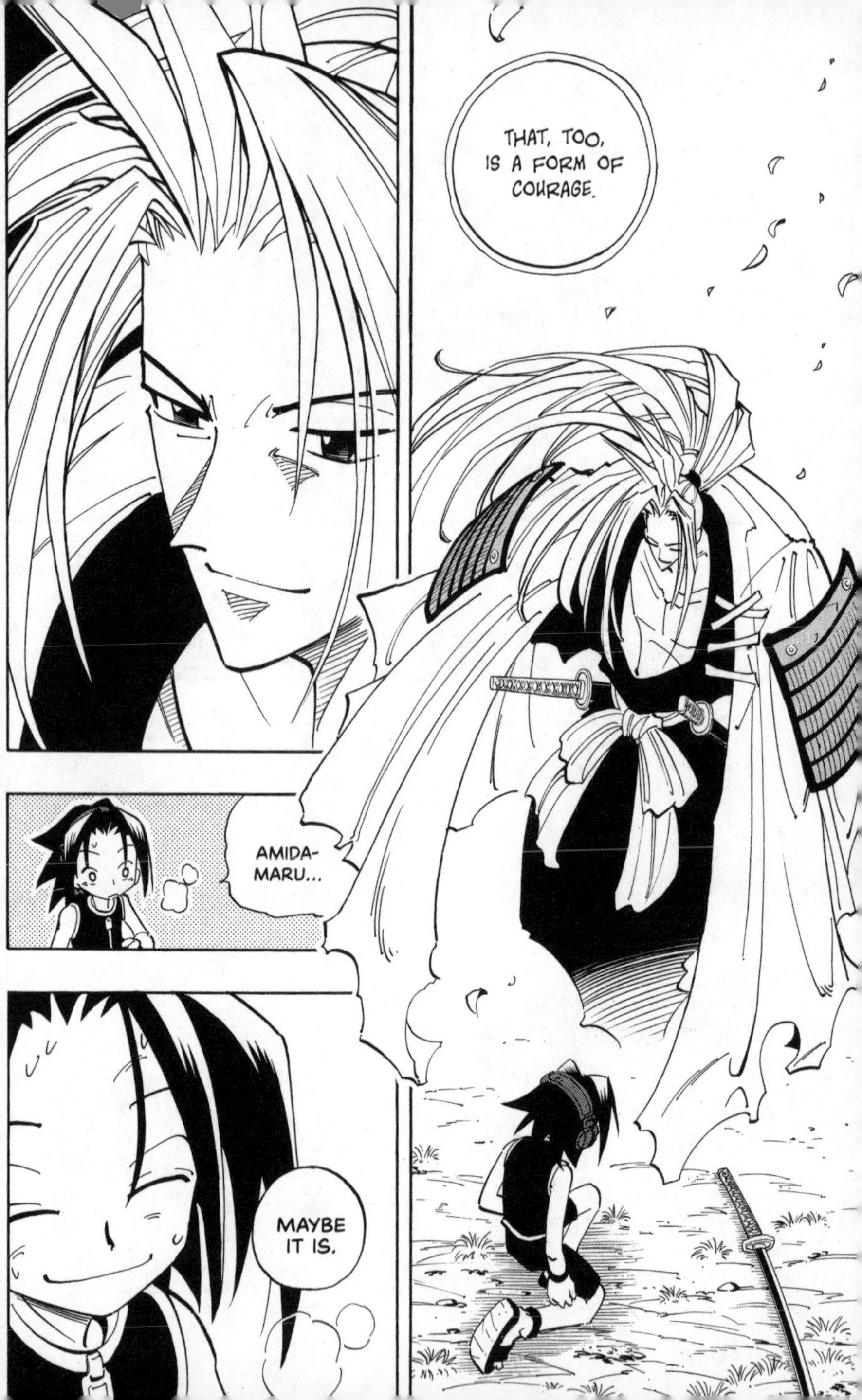
THAT, TOO, IS A FORM OF COURAGE.
AMIDA-MARU...
MAYBE IT IS.

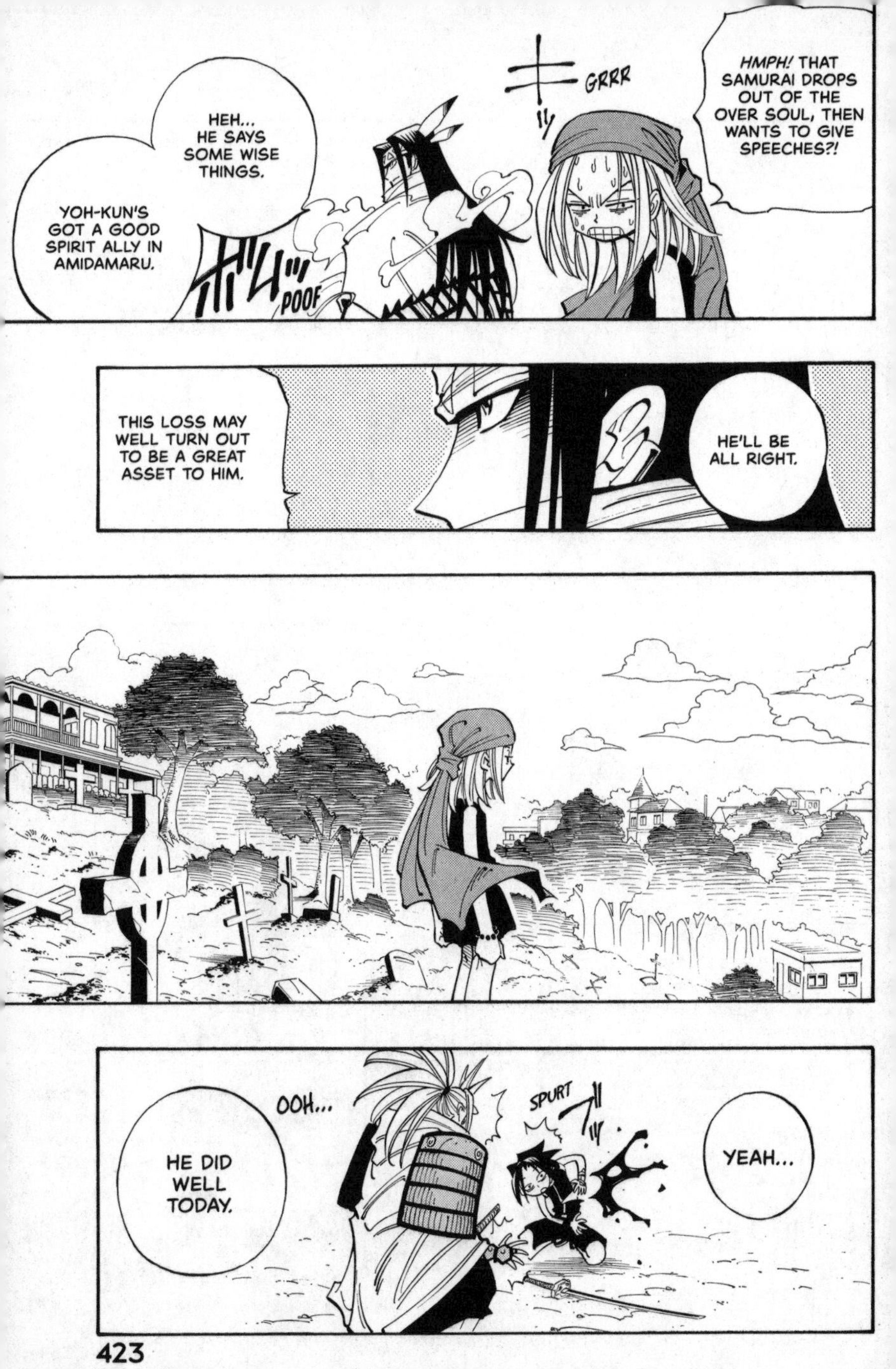
HMPH! THAT SAMURAI DROPS OUT OF THE OVER SOUL, THEN WANTS TO GIVE SPEECHES?!
GRRR
HEH... HE SAYS SOME WISE THINGS.
YOH-KUN'S GOT A GOOD SPIRIT ALLY IN AMIDAMARU.
POOF
HE'LL BE ALL RIGHT.
THIS LOSS MAY WELL TURN OUT TO BE A GREAT ASSET TO HIM.
YEAH...
SPURT
OOH...
HE DID WELL TODAY.

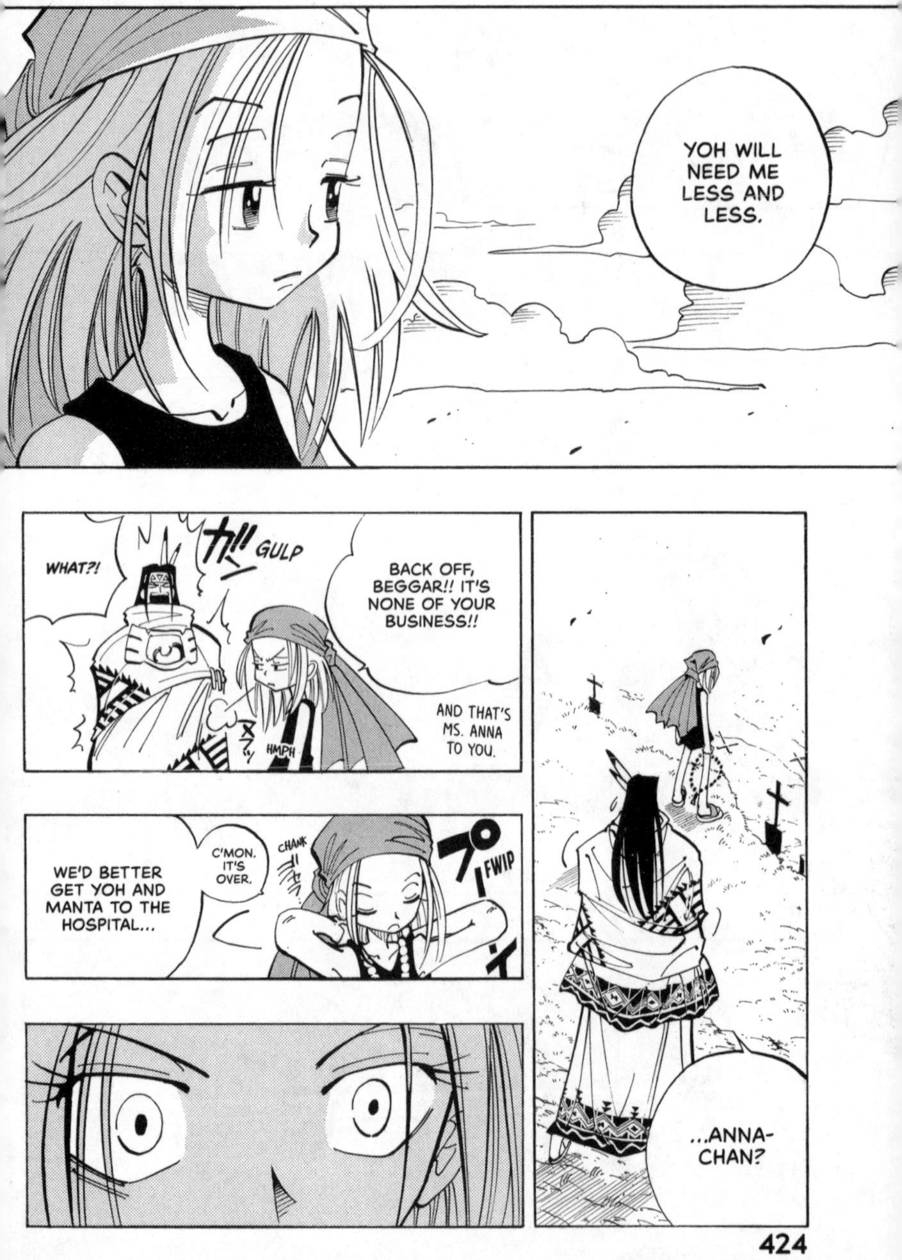
YOH WILL NEED ME LESS AND LESS.
...ANNA-CHAN?
BACK OFF, BEGGAR!! IT'S NONE OF YOUR BUSINESS!!
AND THAT'S MS. ANNA TO YOU.
GULP
WHAT?!
HMPH
FWIP
CHANK
C'MON. IT'S OVER.
WE'D BETTER GET YOH AND MANTA TO THE HOSPITAL...

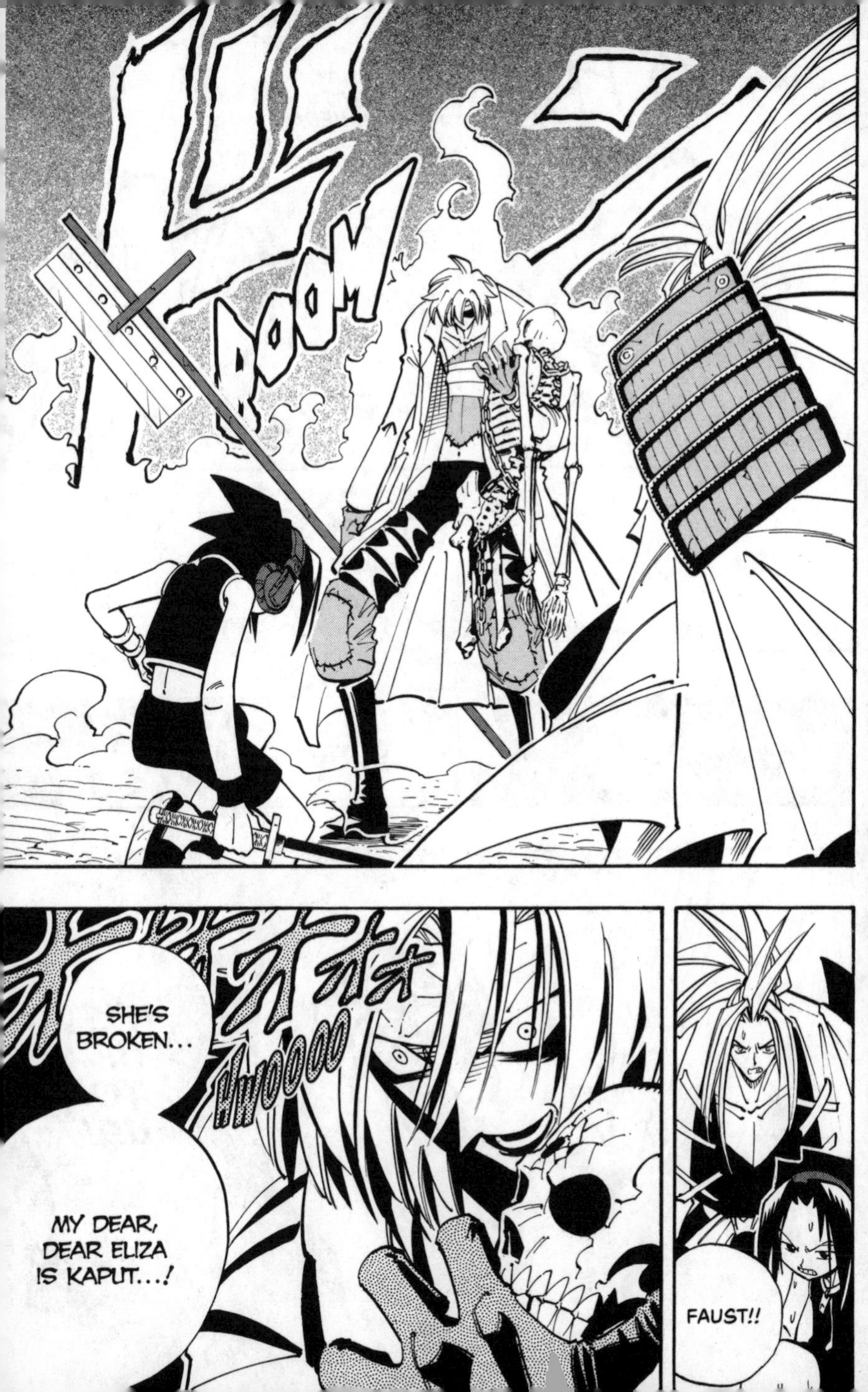
BOOM
FAUST!!
SHE'S BROKEN...
MY DEAR, DEAR ELIZA IS KAPUT...!

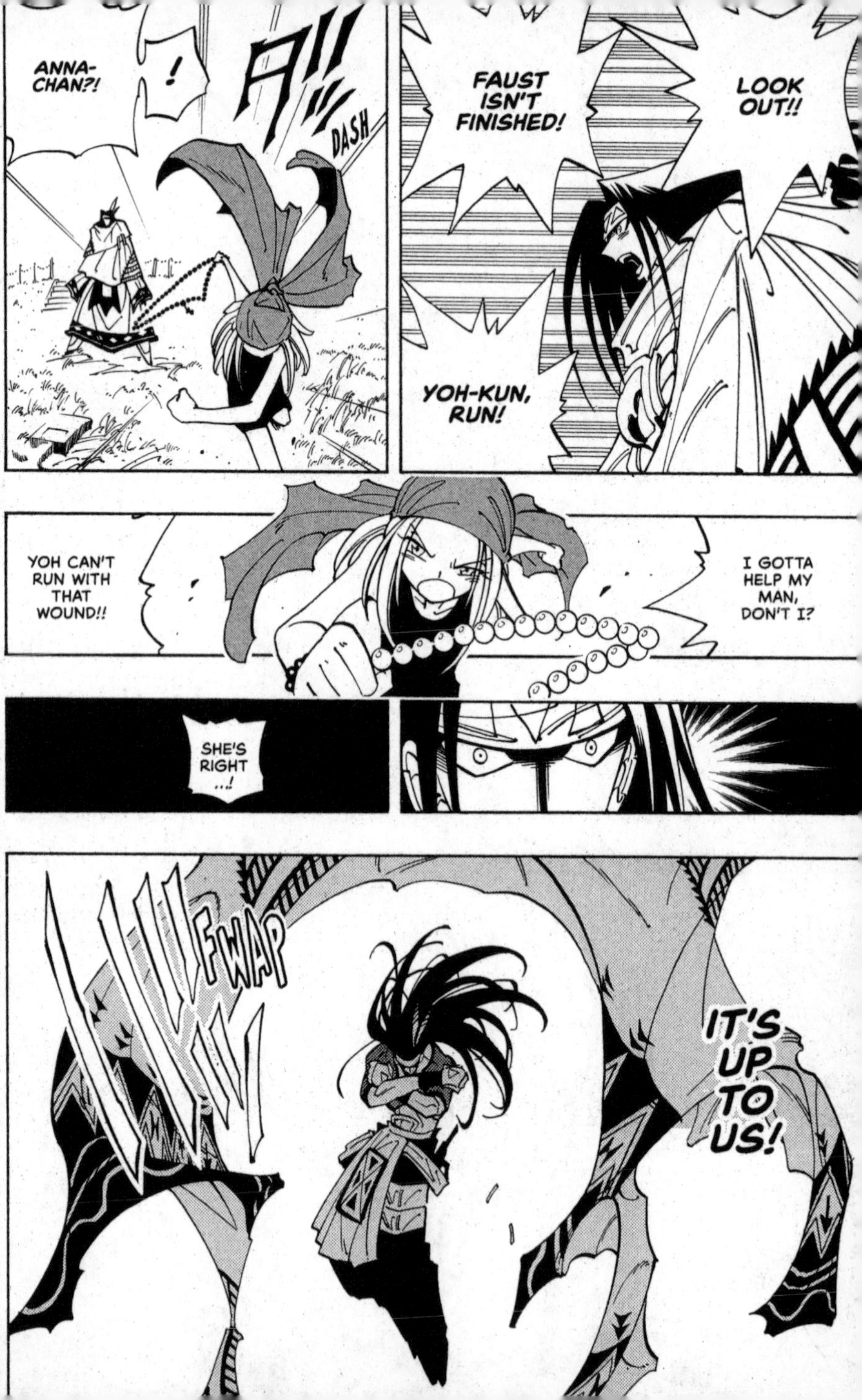
LOOK OUT!!
FAUST ISN'T FINISHED!
YOH-KUN, RUN!
A!!
DASH
!
ANNA-CHAN?!
I GOTTA HELP MY MAN, DON'T I?
YOH CAN'T RUN WITH THAT WOUND!!
SHE'S RIGHT ...!
IT'S UP TO US!
FWAP

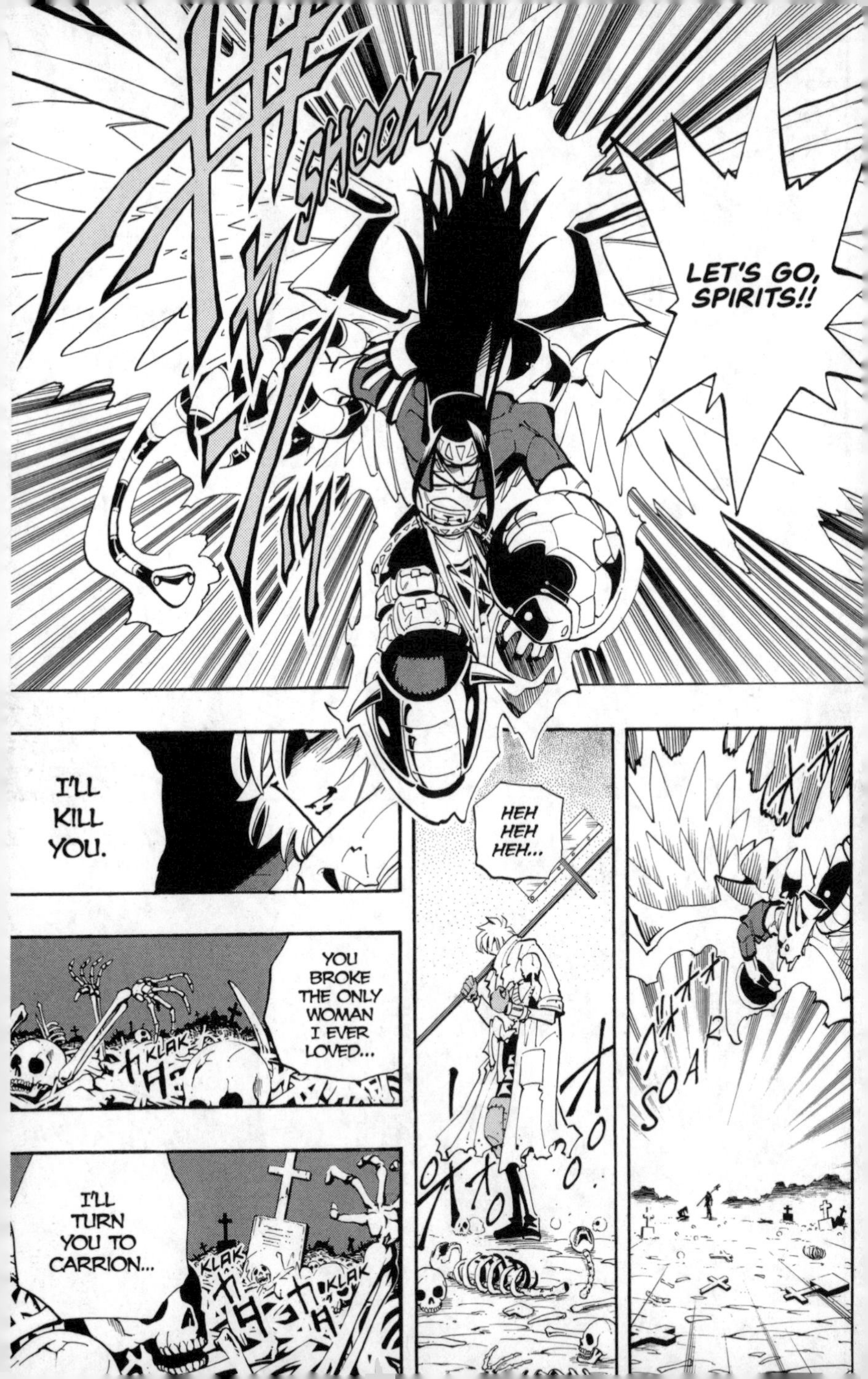
LET'S GO, SPIRITS!!
SHOOM
SOAR
HEH HEH HEH...
I'LL KILL YOU.
YOU BROKE THE ONLY WOMAN I EVER LOVED...
KLAK
I'LL TURN YOU TO CARRION...
KLAK
KLAK

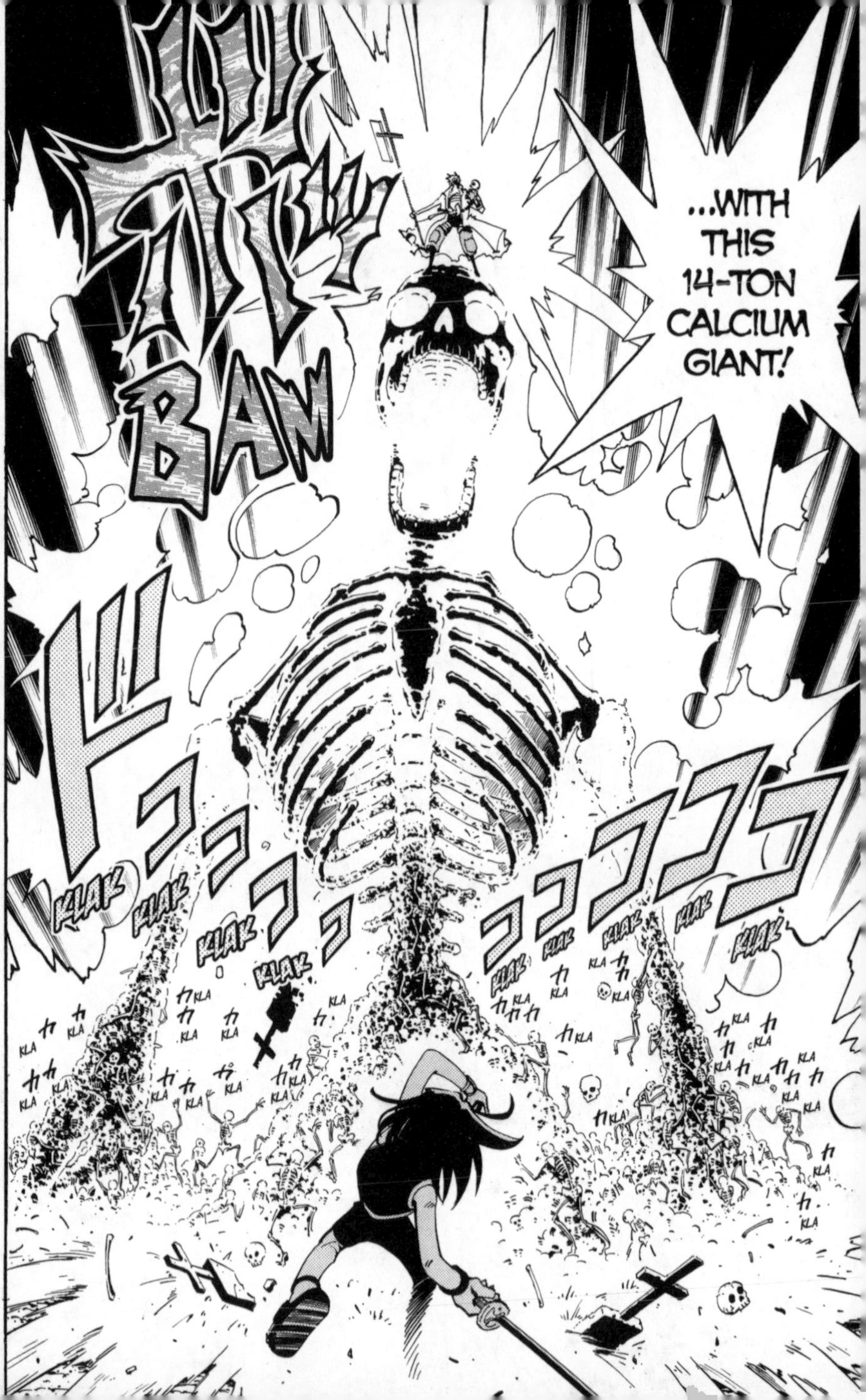
...WITH THIS 14-TON CALCIUM GIANT!
BAM
KLAK
KLA

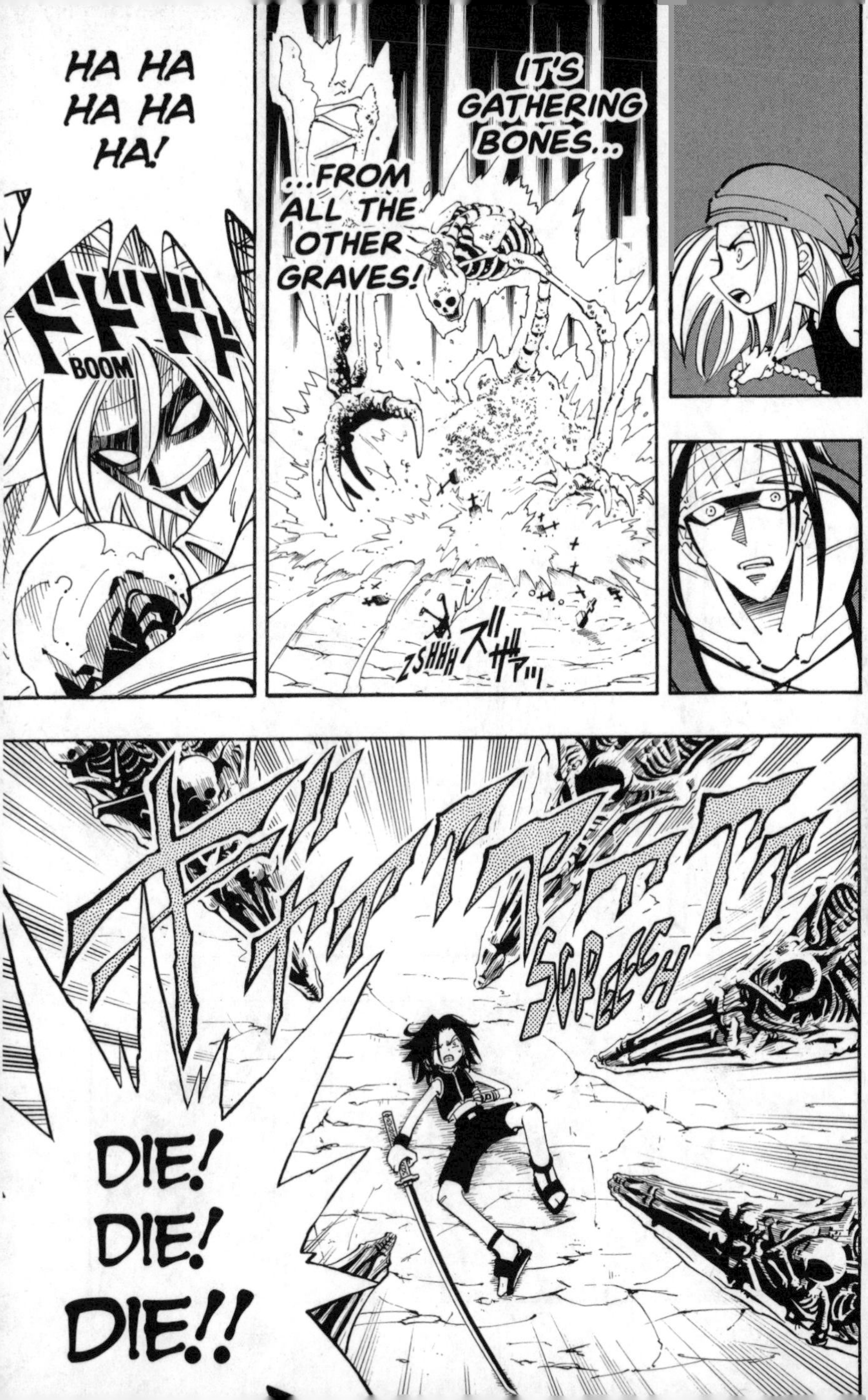
IT'S GATHERING BONES...
...FROM ALL THE OTHER GRAVES!
ZSHHH
HA HA HA HA HA!
BOOM
SCREECH
DIE! DIE! DIE!!

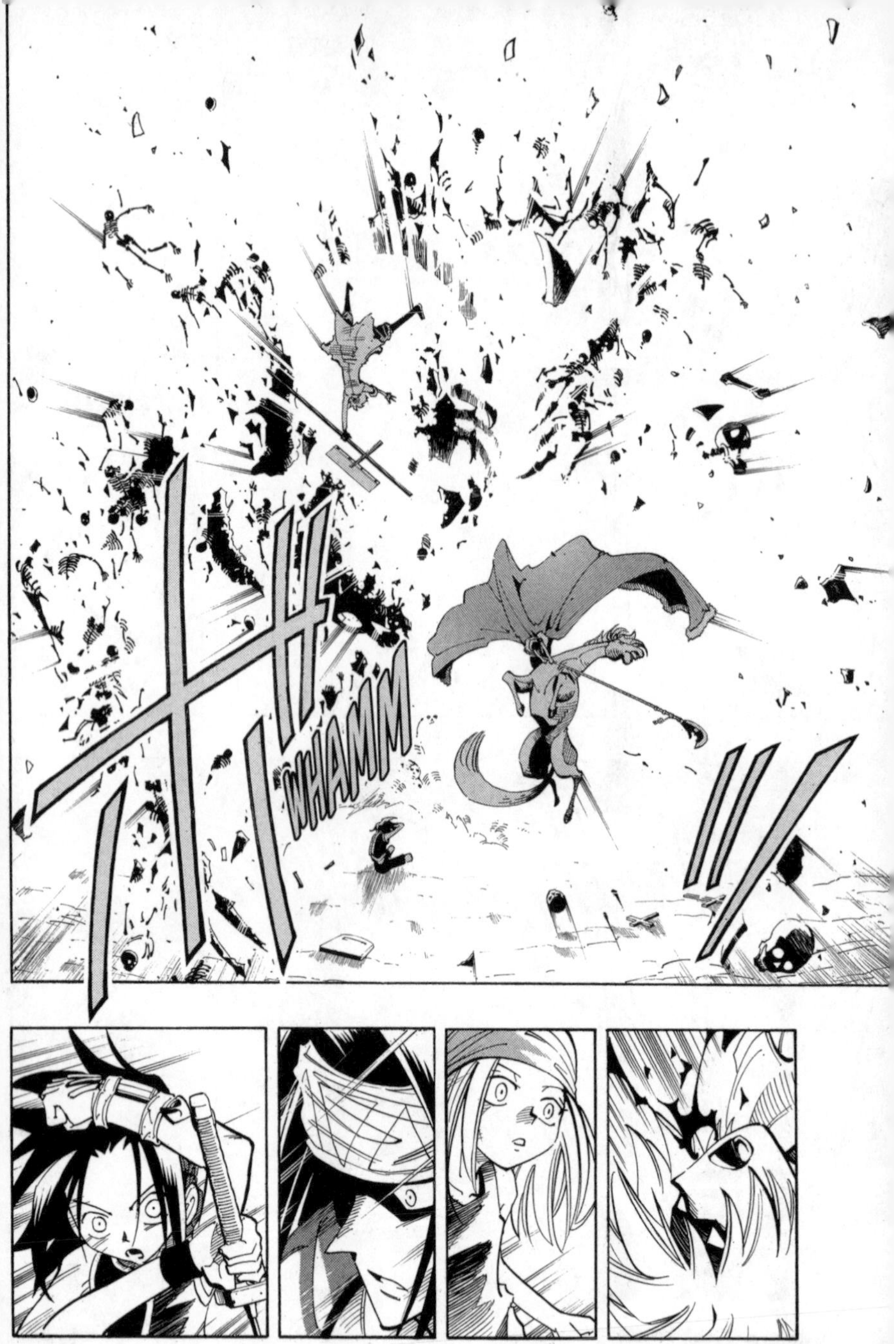
WHAMM

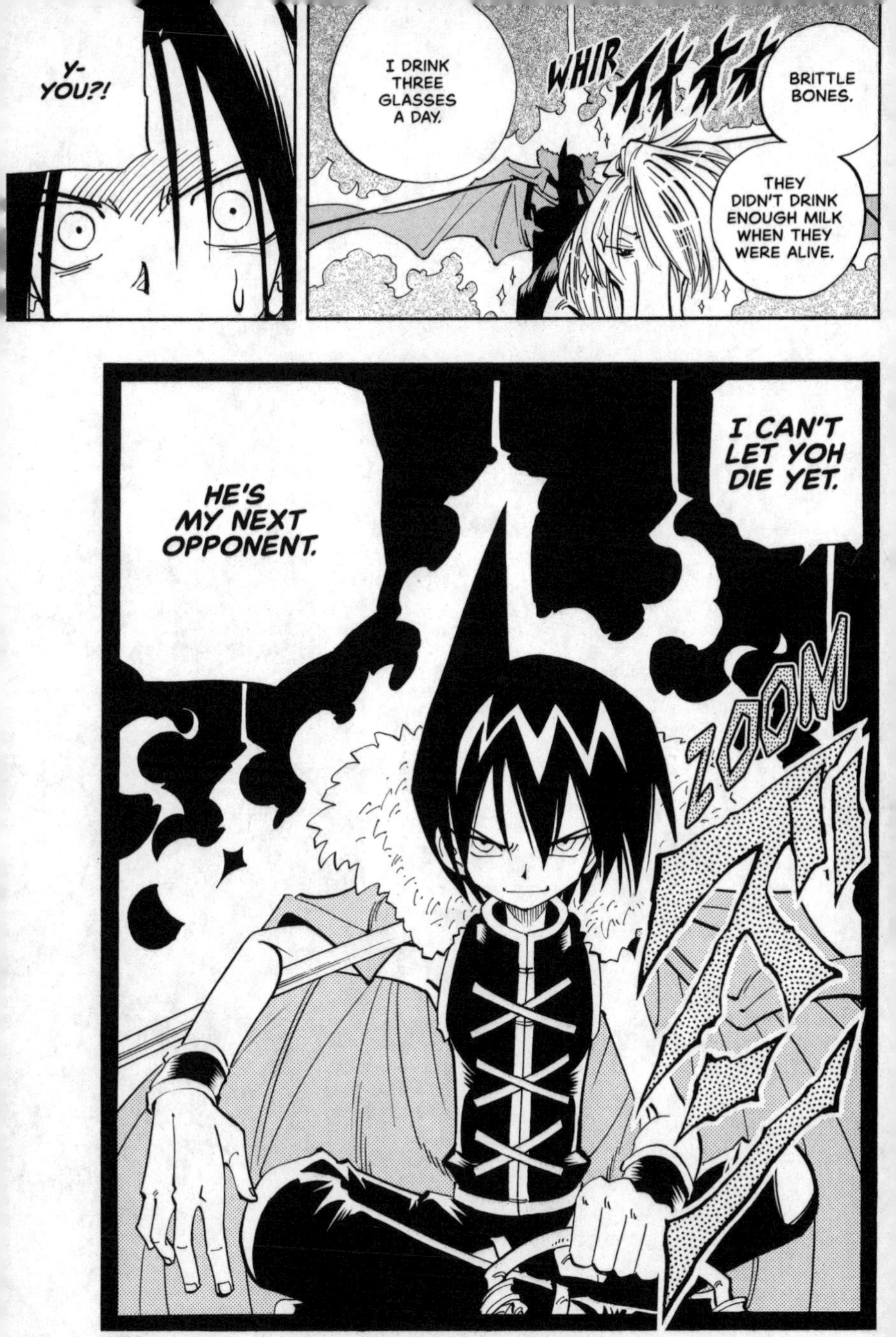
BRITTLE BONES.
THEY DIDN'T DRINK ENOUGH MILK WHEN THEY WERE ALIVE.
WHIR
I DRINK THREE GLASSES A DAY.
Y-YOU?!
I CAN'T LET YOH DIE YET.
HE'S MY NEXT OPPONENT.
ZOOM

SHAMAN
KING
6

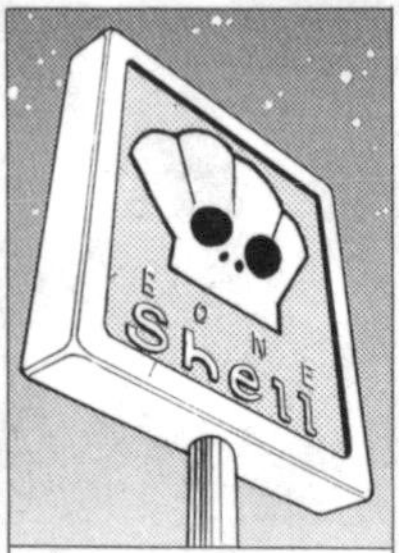
BONE
Shell

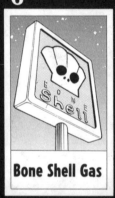

Bone Shell Gas

Chapter 47: June Goodbyes

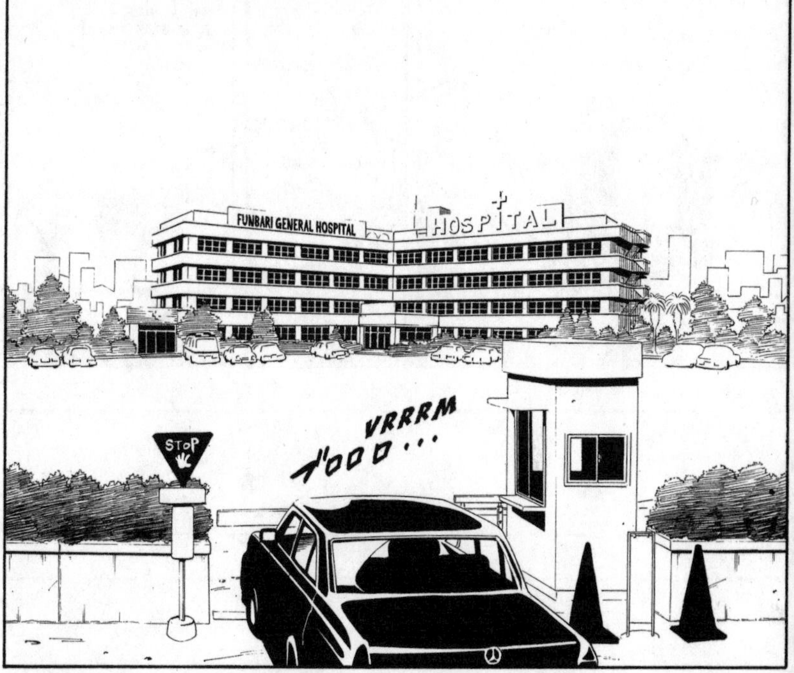
FUNBARI GENERAL HOSPITAL
HOSPITAL
STOP
VRRRM

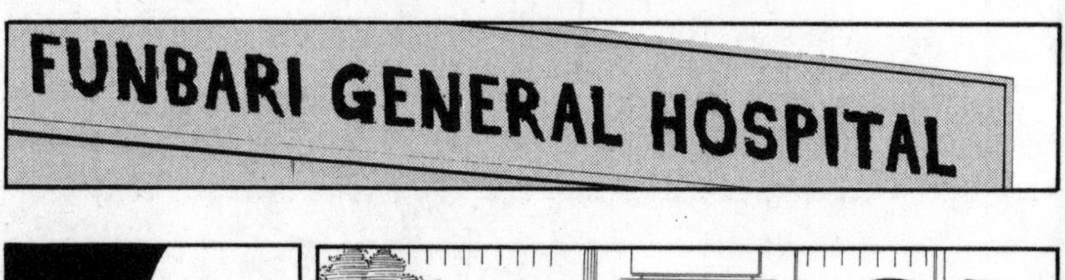
FUNBARI GENERAL HOSPITAL

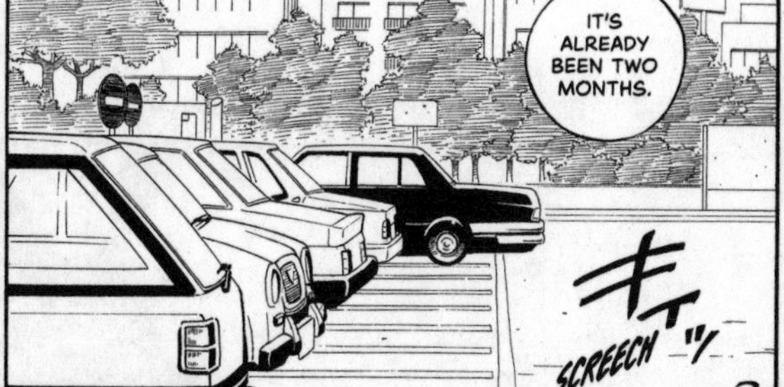
IT'S ALREADY BEEN TWO MONTHS.
SCREECH

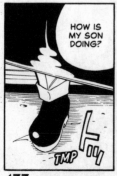

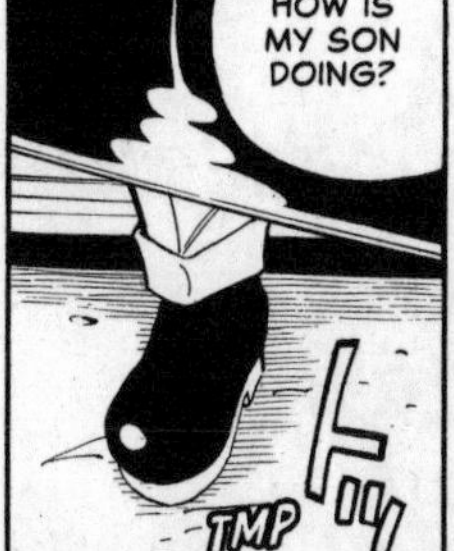
HOW IS MY SON DOING?
TMP

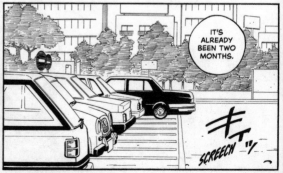

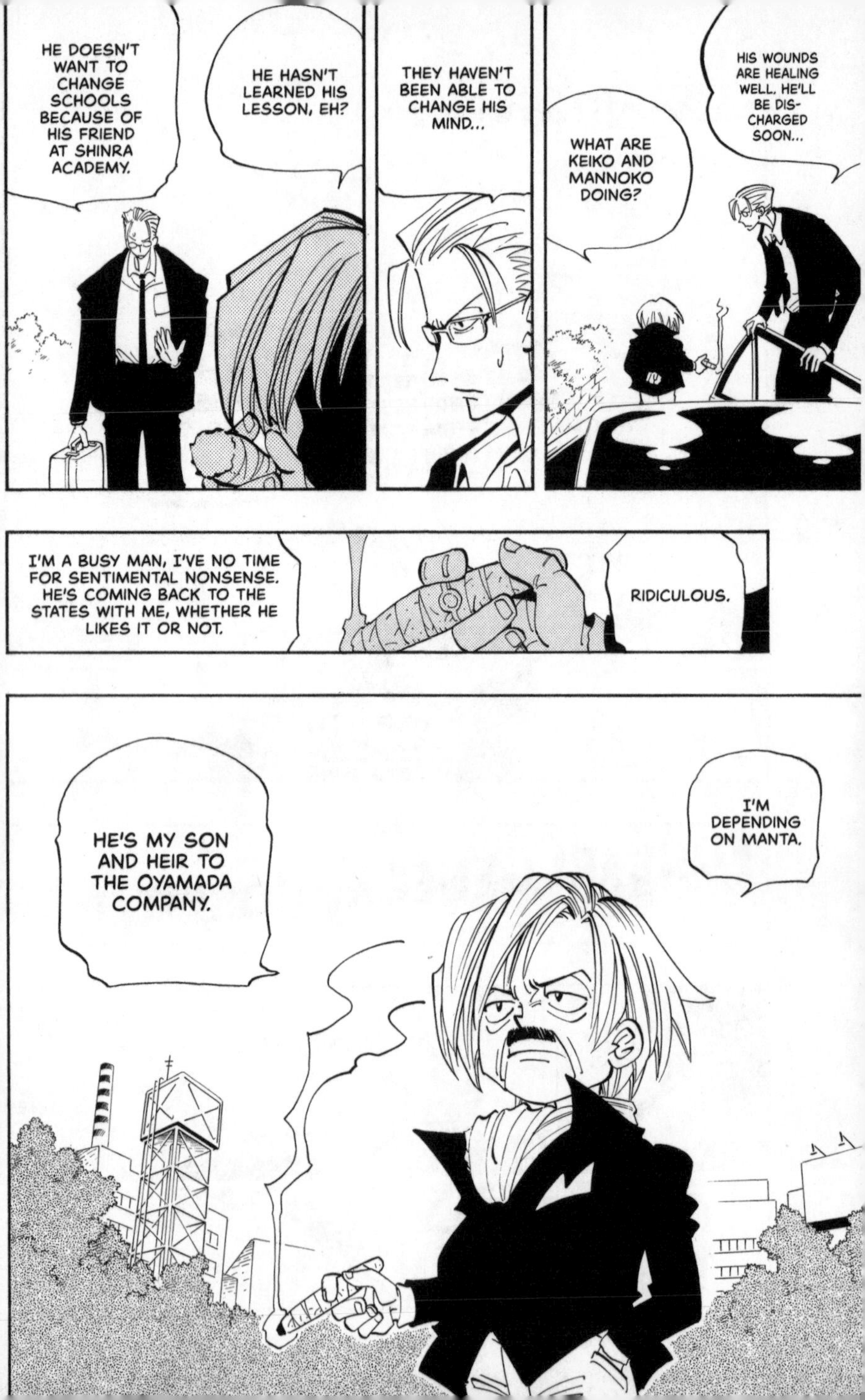
HIS WOUNDS ARE HEALING WELL. HE'LL BE DIS- CHARGED SOON...
WHAT ARE KEIKO AND MANNOKO DOING?
THEY HAVEN'T BEEN ABLE TO CHANGE HIS MIND...
HE HASN'T LEARNED HIS LESSON, EH?
HE DOESN'T WANT TO CHANGE SCHOOLS BECAUSE OF HIS FRIEND AT SHINRA ACADEMY.
RIDICULOUS.
I'M A BUSY MAN, I'VE NO TIME FOR SENTIMENTAL NONSENSE. HE'S COMING BACK TO THE STATES WITH ME, WHETHER HE LIKES IT OR NOT.
I'M DEPENDING ON MANTA.
HE'S MY SON AND HEIR TO THE OYAMADA COMPANY.

June Goodbyes

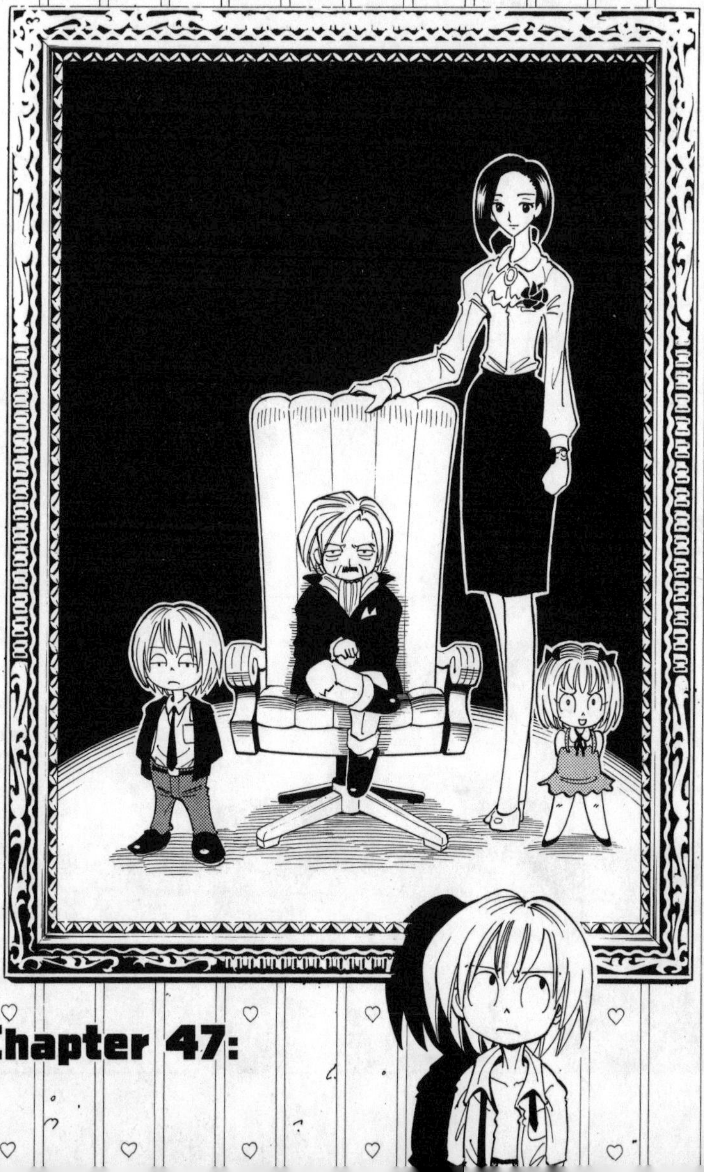

Chapter 47:

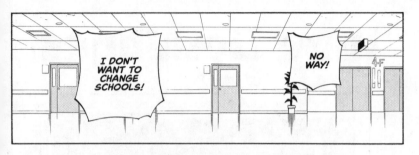

NO WAY!
I DON'T WANT TO CHANGE SCHOOLS!
IT COULD HAVE HAPPENED ANYWHERE! I GOT MUGGED, ALL RIGHT?!
HEY
I WASN'T CAREFUL ENOUGH! HOW MANY TIMES DO I HAVE TO TELL YOU?!
MANTANNIAN DICTIONARY
SANS FAMILLE
THE LITTLE PRINCESS
THE LITTLE
YOU WERE NEARLY DISEMBOW-ELED!
IT'S SO HORRIBLE! I CAN'T EVEN SHOW MY FACE IN PUBLIC.
SOB
FLIP
PLEASE COOP-ERATE, MANTA.
YOU MUSTN'T ASSOCIATE WITH RIFFRAFF ANYMORE.
Keiko Oyamada
(Manta's mother, age 37)

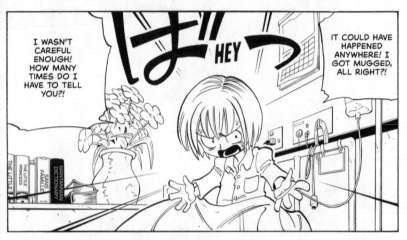

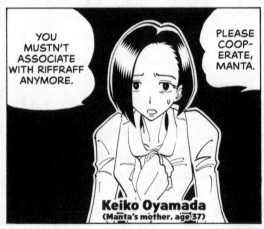

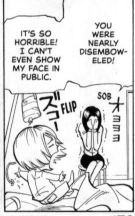

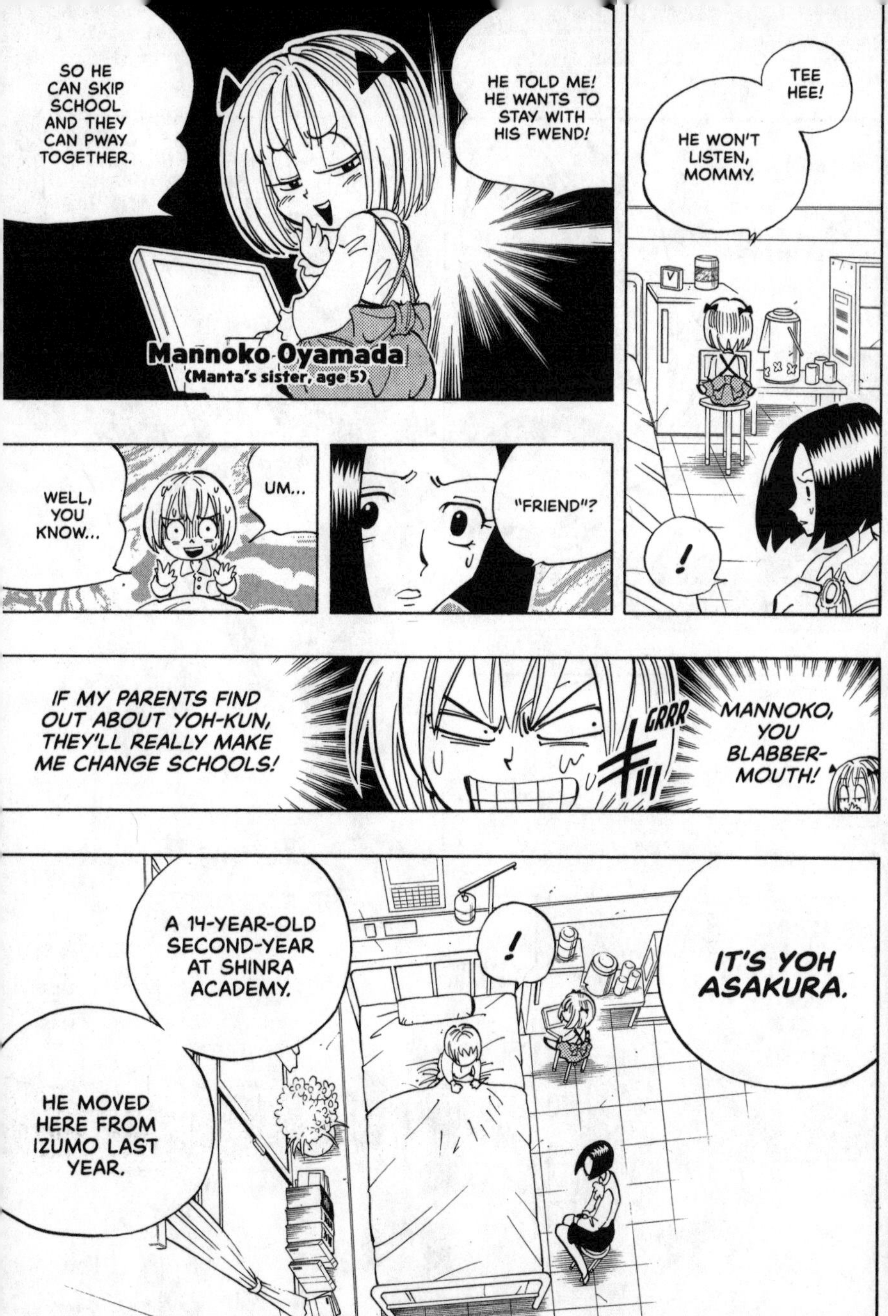
TEE HEE!
HE WON'T LISTEN, MOMMY.
!
HE TOLD ME! HE WANTS TO STAY WITH HIS FWEND!
SO HE CAN SKIP SCHOOL AND THEY CAN PWAY TOGETHER.
Mannoko Oyamada
(Manta's sister, age 5)
"FRIEND"?
UM...
WELL, YOU KNOW...
MANNOKO, YOU BLABBER-MOUTH!
GRRR
IF MY PARENTS FIND OUT ABOUT YOH-KUN, THEY'LL REALLY MAKE ME CHANGE SCHOOLS!
IT'S YOH ASAKURA.
!
A 14-YEAR-OLD SECOND-YEAR AT SHINRA ACADEMY.
HE MOVED HERE FROM IZUMO LAST YEAR.

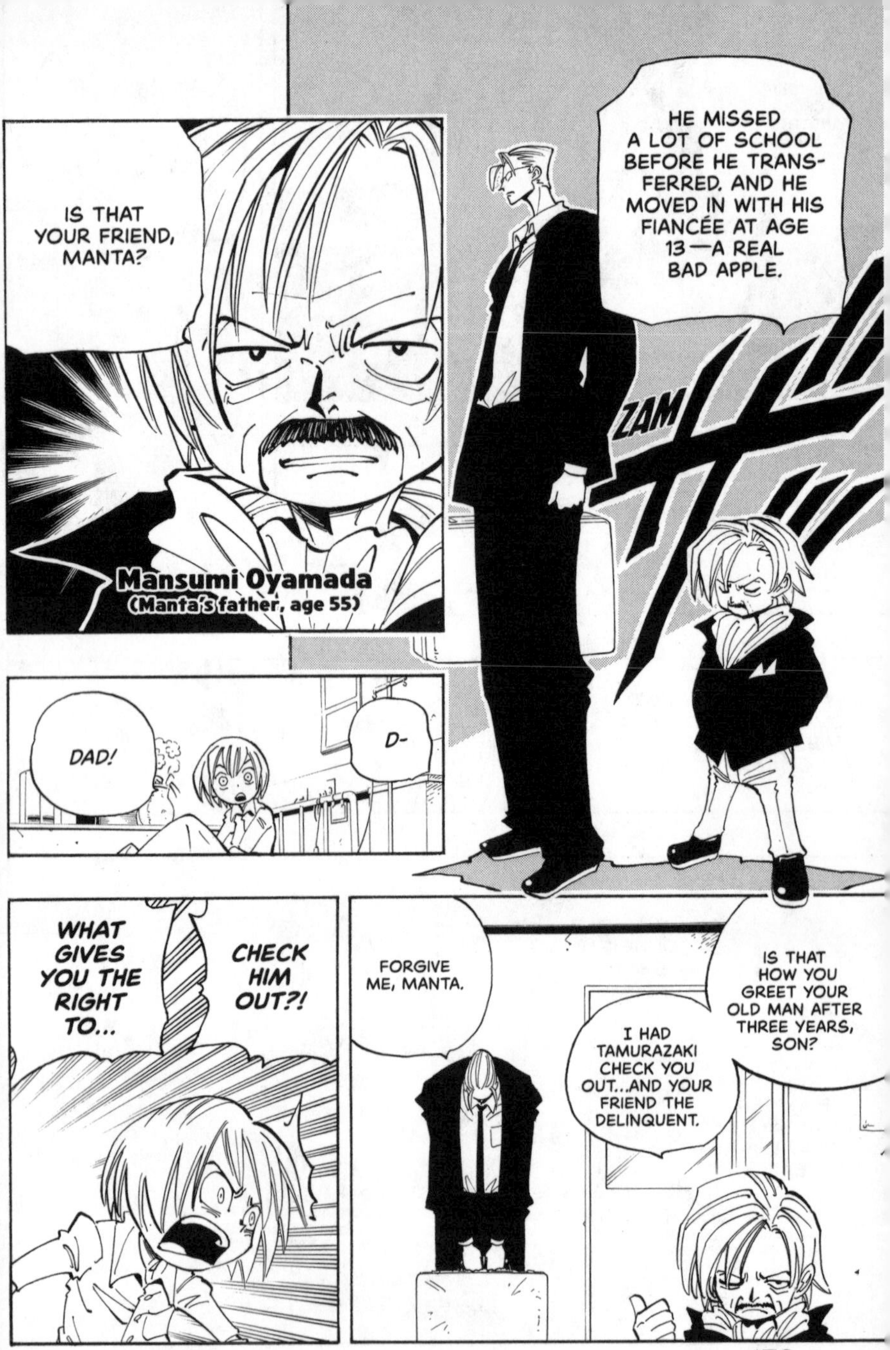
HE MISSED A LOT OF SCHOOL BEFORE HE TRANSFERRED. AND HE MOVED IN WITH HIS FIANCÉE AT AGE 13—A REAL BAD APPLE.
ZAM
IS THAT YOUR FRIEND, MANTA?
Mansumi Oyamada
(Manta's father, age 55)
D-
DAD!
IS THAT HOW YOU GREET YOUR OLD MAN AFTER THREE YEARS, SON?
I HAD TAMURAZAKI CHECK YOU OUT...AND YOUR FRIEND THE DELINQUENT.
FORGIVE ME, MANTA.
WHAT GIVES YOU THE RIGHT TO...
CHECK HIM OUT?!

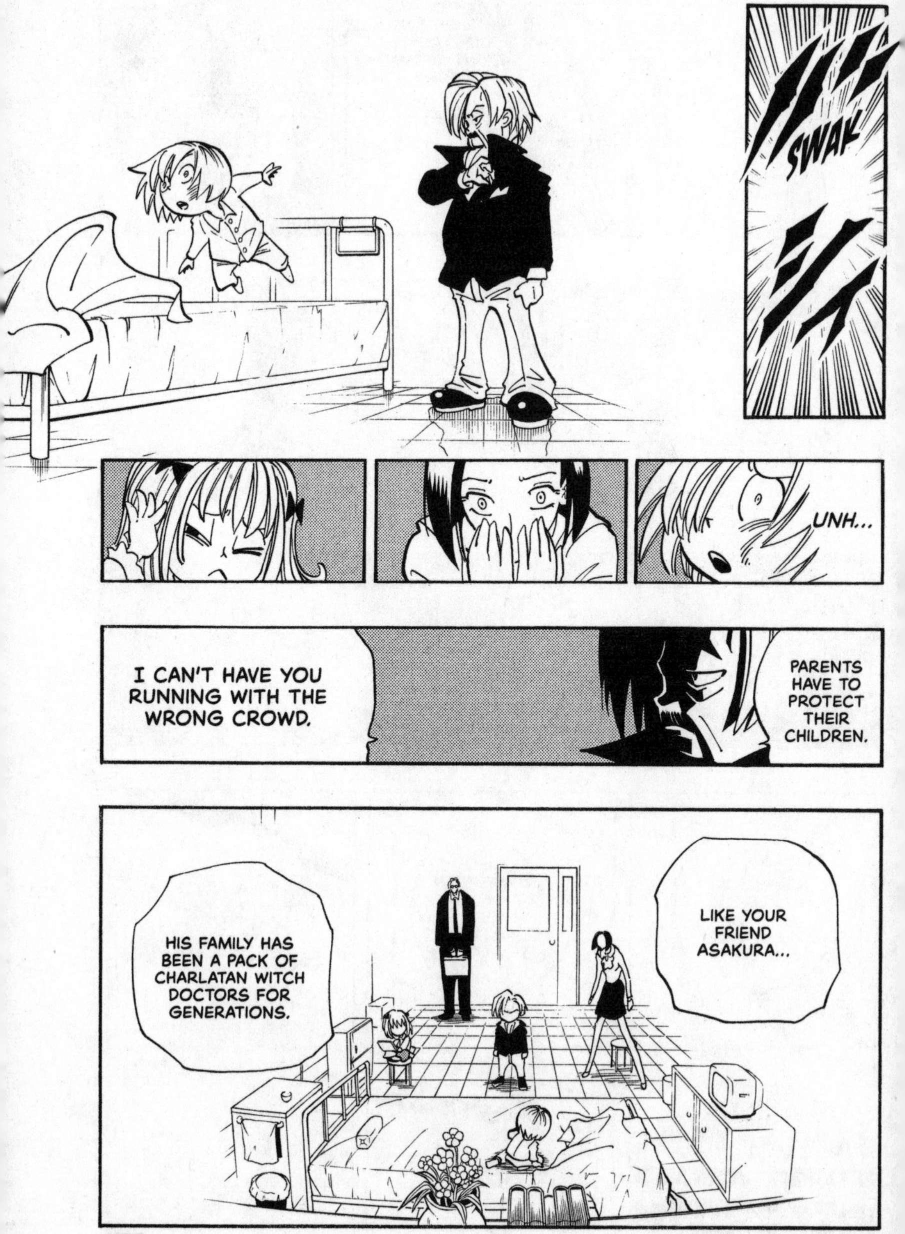
SWAK
UNH...
PARENTS HAVE TO PROTECT THEIR CHILDREN.
I CAN'T HAVE YOU RUNNING WITH THE WRONG CROWD.
LIKE YOUR FRIEND ASAKURA...
HIS FAMILY HAS BEEN A PACK OF CHARLATAN WITCH DOCTORS FOR GENERATIONS.

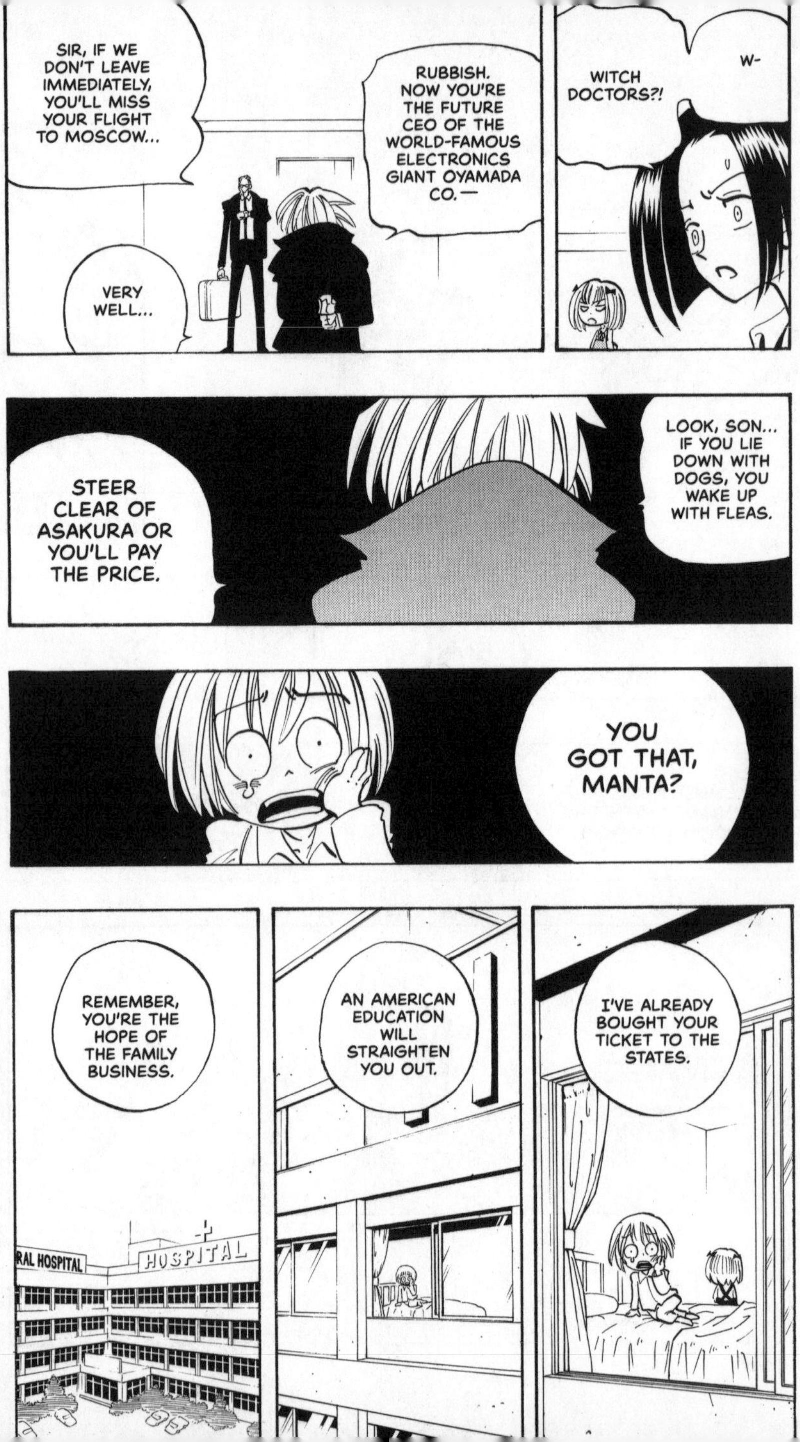
W-
WITCH DOCTORS?!
RUBBISH. NOW YOU'RE THE FUTURE CEO OF THE WORLD-FAMOUS ELECTRONICS GIANT OYAMADA CO.—
SIR, IF WE DON'T LEAVE IMMEDIATELY, YOU'LL MISS YOUR FLIGHT TO MOSCOW...
VERY WELL...
LOOK, SON... IF YOU LIE DOWN WITH DOGS, YOU WAKE UP WITH FLEAS.
STEER CLEAR OF ASAKURA OR YOU'LL PAY THE PRICE.
YOU GOT THAT, MANTA?
I'VE ALREADY BOUGHT YOUR TICKET TO THE STATES.
AN AMERICAN EDUCATION WILL STRAIGHTEN YOU OUT.
REMEMBER, YOU'RE THE HOPE OF THE FAMILY BUSINESS.
HOSPITAL
RAL HOSPITAL

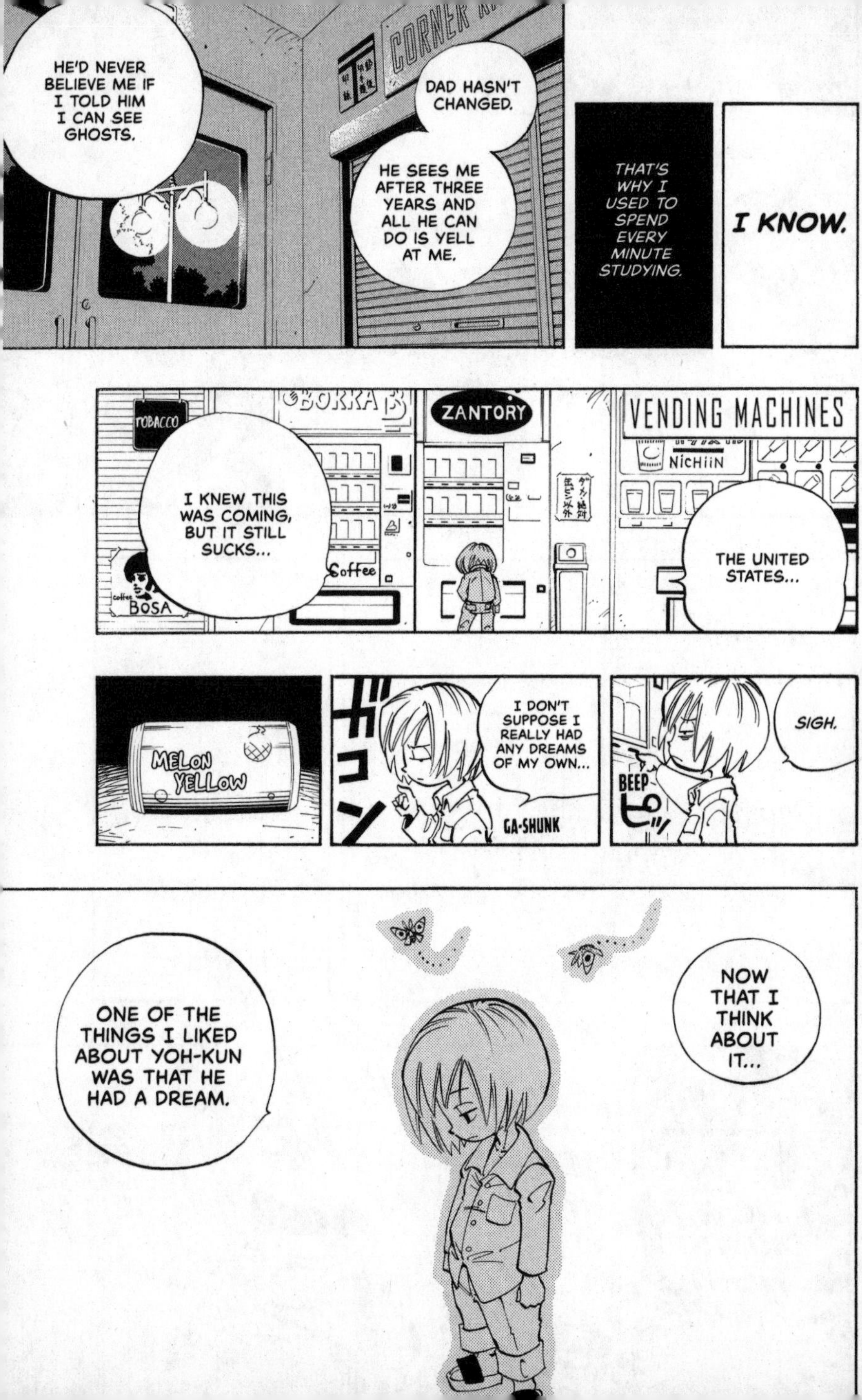

I KNOW.
THAT'S WHY I USED TO SPEND EVERY MINUTE STUDYING.
DAD HASN'T CHANGED.
HE SEES ME AFTER THREE YEARS AND ALL HE CAN DO IS YELL AT ME.
HE'D NEVER BELIEVE ME IF I TOLD HIM I CAN SEE GHOSTS.
VENDING MACHINES
NICHiiN
THE UNITED STATES...
ZANTORY
BOKKA
TOBACCO
I KNEW THIS WAS COMING, BUT IT STILL SUCKS...
Coffee
coffee BOSA
SIGH.
BEEP
ピッ
I DON'T SUPPOSE I REALLY HAD ANY DREAMS OF MY OWN...
GA-SHUNK
ガコン
MELON YELLOW
NOW THAT I THINK ABOUT IT...
ONE OF THE THINGS I LIKED ABOUT YOH-KUN WAS THAT HE HAD A DREAM.

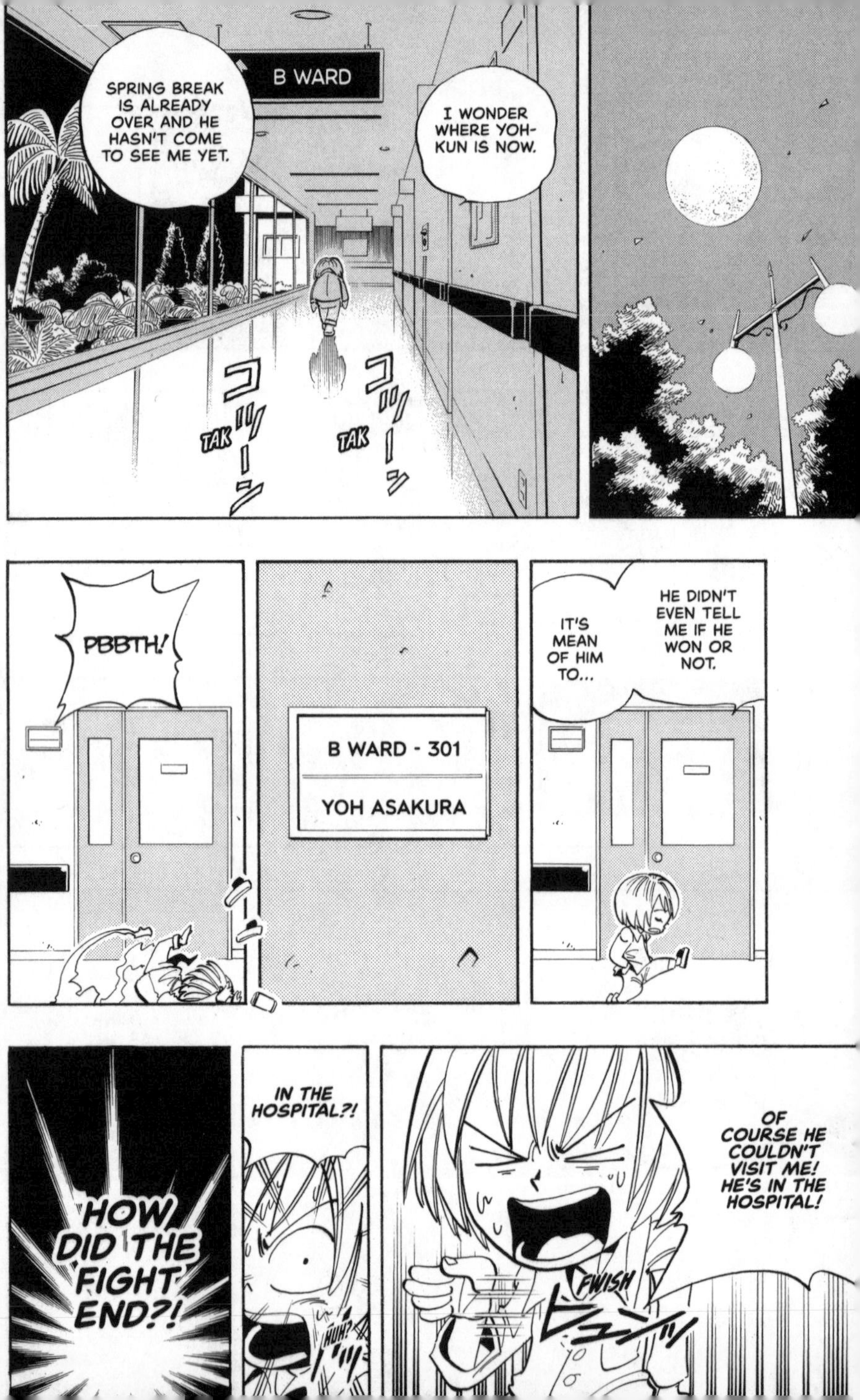
B WARD
I WONDER WHERE YOH-KUN IS NOW.
SPRING BREAK IS ALREADY OVER AND HE HASN'T COME TO SEE ME YET.
TAK
TAK
HE DIDN'T EVEN TELL ME IF HE WON OR NOT.
IT'S MEAN OF HIM TO...
B WARD - 301
YOH ASAKURA
PBBTH!
OF COURSE HE COULDN'T VISIT ME! HE'S IN THE HOSPITAL!
FWISH
IN THE HOSPITAL?!
HUH?
HOW DID THE FIGHT END?!

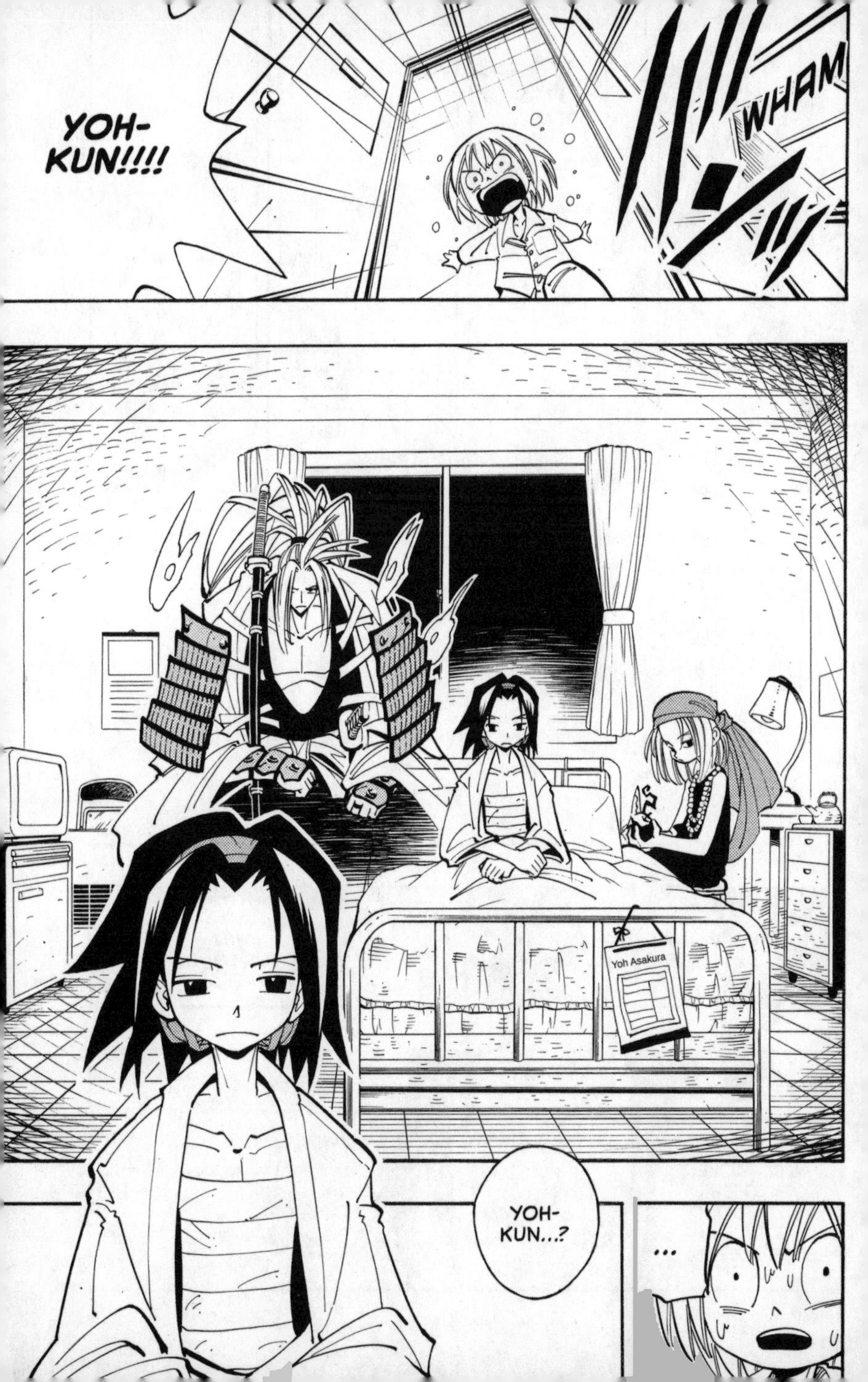
WHAM
YOH-KUN!!!!
Yoh Asakura
...
YOH-KUN...?

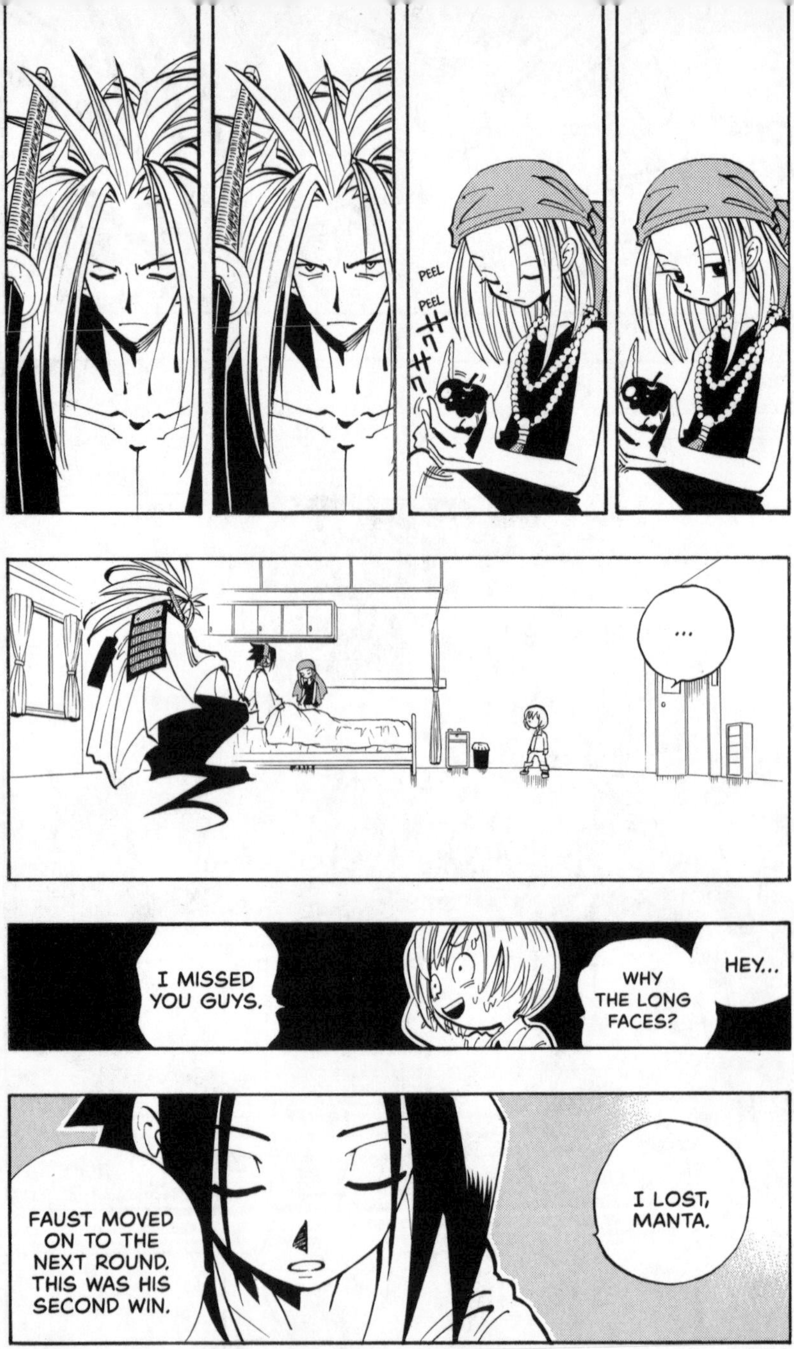
PEEL
PEEL
...
HEY...
WHY THE LONG FACES?
I MISSED YOU GUYS.
I LOST, MANTA.
FAUST MOVED ON TO THE NEXT ROUND. THIS WAS HIS SECOND WIN.

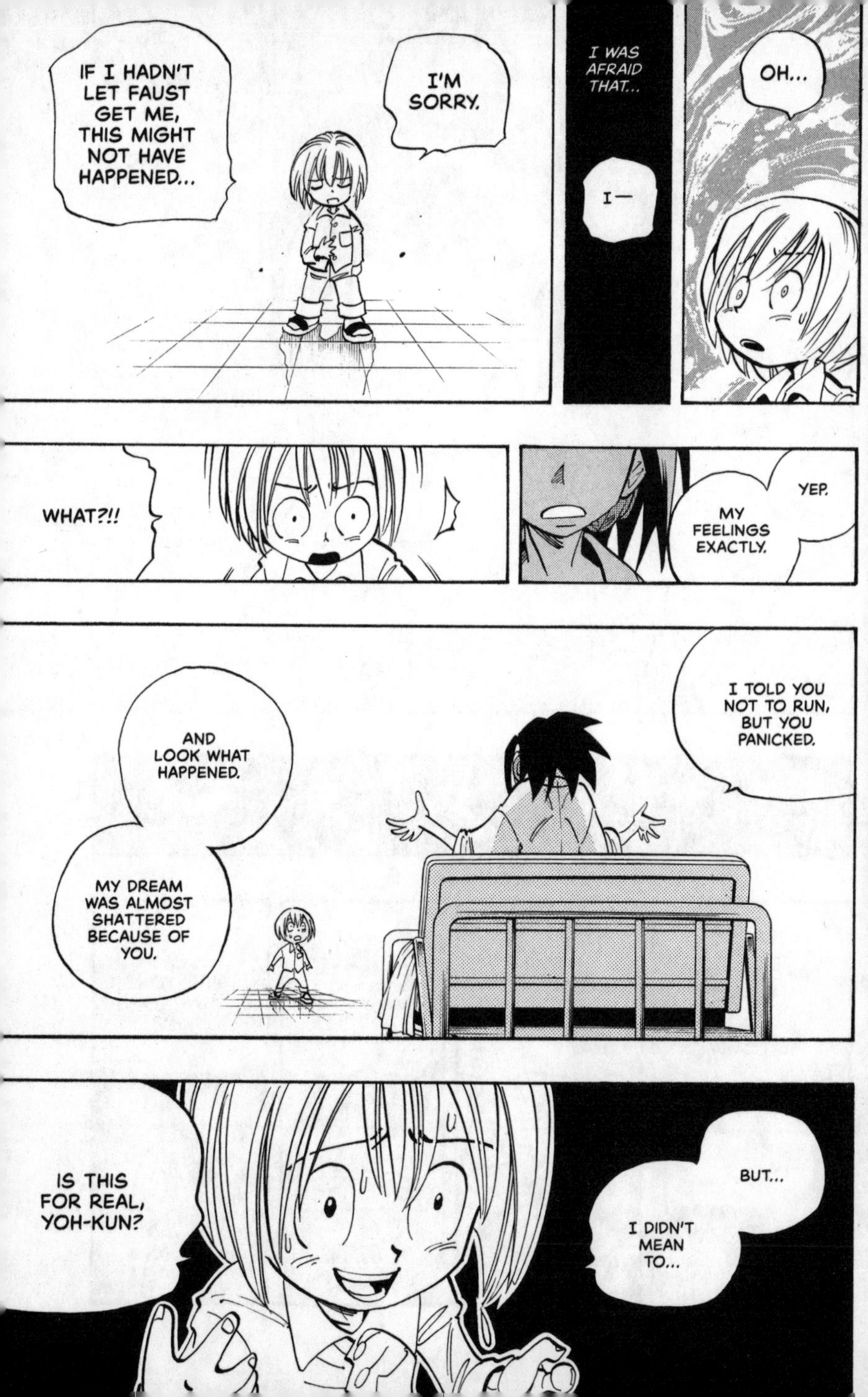
OH...
I WAS AFRAID THAT...
I—
I'M SORRY.
IF I HADN'T LET FAUST GET ME, THIS MIGHT NOT HAVE HAPPENED...
YEP.
MY FEELINGS EXACTLY.
WHAT?!!
I TOLD YOU NOT TO RUN, BUT YOU PANICKED.
AND LOOK WHAT HAPPENED.
MY DREAM WAS ALMOST SHATTERED BECAUSE OF YOU.
BUT...
I DIDN'T MEAN TO...
IS THIS FOR REAL, YOH-KUN?

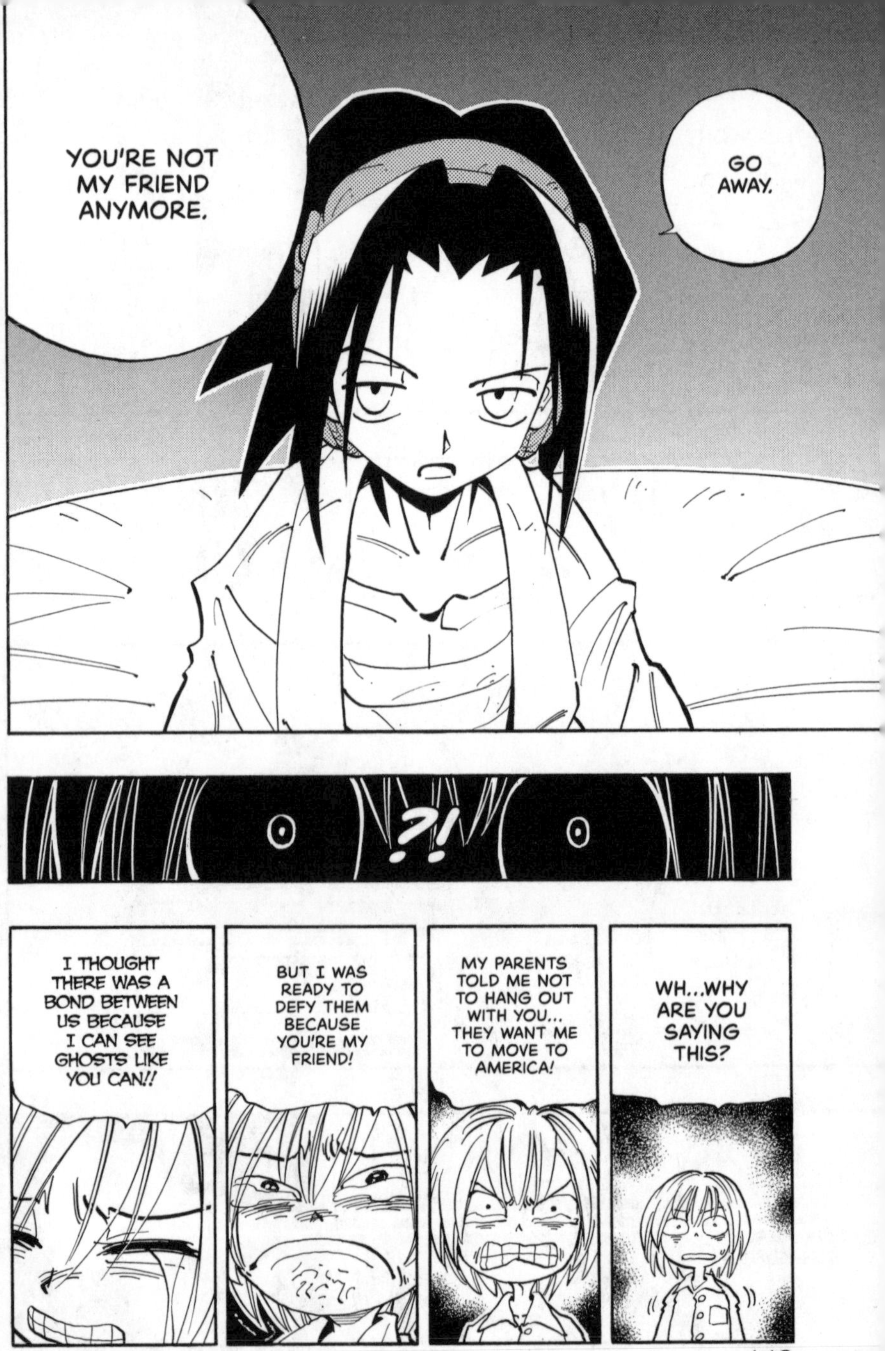
GO AWAY.
YOU'RE NOT MY FRIEND ANYMORE.
?!
WH...WHY ARE YOU SAYING THIS?
MY PARENTS TOLD ME NOT TO HANG OUT WITH YOU... THEY WANT ME TO MOVE TO AMERICA!
BUT I WAS READY TO DEFY THEM BECAUSE YOU'RE MY FRIEND!
I THOUGHT THERE WAS A BOND BETWEEN US BECAUSE I CAN SEE GHOSTS LIKE YOU CAN!!

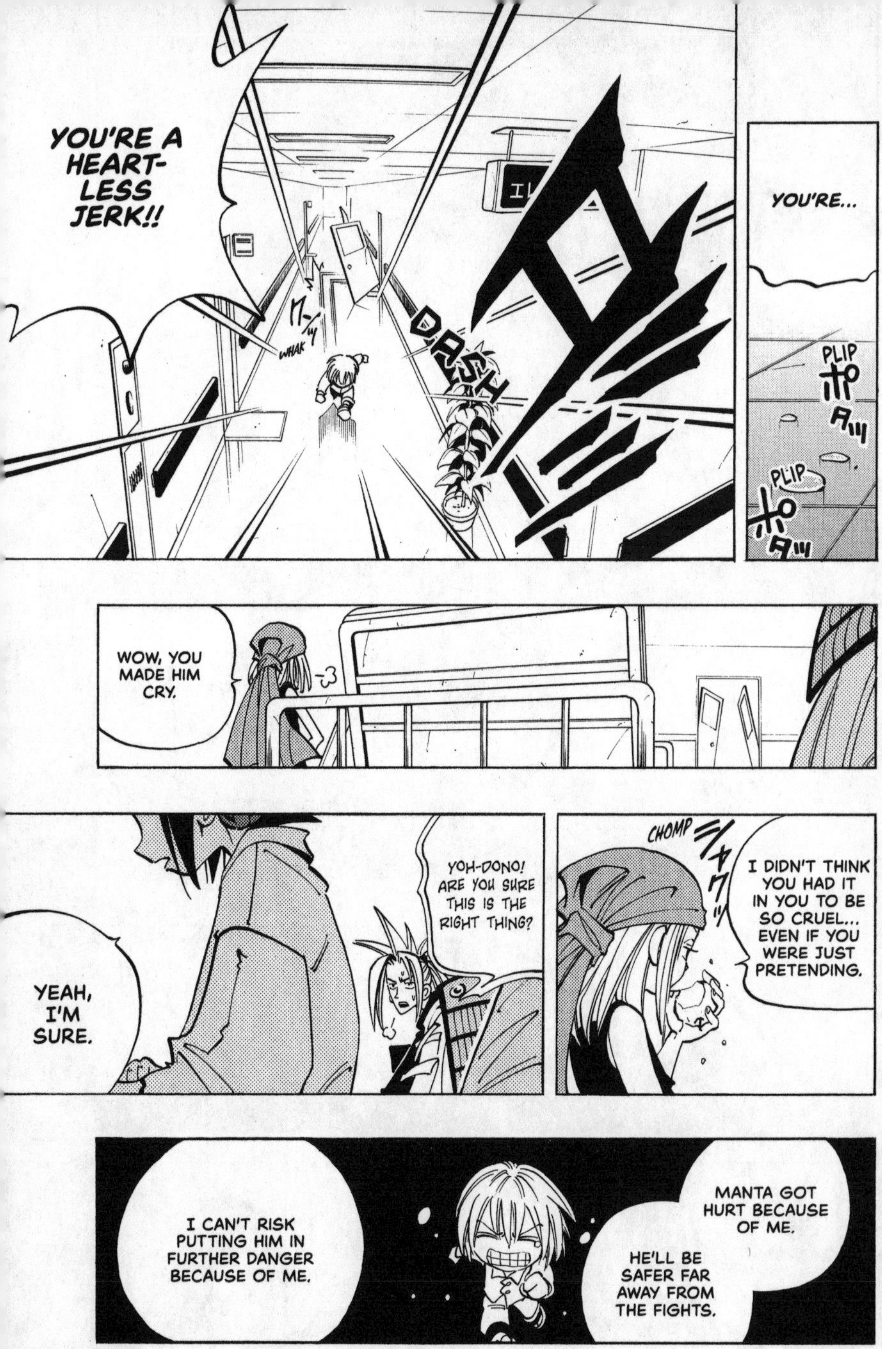
YOU'RE...
PLIP
PLIP
YOU'RE A HEART-LESS JERK!!
DASH
WHAK
WOW, YOU MADE HIM CRY.
I DIDN'T THINK YOU HAD IT IN YOU TO BE SO CRUEL... EVEN IF YOU WERE JUST PRETENDING.
CHOMP
YOH-DONO! ARE YOU SURE THIS IS THE RIGHT THING?
YEAH, I'M SURE.
MANTA GOT HURT BECAUSE OF ME.
HE'LL BE SAFER FAR AWAY FROM THE FIGHTS.
I CAN'T RISK PUTTING HIM IN FURTHER DANGER BECAUSE OF ME.

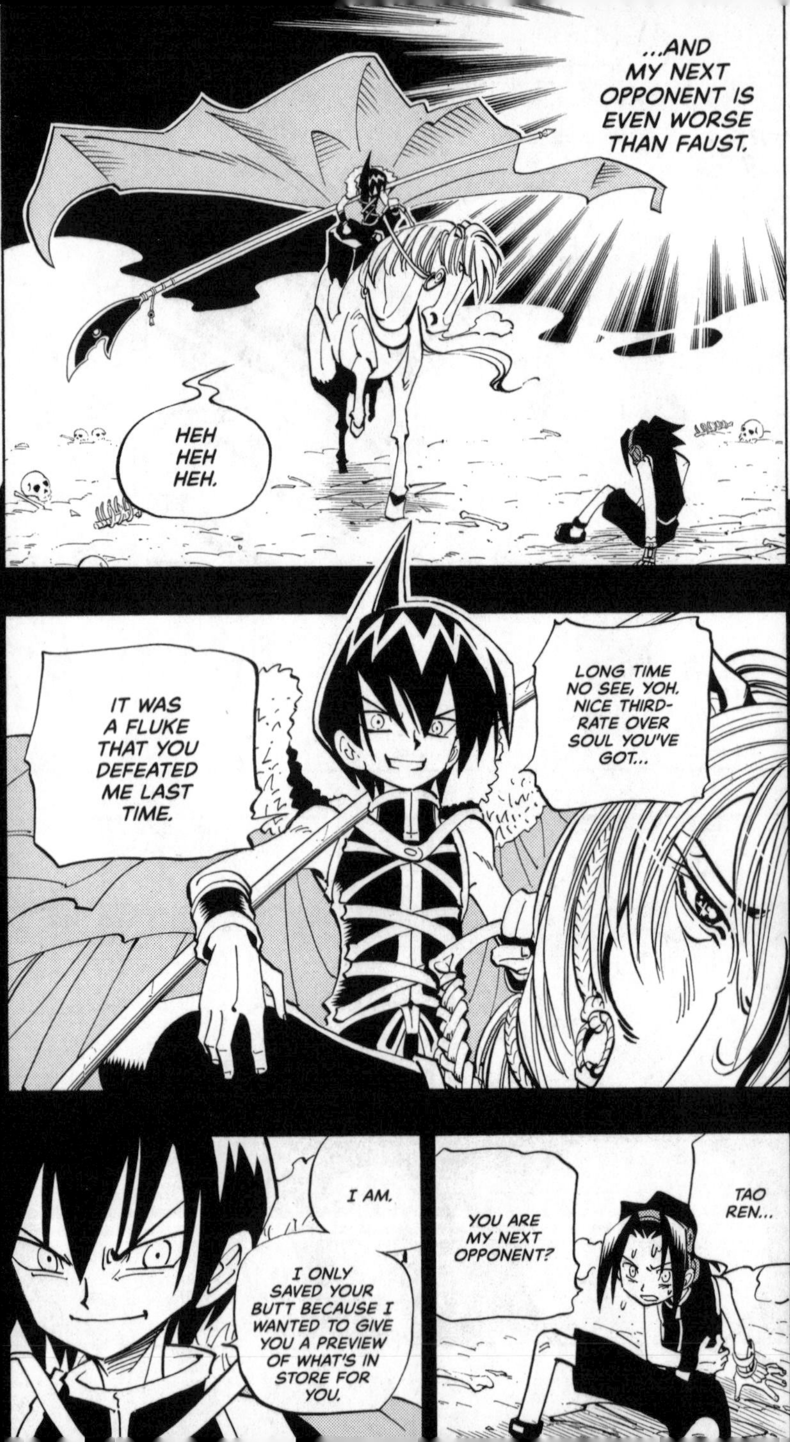
...AND MY NEXT OPPONENT IS EVEN WORSE THAN FAUST.
HEH HEH HEH.
LONG TIME NO SEE, YOH. NICE THIRD-RATE OVER SOUL YOU'VE GOT...
IT WAS A FLUKE THAT YOU DEFEATED ME LAST TIME.
TAO REN...
YOU ARE MY NEXT OPPONENT?
I AM.
I ONLY SAVED YOUR BUTT BECAUSE I WANTED TO GIVE YOU A PREVIEW OF WHAT'S IN STORE FOR YOU.

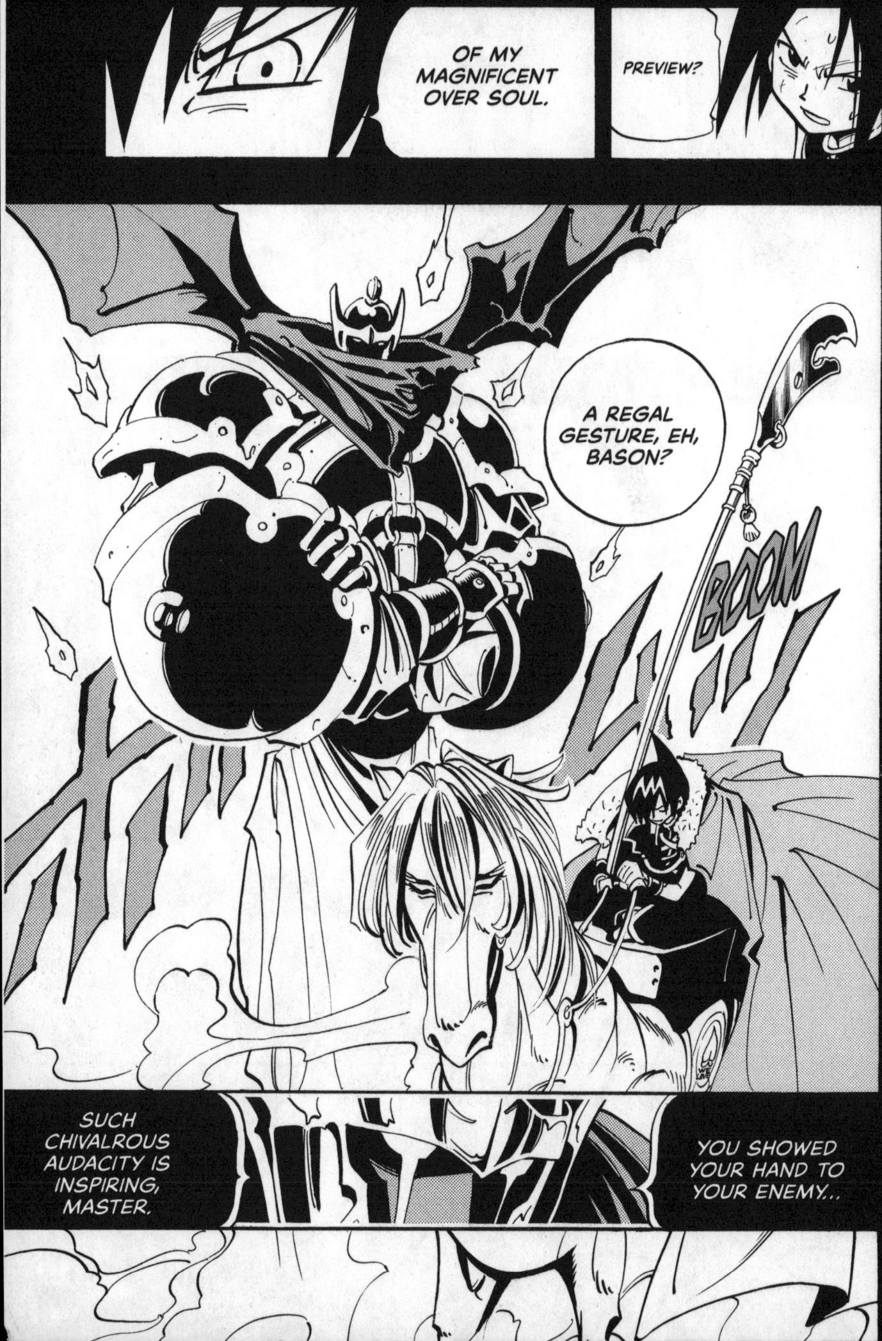
PREVIEW?
OF MY MAGNIFICENT OVER SOUL.
A REGAL GESTURE, EH, BASON?
BOOM
YOU SHOWED YOUR HAND TO YOUR ENEMY...
SUCH CHIVALROUS AUDACITY IS INSPIRING, MASTER.

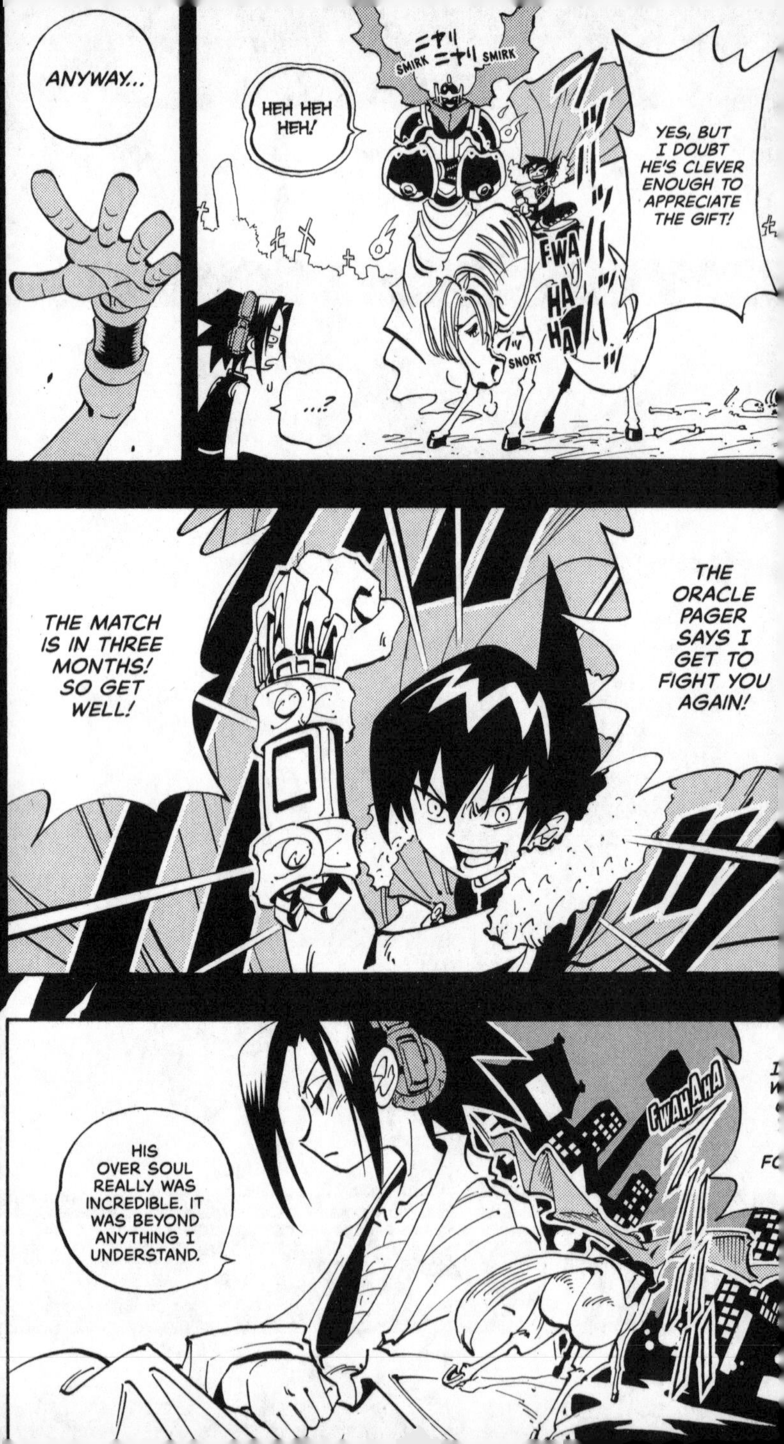
YES, BUT I DOUBT HE'S CLEVER ENOUGH TO APPRECIATE THE GIFT!
FWA HA HA
ニヤリ SMIRK ニヤリ SMIRK
HEH HEH HEH!
SNORT
...?
ANYWAY...
THE ORACLE PAGER SAYS I GET TO FIGHT YOU AGAIN!
THE MATCH IS IN THREE MONTHS! SO GET WELL!
FWAHAHA
HIS OVER SOUL REALLY WAS INCREDIBLE. IT WAS BEYOND ANYTHING I UNDERSTAND.

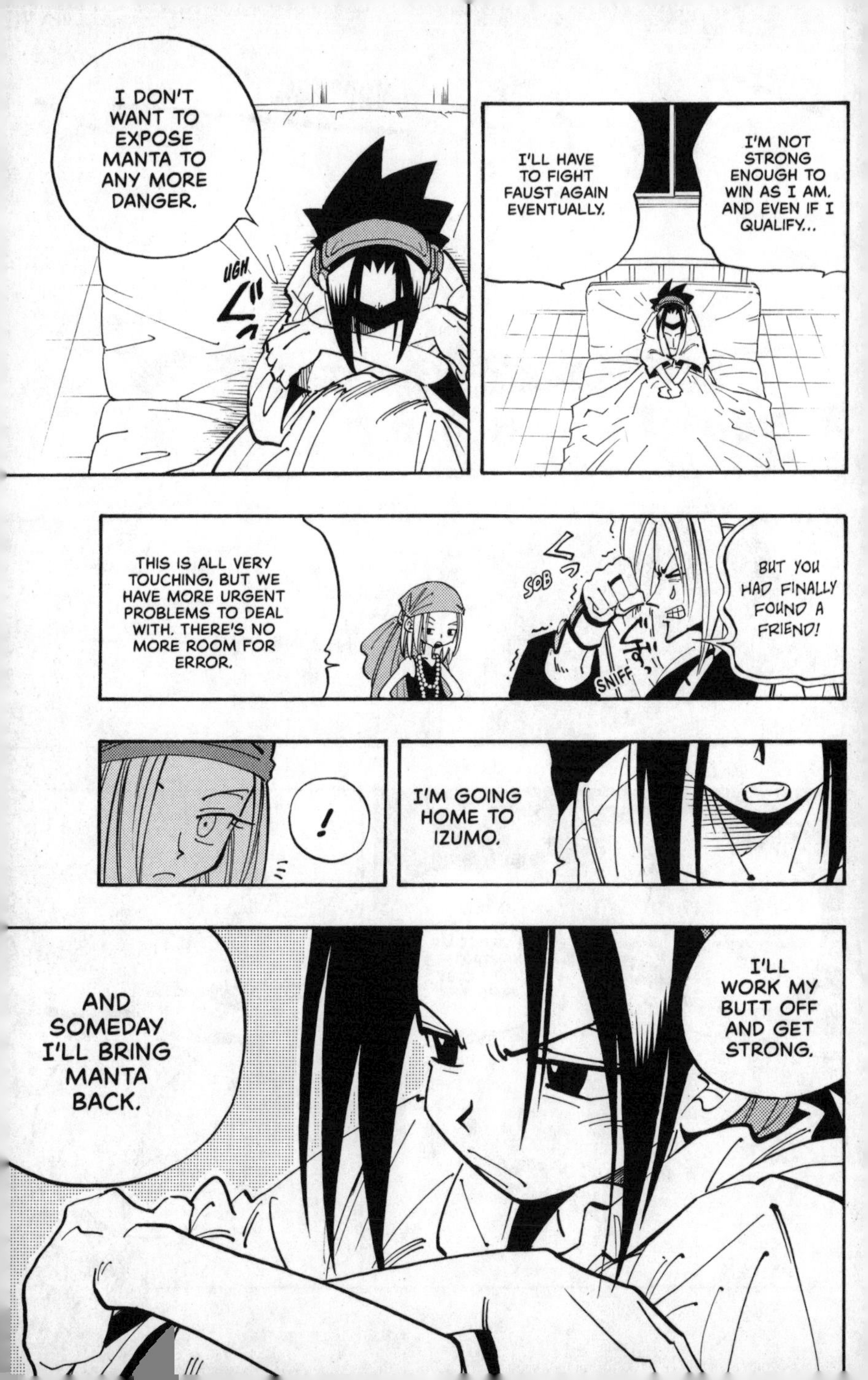
I'M NOT STRONG ENOUGH TO WIN AS I AM. AND EVEN IF I QUALIFY...
I'LL HAVE TO FIGHT FAUST AGAIN EVENTUALLY.
I DON'T WANT TO EXPOSE MANTA TO ANY MORE DANGER.
UGH
BUT YOU HAD FINALLY FOUND A FRIEND!
SOB
SNIFF
THIS IS ALL VERY TOUCHING, BUT WE HAVE MORE URGENT PROBLEMS TO DEAL WITH. THERE'S NO MORE ROOM FOR ERROR.
I'M GOING HOME TO IZUMO.
!
I'LL WORK MY BUTT OFF AND GET STRONG.
AND SOMEDAY I'LL BRING MANTA BACK.

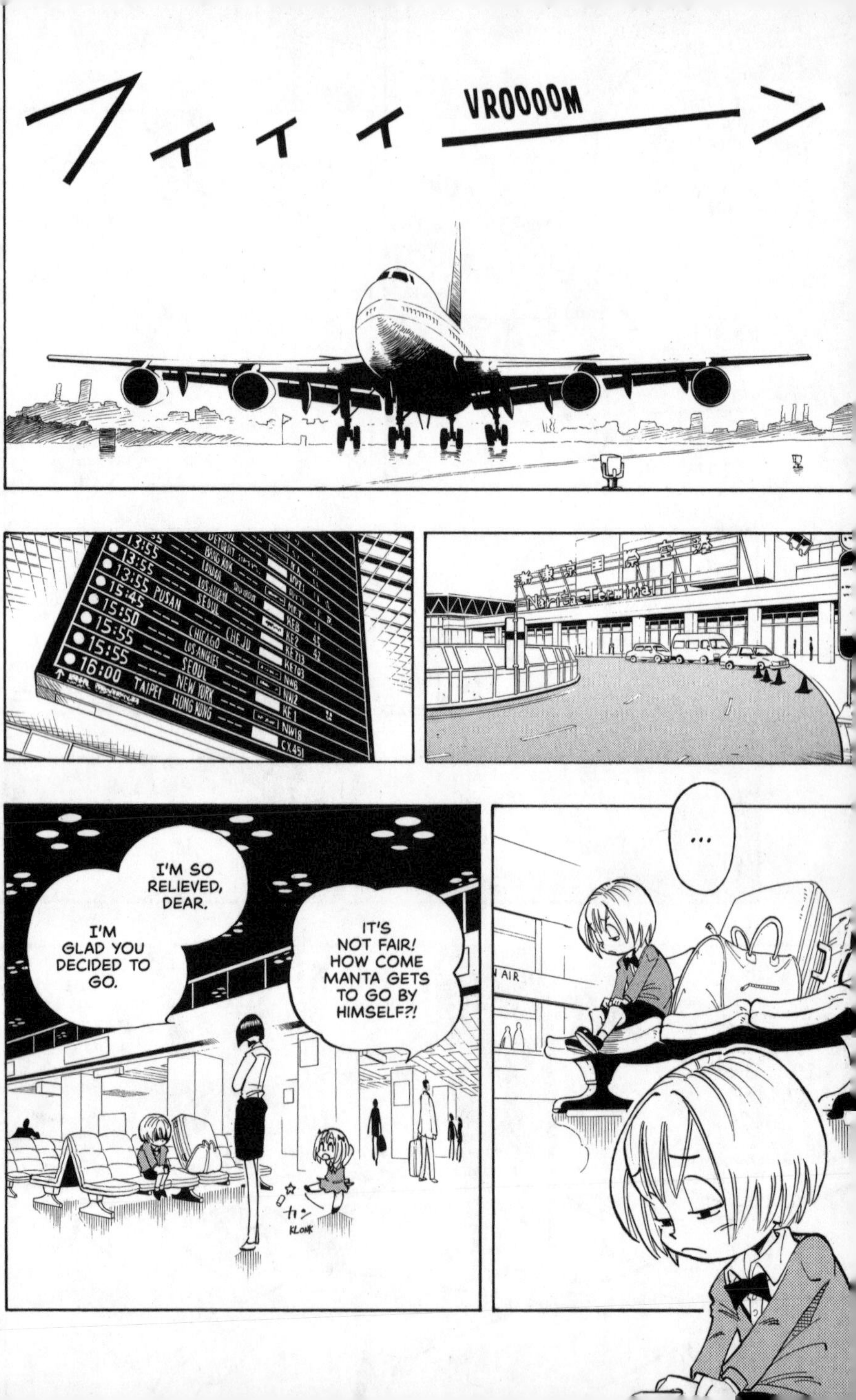
VROOOOM
Narita-Terminal
...
I'M SO RELIEVED, DEAR.
I'M GLAD YOU DECIDED TO GO.
IT'S NOT FAIR! HOW COME MANTA GETS TO GO BY HIMSELF?!
カン
KLONK

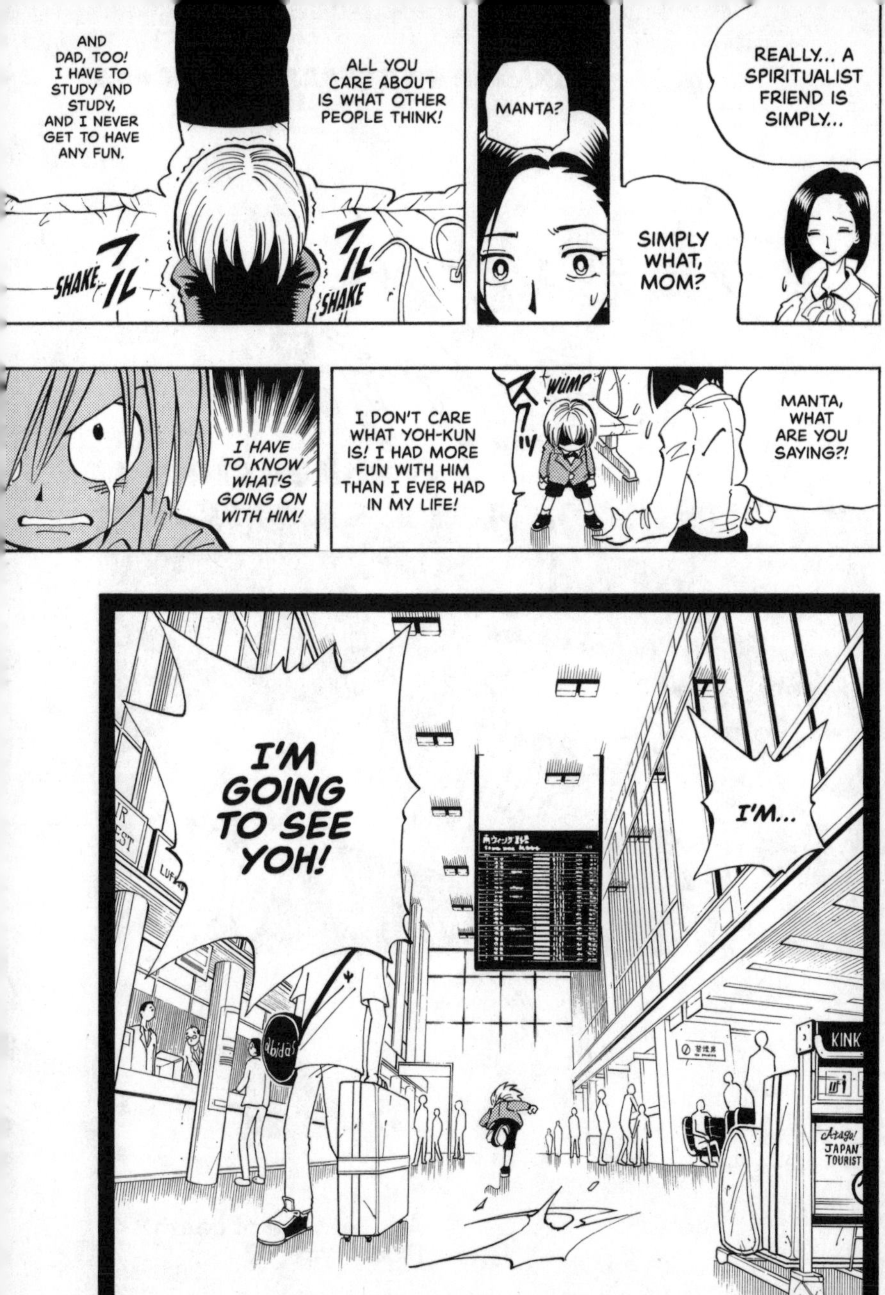
REALLY... A SPIRITUALIST FRIEND IS SIMPLY...
SIMPLY WHAT, MOM?
MANTA?
ALL YOU CARE ABOUT IS WHAT OTHER PEOPLE THINK!
AND DAD, TOO! I HAVE TO STUDY AND STUDY, AND I NEVER GET TO HAVE ANY FUN.
SHAKE
SHAKE
MANTA, WHAT ARE YOU SAYING?!
WUMP
I DON'T CARE WHAT YOH-KUN IS! I HAD MORE FUN WITH HIM THAN I EVER HAD IN MY LIFE!
I HAVE TO KNOW WHAT'S GOING ON WITH HIM!
I'M...
I'M GOING TO SEE YOH!
KINK
JAPAN TOURIST

SHAMAN KING CHARACTER FILE No.25

フランケンシュタイニー

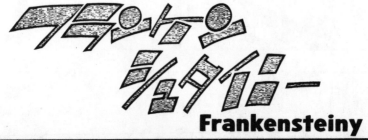

Frankensteiny

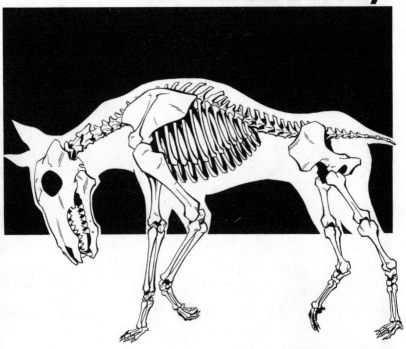

Age (at time of death): 4
Blood Type: D2

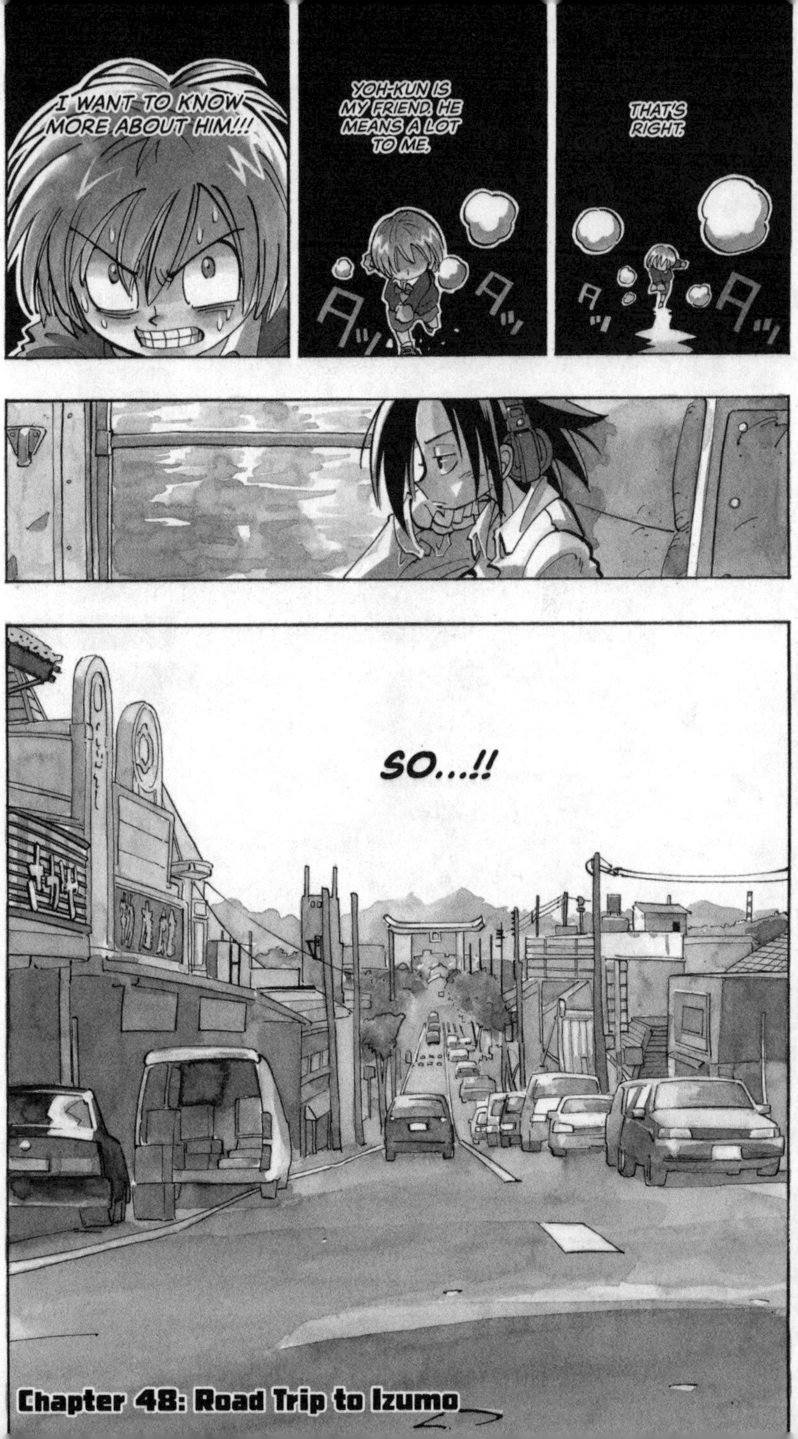
THAT'S RIGHT.
YOH-KUN IS MY FRIEND. HE MEANS A LOT TO ME.
I WANT TO KNOW MORE ABOUT HIM!!!
SO...!!
Chapter 48: Road Trip to Izumo

Chapter 48:

Road Trip to Izumo

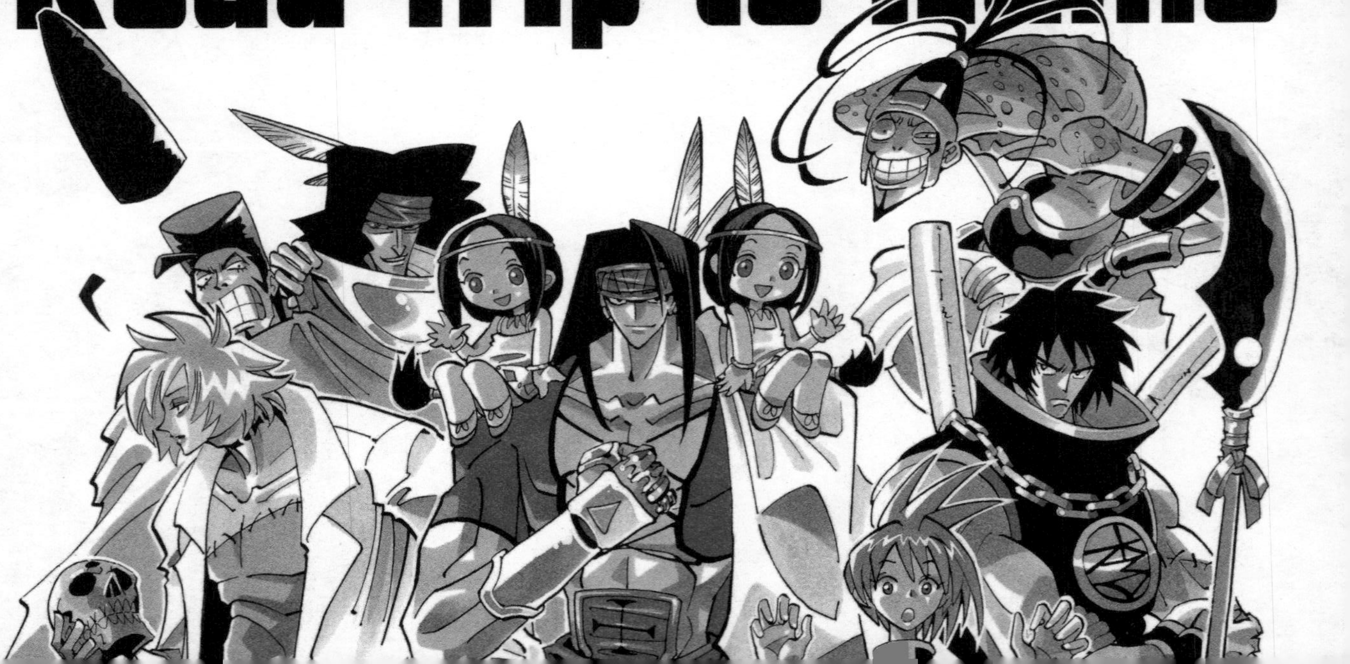

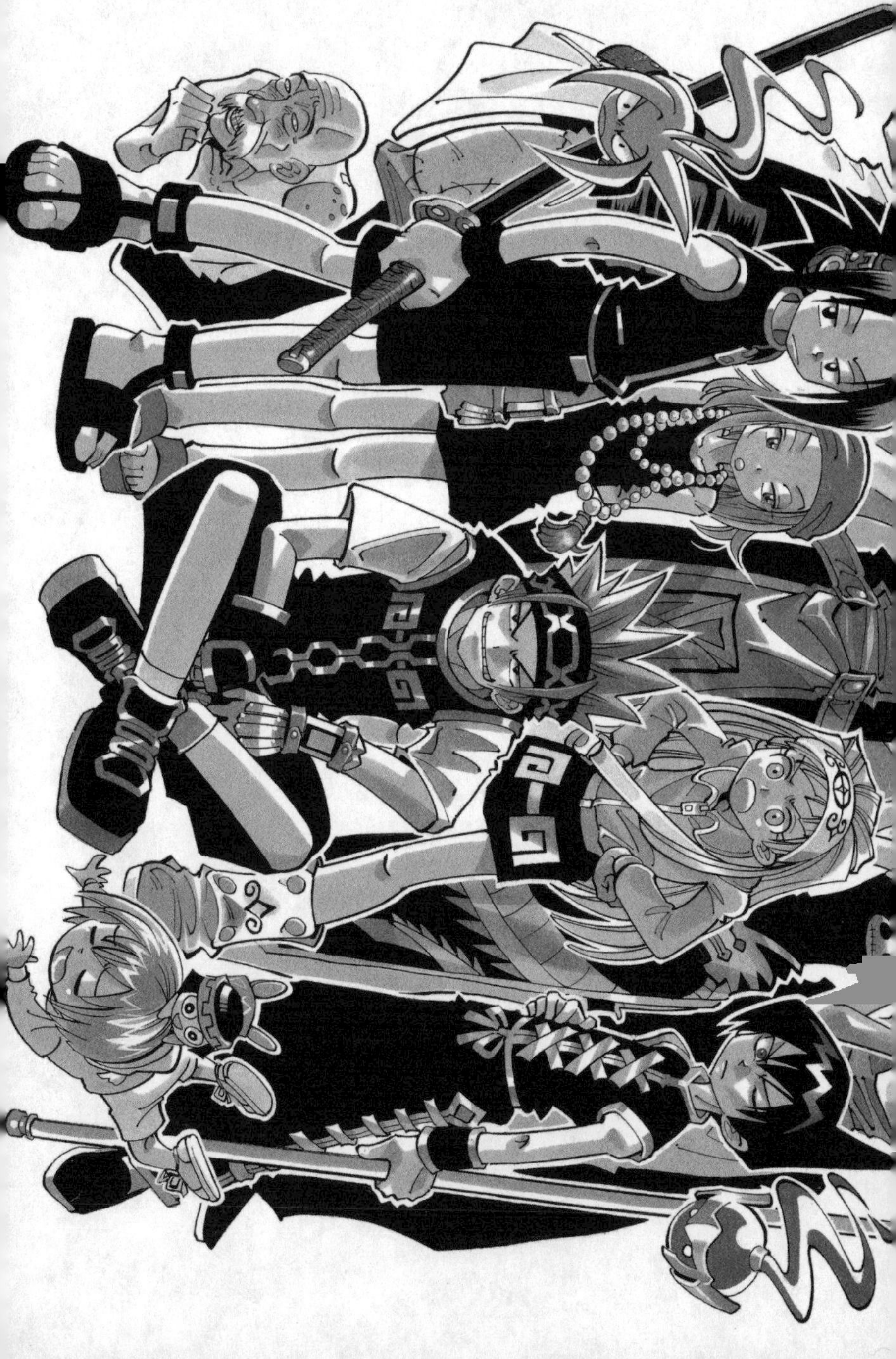

SHAMAN
KING
6

**Ultra Helmet
(Haute Couture)**

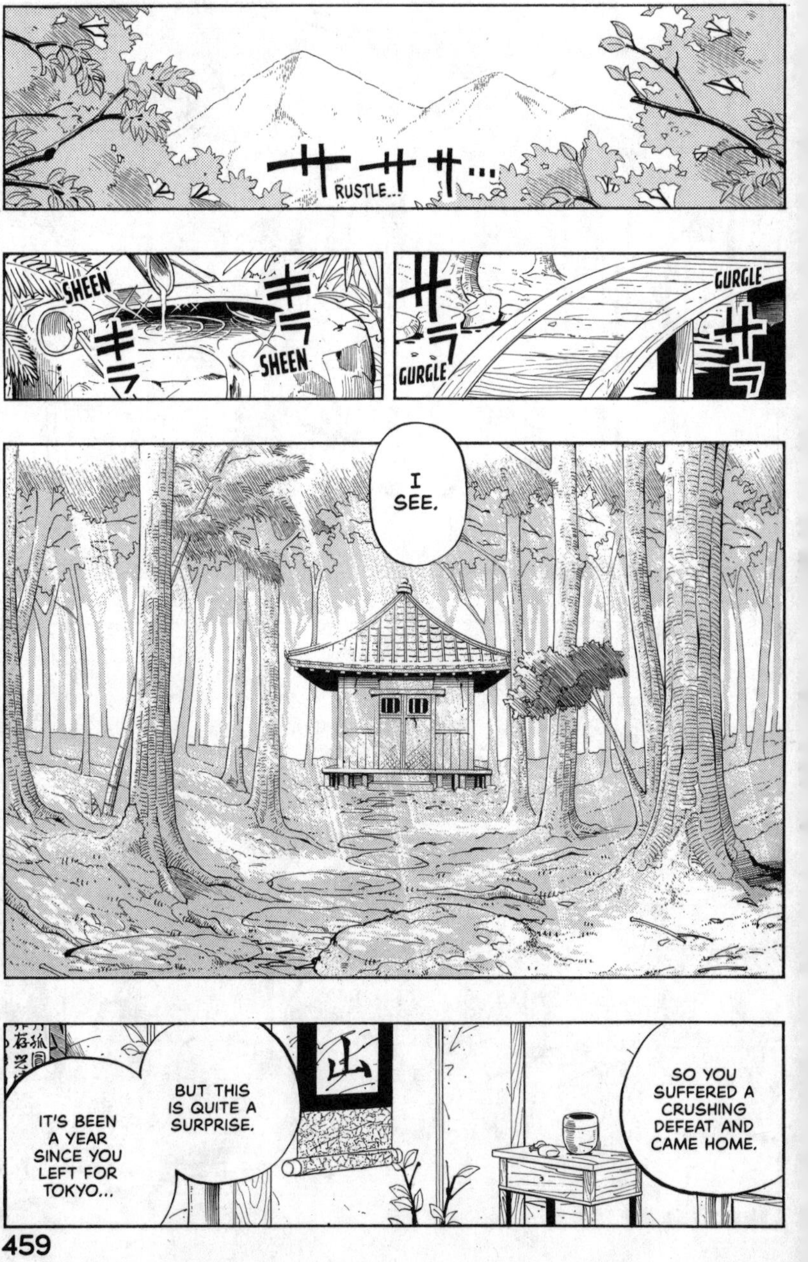
サササ…
RUSTLE...
サラ
GURGLE
サラ
GURGLE
キラ
SHEEN
キラ
SHEEN
I SEE.
SO YOU SUFFERED A CRUSHING DEFEAT AND CAME HOME.
BUT THIS IS QUITE A SURPRISE.
IT'S BEEN A YEAR SINCE YOU LEFT FOR TOKYO...

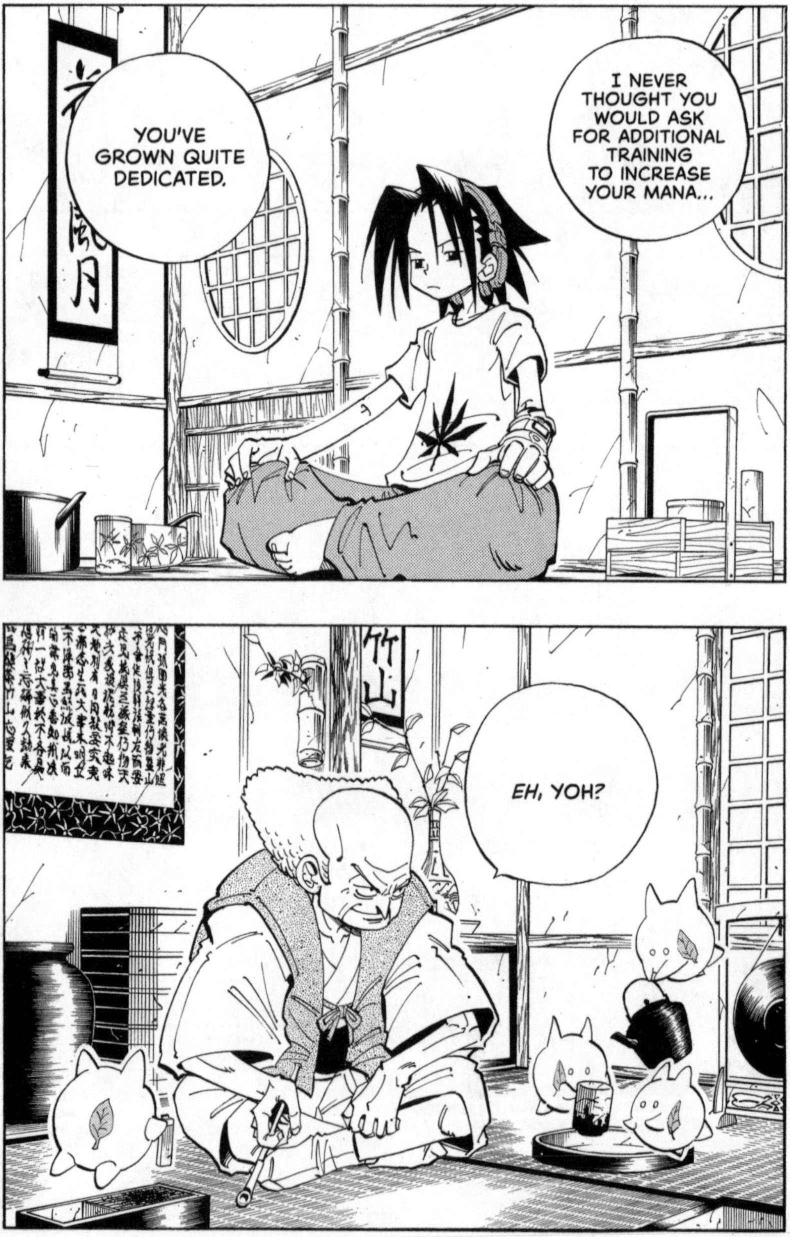
I NEVER THOUGHT YOU WOULD ASK FOR ADDITIONAL TRAINING TO INCREASE YOUR MANA...
YOU'VE GROWN QUITE DEDICATED.
EH, YOH?

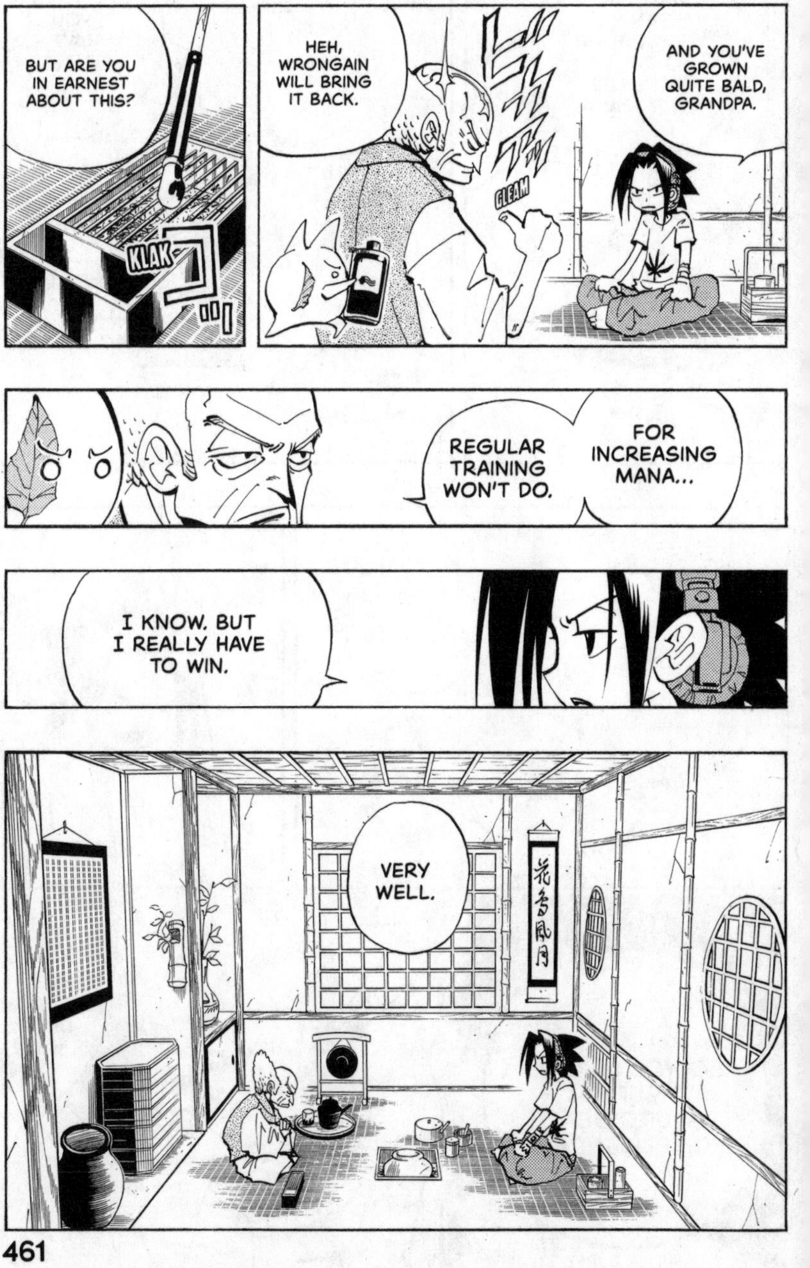
AND YOU'VE GROWN QUITE BALD, GRANDPA.
HEH, WRONGAIN WILL BRING IT BACK.
GLEAM
BUT ARE YOU IN EARNEST ABOUT THIS?
KLAK
FOR INCREASING MANA...
REGULAR TRAINING WON'T DO.
I KNOW. BUT I REALLY HAVE TO WIN.
VERY WELL.

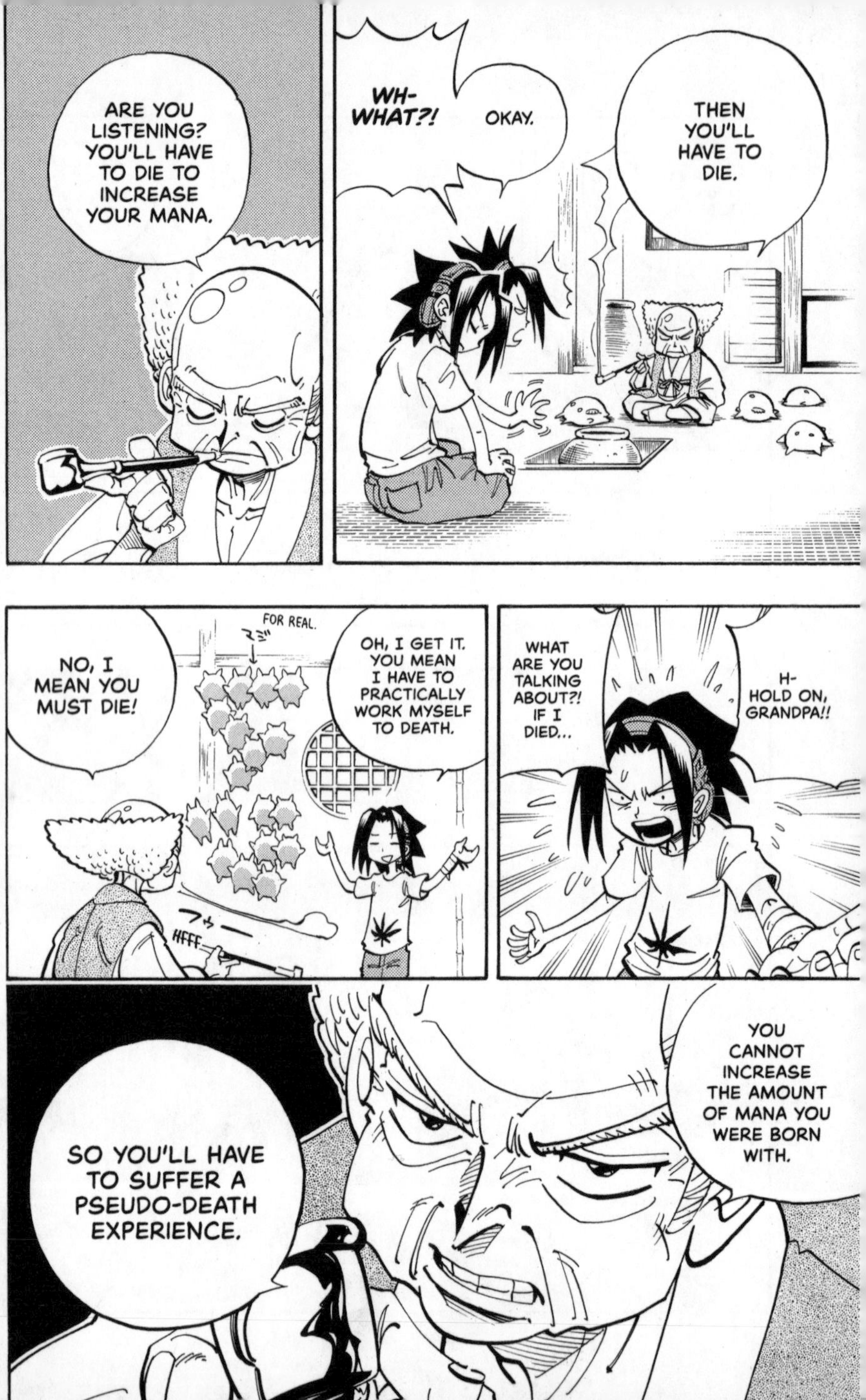
THEN YOU'LL HAVE TO DIE.
OKAY.
WH-WHAT?!
ARE YOU LISTENING? YOU'LL HAVE TO DIE TO INCREASE YOUR MANA.
H-HOLD ON, GRANDPA!!
WHAT ARE YOU TALKING ABOUT?! IF I DIED...
OH, I GET IT. YOU MEAN I HAVE TO PRACTICALLY WORK MYSELF TO DEATH.
FOR REAL.
マジ
NO, I MEAN YOU MUST DIE!
フゥー
HFFF
YOU CANNOT INCREASE THE AMOUNT OF MANA YOU WERE BORN WITH.
SO YOU'LL HAVE TO SUFFER A PSEUDO-DEATH EXPERIENCE.

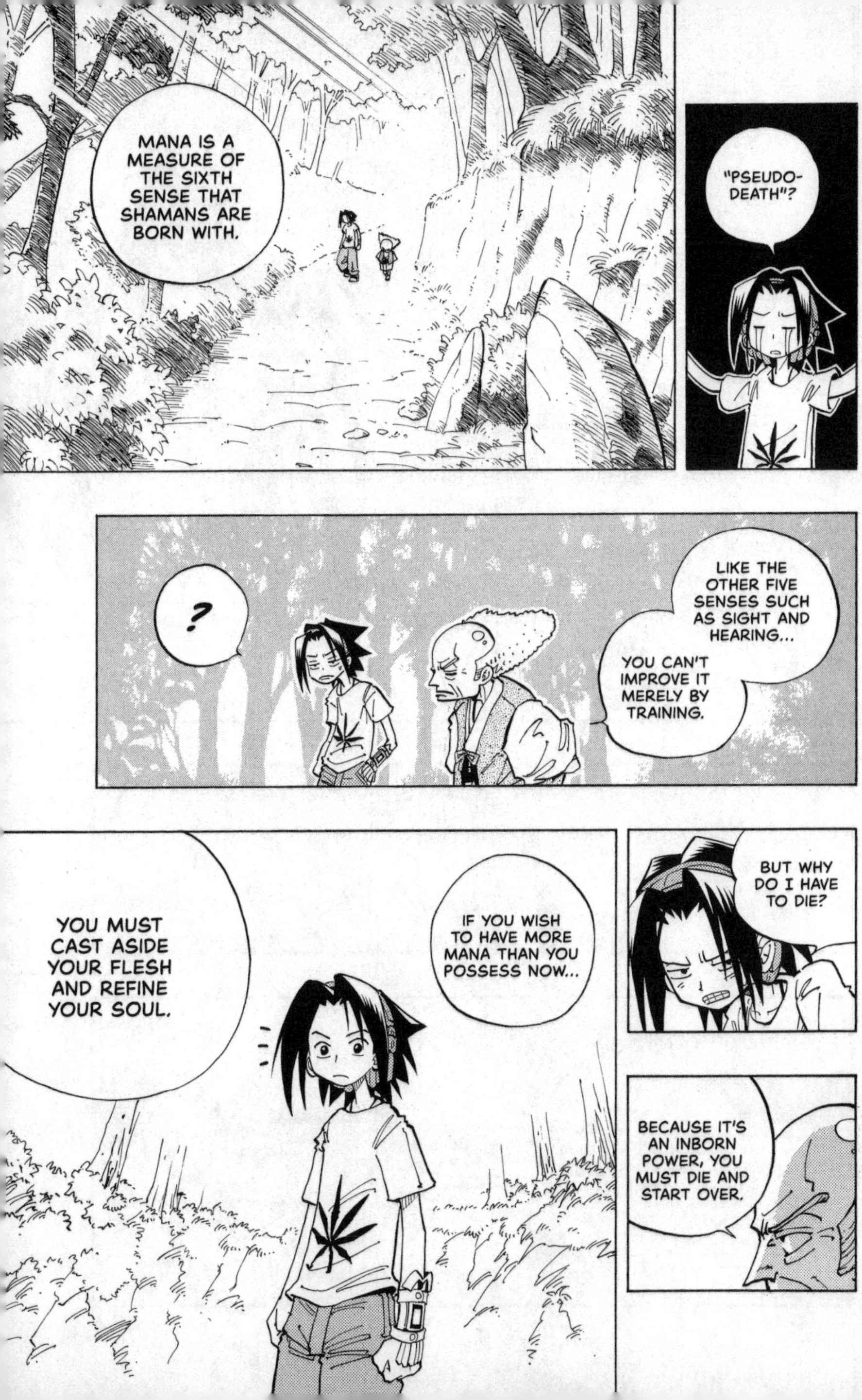
"PSEUDO-DEATH"?
MANA IS A MEASURE OF THE SIXTH SENSE THAT SHAMANS ARE BORN WITH.
LIKE THE OTHER FIVE SENSES SUCH AS SIGHT AND HEARING...
YOU CAN'T IMPROVE IT MERELY BY TRAINING.
?
BUT WHY DO I HAVE TO DIE?
BECAUSE IT'S AN INBORN POWER, YOU MUST DIE AND START OVER.
IF YOU WISH TO HAVE MORE MANA THAN YOU POSSESS NOW...
YOU MUST CAST ASIDE YOUR FLESH AND REFINE YOUR SOUL.

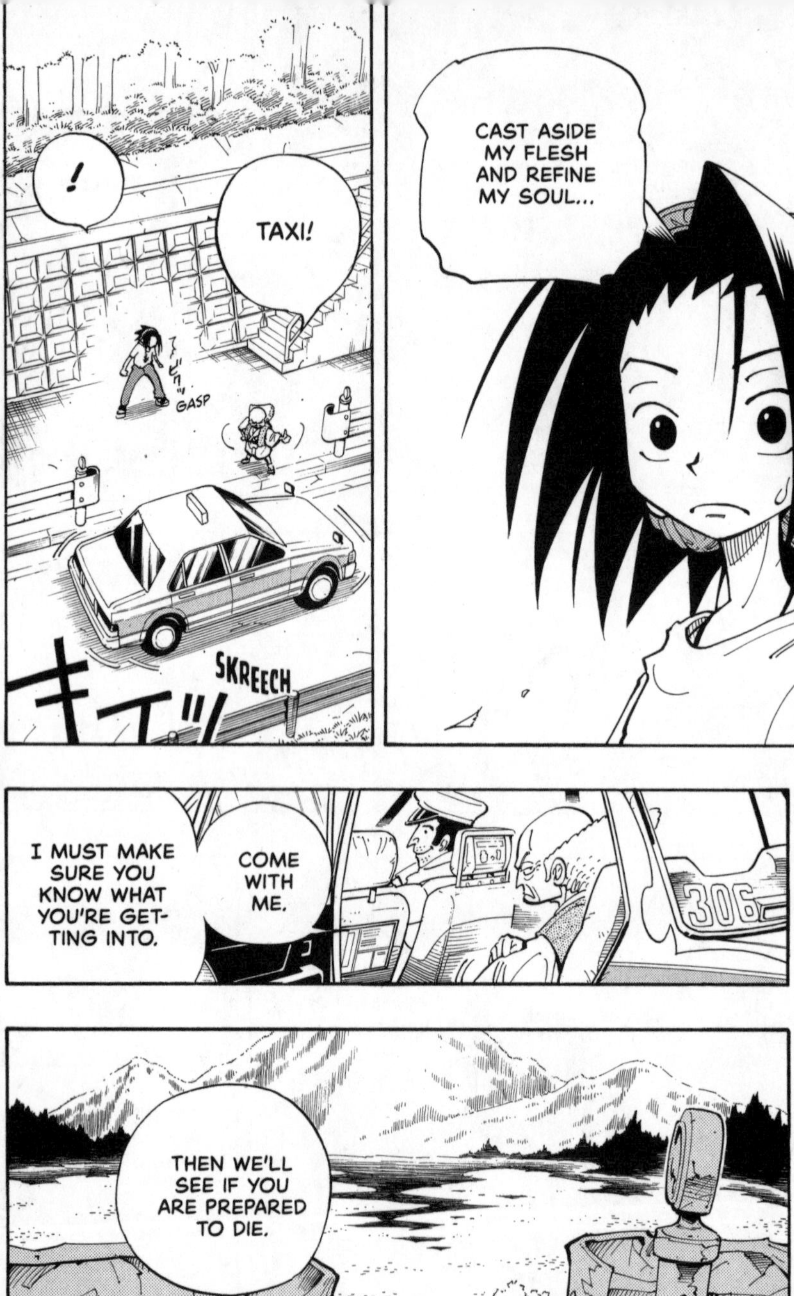
CAST ASIDE MY FLESH AND REFINE MY SOUL...
TAXI!
!
GASP
SKREECH
COME WITH ME.
I MUST MAKE SURE YOU KNOW WHAT YOU'RE GETTING INTO.
THEN WE'LL SEE IF YOU ARE PREPARED TO DIE.

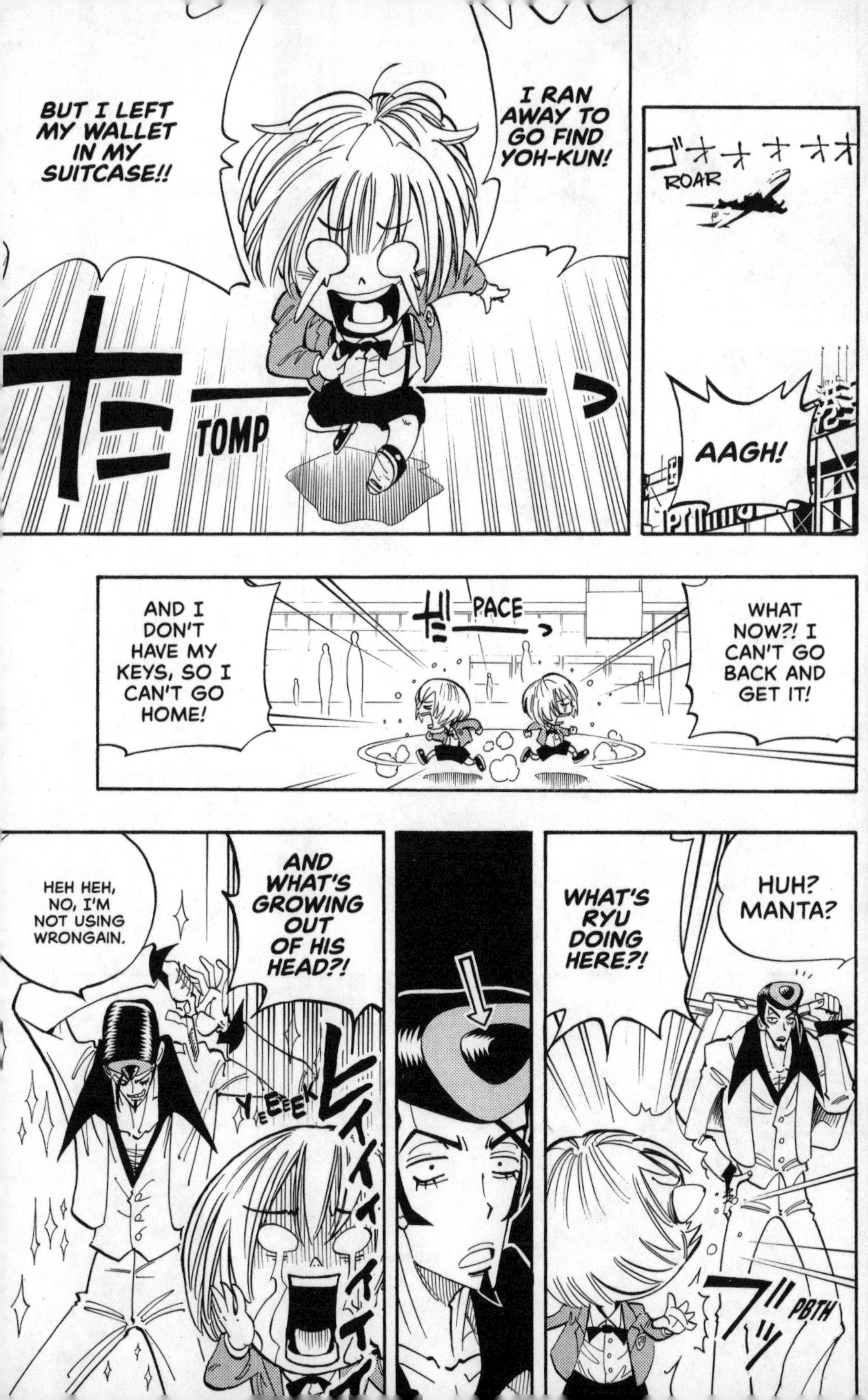
ゴオオオオオ
ROAR
AAGH!
I RAN AWAY TO GO FIND YOH-KUN!
BUT I LEFT MY WALLET IN MY SUITCASE!!
TOMP
WHAT NOW?! I CAN'T GO BACK AND GET IT!
PACE
AND I DON'T HAVE MY KEYS, SO I CAN'T GO HOME!
HUH? MANTA?
PBTH
WHAT'S RYU DOING HERE?!
AND WHAT'S GROWING OUT OF HIS HEAD?!
YEEEEK
HEH HEH, NO, I'M NOT USING WRONGAIN.

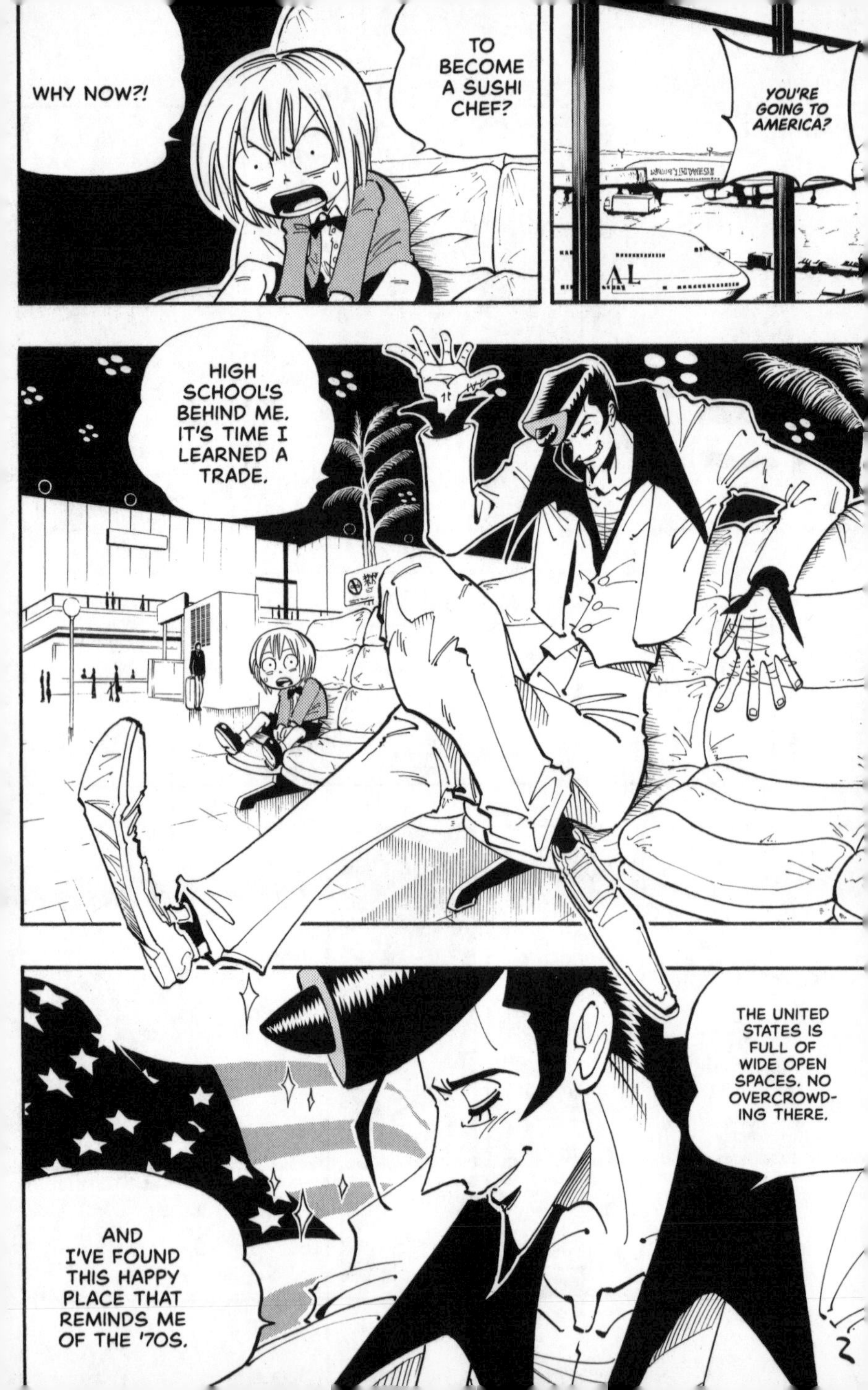
YOU'RE GOING TO AMERICA?
TO BECOME A SUSHI CHEF?
WHY NOW?!
HIGH SCHOOL'S BEHIND ME. IT'S TIME I LEARNED A TRADE.
THE UNITED STATES IS FULL OF WIDE OPEN SPACES. NO OVERCROWD-ING THERE.
AND I'VE FOUND THIS HAPPY PLACE THAT REMINDS ME OF THE '70S.

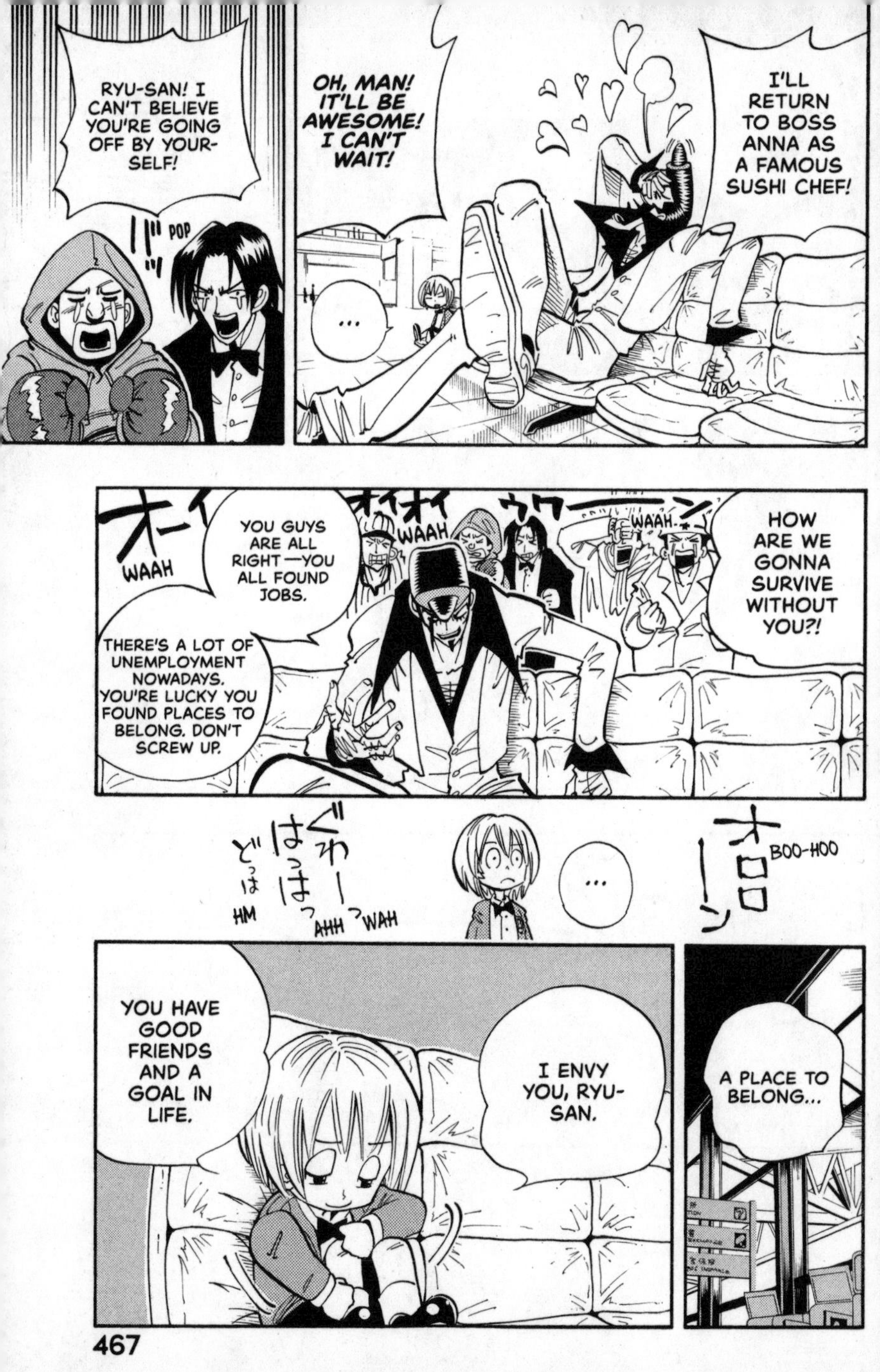

I'LL RETURN TO BOSS ANNA AS A FAMOUS SUSHI CHEF!
OH, MAN! IT'LL BE AWESOME! I CAN'T WAIT!
...
RYU-SAN! I CAN'T BELIEVE YOU'RE GOING OFF BY YOUR-SELF!
POP
HOW ARE WE GONNA SURVIVE WITHOUT YOU?!
WAAH
WAAH
YOU GUYS ARE ALL RIGHT—YOU ALL FOUND JOBS.
WAAH
THERE'S A LOT OF UNEMPLOYMENT NOWADAYS. YOU'RE LUCKY YOU FOUND PLACES TO BELONG. DON'T SCREW UP.
BOO-HOO
...
WAH
AHH
HM
A PLACE TO BELONG...
I ENVY YOU, RYU-SAN.
YOU HAVE GOOD FRIENDS AND A GOAL IN LIFE.

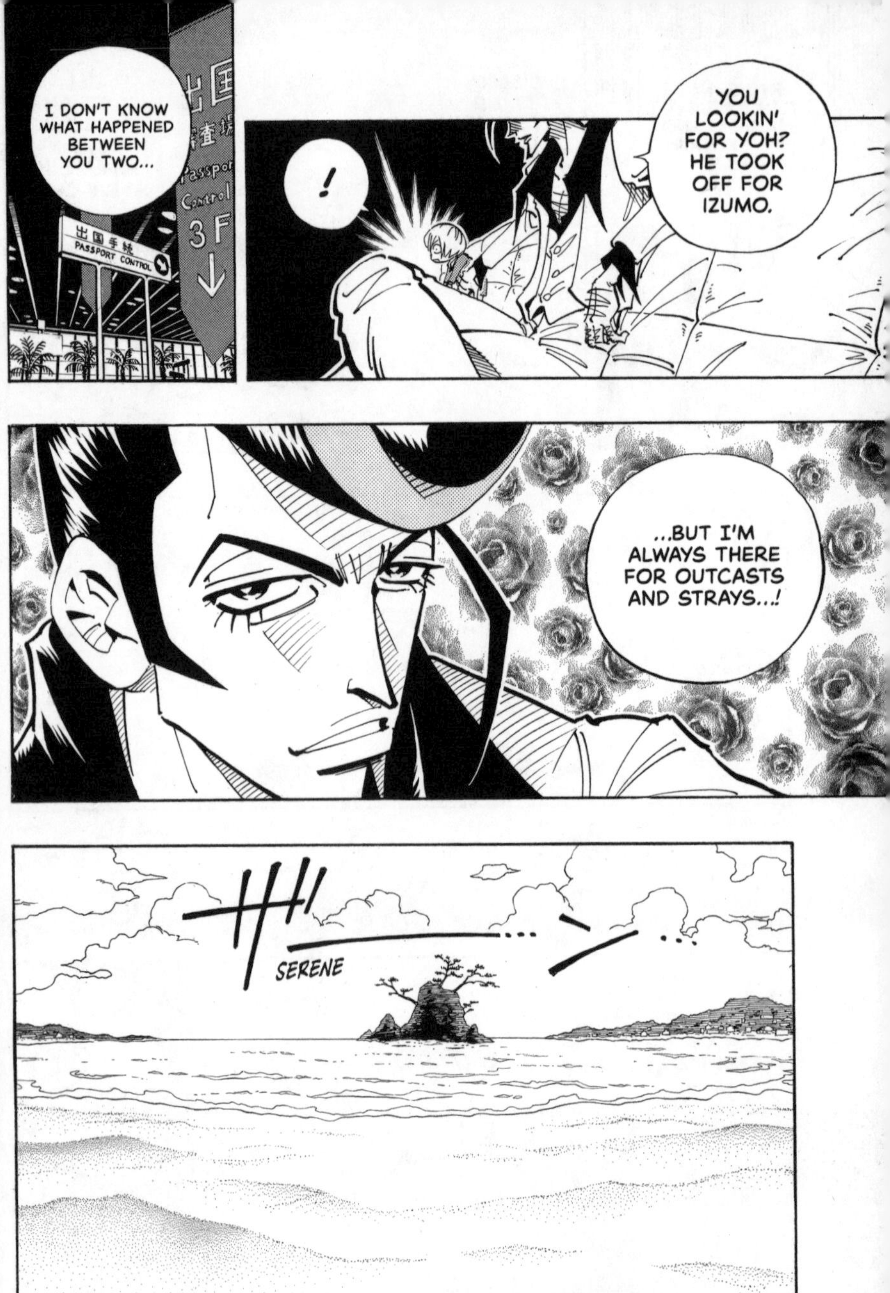

YOU LOOKIN' FOR YOH? HE TOOK OFF FOR IZUMO.
!
I DON'T KNOW WHAT HAPPENED BETWEEN YOU TWO...
出国手続
PASSPORT CONTROL
...BUT I'M ALWAYS THERE FOR OUTCASTS AND STRAYS...!
SERENE

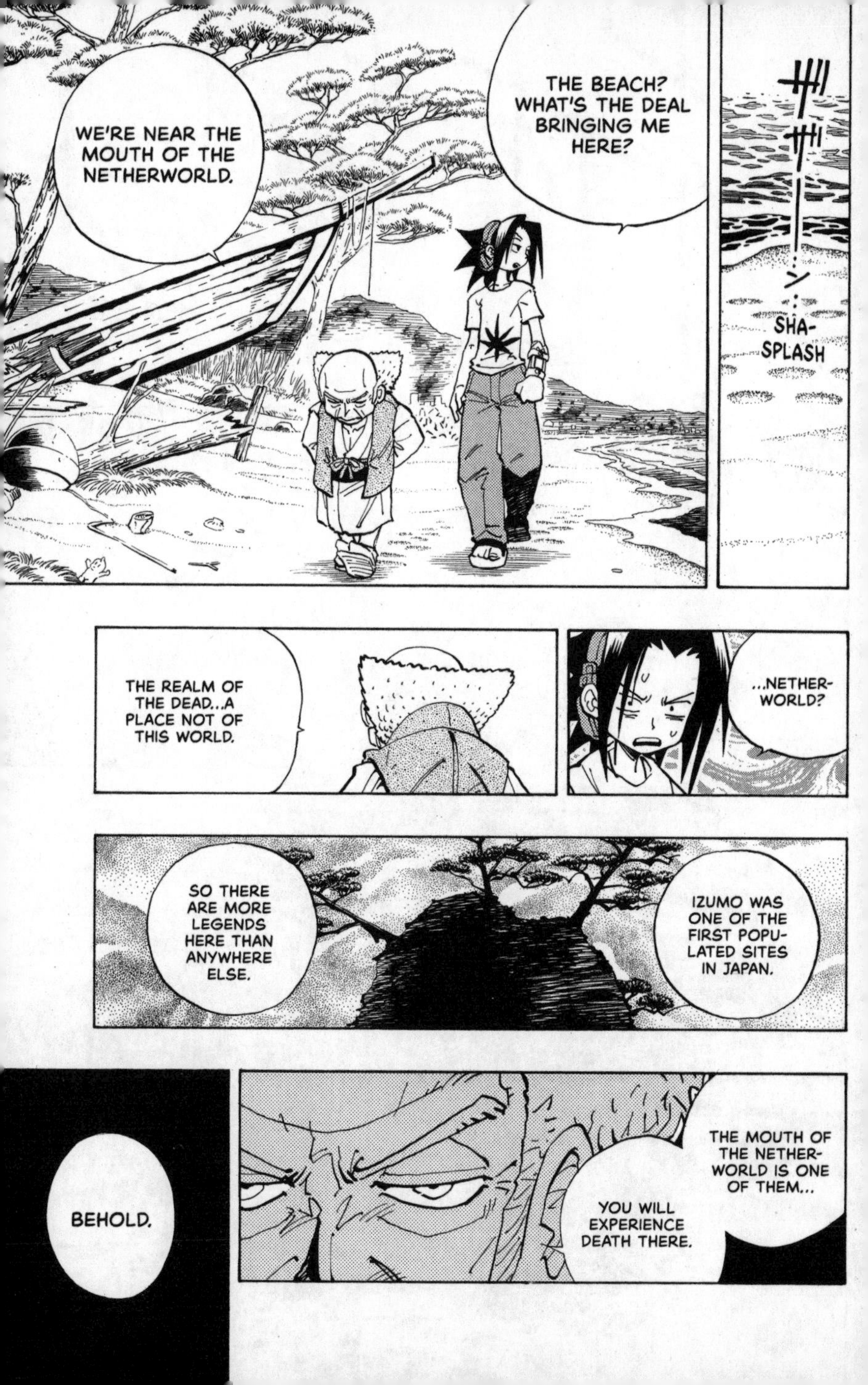
SHA-SPLASH
THE BEACH? WHAT'S THE DEAL BRINGING ME HERE?
WE'RE NEAR THE MOUTH OF THE NETHERWORLD.
...NETHER-WORLD?
THE REALM OF THE DEAD...A PLACE NOT OF THIS WORLD.
IZUMO WAS ONE OF THE FIRST POPU-LATED SITES IN JAPAN.
SO THERE ARE MORE LEGENDS HERE THAN ANYWHERE ELSE.
THE MOUTH OF THE NETHER-WORLD IS ONE OF THEM...
YOU WILL EXPERIENCE DEATH THERE.
BEHOLD.

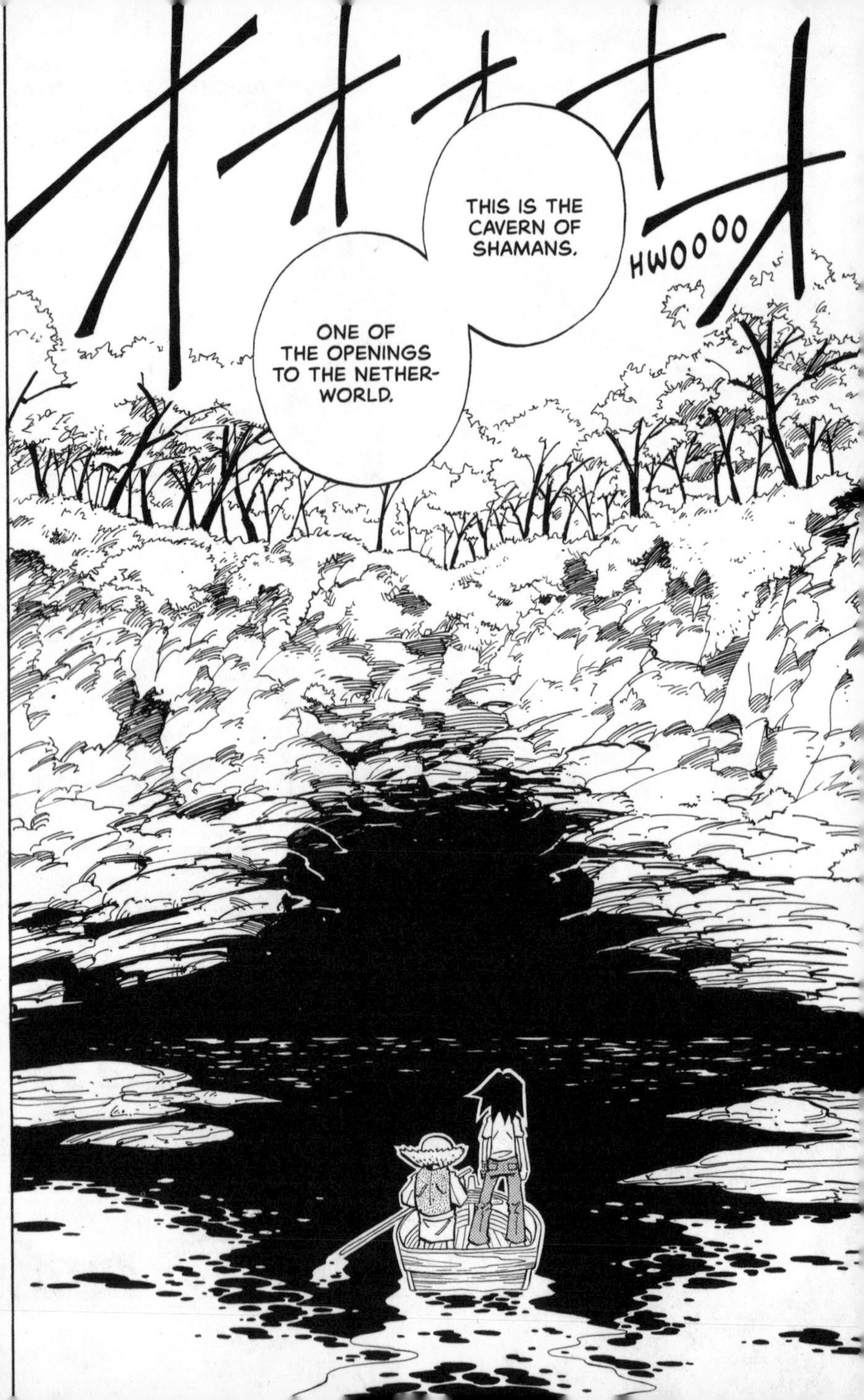

オオオオオ
HWOOOO
THIS IS THE CAVERN OF SHAMANS.
ONE OF THE OPENINGS TO THE NETHER-WORLD.

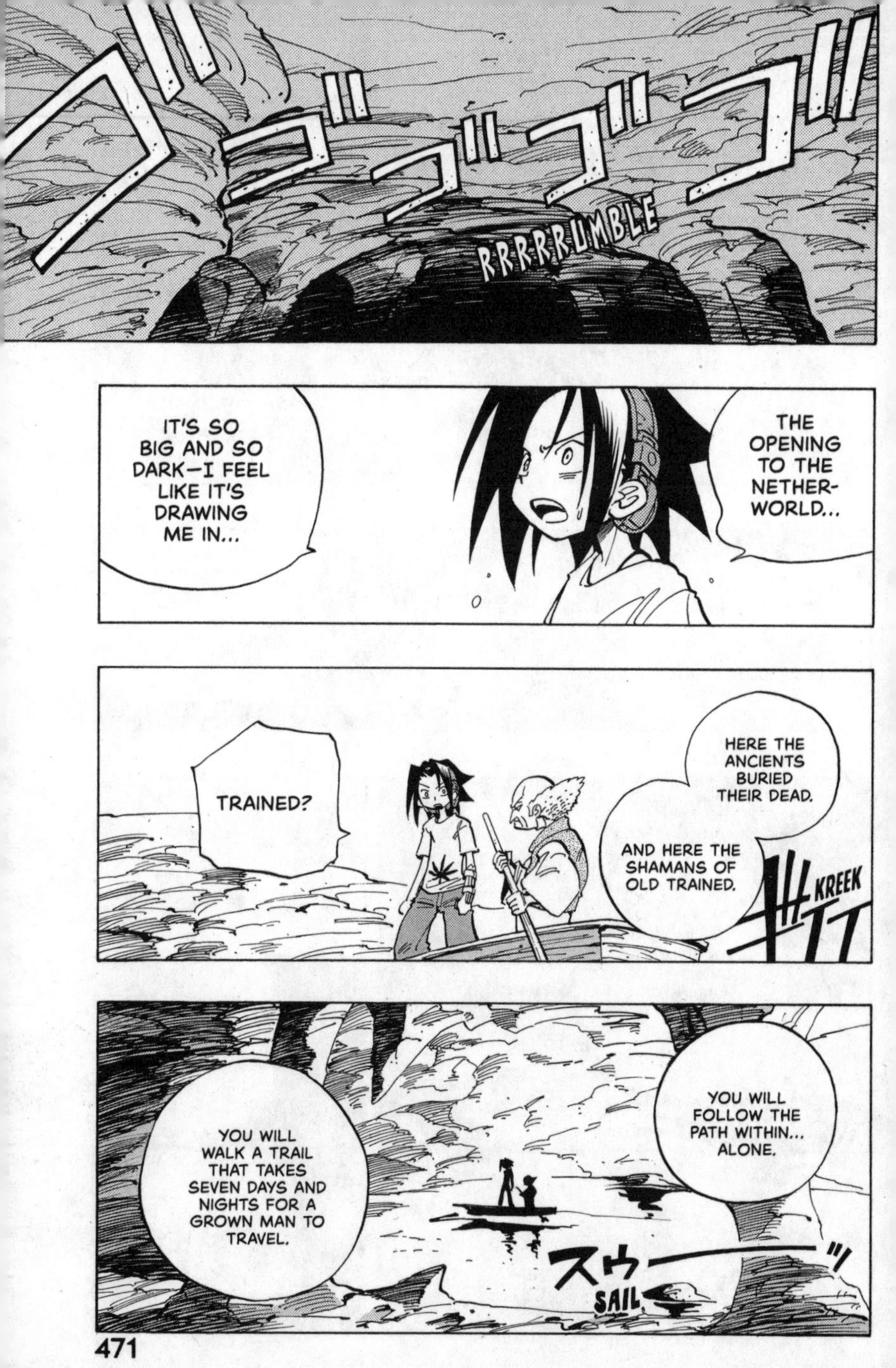
RRRRRUMBLE
THE OPENING TO THE NETHER-WORLD...
IT'S SO BIG AND SO DARK—I FEEL LIKE IT'S DRAWING ME IN...
HERE THE ANCIENTS BURIED THEIR DEAD.
AND HERE THE SHAMANS OF OLD TRAINED.
KREEK
TRAINED?
YOU WILL FOLLOW THE PATH WITHIN... ALONE.
YOU WILL WALK A TRAIL THAT TAKES SEVEN DAYS AND NIGHTS FOR A GROWN MAN TO TRAVEL.
SAIL

SEVEN DAYS AND NIGHTS...
GULP
WELL, I GUESS I CAN DO THAT.
IT'LL BE TOUGH WITHOUT ANY FOOD THOUGH.
YOU THINK YOU'RE JUST GOING FOR A HIKE, YOUNG FOOL?
HERE YOU ENTER A WORLD OF DARKNESS. YOU WON'T BE ABLE TO TELL UP FROM DOWN. HOW WILL THAT AFFECT YOU AFTER SEVEN DAYS?
!
YOUR VISION WILL GO FIRST. THEN YOUR OTHER SENSES WILL DIMINISH...UNTIL ALL THAT REMAINS IS YOUR SIXTH SENSE.
SO BY "DEATH" YOU MEAN...!!
YES, YOU WILL BE STRIPPED OF YOUR PHYSICAL SENSES AND ROAM A WORLD OF THE SPIRIT.
THE FEAR OF NOT SEEING WILL BE OVER-WHELMING...
THERE IS NOTHING MORE FRAGILE THAN A HUMAN SOUL STRIPPED BARE.

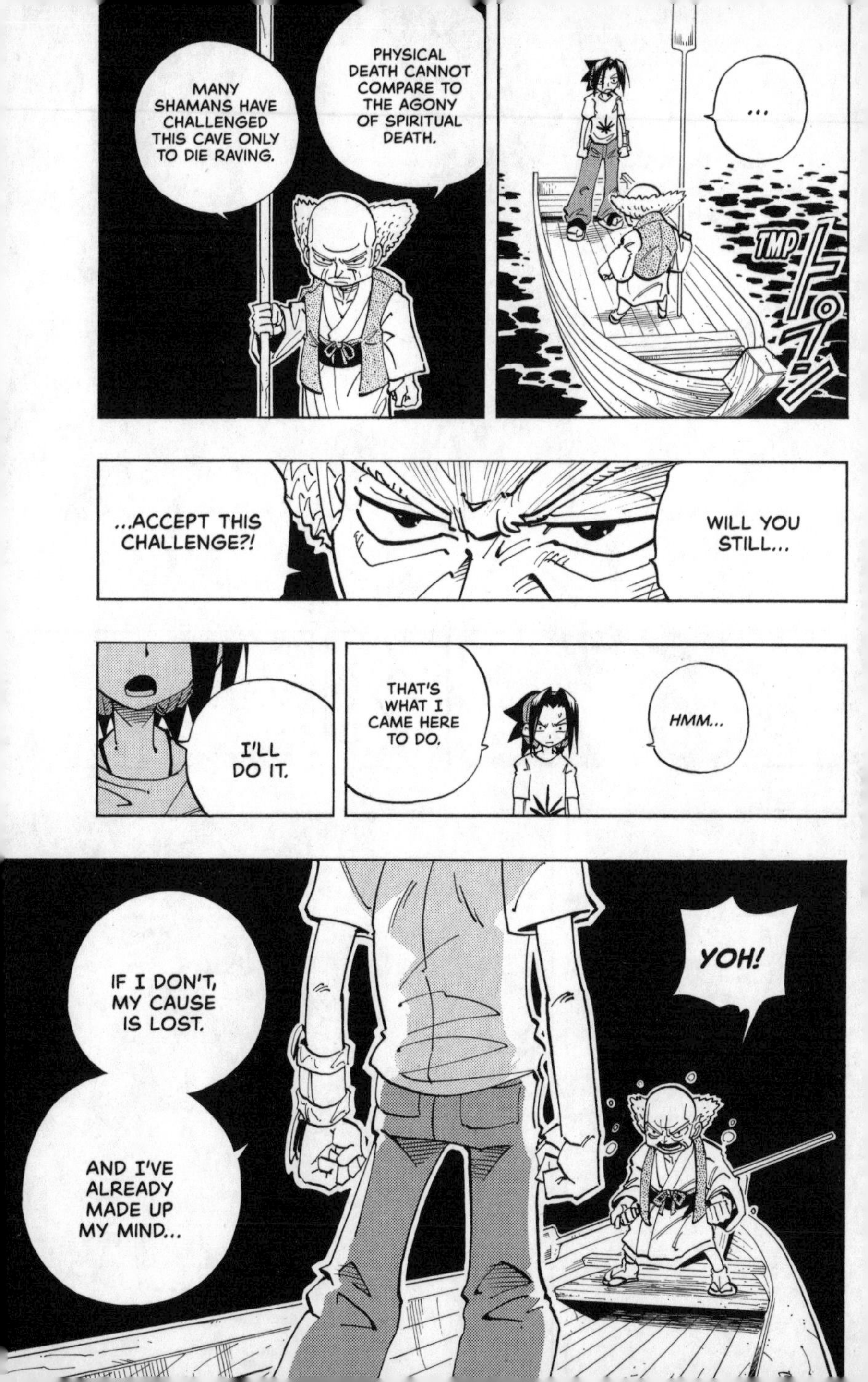
...
TMP
PHYSICAL DEATH CANNOT COMPARE TO THE AGONY OF SPIRITUAL DEATH.
MANY SHAMANS HAVE CHALLENGED THIS CAVE ONLY TO DIE RAVING.
WILL YOU STILL...
...ACCEPT THIS CHALLENGE?!
HMM...
THAT'S WHAT I CAME HERE TO DO.
I'LL DO IT.
YOH!
IF I DON'T, MY CAUSE IS LOST.
AND I'VE ALREADY MADE UP MY MIND...

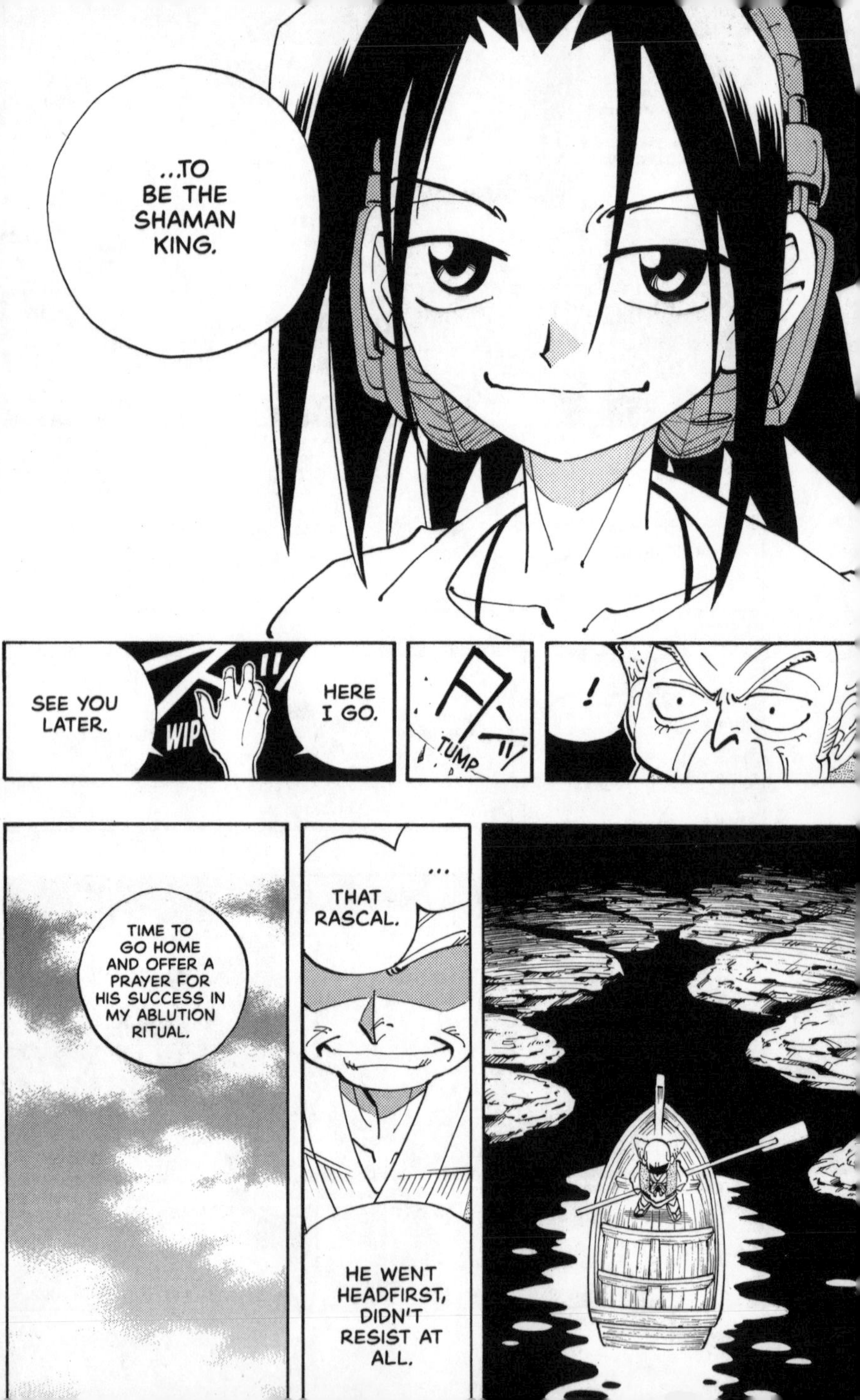
...TO BE THE SHAMAN KING.
!
TUMP
HERE I GO.
WIP
SEE YOU LATER.
...
THAT RASCAL.
HE WENT HEADFIRST, DIDN'T RESIST AT ALL.
TIME TO GO HOME AND OFFER A PRAYER FOR HIS SUCCESS IN MY ABLUTION RITUAL.

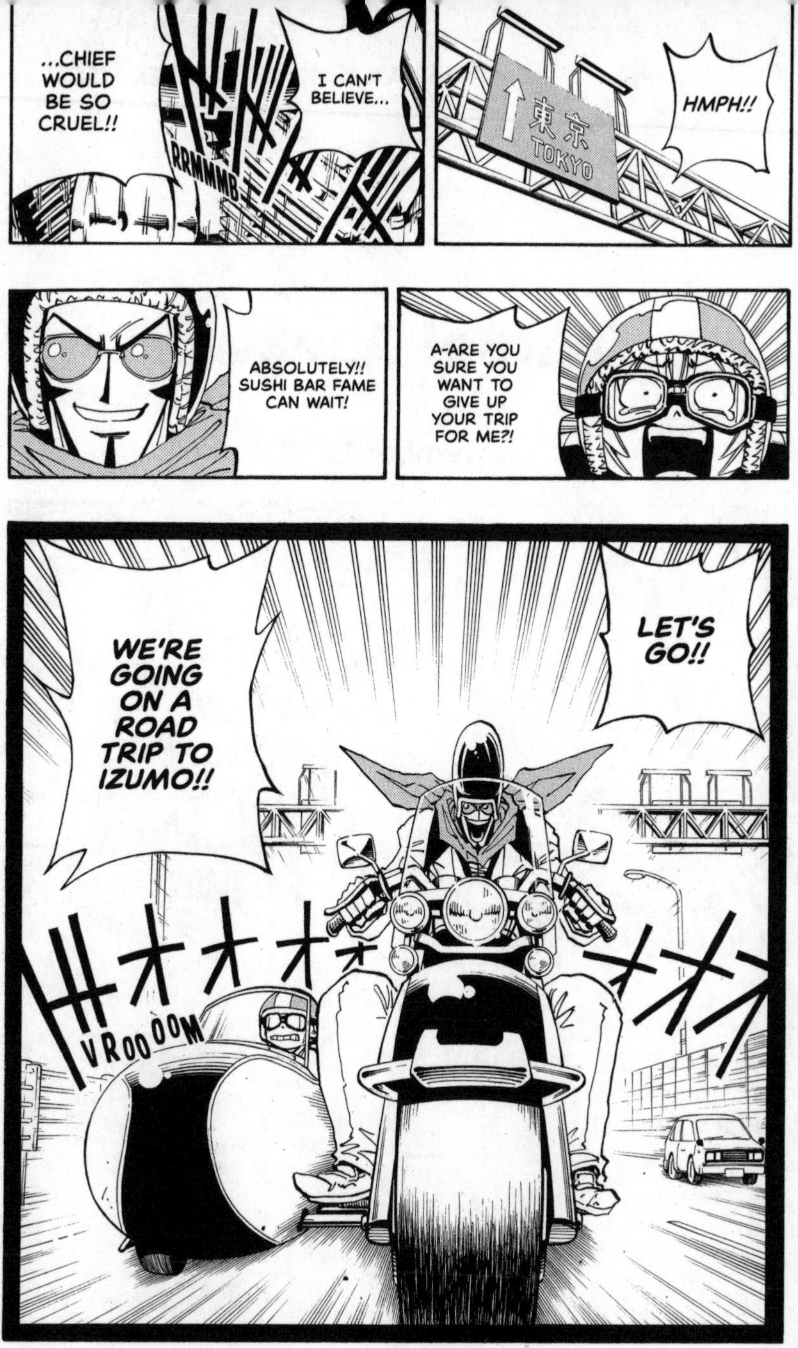
東京
TOKYO
HMPH!!
I CAN'T BELIEVE...
...CHIEF WOULD BE SO CRUEL!!
RRMMMB
A-ARE YOU SURE YOU WANT TO GIVE UP YOUR TRIP FOR ME?!
ABSOLUTELY!! SUSHI BAR FAME CAN WAIT!
LET'S GO!!
WE'RE GOING ON A ROAD TRIP TO IZUMO!!
VROOOOM

Yohmei Asakura

November 1999

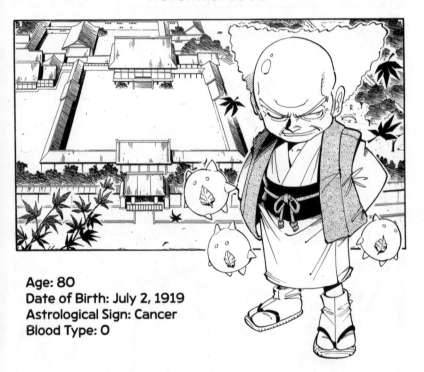

Age: 80
Date of Birth: July 2, 1919
Astrological Sign: Cancer
Blood Type: O

Chapter 49: The "Happy Place" Doctrine

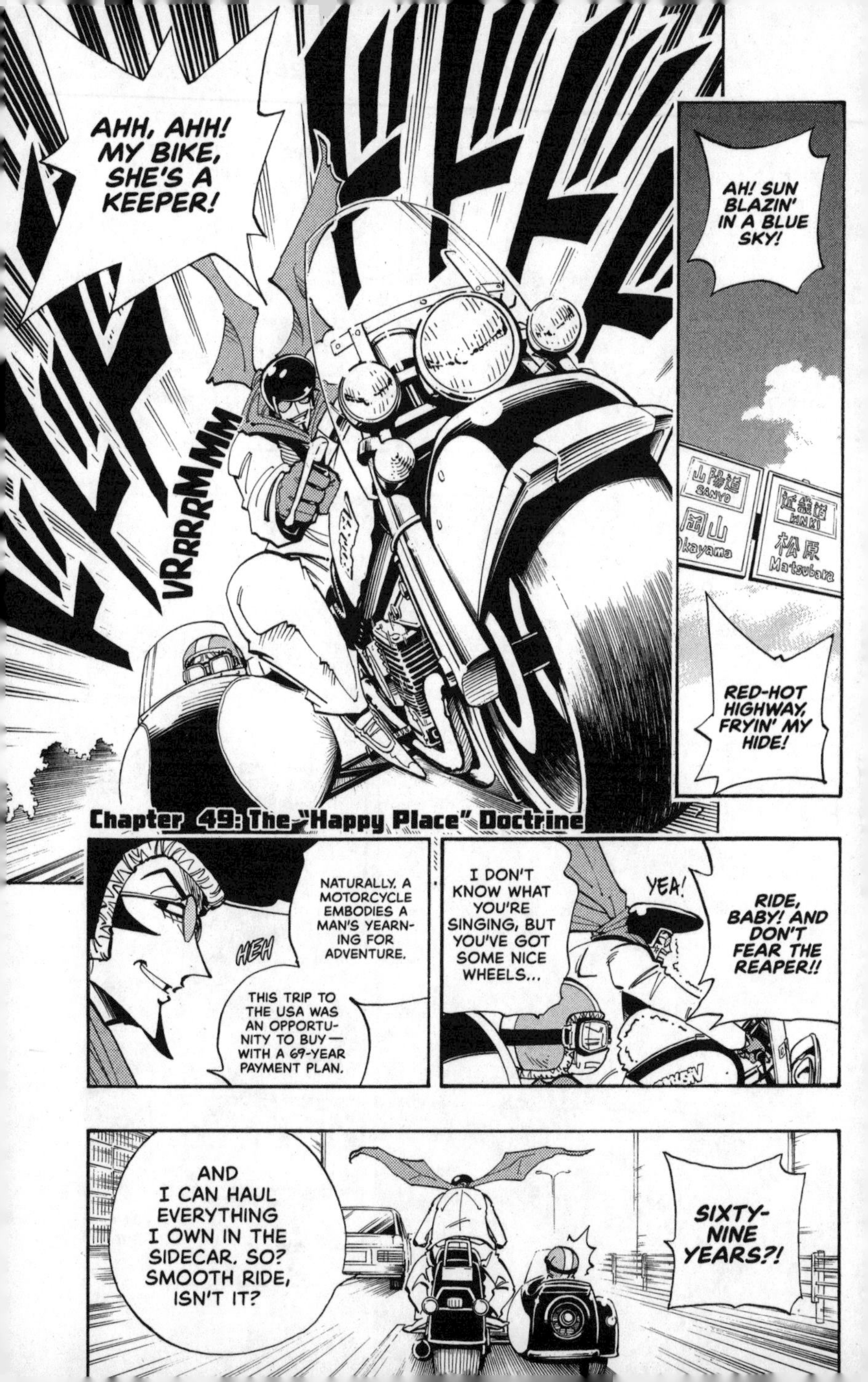
AH! SUN BLAZIN' IN A BLUE SKY!
山陽道
SANYO
岡山
Okayama
近畿道
松原
Matsubara
RED-HOT HIGHWAY, FRYIN' MY HIDE!
AHH, AHH! MY BIKE, SHE'S A KEEPER!
VRRRRMMM
RIDE, BABY! AND DON'T FEAR THE REAPER!!
YEA!
I DON'T KNOW WHAT YOU'RE SINGING, BUT YOU'VE GOT SOME NICE WHEELS...
NATURALLY, A MOTORCYCLE EMBODIES A MAN'S YEARNING FOR ADVENTURE.
HEH
THIS TRIP TO THE USA WAS AN OPPORTUNITY TO BUY—WITH A 69-YEAR PAYMENT PLAN.
SIXTY-NINE YEARS?!
AND I CAN HAUL EVERYTHING I OWN IN THE SIDECAR. SO? SMOOTH RIDE, ISN'T IT?

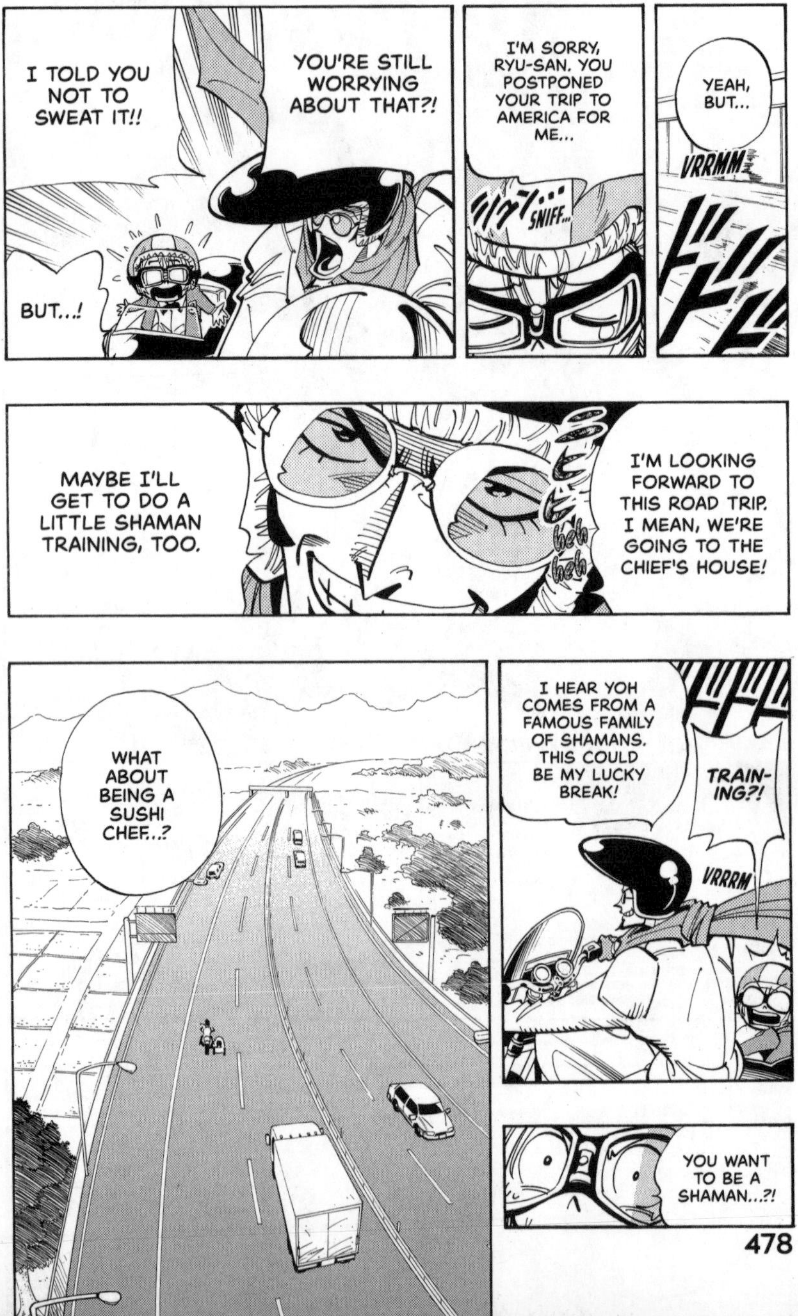
YEAH, BUT...
VRRMM
I'M SORRY, RYU-SAN. YOU POSTPONED YOUR TRIP TO AMERICA FOR ME...
SNIFF...
YOU'RE STILL WORRYING ABOUT THAT?!
I TOLD YOU NOT TO SWEAT IT!!
BUT...!
I'M LOOKING FORWARD TO THIS ROAD TRIP. I MEAN, WE'RE GOING TO THE CHIEF'S HOUSE!
heh heh
MAYBE I'LL GET TO DO A LITTLE SHAMAN TRAINING, TOO.
I HEAR YOH COMES FROM A FAMOUS FAMILY OF SHAMANS. THIS COULD BE MY LUCKY BREAK!
TRAIN-ING?!
VRRRM
YOU WANT TO BE A SHAMAN...?!
WHAT ABOUT BEING A SUSHI CHEF...?

Chapter 49:
The "Happy Place" Doctrine

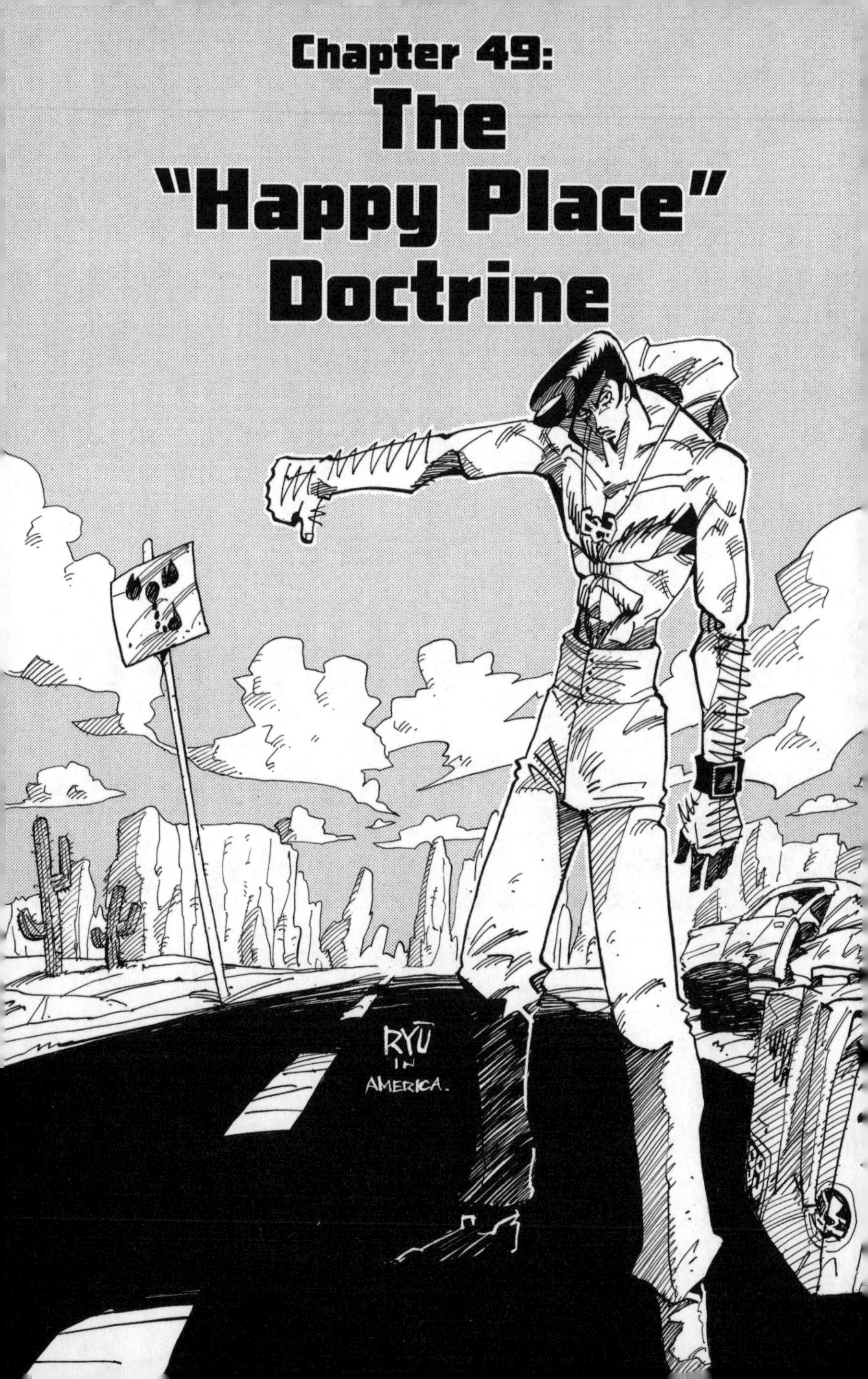
RYU IN AMERICA.

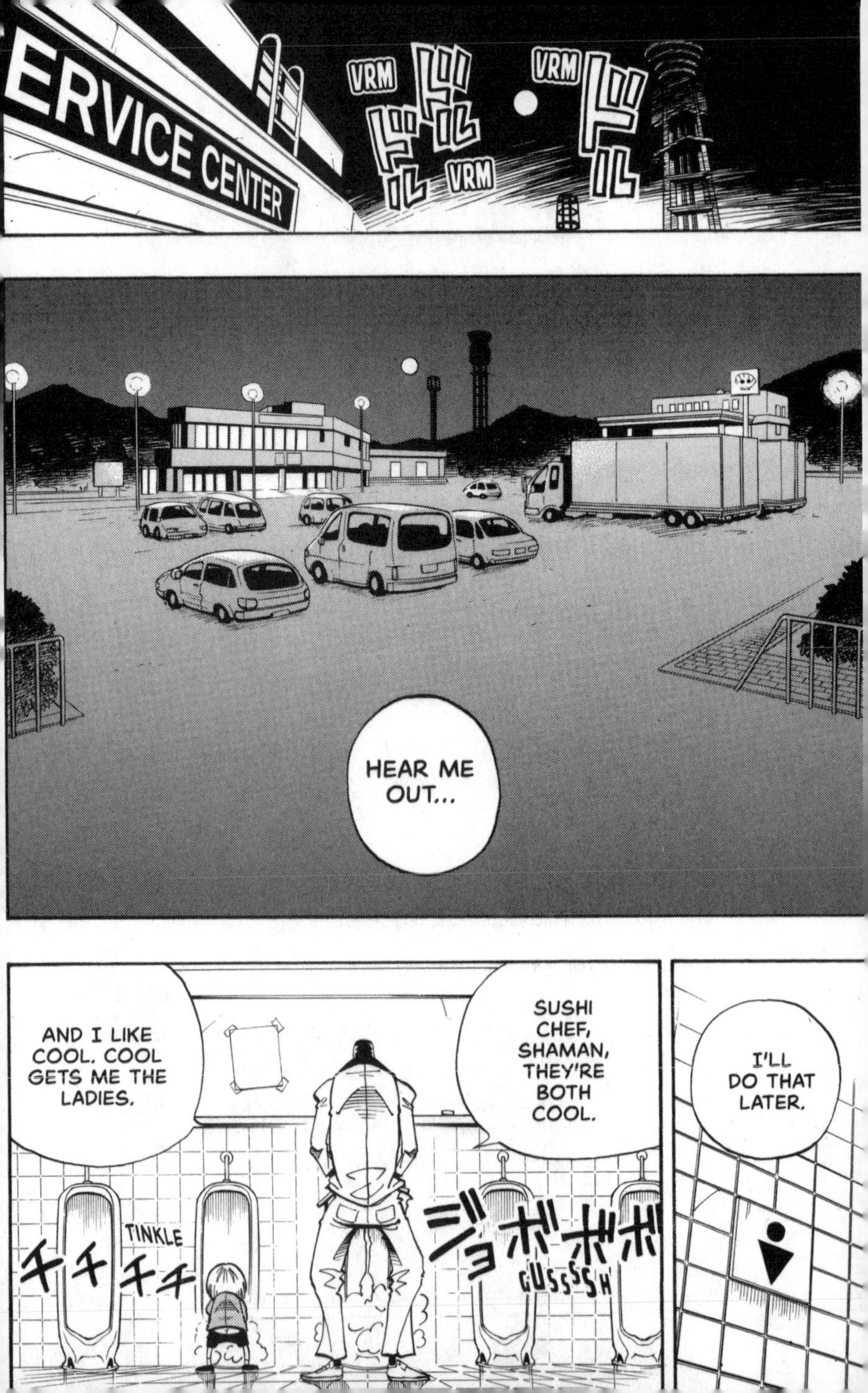
ERVICE CENTER
VRM
VRM
VRM
HEAR ME OUT...
I'LL DO THAT LATER.
SUSHI CHEF, SHAMAN, THEY'RE BOTH COOL.
AND I LIKE COOL. COOL GETS ME THE LADIES.
ジョボボボ
GUSSSSH
チチチチ
TINKLE

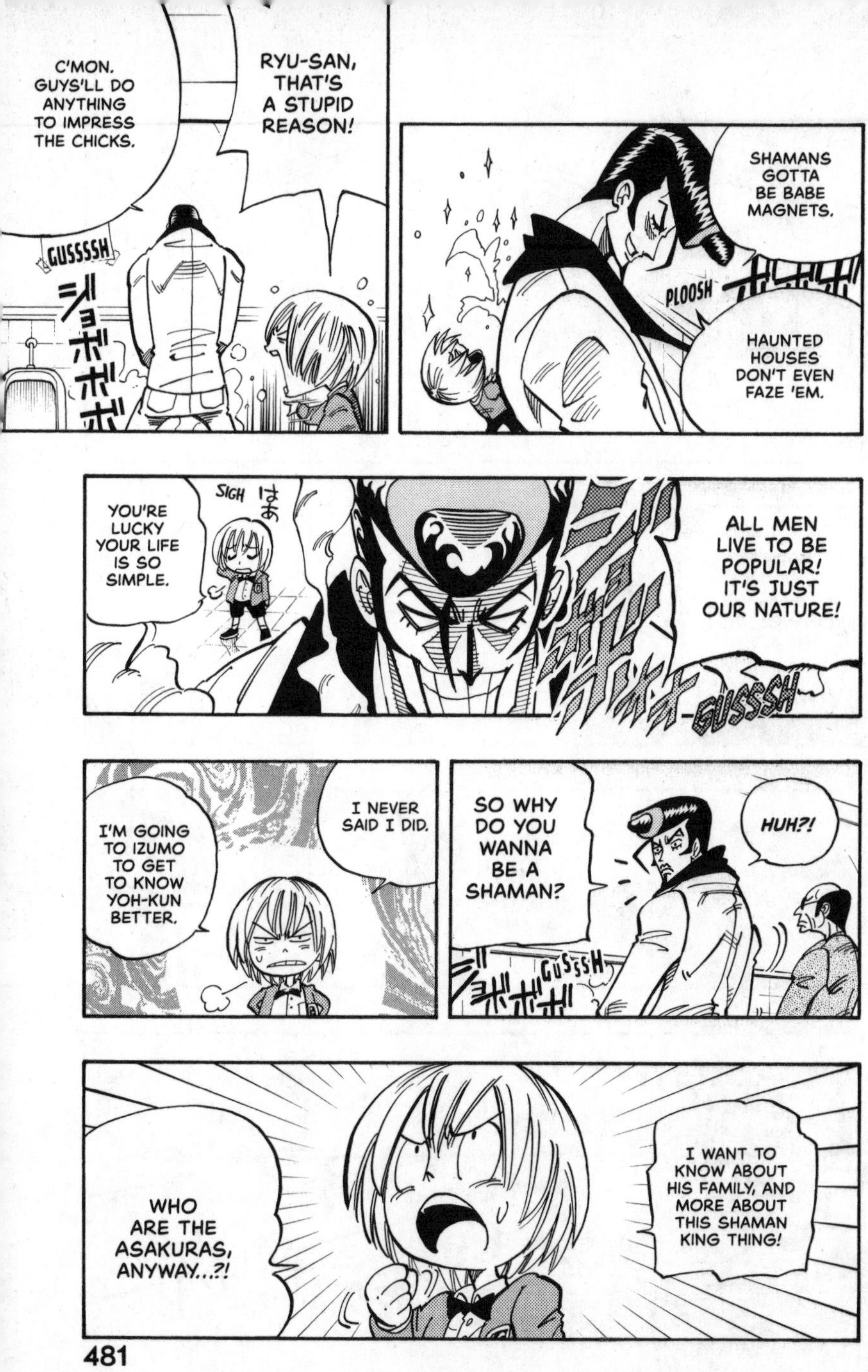
SHAMANS GOTTA BE BABE MAGNETS.
PLOOSH
HAUNTED HOUSES DON'T EVEN FAZE 'EM.
RYU-SAN, THAT'S A STUPID REASON!
C'MON. GUYS'LL DO ANYTHING TO IMPRESS THE CHICKS.
GUSSSSH
ジョボボボ
ALL MEN LIVE TO BE POPULAR! IT'S JUST OUR NATURE!
GUSSSH
SIGH
はあ
YOU'RE LUCKY YOUR LIFE IS SO SIMPLE.
HUH?!
SO WHY DO YOU WANNA BE A SHAMAN?
GUSSSH
I NEVER SAID I DID.
I'M GOING TO IZUMO TO GET TO KNOW YOH-KUN BETTER.
I WANT TO KNOW ABOUT HIS FAMILY, AND MORE ABOUT THIS SHAMAN KING THING!
WHO ARE THE ASAKURAS, ANYWAY...?!

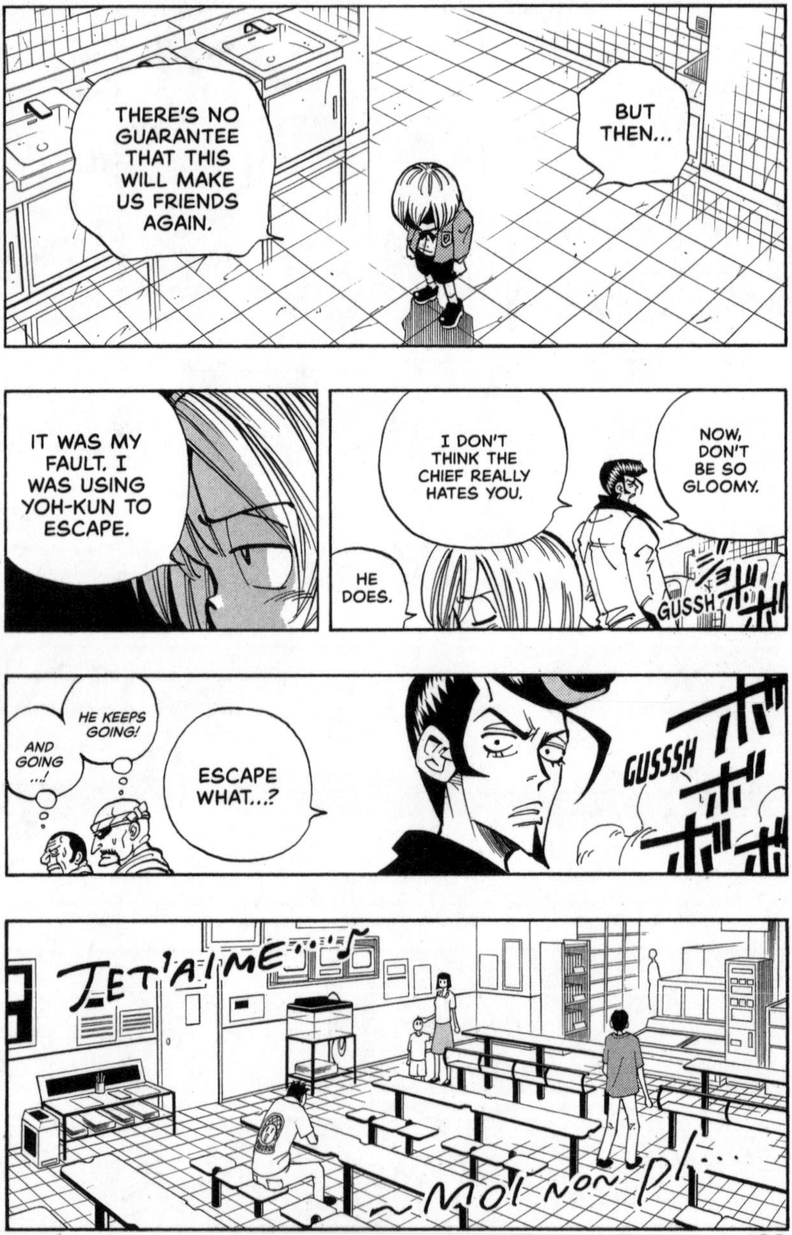
BUT THEN...
THERE'S NO GUARANTEE THAT THIS WILL MAKE US FRIENDS AGAIN.
NOW, DON'T BE SO GLOOMY.
I DON'T THINK THE CHIEF REALLY HATES YOU.
HE DOES.
GUSSH
IT WAS MY FAULT. I WAS USING YOH-KUN TO ESCAPE.
GUSSSH
ESCAPE WHAT...?
HE KEEPS GOING!
AND GOING...!
JE T'AIME...♪
~MOI NON PL...

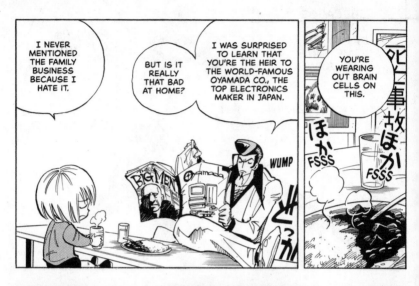

YOU'RE WEARING OUT BRAIN CELLS ON THIS.
FSSS
FSSS
I WAS SURPRISED TO LEARN THAT YOU'RE THE HEIR TO THE WORLD-FAMOUS OYAMADA CO., THE TOP ELECTRONICS MAKER IN JAPAN.
BUT IS IT REALLY THAT BAD AT HOME?
I NEVER MENTIONED THE FAMILY BUSINESS BECAUSE I HATE IT.
WUMP
BUT UNLIKE YOU AND YOH-KUN...
I DON'T HAVE A DREAM.
NO DREAM...?
I TURNED TO YOH-KUN TO FORGET MY REAL LIFE. NO WONDER HE DOESN'T LIKE ME.
YOU'RE BEING AN IDIOT.
WHAT?!
BAM

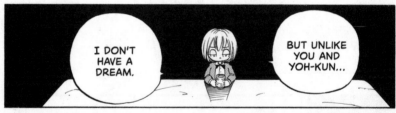

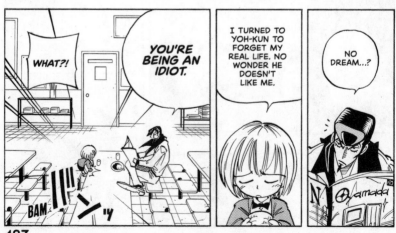

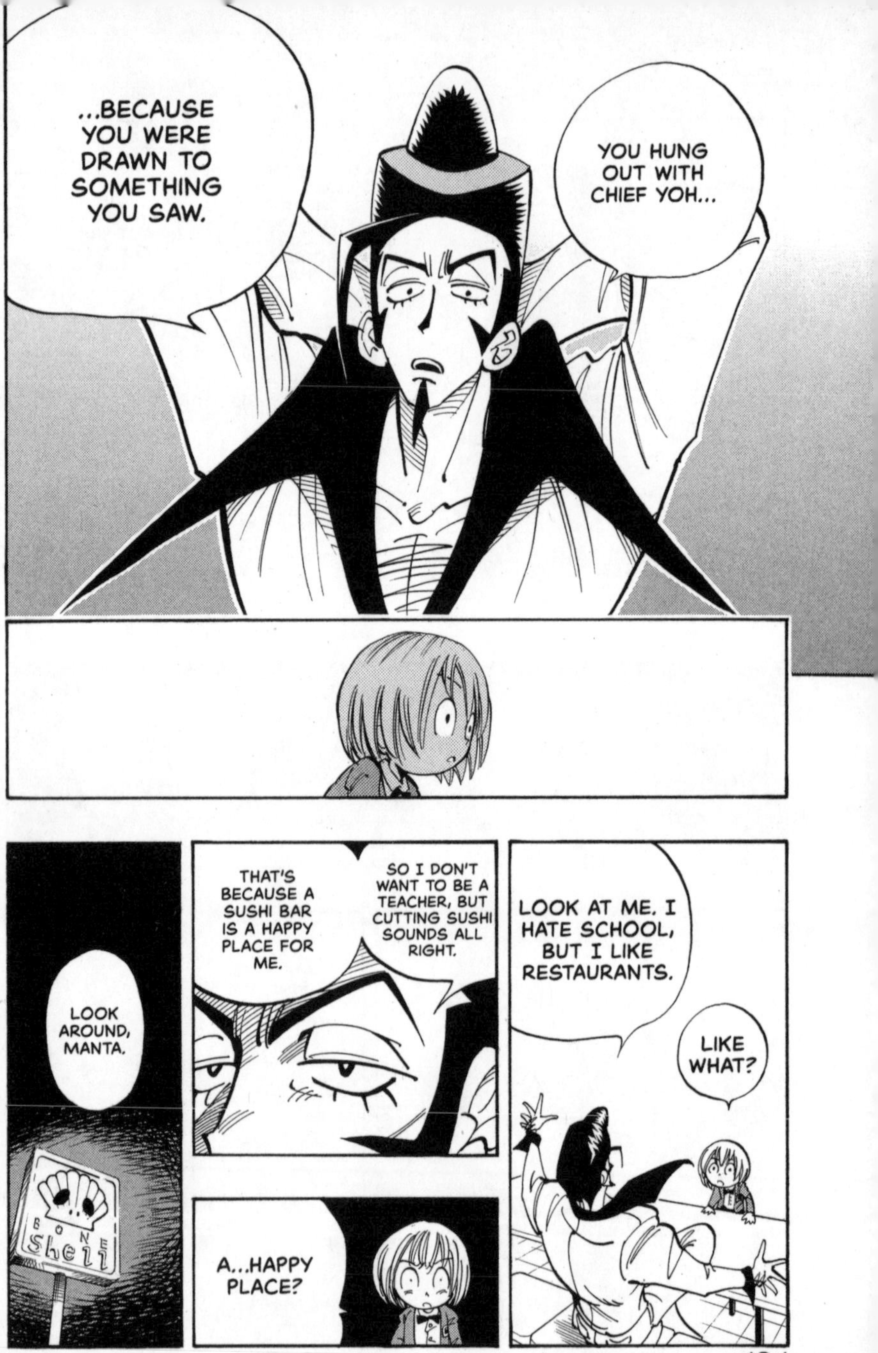
YOU HUNG OUT WITH CHIEF YOH...
...BECAUSE YOU WERE DRAWN TO SOMETHING YOU SAW.
LOOK AT ME. I HATE SCHOOL, BUT I LIKE RESTAURANTS.
LIKE WHAT?
SO I DON'T WANT TO BE A TEACHER, BUT CUTTING SUSHI SOUNDS ALL RIGHT.
THAT'S BECAUSE A SUSHI BAR IS A HAPPY PLACE FOR ME.
A...HAPPY PLACE?
LOOK AROUND, MANTA.
BONE
Shell

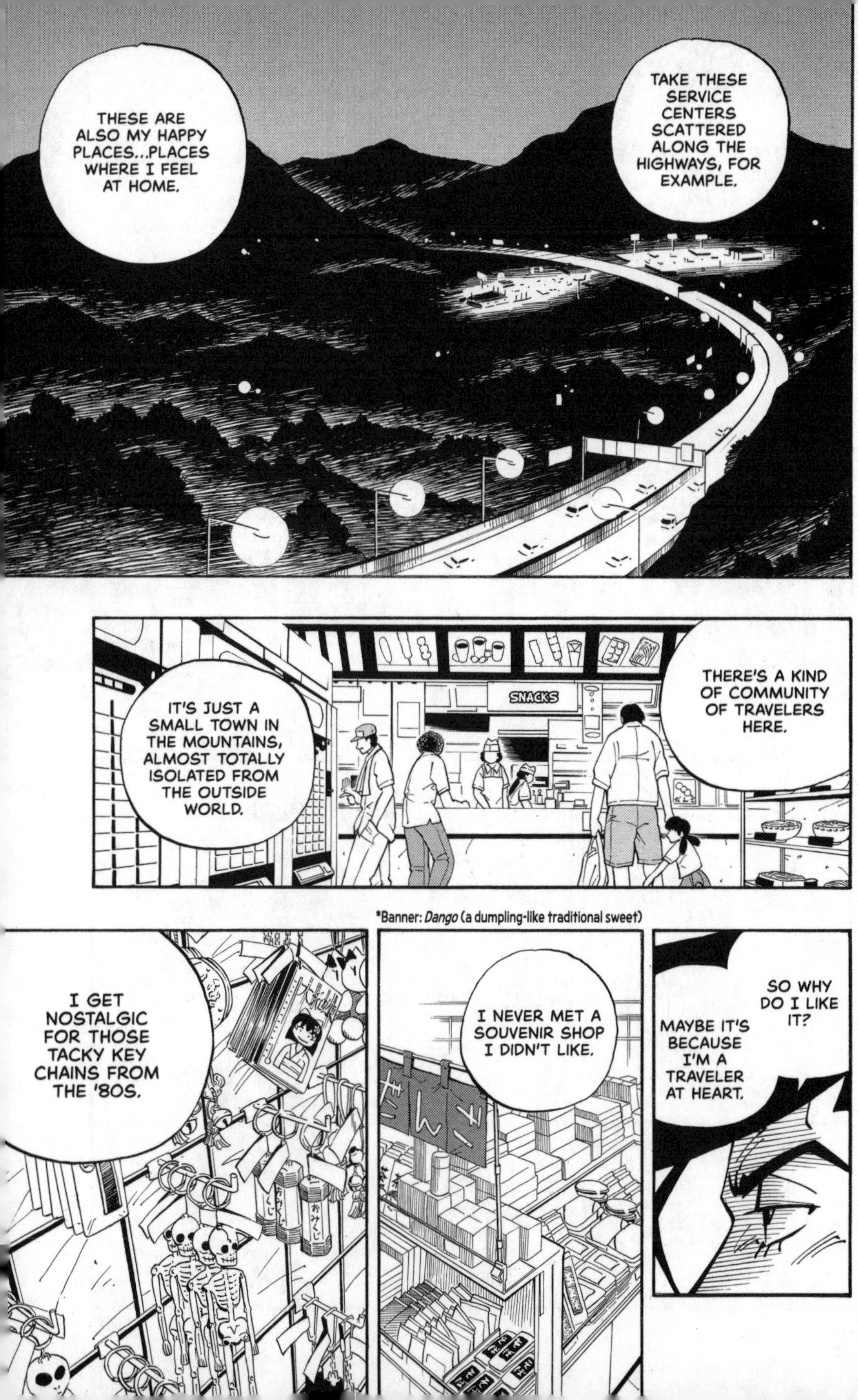
TAKE THESE SERVICE CENTERS SCATTERED ALONG THE HIGHWAYS, FOR EXAMPLE.
THESE ARE ALSO MY HAPPY PLACES...PLACES WHERE I FEEL AT HOME.
THERE'S A KIND OF COMMUNITY OF TRAVELERS HERE.
SNACKS
IT'S JUST A SMALL TOWN IN THE MOUNTAINS, ALMOST TOTALLY ISOLATED FROM THE OUTSIDE WORLD.
SO WHY DO I LIKE IT?
MAYBE IT'S BECAUSE I'M A TRAVELER AT HEART.
I NEVER MET A SOUVENIR SHOP I DIDN'T LIKE.
I GET NOSTALGIC FOR THOSE TACKY KEY CHAINS FROM THE '80S.

*Banner: *Dango* (a dumpling-like traditional sweet)

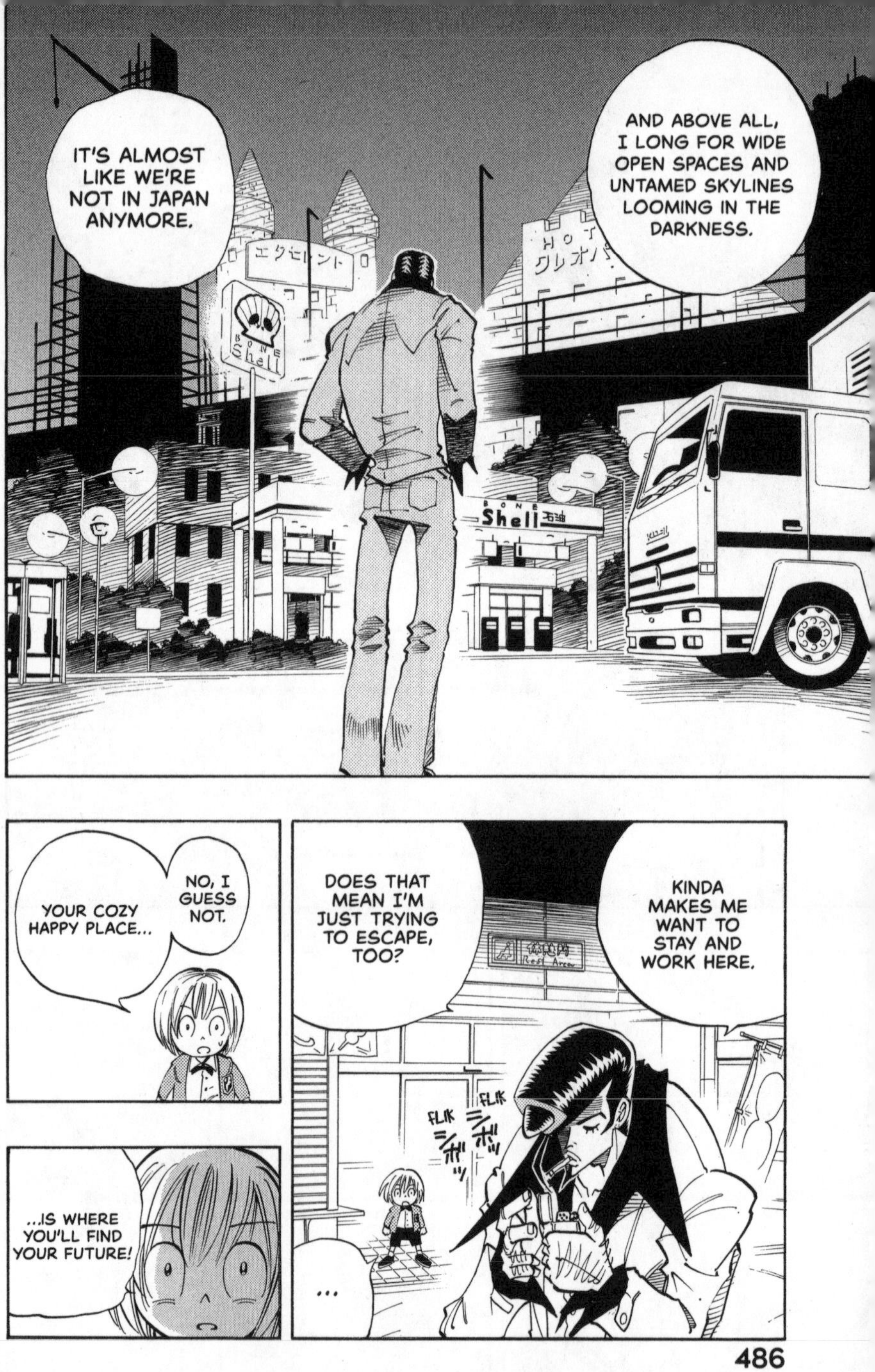
AND ABOVE ALL, I LONG FOR WIDE OPEN SPACES AND UNTAMED SKYLINES LOOMING IN THE DARKNESS.
IT'S ALMOST LIKE WE'RE NOT IN JAPAN ANYMORE.
BONE Shell
Shell 石油
KINDA MAKES ME WANT TO STAY AND WORK HERE.
DOES THAT MEAN I'M JUST TRYING TO ESCAPE, TOO?
FLIK
FLIK
...
NO, I GUESS NOT.
YOUR COZY HAPPY PLACE...
...IS WHERE YOU'LL FIND YOUR FUTURE!

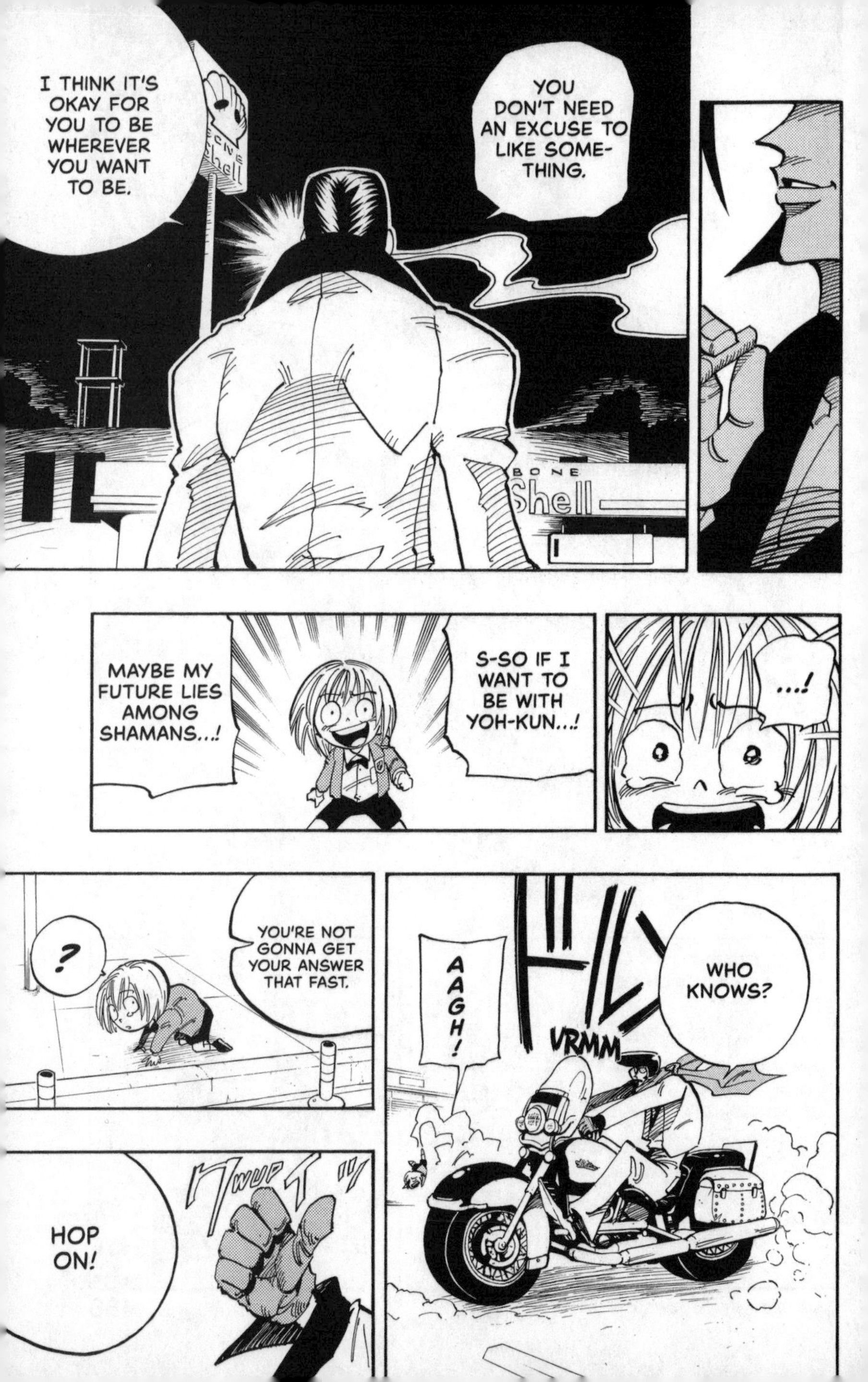

YOU DON'T NEED AN EXCUSE TO LIKE SOME-THING.
I THINK IT'S OKAY FOR YOU TO BE WHEREVER YOU WANT TO BE.
BONE Shell
...!
S-SO IF I WANT TO BE WITH YOH-KUN...!
MAYBE MY FUTURE LIES AMONG SHAMANS...!
WHO KNOWS?
VRMM
AAGH!
YOU'RE NOT GONNA GET YOUR ANSWER THAT FAST.
?
WUP
HOP ON!

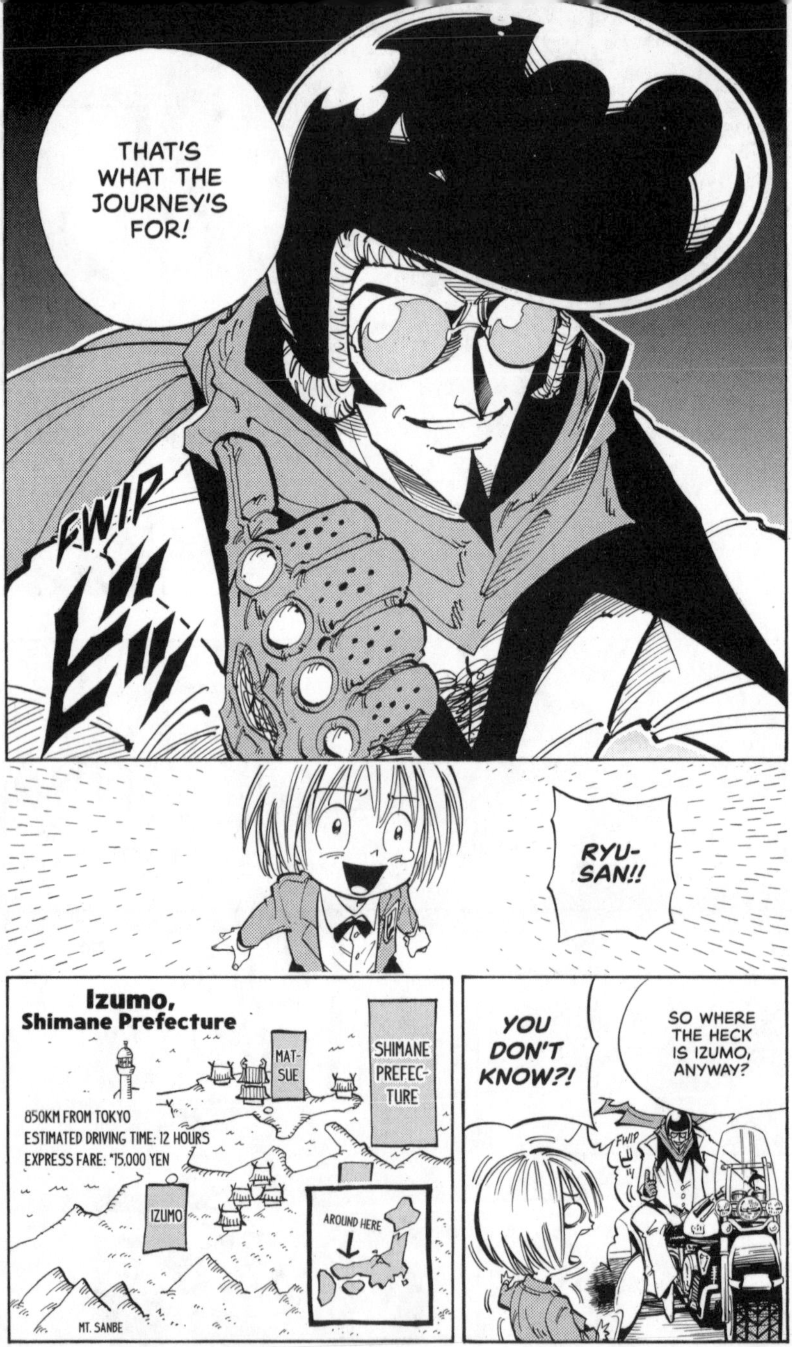
THAT'S WHAT THE JOURNEY'S FOR!
FWIP
RYU-SAN!!
SO WHERE THE HECK IS IZUMO, ANYWAY?
YOU DON'T KNOW?!
FWIP
Izumo, Shimane Prefecture
MAT-SUE
SHIMANE PREFEC-TURE
850KM FROM TOKYO
ESTIMATED DRIVING TIME: 12 HOURS
EXPRESS FARE: *15,000 YEN
IZUMO
AROUND HERE
MT. SANBE

* Approximately 138 dollars as of this writing.

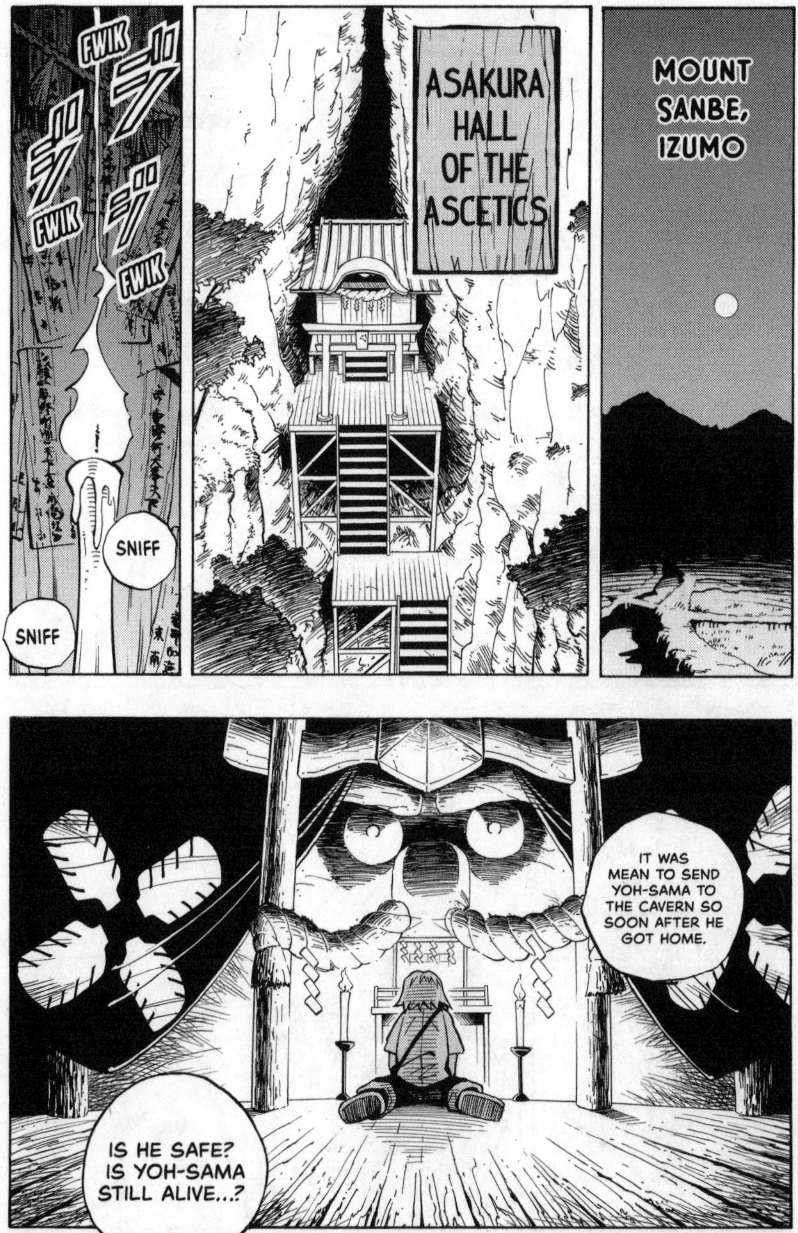
MOUNT SANBE, IZUMO
ASAKURA HALL OF THE ASCETICS
FWIK
FWIK
FWIK
SNIFF
SNIFF
IT WAS MEAN TO SEND YOH-SAMA TO THE CAVERN SO SOON AFTER HE GOT HOME.
IS HE SAFE? IS YOH-SAMA STILL ALIVE...?

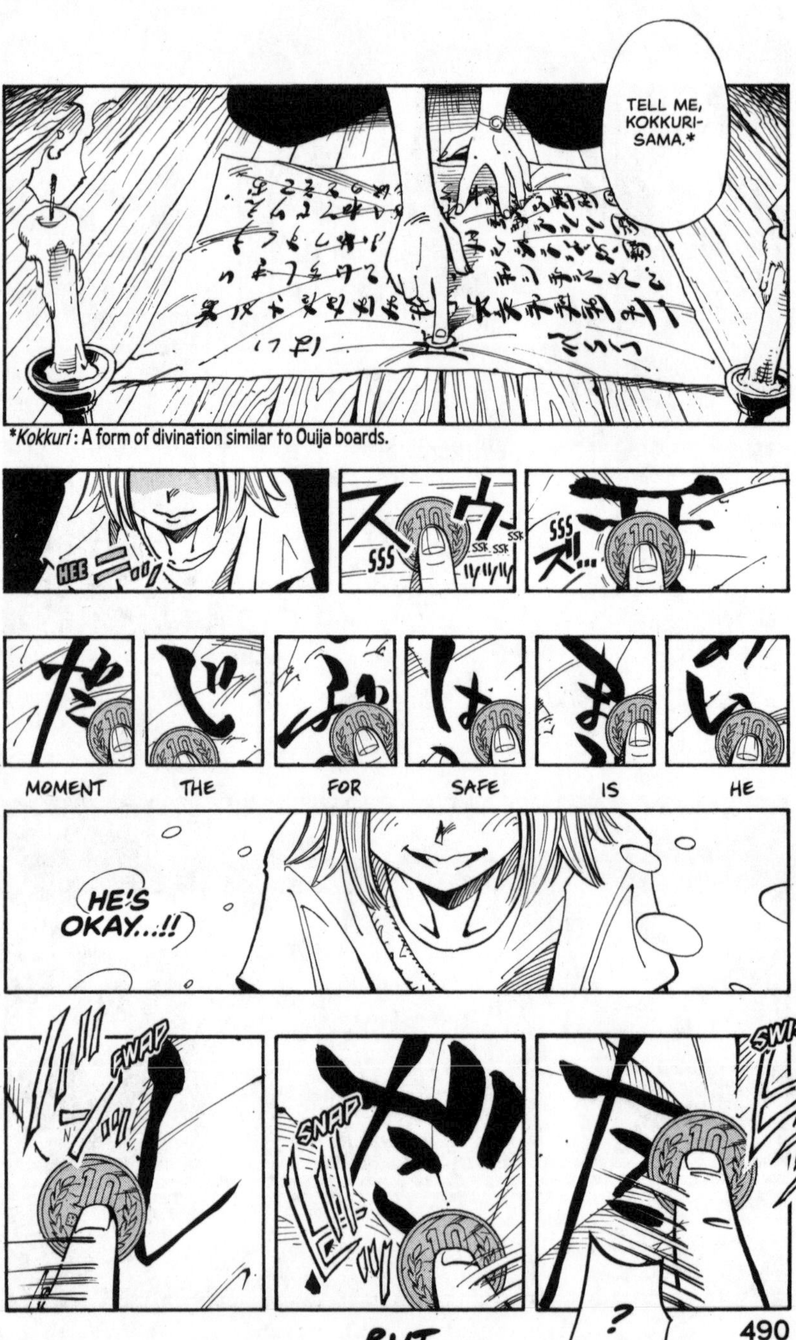
TELL ME, KOKKURI-SAMA.*
*Kokkuri: A form of divination similar to Ouija boards.
SSS
SSS
SSK
SSK
SSK
HEE
HE
IS
SAFE
FOR
THE
MOMENT
HE'S OKAY...!!
SWISH
?
SNAP
FWAP
BUT...

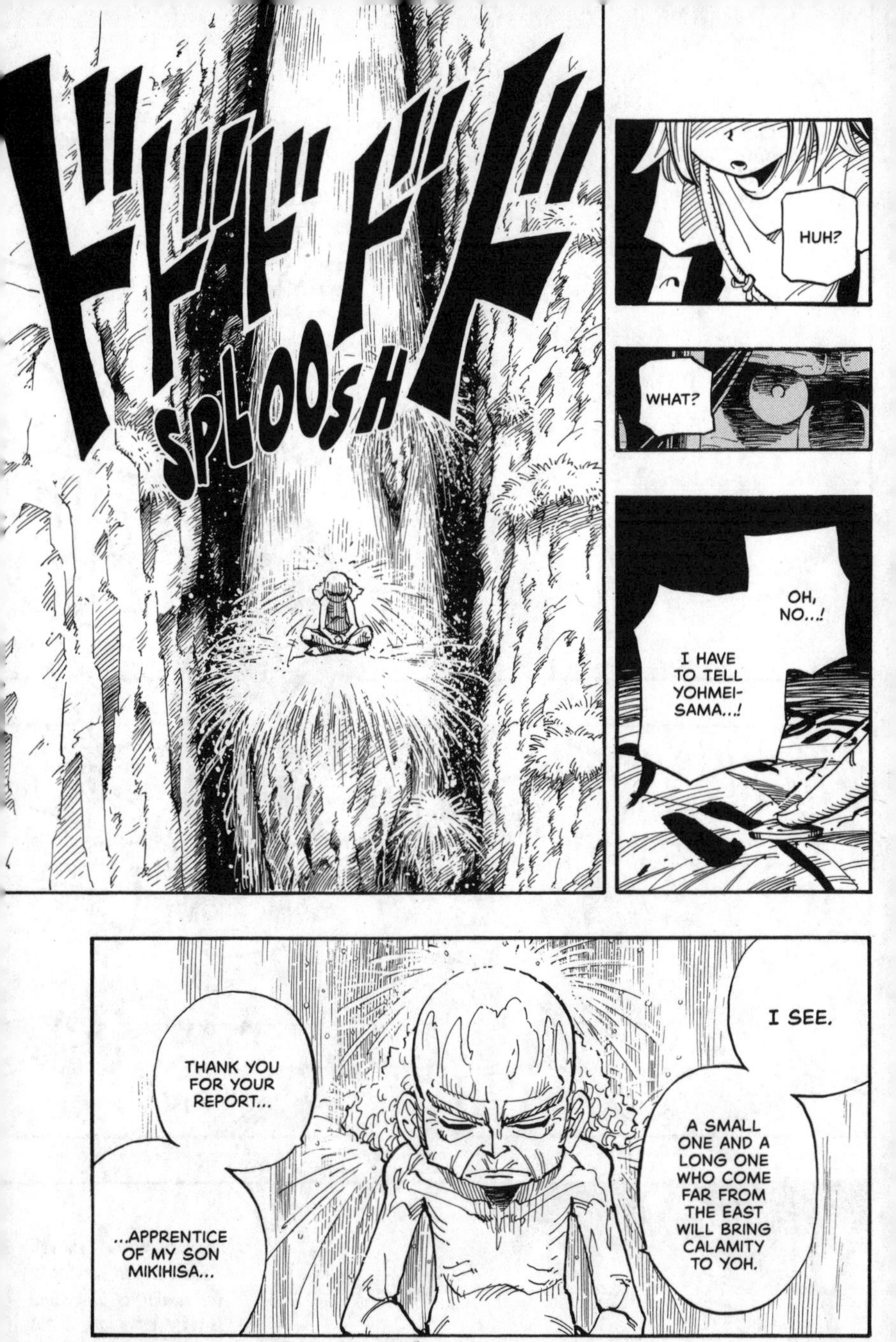
HUH?
WHAT?
OH, NO...!
I HAVE TO TELL YOHMEI-SAMA...!
SPLOOSH
I SEE.
A SMALL ONE AND A LONG ONE WHO COME FAR FROM THE EAST WILL BRING CALAMITY TO YOH.
THANK YOU FOR YOUR REPORT...
...APPRENTICE OF MY SON MIKIHISA...

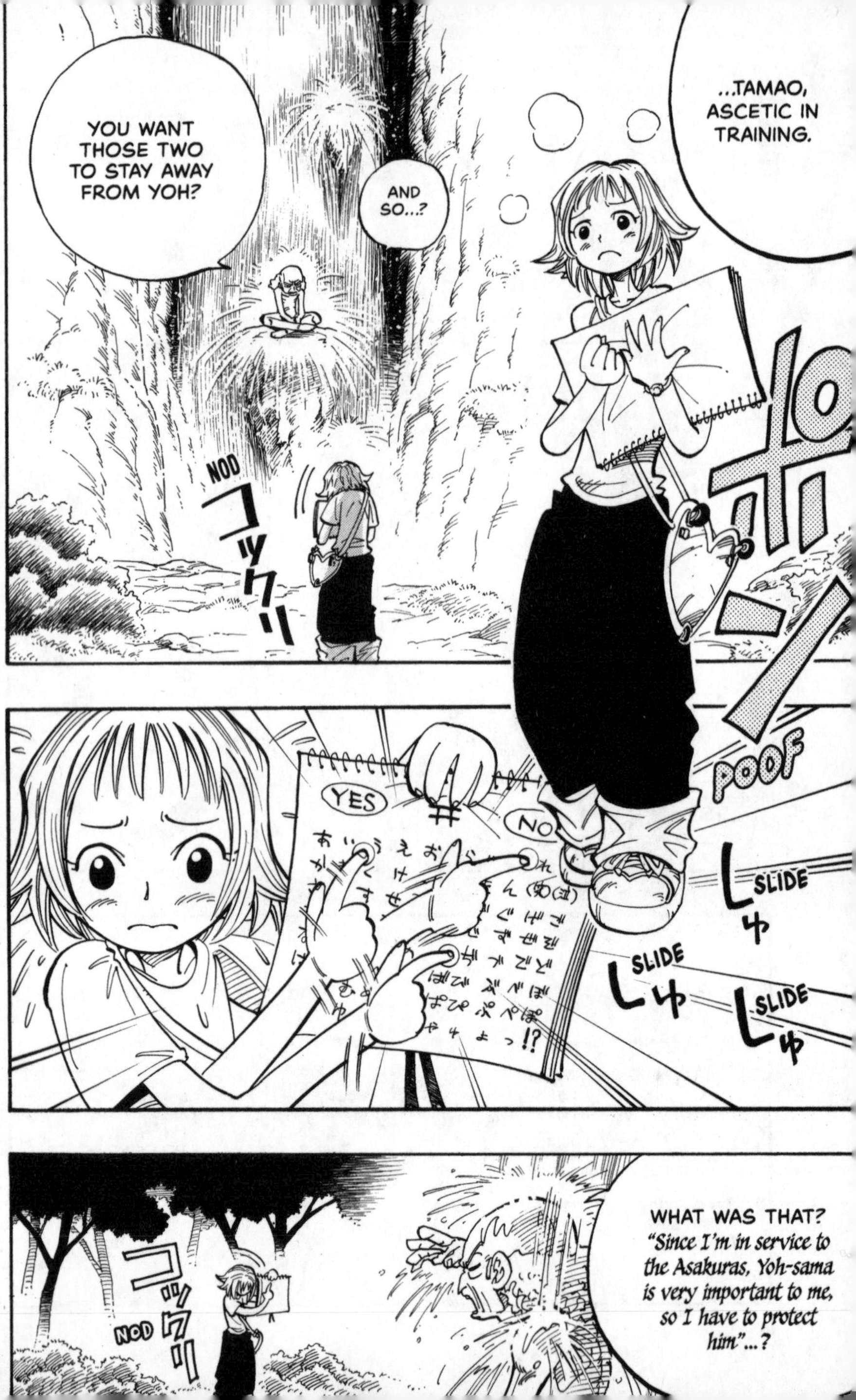

...TAMAO, ASCETIC IN TRAINING.
YOU WANT THOSE TWO TO STAY AWAY FROM YOH?
NOD
コックリ
AND SO...?
ポン
POOF
YES
NO
しゅ
SLIDE
しゅ
SLIDE
しゅ
SLIDE
WHAT WAS THAT? *"Since I'm in service to the Asakuras, Yoh-sama is very important to me, so I have to protect him"...?*
NOD
コックリ

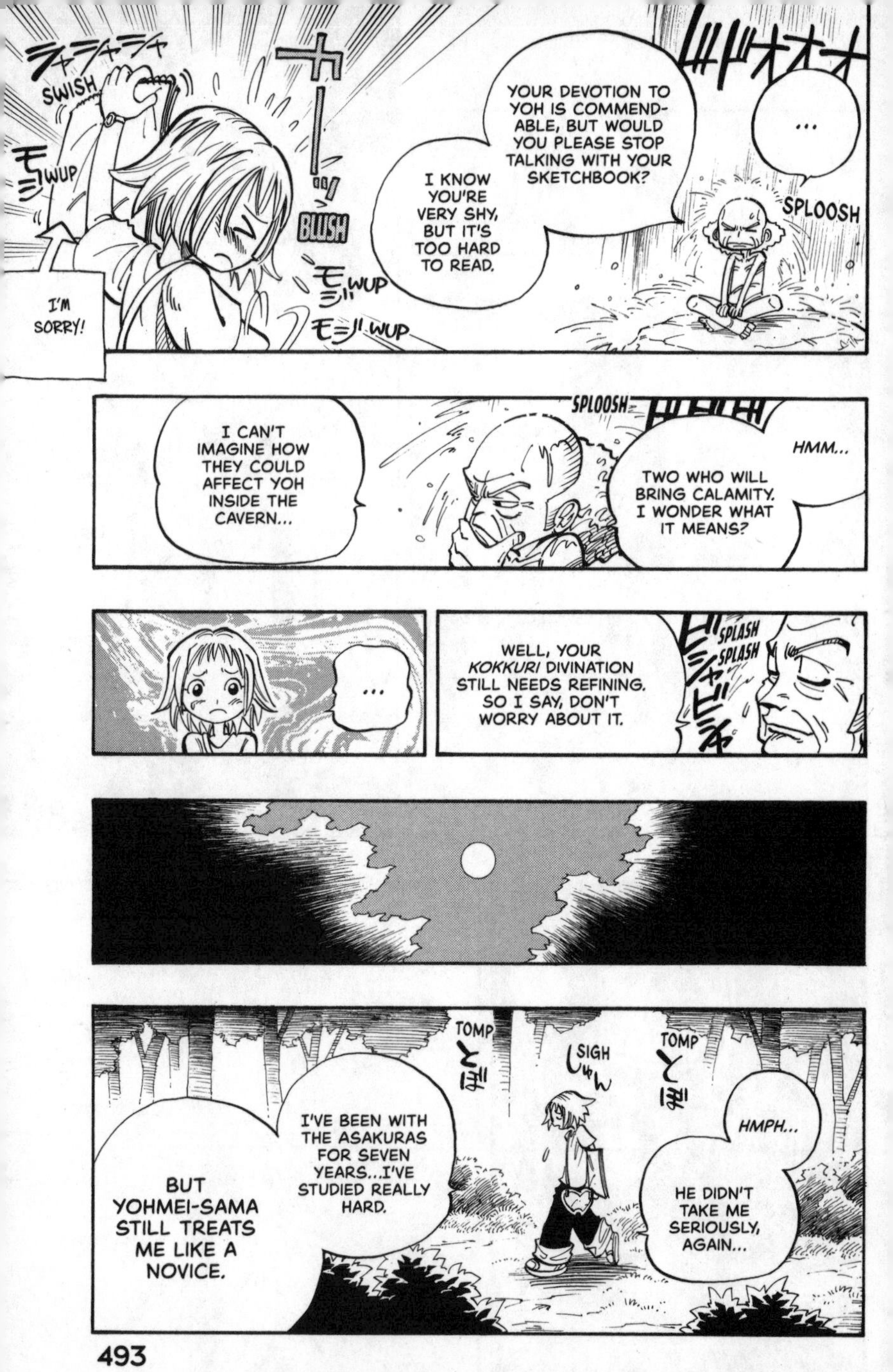
...
SPLOOSH
YOUR DEVOTION TO YOH IS COMMENDABLE, BUT WOULD YOU PLEASE STOP TALKING WITH YOUR SKETCHBOOK?
I KNOW YOU'RE VERY SHY, BUT IT'S TOO HARD TO READ.
BLUSH
WUP
WUP
SWISH
WUP
I'M SORRY!
HMM...
TWO WHO WILL BRING CALAMITY. I WONDER WHAT IT MEANS?
SPLOOSH
I CAN'T IMAGINE HOW THEY COULD AFFECT YOH INSIDE THE CAVERN...
SPLASH SPLASH
WELL, YOUR *KOKKURI* DIVINATION STILL NEEDS REFINING. SO I SAY, DON'T WORRY ABOUT IT.
...
HMPH...
HE DIDN'T TAKE ME SERIOUSLY, AGAIN...
TOMP
SIGH
TOMP
I'VE BEEN WITH THE ASAKURAS FOR SEVEN YEARS...I'VE STUDIED REALLY HARD.
BUT YOHMEI-SAMA STILL TREATS ME LIKE A NOVICE.

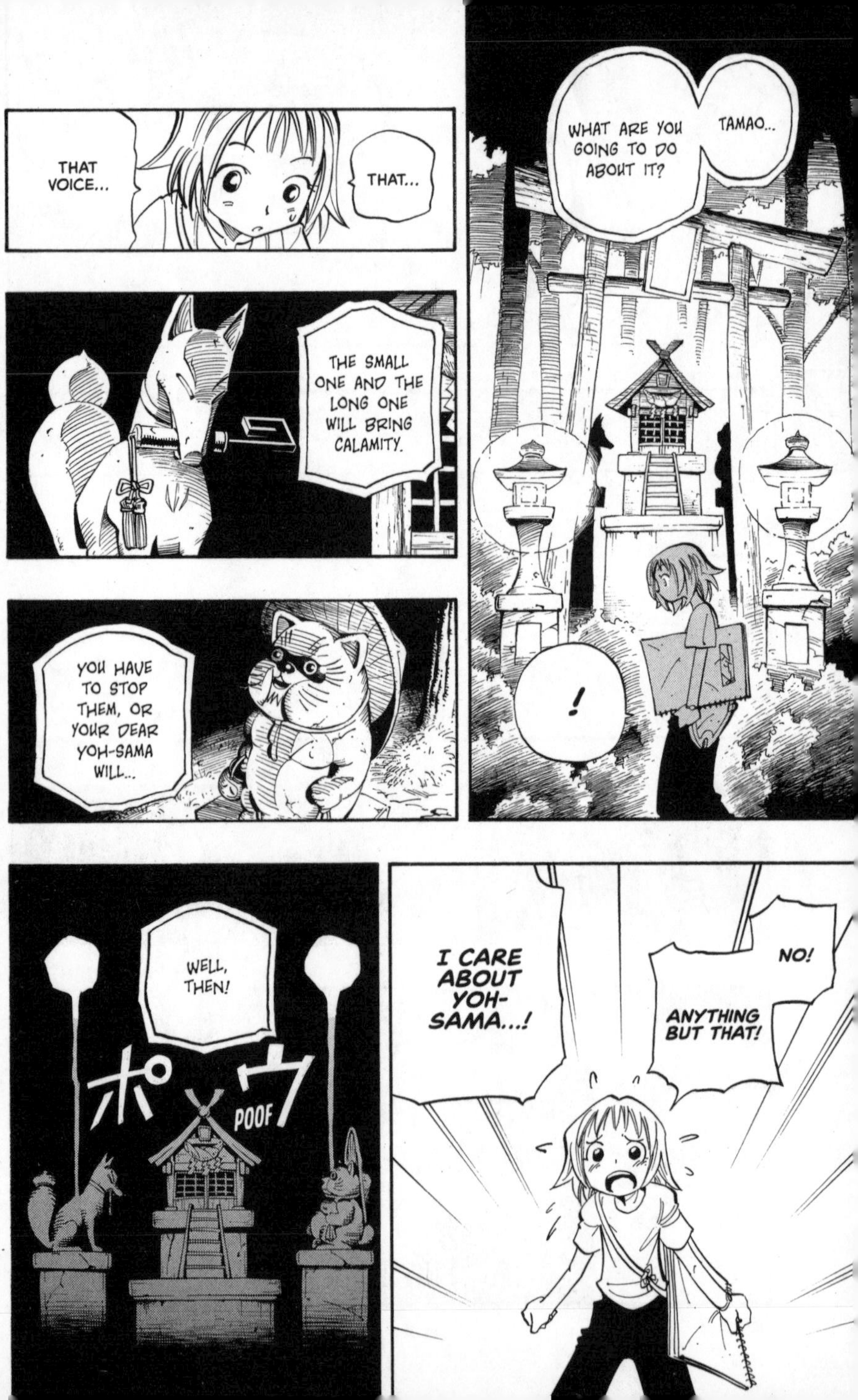
TAMAO...
WHAT ARE YOU GOING TO DO ABOUT IT?
!
THAT...
THAT VOICE...
THE SMALL ONE AND THE LONG ONE WILL BRING CALAMITY.
YOU HAVE TO STOP THEM, OR YOUR DEAR YOH-SAMA WILL...
NO!
ANYTHING BUT THAT!
I CARE ABOUT YOH-SAMA...!
WELL, THEN!
ポウ
POOF

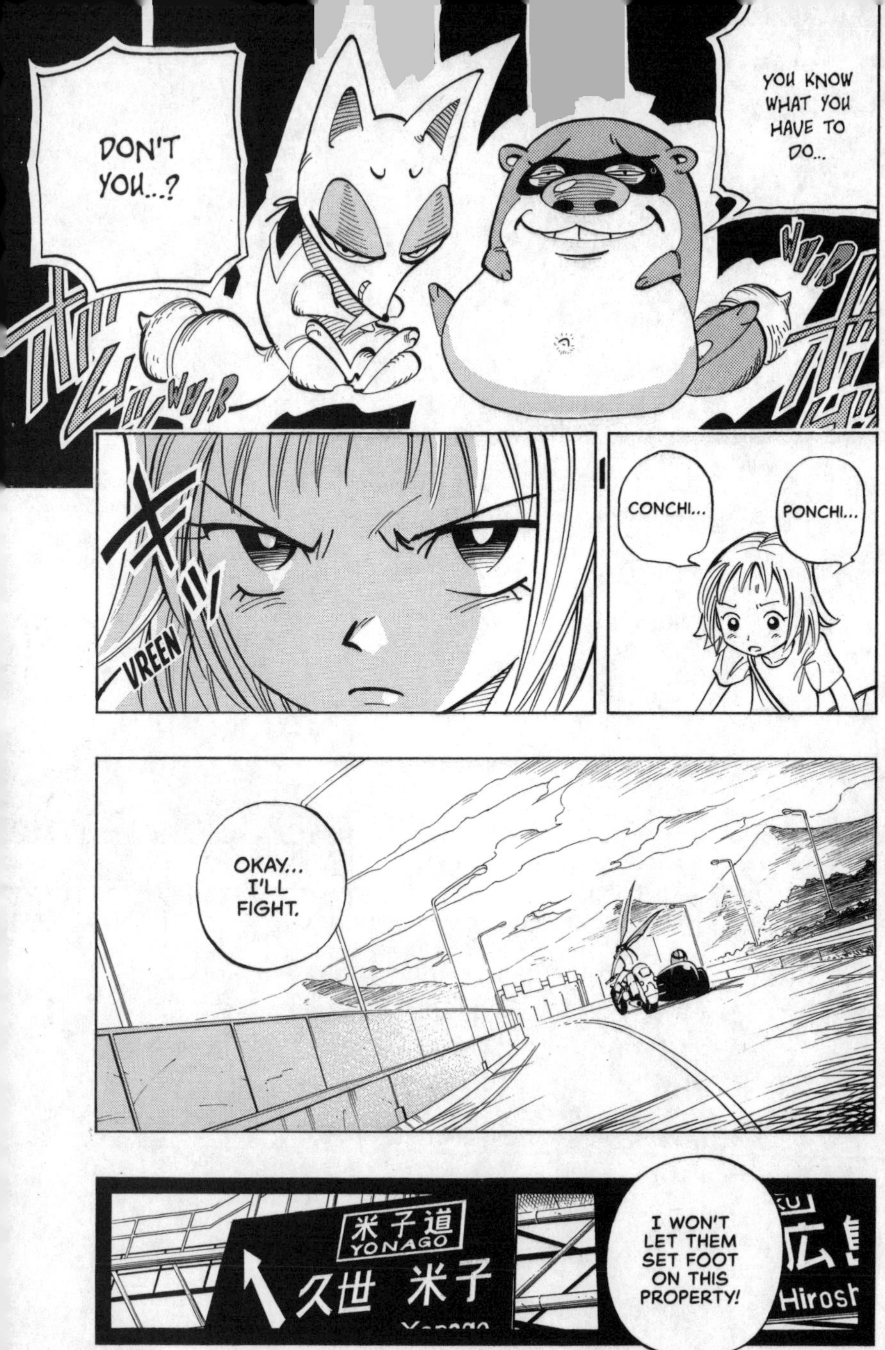
YOU KNOW WHAT YOU HAVE TO DO...
WHIR
DON'T YOU...?
WHIR
PONCHI...
CONCHI...
VREEN
OKAY... I'LL FIGHT.
I WON'T LET THEM SET FOOT ON THIS PROPERTY!
米子道
YONAGO
久世 米子

SHAMAN
KING
6

Sketchbook

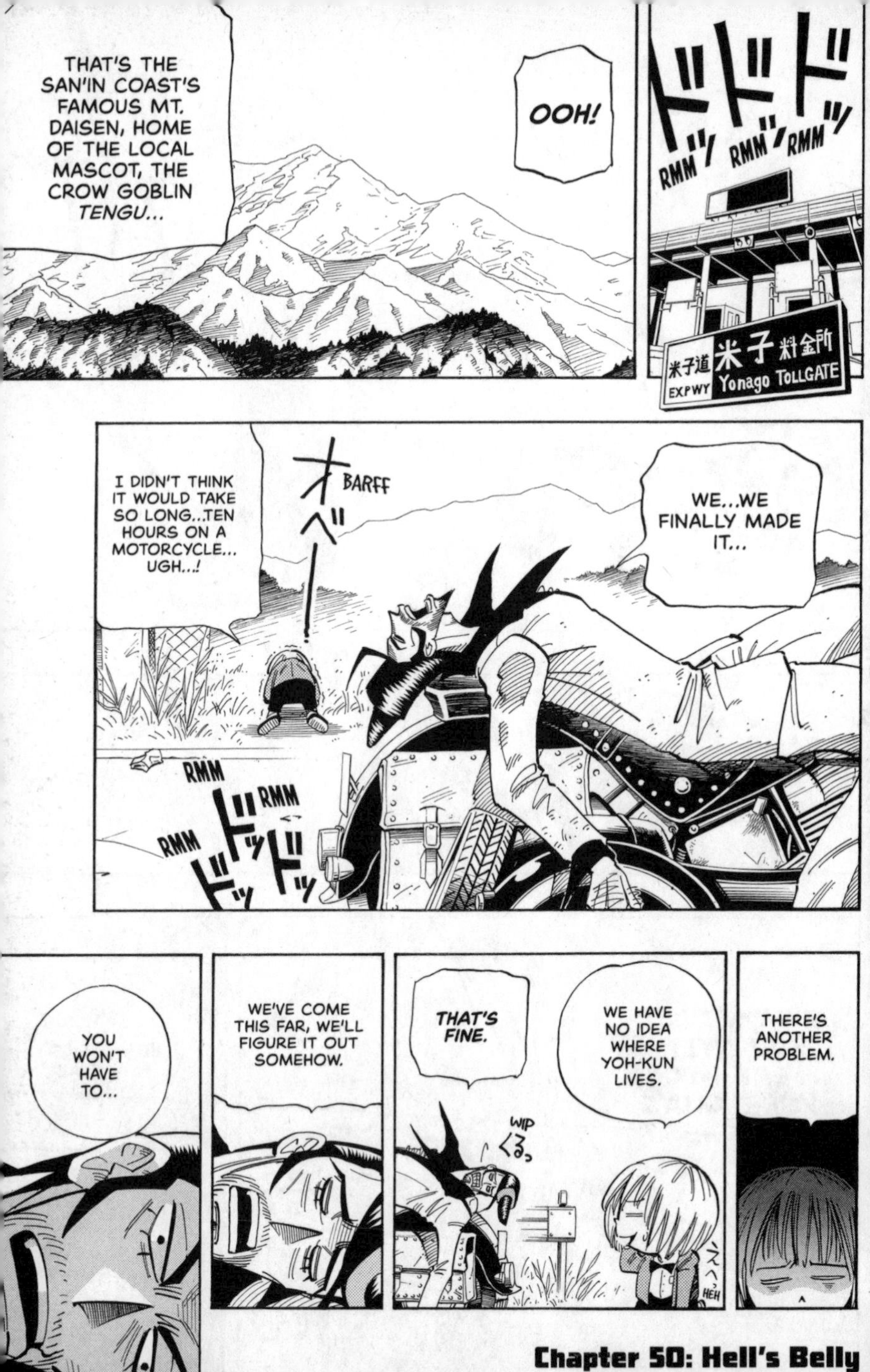
ドドドッ
RMM RMM RMM
米子道 EXPWY
米子料金所 Yonago TOLLGATE
OOH!
THAT'S THE SAN'IN COAST'S FAMOUS MT. DAISEN, HOME OF THE LOCAL MASCOT, THE CROW GOBLIN *TENGU*...
WE...WE FINALLY MADE IT...
オベー
BARFF
I DIDN'T THINK IT WOULD TAKE SO LONG...TEN HOURS ON A MOTORCYCLE... UGH...!
ドッドッドッ
RMM RMM RMM
THERE'S ANOTHER PROBLEM.
WE HAVE NO IDEA WHERE YOH-KUN LIVES.
えへっ
HEH
THAT'S FINE.
くるっ
WIP
WE'VE COME THIS FAR, WE'LL FIGURE IT OUT SOMEHOW.
YOU WON'T HAVE TO...

Chapter 50: Hell's Belly

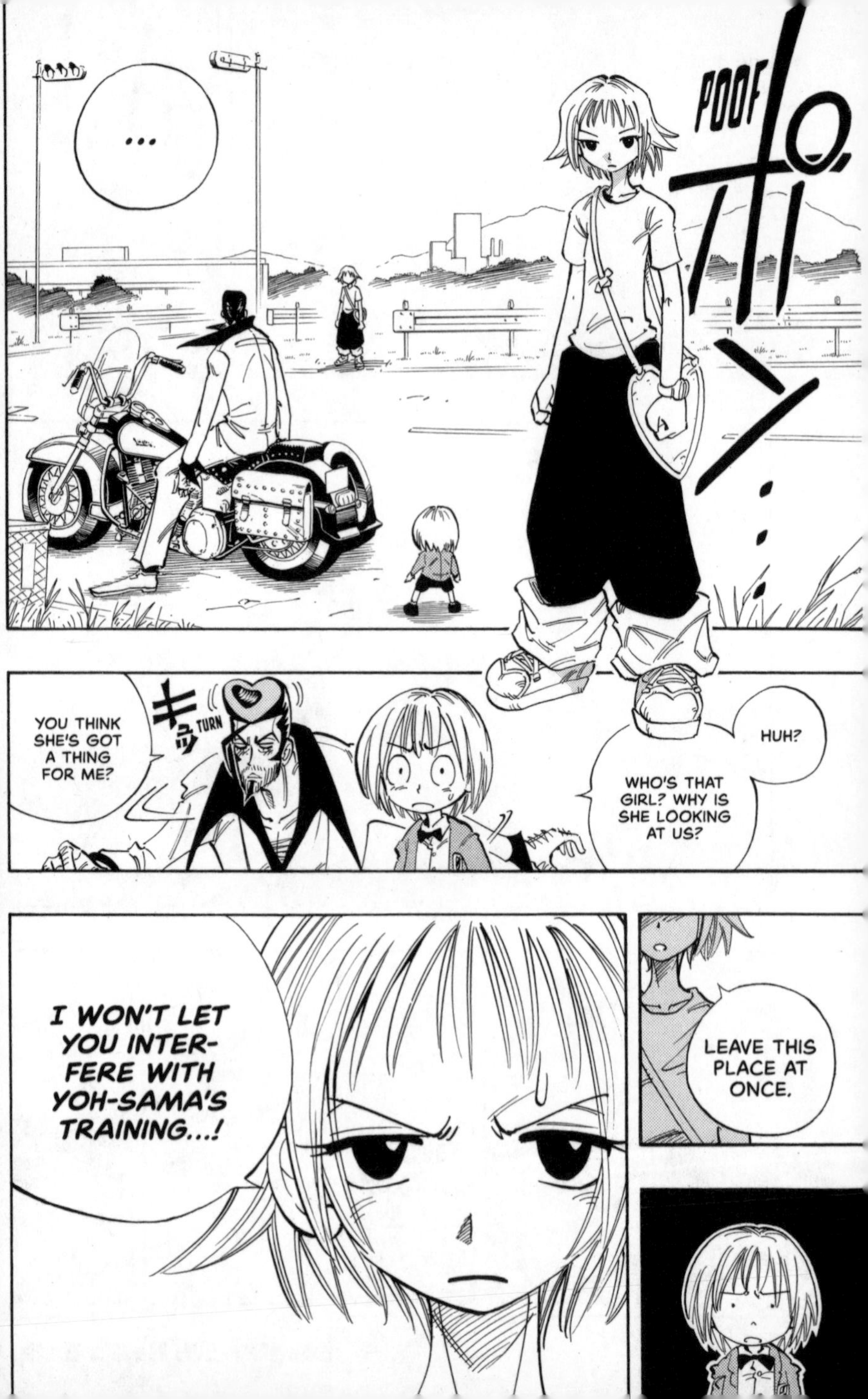
POOF
...
HUH?
WHO'S THAT GIRL? WHY IS SHE LOOKING AT US?
TURN
YOU THINK SHE'S GOT A THING FOR ME?
LEAVE THIS PLACE AT ONCE.
I WON'T LET YOU INTER-FERE WITH YOH-SAMA'S TRAINING...!

Chapter 50:

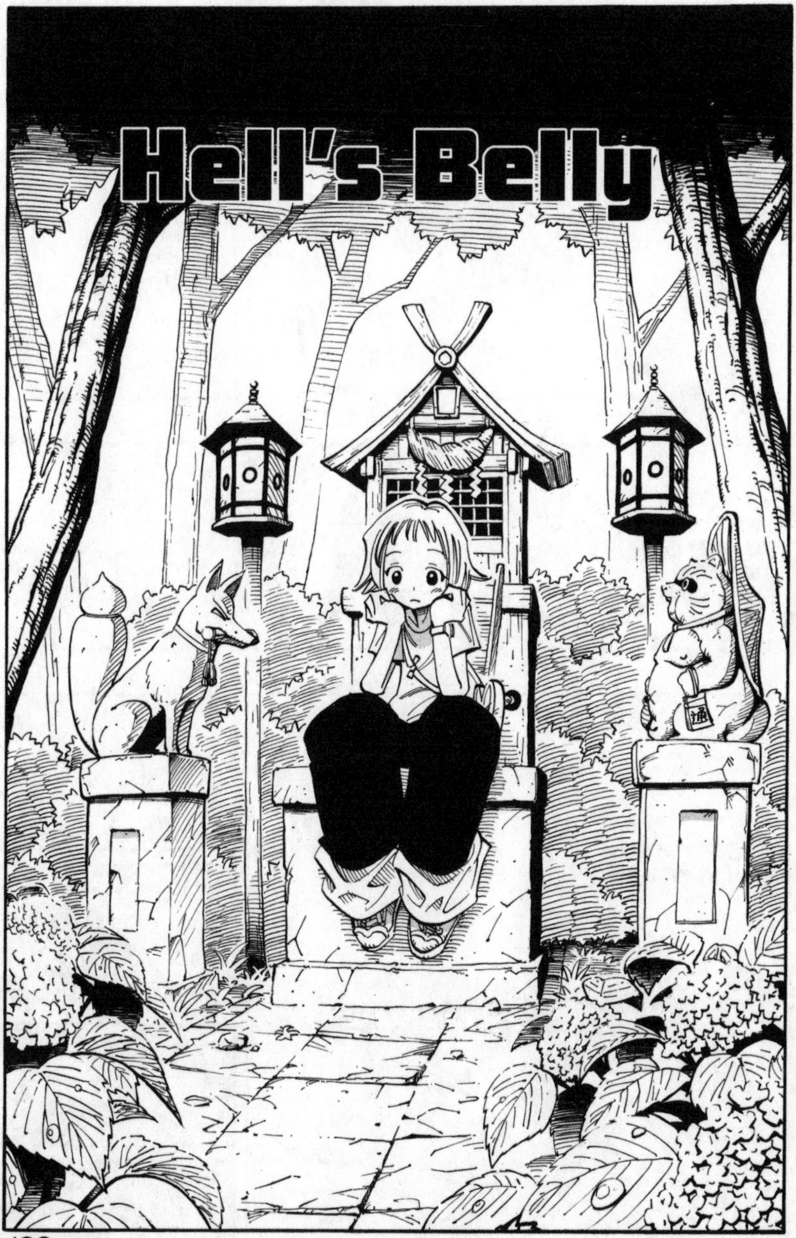
Hell's Belly

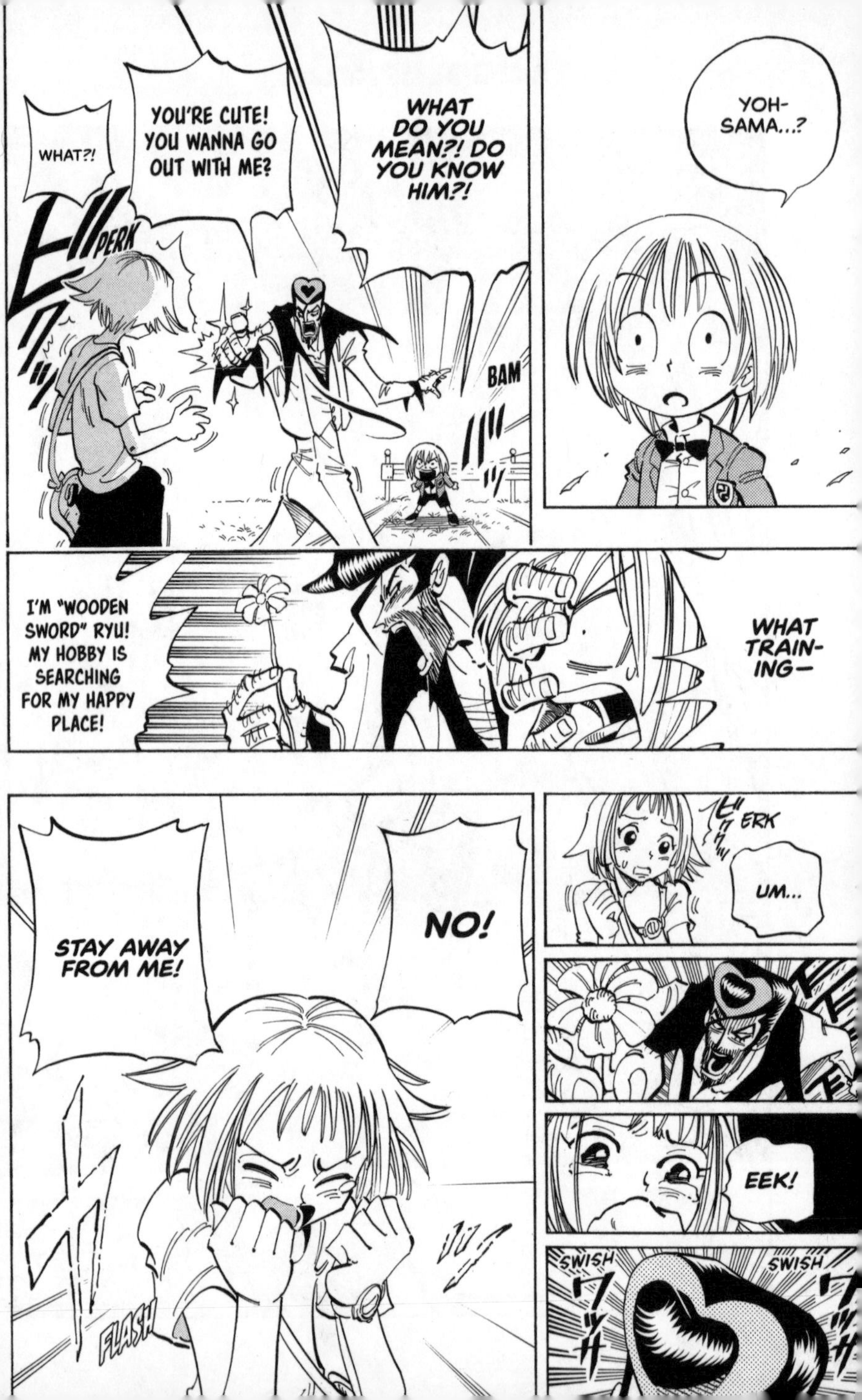
YOH-SAMA...?
WHAT DO YOU MEAN?! DO YOU KNOW HIM?!
YOU'RE CUTE! YOU WANNA GO OUT WITH ME?
WHAT?!
BAM
PERK
WHAT TRAIN-ING—
I'M "WOODEN SWORD" RYU! MY HOBBY IS SEARCHING FOR MY HAPPY PLACE!
ERK
UM...
EEK!
SWISH
SWISH
NO!
STAY AWAY FROM ME!
FLASH

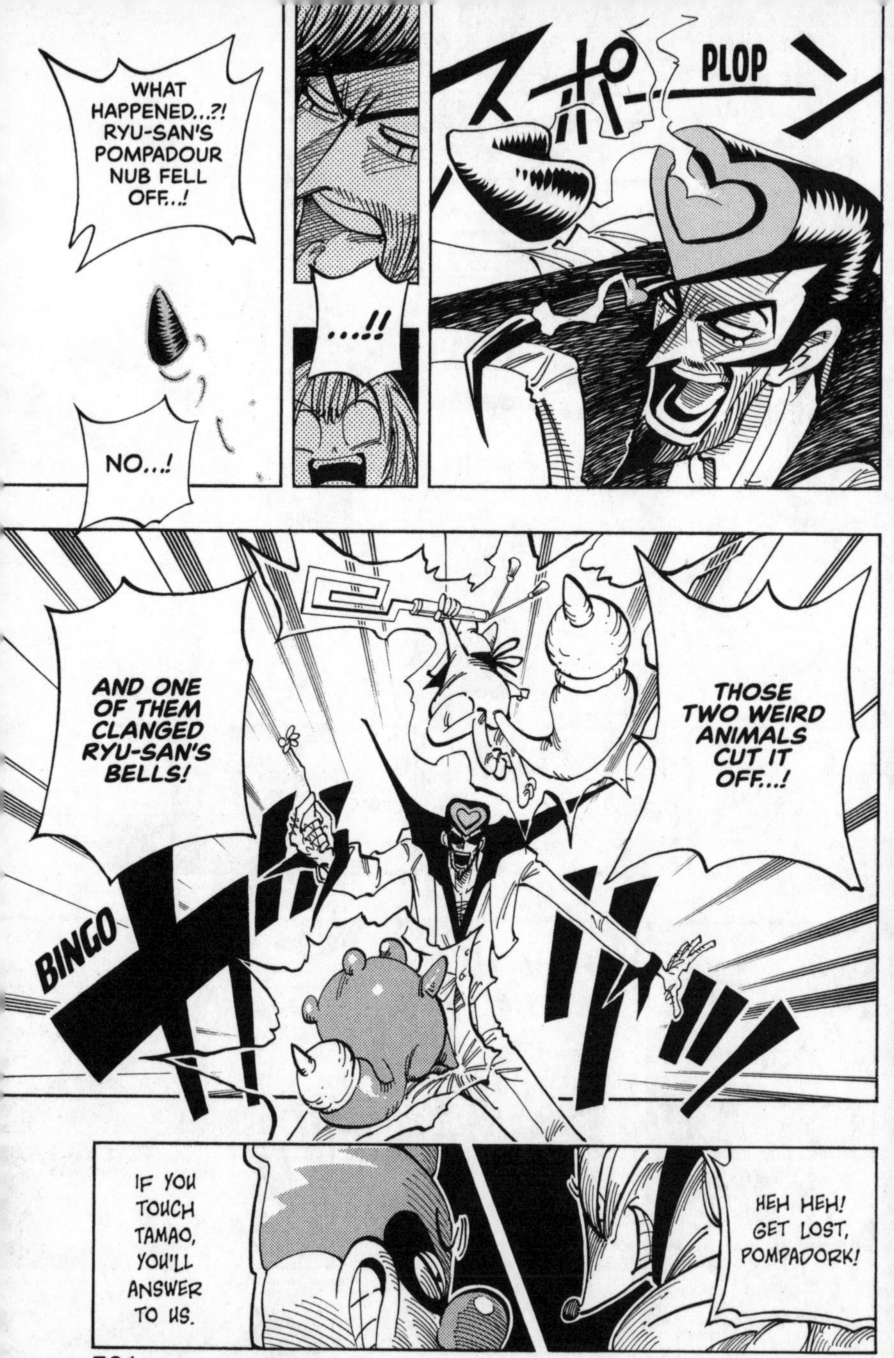
スポーン
PLOP
...!!
WHAT HAPPENED...?! RYU-SAN'S POMPADOUR NUB FELL OFF...!
NO...!
THOSE TWO WEIRD ANIMALS CUT IT OFF...!
AND ONE OF THEM CLANGED RYU-SAN'S BELLS!
BINGO
HEH HEH! GET LOST, POMPADORK!
IF YOU TOUCH TAMAO, YOU'LL ANSWER TO US.

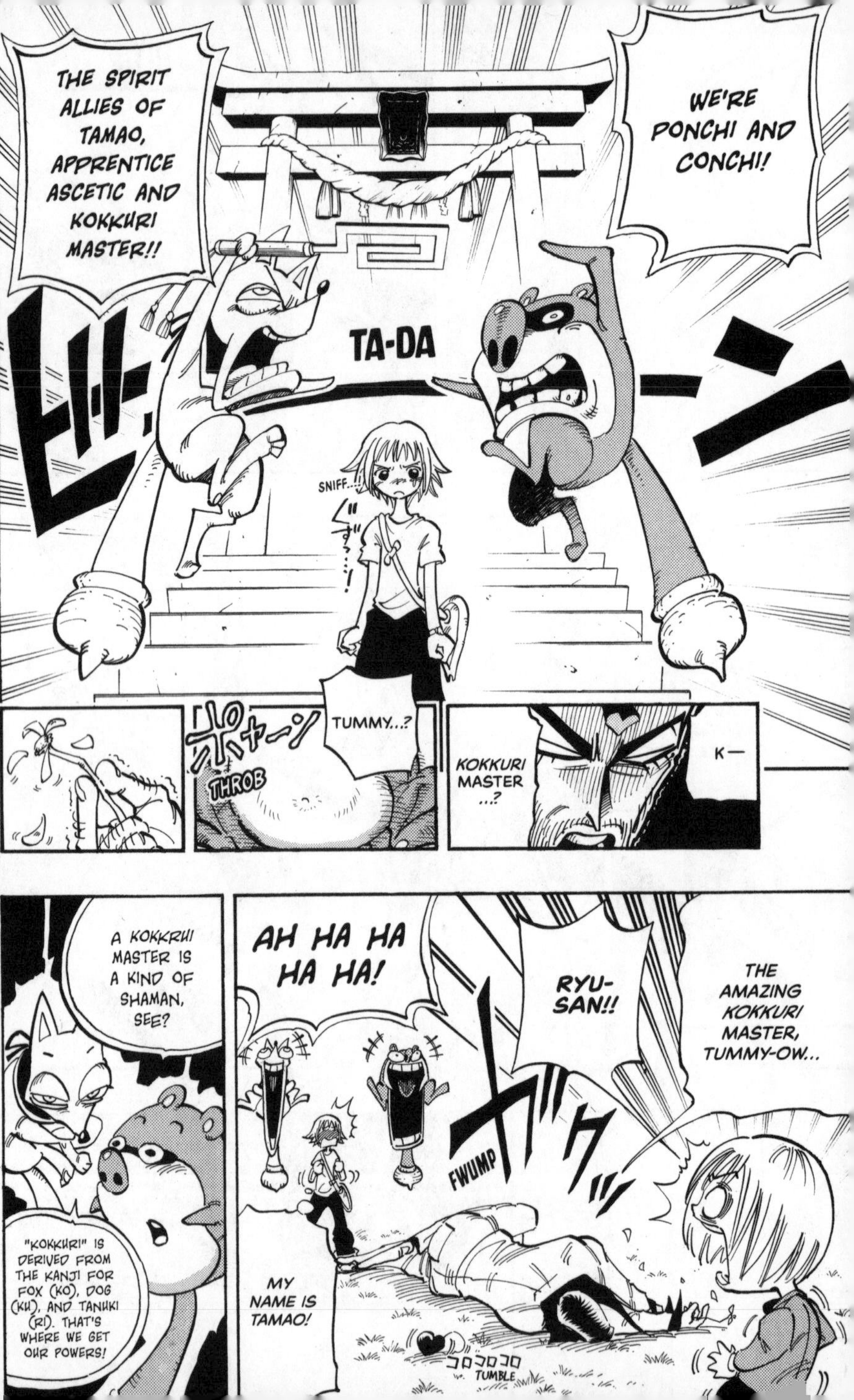
WE'RE PONCHI AND CONCHI!!
THE SPIRIT ALLIES OF TAMAO, APPRENTICE ASCETIC AND KOKKURI MASTER!!
TA-DA
SNIFF...
K—
KOKKURI MASTER ...?
TUMMY...?
THROB
THE AMAZING KOKKURI MASTER, TUMMY-OW...
RYU-SAN!!
AH HA HA HA HA!
FWUMP
MY NAME IS TAMAO!
TUMBLE
A KOKKRUI MASTER IS A KIND OF SHAMAN, SEE?
"KOKKURI" IS DERIVED FROM THE KANJI FOR FOX (KO), DOG (KU), AND TANUKI (RI). THAT'S WHERE WE GET OUR POWERS!

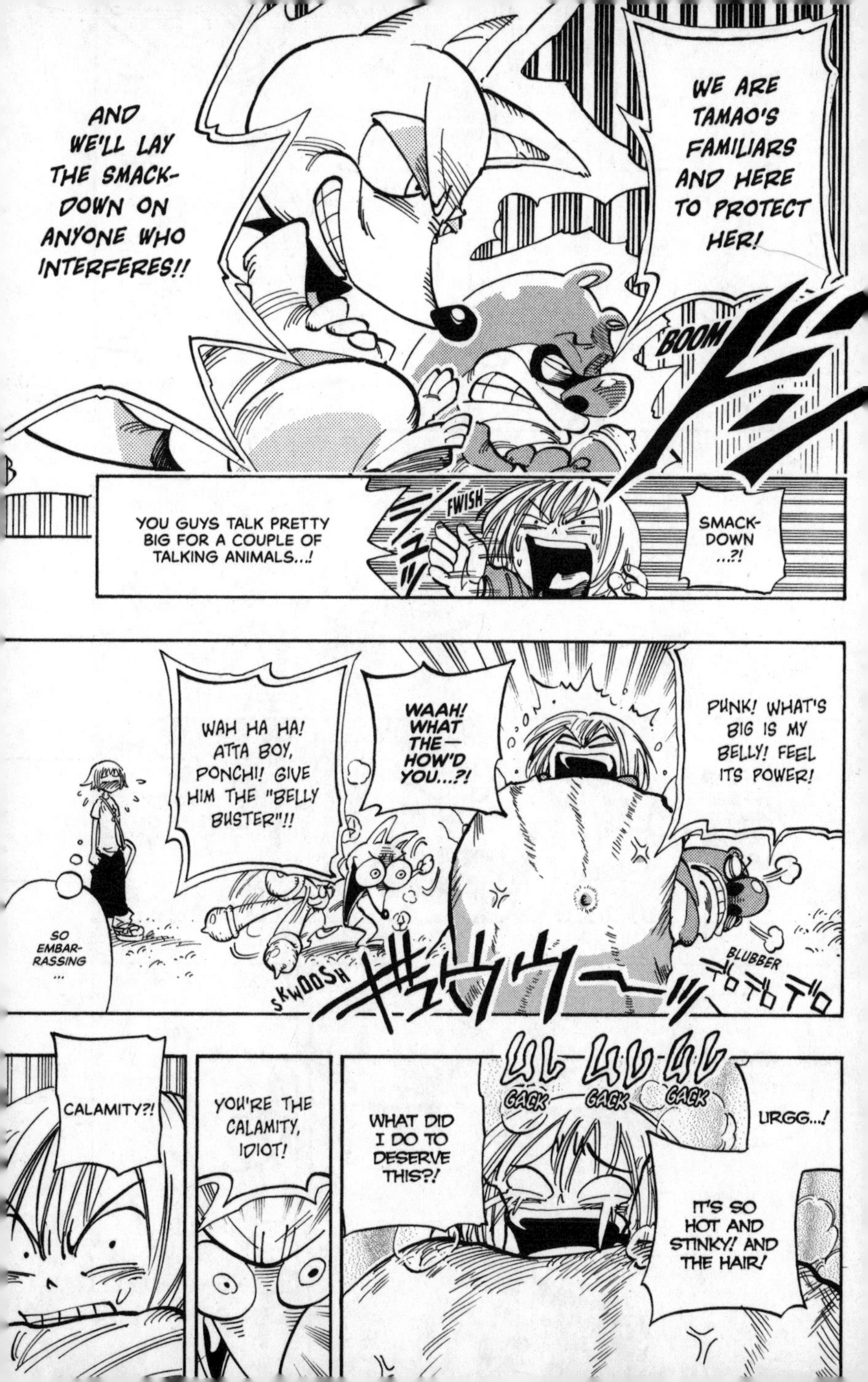
WE ARE TAMAO'S FAMILIARS AND HERE TO PROTECT HER!
AND WE'LL LAY THE SMACK-DOWN ON ANYONE WHO INTERFERES!!
BOOM
SMACK-DOWN ...?!
FWISH
YOU GUYS TALK PRETTY BIG FOR A COUPLE OF TALKING ANIMALS...!
PUNK! WHAT'S BIG IS MY BELLY! FEEL ITS POWER!
WAAH! WHAT THE— HOW'D YOU...?!
WAH HA HA! ATTA BOY, PONCHI! GIVE HIM THE "BELLY BUSTER"!!
BLUBBER
SKWOOSH
SO EMBAR-RASSING ...
GACK GACK GACK
URGG...!
IT'S SO HOT AND STINKY! AND THE HAIR!
WHAT DID I DO TO DESERVE THIS?!
YOU'RE THE CALAMITY, IDIOT!
CALAMITY?!

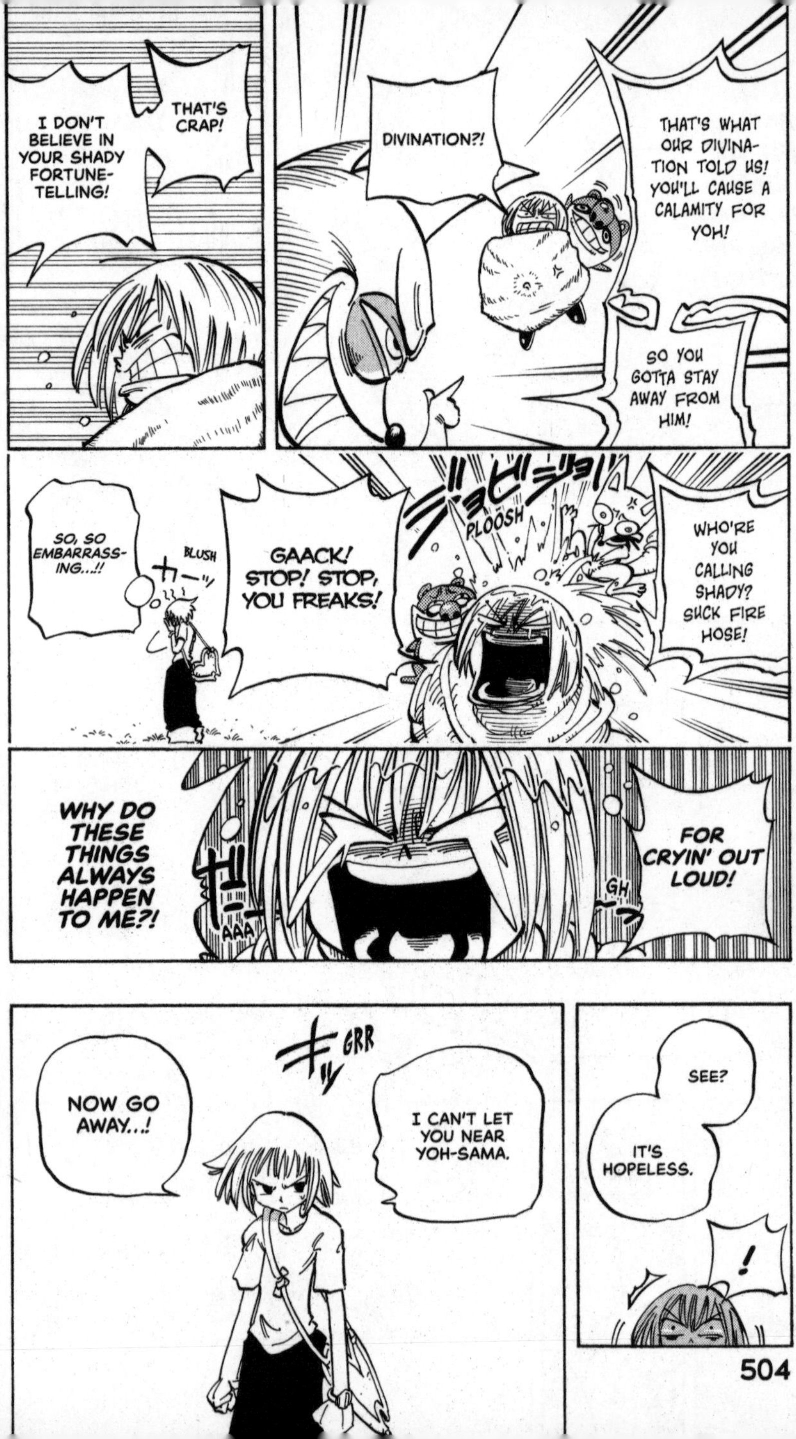
THAT'S WHAT OUR DIVINATION TOLD US! YOU'LL CAUSE A CALAMITY FOR YOH!
SO YOU GOTTA STAY AWAY FROM HIM!
DIVINATION?!
THAT'S CRAP!
I DON'T BELIEVE IN YOUR SHADY FORTUNE-TELLING!
WHO'RE YOU CALLING SHADY? SUCK FIRE HOSE!
PLOOSH
GAACK! STOP! STOP, YOU FREAKS!
BLUSH
SO, SO EMBARRASSING...!!
FOR CRYIN' OUT LOUD!
GH
WHY DO THESE THINGS ALWAYS HAPPEN TO ME?!
AAA
SEE?
IT'S HOPELESS.
!
GRR
I CAN'T LET YOU NEAR YOH-SAMA.
NOW GO AWAY...!

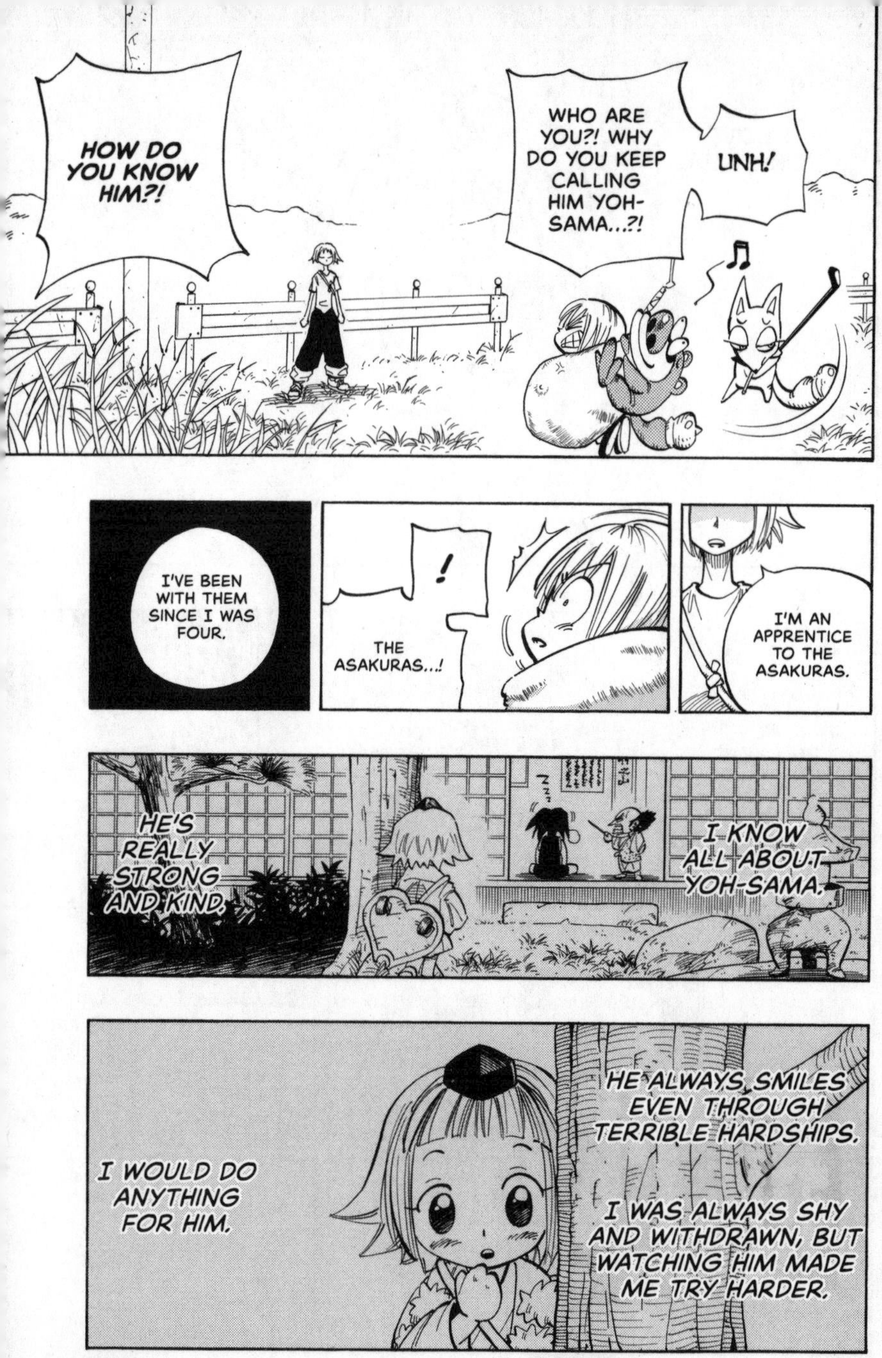
UNH!
WHO ARE YOU?! WHY DO YOU KEEP CALLING HIM YOH-SAMA...?!
HOW DO YOU KNOW HIM?!
I'M AN APPRENTICE TO THE ASAKURAS.
!
THE ASAKURAS...!
I'VE BEEN WITH THEM SINCE I WAS FOUR.
I KNOW ALL ABOUT YOH-SAMA.
HE'S REALLY STRONG AND KIND.
HE ALWAYS SMILES EVEN THROUGH TERRIBLE HARDSHIPS.
I WAS ALWAYS SHY AND WITHDRAWN, BUT WATCHING HIM MADE ME TRY HARDER.
I WOULD DO ANYTHING FOR HIM.

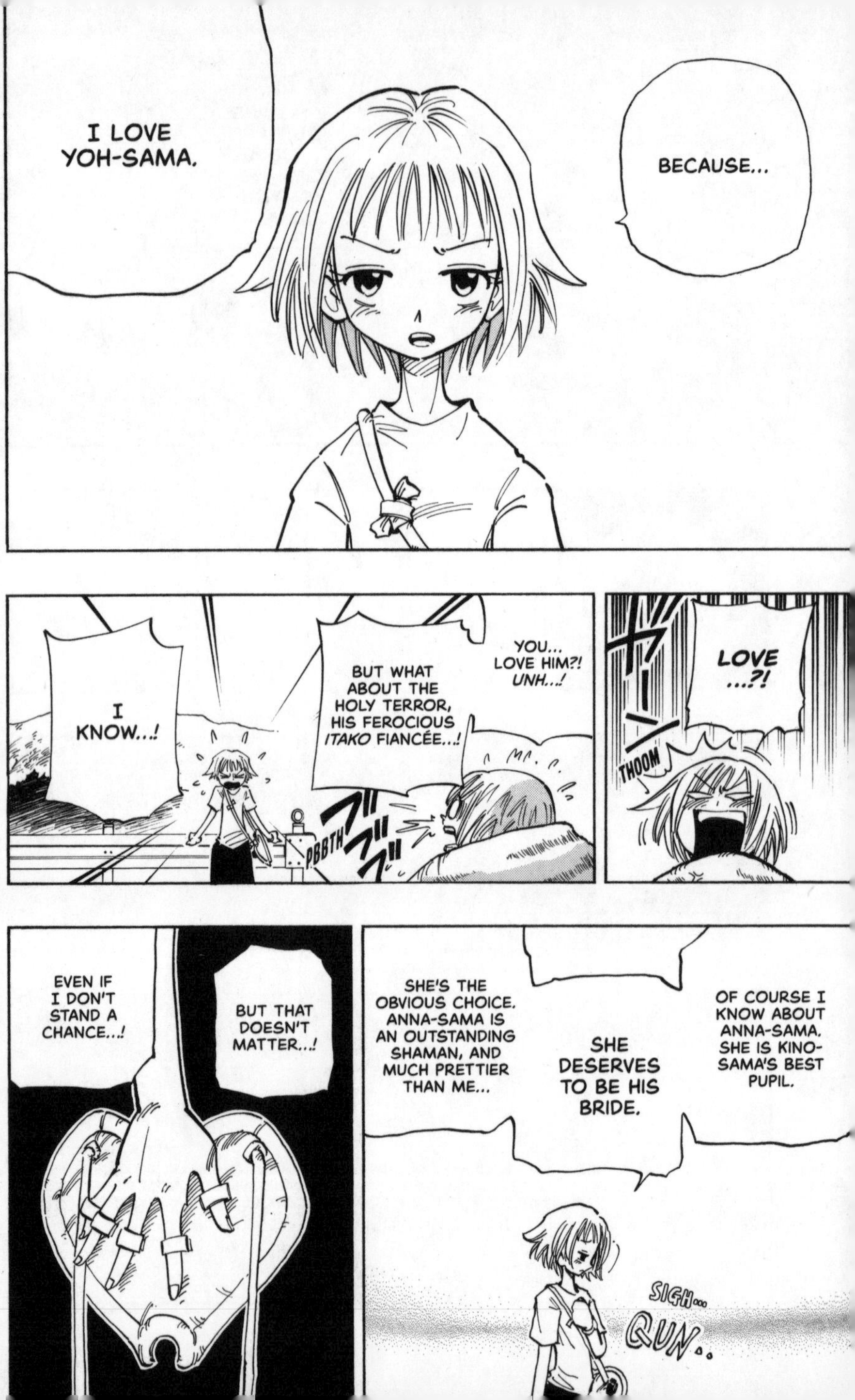
BECAUSE...
I LOVE YOH-SAMA.
LOVE ...?!
THOOM
YOU... LOVE HIM?! UNH...!
BUT WHAT ABOUT THE HOLY TERROR, HIS FEROCIOUS *ITAKO* FIANCÉE...!
PBBTH
I KNOW...!
OF COURSE I KNOW ABOUT ANNA-SAMA. SHE IS KINO-SAMA'S BEST PUPIL.
SHE DESERVES TO BE HIS BRIDE.
SHE'S THE OBVIOUS CHOICE. ANNA-SAMA IS AN OUTSTANDING SHAMAN, AND MUCH PRETTIER THAN ME...
SIGH...
QUN..
BUT THAT DOESN'T MATTER...!
EVEN IF I DON'T STAND A CHANCE...!

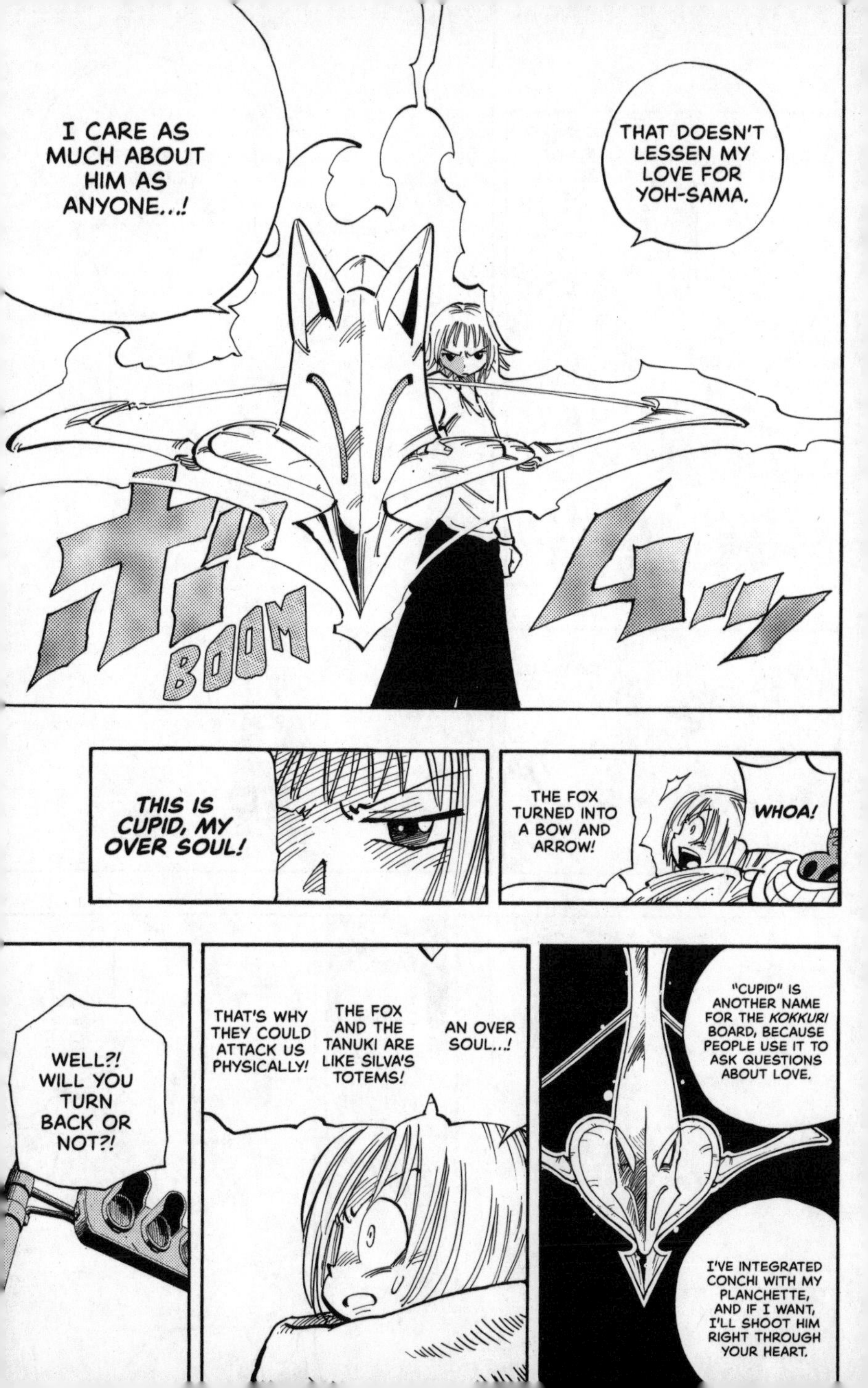
THAT DOESN'T LESSEN MY LOVE FOR YOH-SAMA.
I CARE AS MUCH ABOUT HIM AS ANYONE...!
BOOM
WHOA!
THE FOX TURNED INTO A BOW AND ARROW!
THIS IS CUPID, MY OVER SOUL!
"CUPID" IS ANOTHER NAME FOR THE *KOKKURI* BOARD, BECAUSE PEOPLE USE IT TO ASK QUESTIONS ABOUT LOVE.
I'VE INTEGRATED CONCHI WITH MY PLANCHETTE, AND IF I WANT, I'LL SHOOT HIM RIGHT THROUGH YOUR HEART.
AN OVER SOUL...!
THE FOX AND THE TANUKI ARE LIKE SILVA'S TOTEMS!
THAT'S WHY THEY COULD ATTACK US PHYSICALLY!
WELL?! WILL YOU TURN BACK OR NOT?!

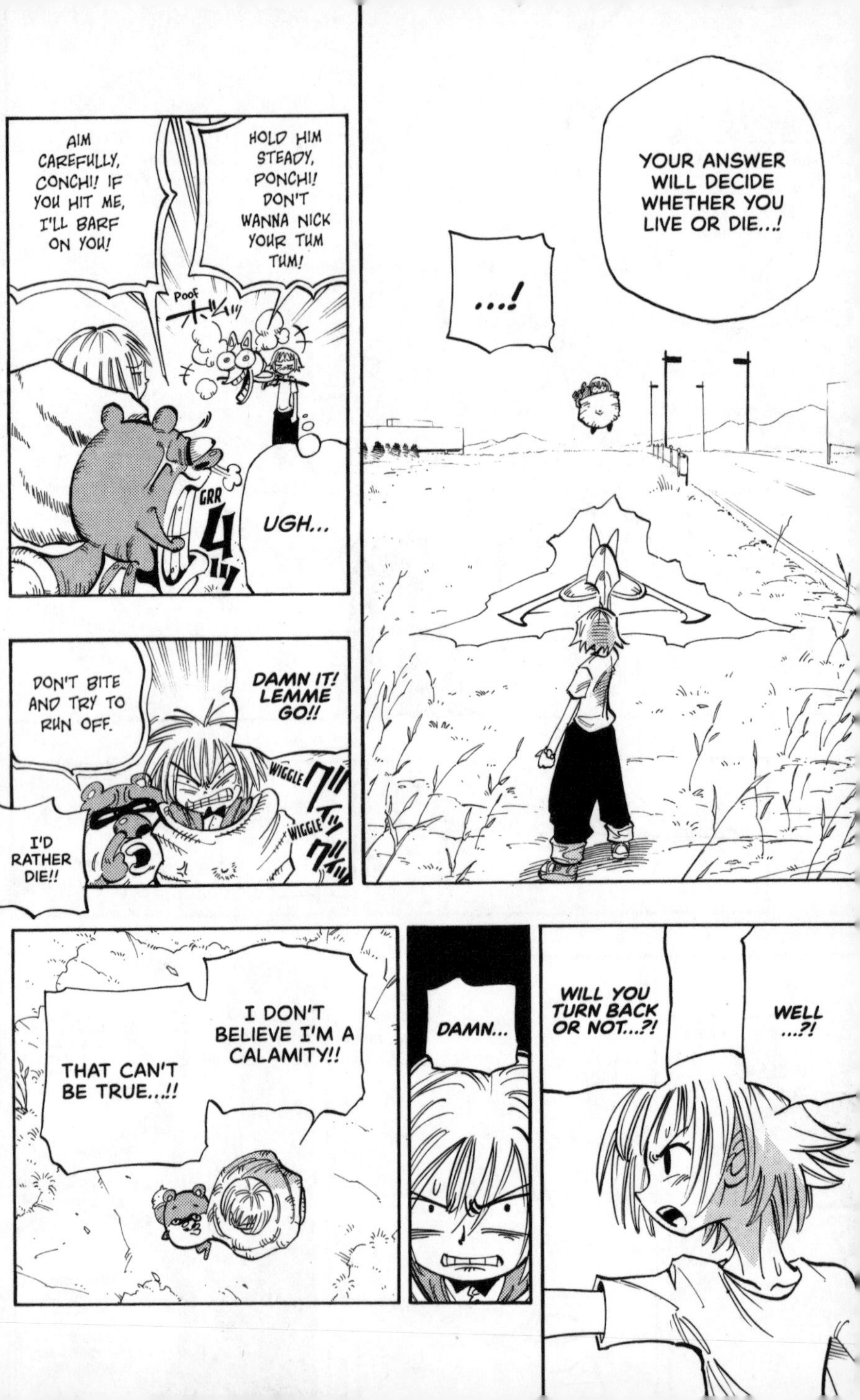
YOUR ANSWER WILL DECIDE WHETHER YOU LIVE OR DIE...!
...!
HOLD HIM STEADY, PONCHI! DON'T WANNA NICK YOUR TUM TUM!
AIM CAREFULLY, CONCHI! IF YOU HIT ME, I'LL BARF ON YOU!
POOF
UGH...
GRR
DAMN IT! LEMME GO!!
DON'T BITE AND TRY TO RUN OFF.
WIGGLE
WIGGLE
I'D RATHER DIE!!
WELL ...?!
WILL YOU TURN BACK OR NOT...?!
DAMN...
I DON'T BELIEVE I'M A CALAMITY!!
THAT CAN'T BE TRUE...!!

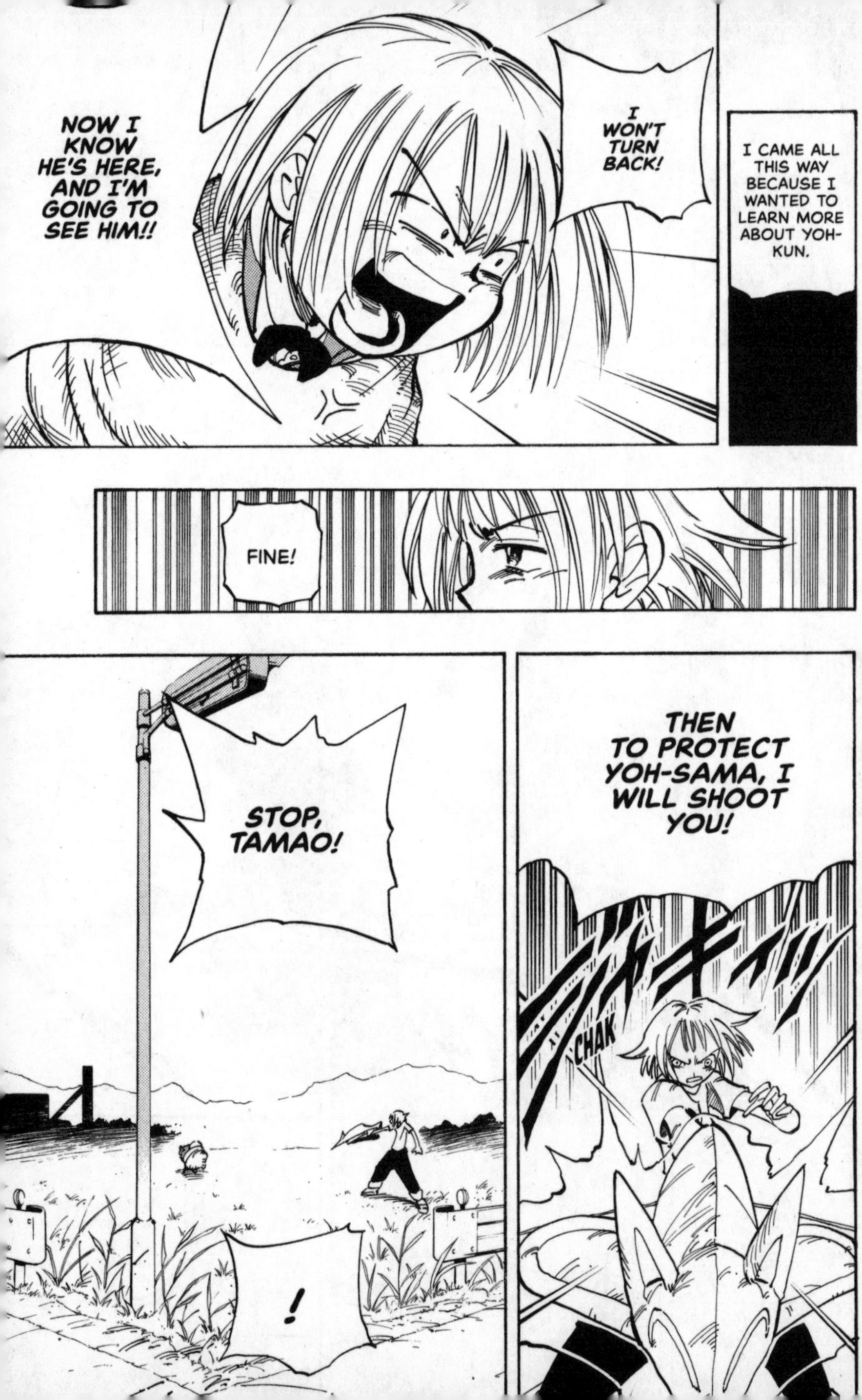
I CAME ALL THIS WAY BECAUSE I WANTED TO LEARN MORE ABOUT YOH-KUN.
I WON'T TURN BACK!
NOW I KNOW HE'S HERE, AND I'M GOING TO SEE HIM!!
FINE!
THEN TO PROTECT YOH-SAMA, I WILL SHOOT YOU!
CHAK
STOP, TAMAO!
!

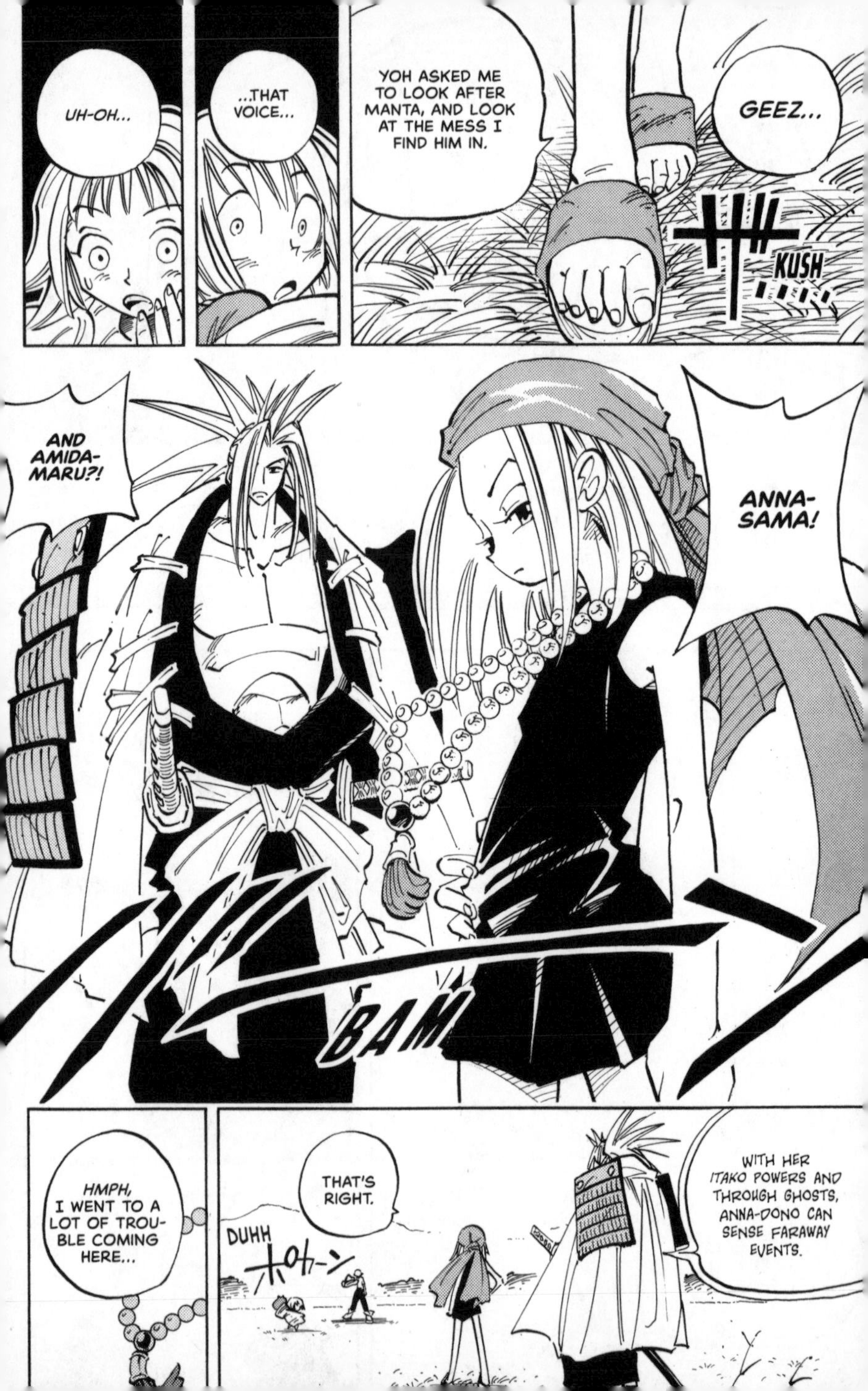
GEEZ...
KUSH
YOH ASKED ME TO LOOK AFTER MANTA, AND LOOK AT THE MESS I FIND HIM IN.
...THAT VOICE...
UH-OH...
ANNA-SAMA!
AND AMIDA-MARU?!
BAM
WITH HER ITAKO POWERS AND THROUGH GHOSTS, ANNA-DONO CAN SENSE FARAWAY EVENTS.
THAT'S RIGHT.
DUHH
HMPH, I WENT TO A LOT OF TROUBLE COMING HERE...

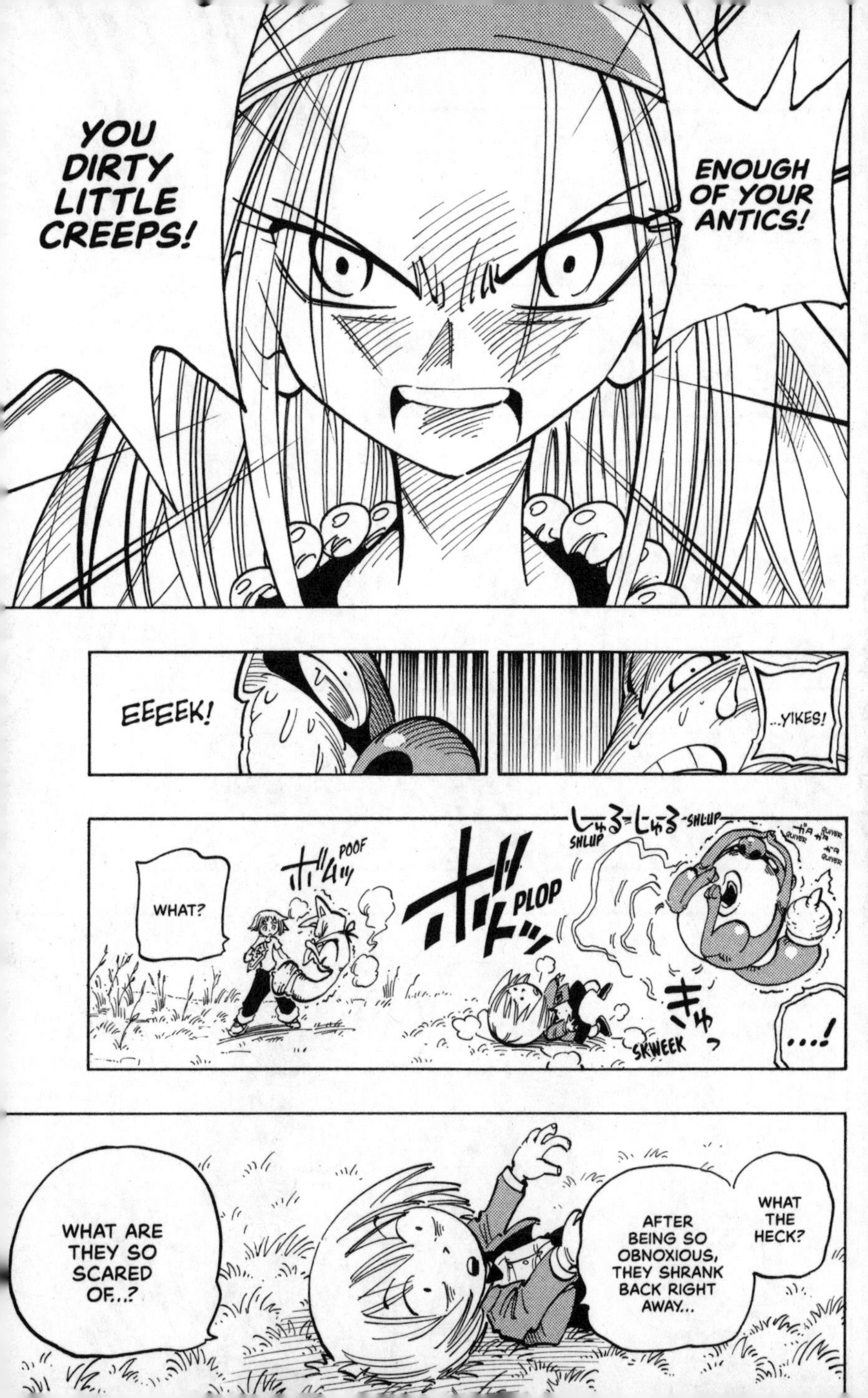

ENOUGH OF YOUR ANTICS!
YOU DIRTY LITTLE CREEPS!
...YIKES!
EEEEK!
QUIVER QUIVER
しゅる SHLUP しゅる SHLUP
...!
きゅっ SKWEEK
PLOP
POOF
WHAT?
WHAT THE HECK?
AFTER BEING SO OBNOXIOUS, THEY SHRANK BACK RIGHT AWAY...
WHAT ARE THEY SO SCARED OF..?

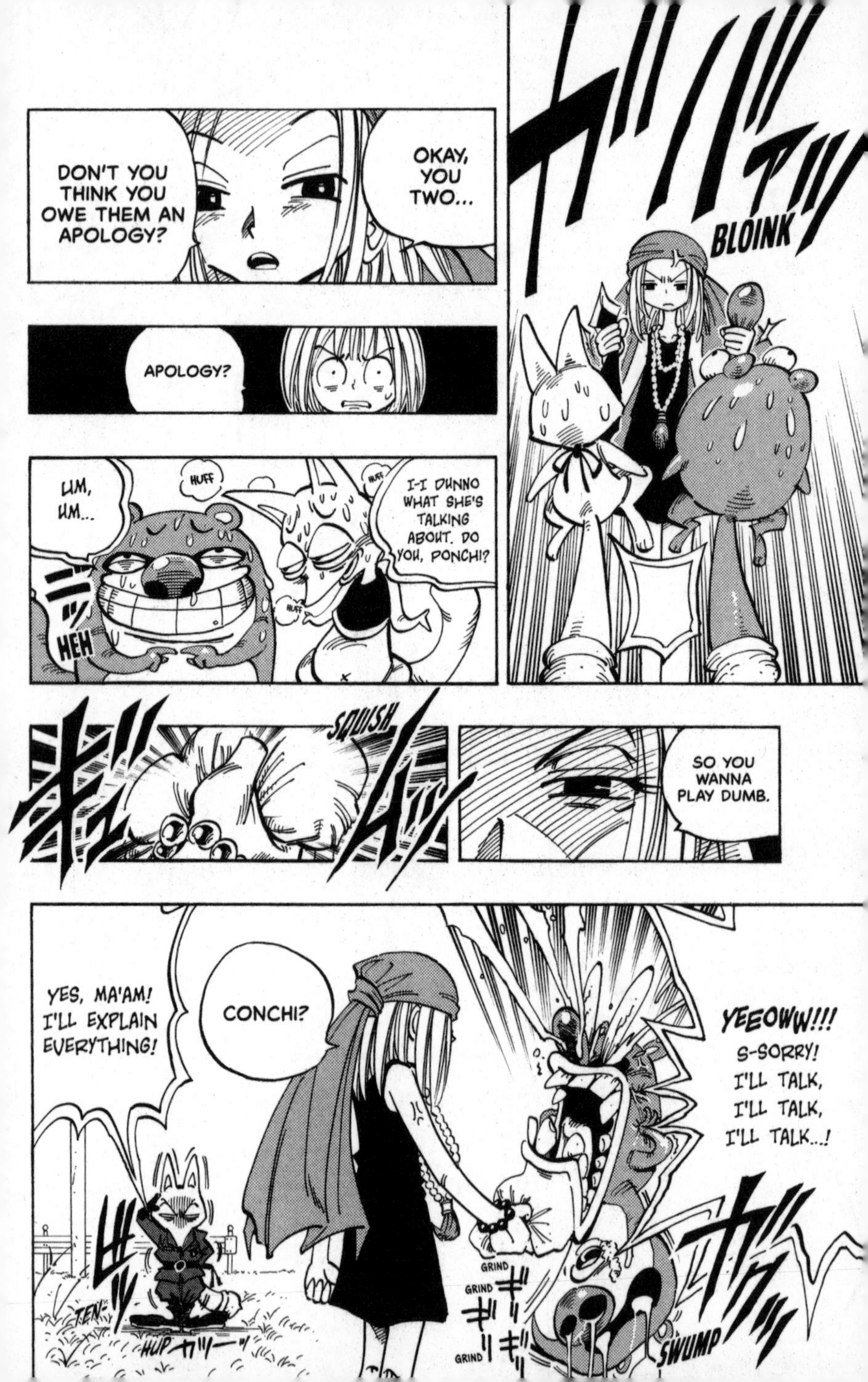
BLOINK
OKAY, YOU TWO...
DON'T YOU THINK YOU OWE THEM AN APOLOGY?
APOLOGY?
HUFF
I-I DUNNO WHAT SHE'S TALKING ABOUT. DO YOU, PONCHI?
HUFF
HUFF
UM, UM...
HEH
SO YOU WANNA PLAY DUMB.
SQUISH
YEEOWW!!!
S-SORRY! I'LL TALK, I'LL TALK, I'LL TALK...!
SWUMP
GRIND
GRIND
GRIND
CONCHI?
YES, MA'AM! I'LL EXPLAIN EVERYTHING!
HUP
TEN-

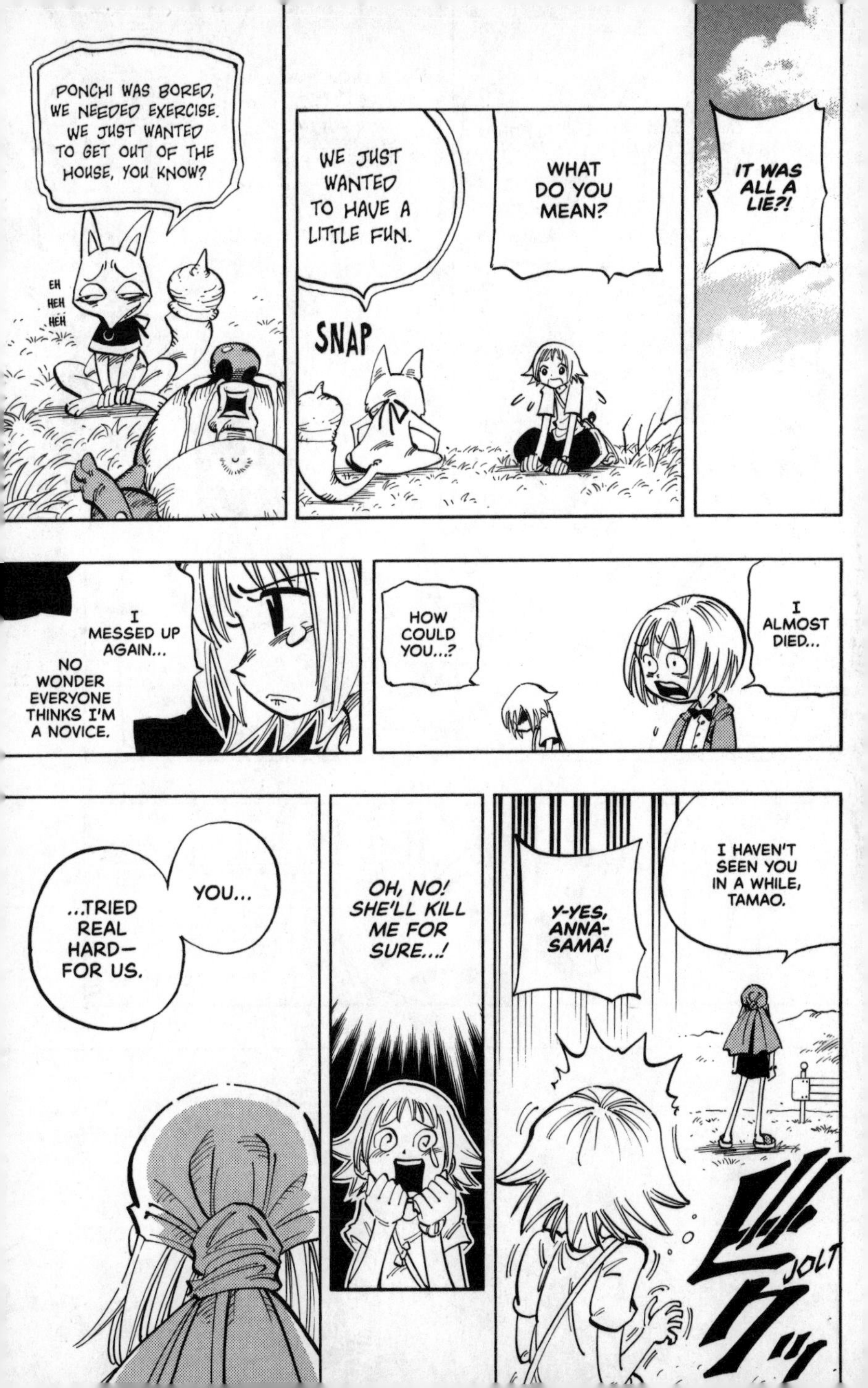
IT WAS ALL A LIE?!
WHAT DO YOU MEAN?
WE JUST WANTED TO HAVE A LITTLE FUN.
SNAP
PONCHI WAS BORED, WE NEEDED EXERCISE. WE JUST WANTED TO GET OUT OF THE HOUSE, YOU KNOW?
EH HEH HEH
I ALMOST DIED...
HOW COULD YOU...?
I MESSED UP AGAIN...
NO WONDER EVERYONE THINKS I'M A NOVICE.
I HAVEN'T SEEN YOU IN A WHILE, TAMAO.
Y-YES, ANNA-SAMA!
JOLT
OH, NO! SHE'LL KILL ME FOR SURE...!
YOU...
...TRIED REAL HARD— FOR US.

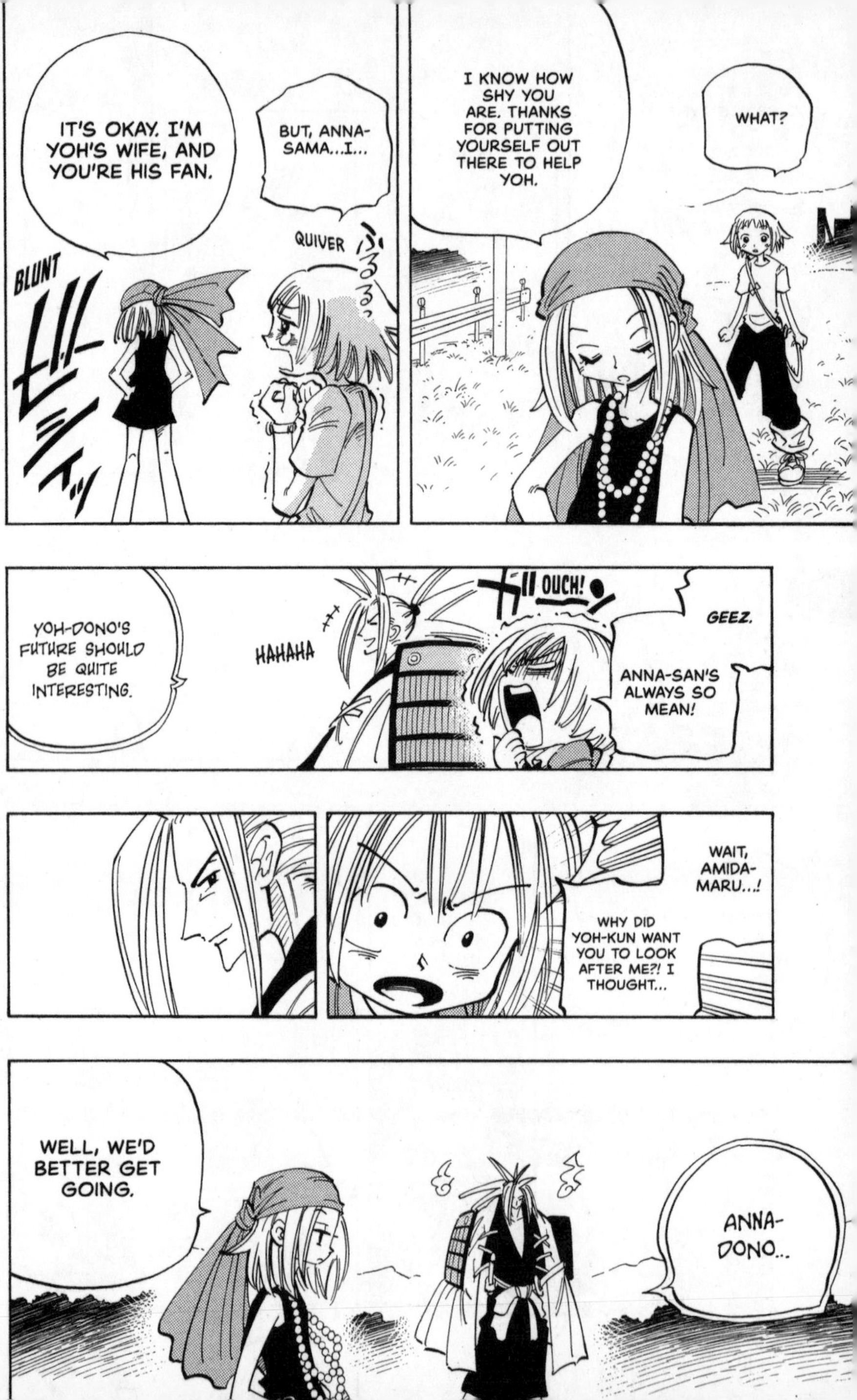
WHAT?
I KNOW HOW SHY YOU ARE. THANKS FOR PUTTING YOURSELF OUT THERE TO HELP YOH.
BUT, ANNA-SAMA...I...
QUIVER
IT'S OKAY. I'M YOH'S WIFE, AND YOU'RE HIS FAN.
BLUNT
GEEZ.
ANNA-SAN'S ALWAYS SO MEAN!
OUCH!
HAHAHA
YOH-DONO'S FUTURE SHOULD BE QUITE INTERESTING.
WAIT, AMIDA-MARU...!
WHY DID YOH-KUN WANT YOU TO LOOK AFTER ME?! I THOUGHT...
ANNA-DONO...
WELL, WE'D BETTER GET GOING.

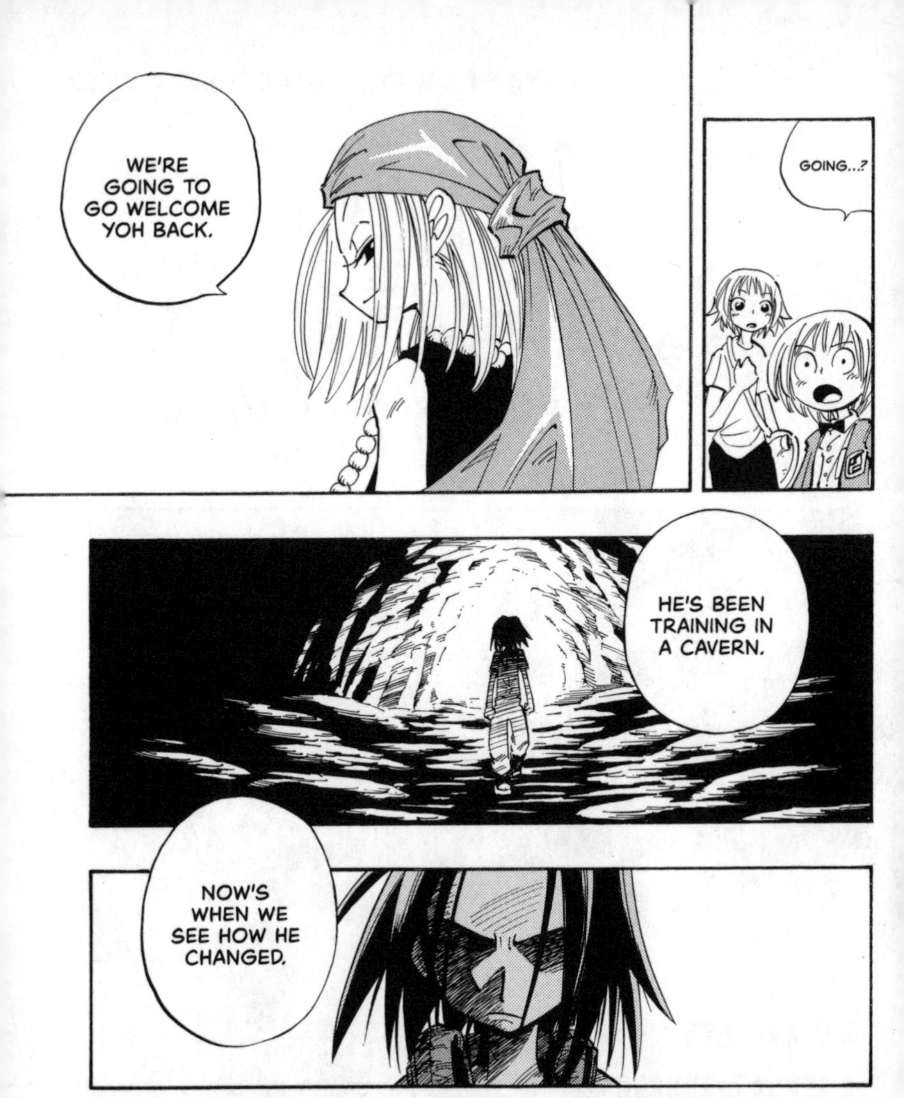
GOING...?
WE'RE GOING TO GO WELCOME YOH BACK.
HE'S BEEN TRAINING IN A CAVERN.
NOW'S WHEN WE SEE HOW HE CHANGED.
ヒュウ
WHOOSH
WHMP
WHMP
WHMP
コロコロコロ

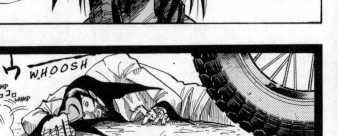

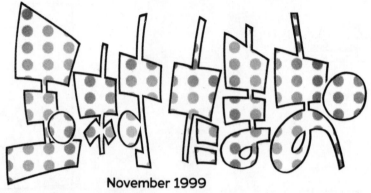

SHAMAN KING CHARACTER FILE No.27

November 1999

さかや
物産館

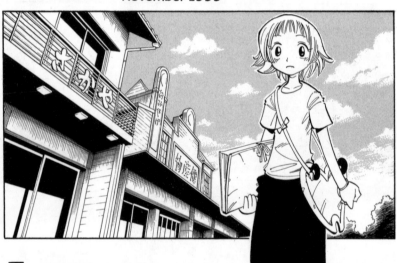

Tamao Tamamura

Age: 11
Date of Birth: June 17, 1988
Astrological Sign: Gemini
Blood Type: A

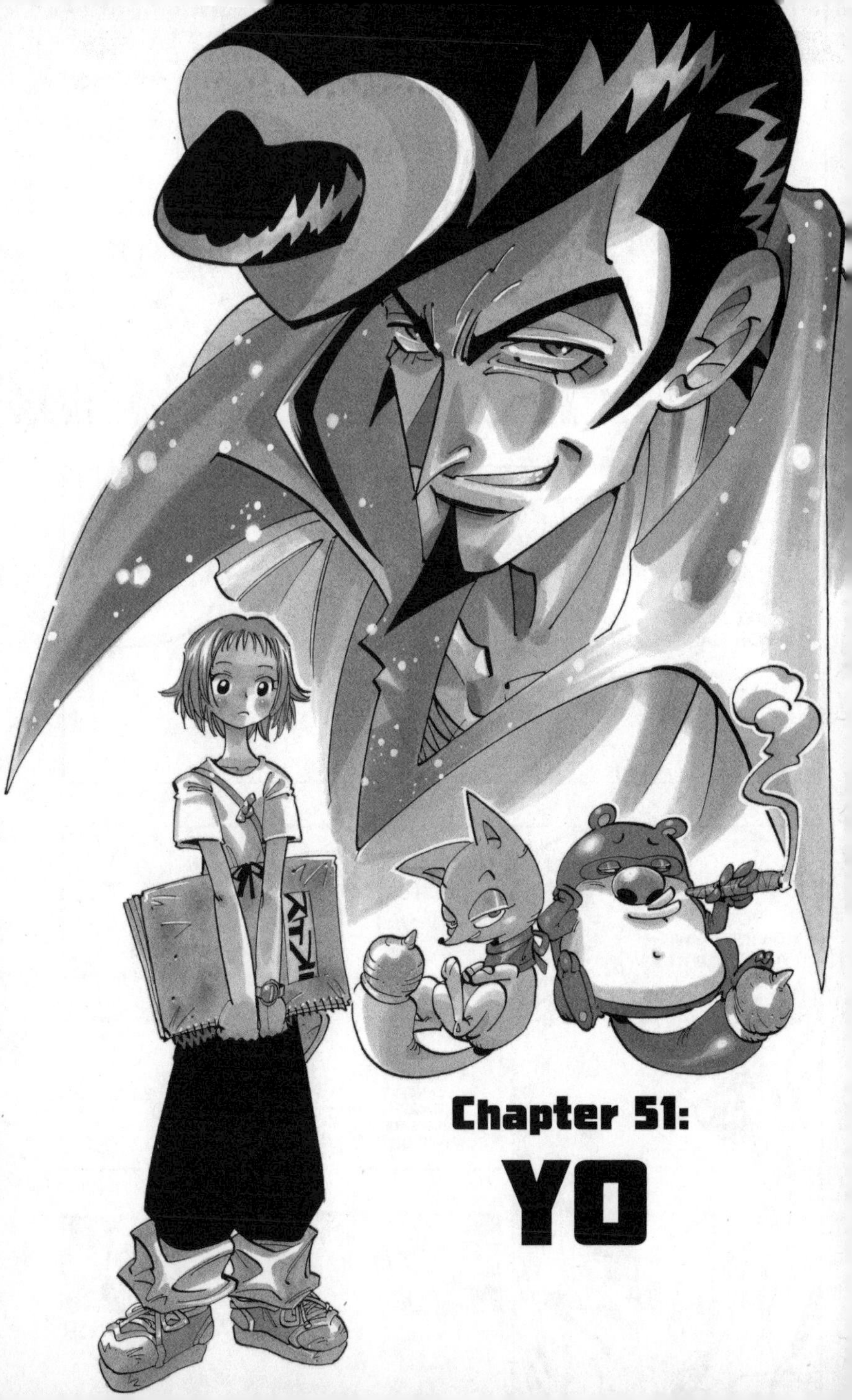

Chapter 51:

YO

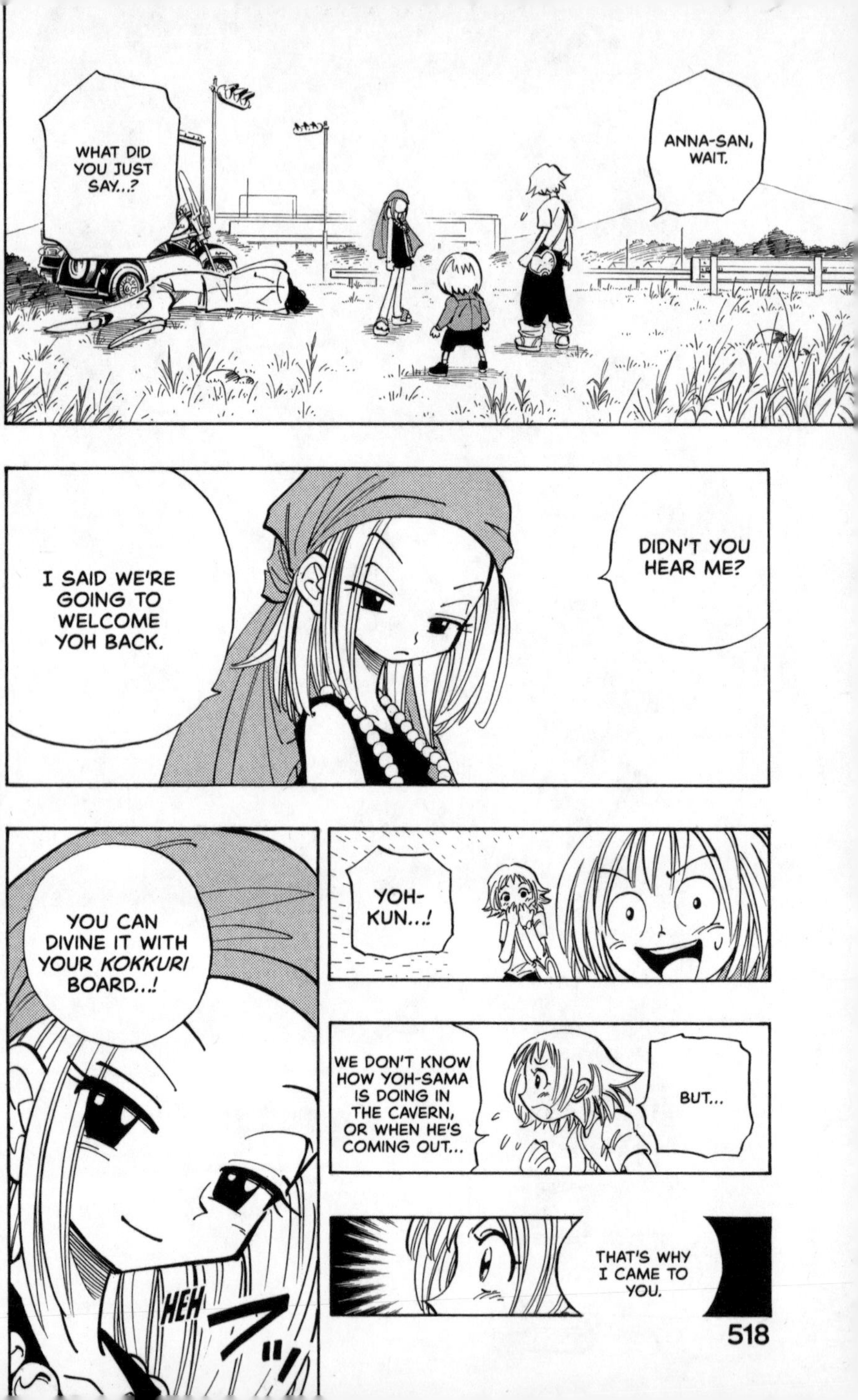
ANNA-SAN, WAIT.
WHAT DID YOU JUST SAY..?
DIDN'T YOU HEAR ME?
I SAID WE'RE GOING TO WELCOME YOH BACK.
YOH-KUN...!
BUT...
WE DON'T KNOW HOW YOH-SAMA IS DOING IN THE CAVERN, OR WHEN HE'S COMING OUT...
THAT'S WHY I CAME TO YOU.
YOU CAN DIVINE IT WITH YOUR KOKKURI BOARD...!
HEH

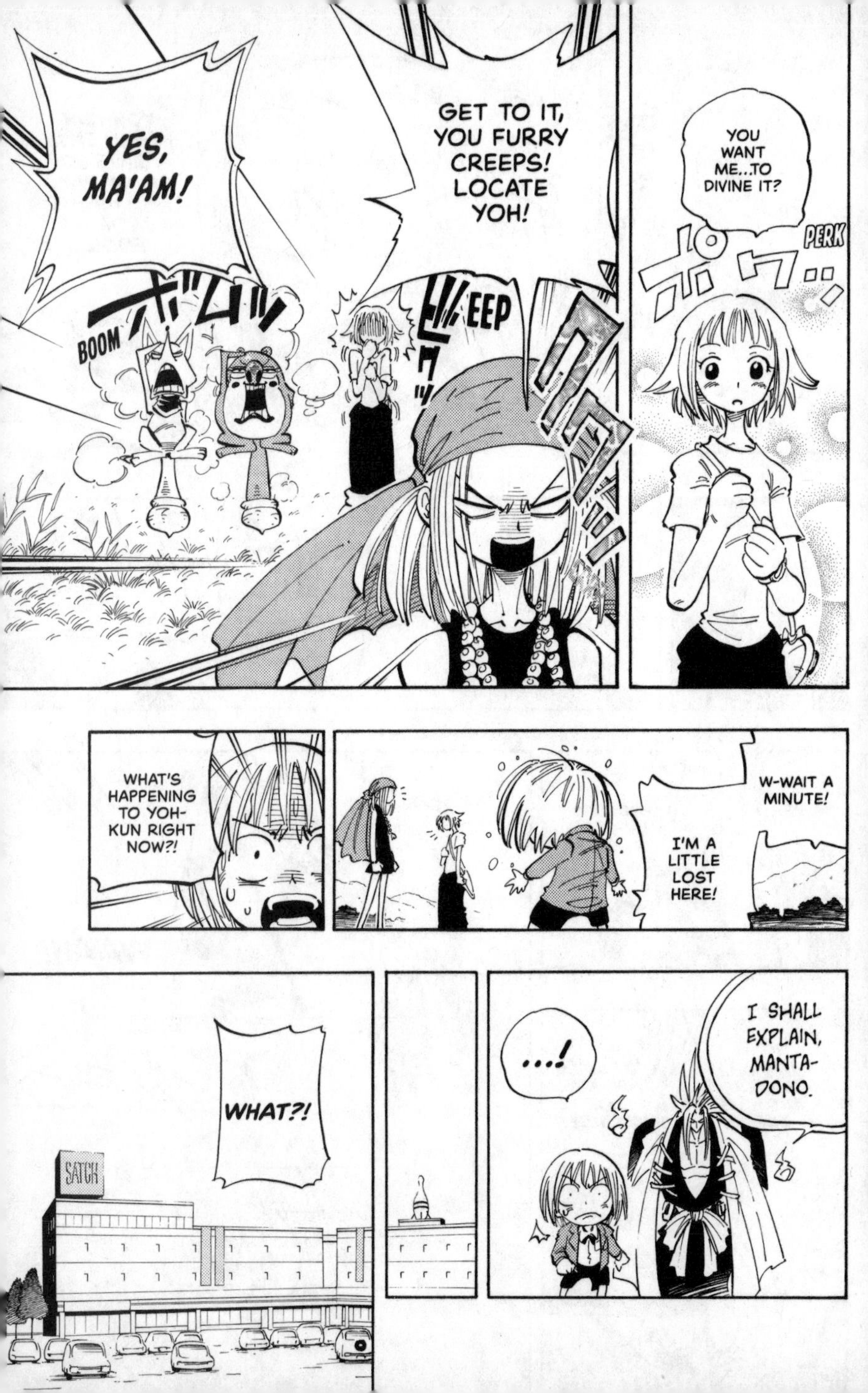
YOU WANT ME...TO DIVINE IT?
PERK
GET TO IT, YOU FURRY CREEPS! LOCATE YOH!
YES, MA'AM!
EEP
BOOM
W-WAIT A MINUTE!
I'M A LITTLE LOST HERE!
WHAT'S HAPPENING TO YOH-KUN RIGHT NOW?!
I SHALL EXPLAIN, MANTA-DONO.
...!
WHAT?!
SATCH

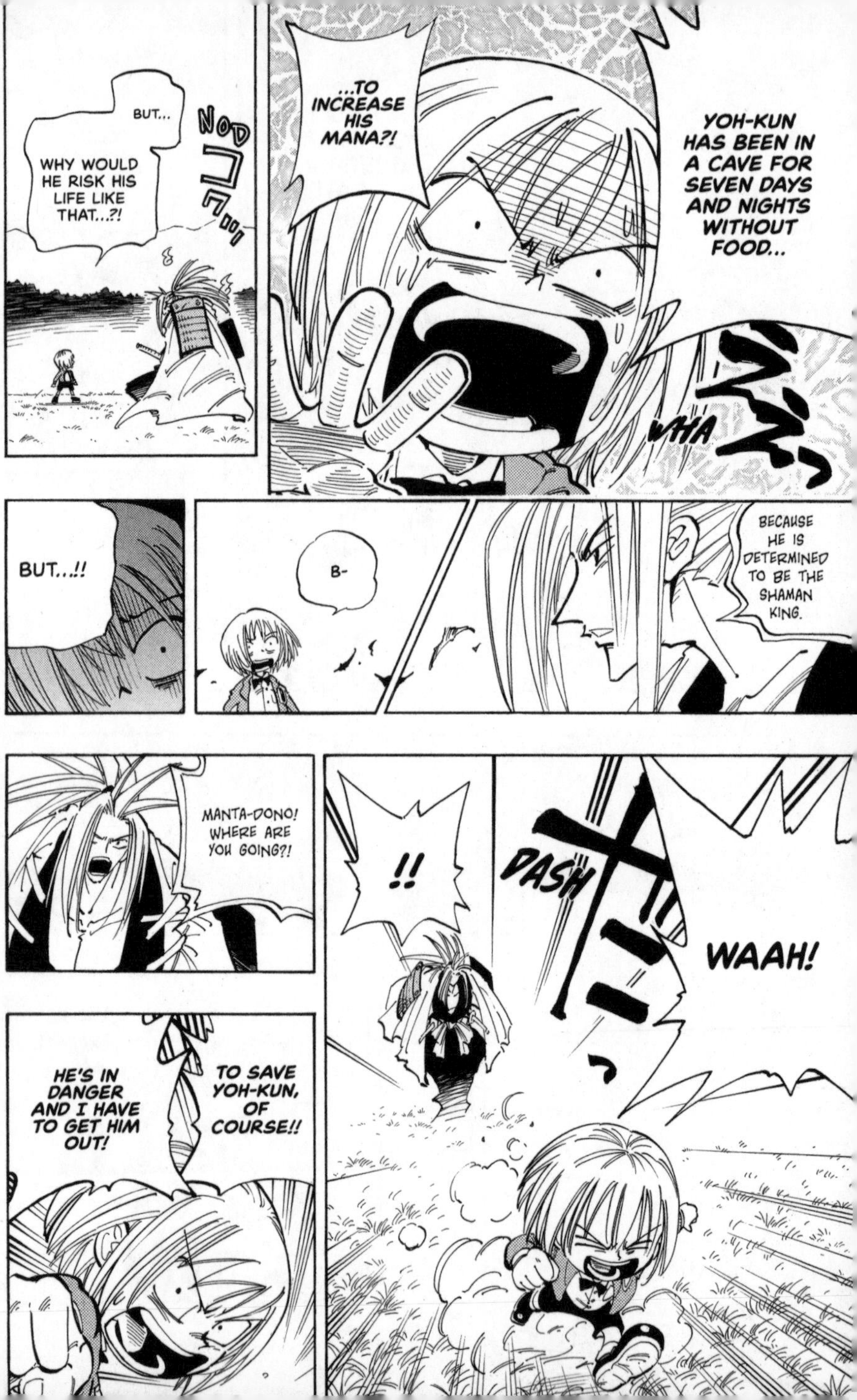
YOH-KUN HAS BEEN IN A CAVE FOR SEVEN DAYS AND NIGHTS WITHOUT FOOD...
...TO INCREASE HIS MANA?!
WHA
NOD
BUT...
WHY WOULD HE RISK HIS LIFE LIKE THAT...?!
BECAUSE HE IS DETERMINED TO BE THE SHAMAN KING.
B-
BUT...!!
WAAH!
DASH
!!
MANTA-DONO! WHERE ARE YOU GOING?!
TO SAVE YOH-KUN, OF COURSE!!
HE'S IN DANGER AND I HAVE TO GET HIM OUT!

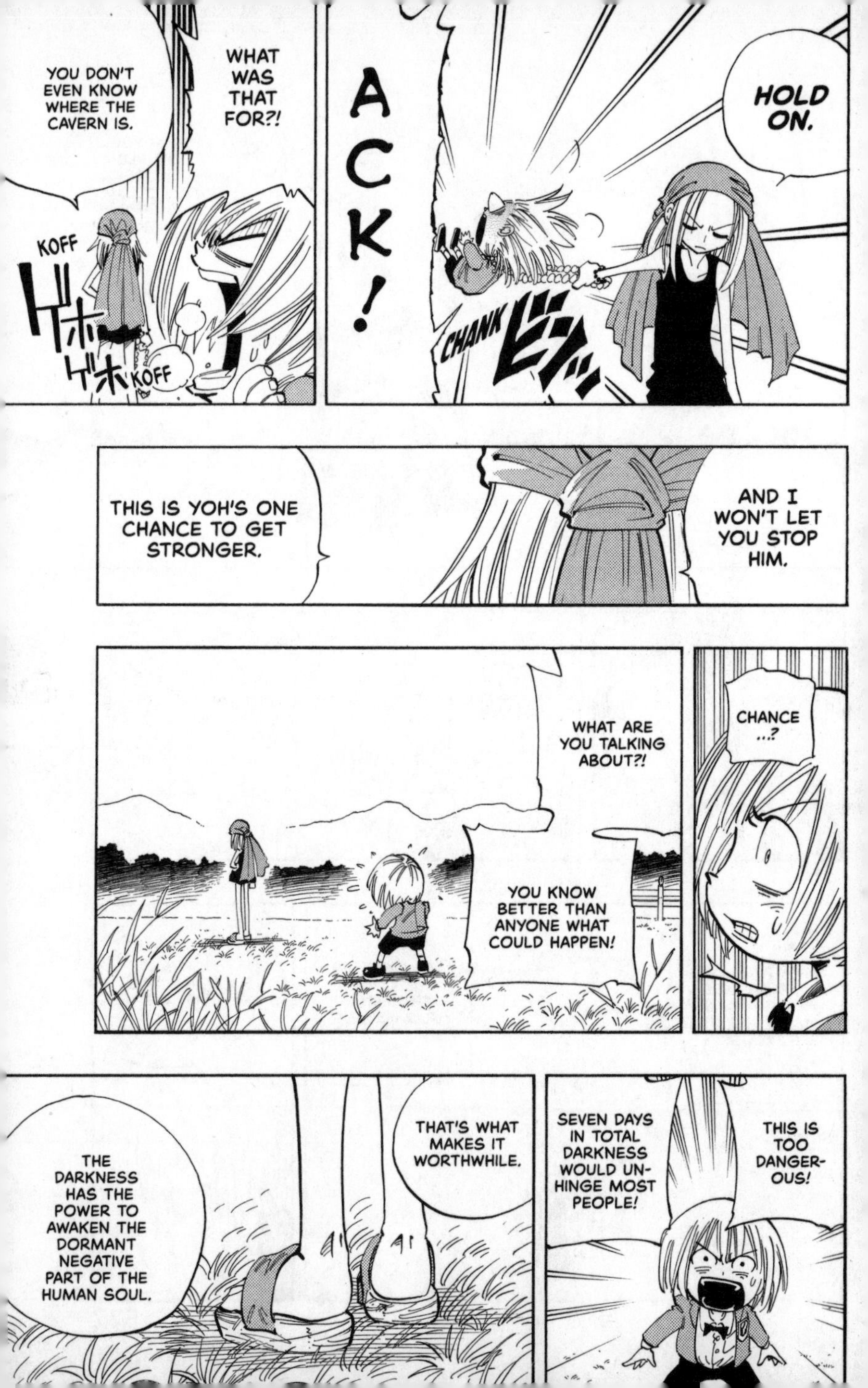

HOLD ON.
ACK!
CHANK
WHAT WAS THAT FOR?!
YOU DON'T EVEN KNOW WHERE THE CAVERN IS.
KOFF
ゲホ
ゲホ
KOFF
AND I WON'T LET YOU STOP HIM.
THIS IS YOH'S ONE CHANCE TO GET STRONGER.
CHANCE ...?
WHAT ARE YOU TALKING ABOUT?!
YOU KNOW BETTER THAN ANYONE WHAT COULD HAPPEN!
THIS IS TOO DANGER-OUS!
SEVEN DAYS IN TOTAL DARKNESS WOULD UN-HINGE MOST PEOPLE!
THAT'S WHAT MAKES IT WORTHWHILE.
THE DARKNESS HAS THE POWER TO AWAKEN THE DORMANT NEGATIVE PART OF THE HUMAN SOUL.

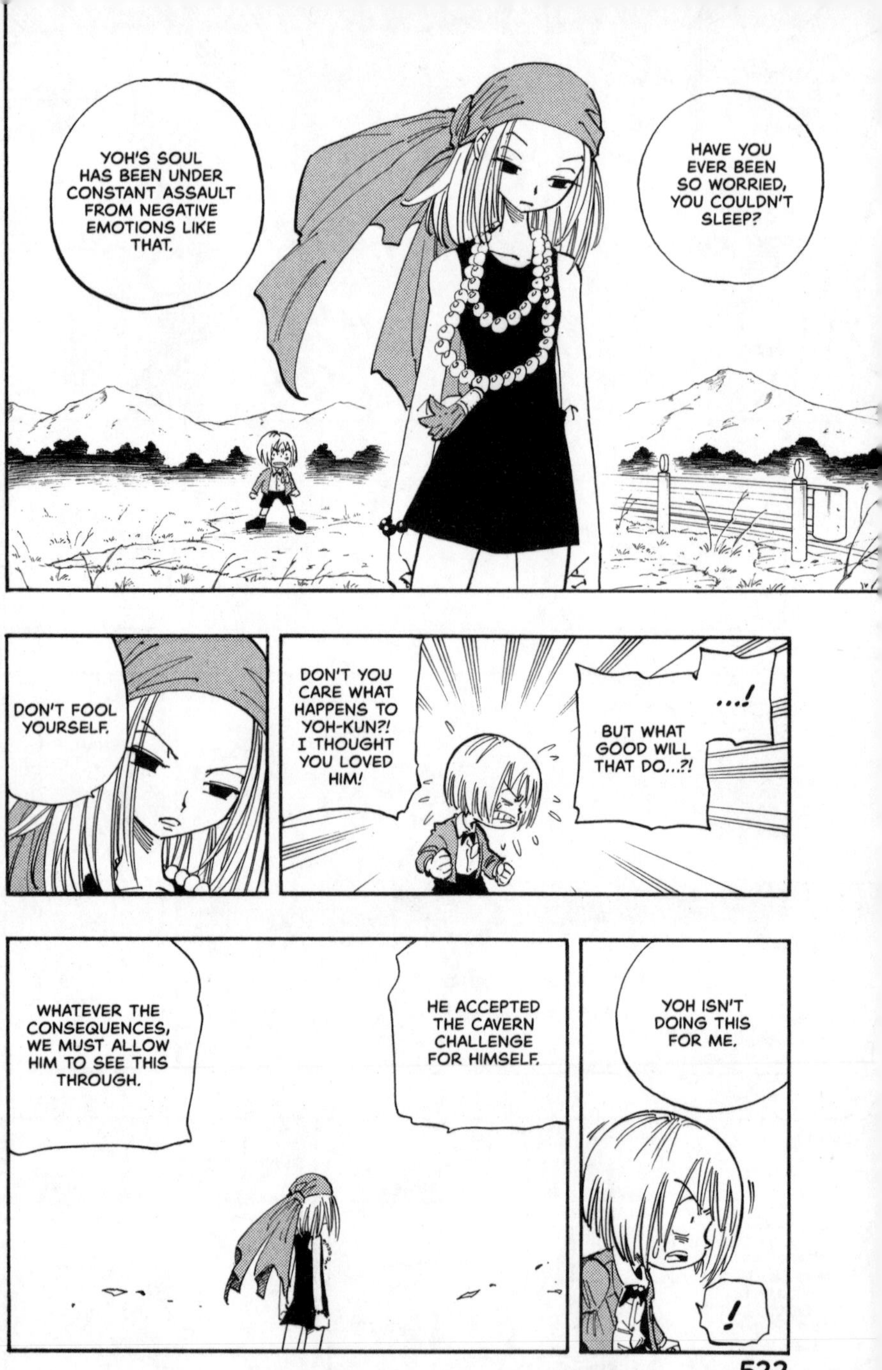
HAVE YOU EVER BEEN SO WORRIED, YOU COULDN'T SLEEP?
YOH'S SOUL HAS BEEN UNDER CONSTANT ASSAULT FROM NEGATIVE EMOTIONS LIKE THAT.
...!
BUT WHAT GOOD WILL THAT DO...?!
DON'T YOU CARE WHAT HAPPENS TO YOH-KUN?! I THOUGHT YOU LOVED HIM!
DON'T FOOL YOURSELF.
YOH ISN'T DOING THIS FOR ME.
!
HE ACCEPTED THE CAVERN CHALLENGE FOR HIMSELF.
WHATEVER THE CONSEQUENCES, WE MUST ALLOW HIM TO SEE THIS THROUGH.

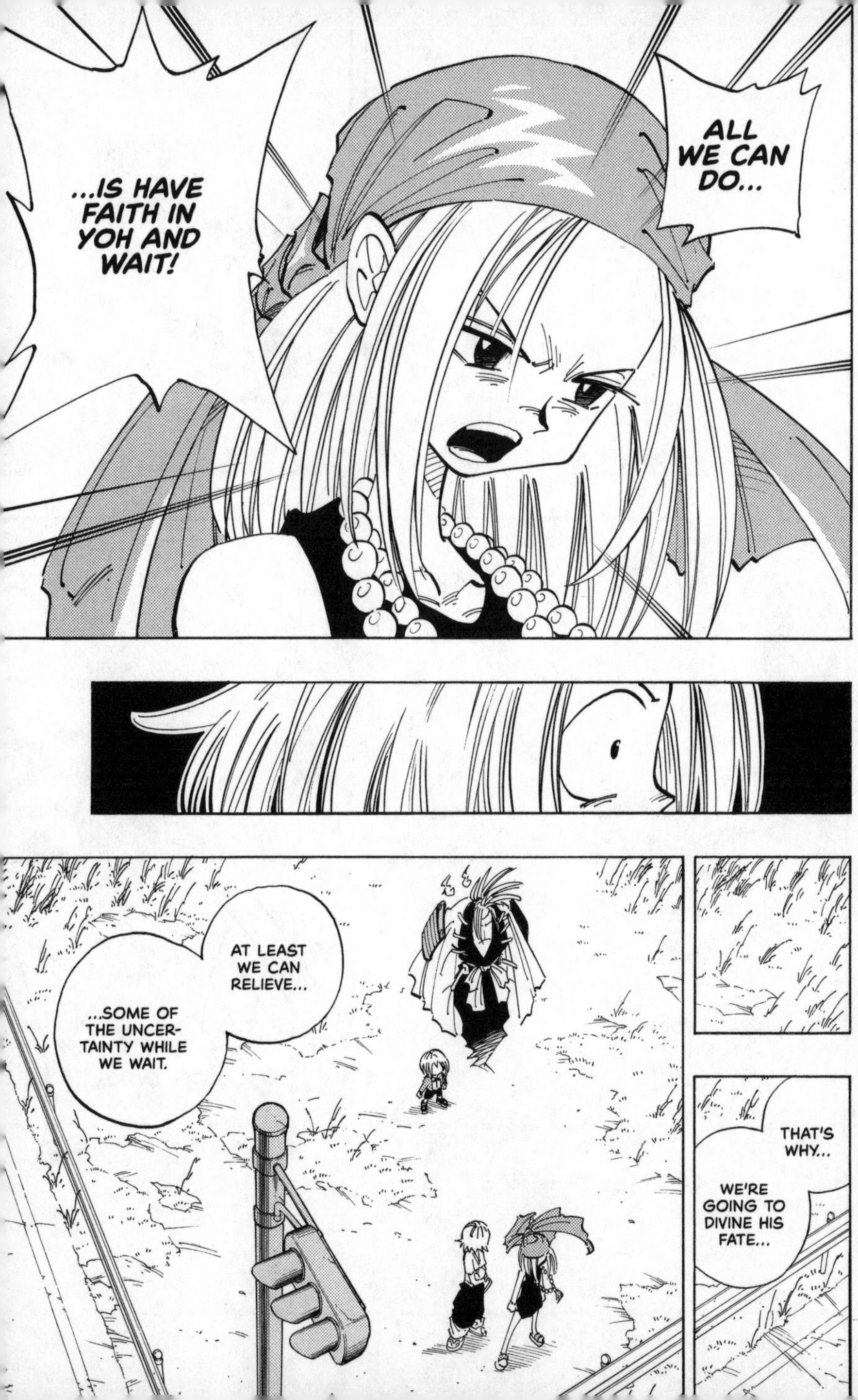
ALL WE CAN DO...
...IS HAVE FAITH IN YOH AND WAIT!
THAT'S WHY...
WE'RE GOING TO DIVINE HIS FATE...
AT LEAST WE CAN RELIEVE...
...SOME OF THE UNCER-TAINTY WHILE WE WAIT.

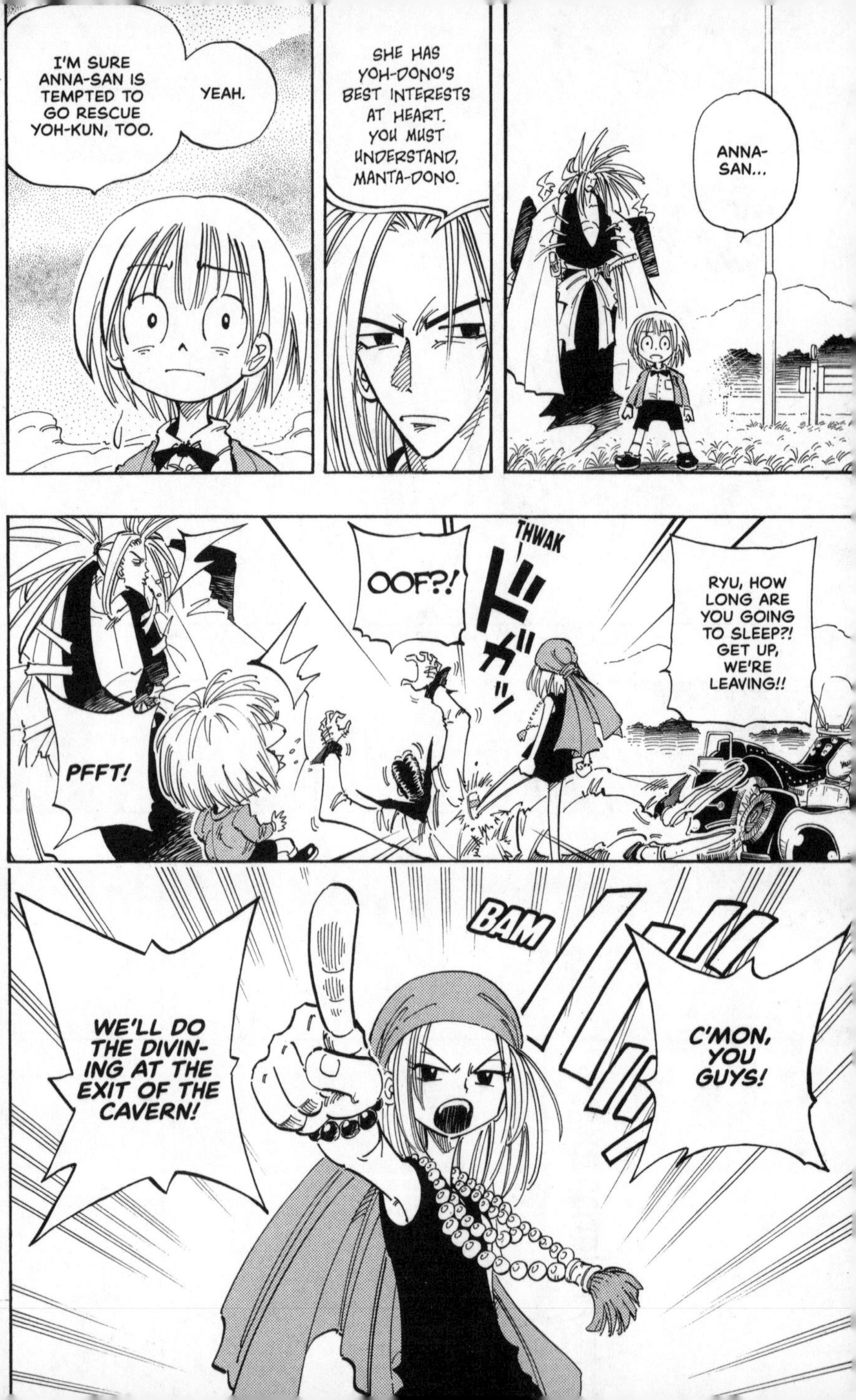
ANNA-SAN...
SHE HAS YOH-DONO'S BEST INTERESTS AT HEART. YOU MUST UNDERSTAND, MANTA-DONO.
I'M SURE ANNA-SAN IS TEMPTED TO GO RESCUE YOH-KUN, TOO.
YEAH.
RYU, HOW LONG ARE YOU GOING TO SLEEP?! GET UP, WE'RE LEAVING!!
THWAK
OOF?!
PFFT!
C'MON, YOU GUYS!
BAM
WE'LL DO THE DIVIN-ING AT THE EXIT OF THE CAVERN!

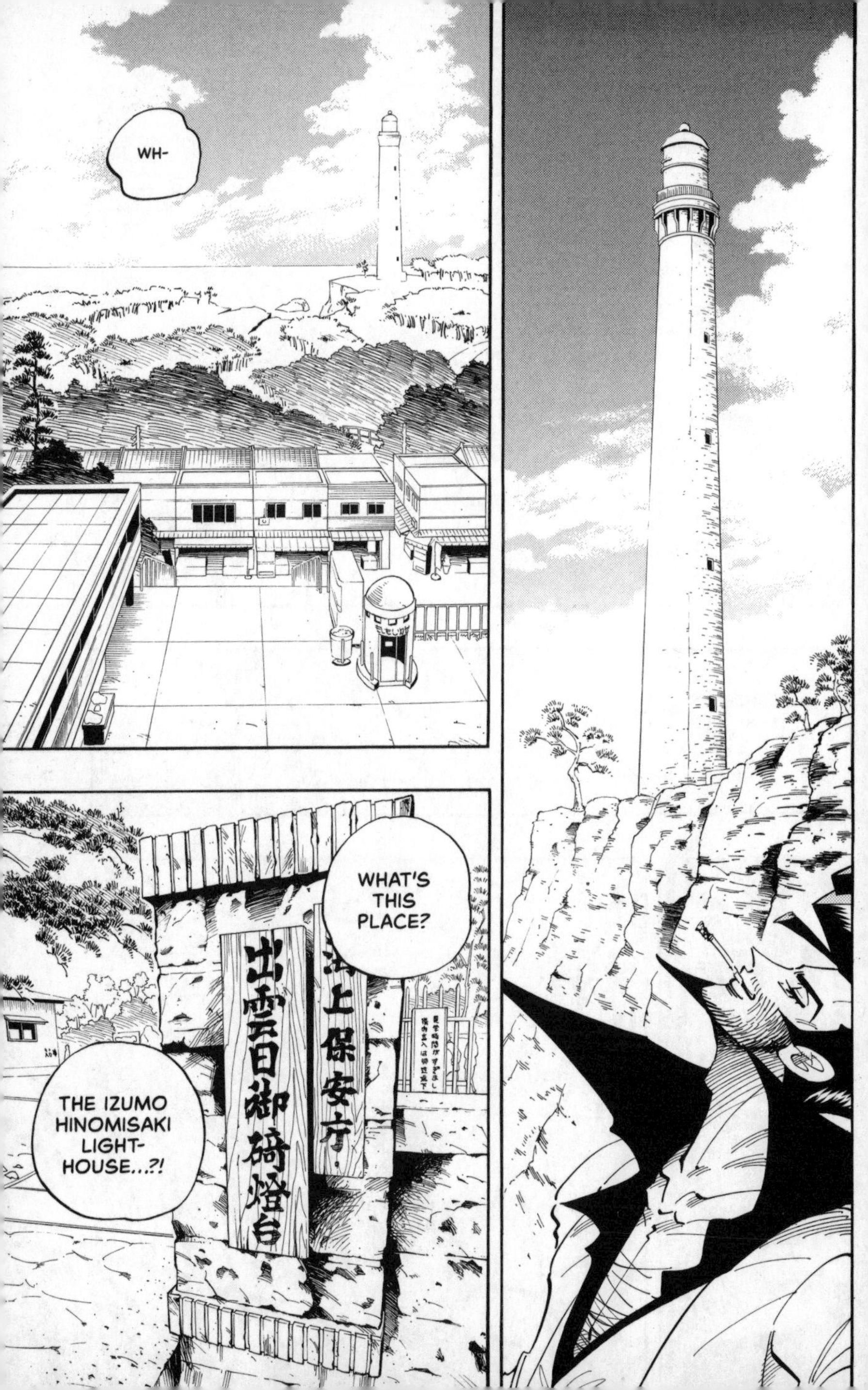
WH-
WHAT'S THIS PLACE?
出雲日御碕燈台
THE IZUMO HINOMISAKI LIGHT-HOUSE...?!

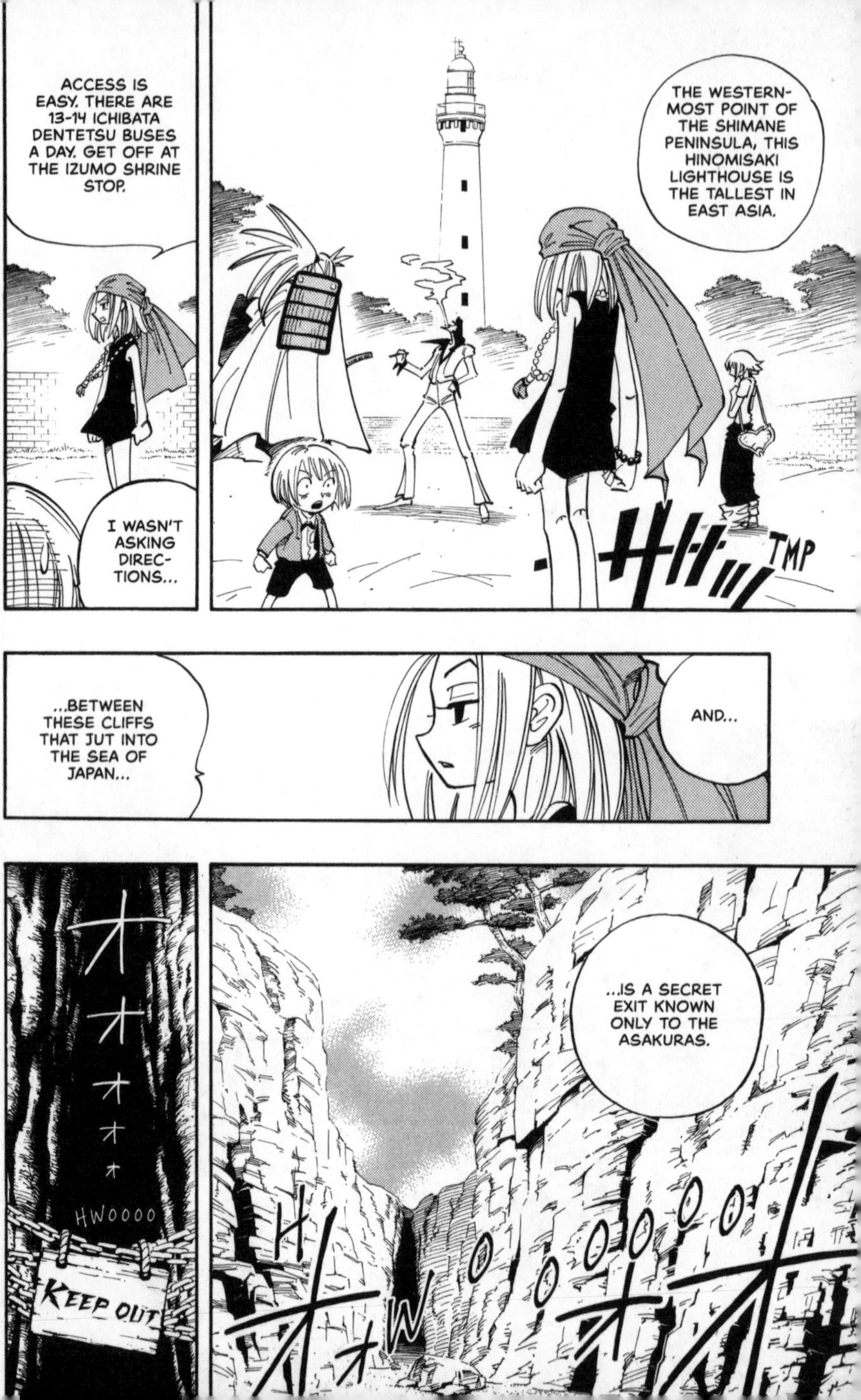
THE WESTERN-MOST POINT OF THE SHIMANE PENINSULA, THIS HINOMISAKI LIGHTHOUSE IS THE TALLEST IN EAST ASIA.
TMP
ACCESS IS EASY. THERE ARE 13-14 ICHIBATA DENTETSU BUSES A DAY. GET OFF AT THE IZUMO SHRINE STOP.
I WASN'T ASKING DIRECTIONS...
AND...
...BETWEEN THESE CLIFFS THAT JUT INTO THE SEA OF JAPAN...
...IS A SECRET EXIT KNOWN ONLY TO THE ASAKURAS.
HWOOOO
KEEP OUT

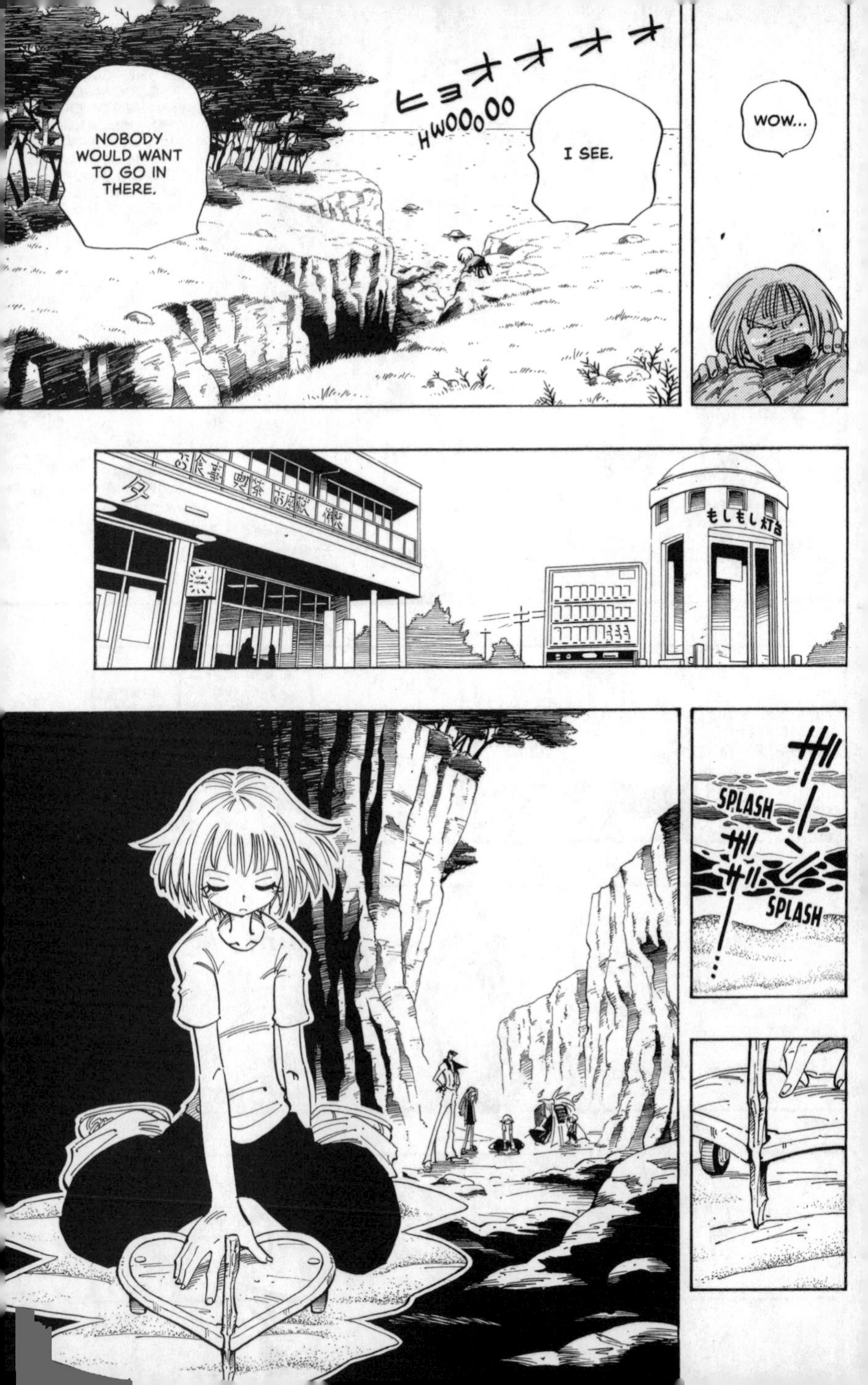
WOW...
ヒョオオオオ
HWOOoOO
I SEE.
NOBODY WOULD WANT TO GO IN THERE.
もしもし灯台
SPLASH
SPLASH

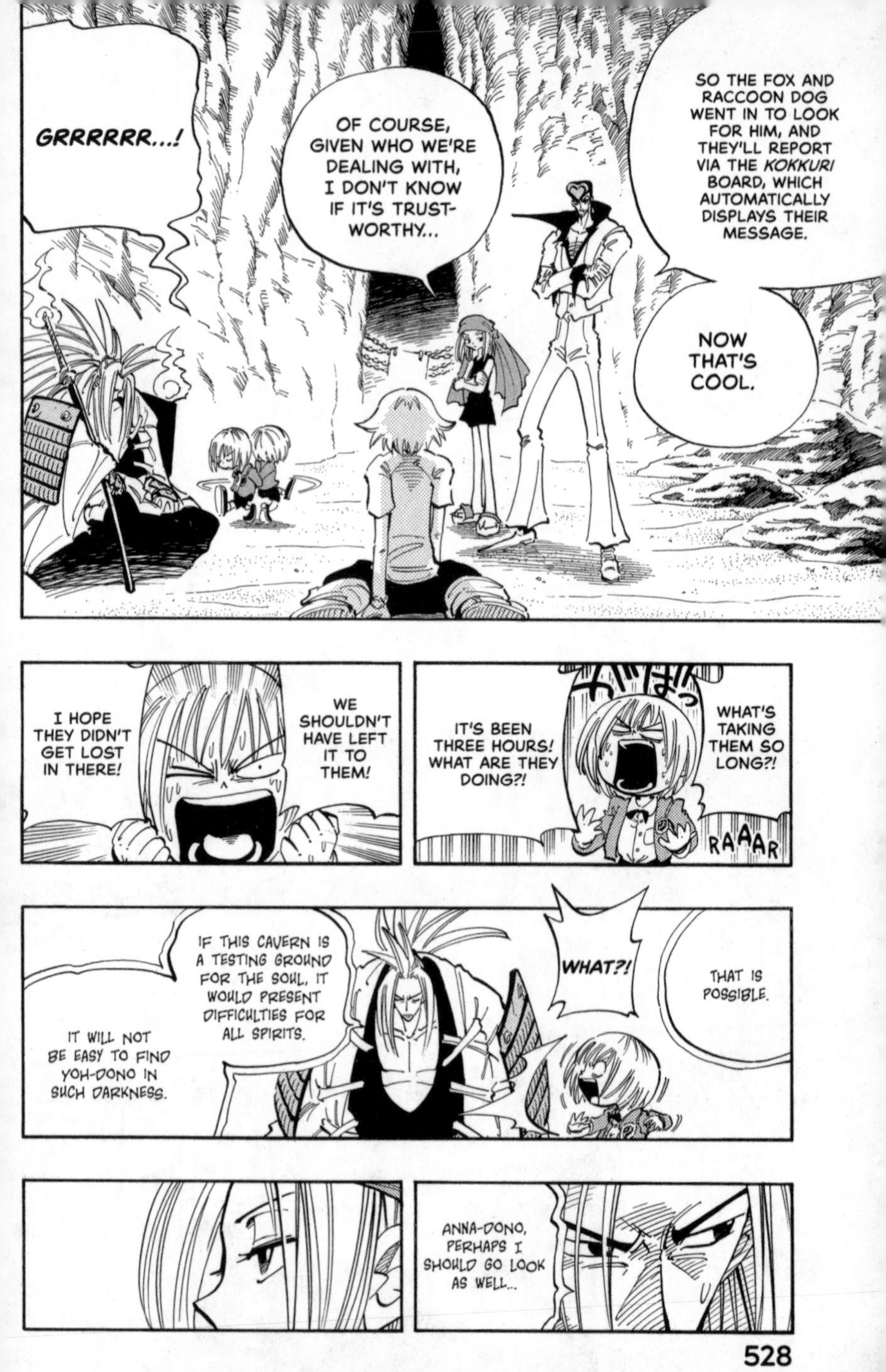
SO THE FOX AND RACCOON DOG WENT IN TO LOOK FOR HIM, AND THEY'LL REPORT VIA THE *KOKKURI* BOARD, WHICH AUTOMATICALLY DISPLAYS THEIR MESSAGE.
NOW THAT'S COOL.
OF COURSE, GIVEN WHO WE'RE DEALING WITH, I DON'T KNOW IF IT'S TRUST-WORTHY...
GRRRRRR...!
WHAT'S TAKING THEM SO LONG?!
IT'S BEEN THREE HOURS! WHAT ARE THEY DOING?!
RAAAR
WE SHOULDN'T HAVE LEFT IT TO THEM!
I HOPE THEY DIDN'T GET LOST IN THERE!
THAT IS POSSIBLE.
WHAT?!
IF THIS CAVERN IS A TESTING GROUND FOR THE SOUL, IT WOULD PRESENT DIFFICULTIES FOR ALL SPIRITS.
IT WILL NOT BE EASY TO FIND YOH-DONO IN SUCH DARKNESS.
ANNA-DONO, PERHAPS I SHOULD GO LOOK AS WELL...

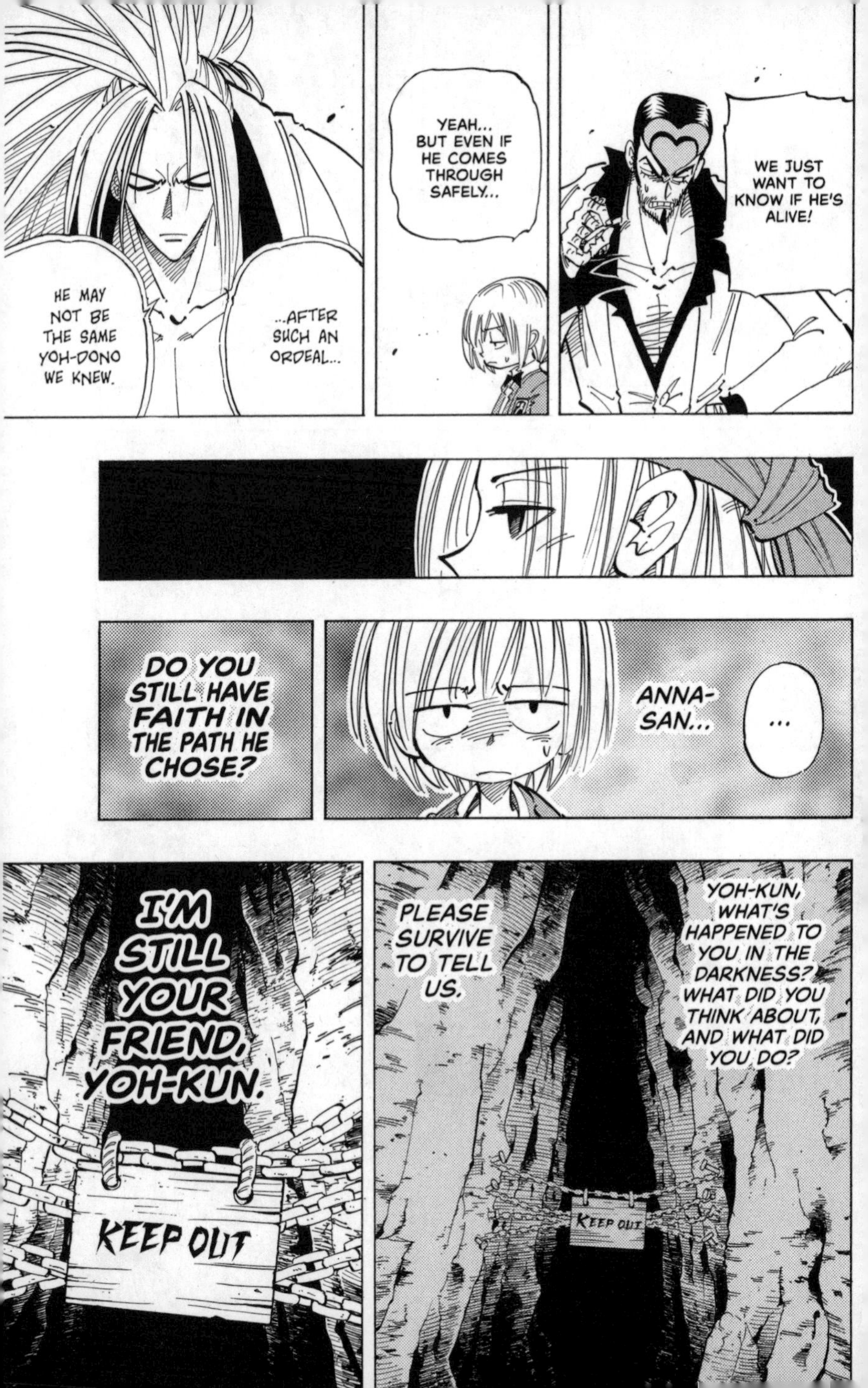
WE JUST WANT TO KNOW IF HE'S ALIVE!
YEAH... BUT EVEN IF HE COMES THROUGH SAFELY...
...AFTER SUCH AN ORDEAL...
HE MAY NOT BE THE SAME YOH-DONO WE KNEW.
...
ANNA-SAN...
DO YOU STILL HAVE FAITH IN THE PATH HE CHOSE?
YOH-KUN, WHAT'S HAPPENED TO YOU IN THE DARKNESS? WHAT DID YOU THINK ABOUT, AND WHAT DID YOU DO?
PLEASE SURVIVE TO TELL US.
KEEP OUT
I'M STILL YOUR FRIEND, YOH-KUN.
KEEP OUT

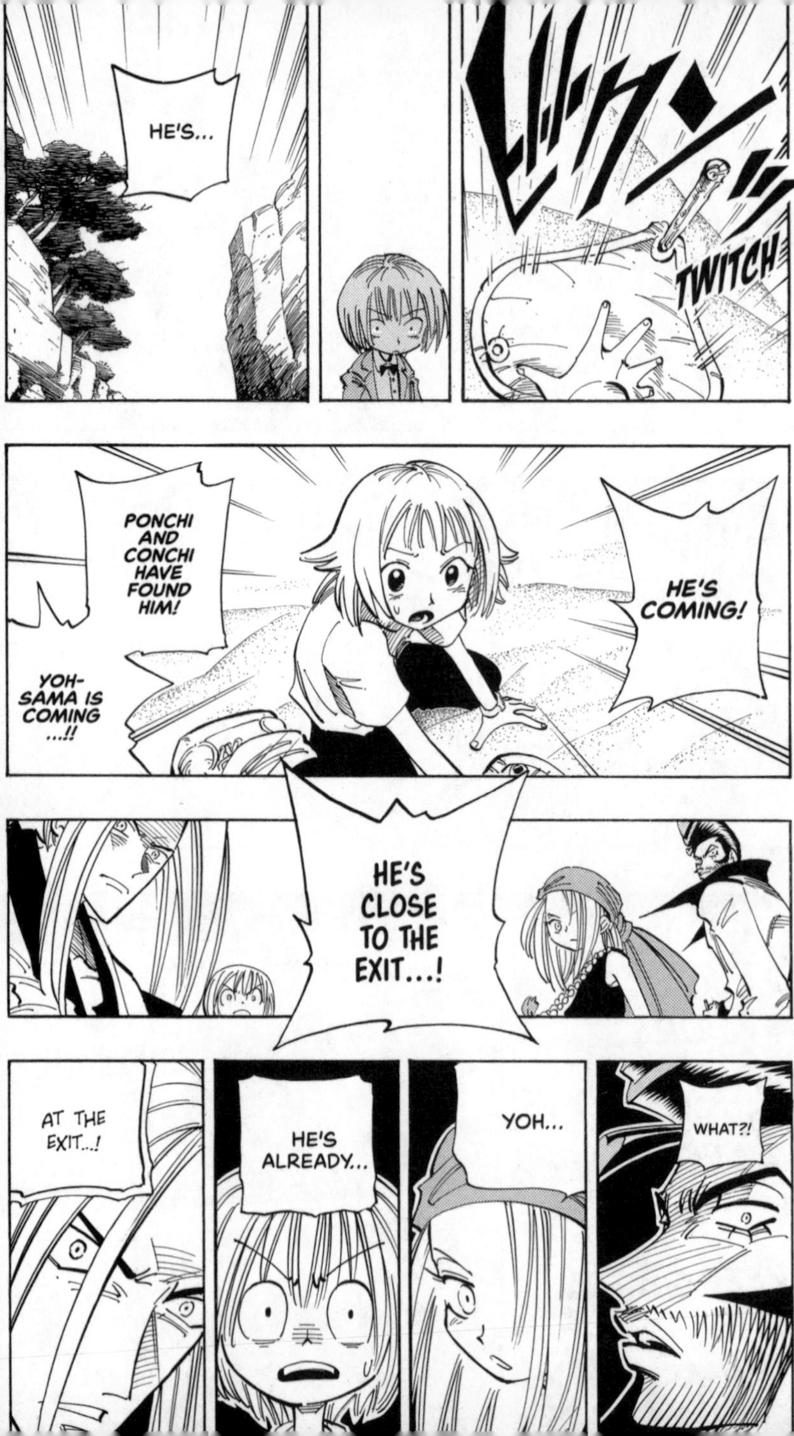
TWITCH
HE'S...
HE'S COMING!
PONCHI AND CONCHI HAVE FOUND HIM!
YOH-SAMA IS COMING...!!
HE'S CLOSE TO THE EXIT...!
WHAT?!
YOH...
HE'S ALREADY...
AT THE EXIT...!

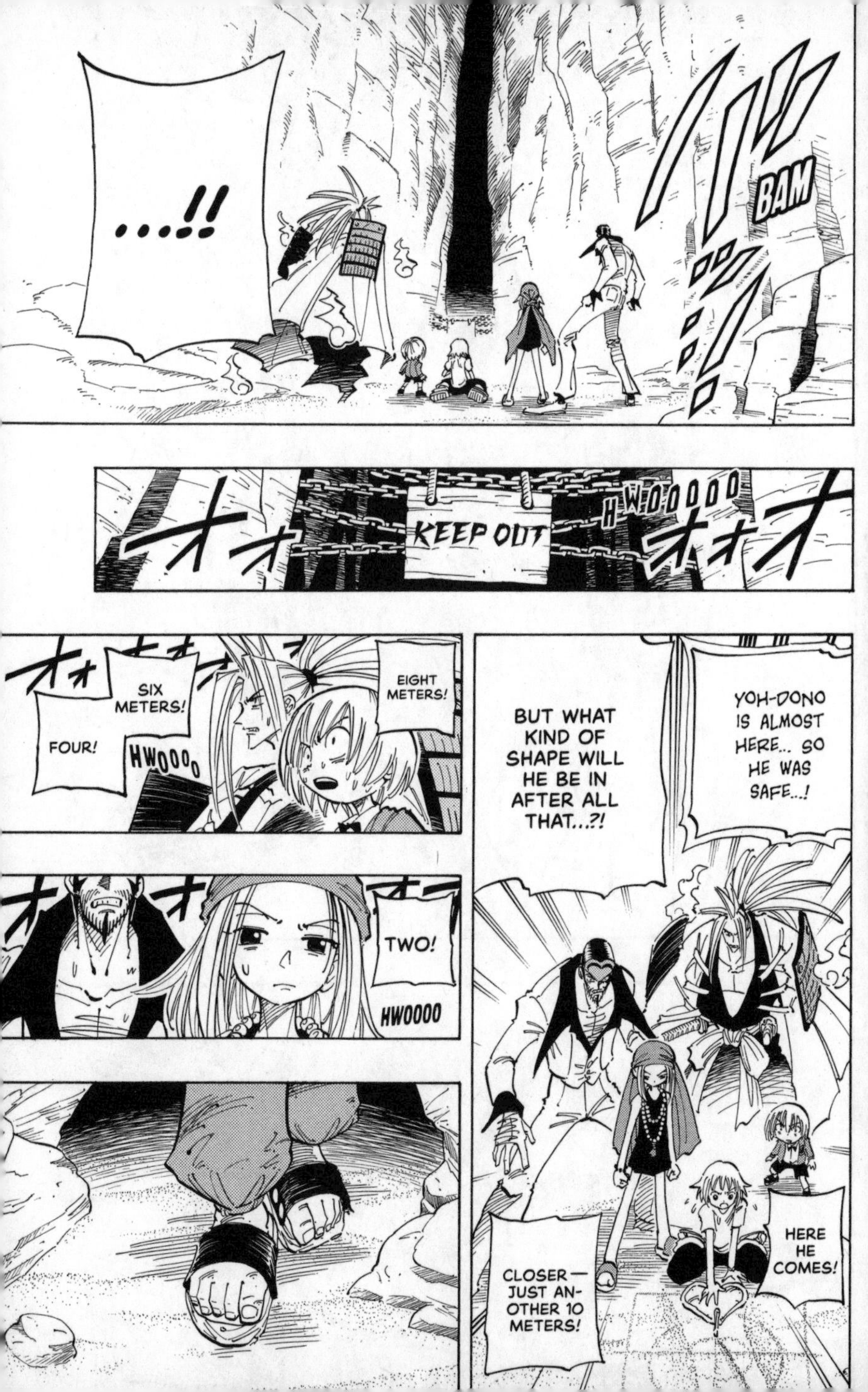
BAM
...!!
HWOOOOO
KEEP OUT
YOH-DONO IS ALMOST HERE... SO HE WAS SAFE...!
BUT WHAT KIND OF SHAPE WILL HE BE IN AFTER ALL THAT...?!
HERE HE COMES!
CLOSER—JUST AN-OTHER 10 METERS!
EIGHT METERS!
SIX METERS!
FOUR!
HWOOOO
TWO!
HWOOOO

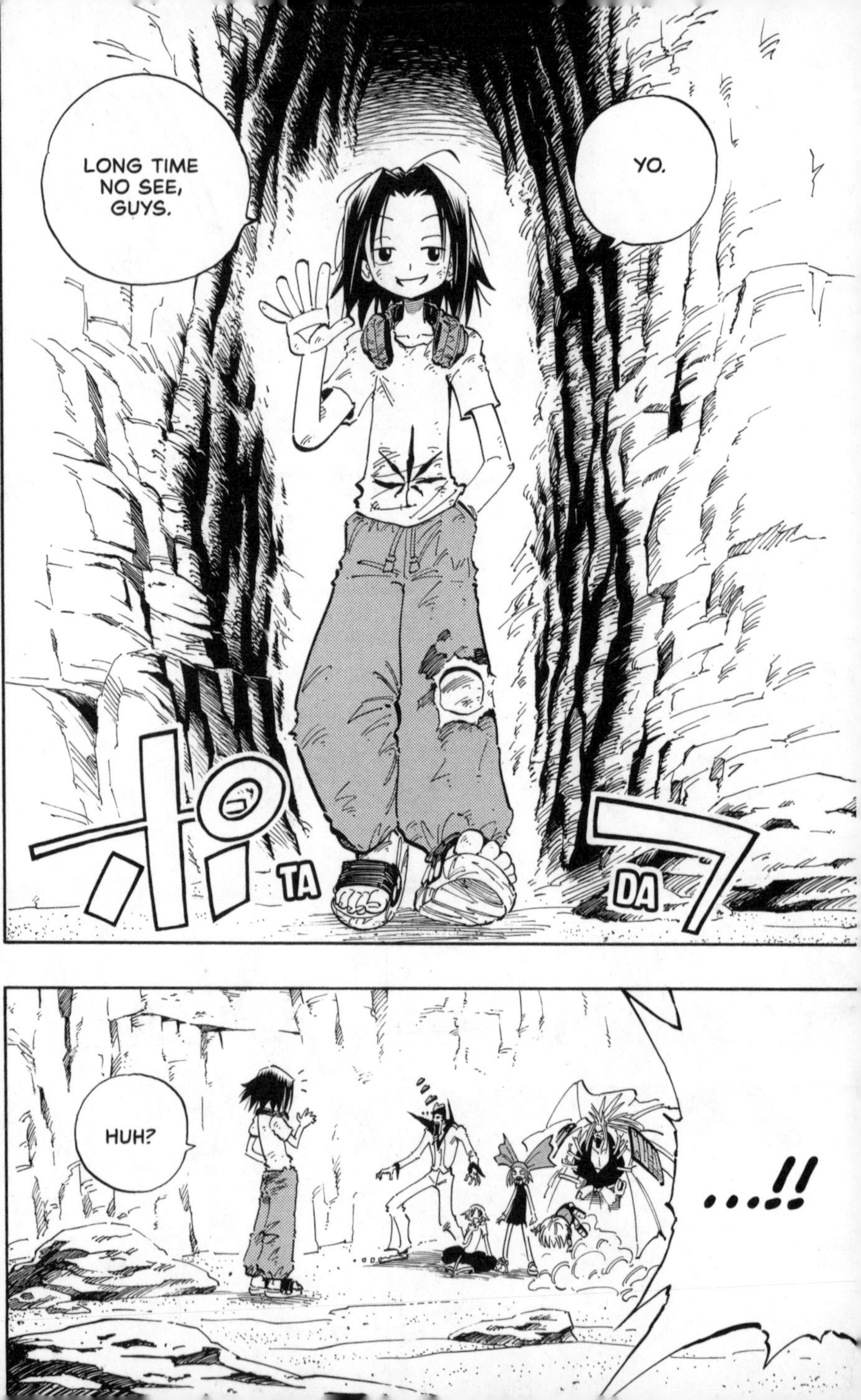
YO.
LONG TIME NO SEE, GUYS.
TA
DA
...!!
HUH?

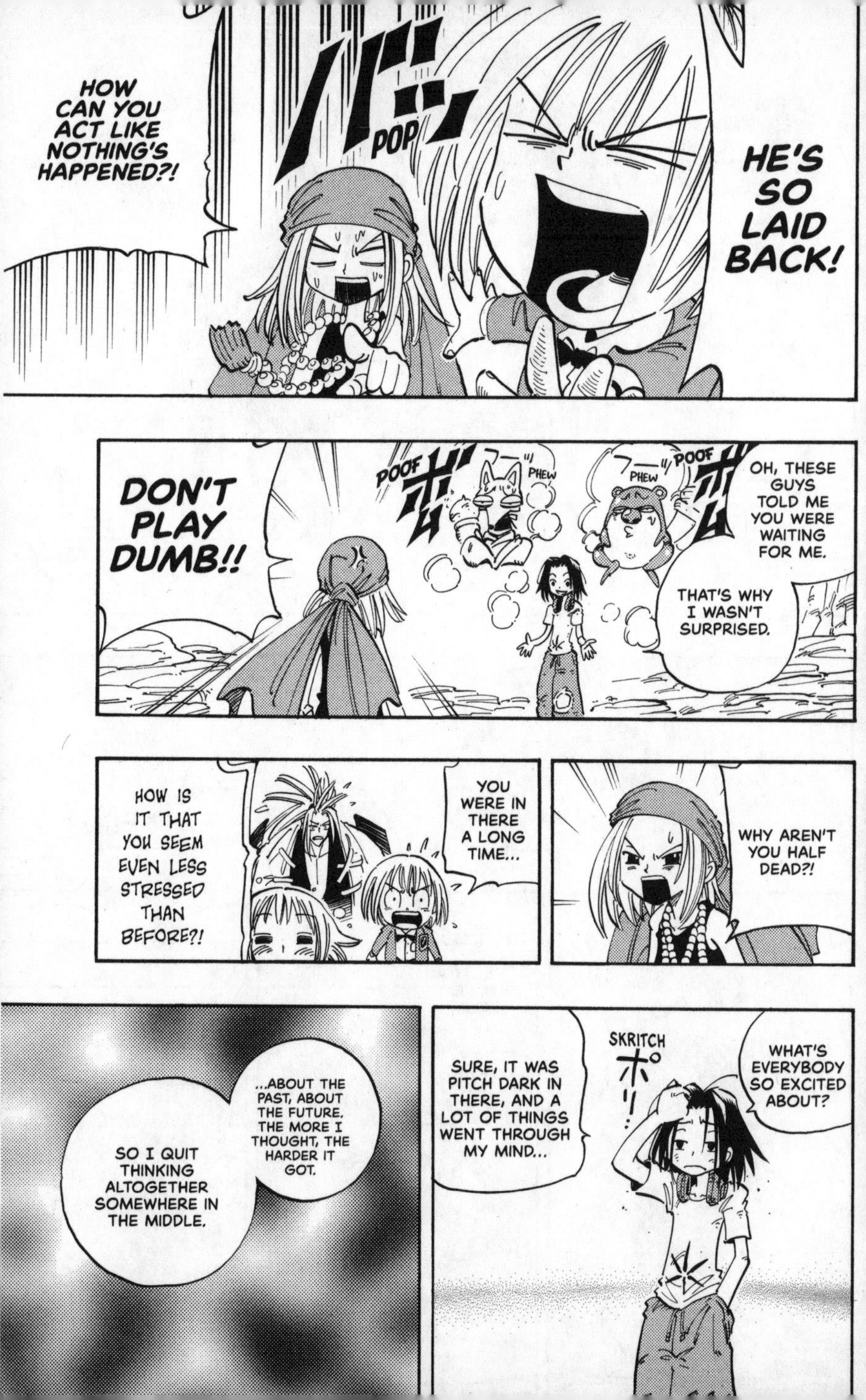
HE'S SO LAID BACK!
POP
HOW CAN YOU ACT LIKE NOTHING'S HAPPENED?!
OH, THESE GUYS TOLD ME YOU WERE WAITING FOR ME.
POOF
PHEW
PHEW
POOF
THAT'S WHY I WASN'T SURPRISED.
DON'T PLAY DUMB!!
WHY AREN'T YOU HALF DEAD?!
YOU WERE IN THERE A LONG TIME...
HOW IS IT THAT YOU SEEM EVEN LESS STRESSED THAN BEFORE?!
WHAT'S EVERYBODY SO EXCITED ABOUT?
SKRITCH
SURE, IT WAS PITCH DARK IN THERE, AND A LOT OF THINGS WENT THROUGH MY MIND...
...ABOUT THE PAST, ABOUT THE FUTURE. THE MORE I THOUGHT, THE HARDER IT GOT.
SO I QUIT THINKING ALTOGETHER SOMEWHERE IN THE MIDDLE.

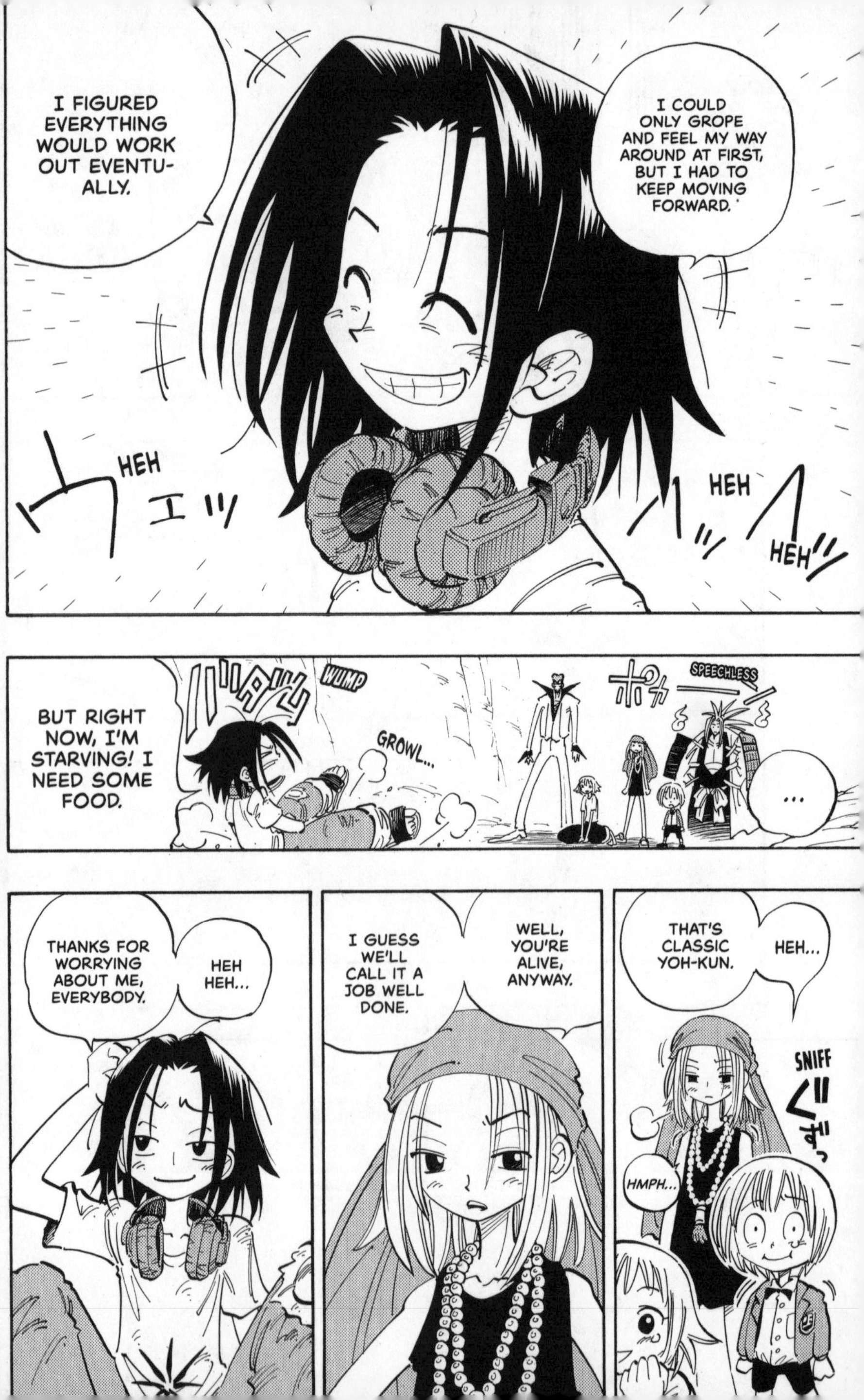
I COULD ONLY GROPE AND FEEL MY WAY AROUND AT FIRST, BUT I HAD TO KEEP MOVING FORWARD.
I FIGURED EVERYTHING WOULD WORK OUT EVENTU-ALLY.
HEH
HEH
HEH
SPEECHLESS
...
GROWL...
WUMP
BUT RIGHT NOW, I'M STARVING! I NEED SOME FOOD.
HEH...
THAT'S CLASSIC YOH-KUN.
SNIFF
HMPH...
WELL, YOU'RE ALIVE, ANYWAY.
I GUESS WE'LL CALL IT A JOB WELL DONE.
HEH HEH...
THANKS FOR WORRYING ABOUT ME, EVERYBODY.

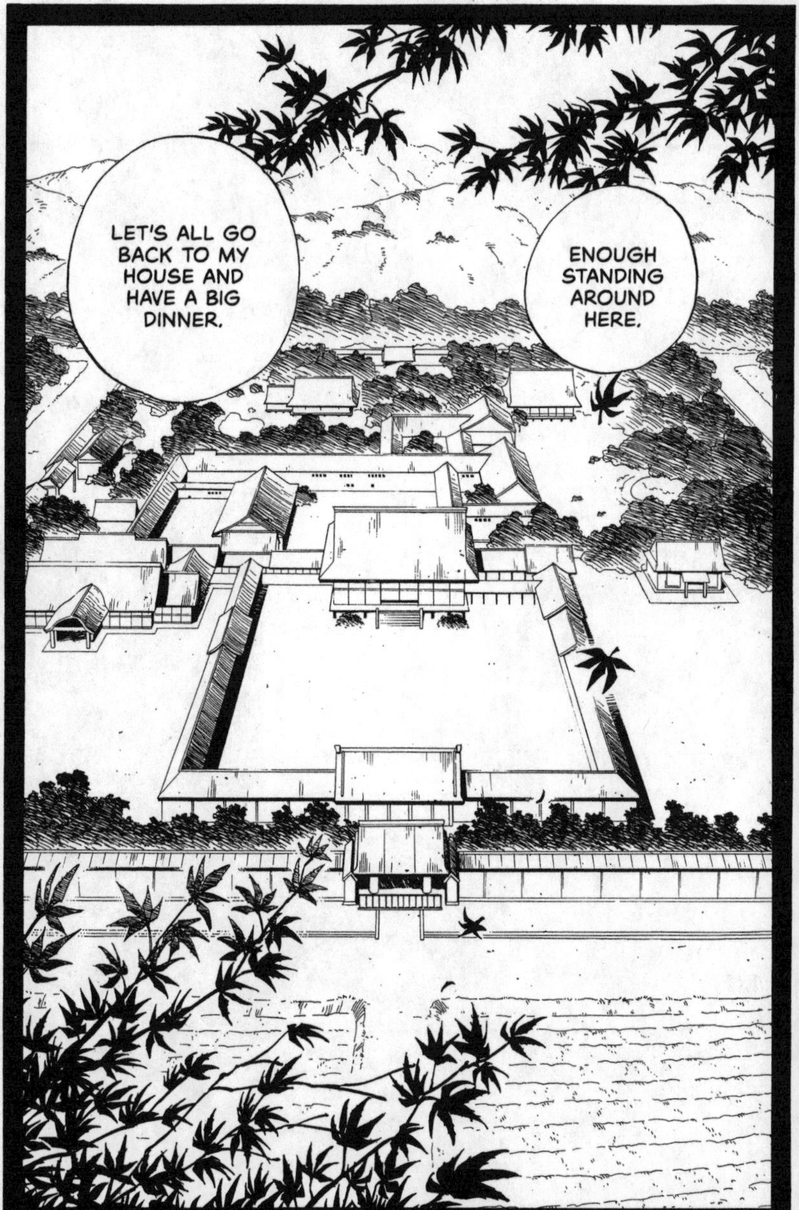
ENOUGH STANDING AROUND HERE.
LET'S ALL GO BACK TO MY HOUSE AND HAVE A BIG DINNER.

SHAMAN
KING
6

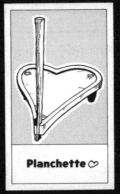

Planchette ♡

Chapter 52: Progress

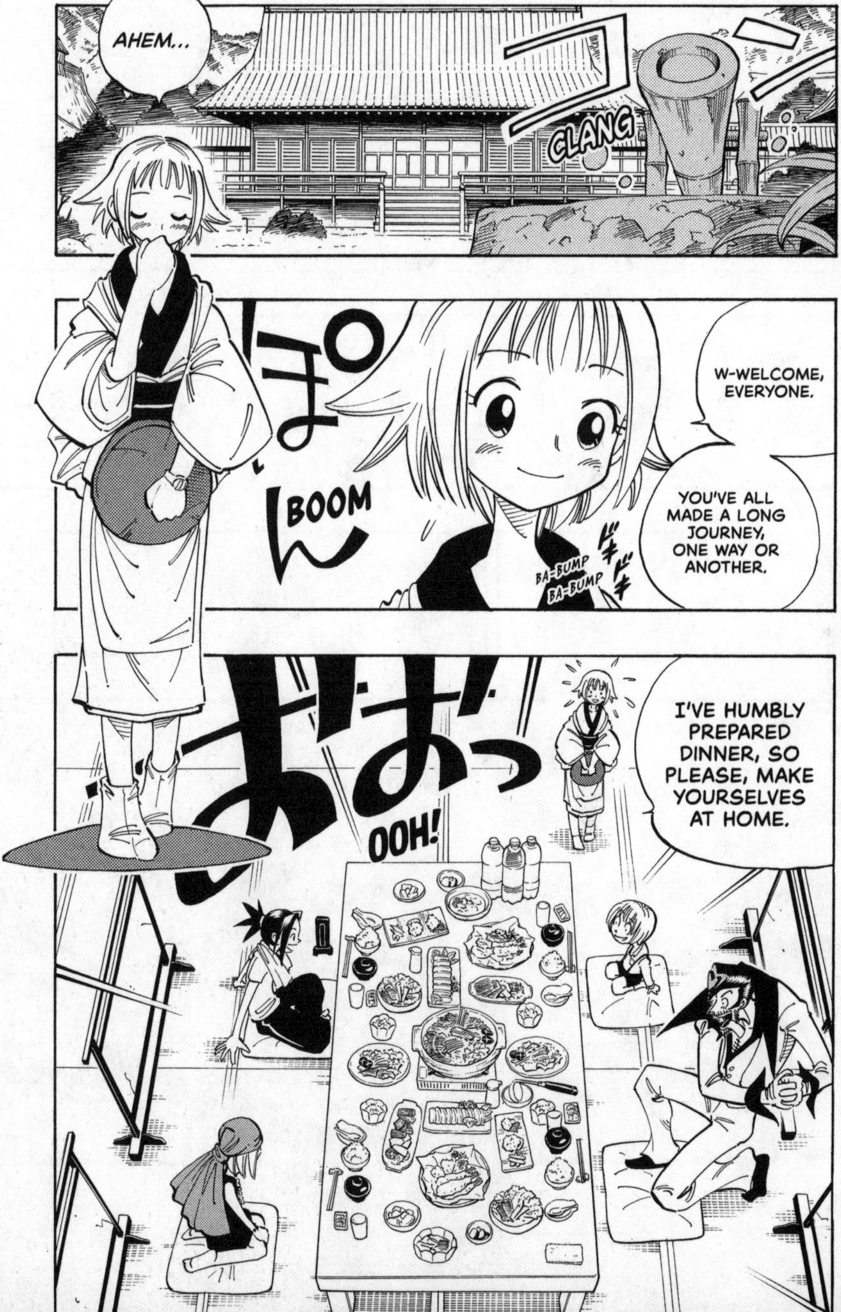
CLANG
AHEM...
W-WELCOME, EVERYONE.
YOU'VE ALL MADE A LONG JOURNEY, ONE WAY OR ANOTHER.
BA-BUMP BA-BUMP
BOOM
I'VE HUMBLY PREPARED DINNER, SO PLEASE, MAKE YOURSELVES AT HOME.
OOH!

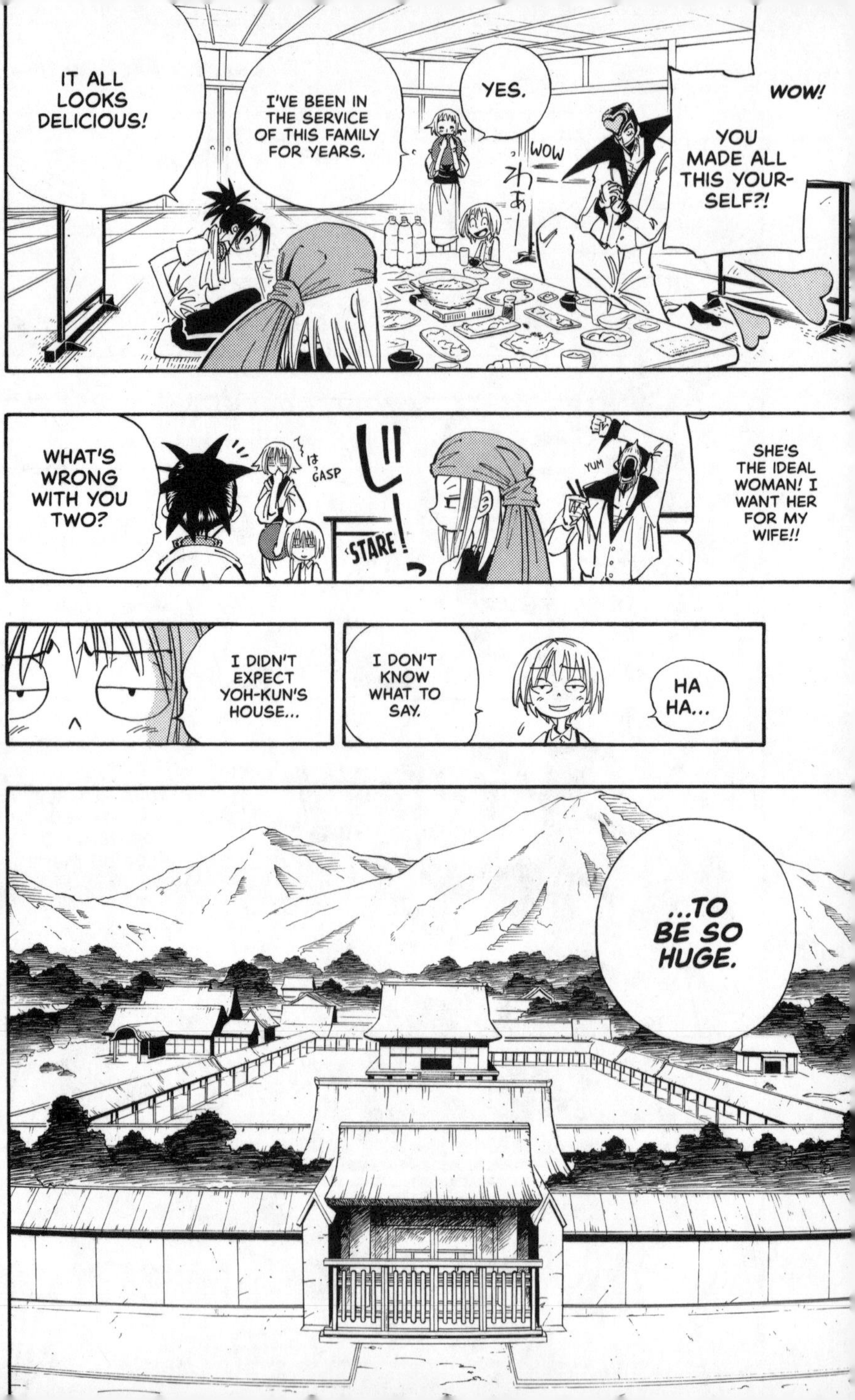
WOW!
YOU MADE ALL THIS YOURSELF?!
WOW
YES.
I'VE BEEN IN THE SERVICE OF THIS FAMILY FOR YEARS.
IT ALL LOOKS DELICIOUS!
SHE'S THE IDEAL WOMAN! I WANT HER FOR MY WIFE!!
YUM
STARE
GASP
WHAT'S WRONG WITH YOU TWO?
HA HA...
I DON'T KNOW WHAT TO SAY.
I DIDN'T EXPECT YOH-KUN'S HOUSE...
...TO BE SO HUGE.

Chapter 52:

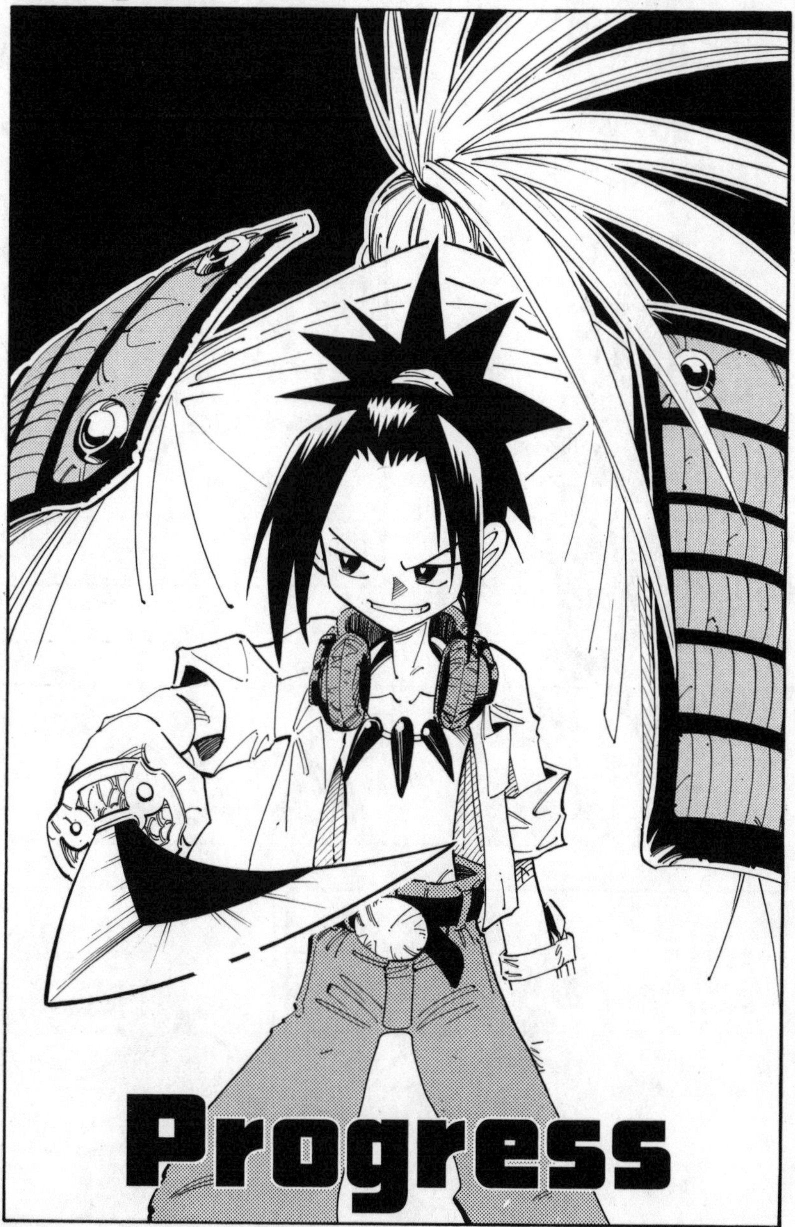
Progress

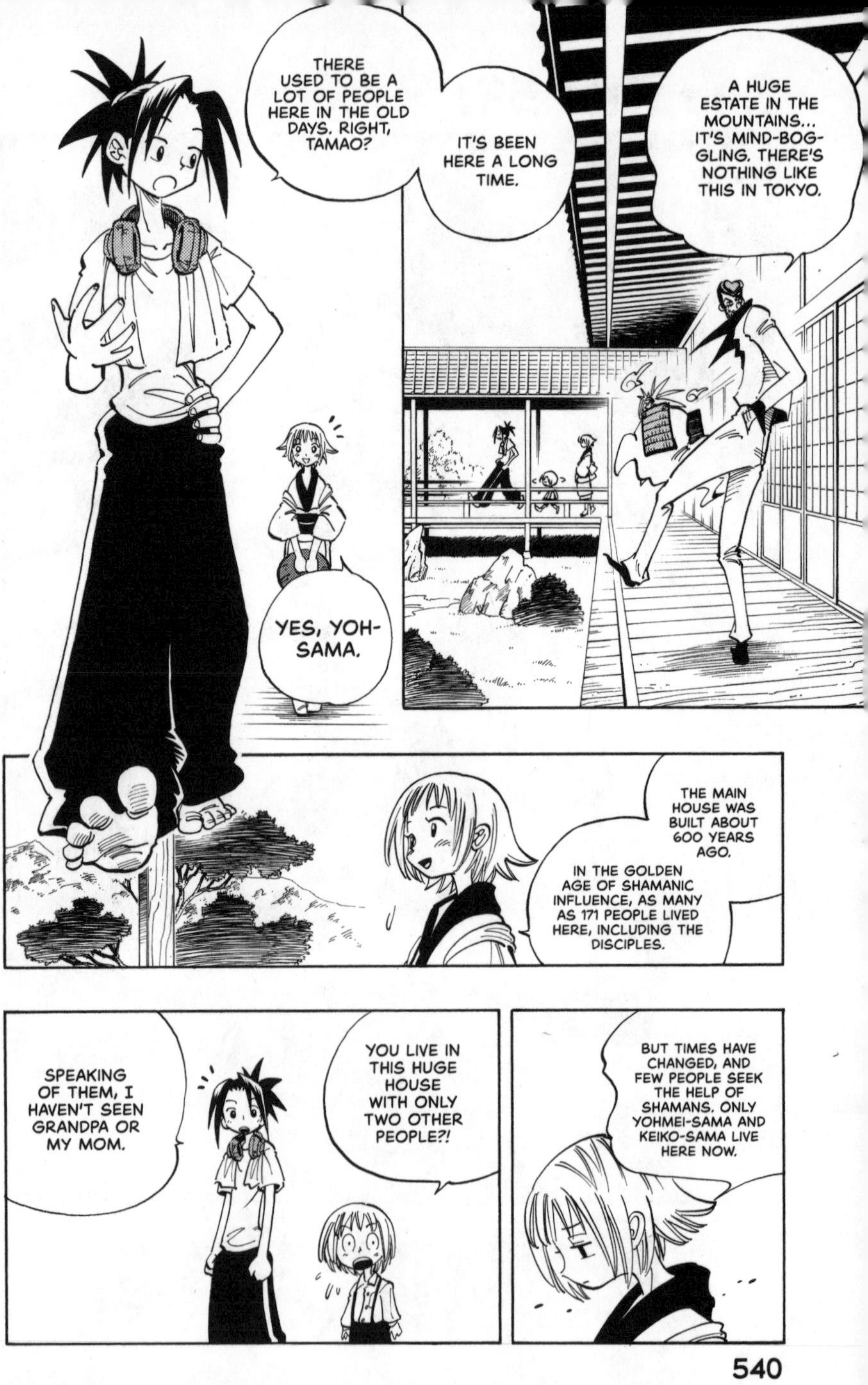
A HUGE ESTATE IN THE MOUNTAINS... IT'S MIND-BOGGLING. THERE'S NOTHING LIKE THIS IN TOKYO.
IT'S BEEN HERE A LONG TIME.
THERE USED TO BE A LOT OF PEOPLE HERE IN THE OLD DAYS. RIGHT, TAMAO?
YES, YOH-SAMA.
THE MAIN HOUSE WAS BUILT ABOUT 600 YEARS AGO.
IN THE GOLDEN AGE OF SHAMANIC INFLUENCE, AS MANY AS 171 PEOPLE LIVED HERE, INCLUDING THE DISCIPLES.
BUT TIMES HAVE CHANGED, AND FEW PEOPLE SEEK THE HELP OF SHAMANS. ONLY YOHMEI-SAMA AND KEIKO-SAMA LIVE HERE NOW.
YOU LIVE IN THIS HUGE HOUSE WITH ONLY TWO OTHER PEOPLE?!
SPEAKING OF THEM, I HAVEN'T SEEN GRANDPA OR MY MOM.

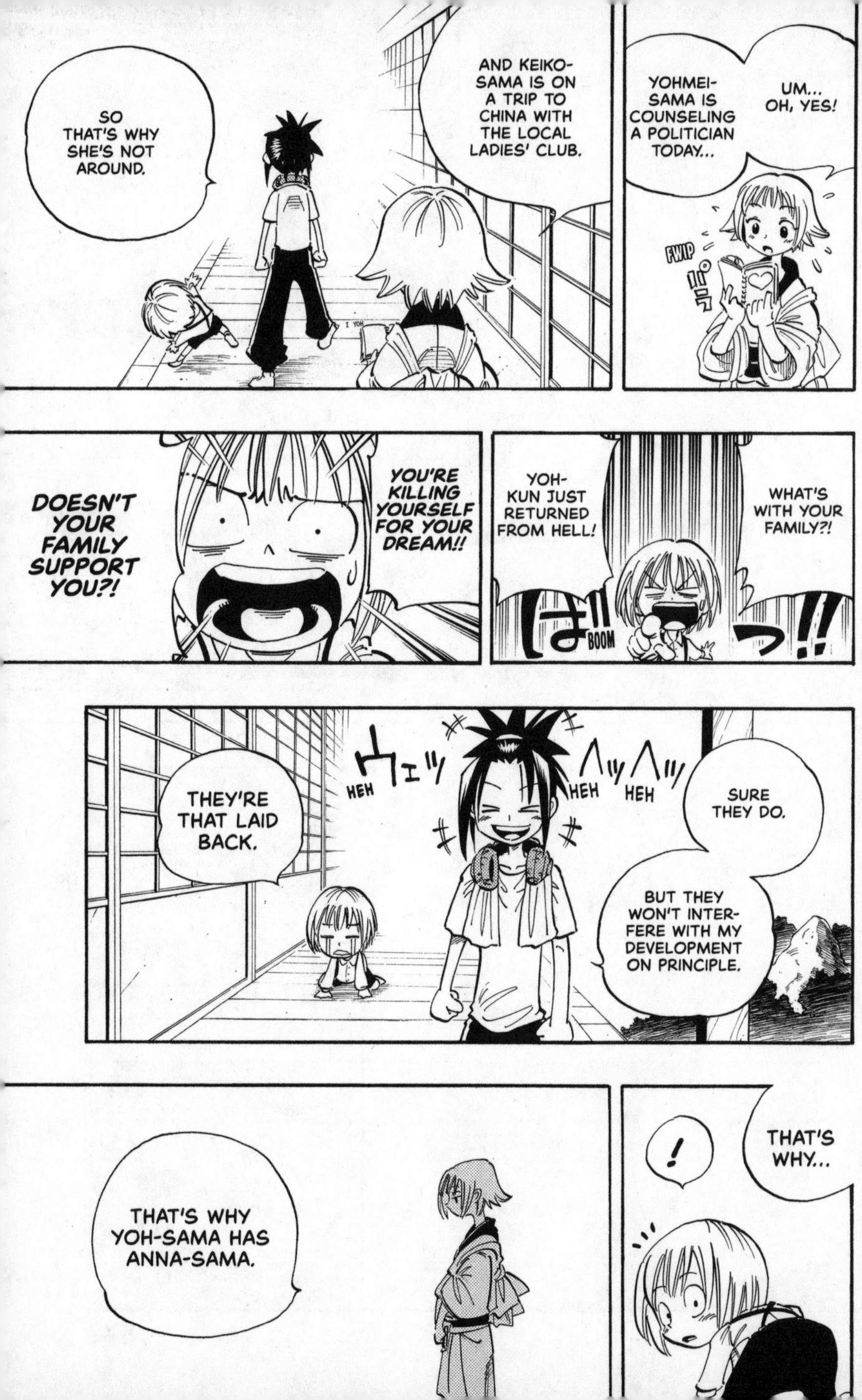
UM... OH, YES!
YOHMEI-SAMA IS COUNSELING A POLITICIAN TODAY...
FWIP
AND KEIKO-SAMA IS ON A TRIP TO CHINA WITH THE LOCAL LADIES' CLUB.
SO THAT'S WHY SHE'S NOT AROUND.
WHAT'S WITH YOUR FAMILY?!
YOH-KUN JUST RETURNED FROM HELL!
ばっ!!
BOOM
YOU'RE KILLING YOURSELF FOR YOUR DREAM!!
DOESN'T YOUR FAMILY SUPPORT YOU?!
SURE THEY DO.
BUT THEY WON'T INTERFERE WITH MY DEVELOPMENT ON PRINCIPLE.
ヘッヘッ
HEH HEH
ウェッ
HEH
THEY'RE THAT LAID BACK.
THAT'S WHY...
!
THAT'S WHY YOH-SAMA HAS ANNA-SAMA.

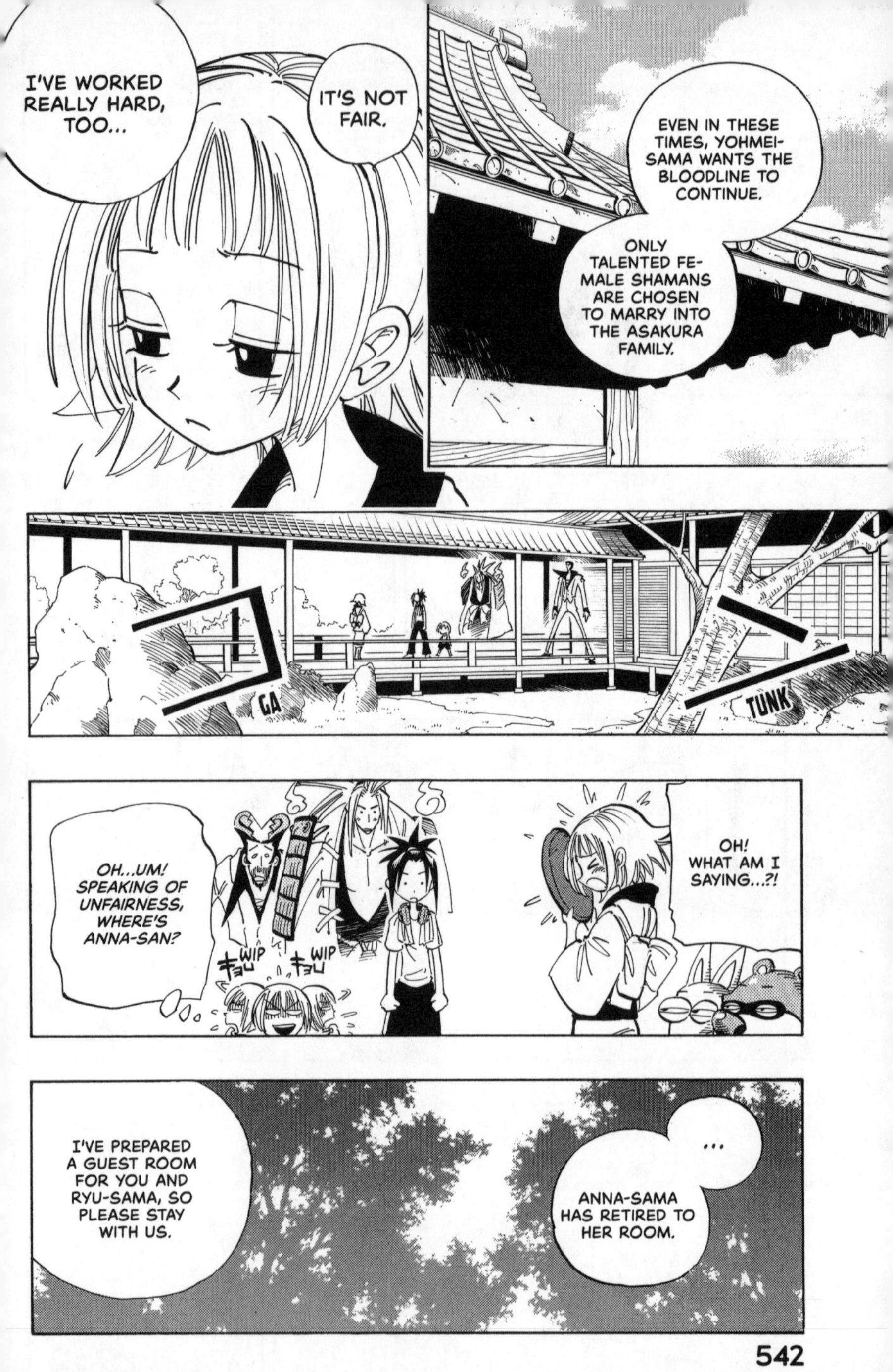
EVEN IN THESE TIMES, YOHMEI-SAMA WANTS THE BLOODLINE TO CONTINUE.
ONLY TALENTED FE-MALE SHAMANS ARE CHOSEN TO MARRY INTO THE ASAKURA FAMILY.
IT'S NOT FAIR.
I'VE WORKED REALLY HARD, TOO...
TUNK
GA
OH! WHAT AM I SAYING...?!
OH...UM! SPEAKING OF UNFAIRNESS, WHERE'S ANNA-SAN?
WIP
WIP
...
ANNA-SAMA HAS RETIRED TO HER ROOM.
I'VE PREPARED A GUEST ROOM FOR YOU AND RYU-SAMA, SO PLEASE STAY WITH US.

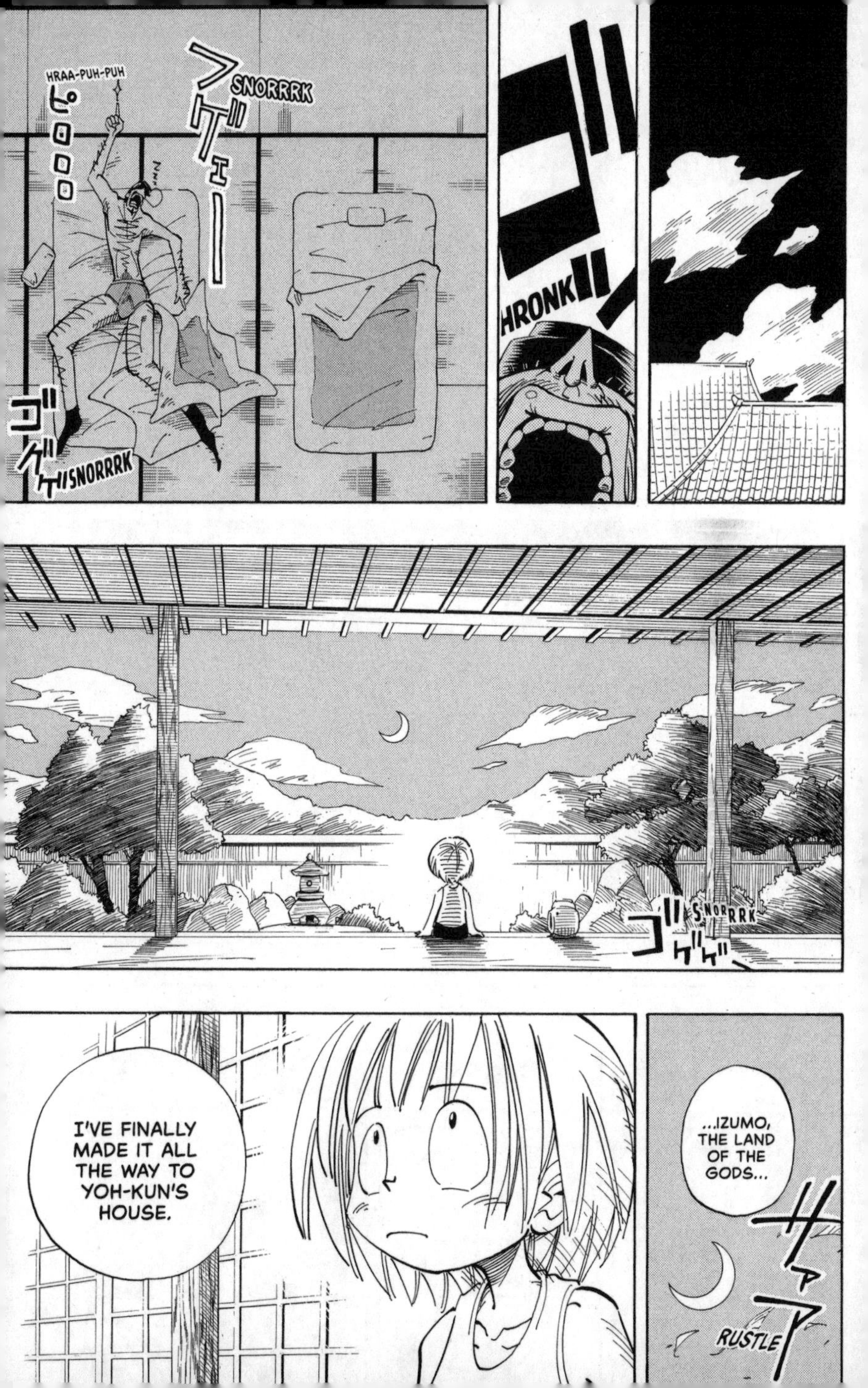

HRONK
SNORRRK
HRAA-PUH-PUH
SNORRRK
SNORRRK
...IZUMO, THE LAND OF THE GODS...
RUSTLE
I'VE FINALLY MADE IT ALL THE WAY TO YOH-KUN'S HOUSE.

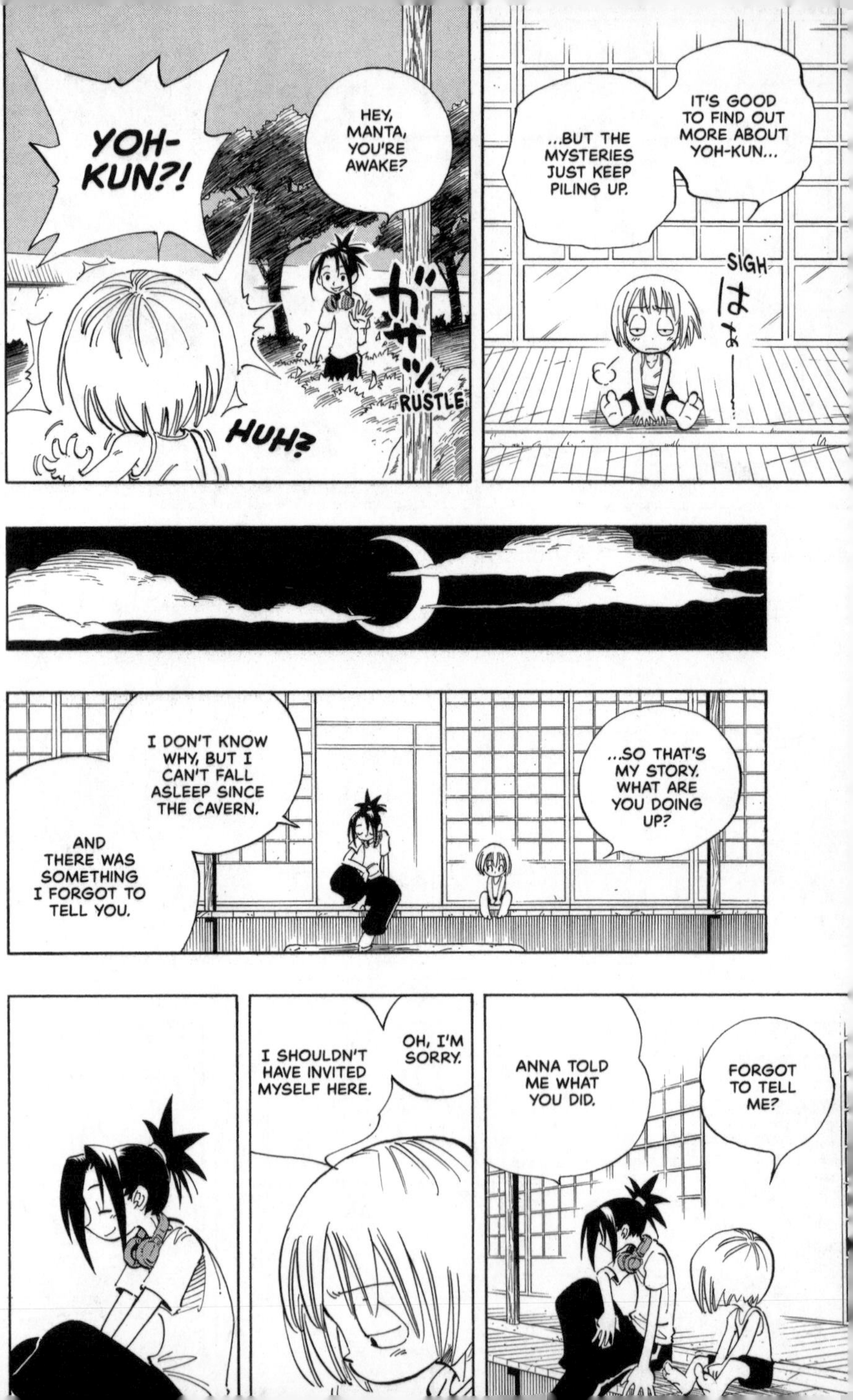
IT'S GOOD TO FIND OUT MORE ABOUT YOH-KUN...
...BUT THE MYSTERIES JUST KEEP PILING UP.
SIGH
はぁー
HEY, MANTA, YOU'RE AWAKE?
YOH-KUN?!
ガサッ
RUSTLE
HUH?
...SO THAT'S MY STORY. WHAT ARE YOU DOING UP?
I DON'T KNOW WHY, BUT I CAN'T FALL ASLEEP SINCE THE CAVERN.
AND THERE WAS SOMETHING I FORGOT TO TELL YOU.
FORGOT TO TELL ME?
ANNA TOLD ME WHAT YOU DID.
OH, I'M SORRY.
I SHOULDN'T HAVE INVITED MYSELF HERE.

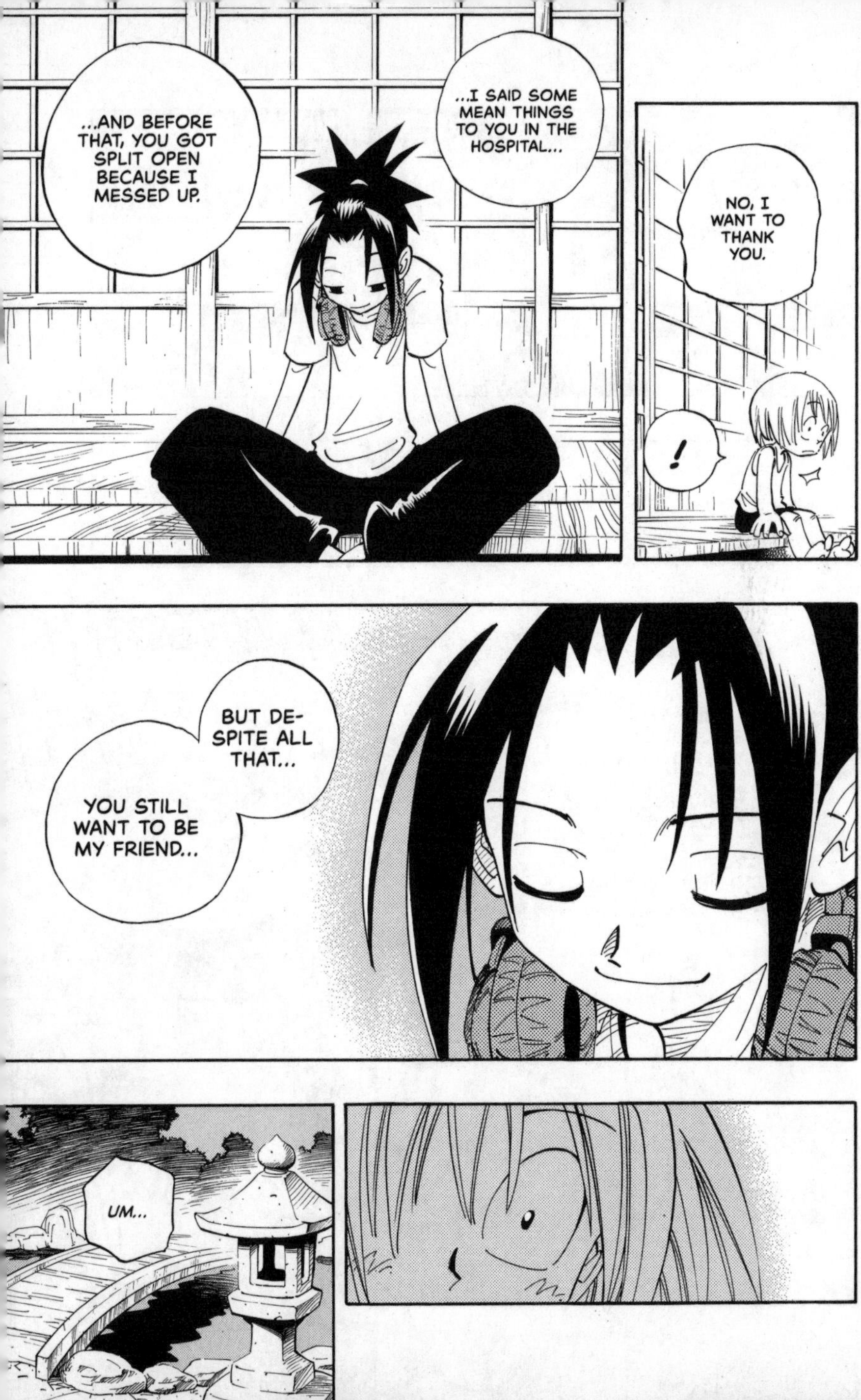
NO, I WANT TO THANK YOU.
!
...I SAID SOME MEAN THINGS TO YOU IN THE HOSPITAL...
...AND BEFORE THAT, YOU GOT SPLIT OPEN BECAUSE I MESSED UP.
BUT DE-SPITE ALL THAT...
YOU STILL WANT TO BE MY FRIEND...
UM...

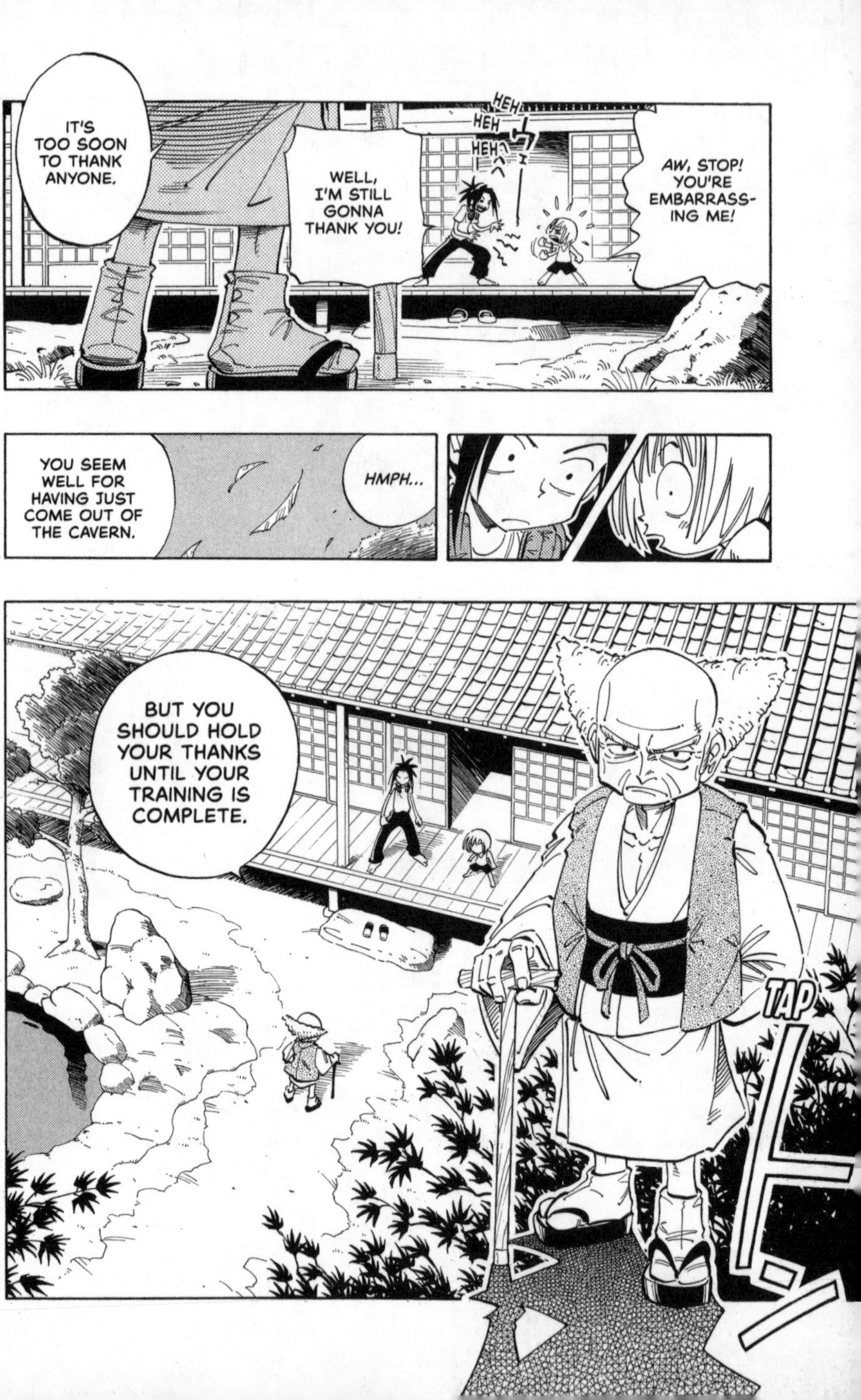
AW, STOP! YOU'RE EMBARRASS-ING ME!
HEH HEH HEH
WELL, I'M STILL GONNA THANK YOU!
IT'S TOO SOON TO THANK ANYONE.
HMPH...
YOU SEEM WELL FOR HAVING JUST COME OUT OF THE CAVERN.
BUT YOU SHOULD HOLD YOUR THANKS UNTIL YOUR TRAINING IS COMPLETE.
TAP

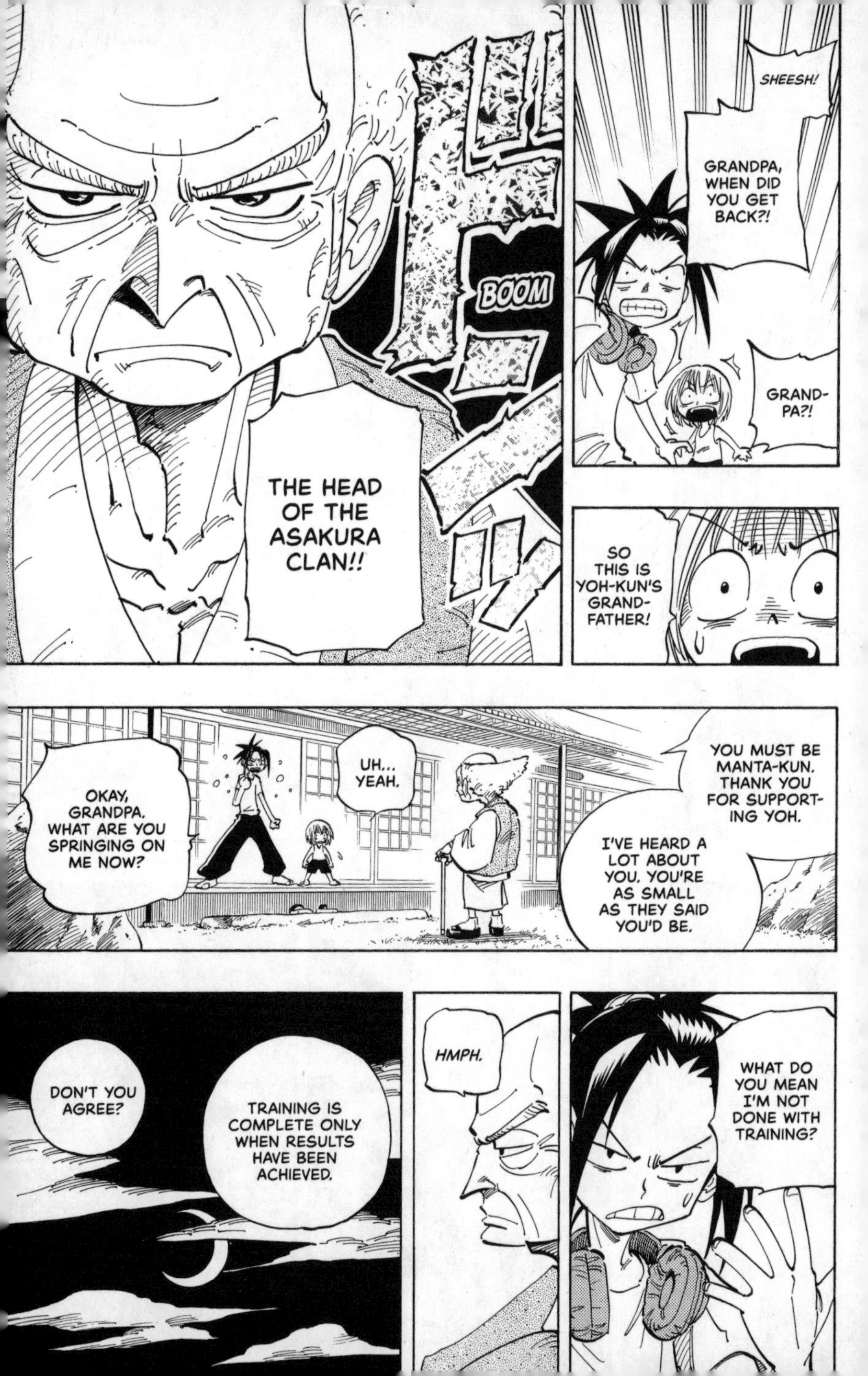
SHEESH!
GRANDPA, WHEN DID YOU GET BACK?!
GRAND-PA?!
SO THIS IS YOH-KUN'S GRAND-FATHER!
BOOM
THE HEAD OF THE ASAKURA CLAN!!
YOU MUST BE MANTA-KUN. THANK YOU FOR SUPPORT-ING YOH.
I'VE HEARD A LOT ABOUT YOU. YOU'RE AS SMALL AS THEY SAID YOU'D BE.
UH... YEAH.
OKAY, GRANDPA, WHAT ARE YOU SPRINGING ON ME NOW?
WHAT DO YOU MEAN I'M NOT DONE WITH TRAINING?
HMPH.
TRAINING IS COMPLETE ONLY WHEN RESULTS HAVE BEEN ACHIEVED.
DON'T YOU AGREE?

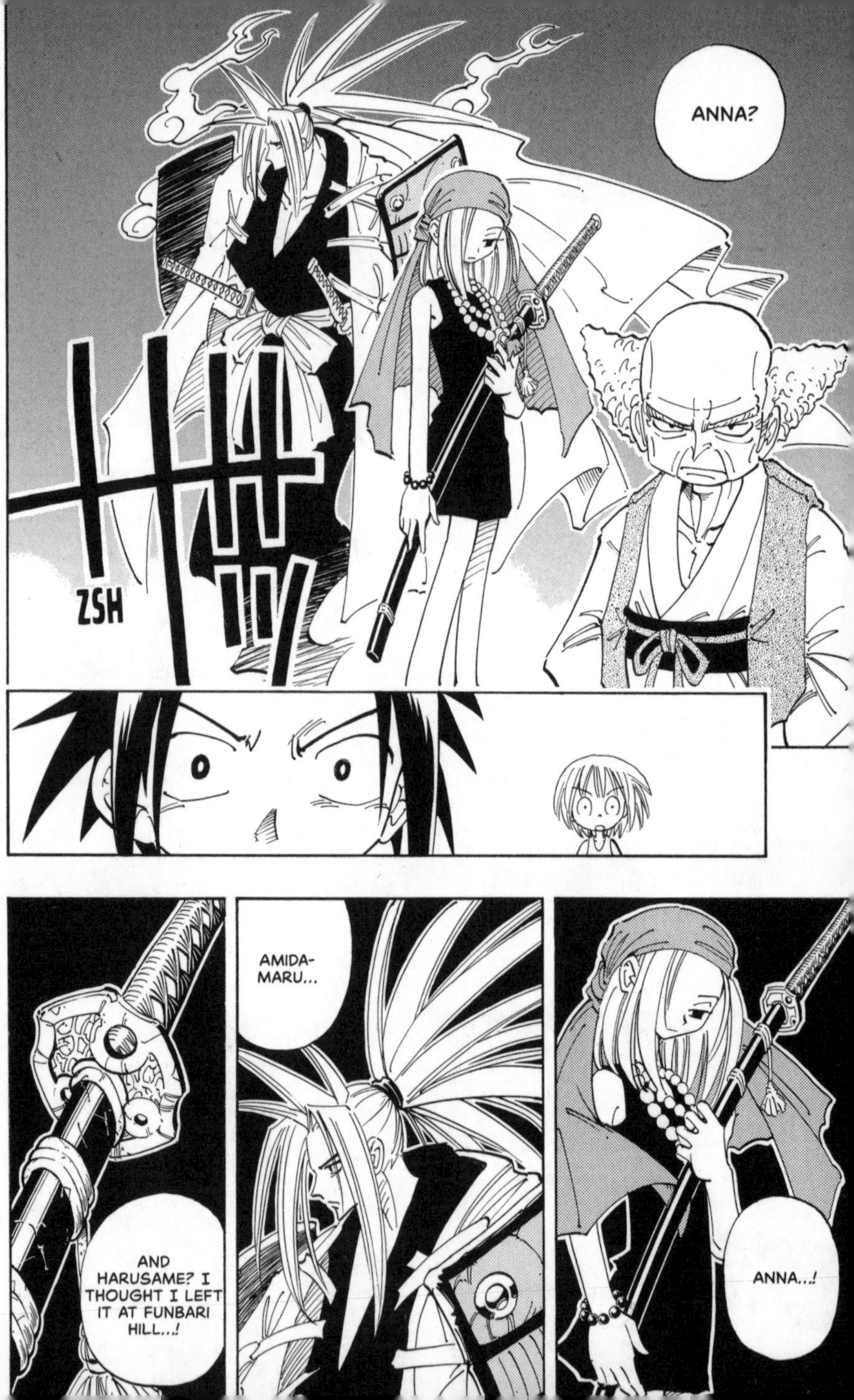
ANNA?
ZSH
ANNA...!
AMIDA-MARU...
AND HARUSAME? I THOUGHT I LEFT IT AT FUNBARI HILL...!

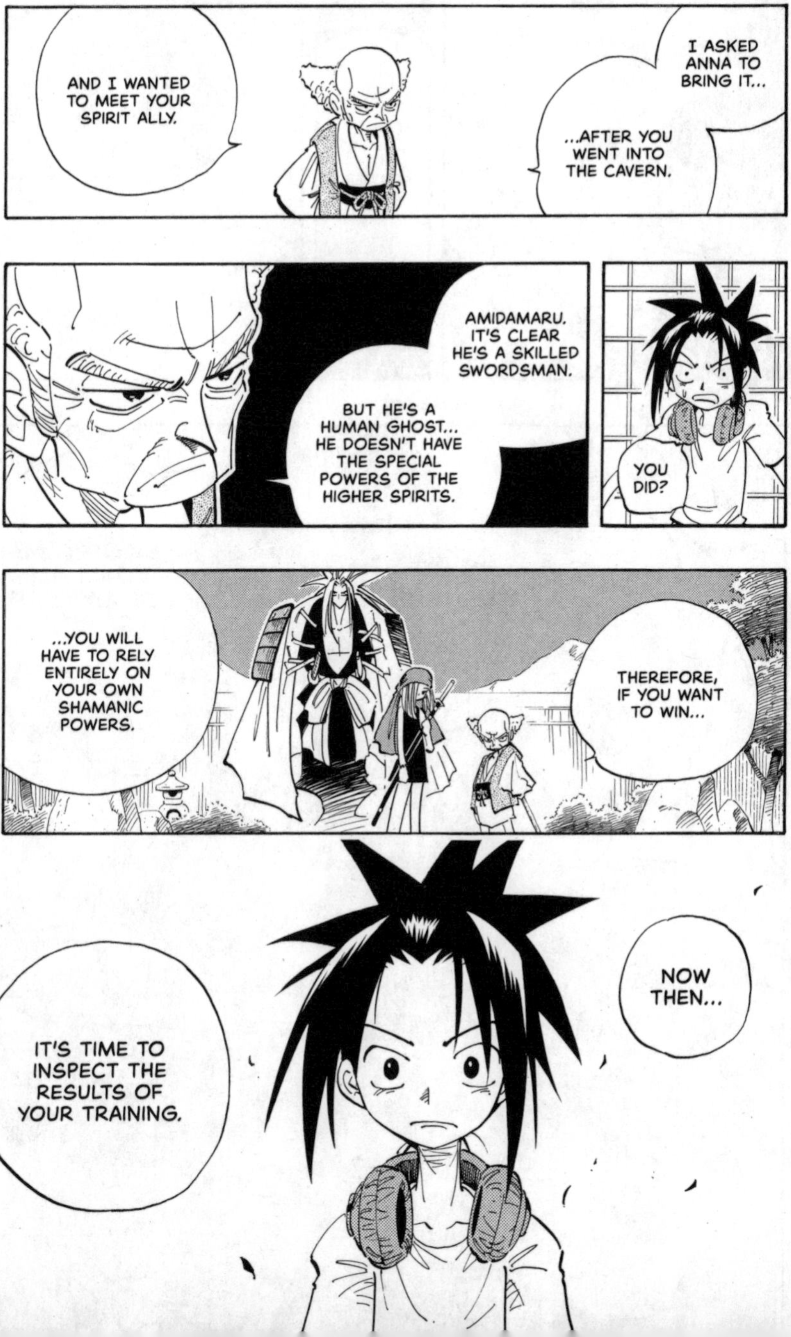
I ASKED ANNA TO BRING IT...
...AFTER YOU WENT INTO THE CAVERN.
AND I WANTED TO MEET YOUR SPIRIT ALLY.
YOU DID?
AMIDAMARU. IT'S CLEAR HE'S A SKILLED SWORDSMAN.
BUT HE'S A HUMAN GHOST... HE DOESN'T HAVE THE SPECIAL POWERS OF THE HIGHER SPIRITS.
THEREFORE, IF YOU WANT TO WIN...
...YOU WILL HAVE TO RELY ENTIRELY ON YOUR OWN SHAMANIC POWERS.
NOW THEN...
IT'S TIME TO INSPECT THE RESULTS OF YOUR TRAINING.

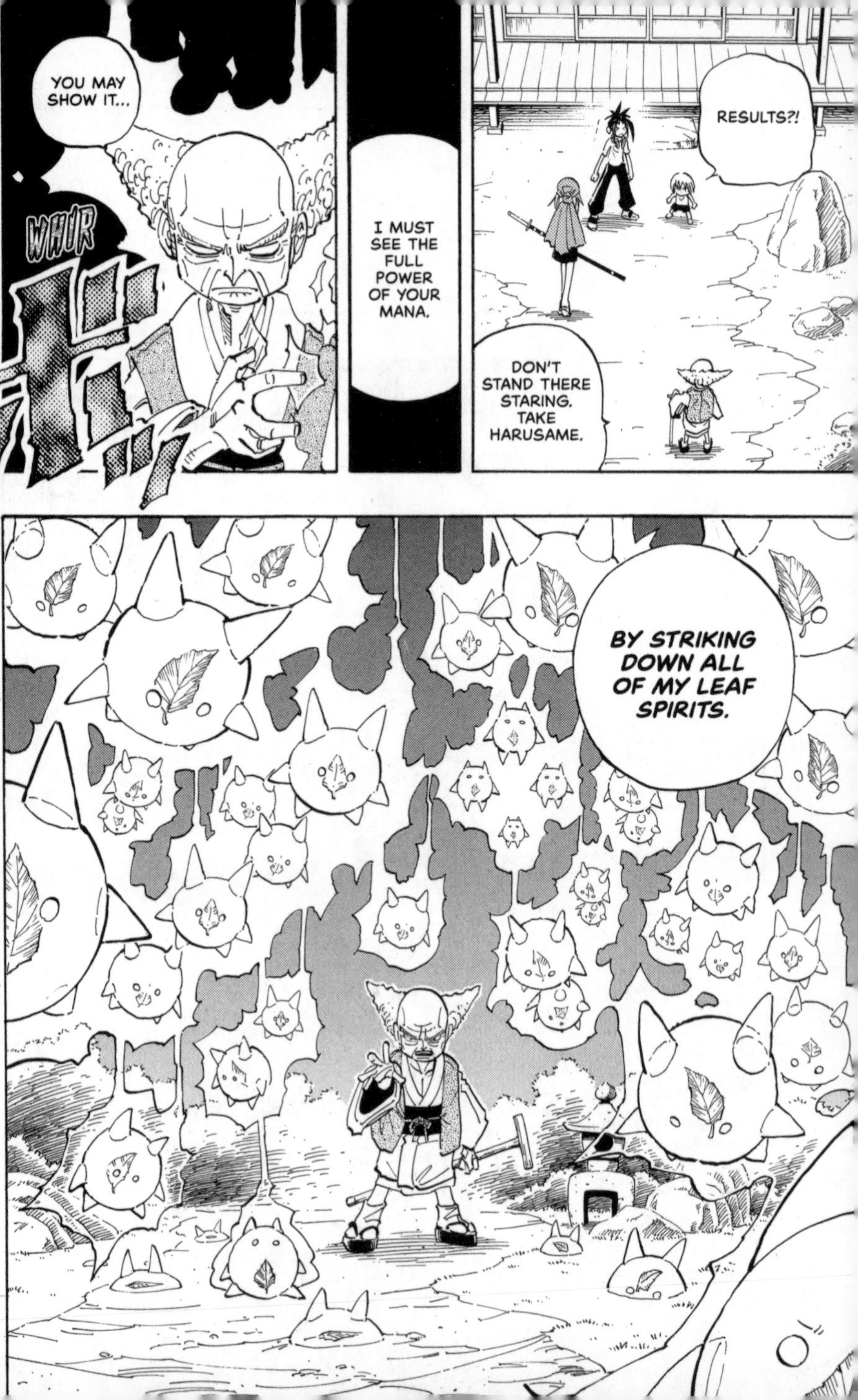
RESULTS?!
DON'T STAND THERE STARING. TAKE HARUSAME.
I MUST SEE THE FULL POWER OF YOUR MANA.
YOU MAY SHOW IT...
WHUR
BY STRIKING DOWN ALL OF MY LEAF SPIRITS.

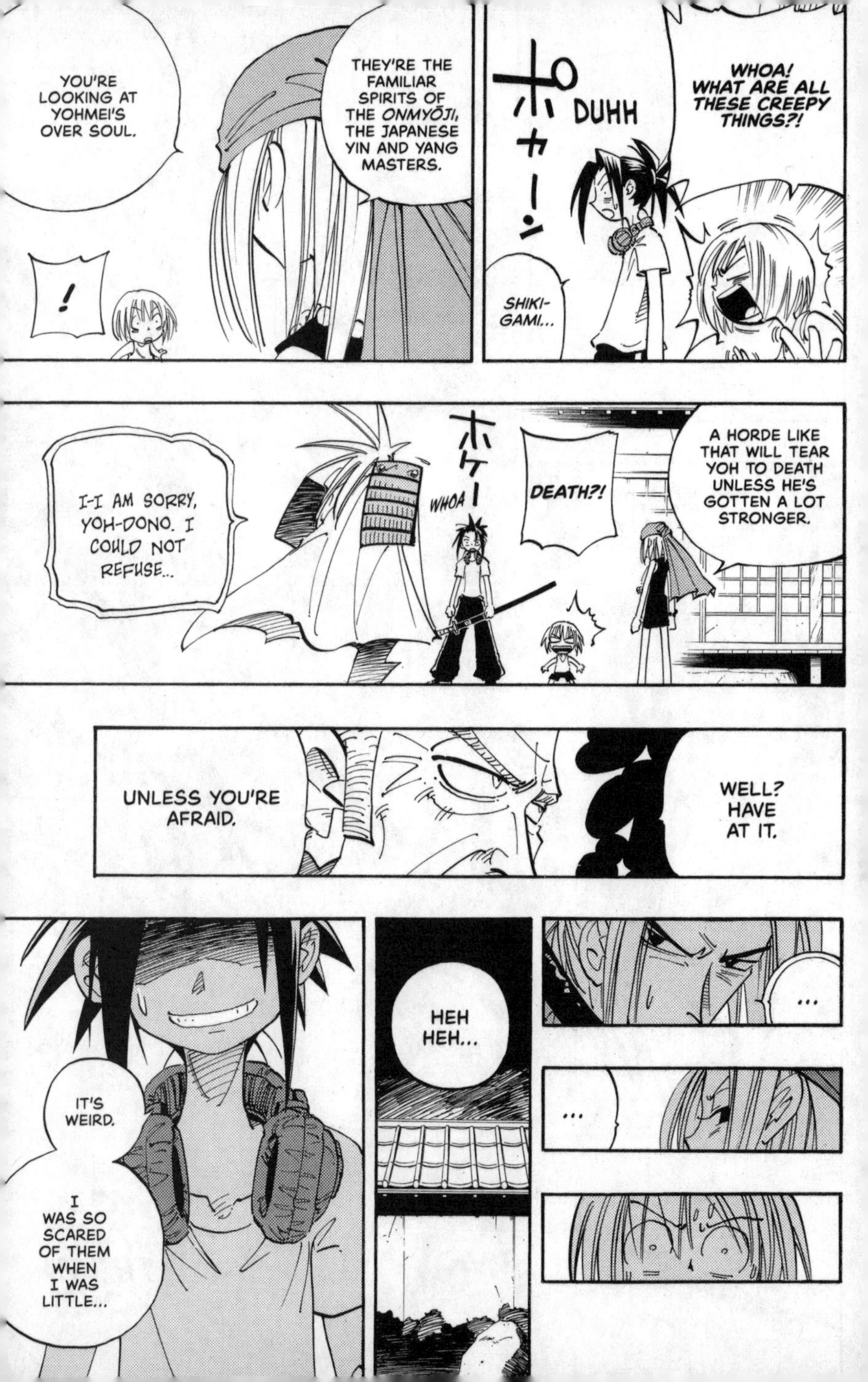
WHOA! WHAT ARE ALL THESE CREEPY THINGS?!
DUHH
SHIKI-GAMI...
THEY'RE THE FAMILIAR SPIRITS OF THE ONMYŌJI, THE JAPANESE YIN AND YANG MASTERS.
YOU'RE LOOKING AT YOHMEI'S OVER SOUL.
!
A HORDE LIKE THAT WILL TEAR YOH TO DEATH UNLESS HE'S GOTTEN A LOT STRONGER.
DEATH?!
WHOA
I-I AM SORRY, YOH-DONO. I COULD NOT REFUSE...
WELL? HAVE AT IT.
UNLESS YOU'RE AFRAID.
...
...
HEH HEH...
IT'S WEIRD.
I WAS SO SCARED OF THEM WHEN I WAS LITTLE...

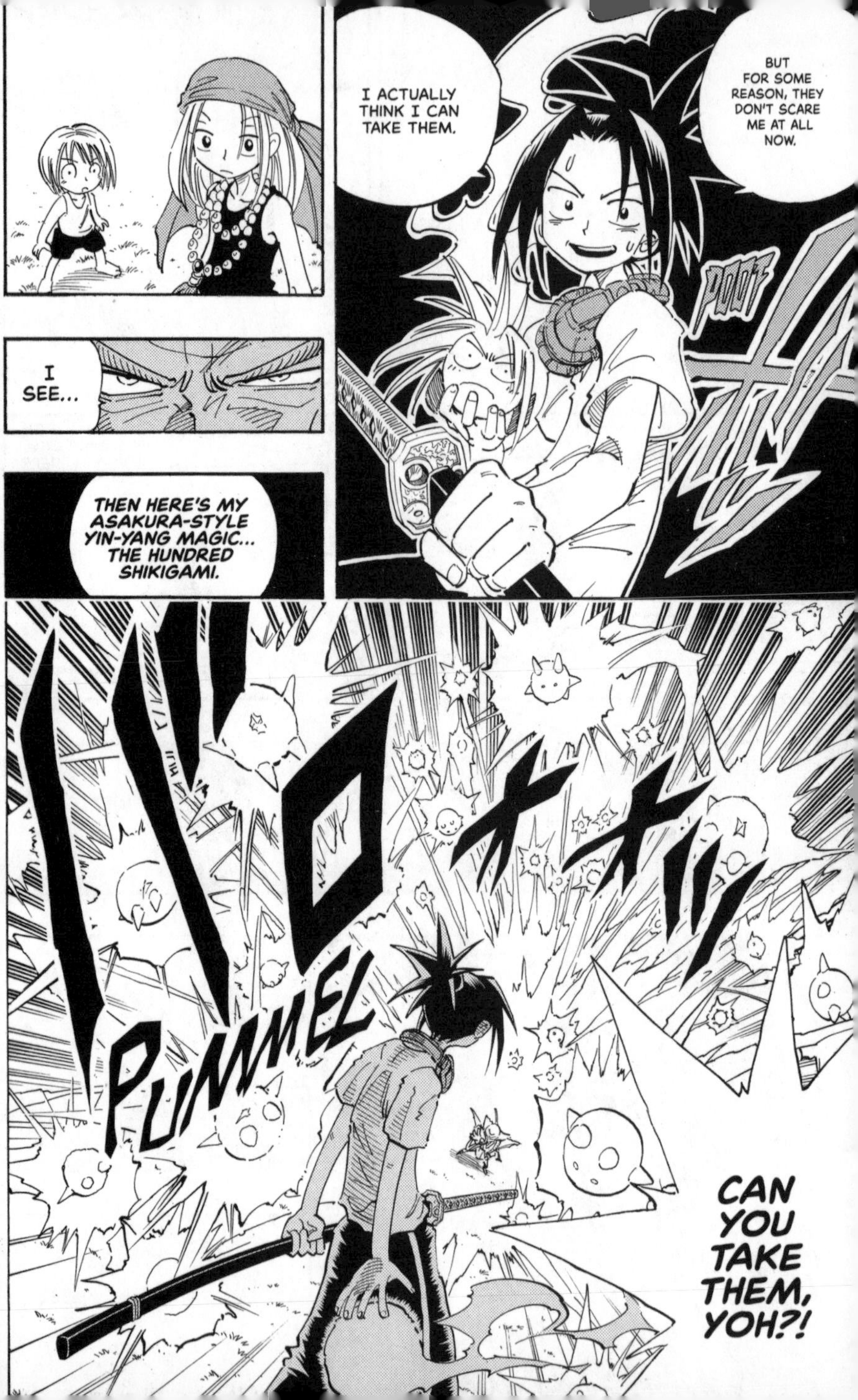
BUT FOR SOME REASON, THEY DON'T SCARE ME AT ALL NOW.
I ACTUALLY THINK I CAN TAKE THEM.
POOF
I SEE...
THEN HERE'S MY ASAKURA-STYLE YIN-YANG MAGIC... THE HUNDRED SHIKIGAMI.
PUMMEL
CAN YOU TAKE THEM, YOH?!

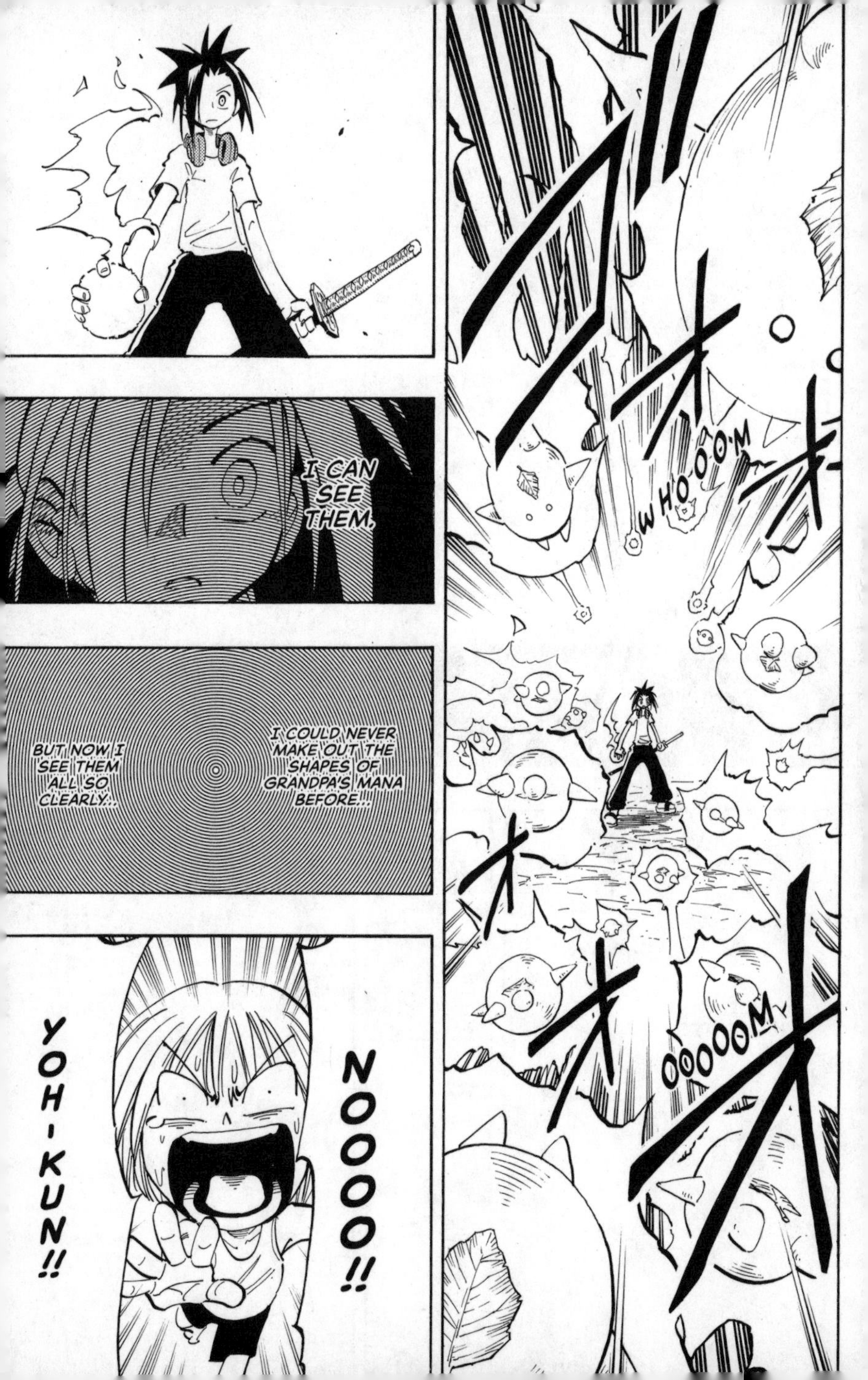
WHOOOM
OOOOOM
I CAN SEE THEM.
I COULD NEVER MAKE OUT THE SHAPES OF GRANDPA'S MANA BEFORE...
BUT NOW I SEE THEM ALL SO CLEARLY...
NOOOOO!!
YOH-KUN!!

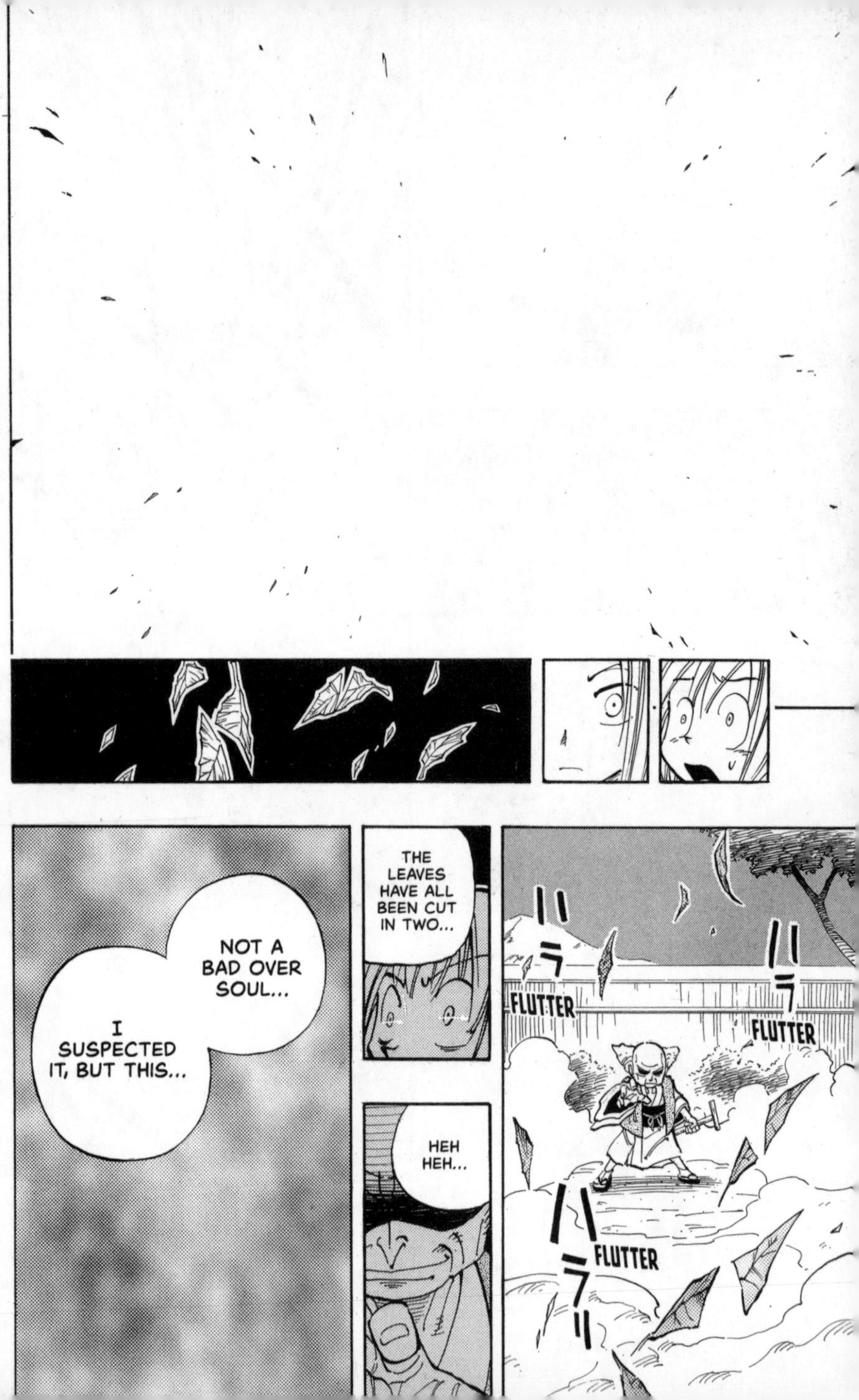
FLUTTER
FLUTTER
FLUTTER
THE LEAVES HAVE ALL BEEN CUT IN TWO...
HEH HEH...
NOT A BAD OVER SOUL...
I SUSPECTED IT, BUT THIS...

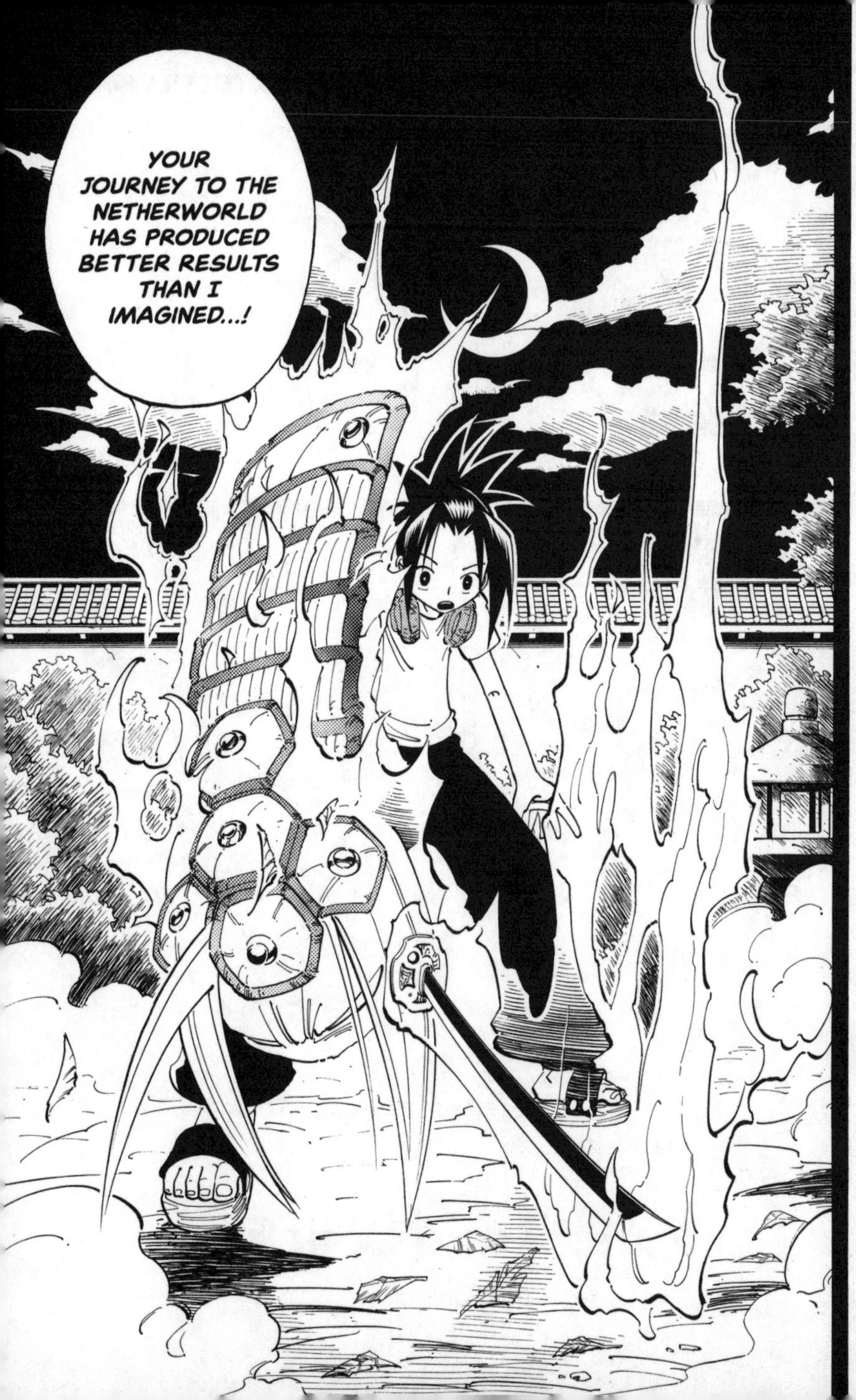
YOUR JOURNEY TO THE NETHERWORLD HAS PRODUCED BETTER RESULTS THAN I IMAGINED...!

SHAMAN KING CHARACTER FILE No.28

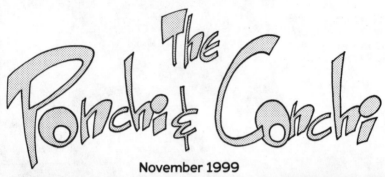

The Ponchi & Conchi

November 1999

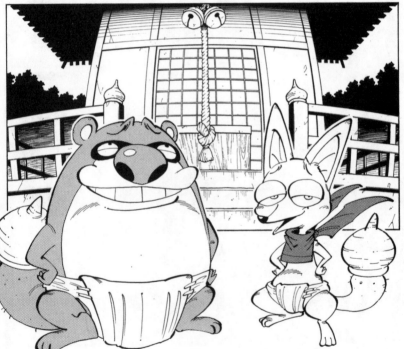

Ponchi and Conchi

Data unknown

Chapter 53: Two Tough Ghosts

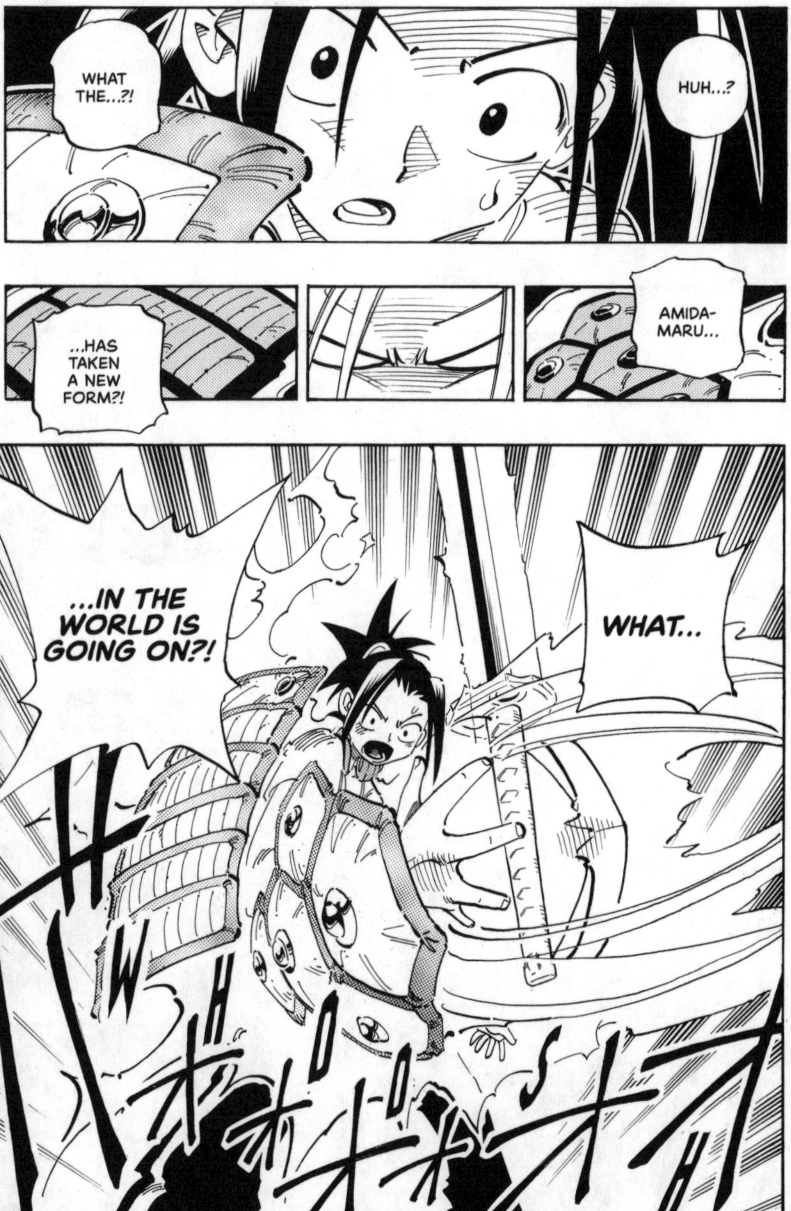
HUH...?
WHAT THE...?!
AMIDA-MARU...
...HAS TAKEN A NEW FORM?!
WHAT...
...IN THE WORLD IS GOING ON?!

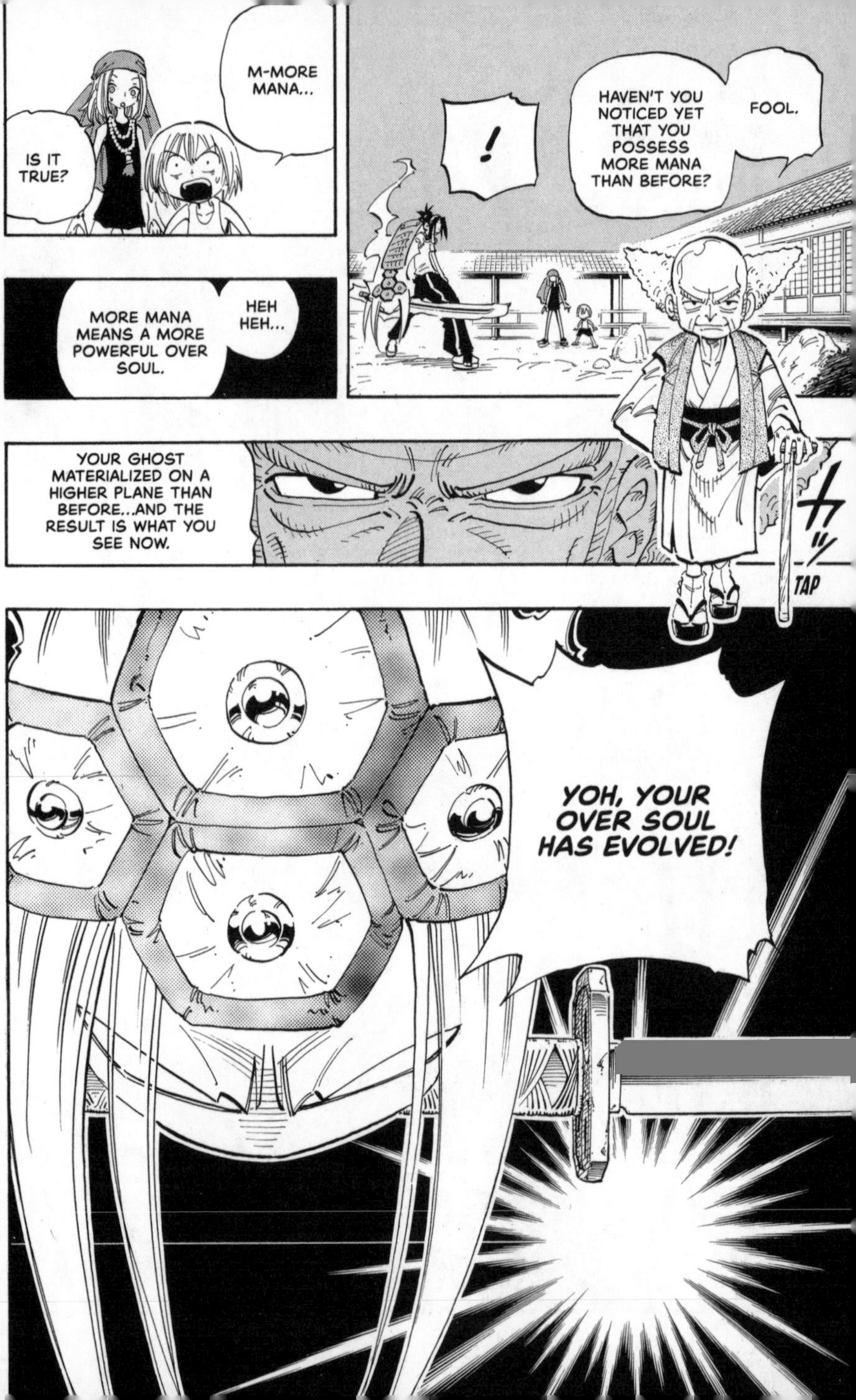
FOOL.
HAVEN'T YOU NOTICED YET THAT YOU POSSESS MORE MANA THAN BEFORE?
!
M-MORE MANA...
IS IT TRUE?
HEH HEH...
MORE MANA MEANS A MORE POWERFUL OVER SOUL.
TAP
YOUR GHOST MATERIALIZED ON A HIGHER PLANE THAN BEFORE...AND THE RESULT IS WHAT YOU SEE NOW.
YOH, YOUR OVER SOUL HAS EVOLVED!

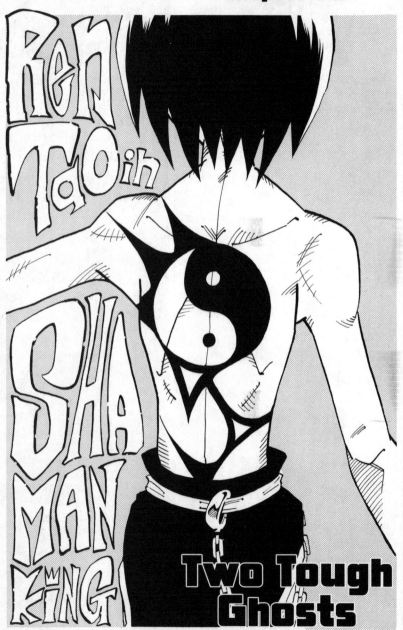

Ren Tao ih
SHAMAN KING

Two Tough Ghosts

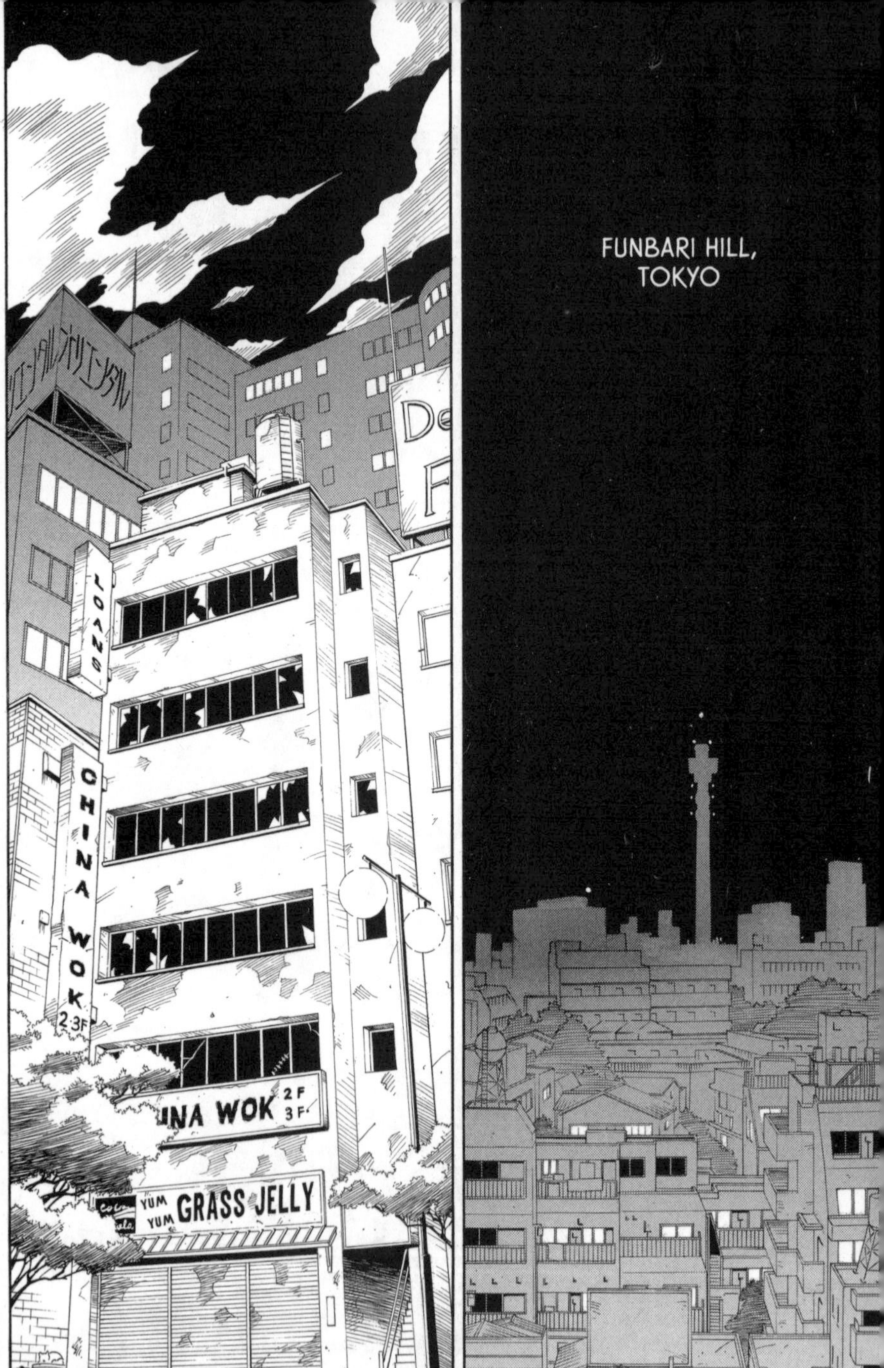
FUNBARI HILL,
TOKYO
LOANS
CHINA WOK
2·3F
INA WOK 2F 3F
YUM YUM GRASS JELLY

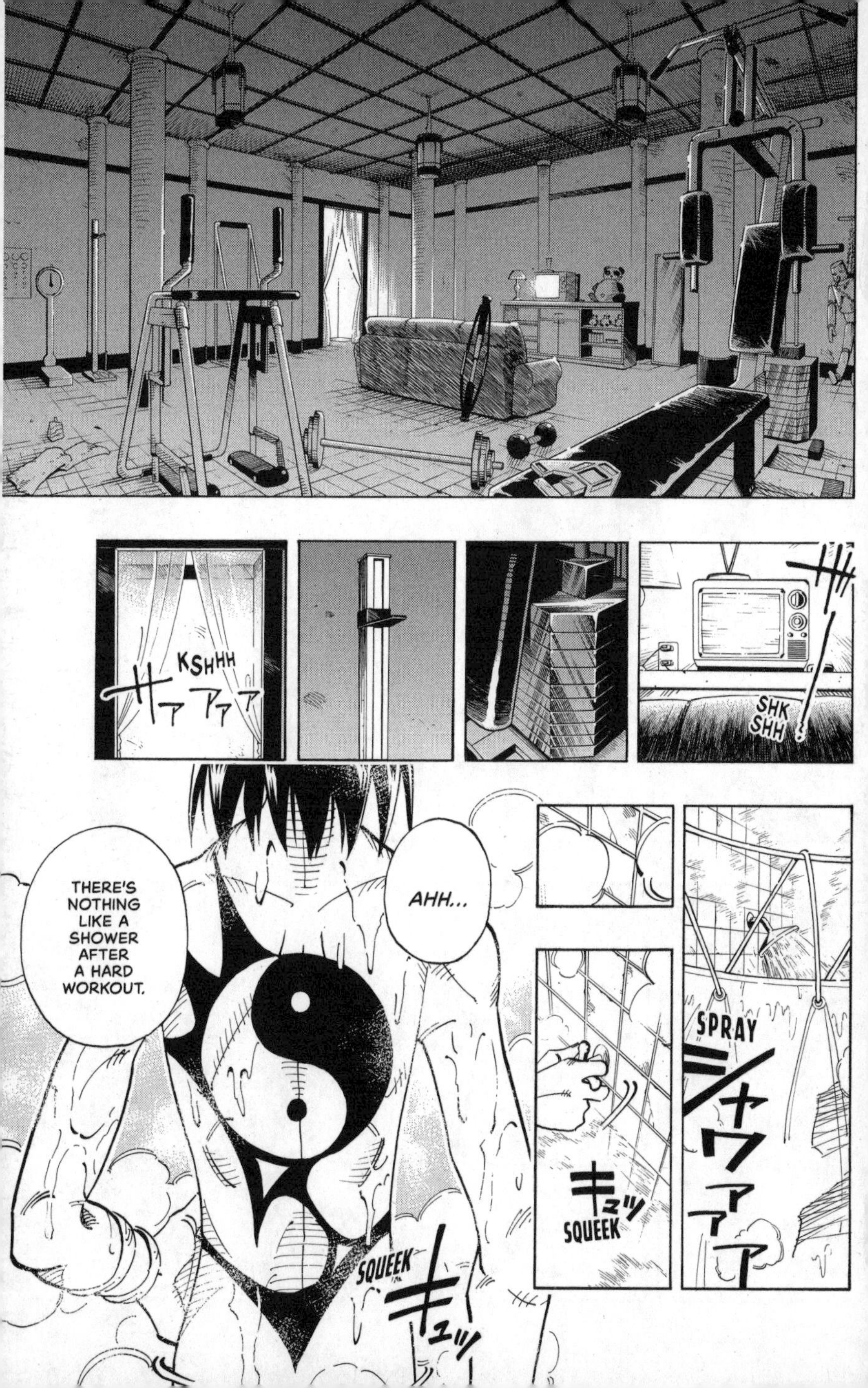
SHK SHH
KSHHH
サァアァア
SPRAY
シャワァアア
キュッ
SQUEEK
AHH...
THERE'S NOTHING LIKE A SHOWER AFTER A HARD WORKOUT.
SQUEEK
キュッ

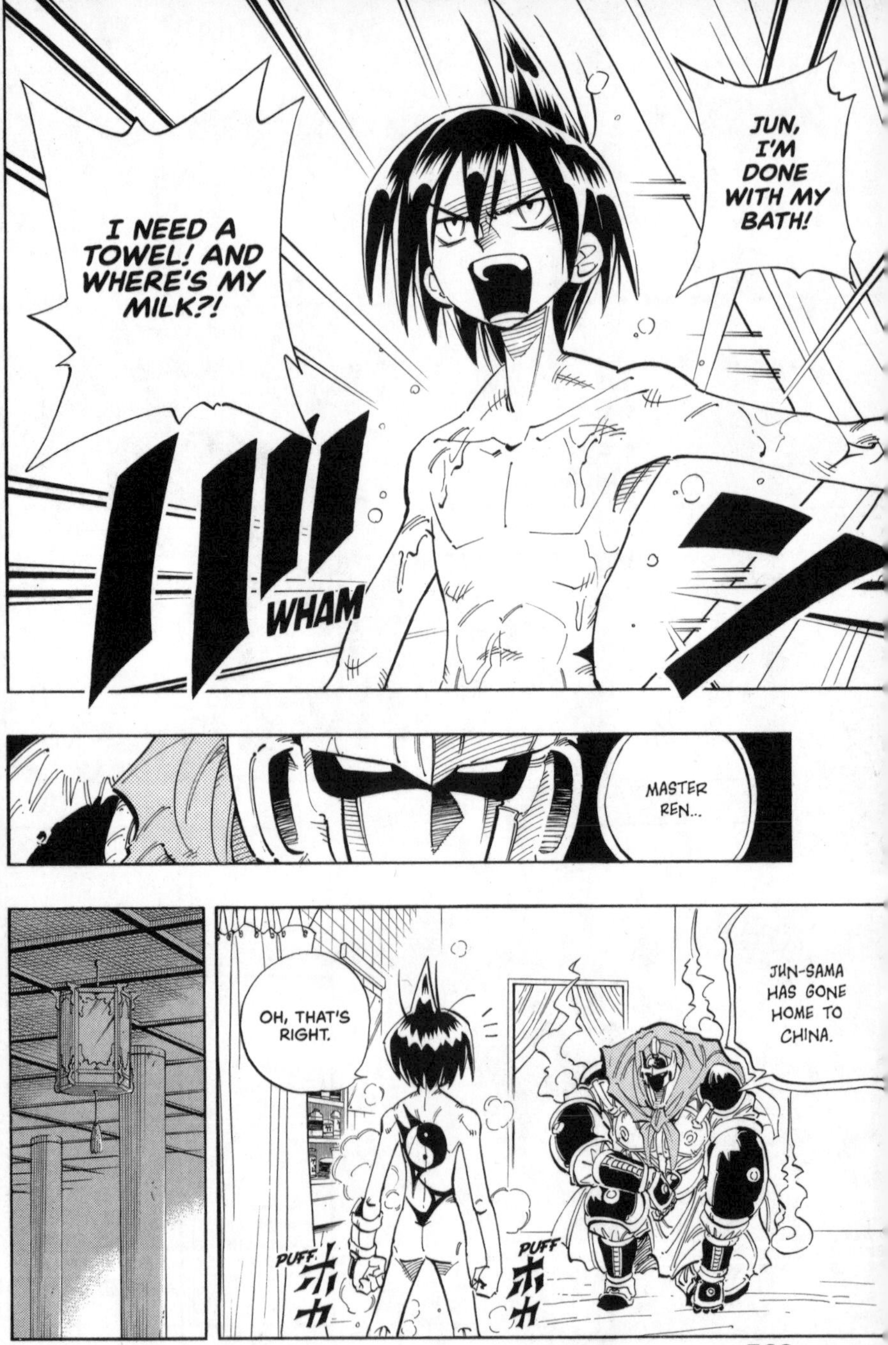
JUN, I'M DONE WITH MY BATH!
I NEED A TOWEL! AND WHERE'S MY MILK?!
WHAM
MASTER REN...
JUN-SAMA HAS GONE HOME TO CHINA.
OH, THAT'S RIGHT.
PUFF
ホカ
PUFF
ホカ

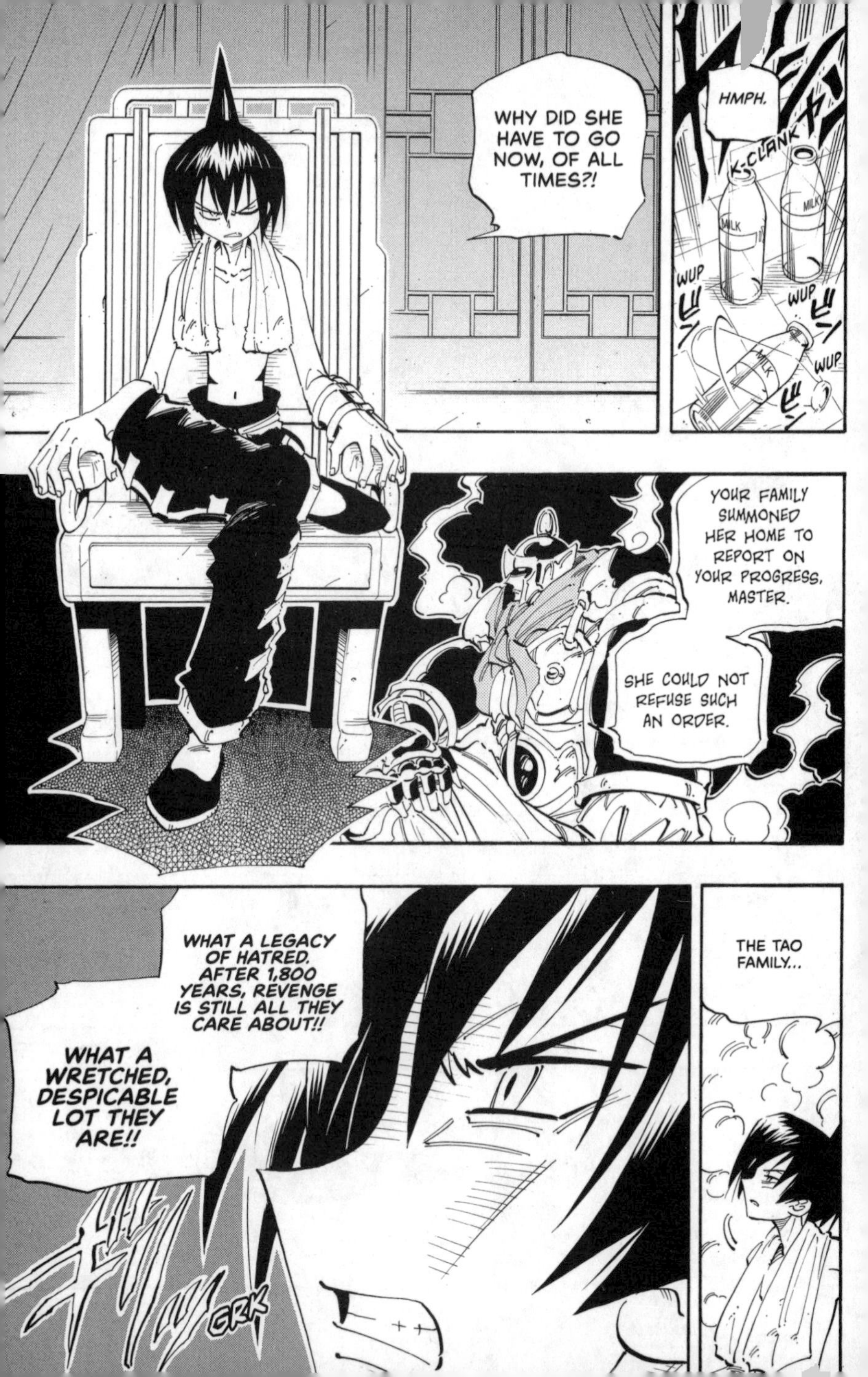
HMPH.
K-CLANK
MILK
MILK
WUP
WUP
MILK
WUP
WHY DID SHE HAVE TO GO NOW, OF ALL TIMES?!
YOUR FAMILY SUMMONED HER HOME TO REPORT ON YOUR PROGRESS, MASTER.
SHE COULD NOT REFUSE SUCH AN ORDER.
THE TAO FAMILY...
WHAT A LEGACY OF HATRED. AFTER 1,800 YEARS, REVENGE IS STILL ALL THEY CARE ABOUT!!
WHAT A WRETCHED, DESPICABLE LOT THEY ARE!!
GRK

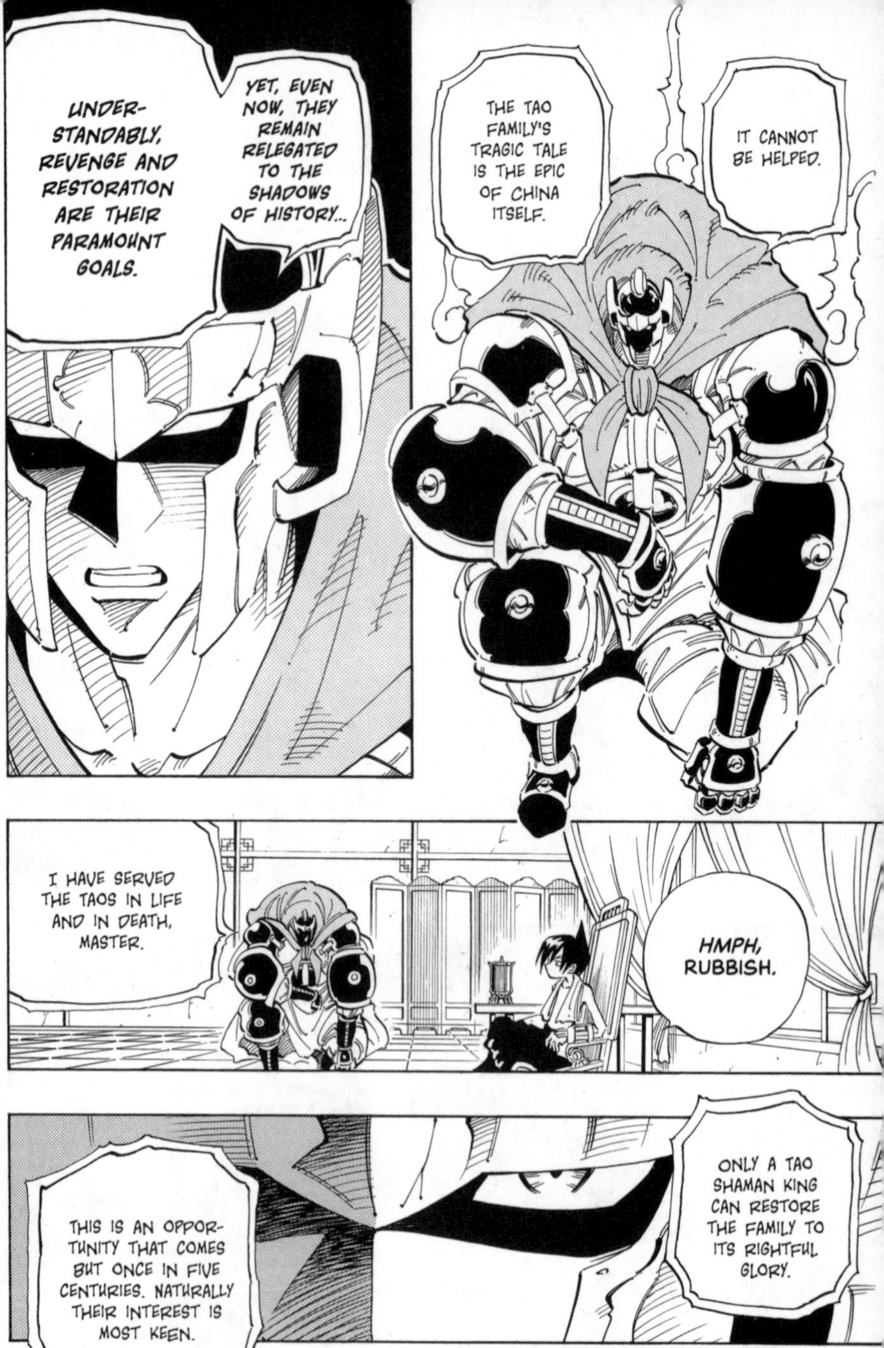
IT CANNOT BE HELPED.
THE TAO FAMILY'S TRAGIC TALE IS THE EPIC OF CHINA ITSELF.
YET, EVEN NOW, THEY REMAIN RELEGATED TO THE SHADOWS OF HISTORY...
UNDER-STANDABLY, REVENGE AND RESTORATION ARE THEIR PARAMOUNT GOALS.
HMPH, RUBBISH.
I HAVE SERVED THE TAOS IN LIFE AND IN DEATH, MASTER.
ONLY A TAO SHAMAN KING CAN RESTORE THE FAMILY TO ITS RIGHTFUL GLORY.
THIS IS AN OPPOR-TUNITY THAT COMES BUT ONCE IN FIVE CENTURIES. NATURALLY THEIR INTEREST IS MOST KEEN.

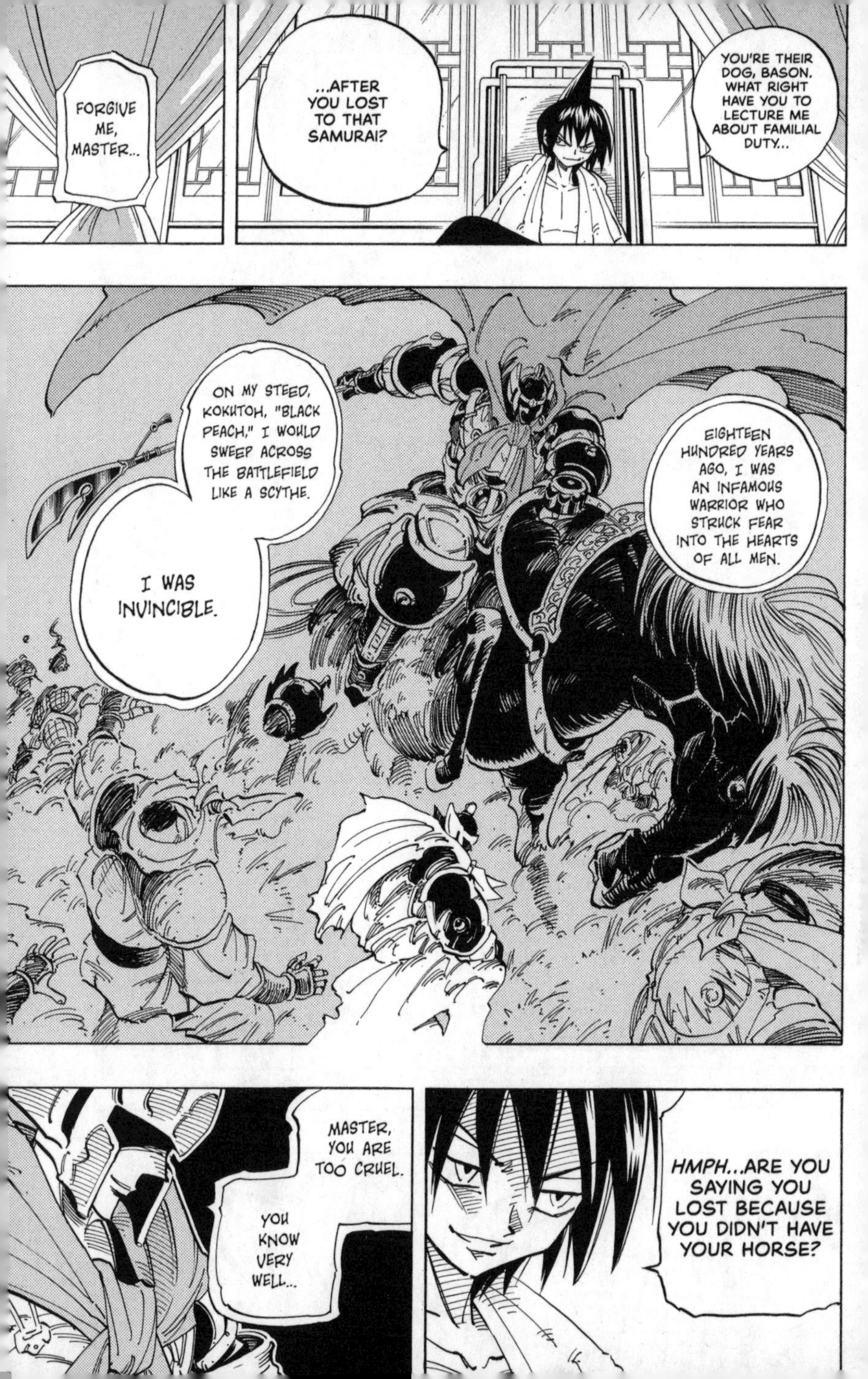
YOU'RE THEIR DOG, BASON. WHAT RIGHT HAVE YOU TO LECTURE ME ABOUT FAMILIAL DUTY...
...AFTER YOU LOST TO THAT SAMURAI?
FORGIVE ME, MASTER...
EIGHTEEN HUNDRED YEARS AGO, I WAS AN INFAMOUS WARRIOR WHO STRUCK FEAR INTO THE HEARTS OF ALL MEN.
ON MY STEED, KOKUTOH, "BLACK PEACH," I WOULD SWEEP ACROSS THE BATTLEFIELD LIKE A SCYTHE.
I WAS INVINCIBLE.
HMPH...ARE YOU SAYING YOU LOST BECAUSE YOU DIDN'T HAVE YOUR HORSE?
MASTER, YOU ARE TOO CRUEL.
YOU KNOW VERY WELL...

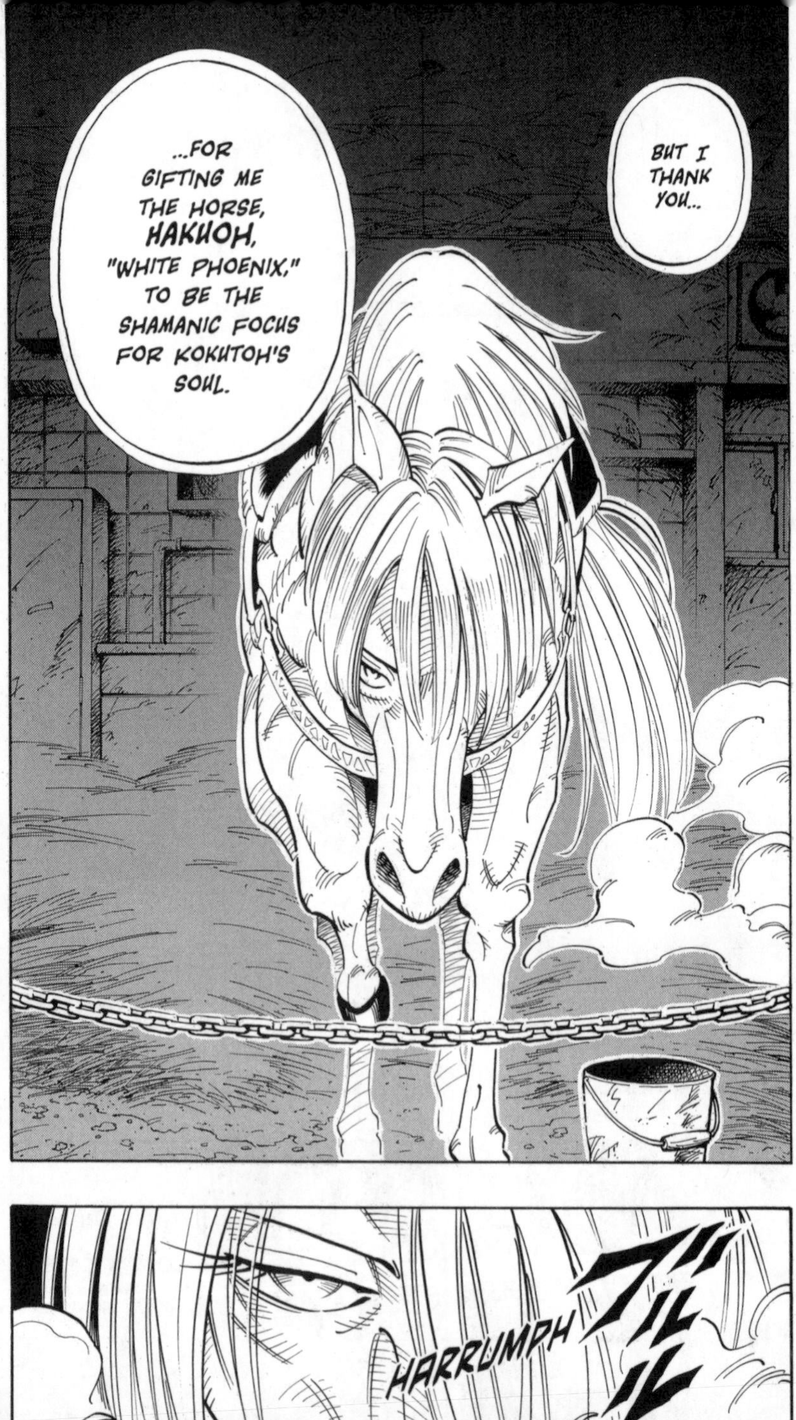
BUT I THANK YOU...
...FOR GIFTING ME THE HORSE, HAKUOH, "WHITE PHOENIX," TO BE THE SHAMANIC FOCUS FOR KOKUTOH'S SOUL.
HARRUMPH

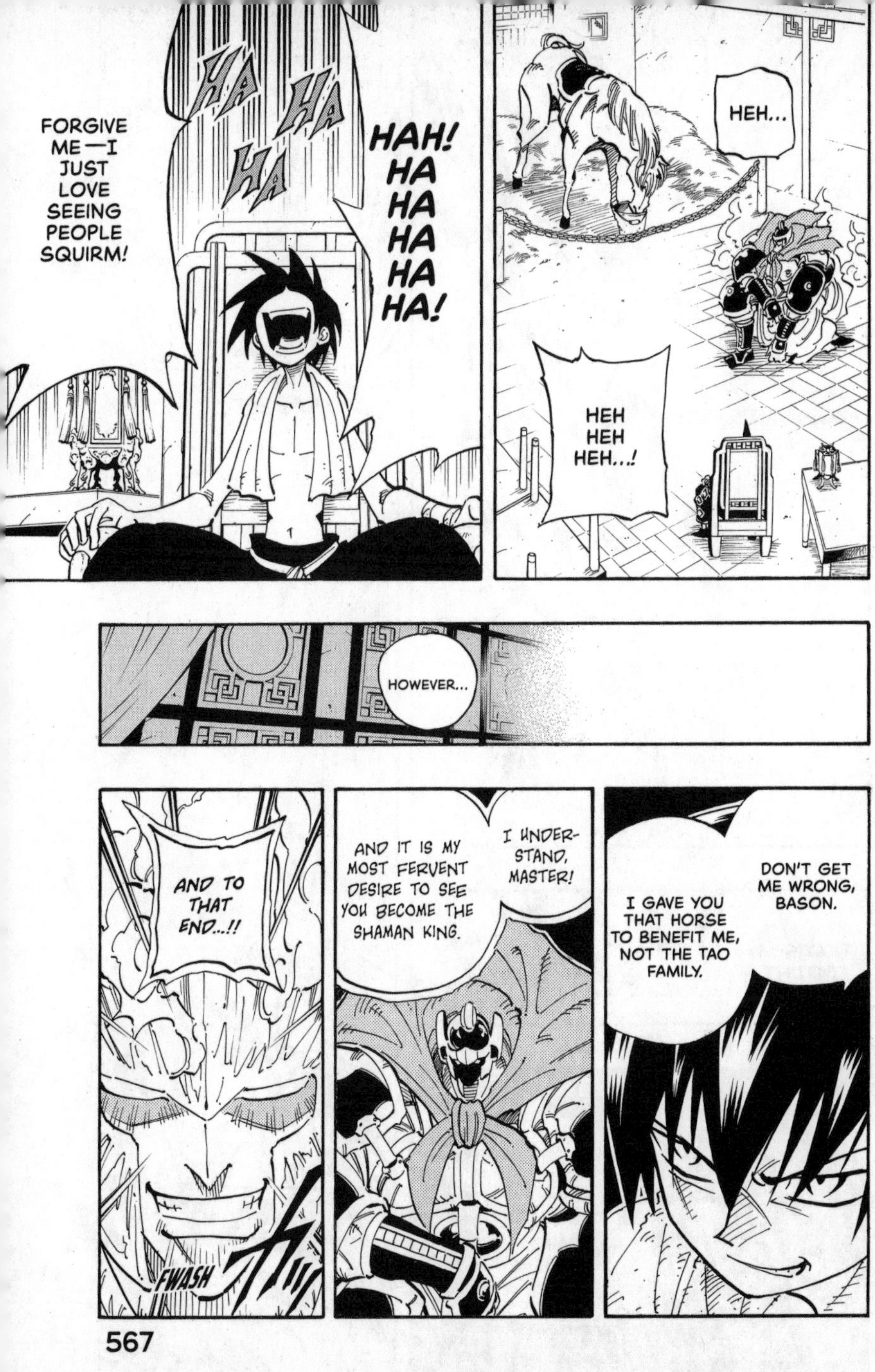
HEH...
HEH HEH HEH...!
HA HA HA HA
HAH! HA HA HA HA HA!
FORGIVE ME—I JUST LOVE SEEING PEOPLE SQUIRM!
HOWEVER...
DON'T GET ME WRONG, BASON.
I GAVE YOU THAT HORSE TO BENEFIT ME, NOT THE TAO FAMILY.
I UNDER-STAND, MASTER!
AND IT IS MY MOST FERVENT DESIRE TO SEE YOU BECOME THE SHAMAN KING.
AND TO THAT END...!!
FWASH

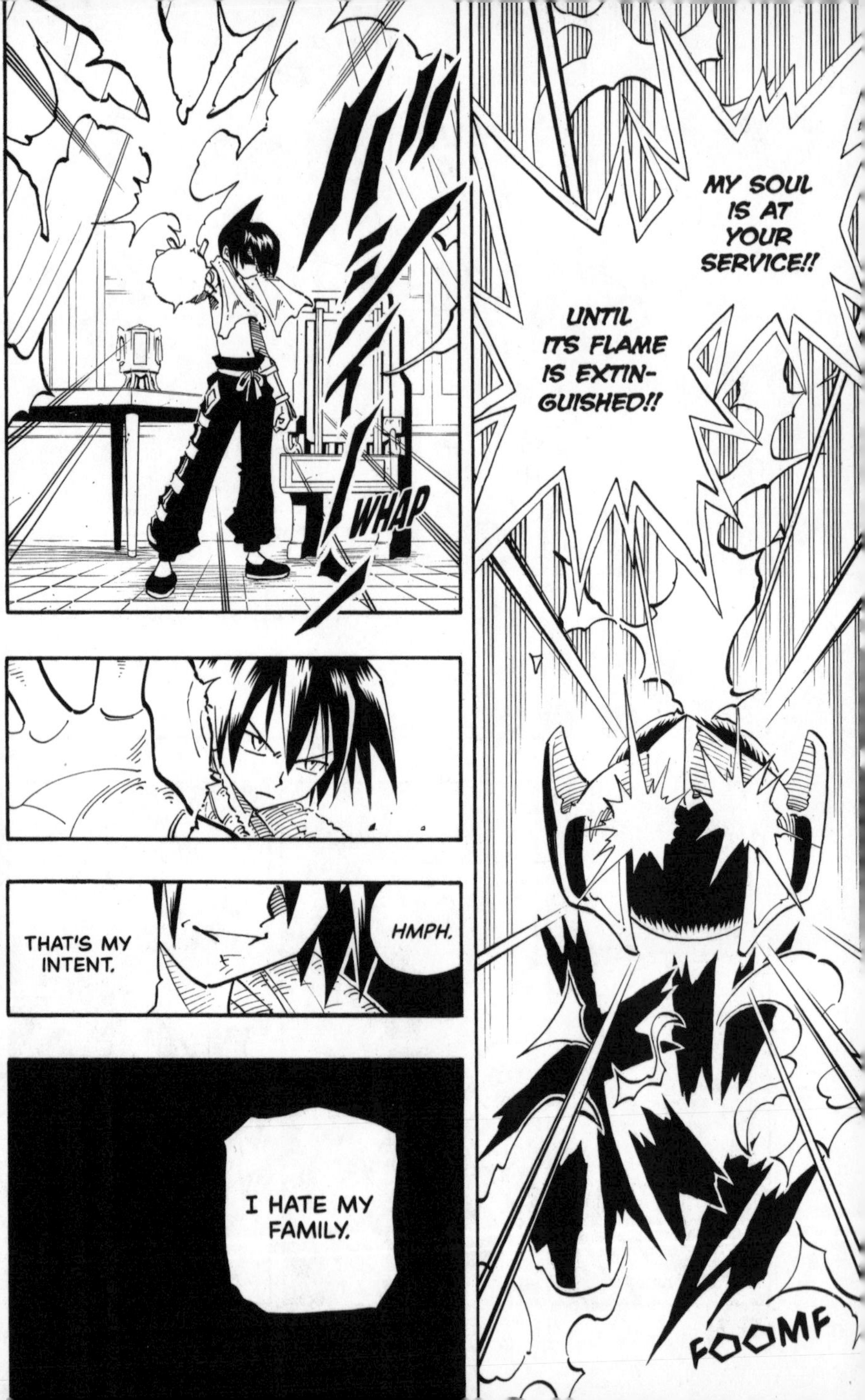
MY SOUL IS AT YOUR SERVICE!!
UNTIL ITS FLAME IS EXTIN-GUISHED!!
FOOMF
WHAP
HMPH.
THAT'S MY INTENT.
I HATE MY FAMILY.

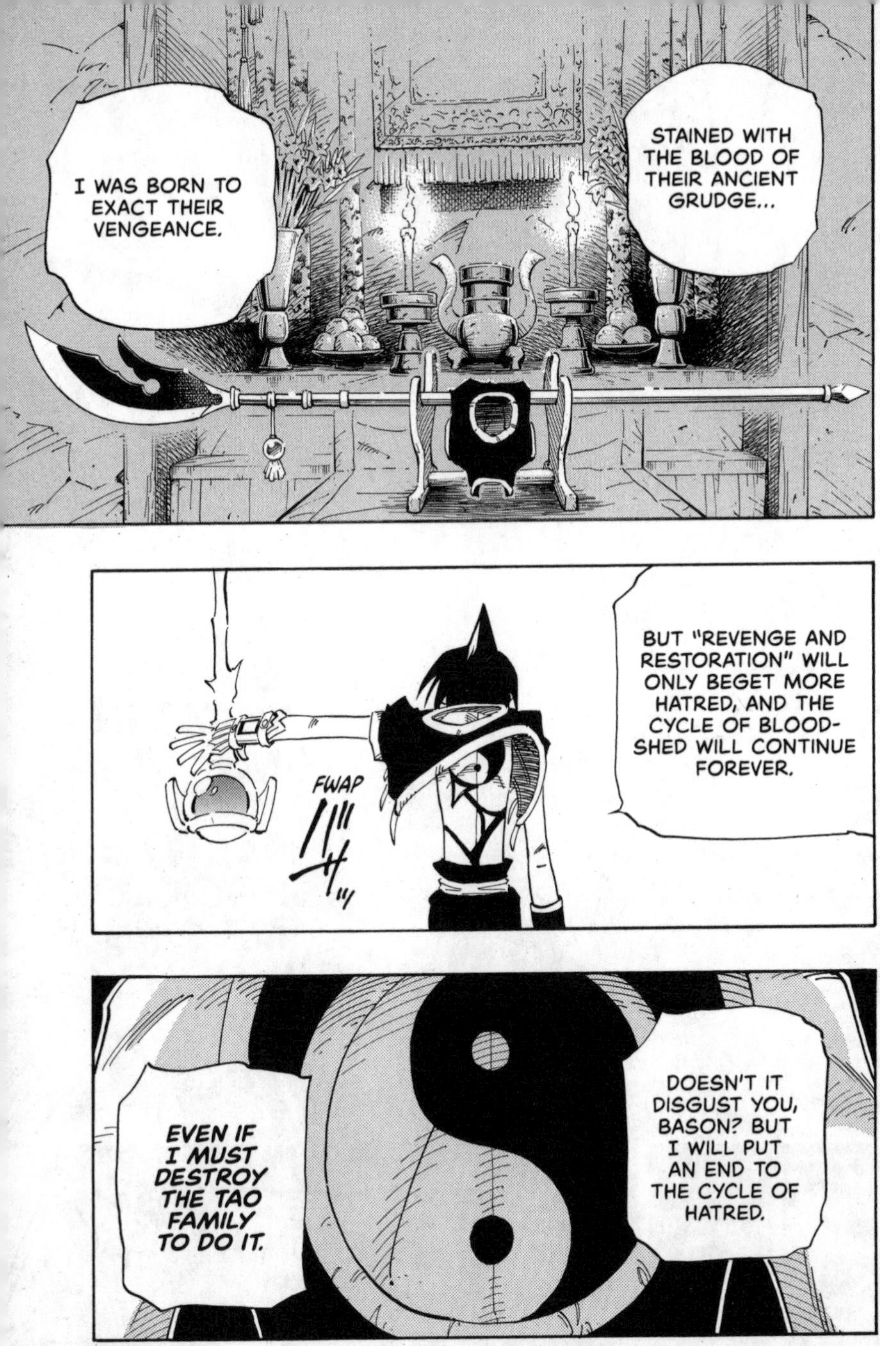
STAINED WITH THE BLOOD OF THEIR ANCIENT GRUDGE...
I WAS BORN TO EXACT THEIR VENGEANCE.
BUT "REVENGE AND RESTORATION" WILL ONLY BEGET MORE HATRED, AND THE CYCLE OF BLOOD-SHED WILL CONTINUE FOREVER.
FWAP
DOESN'T IT DISGUST YOU, BASON? BUT I WILL PUT AN END TO THE CYCLE OF HATRED.
EVEN IF I MUST DESTROY THE TAO FAMILY TO DO IT.

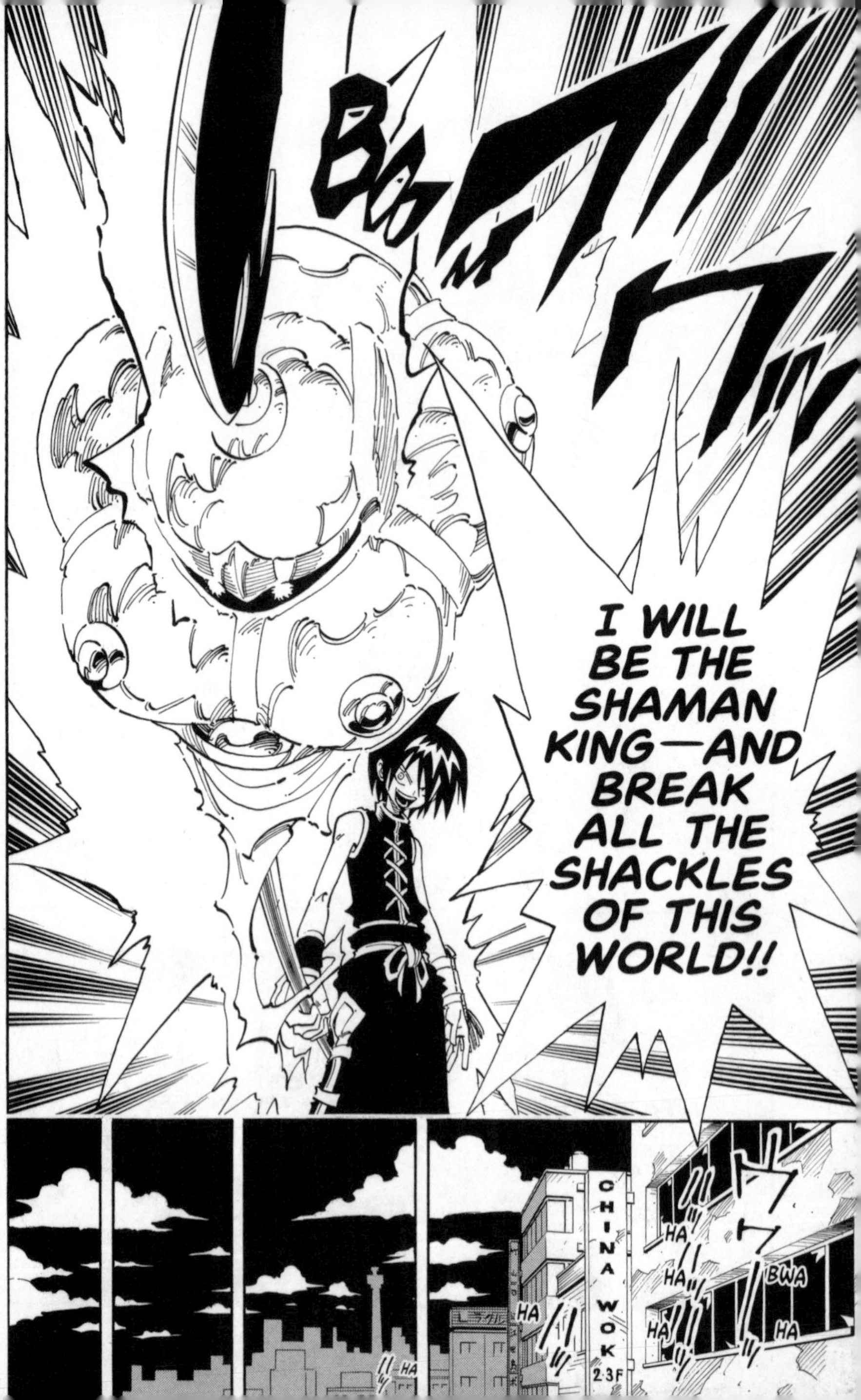
BOOM
I WILL BE THE SHAMAN KING—AND BREAK ALL THE SHACKLES OF THIS WORLD!!
HA
HA
BWA
HA
HA
CHINA WOK
2·3F
HA
HA

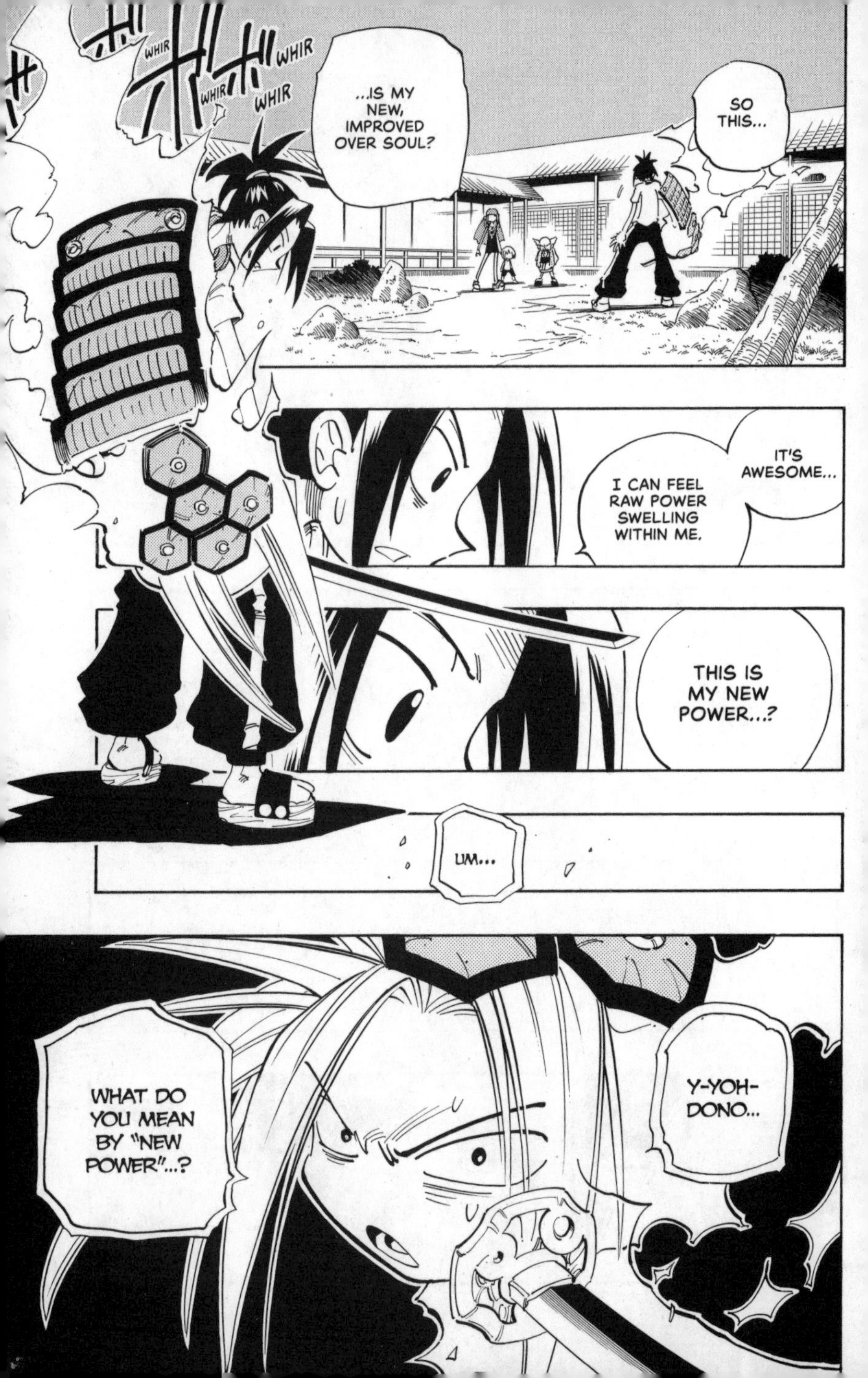
SO THIS...
...IS MY NEW, IMPROVED OVER SOUL?
WHIR
WHIR
WHIR
WHIR
IT'S AWESOME...
I CAN FEEL RAW POWER SWELLING WITHIN ME.
THIS IS MY NEW POWER...?
UM...
Y-YOH-DONO...
WHAT DO YOU MEAN BY "NEW POWER"...?

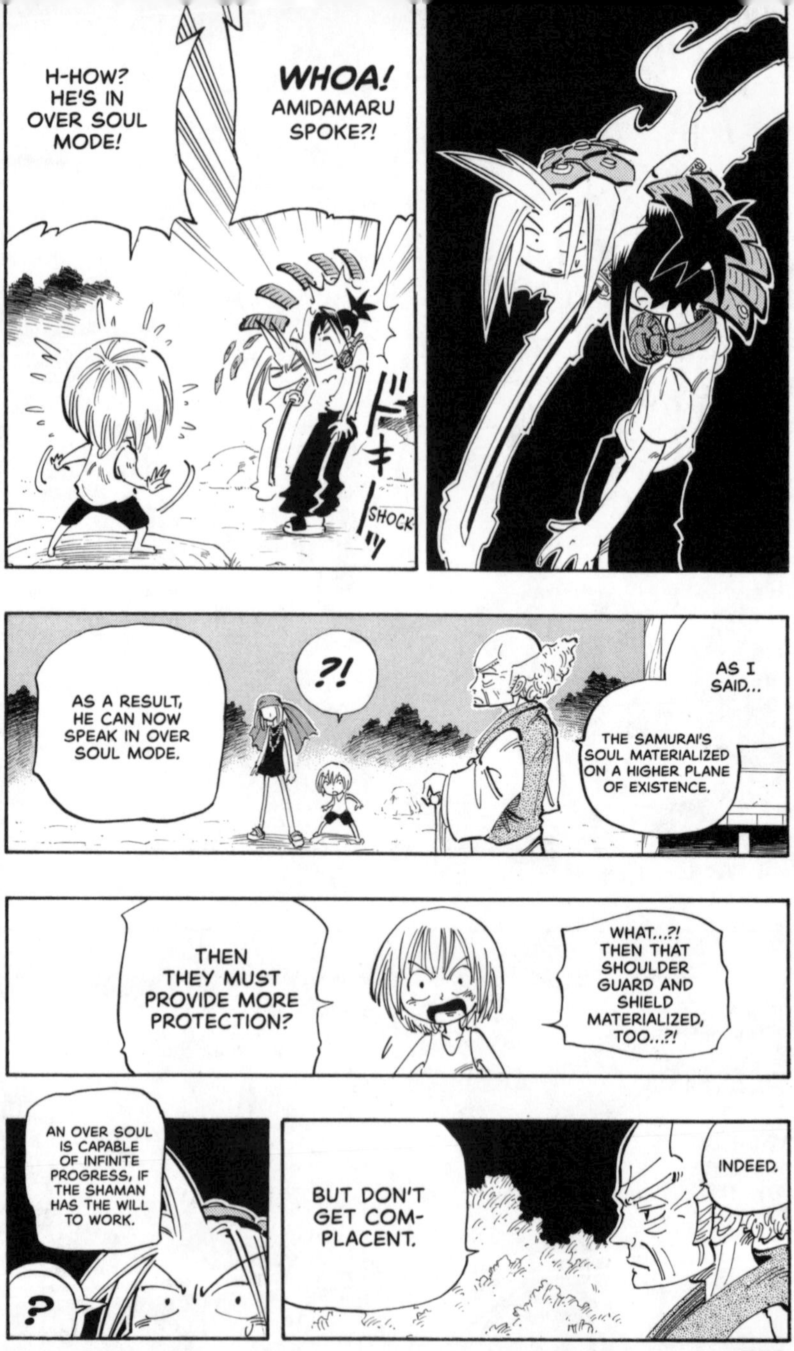
WHOA! AMIDAMARU SPOKE?!
SHOCK
H-HOW? HE'S IN OVER SOUL MODE!
AS I SAID...
THE SAMURAI'S SOUL MATERIALIZED ON A HIGHER PLANE OF EXISTENCE.
?!
AS A RESULT, HE CAN NOW SPEAK IN OVER SOUL MODE.
WHAT...?! THEN THAT SHOULDER GUARD AND SHIELD MATERIALIZED, TOO...?!
THEN THEY MUST PROVIDE MORE PROTECTION?
INDEED.
BUT DON'T GET COM-PLACENT.
AN OVER SOUL IS CAPABLE OF INFINITE PROGRESS, IF THE SHAMAN HAS THE WILL TO WORK.
?

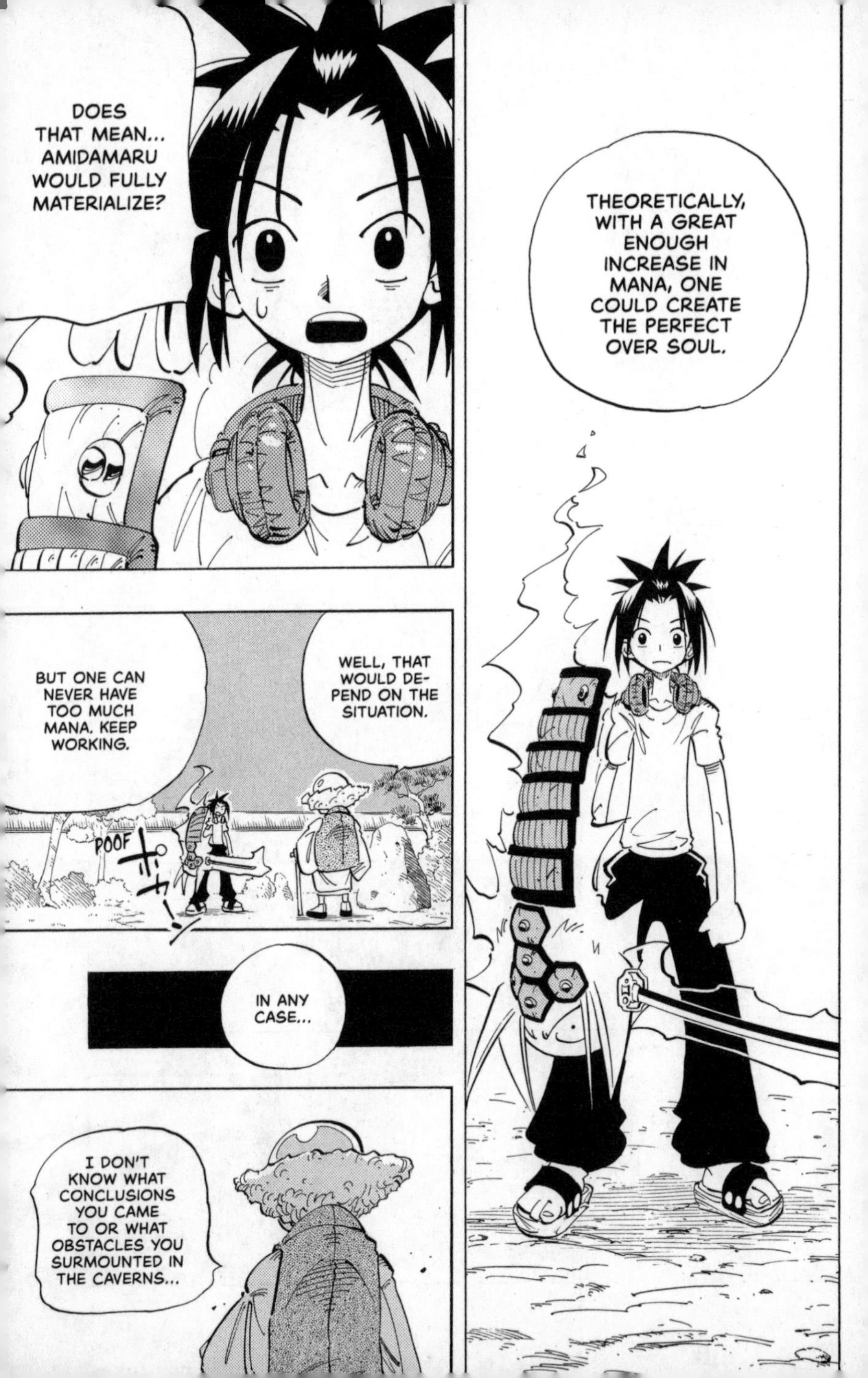
THEORETICALLY, WITH A GREAT ENOUGH INCREASE IN MANA, ONE COULD CREATE THE PERFECT OVER SOUL.
DOES THAT MEAN... AMIDAMARU WOULD FULLY MATERIALIZE?
WELL, THAT WOULD DE-PEND ON THE SITUATION.
BUT ONE CAN NEVER HAVE TOO MUCH MANA. KEEP WORKING.
POOF
IN ANY CASE...
I DON'T KNOW WHAT CONCLUSIONS YOU CAME TO OR WHAT OBSTACLES YOU SURMOUNTED IN THE CAVERNS...

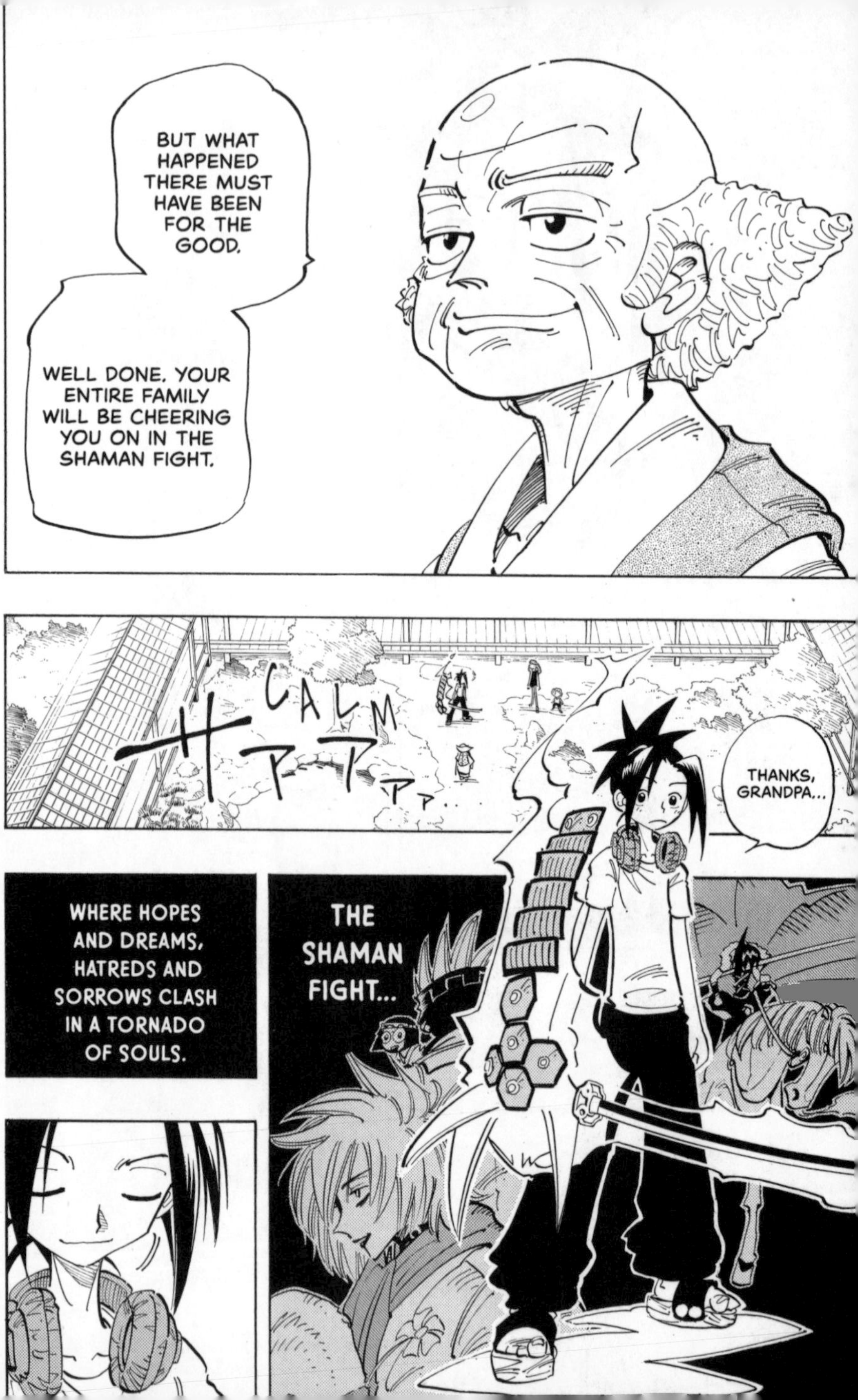
BUT WHAT HAPPENED THERE MUST HAVE BEEN FOR THE GOOD.
WELL DONE. YOUR ENTIRE FAMILY WILL BE CHEERING YOU ON IN THE SHAMAN FIGHT.
THANKS, GRANDPA...
CALM
THE SHAMAN FIGHT...
WHERE HOPES AND DREAMS, HATREDS AND SORROWS CLASH IN A TORNADO OF SOULS.

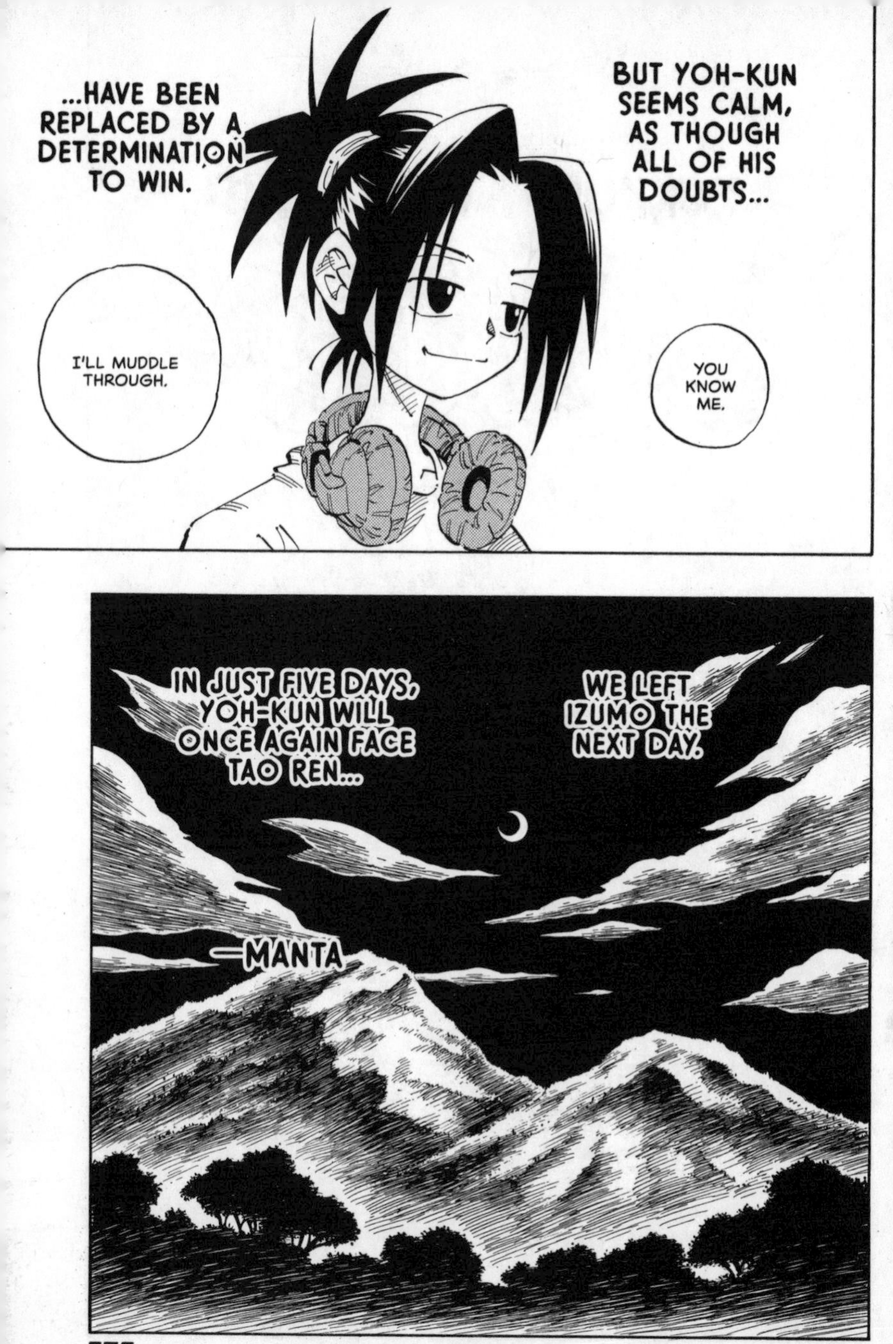
BUT YOH-KUN SEEMS CALM, AS THOUGH ALL OF HIS DOUBTS...
...HAVE BEEN REPLACED BY A DETERMINATION TO WIN.
YOU KNOW ME.
I'LL MUDDLE THROUGH.
WE LEFT IZUMO THE NEXT DAY.
IN JUST FIVE DAYS, YOH-KUN WILL ONCE AGAIN FACE TAO REN...
—MANTA

To be continued in Shaman King Omnibus 3!

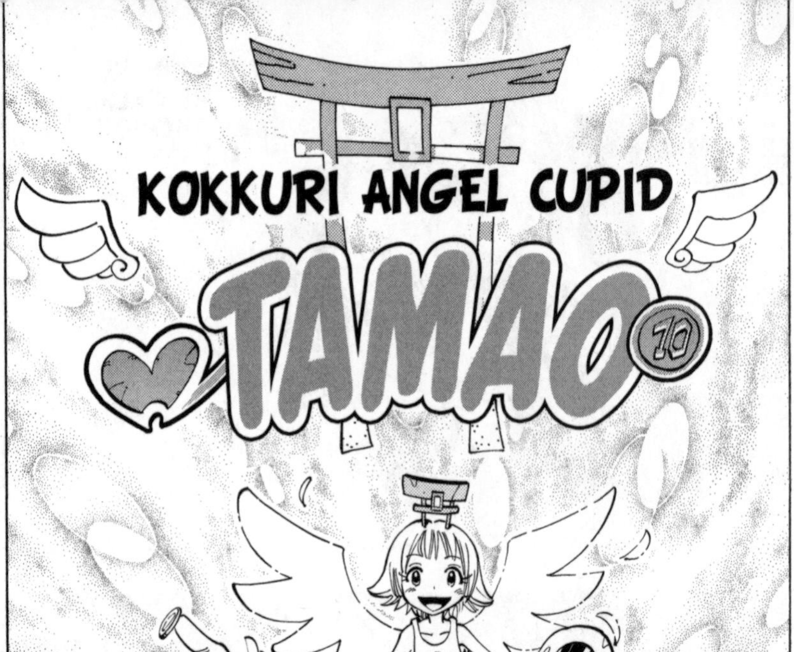
KOKKURI ANGEL CUPID
TAMAO
10
BY HIROYUKI TAKEI

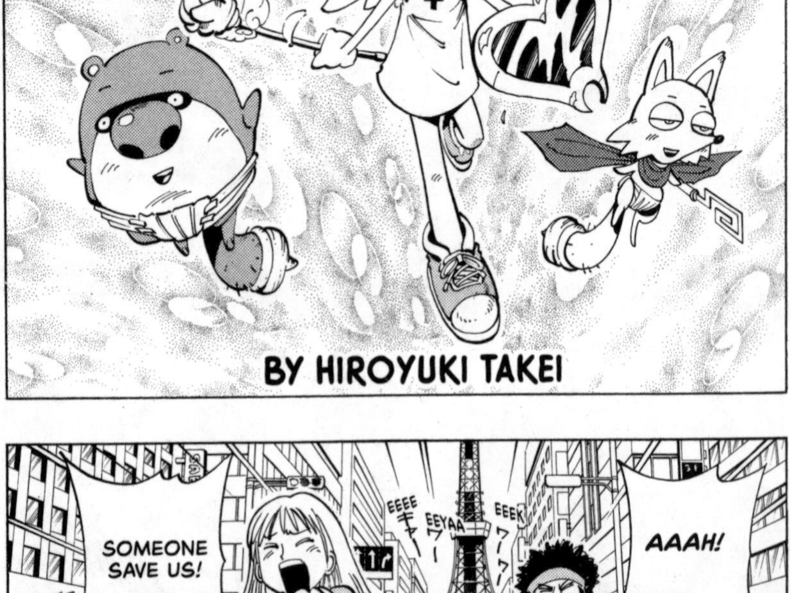
AAAH!
EEEK
EEYAA
EEEE
SOMEONE SAVE US!

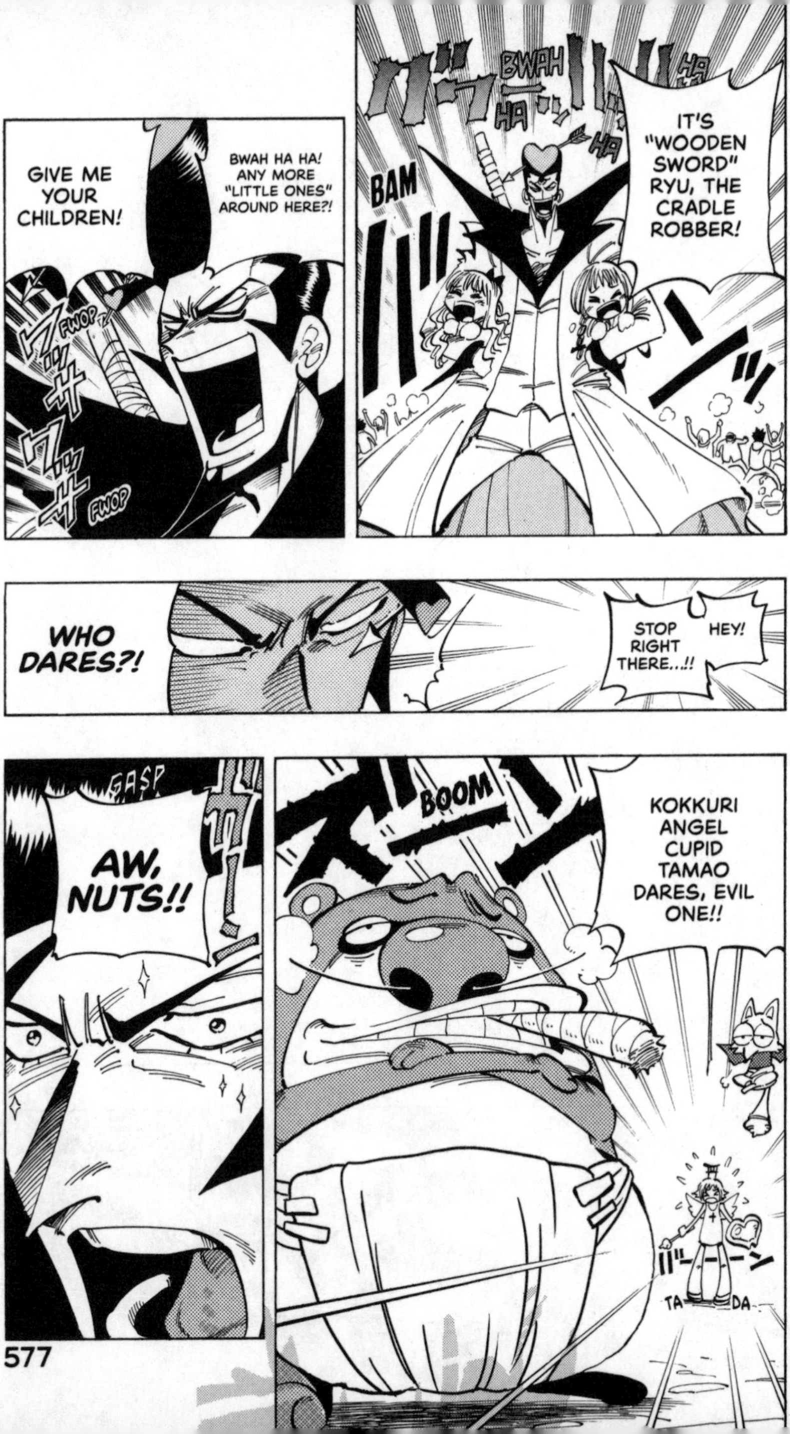

BWAH HA HA HA
IT'S "WOODEN SWORD" RYU, THE CRADLE ROBBER!
BAM
BWAH HA HA! ANY MORE "LITTLE ONES" AROUND HERE?!
GIVE ME YOUR CHILDREN!
FWOP
FWOP
HEY!
STOP RIGHT THERE...!!
WHO DARES?!
BOOM
KOKKURI ANGEL CUPID TAMAO DARES, EVIL ONE!!
TA-DA
GASP
AW, NUTS!!

SHAMAN KING

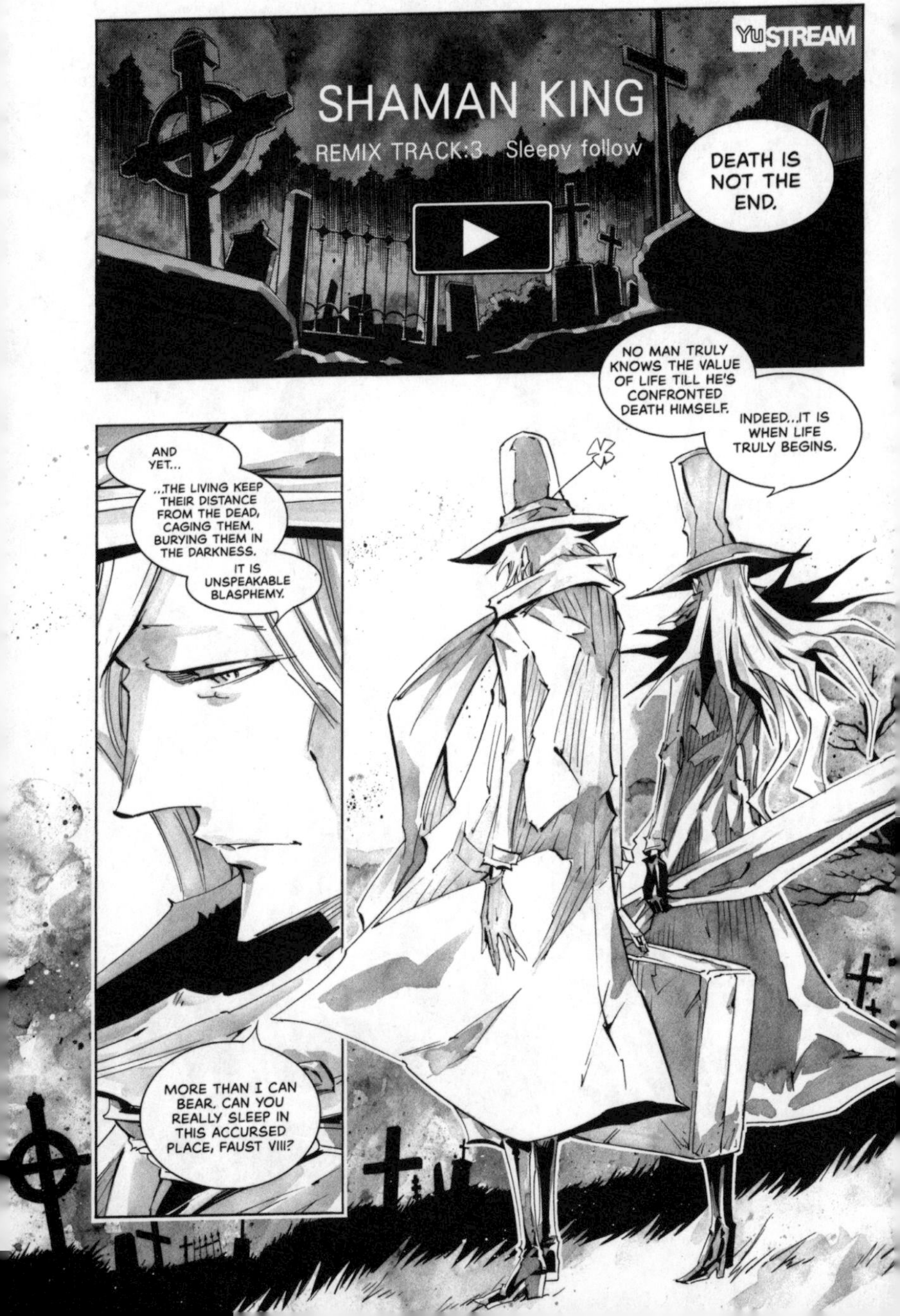
YuSTREAM
SHAMAN KING
REMIX TRACK:3 Sleepy follow
DEATH IS NOT THE END.
NO MAN TRULY KNOWS THE VALUE OF LIFE TILL HE'S CONFRONTED DEATH HIMSELF.
INDEED...IT IS WHEN LIFE TRULY BEGINS.
AND YET...
...THE LIVING KEEP THEIR DISTANCE FROM THE DEAD, CAGING THEM. BURYING THEM IN THE DARKNESS.
IT IS UNSPEAKABLE BLASPHEMY.
MORE THAN I CAN BEAR. CAN YOU REALLY SLEEP IN THIS ACCURSED PLACE, FAUST VIII?

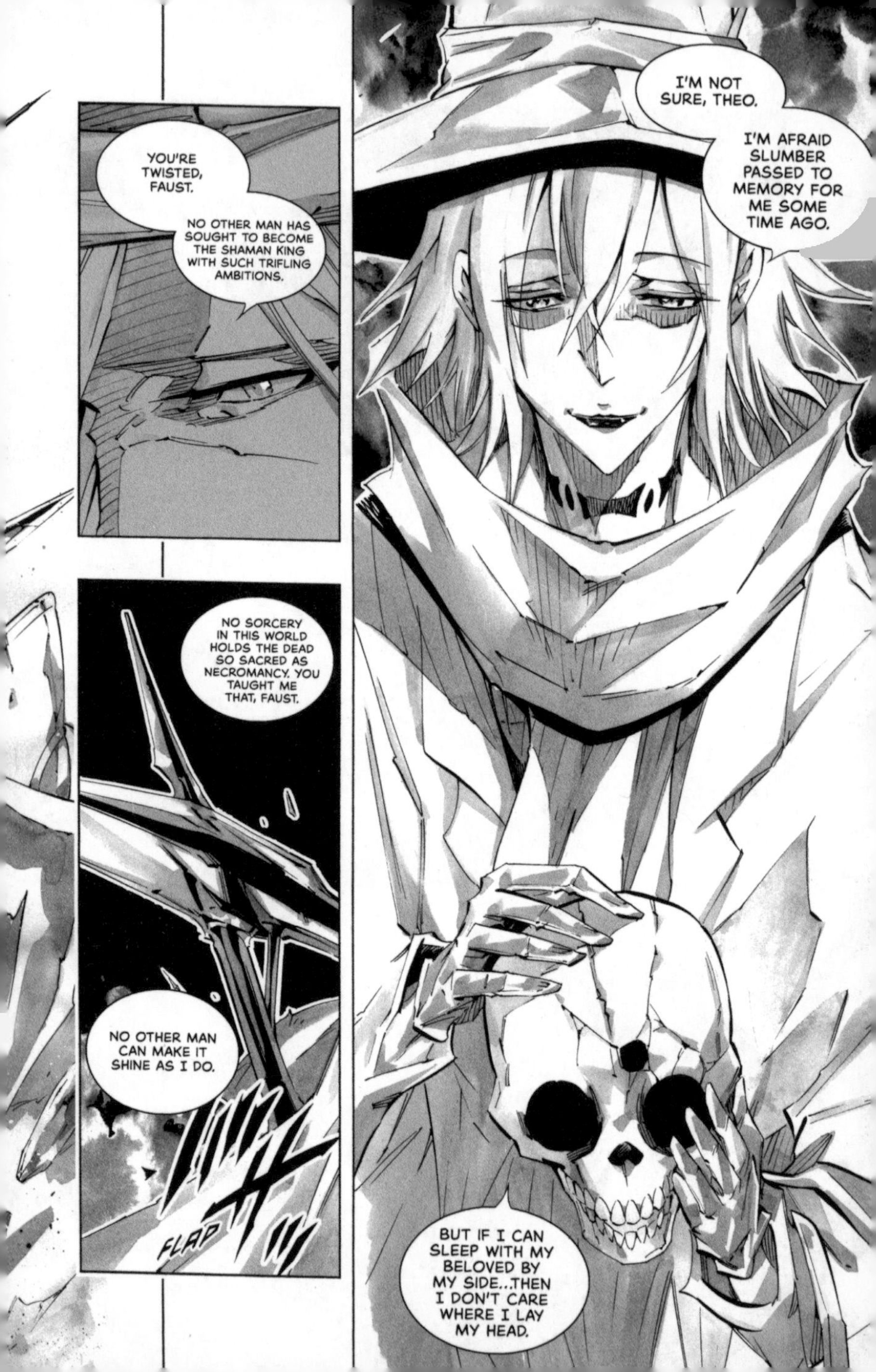
I'M NOT SURE, THEO.
I'M AFRAID SLUMBER PASSED TO MEMORY FOR ME SOME TIME AGO.
BUT IF I CAN SLEEP WITH MY BELOVED BY MY SIDE...THEN I DON'T CARE WHERE I LAY MY HEAD.
YOU'RE TWISTED, FAUST.
NO OTHER MAN HAS SOUGHT TO BECOME THE SHAMAN KING WITH SUCH TRIFLING AMBITIONS.
NO SORCERY IN THIS WORLD HOLDS THE DEAD SO SACRED AS NECROMANCY. YOU TAUGHT ME THAT, FAUST.
NO OTHER MAN CAN MAKE IT SHINE AS I DO.
FLAP

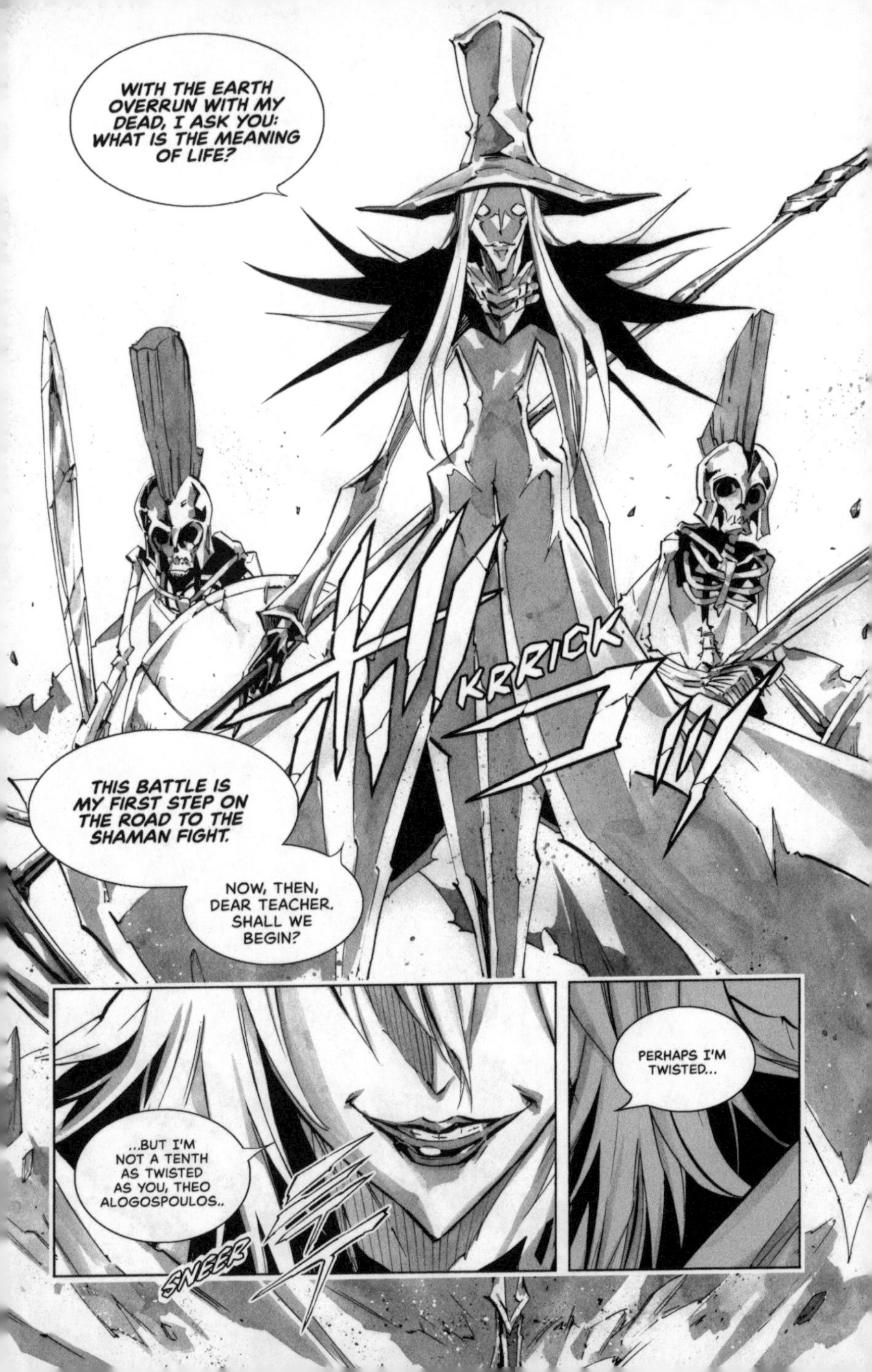
WITH THE EARTH OVERRUN WITH MY DEAD, I ASK YOU: WHAT IS THE MEANING OF LIFE?
KRRICK
THIS BATTLE IS MY FIRST STEP ON THE ROAD TO THE SHAMAN FIGHT.
NOW, THEN, DEAR TEACHER. SHALL WE BEGIN?
PERHAPS I'M TWISTED...
...BUT I'M NOT A TENTH AS TWISTED AS YOU, THEO ALOGOSPOULOS..
SNEER

SHAMAN KING

TRANSLATION NOTES

Honorifics:

Honorifics can be expressions of respect or endearment. They give insight into the nature of the relationship between characters. In this omnibus volume of *Shaman King*, the characters frequently use the following:

-san: Most commonly used to convey general politeness, equivalent to Mr., Ms., etc.

-sama: A level higher than "-san", used to convey greater respect.

-dono: An honorific used for people who are viewed as substantially more important than the speaker, such as samurai, lords, important priests, and so on. -Dono is no longer used much in everyday life, but can easily and quickly lend a sense of antiquity to a scene or character such as Amidamaru.

-kun: An honorific often attached to the names of boys or younger men. As with most honorifics, though, there's some nuance to the exact use of -kun, and it can in principle be used in many cases of superiors addressing or referring to juniors or subordinates, such as a boss mentioning an employee.

-chan: Used to express endearment, mostly toward girls but also to little children, pets, and even among couples. It implies a sense of childish cuteness.

No honorific: The lack of an honorific can also be important. It can indicate that two people are very close, or it may mean the speaker is socially so far above the subject as to owe them no social deference at all. (For example, a ruler would probably not use an honorific in referring to any of their subjects.)

Spirit Flame Mode, page 4

In Japanese, it is *"hitodama mode."* *Hitodama* (literally meaning "human soul") are souls of the dead that have been separated from their bodies and appear in the form of fiery balls.

Itako, page 4

Itako are a kind of shrine maiden particularly in the northern Tōhoku (northeastern) region. They specialize in channeling spirits and performing as mediums for the dead. (In Japanese, a medium is said to perform *kuchiyose,* or "drawing near to the mouth"—that is, speaking for or as the deceased.)

Native American and American Indian, page 7

The website of the National Museum of the American Indian (part of the Smithsonian Institution) states that in referring to the native peoples of the area that is now the United States, the commonly used terms American Indian, Native American, and Native are all considered acceptable. In the original Japanese, all three terms are used throughout in katakana. The NMAI adds that when possible, Native peoples prefer to be referred to by their specific tribal name rather than a general designation. A wide variety of Native tribes historically occupied the land that is now the United States, each with its own culture and often language. The Patch tribe in *Shaman King*, however, is fictional. Mainstream portrayals of shamanism and Native culture sometimes use images that are loosely inspired and may not always be accurate or considered appropriate.

Rahu, page 28
Rahu (pronounced Ragoh in Japanese) and Ketu (pronounced Keito in Japanese) are two of Hindu mythology's nine Navagraha, or celestial bodies. Rahu was the comet that appeared signaling the official start of the Shaman Fight.

Buddha-giri, page 36
Amidamaru's attack name, Buddha-giri, roughly translates to Buddha Slash (with *giri* coming from the Japanese term "to cleave" or "to chop").

Mana, page 44
The term for this inherent power of the shaman is translated from the original Japanese word *furyoku*, whose literal translation is "strength of shamans."

Buddhist exorcism chant, page 55
Priests in Japanese Buddhism may be called upon to perform exorcism of evil spirits, a process that often involves intoning a chant. Chants in Japanese Buddhism are not in the Japanese language as such; rather, they use the Japanese pronunciation of a sequence of Chinese characters, frequently quotations from the Lotus Sutra. Such ceremonies may also include the invocation *"Namu Myōhō Renge-kyō"* ("Glory to the *Lotus Sutra*," a mantra associated with Nichiren Buddhism) or other mantras.

Totem pole, page 76
Totem poles, a widely recognized symbol of Native culture, are chiefly associated with tribes from the Pacific Northwest, including some First Nations peoples from that region in what is now Canada. They can serve a wide variety of purposes, including commemorating ancestors, welcoming visitors, or even shaming someone who has done wrong.

Ikeikebukuro, Karakara Plaza, Sun-Sunshine 60 Building, page 128
These are most likely plays on the names of real locations in Tokyo. "Ikeikebukuro" alludes to Ikebukuro, an important business district. (Although *"ike"* means "lake," *"ike-ike"* means "vibrant" or "bustling.") This area is home to a famous skyscraper called the Sunshine 60 Building.

Ainu, page 129
Manta explains the general background of the Ainu on page 136. The Ainu, a native people of the Japanese islands, now live primarily on Hokkaido and Sakhalin, an island territory of Russia. They speak a unique language, distinct from Japanese. Although several varieties of Ainu language appear to have once existed, including varieties spoken in Sakhalin and possibly in the Kuril islands, another Russian territory, the only remaining extant Ainu tongue is that of Hokkaido, where it's now spoken by only a few elderly tribespeople. Over the past several decades, however, attempts to revitalize the language have begun to be made.

Bear, page 131

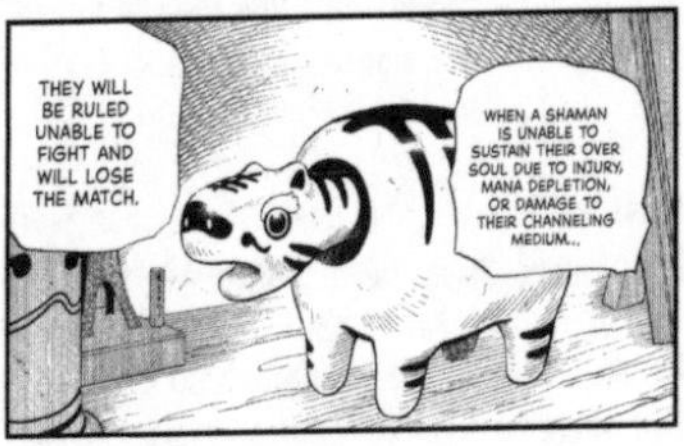
WHEN A SHAMAN IS UNABLE TO SUSTAIN THEIR OVER SOUL DUE TO INJURY, MANA DEPLETION, OR DAMAGE TO THEIR CHANNELING MEDIUM...
THEY WILL BE RULED UNABLE TO FIGHT AND WILL LOSE THE MATCH.

The animal statue depicted on this page may be a bear, and may be of Ainu cultural relevance. The Ainu have a long-standing connection to bears, which they have respected, honored, and perhaps even worshipped throughout their history. The connection was a natural one, both literally and figuratively: The Ainu made much of their living by fishing and foraging, which meant they often crossed paths with these powerful animals doing the same things.

Kamuy, page 136-137

An Ainu term meaning "spirit" or sometimes "god," *kamuy* are similar but by no means identical to the concept of *kami* in Japanese culture. Virtually anything can be a *kamuy*, from bears and deer to salmon and squirrels. Even objects ordinarily considered inanimate, such as tools, might be *kamuy*. These spirits are understood to have a relationship to humans which, if properly respected and honored, they will continually return to Earth to maintain.

Kororo and Koropukkur, pages 156, 159

The character of Kororo belongs to the Koropukkur. Ainu folk belief holds that the Koropukkur are tiny people who live under butterbur *(fuki)* leaves and who reputedly inhabited the Ainu homeland before the Ainu themselves did.

Harusame, page 194

The individual characters that make up the name of Amidamaru's sword come from the words *haru*, meaning spring, and *ame*, meaning rain. Together, the two characters can be read as *harusame*, meaning spring rain, or *shunu*, a type of thin noodles made from bean or potato starch.

Mountain gods, page 214

Perhaps a reference to Kim-un-kamuy, the Ainu mountain god.

Shamanic focus, page 226

Translated from the Japanese, *baikai*, meaning "medium."

En, page 237

The character for the name of the lodge, *En*, means "flame."

Chokohama Foreigner's Cemetery, page 260-261

This location is inspired by the real-life Foreign General Cemetery in Yokohama. Manta's explanation of US Navy Commodore Matthew C. Perry's role in the historical origin is true.

Yuhsuke Takeyama, page 260

This grave is likely a reference to the real-life *mangaka* of this name. Fandom chats mention that he was an assistant to *Shaman King* author Hiroyuki Takei.

Faust VIII, page 270

This character is based on the figure of Dr. Faust, of whom stories and legends have been told since at least the sixteenth century. (The early German legends that form the basis of the tradition may be based on a historical person, Johann Georg Faust.) The basic plot of the story is that Dr. Faust desires knowledge and perhaps magical powers, so he makes a deal with the devil: The devil will give Faust supernatural powers, and in exchange, at the end of his life Faust will be taken to hell where he will be the devil's eternal slave. (This has given rise to the English expression, "a Faustian bargain.")

Bone Shell, page 313

The original is German rendered in katakana: *Schutz des Knochen*, meaning "protection of the bone."

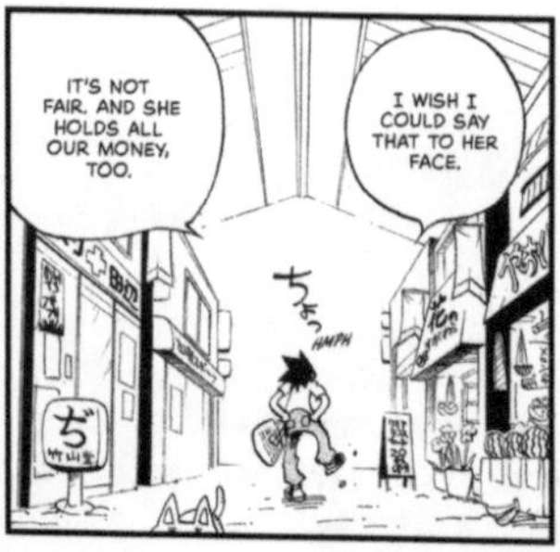
I WISH I COULD SAY THAT TO HER FACE.
IT'S NOT FAIR. AND SHE HOLDS ALL OUR MONEY, TOO.
HMPH

Skull Scrummage, page 334

The original is German rendered in katakana: *Gedränge des Schädel*, "scrummage of the skull."

Store signs, page 378:

From left to right: Clinic, sporting goods, florist, produce. The square sign on the lower left by the clinic reads "hemorrhoids," informing that hemorrhoids are treated here.

Yu Stream, page 381

"Yu" is a transliteration of the Japanese kanji, meaning "ghost."

Faust's pact with Mephistopheles, page 407

As noted above, there are many different versions of the Faust legend. This particular wording of Faust's pact with the devil's representative Mephistopheles seems to be from Goethe's stage play, *Faust*. In Goethe's telling, the bargain was this: If Faust should ever be so pleased with anything Mephistopheles gives him that he wishes to stay in that moment forever, at that moment the devil may take him to hell.

Izumo, page 451

Izumo, Yoh's hometown, is in Shimane Prefecture. Located on the western half of the main Japanese island of Honshu, the ancient province of Izumo (literally "the land of clouds emerging" and now part of Shimane Prefecture) was one of the points of origin of the political powers that would eventually become the modern Japanese state. Moreover, the great shrine at Izumo (Izumo Taisha, or more formally, Izumo Ōyashiro) was and remains one of the most important shrines in Japan's native Shinto religion. In ancient poetry, the area was conventionally known as *yakumo tatsu Izumo*, or "Izumo of the eight clouds rising." This region is known for its tradition both of and in spiritual beliefs and legends. For example, the mouth of the netherworld *(yomi)*, into which the deity Izanagi ventures in search of his deceased wife Izanami in one of Japan's earliest myths, is said to be located in Izumo. (He finds Izanami, but, like Orpheus, he looks upon her when he has been ordered not to, and thereby loses her to the underworld.)

Kokkuri, page 490

Kokkuri is both a game and a form of divination, somewhat like the Ouija board in some Western cultures. (Notice how Tamao uses a 10-yen coin as a guide to the spirit's responses.) The kanji for kokkuri mean "fox-dog-raccoon" *(kitsune-inu-tanuki)*, referring to three important characters in Japanese mythology (see below). "Kokkuri-san" is also the name of the spirit summoned by this game.

Ascetic, page 492

Translated from the the Japanese *shugenja*, a practicioner of *"shugendō,"* an ancient, traditional religion in which monks live in seclusion, often on mountains or in other wilderness areas. A syncretistic religious tradition, *shugendō* borrows elements of both Buddhism and Shinto, among others.

Fox and tanuki, page 494

Ponchi is a tanuki (raccoon-dog), Conchi is a fox *(kitsune)*. Foxes are both tricksters and messengers in Japanese legend, while tanuki frequently cause mischief. Both animals are associated with various magical powers, especially shape-shifting and, in the case of foxes, the tendency to mesmerize human victims.

Mt. Daisen, page 497

Mt. Daisen, along the San'in coast (a stretch of coast along the Sea of Japan encompassing, notably, the Izumo region among others), is a volcano and one of the most important mountains for the *shugendō* religion (see "Ascetic" above). Traditionally, this mountain was said to be the home of Hōkibō, an important *tengu* (a traditional Japanese goblin that sometimes has bird-like characteristics).

Belly buster, page 503

The original Japanese literally translates as "knockout *inarizushi*." Foxes are traditional symbols in Inari shrines in Japan *(Inari* being a messenger of the gods who often takes on a fox's form) and so *"inarizushi"* is associated with foxes. *Inarizushi* is a dish made with a small bag of fried tofu stuffed with rice.

Ichibata Dentetsu Bus, page 526

Ichibata Dentetsu is a local transit system in Izumo, including both train lines and buses.

Moshi-moshi lighthouse, page 527

This is based on real lighthouse-shaped phone booths that exist in Izumo.

Leaf Sprites, shikigami, page 550

Shikigami—the kanji literally mean "ritual-deity"—are, in essence, the familiars of *onmyōji* (see below). They are ghosts or spirits summoned by the practitioner to perform some task, though *shikigami* can be volatile and require careful handling on the part of the conjurer. In this scene, Yohmei Asakura's *shikigami* are leaf sprites, reflecting the kanji used in his and Yoh's name meaning "leaf."

Onmyōji, page 551

Sometimes called yin-yang diviners, *onmyōji* were wonder-workers—somewhere between priests and shamans—who used the forces of yin (the dark, feminine energy) and yang (the bright, masculine energy) to perform spells, divine the future, and exorcise spirits, among other things. Their art was known as *onmyōdo* or *in'yōdō*, both of which mean "the way of yin and yang."

Hakuoh and Kokutoh, pages 565-566

Their names mean "White Phoenix" and "Black Peach," respectively.

SHAMAN KING

Young characters and steampunk setting, like *Howl's Moving Castle* and *Battle Angel Alita*

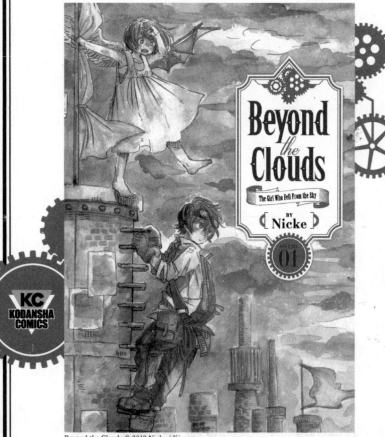

Beyond the Clouds © 2018 Nicke / Ki-oon

A boy with a talent for machines and a mysterious girl whose wings he's fixed will take you beyond the clouds! In the tradition of the high-flying, resonant adventure stories of Studio Ghibli comes a gorgeous tale about the longing of young hearts for adventure and friendship!

Shaman King Omnibus 2 is a work of fiction. Names, characters, places, and incidents are the products of the author's imagination or are used fictitiously. Any resemblance to actual events, locales, or persons, living or dead, is entirely coincidental.

A Kodansha Comics Trade Paperback Original
Shaman King Omnibus 2 copyright © 2020 Hiroyuki Takei
English translation copyright © 2021 Hiroyuki Takei

All rights reserved.

Published in the United States by Kodansha Comics, an imprint of
Kodansha USA Publishing, LLC, New York.

Publication rights for this English edition arranged through
Kodansha Ltd., Tokyo.

First published in Japan in 2020 by Kodansha Ltd., Tokyo.

ISBN 978-1-64651-205-8

Original cover design by Toru Fukushima (Smile Studio)

Printed in the United States of America.

www.kodansha.us

9 8 7 6 5 4 3 2 1
Translation: Lillian Olsen, Erin Procter
Lettering: Jan Lan Ivan Concepcion
Retouching: Jan Lan Ivan Concepcion
Additional Lettering: Nicole Roderick
English Adaptation: Lance Caselman
Editing: Tomoko Nagano, Jason Thompson
YKS Services LLC/SKY Japan, INC.
Kodansha Comics edition cover design by Phil Balsman

Publisher: Kiichiro Sugawara

Director of publishing services: Ben Applegate
Associate director of operations: Stephen Pakula
Publishing services managing editors: Alanna Ruse, Madison Salters
Assistant production managers: Emi Lotto, Angela Zurlo
Logo and character art ©Kodansha USA Publishing, LLC

HOW TO READ MANGA

YOU READ MANGA ***RIGHT TO LEFT*** JAPANESE STYLE

FOLLOW THE NUMBERS BELOW STARTING FROM THE **TOP RIGHT PANEL** AND KEEP IT MOVING FROM THERE! YOU MAY FEEL LIKE YOU'RE READING BACKWARDS, BUT YOU'LL GET THE HANG OF IT FASTER THAN YOU THINK! IF YOU GET LOST ALONG THE WAY, JUST TAKE A LOOK AT THE SAMPLE BELOW! HAPPY READING, AND HAVE FUN!

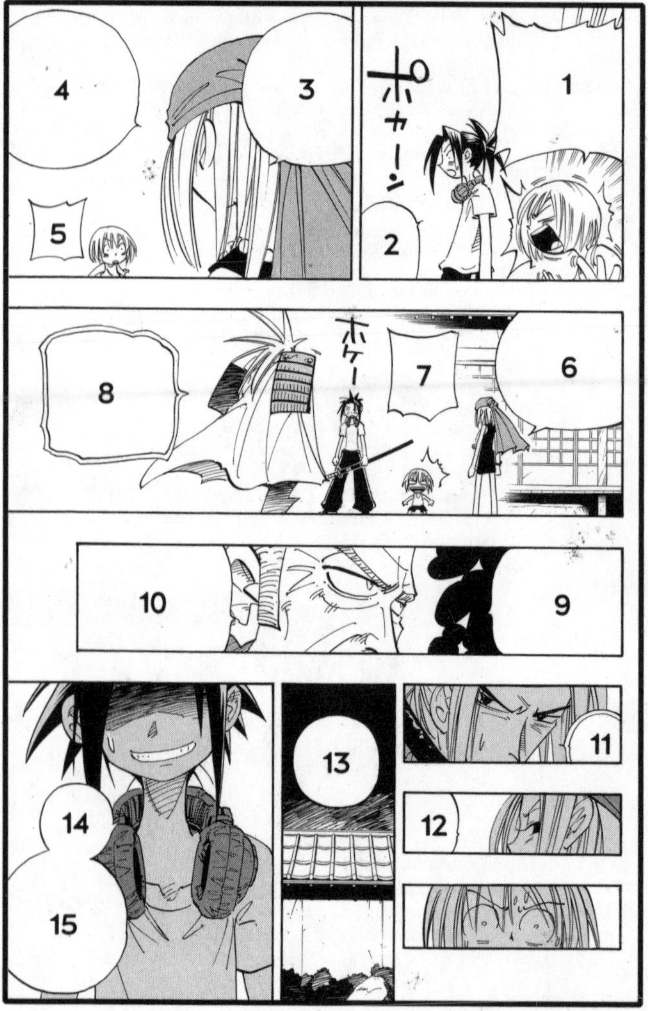

1
ポカーン
2
3
4
5
6
7
ホケー
8
9
10
11
12
13
14
15